Create Your Own Assignments or Use Ours, All with Automatic Grading

An **Assignment** area allows you to create **student homework** and **quizzes** by using **Wiley-provided question banks,** or by writing your own. You may also assign readings, activities and other work you want your students to complete. One of the most powerful features of eGrade Plus is that student assignments will be automatically graded and recorded in your gradebook. This will not only save you time but will provide your students with immediate feedback on their work.

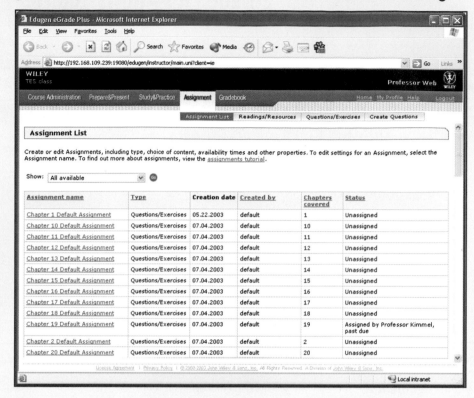

Assess Student Understanding More Closely

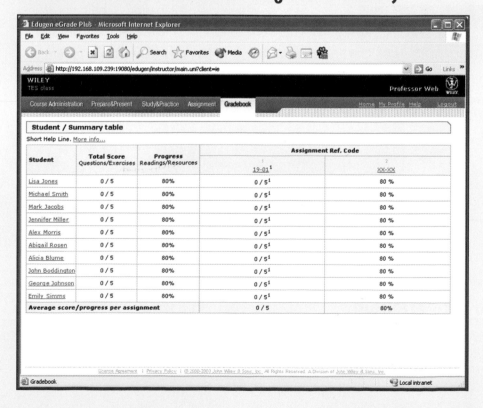

An **Instructor's Gradebook** will keep track of your students' progress and allow you to analyze individual and overall class results to determine their progress and level of understanding

Students,
eGrade Plus Allows You to:

Study More Effectively

Get Immediate Feedback When You Practice on Your Own

eGrade Plus problems link directly to relevant sections of the **electronic book content,** so that you can review the text while you study and complete homework online. Additional resources include **interactive simulations, study guide** and **solutions manual material,** and other problem-solving resources.

Complete Assignments / Get Help with Problem Solving

An **Assignment** area keeps all your assigned work in one location, making it easy for you to stay "on task." In addition, many homework problems contain a **link** to the relevant section of the **multimedia book,** providing you with a text explanation to help you conquer problem-solving obstacles as they arise. You will have access to a variety of **interactive problem-solving tools,** as well as other resources for building your confidence and understanding.

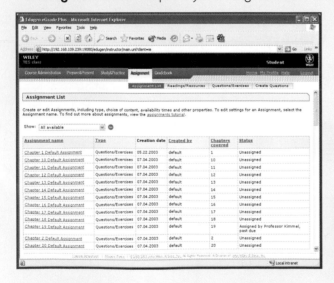

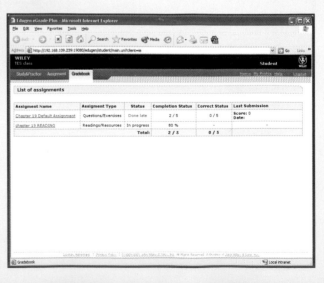

Keep Track of How You're Doing

A **Personal Gradebook** allows you to view your results from past assignments at any time.

eGrade Plus

www.wiley.com/college/schermerhorn
Based on the Activities You Do Every Day

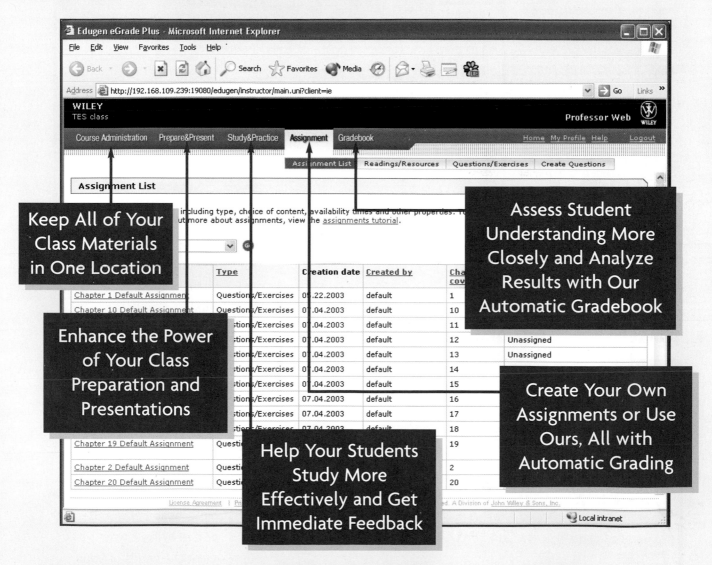

All the content and tools you need, all in one location, in an easy-to-use browser format.

Choose the resources you need, or rely on the arrangement supplied by us.

Now, many of Wiley's textbooks are available with eGrade Plus, a powerful online tool that provides a completely integrated suite of teaching and learning resources in one easy-to-use website. eGrade Plus integrates Wiley's world-renowned content with media, including a multimedia version of the text, PowerPoint slides, and more. Upon adoption of eGrade Plus, you can begin to customize your course with the resources shown here.

See for yourself!

Go to www.wiley.com/college/egradeplus for an online demonstration of this powerful new software.

Keep All of Your Class Materials in One Location

Course Administration tools allow you to manage your class and integrate your eGrade Plus resources with most Course Management Systems, allowing you to keep all of your class materials in one location.

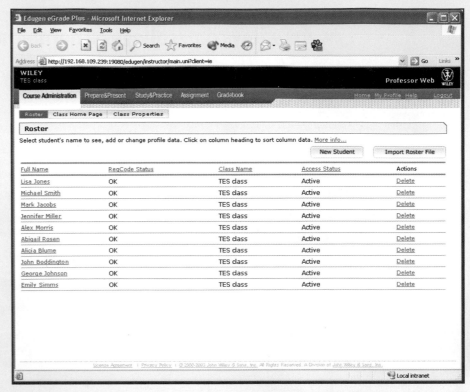

Enhance the Power of Your Class Preparation and Presentations

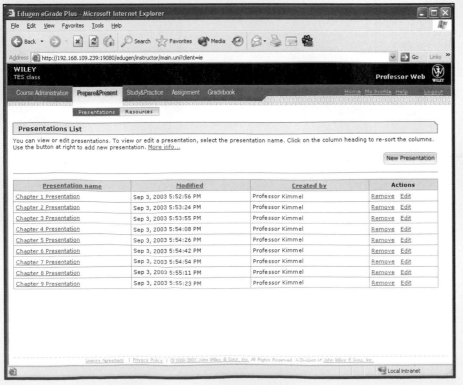

A **Prepare and Present tool** contains all of the Wiley-provided resources, such as **PowerPoint slides** and **student activities,** making your preparation time more efficient. You may easily adapt, customize, and add to Wiley content to meet the needs of your course.

8th EDITION | **Management**

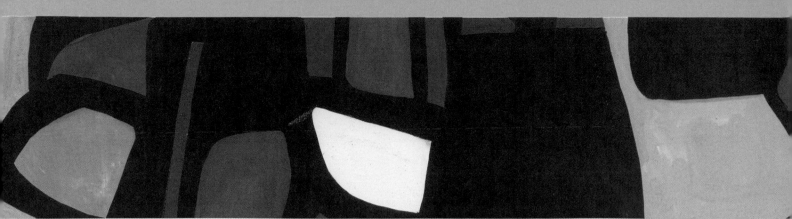

8th EDITION

Management

JOHN R. SCHERMERHORN, JR.

John Wiley & Sons, Inc.

ASSOCIATE PUBLISHER   Judith R. Joseph
PROJECT EDITOR   David Kear
MARKETING MANAGER   David Woodbury
SENIOR PRODUCTION EDITOR   Patricia McFadden
SENIOR DESIGNER   Harry Nolan
SENIOR PHOTO EDITOR   Sara Wight
COVER DESIGN   Harry Nolan
INTERIOR DESIGN   Harry Nolan
ILLUSTRATION COORDINATOR   Sandra Rigby
OUTSIDE PRODUCTION SERVICE   Ingrao Associates

COVER ART   Judith Rothschild
Cummington '41
1946
gouache on board
6 13/16 x 6 3/4 inches
Courtesy of The Judith Rothschild Foundation

CHAPTER OPENER ART   Judith Rothschild
Cummington '41
1946
gouache on board
6 13/16 x 6 3/4 inches
Courtesy of The Judith Rothschild Foundation

This book was set in 10/12 Garamond Book by Progressive Information Technologies
and printed and bound by R.R. Donnelley and Sons. The cover was printed by Lehigh
Press.

This book is printed on acid-free paper. ∞

The paper in this book was manufactured by a mill whose forest management
programs include sustained yield harvesting of its timberlands. Sustained yield
harvesting principles ensure that the number of trees cut each year does not exceed
the amount of new growth.

ISBN: 0-471-45476-1
WIE 0-471 65007-2
Printed in the United States of America
10 9 8 7 6 5 4 3 2 1

About the Author

Dr. John R. Schermerhorn, Jr. is the Charles G. O'Bleness Professor of Management in the College of Business at Ohio University, where he teaches graduate and undergraduate courses in management. Dr. Schermerhorn earned a Ph.D. in organizational behavior from Northwestern University, an MBA (with distinction) in management and international business from New York University, and a BS in business administration from the State University of New York at Buffalo. He has taught at Tulane University, the University of Vermont, and Southern Illinois University at Carbondale, where he also served as Head of the Department of Management and Associate Dean of the College of Business Administration.

Highly dedicated to serving the needs of practicing managers, Dr. Schermerhorn has written *Management 8/e* to help bridge the gaps between the theory and practice of management. At Ohio University Dr. Schermerhorn has been named a University Professor, the university's highest campus-wide honor for excellence in undergraduate teaching. He is committed to instructional excellence and curriculum innovation, and is working extensively with technology utilization in the classroom. He serves as a guest speaker at colleges and universities, lecturing on developments in higher education for business and management, as well as on instructional approaches and innovations.

Dr. Schermerhorn's extensive international experience adds a unique global dimension to his textbooks. He has worked in China, Egypt, Indonesia, Thailand, Malaysia, Vietnam, the Philippines, Poland, Hungary, Venezuela, and Tanzania. He has also served as a Visiting Professor of Management at the Chinese University of Hong Kong, as on-site Coordinator of the Ohio University MBA and Executive MBA programs in Malaysia, and as Kohei Miura visiting professor, Chubu University of Japan. He is also a member of the graduate faculty at Bangkok University, Thailand, serves as advisor to the Lao-American College in Vientiane, Laos, and was recently awarded an honorary doctorate by the University of Pécs Hungary.

A dedicated scholar, Dr. Schermerhorn is a member of the Academy of Management, where he served as chairperson of the Management Education and Development Division. He is known to educators and students alike as senior co-author of *Managing Organizational Behavior 8/e* (Wiley, 2003), *and Core Concepts of Organizational Behavior* (Wiley, 2004). He has also published numerous articles in the *Academy of Management Journal, Academy of Management Review, Academy of Management Executive, Organizational Dynamics, Asia-Pacific Journal of Management,* and the *Journal of Management Development,* among other journals.

To my sons John Christian and Charles Porter

While you played   *It's later now.*   *Think*   *Home,*
I wrote.   *Don't worry.*   *of all the fun*   *now and forever,*
But always,   *Time*   *we have.*   *will always be*
I was listening   *means love shared,*   *Here, there, everywhere,*   *wherever*
and loving   *by you*   *doing things*   *I can be*
you.   *and me.*   *together.*   *with you.*
1984   *1986*   *1989*   *1992*

Time   *Hurry home*   *Songs riding winds.*   *On the mountain,*
has its ways,   *when you can.*   *Mimi,*   *by the Irish lake,*
doesn't it?   *Come laughing, sons.*   *Uncle George,*   *find beauty and*
Not enough,   *Tell us*   *Uncle Nelson.*   *peace.*
not enough,   *your*   *Whispers and choirs.*   *Fairies dance*
I often say.   *wonderful stories.*   *Silence speaks.*   *there.*
1996   *1999*   *2002*   *2004*

Preface

Management today is like the colorful collage featured in the cover art. We live and work in a time of cultural pluralism, globalization, and significant change. Just as a beautiful collage offers the beholder a dynamic mix of colors, forms, and impressions, so too does the new workplace. There is no better time than the present to embrace its rich opportunities and prepare for an exciting future.

MANAGEMENT 8/E PHILOSOPHY

Today's students are tomorrow's leaders and managers. They are the hope of the 21st century. Just as the workplace in this new century will be vastly different from today's, so too must our teaching and learning environments be different from days gone by. Management educators must confidently move students forward on paths toward an uncertain future. New values and management approaches are appearing; the nature of work and organizations is changing; the age of information is not only with us, it is transforming our lives.

Management 8/e is part of the same transformation. This edition has been extensively revised with a sincere commitment to learning in today's complex environment. It is based on four constructive balances that I believe remain essential to the agenda of higher education for business and management.

- *The balance of research insights with formative education.* As educators we must be willing to make choices when bringing the theories and concepts of our discipline to the attention of the introductory student. We cannot do everything in one course. The goal should be to make good content choices and to set the best possible foundations for lifelong learning.

- *The balance of management theory with management practice.* As educators we must understand the compelling needs of students to understand and appreciate the applications of the material they are reading and thinking about. We must continually bring to their attention good, interesting, and recognizable examples.

- *The balance of present understandings with future possibilities.* As educators we must continually search for the directions in which the real world of management is heading. We must select and present materials that can both point students in the right directions and help them develop the confidence and self-respect needed to best deal with them.

- *The balance of what "can" be done with what is, purely and simply, the "right" thing to do.* As educators we are role models; we set the examples. We must be willing to take stands on issues like managerial ethics and corporate social responsibility. We must be careful not to let the concept of "contingency" betray the need for positive "action" and "accountability" in managerial practice.

Today, more than ever before, our students have pressing needs for direction as well as suggestion. They have needs for application as well as information. They have needs for integration as well as presentation. Our instructional approaches and materials must deliver on all of these dimensions and more. My goal is to put into your hands and into those of your students a learning resource that can help meet these needs. *Management 8/e* and its supporting websites are my contributions to the future careers of your students and mine.

MANAGEMENT 8/E HIGHLIGHTS

Management 8/e introduces the essentials of management as they apply within the contemporary work environment. The subject matter is carefully chosen to meet AACSB accreditation guidelines while allowing extensive flexibility to fit various course designs and class sizes. There are many new things to look for in this edition. Along with updates of core material, *Management 8/e* offers a number of changes in the organization, content, and design that respond to current themes and developments in the theory and practice of management.

Organization

- The book is organized into five parts with themes relevant to today's organizations: (1) Introducing Management, (2) Context, (3) Mission, (4) Organization, (5) Leadership.
- *Part 1: Introducing Management*—focuses on understanding managers, what they do, the exciting new workplace, lessons of the past and present, and ethics and social responsibility.
- *Part 2: Context*—explores the contemporary environment in terms of competition, diversity, organization cultures, globalization, cross-cultural management, entrepreneurship, and small business.
- *Part 3: Mission*—addresses how managers use information, information technology, and decision making for planning and controlling, and in the process of strategic management.
- *Part 4: Organization*—reviews traditional and new developments in organization structures, organizational design contingencies and alternatives, as well as systems and work processes.
- *Part 5: Leadership*—presents the major models and current perspectives on leadership, individual behavior and performance, teams and teamwork, communication and interpersonal skills, and change leadership.

Content

In addition to core themes of ethics, diversity, competitive advantage, quality, globalization, and empowerment, specific coverage has been enhanced in *Management 8/e* on the following topics and more:

- Intellectual capital • multicultural organizations • ethnocentrism
- cultural relativism • strategic leadership • competitive advantage
- self-management • crisis management • change leadership • cus-

tomer relationship management • e-business • entrepreneurship • organizational learning • emotional intelligence • horizontal organizations • cross-functional teams • virtual teams • career readiness • virtual organizations • reengineering • work-life balance • strategic human resource planning • boundaryless organizations • performance-based rewards • personality • job stress • alternative work arrangements • cross-cultural communication • conflict management • negotiation • teamwork • innovation processes

Chapter Features

A most important feature of *Management 8/e* is the use of an integrated learning model to help guide students as they read and study for exams. Look for the following features in each chapter.

Planning Ahead—

- Key learning objectives and study questions
- Opening vignette

In Text—

- Learning Preview linking opening vignette to a visual chapter guide
- Learning Checks for each major section and learning objective
- Personal Management feature with recommended self-assessments
- Thematic boxes with current examples on timely themes
- Manager's Notepads with practical guidelines and suggestions
- Reality Checks reporting key facts and surveys
- Take-It-To-The-Case feature introducing chapter case
- Margin photo essays with additional examples
- Margin list identifiers pointing out things to remember
- Margin running glossary with definitions of key terms

End-of-Chapter Study Guide—

- Where We've Been linking back to opening vignette
- The Next Step guide to cases, projects, exercises, and assessments.
- Chapter Summary in bullet-list format
- Key Terms Review for major terms, concepts
- Chapter Self-Test with multiple-choice, short-answer, essay questions

Management Learning Workbook

The expanded Management Learning Workbook in *Management 8/e* provides students and instructors with a rich variety of suggested learning activities.

- Chapter Cases—18 timely cases on well-recognized organizations
- Integrating Cases—two integrating cross-functional cases, including a special focus on ethics and social responsibility

- Active Learning Projects—10 suggestions for student projects (individual or group), including management in popular culture and service learning
- Exercises in Teamwork—30 exercises for in-class and out-of-class use
- Self-Assessments—30 personality and self-reflection instruments
- Student Portfolio Builder—a special guide to building a student portfolio complete with professional résumé and competency documentations

Student Website

An extensive Student Website supports *Management 8/e* both for classroom applications and for distance learning environments. This site, available at www.wiley.com/college/schermerhorn, includes the following special student learning resources.

- PowerPoint downloads for text and supplementary figures
- Interactive on-line versions of in-chapter Reality Checks
- Interactive on-line versions of all cases
- Interactive on-line versions of self-assessments
- An on-line study guide for students, including PowerPoint chapter reviews and chapter self-tests

Instructor's Support

Management 8/e comes with a comprehensive resource package that assists the instructor in creating a motivating and enthusiastic learning environment.

- *Complete Instructor's Resource Guide*—offers helpful teaching ideas, advice on course development, sample assignments, and chapter-by-chapter text highlights, learning objectives, lecture outlines, class exercises, lecture notes, answers to end-of-chapter material, and tips on using cases.
- *The Authors Classroom*—a unique Web resource offering the author's personal classroom materials from special PowerPoint slides to quick-hitting learning activities.
- *Comprehensive Test Bank*—completely updated and linked to the chapter "Learning Checks," questions are categorized by pedagogical element (margin notes, margin terms, or general text knowledge), page number, and type of questions. The entire test bank is available in a computerized version, MICROSOFT Diploma for windows, created by Brownstone Research Group.
- *Video Package*—offering video selections from the business news Nightly Business Report video supplements also available for the integrating cases.
- *Web CT and Blackboard*—full support.

Acknowledgments

Management 8/e was initiated and completed with the support of my new editor Judith Joseph (associate publisher), my superb project editor, David Kear, and the assistance of a talented group of Wiley personnel: Susan Elbe (publisher), Harold Nolan (designer), Sara Wight (photo research), Suzanne Ingrao (Ingrao Associates), Patricia McFadden and Jeanine Furino (production), David Woodbury (marketing), and with the help of Anna Melhorn (illustrations), and Teri Stratford (photos).

Michael K. McCuddy and Wendy Pirie of *Valparaiso University* were the Case Editors for this project. The Integrating Case on Outback Steakhouse is from George Puia of *Indiana State University* and Marilyn Taylor, *University of Missouri,* Kansas City. Michael K. McCuddy also provided the instructor's resource guide and test bank.

Writing and revising *Management 8/e* came during yet further transitions in our family. I remain grateful to Ann, Christian, and Porter for allowing me to continue this project. I sincerely hope the results meet their expectations. I am also grateful for the support by *Chubu University* during my stay as Kohei Miura visiting professor.

I am grateful to the following colleagues whose help with this book at various stages of its life added to my understanding. Allen Amason, *University of Georgia;* Lydia Anderson, *Fresno City College;* Hal Babson, *Columbus State Community College;* Marvin Bates, *Benedictine University;* Joy Benson, *University of Wisconsin–Green Bay;* Peggy Brewer, *Eastern Kentucky University;* Jim Buckenmyer, *Southeast Missouri State University;* William Clark, *Leeward Community College;* Jeanie Diemer, *Ivy Tech State College;* Richard Eisenbeis, *Colorado State University–Pueblo;* Phyllis Flott, *Tennessee State University;* Shelly Gardner, *Augustana College;* Tommy Georgiades, *DeVry University;* Marvin Gordon, *University of Illinois–Chicago;* Carol Harvey, *Assumption College;* Lenie Holbrook, *Ohio University;* Marvin Karlins, *University of South Florida;* Beverly Little, *Western Carolina University;* Kurt Martsolf, *California State University–Hayward;* Brian Maruffi, *Fordham University;* Brenda McAleer, *University of Maine at Augusta;* Donald Mosley, *University of South Alabama;* Behnam Nakhai, *Millersville University of Pennsylvania;* Robert Nale, *Coastal Carolina University;* John Overby, *The University of Tennessee–Martin;* Javier Pagan, *University of Puerto Rico–Piedras;* Diana Page, *University of West Florida;* Wendy Pike, *Benedictine University;* Newman Pollack, *Florida Atlantic University;* Jenny Rink, *Community College of Philadelphia;* Joseph Santora, *Essex County College;* Rajib Sanyal, *The College of New Jersey;* Roy Shin, *Indiana University;* Shanthi Srinivas, *California State Polytechnic University–Pomona;* Howard Stanger, *Canisius College;* William Stevens, *Missouri Southern State College;* Chuck Stubbart, *Southern Illinois University;* Harry Stucke, *Long Island University;* Thomas Thompson, *University of Maryland;* Judy Thompson, *Briar Cliff University;* Michael Troyer, *University of Wisconsin–Green Bay;* Jeffrey Ward, *Edmonds Community College;* James Whitney, *Champlain College;* Garland Wiggs, *Radford University;* Eric Wiklendt, *University of Northern Iowa;* Yichuan Zhao, *Dalian Maritime University.*

How to Use This Book

Each chapter opens with **Planning Ahead**—a set of **study questions** that provides learning objectives for the chapter and a framework for the end-of-chapter review.

Planning Ahead

After reading Chapter 1, you should be able to answer these questions in your own words.

CHAPTER 1 study questions

1. **What are the challenges of working in the new economy?**
2. **What are organizations like in the new workplace?**
3. **Who are managers and what do they do?**
4. **What is the management process?**
5. **How do you learn the essential managerial skills and competencies?**

As the leading global online career site, Monster.com represents the growing field of online job placement services available on the Web. Its founder, Jeff Taylor, describes its birth this way: "One morning I woke up at 4 a.m., and wrote an idea down on a pad of paper I keep next to my bed. I had this dream that I created a bulletin board called the Monster Board. That became the original name for the company. When I got up, I went to a coffee shop, and from 5:30 a.m. until about 10:00 a.m. I wrote the user interface for what today is Monster.com."

Media Metrix has called Monster.com the number-one destination for job seekers and one of the most visited domains on the Internet. It hosts over 36 million job seeker accounts. Job candidates search Monster's 800,000 job postings, some 175 million times each month. They also use Monster for interviewing advice, company research, and even moving tips.

Monster.com represents itself as a "lifelong career network" that serves everyone from recent college graduates all the way up to seasoned executives.

The **Opening Vignette** is a timely, real-world example that highlights chapter themes. The example is visited again in the end-of chapter **Where We've Been**.

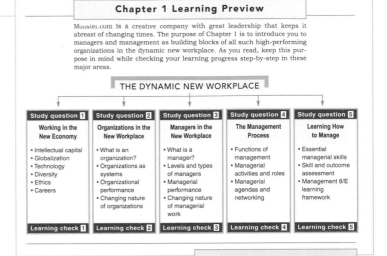

Chapter 1 Learning Preview

Monster.com is a creative company with great leadership that keeps it abreast of changing times. The purpose of Chapter 1 is to introduce you to managers and management as building blocks of all such high-performing organizations in the dynamic new workplace. As you read, keep this purpose in mind while checking your learning progress step-by-step in these major areas.

THE DYNAMIC NEW WORKPLACE

Study question **1**	Study question **2**	Study question **3**	Study question **4**	Study question **5**
Working in the New Economy	**Organizations in the New Workplace**	**Managers in the New Workplace**	**The Management Process**	**Learning How to Manage**
• Intellectual capital • Globalization • Technology • Diversity • Ethics • Careers	• What is an organization? • Organizations as systems • Organizational performance • Changing nature of organizations	• What is a manager? • Levels and types of managers • Managerial performance • Changing nature of managerial work	• Functions of management • Managerial activities and roles • Managerial agendas and networking	• Essential managerial skills • Skill and outcome assessment • Management 8/E learning framework
Learning check **1**	Learning check **2**	Learning check **3**	Learning check **4**	Learning check **5**

The **Learning Preview** links the Opening Vignette with the major topics of the chapter and includes a graphic outline of major topics.

PERSONAL MANAGEMENT

SELF-AWARENESS is one of those concepts that is easy to talk about but very hard to master. What do you really know about yourself? How often do you take a critical look at your attitudes, behaviors, skills, and accomplishments? Do you ever realistically assess your personal strengths and weaknesses—both as you see them and as others do? A high degree of self-awareness is essential for personal adaptability, to be able to grow and develop in changing times. This figure, called the Johari Window, offers a way of comparing what we know about ourselves with what others know about us.[59] Our "open" areas are often small, while the "blind spot," "the unknown," and the "hidden" areas can be quite large. Think about the personal implications of the Johari Window. Are you willing to probe the unknown, uncover your blind spots, and discover talents and weaknesses that may be hidden? As your self-awareness expands, you will find many insights for personal growth and development.

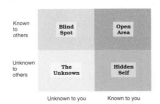

	Unknown to you	Known to you
Known to others	**Blind Spot**	**Open Area**
Unknown to others	**The Unknown**	**Hidden Self**

Get to know yourself better ▶
Complete Self-Assessments #1—**21st Century Manager**, and #2—**Emotional Intelligence**, from the Management Learning Workbook.

The **Personal Management** feature integrates each chapter with personal development issues, including how to "get to know yourself better" by using key learning resources in the end-of-chapter **Management Learning Workbook**.

Thematic Boxes with photo-illustrated examples are embedded in each chapter. Themes are: **Career Connection, Around the World, and In Practice**.

IN PRACTICE

High-performance leadership values people

When Xerox needed to change or go out of business, its Board of Directors turned to an experienced insider for leadership. Their choice was Anne Mulcahy, a company veteran who had worked her way to the top in a 27-year career. With an undergraduate degree in English and journalism, Mulcahy brought a charismatic and hands-on style of leadership to the struggling firm. She began by flying around the world to personally visit Xerox employees in all locations. Her goals were to raise morale and motivation, and refocus on future operations. Named the sixth most powerful woman in the world by *Fortune* magazine, Mulcahy says: "People have to feel engaged, motivated and feel they are making a contribution to something that is important."[9]

www.hudson.org

A Global Perspective
The Hudson Institute is an internationally recognized public policy research organization. Concerns for the digital future, global food issues, and workforce development are active themes in the institute's policy centers.

Margin Photo Essays give short examples relevant to chapter topics

○ **Prejudice** is the display of negative, irrational attitudes toward women or minorities.

○ **Discrimination** actively denies women and minorities the full benefits of organizational membership.

○ The **glass ceiling effect** is an invisible barrier limiting career advancement of women and minorities.

○ **Ethics** set moral standards of what is "good" and "right" in one's behavior.

Boldfaced key terms are called out and defined in the margins, forming a **Margin Running Glossary**.

TAKE IT TO THE CASE

One Every 15 Seconds

Apple Computer Inc.
Where people and design create the future
Innovative design is a mainstay of Apple's business model. But there's more to the company than that. Under the leadership of co-founder Steve Jobs, Apple is a model of operating efficiency and marketing savvy. He claims we are entering the third and "golden age" of personal computing.[41] With this vision, there is no doubt that Jobs brings passion, inventiveness, and a great eye for customer markets to the firm. But the execution comes from people and the team-driven, technology-rich, and talent-based high-performance environment that represents life within Apple. If you want to study a company that operates in the world of the new economy with a new workforce and new organization, take a look at Apple. Even in the intensely competitive computer industry, the wizardry of Apple sets a benchmark for the rest of the pack.

Margin List Notes call attention to key bulleted or numbered lists throughout the text.

← Key personal characteristics for managerial success

A Critical Thinking Case for each chapter is introduced with **Take-It-To-The-Case**, which applies the case to the material being discussed.

Innovative **Reality Checks** in each chapter introduce key facts or survey results relevant to text discussion. Each is linked to an interactive on-line activity that probes further into the issue.

REALITY CHECK 1.1

Barriers to avancement for women of color
A comprehensive three-year study reported by Catalyst identified the four most commonly identified barriers cited by women of color that limit their paths upward in business. Lack of high-visibility assignments was one of the barriers. Take the online "Reality Check" to learn more.

should mean "enabling or her potential." A femal of man environ tributi

Eve be mad study corpora nies w from 8 up fro women force,

Critical survival skills for the new workplace | MANAGER'S NOTEPAD 1.1

- *Mastery:* You need be good at something; you need to be able to contribute something of value to your employer.
- *Contacts:* You need to know people; links with peers and others within and outside the organization are essential to get things done.
- *Entrepreneurship:* You must act as if you are running your own business, spotting ideas and opportunities, and stepping out to embrace them.
- *Love of technology:* You have to embrace technology; you don't have to be a technician, but you must be willing and able to fully utilize IT.
- *Marketing:* You need to be able to communicate your successes and progress, both yours personally and those of your work group.
- *Passion for renewal:* You need to be continuously learning and changing, always updating yourself to best meet future demands.

Manager's Notepads in each chapter offer lists of helpful "do's" and don'ts" of managerial behavior.

Learning check 2

Be sure you can • describe how organizations operate as open systems • explain productivity as a measure of organizational performance • list several ways in which organizations are changing today • distinguish between performance effectiveness and performance efficiency • explain the concept of TQM

At the end of each section, **Learning Checks** prompt you to stop and review the key points you have just studied. If you cannot answer these questions, you should go back and read the section again.

Where We've Been

BACK TO MONSTER.COM

The opening example of Monster.com focused on you, your career, and the great opportunities for career success that exist in today's dynamic environment. You don't need to create your own company like Jeff Taylor did to achieve career success, although you could. What you must do, is discover the learning "monster" within yourself and commit it to academic success and career development. In Chapter 1 you learned about the new work environment, from the challenges of technology utilization, to the forces of globalization, to diversity and ethical behavior, and more. You also gained insight into the nature of organizations, the managerial roles, and the critical importance of developing essential managerial and leadership skills.

Each chapter ends with **Where We've Been**, which looks back at the chapter opening vignette as a helpful reminder for summary and review purposes

---

THE NEXT STEP
INTEGRATED LEARNING ACTIVITIES

Cases/Projects	Self-Assessments	Experiential Exercises
• Apple Computer, Case	• A 21st-Century Manager (#1)	• My Best Manager (#1)
• Outback Steakhouse, Case	• Emotional Intelligence (#2)	• What Managers Do (#2)
• Project 1—Diversity Lessons	• Diversity Awareness (#7)	• Defining Quality (#3)
• Enron and Anderson case	• Are You Cosmopolitan? (#18)	• The Future Workplace (#14)

The Next Step directs you to cases, projects, self-assessments, and experiential exercises included in the **Management Learning Workbook** at the back of the text.

STUDY QUESTIONS SUMMARY

1. What are the challenges of working in the new economy?

• Today's turbulent environment challenges everyone to understand and embrace continuous change and developments in a new information-driven and global economy.
• Work in the new economy is increasingly knowledge based, and people, with their capacity to bring valuable intellectual capital to the workplace, are the ultimate foundation of organizational performance.
• The forces of globalization are bringing increased interdependencies among nations and economies, as customer markets and resource ate intense business competition.

• Ever-present developments in information technology and the continued expansion of the Internet are reshaping organizations, changing the nature of work, and increasing the value of knowledge workers.
• Organizations must value the talents and capabilities of a workforce whose members are increasingly diverse with respect to gender, age, race and ethnicity, able-bodiedness, and lifestyles.
• Society has high expectations for organizations and their members to perform with commitment to high ethical standards and in socially responsible ways, including protection of the natural environment and human rights.

The **Summary** is a bullet list summary of key points for each chapter opening Study Question.

SELF-TEST 1

MULTIPLE-CHOICE QUESTIONS:

1. The process of management involves the functions of planning, _____, leading, and controlling.
   (a) accounting (b) creating (c) innovating (d) organizing

2. An effective manager achieves both high-performance results and high levels of _____ among people doing the required work.
   (a) turnover (b) effectiveness (c) satisfaction (d) stress

3. Performance efficiency is a measure of the _____ associated with task accomplishment.
   (a) resource costs (b) goal specificity (c) product quality (d) product quantity

4. The requirement that a manager answer to a higher-level boss for results achieved by a work team is called _____.
   (a) dependency (b) accountability (c) authority (d) empowerment

An end-of-chapter **Self-Test** helps assess your understanding of key chapter topics, including multiple-choice, short response and essay questions.

KEY TERMS REVIEW

Accountability (p. 17)
Administrators (p. 17)
Conceptual skill (p. 24)
Controlling (p. 21)
Corporate governance (p. 9)
Discrimination (p. 8)
Emotional intelligence (p. 24)
Ethics (p. 8)
Functional managers (p. 17)
General managers (p. 17)
Glass ceiling effect (p. 8)
Globalization (p. 6)
Human skill (p. 24)
Intellectual capital (p. 6)

Knowledge worker (p. 6)
Leading (p. 20)
Lifelong learning (p. 23)
Line managers (p. 17)
Management (p. 19)
Manager (p. 15)
Managerial competency (p. 24)
Middle managers (p. 16)
Open system (p. 12)
Organization (p. 11)
Organizing (p. 20)
Performance effectiveness (p. 12)
Performance efficiency (p. 13)

Planning (p. 20)
Prejudice (p. 8)
Productivity (p. 12)
Project managers (p. 16)
Quality of work life (p. 17)
Skill (p. 23)
Staff managers (p. 17)
Supervisor (p. 16)
Team leader (p. 16)
Technical skill (p. 24)
Top managers (p. 15)
Total quality management TQM (p. 14)
Workforce diversity (p. 7)

The **Key Terms List** is a reminder about key concepts, along with page references where they are defined.

The **Management Learning Workbook** is an end-of-text learning resource complete with a wide variety of cases, active learning projects, experiential exercises, self-assessments, and student portfolio builder to enrich and extend student learning.

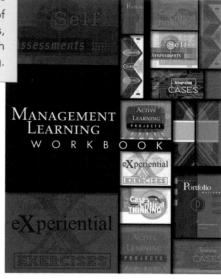

The **Cases for Critical Thinking** section in the *Management Learning Workbook* contains 18 cases, with each based on actual organizations and specifically developed for a text chapter.

Two **Cross-Functional Cases** in the *Management Learning Workbook* extend critical thinking case analysis across management functions. One case focuses on an entrepreneurial business and the other on ethical business decision making.

Ten **Active Learning Projects** in the *Management Learning Workbook* engage students in research and presentation projects on timely management topics, as well as in both service learning and an exploration of management themes in popular culture.

A portfolio of 30 **Experiential Exercises** in the *Management Learning Workbook* help students experience through teamwork a various issues and practical aspects of chapter.

The **Student Portfolio** section of the *Management Learning Workbook* provides students with a template for building a student portfolio to summarize academic outcomes and display career credentials to potential employers.

A set of 30 **Self-assessment** inventories **Exercises** in the *Management Learning Workbook* involves students in exploring their personal managerial tendencies and perspectives.

Brief Contents

Contents

PART TWO ■ CONTEXT

PART THREE ■ MISSION

PART FOUR ■ ORGANIZATION

PART FIVE ■ LEADERSHIP

MANAGEMENT LEARNING WORKBOOK ∎

Experiential Exercises   W-72

Self-Assessments   W-92

Student Portfolio Builder   W-128

Memorandum

To: *Management 8/e Readers*
From: *Professor Schermerhorn*
Subject: *Personal Management*

Welcome to *Management 8/e* and its theme—"personal management."

We live and work today in very complex times. The uncertainties of international relations, the economic forces of globalization, and business ethics scandals are just three of the emerging forces and trends that are having an undeniable impact on our society. The dynamics of ever-present change extend into the workplace and raise for all of us a host of new career challenges. There is no better time than now to commit your energies and intellect to continuous learning and personal development. Indeed, your future depends on it.

Management 8/e is designed with your learning and personal development in mind. A major goal is to help you join the world of work on your terms, and in a positive and progressive way. Importantly, this edition emphasizes *personal management*—the ability to understand yourself individually and in the social context, to assess personal strengths and weaknesses, to exercise initiative, to accept responsibility for accomplishments, to work well with others, and to adapt by continually learning from experience in the quest for self-improvement.

Every chapter of *Management 8/e* contains a Personal Management Box written to help you personalize the topics, theories, and applications. The boxes raise issues, offer tips, ask questions, and suggest learning activities for your professional development. If you take full advantage of them, your confidence will grow and your portfolio of career skills and attitudes will expand.

Management 8/e is a student's book. I teach management every year to undergraduate and graduate students. Just as when I work with them, my goal here is to bring to you the best of my knowledge and experience. Although we can't be in class together, we can meet through the pages and learning activities of *Management 8/e,* and through the resources of the companion website: www.wiley.com/college/schermerhorn

Please join my students and me in working hard to make your introductory study of management a positive and relevant learning experience—one with rich and enduring personal management implications. Get started by reading my attached primer on "Personal Management and Career Readiness."

PERSONAL MANAGEMENT AND CAREER READINESS

In my Memorandum to the Reader, I describe **personal management** as an essential skill, one that is critical for your continued growth and career success. It is the ability to understand yourself individually and in the social context, to assess personal strengths and weaknesses, to exercise initiative, to accept responsibility, to work well with others, and to adapt by continually learning from experience.

One of the best ways to demonstrate personal management is in the way you approach college, your academic courses, and the rich variety of related development opportunities that are available on campus and off. Your introductory course in management offers many ways to explore existing skills and capabilities, and to identify and develop new ones. It will also be rich in ideas and suggestions that can help you find career direction and establish the personal foundations for life-long career success. But always remember: What happens is up to you! Thus, there is no better time than the present to commit to yourself to learning and personal growth.

The Brand Called "You"

The best career advice returns again and again to the message just delivered: What happens is up to you. Don't let yourself down, now or in the future. Step forward and take charge of your continued learning and professional development. Build, refine, and market what author and consultant Tom Peters refers to as the "brand called you." He advises each of us to work hard to create and maintain a unique and timely package of skills and capabilities with career potential. In Peters's words, your personal brand should be "remarkable, measurable, distinguished, and distinctive."[2] It has to set you apart positively from the competition—others who, like you, want good jobs and satisfying careers in today's very challenging economic times.

Building a Student Portfolio

A good way to visualize and package this "brand called you" is in a **student portfolio**—a compendium of materials that document your accomplishments in college and communicate to others your skills and career readiness.[3] In the Management Learning Workbook included with *Management 8/e* you will find an introduction to student portfolios, including a basic template for building one of your own—both in print and in electronic form. A student portfolio will help you begin the process of brand building and to prepare step-by-step your credentials for maximum career impact. Your portfolio, as suggested in this screen shot of the front page from an electronic portfolio, should include at a minimum an up-to-date résumé, a list of courses in your major and related areas, and a summary of relevant skills.

OHIO UNIVERSITY

Resume
Skills
Courses
Contact
Information

Elena Macapagal
copeland@ohio.edu

College of Business

At Ohio University, we use portfolios to help students focus their learning and also to document achievements for both academic and employment purposes. The first thing that building a student portfolio reminds you is that a good résumé is essential. It should present your experiences and accomplishments in a professional and compelling way. Your résumé should catch the attention of potential employers or internship sponsors, and differentiate you from others who want the same positions. A commitment to résumé building and personal management throughout one's college years can create a very substantial foundation of work experience. In the example shown, the résumé helped a student obtain her first choice of full-time employment after graduation. Importantly, her résumé wasn't created for the one interview, and it wasn't created overnight. It was built step-by-step as she progressed through college and used her time well with a goal in mind—getting the job she wanted upon graduation.

WORK EXPERIENCE	**American Express Financial Advisors**, Hudson, Ohio June 2000 - December 2002
	Intern

- Successfully promoted beneficial offerings to existing clients and worked alongside a senior financial advisor in a mentorship program
- Handled advisor projects and assisted client-advisor seminars and meetings
- Planned/managed client-appreciation nights including over 300 clients
- Built relationships with clients through telecommunication
- Supported advisors in various marketing/promotion projects
- Enhanced company communication through the OST and IDSNet database
- Handled and organized accurate and confidential financial documents to help serve clients effectively
- Helped advisors provide clients with an efficient, effective, and comfortable financial portfolio

College Book Store, Athens, Ohio September 2002 - December 2002
Service Desk Representative
- Handled customer questions, complaints, concerns

STUDENT ACTIVITIES	**American Marketing Association** September 2000 - June 2002
	Market Research Committee

- Researched current market conditions and interesting current practices
- Assisted in the organization of various AMA events

A student portfolio is also a way to document how the learning from your courses and other activities creates a core set of personal skills and competencies. As shown in the screenshot example, I encourage my students to document for me and potential employers their competencies in professionalism, leadership, communication, teamwork, critical thinking, and self-management. I also encourage students to be specific and make sure that their unique talents are well described. In the screen shot example, you can see how this student used her study of Japanese language and culture to show readiness for an international business career. Other documentation in her portfolio includes a paper on international relations—demonstrating critical-thinking skills and a letter written to a summer employer offering a proposal for job advancement—demonstrating professionalism and communication skills.

SKILLS

Communication
Demonstrates ability to share ideas and findings clearly in written and oral expression.
Group Contract - I wrote this contract for a group I was a member of after discussing and agreeing upon each issue.
Japanese composition - This composition is written in Japanese. The topic was to describe a person whom we admire.

Critical Thinking
Demonstrates ability to gather and analyze information for creative problem solving.
International Relations - This paper is regarding order and stability in the current international system, based on the international relations theories of realism and liberalism.

Leading
Demonstrates ability to influence and support others to perform complex and ambiguous tasks.
Multinational Business Group Leader - As the group leader for this presentation, I helped direct the research involved and the direction our recommendations took for Umberto Bilancioni (Italian Retailer).

Professionalism
Demonstrates ability to sustain a positive impression, instill confidence and advance in a career.
Job Proposal for advancement - The attached work proposal was presented to my current employers. They had previously asked me of my intentions after graduation. Since this proposal was given to them I was offered a position within the company and have accepted their offer.

Early Career Advice

The management of one's career and career development is extremely challenging in times like ours where change is ever-present, fast-moving, and often unpredictable. The challenges are often magnified at the point of career entry, when one is beginning a new job with a new employer. In terms of early career advice, consider the following lessons taken from my experience and from what my past students have told me.

Lesson one: There is no substitute for performance. No matter what the assignment, you must work hard to quickly establish your credibility and value in any new job.

Lesson two: Be and stay flexible. Don't hide from ambiguity; don't wait for structure. Instead, you must always be able and willing to adapt personally to new work demands, new situations and people, and new organizational forms.

Lesson three: Keep the focus. You can't go forward without talent. You must commit to continuous learning and professional development. In order to get and stay ahead in a career during very competitive times, you must become a talent builder—someone who is always adding to and refining your talents to make them valuable to an employer.

This early career advice places emphasis once again on your commitment to personal management, and on your ability to stay disciplined in continuously taking stock of yourself and seeking the learning available in your daily experiences. You must always be willing to learn. And sometimes, the very best learning comes from situations that you might otherwise turn away from—those that present problems, create anxieties, and otherwise prove difficult for you to deal with.

According to author and consultant Stephen Covey, the foundations for career success are within everyone's grasp. But the motivation and the effort required to succeed must come from within. Only you can make this commitment, and it is best made right from the beginning. Covey's advice is to take charge of your destiny and move your career forward by: (1) behaving like an entrepreneur, (2) seeking feedback on your performance continually, (3) setting up your own mentoring systems, (4) getting comfortable with teamwork, (5) taking risks to gain experience and learn new skills, (6) being a problem solver, and (7) keeping your life in balance.[4]

Sustaining Career Advantage

One of the important things you will learn in *Management 8/e* is the strategic management concept of "competitive advantage"—core competency that delivers high value and is very difficult for competitors to imitate. Just like an organization that must find competitive advantage and then continually innovate to maintain it, you too must adapt and grow with the demands of an ever-changing workplace, economy, and career environment. As shown in the last screen shot, you must achieve a sustainable career advantage—a combination of personal attributes, skills, and capabilities that allows you to consistently outperform others.

Management 8/e is rich with insights into the new workplace, the nature of managerial work, and the great challenges organizations face in a highly competitive global economy. As you move forward in this exciting world of work, you must commit to personal management, continuous learning, and the process of brand building for a satisfying life-long career. Always remember the goal: sustainable career advantage. And you must never forget that its achievement is up to you.

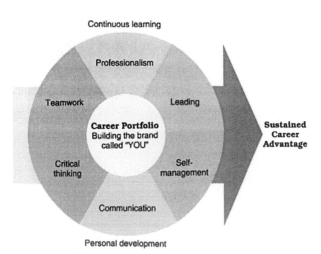

Make the commitment to move forward, right now, in your management course. Get connected with learning and with yourself. Use the personal management resources of *Management 8/e* and its Management Learning Workbook to establish your career readiness and set a strong foundation for personal fulfillment and life-long career success.

[1] Tom Peters, "Is Your Job Your Calling," *Fast Company* (February–March, 1998), p. 108.

[2] Tom Peters, "The Brand Called You," *Fast Company,* (August–September 1997); "The New Wired World of Work," *Business Week* (August 28, 2000), pp. 172–173.

[3] See David S. Chappell and John R. Schermerhorn, Jr., "Electronic Student Portfolios in Management Education," Chapter 5 in Charles Wankel and Robert DeFillipi (Eds.), *Educating Managers with Tomorrow's Technologies* (Greenwich, Conn.: Information Age Publishing, 2003), pp. 101–130.

[4] Stephen Covey, "How to Succeed in Today's Workplace," *USA Weekend* (August 29–31, 1997), pp. 4–5.

1

The dynamic new workplace

CHAPTER 1 study questions

Planning Ahead

After reading Chapter 1, you should be able to answer these questions in your own words.

MONSTER.COM—SMART PEOPLE CREATE THEIR OWN FUTURES

As the leading global online career site, Monster.com represents the growing field of online job placement services available on the Web. Its founder, Jeff Taylor, describes its birth this way: "One morning I woke up at 4 a.m., and wrote an idea down on a pad of paper I keep next to my bed. I had this dream that I created a bulletin board called the Monster Board. That became the original name for the company. When I got up, I went to a coffee shop, and from 5:30 a.m. until about 10:00 a.m. I wrote the user interface for what today is Monster.com."

Media Metrix has called Monster.com the number-one destination for job seekers and one of the most visited domains on the Internet. It hosts over 36 million job seeker accounts. Job candidates search Monster's 800,000 job postings, some 175 million times each month. They also use Monster for interviewing advice, company research, and even moving tips.

Monster.com represents itself as a "lifelong career network" that serves everyone from recent college graduates all the way up to seasoned executives.

There's no complacency here, no becoming comfortable with success. The "Monster" keeps changing as its markets develop. Monster.com provides career advice serving professional development needs; Monstermoving.com helps in planning relocations. Monster users can research companies throughout the United States and overseas in 20 foreign countries, including France, Germany, Singapore, Australia, and others.

Headquartered in Maynard, Massachusetts, Monster.com is the flagship brand of the Interactive division of TMP Worldwide Inc., one of the world's largest search and selection agencies. Its clients include almost all the *Fortune* 500 companies.[1]

> **Get Connected!**
>
> You too can create a monster. Use resources from the end-of-text *Management Learning Workbook* to write your résumé and build a Student Portfolio.

Chapter 1 Learning Preview

Monster.com is a creative company with great leadership that keeps it abreast of changing times. The purpose of Chapter 1 is to introduce you to managers and management as building blocks of all such high-performing organizations in the dynamic new workplace. As you read, keep this purpose in mind while checking your learning progress step-by-step in these major areas.

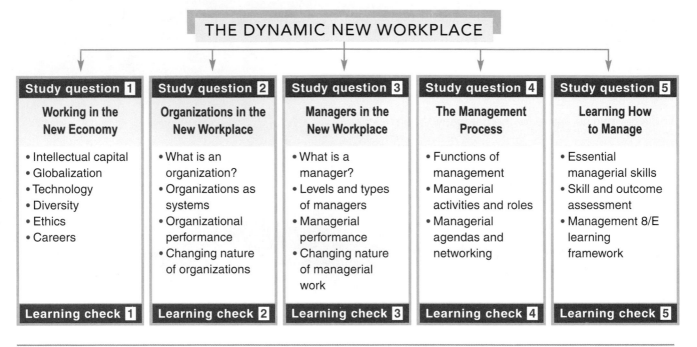

THE DYNAMIC NEW WORKPLACE

Study question 1	Study question 2	Study question 3	Study question 4	Study question 5
Working in the New Economy	**Organizations in the New Workplace**	**Managers in the New Workplace**	**The Management Process**	**Learning How to Manage**
• Intellectual capital • Globalization • Technology • Diversity • Ethics • Careers	• What is an organization? • Organizations as systems • Organizational performance • Changing nature of organizations	• What is a manager? • Levels and types of managers • Managerial performance • Changing nature of managerial work	• Functions of management • Managerial activities and roles • Managerial agendas and networking	• Essential managerial skills • Skill and outcome assessment • Management 8/E learning framework
Learning check 1	Learning check 2	Learning check 3	Learning check 4	Learning check 5

The 21st century has brought with it a new workplace, one in which everyone must adapt to a rapidly changing society with constantly shifting demands and opportunities. Learning and speed are in; habit and complacency are out. Organizations are fast changing, as is the nature of work itself. The economy is global, driven by innovation and technology. Even the concept of success, personal and organizational, is evolving as careers take new forms and organizations transform to serve new customer expectations. These developments, say the editors of *Fast Company* magazine, affect us all, offering both "unparalleled opportunity and unprecedented uncertainty." In this age of continuous challenge, a compelling message must be heard by all of us—smart people and smart organizations create their own futures.[2]

In the quest for the future the best employers share an important commitment—they value people! They offer supportive work environments that allow people's talents to be fully utilized while providing them with both valued rewards and respect for work-life balance. In progressive organizations, employees benefit from flexible work schedules, on-site child care, health and fitness centers, domestic partner benefits, as well as opportunities for profit sharing, cash bonuses, and competitive salaries. In short, the best employers are not just extremely good at attracting and retaining talented employees. They also excel at creating a high-performance context in which everyone's abilities are highly valued.

After studying high-performing companies, management scholars Charles O'Reilly and Jeffrey Pfeffer conclude that success is achieved because they are better than their competitors at getting extraordinary results from the people working for them. "These companies have won the war for talent," they say, "not just by being great places to work—although they are that—but by figuring out how to get the best out of all of their people, every day."[3] This, in large part, is what *Management 8/e* and your management course are all about. Both are designed to introduce you to the concepts, themes, and directions that are consistent with career success and organizational leadership in today's high-performance work settings. As you begin, let your study of management be devoted to learning as much as you can to prepare for a career-long commitment to getting great things accomplished through working with and valuing people.

WORKING IN THE NEW ECONOMY

Yes, we now live and work in a new economy ripe with challenging opportunities and dramatic uncertainty.[4] It is a networked economy in which people, institutions, and nations are increasingly influenced by the Internet and continuing developments in information technology.[5] The chapter opener on Monster.com is but one example of how the Web and its vast networking capabilities are changing our lives. The new economy is global, and the nations of the world are increasingly interdependent. The new economy is also knowledge based, and success is forged in workplaces continually reinvented to unlock the great potential of human intelligence. The themes of the day are "respect," "participation," "empowerment," "involvement," "teamwork," "self-management," and more.

Undoubtedly, too, the new economy is performance driven. Expectations for organizations and their members are very high. Success must be earned in a society that demands nothing less than the best from all its institutions. Organizations are expected to continuously excel on performance criteria that include concerns for ethics and social responsibilities, innovativeness, and employee development, as well as more traditional measures of profitability and investment value. When they fail, customers, investors, and employees are quick to let them know. For individuals, there are no guarantees of long-term employment. Jobs are increasingly earned and re-earned every day through one's performance accomplishments. Careers are being redefined in terms of "flexibility," "free agency," "skill portfolios," and "enterpreneurship." Today, it takes initiative and discipline and continuous learning to stay in charge of your own career destiny. Tomorrow's challenges are likely to be even greater.

Just what are the challenges ahead?

INTELLECTUAL CAPITAL

The dynamic pathways into the future are evident among new benchmarks being set in and by progressive organizations everywhere. At Herman Miller, the innovative manufacturer of designer furniture, respect for employees is a rule of thumb. The firm's core values include the statement: "Our greatest assets as a corporation are the gifts, talents and abili-

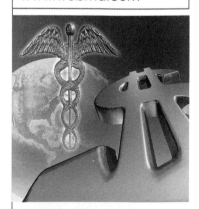

www.webmd.com

WebMD offers online connectivity and a full suite of healthcare services. It is also a global citizen, using the Internet in a plan to deliver medical assistance to people in the world's poorest nations.

High-performance leadership values people

When Xerox needed to change or go out of business, its Board of Directors turned to an experienced insider for leadership. Their choice was Anne Mulcahy, a company veteran who had worked her way to the top in a 27-year career. With an undergraduate degree in English and journalism, Mulcahy brought a charismatic and hands-on style of leadership to the struggling firm. She began by flying around the world to personally visit Xerox employees in all locations. Her goals were to raise morale and motivation, and refocus on future operations. Named the sixth most powerful woman in the world by *Fortune* magazine, Mulcahy says: "People have to feel engaged, motivated and feel they are making a contribution to something that is important."[9]

○ **Intellectual capital** is the collective brainpower or shared knowledge of a workforce.

○ A **knowledge worker** is someone whose mind is a critical asset to employers.

ties of our employee-owners. . . . When we as a corporation invest in developing people, we are investing in our future." Former CEO Max DePree says, "At Herman Miller, we talk about the difference between being successful and being exceptional. Being successful is meeting goals in a good way—being exceptional is reaching your potential."[6]

The point of these examples is clear. People—what they know, what they learn, and what they do with it—are the ultimate foundations of organizational performance. They represent an **intellectual capital** defined as the collective brainpower or shared knowledge of a workforce that can be used to create value.[7] Indeed, the ultimate elegance of the new workplace may well be its ability to combine the talents of many people, sometimes thousands of them, to achieve unique and significant results.

This is the new age of the **knowledge worker**—someone whose mind is a critical asset to employers and who adds to the intellectual capital of the organization.[8] If you want a successful career in the new economy, you must be willing to reach for the heights of personal competency and accomplishment. You must be a self-starter willing to continuously learn from experience even in an environment that grows daily more complex and challenging.

GLOBALIZATION

Japanese management consultant Kenichi Ohmae suggests that the national boundaries of world business have largely disappeared.[10] At the very least we can say that they are fast disappearing. Who can state with confidence where their favorite athletic shoes or the parts for their personal computer were manufactured? More and more products are designed in one country, while their component parts are made in others and the assembly of the final product takes place in still another. Top managers at Ford, IBM, Sony, and other global corporations have no real need for the word "overseas" in everyday business vocabulary. They operate as global businesses that view themselves as equidistant from customers and suppliers, wherever in the world they may be located.

○ **Globalization** is the worldwide interdependence of resource flows, product markets, and business competition.

This is part of the force of **globalization,** the worldwide interdependence of resource flows, product markets, and business competition that characterizes our new economy.[11] This process is described as one in which "improvements in technology (especially in communications and transportation) combine with the deregulation of markets and open borders to bring about vastly expanded flows of people, money, goods, services, and information."[12] In a globalized world, countries and peoples are increasingly interconnected through the news, in travel and lifestyles, in labor markets and employment patterns, and in business dealings. Government leaders now worry about the competitiveness of nations just as corporate leaders worry about business competitiveness.[13] The world is increasingly arranged in regional economic blocs, with Asia, North and Latin America, and Europe as key anchors, and with Africa fast emerging to claim its economic potential. Like any informed citizen, you too must understand the forces of globalization.

TECHNOLOGY

The global economy isn't the only beneficiary of developments with new technology. Who hasn't been affected by the Internet and the World Wide Web? For better or worse, we now live in a technology-driven world increasingly dominated by bar codes, automatic tellers, computerized telemarketing campaigns, electronic mail, Internet resources, electronic commerce, and more.

From the small retail store to the large multinational firm, technology is an indispensable part of everyday operations—whether one is checking inventory, making a sales transaction, ordering supplies, or analyzing customer preferences.[14] And when it comes to communication in organizations, geographical distances hardly matter anymore. Computer networking can bring together almost anyone from anywhere in the world at the mere touch of a keyboard. In "virtual space" people hold meetings, access common databases, share information and files, make plans, and solve problems together—all without ever meeting face-to-face. As the pace and complexities of technological change accelerate, the demand for knowledge workers with the skills to best utilize technology is increasing. Computer literacy must be mastered and continuously updated as a foundation for career success.

> **Get Connected!**
>
> Internet support for *Management 8/e* enriches your learning. Take full advantage of www.wiley.com/college/schermerhorn.

DIVERSITY

When published by the Hudson Institute, the report *Workforce 2000: Work and Workers for the 21st Century* created an immediate stir in business circles, among government policymakers, and in the public eye.[15] It called attention to the slow growth of the American workforce, fewer younger workers entering the labor pool, the higher average age of the workforce, more women entering the workforce, and the increased proportions of minorities and immigrants in the workforce. A follow-up report, *Workforce 2020*, focusing on diversity themes and trends, was referred to as "a wake-up call for American workers, corporations, educators, parents and government officials."[16]

The term **workforce diversity** describes the composition of a workforce in terms of differences among the members.[17] These differences include gender, age, race, ethnicity, religion, sexual orientation, and able-bodiness. In the United States the legal environment (see Chapter 12) is very strict in prohibiting the use of demographic characteristics in human resource management decisions.[18] And indeed, today's increasingly diverse and multicultural workforce is increasingly viewed as an asset of-

○ **Workforce diversity** describes difference among workers in gender, race, age, ethnic culture, able-bodiness, religious affiliation, and sexual orientation.

fering great opportunities for performance gains.[19] By "valuing diversity" organizations can tap a rich talent pool and help everyone work to their full potential. But what does this really mean? According to one consultant, it should mean "enabling every member of your workforce to perform to his or her potential." A female vice president at Avon once posed the challenge of managing diversity this way: "consciously creating an environment where everyone has an equal shot at contributing, participating, and most of all advancing."[20]

Even though progress in valuing diversity continues to be made, lingering inequalities remain in the workplace. A study by Catalyst, a nonprofit research group focusing on corporate women, reports that among *Fortune* 500 companies women held 15.7 percent of top jobs in 2002, up from 8.7 percent in 1995. There were six woman CEOs, up from 1 in 1995.[21] That's quite an increase. But with women comprising about 47 percent of the U.S. labor force, the figures still leave a lot of room for future progress. In terms of wage comparisons, for each $1 earned by men, women earn 86 cents; black women earn 64 cents and Hispanic women earn 52 cents. Catalyst also found that 66 percent of minority women in management are dissatisfied with their career advancement opportunities.[22]

In respect to racial diversity in the workplace, a *Fortune* magazine article once concluded: "The good news is, there's plenty of progress for companies and employees to talk about . . . But what often doesn't get said, especially in mixed-race settings, is how much remains to get done."[24] A recent study revealed, for example, that when resumes are sent to potential employers, those with white-sounding first names, like Brett, received 50 percent more responses than those with black-sounding first names, such as Kareem.[23] The fact that these résumés were created with equal credentials reveals once again that diversity bias can still be a limiting factor in too many work settings.[25] **Prejudice,** or the holding of negative, irrational opinions and attitudes regarding members of diverse populations, sets the stage for bias. It becomes active **discrimination** when minority members are unfairly treated and denied the full benefits of organizational membership. A subtle form of discrimination is called the **glass ceiling effect,** an invisible barrier or "ceiling" that prevents women and minorities from rising above a certain level of organizational responsibility.[26] Scholar Judith Rosener suggests that the organization's loss for any discriminatory practices is "undervalued and underutilized human capital."[27]

ETHICS

Surely you remember the recent sensational cases of ethical failures in business—WorldCom, Enron, and Arthur Andersen, among others.[28] In Chapter 3, **ethics** is defined as a code of moral principles that sets standards of what is "good" and "right" as opposed to "bad" or "wrong" in the conduct of a person or group. There is a lot to be concerned about in the behavior of the corporations and people behind the scandals. Senior executives acted unethically and organizational systems tolerated actions that enriched the few while damaging many—ranging from company employees losing retirement savings, to stockholders whose investments lost value, to customers and society who paid the price as business performance deteriorated.

Even though ethical failures are well publicized, there is a plethora of positive cases and ethical role models to be studied as well. You will find

O **Prejudice** is the display of negative, irrational attitudes toward women or minorities.

O **Discrimination** actively denies women and minorities the full benefits of organizational membership.

O The **glass ceiling effect** is an invisible barrier limiting career advancement of women and minorities.

O **Ethics** set moral standards of what is "good" and "right" in one's behavior.

in this book many examples of people and organizations that are exemplars of ethical leadership and whose integrity is unquestioned. They meet the standards of a new ethical reawakening that places high value on social responsibility in business and organizational practices. The expectations include integrity and ethical leadership at all levels in an organizations, sustainable development and protection of the natural environment, protection of consumers through product safety and fair practices, and protection of human rights in all aspects of society, including employment.[29]

Society is becoming strict in requiring businesses and other social institutions to operate according to high moral standards. Businesses by law must have boards of directors that are elected by stockholders to represent their interests. One of the issues raised by the rash of business ethics failures is the role of **corporate governance,** the active oversight of management decisions and company actions by boards of directors. Many argue that corporate governance failed in cases like Enron and Andersen. The result is more emphasis today on restoring the strength of corporate governance. The expectation is that boards will hold management accountable for ethical and socially responsible behavior by the businesses they are hired to lead. Consider, for example, the ethical framework set by this statement from the credo of Johnson & Johnson:[30]

○ **Corporate governance** is oversight of a company's management by a board of directors.

We are responsible to the communities in which we live and work and to the world community as well. We must be good citizens—support good works and charities and bear our fair share of taxes. We must encourage civic improvements and better health and education. We must maintain in good order the property we are privileged to use, protecting the environment and natural resources.

CAREER CONNECTION

Nonprofit organizations rich in opportunities

"Get Out. Do Good." So reads the slogan of VolunteerMatch, self-described on its website as "the nonprofit, online service that helps interested volunteers get involved with community service organizations throughout the United States." In anyone's career it is important to remember that not all work is for-pay work; not all job satisfaction comes from full-time employment. Nonprofit organizations, from the Red Cross to Goodwill Industries to many others, are essential to the life of our communities and society at large. All depend on volunteers to make their services possible. VolunteerMatch has now handled over 1 million volunteer referrals and continues to grow in its aspiration to partner volunteer skills with the needs of nonprofits.

CAREERS

The career implications of the new economy and the challenges of change make personal initiative and self-renewal hallmarks of the day. British scholar Charles Handy suggests the analogy of the Irish shamrock to describe and understand the new employment patterns characteristic of this dynamic environment.[31] Each of a shamrock's three leaves has a different career implication. In one leaf are the core workers. These full-time employees pursue traditional career paths. With success and the maintenance of critical skills, they can advance within the organization and may remain employed for a long time. In the second leaf are contract workers. They perform specific tasks as needed by the organization and are compensated on a fee-for-services basis rather than by a continuing wage or salary. They sell a skill or service and contract with many different employers over time. In the third leaf are part-time workers hired only as needed and for only the number of hours needed. Employers expand and reduce their part-time staffs as business needs rise and fall. Part-time work can be a training ground or point of entry to the core when openings are available.

You must be prepared to prosper in any of the shamrock's three leaves. The typical career of the 21st century won't be uniformly full-time and limited to a single large employer. It is more likely to unfold opportunistically and involve several employment options over time. Not only must you be prepared to change jobs and employers over time, but your skills must be portable and always of current value in the employment markets. Skills aren't gained once and then forgotten; they must be carefully maintained and upgraded all the time. One career consultant describes this career scenario with the analogy of a surfer: "You're always moving. You can expect to fall into the water any number of times, and you have to get back up to catch the next wave."[32] Handy's advice is that you maintain a "portfolio of skills" that are always up-to-date and valuable to potential employers.

Learning check 1

Be sure you can • describe how intellectual capital, ethics, diversity, globalization, technology, and the changing nature of careers influence working in the new economy • define the terms intellectual capital, workforce diversity, and globalization • explain how prejudice, discrimination, and the glass ceiling effect can hurt people at work

ORGANIZATIONS IN THE NEW WORKPLACE

The new world of work is closely tied to the connectivity made possible by information technology. Management consultant Tom Peters describes it this way:[33]

In the next few years, whether at a tiny company or behemoth, we will be working with an eclectic mix of contract teammates from around the globe, many of whom we'll never meet face-to-face. Every project will call for a new team, composed of specially tailored skills. . . . Every player on this team will be evaluated—pass-by-pass, at-bat by at-bat, for the quality and uniqueness and timeliness and passion of her or his contribution.

Organizations in the new workplace are challenging settings, but exciting for their great opportunities and possibilities. Whether large or small, business or nonprofit, each should make real and positive contributions to society. Everyone has a stake in making sure that they perform up to expectations, including how well they serve as a principal source of careers and economic livelihood. In his article "The Company of the Future," Robert Reich says: "Everybody works for somebody or

Critical survival skills for the new workplace

- *Mastery:* You need be good at something; you need to be able to contribute something of value to your employer.
- *Contacts:* You need to know people; links with peers and others within and outside the organization are essential to get things done.
- *Entrepreneurship:* You must act as if you are running your own business, spotting ideas and opportunities, and stepping out to embrace them.
- *Love of technology:* You have to embrace technology; you don't have to be a technician, but you must be willing and able to fully utilize IT.
- *Marketing:* You need to be able to communicate your successes and progress, both yours personally and those of your work group.
- *Passion for renewal:* You need to be continuously learning and changing, always updating yourself to best meet future demands.

something—be it a board of directors, a pension fund, a venture capitalist, or a traditional boss. Sooner or later you're going to have to decide who you want to work for."[34] In order to make good employment choices and perform well in a career, you must have a fundamental understanding of the nature of organizations in the new workplace. *Manager's Notepad 1.1* provides a first look at some of the critical survival skills that you should acquire to work well in the organizations of today . . . and tomorrow.[35]

WHAT IS AN ORGANIZATION?

An **organization** is a collection of people working together to achieve a common purpose.[36] It is a unique social phenomenon that enables its members to perform tasks far beyond the reach of individual accomplishment. This description applies to organizations of all sizes and types, from large corporations, to the small businesses that make up the life of any community, to nonprofit organizations such as schools, government agencies, and community hospitals.

All organizations share a broad purpsose—providing useful goods or services. Each one should return value to society and satisfy customers' needs in order to justify its continued existence. A clear sense of purpose that is tied to "quality products" and "customer satisfaction" is an important source of organizational strength and performance advantage. At Medtronics, a large Minnesota-based medical products company, for example, employees are noted for innovation and their commitment to a clear and singular corporate mission—helping sick people get well. The sense of common purpose centers attention and focuses their collective talents on accomplishing a compelling goal: improving the health and well-being of those who use Medtronics products.[37]

○ An **organization** is a collection of people working together in a division of labor to achieve a common purpose.

ORGANIZATIONS AS SYSTEMS

○ An **open system** transforms resource inputs from the environment into product outputs.

Organizations are systems composed of interrelated parts that function together to achieve a common purpose.[38] They are **open systems** that interact with their environments in the continual process of transforming resource inputs into product outputs in the form of finished goods and/or services. As shown in *Figure 1.1*, the external environment is a critical element in the open-systems view of organizations. It is both a supplier of resources and the source of customers. Feedback from the environment tells an organization how well it is doing. Without customer willingness to use the organization's products, it is difficult to operate or stay in business over the long run. The recent bankruptcies of Kmart, WorldCom, and Andersen give stark testimony to this fact of the marketplace: without customers, a business can't survive.

ORGANIZATIONAL PERFORMANCE

For an organization to perform well, resources must be well utilized and customers well served. The notion of *value creation* is very important in this context. If operations add value to the original cost of resource inputs, then (1) a business organization can earn a profit—that is, sell a product for more than the cost of making it (e.g., fast-food restaurant meals), or (2) a nonprofit organization can add wealth to society—that is, provide a public service that is worth more than its cost (e.g., fire protection in a community). Value is created when an organization's resources are utilized in the right way, at the right time, and at minimum cost to create for customers high-quality goods and services.

○ **Productivity** is the quantity and quality of work performance, with resource utilization considered.

The best organizations utilize a variety of performance measures. On the customer side, high-performing firms measure customer satisfaction and loyalty, as well as market share. On the employee side, they measure retention, career development, job satisfaction, and task performance. A common measure of overall performance is **productivity,** the quantity and quality of work performance, relative to resources used. Productivity can be measured at the individual and group as well as organizational levels.

○ **Performance effectiveness** is an output measure of task or goal accomplishment.

Figure 1.2 links productivity with two terms commonly used in management, effectiveness and efficiency. **Performance effectiveness** is an output measure of task or goal accomplishment. If you are working in the manufacturing area of a computer firm, for example, performance effectiveness may mean that you meet a daily production target in terms of the quantity and quality of keyboards assembled. By so doing, you help the

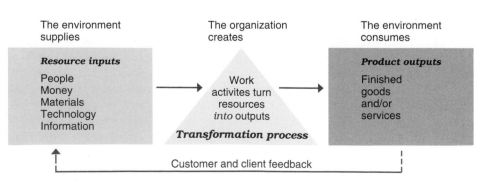

Figure 1.1 Organizations as open systems.

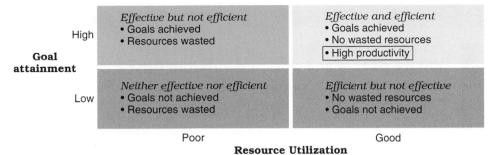

	Poor	Good
High	*Effective but not efficient* • Goals achieved • Resources wasted	*Effective and efficient* • Goals achieved • No wasted resources • High productivity
Low	*Neither effective nor efficient* • Goals not achieved • Resources wasted	*Efficient but not effective* • No wasted resources • Goals not achieved

Goal attainment (High / Low)

Resource Utilization (Poor / Good)

Figure 1.2 Productivity and the dimensions of organizational performance.

company as a whole to maintain its production schedule and meet customer demands for timely delivery and high-quality products.

Performance efficiency is a measure of the resource costs associated with goal accomplishment. Cost of labor is a common efficiency measure. Others include equipment utilization, facilities maintenance, and supplies or materials expenses. Returning to the example of computer assembly, the most efficient production is accomplished at a minimum cost in materials and labor. If you were producing fewer computer keyboards in a day than you were capable of, this amounts to inefficiency. Likewise, if you made a lot of mistakes or wasted materials in the assembly process, this is also inefficient work.

> O **Performance efficiency** is an input measure of resource cost associated with goal accomplishment.

CHANGING NATURE OF ORGANIZATIONS

Change is a continuing theme of this book, and organizations are certainly undergoing dramatic changes today. Among the many trends in the new workplace, the following organizational transitions are important to your study of management:[39]

- *Belief in human capital:* Demands of the new economy place premiums on high-involvement and participatory work settings that rally the knowledge, experience, and commitment of all members.

> ← How organizations are changing

- *Demise of "command-and-control":* Traditional hierarchical structures with "do as I say" bosses are proving too slow, conservative, and costly to do well in today's competitive environments.

- *Emphasis on teamwork:* Today's organizations are less vertical and more horizontal in focus; they are increasingly driven by teamwork that pools talents for creative problem solving.

- *Pre-eminence of technology:* New opportunities appear with each new development in computer and information technology; they continually change the way organizations operate and how people work.

- *Embrace of networking:* Organizations are networked for intense real-time communication and coordination, internally among parts and externally with partners, contractors, suppliers, and customers.

- *New workforce expectations:* A new generation of workers brings to the workplace less tolerance for hierarchy, more informality, and more attention to performance merit than to status and seniority.

- *Concern for work-life balance:* As society increases in complexity, workers are forcing organizations to pay more attention to balance in the often-conflicting demands of work and personal affairs.

Apple Computer Inc.
Where people and design create the future

Innovative design is a mainstay of Apple's business model. But there's more to the company than that. Under the leadership of co-founder Steve Jobs, Apple is a model of operating efficiency and marketing savvy. He claims we are entering the third and "golden age" of personal computing.[41] With this vision, there is no doubt that Jobs brings passion, inventiveness, and a great eye for customer markets to the firm. But the execution comes from people and the team-driven, technology-rich, and talent-based high-performance environment that represents life within Apple. If you want to study a company that operates in the world of the new economy with a new workforce and new organization, take a look at Apple. Even in the intensely competitive computer industry, the wizardry of Apple sets a benchmark for the rest of the pack.

- *Focus on speed:* Everything moves fast today; in business those who get products to market first have an advantage, and in any organization work is expected to be both well done and timely.

There are many force driving these changes in organizations. Key among them is unrelenting demand for quality products and services. Organizations that fail to listen to their customers and fail to deliver quality goods and services at reasonable prices will be left struggling in a highly competitive environment. References will be made throughout this book to the concept of **total quality management (TQM)**—managing with an organization-wide commitment to continuous improvement and meeting customer needs completely.[40] For the moment, the quality commitment can be recognized as a hallmark of enlightened productivity management in any organization.

○ **Total quality management (TQM)** is managing with commitment to continuous improvement, product quality, and customer satisfaction.

Learning check 2

Be sure you can • describe how organizations operate as open systems • explain productivity as a measure of organizational performance • list several ways in which organizations are changing today • distinguish between performance effectiveness and performance efficiency • explain the concept of TQM

MANAGERS IN THE NEW WORKPLACE

In an article entitled "Putting People First for Organizational Success," Jeffrey Pfeffer and John F. Veiga argue forcefully that organizations perform better when they treat their members better. They also point out that too many organizations fail to operate in this manner and, as a consequence, suffer performance failures. Pfeffer uses the term "toxic workplaces" to describe organizations that treat their employees mainly as costs to be reduced. True high-performing organizations are very different. They treat people as valuable strategic assets that should be carefully nurtured.[42]

The themes and concepts of *Management 8/e* support this view that organizations should operate with a commitment to people as their most important assets. Importantly and in the day-to-day flow of events in any workplace, those who serve in managerial roles have a special responsibility for ensuring that this commitment is fulfilled.

WHAT IS A MANAGER?

You find them in all organizations. They work with a wide variety of job titles—team leader, department head, project manager, dean, president, administrator, and more. They always work directly with other persons who rely on them for critical support and assistance in their own jobs. We call them **managers,** people in organizations who directly support and help activate the work efforts and performance accomplishments of others.

> O A **manager** is a person who supports and is responsible for the work of others.

For those serving as managers, the job is challenging and substantial. Any manager is responsible not just for his or her own work but for the overall performance accomplishments of a team, work group, department, or even organization as a whole. Research conducted by the Saratoga Institute reports that the average manager oversees the work of 10.75 other people.[43] Whether they are called direct reports, team members, work associates, or subordinates, these "other people" are the essential human resources whose contributions represent the real work of the organization.

Every manager's job thus entails a key responsibility—to help other people achieve high performance. Those persons working with and reporting to managers are the critical human capital upon whose intellects and efforts the performance of any organization is ultimately built. As pointed out by management theorist Henry Mintzberg, being a manager in this sense is a most important and socially responsible job:[44]

> *No job is more vital to our society than that of the manager. It is the manager who determines whether our social institutions serve us well or whether they squander our talents and resources. It is time to strip away the folklore about managerial work, and time to study it realistically so that we can begin the difficult task of making significant improvement in its performance.*

LEVELS AND TYPES OF MANAGERS

The nature of managerial work is evolving as organizations change and develop with time. A *Wall Street Journal* report described the transition of managers as follows: "Not so long ago they may have supervised 10 people sitting outside their offices. Today they must win the support of scores more—employees of different backgrounds, job titles, and even cultures. These new managers are expected to be skilled at organizing complex subjects, solving problems, communicating ideas, and making swift decisions."[45]

Levels of Managers

At the highest levels of organizations, common job titles are chief executive officer (CEO), president, and vice president. These **top managers** are responsible for the performance of an organization as a whole or for one of its larger parts. They pay special attention to the external environment,

> O **Top managers** guide the performance of the organization as a whole or of one of its major parts.

MANAGERS NOTEPAD 1.2   Nine responsibilities of team leaders

1. Plan meetings and work schedules.
2. Clarify goals and tasks, and gather ideas for improvement.
3. Appraise performance and counsel team members.
4. Recommend pay increases and new assignments.
5. Recruit, train, and develop team to meet performance goals.
6. Encourage high performance and teamwork.
7. Inform team members about organizational goals and expectations.
8. Inform higher levels of team needs and accomplishments.
9. Coordinate with other teams and support the rest of the organization.

are alert to potential long-run problems and opportunities, and develop appropriate ways of dealing with them. The best top managers are future-oriented strategic thinkers who make many decisions under highly competitive and uncertain conditions. They scan the environment, create and communicate long-term vision, and ensure that strategies and objectives are consistent with the organization's purpose and mission. Before retiring as Medtronics' CEO, Bill George crafted "Vision 2010" to position the firm as a client-centered deliverer of medical services. The hours were long and the work demanding, but George also loved his job, saying: "I always dreamed . . . of being head of a major corporation where the values of the company and my own values were congruent, where a company could become kind of a symbol for others, where the product that you represent is doing good for people."[46]

○ **Middle managers** oversee the work of large departments or divisions.

Middle managers are in charge of relatively large departments or divisions consisting of several smaller work units. Examples are clinic directors in hospitals; deans in universities; and division managers, plant managers, and branch sales managers in businesses. Middle managers work with top managers and coordinate with peers to develop and implement action plans to accomplish organizational objectives. They must be team oriented and able to work well with people from all parts of an organization. An important example is the job of **project manager**, someone who coordinates complex projects with task deadlines while working with many persons within and outside the organization. At General Electric, for example, corporate troubleshooting groups solve problems and create change across divisions and geographic boundaries within the company. One cross-functional team brought together managers from marketing, human resources, and field operations to design a new compensation system.[47]

○ **Project managers** coordinate complex projects with task deadlines.

Even though most people enter the workforce as technical specialists, sooner or later they advance to positions of initial managerial responsibility. A first job in management typically involves serving as a **team leader** or **supervisor**—someone in charge of a small work group composed of nonmanagerial workers. Job titles for these *first-line managers* vary greatly but include such designations as department head, group leader, and unit manager. For example, the leader of an auditing team is considered a first-line manager, as is the head of an academic department in a university. *Manager's Notepad 1.2* offers advice on the performance responsibilities of team leaders and supervisors.[48] Such managers ensure that their work

○ **Team leaders** or **supervisors** report to middle managers and directly supervise nonmanagerial workers.

teams or units meet performance objectives that are consistent with higher-level organizational goals. Justine Fritz led a 12-member Medtronics team to launch a new product. "I've just never worked on anything that so visibly, so dramatically changes the quality of someone's life," she says, while noting that the demands are also great. "Some days you wake up, and if you think about all the work you have to do it's so overwhelming, you could be paralyzed." That's the challenge of managerial work at any level. Justine says: "You just have to get it done."[49]

Types of Managers

In addition to serving at different levels of authority, managers work in different capacities within organizations. **Line managers** are responsible for work activities that make a direct contribution to the organization's outputs. For example, the president, retail manager, and department supervisors of a local department store all have line responsibilities. Their jobs in one way or another are directly related to the sales operations of the store. **Staff managers,** by contrast, use special technical expertise to advise and support the efforts of line workers. In a department store, the director of human resources and chief financial officer would have staff responsibilities.

In business, **functional managers** have responsibility for a single area of activity, such as finance, marketing, production, personnel, accounting, or sales. **General managers** are responsible for more complex units that include many functional areas. An example is a plant manager who oversees many separate functions, including purchasing, manufacturing, warehousing, sales, personnel, and accounting. It is common for managers working in public or nonprofit organizations to be called **administrators.** Examples include hospital administrator, public administrator, city administrator, and human-service administrator.

MANAGERIAL PERFORMANCE

All managers help people, working individually and in groups, to achieve productivity while using their talents to accomplish organizational goals. Importantly, managers do this while being held personally "accountable" for results achieved. **Accountability** is the requirement of one person to answer to a higher authority for performance results achieved in his or her area of work responsibility. The team leader is accountable to a middle manager, the middle manager is accountable to a top manager, and even the top manager is accountable to a board of directors.

But the concept of managerial performance is multidimensional. Effective managers help others to *both* achieve high performance by working effectively and efficiently, *and* experience satisfaction in their work. This dual concern for performance and satisfaction is a central theme in the new workplace, and it runs throughout *Management 8/e*. It is represented in the concept of **quality of work life,** an indicator of the overall quality of human experiences in the workplace. A "high-QWL" workplace expresses a true respect for people at work by offering such things as fair pay, safe working conditions, opportunities to learn and use new skills, room to grow and progress in a career, protection of individual rights, and pride in the work itself and in the organization. Part of any manager's accountability is to achieve high-performance outcomes while maintaining a high-quality work life environment.[50] Simply put, in the new workplace, performance, satisfaction, and a high-quality work life can and should go hand in hand.

○ **Line managers** directly contribute to the production of the organization's basic goods or services.

○ **Staff managers** use special technical expertise to advise and support line workers.

○ **Functional managers** are responsible for one area of activity, such as finance, marketing, production, personnel, accounting, or sales.

○ **General managers** are responsible for complex multi-functional units.

○ An **administrator** is a manager in a public or nonprofit organization.

○ **Accountability** is the requirement to show performance results to a supervisor.

○ **Quality of work life** is the overall quality of human experiences in the workplace.

CHANGING NATURE OF MANAGERIAL WORK

In today's organizations the words "coordinator," "coach," and "team leader" are heard as often as "supervisor" or "manager." The work managers perform is less directive and more supportive than in the past. It has to be in a world where high performance comes only to those who truly value and sustain human capital. There is little tolerance or need in today's organizations for those who simply sit back and tell others what to do. The best managers are well informed regarding the needs of those reporting to or dependent on them. They can often be found working alongside those they supervise. They will always be found providing advice and developing the support needed for others to peform to the best of their abilities. High-performing managers are good at building working relationships with others, helping others develop their skills and performance competencies, fostering teamwork, and otherwise creating a work envirnment that is both performance driven and satisfying to those who do the required work.

Among the many changes taking place in managerial work, the concept of the "upside-down pyramid" is insightful. Shown in *Figure 1.3*, it offers an alternative and suggestive way of viewing organizations and the role played by managers within them. The operating workers are at the top of the upside-down pyramid, just below the customers and clients they serve. They are supported in their work efforts by managers located at the bottom. These managers aren't just order-givers; they are there to mobilize and deliver the support others require to best serve customer needs. Each member of the upside-down pyramid is a *value-added worker*—someone who creates eventual value for the organization's customers or clients. The whole organization is devoted to serving the customer, and this is made possible with the support of managers.

Many trends and emerging practices in organizations, such as the upside-down pyramid, require new thinking from people who serve as man-

REALITY CHECK 1.2

Are students ready for work?
In a survey reported by *USA Today*, 66 percent of students said they were well prepared to work in diverse teams. Only 13 percent of employers agreed. Take the online "Reality Check" to further examine differences in student and employer perceptions.

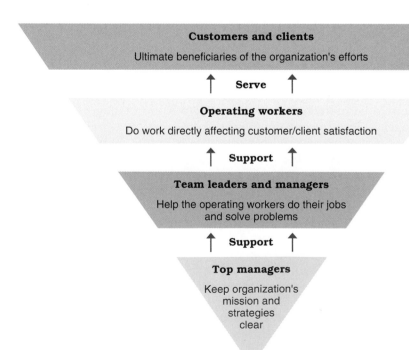

Figure 1.3 The organization viewed as an upside-down pyramid.

agers. As noted earlier, we are in a time when the best managers are known more for "helping" and "supporting" than for "directing" and "order-giving." Even in an age of high technology and "smart" machines, the human resource is indispensable. Worker involvement and empowerment are critical building blocks of organizational success. Full human resource utilization increasingly means changing the way work gets done by pushing decision-making authority to the point where the best information and expertise exist—with the operating workers.

Learning check 3

Be sure you can • describe the various types and levels of managers • define the terms accountability and quality of work life and explain their importance to managerial performance • explain the role of managers in the upside-down pyramid view of organizations, • list several ways managerial work is changing today

THE MANAGEMENT PROCESS

The ultimate "bottom line" in every manager's job is to succeed in helping an organization achieve high performance by best utilizing its human and material resources. If productivity in the form of high levels of performance effectiveness and efficiency is a measure of organizational success, managers are largely responsible for its achievement. It is their job to mobilize technology and talent by creating environments within which people work hard and perform to the best of their abilities.

FUNCTIONS OF MANAGEMENT

Managers must have the capabilities to recognize performance problems and opportunities, make good decisions, and take appropriate actions. They do this through the process of **management**—planning, organizing, leading, and controlling the use of resources to accomplish performance goals. These four management functions and their interrelationships are shown in *Figure 1.4*. All managers, regardless of title, level, type, and organizational setting, are responsible for the four functions.[51] However, they

○ **Management** is the process of planning, organizing, leading, and controlling the use of resources to accomplish performance goals.

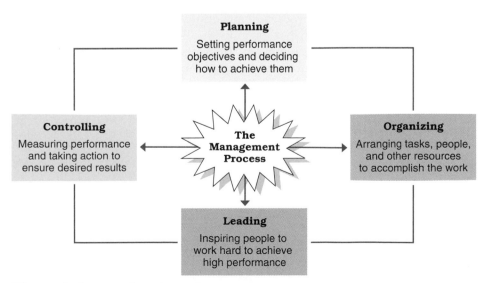

Figure 1.4 Four functions of management.

are not accomplished in linear step-by-step fashion. The reality is that all functions are continually engaged as a manager moves from task to task and opportunity to opportunity in his or her work.

Planning

○ **Planning** is the process of setting objectives and determining what should be done to accomplish them.

In management, **planning** is the process of setting performance objectives and determining what actions should be taken to accomplish them. Through planning, a manager identifies desired results and ways to achieve them. Take, for example, an Ernst & Young initiative that was developed to better meet the needs of the firm's female professionals.[52] Top management grew concerned about the firm's retention rates for women and by a critical report from the research group Catalyst. Chairman Philip A. Laskawy, who personally headed Ernst & Young's Diversity Task Force, responded by setting a planning objective to reduce turnover rates for women. Rates at the time were running some 22 percent per year and costing the firm about 150 percent of each person's annual salary to hire and train new staff.

Organizing

○ **Organizing** is the process of assigning tasks, allocating resources, and coordinating work activities.

Even the best plans will fail without strong implementation. Success begins with **organizing,** the process of assigning tasks, allocating resources, and coordinating the activities of individuals and groups to implement plans. Through organizing, managers turn plans into actions by defining jobs, assigning personnel, and supporting them with technology and other resources. At Ernst & Young, Laskawy organized to meet his planning objective by first creating a new Office of Retention and then hiring Deborah K. Holmes to head it. As retention problems were identified in various parts of the firm, Holmes convened special task forces to tackle them and recommend location-specific solutions. A Woman's Access Program was started to give women access to senior executives for mentoring and career development.

Leading

○ **Leading** is the process of arousing enthusiasm and inspiring efforts to achieve goals.

In management, **leading** is the process of arousing people's enthusiasm to work hard and inspiring their efforts to fulfill plans and accomplish objectives. Through leading, managers build commitments to a common vision, encourage activities that support goals, and influence others to do their best work in the organization's behalf. At Ernst & Young, Deborah Holmes identified a core problem—work at the firm was extremely intense and women were often stressed because their spouses also worked. She became a champion for improved work-life balance and pursued it relentlessly. Although admitting that "there's no silver bullet" in the form of a universal solution, new initiatives from her office supported and encouraged better balance. She started "call-free holidays" where professionals did not check voice mail or e-mail on weekends and holidays. She also started a "travel sanity" program that limited staffers' travel to four days a week so that they could get home for weekends.

Controlling

The management function of **controlling** is the process of measuring work performance, comparing results to objectives, and taking corrective action as needed. Through controlling, managers maintain active contact with people in the course of their work, gather and interpret reports on performance, and use this information to plan constructive action and change. At Ernst & Young, Laskawy and Holmes both knew what the retention rates were when they started the new program, and they were subsequently able to track improvements. Through measurement they were able to compare results with objectives, and track changes in work-life balance and retention rates. They continually adjusted the program to improve it. In today's dynamic times, such control and adjustment are indispensable. Things don't always go as anticipated and plans must be modified and redefined for future success.

○ **Controlling** is the process of measuring performance and taking action to ensure desired results.

MANAGERIAL ACTIVITIES AND ROLES

Although the management process may seem straightforward, things are more complicated than they appear at first glance. In his classic book *The Nature of Managerial Work,* Henry Mintzberg describes the daily work of corporate chief executives as: "There was no break in the pace of activity during office hours. The mail . . . telephone calls . . . and meetings . . . accounted for almost every minute from the moment these executives entered their offices in the morning until they departed in the evenings."[53] Today, we would have to add ever-present e-mail to Mintzberg's list of executive preoccupations.[54]

In trying to systematically describe the nature of managerial work and the demands placed on those who do it, Mintzberg identified the set of 10 roles depicted in *Figure 1.5.* The roles involve managing information, people, and action. The roles are interconnected, and all managers must be prepared to perform all of them.[55] In Mintzberg's framework, a manager's

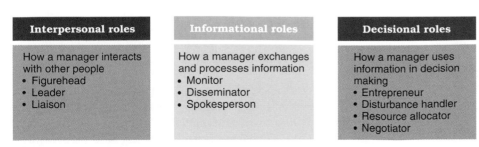

Interpersonal roles	Informational roles	Decisional roles
How a manager interacts with other people	How a manager exchanges and processes information	How a manager uses information in decision making
• Figurehead	• Monitor	• Entrepreneur
• Leader	• Disseminator	• Disturbance handler
• Liaison	• Spokesperson	• Resource allocator
		• Negotiator

Figure 1.5 Mintzberg's 10 managerial roles.

informational roles involve the giving, receiving, and analyzing of information. The *interpersonal roles* involve interactions with people inside and outside the work unit. The *decisional roles* involve using information to make decisions to solve problems or address opportunities.

Mintzberg is careful to note that the manager's day is unforgiving in the intensity and pace of these role requirements. The managers he observed had little free time because unexpected problems and continuing requests for meetings consumed almost all the time that became available. Their workdays were hectic, and the pressure for continuously improving performance was all-encompassing. Says Mintzberg: "The manager can never be free to forget the job, and never has the pleasure of knowing, even temporarily, that there is nothing else to do. . . . Managers always carry the nagging suspicion that they might be able to contribute just a little bit more. Hence they assume an unrelenting pace in their work."[56]

Managerial work is busy, demanding, and stressful not just for chief executives but for managers at all levels of responsibility in any work setting. A summary of research on the nature of managerial work offers this important reminder.[57]

Realities of managerial work ⟶
- Managers work long hours.
- Managers work at an intense pace.
- Managers work at fragmented and varied tasks.
- Managers work with many communication media.
- Managers accomplish their work largely through interpersonal relationships.

PERSONAL MANAGEMENT

SELF-AWARENESS is one of those concepts that is easy to talk about but very hard to master. What do you really know about yourself? How often do you take a critical look at your attitudes, behaviors, skills, and accomplishments? Do you ever realistically assess your personal strengths and weaknesses—both as you see them and as others do? A high degree of self-awareness is essential for personal adaptibility, to be able to grow and develop in changing times. This figure, called the Johari Window, offers a way of comparing what we know about ourselves with what others know about us.[59] Our "open" areas are often small, while the "blind spot," "the unknown," and the "hidden" areas can be quite large. Think about the personal implications of the Johari Window. Are you willing to probe the unknown, uncover your blind spots, and discover talents and weaknesses that may be hidden? As your self-awareness expands, you will find many insights for personal growth and development.

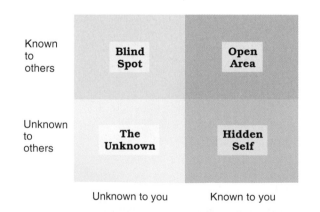

	Unknown to you	Known to you
Known to others	**Blind Spot**	**Open Area**
Unknown to others	**The Unknown**	**Hidden Self**

Get to know yourself better ▶
Complete Self-Assessments #1—**21st Century Manager**, and #2—**Emotional Intelligence**, from the Management Learning Workbook.

MANAGERIAL AGENDAS AND NETWORKING

On his way to a meeting, a GM bumped into a staff member who did not report to him. Using this opportunity, in a two-minute conversation he: (a) asked two questions and received the information he needed; (b) reinforced their good relationship by sincerely complimenting the staff member on something he had recently done; and (c) got the staff member to agree to do something that the GM needed done.

This description of a brief incident provides a glimpse of an effective general manager (GM) in action.[58] It portrays two activities that management consultant and scholar John Kotter considers critical to a general manager's success—agenda setting and networking. Through *agenda setting*, good managers develop action priorities that in-

Be sure you can • define and give examples of each of the four major functions in the management process—planning, organizing, leading, and controlling • explain Mintzberg's view of what managers do, including the key managerial roles • explain how managers use agendas and networks to fulfill their work responsibilities

Learning check 4

clude goals and plans spanning long and short time frames. These agendas are usually incomplete and loosely connected in the beginning, but become more specific as the manager utilizes information continually gleaned from many different sources. The agendas are kept always in mind and are "played out" whenever an opportunity arises, as in the preceding quotation.

Good managers implement their agendas by working with a variety of people inside and outside the organization. In Kotter's example, the GM was getting things done through a staff member who did not report directly to him. This is made possible by *networking,* the process of building and maintaining positive relationships with people whose help may be needed to implement one's work agendas. In this example, the GM's networks would include relationships with peers, a boss, and higher-level executives, subordinates and members of their work teams, as well as with external customers, suppliers, and community representatives. Such networks are indispensable to managerial success in today's complex work environments, and excellent managers devote much time and effort to their development.

LEARNING HOW TO MANAGE

Today's turbulent times present an ever-shifting array of problems, opportunities, and performance expectations to organizations and their members. Change is a way of life, and it demands new organizational and individual reponses. The quest for high performance is relentless, with workers everywhere expected to find ways to achieve high productivity under new and dynamic conditions. They are expected to become involved, participate fully, demonstrate creativity, and find self-fulfillment in their work. They are expected to be team players who understand the needs and goals of the total organization and who use new technologies to their full advantage.

All of this, of course, means that your career success depends on a real commitment to learning—not just formal learning in the classroom, but also **lifelong learning.** This is the process of continuously learning from our daily experiences and opportunities. Especially in a dynamic and ever-changing environment, a commitment to lifelong learning helps us build portfolios of skills that are always up to date, job relevant, and valuable in the emerging economy.

O **Lifelong learning** is continuous learning from daily experiences.

ESSENTIAL MANAGERIAL SKILLS

A **skill** is the ability to translate knowledge into action that results in desired performance. Obviously, many skills are required to master the challenging nature of managerial work. The most important ones are those that allow managers to help others become more productive in their work. Harvard scholar Robert L. Katz has classified the essential skills of managers into three categories: technical, human, and conceptual.[60] Although all three skills are necessary for managers, he suggests that their relative importance tends to vary by level of managerial responsibility, as shown in *Figure 1.6.*

O A **skill** is the ability to translate knowledge into action that results in desired performance.

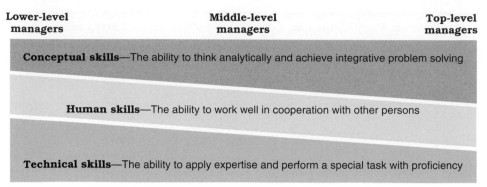

Figure 1.6 Katz's essential managerial skills.

○ A **technical skill** is the ability to use expertise to perform a task with proficiency.

A **technical skill** is the ability to use a special proficiency or expertise to perform particular tasks. Accountants, engineers, market researchers, financial planners, and systems analysts, for example, possess technical skills. These skills are initially acquired through formal education and are further developed by training and job experience. Technical skill in the new economy is also increasingly tied to computer literacy and utilization of the latest information technology. Figure 1.6 shows that technical skills are very important at career entry levels. The critical question to be asked and positively answered by you in this respect and in preparation for any job interview comes down to this simple test: "What can you really do for an employer?"

○ A **human skill** is the ability to work well in cooperation with other people.

The ability to work well in cooperation with other persons is a **human skill.** It emerges in the workplace as a spirit of trust, enthusiasm, and genuine involvement in interpersonal relationships. A manager with good human skills will have a high degree of self-awareness and a capacity to understand or empathize with the feelings of others. An important component of the essential human skills is **emotional intelligence.**[61] Discussed in Chapter 13 for its leadership implications, "EI" is defined by scholar and consultant Daniel Goleman as the "ability to manage ourselves and our relationships effectively."[62] Given the highly interpersonal nature of managerial work, human skills and emotional intelligence are critical for all managers. Figure 1.6 shows that they are consistently important across all the managerial levels. Again, a straightforward question puts your interpersonal skills and emotional intelligence to the test: "How well do you work with others?"

○ **Emotional intelligence** is the ability to manage ourselves and our relationships effectively.

All good managers ultimately have the ability to view situations broadly and to solve problems to the benefit of everyone concerned. This ability to think critically and analytically is a **conceptual skill.** It involves the capacity to break problems into smaller parts, to see the relations between the parts, and to recognize the implications of any one problem for others. As we assume ever-higher responsibilities in organizations, we are called upon to deal with more ambiguous problems that have many complications and longer-term consequences. Figure 1.6 shows that conceptual skills gain in relative importance for top managers. At this point, you should ask: "Am I developing critical thinking and problem-solving capabilities for long-term career success?"

○ A **conceptual skill** is the ability to think analytically and solve complex problems.

SKILL AND OUTCOME ASSESSMENT

○ A **managerial competency** is a skill-based capability for high performance in a management job.

Business and management educators are increasingly interested in helping people acquire the essential skills and develop specific competencies that can help them achieve managerial success. A **managerial competency** is a skill-based capability that contributes to high performance in a management job.[63] A number of these competencies have been implied in the previous discussion of the management process, including those related to planning, organizing, leading, and controlling. Competencies are also implicit in the information, interpersonal, and decision-making demands of managerial roles, as well as in agenda setting and networking as managerial activities.

Listed here are some of the skills and personal characteristics business schools emphasize as foundations for continued professional development and career success. You can use this as a preliminary checklist for assessing your career readiness.

- *Communication*—Ability to share ideas and findings clearly in written and oral expression—includes writing, oral presentation, giving/receiving feedback, technology utilization.

- *Teamwork*—Ability to work effectively as a team member and team leader—includes team contribution, team leadership, conflict management, negotiation, consensus building.

- *Self-management*—Ability to evaluate oneself, modify behavior, and meet performance obligations—includes ethical reasoning and behavior, personal flexibillity, tolerance for ambiguity, performance responsibility.

- *Leadership*—Ability to influence and support others to perform complex and ambiguous tasks—includes diversity awareness, global understanding, project management, strategic action.

- *Critical thinking*—Ability to gather and analyze information for creative problem solving—includes problem solving, judgment and decision making, information gathering and interpretation, creativity/innovation.

- *Professionalism*—Ability to sustain a positive impression, instill confidence, and maintain career advancement—includes personal presence, personal initiative, and career management.

◄———
Key personal characteristics for managerial success

MANAGEMENT 8/e LEARNING FRAMEWORK

Management 8/e introduces management as an academic discipline whose understanding is important for anyone seeking career success in the new workplace. The focus is on helping you to become familiar with key concepts, theories, and terms, and to understand their practical implications. The five major parts of the book are presented in a systematic building-block fashion: (1) Introducing Management, (2) Context, (3) Mission, (4) Organization, (5) Leading. The subject matter in each has been carefully chosen, described, and illustrated in ways that encourage you to actively think about your developing managerial skills and competencies.

As you read *Management 8/e* remember to take full advantage of the built-in learning framework. The chapters are written with an integrated pedagogy that makes it easier for you to do well on assignments and examinations. From the chapter-opening study questions, to the learning preview, to the embedded learning checks, through the many examples, to the end-of-chapter study guide with its summary, key terms review, and self-test, you have the opportunity to learn as you read. If you allow the book's pedagogy to work for you, the learning opportunities summarized in *Figure 1.7* should pay off in solid understanding and enhanced course performance.

www.hudson.org

A Global Perspective

The Hudson Institute is an internationally recognized public policy research organization. Concerns for the digital future, global food issues, and workforce development are active themes in the institute's policy centers.

Part 1 Introducing Management
• The Dynamic New Workplace
• Management—Past to Present
• Ethical Behavior and Social Responsibility

Part 2 Context
• Environment and Diversity
• Global Dimensions
• Entrepreneurship and Small Business

Managerial Skills and Competencies

Management Learning Workbook

Part 3 Mission
• Information and Decision Making
• Planning and Controlling
• Strategic Management

Part 4 Organization
• Organizing
• Organizational Design and Processes
• Human Resource Management

Part 5 Leadership
• Leading
• Motivation–Theory and Practice
• Individual, Behavior and Performance
• Teams and Teamwork
• Communication and Interpersonal Skills
• Change Leadership

Figure 1.7 *Management 8/e*—Understanding Management from Theory to Practice.

A special and unique learning resource is found in the end-of-text (*Management Learning Workbook*). This feature offers the critical "next step" in learning, providing you with a rich variety of resources and activities. Explore the cases, pursue the active learning projects, engage in the experiential exercises, take the self-assessments, and build a student portfolio. Many opportunities for learning are present in the workbook, but only you can take advantage of them. Only you can step forward and take personal responsibility for advancing your managerial skills and career readiness in today's challenging world. *Management 8/e* from cover to cover is a great learning resource. Now is the time to read, study, and benefit from it. Get connected with your future!

Learning check 5

Be sure you can • define three essential managerial skills—technical, human, and conceptual skills • explain Katz's view of how these skills vary in importance across management levels • define emotional intelligence as an important human skill • list and give examples of several personal characteristics important for managerial success

CHAPTER 1 STUDY GUIDE

Where We've Been

BACK TO MONSTER.COM

The opening example of Monster.com focused on you, your career, and the great opportunities for career success that exist in today's dynamic environment. You don't need to create your own company like Jeff Taylor did to achieve career success, although you could. What you must do, is discover the learning "monster" within yourself and commit it to academic success and career development. In Chapter 1 you learned about the new work environment, from the challenges of technology utlization, to the forces of globalization, to diversity and ethical behavior, and more. You also gained insight into the nature of organizations, the managerial roles, and the critical importance of developing essential managerial and leadership skills.

THE NEXT STEP
INTEGRATED LEARNING ACTIVITIES

Cases/Projects	Self-Assessments	Experiential Exercises
• Apple Computer, Case	• A 21st-Century Manager (#1)	• My Best Manager (#1)
• Outback Steakhouse, Case	• Emotional Intelligence (#2)	• What Managers Do (#2)
• Project 1—Diversity Lessons	• Diversity Awareness (#7)	• Defining Quality (#3)
• Enron and Anderson case	• Are You Cosmopolitan? (#18)	• The Future Workplace (#14)

STUDY QUESTIONS SUMMARY

1. What are the challenges of working in the new economy?

- Today's turbulent environment challenges everyone to understand and embrace continuous change and developments in a new information-driven and global economy.
- Work in the new economy is increasingly knowledge based, and people, with their capacity to bring valuable intellectual capital to the workplace, are the ultimate foundation of organizational performance.
- The forces of globalization are bringing increased interdependencies among nations and economies, as customer markets and resource flows create intense business competition.

- Ever-present developments in information technology and the continued expansion of the Internet are reshaping organizations, changing the nature of work, and increasing the value of knowledge workers.
- Organizations must value the talents and capabilities of a workforce whose members are increasingly diverse with respect to gender, age, race and ethnicity, able-bodiedness, and lifestyles.
- Society has high expectations for organizations and their members to perform with commitment to high ethical standards and in socially responsible ways, including protection of the natural environment and human rights.

- Careers in the new economy require great personal initiative to build and maintain skill "portfolios" that are always up-to-date and valuable to employers challenged by the intense competition and the information age.

2. What are organizations like in the new workplace?

- Organizations are collections of people working together to achieve a common purpose.
- As open systems, organizations interact with their environments in the process of transforming resource inputs into product outputs.
- Productivity is a measure of the quantity and quality of work performance, with resource costs taken into account.
- High-performing organizations are both effective, in terms of goal accomplishment, and efficient, in terms of resource utilization.
- Organizations today emphasize total quality management in a context of technology utilization, empowerment and teamwork, and concern for work-life balance, among other trends.

3. Who are managers and what do they do?

- Managers directly support and facilitate the work efforts of other people in organizations.
- Top managers scan the environment, create vision, and emphasize long-term performance goals; middle managers coordinate activities in large departments of divisions; team leaders and supervisors support performance at the team or work-unit level.
- Functional managers work in specific areas such as finance or marketing; general managers are responsible for larger multifunctional units; administrators are managers in public or nonprofit organizations.
- Managers are held accountable for performance results that the manager depends on other persons to accomplish.
- The upside-down pyramid view of organizations shows operating workers at the top serving customer needs while being supported from below by various levels of management.

- The changing nature of managerial work emphasizes being good at "coaching" and "supporting" others, rather than simply "directing" and "order-giving."

4. What is the management process?

- The management process consists of the four functions of planning, organizing, leading, and controlling.
- Planning sets the direction; organizing assembles the human and material resources; leading provides the enthusiasm and direction; controlling ensures results.
- Managers implement the four functions in daily work that is intense and stressful, involving long hours and continuous performance pressures.
- Managerial success in this demanding context requires the ability to perform well in interpersonal, informational, and decision-making roles.
- Managerial success also requires the ability to utilize interpersonal networks to accomplish well-selected task agendas.

5. How do you learn the essential managerial skills and competencies?

- Careers in the new economy demand continual attention to lifelong learning from all aspects of daily experience and job opportunities.
- Skills considered essential for managers are broadly described as technical—ability to use expertise; human—ability to work well with other people; and conceptual—ability to analyze and solve complex problems.
- Skills and outcomes considered as foundations for managerial success include communication, teamwork, self-management, leadership, critical thinking, and professionalism.
- *Management 8/e* focuses attention on building your career potential through understanding the practical implications of important concepts and theories.

KEY TERMS REVIEW

Accountability (p. 17)
Administrators (p. 17)
Conceptual skill (p. 24)
Controlling (p. 21)
Corporate governance
     (p. 9)
Discrimination (p. 8)
Emotional intelligence
     (p. 24)
Ethics (p. 8)
Functional managers
     (p. 17)
General managers (p. 17)
Glass ceiling effect
     (p. 8)
Globalization (p. 6)
Human skill (p. 24)
Intellectual capital
     (p. 6)

Knowledge worker
     (p. 6)
Leading (p. 20)
Lifelong learning
     (p. 23)
Line managers (p. 17)
Management (p. 19)
Manager (p. 15)
Managerial competency
     (p. 24)
Middle managers
     (p. 16)
Open system (p. 12)
Organization (p. 11)
Organizing (p. 20)
Performance
     effectiveness (p. 12)
Performance efficiency
     (p. 13)

Planning (p. 20)
Prejudice (p. 8)
Productivity (p. 12)
Project managers
     (p. 16)
Quality of work life
     (p. 17)
Skill (p. 23)
Staff managers
     (p. 17)
Supervisor (p. 16)
Team leader (p. 16)
Technical skill (p. 24)
Top managers (p. 15)
Total quality
     management TQM
     (p. 14)
Workforce diversity
     (p. 7)

SELF-TEST 1

MULTIPLE-CHOICE QUESTIONS:

1. The process of management involves the functions of planning, _____, leading, and controlling.
    (a) accounting (b) creating (c) innovating (d) organizing

2. An effective manager achieves both high-performance results and high levels of _____ among people doing the required work.
    (a) turnover (b) effectiveness (c) satisfaction (d) stress

3. Performance efficiency is a measure of the _____ associated with task accomplishment.
    (a) resource costs (b) goal specificity (c) product quality (d) product quantity

4. The requirement that a manager answer to a higher-level boss for results achieved by a work team is called _____.
    (a) dependency (b) accountability (c) authority (d) empowerment

5. Productivity is a measure of the quantity and _____ of work produced, with resource utilization taken into account.
   (a) quality (b) cost (c) timeliness (d) value

6. _____ managers pay special attention to the external environment, looking for problems and opportunities and finding ways to deal with them.
   (a) Top (b) Middle (c) Lower (d) First-line

7. The accounting manager for a local newspaper would be considered a _____ manager, whereas the editorial manager would be considered a _____ manager.
   (a) general, functional (b) middle, top (c) staff, line (d) senior, junior

8. When a team leader clarifies desired work targets and deadlines for a work team, he or she is fulfilling the management function of _____.
   (a) planning (b) delegating (c) controlling (d) supervising

9. The process of building and maintaining good working relationships with others who may help implement a manager's work agendas is called _____.
   (a) governance (b) networking (c) authority (d) entrepreneurship

10. In Katz's framework, top managers tend to rely more on their _____ skills than do first-line managers.
    (a) human (b) conceptual (c) decision-making (d) technical

11. The research of Mintzberg and others concludes that managers _____.
    (a) work at a leisurely pace (b) have blocks of private time for planning (c) always live with the pressures of performance responsibility (d) have the advantages of short workweeks

12. When someone with a negative attitude toward minorities makes a decision to deny advancement opportunities to a Hispanic worker, this is an example of _____.
    (a) discrimination (b) emotional intelligence (c) control (d) prejudice

13. Among the trends in the new workplace, one can expect to find _____.
    (a) more order-giving (b) more valuing people as human assets (c) less teamwork (d) reduced concern for work-life balance

14. The manager's role in the "upside-down pyramid" view of organizations is best described as providing _____ so that operating workers can directly serve _____.
    (a) direction, top management (b) leadership, organizational goals (c) support, customers (d) agendas, networking

15. The management function of _____ is being perfomed when a retail manager measures daily sales in the dress department and compares them with daily sales targets.
    (a) planning (b) agenda setting (c) controlling (d) delegating

SHORT-RESPONSE QUESTIONS:

16. List and explain the importance of three pressures of ethics and social responsibility that managers must be prepared to face.

17. Explain how "accountability" operates in the relationship between (a) a manager and her subordinates, and (b) the same manager and her boss.

18. Explain how the "glass ceiling effect" may disadvantage newly hired African-American college graduates in a large corporation.

19. What is "globalization" and what are its implications for working in the new economy?

APPLICATION QUESTION:

20. You have just been hired as the new supervisor of an audit team for a national accounting firm. With four years of experience, you feel technically well prepared for the assignment. However, this is your first formal appointment as a "manager." Things are complicated at the moment. The team has 12 members, of diverse demographic and cultural backgrounds, as well as work experience. There is an intense workload and lots of performance pressure. How will this situation challenge you to develop and use essential managerial skills and related competencies to successfully manage the team to high levels of auditing performance?

www.wiley.com/college/schermerhorn

2

Management—past to present

Planning Ahead →

After reading Chapter 2, you should be able to answer these questions in your own words.

CHAPTER 2 study questions

1. What can be learned from classical management thinking?

2. What ideas were introduced by the human resource approaches?

3. What is the role of quantitative analysis in management?

4. What is unique about the systems view and contingency thinking?

5. What are continuing management themes of the 21st century?

GOOGLE, INC.—PRACTICE MAKES PERFECT

"Googol" is a mathematical term standing for the number 1 followed by 100 zeros. That's a real big number. It's also symbolic of the reach of the popular Web search engine Google, now handling many millions of Web searches everyday. Google's origins trace to 1995 when Larry Page and Sergey Brin met as students at Stanford University. Their conversations led to collaboration on a search engine they called BackRub. It became so popular on campus that they kept refining and expanding the service in Larry's dormitory room.

Google, Inc., was hatched in 1998 with the goal: "to organize the information overload of the Internet in a transparent and superior way." It hasn't stopped running, or growing, since. A search today will examine over 300 billion Web pages to find what you want. Some 75% of website referrals pass through Google. And, it is the engine that drives AOL and Yahoo searches. Talk about success!

What is the Google difference? How did it gain such runaway popularity? The answer is performance excellence based on speed, accuracy, and ease of use. These have been the guiding performance criteria from the beginning, the basis for generating user appeal and competitive advantage in the marketplace. Page and Brin want to create a "perfect search engine" that "understands exactly what you mean and gives you back exactly what you want," says Page. With such goals, talent and motivation drive the system.

In the continuing search for innovation, the firm sticks to its historical roots—an informal culture with a small company feel. At Google creative and happy people diverse in backgrounds, skills, and interests come together to build an ever-better search engine.

The company website describes its approach to talent this way: "Google's hiring policy is aggressively non-discriminatory, and favors ability over experience. The result is a staff that reflects the global audience the search engine serves. In all, 34 languages are spoken by Google staffers—from Turkish to Telugu. Outside of the office, 'Googlers' pursue interests from cross-country cycling to wine tasting, from flying to Frisbee."[1]

Get Connected!

There's more to Google than meets the eye. Optimize your searches by learning more at Google Help Central.

Chapter 2 Learning Preview

Just as a Google search churns through billions of websites, Google's founders and staffers continuously strive to learn from past experience and apply their expertise to continuously improving the company. The same holds as scholars work within the field of management itself. In Chapter 2 you will become acquainted with the historical roots of management and learn how they created the knowledge base that today helps you and others become better managers.

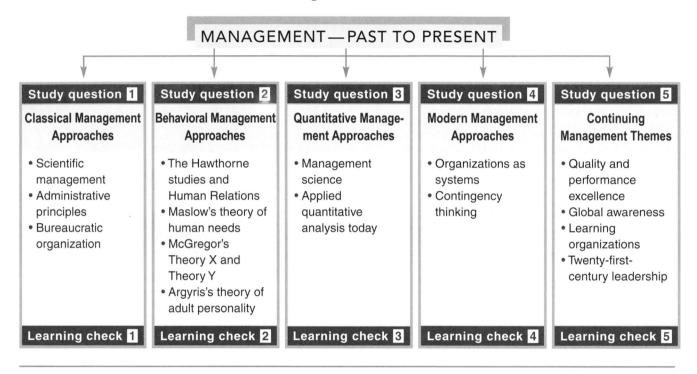

MANAGEMENT—PAST TO PRESENT

Study question 1	Study question 2	Study question 3	Study question 4	Study question 5
Classical Management Approaches	**Behavioral Management Approaches**	**Quantitative Management Approaches**	**Modern Management Approaches**	**Continuing Management Themes**
• Scientific management • Administrative principles • Bureaucratic organization	• The Hawthorne studies and Human Relations • Maslow's theory of human needs • McGregor's Theory X and Theory Y • Argyris's theory of adult personality	• Management science • Applied quantitative analysis today	• Organizations as systems • Contingency thinking	• Quality and performance excellence • Global awareness • Learning organizations • Twenty-first-century leadership
Learning check 1	Learning check 2	Learning check 3	Learning check 4	Learning check 5

The problems and opportunities facing organizations today are complex, ever-present, and always changing. From the anxieties of terrorism to the uncertainties of international politics to the challenges of globalization, all of society's institutions feel the pressures of a new and very challenging environment. The world of work and business as we have known it is being transformed as traditional ways of doing things are replaced by new practices and viewpoints. But even in the rush toward an exciting future, one shouldn't sell history short. Knowledge gained through past experience can and should be used as a foundation for future success.

When Harvard University Press released *Mary Parker Follett—Prophet of Management: A Celebration of Writings from the 1920s*, it clearly reminded us of the wisdom of history.[2] Although Follett wrote in a different day and age, her ideas are rich with foresight. She advocated cooperation and better horizontal relationships in organizations, taught respect for the experience and knowledge of workers, warned against the dangers of too much hierarchy, and called for visionary leadership. Today we pursue similar themes while using terms like "empowerment," "involvement," "flexibility," and "self-management." Rather than naively believe that we are reinventing management practice, it is better to recognize the historical roots of many modern ideas and admit that we are still trying to perfect them.[3]

In *The Evolution of Management Thought*, Daniel Wren traces management as far back as 5000 B.C., when ancient Sumerians used written records to assist in governmental and commercial activities.[4] Management was important to the construction of the Egyptian pyramids, the rise of the Roman Empire, and the commercial success of 14th-century Venice. By the time of the Industrial Revolution in the 1700s, great social changes helped prompt a great leap forward in the manufacture of basic staples and consumer goods. Industrial development was accelerated by Adam Smith's ideas of efficient production through specialized tasks and the division of labor. By the turn of the 20th century, Henry Ford and others were making mass production a mainstay of the emerging economy. Since then, the science and practices of management have been on a rapid and continuing path of development.

CLASSICAL MANAGEMENT APPROACHES

Our study of management begins with the classical approaches: (1) scientific management, (2) administrative principles, and (3) bureaucratic organization.[5] *Figure 2.1* associates each with a prominent person in the history of management thought. These names are important to know since they are still widely used in management conversations today. Also, the figure shows that the classical approaches share a common assumption: People at work act in a rational manner that is primarily driven by economic concerns. Workers are expected to rationally consider opportunities made available to them and do whatever is necessary to achieve the greatest personal and monetary gain.[6]

SCIENTIFIC MANAGEMENT

In 1911 Frederick W. Taylor published *The Principles of Scientific Management*, in which he makes the following statement: "The principal object of management should be to secure maximum prosperity for the employer, coupled with the maximum prosperity for the employee."[7] Taylor, often called the "father of scientific management," noticed that many workers did their jobs their own way and without clear and uniform specifications. He believed that this caused them to lose efficiency and perform below their true capacities. He also believed that this problem could be corrected if workers were taught and then helped by supervisors to always perform their jobs in the right way.

www.maids.com

Maids International conducted systematic studies of high labor turnover. Tasks were redesigned, and time was provided for relaxation. CEO Dan Bishop says: "Fatigue and boredom are what burn people out. We tried to eliminate them."

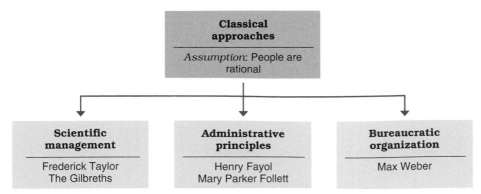

Figure 2.1 Major branches in the classical approach to management.

| MANAGER'S NOTEPAD 2.1 | Practical lessons from scientific management |

- Make results-based compensation a performance incentive.
- Carefully design jobs with efficient work methods.
- Carefully select workers with the abilities to do these jobs.
- Train workers to perform jobs to the best of their abilities.
- Train supervisors to support workers so that they can perform jobs to the best of their abilities.

○ **Scientific management** emphasizes careful selection and training of workers and supervisory support.

Taylor's goal was to improve the productivity of people at work. He used the concept of "time study" to analyze the motions and tasks required in any job and to develop the most efficient ways to perform them.[8] He then linked these job requirements with both training for the worker and support from supervisors in the form of proper direction, work assistance, and monetary incentives. The implications of his efforts are found in many management settings today, as summarized in *Manager's Notepad 2.1.* Taylor's approach is known as **scientific management** and includes these four guiding action principles.

Principles of scientific management

1. Develop for every job a "science" that includes rules of motion, standardized work implements, and proper working conditions.
2. Carefully select workers with the right abilities for the job.
3. Carefully train workers to do the job and give them the proper incentives to cooperate with the job "science."
4. Support workers by carefully planning their work and by smoothing the way as they go about their jobs.

○ **Motion study** is the science of reducing a task to its basic physical motions.

Mentioned in Taylor's first principle, **motion study** is the science of reducing a job or task to its basic physical motions. Two contemporaries of Taylor, Frank and Lillian Gilbreth, pioneered motion studies as a management tool. In one famous study they reduced the number of motions used by bricklayers and tripled their productivity.[9] The Gilbreths' work established the foundation for later advances in the areas of job simplification, work standards, and incentive wage plans—all techniques still used in the modern workplace.

An example of the continuing influence of Taylor and the Gilbreths can be seen at United Parcel Service, where workers are guided by carefully calibrated productivity standards. At regional centers, sorters are timed according to strict task requirements and are expected to load vans at a set number of packages per hour. Delivery stops on regular van routes are studied and carefully timed, and supervisors generally know within a few minutes how long a driver's pickups and deliveries will take. Industrial engineers devise precise routines for drivers, who are trained to knock on customers' doors rather than spend even a few seconds looking for the doorbell. Handheld computers further enhance delivery efficiencies. At UPS, savings of seconds on individual stops add up to significant increases in productivity.

ADMINISTRATIVE PRINCIPLES

A second branch in the classical approaches to management includes attempts to document and understand the experiences of successful managers. Two prominent writers in this school of thought are Henri Fayol and Mary Parker Follett.

Henri Fayol

In 1916, after a career in French industry, Henri Fayol published *Administration Industrielle et Générale*.[10] The book outlines his views on the proper management of organizations and the people within them. It identifies the following five "rules" or "duties" of management, which closely resemble the four functions of management—planning, organizing, leading, and controlling—that we talk about today:

1. *Foresight*—to complete a plan of action for the future.
2. *Organization*—to provide and mobilize resources to implement the plan.
3. *Command*—to lead, select, and evaluate workers to get the best work toward the plan.
4. *Coordination*—to fit diverse efforts together, and ensure information is shared and problems solved.
5. *Control*—to make sure things happen according to plan and to take necessary corrective action.

← Fayol's rules of management

Most importantly, Fayol believed that management could be taught. He was very concerned about improving the quality of management and set forth a number of "principles" to guide managerial action. A number of them are still part of the management vocabulary. They include Fayol's *scalar chain principle*—there should be a clear and unbroken line of communication from the top to the bottom in the organization; the *unity of command principle*—each person should receive orders from only one boss; and the *unity of direction principle*—one person should be in charge of all activities that have the same performance objective.

Mary Parker Follett

Another contributor to the administrative principles school was Mary Parker Follett, who was eulogized at her death in 1933 as "one of the most important women America has yet produced in the fields of civics and sociology."[12] In her writings about businesses and other organizations, Follett displayed an understanding of groups and a deep commitment to human cooperation—ideas that are highly relevant today. For her, groups

AROUND THE WORLD

Quality practices readily travel the world

When Mercedes Benz set up manufacturing in the United States, the best of its German management practices came, too.[11] The German automaker expects and teaches its American workers to follow precise standards known at SMPs (standard methods and procedures). The SMPs specify everything right down to the way a lug nut should be tightened and where a tool should be placed when not in use. Mercedes believes this is the key to maintaining high-quality and high-performance standards, no matter where in the world its automobiles are manufactured. A spokesperson says: "Our success would not have been possible without the great partnership we formed with the State of Alabama and without the strong workforce that we have found here."

were mechanisms through which diverse individuals could combine their talents for a greater good. She viewed organizations as "communities" in which managers and workers should labor in harmony, without one party dominating the other and with the freedom to talk over and truly reconcile conflicts and differences. She believed it was the manager's job to help people in organizations cooperate with one another and achieve an integration of interests.

A review of *Dynamic Administration: The Collected Papers of Mary Parker Follett* helps to illustrate the modern applications of her management insights.[14] Follett believed that making every employee an owner in the business would create feelings of collective responsibility. *Today*, we address the same issues under such labels as "employee ownership," "profit sharing," and "gain-sharing plans." Follet believed that business problems involve a wide variety of factors that must be considered in relationship to one another. *Today*, we talk about "systems" when describing the same phenomenon. Follett believed that businesses were services and that private profits should always be considered vis-à-vis the public good. *Today*, we pursue the same issues under the labels of "managerial ethics" and "corporate social responsibility."

BUREAUCRATIC ORGANIZATION

Max Weber was a late-19th-century German intellectual whose insights have had a major impact on the field of management and the sociology of organizations. His ideas developed somewhat in reaction to what he considered to be performance deficiencies in the organizations of his day. Among other things, Weber was concerned that people were in positions of authority not because of their job-related capabilities, but because of their social standing or "privileged" status in German society. For this and other reasons, he believed that organizations largely failed to reach their performance potential.

At the heart of Weber's thinking was a specific form of organization he believed could correct the problems just described—a **bureaucracy**.[15] This is an ideal, intentionally rational, and very efficient form of organization founded on principles of logic, order, and legitimate authority. The defining characteristics of Weber's bureaucratic organization are as follows:

- *Clear division of labor:* Jobs are well defined, and workers become highly skilled at performing them.
- *Clear hierarchy of authority:* Authority and responsibility are well defined for each position, and each position reports to a higher-level one.
- *Formal rules and procedures:* Written guidelines direct behavior and decisions in jobs, and written files are kept for historical record.
- *Impersonality:* Rules and procedures are impartially and uniformly applied with no one receiving preferential treatment.
- *Careers based on merit:* Workers are selected and promoted on ability and performance, and managers are career employees of the organization.

Weber believed that organizations would perform well as bureaucracies. They would have the advantages of efficiency in utilizing resources

○ A **bureaucracy** is a rational and efficient form of organization founded on logic, order, and legitimate authority.

→ Characteristics of Weber's bureaucracy

and of fairness or equity in the treatment of employees and clients. In his words:

> *The purely bureaucratic type of administrative organization . . . is, from a purely technical point of view, capable of attaining the highest degree of efficiency . . . . It is superior to any other form in precision, in stability, in the stringency of its discipline, and in its reliability. It thus makes possible a particularly high degree of calculability of results for the heads of the organization and for those acting in relation to it. It is finally superior both in intensive efficiency and in the scope of its operations and is formally capable of application to all kinds of administrative tasks.[16]*

This is the ideal side of bureaucracy. However, the terms "bureaucracy" and "bureaucrat" are now often used with negative connotations. The *possible disadvantages of bureaucracy* include excessive paperwork or "red tape," slowness in handling problems, rigidity in the face of shifting customer or client needs, resistance to change, and employee apathy. These disadvantages are most likely to cause problems for organizations that must be flexible and quick in adapting to changing circumstances—a common situation today. Thus researchers now try to determine when and under what conditions bureaucratic features work best. They also want to identify alternatives to the bureaucratic form. Current trends in management include many innovations that seek the same goals as Weber but with different approaches to how organizations can be structured.

Be sure you can • list the principles of Taylor's scientific management • list the key characteristics of bureaucracy and explain why Weber considered it an ideal form of organization • identify possible disadvantages of bureaucracy in today's environment

Learning check 1

BEHAVIORAL MANAGEMENT APPROACHES

During the 1920s, an emphasis on the human side of the workplace began to influence management thinking. Major branches in the behavioral or human resource approaches to management are shown in *Figure 2.2*. They include the famous Hawthorne studies and Maslow's theory of human needs, as well as theories generated from these foundations by Douglas McGregor, Chris Argyris, and others. The behavioral approaches maintain

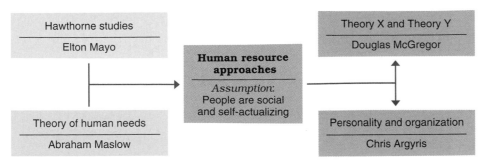

Figure 2.2 Foundations in the behavioral or human resource approaches to management.

that people are social and self-actualizing. People at work are assumed to seek satisfying social relationships, respond to group pressures, and search for personal fulfillment.

THE HAWTHORNE STUDIES AND HUMAN RELATIONS

In 1924, the Western Electric Company (predecessor to today's Lucent Technologies) commissioned a research program to study individual productivity at the Hawthorne Works of the firm's Chicago plant.[17] The initial "Hawthorne studies" had a scientific management perspective and sought to determine how economic incentives and the physical conditions of the workplace affected the output of workers. An initial focus was on the level of illumination in the manufacturing facilities; it seemed reasonable to expect that better lighting would improve performance. After failing to find this relationship, however, the researchers concluded that unforeseen "psychological factors" somehow interfered with their illumination experiments. This finding and later Hawthorne studies directed attention toward human interactions in the workplace and ultimately had a major influence on the field of management.

Relay Assembly Test-Room Studies

In 1927, a team led by Harvard's Elton Mayo began more research to examine the effect of worker fatigue on output. Care was taken to design a scientific test that would be free of the psychological effects thought to have confounded the earlier illumination studies. Six workers who assembled relays were isolated for intensive study in a special test room. They were given various rest pauses, and workdays and workweeks of various lengths, and production was regularly measured. Once again, researchers failed to find any direct relationship between changes in physical working conditions and output. Productivity increased regardless of the changes made.

Mayo and his colleagues concluded that the new "social setting" created for workers in the test room accounted for the increased productivity. Two factors were singled out as having special importance. One was the *group atmosphere;* the workers shared pleasant social relations with one

IN PRACTICE

People hold the keys to long-term performance success

Toronto-based Four Seasons Hotels and Resorts seeks employees who are friendly, committed to teamwork, and, of course, highly talented. The firm declares that quality of service is "so critically important to our guests, and the degree to which we can provide and evolve it, worldwide, is also the degree to which we can differentiate ourselves and stay ahead of the rest." Four Seasons is a leader in the luxury segment of the hospitality industry. Its strengths and reputation are cultivated with leadership commitment to a fundamental principle: The key to sustained performance success is people. Among the guiding values of the firm is: "we believe that each of us needs a sense of dignity, pride and satisfaction in what we do."[18]

another and wanted to do a good job. The other was more *participative supervision*. Test-room workers were made to feel important, were given a lot of information, and were frequently asked for their opinions. This was not the case in their regular jobs elsewhere in the plant.

Employee Attitudes, Interpersonal Relations, and Group Processes

Mayo's research continued until the worsening economic conditions of the Depression forced their termination in 1932. By then, interest in the human factor had broadened to include employee attitudes, interpersonal relations, and group relations. In one study, over 21,000 employees were interviewed to learn what they liked and disliked about their work environment. "Complex" and "baffling" results led the researchers to conclude that the same things (e.g., work conditions or wages) could be sources of satisfaction for some workers and of dissatisfaction for others. The final Hawthorne study was conducted in the bank wiring room and centered on the role of the work group. A surprise finding here was that people would restrict their output in order to avoid the displeasure of the group, even if it meant sacrificing pay that could otherwise be earned by increasing output. Thus, it was recognized that groups can have strong negative, as well as positive, influences on individual productivity.

Lessons of the Hawthorne Studies

As scholars now look back, the Hawthorne studies are criticized for poor research design, weak empirical support for the conclusions drawn, and the tendency of researchers to overgeneralize their findings.[19] Yet their significance as turning points in the evolution of management thought remains intact. The Hawthorne studies helped shift the attention of managers and management researchers away from the technical and structural concerns of the classical approach and toward social and human concerns as keys to productivity. They showed that people's feelings, attitudes, and relationships with coworkers affected their work. They recognized the importance of group influences on individuals. They also identified the **Hawthorne effect**—the tendency of people who are singled out for special attention to perform as anticipated merely because of expectations created by the situation.

> o The **Hawthorne effect** is the tendency of persons singled out for special attention to perform as expected.

The Hawthorne studies contributed to the emergence of the **human relations movement,** which influenced management thinking during the 1950s and 1960s. This movement was largely based on the viewpoint that managers who used good human relations in the workplace would achieve productivity. Importantly, this movement combined with related developments in the social sciences to set the stage for what has now evolved as the field of **organizational behavior,** the study of individuals and groups in organizations.

> o The **human relations movement** suggests that managers using good human relations will achieve productivity.

> o **Organizational behavior** is the study of individuals and groups in organizations.

MASLOW'S THEORY OF HUMAN NEEDS

Among the insights of the human relations movement, the work of psychologist Abraham Maslow in the area of human "needs" is a key foundation.[20] A **need** is a physiological or psychological deficiency a person feels the compulsion to satisfy. This is a significant concept for managers because needs create tensions that can influence a person's work attitudes and behaviors.

> o A **need** is a physiological or psychological deficiency that a person wants to satisfy.

Maslow identified the five levels of human needs, shown in *Figure 2.3.* From lowest to highest in order, they are physiological, safety, social, es-

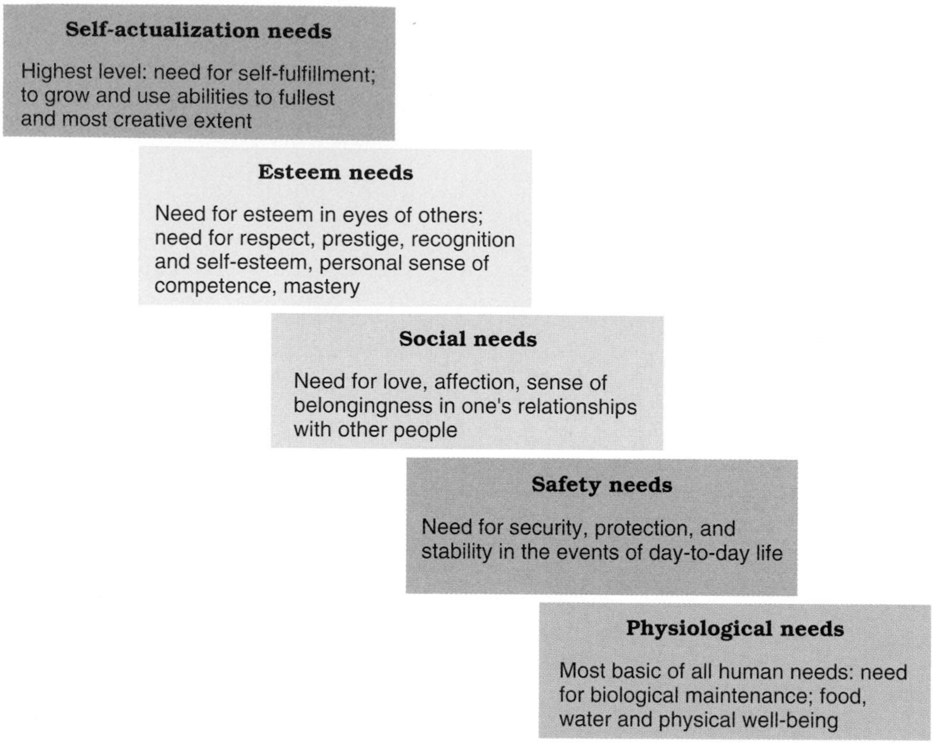

Figure 2.3   Maslow's hierarchy of human needs.

teem, and self-actualization needs. Maslow's theory is based on two underlying principles. The first is the *deficit principle*—a satisfied need is not a motivator of behavior. People act to satisfy "deprived" needs, those for which a satisfaction "deficit" exists. The second is the *progression principle*—the five needs exist in a hierarchy of "prepotency." A need at any level is only activated when the next-lower-level need is satisfied.

According to Maslow, people try to satisfy the five needs in sequence. They progress step by step from the lowest level in the hierarchy up to the highest. Along the way, a deprived need dominates individual attention and determines behavior until it is satisfied. Then, the next-higher-level need is activated. At the level of self-actualization, the deficit and progression principles cease to operate. The more this need is satisfied, the stronger it grows.

Consistent with human relations thinking, Maslow's theory implies that managers who help people satisfy their important needs at work will achieve productivity. Although scholars now recognize that things are more complicated than this, as discussed in Chapter 14 on motivation, Maslow's ideas are still relevant. Consider, for example, the case of volunteer workers who do not receive any monetary compensation. Managers in nonprofit organizations have to create jobs and work environments that satisfy the many different needs of volunteers. If their work isn't fulfilling, the volunteers will lose interest and probably redirect their efforts elsewhere.

McGREGOR'S THEORY X AND THEORY Y

Douglas McGregor was heavily influenced by both the Hawthorne studies and Maslow. His classic book *The Human Side of Enterprise* advances the thesis that managers should give more attention to the social and self-actualizing needs of people at work.[22] McGregor called upon managers to shift their view of human nature away from a set of assumptions he called "Theory X" and toward ones he called "Theory Y."

According to McGregor, managers holding **Theory X** assumptions approach their jobs believing that those who work for them generally dislike work, lack ambition, are irresponsible, are resistant to change, and prefer to be led rather than to lead. McGregor considers such thinking inappropriate. He argues instead for the value of **Theory Y** assumptions in which the manager believes people are willing to work, are capable of self-control, are willing to accept responsibility, are imaginative and creative, and are capable of self-direction.

An important aspect of McGregor's ideas is his belief that managers who hold either set of assumptions can create **self-fulfilling prophecies**— that is, through their behavior they create situations where others act in ways that confirm the original expectations. *Managers with Theory X assumptions,* for example, act in a very directive "command-and-control" fashion that gives people little personal say over their work. These supervisory behaviors create passive, dependent, and reluctant subordinates who tend to do only what they are told to or required to do. This reinforces the original Theory X viewpoint.

In contrast, *managers with Theory Y perspectives* behave in "participative" ways that allow subordinates more job involvement, freedom, and responsibility. This creates opportunities to satisfy esteem and self-actualization needs, and workers tend to perform as expected with initiative and high performance. The self-fulfilling prophecy thus becomes a positive one. Theory Y thinking is consistent with developments in the new workplace and its emphasis on valuing workforce diversity. It is also central to the popular notions of employee participation, involvement, empowerment, and self-management.[23]

o **Theory X** assumes people dislike work, lack ambition, are irresponsible, and prefer to be led.

o **Theory Y** assumes people are willing to work, accept responsibility, are self-directed and creative.

o A **self-fulfilling prophecy** occurs when a person acts in ways that confirm another's expectations.

ARGYRIS'S THEORY OF ADULT PERSONALITY

Ideas set forth by the well-regarded scholar and consultant Chris Argyris also reflect the belief in human nature advanced by Maslow and McGregor. In his book *Personality and Organization,* Argyris contrasts the management practices found in traditional and hierarchical organizations with the needs and capabilities of mature adults.[25] He concludes that some

Positive management style breaks the glass ceiling

When Betsy Holden became the president and CEO of Kraft Foods, Inc., she had earned her way to the top. With a graduate degree from Northwestern's Kellogg School, she rose from division brand manager to CEO in just 16 years. Holden has been praised for "hard work, focus, and creativity," and a "positive, upbeat, enthusiastic, collaborative, and team-oriented" management style. She says: "I think I'm good at inspiring, setting a vision of what we need to go and do—and then engaging the team and putting together the game plan to get there." Career development is important to her. When helping others, she asks: "What skills do you need, what experiences do you need, what development do you need?" Perhaps the most important testimony to her management style is the next question: "How do we help you make that happen?"[21]

practices, especially those influenced by the classical management approaches, are inconsistent with the mature adult personality.

Consider these examples. In scientific management, the principle of specialization assumes that people will work more efficiently as tasks become better defined. Argyris believes that this may inhibit self-actualization in the workplace. In Weber's bureaucracy, people work in a clear hierarchy of authority, with higher levels directing and controlling lower levels. Argyris worries that this creates dependent, passive workers who feel they have little control over their work environments. In Fayol's administrative principles, the concept of unity of direction assumes that efficiency will increase when a person's work is planned and directed by a supervisor. Argyris suggests that this may create conditions for psychological failure; psychological success occurs when people define their own goals.

Like McGregor, Argyris believes that managers who treat people positively and as responsible adults will achieve the highest productivity. His advice is to expand job responsibilities, allow more task variety, and adjust supervisory styles to allow more participation and promote better human relations. He believes that the common problems of employee absenteeism, turnover, apathy, alienation, and low morale may be signs of a mismatch between management practices and mature adult personalities.

Learning check 2	*Be sure you can* • define the term Hawthorne effect • explain how the Hawthorne findings influenced the development of management thought • explain how Maslow's hierarchy of needs operates in the workplace • distinguish between Theory X and Theory Y assumptions, and explain why McGregor favored Theory Y • explain Argyris's criticism that traditional organizational practices are inconsistent with mature adult personalities

QUANTITATIVE MANAGEMENT APPROACHES

About the same time that some scholars were developing human resource approaches to management, others were investigating how quantitative techniques could improve managerial decision making. The foundation of the quantitative approaches is the assumption that mathematical techniques can be used for better problem solving. Today these applications are increasingly supported and driven by computer technology and software programs.

MANAGEMENT SCIENCE

○ **Management science** uses mathematical techniques to analyze and solve management problems.

The terms **management science** and *operations research* are often used interchangeably to describe the scientific applications of mathematical techniques to management problems. A typical approach proceeds as follows. A problem is encountered, it is systematically analyzed, appropriate mathematical models and computations are applied, and an optimum solution is identified. There are a variety of management science applications that can be used in this way. *Mathematical forecasting* helps make future projections that are useful in the planning process. *Inventory modeling* helps control inventories by mathematically establishing how much to order and when. *Linear programming* is used to calculate how best to allocate scarce resources among competing uses. *Queuing theory* helps allocate service personnel or workstations to minimize customer waiting time and service cost. *Network models* break large tasks into smaller components to allow for better analysis, planning, and control of complex projects. *Simulations* create models of problems so different solutions under various assumptions can be tested.

Regardless of the specific technique used, the essence of quantitative management approaches includes these characteristics. There is a focus on rational decision making that has clear action implications. The techniques use "economic" decision criteria, such as costs, revenues, and return on investment. They also involve mathematical models that follow sophisticated rules and formulas.

APPLIED QUANTITATIVE ANALYSIS TODAY

University courses in management science, operations research, and quantitative business analysis provide a good introduction to these quantitative management foundations. Courses in operations management apply them to the physical production of goods and services. Since many of the techniques are highly sophisticated, organizations often employ staff specialists to help managers take advantage of them effectively. Software developments are now making these techniques more readily available through easy-to-use applications for desktop and even handheld personal computers. This greatly expands their use throughout the workplace and makes it even more important for managers to understand the value of each technique. Always, of course, mathematical solutions to problems must be supported by good managerial judgment and an appreciation of the human factor.

www.spss.com

A popular and easy-to-use software program for statistical analysis is SPSS, available from SPSS Inc. The firm supports databased problem solving, with applications to customer relationship management and business intelligence.

Be sure you can • define the term management science • list three quantitative techniques that are used in management today • explain how these techniques help managers solve problems

Learning check 3

MODERN MANAGEMENT APPROACHES

The modern approaches to management grew from the rich foundations established by the classical, human resource, and quantitative schools of thought. According to the modern management approaches, people are complex and variable. They have many varied needs that can change over time. They possess a range of talents and capabilities that can be continually developed. Organizations and managers, therefore, should respond to individual differences with a wide variety of managerial strategies and job opportunities. Key foundations of the modern management approaches thus include the systems view of organizations and contingency thinking. Importantly, they recognize that no one model or theory applies universally in all situations or to the exclusion of the others.

ORGANIZATIONS AS SYSTEMS

Formally defined, a **system** is a collection of interrelated parts that function together to achieve a common purpose. A **subsystem** is a smaller component of a larger system.[26] One of the earliest management writers to adopt a systems perspective was Chester Barnard. His 1938 ground-breaking book *Functions of the Executive* was based on years of experience as a telephone company executive.[27] Barnard described organizations as cooperative sys-

○ A **system** is a collection of interrelated parts working together for a purpose.

○ A **subsystem** is a smaller component of a larger system.

Figure 2.4. Organizations as complex networks of interacting subsystems.

tems that achieve great things by integrating the contributions of many individuals to achieve a common purpose. Importantly, Barnard considered cooperation a "conscious, deliberate, and purposeful" feature of organizations. In other words, it had to be created. For him, using communication to make this cooperation happen was the principle executive responsibility.

Management theory and practice today are influenced by the complexity of organizational systems and subsystems.[28] One application is described in *Figure 2.4,* which is an extension of the systems view of organizations described in Chapter 1. This figure first depicts the larger organization as an **open system** that interacts with its environment in the continual process of transforming inputs from suppliers into outputs for customers. Within the organization any number of critical subsystems can be described as part of the transformation process. In the figure, the operations and service management systems are a central point. They provide the integration among other subsystems, such as purchasing, accounting, sales, and information, that are essential to the work of the organization. Importantly, and as suggested by Barnard, high performance by the organization as a whole occurs only when each subsystem both performs its tasks well and works well in cooperation with others. It is the job of managers throughout the organization to make this coordinated action possible.

> ○ An **open system** interacts with its environment and transforms resource inputs into outputs.

CONTINGENCY THINKING

Modern management is situational in orientation; that is, it attempts to identify practices that are the best fit with the unique demands of a situation. It utilizes **contingency thinking** that tries to match managerial responses with the problems and opportunities specific to different settings, particularly those posed by individual and environmental differences. In the modern management approach, there is no expectation that one can or should find the "one best way" to manage in all circumstances. Rather, the contingency perspective tries to help managers understand situational differences and respond to them in ways appropriate to their unique characteristics.[29]

> ○ **Contingency thinking** tries to match management practices with situational demands.

Contingency thinking is an important theme in this book, and its implications extend to all of the management functions—from planning and controlling for diverse environmental conditions, to organizing for different environments and strategies, to leading in different performance situations. For example, consider again the concept of bureaucracy. Weber offered it as an ideal form of organization. But from a contingency perspective, the strict bureaucratic form is only one possible way of organizing things. What turns out to be the "best" structure in any given situation will depend on many factors, including environmental uncertainty, an organization's primary technology, and the strategy being pursued. The strict bureaucracy works best only when the environment is relatively stable and operations are predictable. In other situations, alternative and more flexible structures are needed. Contingency thinking recognizes that what is a good structure for one organization may not work well for another, and what works well at one time may not work as well in the future as circumstances change.[30] This contingency approach to organization structure and design will be examined further in Chapters 10 and 11.

REALITY CHECK 2.2

Mobility in American society
Management theories and practices should keep pace with changes in society at large. Did you know that some 17 percent of Americans change their residences each year? Take the online "Reality Check" to learn more about mobility in American society. You may be surprised!

Be sure you can • define the terms *system*, *subsystem*, and *open system* • apply these concepts to describe the operations of an organization in your community • define the term *contingency thinking* • explain how contingency thinking might influence a manager's decision to use or not use a bureaucratic approach to organization structure	**Learning check 4**

CONTINUING MANAGEMENT THEMES

The many accumulating insights discussed so far helped set the foundation for important trends and directions in management thought that are well in evidence as we begin the 21st century. Among the most important is the recognition that we live and work in a dynamic and ever-changing environment that puts unique and never-ending pressures on organizations. In this context, the themes reflected throughout *Management 8/e* include quality and performance excellence, ethics and social responsibility, global awareness, and the importance of new leadership in an age of information, knowledge workers, and highly competitive business environments.

QUALITY AND PERFORMANCE EXCELLENCE

The quality theme first introduced in Chapter 1 remains a very important direction in management today.[31] Managers and workers in truly progressive organizations are quality conscious. They understand the basic link between competitive advantage and the ability to always deliver quality goods and services to their customers. The best organizational cultures include quality as a core value and reinforce the quality commitment in all aspects of the work environment.

Every effort is made in total quality management (TQM) to build quality into all aspects of operations from initial acquisition of resources, through the transformation processes and work systems, all the way to ultimate product delivery to customers or clients. *Figure 2.5* describes the systems context for TQM with respect to the **value chain**—a specific sequence of activities that transforms raw materials into a finished good or service.[32] Quality must be maintained at each point in the value chain,

○ A **value chain** is the sequence of activities that transforms raw materials into finished goods or services.

TAKE IT TO THE CASE

The Coca-Cola Company
Coke gets back to business

Talk about history! Coca-Cola for decades has been one of the world's best-known brands. Where in the world can you go and not be able to get a Coke? But the firm's glorious past can't guarantee the same future. Coke must prosper in a highly competitive soft drink industry, and successfully counter all attacks by archrival Pepsi as well as those of discount beverage sellers and new entrants like Virgin Cola. Past achievements (Diet Coke) and failures ("New Coke") provide a learning base from which to craft future strategy and plans. However, like all growth companies, Coke has to deal with the inevitable problems of increasing size, organizational structures, and the management of people.[38]

whether it is performed directly by the organization or is part of its network of relationships with suppliers and contractors.

Closely aligned with the pursuit of quality is management commitment to performance excellence, a theme that rose to special prominence over 20 years ago when *In Search of Excellence: Lessons from America's Best-Run Companies* was published by Thomas Peters and Robert Waterman.[33] Based on case investigations of successful companies, they identified the eight attributes of performance excellence shown in *Manager's Notepad 2.2*. Although we now recognize that these attributes are but modest insights into a far more complex performance picture, they are useful starting points. In them you will find many themes and directions that are now common practice in organizations today.

GLOBAL AWARENESS

We are just emerging from a decade in which the quality and performance excellence themes were reflected in the rise of "process reengineering," "virtual organizations," "agile factories," "network firms," and other concepts introduced in this book. But while the best formulas for success continue to be tested and debated, an important fact remains: Much of the pressure for quality and performance excellence is created by the forces of globalization and a highly competitive global economy. Nowhere is this

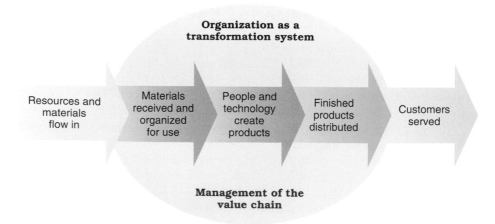

Figure 2.5. The organizational value chain.

Eight attributes of performance excellence

- *Bias toward action*—making decisions and making sure things get done.
- *Closeness to the customers*—knowing their needs and valuing customer satisfaction.
- *Autonomy and entrepreneurship*—supporting innovation, change, and risk taking.
- *Productivity through people*—valuing human resources as keys to quality and performance.
- *Hands-on and value-driven*—having a clear sense of organizational purpose.
- *Sticking to the knitting*—focusing resources and attention on what the organization does best.
- *Simple form and lean staff*—minimizing management levels and staff personnel.
- *Simultaneous loose-tight properties*—allowing flexibility while staying in control.

challenge more evident than in the continuing efforts of businesses around the globe to transform themselves into truly world-class operations.

Like the lessons of performance excellence, current trends and directions in global awareness have ties back to the 1980s. That was a time when the success of Japanese industry caught worldwide attention and both scholars and consultants rushed to identify what could be learned from Japanese management practices. The books *Theory Z*, by William Ouchi, and *The Art of Japanese Management,* by Richard Tanner Pascale and Anthony G. Athos, were among the first that called attention to the possible link between unique Japanese practices and business success.[34] Ouchi used the term "Theory Z" to describe a management framework that uses insights found in the Japanese models.[35] Prominent in the **Theory Z** management approach are such things as long-term employment, slower promotions and more lateral job movements, greater attention to career planning and development, more use of consensus decision making, and high emphasis on use of teamwork and employee involvement. And even though the Japanese economy and management systems face pressures of their own today, these early insights into the Japanese business experience helped to establish a global awareness that continues to enrich management thinking today. This international dimension will be emphasized throughout *Management 8/e.* Chapter 5 gives special attention to understanding cultural influences on management practices.

○ **Theory Z** describes management emphasizing long-term employment, consensus, and teamwork.

LEARNING ORGANIZATIONS

The change and uncertainty in today's environment have given rise to an emphasis on creating **learning organizations,** ones that are able to continually learn and adapt themselves to new circumstances. Such organiza-

○ A **learning organization** continuously changes and improves, using the lessons of experience.

tions are successful because they are uniquely capable of improving themselves by learning from experience. Consultant Peter Senge popularized the concept of the learning organization in his book *The Fifth Discipline,* and he identifies the following as its core ingredients.[36]

→ Core ingredients of a learning organization

1. Mental models—everyone sets aside old ways of thinking.
2. Personal mastery—everyone becomes self-aware and open to others.
3. Systems thinking—everyone learns how the whole organization works.
4. Shared vision—everyone understands and agrees to a plan of action.
5. Team learning—everyone works together to accomplish the plan.

Organizations that meet Senge's criteria for learning organizations offer work settings in which members develop their abilities to learn and are encouraged and helped to make that learning continuously available to everyone else. They have value-driven organizational cultures that emphasize information sharing, teamwork, empowerment, participation, and learning. Importantly, the leaders of learning organizations set an example for others by embracing change and communicating enthusiasm for solving problems and growing with new opportunities.

PERSONAL MANAGEMENT

Now is a very good time for you to examine your **LEARNING STYLE**. Every person a manager deals with is unique; most problem situations are complex; and things are always changing. Success in management only comes to those who thrive on learning. Some people learn by watching; they observe others and model what they see. Others learn by doing; they act and experiment, learning as they go. There is no one best way to learn about managing—there is only the need to learn . . . all the time, from others, from formal training, and from real experiences. An organization development manager at PepsiCo once said: "I believe strongly in the notion that enhancing managers' knowledge of their strengths and particularly their weaknesses is integral to ensuring long-term, sustainable performance improvement and executive success."[24] The problem is that many of us never dig deep enough to both get this depth of personal understanding and use it to set learning goals. You can start here by keeping a personal strengths and weaknesses scorecard.

Strengths

Where I am now	Learning goals

Weaknesses

Where I am now	Learning goals

Get to know yourself better ▶
Complete Self-Assessments #3—**Learning Tendencies,** and #4—**What are Your Managerial Assumptions?,** from the Management Learning Workbook.

21st-CENTURY LEADERSHIP

There is no doubt that today's social, political, and economic forces make it necessary for people and organizations to continually adapt to new situations if they are to survive and prosper over the long run. Learning, learning, and more learning is the new reality of work in the 21st century. This fact carries with it distinctive personal development and leadership challenges. And when it comes to leadership, history once again sets the stage for the future. In his book *No Easy Victories,* John Gardner speaks of leadership as a special responsibility, and his words are well worth considering today.

Leaders have a significant role in creating the state of mind that is the society. They can serve as symbols of the moral unity of the society. They can express the values that hold the society together. Most important, they can conceive and articulate goals that lift people out of their petty preoccupations, carry them above the conflicts that tear a society apart, and unite them in the pursuit of objectives worthy of their best efforts.[37]

Leadership and the new directions of learning organizations are singled out again and again in *Management 8/e* as important keys to personal and organizational performance.

Managers of the 21st century will have to excel as never before to meet the expectations held of them and of the organizations they lead. Importantly, we must all recognize that new managerial outlooks and new managerial competencies appropriate to the new times are requirements for future leadership success. At the very least, the *21st-century manager* must be a:

- *Global strategist*—understanding the interconnections among nations, cultures, and economies; planning and acting with due consideration of them.

- *Master of technology*—comfortable with information technology; understanding technological trends and their implications; able to use technology to best advantage.

- *Inspiring leader*—attracting highly motivated workers and inspiring them with a high-performance culture where individuals and teams can do their best work.

- *Model of ethical behavior*—acting ethically in all ways, setting high ethical standards for others to follow, building a work culture that values ethics and social responsibility.

◄ Characteristics of the 21st-century executive

Management scholar and consultant Peter Drucker calls this the age of information and considers knowledge the principal resource of a competitive society. Drucker also cautions that knowledge constantly makes itself obsolete.[39] In a society where knowledge workers are increasingly important, this means that new managers must be well educated . . . and they must continue that education throughout their careers. Success in turbulent times comes only through learning and continuous improvement.

The new economy requires everyone—you included—to be unrelenting in efforts to develop, refine, and maintain job-relevant skills and competencies. It requires leaders with strong people skills, ones attuned to the nature of an information/service society, ones who understand the international dimensions, and ones who establish commitments to work-life balance. And the new economy places a premium on high-performance leadership. Consider, for example, this comment by former corporate CEO and college president Ralph Sorenson: "It is the *ability to make things happen* that most distinguishes the successful manager from the mediocre or unsuccessful one. . . . The most cherished manager is the one who says 'I can do it,' and then does."[40]

"Do it," advises Sorenson. "Of course," you may quickly answer. But don't forget that the 21st-century manager must also do the "right" things—the things that really count, the things that add value to the organization's goods and/or services, the things that make a real difference in performance results and competitive advantage, and the ethical things. Those are challenging directions for leadership and career success in the new economy.

Be sure you can • define the term value chain • illustrate how the value chain operates in an organization that you know • explain Theory Z • list the characteristics of a learning organization • discuss special characteristics of 21st-century leaders • discuss your personal responsibilities for learning and performance

Learning check 5

CHAPTER 2 STUDY GUIDE

Where We've Been

BACK TO GOOGLE, INC.

The opening example of Google, Inc., introduced you to the world of high technology and the opportunities of getting connected in our digital world. But it is important to remember that Google couldn't have been created without the knowledge made available by the full history of research and development in computer science. Now it's an organization that is turning its founders' commitments to learning into the pathway toward the future. In Chapter 2 you learned the major historical roots that influence the study of management. As you read further in *Management 8/e,* keep the lessons of history in mind. The management theories and concepts we value today have strong links to the past.

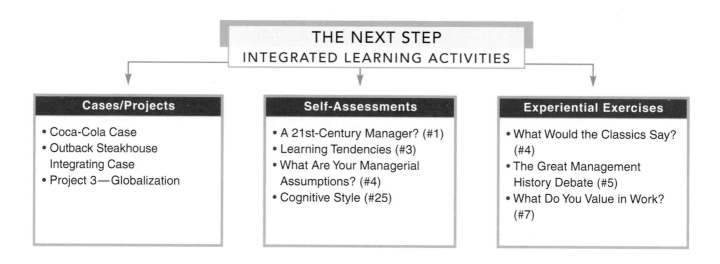

THE NEXT STEP
INTEGRATED LEARNING ACTIVITIES

Cases/Projects
- Coca-Cola Case
- Outback Steakhouse Integrating Case
- Project 3—Globalization

Self-Assessments
- A 21st-Century Manager? (#1)
- Learning Tendencies (#3)
- What Are Your Managerial Assumptions? (#4)
- Cognitive Style (#25)

Experiential Exercises
- What Would the Classics Say? (#4)
- The Great Management History Debate (#5)
- What Do You Value in Work? (#7)

STUDY QUESTIONS SUMMARY

1. What can be learned from classical management thinking?

- Frederick Taylor's four principles of scientific management focused on the need to carefully select, train, and support workers for individual task performance.
- Henri Fayol suggested that managers should learn what are now known as the management functions of planning, organizing, leading, and controlling.
- Max Weber described bureaucracy with its clear hierarchy, formal rules, and well-defined jobs as an ideal form of organization.

2. What ideas were introduced by the human resource approaches?

- The human resource or behavioral approaches shifted attention toward the human factor as a key element in organizational performance.
- The historic Hawthorne studies suggested that work behavior is influenced by social and psychological forces and that work performance may be improved by better "human relations."
- Abraham Maslow's hierarchy of human needs introduced the concept of self-actualization and the potential for people to experience self-fulfillment in their work.

- Douglas McGregor urged managers to shift away from Theory X and toward Theory Y thinking, which views people as independent, responsible, and capable of self-direction in their work.
- Chris Argyris pointed out that people in the workplace are adults and may react negatively when constrained by strict management practices and rigid organizational structures.

3. What is the role of quantitative analysis in management?

- The availability of high-power desktop computing provides new opportunities for mathematical methods to be used for managerial problem solving.
- Many organizations employ staff specialists who are experts in quantitative management science and operations research.
- Quantitative techniques used by managers include forecasting, linear programming, and simulation, among others.

4. What is unique about the systems view and contingency thinking?

- Organizations are complex open systems that interact with their external environments to transform resource inputs into product outputs.

- Resource acquisition and customer satisfaction are important requirements in the organization-environment relationship.
- Organizations are composed of many internal subsystems that must work together in a coordinated way to support the organization's overall success.
- Contingency thinking avoids "one best way" arguments, recognizing the need to understand situational differences and respond appropriately to them.

5. What are continuing management themes of the 21st century?

- The commitment to meet customer needs guides organizations toward total quality management and continuous improvement of operations.
- Interest in Japanese management practices illustrates the opportunities to learn new ways of managing from practices in other countries.
- Changing times place great value on learning organizations, ones that are able to continually learn and adapt themeselves to changing circumstances.
- New managers must accept and excel at 21st-century leadership responsibilities to perform as global strategists, technology masters, sensitive politicians, leader/motivators, and ethical role models.

KEY TERMS REVIEW

Bureaucracy (p. 38)
Contingency thinking (p. 46)
Hawthorne effect (p. 41)
Human relations movement (p. 41)
Learning organization (p. 49)

Management science (p. 44)
Motion study (p. 36)
Need (p. 41)
Open system (p. 46)
Organizational behavior (p. 41)
Scientific management (p. 36)

Self-fulfilling prophecies (p. 43)
Subsystem (p. 45)
System (p. 45)
Theory X (p. 43)
Theory Y (p. 43)
Theory Z (p. 49)
Value chain (p. 47)

SELF-TEST 2

MULTIPLE-CHOICE QUESTIONS:

1. The assumption that people are complex with widely varying needs is most associated with the _____ management approaches.
   (a) classical (b) neoclassical (c) behavioral (d) modern

2. The father of scientific management is _____.
   (a) Weber (b) Taylor (c) Mintzberg (d) Katz

3. The Hawthorne studies are important because they raised awareness of the important influences of _____ on productivity.
   (a) structures (b) human factors (c) physical work conditions (d) pay and rewards

4. Advice to study a job and carefully train workers to do that job with financial incentives tied to job performance would most likely come from _____.
   (a) scientific management (b) contingency management (c) Henri Fayol (d) Abraham Maslow

5. The highest level in Maslow's hierarchy is the level of _____ needs.
   (a) safety (b) esteem (c) self-actualization (d) physiological

6. Conflict between the mature adult personality and a rigid organization was a major concern of _____.
   (a) Argyris (b) Follett (c) Gantt (d) Fuller

7. When people perform in a situation as they are expected to, this is sometimes called the _____ effect.
   (a) Hawthorne (b) bureaucratic (c) contingency (d) open-systems

8. Linear programming and queuing theory are examples of techniques found in the _____ approach to management.
   (a) classical (b) quantitative (c) bureaucratic organization (d) modern

9. Resource acquisition and customer satisfaction are important when an organization is viewed as a(n) _____.
   (a) bureaucracy (b) closed system (c) open system (d) pyramid

10. Long-term employment and consensus decision making are characteristic of the _____ management framework.
    (a) Theory X (b) Theory Y (c) Theory Z (d) contingency

11. When your local bank or credit union is viewed as an open system, the loan-processing department would be considered a _____.
    (a) subsystem (b) closed system (c) resource input (d) value center

12. When a manager notices that Sheryl has strong social needs and puts her in a job that involves customer relations, while also being sure to give Kwabena lots of praise because of his strong ego needs, the manager is displaying _____.
    (a) systems thinking (b) Theory X (c) motion study (d) contingency thinking

13. If you conducted a value chain analysis of a business, you would study _____.
    (a) customer satisfaciton with products (b) how much TQM affect profits (c) the flow of activities that trans-
    form resources into goods and services (d) the links between performance and rewards

14. In a learning organization, as described by Peter Senge, one would expect to find _____.
    (a) priority placed on following rules and procedures (b) promotions based on seniority (c) employees who
    are willing to set aside old thinking and embrace new ways (d) a strict hierarchy of authority

15. 21st-century leaders must, according to Ralph Sorenson, be able to add value to organizations by
    _____.
    (a) taking action to make things happen (b) building efficient structures (c) keeping customers happy (d)
    using mathematics for decision making

SHORT-RESPONSE QUESTIONS:

16. Explain how McGregor's Theory Y assumptions can create self-fulfilling prophecies consistent with the
    current emphasis on participation and involvement in the workplace.

17. How do the deficit and progression principles operate in Maslow's hierarchy-of-needs theory?

18. Define "contingency thinking" and give an example of how it might apply to management.

19. Explain why the external environment is so important in the open-systems view of organizations.

APPLICATION QUESTION:

20. Enrique Temoltzin has just been appointed the new manager of your local college bookstore. Enrique
    would like to make sure the store operates according to Weber's bureaucracy. Describe the characteristics
    of bureaucracy and answer this question: Is the bureaucracy a good management approach for Enrique to
    follow? Discuss the possible limitations of bureaucracy and the implications for managing people as key
    assets of the store.

www.wiley.com/college/schermerhorn

3

Ethical behavior and social responsibility

CHAPTER 3 study questions

1. What is ethical behavior?

2. How do ethical dilemmas complicate the workplace?

3. How can high ethical standards be maintained?

4. What is corporate social responsibility?

5. How do organizations and governments work together in society?

Planning Ahead

After reading Chapter 3, you should be able to answer these questions in your own words.

BEN & JERRY'S—HELP MAKE THE WORLD A BETTER PLACE

You know the ice cream for sure—who hasn't tasted a Ben & Jerry's Cherry Garcia® cone or delighted with a scoop of Chunky Monkey® banana ice cream? But do you really know the company? Ben & Jerry's earned its reputation not just from great ice cream but also from the concept of "linked prosperity," sharing prosperity with its employees and the communities in which it operates.

Flash back to 1977 when two friends, Ben Cohen and Jerry Greenfield, move from Long Island to Burlington, Vermont. Needing a source of income, they take a correspondence course on ice cream making from Pennsylvania State University. Fast forward to 1978, when Ben & Jerry's Homemade, on a $12,000 investment, sold its first ice cream cones from a converted gas station in downtown Burlington. It was a "different" ice cream store right from the start. In 1979 the first Free Cone Day—free ice cream for all day—was held to celebrate the store's first anniversary.

Fast forward to 1985, when the company, with $9 million in annual sales, establishes the Ben & Jerry's Foundation to fund community-oriented projects. Financially, 7.5 percent of the company's annual pre-tax profits are pledged annually to support the foundation. Fast forward to 1988, when the firm, with $47 million in annual sales, receives the Corporate Giving Award from the Council on Economic Priorities for its foundation's philanthropy. Fast forward to 1989—sales are $59 million and the company introduces Rainforest Crunch® ice cream, with sales helping to support rainforest preservation efforts.

Fast forward again to today—what do we find? The now-global company is owned by Unilever and has sales outlets in Europe, the Middle East, Latin America, and Asia. It remains distinguished by a mission statement still devoted to linked prosperity. Its commitments are to quality products, sustainable value for stakeholders, the welfare of employees, and innovation to improve the quality of life in its communities and around the world. The Ben & Jerry's foundation remains committed to "creative problem solving for hopefulness."[1]

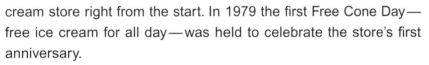

Get Connected!

Shouldn't you know more about business ethics and social responsibility? Check the websites of the Ethics Resource Center and Business for Social Responsibility.

Chapter 3 Learning Preview

You have to appreciate what Ben Cohen and Jerry Greenfield accomplished at Ben & Jerry's. And it isn't just that they were able to forge a well-regarded, global company from a small startup. It is the nature of the company they developed, one with a commitment to ethical behavior and social responsibility, that is the true hallmark. Chapter 3 examines these issues in detail, with the goal of encouraging your understanding of and commitment to ethical and socially responsible behavior. As you read, check your learning progress in these major areas.

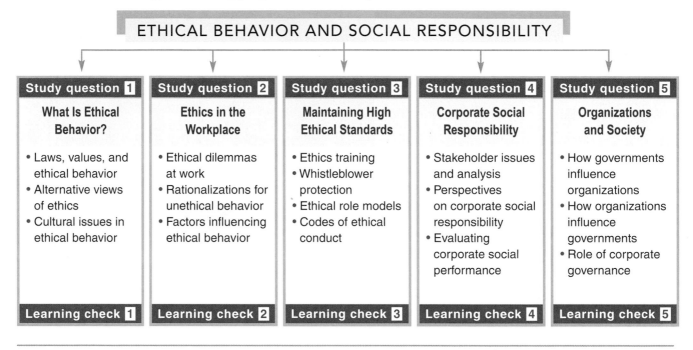

ETHICAL BEHAVIOR AND SOCIAL RESPONSIBILITY

Study question 1	Study question 2	Study question 3	Study question 4	Study question 5
What Is Ethical Behavior?	**Ethics in the Workplace**	**Maintaining High Ethical Standards**	**Corporate Social Responsibility**	**Organizations and Society**
• Laws, values, and ethical behavior • Alternative views of ethics • Cultural issues in ethical behavior	• Ethical dilemmas at work • Rationalizations for unethical behavior • Factors influencing ethical behavior	• Ethics training • Whistleblower protection • Ethical role models • Codes of ethical conduct	• Stakeholder issues and analysis • Perspectives on corporate social responsibility • Evaluating corporate social performance	• How governments influence organizations • How organizations influence governments • Role of corporate governance
Learning check 1	**Learning check 2**	**Learning check 3**	**Learning check 4**	**Learning check 5**

It wasn't very long ago that we were shocked and dismayed when a rash of sensational news reports communicated the worst of business behavior, among them WORLDCOM FACING CHARGES OF FRAUD—HOW ENRON BOSSES CREATED A CULTURE OF PUSHING LIMITS—ANDERSEN'S WRONG TURNS GREW OBVIOUS—A "STELLAR REPUTATION" SHATTERED.[2] The stories behind the headlines revealed ethical failures by prominent businesses and their leaders. They were hard facts of the new century, not just textbook possibilities. In December 2001, three months after the attack on the World Trade Center, Enron declared bankruptcy, the largest in U.S. history. In July 2002, the WorldCom bankruptcy bettered Enron by 60 percent, coming in at $104 billion. Caught in Enron's web of ethical catastrophe, Arthur Andersen, LLP, fell from being one of the largest certified public accounting firms in the world to being out of business.[3]

The root causes of these and many other bankruptcies were not poor business models or bad market calculations. They were failures of ethics. Employees and officers lied and cheated about important financial information. They cajoled and threatened others to do the same. They modeled unethical practices to the point that such behavior became accepted practices within the firms.[4] Such cases can easily leave us feeling cynical, pessimistic, and even helpless regarding the state of ethical leadership in our society. But even in the face of so much bad news, a more positive and promising perspective can be taken. Jana Matthews, founder and CEO of Boulder Quantum Ventures, a consulting firm that helps businesses grow, says:

> After watching WorldCom, Enron, Arthur Andersen and other companies cook the book and artificially inflate profits, I understand the public skepticism about business. But I maintain that there are thousands and thousands of companies employing millions and millions of people who operate honestly, with the right values.[5]

It is time to get serious about the moral aspects and social implications of decision making in organizations. In your career and in the work of any manager, performance goals must always be achieved through ethically and socially responsible action. The following reminder from Desmond Tutu, archbishop of Capetown, South Africa, and winner of the Nobel Peace Prize, is applicable to managers everywhere:

> You are powerful people. You can make this world a better place where business decisions and methods take account of right and wrong as well as profitability. . . . You must take a stand on important issues: the environment and ecology, affirmative action, sexual harassment, racism and sexism, the arms race, poverty, the obligations of the affluent West to its less-well-off sisters and brothers elsewhere.[6]

WHAT IS ETHICAL BEHAVIOR?

For our purposes, **ethics** can be defined as the code of moral principles that sets standards of good or bad, or right or wrong, in one's conduct.[7] Ethics provides principles to guide behavior and help people make moral choices among alternative courses of action. In practice, **ethical behavior** is that which is accepted to be "good" and "right" as opposed to "bad" or "wrong" in the context of the governing moral code.

○ **Ethics** sets standards of good or bad, or right or wrong, in one's conduct.

○ **Ethical behavior** is "right" or "good" in the context of a governing moral code.

LAWS, VALUES, AND ETHICAL BEHAVIOR

It makes sense that anything that is legal should be considered ethical. Yet slavery was once legal in the United States and laws once permitted only men to vote. That doesn't mean the practices were ethical; rather, we consider these laws unethical today. Furthermore, just because an action is not strictly illegal doesn't make it ethical. Living up to the "letter of the law" is not sufficient to guarantee that one's actions will or should be considered ethical.[8] Is it truly ethical, for example, for an employee to take longer than necessary to do a job? To make personal telephone calls on company time? To call in sick to take a day off for leisure? To fail to report rule violations by a coworker? None of these acts are strictly illegal, but many people would consider any one or more of them to be unethical.

Most ethical problems in the workplace arise when people are asked to do or find themselves about to do something that violates their personal beliefs. For some, if the act is legal they proceed with confidence. For others, the ethical test goes beyond the legality of the act alone. The ethical question extends to personal **values**—the underlying beliefs and attitudes

○ **Values** are broad beliefs about what is appropriate behavior.

TAKE IT TO THE CASE!

Tom's of Maine
—Where "doing business" means "doing good"

Values drive the natural-products firm Tom's of Maine. Founded by Tom Chappell and his wife Kate, the company was described by the Council of Economic Priorities as one of the "saints of social responsibility." Tom's products cost more, but customers know they support a company whose products don't pollute. Tom says, "I believe we have been able to expand upon the historical point of view that business is just for making money to a broader view that business is about doing good for others in the process of getting financial gain." The mission states "We believe our company can be profitable and successful while acting in a socially and environmentally responsible manner."[10]

○ **Terminal values** are preferences about desired end states.

○ **Instrumental values** are preferences regarding the means to desired ends.

that help determine individual behavior. To the extent that values vary among people, we can expect different interpretations of what behavior is ethical or unethical in a given situation.

The psychologist Milton Rokeach makes a popular distinction between "terminal" and "instrumental" values.[9] **Terminal values** are preferences about desired ends, such as the goals one strives to achieve in life. Examples of terminal values considered important by managers include self-respect, family security, freedom, inner harmony, and happiness. **Instrumental values** are preferences regarding the means for accomplishing these ends. Among the instrumental values held important by managers are honesty, ambition, courage, imagination, and self-discipline. Both terminal and instrumental values vary from one person to the next, but the value pattern for any one person is very enduring. This variation among value profiles is a reason why different people respond quite differently to a situation with ethical challenges.

ALTERNATIVE VIEWS OF ETHICS

Figure 3.1 shows four views of ethical behavior that philosophers have discussed over the years.[11] Behavior that would be considered ethical

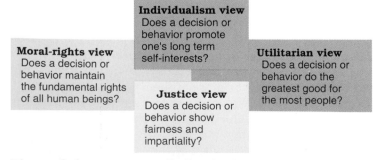

Individualism view
Does a decision or behavior promote one's long term self-interests?

Moral-rights view
Does a decision or behavior maintain the fundamental rights of all human beings?

Utilitarian view
Does a decision or behavior do the greatest good for the most people?

Justice view
Does a decision or behavior show fairness and impartiality?

Figure 3.1 Four views of ethical behavior.

from the **utilitarian view** delivers the greatest good to the greatest number of people. Founded in the work of 19th-century philosopher John Stuart Mill, this results-oriented point of view tries to assess the moral implications of decisions in terms of their consequences. Business decision makers, for example, are inclined to use profits, efficiency, and other performance criteria to judge what is best for the most people. A manager may make a utilitarian decision to cut 30 percent of a plant's workforce in order to keep the plant profitable and save the remaining jobs.

○ In the **utillitarian view** ethical behavior delivers the greatest good to the most people.

The **individualism view** of ethical behavior is based on the belief that one's primary commitment is long-term advancement of self-interests. People supposedly become self-regulating as they pursue long-term individual advantage. For example, lying and cheating for short-term gain should not be tolerated. If one person does it, everyone will do it, and no one's long-term interests will be served. The individualism view is supposed to promote honesty and integrity. But in business practice it may result in a *pecuniary ethic*, described by one executive as the tendency to "push the law to its outer limits" and "run roughshod over other individuals to achieve one's objectives."[12]

○ In the **individualism view** ethical behavior advances long-term self-interests.

Ethical behavior under a **moral-rights view** is that which respects and protects the fundamental rights of people. From the teachings of John Locke and Thomas Jefferson, for example, the rights of all people to life, liberty, and fair treatment under the law are considered inviolate. In organizations, this concept extends to ensuring that employees are always protected in rights to privacy, due process, free speech, free consent, health and safety, and freedom of conscience. The issue of *human rights*, a major ethical concern in the international business environment, is central to this perspective. The United Nations stands by the Universal Declaration of Human Rights passed by the General Assembly in 1948.

○ In the **moral-rights view** ethical behavior respects and protects fundamental rights.

Finally, the **justice view** of moral behavior is based on the belief that ethical decisions treat people impartially and fairly, according to legal rules and standards. This approach evaluates the ethical aspects of any decision on the basis of whether it is "equitable" for everyone affected.[13] **Procedural justice** involves the degree to which policies and rules are fairly administered. For example, does a sexual harassment charge levied against a senior executive receive the same full hearing as one made against a first-level supervisor? **Distributive justice** involves the degree to which outcomes are allocated without respect to individual characteristics based on ethnicity, race, gender, age, or other particularistic criteria. For example, does a woman with the same qualifications and experience as a man receive the same consideration for hiring or promotion? **Interactional justice** involves the degree to which others are treated with dignity and respect. For example, does a bank loan officer take the time to fully explain to an applicant why he or she was turned down for a loan?[14]

○ In the **justice view** ethical behavior treats people impartially and fairly.

○ **Procedural justice** is concerned that policies and rules are fairly applied.

○ **Distributive justice** is concerned that people are treated the same regardless of personal characteristics.

○ **Interactional justice** is the degree to which others are treated with dignity and respect.

CULTURAL ISSUES IN ETHICAL BEHAVIOR

The influence of culture on ethical behavior is increasingly at issue in this time of globalization. Corporate leaders must master difficult challenges when operating across borders that are cultural as well as national. Former Levi CEO Robert Haas once said that an ethical dilemma "becomes even more difficult when you overlay the complexities of different cultures and values systems that exist throughout the world."[15]

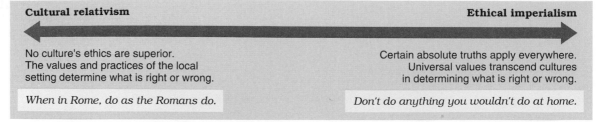

Cultural relativism

No culture's ethics are superior.
The values and practices of the local
setting determine what is right or wrong.

When in Rome, do as the Romans do.

Ethical imperialism

Certain absolute truths apply everywhere.
Universal values transcend cultures
in determining what is right or wrong.

Don't do anything you wouldn't do at home.

Figure 3.2 The extremes of cultural relativism and ethical imperialism in international business ethics.
Source: Developed from Thomas Donaldson, "Values in Tension: Ethics Away from Home," *Harvard Business Review*, vol. 74 (September–October 1996), pp. 48–62.

○ **Cultural relativism** suggests there is no one right way to behave; ethical behavior is determined by its cultural context.

○ **Universalism** suggests ethical standards apply absolutely across all cultures.

○ **Ethical imperialism** is an attempt to impose one's ethical standards on other cultures.

Those who believe that behavior in foreign settings should be guided by the classic rule of "When in Rome, do as the Romans do" reflect an ethical position of **cultural relativism.**[16] This is the belief that there is no one right way to behave and that ethical behavior is always determined by its cultural context. An American international business executive guided by rules of cultural relativism, for example, would argue that the use of child labor is okay in another country if it is consistent with local laws and customs.

Figure 3.2 contrasts cultural relativism with the alternative of **universalism.** This ethical position suggests if a behavior or practice is not okay in one's home environment, it is not acceptable practice anywhere else. In other words, ethical standards are universal and should apply absolutely across cultures and national boundaries. In the former example, the American executive would not do business in a setting where child labor was used, since it is unacceptable at home. Critics of such a universal approach claim that it is a form of **ethical imperialism,** or the attempt to externally impose one's ethical standards on others.

Business ethicist Thomas Donaldson discusses the debate between cultural relativism and ethical imperialism. Although there is no simple answer, he finds fault with both extremes. He argues instead that certain fundamental rights and ethical standards can be preserved while values and traditions of a given culture are respected.[17] The core values or "hyper-norms" that should transcend cultural boundaries focus on human dignity, basic rights, and good citizenship. With a commitment to core values creating a transcultural ethical umbrella, Donaldson believes international business behaviors can be tailored to local and regional cultural contexts. In the case of child labor, again, the American executive might ensure that any children working in a factory under contract to his or her business would be provided schooling as well as employment. *Manager's Notepad 3.1* summaries Donaldson's suggestions on how corporations can respect the core or universal values.[18]

Learning check 1

Be sure you can • define ethics • list and explain four views of ethical behavior • discuss the types of ethical problems faced by people at work • differentiate the implications of cultural relativism and universalism in international business ethics

How international businesses can respect
universal values

MANAGER'S NOTEPAD   3.1

Respect Human Dignity

- Create a culture valuing emloyees, customers, and suppliers.
- Keep a safe workplace.
- Produce safe products and services.

Respect Basic Rights

- Protect rights of employees, customers, and communities.
- Avoid any threats to safety, health, education, living standards.

Be Good Citizens

- Support social institutions, economic and educational systems.
- Work with governments and institutions to protect the environment.

ETHICS IN THE WORKPLACE

A classic quotation states: "Ethical business is good business." The same can be said for all persons and institutions throughout society. But the real test is when a manager or worker encounters a situation that challenges his or her ethical beliefs and standards. Often ambiguous and unexpected, these ethical challenges are inevitable and everyone has to be prepared to deal with them, even students. A college student may get a job offer and accept it, only to get a better offer two weeks later. Is it right for her to renege on the first job to accept the second? A student knows that in a certain course his roommate submitted a term paper purchased on the Internet. Is it right for him not to tell the instructor? One student tells another that a faculty member promised her a high final grade in return for sexual favors. Is it right for him not to vigorously encourage her to inform the instructor's department head?

ETHICAL DILEMMAS AT WORK

An **ethical dilemma** is a situation that requires a choice regarding a possible course of action that, although offering the potential for personal or organizational benefit or both, may be considered unethical. It is often a situation in which action must be taken but for which there is no clear consensus on what is "right" and "wrong." The burden is on the individual to make good choices. An engineering manager speaking from experience sums it up this way: "I define an unethical situation as one in which I have to do something I don't feel good about."[19] Some problem areas where managers can get caught in ethical dilemmas include:[20]

- *Discrimination*—denying promotion or appointment to a job candidate because of the candidate's race, religion, gender, age, or other non-job-relevant criterion.

○ An **ethical dilemma** is a situation that although offering potential benefit or gain is also unethical.

← Ethical problem areas for managers

- *Sexual harassment*—making a coworker feel uncomfortable because of inappropriate comments or actions regarding sexuality; or a manager requesting sexual favors in return for favorable job treatment.

- *Conflicts of interest*—taking a bribe or kickback or extraordinary gift in return for making a decision favorable to the gift giver.

- *Customer confidence*—giving to another party privileged information regarding the activities of a customer.

- *Organizational resources*—using official stationery or a company e-mail account to communicate personal opinions or make requests from community organizations.

In a survey of *Harvard Business Review* subscribers, many of the ethical dilemmas reported by managers involved conflicts with superiors, customers, and subordinates.[21] The most frequent issues involved dishonesty in advertising and communications with top management, clients, and government agencies. Problems in dealing with special gifts, entertainment, and kickbacks were also reported. Significantly, the managers' bosses sometimes pressured them to engage in such unethical activities as supporting incorrect viewpoints, signing false documents, overlooking the boss's wrongdoings, and doing business with the boss's friends.

REALITY CHECK 3.1

Can unethical behavior be controlled?
In a survey by the accounting and consulting firm KPMG LLP, some 75 percent of respondents said they had witnessed unethical acts at work in the last 12 months. The next question is: What did they do about it? Take the online "Reality Check" to learn more.

RATIONALIZATIONS FOR UNETHICAL BEHAVIOR

Why do otherwise reasonable people justify unethical acts? Think back to the earlier examples and to those from your experiences. Consider the possibility of being asked to place a bid for a business contract using insider information, paying bribes to obtain foreign business, falsifying expense account bills, and so on. "How," you should be asking, "do people explain doing things like this?" There are at least four common rationalizations that may be used to justify misconduct in these and other ethical dilemmas.[22]

Four ways of thinking about ethical behavior

- Convincing yourself that the behavior is not really illegal.
- Convincing yourself that the behavior is in everyone's best interests.
- Convincing yourself that nobody will ever find out what you've done.
- Convincing yourself that the organization will "protect" you.

After doing something that might be considered unethical, a rationalizer says, *"It's not really illegal."* This expresses a mistaken belief that one's behavior is acceptable, especially in ambiguous situations. When dealing with shady or borderline situations in which you are having a hard time precisely determining right from wrong, the advice is quite simple: When in doubt about a decision to be made or an action to be taken, don't do it.

Another common statement by a rationalizer is: *"It's in everyone's best interests."* This response involves the mistaken belief that because someone can be found to benefit from the behavior, the behavior is also in the individual's or the organization's best interests. Overcoming this rationalization depends in part on the ability to look beyond short-run results to address longer-term implications, and to look beyond results in general to the ways in which they are obtained. For example, in response to the question "How far can I push matters to obtain this performance goal?," the best answer may be: "Don't try to find out."

Sometimes rationalizers tell themselves, *"No one will ever know about it."* They mistakenly believe that a questionable behavior is really "safe" and will never be found out or made public. Unless it is discovered, the argument implies, no crime was really committed. Lack of accountability, unrealistic pressures to perform, and a boss who prefers "not to know" can all reinforce such thinking. In this case, the best deterrent is to make sure that everyone knows that wrongdoing will be punished whenever it is discovered.

Finally, rationalizers may proceed with a questionable action because of a mistaken belief that *"the organization will stand behind me."* This is misperceived loyalty. The individual believes that the organization's best interests stand above all others. In return, the individual believes that top managers will condone the behavior and protect the individual from harm. But loyalty to the organization is not an acceptable excuse for misconduct; it should not stand above the law and social morality.

FACTORS INFLUENCING ETHICAL BEHAVIOR

It is almost too easy to confront ethical dilemmas from the safety of a textbook or a college classroom. In practice, people are often challenged to choose ethical courses of action in situations where the pressures may be contradictory and great. Sadly, a surprising 56 percent of U.S. workers in one survey reported feeling pressured to act unethically in their jobs.[23] The same survey also revealed that 48 percent had committed questionable acts within the past year. Increased awareness of the factors influencing ethical behavior can help you better deal with them in the future. *Figure 3.3* shows these influences emanating from the person, the organization, and the environment.

The Person

Family influences, religious values, personal standards, and personal needs, financial and otherwise, will help determine a person's ethical conduct in any given circumstance. Managers who lack a strong and clear set of personal ethics will find that their decisions vary from situation to situation as they strive to maximize self-interests. Those with

Figure 3.3 Factors influencing ethical managerial behavior—the person, organization, and environment.

solid *ethical frameworks,* personal rules or strategies for ethical decision making, will be more consistent and confident. Their choices are always guided by a stable set of ethical standards. Personal values that give priority to such virtues as honesty, fairness, integrity, and self-respect provide *ethical anchors* that help people make correct decisions even when circumstances are ambiguous and situational pressures are difficult.

It isn't easy to stand up for what you believe in as a person, especially in a social context full of contradictory or just plain bad advice. Consider these words from a commencement address delivered a few years ago at a well-known school of business administration. "Greed is all right," the speaker said. "Greed is healthy. You can be greedy and still feel good about yourself." The students, it is reported, greeted these remarks with laughter and applause. The speaker was Ivan Boesky, once considered the "king of the arbitragers."[24] It wasn't long after his commencement speech that Boesky was arrested, tried, convicted, and sentenced to prison for trading on inside information.

The Organization

The organization is another important influence on ethics in the workplace. We noted earlier that bosses can have a major impact on their subordinate's behaviors. Just exactly what a supervisor requests, and which actions are rewarded or punished, can certainly affect an individual's decisions and actions. The expectations and reinforcement provided by peers and group norms are likely to have a similar impact. Formal policy statements and written rules are also helpful. They support and reinforce the ethical climate for the organization as a whole.

At the Body Shop, founder Anita Roddick created an 11-point charter to guide the company's employees: "Honesty, integrity and caring form the foundations of the company and should flow through everything we do— we will demonstrate our care for the world in which we live by respecting fellow human beings, by not harming animals, by preserving our forests." The fact that the Body Shop still gets occasional ethical criticisms demonstrates the inadequacy of formal policies alone to guarantee consistent ethical behavior. A visit to the Body Shop website, however, shows the firm's ongoing ethical commitments and provides answers to frequently asked questions regarding such controversial issues as animal testing in the cosmetics industry.[25]

www.manhattan.edu

Through its Center for Professional Ethics, Manhattan College offers training in the recognition of ethical problems, the development of skills for dealing with them, and the building of ethical climates in organizational cultures.

The Environment

Organizations operate in competitive environments influenced by government laws and regulations, and social norms and values. Laws interpret social values to define appropriate behaviors for organizations and their members; regulations help governments monitor these behaviors and keep them within acceptable standards. For example, the recent Enron and Arthur Andersen scandals led to new legislation that attempts to substitute for any lack of ethical leadership at the firm and industry levels in U.S. business. The *Sarbanes-Oxley Act* of 2002 now makes it easier for corporate executives to be tried and sentenced to jail for financial misconduct. It also created The Public Company Accounting Oversight Board and set a new standard (Section 404) for auditors to verify reporting processes in the companies they audit.

The climate of competition in an industry also sets a standard of behavior for those who hope to prosper within it. Sometimes the pressures

Living by personal values makes business sense

You don't need to leave your values at home when you go to work or own your own business. Many people said that Aaron Feurstein was crazy when he kept some 1000 workers on the payroll when his apparel factory burned down. After Malden Mills of Lawrence, Massachusetts, got back in business producing Polartec and Polarfleece knits, owner, president, and CEO Feurstein couldn't have been prouder. He had paid his jobless employees over $15 million during the several months it took to rebuild the plant. He has also gained a loyal workforce dedicated to customers. Feurstein calls his decision just "common sense." Admired for his corporate decency, he hopes other CEOs believe "that there's a moral imperative that they must answer to as well."[26]

of competition contribute further to the ethical dilemmas of managers. Former American Airlines president Robert Crandall once telephoned Howard Putnam, then president of now-defunct Braniff Airlines. Both companies were suffering from money-losing competition on routes from their home base of Dallas. A portion of their conversation follows:[27]

> *Putnam:* Do you have a suggestion for me?
> *Crandall:* Yes. . . . Raise your fares 20 percent. I'll raise mine the next morning.
> *Putnam:* Robert, we—
> *Crandall:* You'll make more money and I will, too.
> *Putnam:* We can't talk about pricing.
> *Crandall:* Oh, Howard. We can talk about anything we want to talk about.

The U.S. Justice Department disagreed. It alleged that Crandall's suggestion of a 20 percent fare increase amounted to an illegal attempt to monopolize airline routes. The suit was later settled when Crandall agreed to curtail future discussions with competitors about fares.

Be sure you can • define an ethical dilemma • list at least three ethical problem areas common in the workplace • list four common rationalizations for unethical behavior • explain how ethics are influenced by . . . the person, the organization, the environment

Learning check 2

MAINTAINING HIGH ETHICAL STANDARDS

The bad news is, as we well know, that news from the corporate world is not always positive. Consider these actual reports from past news stories. *Item:* Firm admits lowering phone contract bid after receiving confidential information from an insider that an initial bid "was not good enough to win." *Item:* Company admits overcharging consumers and in-

MANAGER'S NOTEPAD 3.2

Checklist for dealing with ethical dilemmas

Step 1. Recognize the ethical dilemma.

Step 2. Get the facts.

Step 3. Identify your options.

Step 4. Test each option: Is it legal? Is it right? Is it beneficial?

Step 5. Decide which option to follow.

Step 6. Double-check decision by asking the "spotlight" questions:

"How would I feel if my family found out about my decision?"

"How would I feel about this if my decision were printed in the local newspaper?"

Step 7. Take action.

surers more than $13 million for repairs to damaged rental cars. *Item:* Executives get prison terms for selling adulterated apple juice; the juice, labeled "100% fruit juice," was actually a blend of synthetic ingredients.

The good news is that progressive organizations support a variety of methods for maintaining high ethical standards in workplace affairs. Some of the most important efforts in this area involve ethics training, whistleblower protection, top management support, formal codes of ethics, and strong ethical cultures.

ETHICS TRAINING

○ **Ethics training** seeks to help people understand the ethical aspects of decision making and to incorporate high ethical standards into their daily behavior.

Ethics training, takes the form of structured programs to help participants understand the ethical aspects of decision making. It is designed to help people incorporate high ethical standards into their daily behaviors. An increasing number of college curricula now include required courses on ethics, and seminars on this topic are popular in the corporate world. But it is important to keep ethics training in perspective. An executive at Chemical Bank once put it this way: "We aren't teaching people right from wrong—we assume they know that. We aren't giving people moral courage to do what is right—they should be able to do that anyhow. We focus on dilemmas."[28]

Many ethical dilemmas arise as a result of the time pressures of decisions. Ethics training can help people learn how to deal with ethical issues while under pressure. *Manager's Notepad 3.2* presents a seven-step checklist for dealing with an ethical dilemma. It offers an important reminder to double-check decisions *before* taking action. The key issue in the checklist may well be Step 6—the risk of public disclosure. Asking and answering the "spotlight" questions is a powerful way to test whether a decision is consistent with your personal ethical standards.

WHISTLEBLOWER PROTECTION

Agnes Connolly pressed her employer to report two toxic chemical accidents; Dave Jones reported that his company was using unqualified suppliers in the construction of a nuclear power plant; Margaret Newsham revealed that her firm was allowing workers to do personal business while on government contracts; Herman Cohen charged that the ASPCA in New York was mistreating animals; Barry Adams complained that his hospital followed unsafe practices.[29] They were **whistleblowers,** persons who expose the misdeeds of others in organizations in order to preserve ethical standards and protect against wasteful, harmful, or illegal acts.[30] All were fired from their jobs. Indeed, whistleblowers face the risks of impaired career progress and other forms of organizational retaliation, up to and including termination.

○ A **whistleblower** exposes the misdeeds of others in organizations.

Today, federal and state laws increasingly offer whistleblowers some defense against "retaliatory discharge." But although signs indicate that the courts are growing supportive of whistleblowers, legal protection can still be inadequate. Laws vary from state to state, and federal laws mainly protect government workers. Furthermore, even with legal protection, potential whistleblowers may find it hard to expose unethical behavior in the workplace.

Some organizational barriers to whistleblowing include a *strict chain of command* that makes it hard to bypass the boss; *strong work group identities* that encourage loyalty and self-censorship; and *ambiguous priorities* that make it hard to distinguish right from wrong.[31] A survey by the Ethics Resource Center reports that some 44 percent of workers in the United States still fail to report the wrongdoings they observe at work. The top reasons for not reporting are "(1) the belief that no corrective action would be taken and (2) the fear that reports would not be kept confidential."[32]

In the attempt to remove these and other blocks to the exposure of unethical behaviors, some organizations have formally appointed staff members to serve as *ethics advocates.* One novel proposal suggests the use of *moral quality circles* to help create shared commitments for everyone to work at their moral best.[33]

ETHICAL ROLE MODELS

Gabrielle Melchionda, a young entrepreneur in Portland, Maine, started Mad Gab's Inc., an all-natural skin-care business, while a college student. After her sales had risen to over $300,000, an exporter offered her a deal—sell $2 million of her products abroad. She turned it down. Why? The exporter also sold weapons, and that was against her values. Her values guide all business decisions, right from having an employee profit-sharing plan to hiring disabled adults to using only packaging designs that minimize waste.[34]

Top managers, in large and small enterprises, have the power to shape an organization's policies and set its moral tone. They also have a major responsibility to use this power well by serving as ethical role models. Not only must their day-to-day behavior be the epitome of high ethical conduct, but they must also create ethical cultures and communicate similar expectations throughout the organization.

Even though top managers bear a special responsibility for setting the ethical tone of an organization, all managers are in a position to influence the ethical behavior of the people who work for and with them. All managers must act as ethical role models, and both expect and support ethical behavior by others. The important supervisory act of setting goals and communicating performance expectations is a good case in point. A surprising 64 percent of 238 executives in one study, for exam-

www.ci.sf.ca.us

The City of San Francisco is a social activist, requiring companies that do business with it to offer benefits to domestic partners of their employees the same benefits that spouses would enjoy.

ple, reported feeling stressed to compromise personal standards to achieve company goals. A *Fortune* survey also reported that 34 percent of its respondents felt a company president can create an ethical climate by setting *reasonable* goals "so that subordinates are not pressured into unethical actions."[35] Any manager may unknowingly encourage unethical practices by exerting too much pressure for others to accomplish goals that are too difficult. Part of the manager's ethical responsibility is to be realistic about performance goals.

CODES OF ETHICAL CONDUCT

A **code of ethics** is a formal statement of an organization's values and ethical principles. It offers guidelines on how to behave in situations susceptible to ethical dilemmas. Such codes are important anchor points in professions such as engineering, medicine, law, and public accounting. In organizations they identify expected behaviors in such areas as general citizenship, the avoidance of illegal or improper acts in one's work, and good relationships with customers. Specific guidelines are often set for bribes and kickbacks, political contributions, honesty of books or records, customer–supplier relationships, and confidentiality of corporate information.

In the increasingly complex world of international business, codes of conduct for manufacturers and contractors are becoming more prevalent. At Gap, Inc. global manufacturing is governed by a formal Code of Vendor Conduct.[37] The document specifically deals with *discrimination*—stating "Factories shall employ workers on the basis of their ability to do the job, not on the basis of their personal characteristics or beliefs"; *forced labor*—stating "Factories shall not use any prison, indentured or forced labor"; *working conditions*—stating "Factories must treat all workers with respect and dignity and provide them with a safe and healthy environment"; and *freedom of association*—stating "Factories must not interfere with workers who wish to lawfully and peacefully associate, organize or bargain collectively."

Although codes of ethical conduct are now common, it must be remembered that they have limits. While helpful, codes alone cannot guarantee ethical conduct. Ultimately, the value of any ethics code still rests on the human resource foundations of the organization. There is no replacement for effective hiring practices that staff organizations with honest and moral people. And there is no replacement for leadership by committed managers who set positive examples and always act as ethical role models.

PERSONAL MANAGEMENT

PERSONAL CHARACTER is a foundation for all that we do. It establishes our integrity and provides an ethical anchor for our behavior in the workplace and in life overall. Persons of high integrity can always be confident in the self-respect it provides, even in the most difficult of situations. Those who lack it are destined to perpetual insecurity, acting inconsistently and suffering not only in self-esteem but also in the esteem of others. How strong is your personal character? How well prepared are you to deal with the inevitable ethical dilemmas and challenges in work and in life? Can you give specific examples showing how your behavior lives up to these Six Pillars of Character identified by the Josephson Institute of Ethics?[36]

- *Trustworthiness*—Honesty, integrity, reliability in keeping promises, loyalty
- *Respect*—Civility, courtesy and decency, dignity, tolerance, and acceptance
- *Responsibility*—Sense of accountability, pursuit of excellence, self-restraint
- *Fairness*—Commitment to process, impartiality, equity
- *Caring*—Concern for others, benevolence, altruism
- *Citizenship*—Knowing the law, being informed, volunteering

Get to know yourself better ▶
Complete Self-Assessments #5—**Terminal Values Survey**, and #6—**Instrumental Values Survey**; and Exercises #6—**Confronting Ethical Dilemmas** from the Management Learning Workbook.

○ A **code of ethics** is a formal statement of values and ethical standards.

CORPORATE SOCIAL RESPONSIBILITY

It is now time to shift our interest in ethical behavior from the level of the individual to that of the organization. To begin, it is important to remember that all organizations exist in complex relationship with elements in their external environment. In this context, **corporate social responsibility** is defined as an obligation of the organization to act in ways that serve both its own interests and the interests of society at large.[38]

STAKEHOLDER ISSUES AND ANALYSIS

A popular and useful way to examine the concept of corporate social responsibility is through a stakeholder analysis. *Figure 3.4* describes the environment of a typical business firm as a network of **organizational stakeholders**—those persons, groups, and other organizations directly affected by the behavior of the organization and holding a stake in its performance.[39] In this perspective, the organization has a social responsibility to serve the interests of its many stakeholders, including:

- *Employees*—employees and contractors who work for the organization.
- *Customers*—consumers and clients that purchase the organization's goods and/or use its services.

○ **Corporate social responsibility** is the obligation of an organization to serve its own interests and those of society.

○ **Organizational stakeholders** are directly affected by the behavior of the organization and hold a stake in its performance.

← Major organizational stakeholders

Figure 3.4 Multiple stakeholders in the environment of organization.

- *Suppliers*—providers of the organization's human, information, material, and financial resources.

- *Owners*—stockholders, investors, and creditors with claims on assets and profits of the organization.

- *Competitors*—other organizations producing the same or similar goods and services.

- *Regulators*—the local, state, and national government agencies that enforce laws and regulations.

- *Interest groups*—community groups, activists, and others representing interests of citizens and society.

The unethical practices at WorldCom, Enron, and Andersen, as discussed previously, had an adverse impact on these firms' stakeholders. Everyone from investors to employees to customers suffered, with even competitors feeling the spillover effects as new government regulations were put into place. But even when it seems that "bad" things dominate the news, remember that there are also a lot of good things happening in organization–stakeholder relationships.

Ben Cohen, of Ben & Jerry's fame, has started Hot Fudge, a venture capital fund devoted to community development.[40] The fund supports small business development in depressed communities with the goal of building local economies. Timberland Company provides each full-time employee 40 hours of paid time per year for community volunteer work. It also supports City Year, an organization that promotes community service. One top manager turned down a higher-paying job with another employer, saying: "Timberland's motto is 'when you come to work in the morning, don't leave your values at the door.'"[41] And at Tom's of Maine, founders Tom and Kate Chappell clearly state: "When we founded the company, it was our goal to make a different kind of business, one where people, the environment and animals are seen as inherently worthy and deserving of respect. We remain committed to this mission, now more than ever."[42]

Consumers, activist groups, nonprofit organizations, and governments are increasingly vocal and influential in directing organizations toward socially responsible practices. In today's information age business activities are increasingly transparent. Irresponsible practices are difficult to hide for long, wherever in the world they take place. Not only do news organizations find and disseminate the information, activist organizations also lobby, campaign, and actively pressure organizations to respect and protect everything from human rights to the natural environment. Increasingly important too are investor groups such as the Interfaith Council for Corporate Responsibility that support social causes through share ownership. They pool resources, buy shares in companies, and then advance proxy resolutions and lobby corporate leadership to ensure the businesses perform in socially responsible ways.

Ultimately, leaders exert a critical influence on the behavior of organizations and their members. The leadership beliefs that guide socially responsible practices have been described as:[43]

- *People*—belief that people do their best in healthy work environments with a balance of work and family life.

- *Communities*—belief that organizations perform best when located in healthy communities.

- *Natural environment*—belief that organizations gain by treating the natural environment with respect.

www.cepnyc.org

The Council on Economic Priorities supports a certification system to show that firms do not use child or forced labor, offer safe working conditions, pay sufficient wages, and respect rights to organize.

Leadership beliefs guiding socially responsible practices

- *Long term*—belief that organizations must be managed and led for long-term success.
- *Reputation*—belief that one's reputation must be protected to ensure consumer and stakeholder support.

PERSPECTIVES ON CORPORATE SOCIAL RESPONSIBILITY

Two contrasting views of corporate social responsibility have stimulated debate in academic and public-policy circles.[44] The *classical view* holds that management's only responsibility in running a business is to maximize profits. In other words, "the business of business is business," and the principal concern of management should always be to maximize shareholder value. This view is supported by Milton Friedman, a respected economist and Nobel Laureate. He says, "Few trends could so thoroughly undermine the very foundations of our free society as the acceptance by corporate officials of social responsibility other than to make as much money for their stockholders as possible."[45] The *arguments against corporate social responsibility* include fears that its pursuit will reduce business profits, raise business costs, dilute business purpose, give business too much social power, and do so without business accountability to the public.

By contrast, the *socioeconomic view* holds that management of any organization must be concerned within the broader social welfare and not just with corporate profits. This broadbased stakeholder perspective is supported by Paul Samuelson, another distinguished economist and Nobel Laureate. He states, "A large corporation these days not only may engage in social responsibility, it had damn well better try to do so."[46] Among the *arguments in favor of corporate social responsibility* are that it will add long-run profits for businesses, improve the public image of businesses, and help them avoid government regulation. Furthermore, businesses have the resources and ethical obligation to act responsibly.

REALITY CHECK 3.2

What the world thinks about social responsibility
In a survey of 25,000 people from 23 countries, Environics International Ltd. found that 90 percent wanted businesses to focus on more than profitability. Take the online "Reality Check" to learn more about how citizens of the world view dimensions of corporate social responsibility.

Today, there is little doubt that the public at large wants businesses and other organizations to act with genuine social responsibility. Stakeholder expectations are increasingly well voiced and include demands that organizations integrate social responsibility into their core values and daily activities. And research indicates that social responsibility can be associated with strong financial performance and, at worst, has no adverse financial impact.[47] The argument that acting with a commitment to social responsibility will negatively affect the "bottom line" is hard to defend. Indeed, evidence points toward a *virtuous circle* in which corporate social responsibility leads to improved financial performance for the firm and this in turn leads to more socially responsible actions in the future.[48]

There seems little reason to believe that businesses cannot serve the public good while advancing the financial interests of their shareholders. Even as the research continues on this important concept, these historical comments by management theorist Keith Davis still confirm the importance of corporate social responsibility in our society.[49]

Society wants business as well as all other major institutions to assume significant social responsibility. Social responsibility has become the hallmark of a mature, global organization. . . . The business which

Performance and social responsibility go hand in hand

Business for Social Responsibility summarizes research showing a positive relationship between social responsibility and improved business performance. One study reports that companies making a public commitment to rely on their ethics codes outperformed in market value added over those companies that did not do so. Another finds that environmental initiatives can reduce costs; reducing emissions of gases that contribute to global climate change can increase energy efficiency and reduce utility bills. In a consumer sample, researchers found that 76 percent would switch brands to buy from a firm associated with a good cause. In a study of MBA students, over 50 percent were willing to accept lower salaries to work for socially responsible employers, suggesting that socially responsible practices can assist in employee hiring and retention.[50]

vacillates or chooses not to enter the arena of social responsibility may find that it gradually will sink into customer and public disfavor.

EVALUATING CORPORATE SOCIAL PERFORMANCE

○ A **social responsibility audit** assesses an organization's accomplishments in areas of social responsibility.

A **social responsibility audit** can be used at regular intervals to report on and systematically assess an organization's accomplishments in various areas of corporate social responsibility. You might think of social responsibility audits as attempts to assess the social performance of organizations, much as accounting audits assess their financial performance. Typical audit areas include concerns for ecology and environmental quality, truth in lending, product safety, consumer protection, and aid to education. They also include service to communities, employment practices, diversity practices, progressive labor relations and employee assistance, and general corporate philanthropy, among other possibilities.

Criteria for Evaluating Social Performance

The social performance of business firms and other organizations can be described as driven by *compliance*—acting to avoid adverse consequences, or by *conviction*—acting to create positive impact.[51] Obviously, those of us who highly value corporate social responsibility believe that organizations should act with both. *Figure 3.5* links compliance and conviction with four criteria of social responsibility identified by management scholar Archie Carroll—economic, legal, ethical, and discretionary.[52] An audit of corporate social performance might include questions posed for each criterion. (1) Is the organization's *economic responsibility* met—is it profitable? (2) Is the organization's *legal responsibility* met—does it obey the law? (3) Is the organization's *ethical responsibility* met—is it doing the "right" things? (4) Is the organization's *discretionary responsibility* met—does it contribute to the broader community?

As the audit moves step-by-step through these criteria, the assessment inquires into ever-greater demonstrations of social performance. An organization is meeting its economic responsibility when it earns a profit through the provision of goods and services desired by customers. Legal

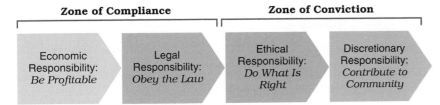

Figure 3.5 Criteria for evaluating corporate social performance.

responsibility is fulfilled when an organization operates within the law and according to the requirements of various external regulations. An organization meets its ethical responsibility when its actions voluntarily conform not only to legal expectations but also to the broader values and moral expectations of society. The highest level of social performance comes through the satisfaction of an organization's discretionary responsibility. Here, the organization voluntarily moves beyond basic economic, legal, and ethical expectations to provide leadership in advancing the well-being of individuals, communities, and society as a whole.

Social Responsibility Strategies

The social performance of organizations can also be analyzed in respect to the apparent "strategy" being followed. *Figure 3.6* describes a continuum of four corporate social responsibility strategies, with the commitment increasing as the strategy shifts from "obstructionist" at the lowest end to "proactive" at the highest.[53]

An **obstructionist strategy** ("Fight the social demands") reflects mainly economic priorities; social demands lying outside the organization's perceived self-interests are resisted. If the organization is criticized for wrongdoing, it can be expected to deny the claims. A **defensive strategy** ("Do the minimum legally required") seeks to protect the organization by doing the minimum legally necessary to satisfy expectations. Corporate behavior at this level conforms only to legal requirements,

○ An **obstructionist strategy** avoids social responsibility and reflects mainly economic priorities.

○ A **defensive strategy** seeks protection by doing the minimum legally required.

Commitment to corporate social responsibilities

Figure 3.6 Four strategies of corporate social responsibility—from obstructionist to proactive behavior.

competitive market pressure, and perhaps activist voices. If criticized, intentional wrongdoing is likely to be denied.

○ An **accommodative strategy** accepts social responsibility and tries to satisfy economic, legal, and ethical critera.

Organizations pursuing an **accommodative strategy** ("Do the minimum ethically required") accept their social responsibilities. They try to satisfy economic, legal, and ethical criteria. Corporate behavior at this level is congruent with society's prevailing norms, values, and expectations. But, it may be so only because of outside pressures. An oil firm, for example, may be willing to "accommodate" with cleanup activities when a spill occurs but remain quite slow in taking actions to prevent them in the first place. The **proactive strategy** ("Take leadership in social initiatives") is designed to meet all the criteria of social performance, including discretionary performance. Corporate behavior at this level takes preventive action to avoid adverse social impacts from company activities, and it takes the lead in identifying and responding to emerging social issues.

○ A **proactive strategy** meets all the criteria of social responsibility, including discretionary performance.

Learning check 4

Be sure you can • define the term *corporate social responsibility* • summarize the arguments for and against social responsibility by businesses • defend a personal preference between these arguments • identify four criteria for measuring corporate social performance • identify these criteria with four possible social responsibility strategies

---

ORGANIZATIONS AND SOCIETY

The fact remains that not all managers and not all organizations accept the challenge of acting with conviction and proactive commitment to social responsibility. Government, as the voice and instrument of the people, is often called upon to step in and act in the public behalf.

HOW GOVERNMENTS INFLUENCE ORGANIZATIONS

Governments influence organizations by passing laws and establishing regulating agencies to control and direct their behavior. It may not be too farfetched to say that behind every piece of legislation—national, state, or local—is a government agency charged with the responsibility of monitoring and ensuring compliance with its mandates. You know these agencies best by their acronyms: FAA (Federal Aviation Administration), EPA (Environmental Protection Agency), OSHA (Occupational Safety and Health Administration), and FDA (Food and Drug Administration), among many others.

Business executives often complain that many laws and regulations are overly burdensome. Public outcries to "dismantle the bureaucracy" and/or "deregulate business" express concerns that some agencies and legislation are not functional. But the reality is that the legal environment is both complex and constantly changing. Managers must stay informed about new and pending laws as well as existing ones. As a reminder, consider four areas in which the U.S. government takes an active role in regulating business affairs.

The first area is *occupational safety and health*. The Occupational Safety and Health Act of 1970 firmly established that the federal government was concerned about worker health and safety on the job. Even though some complain that the regulations are still not strong enough, the act continues to influence the concerns of employers and government policymakers for worker safety. Second is the area of *fair labor practices*. Legislation and regulations that prohibit discrimination in labor practices are discussed in Chapter 12 on human resource management. The Equal Employment Opportunity Act of 1972 and related regulations are designed to reduce barriers to employment based on race, gender, age, national origin, and marital status. Third is *consumer protection*. The Consumer Product Safety Act of 1972 gives government the authority to examine and force a business to withdraw from sale any product that it feels is hazardous to the consumer. Children's toys and flammable fabrics are within the great range of products affected by such regulation. The fourth area concerns *environmental protection*. Several antipollution acts, beginning with the Air Pollution Control Act of 1962, are designed to eliminate careless pollution of the air, water, and land.

AROUND THE WORLD

Nonprofit supports social accountability worldwide

Among the important social contributions of nonprofit organizations, Social Accountability International stands tall for its dedication to workers and their communities around the world. Its mission is described as "setting standards for a just world." In practice this involves the organization's commitment to improving workplaces and combatting sweatshops through the expansion and further development of the international workplace standards known as SA8000 and S8000. The nine dimensions of accountability it measures are child labor, forced labor, health and safety, freedom of association and the right to collective bargaining, discrimination, discipline, working hours, remuneration, and management systems. Certification is voluntary but is highly regarded by unions and nongovernmental organizations (NGOs). At present there are certified firms in more than 30 countries and industries.[54]

HOW ORGANIZATIONS INFLUENCE GOVERNMENTS

Just as governments influence organizations, the leaders of organizations also take action to influence governments. There are a number of ways in which businesses in particular attempt to influence government to adopt and pursue policies favorable to them.

Through *personal contacts and networks* executives get to know important people in government and try to gain their support for special interests. Through *public relations compaigns* executives try to communicate positive images of their organizations to the public at large. Through **lobbying**, often with the assistance of professional lobbyists, executives can have their desires communicated directly to government officials. Executives also seek influence through financial contributions to **political action committees** (PACs) that collect money and donate it to support favored political candidates. Unfortunately, *illegal acts* also occur. Executives sometimes resort to

○ **Lobbying** expresses opinions and preferences to government officials.

○ **Political action committees** collect money for donation to political campaigns.

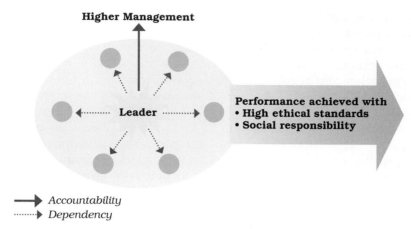

Higher Management

Leader

Performance achieved with
• **High ethical standards**
• **Social responsibility**

→ *Accountability*
┈┈▶ *Dependency*

Figure 3.7   Centrality of ethics and social responsibility in leadership and the managerial role.

bribes or illegal financial campaign contributions in the attempt to gain influence over public officials.

ROLE OF CORPORATE GOVERNANCE

○ **Corporate governance** is the oversight of top management by a board of directors.

In Chapter 1 **corporate governance** was defined as oversight of the top management of an organization by a board of directors. Governance most typically involves hiring, firing, and compensating the CEO, assessing strategy and verifying financial records. One board member describes the responsibilities of corporate governance as: "It's really about setting and maintaining high standards."[55] But even though the purpose is clear, there is a lot of concern that corporate governance can be inadequate and in some cases ineffectual. For example, the news contains critical reports that CEO pay is both too high and too often high when firms perform poorly; we also read about continuing accounting scandals that reveal misuse of corporate assets and wrongful financial reporting.[56] All this raises stakeholder concerns to ensure high standards of ethical conduct by executives and socially responsible behavior by organizations.

There is no doubt that the pressure is on to restore corporate governance to its rightful place as a key guarantor that businesses and other organizations are run properly. And importantly, the responsibilities of "governance" in respect to day-to-day managerial control are being well communicated throughout organizations. Trends in social values are reflected in ever-increasing demands from governments and other stakeholders that managerial decisions reflect ethical as well as high-performance standards. All managers must accept personal responsibility for doing the "right" things. Decisions must be made and problems solved with ethical considerations standing side by side with performance objectives.

Management 8/e focuses your attention throughout on the responsibilities depicted in *Figure 3.7*. It presents the manager's or team leader's challenge this way: to fulfill an accountability for achieving performance objectives, while always doing so in an ethical and socially responsible manner. The full weight of this responsibility holds in every organizational setting from small to large and from private or nonprofit. It holds also at every managerial level, from bottom to top. There is no escaping the ultimate reality—being a manager is a very socially responsible job!

| Learning check 5 | *Be sure you can* • explain and give examples of how governments use legislation to influence business behavior • identify methods used by businesses to influence governments to adopt favorable policies toward them • define corporate governance and discuss its importance in organization–society relationships |

CHAPTER 3 STUDY GUIDE

Where We've Been

BACK TO BEN & JERRY'S

The opening example of Ben & Jerry's provided a clear benchmark for how business performance, ethical behavior, and social responsibility can go hand in hand. Ben & Jerry's, along with other positive examples in the chapter, including that of Tom's of Maine, helps offset the bad side of business and managerial behavior sensationalized in the cases of Enron, Andersen, WorldCom, and others. In Chapter 3 you learned more about the issues and complexities of personal ethics and corporate social responsibility. As you read further in *Management 8/e,* always keep these themes in mind as a learning context. Never forget that there is no substitute for ethical and socially responsible behavior.

THE NEXT STEP
INTEGRATED LEARNING ACTIVITIES

Cases/Projects

- Tom's of Maine Case
- Enron and Arthur Andersen Case
- Project 4—Corporate Social Responsibility
- Project 6—CEO Pay

Self-Assessments

- Terminal Values (#5)
- Instrumental Values (#6)
- Diversity Awareness (#7)
- Internal/External Control (#26)

Exercises in Teamwork

- Confronting Ethical Dilemmas (#7)
- What Do You Value in Work? (#7)
- Case of the Contingency Workforce (#22)

STUDY QUESTION SUMMARY

1. What is ethical behavior?

- Ethical behavior is that which is accepted as "good" or "right" as opposed to "bad" or "wrong."
- Simply because an action is not illegal does not necessarily make it ethical in a given situation.
- Because values vary, the question of "What is ethical behavior?" may be answered differently by different people.
- Four ways of thinking about ethical behavior are the utilitarian, individualism, moral-rights, and justice views.
- Cultural relativism argues that no culture is ethically superior to any other.

2. How do ethical dilemmas complicate the workplace?

- When managers act ethically they have a positive impact on other people in the workplace and on the social good performed by organizations.
- An ethical dilemma occurs when someone must decide whether to pursue a course of action that, although offering the potential for personal or organizational benefit or both, may be considered potentially unethical.
- Managers report that their ethical dilemmas often involve conflicts with superiors, customers,

and subordinates over such matters as dishonesty in advertising and communications as well as pressure from their bosses to do unethical things.

- Common rationalizations for unethical behavior include believing the behavior is not illegal, is in everyone's best interests, will never be noticed, or will be supported by the organization.

3. How can high ethical standards be maintained?

- Ethics training in the form of courses and training programs helps people better deal with ethical dilemmas in the workplace.
- Whistleblowers expose the unethical acts of others in organizations, even while facing career risks for doing so.
- Top management sets an ethical tone for the organization as a whole, and all managers are responsible for acting as positive models of appropriate ethical behavior.
- Written codes of ethical conduct formally state what an organization expects of its employees regarding ethical conduct at work.

4. What is corporate social responsibility?

- Corporate social responsibility is an obligation of the organization to act in ways that serve both its own interests and the interests of its many external publics, often called stakeholders.
- Criteria for evaluating corporate social performance include economic, legal, ethical, and discretionary responsibilities.
- Corporate strategies in response to social demands include obstruction, defense, accommodation, and proaction, with more progressive organizations taking proactive stances.

5. How do organizations and governments work together in society?

- Government agencies are charged with monitoring and ensuring compliance with the mandates of law.
- Managers must be well informed about existing and pending legislation in a variety of social responsibility areas, including environmental protection and other quality-of-life concerns.
- Organizations exert their influence on government in many ways, including interpersonal contacts of executives, use of lobbyists, and financial contributions to PACs.
- All managerial decisions and actions in every workplace should fulfill performance accountability with commitments to high ethical standards and socially responsible means.

KEY TERMS REVIEW

SELF-TEST 3

MULTIPLE-CHOICE QUESTIONS:

1. Values are personal beliefs that help determine whether a behavior will be considered ethical or unethical. An example of terminal value is _____ .
   (a) ambition (b) self-respect (c) courage (d) imagination

2. Under the _____ view of ethical behavior, a businessowner would be considered ethical if she reduced a plant's workforce by 10 percent in order to cut costs and be able to save jobs for the other 90 percent.
   (a) utilitarian (b) individualism (c) justice (d) moral-rights

3. A manager's failure to enforce a late-to-work policy the same way for all employees is an ethical violation of _____ justice.
   (a) ethical (b) moral (c) distributive (d) procedural

4. The Sarbanes-Oxley Act of 2002 makes it easier for corporate executives to _____.
   (a) protect themselves from shareholder lawsuits (b) sue employees who commit illegal acts (c) be tried and sentenced to jail for financial misconduct (d) shift blame for wrongdoing to boards of directors

5. Two "spotlight" questions for conducting the ethics double-check of a decision are: (a) "How would I feel if my family found out about this?" and (b) "How would I feel if _____?"
   (a) my boss found out about this (b) my subordinates found out about this (c) this was printed in the local newspaper (d) this went into my personnel file

6. Research on ethical dilemmas indicates that _____ is/are often the cause of unethical behavior by people at work.
   (a) declining morals in society (b) lack of religious beliefs (c) the absence of whistleblowers (d) pressures from bosses and superiors

7. Customers, investors, employees, and regulators are examples of _____ that are important in the analysis of corporate social responsibility.
   (a) special-interest groups (b) stakeholders (c) ethics advocates (d) whistleblowers

8. A(n) _____ is someone who exposes the ethical misdeeds of others.
   (a) whistleblower (b) ethics advocate (c) ombudsman (d) stakeholder

9. Two employees are talking about their employers. Sean says that ethics training and codes of ethical conduct are worthless; Maura says these are the best ways to ensure ethical behavior in the organization. Who is right and why?
   (a) Sean—no one cares. (b) Maura—only the organization can influence ethical behavior. (c) Neither Sean nor Maura—training and codes can aid but never guarantee ethical behavior. (d) Neither Sean nor Maura—only the threat of legal punishment will make people act ethically.

10. A proponent of the classical view of corporate social responsibility would most likely agree with which of these statements?
    (a) Social responsibility improves the public image of business. (b) The primary responsibility of business is to maximize business profits. (c) By acting responsibly, businesses avoid government regulation. (d) Businesses can and should do "good" while doing business.

11. Which criterion for evaluating corporate social performance ranks highest in terms of conviction to operate in a responsible manner?
    (a) economic (b) legal (c) ethical (d) discretionary

12. An organization that takes the lead in addressing emerging social issues is being _____, showing the most progressive corporate social responsibility strategy.
    (a) accommodative (b) defensive (c) proactive (d) obstructionist

13. The U.S. Equal Opportunity Act of 1972 is an example of government regulation of business with respect to _____.
    (a) fair labor practices (b) consumer protection (c) environmental protection (d) occupational safety and health

14. _____ seek to influence governments to adopt favorable policies toward business by raising money and donating it to support political candidates.
    (a) Stakeholders (b) Lobbyists (c) PACs (d) Auditors

15. In the final analysis, managers must make sure that high-performance goals in and by organizations are achieved by _____ means.
    (a) any possible (b) cultural relativism (c) ethical imperialism (d) ethical and socially responsible

SHORT-RESPONSE QUESTIONS:

16. Explain the difference between the individualism and justice views of ethical behavior.

17. List four common rationalizations for unethical managerial behavior.

18. What are the major elements in the socioeconomic view of corporate social responsibility?

19. What role do government agencies play in regulating the socially responsible behavior of businesses?

APPLICATION QUESTION:

20. A small outdoor clothing company has just received an attractive offer from a business in Bangladesh to manufacture its work gloves. The offer would allow for substantial cost savings over the current supplier. The company manager, however, has read reports that some Bangladeshi businesses break their own laws and operate with child labor. How would differences in the following corporate responsibility strategies affect the manager's decision regarding whether to accept the offer: obstruction, defense, accommodation, and proaction?

www.wiley.com/college/schermerhorn

4

Environment, organizational culture, and diversity

Planning Ahead

After reading Chapter 4, you should be able to answer these questions in your own words.

CHAPTER 4 study questions

1. What is the external environment of organizations?

2. What is a customer-driven organization?

3. What is a quality-driven organization?

4. What is organizational culture?

5. How is diversity managed in a multicultural organization?

HERMAN MILLER—CORE VALUES DRIVE A PERFORMANCE ENVIRONMENT

At Herman Miller, the innovative and award-winning manufacturer of designer furniture, the idea of the corporation goes well beyond its existence as a legal entity. Core values build an internal environment of high performance as the firm embraces a full set of stakeholders, including employees, suppliers, customers, and the community.

Values at Herman Miller drive a unique and high-performance system built on a fundamental belief in "participation." Go to the website and you'll find the firm self-described this way: "For 50 years participation has been central to Herman Miller. It still is. We believe in participation because we value and benefit from the richness of ideas and opinions of thousands of people. Participation enables employee-owners to contribute their unique gifts and abilities to the corporate community."

There's also a unique self-concept at the firm. Herman Miller calls itself "a high-performance, values-driven community of people tied together by a common purpose." Known as the "Herman Miller way," these core values are:

- Making a meaningful contribution to our customers
- Cultivating community, participation, and people development
- Creating economic value for shareholders and employee-owners
- Responding to change through design and innovation
- Living with integrity and respecting the environment

Yes, Herman Miller is a different kind of company, a model of excellence in the new world of work. It is a values-driven company that finds high performance through everyday respect for people. And it works! The firm has been ranked among the 400 best-performing large corporations in America by *Forbes* magazine; *Business Ethics* magazine has ranked it in the top 10 among the "100 Best Corporate Citizens" in America and first among all ranked companies for "Service to the Environment."[1]

Get Connected!

Find out more about Herman Miller's core values. Examine the firm's concept of corporate community. Think about the roles leaders play in building high-performing organizations.

Chapter 4 Learning Preview

Herman Miller keeps its high-performance edge with a unique commitment to environment and diversity. Externally the firm values all stakeholders, including its communities and the natural environment. Internally it values people, respects diversity, and engages employees through participation in the affairs of the enterprise. The purpose of Chapter 4 is to introduce you to the external and internal environments of organizations. As you read, check your learning progress in these major areas.

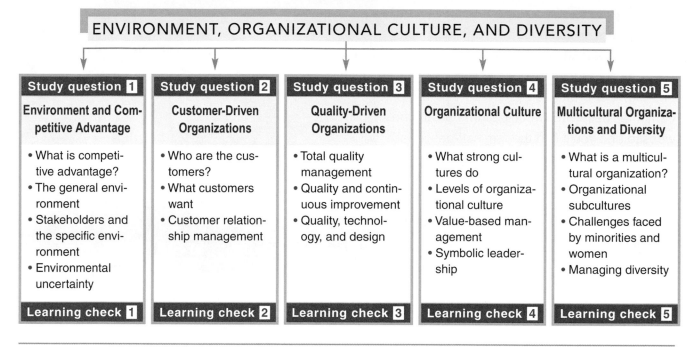

ENVIRONMENT, ORGANIZATIONAL CULTURE, AND DIVERSITY

Study question 1

Environment and Competitive Advantage

- What is competitive advantage?
- The general environment
- Stakeholders and the specific environment
- Environmental uncertainty

Learning check 1

Study question 2

Customer-Driven Organizations

- Who are the customers?
- What customers want
- Customer relationship management

Learning check 2

Study question 3

Quality-Driven Organizations

- Total quality management
- Quality and continuous improvement
- Quality, technology, and design

Learning check 3

Study question 4

Organizational Culture

- What strong cultures do
- Levels of organizational culture
- Value-based management
- Symbolic leadership

Learning check 4

Study question 5

Multicultural Organizations and Diversity

- What is a multicultural organization?
- Organizational subcultures
- Challenges faced by minorities and women
- Managing diversity

Learning check 5

Once a benchmark for science fiction writers, the dawning of the 21st century is now placing unrelenting new demands on organizations and their members. Managers today are learning to operate in a world that places a premium on information, technology utilization, quality, customer service, and speed. They are learning how to succeed in a world of intense competition, continued globalization of markets and business activities, and rapid technological change. And they are facing renewed demands for ethical behavior and social responsibility.

This chapter introduces the external and internal environments of organizations, along with their performance implications. The chapter opening example of Herman Miller sets the stage. It introduces the importance of core values and the belief in people. It raises the question: What must organizations do to remain successful in our dynamic, complex, and ever-changing environment?

ENVIRONMENT AND COMPETITIVE ADVANTAGE

In his book *The Future of Success,* former U.S. Secretary of Labor Robert Reich says: "The emerging economy is offering unprecedented opportunities, an ever-expanding choice of terrific deals, fabulous products, good investments, and great jobs for people with the right talents and skills. Never before in human history have so many had access to so much so easily."[2] In these terms, things couldn't be better for organizations and career seekers. But there are also major challenges to be faced. When looking at things from a business vantage point, IBM's former CEO Louis V. Gerstner, Jr., described the challenge this way: "We believe very strongly that the age-old levers of competition—labor, capital, and land—are being supplemented by knowledge, and that most successful companies in the future will be those that learn how to exploit knowledge—knowledge about customer behavior, markets, economies, technology—faster than their competitors."[3]

Knowledge and speed are indispensable to success in this new economy. Even as managers strive to lead their organizations toward a high-performance edge, they cannot afford for a minute to rest on past laurels. The world is too uncertain and the competition too intense for that. "In order to survive," Reich points out, "all organizations must dramatically and continuously improve—cutting costs, adding value, creating new products."[4]

WHAT IS COMPETITIVE ADVANTAGE?

Astute executives understand the management implications in the prior observations. They are ever-alert to environmental trends that require adjustments in the ways their organizations operate and that offer opportunities to gain **competitive advantage.**[5] This term refers to a core competency that clearly sets an organization apart from its competitors and gives it an advantage over them in the marketplace. Simply put, it comes from an ability to do things better than one's competitors. An organization may achieve competitive advantage in many ways, including through its products, pricing, customer service, cost efficiency, and quality, among other aspects of operating excellence. But regardless of how competitive advantage is achieved, the key result is the same—an ability to consistently do something of high value that one's competitors cannot replicate quickly or do as well.

○ A **competitive advantage** allows an organization to deal with market and environmental forces better than its competitors.

IN PRACTICE

Entrepreneurship + quality = competitive advantage

John Sortino heard the call to competitive advantage and followed the pathways of entrepreneurship. He started Vermont Teddy Bear Company after adding sunglasses to his son's favorite teddy bear, and decided to make more bears of his own and sell them from a peddler's cart in Burlington, Vermont. The firm has grown into a substantial award-winning local employer and maker of more than 350,000 bears a year. It has won the Heritage of New England Award for promoting its products truthfully and operating with exceptional quality; it received the Circle of Excellence award from BizRate for the quality of its online store. Sortino credits the firm's success to highly committed workers, saying "It is everyone working together which creates a successful customer service program." The corporate mission reads: "To make the world a better place . . . one Bear at a time."[6]

Some years ago, at a time when American industry was first coming to grips with fierce competition from Japanese products, American quality pioneer J. M. Juran challenged an audience of Japanese executives with a prediction. He warned them against complacency, suggesting that America would bounce back in business competitiveness and that the words "Made in America" would once again symbolize world-class quality.[7] There seems little doubt today that Juran's prediction was accurate.

Business excellence did resurge in America, with part of the reason coming from better understanding by business leaders of the interdependencies of their organizations with the external environment. Competitive advantage in the demanding global economy can be achieved only by continuously scanning the environment for opportunities and taking effective action based on what is learned.[8] The ability to do this begins with the answer to a basic question: What is in the external environment of organizations?

THE GENERAL ENVIRONMENT

O The **general environment** is comprised of cultural, economic, legal-political, and educational conditions.

→

Elements in the general environment.

The **general environment** consists of all conditions in external environment that form a background context for managerial decision making. Typical external environmental issues include:

- *Economic conditions*—health of the economy in terms of inflation, income levels, gross domestic product, unemployment, and job outlook.
- *Social-cultural conditions*—norms, customs, and social values on such matters as human rights, trends in education and related social institutions, as well as demographic patterns in society.
- *Legal-political conditions*—prevailing philosophy and objectives of the political party or parties running the government, as well as laws and government regulations.
- *Technological conditions*—development and availability of technology, including scientific advancements.
- *Natural environment conditions*—nature and conditions of the natural environment, including levels of public concern expressed through environmentalism.

If we take the natural environment as an example, Japanese automakers seem to be finding the potential for competitive advantage. Both Honda and Toyota have received awards from the Sierra Club for excellence in environmental engineering. The two firms are on the leading edge of new markets for hybrid cars that combine gas and electric power. While America's automakers were betting that customers would stay loyal to large gas-fueled and often gas-hungry vehicles, their Japanese competitors saw the potential for competitive advantage. Now they have experience and a reputation gained from being first to market with the more environmentally friendly vehicles.

In respect to the sociocultural environment, population demographics are a key feature. Managers who understand demographic profiles and trends can anticipate shifts in the customer base and labor markets that affect their organizations. For example, *Manager's Notepad 4.1* highlights important diversity trends in the demographic characteristics of American society.[9] These and other differences in general environment factors are especially noticeable internationally. External conditions vary significantly from one country and culture to the next, and managers must understand these differences. Like many large firms, the pharmaceutical giant Merck derives a substantial portion of its business from overseas operations. Its

Diversity trends in the sociocultural environment

- People of color are an increasing percentage of the workforce.
- More women are working.
- People with disabilities are gaining more access to the workplace.
- More workers come from nontraditional families (e.g., single parents, dual wage earners).
- Average age of workers is increasing.
- Religious diversity of workers is increasing.

executives recognize the need to be well informed about and responsive to differing local conditions. In Europe, for example, they have entered into cooperative agreements with local companies, conducted research with local partners, and worked with local governments on legal matters.

STAKEHOLDERS AND THE SPECIFIC ENVIRONMENT

The **specific environment** consists of the actual organizations, groups, and persons with whom an organization interacts and conducts business. These are environmental elements of direct consequence to the organization as it operates on a day-to-day basis. The specific environment is often described in terms of **stakeholders,** defined in Chapter 3 as the persons, groups, and institutions who are affected in one way or another by the organization's performance. They are key constituencies that have a stake in the organization's performance, are influenced by how it operates, and can influence it in return.

Sometimes called the *task environment,* the specific environment and the stakeholders are distinct for each organization. They can also change over time according to the company's unique customer base, operating needs, and circumstances. Important stakeholders common to the specific environment of most organizations include customers, suppliers, competitors, regulators, and investors/owners from the external environment, as well as employees from the internal environment. Interestingly, a recent study of MBA students shows how differently stakeholders may be valued. In answer to a question regarding what a business's top priorities should be, 75 percent included "maximizing shareholder value" and 71 percent included "satisfying customers." Only 25 percent included "creating value for communities," and only 5 percent "concern for environmentalism."[10]

Figure 4.1 shows the typical business firm as an open system, with the interests of several stakeholder groups linked with stages in the input-transformation-output process. This type of stakeholder analysis can be used to both assess the current performance of organizations vis-à-vis *strategic constituencies* and to develop ideas for improving performance in the future. The analysis helps focus management attention on **value creation,** the extent to which the organization is creating value for and satisfying the needs of important constituencies.

As suggested in the figure, value creation is important to stakeholders from both the specific environment, reflected on the input and output boundaries of the business firm as an open system, and from the

○ The **specific environment** includes the people and groups with whom an organization interacts.

○ **Stakeholders** are the persons, groups, and institutions directly affected by an organization.

○ **Value creation** is creating value for and satisfying needs of constituencies.

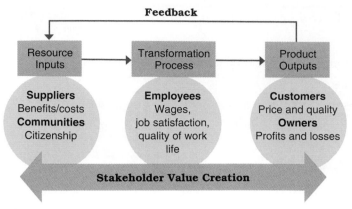

Figure 4.1 Stakeholder analysis of value creation for key constituencies of a business firm: an open-systems approach.

internal environment, reflected in the transformation process itself. In respect to product outputs, for example, businesses create value for customers through product price and quality, and for owners by realized profits and losses. In respect to inputs, businesses create value for suppliers through the benefits of long-term business relationships, and for communities in such areas as the citizenship they display in using and contributing to public services. And in respect to throughputs, businesses create value for employees through the wages and satisfaction gained through their work at transforming resource inputs into product outputs.

ENVIRONMENTAL UNCERTAINTY

○ **Environmental uncertainty** is a lack of complete information about the environment.

The fact is that there is a lot of uncertainty in the external environments of many organizations. **Environmental uncertainty** means that there is a lack of complete information regarding what exists and what developments may occur. This makes it difficult to analyze constituencies and their needs, predict future states of affairs, and understand their potential implications for the organization. *Figure 4.2* describes two dimen-

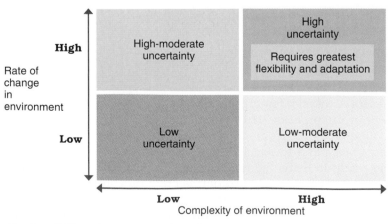

Figure 4.2 Dimensions of uncertainty in organizational environments.

sions of environmental uncertainty: (1) complexity, or the number of different factors in the environment, and (2) the rate of change in these factors.[11]

Environmental uncertainty presents a host of management challenges. Greater uncertainty requires more concentrated attention. An uncertain environment has to be continually studied and monitored to spot emerging trends. Also, the greater the environmental uncertainty, the greater the need for flexibility and adaptability in organizational designs and work practices. Because of uncertainty, organizations must be able to respond quickly as new circumstances arise and information becomes available. Throughout this book you will find many examples of how organizations try to stay adaptable in order to best deal with the high uncertainty that so often prevails in their environments.

Learning check 1

Be sure you can • list key elements in the general and specific environments of organizations • define the terms competitive advantage, stakeholders, and environmental uncertainty • describe the stakeholders for a business in your local community

---

CUSTOMER-DRIVEN ORGANIZATIONS

Question:	What's your job?
Answer:	I run the cash register and sack groceries.
Question:	But isn't it your job to serve the customer?
Answer:	I guess, but it's not in my job description.

This conversation illustrates what often becomes the missing link in the quest for competitive advantage: customer service.[12] Contrast this conversation with the case of a customer who called the Vermont Teddy Bear Company to complain that her new mail-order teddy bear had a problem. The company responded promptly, she said, and arranged to have the bear picked up and replaced. She wrote the firm to say "thank you for the great service and courtesy you gave me."[13]

WHO ARE THE CUSTOMERS?

Figure 4.3 expands the open-systems view of organizations to now depict the complex internal operations of the organization as well as its inter-

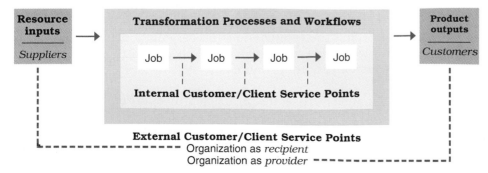

Figure 4.3 The importance of external and internal customers.

www.dell.com

The customer is "captain" of the supply chain for Dell Computer. Founder and chairman Michael Dell firmly believes that customers drive competitive advantage. The firm is a leader in using information technology to efficiently deliver products meeting customer preferences.

dependence with the external environment. In this figure the organization's *external customers* purchase the goods produced or utilize the services provided. They may be industrial customers, that is, other firms that buy a company's products for use in their own operations; or they may be retail customers or clients who purchase or use the goods and services directly. *Internal customers,* by contrast, are found within the organization. They are the individuals and groups who use or otherwise depend on one anothers' work in order to do their own jobs well. The notion of customer service applies equally well to external and internal customers.

WHAT CUSTOMERS WANT

Customers are always key stakeholders; they sit at the top when organizations are viewed as the upside-down pyramids described in Chapter 1. And without any doubt, customers put today's organizations to a very stiff test. They primarily want three things in the goods and services they buy: (1) high quality, (2) low price, and (3) on-time delivery. Offering them anything less is unacceptable.

Organizations that can't meet customer expectations suffer the market consequences; they lose competitive advantage. Some time ago, for example, Intel Corporation faced a crisis in customer confidence when a defect was found in one of its computer chips. At first, top management of this highly regarded company balked at replacing the chips, suggesting that the defect wasn't really important. But customers were angry and unrelenting in their complaints. Eventually the customers won, as they should. Intel agreed to replace the chips without any questions asked. Company executives also learned two important lessons of successful business practices: (1) always protect your reputation for quality products—it is hard to get and easy to lose, and (2) always treat your customers right—they, too, are hard to get and easy to lose.

CUSTOMER RELATIONSHIP MANAGEMENT

A *Harvard Business Review* survey reports that American business leaders rank customer service and product quality as the first and second most important goals in the success of their organizations.[14] In a survey by the market research firm Michelson & Associates, poor service and product dissatisfaction were also ranked #1 and #2 as reasons why customers abandon a retail store.[15] Reaching the goals of providing great service and quality products isn't always easy. But when pursued relentlessly they can be important sources of competitive advantage. Just imagine the ramifications if every customer or client contact for an organization were positive. Not only would they return again and again as customers, they would also tell others and expand the customer base.

Progressive managers use the principles of **customer relationship management** to establish and maintain high standards of customer service. Known as "CRM," this approach uses the latest information technologies to maintain intense communication with customers as well as to gather and utilize data regarding their needs and desires. At Marriott International, for example, CRM is supported by special cus-

○ **Customer relationship management** strategically tries to build lasting relationships with and to add value to customers.

tomer management software that tracks information on customer preferences. When you check in, the likelihood is that your past requests for things like a king-size bed, no smoking room, and computer modem access are already in your record. Says Marriott's chairman: "It's a big competitive advantage."[16]

Just as organizations need to manage their customers on the output side, supplier relationships on the input side must be well-managed, too. The concept of **supply chain management** involves strategic management of all operations involving an organization is suppliers. This includes the use of information technology to improve purchasing, manufacturing, transportation, and distribution.[17] The goals of SCM are straightforward: achieve efficiency in all aspects of the supply chain while ensuring on-time availability of quality resources for customer-driven operations. As retail sales are made at Wal-Mart, for example, an information system updates inventory records and sales forecasts. Suppliers access this information electronically, allowing them to adjust their operations and rapidly ship replacement products to meet the retailer's needs.

○ **Supply chain management** strategically links all operations dealing with resource supplies.

Be sure you can • explain the difference between internal and external customers of a firm • list the three primary things customers want in what they buy • discuss the importance of customer relationship management in a competitive business environment

Learning check 2

QUALITY-DRIVEN ORGANIZATIONS

If managing for high performance and competitive advantage is the theme of the day, "quality" is one of its most important watchwords. Customers want quality whether they are buying a consumer product or receiving a service. The achievement of quality objectives in all aspects of operations is a global criterion of organizational performance in manufacturing and service industries alike. **ISO certification** by the International Standards Organization in Geneva, Switzerland, has been adopted by many countries of the world as a quality benchmark. Businesses that want to compete as "world-class companies" are increasingly expected to have ISO certification at various levels. To do so, they must refine and upgrade quality in all operations and then undergo a rigorous assessment by outside auditors to determine whether they meet ISO requirements.

○ **ISO certification** indicates conformance with a rigorous set of international quality standards.

TOTAL QUALITY MANAGEMENT

The term **total quality management** (TQM) was introduced in Chapter 1. It describes the process of making quality principles part of the organization's strategic objectives, applying them to all aspects of operations, committing to continuous improvement, and striving to meet customers' needs by doing things right the first time.[18]

Most TQM approaches begin with an insistence that the total quality commitment apply to everyone in an organization and to all aspects of op-

○ **Total quality management** is managing with an organization-wide commitment to continuous improvement, product quality, and customer needs.

United Parcel Service
Where technology rules a total quality road

Once named company of the year by *Forbes* magazine, UPS is the world's largest package delivery company. It's also a leader in technology utilization for competitive advantage. Log on the UPS website and the company literally takes you around the world of package delivery. Operating efficiency and customer service are rules of the day every day at UPS. The company claims "a technology infrastructure second to none, enabling customers to link product shipments, services and information throughout the transaction value chain." Customers find IT working for them through an efficient online package tracking system and transit and delivery times. Operations are streamlined through the firm's seamless supply chain. New directions are found in UPS e-Commerce Solutions.

erations, right from resource acquisition through to the production and distribution of finished goods and services.[19] One well-known consultant, Philip Crosby, became quite famous for offering these "four absolutes" of management for total quality control: (1) *quality means conformance to standards*—workers must know exactly what performance standards they are expected to meet; (2) *quality comes from defect prevention, not defect correction*—leadership, training, and discipline must prevent defects in the first place; (3) *quality as a performance standard must mean defect-free work*—the only acceptable quality standard is perfect work; and (4) *quality saves money*—doing things right the first time saves the cost of correcting poor work.[20]

Get Connected!

Visit the website for the Malcolm Baldrige National Quality Awards in business. Learn more about Deming's 14 Points of Quality.

QUALITY AND CONTINUOUS IMPROVEMENT

The work of W. Edwards Deming is a cornerstone of the total quality movement. The story begins in 1951 when he was invited to Japan to explain quality control techniques that had been developed in the United States. The result was a lifelong relationship epitomized in the Deming prize, which is still annually awarded in Japan for excellence in quality. "When Deming spoke," we might say, "the Japanese listened." The principles he taught the Japanese were straightforward . . . and they worked: tally defects, analyze and trace them to the source, make corrections, and keep a record of what happens afterward.[21] Deming's "14 points of quality" emphasize constant innovation, use of statistical methods, and commitment to training in the fundamentals of quality assurance.

○ **Continuous improvement** involves always searching for new ways to improve work quality and performance.

The search for quality is closely tied to the emphasis on **continuous improvement**—always looking for new ways to improve on current performance.[22] The notion is that one can never be satisfied; something always can and should be improved on. Continuous improvement must be a way of life. Another important aspect of total quality operations is *cycle time*—the elapsed time between receipt of an order and delivery of the finished product. The quality objective here is to reduce cycle time by finding ways to serve customer needs more quickly.

One way to combine employee involvement and continuous improvement is through the popular **quality circle** concept.[23] This is a small group of workers that meets regularly to discuss ways of improving the quality of their products or services. Their objective is to assume responsibility for quality and apply every member's full creative potential to ensure that it is achieved. Such worker empowerment can result in cost savings from improved quality and greater customer satisfaction. It can also improve morale and commitment, as the following remarks from quality circle members indicate: "This is the best thing the company has done in 15 years." . . . "The program proves that supervisors have no monopoly on brains." . . . "It gives me more pride in my work."[24]

○ Members of a **quality circle** meet periodically to discuss ways of improving the quality of products or services.

QUALITY, TECHNOLOGY, AND DESIGN

Technology utilization is improving the quality of manufacturing today by helping firms better integrate their operations with customer preferences and by allowing production changes to be made quickly and at low cost. For example, *lean production* uses technologies to streamline systems and allow work to be performed with fewer workers and smaller inventories. *Flexible manufacturing* allows processes to be changed quickly and efficiently to produce different products or modifications to existing ones. Through such techniques as *agile manufacturing* and *mass customization,* organizations are able to make individualized products quickly and with production efficiencies once only associated with the mass production of uniform products.[25]

Another timely and important contribution to quality management is found in *product design.* We are all aware of design differences among products, be they cars, computers, cell phones, stereos, watches, clothes, or whatever. But what may not be recognized is that design makes a difference in how things are produced and at what level of cost and quality. In today's competitive global economy, product designs are strategic weapons. A "good" design has both eye appeal to the customer and is easy to manufacture with productivity. *Design for manufacturing* means that products are styled to lower production costs and smooth the way toward high-quality results in all aspects of the manufacturing processes. A manufacturing approach that shows respect for the natural environment is *design for disassembly.* The goal is to design products while taking into account how their component parts will be recycled at the end of their lives.

Be sure you can • define the term *ISO certification* • explain the role of continuous improvement in TQM • describe what a quality circle is and how its use can increase performance quality • discuss how good use of technology and product design can improve quality

Learning check 3

ORGANIZATIONAL CULTURE

"Culture" is a popular word in management these days. Important differences in national cultures will be discussed in Chapter 5 on the global dimensions of management. Here, it is time to talk about cultural differ-

---

MANAGER'S NOTEPAD 4.2

S·C·O·R·E·S—How to read an organization's culture

S—How tight or loose is the *structure*?

C—Are decisions *change* oriented or driven by the status quo?

O—What *outcomes* or results are most highly valued?

R—What is the climate for *risk taking*, innovation?

E—How widespread is *empowerment*, worker involvement?

S—What is the competitive *style*, internal and external?

○ **Organizational culture** is the system of shared beliefs and values that guides behavior in organizations.

ences in the internal environments of organizations. **Organizational culture** is defined by noted scholar and consultant Edgar Schein as the system of shared beliefs and values that develops within an organization and guides the behavior of its members.[26] Sometimes called the *corporate culture,* it is a key aspect of any organization and work setting. Whenever someone, for example, speaks of "the way we do things here," they are talking about the culture.

WHAT STRONG CULTURES DO

Although it is clear that culture is not the sole determinant of what happens in organizations, it is an important influence on what they accomplish . . . and how. The internal culture has the potential to shape attitudes, reinforce beliefs, direct behavior, and establish performance expectations and the motivation to fulfill them. A widely discussed study of successful businesses concluded that organizational culture made a major contribution to their long-term performance records.[27] Importantly, the cultures in these organizations provided for a clear vision of what the organization was attempting to accomplish, allowing individuals to rally around the vision and work hard to support and accomplish it.[28] *Manager's Notepad 4.2* offers ideas for reading differences among organizational cultures.

Strong cultures, ones that are clear and well defined and widely shared among members, discourage dysfunctional work behaviors and encourage positive ones. They commit members to doing things for and with one another that are in the best interests of the organization. The best organizations are likely to have cultures that are performance oriented, emphasize teamwork, allow for risk taking, encourage innovation, and make the well-being of people a top management priority.[29] Honda is a good example. The firm's culture is tightly focused around what is known as "The Honda Way"—a set of principles emphasizing ambition, respect for ideas, open communication, work enjoyment, harmony, and hard work.

LEVELS OF ORGANIZATIONAL CULTURE

Organizational culture is usually described from the perspective of the two levels shown in *Figure 4.4*—the "observable" culture and the "core" culture.[30] The *observable culture* is visible; it is what one sees and hears when

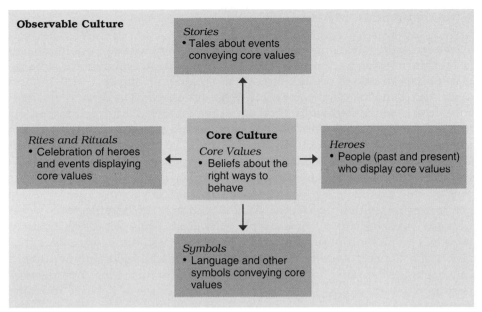

Figure 4.4 Levels of organizational culture—observable culture and core culture.

walking around an organization as a visitor, a customer, or an employee. The observable culture is apparent in the way people dress at work, how they arrange their offices, how they speak to and behave toward one another, the nature of their conversations, and how they talk about and treat their customers. It is also found in the following elements of daily organizational life—through them, new members learn the organization's culture and all members share and reinforce its special aspects over time:

- *Stories*—oral histories and tales, told and retold among members, about dramatic sagas and incidents in the life of the organization.
- *Heroes*—the people singled out for special attention and whose accomplishments are recognized with praise and admiration among members; they include founders and role models.
- *Rites and rituals*—the ceremonies and meetings, planned and spontaneous, that celebrate important occasions and performance accomplishments.
- *Symbols*—the special use of language and other nonverbal expressions to communicate important themes of organizational life.

← Elements in the observable culture of organizations

The second and deeper level of organizational culture is the *core culture*. It consists of the **core values** or underlying assumptions and beliefs that shape and guide people's behaviors, and actually contribute to the aspects of observable culture just described. Strong-culture organizations operate with a small but enduring set of core values. Researchers point out that commitment to core values is a major contributor to long-term success.[31] Highly successful companies typically emphasize the values of performance excellence, innovation, social responsibility, integrity, worker involvement, customer service, and teamwork. Examples of core values that drive the best firms include "service above all else" at Nordstrom; "science-based innovation" at Merck; "encouraging individual initiative and creativity" at SONY; and "fanatical attention to consistency and detail" at Disney.

○ **Core values** are beliefs and values shared by organization members.

VALUE-BASED MANAGEMENT

○ **Value-based management** actively develops, communicates, and enacts shared values.

The core values espoused by organizations are widely publicized in corporate mission statements and on their official websites. But mere testimonies to values are not enough to create a strong core culture and derive its benefits. The values must be practiced. They must be real, they must be shared, and they must be modeled and reinforced by managers from top to bottom. The term **value-based management** describes managers who actively help develop, communicate, and enact shared values within an organization. Importantly, one area where value-based management has a major impact is with respect to ethics and social responsibility. As discussed in the last chapter, core values are powerful influences on the ethical behavior of organization members. At Tom's of Maine, for example, CEO Tom Chappell didn't hesitate to recall a new all-natural deodorant when customers were dissatisfied.[32] It cost the company some $400,000, but Chappell confidently did the "right" thing. His company is founded on values that include fairness and honesty, and he lives up to them, setting a positive example for others to follow.

The responsibility for value-based management extends to all managers and team leaders working at all levels. Like the organization, any work team or group will have a culture. How well this culture operates to support the group and its performance objectives will depend in part on the strength of the core values and the manager's role as a values champion. Just as with the organization as a whole, the value-based management of any work unit or team should meet the test of these criteria.[33]

Criteria for value-based management

→
- *Relevance*—Core values should support key performance objectives.
- *Integrity*—Core values should provide clear, consistent ethical anchors.
- *Pervasiveness*—Core values should be understood by all members.
- *Strength*—Core values should be accepted by everyone involved.

AROUND THE WORLD

Value-based initiative encourages Latin American entrepreneurs

Entrepreneurship accounts for most new job creation, business innovation, and inventions around the world. With the vision of helping Latin America's sagging economies, Linda Rottenberg and Peter Kellner formed the nonprofit organization Endeavor to help owners of small and medium-sized businesses in Latin America to become entrepreneurs. In six years their approach has created over 6000 new jobs and generated more than $400 million in local entrepreneurial revenues. The World Bank's president, James D. Wolfensohn, calls the firm "a model that should be replicated around the world." After examining its successes in Latin America, he wants to support its expansion to Africa. Endeavor's founders Rottenberg and Kellner are committed to the belief that "new ventures create jobs, spread wealth, expand opportunity and increase social mobility."[34]

SYMBOLIC LEADERSHIP

A **symbolic leader** is someone who uses symbols well to establish and maintain a desired organizational culture. Symbolic managers and leaders both act and talk the "language" of the organization. They are always careful to behave in ways that live up to the espoused core values; they are ever-present role models for others to emulate and follow. Symbolic leaders also communicate values in their spoken and written words, taking advantage of every opportunity to do so. They use language very well to describe people, events, and even the competition in ways that reinforce and communicate core values. *Language metaphors*—the use of positive examples from another context—are very powerful in this regard. For example, newly hired workers at Disney World and Disneyland are counseled to always think of themselves as more than employees; they are key "members of the cast," and they work "on stage." After all, they are told, Disney isn't just any business, it is an "entertainment" business.

Good symbolic leaders highlight and even dramatize core values and the observable culture. They tell key stories over and over again, and they encourage others to tell them. They often refer to the "founding story" about the entrepreneur whose personal values set a key tone for the enterprise. They remind everyone about organizational heroes, past and present, whose performances exemplify core values. They often use rites and rituals to glorify the performance of the organization and its members. At Mary Kay Cosmetics, gala events at which top sales performers share their tales of success are legendary. So, too, are the lavish incentive awards presented at these ceremonies, especially the pink luxury cars given to the most successful salespeople.[35]

○ A **symbolic leader** uses symbols to establish and maintain a desired organizational culture.

Learning check 4

Be sure you can • define the term organizational culture and explain the importance of strong cultures to organizations • distinguish between the observable and core cultures • explain the concept of value-added management • discuss how symbolic leaders build high-performance organizational cultures

MULTICULTURAL ORGANIZATIONS AND DIVERSITY

At the very time that we talk about the culture of an organization as a whole, we must also recognize diversity in its membership. Organizations are made up of people, each of whom is as a unique individual. An important key to competitive advantage is respecting this diversity and allowing everyone's talents to be fully utilized.

As first introduced in Chapter 1, **diversity** is a term used to describe differences among people at work. Primary dimensions of diversity include age, race, ethnicity, gender, physical ability, and sexual orientation. But workplace diversity also includes differences in religious beliefs, education, experience, and family status, among others.[36] In his book *Beyond Race and Gender,* consultant R. Roosevelt Thomas, Jr., makes the point that "diversity includes everyone." He says: "In this expanded context, white males are as diverse as their colleagues."[37] Thomas also links diversity with organizational culture, believing that the way people are treated

○ The term **diversity** describes race, gender, age, and other individual differences.

at work—with respect and inclusion, or with disrespect and exclusion—is a direct reflection of the organization's culture.

Thomas's diversity message to those who lead and manage organizations is pointed. Diversity is a potential source of competitive advantage, offering organizations a mixture of talents and perspectives that is ready and able to deal with the complexities and uncertainty in the ever-changing 21st-century environment. If you do the right things in organizational leadership, in other words, you'll gain competitive advantage through diversity. If you don't, you'll lose it. This message is backed by recent research on the relationship of diversity and performance. In a study of the business case for diversity, Thomas Kochan and his colleagues at MIT found that the presence of diversity alone does not guarantee a positive performance impact.[38] Only when diversity is leveraged through training and supportive human resource practices are the advantages gained. The study offers this guidance:

> To be successful in working with and gaining value from diversity requires a sustained, systemic approach and long-term commitment. Success is facilitated by a perspective that considers diversity to be an opportunity for everyone in an organization to learn from each other how better to accomplish their work and an occasion that requires a supportive and cooperative organizational culture as well as group leadership and process skills that can facilitate effective group functioning.

WHAT IS A MULTICULTURAL ORGANIZATION?

○ **Multiculturalism** involves pluralism and respect for diversity.

○ A **multicultural organization** is based on pluralism and operates with inclusivity and respect for diversity.

⟶ Characteristics of multicultural organizations

A key issue in the culture of any organization is *inclusivity*—the degree to which the organization is open to anyone who can perform a job, regardless of their race, sexual preference, gender, or other diversity attribute.[39] The term **multiculturalism** refers to inclusivity, pluralism, and respect for diversity in the workplace. There is no reason why organizational cultures cannot communicate core values that respect and empower the full demographic and cultural diversity that is now characteristic of our workforces. The "best" organizational cultures in this sense are inclusive. They value the talents, ideas, and creative potential of all members. The model in this regard is the truly **multicultural organization** with these characteristics:[40]

- *Pluralism*—Members of both minority cultures and majority cultures are influential in setting key values and policies.
- *Structural integration*—Minority-culture members are well represented in jobs at all levels and in all functional responsibilities.
- *Informal network integration*—Various forms of mentoring and support groups assist in the career development of minority-culture members.
- *Absence of prejudice and discrimination*—A variety of training and task force activities address the need to eliminate culture-group biases.
- *Minimum intergroup conflict*—Diversity does not lead to destructive conflicts between members of majority and minority cultures.

○ Organizational **subcultures** exist among people with similar values and beliefs based on shared work responsibilities and personal characteristics.

ORGANIZATIONAL SUBCULTURES

Like society as a whole, organizations contain a mixture of **subcultures,** that is, cultures common to groups of people with similar values and beliefs based on shared work responsibilities and personal characteristics. Whereas the pluralism that characterizes multicultural organizations conveys respect for different subcultures, working relations in organizations are too often hurt by the opposite tendency. Just as with life in general, **ethnocentrism**—the belief that one's membership group or subculture is superior to all others—can creep into the workplace and adversely affect the way people relate to one another.

The many possible subcultures in organizations include *occupational subcultures*.[41] Salaried professionals such as lawyers, scientists, engineers, and accountants have been described as having special needs for work autonomy and empowerment that may conflict with traditional management methods of top-down direction and control. Unless these needs are recognized and properly dealt with, salaried professionals may prove difficult to integrate into the culture of the larger organization.

There are also *functional subcultures* in organizations, and people from different functions often have difficulty understanding and working well with one another. For example, employees of a business may consider themselves "systems people" or "marketing people" or "manufacturing people" or "finance people." When such identities are overemphasized, members of the functional groups may spend most of their time with each other, develop a "jargon" or technical language that is shared among themselves, and view their role in the organization as more important than the contributions of the other functions.

Differences in *ethnic or national cultures* will be discussed in Chapter 5 on the global dimensions of management.[42] Although it is relatively easy to recognize that people from various countries and regions of the world have different cultures, it is far harder to turn this awareness into the ability to work well with persons whose backgrounds differ from our own. The best understanding is most likely gained through direct contact and being open-minded. The same advice holds in respect to *racial subcultures*. Although one may speak in everyday conversations about "African-American" or "Latino" or "Anglo" cultures, one has to wonder what we really know about them.[43] Importantly, a key question remains largely unanswered: Where can we find frameworks for understanding them? If improved cross-cultural understandings can help people work better across national boundaries, how can we create the same to help people from different racial subcultures work better together?

We live at a time when the influence of *generational subcultures* at work is of growing importance. But the issues are more subtle than young-old issues alone. It is possible to identify "generational gaps" among "baby boomers" now in their 50s, "Generation Xers" now in their 30s and early 40s, "Nexters" now in their 20s, and the "Millennial Generation" in high school at the turn of the century. Members of these generations grew up in quite different worlds and were influenced by different values and opportunities. Their work preferences and attitudes tend to reflect these differences. Someone who is 60 years old today, a common age for senior managers, was a teenager in the 1960s. Such a person may have difficulty understanding, supervising, and working with younger managers who were teens during the 1970s, 1980s, and even the 1990s. And if you are one of the latter generations—perhaps the Millennial Generation—you'll need to ponder how well you will do in the future when working with colleagues who grew up in the early years of the 21st century.[44]

○ **Ethnocentrism** is the belief that one's membership group or subculture is superior to all others.

REALITY CHECK 4.1

How minority employees view their work
In a study by Korn/Ferry International, the reported job satisfaction by black (64%) and white (62%) employees was quite comparable. But, things were far less similar when questions turned to issues of fairness and pay. Take the online "Reality Check" to learn more about the results of this survey.

Issues of relationships and discrimination based on *gender subcultures* also continue to complicate the workplace. Some research shows that when men work together, a group culture forms around a competitive atmosphere. Sports metaphors are common, and games and stories often deal with winning and losing.[45] When women work together, a rather different culture may form, with more emphasis on personal relationships and collaboration.[46]

CHALLENGES FACED BY MINORITIES AND WOMEN

The very term "diversity" basically means the presence of differences. But what does it mean when those differences are distributed unequally in the organizational power structure? What difference does it make when one subculture is in "majority" status while others become "minorities" in respect to representation within the organization? Even though organizations are changing today, most senior executives in large organizations are older, white, and male. There is still likely to be more workforce diversity at lower and middle levels of most organizations than at the top.

○ The **glass ceiling** is a hidden barrier to the advancement of women and minorities.

Take a look at the situation shown by *Figure 4.5*. It depicts the operation of the **glass ceiling,** defined in Chapter 1 as an invisible barrier that limits the advancement of women and minorities in some organizations. What are the implications for minority members, such as women or persons of color, seeking to advance and prosper in organizations traditionally dominated by a majority culture, such as white males? Consider also the situation of Jesse Spaulding as a regional manager for a restaurant chain owned by Shoney's. He says that the firm used to operate on the "buddy system," which "left people of color by the wayside" when it came to promotions. Things changed with new leadership, delighting Spaulding with new opportunity. Shoney's gained ranking among *Fortune* magazine's list of America's 50 Best Companies for Minorities.[47]

The daily work challenges faced by minorities and women can range from misunderstandings and lack of sensitivity on the one hand, to glass

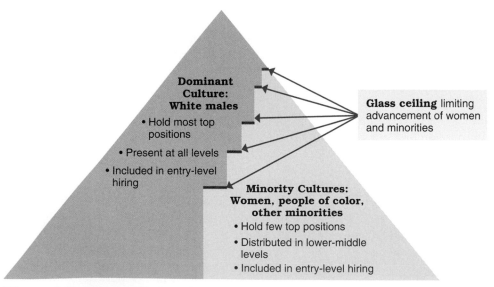

Figure 4.5 Glass ceilings as barriers to women and minority cultures in traditional organizations.

ceiling limitations, to even outright harassment and discrimination. *Sexual harassment* in the form of unwanted sexual advances, requests for sexual favors, and sexually laced communications is a problem female employees in particular may face. Minority workers can also be targets of cultural jokes; one survey reports some 45 percent of respondents had been the targets of such abuse. *Pay discrimination* is also an issue. A senior executive in the computer industry reported her surprise at finding out that the top performer in her work group, an African-American male, was paid 25 percent less than anyone else. This wasn't because his pay had been cut to that level, she said, but because his pay increases over time had always trailed those given to his white coworkers. The differences added up significantly over time, but no one noticed or stepped forward to make the appropriate adjustment.[48] Minority members may also face *job discrimination.* Microsoft, for example, has been criticized for treating the firm's 5000 or more temporary workers unfairly in terms of access to benefits and work assignments. Some temporaries (who wore orange identification badges at work) claimed that they were treated as second-class citizens by the permanent employees (who wore blue badges).[49]

REALITY CHECK 4.2

How does age affect attitude?
Data collected from 4000 executives show correlations between age and personality traits related to work effectiveness. Patience improves with age, blossoming (the data say) after the age of 45. Take the online "Reality Check" to learn more about age and attitude.

Muslims and Arab-Americans fight job bias

There is no room for employment discrimination in the new workplace. But ever since September 11, 2001, the U.S. Equal Employment Opportunity Commission has faced a "worrisome rise" in workplace discrimination complaints filed by Muslims and Arab-Americans. Cases handled range from the firing of an Afghan museum security guard, to the firing of a Muslim nurse for wearing a headscarf, to four Pakistani workers being given poor jobs and ridiculed during their daily prayers. One settlement went as high as $1.1 million in favor of the plaintiffs. The EEOC has been reaching out to workers and employers alike in trying to counter the trend. One of its commissioners, Paul Steven Miller, says: "It is the responsibility of the government and employers to protect these workers from discrimination and to reinforce the principles of equality."[52]

Sometimes the adaptation of minorities to organizations dominated by a majority culture takes the form of tendencies toward **biculturalism.** This is the display by members of minority cultures of majority culture characteristics that seem necessary to succeed in the work environment. For example, one might find gays and lesbians hiding their sexual orientation from coworkers out of fear of prejudice or discrimination. Similarly, one might find an African American carefully training herself to not use at work certain words or phrases that might be considered by white coworkers as subculture slang.

The special economic and work challenges faced by minorities are not always highly visible. The employment gains by Americans of color were hit hard by the post–9/11 economic downturn. Black and Latino workers suffered job losses disproportionate to those for whites, cutting severely

O **Biculturalism** is when minority members adopt characteristics of majority cultures in order to succeed.

into progress made in the previous decade.[50] And as to that period of economic expansion, we all know most Americans benefitted from a growth in jobs and employment opportunities. But how many of us know that disabled workers largely failed to share in the gains? At the same time that demand for workers in general rose, the employment rate of the disabled fell over 10 percent for men and 5 percent for women.[51]

MANAGING DIVERSITY

PERSONAL MANAGEMENT

DIVERSITY MATURITY is essential if you are to work well in today's organizations. It is a cornerstone for personal inclusivity. Consultant Roosevelt Thomas uses the following questions when testing diversity maturity among people in the workplace. Answer the questions. Be honest; admit where you still have work left to do. Use your answers to help set future goals to ensure that your actions, not just your words, consistently display positive diversity values.

- Do you accept responsibility for improving your performance?
- Do you understand diversity concepts?
- Do you make decisions about others based on their abilities?
- Do you understand that diversity issues are complex?
- Are you able to cope with tensions in addressing diversity?
- Are you willing to challenge the way things are?
- Are you willing to learn continuously?

Get to know yourself better ▶
Complete Self-Assessment #7 — **Diversity Awareness,** and **Exercise #7 — What Do You Value in Work?,** from the Management Learning Workbook.

There's no doubt today what minority workers want.[53] They want the same thing everyone wants. They want respect for their talents and a work setting that allows them to achieve to their full potential. It takes the best in diversity leadership at all levels of organizational management to meet these expectations. R. Roosevelt Thomas defines **managing diversity** as building an organizational culture that allows all members, minorities and women included, to reach their full potential.

Figure 4.6 describes a continuum of leadership approaches to diversity. The first is *affirmative action,* in which leadership commits the organization to hiring and advancing minorities and women. The second is *valuing diversity,* in which leadership commits the organization to education and training programs designed to help people better understand and respect individual differences. The third and most comprehensive is *managing diversity,* in which leadership commits to changing the organizational culture to empower and include all people.

Thomas believes that managing diversity holds the most value in respect to competitive advantage.[54] A diverse workforce offers a rich pool of talents, ideas, and viewpoints for solving the complex problems of often-uncertain environments. And a diverse workforce is best aligned with the needs and expectations of a diverse customer and stakeholder base. Organizations that Thomas calls "diversity mature" are well positioned to derive these and other sources of competitive advantage. In these organizations there is a diversity mission as well as an organizational mission; diversity is viewed as a strategic imperative, and the members understand diversity concepts.[55] Ultimately, however, he considers the basic building block of a diversity-mature organization to be the *diversity-mature individual.*[56]

Perhaps the most important word in human resource management today is "inclusiveness." By valuing diversity and building multicultural organizations that include everyone, organizations of all types can be strengthened and brought into better alignment with the challenges and opportunities of today's environment. Research reported in the *Gallup Management Journal,* for example, shows that establishing a racially and

○ **Managing diversity** is building an inclusive work environment that allows everyone to reach their full potential.

| Affirmative Action Create upward mobility for minorities and women | Valuing Differences Build quality relationships with respect for diversity | Managing Diversity Achieve full utilization of diverse human resources |

Figure 4.6 Leadership approaches to diversity—from affirmative action to managing diversity.
Source: Developed from R. Roosevelt Thomas, Jr., *Beyond Race and Gender* (New York: AMACOM, 1991), p. 28.

ethnically inclusive workplace is good for morale.[57] In a study of 2014 American workers, those who felt included were more likely to stay with their employers and recommend them to others. Survey questions asked such things as: "Do you always trust your company to be fair to all employees?" "At work, are all employees always treated with respect?" "Does your supervisor always make the best use of employees' skills?" Clearly, inclusivity counts; it counts in terms of respect for people, and it counts in building organizational capacities for high performance and sustainable competitive advantage. As Michael R. Losey, president of the Society for Human Resource Management (SHRM), says: "Companies must realize that the talent pool includes people of all types, including older workers; persons with disabilities; persons of various religious, cultural, and national backgrounds; persons who are not heterosexual; minorities; and women."[58]

Learning check 5

Be sure you can • explain multiculturalism and list key characteristics of multicultural organizations • identify typical organizational subcultures • discuss the common employment problems faced by minorities and women • explain Thomas's concept of managing diversity • realistically assess your diversity maturity

CHAPTER 4 STUDY GUIDE

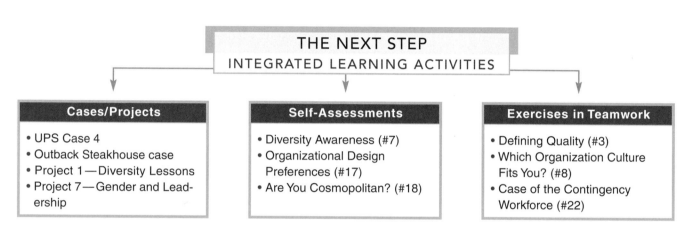

Where We've Been

BACK TO HERMAN MILLER

The opening example describes Herman Miller as a vanguard company noted for its values and performance success. In Chapter 4 you learned more about the complex nature of the external environments faced by organizations like Herman Miller. You also learned how organizations can benefit from strong and positive cultures and from internal environments committed to managing diversity and inclusivity for all employees. All of this, of course, doesn't just happen. Great managers make it happen. And that is what *Management 8/e* is all about.

THE NEXT STEP
INTEGRATED LEARNING ACTIVITIES

Cases/Projects

- UPS Case 4
- Outback Steakhouse case
- Project 1—Diversity Lessons
- Project 7—Gender and Leadership

Self-Assessments

- Diversity Awareness (#7)
- Organizational Design Preferences (#17)
- Are You Cosmopolitan? (#18)

Exercises in Teamwork

- Defining Quality (#3)
- Which Organization Culture Fits You? (#8)
- Case of the Contingency Workforce (#22)

STUDY QUESTION SUMMARY

1. What is the external environment of organizations?

- Competitive advantage and distinctive competency can only be achieved by organizations that deal successfully with dynamic and complex environments.
- The external environment of organizations consists of both general and specific parts.
- The general environment includes background economic, sociocultural, legal-political, technological, and natural environment conditions.
- The specific or task environment consists of suppliers, customers, competitors, regulators, and pressure groups that an organization interacts with.

- Environmental uncertainty challenges organizations and managers to be flexible and responsive to new and changing conditions.

2. What is a customer-driven organization?

- A customer-driven organization recognizes customer service and product quality as foundations of competitive advantage.
- Total quality operations address needs of both internal customers and external customers.
- Customer relationship management builds and maintains strategic relationships with customers.
- Supply chain management builds and maintains strategic relationships with suppliers.

3. What is a quality-driven organization?

- To compete in the global economy, organizations are increasingly expected to meet ISO 9000 quality standards.
- Total quality management makes quality a strategic objective of the organization and supports it by continuous improvement efforts.
- Total quality operations try to meet customers' needs—on time, the first time, and all the time.
- Quality circles are groups of employees working together to solve quality problems.

4. What is organizational culture?

- The organizational culture is an internal environment that establishes a personality for the organization and has a strong influence on the behavior of its members.
- The observable culture is found in the rites, rituals, stories, heroes, and symbols of the organization.
- The core culture consists of the core values and fundamental beliefs on which the organization is based.

- In organizations with strong cultures, members behave with shared understandings that support the organizational objectives.
- Symbolic managers build shared values, and use stories, ceremonies, heroes, and language to reinforce these values.

5. How is diversity managed in a multicultural organization?

- The organizational culture should create a positive ethical climate, or shared set of understandings about what is considered ethical.
- Multicultural organizations operate through a culture that values pluralism and respects diversity.
- Organizations have many subcultures, including those based on occupational, functional, ethnic, racial, age, and gender differences in a diverse workforce.
- Challenges faced by organizational minorities include sexual harassment, pay discrimination, job discrimination, and the glass ceiling effect.
- Managing diversity is the process of developing a work environment that is inclusive and allows everyone to reach their full potential.

KEY TERMS REVIEW

Biculturalism (p. 103)

Competitive advantage (p. 87)

Continuous improvement (p. 94)

Core values (p. 97)

Customer relationship management (p. 92)

Diversity (p. 99)

Environmental uncertainty (p. 90)

Ethnocentrism (p. 101)

General environment (p. 88)

Glass ceiling (p. 102)

ISO certification (p. 93)

Managing diversity (p. 104)

Multicultural organization (p. 100)

Multiculturalism (p. 100)

Organizational culture (p. 96)

Quality circle (p. 95)

Specific environment (p. 89)

Stakeholders (p. 89)

Subcultures (p. 101)

Supply chain management (p. 93)

Symbolic leader (p. 99)

Total quality management (p. 93)

Value-based management (p. 98)

Value creation (p. 89)

SELF-TEST 4

MULTIPLE-CHOICE QUESTIONS:

1. The general environment of an organization would include _____.
   (a) population demographics (b) activist groups (c) competitors (d) customers

2. In terms of value creation for stakeholders, _____ have a major interest in a business firm's profits and losses.
   (a) employees (b) communities (c) owners (d) suppliers

3. Two dimensions that determine the level of environmental uncertainty are the number of factors in the external environment and the _____ of these factors.
   (a) location (b) rate of change (c) importance (d) interdependence

4. Benchmarking, continuous improvement, and reduced cycle times are examples of organizational practices that show a commitment to _____.
   (a) affirmative action (b) total quality management (c) cost containment (d) supply chain management

5. A quality standard that has become essential for world-class companies competing in global markets is _____.
   (a) the Deming prize (b) the Baldrige award (c) CRM (d) ISO certification

6. New computer technologies have made possible _____ that quickly and efficiently produces individualized products for customers.
   (a) flexible manufacturing (b) mass production (c) mass customization (d) design for disassembly

7. Planned and spontaneous ceremonies and celebrations of work achievements illustrate how _____ help build strong corporate cultures.
   (a) rewards (b) heroes (c) rites and rituals (d) core values

8. When managers at Disney World use language metaphors, telling workers they are "on stage" as "members of the cast," they are engaging in _____ leadership.
   (a) symbolic (b) competitive (c) multicultural (d) stakeholder

9. Pluralism and the absence of discrimination and prejudice in policies and practices are two important hallmarks of _____.
   (a) the glass ceiling effect (b) a multicultural organization (c) quality circles (d) affirmative action

10. When members of minority cultures feel that they have to behave in ways similar to the majority, this is called _____.
    (a) biculturalism (b) symbolic leadership (c) the glass ceiling effect (d) inclusivity

11. Wal-Mart's suppliers electronically access inventory data and sales forecasts in the stores and automatically ship replacement products. This is an example of IT utilization in _____.
    (a) supply chain management (b) customer relationship management (c) total quality management (d) strategic constituencies analysis

12. Whether a structure is tight or loose and whether decisions are change oriented or driven by the status quo are indicators of an organization's _____.
    (a) inclusivity (b) culture (c) competitive advantage (d) multiculturalism

13. Performance with honesty, innovation, and social responsibility are among the _____ often espoused in corporate mission statements.
(a) core values (b) stakeholder interests (c) TQM practices (d) ISO standards

14. _____ means that an organization fully integrates members of minority cultures and majority cultures.
(a) Equal employment opportunity (b) Affirmative action (c) Symbolic leadership (d) Pluralism

15. The beliefs that older workers are not creative and are most interested in routine jobs are examples of stereotypes that can create bad feelings among members of different _____ subcultures in organizations.
(a) occupational (b) generational (c) gender (d) functional

SHORT-RESPONSE QUESTIONS:

16. What operating objectives are appropriate for an organization seeking competitive advantage through improved customer service?

17. What is the difference between an organization's external customers and its internal customers?

18. What is value-based management?

19. Why is it important for managers to understand subcultures in organizations?

APPLICATION QUESTION:

20. Two businesswomen, former college roommates, are discussing their jobs and careers over lunch. You overhear one saying to the other, "I work for a large corporation, while you own a small retail business. In my company there is a strong corporate culture and everyone feels its influence. In fact, we are always expected to act in ways that support the culture and serve as role models for others to do so as well. This includes a commitment to diversity and multiculturalism. Because of the small size of your firm, things like corporate culture, diversity, and multiculturalism are not so important to worry about." Do you agree or disagree with this statement? Why?

www.wiley.com/college/schermerhorn

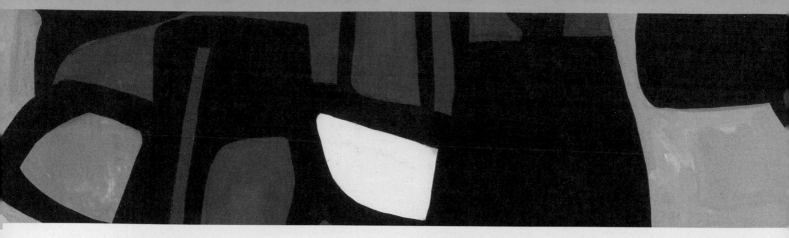

5

Global dimensions of management

Planning Ahead

After reading Chapter 5, you should be able to answer these questions in your own words.

CHAPTER 5 study questions

1. What are the international management challenges of globalization?

2. What are the forms and opportunities of international business?

3. What are multinational corporations and what do they do?

4. What is culture and how does it relate to global diversity?

5. How do management practices and learning transfer across cultures?

LIMITED BRANDS—FASHION THRIVES IN A WORLD OF OPPORTUNITY

What do Victoria's Secret, Express, Bath & Body Works, The Limited, The White Barn Candle Co., Aura Science, and Henri Bendel have in common? They all trace their roots to 1963 and a small women's clothing store in Columbus, Ohio. That single store has grown to more than 4000 now, all part of a company known globally for building a family of the best fashion names in the world—Limited Brands.

Limited Brands was named the world's most admired fashion retailer by *Fortune* magazine in 2003. Founder, chairman, and CEO Leslie Wexner is a member of the retail CEOs all-star team, being cited as a "pioneer of specialty brands" and someone with special retailing "vision and focus." All this has been achieved in a competitive industry described as challenged by "logistics, merchandising, marketing, human resources, property and, in some cases, global expansion."

In the quest for competitive advantage, The Limited has gone global. It sources its products from around the world. To ensure quality and protect its brand the firm's supplier and subcontractor relationships are guided by a "What We Stand For" policy, designed to ensure ethical operations. The policy states: "We will not do business with individuals or suppliers that do not meet our standards. We expect our suppliers to promote an environment of dignity, respect and opportunity; provide safe and healthy working conditions; offer fair compensation through wages and other benefits; hire workers of legal age, who accept employment on a voluntary basis; and maintain reasonable working hours." For its role in helping to expand the apparel manufacturing industry in sub-Saharan Africa to over $1 billion in sales, The Limited was recognized with a Special Recognition Award for Business Enterprise in Africa from the Africa-America Institute.

In respect to his business success, Leslie Wexner sums it up this way: "Better brands. Best brands. I don't believe bigger is better. I believe better is better. Period."[1]

Get Connected!

Browse the Web for information on the retailing industry, at home and around the world. Is The Limited still doing the right things?

Chapter 5 Learning Preview

There is more to Limited Brands than its 4000+ retail stores. Standing behind the displays and the fashion merchandise is a large operation that depends on vast worldwide networks of suppliers and subcontractors to produce its products. But even as The Limited seeks the world's opportunities, its global reach must be well managed and its ethical standards must be maintained. In Chapter 5 you will learn about international management with special attention to multinational corporations and the implications of global cultural diversity.

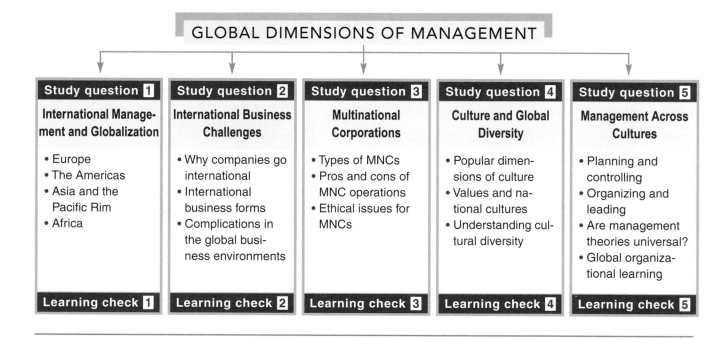

GLOBAL DIMENSIONS OF MANAGEMENT

Study question 1	Study question 2	Study question 3	Study question 4	Study question 5
International Management and Globalization	**International Business Challenges**	**Multinational Corporations**	**Culture and Global Diversity**	**Management Across Cultures**
• Europe • The Americas • Asia and the Pacific Rim • Africa	• Why companies go international • International business forms • Complications in the global business environments	• Types of MNCs • Pros and cons of MNC operations • Ethical issues for MNCs	• Popular dimensions of culture • Values and national cultures • Understanding cultural diversity	• Planning and controlling • Organizing and leading • Are management theories universal? • Global organizational learning
Learning check 1	Learning check 2	Learning check 3	Learning check 4	Learning check 5

There is no doubt about it. We live and work in a global community, one that grows smaller and more immediately accessible by the day. The internet and television bring on-the-spot news from around the world into our homes, 24 hours a day. The world's newspapers from *The New York Times,* to *El Financiero* (Mexico), to *Le Monde* (France), to *The Japan Times* can be read at the touch of a keyboard on your PC. It is possible to board a plane in Minneapolis and fly nonstop to Beijing; it is sometimes less expensive to fly from Columbus, Ohio, to Paris than to Albany, New York. Colleges and universities offer a growing variety of study-abroad programs.

This world of international opportunities isn't just for tourists and travelers; it has major implications for businesses and those who work in them. Just take a look at the automobile industry. The Chrysler PT Cruiser is built in Mexico for Daimler-Chrysler of Germany; Ford owns Volvo; Toyota has produced more than 10 million cars at its American plants; the "big three" Japanese automakers—Honda, Nissan, Toyota—get as much as 80 to 90 percent of their profits from sales in America. And when the last of the original Volkswagen Beetles was made in mid-2003, it wasn't a German band that heralded its departure to the museum. *Mariachi* music greeted the car as it rolled off the line at Volkswagen's Puebla, Mexico, plant.[2] The same trends and patterns are evident in other industries and countries. National boundaries are fast blurring as businesses of all sizes and types now travel the trade routes of the world.

Astute business investors know all this and more. They buy and sell only with awareness of the latest financial news from Hong Kong, London, Tokyo, New York, Sao Paulo, Johannesburg, and other of the world's financial centers. There is no doubt that we live and work today in a truly global village. You, like the rest of us, must get connected with its implications for everyday living and careers.

INTERNATIONAL MANAGEMENT AND GLOBALIZATION

This is the age of the **global economy** in which resource supplies, product markets, and business competition are worldwide rather than purely local or national in scope.[3] It is also a time heavily influenced by the forces of **globalization,** the process of growing interdependence among these components in the global economy.[4] Harvard scholar and consulant Rosabeth Moss Kanter describes it as: "one of the most powerful and pervasive influences on nations, businesses, workplaces, communities, and lives . . .[5]

The global economy offers great opportunities of worldwide sourcing, production, and sales capabilities. But as businesses spread their reach around the world, the processes of globalization also bring many adjustments to traditional patterns.[6] Large multinational businesses are increasingly adopting transnational or "global" identities, rather than being identified with a national home. The growing strength and penetration of these businesses worldwide are viewed by some as a potential threat to national economies and their local business systems, labor markets, and cultures. All this adds up to great uncertainty as executives move into new and uncharted competitive territories. America online's co-founder Stephen M. Case once described the scene: "I sometimes feel like I'm behind the wheel of a race car. One of the biggest challenges is there are no road signs to help navigate. And in fact . . . no one has yet determined which side of the road we're supposed to be on."[7]

The term used to describe management in organizations with business interests in more than one country is **international management.** There is no denying its importance. Procter & Gamble, for example, pursues a global strategy with a presence in more than 70 countries; the majority of McDonald's sales are now coming from outside the United States, with some of its most profitable restaurants located in places like Moscow, Budapest, and Beijing. As the leaders of these and other companies press forward with global initiatives, the international management challenges and opportunities of working across borders—national and cultural—must be mastered. A new breed of manager, the **global manager,** is increasingly sought after. This is someone informed about international developments, transnational in outlook, competent in working with people from different cultures, and always aware of regional developments in a changing world.

What about you? Are you prepared for the challenges of international management? Are you informed about the world and the forces of globalization?

○ In the **global economy** resources, markets, and competition are worldwide in scope.

○ **Globalization** is the process of growing interdependence among elements of the global economy.

○ **International management** involves managing operations in more than one country.

○ A **global manager** is culturally aware and informed on international affairs.

EUROPE

○ The **European Union** is a political and economic alliance of European countries.

The new Europe is a place of dramatic political and economic developments.[8] The **European Union** (EU) is expanding to 22 countries that agree to support mutual economic growth by removing barriers that previously limited cross-border trade and business development. As an economic union, the EU is putting the rest of the world on notice that European business is a global force to be reckoned with. Members are linked through favorable trade and customs laws intended to facilitate the free flow of workers, goods and services, and investments across national boundaries. Businesses in each member country have access to a market of over 375 million consumers, compared to 220 million in the United States and 120 million in Japan.

○ The **euro** is the new common European currency.

Among the important business and economic developments in the EU are agreements to eliminate frontier controls and trade barriers, create uniform minimum technical product standards, open government procurement to businesses from all member countries, unify financial regulations, lift competitive barriers in banking and insurance, and offer a common currency—the **euro.** The growing worldwide impact of the euro is being watched carefully. Although there are still political and economic uncertainties, the expected regional benefits of an expanding EU include higher productivity, lower inflation, and steady growth.

TAKE IT TO THE CASE

Harley Davidson Motor Company
Where style and strategy travel the globe

Harley Davidson motorcycles rule the road these days. Along with the popular "Harley"-branded clothing and accessories, the company is on a roll. It wasn't always that way. During the late 1970s, the firm's sales suffered in the face of new and stiff competition from Japan. The U.S. International Trade Commission granted Harley short-term tariff protection from Japanese motorcycles in 1983; the firm regrouped, put its house in order, and hasn't looked back since. The Harley Owner's Group has over a half-million members worldwide. Harley has a solid market in Japan, where its bikes are a mark of prestige for their owners. Harley is secure in pursuing its mission with a clear sense of its global markets: "We fulfill dreams through the experience of motorcycling."[10]

THE AMERICAS

○ **NAFTA** is the North American Free Trade Agreement linking Canada, the United States, and Mexico in an economic alliance.

The United States, Canada, and Mexico are joined in the North American Free Trade Agreement **(NAFTA).** This agreement largely frees the flow of goods and services, workers, and investments within a region that has more potential consumers than its European rival, the EU. Getting approval of NAFTA from all three governments was not easy. Whereas Canadian firms worried about domination by U.S. manufacturers, American politicians were concerned about the potential loss of jobs to Mexico. Some calls were made for more government legislation and support to protect domestic industries from foreign competition. While Mexicans feared that free trade would bring a further intrusion of U.S. culture and values into their country, Americans complained that Mexican businesses did not operate by the same social standards—particularly with respect to environmental protection and the use of child labor.

At times an issue in NAFTA controversies, **maquiladoras** are foreign manufacturing plants allowed to operate in Mexico with special privileges in return for employing Mexican labor.[9] These firms import materials, components, and equipment duty free. They employ lower-cost Mexican labor to assemble these materials into finished products, which are then exported with duty paid only on the "value added" in Mexico. Critics of *maquiladoras* accuse them of exploiting Mexican workers and giving away jobs that would otherwise go to Americans. They also point to high "social costs" as a continuing influx of workers overburdens services in Mexican border towns and the region becomes increasingly "Americanized." Advocates argue that *maquiladoras* increase employment and prosperity, and help develop skilled local workers.

○ **Maquiladoras** are foreign manufacturing plants that operate in Mexico with special privileges.

Optimism regarding business and economic growth extends throughout the Americas. Countries of the region are cutting tariffs, updating their economic policies, and welcoming foreign investors. An agreement has been reached by trade ministers to create a Free Trade Area of the Americas (FTAA), a proposed free-trade zone that would stretch from Point Barrow, Alaska, all the way to Tierra del Fuego, Chile. In addition, the *MERCOSUR* agreement links Bolivia, Brazil, Paraguay, Uruguay; and Argentina; the Andean Pact links Venezuela; Colombia, Equador, Peru, and Bolivia; and the Carribean Community, CARICOM, is growing as an economic linkage.

ASIA AND THE PACIFIC RIM

When one looks toward Asia, China looms center stage. The country of 1.3 billion people is the world's largest consumer marketplace. Its economy has averaged over 7 percent growth for the past several years and is closely intertwined with the world at large. China's firms are major exporters of apparel and clothing to firms like Limited Brands, featured in the chapter opener. It is also a top exporter of computers, electrical parts and components, telecommunications equipment, and sporting goods, among other products.[11] Some $120+ billion of exports find their way annually from China to America alone. But in Asia, one also has to recognize the historical strength of Japanese businesses—Honda, Toyota, Sony, to name just three—the growing prominence of firms like Samsung and Hyundai of South Korea, as well as other regional powers like Taiwan and Singapore. Together, they add another $200+ billion in exports to the United States.

Elsewhere in Southeast Asia, countries like Malaysia and Thailand are prominent, Vietnam is fast advancing, and the Philippines is making a strategic move. With a high literacy rate, an educated workforce, and a population that speaks English, it intends to become a world center for business process outsourcing. Goals include expanding its growing presence in global markets for medical transcription and accounting services, as well as customer call centers.[12] The 2003 agreement among 10 Southeast Asian nations to form an economic community along the lines of the EU model is designed to further growth in this region.

"Opportunity" is the watchword of the day wherever you travel or do business in Asia. Asian countries already represent a third of the global marketplace and rank as the world's top market for cars and telecommunications equipment. It is not just "low-cost" labor that attracts businesses to Asia; the growing availability of highly skilled "brainpower" is increasingly high on its list of advantages. India, the world's second-most-populated country, is a good example. The country is in the midst of economic expansion, with a high literacy rate and relatively inexpensive skilled labor. It is emerging as a world-class base for technology development and software engineering.

AFRICA

Africa (see *Figure 5.1*) is a continent in the news.[13] Although often the focus of reports on ethnic turmoil and civil strife in countries struggling along pathways to peace and development, the region beckons international investments. Whereas foreign businesses tend to avoid the risk of trouble spots, they are giving increased attention to stable countries with growing economics. One is Ghana, which has established a growing presence in the market for business process outsourcing.[14] On the discouraging side, the rates of economic growth in sub-Saharan Africa are among the lowest in the world; many parts of Africa suffer from terrible problems of poverty and the ravishment of a continuing AIDS epidemic. The region's need for sustained assistance from business investments and foreign aid is well established.

A report by two Harvard professors recently analyzed the foreign investment environment of Africa and concluded that the region's contextual problems are manageable.[15] "In fact they should be viewed as opportunities," says James A. Austin, one of the co-authors. He adds: "If a company has the managerial and organizational capabilities to deal with the region's unique business challenges, then it will be able to enter a promising market."[16]

The Southern Africa Development Community (SADC) links 14 countries of southern Africa in trade and economic development efforts. The objectives of SADC include harmonizing and rationalizing strategies for sustainable development among member countries.[17] Post-apartheid South Africa, in particular, has benefitted from political revival. A country of almost 50 million people and great natural resources, South Africa is experiencing economic recovery and attracting outside investors. It al-

Figure 5.1 Africa, continent of opportunity.

Mozambique is just one of Africa's opportunities

A turnaround is underway in the East African nation of Mozambique as the former Portuguese colony continues to emerge from years of civil war that began with its independence in 1975. Considered the world's poorest country in 1990, Mozambique's new economy offers citizens hope and advancement. A local entrepreneur says, "Mozambicans, sick of war, want a working society."[19] Mozambique is rich with natural resources and is in an ideal trading location. The country is now home to billion-dollar infrastructure projects financed by development agencies. A railroad and highway corridor from the capital of Maputo to South Africa is fast developing. Mozambique is a member of the South African Development Community.

ready accounts for half the continent's purchasing power.[18] Foreign investments in the country increased sharply after minority white rule ended and Nobel-Prize winner Nelson Mandela became the nation's first black president.

Be sure you can • define the terms global economy and globalization • discuss the implications of globalization for international management • illustrate the significance of regional economic alliances by describing how NAFTA and the EU operate • discuss the pros and cons of *maquiladora* operations

Learning check 1

INTERNATIONAL BUSINESS CHALLENGES

John Chambers, CEO of Cisco Systems, Inc., says: "I will put my jobs anywhere in the world where the right infrastructure is, with the right educated workforce, with the right supportive government."[20] Cisco and other firms like it are **international businesses.** They conduct for-profit transactions of goods and services across national boundaries.

O An **international business** conducts commercial transactions across national boundaries.

WHY COMPANIES GO INTERNATIONAL

International businesses of all types and sizes are the foundations of world trade. They are the engines for moving raw materials, finished products, and specialized services from one country to another in the global economy. The reasons *why businesses go international* include these attractions of the marketplaces of the world:

• *Profits*—Global operations offer greater profit potential.

• *Customers*—Global operations offer new markets to sell products.

• *Suppliers*—Global operations offer access to needed raw materials.

• *Capital*—Global operations offer access to financial resources.

• *Labor*—Global operations offer access to lower labor costs.

← Reasons for engaging in international business

The Web is a goldmine of international business information

There's a world of international business resources available on the Web. Start with a visit to the United States Department of Commerce website of the International Trade Commission. Here you'll find "Country Commercial Guides," updated annually and containing business, economic, and political information. Wander more—the Kelley School of Business at Indiana University maintains a comprehensive list of international business resources on the Web. The search engine Colossus will help you find local search engines in other countries. *The Economist* magazine regularly publishes reports and Web updates on the economies of the world, as do other major business periodicals.

FORMS OF INTERNATIONAL BUSINESS

The common forms of international business are shown in *Figure 5.2*. When a business is just getting started internationally, global sourcing, exporting/importing, and licensing and franchising are the usual ways to begin. These are *market entry strategies* that involve the sale of goods or services to foreign markets but do not require expensive capital investments. Joint ventures and wholly owned subsidiaries are *direct investment strategies*. They require major capital commitments but create rights of ownership and control over operations in the foreign country.

Market Entry Strategies

○ In **global sourcing,** materials or services are purchased around the world for local use.

A common first step into international business is **global sourcing**—the process of purchasing materials, manufacturing components or business services from around the world. It is an international division of labor in which activities are performed in countries where they can be done well at the lowest cost. In manufacturing, global sourcing of components for cars may mean purchasing windshields and instrument panels from Mexico, and antilock braking systems from Germany. In services, it may mean setting up toll-free customer support call centers in the Philippines, or contracting for computer software programs in India. The goal of global sourcing is to take advantage of international wage gaps and the availability of skilled labor by contracting for goods and services in low-cost foreign locations.

○ In **exporting,** local products are sold abroad.

○ **Importing** is the process of acquiring products abroad and selling them in domestic markets.

A second form of international business involves **exporting**—selling locally made products in foreign markets, and/or **importing**—buying foreign-made products and selling them in domestic markets. Because the growth of export industries creates local jobs, governments often offer spe-

Market entry strategies			Direct investment strategies	
Global sourcing	Exporting and importing	Licensing and franchising	Joint ventures	Foreign subsidiaries

→ Increasing involvement in ownership and control of foreign operations

Figure 5.2 Common forms of international business—from market entry to direct investment strategies.

Checklist for successful joint ventures

- Choose a partner familiar with your firm's major business.
- Choose a partner with a strong local workforce.
- Choose a partner with future expansion possibilities.
- Choose a partner with a strong local market for its own products.
- Choose a partner with shared interests in meeting customer needs.
- Choose a partner with good profit potential.
- Choose a partner in sound financial standing.

---

cial advice and assistance to businesses that are trying to develop or expand their export markets. Many U.S. policymakers look to export industries, large and small, as one way to correct trade imbalances. One example is an export initiative that came by chance for Franklin Jacobs, founder of St. Louis–based Falcon Products, Inc., a commercial furniture company. While on a tour through Europe, he says, "I discovered that my products were a lot better and a lot cheaper" than those on the market there. An opportunist, Jacobs rented exposition space at the U.S. Embassy in London, shipped a container load of his furniture, and received over US$ 200,000 in orders. His new export initiative resulted in job expansion at the firm.[21]

Another form of international business is the **licensing agreement,** where foreign firms pay a fee for rights to make or sell another company's products in a specified region. The license typically grants access to a unique manufacturing technology, special patent, or trademark. **Franchising** is a form of licensing in which the foreign firm buys the rights to use another's name and operating methods in its home country. As in domestic franchising agreements, firms like McDonald's, Wendy's, Subway, and others sell facility designs, equipment, product ingredients and recipes, and management systems to foreign investors, while retaining certain product and operating controls.

> ○ In a **licensing agreement** one firm pays a fee for rights to make or sell another company's products.

> ○ In **franchising** a fee is paid for rights to use another firm's name and operating methods.

Direct Investment Strategies

To establish a direct investment presence in a foreign country, many firms enter into **joint ventures.** These are co-ownership arrangements that pool resources and share risks and control for business operations. A joint venture may be established by equity purchases and/or direct investments by a foreign partner in an existing operation; it may also involve the creation of an entirely new business by a foreign and local partner. International joint ventures are *strategic alliances* that help partners gain things through cooperation that otherwise would be difficult to achieve independently. In return for its investment in a local operation, for example, the outside or foreign partner often gains both access to new markets and the assistance of a local partner who understands them. In return for its investment, the local partner often gains new technology as well as opportunities for its employees to learn new skills. *Manager's Notepad 5.1* offers a checklist for choosing joint venture partners.[22]

> ○ A **joint venture** operates in a foreign country through co-ownership with local partners.

A **foreign subsidiary** is a local operation completely owned and controlled by a foreign firm. Like joint ventures, foreign subsidiaries may be formed through direct investment in startup operations called *greenfield ven-*

> ○ A **foreign subsidiary** is a local operation completely owned by a foreign firm.

tures, or through equity purchases in existing ones. When making such investments, foreign firms are clearly taking a business risk. They must be confident that they possess the expertise needed to manage and conduct business affairs successfully in the new environment. This is where prior experience gained through joint ventures can prove very beneficial. Although establishing a foreign subsidiary represents the highest level of involvement in international operations, it can make very good business sense. Nissan recently opened a new plant in Canton, Mississippi, with the expectation of producing 400,000 cars a year there. An auto analyst for a Japanese brokerage firm says: "It's a smart strategy to shift production to North America. They're reducing their exposure through building more in their regional markets, as well as being able to meet consumers' needs more quickly."[23]

COMPLICATIONS IN THE GLOBAL BUSINESS ENVIRONMENT

The environment of international business in any form is complex and dynamic—and highly competitive. Global business executives must master task demands of operating with worldwide suppliers, distributors, customers, and competitors. They must understand and deal successfully with general environment differences in economic, legal-political, and educational systems, among other aspects of business infrastructure. Percy Barnevik, when chairman of the global corporation ABB, once said: "Too many people think you can succeed in the long run just by exporting from America to Europe. But you need to establish yourself locally and become, for example, a Chinese, Indonesian, or Indian citizen."[24]

Differences in legal environments among nations create substantial international business challenges. Organizations are expected to abide by the laws of the host country in which they are operating. In the United States, for example, executives of foreign-owned companies must worry about antitrust issues that prevent competitors from regularly talking to one another. They also must deal with a variety of special laws regarding occupational health and safety, equal employment opportunity, sexual harassment, and other matters—all constraints potentially different from those they find at home.

The more home- and host-country laws differ, the more difficult and complex it is for international businesses to adapt to local ways. Common legal problems in international business involve incorporation practices and business ownership; negotiating and implementing contracts with foreign parties; protecting patents, trademarks, and copyrights; and handling foreign exchange restrictions. Intellectual property rights have long been a source of dispute between western businesses and China. Software piracy and copyright violations of CDs and books, for example, are well known. But General Motors recently had its own problems there. The firm's China executives noticed that a new model from a fast-growing local competitor—Chery Automobile, partially owned by GM's Chinese partner—looked very similar to one of their own cars due out in the near future. GM claims in local courts that their design was copied; the competitor denies the charges.[25]

When disputes between nations relate to international trade, they can end up before the **World Trade Organization.** This is a global institution established to promote free trade and open markets around the world. In the WTO some 140+ members agree to give one another **most favored nation status**—the most favorable treatment for imports and exports. Al-

o **World Trade Organization** member nations agree to negotiate and resolve disputes about tariffs and trade restrictions.

o **Most favored nation status** gives a trading partner most favorable treatment for imports and exports.

though members agree to ongoing negotiations and the reduction of tariffs and trade restrictions, trading relationships are often difficult. The WTO offers a mechanism for monitoring international trade and resolving disputes among countries. **Protectionism** in the form of political calls for tariffs and favorable treatments to help protect domestic businesses from foreign competition is a common and complicating theme. Government leaders, such as the president of the United States, face internal political dilemmas involving the often-conflicting goals of seeking freer international trade while still protecting domestic industries. These dilemmas make it difficult to reach international agreement on trade matters, and create controversies for the WTO.

○ **Protectionism** is a call for tariffs and favorable treatments to protect domestic firms from foreign competition.

Be sure you can • list five reasons that companies pursue international business opportunities • describe and give examples of each of these international business strategies—global sourcing, exporting/importing, franchising/licensing, joint ventures, and foreign subsidiaries • explain the operations of the WTO • discuss how differences in legal environments can affect businesses operating internationally

Learning check 2

MULTINATIONAL CORPORATIONS

A true **multinational corporation** (MNC) is a business firm with extensive international operations in more than one foreign country. Premier MNCs found in annual listings such as *Fortune* magazine's Global 500 include such global giants as General Electric, Exxon, and Wal-Mart from the United States; Mitsubishi, Toyota, and NTT DoCoMo of Japan; DaimlerChrysler of Germany and Royal Dutch/Shell Group of the Netherlands and Great Britain. Also important on the world scene are *multinational organizations* (MNOs)—like the International Federation of Red Cross and Red Crescent Societies, the United Nations, and the World Bank—whose nonprofit missions and operations span the globe.

○ A **multinational corporation** is a business with extensive international operations in more than one foreign country.

TYPES OF MULTINATIONAL CORPORATIONS

A typical MNC operates in many countries but has corporate headquarters in one home or host country. Microsoft, Apple Computer, and McDonald's are among the ready examples. Although deriving substantial sales and profits from international sources, these firms and others like them typically also have strong national identifications. But as the global economy grows more competitive, many multinationals are acting more like **transnational corporations.** They increasingly try to operate worldwide without being identified with one national home.[26] Executives of transnationals view the entire world as their domain for acquiring resources, locating production facilities, marketing goods and services, and for brand image. They seek total integration of global operations, try to operate across borders without home-based prejudices, make major decisions from a global perspective, distribute work among worldwide points of excellence, and employ senior executives from many different countries. Nestlé is a good example in foods; Asea Brown Boveri (ABB) is another in diversified conglomerates. When one buys a Nestlé product in Brazil or has a neighbor working for ABB in Columbus, Ohio, who would know that both are actually registered Swiss companies?

○ A **transnational corporation** is an MNC that operates worldwide on a borderless basis.

PROS AND CONS OF MULTINATIONAL CORPORATIONS

www.kemet.com

The town of Shelby, North Carolina, knows how cut-throat the global economy can be. When Kemet Electronics laid off local employees to shift jobs to Mexico, one said: "I worked all this time to get what I've got, and now it's gone. I thought I had found security."

In this time when consumer demand, resource supplies, product flows, and labor markets increasingly span national boundaries, the actions of MNCs are increasingly influential in the global economy. The United Nations has reported that MNCs hold one-third of the world's productive assets and control 70 percent of world trade. Furthermore, more than 90 percent of these MNCs are based in the Northern Hemisphere. While this may bring a sense of both accomplishment and future opportunity to business leaders, it can also be very threatening to small and less-developed countries and their domestic industries.

Host-Country Issues

Ideally, global corporations and the countries that "host" their foreign operations should both benefit. *Figure 5.3* shows how things can and do go both right and wrong in MNC–host country relationships. The *potential host-country benefits* include larger tax bases, increased employment opportunities, technology transfers, the introduction of new industries, and the development of local resources. The *potential host-country costs* include complaints that MNCs extract excessive profits, dominate the local economy, interfere with the local government, do not respect local customs and laws, fail to help domestic firms develop, hire the most talented of local personnel, and do not transfer their most advanced technologies.[27]

Of course executives of MNCs sometimes feel exploited as well in their relations with host countries. Consider China once again, a setting where major cultural, political, and economic differences confront the outsider.[28] Profits have proved elusive for some foreign investors; some have found it difficult to take profits out of the country; some have struggled to get the raw materials needed for operations.[29] The protection of intellectual property was mentioned earlier as an ongoing concern of foreign manufacturers, and managing relationships with Chinese government agencies can be very complicated.

Home-Country Issues

MNCs may also encounter difficulties in the "home" country where their headquarters are located. Even as many MNCs try to operate more globally, home-country governments and citizens still tend to identify them

MNC host-country relationships		MNC host-country relationships	
What should go right		What can go wrong	
Mutual benefits		**Host-country complaints about MNCs**	**MNC complaints about host countries**
Shared opportunities with potential for • Growth • Income • Learning • Development		• Excessive profits • Economic domination • Interference with government • Hire best local talent • Limited technology transfer • Disrespect for local customs	• Profit limitations • Overpriced resources • Exploitative rules • Foreign exchange restrictions • Failure to uphold contracts

Figure 5.3 What should go right and what can go wrong in MNC–host country relationships.

with local and national interests. When an MNC outsources, cuts back, or closes a domestic operation to shift work to lower-cost international destinations, the loss of local jobs is controversial. Corporate decision makers are likely to be engaged by government and community leaders in critical debate about a firm's domestic social responsibilities. *Home-country criticisms of MNCs* include complaints about transferring jobs out of the country, shifting capital investments abroad, and engaging in corrupt practices in foreign settings.

ETHICAL ISSUES FOR MULTINATIONAL CORPORATIONS

The ethical aspects of international business deserve special attention and were introduced in Chapter 3 on ethics and social responsibility. **Corruption,** engaging in illegal practice to further one's business interests, is a source of continuing controversy. The Foreign Corrupt Practices Act makes it illegal for firms and their managers to engage in U.S. corrupt practices overseas, including giving bribes and excessive commissions to foreign officials in return for business favors. This law specifically bans payoffs to foreign officials to obtain or keep business, provides punishments for executives who know about or are involved in such activities, and requires detailed accounting records for international business transactions. Critics, however, believe the law fails to recognize the "reality" of business as practiced in many foreign nations. They complain that American companies are at a competitive disadvantage because they can't offer the same "deals" as competitors from other nations—deals that locals may regard as standard business practices.

> **Corruption** involves illegal practices to further one's business interests.

Sweatshops, business operations that employ workers at low wages for long hours and in poor working conditions, are another concern in the global business arena. Networks of outsourcing contracts are now common as manufacturers follow the world's low-cost labor supplies—countries like the Philippines, Sri Lanka, and Vietnam are popular destinations. Yet Nike, Inc., has learned that a global company will be held publicly accountable for the work standards and employment practices of its foreign subcontractors. Facing activist criticism, the company revised its labor practices after a review by the consulting firm Goodworks International. Nike now offers a special website, Transparency 101, with reports and audit results on its international labor practices. Nike's international business Web is extensive, including more than 750 manufacturing sites and contractors in some 50 countries.[30]

> **Sweatshops** employ workers at very low wages, for long hours, and in poor working conditions.

Child labor, the full-time employment of children for work otherwise done by adults, is another international business ethics issue. It has been made especially visible by activist concerns regarding the manufacture of handmade carpets in countries like Pakistan. Initiatives to eliminate child labor include an effort by the Rugmark Foundation to discourage purchases of carpets that do not carry its label. The "Rugmark" label is earned by a certification process to guarantee that a carpet manufacturer does not use illegal child labor.[31]

> **Child labor** is the full-time employment of children for work otherwise done by adults.

Yet another ethical issue relates to global concerns for environmental protection. Not only is the world's citizenry worried about disasters such as the pollution aftermath of the Gulf War, but more generally it expects global corporations to respect the natural environment. Industrial pollution of cities, hazardous waste, depletion of natural resources, and related concerns are now worldwide issues. The concept of **sustainable development** is a popular guideline advanced by activist groups. It is "develop-

> **Sustainable development** meets the needs of the present without hurting future generations.

ment that meets the needs of the present without compromising the ability of future generations to meet their own needs."[32] As global corporate citizens, MNCs are increasingly expected to uphold high standards in dealing with sustainable development and protection of the natural environment—whenever and wherever they operate. The available guidelines for responsible environmental policies include **ISO 14000** certification standards of the International Standards Organization.

O **ISO 14000** offers a set of certification standards for responsible environmental policies.

Learning check 3

Be sure you can • differentiate a multinational corporation from a transnational corporation • list at least three host-country complaints and three home-country complaints about MNC operations • define the terms corruption, sweatshop, and child labor, • illustrate how each of these practices can create ethical problems for international businesses

CULTURE AND GLOBAL DIVERSITY

O **Culture** is a shared set of beliefs, values, and patterns of behavior common to a group of people.

O **Culture shock** is the confusion and discomfort a person experiences when in an unfamiliar culture.

Culture is the shared set of beliefs, values, and patterns of behavior common to a group of people. Anyone who has visited another country knows that cultural differences exist. **Culture shock,** the confusion and discomfort a person experiences when in an unfamiliar culture, is a reminder that many of these differences must be mastered just to travel comfortably around the world. But the business implications of cultural differences are also important to understand. An American exporter, for example, once went to see a Saudi Arabian official. He sat in the office with crossed legs and the sole of his shoe exposed—an unintentional sign of disrespect in the local culture. He passed documents to the host using his left hand, which Muslims consider unclean. And he refused to accept coffee when it was offered, suggesting criticism of the Saudi's hospitality. What was the price for these cultural miscues? He lost a $10 million contract to a Korean executive better versed in Arab ways.[33]

O **Ethnocentrism** is the tendency to consider one's culture as superior to others.

Ethnocentrism, the tendency to view one's culture as superior to others, is surprisingly common in international business. Local customs vary in too many ways for most of us to become true experts in the many cultures of our diverse world. Yet there are things we can do to respect differences, successfully conduct business abroad, and minimize culture shock. Self-awareness and reasonable sensitivity are the basic building blocks of cultural awareness, as suggested in *Manager's Notepad 5.2.*[34]

POPULAR DIMENSIONS OF CULTURE

The first impressions of an international traveler often relate to language differences and difficulties. But other dimensions of popular culture quickly follow, including use of space, time orientation, religion, and contracts and agreements.[35] When executives at British Airways surveyed international customers, for example, a simple lesson emerged—don't assume people from different cultures will have the same dining habits and preferences. Japanese, for example, commented that BA's food was "not bad for Westerners." They also pointed out that the white china dishes were similar to those used in Japanese hospitals and prisons. "The further away from our Western culture we go, the less satisfied our customers are," said one BA marketing manager, "people from other cultures have felt looked down upon."[36]

Stages in adjusting to a new culture

- *Confusion:* First contacts with the new culture leave you anxious, uncomfortable, and in need of information and advice.
- *Small victories:* Continued interactions bring some "successes," and your confidence grows in handling daily affairs.
- *The honeymoon:* A time of wonderment, cultural immersion, and even infatuation, with local ways viewed positively.
- *Irritation and anger:* A time when the "negatives" overwhelm the "positives," and the new culture becomes a target of your criticism.
- *Reality:* A time of rebalancing; you are able to enjoy the new culture while accommodating its less desirable elements.

Language

Language is a medium of culture. It provides access to the cultural understanding needed to conduct business and develop personal relationships. Not only do languages vary around the world; the same language (such as English) can vary in usage from one country to the next (as it does from America to England to Australia). Although it isn't always possible to know a local language, such as Hungarian, it is increasingly usual in business dealings to find some common second language in which to communicate, such as English, French, German, or Spanish. The importance of good foreign language training is critical for the truly global manager. When Larry Johnston arrived in Paris to head up GE's medical equipment operations in Europe, the Middle East, and Africa, the first thing he did was study French intensively for a month. "I went from 7 A.M. to 8 P.M. and learned enough to converse," he says.[37]

According to anthropologist Edward T. Hall, there are systematic and important differences in the way cultures utilize language in communication.[38] He describes **low-context cultures** as those in which most communication takes place via the written or spoken word. In places like the United States, Canada, and Germany, the message is delivered in very precise wording. One has to listen and read carefully to best understand what the message sender intends. Things are quite different in **high-context cultures,** where much communication takes place through nonverbal and situational cues. In these cultures words communicate only a (sometimes small) part of the message. The rest must be interpreted from the situational "context"—body language, physical setting, and even the past relationships among those involved. This process is often time consuming and very deliberate. In high-context Japan, for example, much emphasis is given to social settings in which potential business partners develop a relationship and get to know one another; once this is accomplished, future deals can then be formed.

○ **Low-context cultures** emphasize communication via spoken or written words.

○ **High-context cultures** rely on nonverbal and situational cues as well as spoken or written words in communication.

Interpersonal Space

Hall considers the use of interpersonal space as one of the important "silent languages" of culture.[39] Arabs and many Latin Americans, for example, prefer to communicate at much closer distances than is standard in American practice. Misunderstandings are possible if one person moves back as another moves forward to close the interpersonal distance between them. Some cultures of the world also value space more highly than others. Americans tend to value large and private office space. The Japanese are highly efficient in using space; even executive offices are likely to be shared in major corporations.

Time Orientation

Time orientation is another of the silent languages of culture.[40] The way people approach and deal with time tends to vary widely. Mexicans, for example, may specify *hora Americana* on invitations if they want guests to appear at the appointed time; otherwise, it may be impolite to arrive punctually for a scheduled appointment. When working in Vietnam, punctuality is important and communicates respect for one's host.[41] Hall describes **monochronic cultures** in which people tend to do one thing at a time. The standard American business practice is to schedule a meeting and give the visitor one's undivided attention for the allotted time.[42] In **polychronic cultures,** time is used to accomplish many different things at once. The American visitor to an Egyptian client may be frustrated by continued interruptions as people flow in and out of the office and various transactions are made.

○ In **monochronic cultures** people tend to do one thing at a time.

○ In **polychronic cultures** time is used to accomplish many different things at once.

Religion

One should always be aware of religious traditions when visiting and working in other cultures. Religion is a major influence on many people's lives, and its impact may extend to practices regarding dress, food, and interpersonal behavior. It is a source of ethical and moral teaching, with associated personal and institutional implications. "Islamic banks" in the Middle East, for example, service their customers without any interest charges to remain consistent with teachings of the *Koran.* The traveler and businessperson should always be sensitive to the rituals, holy days, and sabbath schedules of alternative religions. When working in Malaysia, for example, it is polite to schedule business dinners after 8 P.M. This allows Muslims to complete the evening prayer before dining. Similarly, it should be remembered that the Islamic holy month of Ramadan is a dawn-to-dusk time of fasting.

Contracts and Agreements

Cultures vary in their use of contracts and agreements. In the United States a contract is viewed as a final and binding statement of agreements. This tends to be consistent with practices of low-context cultures. But, in high-context cultures the written contract may be viewed as more of a starting point. Once in place it will continue to emerge and be modified as the parties work together over time. McDonald's once found this out when the Chinese government ignored the firm's lease on a restaurant site in downtown Beijing and tore down the building to make room for a development project. In the United States, furthermore, contracts are expected to be in writing. Requesting a written agreement from an Indonesian who has given his "word" may be considered disrespectful.

VALUES AND NATIONAL CULTURES

As companies go global, their managers must become more global in viewpoints, experiences, and cultural appreciation. A German who travels frequently in the United States on business, for example, once told a *Wall*

Street Journal reporter that he was surprised at how few of his American counterparts had traveled abroad and at how generally "nonglobal" they were. But he enjoyed the "friendliness and openness" of his American counterparts, as well as their tendency of "make quick decisions." Similarly, when Bob Hendry was sent to Germany to head General Motors' Opel Division he encountered work-style differences. The American emphasis on short-term monthly and quarterly performance targets, for example, clashed with the German focus on one-year and longer results.[43]

It is helpful to have a framework for understanding how cultural differences can influence management and organizational practices. Geert Hofstede, a Dutch scholar and international management consultant, studied personnel from a U.S.-based MNC operating in 40 countries. First published in his book *Culture's Consequences: International Differences in Work-Related Values*, his research offers preliminary insights for understanding broad differences in national cultures.[44] *Figure 5.4* shows how selected countries rank on the five dimensions Hofstede now uses in his model.

1. *Power distance*—the degree to which a society accepts or rejects the unequal distribution of power among people in organizations and the institutions of society.
2. *Uncertainty avoidance*—the degree to which a society is uncomfortable with risk, change and situational uncertainty, versus having tolerance for them.
3. *Individualism-collectivism*—the degree to which a society emphasizes individual accomplishments and self-interests, versus collective accomplishments and the interests of groups.
4. *Masculinity-femininity*—the degree to which a society values assertiveness and material success, versus feelings and concern for relationships.[45]
5. *Time orientation*—the degree to which a society emphasizes the short-term versus greater concern for the future.[46]

← Hofstede's dimensions of national cultures

Hofstede's framework helps identify managerial implications of these potential cultural differences. For example, workers from high power-

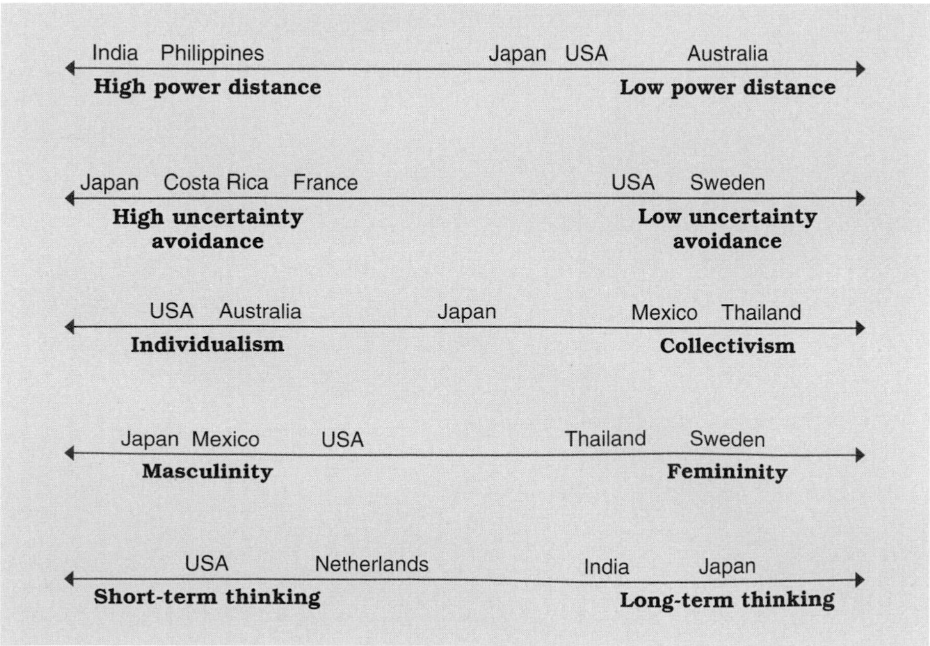

Figure 5.4 How countries compare on Hofstede's dimensions of national culture.

distance cultures such as Singapore can be expected to show great respect to elders and those senior in authority. In the more uncertainty-avoidance cultures like France, employment practices that increase job security are likely to be favored. In highly individualistic societies like the United States, workers may be expected to emphasize self-interests more than group loyalty. Outsiders may also find that the workplace in masculine societies such as Japan displays more rigid gender stereotypes. Also, corporate strategies in more long-term cultures are likely to be just that—more long-term oriented.

UNDERSTANDING CULTURAL DIVERSITY

Consider this scene.[47] Interbrew SA of Belgium purchased 50 percent ownership in Oriental Brewery of South Korea, putting four of its senior managers into the Korean operation. "It was a new experience," said Ms. Park, one of Oriental's local staff. It was also a clash of business cultures. The newcomers wanted locals to express their ideas and work toward clear objectives; the locals were used to following orders and working through relationships. After two years Ms. Park finally agreed that the western and local staff were making progress toward learning how to work together.

Stepping into cross-cultural work and managerial situations of any sort is complicated. It takes all of one's understanding and skills to best deal with the challenges. In addition to the descriptions of popular and national cultures already discussed, the integrative framework of management scholar Fons Trompenaars can be helpful. In research with some 15,000 respondents from 47 countries, he identifies systematic cultural differences in the ways relationships are handled among people, attitudes toward time, and attitudes toward the environment.[48] By better understanding these patterns of difference, he suggests we can improve our effectiveness when working across cultures.

Relationships with People

According to Trompenaars's framework, there are five major cultural differences in how people handle relationships with one another.

Quicksilver Enterprises, Inc., licensed a Brazilian distributor to build and sell its ultra-light airplanes. After six months, royalty payments stopped. The Brazilian company claimed it had changed the design and created a new plane.

How different cultures view relationships

1. *Universalism vs. particularism*—the degree to which a culture emphasizes rules and consistency in relationships, or accepts flexibility and the bending of rules to fit circumstances.
2. *Individualism vs. collectivism*—the degree to which a culture emphasizes individual freedoms and responsibilities in relationships, or focuses more on group interests and consensus.
3. *Neutral vs. affective*—the degree to which a culture emphasizes objectivity and reserved detachment in relationships, or allows more emotionality and expressed feelings.
4. *Specific vs. diffuse*—the degree to which a culture emphasizes focused and in-depth relationships, or broader and more superficial ones.
5. *Achievement vs. prescription*—the degree to which a culture emphasizes an earned or performance-based status in relationships, or awards status based on social standing and nonperformance factors.

Attitudes Toward Time

Attitudes toward time in the Trompenaars framework differ in the relative emphasis given to the present versus the past and future. In cultures that take a *sequential view*, time is considered a continuous and passing series of events. This view of time may be represented by a circle and the notion that time is recycling, a moment passed will return again. In cultures that take a *synchronic view*, by contrast, time takes on a greater sense of urgency. It is more linear, with a great interest in moving, from present to future. Pressures to resolve problems quickly so that time won't be "lost" are characteristic of synchronic cultures.

Attitudes Toward the Environment

Trompenaars also recognizes that cultures vary in their approach to the environment. In cultures that are *inner-directed*, people tend to view themselves as quite separate from nature. They are likely to consider the environment as something to be controlled or used for personal advantage. In cultures that are *outer-directed*, people tend to view themselves as part of nature. They are more likely to try to blend with or go along with the environment than to try to control it.

Be sure you can • define the term culture • explain how ethnocentrism can create difficulties for people working across cultures • differentiate between low-context and high-context cultures, and between monochronic and polychronic cultures • define Hofstede's five dimensions of value differences among national cultures • illustrate each dimension by contrasting America culture with those of other countries • identify the major components in Trompenaars's model of cultural differences

Learning check 4

MANAGEMENT ACROSS CULTURES

The management process—planning, organizing, leading, and controlling—is as relevant to international operations as to domestic ones. Yet as the preceding discussion of environment and culture should suggest, these functions must be applied appropriately from one country and culture to the next. **Comparative management** is the study of how management systematically differs among countries and/or cultures. Today we recognize the importance of learning about how management is practiced around the world. Competition and the global economy have given rise to *global managers*, defined earlier as managers comfortable with cultural diversity, quick to find opportunities in unfamiliar settings, and able to marshal economic, social, technological, and other forces for the benefit of the organization.[49] Says Robin Willett, group deputy chairman of Willet Systems, Ltd. of the United Kingdom: "Our aim has always been to be a truly global company, not simply an exporter. We work very hard at developing and maintaining an international mindset that is shared by everyone—from senior management to staff."[50]

○ **Comparative management** studies how management practices differ among countries and cultures.

PLANNING AND CONTROLLING

Planning and controlling are especially challenging in the complex environment of international businesses. Picture a home office somewhere in the United States, say Chicago. Foreign operations are scattered in Asia, Africa, South America, and Europe. Planning must somehow link the home office and foreign affiliates, while taking into account different countries, cultures, and needs. Increasingly, new technology facilitates the

Get ready, your next job may be with a foreign employer

People were skeptical when Honda opened its first U.S. automobile plant in Marysville, Ohio, in 1982. But not only did American consumers embrace the firm's products—local workers did, too. There are over 13,000 people employed by Honda in its multiple U.S. plants. Allen Kinzer, now retired, was the first American manager Honda hired in its Marysville plant. Although people were worried whether or not U.S. workers could adapt to the Japanese firm's production methods, technology, and style, it all worked out. Says Kinzer: "It wasn't easy blending the cultures; anyone who knew anything about the industry at the time would have to say it was a bold move." Bold move indeed! Honda now produces almost 500,000 cars per year in America. It is only one among hundreds of foreign firms offering employment opportunities to U.S. workers.[51]

planning and control of global operations through vastly improved communications systems. Computer-based global networks and secure Web portals allow home and field offices to share databases, electronically transfer documents, hold virtual conferences, and make group decisions without face-to-face meetings.

Firms with investments in foreign countries must also factor into their planning the risks of doing business across political and economic borders. One risk is **currency risk.** Companies like McDonald's, for example, must eventually convert their foreign currency earnings into dollars. But exchange rates vary, and the dollar value of revenues earned and expenses incurred in other currencies changes over time. When the euro strengthened recently, the dollar lost more than 20 percent of its value. This hurt Europeans with dollar-denominated assets, but American companies like McDonalds gained because profits earned by their stores in Europe bought more dollars. American exporters gained also because the stronger euro made their products cheaper in European markets and encouraged more sales.

Another risk of international business is **political risk,** the potential loss of one's investment in or managerial control over a foreign asset because of instability and political changes in the host country. The major threats of political risk today come from terrorism, civil wars, armed conflicts and military disruptions, shifting government systems through elections or forced takeovers, and new laws and economic policies. **Political-risk analysis** is a planning process that forecasts the probability of disruptive events that can threaten the security of a foreign investment. The stakes in political risk analysis are quite high. It is obvious that some foreign investors, particularly French and Russian companies, suffered when the United States and Great Britain went to war with Iraq. It may be less obvious that other companies suffered when anti-American and anti-British sentiments led to boycotts of their products.

○ **Currency risk** is possible loss because of fluctuating exchange rates.

○ **Political risk** is the possible loss of investment in or control over a foreign asset because of instability and political changes in the host country.

○ **Political-risk analysis** forecasts how political events may impact foreign investments.

ORGANIZING AND LEADING

The same factors that challenge planning and controlling in the international arena also affect managerial efforts to organize and lead. The forces of globalization are complex indeed. For Caltex, it has meant closing a corporate headquarters in Dallas, Texas, and moving to Singapore. It has meant setting up a website development division in South Africa and an accounting division in the Philippines. Now part of Chevron-Texaco, the firm's goal is to leverage advancing technology and communications to build centers of excellence around the world.[52]

A common organizing approach for organizations just getting started in international business is to appoint a vice president or other senior manager to oversee all foreign operations. This may be fine for limited international activity, but as global involvement expands, it usually requires a more complex arrangement. The *global area structure* shown in *Figure 5.5* arranges production and sales functions into separate geographical units. This allows activities in major areas of the world to be given special executive attention. Another organizing option is the *global product structure,* also shown in the figure. It gives worldwide responsibilities to product group managers, who are assisted by area specialists on the corporate staff. These specialists provide expert guidance on the unique needs of various countries or regions. When Carly Fiorina became CEO of Hewlett-Packard, for example, she found the firm losing touch with its international customers. Wanting to make it easier for them to buy HP products from anywhere in the world, she reorganized the firm into global sales and marketing groups to better match global services with local needs.[53]

A rule of thumb for staffing international operations can be stated this way: "Hire competent locals, use competent locals, and listen to competent locals." But in addition, global success also frequently depends on the work of **expatriates**—employees who live and work in foreign countries on short-term or long-term assignments. For progressive firms, assigning home office personnel to foreign operations is increasingly viewed as a strategic opportunity.[54] Not only does this offer the individuals challenging work experiences, it also helps bring into the executive suite culturally aware managers with truly global horizons and interpersonal networks of global contacts. Of course, not everyone performs well in an overseas assignment. Among the foundations for success are such personal attributes as a high degree of self-awareness and cultural sensitivity, a real desire to live and work abroad, family flexibility and support, as well as technical competence in one's job.

○ An **expatriate** lives and works in a foreign country.

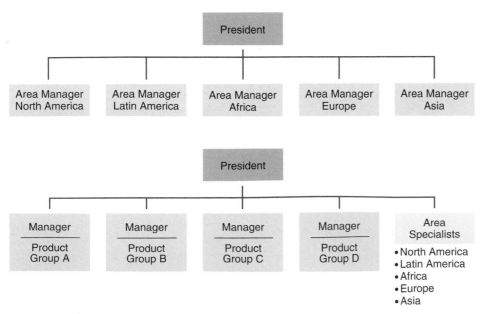

Figure 5.5 Alternative multinational structures for global operations.

ARE MANAGEMENT THEORIES UNIVERSAL?

Management practices in North America and Western Europe frequently have been used as models around the world. Increasingly, however, a significant question is asked: "Are management theories universal?" Geert Hofstede, whose framework for understanding national cultures was introduced earlier, believes the answer is "No."[55] He worries that many theories are ethnocentric and fail to take into account cultural differences. For example, he argues that the American emphasis on participation in leadership reflects the culture's moderate stance on power distance. National cultures with lower scores, such as Sweden and Israel, are characterized by even more "democratic" leadership initiatives. By contrast, the cultures of France and some Asian countries with higher power-distance scores are comfortable with hierarchy and less concerned with participative leadership.

Hofstede also points out that the motivation theories of American scholars tend to value individual performance. This is consistent with the high individualism found in Anglo-American countries such as the United States, Canada, and the United Kingdom. Elsewhere, where values are more collectivist, the theories may be less applicable. Even a common value, such as the desire for increased humanization of work, may lead in different management directions. Until recently, practices in the United States largely emphasized redesigning jobs for individuals. Elsewhere in the world, such as in Sweden, the emphasis has been on redesigning jobs for groups of workers.

Consider as well the implications of transferring to the United States and other Western countries some of the Japanese management practices that have attracted great interest over the years.[56] Lifetime employment, gradual career advancement, and collective decision making have all been associated in one way or another with past successes in Japanese industry.[57] But as interesting as the practices may be, attempts to transfer them elsewhere must take into account the distinctive Japanese cultural traditions in which they emerged—such as long-term orientation, collectivism, and high power distance.[58]

GLOBAL ORGANIZATIONAL LEARNING

In the dynamic and ever-expanding global economy, cultural awareness is helping to facilitate more informed transfers of management and organizational practices. We live at a fortunate time when managers around the world are realizing they have much to share with and learn from one another. Global organizational learning is a timely and relevant theme. This point is evident in the following words of Kenichi Ohmae, noted Japanese management consultant and author of *The Borderless World*:

> Companies can learn from one another, particularly from other excellent companies, both at home and abroad. The industrialized world is becoming increasingly homogeneous in terms of customer needs and social infrastructure, and only truly excellent companies can compete effectively in the global marketplace.[61]

Yes, we do have a lot to learn from one another.[62] Yet it must be learned with full appreciation of the constraints and opportunities of different cultures and country environments. Like the American management practices

---

REALITY CHECK 5.2

What happens when the expatriate comes home?
International experience is supposed to be a big plus in today's corporations. But in research by the Center for Global Assignments, 60 percent of returning American expatriates reported that the adjustment to coming home was harder than going overseas. Take the online "Reality Check" to learn more about executive experiences with international assignments.

○ **Ethnocentric attitudes** consider practices of the home country the best.

before them, Japanese approaches and those from other cultures must be studied and adapted for local use very carefully. This applies to the way management is practiced in Mexico, South Africa, Indonesia, Hungary, or any other part of the world. As Hofstede states: "Disregard of other cultures is a luxury only the strong can afford. . . . increase in cultural awareness represents an intellectual and spiritual gain.[63]

○ **Polycentric attitudes** assume locals know best ways to manage in their countries.

When it comes to global organizational learning, however, not everyone and not every organization is ready. In some international businesses **ethnocentric attitudes** still predominate.[64] Managers tend to view things from the perspective that the best approaches are always found at home. They fail to respect other practices and people, they tend to keep control of foreign operations at home, and they find little to learn from their international experiences. In other businesses, **polycentric attitudes** predominate. In these settings, managers respect the knowledge and practices of locals and allow them to largely run the operation in their countries. Learning, however, is still limited in that there is little transfer of experience from one location to the next. In the truly global business, **geocentric attitudes** create a rich global learning environment. Managers show a collaborative approach that links all international operations into a vast learning network, rich in information sharing. The emphasis is on deriving maximum advantage from best practices and the best people, wherever in the world they may be located.

Geocentric attitudes, displayed by managers and instilled in the corporate culture, offer the most opportunities for truly global organizational learning. Always, however, the approach to learning should be an alert, open, inquiring, and cautious one. It is important to both identify the potential merits of management practices found in other countries and understand how cultural differences may affect their success or failure when applied elsewhere. We should always be looking everywhere for new ideas. But we should hesitate to accept any practice, no matter how well it appears to work somewhere else, as a universal prescription to action. Indeed, the goal of comparative management studies is not to find universal principles. It is to help develop creative and critical thinking about the way managers around the world do things and about whether they can and should be doing them better.

○ **Geocentric attitudes** value talent and best practices from all over the world.

PERSONAL MANAGEMENT

The complications of world events are ever-present reminders that **CULTURAL AWARENESS** is one of the great challenges of the 21st century. Consultant Richard Lewis warns of "cultural spectacles" that limit our vision, causing us to see and interpret things with the biases of our own culture.[59] You must learn to take off the spectacles and broaden your cultural horizons. The college campus is a great place to start. Its rich community of international students can take you around the world every day. Do you know for example that in Asian cultures Confucian values like the following are very influential?[60]

- *Harmony*—works well in a group, doesn't disrupt group order, puts group before self-interests.
- *Hierarchy*—accepts authority and hierarchical nature of society, doesn't challenge superiors.
- *Benevolence*—acts kind and understanding toward others, paternalistic, willing to teach and help subordinates.
- *Loyalty*—loyal to organization and supervisor, dedicated to job, grateful for job and support of superior.
- *Learning*—eager for new knowledge, works hard to learn new job skills, strives for high performance.

Get to know yourself better ▶
Complete Self-Assessments #8—**Global Time Orientation Readiness Index**, and #9—from the Management Learning Workbook.

Learning check 5

Be sure you can • discuss the international management implications of political risk • discuss the challenges of expatriate work • describe the differences between a global area structure and global product structure as ways of organizing for international operations • defend an answer to the question: "Do American management theories apply universally around the world?"

CHAPTER 5 STUDY GUIDE

Where We've Been

BACK TO LIMITED BRANDS

The opening example of Limited Brands described the growth of a hallmark firm in the fashion industry. It also shows that The Limited embraces the opportunities of a global economy, being a leader in deriving competitive advantage from global sourcing and other forms of international business. In Chapter 5 you learned about regional economic alliances and the complexities of international business, including the ethical issues faced by MNCs. You also learned about culture and how to examine differences among national cultures. Perhaps most importantly, you have been well introduced to a theme that must stay with you throughout your study of management—the importance of cross-cultural understanding and sensitivity.

THE NEXT STEP
INTEGRATED LEARNING ACTIVITIES

Cases/Projects

- Harley Davidson Case
- Project 3—Globalization
- Project 9—Management in Popular Culture

Self-Assessments

- Global Readiness Index (#8)
- Time Orientation (#9)
- Organizational Design Preference (#17)

Exercises in Teamwork

- What Do You Value in Work? (#7)
- Which Organization Culture Fits you? (#8)
- The "Best" Job Design (#23)

STUDY QUESTIONS SUMMARY

1. What are the international management challenges of globalization?

- International management is practiced in organizations that conduct business in more than one country.
- Global managers are informed about international developments, transnational in outlook, competent in working with people from different cultures, and always aware of regional developments in a changing world.
- The global economy is making the diverse countries of the world increasingly interdependent regarding resource supplies, product markets, and business competition.
- The global economy is now strongly influenced by regional developments that involve growing economic integration in Europe, the Americas, and Asia, and the economic emergence of Africa.

2. What are the forms and opportunities of international business?

- Five forms of international business are global sourcing, exporting and importing, licensing and franchising, joint ventures, and wholly owned subsidiaries.
- The market entry strategies of global sourcing, exporting/importing, and licensing are common for firms wanting to get started internationally.
- Direct investment strategies to establish joint ventures or wholly owned subsidiaries in foreign countries represent substantial commitments to international operations.
- Global operations are influenced by important environmental differences among the economic, legal-political, and educational systems of countries.

3. What are multinational corporations and what do they do?

- A multinational corporation (MNC) is a business with extensive operations in more than one foreign country.
- True MNCs are global firms with worldwide missions and strategies that earn a substantial part of their revenues abroad.
- MNCs offer potential benefits to host countries in broader tax bases, new technologies, employment opportunities; MNCs can also disadvantage host countries if they interfere in local government, extract excessive profits, and dominate the local economy.
- The Foreign Corrupt Practices Act prohibits American MNCs from engaging in corrupt practices abroad.

4. What is culture and how does it relate to global diversity?

- The dimensions of popular culture include language, use of space, time orientation, religion, and the nature of contracts.
- Hofstede's dimensions of value differences in national cultures include power distance, uncertainty avoidance, individualism-collectivism, masculinity-femininity, and time orientation.
- Trompenaars' framework of cultural differences focuses on how people handle relationships with one another, their attitudes toward time, and their attitudes toward the environment.

5. How do management practices and learning transfer across cultures?

- The management process must be used appropriately and applied with sensitivity to local cultures and situations.
- The field of comparative management studies how management is practiced around the world and how management ideas are transferred from one country or culture to the next.
- Management practices are influenced by cultural values; practices that are successful in one culture may work less well in others.
- The concept of global management learning has much to offer as the "borderless" world begins to emerge and as the management practices of diverse countries and cultures become more visible.

KEY TERMS REVIEW

Child labor (p. 123)
Comparative management (p. 129)
Corruption (p. 123)
Culture (p. 124)
Culture shock (p. 124)
Currency risk (p. 130)
Ethnocentric attitudes (p. 132)
Ethnocentrism (p. 124)
Euro (p. 114)
European Union (p. 114)
Expatriates (p. 131)
Exporting (p. 118)

Foreign subsidiary (p. 119)
Franchising (p. 119)
Geocentric attitudes (p. 133)
Global economy (p. 113)
Global manager (p. 113)
Global sourcing (p. 118)
Globalization (p. 113)
High-context culture (p. 125)
Importing (p. 118)
International business (p. 117)

International management (p. 113)
ISO 14000 (p. 126)
Joint ventures (p. 119)
Licensing agreement (p. 119)
Low-context culture (p. 125)
Maquiladora (p. 115)
Monochronic cultures (p. 126)
Most favored nation status (p. 120)

SELF-TEST 5

MULTIPLE-CHOICE QUESTIONS:

1. In addition to gaining new markets, the reasons why businesses go international include the search for _____.
   (a) political risk (b) protectionism (c) lower labor costs (d) most favored nation status

2. A _____ is a foreign firm that operates with special privileges in Mexico in return for agreeing to employ Mexican labor.
   (a) *keiretsu* (b) *maquiladora* (c) *jacaranda* (d) *zapatista*

3. A common form of international business that falls into the category of a direct investment strategy is _____.
   (a) exporting (b) joint venturing (c) licensing (d) global sourcing

4. The World Trade Organization, or WTO, would most likely become involved in disputes between countries over _____.
   (a) exchange rates (b) Lethnocentrism (c) nationalization (d) tariffs and protectionism

5. If a new government seizes all foreign assets in the country and nationalizes them, the loss to foreign firms is a _____ risk of international business.
   (a) multinational (b) political (c) currency (d) social

6. In _____ cultures, members tend to do one thing at a time; in _____ cultures, members tend to do many things at once.
   (a) monochronic, polychronic (b) polycentric, geocentric (c) collectivist, individualist (d) neutral, affective

7. Business complaints about copyright protection and intellectual property rights in some countries illustrate how differences in _____ can impact international operations.
   (a) legal environments (b) political stability (c) sustainable development (d) economic systems

8. A firm operating with separate vice presidents for Asian, African, and European divisions is using a global _____ structure.
   (a) product (b) functional (c) area (d) matrix

9. In Hofstede's study of national cultures, America was found to be highly _____ compared with other countries in his sample.
   (a) individualistic (b) collectivist (c) feminine (d) long-term oriented

10. It is considered _____ when a foreign visitor takes offense at a local custom such as dining with one's fingers, considering it inferior to practices of his or her own culture.
(a) universalist (b) prescriptive (c) monochronic (d) enthnocentric

11. When Limited Brands buys cotton in Egypt and has pants sewn from it in Sri Lanka according to designs made in Italy for sale in the United State by catalog orders, this form of international business is known as _____.
(a) licensing (b) importing (c) joint venturing (d) global sourcing

12. The difference between an international business and a transnational corporation is that the transnational _____.
(a) operates without a strong national identity (b) does business in only one or two foreign countries (c) is led by managers with ethnocentric attitudes (d) is ISO 14000 certified

13. The Foreign Corrupt Practices Act makes it illegal for _____.
(a) Americans to contract with sweatshop operations abroad (b) foreign businesses to pay bribes to U.S. government officials (c) U.S. businesses to make "payoffs" abroad to gain international business contracts (d) foreign businesses to steal intellectual property from U.S. firms operating in their countries

14. In a high-context culture one would expect to find _____.
(a) low uncertainty avoidance (b) belief in achievement (c) an inner-directed orientation toward nature (d) emphasis on nonverbal as well as verbal communication

15. Hofstede would describe a culture in which members respect age and authority and in which workers defer to the preferences of their supervisors or team leaders as _____.
(a) low masculinity (b) high particularism (c) high power distance (d) monochronic

SHORT-RESPONSE QUESTIONS:

16. Why is NAFTA important for American businesses?

17. Why do host countries sometimes complain about the operations of MNCs within their borders?

18. In what ways is the "power-distance" dimension of national culture important in management?

19. Choose a region of the world (Europe, the Americas, Africa, Asia) and describe its significance in the global economy.

APPLICATION QUESTION:

20. Kim has just returned from her first business trip to Japan. While there, she was impressed with the use of quality circles and work teams. Now back in Iowa, she would like to start the same practices in her canoe-manufacturing company of 75 employees. Based on the discussion of culture and management in this chapter, what advice would you offer Kim?

6

Entrepreneurship and small business

Planning Ahead →

After reading Chapter 6,
you should be able to
answer these questions
in your own words.

CHAPTER 6 study questions

1. What is entrepreneurship?

2. What is special about small businesses?

3. How does one start a new venture?

4. What resources support entrepreneurship and business development?

COUNT-ME-IN FOR WOMEN'S ECONOMIC INDEPENDENCE—INVEST IN PEOPLE AND IDEAS

Each year people with good ideas don't get the chance to turn them into reality. A good percentage of them are women.

Count-Me-In for Women's Economic Independence is out to turn the tables and give female entrepreneurs a chance to get started. Co-founded by Nell Merlino, also creator of Take Our Daughters to Work Day, and Iris Burnett, Count-Me-In uses the Internet to raise money for loans to female entrepreneurs.

The firm operates a website that solicits contributions as small as $5 that are put into a revolving loan fund. The fund is then tapped to provide "microcredit" loans in amounts from $500 to $10,000 to help women start and expand small businesses. Women qualify for the loans by a unique credit scoring system that doesn't hold against them things like a divorce, time off to raise a family, or age that might discourage conventional lenders.

Geneva Francais got a $1,500 loan to build storage shelves for her special cooking sauce "Geneva's Splash," brewed and bottled in her kitchen. Francais is a 65-year-old widow. She says: "A bank would not loan a woman money when she is 65 years old. It's as simple as that." With her loan, she hopes to double the $400 per month Social Security income that she presently lives on. Heather McCartney is married to a high school principal in New York. She received a $5,000 loan to expand "Ethnic Edibles," her line of cookies and cookie cutters designed along traditional African motifs. The money will be used for packaging and marketing.

Merlino says: "Women own 38 percent of all businesses in this country, but still have far less access to capital than men because of today's process." Count-Me-In is out to change all that.[1]

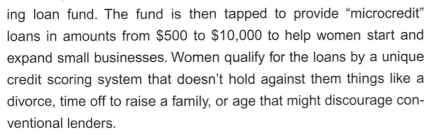

Get Connected!

Imagine what people can do just given the chance. Check out the resources for entrepreneurship online and in your community.

Chapter 6 Learning Preview

When Nell Merino and Iris Burnett got together to create Count-Me-In, they took a risk—in fact, they took more than one. They risked their own time and resources to start the firm; they risked the firm's capital on the women they helped to start new businesses. In Chapter 6 you will learn about entrepreneurship and the taking of business risks to pursue one's dreams. The chapter gives special attention to the small business context and the many opportunities it offers for people, including you, to one day start and own their own businesses.

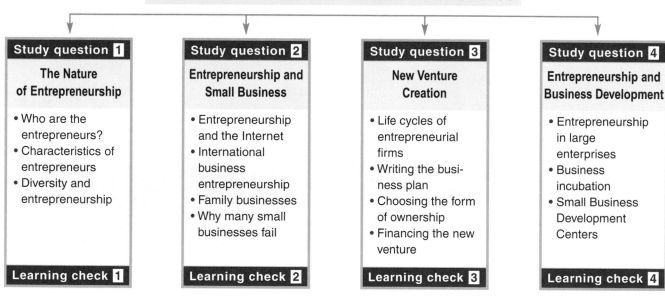

ENTREPRENEURSHIP AND SMALL BUSINESS

Study question 1

The Nature of Entrepreneurship

- Who are the entrepreneurs?
- Characteristics of entrepreneurs
- Diversity and entrepreneurship

Learning check 1

Study question 2

Entrepreneurship and Small Business

- Entrepreneurship and the Internet
- International business entrepreneurship
- Family businesses
- Why many small businesses fail

Learning check 2

Study question 3

New Venture Creation

- Life cycles of entrepreneurial firms
- Writing the business plan
- Choosing the form of ownership
- Financing the new venture

Learning check 3

Study question 4

Entrepreneurship and Business Development

- Entrepreneurship in large enterprises
- Business incubation
- Small Business Development Centers

Learning check 4

Count-Me-In is an innovative organization. Its founders have done their homework. They've spotted a market niche missed or ignored by conventional lenders—small credit requests by women wanting to start or expand a small business. They've designed an Internet-driven way to address this niche and play an important social role. In short, they're in the business of doing good. Count-Me-In has the strategic focus, organization, and leadership that appear capable of bringing it long-term success. It is an interesting example of what one can do with creativity and initiative in the world of work today. In fact, this is a chapter of examples. The goal is not only to inform, to better familiarize you with the nature of entrepreneurship, small business, and new venture creation. It's also to enthuse, to stimulate you to consider starting your own business, being your own boss, and making your own special contribution to society.

Consider Count-Me-In again. Not only is it an interesting enterprise, the name itself is enlightening. It suggests both hope and inclusion, the desire to bring everyone and anyone to the point of benefitting from the pursuit of their business ideas. This should be motivating to you, suggesting that there are no excuses for not trying . . . for not giving your ideas a chance. What about it? Can we count you into the world of entrepreneurship and small business?

THE NATURE OF ENTREPRENEURSHIP

Today's dynamic environment demands that organizations and their managers adapt and renew themselves continually to succeed over time. People and organizations must change frequently and at a rapidly accelerating pace. Success in a highly competitive business environment, in particular, depends on **entrepreneurship.** This term is used to describe strategic thinking and risk-taking behavior that result in the creation of new opportunities for individuals and/or organizations. H. Wayne Huizenga, featured below, and a member of the Entrepreneurs' Hall of Fame, describes it this way: "An important part of being an entrepreneur is a gut instinct that allows you to believe in your heart that something will work even though everyone else says it will not." You say, "I am going to make sure it works. I am going to go out there and make it happen."[2] These opportunities are illustrated in the success stories of business ventures that grew into large companies, such as the now-familiar Domino's Pizza and Federal Express, or of great new products like 3M's the popular Post-it® notes.

O **Entrepreneurship** is dynamic, risk-taking, creative, growth-oriented behavior.

WHO ARE THE ENTREPRENEURS?

An **entrepreneur** is a risk-taking individual who takes action to pursue opportunities others fail to recognize, or even view as problems or threats. In the business context, an entrepreneur starts new ventures that bring to life new product or service ideas. Researchers are interested in the characteristics of entrepreneurs. They want to know what it takes to achieve entrepreneurial success.

O An **entrepreneur** is willing to pursue opportunities in situations others view as problems or threats.

Before examining the findings, though, let's meet some real, high-profile entrepreneurs. Their stories are rich with ideas for all of us to consider. Although the people and accomplishments are different, they share something in common. These entrepreneurs each built successful long-term businesses from good ideas and hard work.[3]

After a career in sales, Mary Kay "retired" for a month. The year was 1963. When starting to write a book to help women compete in the male-dominated business world she realized she was writing a business plan. From that plan arose Mary Kay Cosmetics. Launched on $5,000, the company now operates worldwide and has been named one of the best companies to work for in America. Mary Kay's goal beginning has always been "to help women everywhere reach their full potential."

Mary Kay Ash

Richard Branson

Want to start an airline? Richard Branson did, calling it Virgin Atlantic. But he started first in his native England with a student literary magazine and small mail-order record business. Since, he's built "Virgin" into one of the world's most recognized brand names. Today, the Virgin Group is a business conglomerate employing some 25,000 people around the globe. It holds over 200 companies, including Virgin Mobile, Virgin Records, and even Virgin Cola. It's all very creative and ambitious. But that's Branson. "I love to learn things I know little about," he says.

Earl Graves

With a vision and a $175,000 loan, Earl Graves started *Black Enterprise* magazine in 1970. That success grew into the diversified business information company Earl G Graves, Ltd., including BlackEnterprise.com. Growing up in Brooklyn, New York, at the age of 6 he was selling Christmas cards to neighbors. Today the business school at his college alma mater, Baltimore's Morgan State University, is named after him. Graves says: "I feel that a large part of my role as publisher of *Black Enterprise* is to be a catalyst for black economic development in this country."

H. Wayne Huizenga

What do Waste Management, Inc., the Miami Dolphins football team, AutoNation, Inc., and Blockbuster Video have in common? They have all at one time been owned by entrepreneur Wayne Huizenga. How did it all start? In 1962, aged 25, he borrowed $5,000 from his father-in-law, got a used truck, and acquired a few trash-hauling accounts. He then built the world's largest waste disposal company, Waste Management. He's been buying, building, and selling businesses ever since . . . and reaping the benefits. Huizenga says: "Success depends on seizing the moment and sometimes creating your own opportunity."

Anita Roddick

In 1973 Anita Roddick was a 33-year-old housewife looking for a way to support herself and her two children. She spotted a niche for natural-based skin and health care products, and started mixing and selling her own from a small shop in Brighton, England. The Body Shop PLC has grown to some 1500 outlets in 47 countries with 24 languages, selling a product every half-second to one of its 86+ million customers. Known for her commitment to human rights, the environment, and economic development, Roddick believes in business social responsibility. She says: "If you think you're too small to have an impact, try going to bed with a mosquito."

Have you had your Wendy's today? A lot of people have, and there's quite a story behind it. The first Wendy's restaurant opened in Columbus, Ohio, in November 1969. It's still there; there are also about 5000 others now operating around the world. What began as founder David Thomas's dream to own one restaurant grew into a global enterprise. He went on to become one of the world's best-known entrepreneurs: "the world's most famous hamburger cook." But there's more to Wendy's than profits and business performance alone; social responsibility counts, too. Wendy's strives to be in touch with its communities, with a special focus on helping schools and schoolchildren. In 1992 Dave founded the Dave Thomas Foundation for Adoption.

David Thomas

CHARACTERISTICS OF ENTREPRENEURS

Do you find any common patterns in the prior examples? A common image of an entrepreneur is as the founder of a new business enterprise that achieves large-scale success, like the ones just mentioned. But, entrepreneurs also operate on a smaller and less public scale. Those who take the risk of buying a local McDonald's or Subway Sandwich franchise, opening a small retail shop, or going into a self-employed service business are also entrepreneurs. Similarly, anyone who assumes responsibility for introducing a new product or change in operations within an organization is also demonstrating the qualities of entrepreneurship.

Obviously there's a lot to learn about entrepreneurs and entrepreneurship. Starting with the individual, however, indications are that entrepreneurs tend to share certain attitudes and personal characteristics. The general profile is of an individual that is very self-confident, determined, resilient, adaptable, and driven by excellence.[4] You should be able to identify these attributes in the prior examples. As shown in *Figure 6.1,* the typ-

Figure 6.1 Personal traits and characteristics of entrepreneurs.

ical personality traits and characteristics of entrepreneurs include the following:[5]

Characteristics of entrepreneurs →

- *Internal locus of control:* Entrepreneurs believe that they are in control of their own destiny; they are self-directing and like autonomy.

- *High energy level:* Entrepreneurs are persistent, hard working, and willing to exert extraordinary efforts to succeed.

- *High need for achievement:* Entrepreneurs are motivated to accomplish challenging goals; they thrive on performance feedback.

- *Tolerance for ambiguity:* Entrepreneurs are risk takers; they tolerate situations with high degrees of uncertainty.

- *Self-confidence:* Entrepreneurs feel competent, believe in themselves, and are willing to make decisions.

- *Passion and action orientation:* Entrepreneurs try to act ahead of problems; they want to get things done and not waste valuable time.

- *Self-reliance and desire for independence:* Entrepreneurs want independence; they are self-reliant; they want to be their own boss, not work for others.

- *Flexibility:* Entrepreneurs are willing to admit problems and errors, and to change a course of action when plans aren't working.

In addition, research also suggests that entrepreneurs have unique backgrounds and personal experiences.[6] *Childhood experiences and family environment* seem to make a difference. Evidence links entrepreneurs with parents who were entrepreneurial and self-employed. Similarly, entrepreneurs are often raised in families that encourage responsibility, initiative, and independence. Another issue is *career or work history.* Entrepreneurs who try one venture often go on to others. Prior work experience in the business area or industry is helpful. Entrepreneurs also tend to emerge during certain *windows of career opportunity.* Most start their businesses between the ages of 22 and 45, an age spread that seems to allow for risk taking. However, age is no barrier. When Tony DeSio was 50 he founded the Mail Boxes Etc. chain. He sold it for $300 million when he was 67 and suffering heart problems. Within a year he launched PixArts, another franchise chain based on photography and art.[7]

Finally, a report in the *Harvard Business Review* suggests that entrepreneurs may have unique and *deeply embedded life interests.* The article describes entrepreneurs as having strong interests in creative production—enjoying project initiation, working with

PERSONAL MANAGEMENT

Not everyone is comfortable with **RISK TAKING**. The uncertainty of risky situations is unsettling, and the anxieties are threatening for some of us. But risks, small and large, are a part of everyday living. In school and around campus there are many opportunities to explore your openness to risk and entrepreneurial tendencies. What will it take for you to start your own business or propose a new venture to your employer? Two former managers of Footlocker stores took the risk, and it paid off handsomely.[10] After noticing that customers kept asking for sports caps unavailable in stores, Glenn Campbell and Scott Molander decided to start a store of their own—Hat World. "People thought we were crazy," Campbell says. But Hat World took off, selling over 6000 caps in two months. The entrepreneurs opened four more stores within a year. At last check, Campbell and Molander's risk turned into a firm with annual sales of $150+ million. Could this story be yours someday?

Entrepreneur's Hall of Fame

Get to know yourself better ►
Complete Self-Assessment #10—**Entrepreneurship Orientation,** and Exercise #8—**Which Orgnization Culture Fits You?,** from the Management Learning Workbook.

Challenging the myths about entrepreneurs

MANAGER'S NOTEPAD 6.1

- *Entrepreneurs are born, not made.* Not true! Talent gained and enhanced by experience is a foundation for entrepreneurial success.

- *Entrepreneurs are gamblers.* Not true! Entrepreneurs are risk takers, but the risks are informed and calculated.

- *Money is the key to entrepreneurial success.* Not true! Money is no guarantee of success: There's a lot more to it than that; many entrepreneurs start with very little.

- *You have to be young to be an entrepreneur.* Not true! Age is no barrier to entrepreneurship; with age often comes experience, contacts, and other useful resources.

- *You have to have a degree in business to be an entrepreneur.* Not true! You may not need a degree at all; although a business degree is not necessary, it helps to study and understand business fundamentals.

---

the unknown, and finding unconventional solutions. They also have strong interests in enterprise control—finding enjoyment from running things. The combination of creative production and enterprise control is characteristic of people who want to start things and move things toward a goal.[8]

Undoubtedly, entrepreneurs seek independence and the sense of mastery that comes with success. That seems to keep driving Tony DeSio in the example above. When asked by a reporter what he liked most about entrepreneurship, he replied: "Being able to make decisions without having to go through layers of corporate hierarchy—just being a master of your own destiny."[9]

DIVERSITY AND ENTREPRENEURSHIP

Entrepreneurship is rich with diversity, and it grows richer by the day with the efforts of Count-Me-In and other organizations like it. The National Foundation for Women Business Owners (NFWBO) reports there are over 9 million businesses in the United States that are owned by women, creating jobs for 27.5 million people. This represents about 38 percent of all U.S. businesses. Its website offers substantial Web-based support for and facts about female entrepreneurs.[11] The NFWBO also reports that women are starting new businesses at twice the rate of the national average. Most indicate being motivated by a new idea or by realizing that they could do for themselves what they were already doing for other employers.

Clearly, entrepreneurship offers women opportunities of striking out on their own; it is also a pathway to opportunity that may be blocked otherwise. Among women leaving private-sector employment to strike out on their own, 33 percent said they were not being taken seriously by their prior employer; 29 percent said they had experienced "glass ceiling" issues.[12] In *Women Business Owners of Color: Challenges and Accomplishments,* the NFWBO discusses the motivations of women of color to pursue entrepreneurship because of glass ceiling problems. These include not being recognized or valued by their prior employers, not being taken seriously, and seeing others promoted ahead of them.[13]

Data reported by the Small Business Administration show that entrepreneurship is opening business doors for minorities. Minority-owned businesses are one of the fastest-growing sectors of the economy. Businesses created by minority entrepreneurs employ over 4 million American workers and generate over $500 billion in annual revenues. And the numbers are growing daily. SBA data on businesses' growth rates for 1987–1997 show that the number of African-American-owned businesses grew by 103 percent. Asian and other minority-owned firms grew 180 percent; Hispanic-owned firms grew 232 percent.[14] See *Manager's Notepad 6.1* for some challenges to common myths about entrepreneurship.[15]

Learning check 1

Be sure you can • define the term *entrepreneurship* • list key personal characteristics of entrepreneurs • explain the influence of background and experience on entrepreneurs • discuss opportunities for entrepreneurship by women and minorities

---

ENTREPRENEURSHIP AND SMALL BUSINESS

O A **small business** has fewer than 500 employees, is independently owned and operated, and does not dominate its industry.

The U.S. Small Business Administration defines a **small business** as one with 500 or fewer employees, with the definition varying a bit by industry. The SBA also states that a small business is one that is independently owned and operated and that does not dominate its industry.[16] Almost 99 percent of American businesses meet this definition, and some 87 percent employ fewer than 20 persons.

The small business sector is very important in most nations of the world. Among other things, small businesses offer major economic advantages. In the United States, for example, they employ some 52 percent of private workers, provide 51 percent of private-sector output, receive 35 percent of federal government contract dollars, and provide as many as 7 out of every 10 new jobs in the economy.[17] Smaller businesses are especially prevalent in the service and retailing sectors of the economy. Higher costs of entry make them less common in other industries such as manufacturing and transportation.

There are many reasons why people pursue entrepreneurship and launch their own businesses. One study reports the following motivations: #1—wanting to be your own boss and control your future; #2—going to work for a family-owned business; and #3—seeking to fulfill a dream.[18] Only a very small percentage of respondents indicated that they had no other choice, such as having been laid off when their employer downsized.

Once a decision is made to go the small business route, the most common ways to get involved are: (1) start one, (2) buy an existing one, or (3) buy and run a **franchise**—where a business owner sells to another the right to operate the same business in another location. A franchise runs under the original owner's business name and guidance. In return, the franchise parent receives a share of income or a flat fee from the franchisee.

○ A **franchise** is when one business owner sells to another the right to operate the same business in another location.

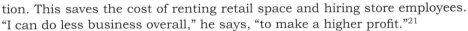

CAREER CONNECTION

Hispanic ad agency helps others bridge the gap

After moving to the United States from Venezuela some 20 years ago, Anita Santiago said: "I'll never be able to land a job." But she did, in the advertising business. Four years later she started Anita Santiago Advertising, Inc. to focus on the Latin community and help communicate her culture to large companies. *Que gran idioma tengo,* reads the front page of her website, quoting Chilean poet Pablo Neruda: "What a great language I have." Says Santiago: "I can see culture from both sides. You can't learn that from a book." Anita's advice to the about-to-be entrepreneur is: "Be the expert—as we are in biculturalism. . . . Be creative." She adds: "Lastly, hire the best people."[19]

ENTREPRENEURSHIP AND THE INTERNET

Have you started a "dot-com" today? The Internet has opened a whole new array of entrepreneurial possibilities. Just take a look at the action on eBay and imagine how many people are now running small trading businesses from their homes. The SBA has predicted that already some 85 percent of small firms are conducting business over the Internet.[20] Many of these firms are existing firms that modified traditional ways to pursue new Internet-driven opportunities. For some of these, the old ways of operating from a bricks-and-mortar retail establishment have given way to entirely online business activities. That's what happened to Rod Spencer and his S&S Sportscards store in Worthington, Ohio. He closed his store not because business was bad, it was really good. But the nature of the business was shifting into cyberspace. When sales over the Internet became much greater than in-store sales, Spencer decided to follow the world of e-commerce. He now works from his own home with a computer and high-speed Internet connection. This saves the cost of renting retail space and hiring store employees. "I can do less business overall," he says, "to make a higher profit."[21]

✓ REALITY CHECK 6.1

How entrepreneurs get started
In a survey of 448 business owners, some 18 percent indicated they began while working for a larger company. How did the rest of the entrepreneurs get started? Take the online "Reality Check" to learn more.

Internet entrepreneurship isn't limited to trading through eBay or trying to create the next Amazon.com. A growing area for Internet entrepreneurship is B2B, specialized business-to-business websites that link buyers and sellers. It used to be that the Fagan Cadillac dealership in Janesville, Wisconsin, would get most of its used cars by sending a buyer to several used car auctions per month. Now, the buyer does most of his work on the Internet, using General Motors' Smart-Auction website to browse an ever-changing selection of cars returned from lease. His activities are part of an online business-to-business industry that now exceeds $480 billion per year. The opportunities for B2B entrepreneurship are many. If interested, you just need to let your creativity go to work.[22]

> Get Connected!
>
> Want to know more about Hispanic businesses? Check out Hispanic Business online.

INTERNATIONAL BUSINESS ENTREPRENEURSHIP

In the last chapter the reasons why businesses go international were discussed. The same global opportunities exist for smaller businesses. They also often find that international business brings opportunities for expanded markets, additional financing, access to quality and possibly lower-cost resources, access to labor and technical expertise, and locations for low-cost manufacturing or outsourcing. The Internet now makes selling abroad relatively easy; today's advanced distribution systems also make product delivery quick and efficient. Additionally, smaller businesses can find alliance opportunities in strategic ventures with foreign partners.

As the economies of the world's countries improve and the overall standards of living rise, consumer demand for goods and services grows as well. Governments, federal and state, encourage small businesses to explore and expand export activities. Like most states, the Ohio state government offers export development assistance to entrepreneurs through its International Trade Division. At the national level, the International Trade Administration of the U.S. Department of Commerce provides similar services. Small Business Administration loan guarantees for small business exporters grew 600 percent over a recent five-year period.[23]

Many smaller companies are seeking diversification opportunities abroad. With diversification comes some insurance against the risk of economic slowdown in any one area. If domestic business declines, the hope is that international business will take up the slack. Of course, it takes investment to move any business, small or large, toward international opportunities. One has to invest in travel, communication, and time to build relationships and gain expertise. But there is considerable support available. Small manufacturers seeking to attract foreign customers may begin, for example, by joining the Thomas Register of American Companies. It provides an Internet search engine for prospective customers to locate American business suppliers. Through its Trade Net Export Advisor service, the SBA also offers potential exporters everything from expert advice on getting started to lists of actual trade leads around the world. Many other resources are available to those trying to get started in international business. You just have to look.

FAMILY BUSINESSES

○ A **family business** is owned and controlled by members of a family.

Family businesses, ones owned and financially controlled by family members, represent the largest percentage of businesses operating worldwide. The Family Firm Institute reports that family businesses account for 78 percent of new jobs created in the United States and provide 60 percent of the nation's employment.[24] Family businesses must solve the same problems of other small or large businesses—meeting the challenges of strategy, competitive advantage, and operational excellence. When everything goes right, the family firm is almost an ideal situation—everyone working together, sharing values and a common goal, and knowing that what they do benefits the family. But it doesn't always work out this way or stay this way as a business changes hands over successive generations. Indeed, family businesses often face quite unique problems.

"Okay, Dad, so he's your brother. But does that mean we have to put up with inferior work and an erratic schedule that we would never tolerate from anyone else in the business?"[25] This conversation introduces a problem that can all too often set the stage for failure in a family business—the *family business feud.* Simply put, members of the controlling family get into disagreements about work responsibilities, business strategy, operating approaches, finances, or other matters. The example is indicative of an intergenerational problem, but the feud can be between spouses, among siblings, between parents and children. It really doesn't matter. Unless disagreements are resolved satisfactorily among family members and to the benefit of the business itself, the firm will have difficulty surviving in a highly competitive environment.

Another significant problem faced by family businesses is the **succession problem**—transferring leadership from one generation to the next. A survey of small and midsized family businesses indicated that 66 percent planned on keeping the business within the family.[26] The management question is: How will the assets be distributed and who will run the business when the current head leaves? Although this problem is not specific to the small firm, it is especially significant in the family business context. The data on succession are eye-opening. About 30 percent of family firms survive to the second generation; only 12 percent survive to the third; only 3 percent are expected to survive beyond that.[27]

A family business that has been in operation for some time is a source of both business momentum and financial wealth. Both must be maintained in the succession process. Business advisors recommend a **succession plan**—a formal statement that describes how the leadership transition and related financial matters will be handled when the time for changeover arrives. *A succession plan should include* at least procedures

> O The **succession problem** is the issue of who will run the business when the current head leaves.

> O A **succession plan** describes how the leadership transition and related financial matters will be handled.

AROUND THE WORLD

Chamber of Commerce connects businesses across borders

Through a special program called "Wiring the Border," the United States–Mexico Chamber of Commerce is helping border companies tap the e-commerce marketplace. The Chamber's president, Albert C. Zapanta, says: "This initiative will help small businesses reach the international marketplace and compete effectively around the world." Major U.S. and Mexican corporations, including IBM and TelMex, are helping to sponsor the program. The partners are contributing Web-enabling components. The member small businesses will be joined in a virtual network that will utilize e-commerce to increase sales, profits, and employment. Zapanta says: "Communities along the border have not shared in the economic growth enjoyed by most Americans the past several years, but they have borne a disproportionate share of the burden." Through "Wiring the Border," the Chamber and its partners hope to bring positive change to both sides of the border.[28]

for choosing or designating the firm's new leadership, legal aspects of any ownership transfer, and any financial and estate plans relating to the transfer. The foundations for effective implementation of a succession plan are set up well ahead of the need to use it. The plan should be shared and understood among all affected by it. The chosen successor should be prepared through experience and training to perform the new role when needed.

WHY MANY SMALL BUSINESSES FAIL

Small businesses have a high failure rate—one high enough to be scary. The SBA reports that as many as 60 to 80 percent of new businesses fail in their first five years of operation.[29] Part of this is a "counting" issue—the government counts as a "failure" any business that closes, whether it is due to the death or retirement of an owner, sale to someone else, or the inability to earn a profit.[30] Nevertheless, the fact remains: A lot of small business startups don't make it. And as shown in *Figure 6.2,* most of the failures are due to bad judgment and management mistakes made by entrepreneurs and owners. The following errors are common causes of small business failures.[31]

Reasons for new business failures

- *Lack of experience*—not having sufficient know-how to run a business in the chosen market or area.
- *Lack of expertise*—not having expertise in the essentials of business operations, including finance, purchasing, selling, and production.
- *Lack of strategy and strategic leadership*—not taking the time to craft a vision and mission, and formulate and properly implement strategy.
- *Poor financial control*—not keeping track of the numbers and failure to control business finances.
- *Growing too fast*—not taking the time to consolidate a position, fine-tune the organization, and systematically meet the challenges of growth.
- *Insufficient commitment*—not devoting enough time to the requirements of running a competitive business.
- *Ethical failure*—falling prey to the temptations of fraud, deception, and embezzlement.

Figure 6.2 Eight reasons why many small businesses fail.

NEW VENTURE CREATION

Now that the reasons for business failure have been described, let's talk about doing it right. Whether your interest is low-tech or high-tech, online or offline, opportunities for new ventures are always there for the true entrepreneur. To pursue entrepreneurship and start a new venture, you need good ideas and the courage to give them a chance. But you must also be prepared to meet and master the test of strategy and competitive advantage. Can you identify a *market niche* that is being missed by other established firms? Can you identify a *new market* that has not yet been discovered by existing firms? Can you generate **first-mover advantage** by exploiting a niche or entering a market before competitors? These are among the questions that entrepreneurs must ask and answer in the process of beginning a new venture. Of course, a focus on the customer is critical, too, as suggested in *Manager's Notepad 6.2.*[32]

○ A **first-mover advantage** comes from being first to exploit a niche or enter a market.

LIFE CYCLES OF ENTREPRENEURIAL FIRMS

Figure 6.3 describes the stages common to the life cycles of entrepreneurial companies. It shows the relatively predictable progression of the small business.[33] The firm begins with the *birth stage*—where the entrepreneur struggles to get the new venture established and survive long enough to test the viability of the underlying business model in the marketplace. The firm then passes into the *breakthough stage*—where the business model begins to work well, growth is experienced, and the complexity of managing the business operation expands significantly. Next comes the *maturity stage*—where the entrepreneur experiences the advantages of market success and financial stability, while also facing continuing management challenges of remaining competitive in a changing environment.

Entrepreneurs often face control and management dilemmas when their firms experience growth, including possible diversification or global

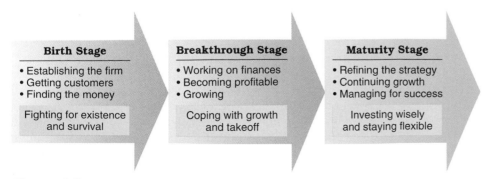

Figure 6.3 Stages in the life cycle of an entrepreneurial firm.

MANAGER'S NOTEPAD 6.2	Questions that keep a new venture focused on its customers

- Who is your customer?
- How will you reach customers in key market segments?
- What determines customer choices to buy your product/service?
- Why is your product/service a compelling choice for the customer?
- How will you price your product/service for the customer?
- How much does it cost to make and deliver your product/service?
- How much does it cost to attract a customer?
- How much does it cost to support and retain a customer?

expansion. They encounter a variation of the succession problem described earlier for family businesses. This time the problem is succession from entrepreneurial leadership to professional strategic leadership. The former brings the venture into being and sees it through the early stages of life; the latter manages and leads the venture into maturity as an ever-evolving and perhaps still-growing corporate enterprise. If the entrepreneur is incapable of meeting or unwilling to meet the firm's leadership needs in later life-cycle stages, continued business survival and success may well depend on the business being sold or management control being passed to professionals.

WRITING THE BUSINESS PLAN

O A **business plan** describes the direction for a new business and the financing needed to operate it.

When people start new businesses, or even start new units within existing ones, they can greatly benefit from a good **business plan.** This is a plan that describes the details needed to obtain startup financing and operate a new business.[34] Banks and other financiers want to see a business plan before they loan money or invest in a new venture; senior managers want to see a business plan before they allocate scarce organizational resources to support a new entrepreneurial project. Importantly, the detailed thinking required to prepare a business plan can contribute to the success of the new initiative. Says Ed Federkeil, who founded a small business called California Custom Sport Trucks: "It gives you direction instead of haphazardly sticking your key in the door every day and saying—'What are we going to do?'"[35]

Although there is no single template for a successful business plan, there is general agreement on the framework presented in *Manager's Notepad 6.3.*[36] Any business plan should have an executive summary, cover certain business fundamentals, be well-organized with headings, be easy to read, and be no more than about 20 pages in length. One of the great advantages of a business plan, of course, is forcing the entrepreneur to think through important issues and challenges before starting out. In addition to advice you find in books and magazines, there are many online resources available to assist in the development of a business plan. Among the alternatives are American Express Small Business Services, Business Town.com, and BizPlanIt.com.

What to include in a business plan

- *Executive summary*—overview of business purpose and highlight of key elements of the plan.
- *Industry analysis*—nature of the industry, including economic trends, important legal or regulatory issues, and potential risks.
- *Company description*—mission, owners, and legal form.
- *Products and services description*—major goods or services, with special focus on uniqueness vis-à-vis competition.
- *Market description*—size of market, competitor strengths and weaknesses, five-year sales goals.
- *Marketing strategy*—product characteristics, distribution, promotion, pricing, and market research.
- *Operations description*—manufacturing or service methods, supplies and suppliers, and control procedures.
- *Staffing description*—management and staffing skills needed and available, compensation, human resource systems.
- *Financial projection*—cash flow projections for one to five years, break-even points, and phased investment capital.
- *Capital needs*—amount of funds needed to run the business, amount available, amount requested from new sources.
- *Milestones*—a time table of dates showing when key stages of new venture will be completed.

www.fambiz.com

Many universities have centers that specialize in family businesses. They offer research results, information, and advice on handling special problems. Fambiz.com is a good source of information on family businesses, as is The Family Firm Institute.

CHOOSING THE FORM OF OWNERSHIP

One of the important planning choices that must be made in starting a new venture is the legal form of ownership. There are a number of alternatives, and the choice among them involves careful consideration of their respective advantages and disadvantages. Briefly, the ownership forms include the following.

A **sole proprietorship** is simply an individual or a married couple pursuing business for a profit. This does not involve incorporation. One does business, for example, under a personal name—such as "Tiana Lopez Designs." A sole proprietorship is simple to start, run, and terminate. However, the business owner is personally liable for business debts and claims. This is the most common form of small business ownership in the United States.

A **partnership** is formed when two or more people agree to contribute resources to start and operate a business together. Most typically it is backed by a legal and written partnership agreement. Business partners agree on the contribution of resources and skills to the new venture and on the sharing of profits and losses. In a *general partnership,* the simplest and most common form, they also share management responsibilities. A *limited partnership* consists of a general partner and one or more "limited" partners who

○ A **sole proprietorship** is an individual pursuing business for a profit.

○ A **partnership** is when two or more people agree to contribute resources to start and operate a business together.

do not participate in day-to-day business management. They share in profits, but their losses are limited to the amount of their investment. *A limited liability partnership,* common among professionals such as accountants and attorneys, limits the liability of one partner for the negligence of another.

○ A **corporation** is a legal entity that exists separately from its owners.

A **corporation,** commonly identified by the "Inc." designation in a name, is a legal entity that is chartered by the state and exists separately from its owners. The corporation can be for-profit, such as Microsoft Inc., or not-for-profit, such as Count-Me-In, Inc. The corporate form offers two major advantages: (1) it grants the organization certain legal rights (e.g., to engage in contracts), and (2) the corporation becomes responsible for its own liabilities. This separates the owners from personal liability and gives the firm a life of its own that can extend beyond that of its owners. The disadvantage of incorporation rests largely with the cost of incorporating and the complexity of the documentation required to operate an incorporated business.

○ A **limited liability corporation (LLC)** is a hybrid business form combining advantages of the sole propietorship, partnership, and corporation.

Recently, the **limited liability corporation (LLC)** has gained popularity. A limited liability corporation combines the advantages of the other forms—sole proprietorship, partnership, and corporation. For liability purposes, it functions like a corporation, protecting the assets of owners against claims made against the company. For tax purposes, it functions as a partnership in the case of multiple owners and as a sole proprietorship in the case of a single owner.

FINANCING THE NEW VENTURE

Starting a new venture takes money, and that money often must be raised. The cost of startup will most likely exceed the amount available from personal sources. There are two major ways the entrepreneur can obtain outside financing for a new venture. **Debt financing** involves going into debt by borrowing money from another person, a bank, or a financial institution. This loan must be paid back over time with interest. A loan also requires collateral that pledges business assets or personal assets, such as a home, to secure the loan in case of default. **Equity financing** involves giving ownership shares in the business to outsiders in return for outside investment monies. This money does not need to be paid back. It is an investment, and the investor assumes the risk for potential gains and losses. In return for taking that risk, the equity investor gains some proportionate ownership control.

○ **Debt financing** involves borrowing money that must be repaid over time with interest.

○ **Equity financing** involves exchanging ownership shares for outside investment monies.

○ **Venture capitalists** make large investments in new ventures in return for an equity stake in the business.

Equity financing is usually obtained from **venture capitalists,** companies that pool capital and make investments in new ventures in return for an equity stake in the business. Typically, venture capitalists finance only a very small proportion of new ventures. They tend to focus on relatively large investments, such as $1 million or more, and they usually take a management role in order to grow the business and add value as soon as possible. Sometimes that value is returned when a fast-growing firm that gains a solid market base and becomes a candidate for an **initial public offering**, or **IPO.** This is when shares of stock in the business are first sold to the public and then begin trading on a major stock exchange. When an IPO is successful and the share prices are bid up by the market, the original investments of the venture capitalist and entrepreneur rise in value. The anticipation of such return on investment is a large part of the venture capitalist's motivation; indeed, it is the nature of the venture capital business.

○ An **initial public offering (IPO)** is an initial selling of shares of stock to the public at large.

Of the many venture capital firms in the United States, very few specifically seek investments in women-owned companies. It's an accepted fact that even though women are starting more new businesses than ever before, they don't get as much of the available venture capital as men. When ven-

TAKE IT TO THE CASE

Domino's Pizza
Customer-driven strategy brings pizzas to your door

"Hello, Domino's Pizza, may I have your telephone number?" So begins a typical conversation when you telephone an order for a home delivery from Domino's Pizza. Within minutes, it seems, the pizza is at your door. Behind this seemingly simple transaction stands a customer-driven strategy and sophisticated use of technology. Domino's franchise stores depend upon quality and timely service from a complex chain of suppliers and distribution points. Over 6600 stores, including those in 64 countries, must be kept in stock with hundreds of products, ranging from food items to pizza boxes to business forms to cleaning supplies. Domino's is committed to customer relationship management and supply chain management to support its franchise stores and better serve customers.[37]

ture capital isn't available to the entrepreneur, male or female, another important financing option is the **angel investor.** This is a wealthy individual who is willing to make an investment in return for equity in a new venture. Angel investors are especially common and helpful in the very early startup stage. Their presence can help raise the confidence and interests of other venture capitalists, and attract additional venture funding that would otherwise not be available. For example, when Liz Cobb wanted to start her sales compensation firm, Incentive Systems, she contacted 15 to 20 venture capital firms. She was interviewed by 10 and turned down by all of them. After she located $250,000 from two angel investors, the venture capital firms got interested again. She was able to obtain her first $2 million in financing and has since built the firm into a 70-plus employee business.[38]

○ An **angel investor** is a wealthy individual willing to invest in return for equity in a new venture.

Be sure you can • explain the concept of first-mover advantage in new venture creation • illustrate new venture life-cycle stages from birth to breakthrough to maturity • identify the major elements in a business plan • differentiate between common forms of small business ownership—sole proprietorship, partnership, and corporation • differentiate between debt financing and equity financing • explain the roles of venture capitalists and angel investors in new venture financing

Learning check 3

ENTREPRENEURSHIP AND BUSINESS DEVELOPMENT

Entrepreneurship is indispensable to a healthy and growing economy, whether one is talking about a local community or an entire nation. It provides the creative spark to launch the small businesses and new ventures that are so important to job creation and economic development. It also provides the engine that drives innovation and business development within large enterprises.

African-American entrepreneurs lead the way

At a small brick church in Montgomery, Alabama, in 1956 Martin Luther King, Jr., told African Americans to "work within the framework of democracy to bring about a better distribution of wealth." King's call is being answered by entrepreneurship within the black community. Among 25- to 35-year-olds starting businesses in America, African Americans lead the way; there are three startups of African-American–owned companies for each headed by someone of another ethnicity. Gwen Day Richardson once viewed politics as the way to make a positive impact. Now she's pursuing the business route, starting cushcity.com, an online bookstore selling African-American merchandise. Fred Terrell started the venture capital fund Provender Capital. He believes that having more African-American–owned venture capital funds makes it easier for black entrepreneurs to get started. John Butler, professor of business at the University of Texas at Austin says: "The history of black Americans has always been self-employment and entrepreneurship."[39]

ENTREPRENEURSHIP IN LARGE ENTERPRISES

Just like their smaller counterparts, large organizations depend on the entrepreneurial spirit to drive innovation for sustained competitive advantage. High performance in dynamic and competitive environments increasingly depends on the creative contributions of workers who are willing to assume risk and take initiative. Yet paradoxically, the natural tendencies of very large and complex systems may be toward stability, rigidity, and avoidance of risk.

> ○ **Intrapreneurship** is entrepreneurial behavior displayed by people or subunits within large organizations.

The concept of **intrapreneurship** describes entrepreneurial behavior by people and subunits operating within large organizations.[40] Through the efforts of *intrapreneurs,* large organizations are able to turn new ideas into profitable new products, services, and business ventures. At Trilogy Software, Inc., in Austin, Texas, for example, talented engineers are hired directly from college. They attend Trilogy University for three months, learning about the company and its mission, executives, and expectations. They are told that they are responsible for creating the company's new revenues. The "university" experience is designed to start the creative process and build networks for entrepreneurship and internal business development. So far Trilogy has created from within itself six successful new ventures.[41]

> ○ **Skunkworks** are teams allowed to work creatively together, free of constraints from the larger organization.

Managers often find that gaining a competitive edge and success through intrapreneurship depends on the ability of large organizations to act like small ones. To do this, they create small subunits, often called **skunkworks**, in which teams are allowed to work together in a unique setting that is highly creative and free of the operating restrictions of the larger parent organization. A classic example occurred at Apple Computer, Inc., where a small group of enthusiastic employees was once sent off to a separate facility in Cupertino, California. Their mandate was straightforward: to create a state-of-the-art, user-friendly personal computer. The group operated free of the firm's normal product development bureaucracy, set its own norms, and worked together without outside interference. The "Jolly Roger" was even raised over their building as a symbol of independence. It worked. This team brought the now-famous Macintosh computer into being.

BUSINESS INCUBATION

One of the advantages of intrapreneurship is that it takes place in a larger organizational environment that can be highly supportive in terms of money and other startup resources. Individual entrepreneurs who must start on their own face quite a different set of challenges. Even though entrepreneurship and new venture creation are creative and exciting prospects, they are also potentially daunting in complexity and required resources.

One way that the motivation toward entrepreneurship can be maintained is through the support of a **business incubator.** This is a special facility that offers space, a variety of shared administrative services, and management advice to help small businesses get started. Some incubators are focused on specific businesses such as technology, manufacturing, or services; some are in more rural areas, others are city based. But regardless of focus and location, incubators share the common goal of helping to build successful new businesses that create jobs and improve economic development. They pursue this goal by nurturing startup businesses in the incubators to help them to grow more quickly and become healthy enough to survive on their own. And, of course, the expected benefits include job and wealth creation in the economies of local communities.

○ **Business incubators** offer space, shared services, and advice to help small businesses get started.

SMALL BUSINESS DEVELOPMENT CENTERS

With small business playing such an important economic role, a variety of resources are available to promote their development. At the level of the federal government, the United States Small Business Administration works with state and local agencies to support a network of over 1000 **Small Business Development Centers** nationwide. These SBDCs offer guidance to entrepreneurs and small business owners—actual and prospective—in how to set up and successfully run a business operation. Often these centers are associated with universities or colleges. They offer opportunities for students to become involved as consultants and learn first-hand the nature of small business and entrepreneurship.

○ **Small Business Development Centers** offer guidance and support to small business owners in how to set up and run a business operation.

This has been a chapter of examples. Other than doing it, the best way to learn about entrepreneurship and venturing is to study and ponder the experiences of others. Here's a final example for you. When they joined the Silicon Valley Small Business Development Center, Jean Jaffess and her partners in Mambo Design & Consulting were able to find assistance in writing a business plan. They were also tutored in understanding financial reports and tax requirements.[42] The SBDC helped Mambo get started in the business of Web design and consulting services. Without its support, Jaffress might never have gotten Mambo up and running. But with it, the risks of entrepreneurship became manageable and she was able to pursue the dream of owning her own business.

Be sure you can • define the term intrapreneurship and differentiate it from entrepreneurship • explain the purpose of business incubators • explain how Small Business Development Centers try to help people start and operate small businesses

Learning check 4

CHAPTER 6 STUDY GUIDE

Where We've Been

BACK TO COUNT-ME-IN

The opening example of Count-Me-In introduced entrepreneurship from the perspective of a firm devoted to serving as a champion for women who want to start their own businesses. In Chapter 6 and through its many examples, you learned about entrepreneurship and the characteristics of entrepreneurs. You learned some of the basic elements of starting a new venture, and you learned about the nature of business ownership. Importantly, throughout the chapter you have been exposed to many issues and examples that introduce the world of career opportunity that exists in entrepreneurship and small business ownership.

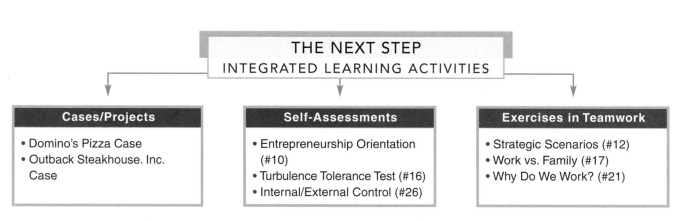

THE NEXT STEP
INTEGRATED LEARNING ACTIVITIES

Cases/Projects	Self-Assessments	Exercises in Teamwork
• Domino's Pizza Case • Outback Steakhouse. Inc. Case	• Entrepreneurship Orientation (#10) • Turbulence Tolerance Test (#16) • Internal/External Control (#26)	• Strategic Scenarios (#12) • Work vs. Family (#17) • Why Do We Work? (#21)

STUDY QUESTIONS SUMMARY

1. What is entrepreneurship?

• Entrepreneurship is risk-taking behavior that results in the creation of new opportunities for individuals and/or organizations.

• An entrepreneur is someone who takes risks to pursue opportunities in situations others may view as problems or threats.

• The examples of entrepreneurs like Mary Kay Ash, Richard Branson, Earl Graves, and Anita Roddick can be a source of learning and inspiration for others.

• Entrepreneurs tend to be creative people who are self-confident, determined, resilient, adaptable, and driven to excel; they like to be masters of their own destinies.

• Entrepreneurship is rich with diversity, with women and minority-owned business startups increasing in numbers.

2. What is special about small businesses?

• Entrepreneurship results in the founding of many small business enterprises that offer job creation and other benefits to economies.

• The Internet has opened a whole new array of entrepreneurial possibilities, including online buying and selling and the more formal pursuit of dot.com businesses.

• Smaller businesses are pursuing more global opportunities in the quest for expanded markets, access to labor and technical expertise, and locations for low-cost manufacturing or outsourcing.

• Family businesses that are owned and financially controlled by family members represent the largest percentage of businesses operating worldwide.

- A significant problem faced by family businesses is the succession problem of transferring leadership from one generation to the next.
- Small businesses have a high failure rate; as many as 60 to 80 percent of new businesses fail in their first five years of operation.
- Small business failures are largely due to poor management, when owners make bad decisions on major business matters.

3. How does one start a new venture?

- Entrepreneurial firms tend to follow the life-cycle stages of birth, breakthrough, and maturity, with each stage offering different management challenges.
- New startups should be guided by a good business plan that describes the intended nature of the business, how it will operate, and how financing will be obtained.
- An important choice is the form of business ownership, with the proprietorship, corporate and limited liability forms offering different advantages and disadvantages.

- Two basic ways of financing a new venture are through debt financing, by taking loans, and equity financing, which exchanges ownership shares in return for outside investment.
- Venture capitalists pool capital and make investments in new ventures in return for an equity stake in the business.
- The angel investor is a wealthy individual who is willing to invest money in return for equity in a new venture.

4. What resources support entrepreneurship and business development?

- Intrapreneurship, or entrepreneurial behavior within larger organizations, is important in today's competitive environment.
- Business incubators offer space, shared services, and advice to small businesses in the startup stages.
- Small businesses can get a variety of forms of support and assistance from Small Business Development Centers funded by U.S. government sources.

KEY TERMS REVIEW

Angel investor (p. 155)
Business incubator
    (p. 157)
Business plan (p. 152)
Corporation (p. 154)
Debt financing (p. 154)
Entrepreneur (p. 141)
Entrepreneurship
    (p. 141)
Equity financing (p. 154)
Family business (p. 148)

First-mover advantage
    (p. 151)
Franchise (p. 147)
Initial Public Offering
    (IPO) (p. 154)
Intrapreneurship
    (p. 156)
Limited Liability
    Corporation (154)
Partnership (p. 153)
Skunkworks (p. 156)

Small business (p. 146)
Small Business
    Development Center
    (p. 157)
Sole proprietorship
    (p. 153)
Succession plan (p. 149)
Succession problem
    (p. 149)
Venture capitalists
    (p. 154)

SELF-TEST 6

MULTIPLE-CHOICE QUESTIONS:

1. _____ is among the personality characteristics commonly found among entrepreneurs.
    (a) External locus of control (b) Inflexibility (c) Self-confidence

2. When an entrepreneur is comfortable with uncertainty and willing to take risks, these are indicators of someone with a(n) _____.
(a) high tolerance for ambiguity (b) internal locus of control (c) need for achievement (d) action orientation

3. Almost _____ percent of American businesses meet the definition of "small business" used by the Small Business Administration.
(a) 40 (b) 99 (c) 75 (d) 81

4. When a business owner sells to another person the right to operate that business in another location, this is a _____.
(a) conglomerate (b) franchise (c) joint venture (d) limited partnership

5. A small business owner who is concerned about passing the business on to heirs after retirement or death should prepare a formal _____ plan.
(a) retirement (b) succession (c) franchising (d) liquidation

6. Among the most common reasons that new small business startups often fail is _____.
(a) lack of business expertise (b) strict financial controls (c) slow growth (d) high ethical standards

7. When a new business is quick to capture a market niche before competitors, this is called _____.
(a) Intrapreneurship (b) an initial public offering (c) succession planning (d) first-mover advantage

8. When a small business is just starting, the business owner is typically struggling to _____.
(a) gain acceptance in the marketplace (b) find partners for expansion (c) prepare an initial public offering (d) bring professional skills into the management team

9. A venture capitalist who receives an ownership share in return for investing in a new business is providing _____ financing.
(a) debt (b) equity (c) corporate (d) partnership

10. _____ is a term used to describe a small group of people operating with independence and in the expectation of being highly creative within a large organization.
(a) Skunkworks (b) Product team (c) Focus group (d) Leadership council

11. _____ take ownership shares in a new venture in return for providing the entrepreneur with critical startup funds.
(a) Business incubators (b) Angel investors (c) SBDCS (d) Intrapreneurs

12. Among the forms of small business ownership, only a _____ protects the owners from any personal liabilities for business losses.
(a) sole proprietorship (b) franchise (c) limited partnership (d) corporation

13. The first component of a good business plan is usually_____.
(a) an industry analysis (b) a marketing strategy (c) an executive summary (d) a set of milestones

14. Data on current trends in small business ownership in the United States would most likely show that _____.
(a) the numbers of women- and minority-owned businesses are declining (b) the majority of small businesses conduct some business by Internet (c) large businesses create more jobs than small businesses (d) very few small business engage in international import/export activities

15. In _____ financing, the entrepreneur borrows money as a loan that must eventually be paid back to the lender.
   (a) debt (b) equity (c) partnership (d) IPO

SHORT-RESPONSE QUESTIONS:

16. What is the relationship between diversity and entrepreneurship?

17. What are the major stages in the life cycle of an entrepreneurial firm, and what are the leadership challenges at each stage?

18. What are the advantages of choosing a limited partnership form of small business ownership?

19. How can a large corporation stimulate entrepreneurship within itself?

APPLICATION QUESTION:

20. Assume for the moment that you have a great idea for a potential Internet-based startup business. In discussing the idea with a friend, she advises you to be very careful to tie your business idea to potential customers and then describe it well in a business plan. "After all," she says, "you won't succeed without customers and you'll never get a chance to succeed if you can't attract financial backers through a good business plan." With these words to the wise, you proceed. What questions will you ask and answer to ensure that you are customer-focused in this business? What are the major areas that you would address in writing your initial business plan?

www.wiley.com/college/schermerhorn

7

Information and decision making

Planning Ahead

After reading Chapter 7, you should be able to answer these questions in your own words.

CHAPTER 7 study questions

1. How is information technology changing the workplace?

2. What is the role of information in the management process?

3. How do managers use information to make decisions?

4. What are the steps in the decision-making process?

5. What are the current issues in managerial decision making?

MOTOWN.COM—STAY TUNED IN TO THE ENVIRONMENT

Stay tuned in to the environment? Berry Gordy, founder of Motown Records sure did. His Motown trip has been one decision after another . . . good ones at that. And the songs he produced from "Motor City" help tell the story. Turn on your PC to the Motown jukebox and punch in the 1950s. Let the music steer your way back to the 1960s—Lionel Richie, Mary Welles, Martha and the Vandellas . . . to the 1970s—Marvin Gaye, Gladys Knight and the Pips, Stevie Wonder, Diana Ross. And still, the beat goes on. Grab the new award-winning DVD *Standing in the Shadows of Motown* and learn the story of the Funk Brothers Uriel Junes, Joe Hunter, and the other musicians who shaped the Motown sound at "Hitsville U.S.A."

An entrepreneur by nature, Gordy started Motown Records in 1957. He had been writing songs with his friend Smokey Robinson while working on the assembly line at a Detroit Ford plant. Encouraged by Robinson, he took the risk and started his own studio, using local talent with a distinctive sound. His strategy was to make a total package of background musicians and singers available to new artists from the Detroit neighborhoods. He had an ear for the marketplace and great business sense. By 1973 Motown was hailed by the *Detroit Free Press* as the "nation's largest black-owned entertainment conglomerate."

Berry Gordy sold Motown in 1988 and was inducted into the Rock and Roll Hall of Fame. Motown today is part of Universal Music Studios, living on, making the turn into the 21st century.[1]

Get Connected!

Take an online look at developments in the music industry. What do you see as challenges and business opportunities of selling music in a digital age?

Chapter 7 Learning Preview

Berry Gordy made many many decisions over the years while creating the Motown sound and forging a successful career in music and entertainment. At each step of the way he combined talent and business insight with risk and environmental awareness. He was a master at gathering information and turning it into plans that met market needs. In Chapter 7 you will learn about information and decision making, with special attention to developments in information technology.

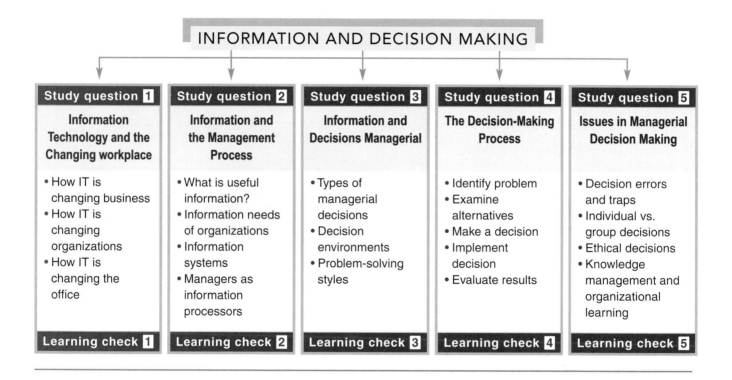

INFORMATION AND DECISION MAKING

Study question 1	Study question 2	Study question 3	Study question 4	Study question 5
Information Technology and the Changing workplace	**Information and the Management Process**	**Information and Decisions Managerial**	**The Decision-Making Process**	**Issues in Managerial Decision Making**
• How IT is changing business • How IT is changing organizations • How IT is changing the office	• What is useful information? • Information needs of organizations • Information systems • Managers as information processors	• Types of managerial decisions • Decision environments • Problem-solving styles	• Identify problem • Examine alternatives • Make a decision • Implement decision • Evaluate results	• Decision errors and traps • Individual vs. group decisions • Ethical decisions • Knowledge management and organizational learning
Learning check 1	Learning check 2	Learning check 3	Learning check 4	Learning check 5

When Berry Gordy founded Motown Records, it was just that— a world of records cut by musicians playing together and recording in real time. The music industry has since changed, following the pathways of our new economy. One would have to guess that if Gordy were starting Motown now, he would be riding the digital wave, taking the best the new environment has to offer and turning it, as always, into a sound with a soul.

Society today is different. It is in what futurist Alvin Toffler calls the *third wave* of development—information-driven, digital, networked, and continuously evolving.[2] An important key to performance in this new world is information technology, or "IT," and the way it is utilized. We live and work at a time when computers make more information about more things available to more people more quickly than ever before. The question is: How well do we take advantage of it? Consider this description of how the world of business has been competitively changed by fast-paced developments.[3]

Product life cycles are compressing and windows of market opportunity are slamming shut faster than ever before. Streamlined businesses are collapsing two and three jobs into one and asking managers to supervise more operations, across larger geographic expanses. Customers are demanding instant answers, personalized attention, and customized solutions. The only way for companies to maintain momentum, stay ahead of the market, and compete successfully in this unforgiving business environment is to find new and faster ways of sharing critical information and leveraging knowledge resources.

INFORMATION TECHNOLOGY AND THE CHANGING WORKPLACE

Management scholar and consultant Peter Drucker says that in our IT-driven economy "the productivity of knowledge and knowledge workers" is the decisive competitive factor.[4] A **knowledge worker** is one whose value to organizations rests with intellect, not physical capabilities. Knowledge workers add to an organization's **intellectual capital,** first defined in Chapter 1 as the collective brainpower or shared knowledge of a workforce that can be used to create wealth.[5]

> **O Knowledge workers** add value to organizations through intellect.

> **O Intellectual capital** is the collective brainpower or shared knowledge of a workforce.

Both knowledge and intellectual capital are irreplaceable organizational resources. They grow from information that, today, increasingly moves at high speed through electronic networks that link each of us to the world at large with an access and intensity never before possible. Thus, what Drucker called "the productivity of knowledge and knowledge workers" depends on two "must have" competencies: (1) *computer competency*—the ability to understand computers and to use them to their best advantage; and (2) *information competency*—the ability to utilize technology to locate, retrieve, evaluate, organize, and analyze information for decision making.

HOW IT IS CHANGING BUSINESS

One of the most significant business developments of all time is **electronic commerce,** or "e-commerce." This is the process of buying and selling goods and services electronically through use of the Internet. Business transactions between buyers and sellers are completed online rather than face-to-face. In *business-to-consumer e-commerce,* or "B2C," businesses like Amazon.com and Dell.com engage in e-retailing, selling directly to customers over the Internet. In *business-to-business e-commerce,* or

> **O Electronic commerce** is buying and selling goods and services through use of the Internet.

Doing what they say can't be done

"Discover books you'll love at Amazon.com" reads the note that arrives with the gift—a book from your friend. The book comes by priority mail, was ordered online, paid for by credit card, and shipped immediately. The package is even gift wrapped and carries a personal note from the gift giver—entered online of course. Amazon invites you to shop in its bookstore anytime you want day or night, 365 days a year. After all, the bookstore has put a capital E on the term E-business! Along the way, it has also established a new level and form of business competition. And at Amazon the growth goes on. Log on today and you can also buy everything from health and beauty aids to tools and hardware, to toys and videogames, and more. What began as a firm advertising that "Your next book is only a click away" is a huge and diverse consumer marketplace.[7]

"B2B," businesses use the Internet to collaborate and make transactions with one another. The stages of development in e-commerce are:[6]

Steps in developing an e-business →

1. *Secure an online identity:* Firms have a Web address and most likely a posted home page.
2. *Establish a Web presence:* Firms use their home page for advertising or promotional purposes but do not allow online queries or ordering.
3. *Enable e-commerce:* Firms engage in e-commerce with websites allowing visitors to order products online.
4. *Provide e-commerce and customer relationship management:* Firms use their websites to serve customers, for example, checking orders or inventory levels online.
5. *Utilize a service application model:* Firms use advanced websites to serve business functions such as financial and operations management.

HOW IT IS CHANGING ORGANIZATIONS

Information technology is changing organizations by breaking down barriers.[8] As shown in *Figure 7.1,* within organizations, this means that people working in different departments, levels, and physical locations can more easily communicate and share information. It also means that the organization can operate with fewer middle managers whose jobs otherwise would be to facilitate these information flows; computers now do the job. IT-intensive organizations are "flatter" and operate with fewer levels than their more traditional organizational counterparts. This creates opportunities for competitive advantage by faster decision making, better use of timely information, and better coordination of decisions and actions.

IT also breaks barriers between organizations and key elements in the external environment. It plays an important role in *customer relationship management* by quickly and accurately providing information for decision makers regarding customer needs, preferences, and satisfactions. It helps

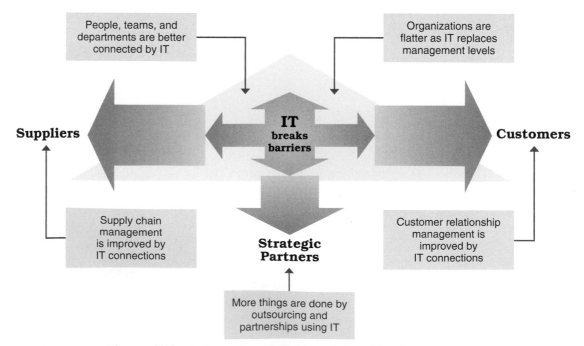

Figure 7.1 Information technology is breaking barriers and changing organizations.

manage and control costs in all aspects of supply *chain management* from initiation of purchase to logistics and transportation to point of delivery and ultimate use. IT also allows outsourcing and other business contracts to be continuously and efficiently monitored.

HOW IT IS CHANGING THE OFFICE

Progressive organizations are doing all they can to design work settings for high performance in an environment where "speed to market," "quick response," "fast cycle time," and "time-based competition" are top priorities.[9] They drive investments in IT that have dramatically changed what most of us still call "the office."

CHECK 7.1

Insights into the digital divide

This won't surprise you: Whites are more likely than minorities to have Internet access. But who uses the Web the most among those who do have Internet access? Take the online "Reality Check" to learn more about the results of a "digital divide" survey by Forrester Research.

People work at "smart" stations with sophisticated voice, image, text, and other data-handling operations. Many of these stations are temporary spaces that telecommuters "visit" during those times when they are in the main office; otherwise they work from virtual offices—on the road, anywhere. Databases are easily accessed and shared to solve problems, and prepare and analyze reports. Filing cabinets are few, and little paper is found. Meeting notes are written on electronic pads or jotted in palm-held electronic diaries. All are easily up-loaded into computer files. E-mail is automatically prioritized and linked to relevant databases to speed problem solving. Computer conferencing and videoconferencing are commonplace; people separated by great distances collaborate on projects without meeting face-to-face.

And that's not all. There are more developments coming to the networked office every day, and you most probably are already familiar with them. **Instant messaging,** instantaneous communication among persons online at the same time, isn't just for friends; it is a work facilitator as well. **Peer-to-peer file sharing** (P2P), PCs connected directly to one another over the Internet, gained fame as a way for friends to swap music and video files. It is now becoming indispensable as a way for workers to share information and otherwise collaborate "peer-to-peer."

○ **Instant messaging** is instantaneous communication between people online at the same time.

○ **Peer-to-peer file sharing** connects PCs directly to one another over the Internet.

Learning check 1

Be sure you can • define the terms "electronic commerce", "B2B", and "B2C" • discuss how IT is breaking barriers within organizations and between organizations and their environments • describe the way IT is changing the office

---

INFORMATION AND THE MANAGEMENT PROCESS

Organizations are changing as continuing developments in information technology exert their influence. Information departments or centers are now mainstream on organization charts. The number and variety of information career fields is rapidly expanding. Managers are increasingly expected to excel in their information processing roles. All of this, and more, is characteristic of the great opportunities of an information age.

WHAT IS USEFUL INFORMATION?

O **Data** are raw facts and observations.

O **Information** is data made useful for decision making.

Data are raw facts and observations. **Information** is data made useful and meaningful for decision making. In the music industry, for example, lots of data are available on the demographic profiles of customers—such as which age groups are buying which CDs and where they are buying them. Not everyone with access to this data, however, uses it well. But those who do may gain competitive advantage, perhaps by changing their advertising because younger customers do a lot of buying on the Internet while older customers shop mainly in retail stores.

The management process of planning, organizing, leading, and controlling is ultimately driven by information, not data alone. Managers need good information, and they need it all the time. Information that is truly useful meets the test of these five criteria:

Criteria of useful information

1. *Timely*—the information is available when needed; it meets deadlines for decision making and action.
2. *High quality*—the information is accurate, and it is reliable; it can be used with confidence.
3. *Complete*—the information is complete and sufficient for the task at hand; it is as current and up-to-date as possible.
4. *Relevant*—the information is appropriate for the task at hand; it is free from extraneous or irrelevant materials.
5. *Understandable*—the information is clear and easily understood by the user; it is free from unnecessary detail.

INFORMATION NEEDS IN ORGANIZATIONS

Driven largely by IT, information serves the variety of needs described in *Figure 7.2*. At the organization's boundaries, information in the external environment is accessed. Managers use this *intelligence information* to deal effectively with competitors and key stakeholders such as government agencies, creditors, suppliers, and stockholders. Peter Drucker says that "a winning strategy will require information about events and conditions outside the institution," and that organizations must have "rigorous methods for gathering and analyzing outside information."[10] Organizations also send many types of *public information* to stakeholders and the external environment. This serves a variety of purposes ranging from image building to product advertising to financial reporting for taxes.

Within organizations, people need vast amounts of information to make decisions and solve problems in their daily work. The ability of IT to gather and move information quickly allows top levels to stay informed while freeing lower levels to make speedy decisions and take the actions they need to best perform their jobs. Silicon valley pioneer and Cisco Systems CEO John Chambers, for example, points out that he always has the information he needs to be in control—be it information on earnings, expenses, profitability, gross margins, and more. He also says, importantly: "Because I have my data in that format, every one of my employees can make decisions that might have had to come all the way to the president. . . . Quicker decision making at lower levels will translate into higher profit margins.. . . Companies that don't do that will be noncompetitive."[11]

INFORMATION SYSTEMS

In order to perform well, people in any work setting, large or small, must have available to them the right information at the right time and in the

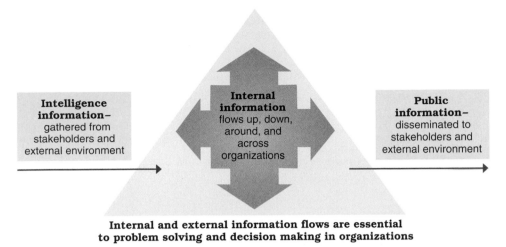

Figure 7.2 External and internal information needs of organizations.

right place. **Information systems** use the latest in information technology to collect, organize, and distribute data in such a way that they become meaningful as information. **Management information systems,** or MIS, meet the specific information needs of managers as they make a variety of day-to-day decisions. Although it is important to avoid common mistakes (*see Manager's Notepad 7.1*), today's developments in MIS make possible performance levels that are truly extraordinary. C.R. England, Inc., a long-haul refrigerated trucking company, for example, uses a computerized MIS to monitor more than 500 aspects of organizational performance. The system tracks everything from billing accuracy to arrival times to driver satisfaction with company maintenance on their vehicles. Says CEO Dan England: "Our view was, if we could measure it, we could manage it."[12]

○ **Information systems** use IT collect, organize, and distribute data for use in decision making.

○ **Management information systems** to meet the information needs of managers in daily decisions

Decision Support and Expert Systems

A **decision support system** (DSS) is an interactive information system that allows users to organize and analyze data for solving complex and sometimes unstructured problems. Decision support systems are now available to assist in such business decisions as mergers and acquisitions, plant expansions, new product developments, and stock portfolio management, among many others. A fast-growing application involves *group decision support systems* (GDSS) that facilitate group efforts to solve complex and unstructured problems. GDSS software, called **groupware,** allows several people to simultaneously access a file or database and work together virtually. It facilitates information exchange, group decision making, work scheduling, and other forms of group activity without the requirement of face-to-face meetings.

An exciting area is *artificial intelligence* (AI), a field of science that is interested in building computer systems with the capacity to reason the way people do. **Expert systems** use AI to mimic the thinking of human experts, even to the point of dealing with ambiguities and difficult issues of judgment. In so doing, they offer consistent and "expert" decision-making advice to the user. Some use a complicated set of "if . . . then" rules developed by human experts to analyze problems. A good example is automatic approval for credit card purchases. Behind this system is an AI platform that analyzes the purchaser's credit worthiness using a

○ **Decision support systems** help users organize and analyze data for problem solving.

○ **Groupware** is software that facilitates group collaboration and problem solving.

○ **Expert systems** allow computers to mimic the thinking of human experts for applied problem solving.

MANAGER'S NOTEPAD 7.1

Avoiding common information systems mistakes

- Don't assume more information is always better.
- Don't assume that computers eliminate human judgment.
- Don't assume the newest technology is always best.
- Don't assume nothing will ever go wrong with your computer.
- Don't assume that everyone understands how the system works.

set of predetermined rules, the same ones that a human expert would apply.

Web Portals and Networks

The growth of the World Wide Web has created many advantages in the area of information systems. Rather than relying solely on their own networks for computer interfacing, organizations are actively utilizing Web portals to facilitate information processing. It is now very common for organizations to have **intranets** and **corporate portals** that allow employees, by password access, to share databases and communicate electronically. The goal is to efficiently improve integration and communication throughout the organization, while making it easy for employees to access key services. At Hewlett-Packard, for example, a corporate portal has saved over $50 million in reduced paperwork and administrative costs. Employees use the portal to stay up to date on company news, access benefit information, participate in focus groups and special surveys, and locate one another for business communications.[13]

○ **Intranets** and **corporate portals** use the Web for communication and data sharing within an organization.

Extranets and enterprise portals allow communication and data sharing between the organization and special elements in its external environment. They typically link organizations with strategic partners, vendors, outsourcers, suppliers, and consultants. An important and rapidly expanding development in this area is called **electronic data interchange,** or EDI. It uses controlled access to enterprise portals and supporting software to enable firms to electronically transact business with one another, for example by sharing purchase orders, bills, receipt confirmations, and payments. The goals of EDI include improved transaction speed and cost savings. In the retailing industry where profit margins are tiny, Wal-Mart aggressively pursues these goals as a state-of-the art user of EDI. Its suppliers are required to purchase the necessary software and then electronically work with the firm to handle all order, purchasing, and delivery details.

○ **Extranets and enterprise portals** use the Web for communication and data sharing between the organization and its environment.

○ **Electronic data interchange** uses controlled access to enterprise portals to enable firms to electronically transact business with one another.

MANAGERS AS INFORMATION PROCESSORS

The manager's job as shown in *Figure 7.3* is a nerve center of information flows, with information being continually gathered, given, and received from many sources. All of the managerial roles identified by Henry Mintzberg and discussed in Chapter 1—interpersonal, decisional, and informational—involve communication and information processing.[15] So too, do all aspects of the management process—planning, organizing, leading, and controlling. Success in management is increasingly tied to the opportunities of IT.

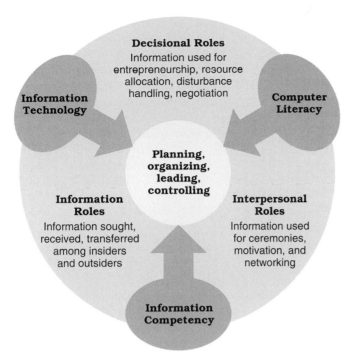

Figure 7.3 The manager as an information-process-ing nerve center.

- *Planning advantages*—better and more timely access to useful informa-tion, involving more people in the planning process.

- *Organizing advantages*—more ongoing and informed communication among all parts, improving coordination and integration.

- *Leading advantages*—more frequent and better communication with staff and stakeholders, keeping objectives clear.

- *Controlling advantages*—more immediate measures of performance re-sults, allowing real-time solutions to problems.

Advantages of IT utilization by managers

Be sure you can • differentiate data and information • list the criteria of useful infor-mation • describe the information needs of organizations • explain the role of in-formation systems in organizations • illustrate the use of corporate portals and en-terprise portals • describe how IT influences the four functions of management

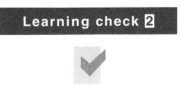

Learning check **2**

INFORMATION AND MANAGERIAL DECISIONS

One way to describe what managers do is that they use information to solve a continuous stream of daily problems. The most obvious problem situation is a *performance deficiency*, that is, when actual performance is less than desired. For example, a manager faces a possible problem when turnover or absenteeism suddenly increases in the work unit, when a sub-ordinate's daily output decreases, or when a higher executive complains about something that has been said or done. Another important problem situation emerges as a *performance opportunity* when an actual situation either turns out better than anticipated or offers the potential to be so.

The challenge in dealing with any performance deficiency or perfor-mance opportunity is to proceed with effective **problem solving**—the

○ **Problem solving** involves identifying and taking ac-tion to resolve problems.

○ A **decision** is a choice among possible alternative courses of action.

process of identifying a discrepancy between an actual and desired state of affairs and then taking action to resolve the deficiency or take advantage of the opportunity. Success in problem solving is dependent on the right information being available to the right people at the right times so that they can make good problem-solving decisions. A **decision,** to be precise, is a choice among alternative possible courses of action. In today's IT-enriched organizations, information systems assist managers in gathering data, turning them into useful information, and utilizing that information individually and collaboratively to make problem-solving decisions.

TYPES OF MANAGERIAL DECISIONS

○ A **programmed decision** applies a solution from past experience to a routine problem.

○ **Structured problems** are straightforward and clear in information needs.

Managers make different types of decisions in their day-to-day work. **Programmed decisions** use solutions already available from past experience to solve **structured problems**—ones that are familiar, straightforward, and clear with respect to information needs. These problems are routine; although perhaps not predictable, they can at least be anticipated. This means that decisions can be planned or programmed in advance to be implemented as needed. In human resource management, for example, problems are common whenever decisions are made on pay raises and promotions, vacation requests, committee assignments, and the like. Knowing this, forward-looking managers plan ahead on how to handle complaints and conflicts when and if they should arise.

○ **Unstructured problems** have ambiguities and information deficiencies.

○ A **nonprogrammed decision** applies a specific solution crafted for a unique problem.

Managers must also deal with new or unusual situations that present **unstructured problems,** full of ambiguities and information deficiencies. These problems require **nonprogrammed decisions** that craft novel solutions to meet the demands of the unique situation at hand. Most problems faced by higher-level managers are of this type, often involving choice of strategies and objectives in situations of some uncertainty.

○ A **crisis** is an unexpected problem that can lead to disaster if not resolved quickly and appropriately.

An extreme type of nonprogrammed decision must be made in times of **crisis**—the occurrence of an unexpected problem that can lead to disaster if not resolved quickly and appropriately. Terrorism in a post–9/11 world, outbreaks of workplace violence, man-made environmental catastrophes, ethical scandals, and IT failures are examples. The ability to handle crises (see *Manager's Notepad 7.2*) may be the ultimate test of a manager's problem-solving capabilities. Unfortunately, research indicates that managers may react to crises by doing the wrong things. They isolate themselves and try to solve the problem alone or in a small "closed" group.[16] This denies them access to crucial information and assistance at the very time they are most needed. The crisis can even be accentuated when more problems are created because critical decisions are made with poor or inadequate information and from a limited perspective. The organizational consequences of alienated customers, lost profits, damaged reputation, and increased costs can be very severe.

○ **Crisis management** is preparation for the management of crises that threaten an organization's health and well-being.

For these and other reasons, many organizations are developing formal **crisis management** programs. They are designed to help managers and others prepare for unexpected high-impact events that threaten an organization's health and well-being. Anticipation is one aspect of crisis management; preparation is another. People can be assigned ahead of time to *crisis management teams,* and *crisis management plans* can be developed to deal with various contingencies. Just as police departments and community groups plan ahead and train to best handle civil and natural disasters, so too can managers and work teams plan ahead and train to best deal with organizational crises.[7]

MANAGER'S NOTEPAD 7.2

Six rules for crisis management

1. *Figure out what is going on*—Take the time to understand the situation, what's happening, and the conditions under which the crisis must be resolved.
2. *Remember that speed matters*—Attack the crisis as quickly as possible, trying to catch it when it is as small as possible.
3. *Remember that slow counts, too*—Know when to back off and wait for a better opportunity to make progress with the crisis.
4. *Respect the danger of the unfamiliar*—Understand that the most dangerous crisis is the all-new territory where you and others have never been before.
5. *Value the skeptic*—Don't look for and get too comfortable with agreement; appreciate skeptics and let them help you to see things differently.
6. *Be ready to "fight fire with fire"*—When things are going wrong but others don't seem to care, you may have to start a crisis of your own to get their attention.

DECISION ENVIRONMENTS

Figure 7.4 shows three different decision environments—certainty, risk, and uncertainty. Although managers make decisions in each, the conditions of risk and uncertainty are common at higher management levels where problems are more complex and unstructured. Former Coca-Cola CEO Roberto Goizueta, for example, was known as a risk taker. Among his risky moves were introducing Diet Coke to the market, changing the formula of Coca-Cola to create New Coke, and then reversing direction after New Coke flopped.[18]

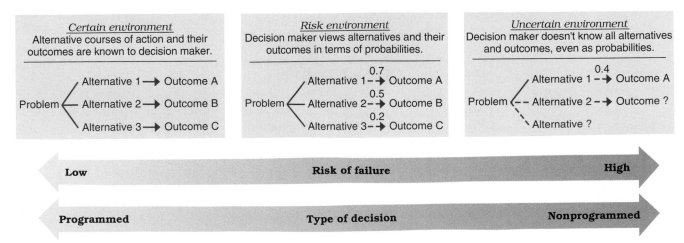

Figure 7.4   Three environments for managerial decision making and problem solving.

○ A **certain environment** offers complete information on possible action alternatives and their consequences

○ A **risk environment** lacks complete information but offers "probabilities" of the likely outcomes for possible action alternatives.

○ An **uncertain environment** lacks so much information that it is difficult to assign probabilities to the likely outcomes of alternatives.

The decision to market any new Coke is made in conditions quite different from the relative predictability of a **certain environment.** This is an ideal decision situation where factual information is available about the possible alternative courses of action and their outcomes. The decision makers task is simply to study the alternatives and choose the best solution. But very few managerial problems are like this. It is more common to face a **risk environment** where facts and information on action alternatives and their consequences are incomplete, but some estimates of "probabilities" can be made. A *probability* is the degree of likelihood (e.g., 4 chances out of 10) that an event will occur. Risk is typical for entrepreneurs and organizations that depend on ideas and continued innovation for their success. Steps can be taken to reduce risk in many situations. In the case of a new coke product for example, the firm can make the go-ahead decision only after receiving favorable reports from special focus groups testing it.

When facts are few and information is so poor that managers are unable even to assign probabilities to the likely outcomes of alternatives, an **uncertain environment** exists. This is the most difficult decision condition.[19] The high level of uncertainty forces managers to rely heavily on creativity in solving problems. Because uncertainty requires unique, novel, and often totally innovative alternatives, groups are frequently used for problem solving. In all cases, the responses to uncertainty depend greatly on intuition, judgment, informed guessing, and hunches—all of which leave considerable room for error.

Specialty talents can lead to specialty careers

Ariane Daguin and George Faison know the concept of risk quite well. In their former jobs as sales manager and general manager for a New York pâté producer, they located a foie gras supplier as good as any in France. When their boss balked at contracting for all the farmer's output, they took a risk. Betting that there was a market, they quit their jobs, signed the foie gras supplier, and invested $15,000 to start D'Artagnan, Inc. Their company now far outshines their former employer. It is America's leading purveyor of foie gras, pâtés, sausages, smoked delicacies, and organic game and poultry. Its products are used by the world's top restaurants, hotels, retailers, cruise ships, and airlines. D'Artagnan's founders found a market niche for their special talents.[20]

PROBLEM-SOLVING STYLES

In practice, managers display three quite different approaches or "styles" in the way they process information and deal with problems. Some are *problem avoiders* who ignore information that would otherwise signal the presence of an opportunity or performance deficiency. They are inactive in information gathering, not wanting to make decisions and deal with problems. *Problem solvers,* by contrast, are willing to make decisions and try to solve problems, but only when forced to by the situation. They are reactive in gathering information and responding to problems after they occur. They may deal reasonably well with performance deficiencies, but they miss many performance opportunities. Problem *seekers* actively process information and constantly look for problems to solve or opportunities to explore. True problem seekers are proactive and forward thinking. They anticipate problems and opportunities and take appropriate action to gain the advantage. Success at problem seeking is one of the ways exceptional managers distinguish themselves from the merely good ones.

Managers also differ in tendencies toward "systematic" and "intuitive" thinking. In **systematic thinking** a person approaches problems in a rational, step-by-step, and analytical fashion. This type of thinking involves breaking a complex problem into smaller components and then addressing them in a logical and integrated fashion. Managers who are systematic can be expected to make a plan before taking action and then to search for information to facilitate problem solving in a step-by-step fashion.

Someone using **intuitive thinking,** by contrast, is more flexible and spontaneous and also may be quite creative.[21] This type of thinking allows us to respond imaginatively to a problem based on a quick and broad evaluation of the situation and the possible alternative courses of action. Managers who are intuitive can be expected to deal with many aspects of a problem at once, jump quickly from one issue to another, and consider "hunches" based on experience or spontaneous ideas. This approach tends to work best in situations of high uncertainty where facts are limited and few decision precedents exist.

Senior managers, in particular, must deal with portfolios of problems and opportunities that consist of multiple and interrelated issues. This requires *multidimensional thinking,* or the ability to view many problems at once, in relationship to one another, and across long and short time horizons.[22] The best managers "map" multiple problems into a network that can be actively managed over time as priorities, events, and demands continuously change. And importantly, they are able to make decisions and take actions in the short run that benefit longer-run objectives. They avoid being sidetracked while sorting through a shifting mix of daily problems. This requires skill at **strategic opportunism**—the ability to remain focused on long-term objectives while being flexible enough to resolve short-term problems and opportunities in a timely manner.[23]

○ **Systematic thinking** approaches problems in a rational and analytical fashion.

○ **Intuitive thinking** approaches problems in a flexible and spontaneous fashion.

○ **Strategic opportunism** focuses on long-term objectives while being flexible in dealing with short-term problems.

Learning check 3

Be sure you can • define the terms "problem solving" and "decision" • differentiate among programmed, nonprogrammed, and crisis decisions • explain the challenges of decision making in certain, risk, and uncertain environments • describe three problem-solving styles of managers • discuss the differences between systematic and intuitive thinking

---

THE DECISION-MAKING PROCESS

The **decision-making process** involves a set of activities that begins with identification of a problem, includes making a decision, and ends with the evaluation of results.[24] As shown in *Figure 7.5,* the steps in managerial decision making are: (1) identify and define the problem, (2) generate and evaluate alternative solutions, (3) choose a preferred course of action and conduct the "ethics double-check," (4) implement the decision, and (5) evaluate results. Importantly, Step 3 in this model includes a built-in "checkpoint" as a way to verify the ethical aspects of a decision before any action is taken. Working with the following short-but-true case will help put all five steps into perspective.

○ The **decision-making process** begins with identification of a problem and ends with evaluation of implemented solutions.

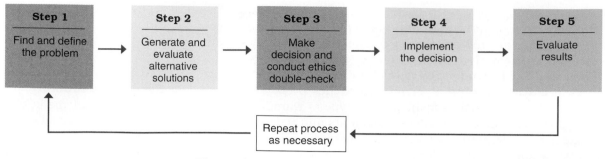

Figure 7.5 Steps in managerial decision making and problem solving.

The Ajax Case. On December 31, the Ajax Company decided to close down its Murphysboro plant. Market conditions were forcing layoffs, and the company could not find a buyer for the plant. Of 172 employees, some had been with the company as long as 18 years, others as little as 6 months. All were to be terminated. Under company policy, they would be given serverance pay equal to one week's pay per year of service. Top management faced a difficult problem: how to minimize the negative impact of the plant closing on employees, their families, and the small town of Murphysboro.

This case reflects how competition, changing times, and the forces of globalization can take their toll on organizations, the people that work for them, and the communities in which they operate. Think about how you would feel as one of the affected employees. Think about how you would feel as the mayor of this small town. Think about how you would feel as a corporate executive having to make the required decisions.

IDENTIFY AND DEFINE THE PROBLEM

The first step in decision making is to find and define the problem. This is a stage of information gathering, information processing, and deliberation.[25] It is important at this step to clarify goals by identifying exactly what a decision should accomplish. The more specific the goals, the easier it is to evaluate results after the decision is actually implemented. Importantly, the way a problem is defined can have a major impact on how it is resolved.

Three common mistakes occur in this critical first step in decision making. *Mistake number 1* is defining the problem too broadly or too narrowly. To take a classic example, the problem stated as "Build a better mousetrap" might be better defined as "Get rid of the mice." That is, managers should define problems in ways that give them the best possible range of problem-solving options. *Mistake number 2* is focusing on symptoms instead of causes. Symptoms are indicators that problems may exist, but they shouldn't be mistaken for the problems themselves. Managers should be able to spot problem symptoms (e.g., a drop in performance). But instead of treating symptoms (such as simply encouraging higher performance), managers should address their root causes (such as discovering the worker's need for training in the use of a complex new computer system). *Mistake number 3* is choosing the wrong problem to deal with. Managers should set priorities and deal with the most important problems first. They should also give priority to problems that are truly solvable.

Back to the Ajax Case. Closing the Ajax plant will put a substantial number of people from this small community of Murphysboro out of work. The unemployment created will have a negative impact on individuals, their families, and the community as a whole. The loss of the Ajax tax base will further hurt the community. The local financial implications of the plant closure will be great. The problem for Ajax management is how to minimize the adverse impact of the plant closing on the employees, their families, and the community.

GENERATE AND EVALUATE ALTERNATIVE COURSES OF ACTION

Once the problem is defined, it is time to assemble the facts and information that will be helpful for problem solving. It is important here to clarify exactly what is known and what needs to be known. Extensive information gathering should identify alternative courses of action, as well as their anticipated consequences. The process of evaluating alternatives often benefits from a *stakeholder analysis.* Key stakeholders in the problem should be identified and the effects of each possible course of action on them considered. Another useful approach for the evaluation of alternatives is **cost-benefit analysis,** the comparison of what an alternative will cost in relation to the expected benefits. At a minimum, the benefits of an alternative should be greater than its costs. Typical criteria for evaluating alternatives include the following:

○ **Cost-benefit analysis** involves comparing the costs and benefits of each potential course of action.

◀

Criteria for evaluating alternatives

- *Benefits:* What are the "benefits" of using the alternative to solve a performance deficiency or take advantage of an opportunity?
- *Costs:* What are the "costs" of implementing the alternative, including resource investments as well as potential negative side effects?
- *Timeliness:* How fast will the benefits occur and a positive impact be achieved?
- *Acceptability:* To what extent will the alternative be accepted and supported by those who must work with it?
- *Ethical soundness:* How well does the alternative meet acceptable ethical criteria in the eyes of the various stakeholders?

The end result of this step can only be as good as the quality of the options considered; the better the pool of alternatives, the more likely that a good solution will be achieved. A common error is abandoning the search for alternatives too quickly. This often happens under pressures of time and other circumstances. But just because an alternative is convenient doesn't make it the best. It could have damaging side effects, or it could be less good than others that might be discovered with extra effort. One way to minimize this error is through participation and involvement, bringing more people into the process, and bringing more information and perspectives to bear on the problem.

Back to the Ajax Case. The Ajax plant is going to be closed. Among the possible alternatives that can be considered are: (1) close the plant on schedule and be done with it; (2) delay the plant closing until all efforts have been made to sell it to another firm; (3) offer to sell the plant to the employees and/or local interests; (4) close the plant and offer transfers to other Ajax plant locations; or (5) close the plant, offer transfers, and help the employees find new jobs in and around Murphysboro.

DECIDE ON A PREFERRED COURSE OF ACTION

○ The **classical decision model** describes decision making with complete information.

This is the point of choice, where an actual decision is made to select a preferred course of action. Just how this is done and by whom must be successfully resolved in each problem situation. Management theory recognizes differences between the classical and behavioral models of decision making shown in *Figure 7.6*. The **classical decision model** views the manager as acting rationally in a certain world. Here, the manager faces a clearly defined problem and knows all possible action alternatives as well as their consequences. As a result, he or she makes an **optimizing decision** that gives the absolute best solution to the problem. The classical approach is a rational model that assumes perfect information is available for decision making.

○ An **optimizing decision** chooses the alternative giving the absolute best solution to a problem.

○ The **behavioral decision model** describes decision making with limited information and bounded rationality.

○ A **satisficing decision** chooses the first satisfactory alternative that comes to one's attention.

Behavioral scientists question these assumptions. Perhaps best represented by the work of Herbert Simon, they recognize limits to our human information-processing capabilities.[26] These *cognitive limitations* make it hard for managers to become fully informed and make perfectly rational decisions. They create a *bounded rationality* such that managerial decisions are rational only within the boundaries defined by the available information. The **behavioral decision model,** accordingly, assumes that people act only in terms of what they perceive about a given situation. Because such perceptions are frequently imperfect, the decision maker has only partial knowledge about the available action alternatives and their consequences. Consequently, the first alternative that appears to give a satisfactory resolution of the problem is likely to be chosen. Simon, who won a Nobel Prize for his work, calls this the tendency toward **satisficing decisions**—choosing the first satisfactory alternative that comes to your attention. This model seems especially accurate in describing how people make decisions about ambiguous problems in risky and uncertain conditions.

Back to the Ajax Case. Management at Ajax decided to follow alternative 5 as described in Step 2 of the decision-making process. They would close the plant, offer transfers to company plants in another state, and offer to help displaced employees find new jobs in and around Murphysboro.

IMPLEMENT THE DECISION

Once a preferred solution is chosen, actions must be taken to fully implement it. Nothing new can or will happen unless action is taken to actually solve the problem. Managers not only need the determination and creativity to arrive at a decision, they also need the ability and willingness to implement it.

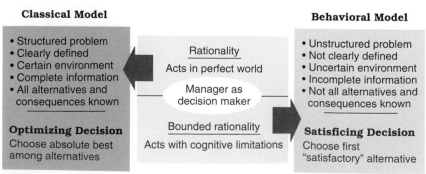

Classical Model

- Structured problem
- Clearly defined
- Certain environment
- Complete information
- All alternatives and consequences known

Optimizing Decision
Choose absolute best among alternatives

Rationality
Acts in perfect world

Manager as decision maker

Bounded rationality
Acts with cognitive limitations

Behavioral Model

- Unstructured problem
- Not clearly defined
- Uncertain environment
- Incomplete information
- Not all alternatives and consequences known

Satisficing Decision
Choose first "satisfactory" alternative

Figure 7.6 Differences in the classical and behavioral models of managerial decision making.

The "ways" in which previous steps have been accomplished can have a powerful impact on this stage of implementation. Difficulties encountered at this point often trace to the *lack-of-participation error.* This is a failure to adequately involve in the process those persons whose support is necessary to implement the decision. Managers who use participation wisely get the right people involved in problem solving right from the beginning. When they do, implementation typically follows quickly, smoothly, and to everyone's satisfaction. Participation in decision making not only makes everyone better informed, it also builds the commitments needed for implementation.

Back to the Ajax Case. Ajax ran an ad in the local and regional newspapers for several days. The ad called attention to an "Ajax skill bank" composed of "qualified, dedicated, and well-motivated employees with a variety of skills and experiences." Interested employers were urged to contact Ajax for further information.

EVALUATE RESULTS

The decision-making process is not complete until results are evaluated. If the desired results are not achieved and/or if undesired side effects occur, corrective action should be taken. In this sense, evaluation is a form of managerial control. It involves gathering data to measure performance results against goals. Both the positive and negative outcomes should be examined. If the original choice appears inadequate, it is time to reassess and return to earlier steps. In this way, problem solving becomes a dynamic and ongoing activity within the management process. Evaluation is always easier, furthermore, when clear goals, measurable targets, and timetables were established to begin with.

Back to the Ajax Case. The advertisement ran for some 15 days. The plant's industrial relations manager commented, "I've been very pleased with the results." That's all we know. You can look back on the case and problem-solving process just described and judge for yourself. How well did Ajax management do in dealing with this very difficult problem? Perhaps you would have approached the situation and the five steps in decision making somewhat differently.

PERSONAL MANAGEMENT

Managers must have the **SELF-CONFIDENCE** to not only make decisions but also to implement them. Too many of us find all sorts of excuses for doing everything but that— we have difficulty deciding and we have difficulty acting. Opportunities to improve and develop your self-confidence abound, especially through involvement in the many student organizations on your campus. Carole Clay Winters was the first member of her family to go to college. On the encouragement of an economics professor, she joined Students in Free Enterprise (SIFE) and ended up on a team teaching business concepts to elementary school children in the local community.[27] Her team was chosen to participate in a national competition. They didn't win, but Carole did. "I felt my life had changed," she said. "I realized that if I could answer all the questions being posed by some of the country's most powerful executives, I had what I needed to become an executive myself." Carole went on to become manager in the Washington, D.C., office of KPMG. What about you? Do you have the self-confidence to make decisions relating to your career goals and future success? Are you taking full advantage of opportunities, on campus and off, to experience the responsibilities of leadership and gain confidence in your decision-making capabilities?

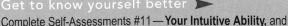

Get to know yourself better ➤
Complete Self-Assessments #11—**Your Intuitive Ability,** and #12—**Assertiveness,** from the Management Learning Workbook.

Learning check 4

Be sure you can • list the steps in the decision-making process • apply these steps to a sample decision-making situation • explain stakeholder analysis and cost-benefit analysis • discuss the differences between the classical and behavioral decision models • define the terms "optimizing" and "satisficing"

ISSUES IN MANAGERIAL DECISION MAKING

In settings rich in information technology but complicated by risk and uncertainty, managers with their limited human capacities face many decision-making challenges. It helps to be aware of the common decision-making errors and traps, the advantages and disadvantages of individual and group decision making, the imperative of ethical decision making, and the growing importance of knowledge management and organizational learning.

DECISION-MAKING ERRORS AND TRAPS

O **Heuristics** are strategies for simplifying decision making.

Faced with limited information, time and even energy, people often use simplifying strategies for decision making. These strategies, known as **heuristics,** can cause decision-making errors.[28] The *availability heuristic* occurs when people use information "readily available" from memory as a basis for assessing a current event or situation. An example is deciding not to invest in a new product based on your recollection of how well a similar new product performed in the recent past. The potential bias is that the readily available information may be fallible and irrelevant. The new product that recently failed may have been a good idea that was released to market at the wrong time of year.

The *representativeness heuristic* occurs when people assess the likelihood of something occurring based on its similarity to a stereotyped set of occurrences. An example is deciding to hire someone for a job vacancy simply because he or she graduated from the same school attended by your last and most successful new hire. The potential bias is that the representative stereotype may mask the truly important factors relevant to the decision. For instance, the abilities and career expectations of the newly hired person may not fit the job requirements.

The *anchoring and adjustment heuristic* involves making decisions based on adjustments to a previously existing value or starting point. An example is setting a new salary level for an employee by simply raising the prior year's salary by a reasonable percentage. This may inappropriately bias a decision toward only incremental movement from the starting point. For instance, the individual's market value may be substantially higher than the existing salary. An incremental adjustment won't keep this person from looking for another job.

O **Framing error** is solving a problem in the context perceived.

In addition to the biases of judgmental heuristics, managers can suffer from **framing error** when making decisions. Framing occurs when a problem is evaluated and resolved in the context in which it is perceived—either positive or negative. An example from the world of marketing is a product that data show has a 40 percent market share. A negative frame views the product as being deficient because it is missing 60 percent of the market. The likely discussion and problem solving in this frame would focus on the question: "What are we doing wrong?" Alternatively, the frame could be a positive one, looking at the 40 percent share as a good accomplishment. In this case the discussion is more likely to proceed with the question: "How do we do things better?" Sometimes people use framing as a tactic for presenting information in a way that gets other people to think inside the desired frame. In politics this is often referred to as "spinning" the data. In the marketing example, the data could be 'spun' to the negative or positive by a presenter in an attempt to influence the decision-making process one way or the other.

O **Escalating commitment** is the continuation of a course of action even though it is not working.

Good managers are also aware of another decision-making trap known as **escalating commitment.** This is a decision to increase effort and per-

---

How to avoid the escalation trap

- Set advance limits on your involvement and commitment to a particular course of action; stick with these limits.
- Make your own decisions; don't follow the lead of others, since they are also prone to escalation.
- Carefully determine just why you are continuing a course of action; if there are insufficient reasons to continue, don't.
- Remind yourself of what a course of action is costing; consider saving these costs as a reason to discontinue.
- Watch for escalation tendencies; be on guard against their influence on both you and others involved in the course of action.

---

haps apply more resources to pursue a course of action that is not working.[29] In such cases, managers let the momentum of the situation overwhelm them. They are unable to decide to "call it quits," even when experience otherwise indicates that this is the most appropriate thing to do. *Manager's Notepad 7.3* offers advice on avoiding tendencies toward escalating commitments to previously chosen courses of action.

INDIVIDUAL VS. GROUP DECISION MAKING

One of the important issues in decision making is the choice of whether to make the decision individually or with the participation of a group. The best managers and team leaders don't limit themselves to just one way. Instead, they switch back and forth among individual and group decision making to best fit the problems at hand. A managerial skill is the ability to choose the "right" decision method—one that provides for a timely and quality decision, and one to which people involved in the implementation will be highly committed. To do this well, however, managers must understand both the potential assets and potential liabilities of moving from individual to more group-oriented decision making.[30]

The potential *advantages of group decision making* are highly significant, and they should be actively sought whenever time and other circumstances permit. Team decisions make greater amounts of information, knowledge, and expertise available to solve problems. They expand the number of action alternatives that are examined; they help to avoid tunnel vision and consideration of only limited options. Team decisions increase the understanding and acceptance of outcomes by members. And importantly, team decisions increase the commitments of members to work hard to implement final plans.

The *potential disadvantages of group decision making* trace largely to the difficulties that can be experienced in a group process. In a team decision there may be social pressure to conform. Some individuals may feel intimidated or compelled to go along with the apparent wishes of others. There may be minority domination, where some members feel forced or "railroaded" to accept a decision advocated by one vocal individual or small coalition. Also, there is no doubt that the time required to make team decisions can sometimes be a disadvantage. As more people are involved in the dia-

TAKE IT TO THE CASE

Kate Spade turns risk into opportunities

If you start with an idea to create a better handbag, a vacation in Provincetown, Massachusetts, and a woman's first name and her future husband's last, what do you get? Kate Spade—one of the best-known and fastest-growing brands in the fashion business. Kate wanted to start her own business and believed she knew what the fashion handbag market was missing. The risk was high; the odds were against her. But starting in 1992 with six construction paper design mock-ups, she hasn't looked back since. Her company is now a $70 million business, with retail stores in the United States, Canada, and Japan, and products sold globally at high-quality department and specialty stores. Her brand communicates sophistication. And with a continued and laser-sharp eye on the market, Kate Spade continues to grow. Her lines now include luggage, shoes, glasses, and paper products; more are on the way. And then there's husband Jack—watch out for Jack Spade, he's on the move too.[32]

logue and discussion, decision making takes longer. This added time may be costly, even prohibitively so, in certain circumstances.[31]

ETHICAL DECISION MAKING

Chapter 3 was devoted to ethics and social responsibility issues in management. As a reminder, however, it is important to restate the expectation that any decision should be ethical. It should at least meet the test described in Step 3 of decision making as the "ethics double-check." This involves asking and answering two straightforward but powerful *spotlight questions*: (1) "How would I feel if my family found out about this decision?" (2) "How would I feel if this decision were published in the local newspaper?" The Josephson Institute model for ethical decision making suggests a third question to further strengthen the ethics double-check: "Think of the person you know or know of (in real life or fiction) who has the strongest character and best ethical judgment. Then ask yourself—what would that person do in your situation?"[33]

Although it adds time to decision making, the ethics double-check is necessary to ensure that the ethical aspects of a problem are properly considered in all situations. It is also consistent with the demanding moral standards of modern society. A willingness to pause to examine the ethics of a proposed decision may well result in both a better decision and the prevention of costly litigation. Ethicist Gerald Cavanaugh and his associates suggest that managers can proceed with the most confidence when the following criteria are met.[34]

Ethical criteria for decision making

1. *Utility*—Does the decision satisfy all constituents or stakeholders?
2. *Rights*—Does the decision respect the rights and duties of everyone?
3. *Justice*—Is the decision consistent with the canons of justice?
4. *Caring*—Is the decision consistent with my responsibilities to care?

KNOWLEDGE MANAGEMENT AND ORGANIZATIONAL LEARNING

Now that the process of managerial decision making is clear, let's return to its context—a technology-driven world rich with information and demanding in the pace and uncertainty of change. This is the setting in which knowl-

Global sourcing rules computer software services

It's hard to find an executive conversation about computer software today without hearing a reference to India. The country's talented computer scientists offer great advantages to organizations willing to invest in global sourcing. Wipro Technologies, based in the Indian high-tech capital of Bangalore, is one of India's most valuable companies. It was named by *Business Week* magazine as one of the seven top software services firms in the world. Wipro's website includes this testimonial from former GE CEO Jack Welch: "From the first day in dealing with Wipro, there's been nothing but quality, character, highest integrity, highest quality work. As a joint venture, you wouldn't find a better partner. As a supplier, you wouldn't find a higher quality partner."[37]

edge workers with intellectual capital become the most critical assets of organizations. Management theorist Peter Drucker, however, warns us that "knowledge constantly makes itself obsolete."[35] His message must be taken to heart. People and organizations cannot rest on past laurels; future success will be earned only by those who continually learn through experience.

The term **knowledge management** describes the processes through which organizations develop, organize, and share knowledge to achieve competitive advantage.[36] The significance of knowledge management as a strategic and integrating force in organizations is represented by the emergence of a new executive job title—*chief knowledge officer* (CKO). The CKO is responsible for energizing learning processes and making sure that an organization's portfolio of intellectual assets are well managed and continually enhanced. These assets include such things as patents, intellectual property rights, trade secrets, and special processes and methods, as well as the accumulated knowledge and understanding of the entire workforce.

○ **Knowledge management** is the processes using intellectual capital for competitive advantage.

Knowledge management requires the creation of an organizational culture that truly values learning. BP Amoco's CEO John Browne says: "Learning is at the heart of a company's ability to adapt to a rapidly changing environment." He goes on to add, "In order to generate extraordinary value for its shareholders, a company must learn better than its competitors and apply that knowledge throughout its businesses faster and more widely than they do."[38] Like other progressive organizations today, BP is striving to build the foundations of what a consultant Peter Senge calls true **learning organization.** This is an organization, first described in Chapter 2, as one that "by virtue of people, values, and systems is able to continuously change and improve its performance based upon the lessons of experience."[39] Browne says that organizations can learn from many sources. They can learn from their own experience. They can learn from the experiences of their contractors, suppliers, partners, and customers. And they can learn from firms in unrelated businesses.[40] All of this, of course, depends on a willingness to seek out learning opportunities from these sources and to make information sharing an expected and valued work behavior.

○ A **learning organization** continuously changes and improves using the lessons of experience.

Learning check 5

Be sure you can • explain the availability, representativeness, anchoring, and adjustment heuristics • illustrate framing error and escalating commitment in decision making • list questions that can be asked to double check the ethics of a decision • discuss why the best organizations today give high priority to knowledge management and organizational learning

CHAPTER 7 STUDY GUIDE

Where We've Been

BACK TO MOTOWN

The opening example of Motown introduced you to the importance of staying informed about the environment and making good decisions that keep you and your organization well positioned for continued success. In Chapter 7 you learned about the information needs of organizations and how new developments in information technology are changing organizations and the way people work. You have also learned how managers use information in the decision-making process, with special attention to decision errors and traps, ethical decision making, and decision making by individuals and groups.

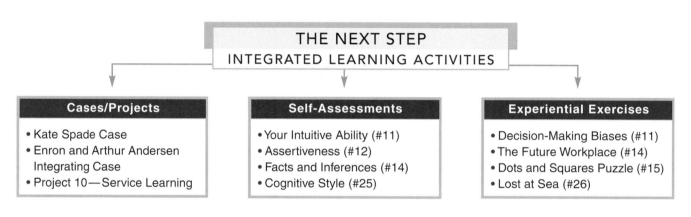

THE NEXT STEP
INTEGRATED LEARNING ACTIVITIES

Cases/Projects	Self-Assessments	Experiential Exercises
• Kate Spade Case • Enron and Arthur Andersen Integrating Case • Project 10—Service Learning	• Your Intuitive Ability (#11) • Assertiveness (#12) • Facts and Inferences (#14) • Cognitive Style (#25)	• Decision-Making Biases (#11) • The Future Workplace (#14) • Dots and Squares Puzzle (#15) • Lost at Sea (#26)

STUDY QUESTIONS SUMMARY

1. How is information technology changing the workplace?

• A major and rapidly growing force in the economy are e-businesses, which use the Internet to engage in business-to-consumer and business-to-business electronic commerce.

• Within organizations and between organizations IT is breaking barriers to speed work flows and cut costs.

• Today's "electronic" offices with e-mail, instant messaging, and networked computer systems are changing the way work is accomplished in and by organizations.

2. What is the role of information in the management process?

• Information is data made useful for decision making.

• Organizations need and use internal, public, and intelligence information.

• Management information systems (MIS) collect, organize, store, and distribute data to meet the information needs of managers.

• Intranets, extranets and Web portals allow people to share databases and communicate electronically within an organization and between the organization and its environment.

3. How do managers use information to make decisions?

• A problem is a discrepancy between an actual and a desired state of affairs.

• The most threatening type of problem is the crisis, which occurs unexpectedly and can lead to disaster if it is not handled quickly and properly.

• Managers face structured and unstructured problems in environments of certainty, risk, and uncertainty.

- Managers vary in their willingness to deal with problems, and in their use of systematic and intuitive thinking.

4. What are the steps in the decision-making process?

- The steps in the decision-making process are: find and define the problem, generate and evaluate alternatives, decide on the preferred course of action, implement the decision, and evaluate the results.
- An optimizing decision, following the classical model, chooses the absolute best solution from a known set of alternatives.
- A satisficing decision, following the administrative model, chooses the first satisfactory alternative to come to attention.

5. What are the current issues in managerial decision making?

- Judgmental heuristics, framing errors, and escalating commitment can bias decision making.
- Group decisions offer the potential advantages of greater information and expanded commitment, but they are often slower than individual decisions.
- Decision makers should always take time to double-check the ethics of their decisions.
- Knowledge management captures, develops, and uses knowledge for competitive advantage; a learning organization is committed to continuous change and improvement based on the lessons of experience.

KEY TERMS REVIEW

Behavioral decision model (p. 178)

Certain environment (p. 174)

Classical decision model (p. 178)

Corporate portals (p. 170)

Cost-benefit analysis (p. 177)

Crisis (p. 172)

Crisis management (p. 172)

Data (p. 168)

Decision (p. 172)

Decision-making process (p. 175)

Decision support system (p. 169)

Electronic commerce (p. 165)

Electronic data interchange (p. 170)

Enterprise portals (p. 170)

Escalating commitment (p. 180)

Expert system (p. 169)

Extranet (p. 170)

Framing error (p. 180)

Groupware (p. 169)

Heuristics (p. 180)

Information (p. 168)

Information system (p. 169)

Information technology (p. 169)

Instant messaging (p. 167)

Intellectual capital (p. 165)

Intranet (p. 170)

Intuitive thinking (p. 175)

Knowledge management (p. 183)

Knowledge worker (p. 165)

Learning organization (p. 183)

Management information system (p. 169)

Nonprogrammed decision (p. 172)

Optimizing decision (p. 178)

Peer-to-peer file sharing (p. 167)

Problem solving (p. 171)

Programmed decision (p. 172)

Risk environment (p. 174)

Satisficing decision (p. 178)

Strategic opportunism (p. 175)

Structured problems (p. 172)

Systematic thinking (p. 175)

Uncertain environment (p. 174)

Unstructured problems (p. 172)

SELF-TEST 7

MULTIPLE-CHOICE QUESTIONS:

1. _____ is the collective brainpower or shared knowledge of an organization and its workforce.
   (a) Artificial intelligence (b) Groupware (c) Intellectual capital (d) Intelligence information

2. _____ are special computer programs that use "if . . . then" rules to help users analyze and solve problems.
   (a) Expert systems (b) Heuristics (c) Intranets (d) Web portals

3. A manager who is reactive and works hard to address problems after they occur is known as a _____.
   (a) problem seeker (b) problem avoider (c) problem solver (d) problem manager

4. When businesses like Amazon.com and Dell.com use the Internet to sell products directly to customers, they are pursuing a form of e-commerce known as _____.
   (a) optimizing (b) B2B (c) B2C (d) networking

5. A problem is a discrepancy between a(n) _____ situation and a desired situation.
   (a) unexpected (b) past (c) actual (d) anticipated

6. A(n) _____ thinker approaches problems in a rational and analytic fashion.
   (a) systematic (b) intuitive (c) internal (d) external

7. The first step in the decision-making process is to _____.
   (a) identify alternatives (b) evaluate results (c) find and define the problem (d) choose a solution

8. Being asked to develop a plan to increase international sales of a product is an example of the types of _____ problems that managers must be prepared to deal with.
   (a) routine (b) unstructured (c) crisis (d) structured

9. Costs, timeliness, and _____ are among the recommended criteria for evaluating alternative courses of action.
   (a) ethical soundness (b) competitiveness (c) availability (d) simplicity

10. The _____ decision model views managers as making optimizing decisions, whereas the _____ decision model views them as making satisficing decisions.
    (a) behavioral, human relations (b) classical, behavioral (c) heuristic, humanistic (d) quantitative, behavioral

11. Top managers in organizations commonly use information to make decisions about _____.
    (a) strategy formulation (b) operational plans (c) day-to-day operations (d) short-term plans

12. Among the ways IT is changing organizations today, _____ is one of its most noteworthy characteristics.
    (a) eliminating the need for top managers (b) reducing the amount of information available for decision making (c) breaking down barriers internally and externally (d) decreasing the need for environmental awareness

13. When a problem is addressed according to the positive or negative context in which it is presented, this is an example of _____.
    (a) framing error (b) escalating commitment (c) availability and adjustment (d) strategic opportunism

14. A manager who asks whether or not the decision will satisfy all stakeholders is using the criterion of _____ to check the ethical soundness of the intended course of action.
    (a) justice (b) rights (c) cost vs. benefit (d) utility

15. Among the environments for managerial decision making, certainty is the most favorable and it can be addressed through _____ decisions.
    (a) programmed (b) risk (c) satisficing (d) intuitive

SHORT-RESPONSE QUESTIONS:

16. What is the difference between an optimizing decision and a satisficing decision?

17. How can a manager double-check the ethics of a decision?

18. How would a manager use systematic thinking and intuitive thinking in problem solving?

19. How can the members of an organization be trained in crisis management?

APPLICATION QUESTION:

20. As a participant in a new "mentoring" program between your university and a local high school, you have volunteered to give a presentation to a class of sophomores on the challenges in the new "electronic office." The goal is to sensitize them to developments in IT and motivate them to take the best advantage of their high school program so as to prepare themselves for the workplace of the future. What will you say to them?

www.wiley.com/college/schermerhorn

8

Planning and controlling

Planning Ahead

After reading Chapter 8, you should be able to answer these questions in your own words.

CHAPTER 8 study questions

1. How do managers plan?

2. What types of plans do managers use?

3. What are the useful planning tools and techniques?

4. What is the control process?

5. What are the common organizational controls?

KINKO'S—KNOW WHAT YOU WANT TO ACCOMPLISH

The next time you visit a Kinko's, look around and consider the operation. Make your visit a trip into both the past and the future. It all started in 1970 when Paul Orfalea, recently graduated from college, decided to put a photocopier, film-processing equipment, and a small selection of stationery supplies in a shop near the University of California at Santa Barbara. He called his business "Kinko's"—the nickname given to him by friends.

In business, timing means a lot, and Orfalea's timing was perfect. Copying was in; he was so busy at times that the photocopier had to be moved out into the street, where customers served themselves. Location counts, too, and there was no better place than next door to a university. What began as a single small shop is now self-proclaimed to be "the world's leading provider of document solutions and business services." Kinko's, recently purchased by Federal Express, employs more than 20,000 "team members" worldwide and operates in more than 1100 locations and nine countries.

Orfalea began with a good idea; the firm he started has never looked back. In fact, Kinko's leadership has been very good at looking ahead. What started as a photocopy business has transformed itself many times in Kinko's continuous march toward the future. Today you'll find Kinko's locations digitally connected, with services ranging from the latest technology for color printing and photo finishing to videoconferencing. Kinko's also offers business customers outsourcing solutions, allowing them to avoid expensive investments in document-processing technology. Using Kinkonet, customers can submit orders from homes or offices to any Kinko's location. Kinkos.com offers further easy access to the firm's wide and growing array of business services. As further trends in technology unfold, one wonders what Kinko's will do next.[1]

Get Connected!

In business and in a career you need to look ahead. Visit *Fortune* or *Business Week* or *The Economist* magazines online to find current business or economic forecasts.

Chapter 8 Learning Preview

The story is that Paul Orfalea got the idea for Kinko's when he saw so many students lining up to use the photocopy machine in his university's library. That's insight—spotting opportunity in one's environment. In Chapter 8 you will learn how managers use planning to help turn insight and opportunity into real performance accomplishments. You will find also that what you learn about planning has important personal applications. And you will learn why the management function of controlling is essential if we are to ensure that things do, in fact, happen according to plans.

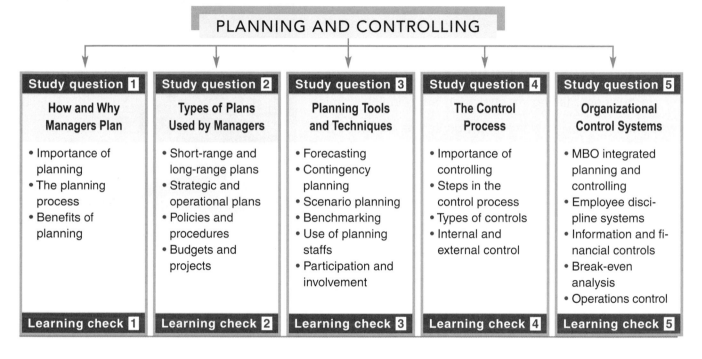

PLANNING AND CONTROLLING

Study question 1

How and Why Managers Plan

- Importance of planning
- The planning process
- Benefits of planning

Learning check 1

Study question 2

Types of Plans Used by Managers

- Short-range and long-range plans
- Strategic and operational plans
- Policies and procedures
- Budgets and projects

Learning check 2

Study question 3

Planning Tools and Techniques

- Forecasting
- Contingency planning
- Scenario planning
- Benchmarking
- Use of planning staffs
- Participation and involvement

Learning check 3

Study question 4

The Control Process

- Importance of controlling
- Steps in the control process
- Types of controls
- Internal and external control

Learning check 4

Study question 5

Organizational Control Systems

- MBO integrated planning and controlling
- Employee discipline systems
- Information and financial controls
- Break-even analysis
- Operations control

Learning check 5

I n his book *Leading the Revolution,*[2] management consultant Gary Hamel argues that many of today's companies won't make it for the long run. "Organizations that succeed in this new century will be as different from industrial-era organizations as those companies themselves were different from craft-based industries," he says. "Companies are going to have to re-invent themselves much more frequently than before.[3] Kinko's seems to be meeting this challenge. Although there are no guarantees about the future, it keeps changing to stay on top of its markets.

Managers need the ability to look ahead, make good plans, and then help others meet the challenges of the future. With the future uncertain, however, the likelihood is that even the best of plans will have to be changed at some point. Thus, managers also need the courage to be flexible in response to new circumstances and the discipline to maintain control even as situations become hectic and the performance pressures stay unrelenting. In the ever-changing technology industry, for example, CEO T. J. Rodgers of Cypress Semiconductor Corp. is known for valuing both performance goals and accountability. Cypress employees work with clear and quantified work goals, which they help set. Rodgers believes the system helps find problems before they interfere with performance. He says:

"Managers monitor the goals, look for problems, and expect people who fall behind to ask for help before they lose control of or damage a major project."[4]

HOW AND WHY MANAGERS PLAN

In Chapter 1 the management process was described as planning, organizing, leading, and controlling the use of resources to achieve performance objectives. The first of these functions, **planning,** sets the stage for the others by providing a sense of direction. It is a process of setting objectives and determining how to best accomplish them. Said a bit differently, planning involves deciding exactly what you want to accomplish and how to best go about it.

○ **Planning** is the process of setting objectives and determining how to accomplish them.

IMPORTANCE OF PLANNING

When planning is done well it creates a solid platform for the other management functions: *organizing*—allocating and arranging resources to accomplish tasks; *leading*—guiding the efforts of human resources to ensure high levels of task accomplishment; and *controlling*—monitoring task accomplishments and taking necessary corrective action.

The centrality of planning in management, as shown in *Figure 8.1,* is important to understand. In today's demanding organizational and career environments it is essential to stay one step ahead of the competition. This involves striving always to become better at what you are doing and to be action oriented. An Eaton Corporation annual report, for example, once stated: "Planning at Eaton means taking the hard decisions before events force them upon you, and anticipating the future needs of the market before the demand asserts itself."[5]

THE PLANNING PROCESS

In the planning process, **objectives** identify the specific results or desired outcomes that one intends to achieve. The **plan** is a statement of action steps to be taken in order to accomplish the objectives. The steps in the systematic planning process include the following:

○ **Objectives** are specific results that one wishes to achieve.

○ A **plan** is a statement of intended means for accomplishing objectives.

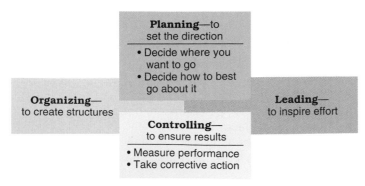

Figure 8.1 The roles of planning and controlling in the management process.

Five steps in the planning process

1. *Define your objectives:* Identify desired outcomes or results in very specific ways. Know where you want to go; be specific enough that you will know you have arrived when you get there, or know how far off the mark you are at various points along the way.

2. *Determine where you stand vis-à-vis objectives:* Evaluate current accomplishments relative to the desired results. Know where you stand in reaching the objectives; know what strengths work in your favor and what weaknesses may hold you back.

3. *Develop premises regarding future conditions:* Try to anticipate future events. Generate alternative "scenarios" for what may happen; identify for each scenario things that may help or hinder progress toward your objectives.

4. *Analyze and choose among action alternatives:* List and carefully evaluate the possible actions that may be taken. Choose the alternative(s) most likely to accomplish your objectives; describe step by step what must be done to follow the chosen course of action.

5. *Implement the plan and evaluate results:* Take action and carefully measure your progress toward objectives. Do what the plan requires; evaluate results; take corrective action, and revise plans as needed.

The planning process just described is an application of the decision-making process just discussed in Chapter 7. It is a systematic way to approach two important tasks: (1) setting performance objectives and (2) deciding how to best achieve them. This is not something managers do while working alone in quiet rooms, free from distractions, and at scheduled times. Planning should be ongoing, continuously done even while dealing with an otherwise hectic and demanding work setting.[6] Importantly, the best planning is always done with the active participation and involvement of those people whose work efforts will eventually determine whether or not the objectives are accomplished.

CAREER CONNECTION

Business schools plan better curricula to improve students' ethics

With the ethics scandals of Enron, WorldCom, Andersen, and others in the news, business school faculties are reviewing the role of ethics in their curricula.[7] Some are opting to install required ethics courses, believing that this will ensure that all graduates have a thorough and intensive grounding in ethical thinking. Others are integrating ethics into all courses and functional areas, stressing the need to anchor ethical issues in decision making in all working contexts. Regardless of the approach taken, students and society will surely benefit. One has to wonder, though, about the timing. Wouldn't it have been better if the business schools had better anticipated the emergence of ethical challenges in the modern workplace, planned ahead for them, and put these ethics curricula into place long ago? At least some of the principal players in recent scandals were MBA graduates from top business schools.

BENEFITS OF PLANNING

Organizations in today's dynamic times are facing pressures from many sources. Externally, these include ethical expectations, government regulations, ever-more-complex technologies, the uncertainties of a global economy, changing technologies, and the sheer cost of investments in labor, capital, and other supporting resources. Internally, they include the quest for operating efficiencies, new structures and technologies, alternative work arrangements, greater diversity in the workplace, and related managerial challenges. As you would expect, planning in such conditions offers a number of benefits.

Planning Improves Focus and Flexibility

Good planning improves focus and flexibility, both of which are important for performance success. An *organization with focus* knows what it does best, knows the needs of its customers, and knows how to serve them well. An *individual with focus* knows where he or she wants to go in a career or situation, and is able to retain that objective even when difficulties arise. An *organization with flexibility* is willing and able to change and adapt to shifting circumstances and operates with an orientation toward the future rather than the past. An *individual with flexibility* adjusts career plans to fit new and developing opportunities.

Planning Improves Action Orientation

Planning is a way for people and organizations to stay ahead of the competition and always become better at what they are doing. It helps avoid the complacency trap of simply being carried along by the flow of events or being distracted by successes or failures of the moment. It keeps the future visible as a performance target and reminds us that the best decisions are often made before events force them upon us.

Management consultant Stephen R. Covey talks about the importance of priorities. He points out that the most successful executives "zero in on what they do that 'adds value' to an organization." Instead of working on too many things, they work on the things that really count. Corey says that good planning makes us more (1) *results oriented*—creating a performance-oriented sense of direction; (2) *priority oriented*—making sure the most important things get first attention; (3) *advantage oriented*—ensuring that all resources are used to best advantage; and (4) *change oriented*—anticipating problems and opportunities so they can be best dealt with.[9]

www.army.mil/

Continuous improvement is a priority with the U.S. Army. In the After-Action Review program, training exercises are videotaped and results are peer reviewed, with participants commenting on one another's performances. Expert observers give immediate feedback.

Planning Improves Coordination

Planning improves coordination. The many different individuals, groups, and subsystems in organizations are each doing many different things at the same time. But even as they pursue their specific tasks and objectives, their accomplishments must add up to meaningful contributions to the needs of the organization as a whole. Good planning throughout an organization creates a **means-ends chain** or *hierarchy of objectives* in which lower-level objectives lead to the accomplishment of higher-level ones. Higher-level objectives as *ends* are directly tied to

○ In a **means-ends chain,** lower-level objectives help accomplish higher-level ones.

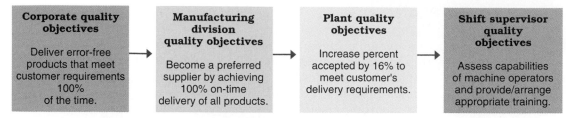

Figure 8.2 A sample means-ends chain for total quality management.

lower-level objectives as the *means* for their accomplishment. *Figure 8.2* uses the example of quality management to show how a means-ends chain helps guide and integrate quality efforts within a large manufacturing firm.

Planning Improves Time Management

One of the side benefits that planning offers is better time management. Lewis Platt, former chairman of Hewlett-Packard, says: "Basically, the whole day is a series of choices."[10] These choices have to be made in ways that allocate your time to the most important priorities. Platt says that he was "ruthless about priorities" and that you "have to continually work to optimize your time."

Most of us have experienced the difficulties of balancing available time with the many commitments and opportunities we would like to fulfill. It is easy to lose track of time and fall prey to what consultants identify as "time wasters." Too many of us allow our time to be dominated by other people and/or by nonessential activities.[11] "To do" lists can help, but they have to contain the right things. In daily living and in management, it is important to distinguish between things that you *must do* (top priority), *should do* (high priority), would be *nice to do* (low priority), and really *don't need to do* (no priority).

Planning Improves Control

When planning is done well it facilitates control, making it easier to measure performance results and take action to improve things as necessary. Planning helps make this possible by defining the objectives along with the specific actions through which they are to be pursued. If results are less than expected, either the objectives or the action being taken, or both, can be evaluated and then adjusted in the control process. In this way planning and controlling work closely together in the management process. Without planning, control lacks a framework for measuring how well things are going and what could be done to make them go better. Without control, planning lacks the follow-through needed to ensure that things work out as planned.

Learning check 1

Be sure you can • define planning as a management function • list the steps in the formal planning process • illustrate the benefits of planning for a business or organization that is familiar to you • illustrate the benefits of planning for personal career development

TYPES OF PLANS USED BY MANAGERS

Managers face different planning challenges in the flow and pace of activities in organizations. In some cases the planning environment is stable and quite predictable; in others it is more dynamic and uncertain. A variety of plans are available to meet these different needs.

SHORT-RANGE AND LONG-RANGE PLANS

A rule of thumb is that *short-range plans* cover one year or less, *intermediate-range plans* cover one to two years, and *long-range plans* look three or more years into the future. Top management is most likely to be involved in setting long-range plans and directions for the organization as a whole, while lower management levels focus more on short-run plans that help achieve long-term objectives. But everyone should understand an organization's long-term plans. In the absence of a hierarchy of objectives tied to a long-range plan, there is always risk that the pressures of daily events may create confusion and divert attention from important tasks. In other words, without a sense of long-term direction, people can end up working hard but without achieving significant results.

Management researcher Elliot Jaques suggests that people vary in their capability to think out, organize, and work through events of different time horizons.[13] In fact, he believes that most people work comfortably with only three-month time spans; a smaller group works well with a one-year span; and only about one person in several million can handle a 20-year time frame. These are provocative ideas. Although a team leader's planning challenges may rest mainly in the weekly or monthly range, a chief executive is expected to have a vision extending several years into the future. Career progress to higher management levels requires the conceptual skills to work well with longer-range time frames.[14]

Complexities and uncertainties in today's environments are putting pressure on these planning horizons. In an increasingly global economy, planning opportunities and challenges are often worldwide in scope, not just local. And, of course, the information age is ever present in its planning implications. We now talk about planning in *Internet time,* where businesses are continually changing and updating plans. Even top managers now face the reality that Internet time keeps making the "long" range of planning shorter and shorter.

STRATEGIC AND OPERATIONAL PLANS

○ A **strategic plan** identifies long-term directions for the organization.

Plans differ not only in time horizons but also in scope. **Strategic plans** set broad, comprehensive, and longer-term action directions. Strategic planning by top management involves determining objectives for the entire organization, describing what and where it wants to be in the future. There was a time, for example, when many large businesses strategically sought to diversify into unrelated areas. A successful oil firm might have acquired an office products company or a successful cereal manufacturer might have acquired an apparel company. In the next chapter on strategic management we will examine the process through which such strategic choices are made and how they can be analyzed. For now, suffice it to say that diversification strategies haven't always proved successful. Many companies following them have since reversed course, choosing instead to strategically focus on core areas of expertise.

○ An **operational plan** identifies activities to implement strategic plans.

Operational plans define what needs to be done in specific functions or work units to implement strategic plans. Typical operational plans in a business firm include: *production plans*—dealing with the methods and technology needed by people in their work; *financial plans*—dealing with money required to support various operations; *facilities plans*—dealing with facilities and work layouts *marketing plans*—dealing with the requirements of selling and distributing goods or services; and *human resource plans*—dealing with the recruitment, selection, and placement of people into various jobs.

REALITY ✓
CHECK 8.1

Low-fare airlines are beating other carriers.
No-frills airlines like Ireland's Ryanair are driving their competitors crazy. By eliminating free beverages and food, the cost savings offset the equivalent of flying with 15 empty seats. Take the online "Reality Check" to find out more about how LFAs save costs and boost profits.

POLICIES AND PROCEDURES

○ A **policy** is a standing plan that communicates broad guidelines for decisions and action.

Among the many plans in organizations, *standing plans* in the form of organizational policies and procedures are designed for use over and over again. A **policy** communicates broad guidelines for making decisions and taking action in specific circumstances. For example, typical human resource policies address such matters as employee hiring, termination, performance appraisals, pay increases, promotions, and discipline. Another policy area of special organizational consequence is sexual harassment. Enlightened employers take great pains to clearly spell out their policies on sexual harassment and the methods for implementing them. When Judith Nitsch started her own engineering consulting business, for example, she defined a sexual harassment policy, took a hard line in its enforcement, and appointed both a male and a female employee for others to talk with about sexual harassment concerns.[15]

○ A **procedure** or **rule** precisely describes actions that are to be taken in specific situations.

Rules or **procedures** describe exactly what actions are to be taken in specific situations. They are often found stated in employee handbooks or manuals as "SOPs"—standard operating procedures. Whereas a policy sets a broad guideline for action, procedures define precise actions to be taken. In the prior example, Judith Nitsch will want to put in place procedures that ensure everyone receives fair, equal, and nondiscriminatory treatment under the sexual harassment policy. Everyone should know how to file a sexual harassment complaint and how that complaint will be handled.

BUDGETS AND PROJECTS

In contrast to standing plans, *single-use plans* are used once, serving the needs and objectives of well-defined situations in a timely manner. **Budgets** are single-use plans that commit resources to activities, projects, or programs. They are powerful tools that allocate scarce resources among multiple and often competing uses. Good managers are able to bargain for and obtain adequate budgets to support the needs of their work units or teams. They also achieve performance objectives while keeping within the allocated budget.

> O A **budget** is a plan that commits resources to projects or activities.

A *fixed budget* allocates a fixed amount of resources for a specific purpose. For example, a manager may have a $25,000 budget for equipment purchases in a given year. A *flexible budget* allows the allocation of resources to vary in proportion with various levels of activity. For example, a manager may have flexibility to hire extra temporary workers if production orders exceed a certain volume.

A common problem with budgets is that resource allocations get "rolled over" from one budgeting period to the next, often without a rigorous performance review. A **zero-based budget** deals with this problem by approaching each new budget period as it if were brand new. There is no guarantee that any past funding will be renewed; all proposals compete anew for available funds at the start of each new budget cycle. In a major division of Campbell Soups, for example, managers using zero-based budgeting once discovered that 10 percent of the marketing budget was going to sales promotions no longer relevant to current product lines.

> O A **zero-based budget** allocates resources as if each budget was brand new.

A lot of work in organizations takes the form of **projects,** one-time activities that have clear beginning and end points. Examples are the completion of a new student activities building on a campus, the development of a new computer software program, or the implementation of a new advertising campaign for a sports team. **Project management** involves making sure that the activities required to complete a project are completed on time, within budget, and in ways that otherwise meet objectives. Managers of projects make extensive use of *project schedules* that define specific task objectives, link activities to be accomplished with due dates, and identify the amounts and time of resource requirements.

> O **Projects** are one-time activities that have clear beginning and end points.

> O **Project management** makes sure that activities required to complete a project are accomplished on time and correctly.

PLANNING TOOLS AND TECHNIQUES

The benefits of planning are best realized when the foundations are strong. The useful tools and techniques of managerial planning include forecasting, contingency planning, scenarios, benchmarking, participative planning, and the use of staff planners.

FORECASTING

O **Forecasting** attempts to predict the future.

Forecasting is the process of predicting what will happen in the future.[16] All plans involve forecasts of some sort. Periodicals such as *Business Week, Fortune,* and *The Economist* regularly report forecasts of economic conditions, interest rates, unemployment, and trade deficits, among other issues. Some are based on *qualitative forecasting,* which uses expert opinions to predict the future. Others involve *quantitative forecasting,* which uses mathematical models and statistical analysis of historical data and surveys to predict future events. Although useful, all forecasts should be treated cautiously. They are planning aids, not substitutes. It is said that a music agent once told Elvis Presley: "You ought to go back to driving a truck because you ain't going nowhere." He was obviously mistaken. That's the problem with forecasts—they can be wrong. In the final analysis forecasting always relies on human judgment. Planning involves deciding what to do about the implications of forecasts once they are made.

CONTINGENCY PLANNING

Planning by definition involves thinking ahead. But the more uncertain the planning environment, the more likely that one's original assumptions, forecasts, and intentions may prove inadequate or wrong.

AROUND THE WORLD

There may be more to competition than meets the eye

Coke and Pepsi spend hundreds of millions of dollars on advertising as they engage one another in the ongoing "Cola War." It may seem that they have nothing to worry about but each other and a few discounters. Not so. There is an ever-changing world out there, and more than 50 percent of their revenues come internationally. Now factor into the planning equation current events, and what do you get? Mecca Cola and Qibla Cola for one thing! Both new colas entered European markets riding a wave of resentment of U.S. brands and multinationals. The founder of Qibla says: "By choosing to boycott major brands, consumers are sending an important signal: that the exploitation of Muslims cannot continue unchecked."[17] Although Coke and Pepsi may have little to fear from these competitors, the emerging international consumer voice has to be heard inside the executive suites of all multinational companies.

Contingency planning identifies alternative courses of action that can be implemented to meet the needs of changing circumstances. Although one can't always predict when things will go wrong, it can be anticipated that they will. It is highly unlikely that any plan will ever be perfect; changes in the environment will sooner or later occur, as will crises and emergencies. And when they do, the best managers and organizations have contingency plans ready to be implemented. Contingency plans contain "trigger points" that indicate when preselected alternative plans should be activated.

○ **Contingency planning** identifies alternative courses of action to take when things go wrong.

SCENARIO PLANNING

A long-term version of contingency planning, called **scenario planning,** involves identifying several alternative future scenarios or states of affairs that may occur. Plans are then made to deal with each should it actually occur.[18] At Royal Dutch/Shell scenario planning began years ago when top managers asked themselves a perplexing question: "What would Shell do after its oil supplies ran out?" Identifying different possible scenarios ahead of time helps organizations like Shell plan ahead to make major adjustments in strategies and operations. Although recognizing that scenario planning can never be inclusive of all future possibilities, a Shell executive once said that it helps "condition the organization to think" and better prepare for "future shocks." At Shell this meant planning for such issues as climate change, sustainable development, human rights, and biodiversity, among others.[19]

○ **Scenario planning** identifies alternative future scenarios and makes plans to deal with each.

BENCHMARKING

All too often planners become too comfortable with the ways things are going and overconfident that the past is a good indicator of the future. Successful planning must challenge the status quo; it cannot simply accept things as they are. One way to do this is through **benchmarking,** a technique that makes use of external comparisons to better evaluate one's current performance and identify possible actions for the future.[20] The purpose of benchmarking is to find out what other people and organizations are doing very well, and plan how to incorporate these ideas into one's own operations. One benchmarking technique is to search for **best practices,** those things done by competitors and noncompetitors alike that help them to achieve superior performance. This powerful planning technique is a way for progressive companies to learn from other "excellent" companies. The best-run organizations also emphasize internal benchmarking that encourages all members and work units to learn and improve by sharing one another's best practices.

○ **Benchmarking** uses external comparisons to gain insights for planning.

○ **Best practices** are things that lead to superior performance.

USE OF STAFF PLANNERS

As organizations grow, there is a corresponding need to increase the sophistication of the planning system itself. In some cases, staff planners are employed to help coordinate planning for the organization as a whole or for one of its major components. These planning specialists are skilled in all steps of the planning process, as well as planning tools and techniques. They can help bring focus and energy to accomplish important, often strategic, planning tasks. But one risk is a tendency for a communication "gap" to develop between staff planners and line managers. Unless everyone works closely together, the resulting plans may be inadequate and people may lack commitment to implement the plans no matter how good they are.

PARTICIPATION AND INVOLVEMENT

○ **Participatory planning** includes the persons who will be affected by plans and/or who will implement them.

"Participation" is a key word in the planning process. **Participatory planning** includes in all planning steps the people who will be affected by the plans and/or who will be asked to help implement them. This process, as shown in *Figure 8.3*, brings to the organization many benefits. Participation can increase the creativity and information available for planning. It can also increase the understanding and acceptance of plans, as well as commitment to their success. Even though participatory planning takes more time, it can improve results by improving implementation. When 7-Eleven executives planned for new "up-scale" products and services such as selling fancy meals-to-go, they received a hard lesson. Although their ideas sounded good at the top, franchisees balked at the shop level. The executives learned the value of taking time to involve franchise owners in the process of planning new corporate strategies.[21]

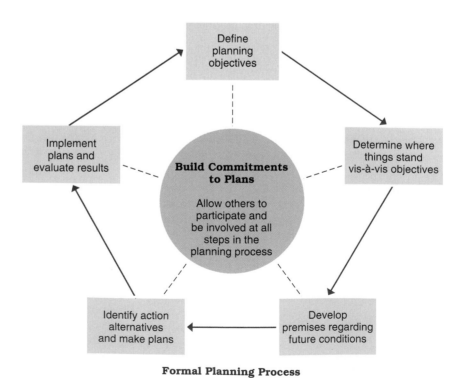

Formal Planning Process

Figure 8.3 How participation and involvement help build commitments to plans.

Be sure you can • define the terms "forecasting," "contingency planning," "scenario planning," and "benchmarking" • explain the value of contingency planning and scenario planning • explain the concept of participatory planning and defend its importance in organizations today

Learning check 3

THE CONTROL PROCESS

"Keeping in touch . . . Staying informed . . . Being in control." In addition to planning, these are important responsibilities for every manager. But "control" is a word like "power." If you aren't careful when it is used, it leaves a negative connotation. But control plays a positive and necessary role in the management process. To have things "under control" is good; for things to be "out of control" is generally bad.

IMPORTANCE OF CONTROLLING

In the management process, **controlling** is a process of measuring performance and taking action to ensure desired results. Its purpose is straightforward—to make sure that plans are achieved, that actual performance meets or surpasses objectives. The foundation of control is information. Henry Schacht, former CEO of Cummins Engine Company, once discussed control in terms of what he called "friendly facts." He stated, "Facts that reinforce what you are doing . . . are nice, because they help in terms of psychic reward. Facts that raise alarms are equally friendly, because they give you clues about how to respond, how to change, where to spend the resources."[22]

> **Controlling** is the process of measuring performance and taking action to ensure desired results.

If you refer back to Figure 8.1, it shows how controlling fits in with the other management functions. Planning sets the directions and allocates resources. Organizing brings people and material resources together in working combinations. Leading inspires people to best utilize these resources. Controlling sees to it that the right things happen, in the right way, and at the right time. It helps ensure that performance by individuals and groups is consistent with plans. It helps ensure that accomplishments throughout an organization are coordinated in means–ends fashion. And, it helps ensure that people comply with organizational policies and procedures.

Effective control is also important to organizational learning. It offers the great opportunity of learning from experience. Consider, for example, the program of **after-action review** pioneered by the U.S. Army and now utilized in many corporate settings. This is a structured review of lessons learned and results accomplished on a completed project, task force, or special operation. Participants are asked to answer questions like: "What was the intent?" "What actually happened?" "What did we learn?"[23] The review helps make continuous improvement a part of the organizational culture. It encourages everyone involved to take responsibility for their performance efforts and accomplishments.

> An **after-action review** identifies lessons learned in a completed project, task force, or special operation.

STEPS IN THE CONTROL PROCESS

The process of management control involves the four steps shown in *Figure 8.4*: (1) establish objectives and standards; (2) measure actual perfor-

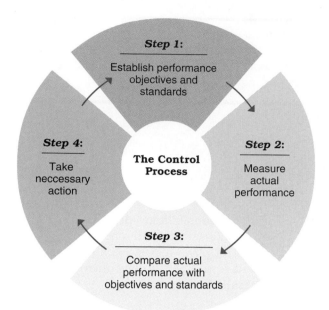

Figure 8.4 Four steps in the control process.

mance; (3) compare results with objectives and standards; and (4) take corrective action as needed. While essential to management, the process applies equally well to personal affairs and careers. Think about it. Without career objectives, how do you know where you really want to go? How can you allocate your time and other resources to take best advantage of available opportunities? Without measurement, how can you assess any progress being made? How can you adjust current behavior to improve prospects for future results?

Step 1: Establish Objectives and Standards

The control process begins with planning, when performance objectives and standards for measuring them are set. It can't start without them. Performance objectives should represent key results that one wants to accomplish. The word "key" in the prior sentence is important. The focus in planning should be on describing "critical" or "essential" results that will make a substantial difference in the success of the organization. Standards are important too. As key results are identified, one also has to specify the standards and measures that will be used to evaluate their accomplishment. Allstate Corporation, for example, has used a "diversity index" to quantify performance on diversity issues. The standards include how well employees meet goals of bias-free customer service, and how well managers meet diversity expectations.[24]

○ An **output standard** measures performance results in terms of quantity, quality, cost, or time.

○ An **input standard** measures work efforts that go into a performance task.

In the control process, **output standards** measure performance results in terms of outcomes like quantity, quality, cost, or time of accomplished work. Allstate's use of the diversity index to rate managerial behavior is one example; others include percentage error rate, dollar deviation from budgeted expenditures, and the number of units produced or customers serviced in a time period. **Input standards,** by contrast, measure effort in terms of the amount of work expended in task performance. They are used in situations where outputs are difficult or expensive to measure. Examples of input standards include conformance to rules and procedures, efficiency in the use of resources, and work attendance or punctuality.

Professional management brings stronger controls

Colorado ski maker Volant Skis, Inc., founded by Hank and Bucky Kashiwa, was in trouble when consultant Mark Soderberg was hired. Half-finished skis were stacked everywhere; up to 40 percent of a day's production was being scrapped. Customers were dissatisfied with unfilled orders. Soderberg's approach was to admit the facts, stop production, analyze systems, and address quality problems. Within two years, orders were flowing again and production was smooth and efficient. As quality went up, costs went down. And with the ski business under control, management was able to consider strategic moves to counter the seasonality of skis, such as entering the golf or biking markets.[25]

Step 2: Measure Actual Performance

The second step in the control process is to measure actual performance. The goal is to accurately measure the performance results (output standards) and/or the performance efforts (input standards). Measurement must be accurate enough to spot significant differences between what is really taking place and what was originally planned. Without it, effective control is not possible. When Linda Sanford was appointed head of IBM's sales force, she came with an admirable performance record earned during a 22-year career with the company. Notably, Sanford grew up on a family farm, where she developed an appreciation for measuring results. "At the end of the day, you saw what you did, knew how many rows of strawberries you picked." At IBM she was known for walking around the factory just to see "at the end of the day how many machines were going out of the back dock."[26]

Step 3: Compare Results with Objectives and Standards

Step 3 in the control process is to compare objectives with results. This step can be expressed as the following *control equation:* Need for action = Desired performance − Actual performance. Sometimes managers make a *historical comparison,* using past performance as a basis for evaluating current performance. A *relative comparison* uses the performance achievements of other persons, work units, or organizations as the evaluation benchmarks. An *engineering comparison* uses standards set scientifically through such methods as time and motion studies. The delivery routines of UPS drivers, for example, are carefully measured in terms of expected minutes per delivery on various routes.

Step 4: Take Corrective Action

The final step in the control process is to take any action necessary to correct problems or make improvements. **Management by exception** is the practice of giving attention to situations that show the greatest need for action. It can save valuable time, energy, and other resources by focusing attention on high-priority areas. Managers should be alert to two types of exceptions. The first is a *problem situation* in which actual performance is below the standard. The reasons for this must be understood so corrective action can restore performance to the desired level. The second is an *opportunity situation* in which actual performance is above the standard. The

o **Management by exception** focuses attention on substantial differences between actual and desired performance.

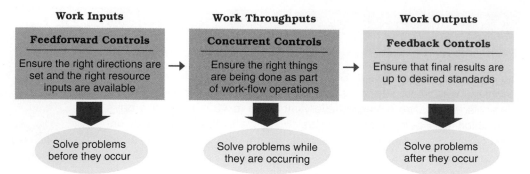

Figure 8.5 The role of feedforward, concurrent, and feedback controls in organizations.

reasons for this must also be understood, with the goal of continuing high level of accomplishment in the future.

TYPES OF CONTROLS

Figure 8.5 shows three major types of managerial controls—feedforward, concurrent, and feedback.[27] Each equates to a different phase of the organization's input-throughput-output cycle. And each offers significant opportunities for taking action to ensure high performance.

Feedforward Controls

○ **Feedforward control** ensures that directions and resources are right before the work begins.

Feedforward controls, also called *preliminary controls,* take place before a work activity begins. They ensure that objectives are clear, that proper directions are established, and that the right resources are available to accomplish them. Feedforward controls are preventive in nature. The goal is to solve problems before they occur by asking an important but often-neglected question: "What needs to be done before we begin?" This is a forward-thinking and proactive approach to control. At McDonald's, for example, preliminary control of food ingredients plays an important role in the firm's quality program. The company requires that suppliers of its hamburger buns produce them to exact specifications, covering everything from texture to uniformity of color. Even in overseas markets, the firm works hard to develop local suppliers that can offer dependable quality.[28]

Concurrent Controls

○ **Concurrent control** focuses on what happens during the work process.

Concurrent controls focus on what happens during the work process. Sometimes called *steering controls,* they make sure things are being done according to plan. The goal is to solve problems as they are occurring. The key question is "What can we do to improve things right now? At McDonald's, ever-present shift leaders provide concurrent control through direct supervision. They constantly observe what is taking place even while helping out with the work. They are trained to intervene immediately when something is not done right and to correct things on the spot. Detailed instruction manuals also "steer" workers in the right directions as their jobs are performed.

TAKE IT TO THE CASE!

Wal-Mart Stores, Inc.
Self-management works at the number-one retailer

Numbers count at Wal-Mart, a firm that takes its financial performance very seriously. Top management at the firm founded by Sam Walton has to; that's part of the deal when you're number one in a global industry. And that company has no intention of resting on its past laurels. A recent observer says: "Wal-Mart is gaining momentum. This fast company is becoming a faster company. Wal-Mart grows a Fortune 100 corporation each year. The company's is as strong as ever." Nancy Handley once supervised the men's department at a suburban St. Louis Wal-Mart store. She put in long hours but liked the responsibility and recognition that came with the job. "I'm proud of who I've made myself into and the department I've created," she said.[30]

Feedback Controls

Feedback controls, also called *postaction controls,* take place after work is completed. They focus on the quality of end results rather than on inputs and activities. The goals are to solve problems after they occur and prevent future ones. They ask the question "Now that we are finished, how well did we do?" Restaurants, for example, ask how you liked a meal . . . after it is eaten; final course evaluations tell instructors how well they performed . . . after the course is over; a budget summary identifies cost overruns . . . after a project is completed. In these and other circumstances the feedback provided by the control process is useful information for improving things in the future.

○ **Feedback control** takes place after an action is completed.

INTERNAL AND EXTERNAL CONTROL

Managers have two broad options with respect to control. They can rely on people to control their own behavior. This strategy of **internal control** allows motivated individuals and groups to exercise self-discipline in fulfilling job expectations. Alternatively, managers can take direct action to control the behavior of others. This strategy of **external control** occurs through personal supervision and the use of formal administrative systems. Effective control typically involves a combination of both. However, the new workplace with its emphasis on participation, empowerment, and involvement places increased reliance on internal control.

○ **Internal control** occurs through self-discipline and self-control.

○ **External control** occurs through direct supervision or administrative systems.

An internal control strategy requires a high degree of trust. When people are expected to work on their own and exercise self-control, managers must give them the freedom to do so. According to Douglas McGregor's Theory Y perspective, introduced in Chapter 2, people are ready and willing to exercise self-control in their work.[29] But he also points out that they are most likely to do this when they participate in setting performance objectives and standards. Furthermore, the potential for self-control is increased when capable people have a clear sense of organizational mission, know their goals, and have the resources necessary to do their jobs well. It is also enhanced by participative organizational cultures in which everyone treats each other with respect and consideration.

Be sure you can • define controlling as a management function • list the steps in the control process • explain where and why planning is important to controlling • explain the difference between output standards and input standards • illustrate how a fast-food restaurant utilizes three types of controls—feedforward, concurrent, and feedback • explain the difference between internal control and external control

ORGANIZATIONAL CONTROL

Organizations benefit from the use of comprehensive and systemwide controls. Among the approaches are management by objectives, employee discipline systems, information and financial analysis, break-even analysis, and the techniques of operations management.

MBO: INTEGRATED PLANNING AND CONTROLLING

○ **MBO** is a process of joint objective setting between a superior and subordinate.

A useful technique for integrating planning and controlling in day-today practice is **management by objectives (MBO).** This is a structured process of regular communication in which a supervisor/team leader and subordinates/team members jointly set performance objectives and review results accomplished.[31] As shown in *Figure 8.6,* MBO creates an agreement between the two parties regarding (1) performance objectives for a given time period, (2) plans through which they will be accomplished, (3) standards for measuring whether they have been accomplished, and (4) procedures for reviewing performance results. Both parties work closely together to fulfill the terms of the agreement.

Performance Objectives in MBO

The way objectives are described and how they are established will both influence the success of MBO. Three types of objectives may be specified in an MBO contract. *Improvement objectives* document intentions for improving performance in a specific way. An example is "to reduce quality rejects by 10 percent." *Personal development objectives* pertain to personal growth activities, often those resulting in expanded job knowledge or

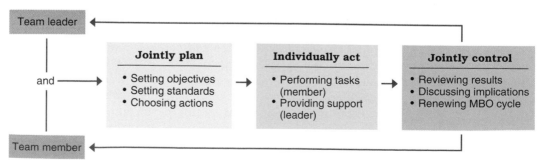

Figure 8.6 Management by objectives as an integrated planning and control framework.

skills. An example is "to learn the latest version of a computer spreadsheet package." Some MBO contracts also include *maintenance objectives* that formally express intentions to maintain performance at an existing level. In all cases, performance objectives in MBO are written and formally agreed upon. They also meet the following four *criteria of a good performance objective:*

1. *Specific*—targets a key result to be accomplished.
2. *Time defined*—identifies a date for achieving results.
3. *Challenging*—offers a realistic and attainable challenge.
4. *Measurable*—is as specific and quantitative as possible.

← Criteria of a good performance objective

One of the more difficult aspects of MBO relates to the last criterion—the need to state performance objectives as specifically and quantitatively as possible. Ideally this involves agreement on a *measurable end product,* for example: "to reduce housekeeping supply costs by 5 percent by the end of the fiscal year." But performance in some jobs, particularly managerial ones, is hard to quantify. Rather than abandon MBO in such cases, it is often possible to agree on performance objectives that are stated as *verifiable work activities*. The accomplishment of the activities serves as an indicator of progress under the performance objective. An example is "to improve communications with my subordinates in the next three months by holding weekly group meetings." Whereas it can be difficult to measure "improved communications," it is easy to document whether the "weekly group meetings" have been held.

MBO Pros and Cons

MBO is one of the most talked about and debated management concepts.[32] As a result, good advice is available. Things to avoid include tying MBO to pay, focusing too much attention on easy objectives, requiring excessive paperwork, and having supervisors simply *tell* subordinates their objectives. The advantages are also clear. MBO focuses workers on the most important tasks and objectives. And it focuses supervisor on areas of support that can truly help their subordinates meet the agreed-upon objectives. Because the process involves direct face-to-face communication, MBO contributes to relationship building. By giving people the opportunity to participate in decisions that affect their work, MBO encourages self-management.[33] One of the things that research is most clear about, in fact, is that participation in goal setting creates motivation to fulfill one's performance obligations.[34]

REALITY CHECK 8.2

Percentage of women as corporate officers
Catalyst reports that 50 of the *Fortune* 500 companies had women holding a quarter or more of the top jobs in 2000, a 100 percent increase since 1995. But 90 companies had none. Take the online "Reality Check" to learn more about women at the top ranks of corporations.

EMPLOYEE DISCIPLINE SYSTEMS

Absenteeism . . . tardiness . . . sloppy work . . . the list of undesirable conduct can go on to even more extreme actions: falsifying records . . . sexual harassment . . . embezzlement. All are examples of behaviors that can and should be formally addressed through **discipline,** the act of influencing behavior through reprimand. When discipline is handled in a fair, consistent, and systematic way, it is a useful form of managerial control. One way to be consistent in disciplinary situations is to remember the "hot stove rules" in *Manager's Notepad 8.1*. They rest on a simple understand-

○ **Discipline** is the act of influencing behavior through reprimand.

MANAGER'S NOTEPAD 8.1

"Hot stove rules" of employee discipline

- A reprimand should be immediate; a hot stove burns the first time you touch it.
- A reprimand should be directed toward someone's actions, not the individual's personality; a hot stove doesn't hold grudges, doesn't try to humiliate people, and doesn't accept excuses.
- A reprimand should be consistently applied; a hot stove burns anyone who touches it, and it does so every time.
- A reprimand should be informative; a hot stove lets a person know what to do to avoid getting burned in the future—"don't touch."
- A reprimand should occur in a supportive setting; a hot stove conveys warmth but with an inflexible rule—"don't touch."
- A reprimand should support realistic rules; the don't-touch-a-hot-stove rule isn't a power play, a whim, or an emotion of the moment; it is a necessary rule of reason.

ing: "When a stove is hot, don't touch it." Everyone knows that when this rule is violated, you get burned—immediately, consistently, but usually not beyond the possibility of repair.[35]

O **Progressive discipline** ties reprimands to the severity and frequency of misbehavior.

Progressive discipline ties reprimands to the severity and frequency of the employee's infractions. Penalties for misbehavior vary according to how significant it is and how often it occurs. The goal is to achieve compliance with organizational expectations through the least extreme reprimand possible. For example, the ultimate penalty of "discharge" would be reserved for the most severe behaviors (e.g., any felony crime) or for repeated infractions of a less severe nature (e.g., being continually late for work and failing to respond to a series of written reprimands and/or suspensions).

INFORMATION AND FINANCIAL CONTROLS

The pressure is ever present for all organizations to use their resources well and to achieve high performance. In business the analysis of a firm's financial performance is an important aspect of managerial control. At a minimum, managers should be able to understand the following financial performance measures: (1) *liquidity*—ability to generate cash to pay bills; (2) *leverage*—ability to earn more in returns than the cost of debt; (3) *asset management*—ability to use resources efficiently and operate at minimum cost; and (4) *profitability*—ability to earn revenues greater than costs.

These financial performance indicators can be assessed using a variety of financial ratios, including those shown in *Manager's Notepad 8.2.* Such ratios provide a framework for historical comparisons within the firm and for external benchmarking relative to industry performance. They can also be used to set financial targets or goals to be shared with employees and tracked to indicate success or failure in

| Popular financial ratios [with preferred directions ↑ or ↓] | MANAGER'S NOTEPAD 8.2 |

Liquidity:

- Current ratio = Current assets/Current liabilities
- ↑ You want more assets and fewer liabilities.

Leverage:

- Debt ratio = Total debts/Total assets
- ↓ You want fewer debts and more assets.

Asset Management:

- Inventory turnover = Sales/Average inventory
- ↑ You want more sales and lower Inventory.

Profitability:

- Net margin = Net profit after taxes/Sales
- Return on investment (ROI) = Net profit after taxes/Total assets
- ↑ You want as much profit as possible.

their accomplishment. At Civco Medical Instruments, for example, a financial scorecard is distributed monthly to all employees. They always know factually how well the firm is doing. This helps them focus on what they can do differently and better, and strengthens personal commitments to future improvements in the firm's "bottom line."[36]

BREAK-EVEN ANALYSIS

A very common method for maintaining control over business operations is **break-even analysis**—the calculation of the point at which sales revenues are sufficient to cover costs. The graph in *Figure 8.7* shows the *break-even point* where losses end and one begins to make a profit. Obviously, the lower the break-even point, the better; the further one moves beyond the break-even point in actual performance, the better. A break-even point (BEP) is calculated by dividing total fixed costs (FC) by price (P) minus variable costs (VC). The formula is: BEP = FC/(P − VC).

Managers use break-even analysis in many ways. A very common situation is for someone in a firm to propose a new product or a new program initiative. Before giving approval, higher managers often ask: "What is your break-even point?" Familiarity with basic accounting principles is helpful in performing the analysis required to answer this question. For example, for a proposed new product you can calculate the sales volume required to break even at a targeted pricing point and also examine the impact of measures to control costs. Set up a spreadsheet with the target price of $8 per unit, fixed costs of $10,000, and variable costs of $4 per unit. According to the formula, the break-even point for these numbers is 2500 units. But if you can reduce the variable costs to $3 per unit, the break-even point falls to 2000 units, allowing you to earn profits much earlier in the cycle. Try experimenting with

○ **Break-even analysis** calculates the point at which sales revenues cover costs.

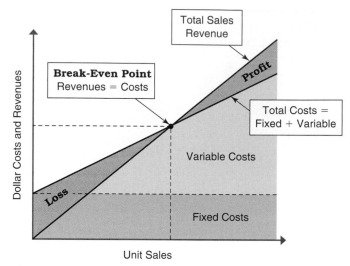

Figure 8.7 Graphical approach to break-even analysis.

different "what-if" scenarios on your spreadsheet. This is exactly the type of analysis that will be expected of you as a matter of routine in business.

OPERATIONS MANAGEMENT AND CONTROL

Control is integral to operations management, where the emphasis is on the efficient transformation of resource inputs into product or service outputs. The areas of purchasing control, inventory control, and statistical quality control are all operations management priorities.

Purchasing Control

Rising costs of materials are a fact of life in today's economy. Controlling these costs through efficient purchasing management is an important productivity tool. Like any individual, a thrifty organization must be concerned about how much it pays for what it buys. To leverage buying power, more organizations are centralizing purchasing to allow buying in volume. They are focusing on a small number of suppliers with whom they negotiate special contracts, gain quality assurances, and get preferred service. They are also finding ways to work together in supplier–purchaser partnerships. It is now more common, for example, that parts suppliers keep warehouses in their customer's facilities. The customer provides the space; the supplier does the rest. The benefits to the customer are lower purchasing costs and preferred service; the supplier gains an exclusive customer contract and more sales volume.

Inventory Control

Inventory is the amount of materials or products kept in storage. Organizations maintain inventories of raw materials, work in process, and finished goods. The goal of inventory control is to make sure that an inventory is just the right size to meet performance needs, thus minimizing the cost. The **economic order quantity** (EOQ) method of inventory control involves ordering a fixed number of items every time an inventory level falls to a predetermined point. When this point is reached, a decision is auto-

www.shrm.org/

The Society for Human Resource Management reports that up to 25 percent of job applications and résumés contain errors. It is always important to check the references of job applicants to make sure that you get the right person to fill openings.

○ Inventory control by **economic order quantity** orders replacements whenever inventory level falls to a predetermined point.

matically made (typically by computer) to place a standard order to replenish the stock. The order sizes are mathematically calculated to minimize costs of inventory. The best example is the local supermarket, where hundreds of daily orders are routinely made on this basis. Another approach to inventory control is **just-in-time scheduling** (JIT), made popular by the Japanese. JIT systems reduce costs and improve workflow by scheduling materials to arrive at a workstation or facility "just in time" to be used. Because almost no inventories are maintained, the just-in-time approach is an important productivity tool.

○ **Just-in-time scheduling** minimizes inventory by routing materials to workstations "just in time" to be used.

Statistical Quality Control

Consistent with the total quality management theme in today's workplace, the practice of **quality control** involves checking processes, materials, products, and services to ensure that they meet high standards. This responsibility applies to all aspects of operations, from the selection of raw materials and supplies right down to the last task performed to deliver the finished good or service. In *statistical quality control,* the process is supported by rigorous statistical analysis. Typically this means taking samples of work, measuring quality in the samples, and then determining the acceptability of results. Unacceptable results in a sample trigger the need for investigation and corrective action. The power of statistics allows the sampling to be efficiently used as the basis for decision making. At General Electric, for example, a Six Sigma program means that statistically the firm's quality performance will tolerate no more than 3.4 defects per million—a perfection rate of 99.9997 percent! As tough as it sounds, "Six Sigma" is a common quality standard for the new workplace.

○ **Quality control** checks processes, materials, products, and services to ensure that they meet high standards.

| Learning check 5 | *Be sure you can* • define the term "management by objectives" • illustrate how MBO operates in the relationship between a team leader and a team member • explain how a progressive discipline system operates • name the common financial ratios used in organizational control • complete a break-even analysis • define the terms "economic order quantity" and "just-in-time delivery" • explain the importance of purchasing control, inventory control, and statistical quality control in organizations |

CHAPTER 8 STUDY GUIDE

Where We've Been

BACK TO KINKO'S

The opening example of Kinko's showed how planning and the willingness to set stretch goals lead to business success. It also showed the importance of staying in touch with an ever-changing environment and updating plans to keep pace with new opportunities. In Chapter 8 you learned about planning and controlling as management functions. You learned about the different types of plans, as well as the important planning tools and techniques. You also learned how control systems facilitate organizational performance. Importantly, you have also gained awareness of how planning and controlling can help with your personal affairs and career development.

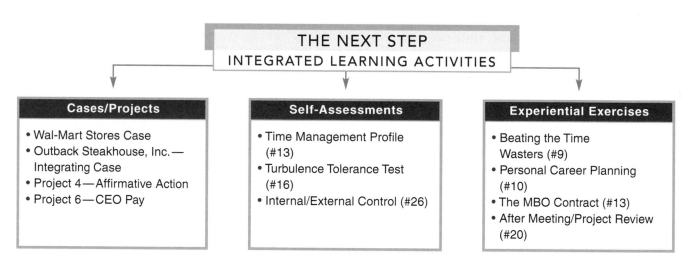

THE NEXT STEP
INTEGRATED LEARNING ACTIVITIES

Cases/Projects	Self-Assessments	Experiential Exercises
• Wal-Mart Stores Case • Outback Steakhouse, Inc.—Integrating Case • Project 4—Affirmative Action • Project 6—CEO Pay	• Time Management Profile (#13) • Turbulence Tolerance Test (#16) • Internal/External Control (#26)	• Beating the Time Wasters (#9) • Personal Career Planning (#10) • The MBO Contract (#13) • After Meeting/Project Review (#20)

STUDY QUESTIONS SUMMARY

1. How do managers plan?

• Planning is the process of setting performance objectives and determining what should be done to accomplish them.

• A plan is a set of intended actions for accomplishing important objectives.

• Planning sets the stage for the other management functions—organizing, leading, and controlling.

• The steps in the planning process are (1) define your objectives, (2) determine where you stand vis-à-vis objectives, (3) develop your premises regarding future conditions, (4) identify and choose among alternative ways of accomplishing objectives, and (5) implement action plans and evaluate results.

• The benefits of planning include better focus and flexibility, action orientation, coordination, control, and time management.

2. What types of plans do managers use?

• Short-range plans tend to cover a year or less, while long-range plans extend up to five years or more.

• Strategic plans set critical long-range directions; operational plans are designed to implement strategic plans.

• Organizational policies, such as a sexual harassment policy, are plans that set guidelines for the behavior of organizational members.

- Organizational procedures and rules are plans that describe actions to be taken in specific situations, such as the steps to be taken when persons believe they have been sexually harassed.
- Organizational budgets are plans that allocate resources to activities or projects.

3. What are the useful planning tools and techniques?

- Forecasting, which attempts to predict what might happen in the future, is a planning aid but not a planning substitute.
- Contingency planning identifies alternative courses of action that can be implemented if and when circumstances change.
- Scenario planning analyzes the implications of alternative versions of the future.
- Planning through benchmarking utilizes external comparisons to identify desirable action directions.
- Participation and involvement open the planning process to valuable inputs from people whose efforts are essential to the effective implementation of plans.

4. What is the control process?

- Controlling is the process of measuring performance and taking corrective action as needed.
- The four steps in the control process are (1) establish performance objectives, (2) measure actual performance, (3) compare results with objectives, (4) take action to resolve problems or explore opportunities.
- Feedforward controls are accomplished before a work activity begins; they ensure that direc-

tions are clear and that the right resources are available to accomplish them.
- Concurrent controls make sure that things are being done correctly; they allow corrective actions to be taken while the work is being done.
- Feedback controls take place after an action is completed; they address the question "Now that we are finished, how well did we do and what did we learn for the future?"
- External control is accomplished through personal supervision and administrative systems.
- Internal control is self-control and occurs as people take personal responsibility for their work.

5. What are the common organizational controls?

- Management by objectives is a process through which supervisors work with their subordinates to "jointly" set performance objectives and review performance results.
- The MBO process is highly participatory and should clarify performance objectives for a subordinate while identifying support that should be provided by a supervisor.
- Discipline is the process of influencing behavior through reprimand; it should be handled in a fair and progressive way.
- Financial control of business performance is facilitated by analysis of financial ratios, such as those dealing with liquidity, assets, and profitability.
- Operations control focuses on efficiencies in purchasing and inventory management, as well as on statistical approaches to quality control.

KEY TERMS REVIEW

After-action review (p. 201)
Benchmarking (p. 199)
Best practices (p. 199)
Break-even analysis (p. 209)
Budget (p. 197)

Concurrent control (p. 204)
Contingency planning (p. 199)
Controlling (p. 201)
Discipline (p. 207)
Economic order quantity (p. 210)

External control (p. 205)
Feedback control (p. 205)
Feedforward control (p. 204)
Forecasting (p. 198)
Input standards (p. 202)

SELF-TEST 8

MULTIPLE-CHOICE QUESTIONS:

1. Planning is the process of _____ and _____.
   (a) developing premises about the future, evaluating them (b) measuring results, taking corrective action (c) measuring past performance, targeting future performance (d) setting objectives, deciding how to accomplish them

2. The benefits of planning include _____.
   (a) improved focus (b) lower labor costs (c) more accurate forecasts (d) guaranteed profits

3. In order to help implement its strategy, a business firm would likely develop a(n) _____ plan for the marketing function.
   (a) IT (b) operational (c) productivity (d) zero-based

4. _____ planning identifies alternative courses of action that can be taken if and when certain situations arise.
   (a) Benchmark (b) Participative (c) Strategic (d) Contingency

5. The first step in the control process is to _____.
   (a) measure actual performance (b) establish objectives and standards (c) compare results with objectives (d) take corrective action

6. The practice of giving attention to situations showing the greatest need for action is called management by _____.
   (a) objectives (b) results (c) efficiency (d) exception

7. A "No Smoking" rule and a sexual harassment policy are examples of _____ plans used by organizations.
   (a) long-range (b) single-use (c) standing-use (d) operational

8. A manager following the "hot stove rules" of progressive discipline would _____.
   (a) avoid giving the employee too much information about what was done wrong (b) stay flexible, reprimanding only at random (c) focus the reprimand on actions, not personality (d) delay reprimands until something positive can also be discussed.

9. Review of an employee's performance accomplishments in an MBO system is done by _____.
   (a) the employee (b) the employee's supervisor (c) the employee and the supervisor (d) the employee, the supervisor, and a lawyer

10. A good performance objective is written in such a way that it _____.
    (a) has no precise timetable (b) is general and not too specific (c) is almost impossible to accomplish (d) can be easily measured

11. When a manager is asked to justify a new budget proposal on the basis of projected activities rather than past practices, this is an example of _____ budgeting.
    (a) zero-based (b) variable (c) fixed (d) contingency

12. One of the benefits of participatory planning is _____.
    (a) reduced time for planning (b) less need for forecasting (c) greater attention to contingencies (d) more commitment to implementation

13. When an automobile manufacturer is careful to purchase only the highest-quality raw materials to be used in production, this is an example of _____ control.
    (a) concurrent (b) statistical (c) inventory (d) feedforward

14. In break-even analysis, the break-even point occurs where _____.
    (a) fixed costs = variable costs (b) profits = expenses (c) assets = liabilities (d) revenues = total costs

15. A manager is failing to live up to the concept of MBO when he or she _____.
    (a) sets performance objectives for subordinates (b) actively supports subordinates in their work (c) jointly reviews performance results with subordinates (d) keeps a written record of subordinates' performance objectives

SHORT-RESPONSE QUESTIONS:

16. List the five steps in the planning process, and give examples of each.
17. How might planning through benchmarking be used by the owner/manager of a local bookstore?
18. How does Douglas McGregor's Theory Y relate to the concept of internal control?
19. How does a progressive discipline system work?

APPLICATION QUESTION:

20. Put yourself in the position of a management trainer. You are asked to make a short presentation to the local Small Business Enterprise Association at its biweekly luncheon. The topic you are to speak on is "How Each of You Can Use Management by Objectives for Better Planning and Control." What will you tell them and why?

www.wiley.com/college/schermerhorn

9

Strategic management

Planning Ahead
—→

After reading Chapter 9,
you should be able to
answer these questions
in your own words.

CHAPTER 9 study questions

1. What are the foundations of strategic competitiveness?

2. What is the strategic management process?

3. What types of strategies are used by organizations?

4. How are strategies formulated?

5. What are current issues in strategy implementation?

STARBUCKS COFFEE COMPANY—GET AND STAY AHEAD WITH STRATEGY

Coffee just might be the most popular drink in the world. And the well-known Starbucks may hold claim to the most valuable brand name in the industry. The strategic question is, How long can Starbucks keep brewing a better cup of coffee?

"Forever," might answer Howard Schultz, chairman and chief global strategist of the company. When he joined Starbucks in 1982 as director of retail operations, the firm was a small coffee retailer in Seattle. But Schultz had the idea to build a coffee bar culture with Starbucks at its center. The rest is Starbucks history.

Schultz's vision was of Starbucks becoming a national chain of stores offering the finest coffee drinks and "educating consumers everywhere about fine coffee." Not only has Starbucks fulfilled this vision on the national scene, it has stuck to its values in the process. Employees are featured in guiding principles: (1) "Provide a great work environment and treat each other with respect and dignity. (2) Embrace diversity as an essential component in the way we do business." You'll also find a strong commitment to the natural environment, the community, and coffee origin countries.

Today Starbucks is more than just another coffee bar retailer. Visit a store or go online and you'll find it now selling tea, chocolates, a variety of gift items, and even music. It's all part of a global strategy for growth. Schultz says: "Moving forward, we will continue to pursue opportunities that increase long-term value for our shareholders and our partners, provide unique experiences for our customers, and bring us ever closer to our goal of becoming the most recognized and respected brand of coffee in the world."[1]

Get Connected!

What are the risks of an aggressive growth strategy? Look at Starbucks's financial reports; check its competitors. Enter the world of the corporate strategist.

Chapter 9 Learning Preview

How far are you from a cup of Starbucks coffee? Most likely, you're not very far away. With more than 6000 locations around the world, the firm is a growth business in more ways than one. There is a continually evolving line of packaged beverages available in retail outlets; there is also a line of music CDs produced by Hear Music, owned by Starbucks. This chapter introduces you to the issues of strategy and strategic management, which Starbucks's leadership struggles with daily. The chapter discusses strategy formulation and implementation, with special attention to alternative types of strategies and frameworks for strategy selection.

STRATEGIC MANAGEMENT

Study question **1**	Study question **2**	Study question **3**	Study question **4**	Study question **5**
Strategic Competitiveness	**The Strategic Management Process**	**Strategies Used by Organizations**	**Strategy Formulation**	**Strategy Implementation**
• What is strategy? • Strategic management • Strategic management goals	• Analysis of mission, values, and objectives • Analysis of Resources and capabilities • Analysis of industry and environment	• Levels of strategy • Growth and diversification • Restructuring and divestiture • Global strategies • Cooperation • E-business	• Porter's generic strategies • Portfolio planning • Adaptive strategies • Incrementalism and emergent strategy	• Management practices and systems • Corporate governance • Strategic leadership
Learning check **1**	Learning check **2**	Learning check **3**	Learning check **4**	Learning check **5**

Let's change industries for a moment and move from Starbucks Coffee to the retailing world. Surely you are familiar with Wal-Mart, America's largest retailer and the recommended case study for Chapter 8. Wal-Mart's master plan is elegant in its simplicity: to deliver consistently low prices and high customer service. An important foundation is use of the latest technology. Inventories are monitored around the clock, and a world-class distribution system ensures that stores are rarely out of the items customers are seeking. All systems are rallied around Wal-Mart's goals—low prices, high customer service. While the firm's competitors are asking, "How can we keep up?" the strategic visionaries at Wal-Mart are asking "How can we stay ahead?"

Even Wal-Mart can't rest on past laurels.[2] Success today is no guarantee of success tomorrow. We will surely see many changes in competitive retailing in the years ahead; we're already seeing many today. Similar forces and challenges confront managers in all settings, Starbucks among them. Today's environment places a great premium on effective "strategy" and "strategic management" as prerequisites for organizational success. "If you want to make a difference as a leader," says *Fast Company* magazine, "you've got to make time for strategy."[3]

STRATEGIC COMPETITIVENESS

An organization with **competitive advantage** operates with an attribute or combination of attributes that allows it to outperform its rivals. At Wal-Mart, for example, one source of such an advantage is information technology that allows the retailer to quickly track sales and monitor inventories. In other industries, Dell Computer eliminates wholesale supplier markups by marketing directly to consumers; Toyota's shorter cycle times allow it to carry smaller amounts of work-in-process inventory. The goal for any organization, however, is not just to achieve competitive advantage. It is to make it sustainable, even as rivals attempt to duplicate and copy a success story. A *sustainable competitive advantage* is one that is difficult for competitors to imitate. At Wal-Mart again, the firm's use of IT is continuously improved. Competitors have trouble catching up, let alone getting ahead.

○ A **competitive advantage** comes from operating in successful ways that are difficult to imitate.

WHAT IS STRATEGY?

A **strategy** is a comprehensive action plan that identifies long-term direction for an organization and guides resource utilization to accomplish goals with sustainable competitive advantage. It focuses attention on the competitive environment and represents a "best guess" about what must be done to ensure future success in the face of rivalry and even as conditions change. Importantly, a strategy provides the plan for allocating and using resources with consistent **strategic intent**—that is, with all organizational energies directed toward a unifying and compelling target or goal.[4] At Coca-Cola, for example, strategic intent has been described as "To put a Coke within 'arm's reach' of every consumer in the world." Given the focus provided by this strategic intent, we would not expect Coca-Cola to be diversifying by investing in snack foods, as does its archrival PepsiCo.

In our fast-paced world of globalization and changing technologies, the "long-term" aspect of strategy is becoming ever shorter. As it does so, the challenges to the strategist become even greater. It used to be that companies could count on traditional "build-and-sell" business models that put them in control. In the early days of the automobile industry, for example, Henry Ford once said: "The customer can have any color he wants as long as it's back." His firm, quite literally, was in the driver's seat. Today things have changed and strategy is increasingly driven by customers and flexibility. Stephen Haeckel, director of strategic studies at IBM's Advanced Business Institute, once described the shift this way: "It's a difference between a bus, which follows a set route, and a taxi, which goes where customers tell it to go."[5]

○ A **strategy** is a comprehensive plan guiding resource allocation to achieve long-term organization goals.

○ **Strategic intent** focuses and applies organizational energies on a unifying and compelling goal.

STRATEGIC MANAGEMENT

In the case of Starbucks and Wal-Mart, crafting strategy may seem a deceptively simple task: find out what customers want, then provide it for them at the best prices and service. In practice, this task is made complex and risky by the forces and uncertainties of competitive environments.[6] Every strategist must remember that at the same time one is trying to create competitive advantage for an organization, competitors are always trying to do the same. This gives rise to demands for strategies that are

TAKE IT TO THE CASE

Reach for the sky in the new economy

"You've got one go in life, so make the most of it" were words of advice from Richard Branson's 99-year-old grandmother. He has. Described as having "a craving for turning possibilities, even unlikely ones, into raging successes," "Branson has built the Virgin Group Ltd. into a global empire of some 200 businesses. British-born and -based Branson has made Virgin into a highly diversified portfolio of companies ranging from Virgin Megastores to Virgin Atlantic Airlines to Virgin Mobile to . . . well, there are many more and no one really knows what will come next. Branson manages this vast network of organizations with only a minimum of corporate hierarchy and with an emphasis on empowerment and trust. "It all comes down to people," says Branson, "nothing else even comes close." Branson has managed growth well so far, betting that giving the diverse business units autonomy will keep both them and the conglomerate strong and profitable.[7]

"bold," "aggressive," "fast-moving," and "innovative." But call them what you will, strategies don't just happen. They must be created. And strategies alone don't automatically bring success. They must be both well chosen and well implemented.

○ **Strategic management** is the process of formulating and implementing strategies.

Strategic management is the process of formulating and implementing strategies to accomplish long-term goals and sustain competitive advantage. The essence of strategic management is looking ahead, understanding the environment and the organization, effectively positioning the organization for competitive advantage in changing times, and then achieving it.

STRATEGIC MANAGEMENT GOALS

Michael Porter, Harvard scholar and strategy consultant, says that "sound strategy starts with having the right goal."[8] He argues that the ultimate goal for any business should be superior profitability. This creates value for investors in the form of **above-average returns,** returns that exceed what an investor could earn by investing in alternative opportunities of equivalent risk.[9]

○ **Above-average returns** exceed what could be earned from alternative investments of equivalent risk.

The ability to earn above-average returns is based in part on the competitive nature of organizational environments. Businesses compete in environments that vary in the following ways.[10] In a *monopoly environment,* there is only one player and no competition. This creates absolute competitive advantage that delivers sustainable and even excessive business profits. The U.S. Justice Department's antitrust lawsuit against Microsoft Corporation argued that the firm achieved actual or close to monopoly status in respect to the market for computer operating systems. An *oligopoly environment* contains a few players who do not directly compete against one another. Firms within an oligopoly sustain long-term competitive advantages within defined market segments. In the absence of competition within these segments, they can also reap excessive business profits. This describes conditions in the breakfast cereals market, for example. The industry is dominated by large players—Kellogg's, General Mills, and Quaker Oats—that control much of the market. It is difficult for new players to break in. From the customer's standpoint, both monopoly and oligopoly are disadvantageous. The lack of competition may keep prices high and product/service innovations low.

The global economy has helped to create for many businesses today an *environment of hypercompetition*.[11] This is an environment in which there are at least several players who directly compete with one another. An example is the fast-food industry, where McDonald's, Burger King, Wendy's, and many other restaurant chains all compete for largely the same customers. Because the competition is direct and intense, any competitive advantage that is realized is temporary. Successful strategies are often copied and firms must continue to find new strategies that deliver new sources of competitive advantage, even while trying to defend existing ones. McDonald's, for example, had to mount an aggressive campaign to defend its french fries—advertised as "America's Favorite Fries"—from a copycat attack by Burger King.[12] In hypercompetition, there are always some winners and losers. Business profits can be attractive but intermittent. The customer generally gains in this environment through lower prices and more product/service innovation.

<table>
<tr><td>*Be sure you can* • define the terms competitive advantage, strategy, and strategic management • explain the concept of sustained competitive advantage • explain the significance of above-average returns as strategic business goals • differentiate monopoly, oligopoly, and hypercompetition as competitive environments</td><td>**Learning check 1**
</td></tr>
</table>

THE STRATEGIC MANAGEMENT PROCESS

Strategic management is successful when good strategies are crafted from insightful understandings of the competitive environment of the organization, and these strategies are well implemented. *Figure 9.1* describes the steps involved in fulfilling the two major responsibilities of the strategic management process—strategy formulation and strategy implementation.

The first strategic management responsibility is **strategy formulation,** the process of creating strategy. This involves assessing existing strategies, organization, and environment to develop new strategies capable of

○ **Strategy formulation** is the process of creating strategies.

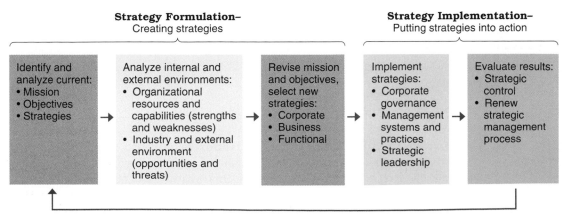

Figure 9.1 Strategy formulation and implementation in the strategic management process.

MANAGER'S NOTEPAD 9.1 Five strategic management tasks

1. Identify organizational mission and objectives.

   Ask: "What business are we in? Where do we want to go?"

2. Assess current performance vis-à-vis mission and objectives.

   Ask: "How well are we currently doing?"

3. Create strategic plans to accomplish purpose and objectives.

   Ask: "How can we get where we really want to be?"

4. Implement the strategic plans.

   Ask: "Has everything been done that needs to be done?"

5. Evaluate results; change strategic plans and/or implementation processes as necessary.

   Ask: "Are things working out as planned? What can be improved?"

---

delivering future competitive advantage. Peter Drucker associates this process with a set of five strategic questions: (1) *What is our business mission?* (2) *Who are our customers?* (3) *What do our customers consider value?* (4) *What have been our results?* (5) *What is our plan?*[13]

○ **Strategy implementation** is the process of putting strategies into action.

The second strategic management responsibility is **strategy implementation,** the process of allocating resources and putting strategies into action. Once strategies are created, they must be successfully acted upon to achieve the desired results. As Drucker says, "The future will not just happen if one wishes hard enough. It requires decision—now. It imposes risk—now. It requires action—now. It demands allocation of resources, and above all, of human resources—now. It requires work—now."[14] Every organizational and management system must be mobilized to support and reinforce the accomplishment of strategies. All resources must be well utilized to achieve maximum impact on performance. All of this, in turn, requires a commitment to the full range of strategic management tasks posed in *Manager's Notepad 9.1.*[15]

ANALYSIS OF MISSION, VALUES, AND OBJECTIVES

The strategic management process begins with a careful review and clarification of organizational mission, values, and objectives.[16] This sets the stage for critically assessing the organization's resources and capabilities as well as competitive opportunities and threats in the external environment.

Mission

○ The **mission** is the organization's reason for existence in society.

As first discussed in Chapter 1, the **mission** or purpose of an organization may be described as its reason for existence in society. Strategy consultant Michael Hammer believes that a mission should represent what the strategy or underlying business model is trying to accomplish. He suggests asking: "What are we moving to?" "What is our dream?" "What kind of a difference do we want to make in the world?" "What do we want to be known for?"[17]

The best organizations have a clear sense of mission, and they utilize resources with clear strategic intent in respect to its fulfillment. At Mary Kay, Inc., for example, the firm's mission is defined as "To enrich women's lives." Starbucks's mission is to be "the premier purveyor of the finest coffee in the world while maintaining our uncompromising principles as we grow." The mission of the American Red Cross is to "provide relief to victims of disasters and help people prevent, prepare for, and respond to emergencies."[18]

A good *mission statement* identifies the *domain* in which the organization intends to operate—including the *customers* it intends to serve, the *products* and/or *services* it intends to provide, and the *location* in which it intends to operate. The mission statement should also communicate the underlying philosophy that will guide employees in these operations. An important test of a mission is how well it serves the organization's **stakeholders.** You should recall that these are individuals and groups—including customers, shareholders, suppliers, creditors, community groups, and others who are directly affected by the organization and its strategic accomplishments. In the strategic management process, the stakeholder test can be done as a *strategic constituencies analysis.* Here, the specific interests of each stakeholder are assessed along with the organization's record in responding to them. *Figure 9.2* gives an example of how stakeholder interests can be reflected in the mission of a business firm.

○ **Stakeholders** are individuals and groups directly affected by an organization and its accomplishments.

Core Values

Behavior in and by organizations will always be affected in part by *values,* which are broad beliefs about what is or is not appropriate. **Organizational culture** was first defined in Chapter 4 as the predominant value system of the organization as a whole.[19] Through organizational cultures, the values of managers and other members are shaped and pointed in common directions. In strategic management, the presence of strong core values for an organization helps build institutional identity. It gives character to an organization in the eyes of its employees and external stakeholders, and it backs up the mission statement. Shared values also help guide the behavior of organization members in meaningful and consistent ways. For example, Merck backs up its mission with a public commitment to core values that include preservation and improvement of human life, scientific excellence, ethics and integrity, and profits from work that benefits humanity.

○ **Organizational culture** is the predominant value system for the organization as a whole.

Employees

We respect the individuality of each employee . . . creativity and productivity are encouraged, valued, and rewarded.

Communities

We are committed to being caring and supportive corporate citizens within the worldwide communities in which we operate.

Mission

Shareholders

We are dedicated to . . . performing in a manner that will enhance returns on investments.

Customers

We are committed to providing superior value in our products and services.

Suppliers

We think of our suppliers as partners who share our goal of . . . highest quality.

Figure 9.2 How external stakeholders can be valued as strategic constituencies of organizations.

Objectives

○ **Operating objectives** are specific results that organizations try to accomplish.

Whereas a mission statement sets forth an official purpose for the organization and the core values describe appropriate standards of behavior for its accomplishment, **operating objectives** direct activities toward key and specific performance results. These objectives are shorter-term targets against which actual performance results can be measured as indicators of progress and continuous improvement. According to Peter Drucker, the *operating objectives of a business* might include the following:[20]

→ Operating objectives of a business

- *Profitability*—producing at a net profit in business.
- *Market share*—gaining and holding a specific market share.
- *Human talent*—recruiting and maintaining a high-quality workforce.
- *Financial health*—acquiring capital; earning positive returns.
- *Cost efficiency*—using resources well to operate at low cost.
- *Product quality*—producing high-quality goods or services.
- *Innovation*—developing new products and/or processes.
- *Social responsibility*—making a positive contribution to society.

ANALYSIS OF ORGANIZATIONAL RESOURCES AND CAPABILITIES

○ A **SWOT analysis** examines organizational strengths and weaknesses and environmental opportunities and threats.

○ A **core competency** is a special strength that gives an organization a competitive advantage.

The strategic management process always involves careful analysis of organizational resources and capabilities. This can be approached by a technique known as **SWOT analysis:** the internal analysis of organizational Strengths and Weaknesses as well as the external analysis of environmental Opportunities and Threats.

As shown in *Figure 9.3*, a SWOT analysis begins with a systematic evaluation of the organization's resources and capabilities. A major goal is to identify **core competencies** in the form of special strengths that the organization has or does exceptionally well in comparison with competitors.

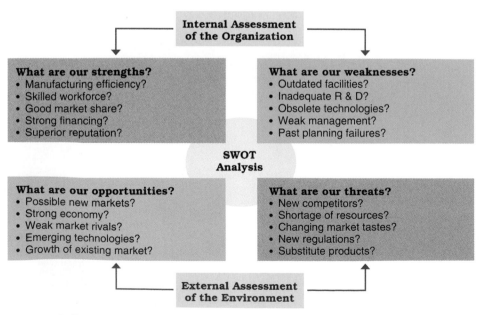

Figure 9.3 SWOT analysis of strengths, weaknesses, opportunities, and threats.

They are capabilities that by virtue of being rare, costly to imitate, and nonsubstitutable, become viable sources of competitive advantage.[21] Core competencies may be found in special knowledge or expertise, superior technologies, efficient manufacturing technologies, or unique product distribution systems, among many other possibilities. But always, and as with the notion of strategy itself, they must be viewed relative to the competition. Organizations need core competencies that do important things better than the competition and that are very difficult for competitors to duplicate. Organizational weaknesses, of course, are the other side of the picture. They must also be identified to gain a realistic perspective on the formulation of strategies. The goal in strategy formulation is to create strategies that leverage core competencies for competitive advantage by building upon organizational strengths and minimizing the impact of weaknesses.

ANALYSIS OF INDUSTRY AND ENVIRONMENT

A SWOT analysis is not complete until opportunities and threats in the external environment are also analyzed. They can be found among *macroenvironment* factors such as technology, government, social structures, population demographics, the global economy, and the natural environment. They can also include developments in the *industry environment* of resource suppliers, competitors, and customers. As shown in the Figure 9.3, opportunities may exist as possible new markets, a strong economy, weaknesses in competitors, and emerging technologies. Weaknesses may be identified in such things as the emergence of new competitors, resource scarcities, changing customer tastes, and new government regulations, among other possibilities.

Scholar and consultant Michael Porter believes that the critical issue in respect to the external environment is how it impacts competition within the industry. He offers the five forces model shown in *Figure 9.4* as a way of adding sophistication to a strategic analysis of the environment.[22] His framework for competitive industry analysis directs attention toward understanding the following forces:

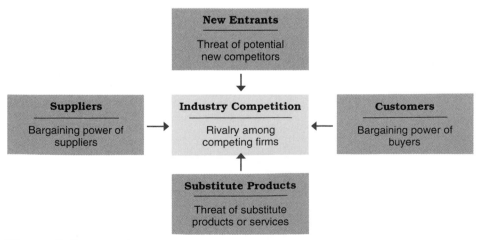

Figure 9.4 Porter's model of five strategic forces affecting industry competition.
Source: Developed from Michael E. Porter, *Competitive Strategy* (New York: Free Press, 1980).

Porter's five competitive forces

1. *Industry competitors*—intensity of rivalry among firms in the industry.
2. *New entrants*—threats of new competitors entering the market.
3. *Suppliers*—bargaining power of suppliers.
4. *Customers*—bargaining power of buyers.
5. *Substitutes*—threats of substitute products or services.

From Porter's perspective, the foundations for any successful strategy rest with a clear understanding of these competitive environmental forces. He calls this the "industry structure." The strategic management challenge is to position an organization strategically within its industry, taking into account the implications of forces that make it more or less attractive. In general, an *unattractive industry* is one in which rivalry among competitors is intense, substantial threats exist in the form of possible new entrants and substitute products, and suppliers and buyers are very powerful in bargaining over such things as prices and quality. An *attractive industry,* by contrast, has less existing competition, few threats from new entrants or substitutes, and low bargaining power among suppliers and buyers. By systematically analyzing industry attractiveness in respect to the five forces, Porter believes that strategies can be chosen to give the organization a competitive advantage relative to its rivals.

Learning check 2

Be sure you can • differentiate strategy formulation from strategy implementation • list the major components in the strategic management process • explain what a mission statement is and illustrate how a good mission statement appeals to stakeholders • list several operating objectives of organizations • define the term "core competencies" • explain a SWOT analysis and use it to assess the strategic situation of an organization familiar to you • explain how Porter's five forces model can be used to assess the attractiveness of an industry

---

STRATEGIES USED BY ORGANIZATIONS

The strategic management process encompasses the three levels of strategy shown in *Figure 9.5*. Strategies are formulated and implemented at the organizational or corporate level, business level, and functional level. All should be integrated in means-end fashion to accomplish objectives and create sustainable competitive advantage.

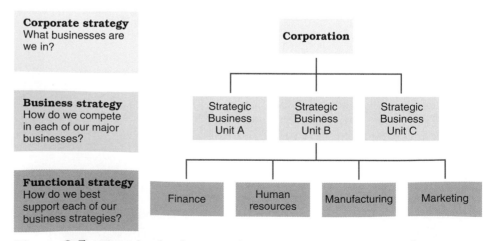

Figure 9.5 Three levels of strategy in organizations—corporate, business, and functional strategies.

Make sure the business strategy has a career payoff

You should know enough about business strategy to be able to make good employment decisions and career choices. For example, there's a lot more to e-business success than simply mastering the technological requirements of going online and the logistical/distribution requirements of delivering products once purchased. This is an intense arena where competitive strategy is fought out day after day. Today's high fliers can easily become tomorrow's losers. There was a time when eToys, Inc. was a high flier, with over 100,000 items in stock and employing some 1000 persons. For a time it seemed that eToys was ready to beat the old economy stalwart, Toys R Us. Well, eToys is gone now; Toys R Us is still around, with its own dot.com component. What was eToys's problem? Profits. At the same time that it was selling $150 million worth of toys on the Web, it was losing over $180 million. No doubt there are winning e-business strategies out there, and such firms should be in your career horizons. But be careful—we'll see a lot more "dot.bombs," too.

LEVELS OF STRATEGY

The level of **corporate strategy** directs the organization as a whole toward sustainable competitive advantage. For a business it describes the scope of operations by answering the following *strategic question:* "In what industries and markets should we compete?" The purpose of corporate strategy is to set direction and guide resource allocations for the entire enterprise. In large, complex organizations, corporate strategy identifies how the company intends to compete across multiple industries and markets. At GE, for example, the firm pursues global business interests in aircraft engines, appliances, capital services, lighting, medical systems, broadcasting, plastics, and power systems, among others. Typical strategic decisions at the corporate level relate to the allocation of resources for acquisitions, new business development, divestitures, and the like across this business portfolio.

Business strategy is the strategy for a single business unit or product line. It describes strategic intent to compete within a specific industry or market. Large *conglomerates* like General Electric are composed of many businesses, with many differences among them in product lines and even industries. The term **strategic business unit (SBU)** is often used to describe a single business firm or a component that operates with a major business line within a larger enterprise. The selection of strategy at the business level involves answering the *strategic question:* "How are we going to compete for customers in this industry and market?" Typical business strategy decisions include choices about product/service mix, facilities locations, new technologies, and the like. In single-business enterprises, business strategy is the corporate strategy.

Functional strategy guides the use of organizational resources to implement business strategy. This level of strategy focuses on activities within a specific functional area of operations. Figure 9.5, the standard business functions of marketing, manufacturing, finance, and human resources, illustrates this level of strategy. The *strategic question* to be answered in selecting functional strategies is: "How can we best utilize resources to implement our business strategy?" Answers to this question

O A **corporate strategy** sets long-term direction for the total enterprise.

O A **business strategy** identifies how a division or strategic business unit will compete in its product or service domain.

O An **SBU** is a major business area that operates with some autonomy.

O A **functional strategy** guides activities within one specific area of operations.

typically involve the choice of management practices within each function that improves operating efficiency, product or service quality, customer service, or innovativeness.

GROWTH AND DIVERSIFICATION STRATEGIES

One of the most common and popular of the grand or master strategies followed by organizations at the corporate or business levels is growth.[23] **Growth strategies** pursue an increase in size and the expansion of current operations. They are popular in part because growth is viewed as necessary for long-run survival in some industries. One approach to growth is through **concentration,** where expansion is within the same business area. McDonald's, Wal-Mart, Starbucks, and others are pursuing aggressive growth strategies while still concentrating on their primary business areas. And importantly, they recognize the limits to growth in domestic markets and are expanding globally into markets and countries around the world.

Growth can also be pursued through **diversification,** where expansion takes place through the acquisition of or investment in new and different business areas. A strategy of *related diversification* involves growth by acquiring new businesses or entering business areas that are related to what one already does. This strategy seeks the advantages of growth in areas that utilize core competencies and existing skills. An example is the acquisition of Tropicana by PepsiCo. Although Tropicana specializes in fruit juices, the business is related to PepsiCo's expertise in the beverages industry. A strategy of *unrelated diversification* involves growth by acquiring businesses or entering business areas that are different from what one already does.

Diversification can also take the form of **vertical integration,** where a business acquires suppliers (*backward vertical integration*) or distributors (*forward vertical integration*). Backward vertical integration has been common in the automobile industry as firms purchased suppliers to ensure quality and control over the availability of key parts. In beverages, both Coca-Cola and PepsiCo have pursued forward vertical integration by purchasing some of their major bottlers.

There is a tendency to equate growth with effectiveness, but that is not necessarily true. Any growth strategy, whether by concentration or some form of diversification, must be well planned and well managed to achieve the desired results. Increased size of operation in any form adds challenge to the management process. Diversification, in particular, brings the difficulties of complexity and the need to manage and integrate very dissimilar operations. Research indicates that business performance may decline with too much unrelated diversification.[24]

RESTRUCTURING AND DIVESTITURE STRATEGIES

When organizations are in trouble, perhaps experiencing problems brought about by difficulties managing growth, some sort of readjustment must be made. Among the master strategies used by organizations, a **retrenchment strategy** seeks to correct weaknesses by making changes to current ways of operating. The goal is most often to reverse or change an approach that isn't working and to reorganize to compete better in the fu-

○ A growth strategy involves expansion of the organization's current operations.

○ Growth through **concentration** is within the same business area.

○ Growth through **diversification** is by acquisition of or investment in new and different business areas.

○ Growth through **vertical integration** is by acquiring suppliers or distributors.

○ A retrenchment strategy changes operations to correct weaknesses.

ture. The most extreme form of retrenchment is *liquidation*, where business ceases and assets are sold to pay creditors. Less extreme and more common is **restructuring** of some sort. This involves making major changes to reduce the scale and/or mix of operations, with the twin goals of consolidating to gain short-term efficiencies and gaining time to prepare new strategies to improve future success.

> ○ **Restructuring** reduces the scale/or mix of operations.

Restructuring is sometimes accomplished by **downsizing,** which decreases the size of operations.[25] The expected benefits are reduced costs and improved operating efficiency. A common way to downsize is cutting the size of the workforce. Research has shown that this is most successful when the workforce is reduced strategically or in a way that improves focus on key performance objectives.[26] Downsizing with a strategic focus is sometimes referred to as *rightsizing.* This contrasts with the less-well-regarded approach of simply cutting staff "across the board."

> ○ **Downsizing** decreases the size of operations.

Restructuring by **divestiture** involves selling off parts of the organization to refocus on core competencies, cut costs, and improve operating efficiency. This is a common strategy for organizations that find they have become overdiversified and are encountering problems managing the complexity of operations. It is also a way for organizations to take advantage of the value of internal assets by selling to a component that can stand on its own as an independent business.

> ○ **Divestiture** sells off parts of the organization to refocus attention on core business areas.

GLOBAL STRATEGIES

Very few businesses operate today without some exposure to and direct involvement in international operations. A key aspect of strategy, therefore, becomes how the firm approaches the global economy and its mix of business risks and opportunities. Very often, a grand or master strategy of growth is pursued with the support of an accompanying global strategy.[27]

An easy way to spot differences in global strategies is to notice how products are developed and advertised around the world. A firm pursuing a **globalization strategy** tends to view the world as one large market, trying as much as possible to standardize products and their advertising for use everywhere. Authority for major management decisions will largely reside with corporate headquarters. The latest Gillette razors, for example, are typically sold and advertised similarly around the world. This reflects a somewhat *ethnocentric view* that assumes that everyone everywhere wants the same thing that one has developed and sold successfully at home.

> ○ A **globalization strategy** adopts standardized products and advertising for use worldwide.

Firms using a **multidomestic strategy** try to customize products and their advertising as much as possible to fit the local needs of different countries or regions. They distribute authority for major decisions to local and area managers to provide this differentiation. This is a popular strategy for many consumer goods companies—Bristol Myers, Procter & Gamble, Unilever—that vary their products according to consumer preferences in different countries and cultures. This reflects a more *polycentric view,* one showing respect for both market diversity and the capabilities of locals to best interpret their strategic implications.

> ○ A **multidomestic strategy** customizes products and advertising to best fit local needs.

A third approach to international business is the **transnational strategy** that seeks balance among efficiencies in global operations and responsiveness to local markets. The *transnational firm,* first described in Chapter 5, tries to operate without a strong national identity and to blend with the global economy to fully tap its business potential. Material re-

> ○ A **transnational strategy** seeks efficiencies of global operations with attention to local markets.

sources and human capital are acquired worldwide; manufacturing and other business functions are performed wherever in the world they can be done best at lowest cost. Ford, for example, draws upon design, manufacturing, and distribution expertise all over the world to build car "platforms" that can then be efficiently modified to meet regional tastes. Such a transnational strategy reflects a *geocentric view* that respects diversity and values talents around the world. Transnational firms typically operate in a highly networked way, with information and learning continually flowing between headquarters and subsidiaries, and among the subsidiaries themselves.

COOPERATIVE STRATEGIES

○ In a **strategic alliance** organizations join together in partnership to pursue an area of mutual interest.

One of the trends today is toward more cooperation among organizations, and *international joint ventures* are a common form of international business. They are one among many forms of **strategic alliances** in which two or more organizations join together in partnership to pursue an area of mutual interest. One way to cooperate strategically is through *outsourcing alliances,* contracting to purchase important services from another organization. Many organizations today, for example, are outsourcing their IT function to firms like EDS and IBM in the belief that these services are better provided by a firm that specializes and maintains its expertise in this area. Cooperation in the supply chain also takes the form of *supplier alliances,* in which preferred supplier relationships guarantee a smooth and timely flow of quality supplies among alliance partners. Another common approach today is cooperation in *distribution alliances,* in which firms join together to accomplish product or services sales and distribution.

○ An **e-business strategy** strategically uses the Internet to gain competitive advantage.

○ A **B2B business strategy** uses IT and Web portals to link organizations vertically in supply chains.

E-BUSINESS STRATEGIES

REALITY CHECK 9.1

B2B changes the world of outsourcing
It is reported that businesses purchasing supplies in online auctions save as much as 20 percent. To date the biggest users are found in the computer and electronics industry. Take the online "Reality Check" to learn more about the use of B2B auctions.

Without a doubt, one of the most frequently asked questions these days for the business executive is: "What is your **e-business strategy**?" This is the strategic use of the Internet to gain competitive advantage.[28] As introduced in Chapter 7, popular e-business strategies involve B2B (business-to-business) and B2C (business-to-customer) applications. **B2B business strategies** use IT and Web portals to vertically link organizations with members of their supply chains. When Dell Computer sets up special website services that allow its major corporate customers to manage their accounts online, when Wal-Mart suppliers are linked to the firm's information systems and manage inventories for their own products electronically, and even when a business uses an online auction site to bid for supplies at the cheapest prices, they are utilizing B2B in various forms. B2B is the largest e-business component in the economy, and its benefits apply to large and small organizations alike.

Most of us probably are more aware of **B2C business strategies** that use IT and Web portals to link organizations with their customers. A common B2C strategy has already been illustrated several times in

○ A **B2C business strategy** uses IT and Web portals to link businesses with customers.

Web-based business models

- *Brokerage*—bringing buyers and sellers together to make transactions (e.g., CarsDirect.com).
- *Advertising*—providing information or services while generating revenue from advertising (e.g., Yahoo!).
- *Merchant model*—selling products wholesale and retail through the Web, e-tailing (e.g., Bluelight.com).
- *Subscription model*—selling access to a website through subscription (e.g., *Wall Street Journal* Interactive).
- *Infomediary model*—collecting information on users and selling it to other businesses (e.g., ePinions.com).
- *Community model*—supporting sites by donations from community of users (e.g., National Public Radio Online).

this book—*e-tailing,* or the sale of goods directly to customers via the Internet. But, importantly, there is more to success with B2C than simply having a website that advertises products for customer purchase. The B2C strategy must be fully integrated with supporting functional strategies and operations. Among the e-tailers, for example, Dell has set a benchmarking standard that is very hard for competitors to duplicate. The easy-to-use Dell website allows customization of an individual's computer order, in effect offering a design-your-own-product capability. Then a highly efficient and streamlined manufacturing and distribution system takes over to build and ship the computer within three business days. And all this is backed by highly efficient customer service. Although many have tried copycat strategies, Dell sustains its competitive advantage with continual improvements to a state-of-the-art and fully integrated e-business strategy.

Manager's Notepad 9.2 lists some of the more common Web-based business models that are available, along with examples of each.[29] In considering the opportunities, however, it is important to keep the Dell story in mind. A lot more is required to achieve success with e-business than simply having IT support and a good website. Whether one is talking B2B or B2C, success with e-business requires both a good strategy and the capacity to implement the strategy extremely well.

Be sure you can • differentiate the three levels of strategy—corporate, business, and functional • list and explain the major types of growth and diversification strategies, and restructuring and divestiture strategies • list and give examples of major global strategies • define the term "strategic alliance" and explain how cooperation is used as a business strategy • explain B2B and B2C as forms of e-business strategy

STRATEGY FORMULATION

Michael Porter says: "The company without a strategy is willing to try anything."[30] With a good strategy in place, by contrast, the resources of the entire organization can be focused on the overall goal—superior profitability or above-average returns. Whether one is talking about building e-business strategies for the new economy or crafting strategies for more traditional operations, it is always important to remember this goal and the need for sustainable competitive advantage. The major *opportunities for competitive advantage* are found in the following areas, which should always be considered in the strategy formulation process:[31]

Opportunities for sustainable competitive advantage

- *Cost and quality*—where strategy drives an emphasis on operating efficiency and/or product or service quality.
- *Knowledge and speed*—where strategy drives an emphasis on innovation and speed of delivery to market for new ideas.
- *Barriers to entry*—where strategy drives an emphasis on creating a market stronghold that is protected from entry by others.
- *Financial resources*—where strategy drives an emphasis on investments and/or loss sustainment that competitors can't match.

It is important to remember that advantages gained in today's global and information-age economy of intense competition must be considered temporary, at best. Things change too fast. Any advantage of the moment will sooner or later be eroded as new market demands, copycat strategies, and innovations by rivals take their competitive tolls.[32] The challenge of achieving sustainable competitive advantage is thus a dynamic one. Strategies must be continually revisited, updated, and changed. This process of strategy formulation is facilitated by a number of strategic planning models or approaches.

PORTER'S GENERIC STRATEGIES

Michael Porter's five forces model for industry analysis (refer back to Figure 9.4) helps answer the question: "Is this an attractive industry for us to compete in?" Within an industry, however, the strategic challenge becomes positioning one's firm and products relative to competitors. The question for strategy formulation becomes: "How can we best compete for customers in this industry?" Porter advises managers to answer this question by using his generic strategies framework, shown in *Figure 9.6*.[33]

According to Porter, business-level strategic decisions are driven by two basic factors: (1) *market scope*—ask: "How broad or narrow is your market or target market?" (2) *source of competitive advantage*—ask: "Will you compete for competitive advantage by lower price or product uniqueness?" As shown in the figure, these factors combine to create the following four generic strategies that organizations can pursue. The examples in the figure and shown here are of competitive positions within the soft-drink industry.

Porter's generic business strategies

1. **Differentiation**—where the organization's resources and attention are directed toward making its products appear different from those of the competition (*example:* Coke, Pepsi).
2. **Cost leadership**—where the organization's resources and attention are directed toward minimizing costs to operate more efficiently than the competition (*example:* Big K Kola, discounter cola brands).

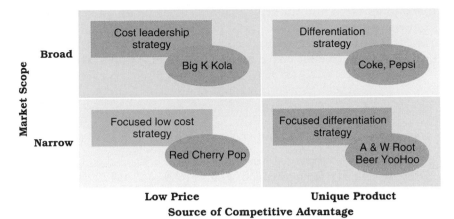

Figure 9.6 Porter's generic strategies framework: soft-drink industry examples.

3. **Focused differentiation**—where the organization concentrates on one special market segment and tries to offer customers in that segment a unique product (*example:* A&W Root Beer, YooHoo).

4. **Focused cost leadership**—where the organization concentrates on one special market segment and tries in that segment to be the provider with lowest costs (*example:* Red Cherry Pop).

Organizations pursuing a **differentiation strategy** seek competitive advantage through uniqueness. They try to develop goods and services that are clearly different from the competition. The objective is to attract customers who become loyal to the organization's products and lose interest in those of competitors. This strategy requires organizational strengths in marketing, research and development, and creativity. Its success depends on continuing customer perceptions of product quality and uniqueness. An example in the apparel industry is Polo Ralph Lauren, retailer of upscale classic fashions and accessories. In Ralph Lauren's words, "Polo redefined how American style and quality is perceived. Polo has always been about selling quality products by creating worlds and inviting our customers to be part of our dream."[34]

Organizations pursuing a **cost leadership strategy** try to have lower costs than competitors and therefore achieve higher profits. The objective is to continuously improve the operating efficiencies of production, distribution, and other organizational systems. This requires tight cost and managerial controls as well as products that are easy to manufacture and distribute. In retailing, Wal-Mart aims to keep its costs so low that it can always offer customers the lowest prices and still make a reasonable profit. Most discounters operate with 18 to 20 percent gross margins. Wal-Mart can accept less and still make the same or higher returns. In financial services, Vanguard Group has succeeded with a strategy based on keeping its costs low and therefore offering mutual funds to customers with minimum fees. Its website proudly proclaims that Vanguard is the industry leader in having the lowest average expense ratios.

Organizations pursuing **focus strategies** concentrate on a special market segment with the objective of serving its needs better than anyone else. The strategies focus organizational resources and expertise on a particular customer group, geographical region, or product or service line. They seek competitive advantage in that market segment through product differentiation or cost leadership. Low-fare airlines, for example, offer

○ A **differentiation strategy** offers products that are unique and different from the competition.

○ A **cost leadership strategy** seeks to operate with lower costs than competitors.

○ A **focused differentiation strategy** offers a unique product to a special market segment.

○ A **focused cost leadership strategy** seeks the lowest costs of operations within a special market segment.

heavily discounted fares and "no frills" service. They focus on serving customers who want to travel point-to-point for the lowest prices. They profit by lowering their costs—for example, by flying to regional airports and eliminating traditional free on-board services such as meals and drinks.

IN PRACTICE

Where selling a better rose makes the difference

A family-owned company in New Philadelphia, Ohio, Endres Floral Company has found its niche by selling "a better rose." And sell it does, shipping millions of roses per year to wholesalers. With 50 employees and 6 acres of greenhouses, the firm grows 170,000 rose bushes and harvests twice each day. To compete with lower-cost producers from South America, the firm differentiates itself on quality. Endres red roses are supposed to last 10 days to 2 weeks without drooping. They are stored in computer-controlled coolers and shipped in special containers. No Endres rose is out of water more than 10 minutes after cutting. A genuine Endres rose can be in a customer's home within 24 hours. The company was founded by Eugene V. Endres, now in the Ohio Agricultural Hall of Fame.[35]

PORTFOLIO PLANNING

In a single-product or single-business firm, the strategic context is one industry. Corporate strategy and business strategy are the same, and resources are allocated on that basis. When firms operate in multiple industries with many products or services, they become internally more complex and often larger in size. This makes resource allocation a more challenging strategic management task, since the mix of businesses must be well managed. The strategy problem is similar to that faced by an individual with limited money who must choose among alternative stocks, bonds, and real estate in a personal investment portfolio. In multibusiness situations, strategy formulation also involves **portfolio planning** to allocate scarce resources among competing uses.[36]

○ A **portfolio planning** approach seeks the best mix of investments among alternative business opportunities.

○ The **BCG matrix** analyzes business opportunities according to market growth rate and market share.

BCG Matrix

Figure 9.7 summarizes an approach to business portfolio planning developed by the Boston Consulting Group and known as the **BCG matrix.** This framework analyzes business opportunities according to industry or market growth rate and market share.[37] As shown in the figure, this comparison results in four possible business conditions, with each being associated with a strategic implication: (1) *stars*—high-market-share/high-growth businesses; (2) *cash cows*—high-market-share/low-growth businesses; (3) *question marks*—low-market-share/high-growth businesses; and (4) *dogs*—low-market-share/ low-growth businesses.

Stars are high-market-share businesses in high-growth markets. They produce large profits through substantial penetration of expanding markets. The preferred strategy for stars is growth, and further resource investments in them are recommended. *Question marks* are low-market-share businesses in high-growth markets. They do not produce much profit but compete in rapidly growing markets. They are the source of difficult strategic decisions. The preferred strategy is growth, but the risk exists that further investments will not result in improved market share.

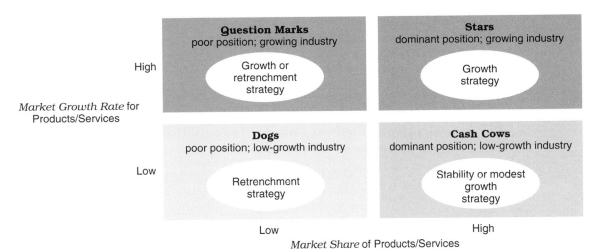

Figure 9.7 The BCG matrix approach to corporate strategy formulation.

Only the most promising question marks should be targeted for growth; others are candidates for retrenchment by restructuring or divesiture.

Cash cows are high-market-share businesses in low-growth markets. They produce large profits and a strong cash flow. Because the markets offer little growth opportunity, the preferred strategy is stability or modest growth. "Cows" should be "milked" to generate cash that can be used to support investments in stars and question marks. *Dogs* are low-market-share businesses in low-growth markets. They do not produce much profit, and they show little potential for future improvement. The preferred strategy for dogs is retrenchment by divestiture.

ADAPTIVE STRATEGIES

The Miles and Snow adaptive model of strategy formulation suggests that organizations pursue strategies that best fit with their external environments.[38] A well-chosen strategy allows an organization to successfully adapt to environmental challenges. The *prospector strategy* involves pursuing innovation and new opportunities in the face of risk and with prospects for growth. This is best suited to a dynamic and high-potential environment. A prospector "leads" an industry by using existing technology to new advantage and creating new products to which competitors must respond. This contrasts with a *defender strategy,* in which an organization tries to protect current market share by emphasizing existing products and without seeking growth. Defenders, like many small local retailers, try to maintain their operating domains with only slight changes over time. As a result, many suffer long-term decline in the face of competition. Defense is a protective strategy suited only for a stable environment and perhaps declining industries.

The *analyzer strategy* seeks to maintain the stability of a core business while exploring selective opportunities for innovation and change. This strategy lies between the prospector and reactor strategies. It is a "follow-the-leader-when-things-look-good" approach. Many of the "clone" makers in the personal computer industry are analyzers; that is, they wait to see what the industry leaders do and how well it works out before modifying their own operations. Organizations pursuing a *reactor strategy* have no real strategy of their own. They simply respond to competitive pressures in order to survive.

www.worthington industries.com

Worthington Industries pursues a human resource strategy based on trust. There are no time clocks. All full-time employees are on salaries. The firm provides free coffee, in-plant barbershops, and medical-wellness centers.

This is a "change-as-last-resort" approach. Reactors are slow to adapt to environmental changes and are the least desirable types in the Miles and Snow model.

A great business model travels the trade routes of the world

In the world of the Internet, eBay, Inc. lives up to its billing as "the world's online marketplace." On any given day over 12 million items are for sale on its website, the most visited on the Internet; online members transact over $15 billion in sales annually, worldwide. Not bad for a company that started in 1995 with a business model that almost seemed too simple to be right: Carry no inventory; just offer an electronic means for buyers and sellers to meet—for a fee. CEO Meg Whitman describes eBay's mission as: "to provide a global trading platform where practically anyone can trade practically anything." The company maintains dedicated local sites in many countries from Singapore to Spain. Although others may try to copy the eBay strategy, its first-mover advantage and global brand make it hard to beat.[39]

INCREMENTALISM AND EMERGENT STRATEGY

Not all strategies are created in systematic and deliberate fashion and then implemented step by step. Instead, strategies sometimes take shape, change, and develop over time as modest adjustments to past patterns. James Brian Quinn calls this a process of *incrementalism,* whereby modest and incremental changes in strategy occur as managers learn from experience and make adjustments.[40] This approach has much in common with Henry Mintzberg's and John Kotter's descriptions of managerial behavior, as described in Chapter 1.[41] They view managers as planning and acting in complex interpersonal networks and in hectic, fast-paced work settings. Given these challenges, effective managers must have the capacity to stay focused on long-term objectives while still remaining flexible enough to master short-run problems and opportunities as they occur.

○ An **emergent strategy** develops over time as managers learn from and respond to experience.

Such reasoning has led Mintzberg to identify what he calls **emergent strategies.**[42] These are strategies that develop progressively over time as "streams" of decisions made by managers as they learn from and respond to work situations. There is an important element of "craftsmanship" here that Mintzberg worries may be overlooked by managers who choose and discard strategies in rapid succession while using the formal planning models. He also believes that incremental or emergent strategic planning allows managers and organizations to become really good at implementing strategies, not just formulating them.

Be sure you can • explain the four generic strategies in Porter's model • illustrate how these strategies use products in a market familiar to you • describe the BCG matrix for portfolio planning and use it to analyze strategic opportunities for a business • differentiate among the prospector, defender, analyzer, and reactor strategies • explain the concepts of incrementalism and emergent strategy

STRATEGY IMPLEMENTATION

No strategy, no matter how well formulated, can achieve long-term success if it is not properly implemented. This includes the willingness to exercise control and make modifications as required to meet the needs of changing conditions. Current issues in strategy implementation include excellence in all management systems and practices, the responsibilities of corporate governance, and the importance of strategic leadership.

MANAGEMENT PRACTICES AND SYSTEMS

The rest of *Management 8/e* is about strategy implementation. In order to successfully put strategies into action, the entire organization and all of its resources must be mobilized in support of them. This, in effect, involves the complete management process from planning and controlling through organizing and leading. No matter how well or elegantly selected, a strategy requires supporting structures, the right technology, a good allocation of tasks and workflow designs, and the right people to staff all aspects of operations. The strategy needs to be enthusiastically supported by leaders who are capable of motivating everyone, building individual performance commitments, and utilizing teams and teamwork to their best advantage. And the strategy needs to be well- and continually communicated to all relevant persons and parties. Only with such total system support for implementation can strategies succeed in today's challenging and highly competitive environments.

Failures of substance and failures of process are common pitfalls that hinder strategy implementation. *Failures of substance* reflect inadequate attention to the major strategic planning elements—analysis of mission and purpose, core values and corporate culture, organizational strengths and weaknesses, and environmental opportunities and threats. *Failures of process* reflect poor handling of the ways in which the various aspects of strategic planning were accomplished. An important process failure is the *lack of participation error.* This is failure to include key persons in the strategic planning effort.[43] As a result, their lack of commitment to all-important action follow-through may severely hurt strategy implementation. Process failure also occurs with too much centralization of planning in top management or too much delegation of planning activities to staff planners or separate planning departments. Another process failure is the tendency to get so bogged down in details that the planning process becomes an end in itself instead of a means to an end. This is sometimes called "goal displacement."

www.americawest.com

America West Airlines competes as a low-cost, full-service airline. The firm strives to sustain financial strength and profitability by careful management of operations and focused route structures.

CORPORATE GOVERNANCE

In the wake of the ethics scandals in business, organizations today are experiencing new pressures at the level of **corporate governance.** As discussed in earlier chapters, this is the system of control and performance monitoring of top management that is maintained by boards of directors and other major stakeholder representatives. In businesses, for example, corporate governance is enacted by boards, institutional investors in a firm's assets, and other ownership interests. Each in its own way is a point of accountability for top management.[44]

Boards of directors play major roles in corporate governance. They are formally charged with ensuring that an organization operates in the best interests of its owners and/or the representative public in the case of non-

O **Corporate governance** is the system of control and performance monitoring of top management.

profit organizations. Controversies sometimes arise over the role of *inside directors,* who are chosen from the senior management of the organization, and *outside directors,* who are chosen from other organizations and positions external to the organization. In some cases insiders may have too much control; in others the outsiders may be selected because they are friends of top management or at least sympathetic to them. The concern is that the boards may be too compliant in endorsing or confirming the strategic initiatives of top management. Today board members are increasingly expected to exercise control and take active roles in ensuring that the stratgic management of an enterprise is successful. They are also being selected because of special expertise that they can bring to the governance process.

If anything, the current trend is toward greater emphasis on the responsibilities of corporate governance. Top managers probably feel more performance accountability today than ever before to boards of directors and other stakeholder interest groups. Furthermore, this accountability relates not only to financial performance but also to broader ethical and social responsibility concerns. At GE, for example, CEO Jeffrey Immelt makes it a practice to absent himself at times from director's meetings.[45] His predecessor, Jack Welch, always wanted to be present when directors met, but Immelt believes differently. His practice helps ensure that the governance responsibilities of the board, including oversight of the CEO's decisions and actions, are independently exercised.

STRATEGIC LEADERSHIP

Effective strategy implementation depends on the full commitment of all managers to support and lead strategic initiatives within their areas of supervisory responsibility. In our dynamic and often-uncertain environment, the premium is on **strategic leadership**—the capability to inspire people to successfully engage in a process of continuous change, performance enhancement, and implementation of organizational strategies.[46] The broad issues associated with strategic leadership are so important that Part 5 of *Management 8/e* is devoted in its entirety to leadership and issues related to leadership development—including leadership models, motivation, communication, interpersonal dynamics, teamwork, and change leadership.

Porter argues that the CEO of a business has to be the chief strategist, someone who provides strategic leadership.[47] He describes the task in the following way. A strategic leader has to be the *guardian of trade-offs.* It is the leader's job to make sure that the organization's resources are allo-

○ **Strategic leadership** inspires people to continuously change, refine, and improve strategies and their implementation.

cated in ways consistent with the strategy. This requires the discipline to sort through many competing ideas and alternatives to stay on course and not get sidetracked. A strategic leader also needs to *create a sense of urgency,* not allowing the organization and its members to grow slow and complacent. Even when doing well, the leader keeps the focus on getting better and being alert to conditions that require adjustments to the strategy. A strategic leader needs to *make sure that everyone understands the strategy.* Unless strategies are understood, the daily tasks and contributions of people lose context and purpose. Everyone might work very hard, but without alignment to strategy the impact is dispersed rather than advancing in a common direction to accomplish the goals. Importantly, a strategic leader must *be a teacher.* It is the leader's job to teach the strategy and make it a "cause," says Porter. In order for strategy to work, it must become an ever-present commitment throughout the organization. This means that a strategic leader must *be a great communicator.* Everyone must understand the strategy and how it makes their organization different from others.

Finally, it is important to note that the challenges faced by organizations today are so complex that it is difficult for any one individual to fulfill all strategic leadership needs. Strategic management is increasingly viewed as a team leadership responsibility. When Michael Dell founded Dell Computer, he did it in his dormitory room at college. Now the firm operates globally with $30 billion in sales. Dell is still Chairman and CEO, but he operates with a top management team. "I don't think you could do it with one person," he says, "there's way too much to be done."[48] As discussed in Chapter 16 on teams and teamwork, it takes hard work and special circumstances to create a real team, at the top or anywhere else in the organization.[49] Top management teams must work up to their full potential in order to bring the full advantages of teamwork to strategic leadership. Dell believes his top management team has mastered the challenge. "We bounce ideas off each other," he says, "and at the end of the day if we say who did this, the only right answer is that we all did. Three heads are better than one."

✔REALITY CHECK 9.2

Importance of leadership qualities

Fast Company magazine and Digital Marketing Services asked 1000 college graduates to think about success and business leadership in the future. At the top of their list of very important leadership capabilities was "technology smarts." Take the online "Reality Check" to learn more about the qualities that make a difference in strategic leadership.

Be sure you can • explain how the management process supports strategy implementation • define the term "corporate governance" • explain why boards of directors sometimes fail in their governance responsibilities • define the term "strategic leadership" • list the responsibilities of a strategic leader in today's organizations

Learning check 5

CHAPTER 9 STUDY GUIDE

Where We've Been

BACK TO STARBUCKS

The opening example of Starbucks introduced a firm that has successfully and aggressively followed a growth strategy. In Chapter 9 you learned more about the concept of strategy and its relationship to the achievement of sustainable competitive advantage. You also learned how the strategic management process analyzes organization and environment, and utilizes various frameworks to select effective strategies. Finally, you learned that even the best strategies deliver high-performance results only when they are well implemented.

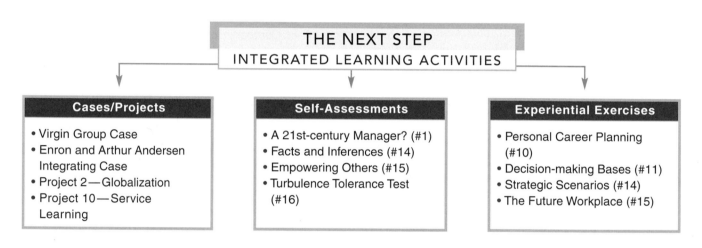

THE NEXT STEP
INTEGRATED LEARNING ACTIVITIES

Cases/Projects	Self-Assessments	Experiential Exercises
• Virgin Group Case • Enron and Arthur Andersen Integrating Case • Project 2—Globalization • Project 10—Service Learning	• A 21st-century Manager? (#1) • Facts and Inferences (#14) • Empowering Others (#15) • Turbulence Tolerance Test (#16)	• Personal Career Planning (#10) • Decision-making Bases (#11) • Strategic Scenarios (#14) • The Future Workplace (#15)

STUDY QUESTIONS SUMMARY

1. What are the foundations of strategic competitiveness?

- Competitive advantage is achieved by operating in ways difficult for competitors to imitate.
- A strategy is a comprehensive plan that sets long-term direction and guides resource allocation for sustainable competitive advantage.
- Strategic intent directs organizational resources and energies toward a compelling goal.
- The strategic goals of a business should include superior profitability and the generation of above-average returns for investors.

2. What is the strategic management process?

- Strategic management is the process of formulating and implementing strategies that achieve goals in a competitive environment.
- The strategic management process begins with analysis of mission, clarification of core values, and identification of objectives.
- A SWOT analysis systematically assesses organizational resources and capabilities and industry/environmental opportunities and threats.
- Porter's five forces model analyzes industry attractiveness in terms of competititors, new entrants, substitute products, and the bargaining powers of suppliers and buyers.

3. What types of strategies are used by organizations?

- Corporate strategy sets direction for an entire organization; business strategy sets direction for a business division or product/service line; functional strategy sets direction for the operational support of business and corporate strategies.

- The grand or master strategies used by organizations include growth—pursuing expansion through concentration and diversification; they also include retrenchment—pursuing ways to scale back operations through restructuring and divestiture.
- Global strategies take advantage of international business opportunities; cooperative strategies, such as international joint ventures, use strategic alliances for performance gains.
- E-business strategies use IT and the Internet to pursue competitive advantage.

4. How are strategies formulated?

- The three options in Porter's model of competitive strategy are: differentiation—distinguishing one's products from the competition; cost leadership—minimizing costs relative to the competition; and focus—concentrating on a special market segment.
- The BCG matrix is a portfolio planning approach that classifies businesses or product lines as "stars," "cash cows," "question marks," or "dogs."
- The adaptive model focuses on the congruence of prospector, defender, analyzer, or reactor strategies with demands of the external environment.

- The incremental or emergent model recognizes that many strategies are formulated and implemented incrementally over time.

5. What are current issues in strategy implementation?

- Management practices and systems—including the functions of planning, organizing, leading, and controlling—must be mobilized to support strategy implementation.
- Pitfalls that inhibit strategy implementation include failures of substance—such as poor analysis of the environment, and failures of process- such as lack of participation in the planning process.
- Boards of directors play important roles in corporate governance, monitoring top management, and organizational strategies and performance.
- Strategic leadership inspires the process of continuous evaluation and improvement of strategies and their implementation.
- Success in strategic leadership requires the ability to manage trade-offs in resource allocations, maintain a sense of urgency in strategy implementation, and effectively communicate the strategy to key constituencies.

KEY TERMS REVIEW

Above-average returns (p. 220)
B2B business strategy (p. 230)
B2C business strategy (p. 230)
BCG matrix (p. 234)
Business strategy (p. 227)
Competitive advantage (p. 219)
Concentration (p. 228)

Core competencies (p. 224)
Corporate governance (p. 237)
Corporate strategy (p. 227)
Cost leadership strategy (p. 233)
Differentiation strategy (p. 233)
Diversification (p. 228)
Divestiture (p. 229)

Downsizing (p. 229)
E-business strategy (p. 230)
Emergent strategy (p. 236)
Focused cost leadership strategy (p. 233)
Focused differentiation strategy (p. 233)
Functional strategy (p. 227)
Globalization strategy (p. 229)

SELF-TEST 9

MULTIPLE-CHOICE QUESTIONS:

1. The most appropriate first question to ask in strategic planning is _____.
   (a) "Where do we want to be in the future?" (b) "How well are we currently doing?" (c) "How can we get where we want to be?" (d) "Why aren't we doing better?"

2. The ability of a firm to consistently outperform its rivals is called _____.
   (a) vertical integration (b) competitive advantage (c) incrementalism (d) strategic intent

3. In a complex conglomerate business such as General Electric, a(n) _____ -level strategy sets strategic direction for a strategic business unit or product division.
   (a) institutional (b) corporate (c) business (d) functional

4. An organization that is downsizing to reduce costs is implementing a grand strategy of _____.
   (a) growth (b) cost differentiation (c) retrenchment (d) stability

5. The _____ is a predominant value system for an organization as a whole.
   (a) strategy (b) core competency (c) mission (d) corporate culture

6. A _____ in the BCG matrix would have a high market share in a low-growth market.
   (a) dog (b) cash cow (c) question mark (d) star

7. In Porter's five forces framework, which of the following increases industry attractiveness?
   (a) many rivals (b) many substitute products (c) low bargaining power of suppliers (d) few barriers to entry

8. When PepsiCo acquired Tropicana, a maker of orange juice, the firm's strategy was one of _____.
   (a) related diversification (b) concentration (c) vertical integration (d) cooperation

9. Cost efficiency and product quality are two examples of _____ objectives of organizations.
   (a) official (b) operating (c) informal (d) institutional

10. The customer generally gains through the lower prices and greater innovation characteristic of _____ environments.
    (a) monopoly (b) oligopoly (c) hypercompetition (d) central planning

11. In the Miles and Snow model of adaptive strategy, the _____ strategy is largely a copycat approach that seeks to do whatever seems to be working well for someone else.
    (a) prospector (b) reactor (c) defender (d) analyzer

12. The role of the board of directors as an oversight body that holds top executives accountable for the success of business strategies is called _____.
    (a) strategic leadership (b) corporate governance (c) logical incrementalism (d) strategic opportunism

13. Among the global strategies that might be pursued by international businesses, the _____ strategy is the most targeted on local needs, local management, and local products.
    (a) ethnocentric (b) transnational (c) geocentric (d) multidomestic

14. Restructuring by downsizing operations and reducing stuff is a form of _____ strategy.
    (a) retrenchment (b) growth (c) concentration (d) incremental

15. According to Porter's model of generic strategies, a firm that wants to compete with its rivals by selling a very low priced product would need to succesfully implement a _____ strategy.
    (a) retrenchment (b) differentiation (c) cost leadership (d) diversification

SHORT-RESPONSE QUESTIONS:

16. What is the difference between corporate strategy and functional strategy?

17. How would a manager perform a SWOT analysis?

18. Explain the difference between B2B and B2C as e-business strategies.

19. What is strategic leadership?

APPLICATION QUESTION:

20. Kim Harris owns and operates a small retail store selling the outdoor clothing of an American manufacturer to a predominately college student market. Lately, a large department store outside of town has started selling similar but lower-priced clothing manufactured in China, Thailand, and Bangladesh. Kim believes he is starting to lose business to this store. Assume you are part of a student team assigned to do a management class project for Kim. His question for the team is: "How can I best deal with my strategic management challenges in this situation?" How will you reply?

www.wiley.com/college/schermerhorn

10

Organizing

CHAPTER 10 study questions

1. What is organizing as a management function?

2. What are the major types of organization structures?

3. What are the new developments in organization structures?

4. What organizing trends are changing the workplace?

Planning Ahead

After reading Chapter 10, you should be able to answer these questions in your own words.

EDWARD JONES—STRUCTURES MUST SUPPORT STRATEGIES

Management scholar and consultant Peter Drucker once called brokerage firm Edward Jones "the Wal-Mart of Wall Street." He describes the firm as having a clear strategy and an innovative structure that directly supports it.

Like Wal-Mart, Edward Jones established itself in rural America. The structure is unique, with a strong core surrounded by largely independent satellite units. Drucker likens it to a "confederation of highly autonomous entrepreneurial units bound together by a highly centralized core of values and services."

The St. Louis-based firm has been called the "last 'not-com' brokerage." Managing partner John Bachman believes the firm succeeds by being different, and he is not interested in becoming an online broker. If you visit the firm's *modest website,* you can't trade online. But you can easily locate one of Edward Jones's nearby branches.

A values-driven commitment to the customer is a common bond among the entrepreneurial Edward Jones brokers, as is a focus on long-term investing and a safety-first orientation. The business strategy is face-to-face and customer-oriented brokerage. Given that, the brokers have the freedom to deal with customers in their own way and in their local setting. Bachman says: "I'm comfortable with our strategy. There's a difference between being part of a market and being the total market. We're the leader in what we do."

Called "America's Main Street Broker" by *Forbes* magazine, Edward Jones ranked on *Fortune* magazine's list of the best companies to work for in America for two years; it has also been ranked highly on *Working Mother* magazine's list of the best firms for working mothers.[1]

Get Connected!

Examine the financial services industry. What are the differences among major firms? Make sure you can manage personal finances.

Chapter 10 Learning Preview

The opening example of Edward Jones shows how one firm has organized itself for high performance in the financial services industry. Part of the challenge faced by the company is to maintain success with its entrepreneurial strategy and small-firm ways even while experiencing the pressures of growth. This chapter introduces you to organizing as a management function. It reviews the traditional ways of structuring organizations as well as new directions such as those taken by Edward Jones. Current trends and organizing practices in the new workplace are also described.

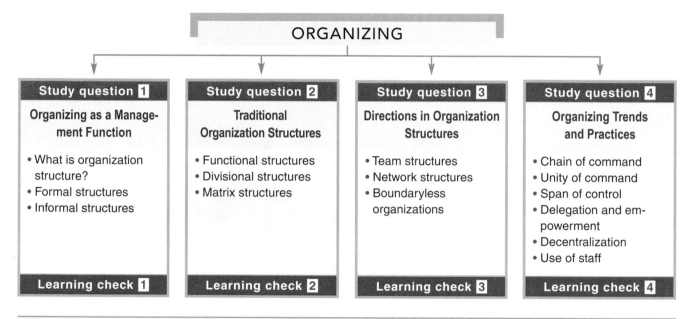

ORGANIZING

Study question 1

Organizing as a Management Function

• What is organization structure?
• Formal structures
• Informal structures

Learning check 1

Study question 2

Traditional Organization Structures

• Functional structures
• Divisional structures
• Matrix structures

Learning check 2

Study question 3

Directions in Organization Structures

• Team structures
• Network structures
• Boundaryless organizations

Learning check 3

Study question 4

Organizing Trends and Practices

• Chain of command
• Unity of command
• Span of control
• Delegation and empowerment
• Decentralization
• Use of staff

Learning check 4

M anagement scholar and consultant Henry Mintzberg points out that organizations are changing very fast in today's world and people within them are struggling to find their place.[2] His point is that people need to understand how their organizations work if they are to work well within them. Mintzberg notes some common questions: "What parts connect to one another?" "How should processes and people come together?" "Whose ideas have to flow where?" These and related questions raise critical issues about organization structures and how well they meet an organization's performance needs.

The organizing approach of Edward Jones—management through a strong central core surrounded by small and autonomous units—is one entrepreneurial benchmark. By building a well-focused yet market-responsive structure, the firm has established and sustained a niche in the highly competitive financial services industry. But this is only one of the ways to structure for success. There are many options as organizations in all industries try new forms in the quest for sustained competitive advantage. Some are using designs that we will discuss as team, network, or even "boundaryless" and "virtual" organizations. Others involve downsizing, rightsizing, and delayering organizations in the search for productivity gains.

Among the best organizations, those that consistently deliver above-average returns and outperform their competitors, one does find consistent themes.[3] They emphasize empowerment, support for employees, responsiveness to client or customer needs, flexibility in dealing with a dynamic environment, and continual attention to quality improvements. They strive for positive cultures and high-quality-of-work-life experiences for members and employees. And importantly, they accept that nothing is constant, at least not for long. They are always seeking new ways of organizing the workplace to best support strategies and achieve high-performance goals.

ORGANIZING AS A MANAGEMENT FUNCTION

Organizing is the process of arranging people and other resources to work together to accomplish a goal. As one of the basic functions of management, it involves both creating a division of labor for tasks to be performed and then coordinating results to achieve a common purpose. *Figure 10.1* shows the central role that organizing plays in the management process. Once plans are created, the manager's task is to see to it that they are carried out. Given a clear mission, core values, objectives, and strategy, *organizing* begins the process of implementation by clarifying jobs and working relationships. It identifies who is to do what, who is in charge of whom, and how different people and parts of the organization relate to and work with one another. All of this, of course, can be done in different ways. The strategic leadership challenge is to choose the best organizational form to fit the strategy and other situational demands.

○ **Organizing** arranges people and resources to work toward a goal.

WHAT IS ORGANIZATION STRUCTURE?

The way in which the various parts of an organization are formally arranged is usually referred to as the **organization structure.** It is the system of tasks, workflows, reporting relationships, and communication channels that link together the work of diverse individuals and groups. Any structure should both allocate tasks through a division of labor and provide for the coordination of performance results. A structure that does both of these things well is an important asset, helping to implement an organization's strategy.[4] Unfortunately, it is easier to talk about good structures than it is to actually create them. This is why you often read and hear about organizations changing their structures in an attempt to improve performance. There is no one best structure that meets the needs of all circumstances; structure must be addressed in a contingency fashion. As environments and situations change,

○ **Organization structure** is a system of tasks, reporting relationships, and communication linkages.

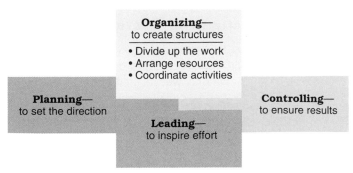

Figure 10.1 Organizing viewed in relationship with the other management functions.

structures must often be changed too. To make good choices, a manager must understand how structures work and know the available alternatives.

FORMAL STRUCTURES

○ An **organization chart** describes the arrangement of work positions within an organization.

○ **Formal structure** is the official structure of the organization.

What you can learn from an organization chart

You may know the concept of structure best in the form of an **organization chart.** This is a diagram that shows reporting relationships and the formal arrangement of work positions within an organization.[5] A typical organization chart identifies various positions and job titles as well as the lines of authority and communication between them. This is the **formal structure,** or the structure of the organization in its official state. It represents the way the organization is intended to function. By reading an organization chart, you can learn the basics of an organization's formal structure, including:

- *Division of work:* Positions and titles show work responsibilities.
- *Supervisory relationships:* Lines show who reports to whom.
- *Communication channels:* Lines show formal communication flows.
- *Major subunits:* Positions reporting to a common manager are shown.
- *Levels of management:* Vertical layers of management are shown.

INFORMAL STRUCTURES

○ **Informal structure** is the set of unofficial relationships among an organization's members.

Behind every formal structure typically lies an **informal structure.** This is a "shadow" organization made up of the unofficial, but often critical, working relationships between organizational members. If the informal structure could be drawn, it would show who talks to and interacts regularly with whom regardless of their formal titles and relationships. The lines of the informal structure would cut across levels and move from side to side. They would show people meeting for coffee, in exercise groups, and in frendship cliques, among other possibilities. Importantly, no organization can be fully understood without gaining insight into the informal structure as well as the formal one.[7]

Informal structures can be very helpful in getting work accomplished. Indeed, they may be essential in many ways to organizational success. This is especially true during times of change, when out-of-date formal structures may fail to provide the support people need to deal with new or unusual situations. Because it takes time to change or modify formal struc-

IN PRACTICE

You can design organizations for informal learning

When the Center for Workforce Development conducted a study at a Siemens factory in North Carolina, the focus was on informal learning. What they found was that the cafeteria was a "hotbed" of learning as workers shared ideas, problems, and solutions with one another over snacks and meals. The Director of Training for Siemens said: "The assumption was made that this was chit chat, talking about the golf game. But there was a whole lot of work activity." For Seimens and other organizations the lesson is to mobilize informal learning opportunities as a resource for continuous organizational improvement.[6]

tures, this happens quite often. In many cases, the informal structure helps fill the void. Through the emergent and spontaneous relationships of informal structures, people benefit in task performance by being in personal contact with others who can help them get things done when necessary. They gain the advantages of *informal learning* that takes place while working and interacting together throughout the workday. Informal structures are also helpful in giving people access to interpersonal networks of emotional support and friendship that satisfy important social needs.

Of course, informal structures also have potential disadvantages. Because they exist outside the formal authority system, the activities of informal structures can sometimes work against the best interests of the organization as a whole. They can be susceptible to rumor, carry inaccurate information, breed resistance to change, and even divert work efforts from important objectives. Also, "outsiders" or people who are left out of informal groupings may feel less a part of daily activities and suffer a loss of satisfaction. Some American managers of Japanese firms, for example, have complained about being excluded from what they call the "shadow cabinet"—an informal group of Japanese executives who hold the real power to get things done and sometimes act to the exclusion of others."[8]

REALITY CHECK 10.1

Structural changes for global businesses
An *Industry Week* survey of 175 CEOs and corporate officers focused on structural changes needed to survive in the tough global economy. They ranked #1 as focusing more on core business areas. Take the online "Reality Check" to learn more about what executives say about changing organizational structures.

Be sure you can • define organizing as a management function • explain the difference between formal and informal structures • discuss the potential advantages and disadvantages of informal structures in organizations

Learning check 1

TRADITIONAL ORGANIZATION STRUCTURES

A traditional principle of organizing is that performance improves when people are allowed to specialize and become expert in specific jobs or tasks. Given this division of labor, however, decisions must then be made on **departmentalization,** how to group work positions into formal teams or departments that are linked together in a coordinated way. These decisions have traditionally resulted in three major types of organizational structures—the functional, divisional, and matrix structures.[9]

○ **Departmentalization** is the process of grouping together people and jobs into work units.

FUNCTIONAL STRUCTURES

In **functional structures,** people with similar skills and performing similar tasks are grouped together into formal work units. Members of functional departments share technical expertise, interests, and responsibilities. The first example in *Figure 10.2* shows a functional structure common in business firms: Top management is arranged by the functions of marketing, finance, production, and human resources. In this functional structure, manufacturing problems are the responsibility of the production vice president, marketing problems are the province of the marketing vice president, and so on. The key point is that members of each function work within their areas of expertise. If each function does its work properly, the expectation is that the business will operate successfully.

○ A **functional structure** groups together people with similar skills who perform similar tasks.

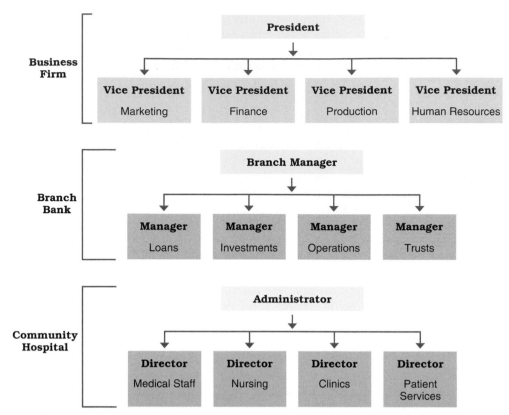

Figure 10.2   Functional structures in a business, branch bank, and community hospital.

Functional structures are not limited to businesses. The figure also shows how this form of departmentalization can be used in other types of organizations, such as banks and hospitals. Functional structures typically work well for small organizations that produce only one or a few products or services. They also tend to work best in relatively stable environments where problems are predictable and the demands for change and innovation are limited. The major *advantages of a functional structure* include the following:

Advantages of functional structures →

- Economies of scale with efficient use of resources.
- Task assignments consistent with expertise and training.
- High-quality technical problem solving.
- In-depth training and skill development within functions.
- Clear career paths within functions.

There are also potential *disadvantages of functional structures.* Common problems include difficulties in pinpointing responsibilities for things like cost containment, product or service quality, timeliness, and innovation. A significant concern is with the **functional chimneys problem**—lack of communication, coordination, and problem solving across functions. Because the functions become formalized not only on an organization chart but also in the mindsets of people, the sense of cooperation and common purpose breaks down. The total system perspective is lost to self-centered and narrow viewpoints. When problems occur between functions, they are too often referred up to higher levels for resolution rather than being addressed by people at the same level. This slows decision making and problem solving and can result in a loss of advantage in competitive situations. For example,

○ The **functional chimneys problem** is a lack of communication and coordination across functions.

when Ford took over as the new owner of Jaguar it had to resolve many quality problems. The quality turnaround took longer than anticipated, in part because of what Jaguar's chairman called "excessive compartmentalization." In building cars, the different departments did very little talking and working with one another. Ford's response was to push for more interdepartmental coordination and consensus decision making.[10]

DIVISIONAL STRUCTURES

A second organizational alternative is the **divisional structure.** It groups together people who work on the same product or process, serve similar customers, and/or are located in the same area or geographical region. As illustrated in *Figure 10.3,* divisional structures are common in complex organizations with diverse operations that extend across many products, territories, customers, and work processes.[11]

Divisional structures attempt to avoid problems common to functional structures. The potential *advantages of divisional structures* include:

- More flexibility in responding to environmental changes.
- Improved coordination across functional departments.
- Clear points of responsibility for product or service delivery.
- Expertise focused on specific customers, products, and regions.
- Greater ease in changing size by adding or deleting divisions.

As with other alternatives, there are potential *disadvantages of divisional structures.* They can reduce economies of scale and increase costs through the duplication of resources and efforts across divisions. They can also create unhealthy rivalries as divisions compete for resources and top mangement attention, and as they emphasize division needs to the detriment of the goals of the organization as a whole.

○ A **divisional structure** groups together people working on the same product, in the same area, with similar customers, or on the same processes.

← Advantages of divisional structures

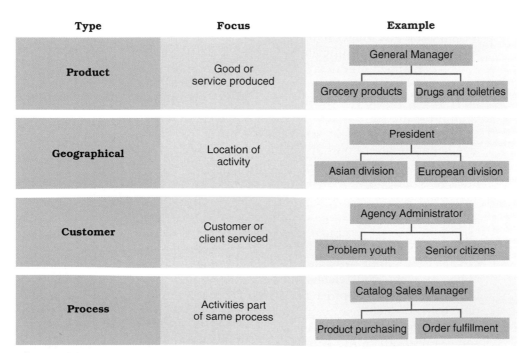

Figure 10.3 Divisional structures based on product, geography, customer, and process.

Product Structures

○ A **product structure** groups together people and jobs working on a single product or service.

Product structures, sometimes called *market structures,* group together jobs and activities working on a single product or service. They clearly identify costs, profits, problems, and successes in a market area with a central point of accountability. Consequently, managers are encouraged to be responsive to changing market demands and customer tastes. Common in large organizations, product structures may even extend into global operations. When taking over as H.J. Heinz's new CEO, William R. Johnson became concerned about the company's international performance. He decided a change in structure could help improve performance. The existing structure that emphasized countries and regions was changed to global product divisions. The choice was based on his belief that a product structure would bring the best brand management to all countries and increase cooperation around the world within product businesses.

Geographical Structures

○ A **geographical structure** groups together people and jobs performed in the same location.

Geographical structures, sometimes called *area structures,* group together jobs and activities being performed in the same location or geographical region. They are typically used when there is a need to differentiate products or services in various locations, such as in different regions of a country. They are also quite common in international operations, where they help to focus attention on the unique cultures and requirements of particular regions. As UPS operations expanded worldwide, for example, the company announced a change from a product to geographical organizational structure. Two geographical divisions were created—the Americas and Europe/Asia. Each area was given responsibility for its own logistics, sales, and other business functions.

Customer Structures

○ A **customer structure** groups together people and jobs that serve the same customers or clients.

Customer structures, sometimes called *market structures,* group together jobs and activities that are serving the same customers or clients. The major appeal is the ability to best serve the special needs of the different customer groups. This is a common form of structure for complex businesses in the consumer products industries. 3M corporation structures itself to focus attention around the world on such diverse markets as consumer and office, speciality materials, industrial, health care, electronics and communications, transportation, graphics, and safety. Customer structures are also useful in services, for example, where banks use them to give separate attention to consumer and commercial customers for loans. The example used in Figure 10.3 also shows a government agency serving different client populations.

Process Structures

○ A **process structure** groups jobs and activities that are part of the same processes.

A *work process* is a group of tasks related to one another that collectively creates something of value to a customer.[12] An example is order fulfillment, as when you telephone a catalog retailer and request a particular item. The process of order fulfillment takes the order from point of initiation by the customer to point of fulfillment by a delivered product. A **process structure** groups together jobs and activities that are part of the same processes. In the example of Figure 10.3, this might take the form of product-purchasing teams, order-fulfillment teams, and systems-support teams for the mail-order catalog business. The importance of understanding work processes and designing process-driven organizations has been popularized by management consultant and author Michael Hammer.[13] The essentials of Hammer's ideas on work process design are discussed in the next chapter.

MATRIX STRUCTURES

The **matrix structure,** often called the *matrix organization,* combines the functional and divisional structures just described. In effect, it is an attempt to gain the advantages and minimize the disadvantages of each. This is accomplished in the matrix by using permanent cross-functional teams to support specific products, projects, or programs.[14] As shown in *Figure 10.4,* workers in a matrix structure belong to at least two formal groups at the same time—a functional group and a product, program, or project team. They also report to two bosses—one within the function and the other within the team.

The matrix organization has gained a strong foothold in the workplace, with applications in such diverse settings as manufacturing (e.g., aerospace, electronics, pharmaceuticals), service industries (e.g., banking, brokerage, retailing), professional fields (e.g., accounting, advertising, law), and the nonprofit sector (e.g., city, state, and federal agencies, hospitals, universities). Matrix structures are also found in multinational corporations, where they offer the flexibility to deal with regional differences as well as multiple product, program, or project needs.

The main contribution of matrix structures to organizational performance lies with the cross-functional teams whose members work closely together to share expertise and information in a timely manner to solve problems. The potential *advantages of matrix structures* include the following:

○ A **matrix structure** combines functional and divisional approaches to emphasize project or program teams.

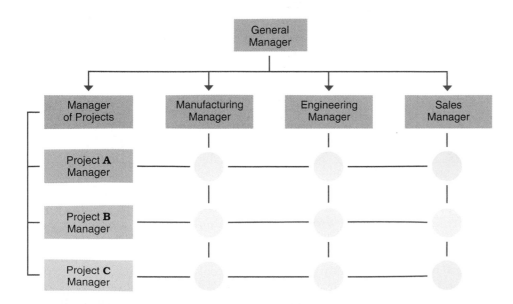

Functional personnel assigned to both projects and functional departments

Figure 10.4 Matrix structure in a small multiproject business firm.

Advantages of a matrix
structure

- Better cooperation across functions.
- Improved decision making as problem solving takes place at the team level, where the best information is available.
- Increased flexibility in adding, removing, and/or changing operations to meet changing demands.
- Better customer service, since there is always a program, product, or project manager informed and available to answer questions.
- Better performance accountability through the program, product, or project managers.
- Improved strategic management, since top managers are freed from unnecessary problem solving to focus time on strategic issues.

Predictably, there are also potential *disadvantages of matrix structures.* The two-boss system is susceptible to power struggles, as functional supervisors and team leaders vie with one another to exercise authority. The two-boss system can also be frustrating for matrix members if it creates task confusion and conflicting work priorities. Team meetings in the matrix are also time consuming. Teams may develop "groupitis," or strong team loyalties that cause a loss of focus on larger organizational goals. And the requirements of adding the team leaders to a matrix structure can result in increased costs.[15]

Learning check 2

Be sure you can • explain the differences between functional, divisional, and matrix structures • list advantages and disadvantages of a functional structure, and draw a chart to show its use in an organization familiar to you • list advantages and disadvantages of a divisional structure • draw a chart to show use of each divisional type in an organization familiar to you • list advantages and disadvantages of a matrix structure, and draw a chart to show its use in an organization familiar to you

---

DIRECTIONS IN ORGANIZATION STRUCTURES

The realities of a global economy and the demands of strategies driven by hypercompetition are putting increasing pressures on organization structures. The performance demands are for more speed to market, greater customer orientation, constant productivity improvements, better technology utilization, and more. The environment is unrelenting in such demands. As a result, managers are continually searching for new ways to better structure their organizations.

Structural innovation is always important in the search for productivity improvement and competitive advantage. The right structure is a performance asset; the wrong one is a liability. Today, the vertical and control-oriented structures of the past are proving less and less sufficient to master the tasks at hand. The matrix structure was a first step toward improving flexibility and problem solving through better cross-functional integration. It is now part of a broader movement toward more horizontal structures that decrease hierarchy, increase empowerment, and better mobilize technology and the talents of people to drive organizational performance. *Manager's Notepad 10.1* offers guidelines for tapping the opportunities of horizontal structures.[17]

TEAM STRUCTURES

As the traditional vertical structures give way to more horizontal ones, teams are serving as the basic building blocks.[18] Organizations with **team structures** extensively use both permanent and temporary teams to solve problems, complete special projects, and accomplish day-to-day tasks.[19] As illustrated in *Figure 10.5,* these are often **cross-functional teams** composed of members from different areas of work responsibility.[20] The intention is to break down the functional chimneys or barriers inside the organization and create more effective lateral relations for problem solving and work performance. They are also often **project teams** that are convened for a particular task or "project" and that disband once it is completed. The intention here is to quickly convene people with the needed talents and focus their efforts intensely to solve a problem or take advantage of a special opportunity.

There are many potential *advantages of team structures.* They help eliminate difficulties with communication and decision making due to the functional chimneys problem described earlier. Team assignments help to break down barriers between operating departments as people from different parts of an organization get to know one another. They can also boost morale. People working in teams often experience a greater sense of involvement and identification, increasing their enthusiasm for the job. Be-

o A **team structure** uses permanent and temporary cross-functional teams to improve lateral relations.

o A **cross-functional team** brings together members from different functional departments.

o **Project teams** are convened for a particular task or project and disband once it is completed.

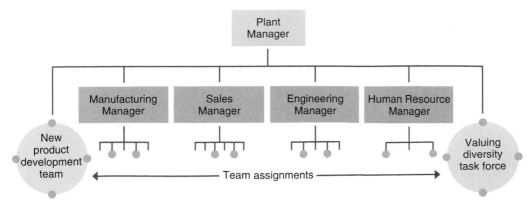

Figure 10.5 How a team structure uses cross-functional teams for improved lateral relations.

Team organization becomes part of borderless world

Intel is a well-known global competitor in the dynamic computer chip industry. But a visit to the firm's website is an eye opener. A quick look finds a listing of over 70 worldwide locations, from Belarus to the Philippines to Tajikistan. A fast-moving company in an industry that never sleeps, the firm taps the talents of the globe to keep its chips ahead of the pack. Intel relies heavily on a team organization; hierarchy takes a back seat to teamwork. Says one team member, "We report to each other." This commitment knows no boundaries. The County Kildare plant in Ireland was named recently by *Fortune* magazine as one of ten "Great Companies to Work For" in Europe. Judges highlighted the importance of egalitarianism at the Irish facility, stating: "Intel has brought to Ireland the Silicon Valley culture of no reserved parking spaces, no executive dining rooms, and small cubicles for all employees. Everyone is on a first-name basis.[16]

cause teams focus shared knowledge and expertise on specific problems, they can also improve the speed and quality of decisions in many situations. After a research team at Polaroid Corporation developed a new medical imaging system in three years, when most had predicted it would take six, a senior executive said, "Our researchers are not any smarter, but by working together they get the value of each other's intelligence almost instantaneously."[21]

The complexities of teams and teamwork contribute to the potential *disadvantages of team structures.* These include conflicting loyalties for persons with both team and functional assignments. They also include issues of time management and group process. By their very nature, teams spend a lot of time in meetings. Not all of this time is productive. How well team members spend their time together often depends on the quality of interpersonal relations, group dynamics, and team management. All of these concerns are manageable, as will be described in Chapter 16 on teams and teamwork.

NETWORK STRUCTURES

○ A **network structure** uses IT to link with networks of outside suppliers and service contractors.

Organizations using a **network structure** operate with a central core that is linked through "networks" of relationships with outside contractors and suppliers of essential services.[22] The old model was for organizations to own everything. The new model is to own only the most essential or "core" components of the business, and to engage in strategic alliances and "outsourcing," to provide the rest. The *strategic alliance,* discussed in the last chapter, is a cooperative strategy through which partners do things of mutual value for one another. **Outsourcing**

○ **Outsourcing** is when a business function is contracted to an outside supplier.

is the contracting of business functions to outside suppliers. For example, a bank may contract with local firms to provide mailroom, cafeteria, and legal services; an airline might contract out customer service jobs at various airports.

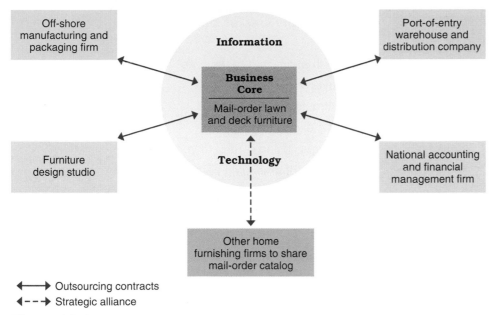

Figure 10.6 A network structure for a Web-based retail business.

Figure 10.6 illustrates a network structure as it might work for a mail-order company selling lawn and deck furniture through a catalog. The firm itself is very small, consisting of a relatively few full-time core employees working from a central headquarters. Beyond that, it is structured as a network of outsourcing and partner relationships, maintained operationally using the latest in information technology. Merchandise is designed on contract with a furniture design firm—which responds quickly as designs are shared and customized via computer networking; it is manufactured and packaged by subcontractors located around the world—wherever materials, quality, and cost are found at best advantage; stock is maintained and shipped from a contract warehouse—ensuring quality storage and on-time expert shipping; all of the accounting and financial details are managed on contract with an outside firm—providing better technical expertise than the firm could afford to employ on a full-time basis; and the quarterly catalog is designed, printed, and mailed cooperatively as a strategic alliance with two other firms that sell different home furnishings with a related price appeal. All of this, of course, is supported by a company website also maintained by an outside contractor.

The creative use of information technology adds to the potential *advantages of network structures.* With the technological edge the mail-order company in the prior example can operate with fewer full-time employees and less-complex internal systems. Network structures are thus very lean and streamlined. They help organizations stay cost competitive through reduced overhead and increased operating efficiency. Network concepts allow organizations to employ outsourcing strategies and contract out specialized business functions rather than maintain full-time staff to do them. Information technology now makes it easy to manage these contracts and business alliances, even across great distances. Within the operating core of a network structure, furthermore, a variety of interesting jobs are created for those who must coordinate the entire system of relationships.

The potential *disadvantages of network structures* largely lie with the demands of new management responsibilities. The more complex the business or mission of the organization, the more complicated the network of contracts and alliances that must be maintained. It may be diffi-

---

MANAGER'S NOTEPAD 10.2

Seven deadly sins of outsourcing

1. Outsourcing activities that are part of the core.
2. Outsourcing to untrustworthy vendors.
3. Not having good contracts with the vendor.
4. Overlooking impact on existing employees.
5. Not maintaining oversight; losing control to vendors.
6. Overlooking hidden costs of managing contracts.
7. Failing to anticipate need to change vendors, cease outsourcing.

---

cult to control and coordinate among them. If one part of the network breaks down or fails to deliver, the entire system suffers the consequences. Also, there is the potential for loss of control over activities contracted out and for a lack of loyalty to develop among contractors who are used infrequently rather than on a long-term basis. Some worry that outsourcing can become so aggressive as to be dangerous to the firm, especially when ever-more-critical activities such as finance, logistics, and human resources management are outsourced. *Manager's Notepad 10.2* lists "seven deadly sins" of outsourcing that were developed by research on the practice.[23] Overall, the conclusion is that outsourcing works well, but like anything else, it must be strategically directed and then controlled for results.

BOUNDARYLESS ORGANIZATIONS

○ A **boundaryless organization** eliminates internal boundaries among subsystems and external boundaries with the external environment.

It is popular today to speak about creating a **boundaryless organization** that eliminates internal boundaries among subsystems and external boundaries with the external environment.[25] The boundaryless organization can be viewed as a combination of the team and network structures just described, with the addition of "temporariness." Within the organization, teamwork and communication—spontaneous, as needed, and intense—replace formal lines of authority. There is an absence of boundaries that traditionally and structurally separate organizational members from one another. In the external context, organizational needs are met by a shifting mix of outsourcing contracts and operating alliances that form and disband with changing circumstances. A "photograph" that documents an organization's configuration of external relationships today will look different from one taken tomorrow, as the form naturally adjusts to new pressures and circumstances. *Figure 10.7* shows how the absence of internal and external barriers helps people work in ways that bring speed and flexibility to the boundaryless firm.

Key requirements of boundaryless organizations are the absence of hierarchy, empowerment of team members, technology utilization, and acceptance of impermanence. Work is accomplished by empowered people who come together voluntarily and temporarily to apply their expertise to a task, gather additional expertise from whatever sources may be required to perform it successfully, and stay together only as long as the task is a work in process. The focus is on talent for task. The assumption is that empowered people working together without bureaucratic restrictions can accomplish great things. Such a work setting is supposed to encourage

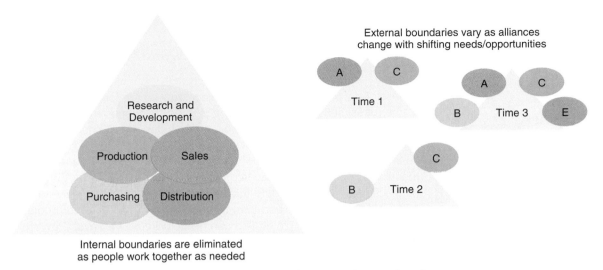

Figure 10.7 The boundaryless organization eliminates internal and external barriers.

creativity, quality, timeliness, and flexibility, while reducing inefficiencies and increasing speed. At General Electric, for example, the drive toward boundaryless operations is supported in part by aggressive "digitization." The firm is moving more and more administrative work onto the Web—where it can be done faster and by persons directly involved. Intermediaries in the form of support personnel are not needed.[26]

Knowledge sharing is both a goal and an essential component of the boundaryless organization. One way to think of this is in the context of a very small organization, perhaps a startup. In the small firm, everyone pitches in to help out as needed and when appropriate to get things done. There are no formal assignments, and there are no job titles or job descriptions standing in the way. People with talent work together as needed to get the job done. The boundaryless organization, in its pure form, is just like that. Even in the larger organizational context, meetings and spontaneous sharing are happening continuously; perhaps thousands of people working together in hundreds of teams form and disband as needed. At consulting giant PricewaterhouseCoopers, for example, knowledge sharing brings together 160,000 partners spread across 150 countries in a vast virtual learning and problem-solving network. Partners collaborate electronically through online databases where information is stored, problems posted, and questions asked and answered in real time by those with experience and knowledge relevant to the problem at hand. Technology makes collaboration instantaneously and always possible, breaking down boundaries that might otherwise slow or impede the firm's performance.[27]

In the organization/environment interface, boundaryless operations emerge in a special form that is sometimes called the **virtual organization**.[28] This is an organization that operates in a shifting network of external alliances that are engaged as needed using IT and the Internet. The boundaries that traditionally separate a firm from its suppliers, customers, and even competitors are largely eliminated, temporarily and in respect to a given transaction or business purpose. Virtual organizations come into being "as needed" when alliances are called into action to meet specific operating needs and objectives. When the work is complete, the alliance rests until next called into action. The virtual organization operates in this manner with the mix of mobilized alliances continuously shifting

o A **virtual organization** uses IT and the Internet to engage a shifting network of strategic alliances.

Harnessing knowledge and networks for economic development

June Holley, president of the Appalachian Center for Economic Networks, uses network organization concepts to support rural economic development. ACEnet is a networking hub for small businesses and micro-enterprises in rural Appalachian Ohio, linking them to develop new business initiatives. Holley began ACEnet to tap local ingenuity and resources for economic development. The pathway to progress was connection—bringing people into contact with one another. By helping people find one another and then by supporting their skills and products, Holley believes economic growth can be unlocked. She says: "Poverty is due to isolation." By breaking the isolation, ACEnet's networking model provides a valuable community service.[24]

and with an expansive pool of potential alliances always ready to be called upon as needed.

Learning check 3	*Be sure you can* • describe how organizations can include cross-functional teams and project teams in their structures • define the term network structure • illustrate how a new venture, such as a Web-based retailer, might use a network structure to organize its various operations • discuss the potential advantages and disadvantages of following a network approach • explain the concept of the boundaryless organization

ORGANIZING TRENDS AND PRACTICES

○ The **upside-down pyramid** puts customers at the top, served by workers whose managers support them.

When structures are modified, refined, and abandoned in the search for new ones, the organizing practices that create and implement them must change too. In Chapter 1 the concept of the **upside-down pyramid** was introduced as an example of the new directions in management. By putting customers on top, served by workers in the middle, who are in turn supported by managers at the bottom, this notion tries to refocus attention on the marketplace and customer needs. Although more of a concept than a depiction of an actual structure, such thinking is representative of forces shaping new directions in how the modern workplace is organized. Among the organizing trends to be discussed next, a common theme runs throughout—making the adjustments needed to streamline operations for cost efficiency, higher performance, and increased participation by workers.

SHORTER CHAINS OF COMMAND

○ The **chain of command** links all persons with successively higher levels of authority.

A typical organization chart shows the **chain of command,** or the line of authority that vertically links each position with successively higher levels of management. The classical school of management suggests that the chain of command should operate according to the *scalar principle*: There should be a clear and unbroken chain of command linking every person in the organization with successively higher levels of authority up to and including the top manager.

TAKE IT TO THE CASE

Strong roots grow enduring brands and great companies

It's hard to resist the sign in the window—"Hot Donuts Now." That sign has been hanging for a long time at Krispy Kreme franchises. Starting in 1937, the company has grown from a small wholesale shop to a publicly traded company with over 270 stores in the United States. CEO Scott Livengood is proud of the firm's history, including its place in a Smithsonian Museum exhibition: "Krispy Kreme: Taking a Bite Out of History." He believes that quality products and customer service provided the springboards for past success and remain the keys to a great future. In just four years the number of stores almost doubled, and there are no plans to cut back. Krispy Kreme stores are open in Canada and the United Kingdom, and international expansion plans include Japan, South Korea, New Zealand, and Spain. Livengood is betting that past lessons and the "Krispy Kreme experience" can successfully master future challenges.[29]

When organizations grow in size they tend to get taller, as more and more levels of management are added to the chain of command. This increases overhead costs; it tends to decrease communication and access between top and bottom levels; it can greatly slow decision making; and it can lead to a loss of contact with the client or customer. These are all reasons why "tall" organizations with many levels of management are often criticized for inefficiencies and poor productivity. The current trend is toward shorter chains of command.

Trend. Organizations are being "streamlined" by cutting unnecessary levels of management; flatter and more horizontal structures are viewed as a competitive advantage.

LESS UNITY OF COMMAND

Another classical management principle describes how the chain of command should operate in daily practice. The *unity-of-command principle* states that each person in an organization should report to one and only one supervisor. This notion of "one person–one boss" is a foundation of the traditional pyramid form of organization. It is intended to avoid the confusion potentially created when a person gets work directions from more than one source. Unity of command is supposed to ensure that everyone clearly understands assignments and does not get conflicting instructions. It is violated, for example, when a senior manager bypasses someone's immediate supervisor to give him or her orders. This can create confusion for the subordinate and also undermine the supervisor's authority.

The "two-boss" system of matrix structure is a clear violation of unity of command. Whereas the classical advice is to avoid creating multiple reporting relationships, the matrix concept creates them by design. It does so in an attempt to improve lateral relations and teamwork in special programs or projects. Unity of command is also less predominant in the team structure and in other arrangements that emphasize the use of cross-functional teams and task forces. The current trend is for less, not more, unity of command in organizations.

Trend. Organizations are using more cross-functional teams, task forces, and horizontal structures, and they are becoming more customer conscious; as they do so, employees often find themselves working for more than one "boss."

WIDER SPANS OF CONTROL

○ **Span of control** is the number of subordinates directly reporting to a manager.

The **span of control** is the number of persons directly reporting to a manager. When span of control is "narrow," only a few people are under a manager's immediate supervision; a "wide" span of control indicates that the manager supervises many people. There was a time in the history of management thought when people searched for the ideal span of control. Although the magic number was never found, this *span-of-control principle* evolved: there is a limit to the number of people one manager can effectively supervise; care should be exercised to keep the span of control within manageable limits.

Figure 10.8 shows the relationship between span of control and the number of levels in the chain of command. *Flat structures* have wider spans of control and fewer levels of management; *tall structures* have narrow spans of control and many levels of management. Because tall organizations have more managers, they are more costly. They are also generally viewed as less efficient, less flexible, and less customer sensitive than flat organizations. Before making spans of control smaller, therefore, serious thought should always be given to both the cost of the added management overhead and the potential disadvantages of a taller chain of command. When spans of control are increased, by contrast, overhead costs are reduced. Workers with less direct supervision in flatter structures also benefit from more empowerment and independence.[30]

Trend. Many organizations are shifting to wider spans of control as levels of management are eliminated; managers are taking responsibility for larger numbers of subordinates who operate with less direct supervision.

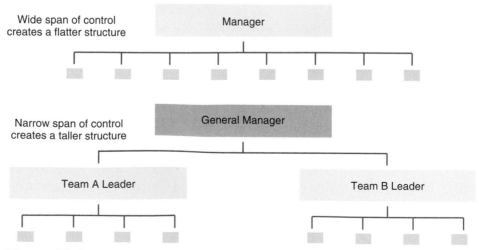

Figure 10.8 Spans of control in "flat" versus "tall" structures.

MORE DELEGATION AND EMPOWERMENT

All managers must decide what work they should do themselves and what should be left for others. At issue here is **delegation**—the process of entrusting work to others by giving them the right to make decisions and take action. There are three steps to delegation. In *step 1, the manager assigns responsibility* by carefully explaining the work or duties someone else is expected to do. This *responsibility* is an expectation for the other person to perform assigned tasks. In *step 2, the manager grants authority to act.* Along with the assigned task, the right to take necessary actions (for example, to spend money, direct the work of others, use resources) is given to the other person. *Authority* is a right to act in ways needed to carry out the assigned tasks. In *step 3, the manager creates accountability.* By accepting an assignment, the person takes on a direct obligation to the manager to complete the job as agreed upon. *Accountability,* originally defined in Chapter 1, is the requirement to answer to a supervisor for performance results.

A classical principle of organization warns managers not to delegate without giving the subordinate sufficient authority to perform. When insufficient authority is delegated, it will be very hard for someone to live up to performance expectations. They simply don't have the authority needed to get the job done. The *authority-and-responsibility principle* states: Authority should equal responsibility when work is delegated from a supervisor to a subordinate. Useful guidelines for delegating are offered in *Manager's Notepad 10.3.*[31]

A common management failure is unwillingness to delegate. Whether due to a lack of trust in others or to a manager's inflexibility in the way things get done, failure to delegate can be damaging. It overloads the manager with work that could be done by others; it also denies others many opportunities to fully utilize their talents on the job. When well done, by contrast, delegation leads to empowerment, in that people have the freedom to contribute ideas and do their jobs in the best possible ways. This involvement can increase job satisfaction for the individual and frequently results in better job performance.

○ **Delegation** is the process of distributing and entrusting work to other persons.

PERSONAL MANAGEMENT

It takes a lot of trust to be comfortable with **EMPOWERMENT**. But if you aren't willing and able to empower others, you'll not only compromise your own performance but also add to the stress of daily work. Empowerment involves allowing and helping others to do things, even things that you might be very good at doing yourself. The beauty of organizations is synergy—bringing together the contributions of many people to achieve something that is much greater than what any individual can accomplish alone. Empowerment gives synergy a chance. But many people, perhaps even you, suffer from control anxiety. They don't empower others because they fear losing control over a task or situation. In groups, they want or try to do everything by themselves; they are afraid to trust other team members with important tasks. Being "unwilling to let go," they try to do too much, with the risk of missed deadlines and even poor performance; they deny others opportunities to contribute, losing the benefits of their talents and often alienating them in the process. Does this description apply to you? Now is a good time to think seriously about your personal style: Are you someone who empowers others, or do you suffer from control anxiety and an unwillingness to delegate?

Get to know yourself better ➤
Complete Assessments #15—**Empowering Others,** and
Exercise #15—**Leading Through Participation** from the Management Learning Workbook.

Trend. Managers in progressive organizations are delegating more; they are finding more ways to empower people at all levels to make more decisions affecting themselves and their work.

MANAGER'S NOTEPAD 10.3

Ground rules for effective delegation

- Carefully choose the person to whom you delegate.
- Define the responsibility; make the assignment clear.
- Agree on performance objectives and standards.
- Agree on a performance timetable.
- Give authority; allow the other person to act independently.
- Show trust in the other person.
- Provide performance support.
- Give performance feedback.
- Recognize and reinforce progress.
- Help when things go wrong.
- Don't forget *your* accountability for performance results.

DECENTRALIZATION WITH CENTRALIZATION

O **Centralization** is the concentration of authority for most decisions at the top level of an organization.

O **Decentralization** is the dispersion of authority to make decisions throughout all organization levels.

A question frequently asked is: "Should most decisions be made at the top levels of an organization, or should they be dispersed by extensive delegation throughout all levels of management?" The former approach is referred to as **centralization;** the latter is called **decentralization.** There is no classical principle on centralization and decentralization. The traditional pyramid form of organization may give the impression of being a highly centralized structure, while decentralization is characteristic of newer structures and many recent organizing trends. But the issue doesn't have to be framed as an either/or choice. Today's organizations can operate with greater decentralization without giving up centralized control. This is facilitated by developments in information technology.

With computer networks and advanced information systems, managers at higher levels can more easily stay informed about a wide range of day-to-day performance matters. Because they have information on results readily available, they can allow more decentralization in decision making.[32] If something goes wrong, presumably the information systems will sound an alarm and allow corrective action to be taken quickly. At BancOne, Inc., for example, the demands of growth and an expanding geographical base have not blurred the lines of authority and accountability. Individual banks in widely dispersed locations are closely monitored for performance results. With the guiding theme of "centralizing paper and decentralizing people," BancOne decentralized its branch bank operations while retaining central control.

Trend. Whereas delegation, empowerment, and horizontal structures are contributing to more decentralization in organizations, advances in information technology simultaneously allow for the retention of centralized control.

REDUCED USE OF STAFF

When it comes to coordination and control in organizations, the issue of line-staff relationships is important. Chapter 1 described the role of staff as providing expert advice and guidance to line personnel. This can help ensure that performance standards are maintained in areas of staff expertise. **Specialized staff** perform a technical service or provide special problem-solving expertise for other parts of the organization. This could be a single person, such as a corporate safety director, or a complete unit, such as a corporate safety department. Many organizations rely on staff specialists to maintain coordination and control over a variety of matters. In a large retail chain, line managers in each store typically make daily operating decisions regarding direct sales of merchandise. But staff specialists at the corporate or regional levels provide direction and support so that all the stores operate with the same credit, purchasing, employment, and advertising procedures.

O **Specialized staff** provide technical expertise for other parts of the organization.

Organizations may also employ **personal staff,** individuals appointed in "assistant-to" positions with the purpose of providing special support to higher-level managers. Such assistants help by following up on administrative details and performing other duties as assigned. They can benefit also in terms of career development through the mentoring relationships that such assignments offer. An organization, for example, might select promising junior managers as temporary administrative assistants to senior managers. This helps them gain valuable experience at the same time that they are facilitating the work of executives.

O **Personal staff** are "assistant-to" positions that support senior managers.

Problems in line-staff distinctions can and do arise. In too many cases, organizations find that the staff grows to the point where it costs more in administrative overhead than it is worth. This is why staff cutbacks are common in downsizing and other turnaround efforts. There are also cases where conflicts in line-staff relationships cause difficulties. This often occurs when line and staff managers disagree over the extent of staff authority. At the one extreme, staff has purely *advisory authority* and can "suggest" but not "dictate." At the other extreme, it has *functional authority* to actually "require" that others do as requested within the boundaries of staff expertise. For example, a human resource department may advise line managers on the desired qualifications of new workers being hired (advisory authority); the department will likely require the managers to follow equal-employment-opportunity guidelines in the hiring process (functional authority).

CHECK 10.2

Growth drivers in business strategy
A survey by Mercer Management Consulting identified new product development as the #1 growth driver behind business strategies. Take the online "Reality Check" to learn more about what executives say about strategies for growing their businesses.

There is no one best solution to the problem of how to divide work between line and staff responsibilities. What is best for any organization will be a cost-effective staff component that satisfies, but doesn't overreact to, needs for specialized technical assistance to line operations.

Trend. Organizations are reducing the size of staff; they are seeking lower costs and increased operating efficiency by employing fewer staff personnel and using smaller staff units.

Be sure you can • define the terms chain of command, unity of command, span of control, delegation, empowerment, decentralization, centralization, and staff • describe the organizational trends that relate to each term • discuss the significance of these trends and practices for people and the new workplace

Learning check 4

CHAPTER 10 STUDY GUIDE

Where We've Been

BACK TO EDWARD JONES

The opening example of Edward Jones described the challenges of organizing to achieve competitive advantage. It suggests that any structure must meet the needs of the organization with respect to situational demands and opportunities. In this chapter you learned the traditional types of organizational structures—functional, divisional, and matrix. You learned about the new team, network, and boundaryless structures that are appearing. And you learned the current trends and practices that are changing the way people work together in today's organizations.

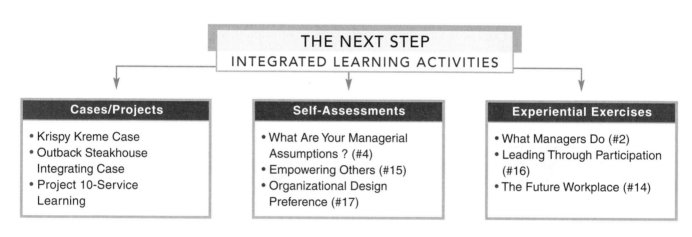

THE NEXT STEP
INTEGRATED LEARNING ACTIVITIES

Cases/Projects	Self-Assessments	Experiential Exercises
• Krispy Kreme Case • Outback Steakhouse Integrating Case • Project 10-Service Learning	• What Are Your Managerial Assumptions ? (#4) • Empowering Others (#15) • Organizational Design Preference (#17)	• What Managers Do (#2) • Leading Through Participation (#16) • The Future Workplace (#14)

STUDY QUESTIONS SUMMARY

1. What is organizing as a management function?

- Organizing is the process of arranging people and resources to work toward a common goal.
- Organizing decisions divide up the work that needs to be done, allocate people and resources to do it, and coordinate results to achieve productivity.
- Structure is the system of tasks, reporting relationships, and communication that links people and positions within an organization.
- The formal structure, such as shown on an organization chart, describes how an organization is supposed to work.
- The informal structure of organization consists of the unofficial relationships that develop among members.

2. What are the major types of organization structures?

- Departmentalization is the process of grouping people together in formal work units or teams.
- In functional structures, people with similar skills who perform similar activities are grouped together under a common manager.
- In divisional structures, people who work on a similar product, work in the same geographical region, serve the same customers, or participate in the same work process are grouped together under common managers.
- A matrix structure combines the functional and divisional approaches to create permanent cross-functional project teams.

3. What are the new developments in organization structures?

- Increasing complexity and greater rates of change in the environment are challenging the performance capabilities of traditional organization structures.
- New developments emphasize more horizontal structures that utilize teams and technology to best advantage.
- Team structures use cross-functional teams and task forces to improve lateral relations and improve problem solving at all levels.
- Network structures use contracted services and strategic alliances to support a core business or organizational center.
- Boundaryless organizations combine team and network structures with the advantages of technology to accomplish temporary tasks and projects.
- Virtual organizations utilize IT and the Internet to mobilize a shifting mix of strategic alliances to accomplish specific tasks and projects.

4. What organizing trends are changing the workplace?

- Traditional vertical command-and-control structures are giving way to more horizontal structures emphasizing employee involvement and flexibility.
- Many organizations are now operating with shorter chains of command and less unity of command.
- Many organizations are now operating with wider spans of control and fewer levels of management.
- The emphasis in more organizations today is on effective delegation and empowerment.
- Advances in information systems make it possible to operate with decentralization while still maintaining centralized control.
- Reducing the size of staff is a trend in organizations seeking cost savings and greater efficiency.

KEY TERMS REVIEW

Boundaryless organization (p. 258)

Centralization (p. 264)

Chain of command (p. 260)

Cross-functional teams (p. 255)

Customer structure (p. 252)

Decentralization (p. 264)

Delegation (p. 263)

Departmentalization (p. 249)

Divisional structure (p. 251)

Formal structure (p. 248)

Functional chimneys problem (p. 250)

Functional structure (p. 249)

Geographical structure (p. 252)

Informal structure (p. 248)

Matrix structure (p. 253)

Network structure (p. 256)

Organization chart (p. 248)

Organization structure (p. 247)

Organizing (p. 247)

Outsourcing (p. 256)

Personal staff (p. 265)

Process structure (p. 252)

Product structure (p. 252)

Project teams (p. 255)

Span of control (p. 262)

Specialized staff (p. 265)

Team structure (p. 255)

Upside-down pyramid (p. 260)

Virtual organization (p. 259)

SELF-TEST 10

MULTIPLE-CHOICE QUESTIONS:

1. The main purpose of organizing as a management function is to _____.
(a) make sure that results match plans (b) arrange people and resources to accomplish work (c) create enthusiasm for the work to be done (d) match strategies with operational plans

2. _____ is the system of tasks, reporting relationships, and communication that links together the various parts of an organization.
(a) Structure (b) Staff (c) Decentralization (d) Differentiation

3. Transmission of rumors and resistance to change is a potential disadvantage often associated with _____.
(a) virtual organizations (b) informal structures (c) delegation (d) specialized staff

4. An organization chart showing vice presidents of marketing, finance, manufacturing, and purchasing all reporting to the president is depicting a _____ structure.
(a) functional (b) matrix (c) network (d) product

5. The "two-boss" system of reporting relationships is found in the _____ structure.
(a) functional (b) matrix (c) network (d) product

6. A manufacturing business with a functional structure has recently developed two new product lines. The president of the company might consider shifting to a/an _____ structure to gain a stronger focus on each product.
(a) virtual (b) informal (c) divisional (d) network

7. Better lower-level teamwork and more top-level strategic management are among the expected advantages of a _____ structure.
(a) divisional (b) matrix (c) geographical (d) product

8. "Tall" organizations tend to have long chains of command and _____ spans of control.
(a) wide (b) narrow (c) informal (d) centralized

9. The unity-of-command principle is intentionally violated in the _____ structure.
(a) network (b) matrix (c) geographical (d) product

10. In delegation, _____ is the right of a subordinate to act in ways needed to carry out the assigned tasks.
(a) authority (b) responsibility (c) accountability (d) centrality

11. The functional chimneys problem occurs when people in different functions _____.
(a) fail to communicate with one another (b) try to help each other work with customers (c) spend too much time coordinating decisions (d) focus on products rather than functions

12. A _____ structure tries to combine the best elements of the functional and divisional forms.
(a) matrix (b) boundaryless (c) team (d) virtual

13. Outsourcing plays a central role in the _____ organization.
(a) functional (b) divisional (c) network (d) team

14. A student volunteers to gather information on a company for a group case analysis project. The other members of the group agree and tell her that she can choose the information sources. This group is giving the student _____ to fulfill the agreed-upon task.
(a) responsibility (b) accountability (c) authority (d) decentralization

15. The current trend in the use of staff in organizations is to _____.
(a) give staff personnel more functional authority over line operations (b) reduce the number of staff personnel overall (c) better utilize IT to give staff more centralized control (d) combine all staff functions in one department

SHORT-RESPONSE QUESTIONS:

16. What is the difference between a product divisional structure and a geographical or area divisional structure?

17. What are symptoms that might indicate a functional structure is causing problems for the organization?

18. Explain by example the concept of a network organization structure.

19. What positive results might be expected when levels of management are reduced and the chain of command shortened in an organization?

APPLICATION QUESTION:

20. Faisal Sham supervises a group of seven project engineers. His unit is experiencing a heavy workload as the demand for different versions of one of his firm's computer components is growing. Faisal finds that he doesn't have time to follow up on all design details for each version. Up until now he has tried to do this all by himself. Two of the engineers have shown interest in helping him coordinate work on the various designs. As a consultant, what would you advise Faisal in terms of delegating work to them?

www.wiley.com/college/schermerhorn

11

Organization design and work processes

Planning Ahead

After reading Chapter 11, you should be able to answer these questions in your own words.

CHAPTER 11 study questions

1. What are the essentials of organizational design?

2. How do contingency factors influence organizational design?

3. What are the major issues in subsystems design?

4. How can work processes be reengineered?

KPMG INTERNATIONAL—DESIGN FOR INTEGRATION, EMPOWERMENT, FLEXIBILITY

The business is professional services; the name is KPMG International, known typically as "KPMG." Positions with the firm are highly sought after by college graduates, especially those in the business disciplines. It offers great handson training and experience for those who want to apply their learning to work in professional business services, especially the areas of assurance, tax and legal, and financial advisory services. KPMG is an international network of affiliated member firms with locations in more than 150 countries and employing some 100,000 professional workers. It is considered one of the world's best. And to stay the best, KPMG organizes for high performance and staffs its business with talented professionals committed to excellence.

Leadership at KPMG recognizes the design challenges of matching the career opportunities of the new workplace with the diversity of today's generation of college graduates. Take a look at the section of the firm's website devoted to careers—KPMG Campus. The site asks you to "choose your shoes," an analogy for indicating personal preferences and career inclinations. If you choose "hiking boots," the KPMG message is about promoting from within, rewards, and advancement possibilites; choose "sandals" and it points out the importance of volunteer opportunities and community responsibility; choose "dress shoes" and the theme is hard work, dependability, and service to clients; choose "mountain climbing boots" and the point is KPMG's commitment to challenging you with high expectations.

Which shoes would you choose? As with all progressive employers, KPMG knows that "one style doesn't fit all"— whether you are talking about shoes or about organizations. KPMG obviously values a good fit between its employees and the firm. By doing so, it also keeps talent a main source of competitive advantage.[1]

Get Connected!

Could your career be in professional services? Find out more about KPMG and firms like it. Web surfing for career options can be time well spent.

Chapter 11 Learning Preview

The example of KPMG shows how top organizations pay attention to the special interests of prospective employees. The message is that the firm will be adaptable and do its best to fit work opportunities to the goals of talented persons. In this chapter you will learn about contingency factors in organizational design, including environment, strategy, technology, size and life cycle, and people. You will also learn the major design differences between bureaucratic and adaptive organizations, the dynamics of differentiation and integration in subsystems design, and the concept of process reengineering as an approach to work process design.

ORGANIZATION DESIGN AND WORK PROCESSES

Study question **1**	Study question **2**	Study question **3**	Study question **4**
Organizational Design Essentials	**Contingencies in Organizational Design**	**Subsystem Design and Integration**	**Work Process Design**
• What is organization design? • Organizational effectiveness • Organizational design choices	• Environment • Strategy • Technology • Size and life cycle • Human resources	• Subsystem differentiation • Subsystem integration	• What is a work process? • How to reengineer core processes • Process-driven organizations
Learning check **1**	Learning check **2**	Learning check **3**	Learning check **4**

If you are in London, don't be surprised to find that St. Luke's isn't a church, it's an advertising agency. But it's also a unique one. Every employee is a part owner; a six-member board elected by staff members governs the company. Everyone's name is listed on the stationery—from the creative director to receptionist. The culture is informal, permeated by creativity. Workspaces are designed with common areas to maximize interaction and connectivity. Everyone focuses on great service to customers. One member of the firm describes working there as like "the difference between going to grade school and going to the university. At school the bell goes 'ding' and tells you what to do. We have no bell. Like the university, as long as you create great stuff, we don't care how you do it." You can expect this configuration—small in size and locally focused—to make St. Luke's quick, nimble, and creative.[2]

Now travel to Switzerland and visit the headquarters of Nestlé.[3] The global food giant has a product mix of beverages, ice cream, prepared foods, chocolates, pet care, and pharmaceuticals. It sells around the world—33 percent in the Americas, 32 percent in Europe, 17 percent in Asia and Africa, and 18 percent elsewhere. A stark contrast to St. Luke's in size and global reach, Nestlé might be described as one of the world's greatest organization design challenges. CEO Peter Brabeck, a 35-year career veteran of the firm, recently reorganized in an attempt to boost profits and improve focus in its worldwide operations. In the past the firm was decentralized into national companies. The new structure reconfigures them into three world regions, with the goal of gaining more cooperation and greater efficiencies. A corporate IT initiative supports the new structure, linking employees worldwide in a knowledge management and information system. In Nestlé's competitive environment, just as with St. Luke's, success depends on the ability to continuously achieve integration, empowerment, and flexibility.

Organizations everywhere are adjusting to best meet new competitive demands. Changing times require flexible and well-integrated organizations that can deliver high-quality products and services while still innovating for sustained future performance. Traditional structures are being flattened, networks are being developed, IT is being utilized, and decision making is being moved to the points where knowledge exists. The goals are clear: improved teamwork, more creativity, shorter product development cycles, better customer service, and higher performance overall. Yet organizations still face widely varying problems and opportunities. There is no one best way to structure and manage them. The key to success is finding the best design to master the unique situational needs and challenges for each organization.[4]

ORGANIZATIONAL DESIGN ESSENTIALS

Just as organizations vary in size and type, so too do the variety of problems and opportunities they face. This is why they use the different types of structures described in Chapter 10—from the traditional functional, divisional, and matrix structures, to the team and network structures, and even beyond to the boundaryless organization. It is why they change structures to try to best fit the demands of new circumstances in a dynamic environment. And it is why we see more and more organizations trying to operate in ways that improve problem solving and flexibility—more sharing of tasks, reduced emphasis on hierarchy, greater emphasis on lateral communication, more teamwork, and more decentralization of decision making and empowerment.

WHAT IS ORGANIZATIONAL DESIGN?

Organizational design is the process of choosing and implementing structures that best arrange resources to accomplish the organization's mission and objectives.[5] Because every organization faces its own set of unique problems and opportunities, the best design at any moment is the one that achieves a good match between structure and situation. As shown in *Figure 11.1,* this includes taking into consideration the implications of environment, strategies, people, technology, and size.[6] The process of organizational design is thus a problem-solving activity, one that should be approached in a contingency fashion that takes all of these factors into account. There is no universal design that applies in all circumstances. The goal is to achieve a best fit among structure and the unique situation faced by each organization.

o **Organizational design** is the process of creating structures that accomplish mission and objectives.

ORGANIZATIONAL EFFECTIVENESS

The ultimate goal of organizational design should be to achieve **organizational effectiveness**—sustainable high performance in using resources to accomplish mission and objectives. Theorists view and analyze organi-

o **Organizational effectiveness** is sustainable high performance in accomplishing mission and objectives.

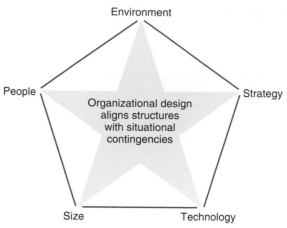

Figure 11.1 A framework for organizational design—aligning structures with situational contingencies.

zational effectiveness from different perspectives.[7] The *systems resource approach* looks at the input side and defines effectiveness in terms of success in acquiring needed resources from the organization's environment. The *internal process approach* looks at the transformation process and examines how efficiently resources are utilized to produce goods and/or services. The *goal approach* looks at the output side to measure achievement of key operating objectives. And the *strategic constituencies approach* looks to the environment to analyze the impact of the organization on key stakeholders and their interests. Although they point in different directions, each of these approaches offers a framework for assessing how well an actual or proposed design is working.

Organizational effectiveness can also be evaluated according to specific criteria that set important performance benchmarks over time.[8] In the short run, the criteria focus on performance effectiveness in goal accomplishment and performance efficiency in resource utilization, as well as stakeholder satisfactions—including customers, employees, owners, and society at large. In the medium term two more criteria become important: adaptability in the face of changing environments, and development of people and systems to meet new challenges. And in the long run, the effectiveness criterion is survival under conditions of uncertainty.

Any organizational design should advance organizational effectiveness. Although there is no one universal design that applies in all circumstances, this does not mean that a given design—one in use or proposed—shouldn't be rigorously evaluated. In fact, quite the opposite applies. A design is choice, and that choice can be for the better or for the worse. Managers as decision makers need to make good organizational design choices; they need to make them with the goal of organizational effectiveness always in mind; and they need to make them with the assistance of an analytical framework that helps them sort through the many design alternatives that exist. In organization theory, these alternatives are broadly framed in the distinction between bureaucratic designs at one extreme and adaptive designs at the other.

ORGANIZATIONAL DESIGN CHOICES

○ A **bureaucracy** emphasizes formal authority, order, fairness, and efficiency.

As first introduced in the discussion on historical foundations of management in Chapter 2, a **bureaucracy** is a form of organization based on logic,

TAKE IT TO THE CASE

World-class entrepreneur places his "BET" on the future

It takes an entrepreneur to start a business, but it takes quality people and the right design to keep it running . . . and growing. Robert Johnson, founder of BET Holdings, knows that for sure. His firm is the first African-American owned and operated media and entertainment company to provide quality television programming, entertainment products, publishing, and Internet services specifically designed to appeal to African-American interests. The company owns and operates four television networks, including BET cable network; it owns Arabesque Books, the leading African-American line of romance novels; and it owns BET.com, the top African-American Internet portal. Johnson sold BET holdings to Viacom for $3 billion and remains chairman and CEO.[9]

order, and the legitimate use of formal authority. Its distinguishing features include a clear-cut division of labor, strict hierarchy of authority, formal rules and procedures, and promotion based on competency. According to sociologist Max Weber, bureaucracies were supposed to be orderly, fair, and highly efficient.[10] In short, they were a model form of organization. Yet if you use the term "bureaucracy" today, it may well be interpreted with a negative connotation. If you call someone a "bureaucrat," it may well be considered an insult. Instead of operating efficiency, the bureaucracies that we know are often associated with "red tape"; instead of being orderly and fair, they are often seen as cumbersome and impersonal to the point of insensitivity to customer or client needs. And the bureaucrats? Don't we assume that they work only according to rules, diligently following procedures and avoiding any opportunities to take initiative or demonstrate creativity?

Research recognizes that there are limits to bureaucracy, particularly in their tendencies to become unwieldy and rigid.[11] Instead of viewing all bureaucratic structures as inevitably flawed, however, management theory asks the contingency questions: (1) When is a bureaucratic form a good choice for an organization? (2) What alternatives exist when it is not a good choice?

Pioneering research conducted in England during the early 1960s by Tom Burns and George Stalker helps answer these questions.[12] After investigating 20 manufacturing firms, they concluded that two quite different organizational forms could be successful, depending on the nature of a firm's external environment. A more bureaucratic form, which Burns and Stalker called *mechanistic*, thrived when the environment was stable. But it experienced difficulty when the environment was rapidly changing and uncertain. In these dynamic situations, a much less bureaucratic form, called *organic*, performed best. *Figure 11.2* portrays these two approaches as opposite extremes on a continuum of organizational design alternatives.

Mechanistic Designs

Organizations with more **mechanistic designs** are highly bureaucratic in nature. As shown in the figure, they typically operate with more central-

Reasons for unscheduled absences
People can't contribute if they don't come to work. A survey of absence patterns experienced by 305 employers by CCH International showed that absences due to work stress increased 14 percent in a five-year period. Take the online "Reality Check" to learn more about absence patterns in the workforce.

○ A **mechanistic design** is centralized with many rules and procedures, a clear-cut division of labor, narrow spans of control, and formal coordination.

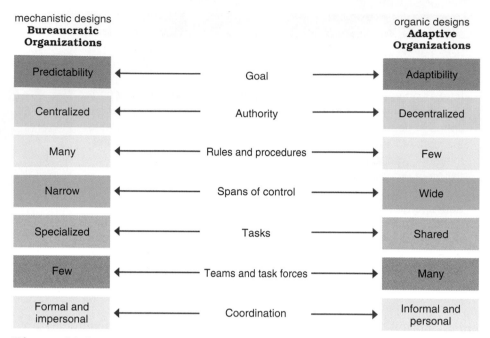

Figure 11.2 A continuum of organizational design alternatives: from bureaucratic to adaptive organizations.

ized authority, many rules and procedures, a precise division of labor, narrow spans of control, and formal means of coordination. Mechanistic designs are described as "tight" structures of the traditional vertical or pyramid form.[13] For a good example, visit your local fast-food restaurant. A relatively small operation, each store operates quite like others in the franchise chain and according to rules established by the corporate management. You will notice that service personnel work in orderly and disciplined ways, guided by training, rules and procedures, and close supervision by crew leaders who work alongside them. Even their appearances are carefully regulated, with everyone working in a standardized uniform. These restaurants perform well as they repetitively deliver items that are part of their standard menus. You quickly encounter the limits, however, if you try to order something not on the menu. The chains also encounter difficulty when consumer tastes change or take on regional preferences that are different from what the corporate menu provides. Adjustments to the system take a long time.

The limits of mechanistic designs and their tight vertical structures are especially apparent in organizations that must operate in dynamic, often uncertain, environments. It's hard, for example, to find a technology company, consumer products firm, financial services business, or dot.com retailer that isn't making continual adjustments in operations and organizational design. Things keep changing on them, and organizational effectiveness depends on being able to change with the times. Mechanistic designs find this hard to do.

Organic Designs

Dee Hock, the founder of Visa International, says: "We can't run 21st-century society with 17th-century notions of organization."[14] Harvard scholar and consultant Rosabeth Moss Kanter notes that the ability to respond quickly to shifting environmental challenges often distinguishes successful organizations from less successful ones. Specifically, Kanter states,

The organizations now emerging as successful will be, above all, flexible; they will need to be able to bring particular resources together quickly, on the basis of short-term recognition of new requirements and the necessary capacities to deal with them . . . The balance between static plans—which appears to reduce the need for effective reaction—and structural flexibility needs to shift toward the latter.[15]

CAREER CONNECTION

Communication across functions is the lifeblood of high performance

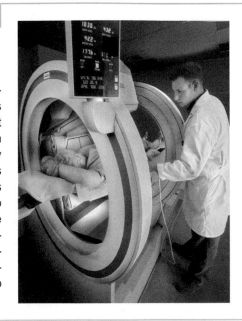

In health care the Mayo Clinic stands in a class all by itself, known worldwide for quality treatment. Founded some 100 years ago by Dr. Charles and Dr. Will Mayo, the clinic is unique in its horizontal approach to patient care. Medical professionals work together in a system that allows them time to thoroughly investigate patient problems and to quickly and easily assist one another. An early emphasis acknowledged that "two heads are better than one and five are even better." Even today, as it continues to grow and change with advancing medical understanding, the Mayo Clinic is still guided by the original vision: "thorough diagnosis, accurate answers and effective treatment through the application of collective wisdom to the problems of each patient." More than 40,000 Mayo employees and 500,000 patients annually rely on an open flow of communication and continual sharing of ideas to meet the commitment to excellence.[18]

The trend is toward **organic designs,** as portrayed in Figure 11.2, having more decentralized authority, fewer rules and procedures, less precise division of labor, wider spans of control, and more personal means of coordination. These create more **adaptive organizations** that operate with horizontal structures and with cultures that encourage worker empowerment and teamwork. They are described as relatively loose systems in which a lot of work gets done through informal structures and networks of interpersonal contacts.[16] Organic designs work well for organizations facing dynamic environments that demand flexibility in dealing with changing conditions. They are also increasingly popular in the new workplace, where the demands of total quality management and competitive advantage place more emphasis on internal teamwork and responsiveness to customers.

Above all, adaptive organizations are built upon a foundation of trust that people will do the right things on their own initiative. They move organizational design in the direction of what some might call *self-organization,* where the focus is on freeing otherwise capable people from unnecessarily centralized control and restrictions. Moving toward the adaptive form means letting workers take over production scheduling and problem solving; it means letting workers set up their own control systems; it means letting workers use their ideas to improve customer service. In the ultimately adaptive organizations, it means that members are given the freedom to do what they can do best—get the job done. This helps create what has been described in earlier chapters as a **learning organization,** one designed for continuous adaptation through problem solving, innovation, and learning.[17]

○ An **organic design** is decentralized with fewer rules and procedures, open divisions of labor, wide spans of control, and more personal coordination.

○ An **adaptive organization** operates with a minimum of bureaucratic features and encourages worker empowerment and teamwork.

○ A **learning organization** is designed for continuous adaptation through problem solving, innovation, and learning.

CONTINGENCIES IN ORGANIZATIONAL DESIGN

Good organizational design decisions should result in supportive structures that satisfy situational demands and advance organizational effectiveness. This is true contingency thinking. Among the contingency factors in the organizational design checklist featured in *Manager's Notepad 11.1* are the environment, strategy, technology, size and life cycle, and human resources.

ENVIRONMENT

The organization's external environment and the degree of uncertainty it offers are of undeniable importance in organizational design.[19] A *certain environment* is composed of relatively stable and predictable elements. As a result, an organization can succeed with relatively few changes in the goods or services produced or in the manner of production over time. Bureaucratic organizations and mechanistic designs are quite adequate under such conditions. An *uncertain environment* will have more dynamic and less predictable elements. Changes occur frequently and may catch decision makers by surprise. As a result, organizations must be flexible and responsive over relatively short time horizons. This requires more adaptive organizations and organic designs. *Figure 11.3* summarizes these relationships, showing how increasing uncertainty in organizational environments calls for more horizontal and adaptive designs.

STRATEGY

The nature of organizational strategies and objectives are important design contingencies. Research on these contingency relationships is often traced to the pioneering work of Alfred Chandler Jr., who analyzed the histories of DuPont, General Motors, Sears, and Standard Oil of New Jersey.[20] Chandler's conclusion that "structure follows strategy" is a key element of

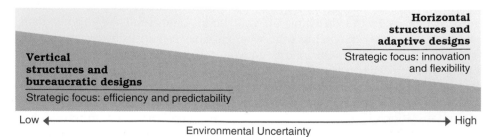

Figure 11.3 Environmental uncertainty and the performance of vertical and horizontal designs.

| Organizational design checklist | MANAGER'S NOTEPAD 11.1 |

Check 1: Does the design fit well with the major problems and opportunities of the external environment?

Check 2: Does the design support the implementation of strategies and the accomplishment of key operating objectives?

Check 3: Does the design support core technologies and allow them to be used to best advantage?

Check 4: Can the design handle changes in organizational size and different stages in the organizational life cycle?

Check 5: Does the design support and empower workers and allow their talents to be used to best advantage?

organizational design. An organization's structure must support its strategy if the desired results are to be achieved.[21]

When strategy is stability oriented, the choice of organizational design is based on the premise that little significant change will be occurring in the external environment. This means that plans can be set and operations programmed to be routinely implemented. To best support this strategic approach, the organization should be structured to operate in well-defined and predictable ways. This is most characteristic of bureaucratic organizations that use more mechanistic design alternatives.

When strategy is growth oriented and when strategy is likely to change frequently, the situation as a whole becomes more complex, fluid, and uncertain. Operating objectives are likely to include the need for innovation and flexible responses to changing competition in the environment. Operations and plans are likely to have short life spans and require frequent and even continuous modification over time. The most appropriate structure is one that allows for internal flexibility and freedom to create new ways of doing things. This is most characteristic of the empowerment found in adaptive organizations using more organic design alternatives.

TECHNOLOGY

Technology is the combination of knowledge, skills, equipment, computers, and work methods used to transform resource inputs into organizational outputs. It is the way tasks are accomplished using tools, machines, techniques, and human know-how. The availability of appropriate technology is a cornerstone of productivity, and the nature of the core technologies in use must be considered in organizational design.

In the early 1960s, Joan Woodward conducted a study of technology and structure in over 100 English manufacturing firms. She classified core *manufacturing technology* into three categories.[22] In **small-batch production,** such as a racing bicycle shop, a variety of custom products are tailor-made to order. Each item or batch of items is made somewhat differently to fit customer specifications. The equipment used may not be elaborate, but a high level of worker skill is often needed. In **mass production,** the organization produces a large number of uniform products in an assembly-line system. Workers are highly dependent on one another, as the product passes

o **Technology** includes equipment, knowledge, and work methods that transform inputs into outputs.

o **Small-batch production** manufactures a variety of products crafted to fit customer specifications.

o **Mass production** manufactures a large number of uniform products with an assembly-line system.

○ In **continuous-process production** raw materials are continuously transformed by an automated system.

from stage to stage until completion. Equipment may be sophisticated, and workers often follow detailed instructions while performing simplified jobs. Organizations using **continuous-process production** are highly automated. They produce a few products by continuously feeding raw materials—such as liquids, solids, and gases—through a highly automated production system with largely computerized controls. Such systems are equipment intensive, but can often be operated by a relatively small labor force. Classic examples are automated chemical plants, steel mills, oil refineries, and power plants.

Woodward found that the right combination of structure and technology was critical to organizational success. The best small-batch and continuous-process plants in her study had more flexible organic structures; the best mass-production operations had more rigid mechanistic structures. The implications of this research have become known as the *technological imperative:* technology is a major influence on organizational structure.

The importance of technology for organizational design applies in services as well as manufacturing, although the core *service technologies* are slightly different.[23] In health care, education, and related services, an **intensive technology** focuses the efforts of many people with special expertise on the needs of patients or clients. In banks, real estate firms, insurance companies, employment agencies, and others like them, a **mediating technology** links together parties seeking a mutually beneficial exchange of values—typically a buyer and seller. Finally, a **long-linked technology** can function like mass production, where a client is passed from point to point for various aspects of service delivery.

PERSONAL MANAGEMENT

It is easy to make decisions when you have perfect information. But in the new world of work, you will often face unstructured problems and have to make decisions with incomplete information under uncertain conditions. Depending on your **TOLERANCE FOR AMBIGBUITY**, you may be comfortable or uncomfortable dealing with these new realities. It takes personal flexibility and lots of confidence to cope well with unpredictability. Some people have a hard time dealing with the unfamiliar. They prefer to work with directions that minimize ambiguity and provide clear decision-making rules; they like the structure of mechanistic organizations with bureaucratic features. Other people are willing and able to perform in less-structured settings that give them lots of flexibility in responding to changing situations; they like the freedom of organic organizations designed for adaptation. You must find a good fit between your personal preferences and the nature of the organizations in which you choose to work. To achieve this fit, you have to both know yourself and be able to read organizational cultures and structures. And whatever your tolerance for ambiguity may be, the best time to explore these issues of person-organization fit is now, before you take your first or next job.

Get to know yourself better ▶
Complete Self-Assessments #16—**Turbulence Tolerance Test,** *and* #17—**Organizational Design Preferences,** from the Management Learning Workbook.

SIZE AND LIFE CYCLE

Typically measured by number of employees, *organizational size* is another contingency factor in organizational design.[25] Although research indicates that larger organizations tend to have more mechanistic structures than smaller ones, it is also clear that this is not always best for them.[26] In fact, a perplexing managerial concern is that organizations tend to become more bureaucratic as they grow in size and consequently have more difficulty adapting to changing environments. It is especially important to understand the design implications of the **organizational life cycle,** or the evolution of an organization over time through different stages of growth. The *stages in the organizational life cycle* can be described as:

Stages in the organizational life cycle →

1. *Birth stage*—when the organization is founded by an entrepreneur.
2. *Youth stage*—when the organization starts to grow rapidly.

IN PRACTICE

Tough times make it hard to keep a small job shop afloat

Running a small business is hard in the best of circumstances. But it takes a master manager to keep things on course through an economic downturn. At Carl Bogatay's Magnum Machine & Fab, Inc., in Washington, Pennsylvania, the employees know the meaning of hard work. They build to order metal parts crafted to specifications provided by the firm's customers. It's a classic "job shop" where each order becomes a new job to be tackled and completed by skilled craftworkers. When there are lots of pallets of raw steel stacked up, times are good; when there aren't, things are getting bad. In good times Bogatay's skilled workers are in high demand. But caught in a downturn, he worries about layoffs affecting his workers and the health of his community. With things tight, Bogatay says his immediate goals are to "get out of debt and have enough to get the parking lot paved."[24]

3. *Midlife stage*—when the organization has grown large with success.
4. *Maturity stage*—when the organization stabilizes at a large size.[27]

In its *birth stage* the founder usually runs the organization. It stays relatively small, and the structure is quite simple. The organization starts to grow rapidly during the *youth stage*, and management responsibilities extend among more people. Here, the simple structure begins to exhibit the stresses of change. An organization in the *midlife stage* is even larger, with a more complex and increasingly formal structure. More levels appear in the chain of command, and the founder may have difficulty remaining in control. In the *maturity stage*, the organization stabilizes in size, typically with a mechanistic structure. It runs the risk of becoming complacent and slow in competitive markets. Bureaucratic tendencies toward stability may lead an organization at this stage toward decline. Steps must be taken to counteract these tendencies and provide for needed creativity and innovation.

One way of coping with the disadvantages of bigness is *downsizing*, that is, taking actions to reduce the scope of operations and number of employees. This response is often used when top management is challenged to reduce costs quickly and increase productivity.[28] But, perhaps more significantly, good managers in many organizations find unique ways to overcome the disadvantages of large size before the crisis of downsizing hits. They are creative in fostering **intrapreneurship,** described in Chapter 6 as the pursuit of entrepreneurial behavior by individuals and subunits within large organizations.[29] They also find ways for smaller entrepreneurial units to operate with freedom and autonomy within the larger organizational framework. **Simultaneous systems,** for example, are organizations that utilize both mechanistic and organic designs to meet the need for production efficiency and continued innovation. This "loose-tight" concept in organizational design is depicted in *Figure 11.4.*

○ **Intensive technology** focuses the efforts and talents of many people to serve clients.

○ **Mediating technology** links together people in a beneficial exchange of values.

○ In **long-linked technology** a client moves from point to point during service delivery.

○ In the **organizational life cycle** an organization passes through different stages from birth to maturity.

○ **Intrapreneurship** is entrepreneurial behavior by individuals and subunits within large organizations.

○ In **simultaneous systems** mechanistic and organic designs operate together in an organization.

HUMAN RESOURCES

Another contingency factor in organizational design is people—the human resources that staff the organization for action. A good organizational design provides people with the supporting structures they need to achieve both high performance and satisfaction in their work. Modern manage-

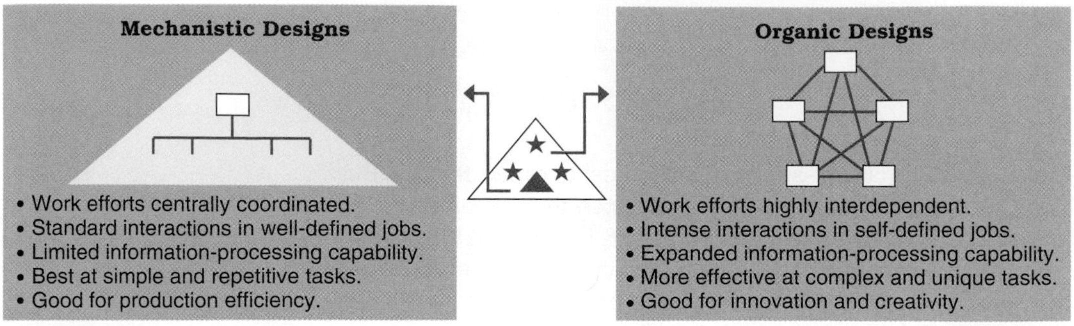

Mechanistic Designs

- Work efforts centrally coordinated.
- Standard interactions in well-defined jobs.
- Limited information-processing capability.
- Best at simple and repetitive tasks.
- Good for production efficiency.

Organic Designs

- Work efforts highly interdependent.
- Intense interactions in self-defined jobs.
- Expanded information-processing capability.
- More effective at complex and unique tasks.
- Good for innovation and creativity.

Figure 11.4 Simultaneous "loose-tight" properties of team structures support efficiency and innovation.

ment theory views people–structure relationships in a contingency fashion. The prevailing argument is that there should be a good "fit" between organizational structures and the human resources.[31]

An important human resource issue in organizational design is skill. Any design should allow the expertise and talents of organizational members to be unlocked and utilized to the fullest. Especially in the age of information and knowledge workers, high-involvement organic designs with their emphasis on empowerment are crucial. When IBM purchased the software firm Lotus, for example, the intention was to turn it into a building block for the firm's networking business. But Lotus was small, and IBM was huge. The whole thing had to be carefully handled or IBM might lose many of the talented people who created the popular LotusNotes and related products. The solution was to adapt the design to fit the people. IBM gave Lotus the space it needed to retain the characteristics of a creative software house. Said the firm's head of software at the time: "You have to keep the people, so you have to ask yourself why it is they like working there."[32]

Learning check 2

Be sure you can • explain the contingency relationships between strategy and organizational design • differentiate among small-batch production, mass production, and continuous-process production • differentiate among intensive, mediating, and long-linked technologies in service industries • explain the concept of simultaneous systems and the loose–tight concept in organizational design

SUBSYSTEMS DESIGN AND INTEGRATION

○ A **subsystem** is a work unit or smaller component within a larger organization.

Organizations are composed of **subsystems,** such as a department or work unit headed by a manager, that operate as smaller parts of a larger and total organizational system. Ideally, the work of subsystems serves the needs of the larger organization. Ideally, too, the work of each subsystem supports the work of others. Things don't always work out this way, however. Another challenge of organizational design is to create subsystems and coordinate relationships so that the entire organization's interests are best met.

Important research in this area was reported in 1967 by Paul Lawrence and Jay Lorsch of Harvard University.[33] They studied 10 firms in three different industries—plastics, consumer goods, and containers. The firms were chosen because they differed in performance. The industries were chosen because they faced different levels of environmental uncertainty. The plastics industry was uncertain; the containers industry was more certain; the consumer goods industry was moderately uncertain. The results of the Lawrence and Lorsch study can be summarized as follows.

First, the total system structures of successful firms in each industry matched their respective environmental challenges. Successful plastics firms in uncertain environments had more organic designs; successful container firms in certain environments had more mechanistic designs. This result was consistent with the earlier research by Burns and Stalker already discussed in this chapter.[34] Second, Lawrence and Lorsch found that subsystem structures in the successful firms matched the challenges of their respective subenvironments. Subsystems within the successful firms assumed different structures to accommodate the special problems and opportunities of their operating situations. Third, the researchers found that subsystems in the successful firms worked well with one another, even though they were also very different from one another.

Family firm builds a global future around customer service

In the competitive arena of business strategy, Enterprise Rent-a-Car has achieved success by pursuing a market that its rivals chose to ignore—renting cars to people whose cars are being serviced or out of commission because of accidents. Started in St. Louis by Jack Taylor in 1957, the privately held company is now bigger than Hertz and Avis. Its 500,000-vehicle fleet is run through some 5000 offices by 50,000 employees spread around North America and now gaining ground in Europe as well. Current Chairman and CEO Andy Taylor says his father built the company around a culture devoted to customer service and satisfaction. The culture is backed by staff selection and extensive training to put the right people in the field. And the Enterprise design ensures effectiveness by blending decentralization of operations with central control. Each branch gets a financial statement and customer satisfaction score every month. Says Taylor: "Our branch managers know exactly how well they did. They've got their bottom line."[30]

SUBSYSTEM DIFFERENTIATION

Figure 11.5 depicts operating differences between three divisions in one of the firms studied by Lawrence and Lorsch. It shows how research and development, manufacturing, and sales subunits operate differently in response to unique needs. This illustrates **differentiation,** which is the degree of difference that exists between the internal components of the organization.

There are four common *sources of subsystems differentiation.* First, the subsystems may have *differences in time orientation.* In a business firm, for example, the manufacturing subsystem may have a shorter-term outlook than does the research and development group. These differences can make it difficult for personnel from the two units to work well together. Second, the different tasks assigned to work units may also result in *differences in objectives.* For example, cost-conscious production managers and volume-conscious marketing managers may have difficulty agreeing on solutions to

○ **Differentiation** is the degree of difference between subsystems in an organization.

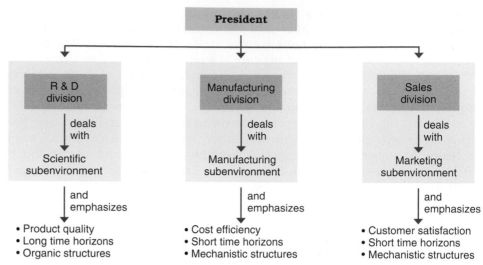

Figure 11.5 Subsystems differentiation among research and development (R&D), manufacturing, and sales divisions.

common problems. Third, *differences in interpersonal orientation* can affect subsystem relations. To the extent that patterns of communication, decision making, and social interaction vary, it may be harder for personnel from different subsystems to work together. And fourth, *differences in formal structure* can also affect subsystem behaviors. Someone who is used to flexible problem solving in an organic setting may find it very frustrating to work with a manager from a mechanistic setting who is used to strict rules.

SUBSYSTEM INTEGRATION

O **Integration** is the level of coordination achieved between subsystems in an organization.

The term **integration** in organization theory refers to the level of coordination achieved among an organization's internal components. Organizational design involves the creation of both differentiated structures and appropriate integrating mechanisms. A basic *organizational design paradox,* however, makes this a particularly challenging managerial task. Increased differentiation among organizational subsystems creates the need for greater integration; however, integration becomes harder to achieve as differentiation increases.

Manager's Notepad 11.2 identifies several mechanisms for achieving subsystem integration.[35] Integrating mechanisms that rely on vertical coordination and the use of authority relationships work best when differentiation is low. They include use of rules and procedures, hierarchical referral, and planning. Integrating mechanisms that emphasize horizontal coordination and improved lateral relations work better when differentiation is high.[36] They include the use of direct contact between managers, liaison roles, task forces, teams, and matrix structures.

Learning check 3

Be sure you can • explain the difference between a system and a subsystem • define the terms differentiation and integration • discuss the implications of the Lawrence and Lorsch study for subsystem design • illustrate how subsystem differentiation might operate in a typical business • list several ways to improve subsystem integration in organizations

How to improve subsystems integration

- *Rules and procedures:* Clearly specify required activities.
- *Hierarchical referral:* Refer problems upward to a common superior.
- *Planning:* Set targets that keep everyone headed in the same direction.
- *Direct contact:* Have subunit managers coordinate directly.
- *Liaison roles:* Assign formal coordinators to link subunits together.
- *Task forces:* Form temporary task forces to coordinate activities and solve problems on a timetable.
- *Teams:* Form permanent teams with the authority to coordinate and solve problems over time.
- *Matrix organizations:* Create a matrix structure to improve coordination on specific programs.

WORK PROCESS DESIGN

From the emphasis on subsystems integration and more cross-functional collaboration in organizational design has come a popular development known as business **process reengineering**.[37] This is defined by consultant Michael Hammer as the systematic and complete analysis of work processes and the design of new and better ones.[38] The goal of a reengineering effort is to focus attention on the future, on customers, and on improved ways of doing things. It tries to break people and mindsets away from habits, preoccupation with past accomplishments, and tendencies to continue implementing old and outmoded ways of doing things. Simply put, reengineering is a way of changing the way work is carried out in organizations.

○ **Process reengineering** systematically analyzes work processes to design new and better ones.

WHAT IS A WORK PROCESS?

In his book *Beyond Reengineering,* Michael Hammer defines a **work process** as "a related group of tasks that together create a result of value for the customer."[39] They are the things people do to turn resource inputs into goods or services for customers. Hammer highlights the following key words in the implications of his definition: (1) *group*—tasks are viewed as part of a group rather than in isolation; (2) *together*—everyone must share a common goal; (3) *result*—the focus is on what is accomplished, not on activities; (4) *customer*—processes serve customers, and their perspectives are the ones that really count.

○ A **work process** is a related group of tasks that together create a value for the customer.

The concept of **workflow,** or the way work moves from one point to another in manufacturing or service delivery, is central to the understanding of processes.[40] The various parts of a work process must all be completed to achieve the desired results, and they must typically be completed in a given order. An important starting point for a reengineering effort is to diagram or map these workflows as they actually take

○ **Workflow** is the movement of work from one point to another in a system.

place. Then each step can be systematically analyzed to determine whether it is adding value, to consider ways of eliminating or combining steps, and to find ways to use technology to improve efficiency. At PeopleSoft, for example, paper forms are definitely out; the goal is to eliminate them as much as possible. Employees are even able to order their own supplies through a direct Web link to Office Depot. The firm's chief information officer once said: "Nobody jumps out of bed in the morning and says, 'I want to go to work and fill out forms.' We create systems that let people be brilliant rather than push paper."[41]

HOW TO REENGINEER CORE PROCESSES

Given the mission, objectives, and strategies of an organization, business process reengineering can be used to regularly assess and fine-tune work processes to ensure that they directly add value to operations. Through a technique called **process value analysis,** core processes are identified and carefully evaluated for their performance contributions. Each step in a workflow is examined. Unless a step is found to be important, useful, and contributing to the value added, it is eliminated. Process value analysis typically involves the following steps.[42]

○ **Process value analysis** identifies and evaluates core processes for their performance contributions.

Steps in process value analysis →

1. Identify the core processes.
2. Map the core processes in respect to workflows.
3. Evaluate all tasks for the core processes.
4. Search for ways to eliminate unnecessary tasks or work.
5. Search for ways to eliminate delays, errors, and misunderstandings.
6. Search for efficiencies in how work is shared and transferred among people and departments.

Figure 11.6 shows an example of how reengineering and better use of computer technology can streamline a purchasing operation. A purchase

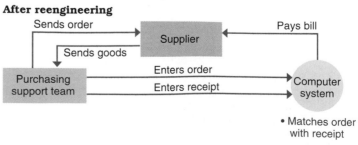

Before reengineering

After reengineering

Figure 11.6 How reengineering can streamline core business processes.

order should result in at least three value-added outcomes: order fulfillment, a paid bill, and a satisfied supplier. Work to be successfully accomplished includes such things as ordering, shipping, receiving, billing, and payment. A traditional business system might have purchasing, receiving, and accounts payable as separate functions, with each communicating with each other and the supplier. Alternatively, process value analysis might result in reengineering that designs a new purchasing support team whose members handle the same work more efficiently with the support of the latest computer technology.[43]

PROCESS-DRIVEN ORGANIZATIONS

Customers, teamwork, and efficiency are central to Hammer's notion of process reengineering. He describes the case of Aetna Life & Casualty Company, where a complex system of tasks and processes once took as much as 28 days to accomplish.[44] Customer service requests were handled in step-by-step fashion by many different persons. After an analysis of workflows, the process was redesigned into a "one and done" format where a single customer service provider handled each request from start to finish. One of Aetna's customer account managers said after the change was made: "Now we can see the customers as individual people. It's no longer 'us' and 'them.'"[45]

Hammer also describes reengineering at a unit of Verizon Communications. Before reengineering, customer inquiries for telephone service and repairs required extensive consultation between technicians and their supervisors. After process value analysis, technicians were formed into geographical teams that handled their own scheduling, service delivery, and reporting. They were given celluar telephones and laptop computers to assist in managing their work, resulting in the elimination of a number of costly supervisory jobs. The technicians enthusiastically responded to the changes and opportunities. "The fact that you've got four or five people zoned in a certain geographical area," said one, "means that we get personally familiar with our customers' equipment and problems."[46]

Americans working longer
The United Nations' International Labor Organization (ILO) reports that the average American adult works some 2000 hours per year for pay. Take the online "Reality Check" to learn how this compares with workers in other parts of the world.

The essence of process reengineering is to locate control for processes with an identifiable group of people, and to focus each person and the entire system on meeting customer needs and expectations. It tries to eliminate duplication of work and systems bottlenecks to reduce costs, increase efficiency, and build capacity for change. As Hammer says about the *process-driven organization:*

> Its intrinsic customer focus and its commitment to outcome measurement make it vigilant and proactive in perceiving the need for change; the process owner, freed from other responsibilities and wielding the power of process design, is an institutionalized agent of change; and employees who have an appreciation for customers and who are measured on outcomes are flexible and adaptable.[47]

Be sure you can • define the terms process reengineering and work process • draw a map of the workflow in an organization familiar to you • explain how process value analysis can be used to streamline workflows and improve work performance

Learning check 4

CHAPTER 11 STUDY GUIDE

Where We've Been

BACK TO KPMG

The opening example of KPMG International highlighted the importance of fitting organizational design with the people who ultimately deliver high-performance outcomes. In Chapter 11 you learned the differences between bureaucratic and adaptive organizations, including the notions of mechanistic and organic designs. You also learned more about the concept of contingency thinking in management, with a special focus on how designs must successfully fit environment, strategy, technology, size and life cycle, and people. You also learned about subsystem design and process reengineering in organizations.

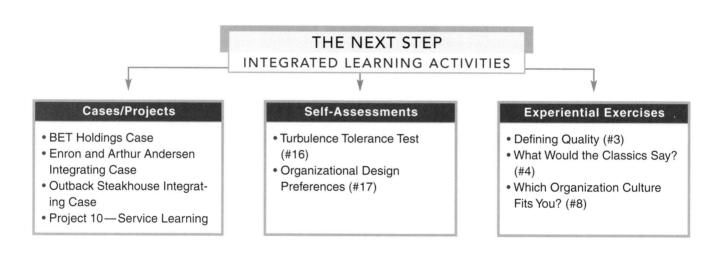

THE NEXT STEP
INTEGRATED LEARNING ACTIVITIES

Cases/Projects	Self-Assessments	Experiential Exercises
• BET Holdings Case • Enron and Arthur Andersen Integrating Case • Outback Steakhouse Integrating Case • Project 10—Service Learning	• Turbulence Tolerance Test (#16) • Organizational Design Preferences (#17)	• Defining Quality (#3) • What Would the Classics Say? (#4) • Which Organization Culture Fits You? (#8)

STUDY QUESTIONS SUMMARY

1. What are the essentials of organizational design?

• Organizational design is the process of choosing and implementing structures that best use resources to serve mission and purpose.

• Bureaucratic organizational designs are vertical and mechanistic; they perform best for routine and predictable tasks.

• Adaptive organizational designs are horizontal and organic; they perform best in conditions requiring change and flexibility.

2. How do contingency factors influence organizational design?

• Environment, strategy, technology, size, and people are all contingency factors influencing organizational design.

• Certain environments lend themselves to vertical and mechanistic organizational designs; uncertain environments require more horizontal and adaptive organizational designs.

• Technology—including the use of knowledge, equipment, and work methods in the transformation process—is an important consideration in organizational design.

• Although organizations tend to become more mechanistic as they grow in size, design efforts must be used to allow for innovation and creativity in changing environments.

3. What are the major issues in subsystems design?

• Organizations are composed of multiple subsystems that must work well together.

- Differentiation is the degree of difference that exists between various subsystems; integration is the level of coordination achieved among them.
- As organizations become more highly differentiated, they have a greater need for integration, but as differentiation increases, integration is harder to accomplish.
- Low levels of differentiation can be integrated through authority relationships and vertical organizational designs.
- Greater differentiation requires more intense integration through horizontal designs, with an emphasis on cross-functional teams and lateral relations.

4. How can work processes be reengineered?

- A work process is a related group of tasks that together create value for a customer.
- Business process engineering is the systematic and complete analysis of work processes and the design of new and better ones.
- In process value analysis all elements of a process and its workflows are examined to identify their exact contributions to key performance results.
- Reengineering eliminates unnecessary work-steps, combines others, and uses technology to gain efficiency and reduce costs.

KEY TERMS REVIEW

Adaptive organization (p. 277)
Bureaucracy (p. 274)
Continuous-process production (p. 280)
Differentiation (p. 283)
Integration (p. 284)
Intensive technology (p. 281)
Intrapreneurship (p. 281)
Learning organization (p. 277)

Long-linked technology (p. 281)
Mass production (p. 279)
Mechanistic design (p. 275)
Mediating technology (p. 281)
Organic design (p. 277)
Organizational design (p. 273)
Organizational effectiveness (p. 273)

Organizational life cycle (p. 281)
Process reengineering (p. 285)
Process value analysis (p. 286)
Simultaneous systems (p. 281)
Small-batch production (p. 279)
Subsystem (p. 282)
Technology (p. 279)
Work process (p. 285)
Workflow (p. 285)

SELF-TEST 11

MULTIPLE-CHOICE QUESTIONS:

1. The bureaucratic organization described by Max Weber is similar to the _____ organization described by Burns and Stalker.
   (a) adaptive (b) mechanistic (c) organic (d) adhocracy

2. Teamwork, task forces, and empowerment are common in organizations operating with _____.
   (a) mechanistic designs (b) strict bureaucracy (c) vertical structures (d) organic designs

3. The production method characteristic of an oil refinery is an example of what Woodward referred to as _____ technology.
   (a) intensive (b) continuous-process (c) mass-production (d) small-batch

4. As organizations grow in size, they tend to become more _____ in design, although this is not always best for them.
   (a) mechanistic (b) organic (c) adaptive (d) simultaneous

5. A basic paradox in subsystem design is that as differentiation increases, the need for _____ also increases but is harder to accomplish.
   (a) cost efficiency (b) innovation (c) integration (d) transformation

6. A(n) _____ organizational design works best in _____ environments.
   (a) flexible, stable (b) adaptive, uncertain (c) mechanistic, dynamic (d) organic, certain

7. A simple structure tends to work well when an organization is in the _____ stage of its life cycle.
   (a) birth (b) midlife (c) maturity (d) decline

8. When the members of a marketing department pursue sales volume objectives and those in manufacturing pursue cost efficiency objectives, this is an example of _____.
   (a) simultaneous systems (b) subsystems differentiation (c) long-linked technology (d) small-batch production

9. A work process is defined as a related group of tasks that together create value for _____.
   (a) shareholders (b) customers (c) workers (d) society

10. The first step in process value analysis is to _____.
    (a) look for ways to eliminate unnecessary tasks (b) map or diagram the workflows (c) identify core processes (d) look for efficiencies in transferring work among people and departments

11. In the _____ approach to organizational effectiveness, the focus is on how well an organization satisfies customers and external stakeholders.
    (a) systems resource (b) strategic constituencies (c) process reengineering (d) goal

12. After the short-term criteria of performance effectiveness and efficiency are met, an organizational design should next satisfy the organizational effectiveness criteria of _____ .
    (a) cost and quality control (b) stability and survival (c) adaptability and development (d) shareholder value and profit maximization

13. A traditional vertical structure is the most appropriate choice when an organization is pursuing a strategic focus on _____ .
    (a) intrapreneurship (b) innovation (c) stability (d) flexibility

14. A small Web design firm that creates one-of-a-kind websites for customers is an example of a _____ technology in Woodward's classification scheme.
    (a) small-batch (b) continuous-process (c) long-linked (d) mediating

15. The major situational contingencies that affect the choice of organizational design include strategy, size, environment, technology, and _____.
    (a) performance (b) people (c) differentiation (d) workflow

SHORT-RESPONSE QUESTIONS:

16. Explain the practical significance of this statement: "Organizational design should always be addressed in contingency fashion."

17. What difference does environment make in organizational design?

18. Describe the relationship between differentiation and integration as issues in subsystem design.

19. If you were a reengineering consultant, how would you describe the steps in a typical approach to process value analysis?

APPLICATION QUESTION:

20. Two business women, former college roommates, are discussing their jobs and careers over lunch. You overhear one saying to the other: "I work for a large corporation. It is bureaucratic and very authority driven. However, I have to say that it is also very successful. I like working there." Her friend responded: "My, I wouldn't like working there at all. In my organization things are very flexible and the structures are loose. We have a lot of freedom and the focus on operations is much more horizontal than vertical. And we, too, are very successful." After listening to the conversation and using insights from management theory, how can these two very different "success stories" be explained?

www.wiley.com/college/schermerhorn

12 | Human resource management

Planning Ahead

After reading Chapter 12, you should be able to answer these questions in your own words.

CHAPTER 12 study questions

1. Why do people make the difference?

2. What is strategic human resource management?

3. How do organizations attract a quality workforce?

4. How do organizations develop a quality workforce?

5. How do organizations maintain a quality workforce?

WORKING MOTHER MEDIA—PEOPLE ARE VALUABLE ASSETS, NOT COSTS

Working Mother magazine's annual listing of the "100 Best Companies for Working Mothers" has become an important management benchmark—both for employers that want to be able to say that they are among the best, and for potential employees who only want to work for the best. The magazine was founded in 1979 and has grown to prominence as a major supporter of mothers with work careers. Monthly topics cover the full gamut from kids to health to personal motivation and more. Self-described as helping women to "integrate their professional lives, their family lives and their inner lives," *Working Mother* mainstreams coverage of work-life balance issues and needs for women. Its focus has garnered a monthly readership of over 3 million.

   Working Mother magazine is part of Working Mother Media, a conglomerate headed by CEO Carol Evans and including the National Association for Female Executives (NAFE)—the country's largest women's professional organization. NAFE focuses on "education, networking, and public advocacy, to empower its members to achieve career success and financial security." Working Mother Media also operates Business Advisory Services for women business owners and a Conference Division.

   Not content to rest on past laurels, the magazine recently added a listing of "Best Companies for Women of Color." In advertising a recent Women of Color Town Hall meeting in Chicago, Working Mother Conferences reminded its readers that: "Women of color hold less than 2% of corporate board seats on the Fortune 500. . . . Black women earn 64 cents to the white man's dollar; Hispanic women earn 52 cents to the white man's dollar . . . while women of color have made recent advances in corporate America, they are not optimistic about continued successes."[1]

> **Get Connected!**
>
> For women, *Working Mother* is a great place to explore the challenges of blending motherhood with a career. For anyone, it offers an up-to-date look at family and career issues.

Chapter 12 Learning Preview

Working Mother Media has made a mark with its focus on the needs of mothers in the new workplace. Pick up any copy of *Working Mother* magazine or browse the online version. You'll find informative and motivating articles dealing with the challenges and opportunities faced by women at work. In this chapter you will learn more about diversity and the primacy of people to organizational performance. You will learn about the process of human resource management through which managers attract, develop, and maintain a talented workforce. You will also learn about the complex legal environment within which such human resource management decisions are made.

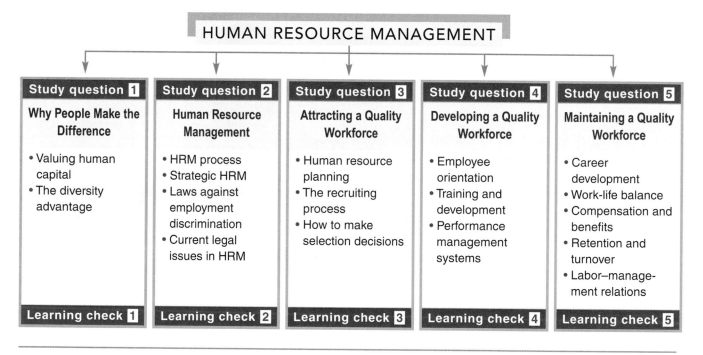

HUMAN RESOURCE MANAGEMENT

Study question 1	Study question 2	Study question 3	Study question 4	Study question 5
Why People Make the Difference	**Human Resource Management**	**Attracting a Quality Workforce**	**Developing a Quality Workforce**	**Maintaining a Quality Workforce**
• Valuing human capital • The diversity advantage	• HRM process • Strategic HRM • Laws against employment discrimination • Current legal issues in HRM	• Human resource planning • The recruiting process • How to make selection decisions	• Employee orientation • Training and development • Performance management systems	• Career development • Work-life balance • Compensation and benefits • Retention and turnover • Labor–management relations
Learning check 1	**Learning check 2**	**Learning check 3**	**Learning check 4**	**Learning check 5**

○ The **social contract** reflects expectations in the employee–employer relationship.

Today, perhaps more than ever before, the pressures of global competition and social change are influencing not just the organizations in which we work but the very nature of employment itself. In his book *The Future of Success,* Robert Reich calls this "the age of the terrific deal."[2] He also describes a shift away from a system in which people work loyally as traditional "employees" for "employers" who provide them career-long job and employment security.[3] In the emerging system we become sellers of our services (talents) to those buyers (employers) who are willing to pay for them. Those who do "buy" are looking for the very best people, whose capabilities and motivations match the demands of high-performance organizations. Reich is talking about changes to the **social contract,** or expectations of the employee–employer relationship. As today's organizations reconfigure around networks, teams, projects, flexibility, speed, and efficiency, the social contract is changing. For the individual, this means an emphasis on skills, responsibility, continuous learning, and mobility. For the organization, it means providing development opportunities, challenging work assignments, the best in resource support, and incentive compensation.[4]

All of this, of course, affects your future career. "Create a brand called 'You,'" "Build a portfolio of skills," "Protect your mobility," "Take charge of your destiny," "Add value to your organization" advise the career gurus.[5] The advice is on target, but the really tough question is: "Are you ready?" Test yourself by asking and answering these *career readiness questions:* Who am I? What do I want? What have I done? What do I know? What can I do? Why should someone hire me?

WHY PEOPLE MAKE THE DIFFERENCE

People have to be a top priority in any organization with high-performance aspirations. Testimonials like these say it all: "*People* are our most important asset"; "It's *people* who make the difference"; "It's the *people* who determine whether our company thrives or languishes." Found on websites, in annual reports, and in executive speeches, they communicate respect for people and the talents they bring to organizations.

VALUING HUMAN CAPITAL

A strong foundation of **human capital**—the economic value of people with job-relevant abilities, knowledge, experience, ideas, energies, and commitments—is essential to any organization's long-term performance success. Consider the strategic leadership implications of these comments made by Jeffrey Pfeffer in his book *The Human Equation: Building Profits by Putting People First.*[6]

> O **Human capital** is the economic value of people with job-relevant abilities, knowledge, ideas, energies, and commitments.

> *The key to managing people in ways that lead to profit, productivity, innovation, and real organizational learning ultimately lies in how you think about your organization and its people. . . . When you look at your people, do you see costs to be reduced? . . . Or, when you look at your people do you see intelligent, motivated, trustworthy individuals—the most critical and valuable strategic assets your organization can have?*

In an Academy of Management Executive article entitled "Putting People First for Organizational Success," Jeffrey Pfeffer and John F. Veiga state: "There is a substantial and rapidly expanding body of evidence . . . that speaks to the strong connection between how firms manage their people and the economic results achieved."[7] They forcefully argue that organizations perform better when they treat their members better. The management practices associated with successful organizations are employment security, decentralization, use of teams, good compensation, extensive training, and information sharing.[8] James Baron and David Kreps also highlight the primacy of people in their book *Strategic Human Resources: Frameworks for General Managers.*[9] Stating that "human resources are key to organizational success or failure," they summarize empirical research showing a relationship between positive human resource policies and higher organizational performance.

REALITY CHECK 12.1

Graduating students' expectations for work
A WetFeet.Com study of some 1600 undergraduate and graduate students shows men expecting almost $7,000 per year more in salary than women. Take the online "Reality Check" to learn more about gender differences in work expectations.

THE DIVERSITY ADVANTAGE

The best employers and the best managers know that to succeed in to-day's challenging times they must place a primacy on people.[10] This means valuing diversity and being fully inclusive of all people with the talent and desire to do good work. Job-relevant talent is not restricted because of anyone's race, gender, religion, marital or parental status, sexual orientation, ethnicity, or other diversity characteristics. And anytime these characteristics interfere with finding, hiring, and utilizing the best employees, the loss will be someone else's gain.

Respect for people in all of their diversity is a major theme in the book *Proversity: Getting Past Face Value and Finding the Soul of People,* by author and consultant Lawrence Otis Graham.[11] He suggests that managers committed to building high-performance work environments should take a simple test. The question is: Which of the following qualities would you look for in anyone who works for you—work ethic, ambition and energy, knowledge, creativity, motivation, sincerity, outlook, collegiality and collaborativeness, curiosity, judgment and maturity, and integrity? In answering, you most likely selected all of these qualities, or at least you should have. The next test question is: "Where can you find people with these workplace qualities?" The correct answer is "everywhere."[12]

Diversity consultant and author R. Roosevelt Thomas puts the challenge this way: "Managers must find ways to get the highest level of contribution from their workers. And they will not be able to do that unless they are aware of the many ways that their understanding of diversity relates to how well, or how poorly, people contribute." Thomas goes further to identify what he calls the *diversity rationale* that must drive organizations today:

> To thrive in an increasingly unfriendly marketplace, companies must make it a priority to create the kind of environment that will attract the best new talent and will make it possible for employees to make their fullest contributions.[13]

www.sap.com

The popular musician Stevie Wonder joined with SAP America, an enterprise-integration software company, to offer the Stevie Wonder Vision Awards. These go to companies that provide employment opportunities for the visually impaired.

Learning check 1

Be sure you can • define the terms social contract and human capital • explain the logic behind this position: Organizations perform better when they treat their people better • discuss how and why workforce diversity can be a source of performance advantage

---

HUMAN RESOURCE MANAGEMENT

A marketing manager at Ideo, a Palo Alto–based industrial design firm, once said: "If you hire the right people . . . if you've got the right fit . . . then everything will take care of itself."[14] It really isn't quite that simple, but one fact of management remains very clear: If an organization doesn't have the right people available to do the required work, it has very little chance of long-term success.

o **Human resource management** is the process of attracting, developing, and maintaining a high-quality workforce.

HUMAN RESOURCE MANAGEMENT PROCESS

The process of **human resource management,** or HRM, involves attracting, developing, and maintaining a talented and energetic workforce. The basic goal of human resource management is to build organizational performance capacity by raising human capital, to ensure that highly capable and enthusiastic people are always available. The three major responsibilities of human resource management are:

1. *Attracting a quality workforce*—involves human resource planning, employee recruitment and selection.
2. *Developing a quality workforce*—involves employee orientation, training and development, and performance appraisal.
3. *Maintaining a quality workforce*—involves career development, work-life balance, compensation and benefits, retention and turnover, and labor-management relations.

← The human resource management process

The area of human resource management provides many career opportunities. HRM departments are common in most organizations. HRM specialists are increasingly important in an environment complicated by legal issues, labor shortages, economic turmoil, changing corporate strategies, changing personal values, new expectations, and more. As outsourcing of professional services becomes more popular, a growing number of firms provide specialized HRM services such as recruiting, compensation, outplacement, and the like. The Society for Human Resource Management, or SHRM, is a professional organization dedicated to keeping its membership up to date in all aspects of HRM and its complex legal environment.

STRATEGIC HUMAN RESOURCE MANAGEMENT

All organizations at all times need to have the right people available to do the work required to achieve and sustain competitive advantage. Today, this challenge is increasingly addressed by making the human resources function an integral component of strategic management. **Strategic human resource management** mobilizes human capital through the HRM process to best implement organizational strategies.[15] One indicator that the HRM process is truly strategic to the organization is when the HRM function is headed by a senior executive reporting directly to the chief executive officer. When Robert Nardelli took over as new CEO of Home Depot, for example, the first person he hired into the senior executive suite was Denis Donovan, who became the firm's executive vice president for human resources. Donovan says: "CEOs and boards of directors are learning that human resources can be one of your biggest game-changers in terms of competitive advantage."[16] The strategic importance of HRM has been further accentuated by the spate of corporate ethics scandals. "It was a failure of people and that isn't lost on those in the executive suite," says Susan Meisinger, president of the Society for Human Resource Development.[17]

PERSONAL MANAGEMENT

PROFESSIONALISM! What does this term mean? If you are in human resource management, the code of ethics of the Society for Human Resource Management offers a framework for consideration.[18] SHRM defines "Professional Responsibility" as:

- adding value to your organization
- contributing to its ethical success
- serving as a leadership role model for ethical conduct
- accepting personal responsibility for one's decisions and actions
- promoting fairness and justice in the workplace
- being truthful in communications
- protecting the rights of individuals
- striving to meet high standards of competence
- strengthening one's competencies continually

Although for human resource professionals, these guidelines are a good starting point for anyone who wants to meet high standards of professionalism at work. What about you? How well do you score? Would you add anything to make this list more meaningful to your career?

Get to know yourself better ►
Complete Self-Assessments #18—**Are You Cosmopolitan?** and #19—**Performance Appraisal Assumptions** from the Management Learning Workbook.

○ **Strategic human resource management** mobilizes human capital to implement organizational strategies.

LAWS AGAINST EMPLOYMENT DISCRIMINATION

O **Discrimination** occurs when someone is denied a job or job assignment for reasons not job relevant.

O **Equal employment opportunity** is the right to employment and advancement without regard to race, sex, religion, color, or national origin.

O **Affirmative action** is an effort to give preference in employment to women and minority group members.

Discrimination in employment occurs when someone is denied a job or a job assignment for reasons that are not job relevant. A sample of major U.S. laws prohibiting job discrimination is provided in *Figure 12.1*. An important cornerstone of this legal protection is *Title VII of the Civil Rights Act of 1964,* as amended by the *Equal Employment Opportunity Act of 1972* and the *Civil Rights Act (EEOA) of 1991.* These acts provide for **equal employment opportunity** (EEO)—the right to employment without regard to race, color, national origin, religion, gender, age, or physical and mental ability. The intent is to ensure all citizens the right to gain and keep employment based only on their ability to do the job and their performance once on the job. EEO is federally enforced by the Equal Employment Opportunity Commission (EEOC), which has the power to file civil lawsuits against organizations that do not provide timely resolution of any discrimination charges lodged against them. These laws generally apply to all public and private organizations employing 15 or more people.

Under Title VII, organizations are expected to show **affirmative action** in setting goals and having plans to ensure equal employment opportunity for members of *protected groups,* those historically underrepresented in the workforce. The purpose of *affirmative action plans* is to ensure that women and minorities are represented in the workforce in proportion to their labor market availability.[19] The pros and cons of affirmative action are debated at both the federal and state levels. Criticisms tend to focus on the use of group membership (e.g., female or minority status) as a criterion in employment decisions.[20] The issues raised include claims of *reverse discrimination* by members of majority

Equal Pay Act of 1963	Requires equal pay for men and women performing equal work in an organization.
Title VII of the Civil Rights Act of 1964 (as amended)	Prohibits discrimination in employment based on race, color, religion, sex, or national origin.
Age Discrimination in Employment Act of 1967	Prohibits discrimination against persons over 40; restricts mandatory retirement.
Occupational Health and Safety Act of 1970	Establishes mandatory health and safety standards in workplaces.
Pregnancy Discrimination Act of 1978	Prohibits employment discrimination against pregnant workers.
Americans with Disabilities Act of 1990	Prohibits discrimination against a qualified individual on the basis of disability.
Civil Rights Act of 1991	Reaffirms Title VII of the 1964 Civil Rights Act; reinstates burden of proof by employer, and allows for punitive and compensatory damages.
Family and Medical Leave Act of 1993	Allows employees up to 12 weeks of unpaid leave with job guarantees for childbirth, adoption, or family illness.

Figure 12.1 A sample of U.S. laws against employment discrimination.

populations. White males, for example, may claim that preferential treatment given to minorities in a particular situation interferes with their individual rights.

As a general rule EEO legal protections do not restrict an employer's right to establish **bona fide occupational qualifications.** These are criteria for employment that can be clearly justified as being related to a person's capacity to perform a job. The use of bona fide occupational qualifications based on race and color is not allowed under any circumstances; those based on sex, religion, and age are very difficult to support.[21] Legal protection against employment discrimination is extensive. Listed below are four examples and brief summaries of their supporting laws.

○ **Bona fide occupational qualifications** are employment criterians justified by capacity to perform a job.

- *Disabilities:* The *Americans with Disabilities Act of 1990* prevents discrimination against people with disabilities. The law forces employers to focus on abilities and what a person can do.

◄
U.S. laws protecting against job discrimination

- *Age:* The *Age Discrimination in Employment Act of 1967 as amended in 1978 and 1986* protects workers against mandatory retirement ages. Age discrimination occurs when a qualified individual is adversely affected by a job action that replaces him or her with a younger worker.

- *Pregnancy:* The *Pregnancy Discrimination Act of 1978* protects female workers from discrimination because of pregnancy. A pregnant employee is protected against termination or adverse job action because of the pregnancy, and is entitled to reasonable time off work.

- *Family matters:* The *Family and Medical Leave Act of 1993* protects workers who take unpaid leaves for family matters from losing their jobs or employment status. Workers are allowed up to 12 weeks' leave for childbirth, adoption, personal illness, or illness of a family member.

CURRENT LEGAL ISSUES IN HUMAN RESOURCE MANAGEMENT

All aspects of human resource management must be accomplished within the legal framework. Failure to do so is not only unjustified in a free society, it can also be a very expensive mistake resulting in fines and penalties. As a reminder, *Manager's Notepad 12.1* identifies questions that are considered illegal—or at least inappropriate—for an interviewer to ask during a job interview.[22] Of course, the American legal and regulatory environment is constantly changing. A committed manager or human resource professional should always stay informed on the following and other issues of legal and ethical consequence.[23]

Sexual harassment occurs when a person experiences conduct or language of a sexual nature that affects their employment situation. According to the EEOC, sexual harassment is behavior that creates a hostile work environment, interferes with their ability to do a job, or interferes with their promotion potential. Organizations should have clear sexual harassment policies in place along with fair and equitable procedures for implementing them.

○ **Sexual harassment** is behavior of a sexual nature that affects a person's employment situation.

The *Equal Pay Act of 1963* provides that men and women in the same organization should be paid equally for doing equal work in terms of required skills, responsibilities, and working conditions. But a linger-

MANAGER'S NOTEPAD 12.1

Illegal or inappropriate [and acceptable] questions when interviewing a job candidate

- National Origin—What is the ethnic origin of your name? [*Okay:* Are you authorized to work in the United States?]
- Family—Are you married? [*Okay:* Would you be willing to relocate?]
- Family—Do you plan to have children? [*Okay:* Are you willing to travel as needed?]
- Family—Who lives with you? [*Okay:* This job requires occasional overtime. Is that acceptable?]
- Age—How old are you? [*Okay:* Are you over 18?]
- Religion—Do you practice a religion? [*Okay:* Nothing.]
- Arrest Record—Have you ever been arrested? [*Okay:* Have you ever been convicted of (crime relevant to job performance)?]
- Disability—Do you have any disabilities? [*Okay:* Can you perform (described in detail) as an essential part of the job?]

○ **Comparable worth** holds that persons performing jobs of similar importance should be paid at comparable levels.

ing issue involving gender disparities in pay involves **comparable worth,** the notion that persons performing jobs of similar importance should be paid at comparable levels. Why should a long-distance truck driver, for example, be paid more than an elementary teacher in a public school? Does it make any difference that the former is a traditionally male occupation and the latter a traditionally female occupation? Advocates of comparable worth argue that such historical disparities are due to gender bias. They would like to have the issue legally resolved.

○ **Independent contractors** are hired on temporary contracts and are not part of the organization's permanent workforce.

The legal status and employee entitlements of *part-time workers* and **independent contractors** are also being debated. In today's era of downsizing, outsourcing, and projects, more and more persons are hired as temporary workers who work under contract to an organization and do not become part of its permanent workforce. They work only "as needed." But, a problem occurs when they are engaged regularly by the same organization and become what many now call *permatemps*. Even though regularly employed they work without benefits such as health insurance and pension eligibilities. A number of legal cases are now before the courts seeking to make such independent contractors eligible for benefits.

○ **Workplace privacy** is the right to privacy while at work.

Workplace privacy is the right of individuals to privacy on the job.[24] It is quite acceptable for employers to monitor the work performance and behavior of their employees. But employer practices can become invasive and cross legal and ethical lines, especially with the capabilities of information technology. Computers can easily monitor e-mails and Internet searches to track personal and unauthorized usage; they can identify who is called by telephone and how long conversations last; they can document work performance moment to moment; and they can easily do more. All of this information, furthermore, can be stored in vast databases that make it available to others, even without the individual's permission. The legal status of such IT surveillance is being debated. Until things are cleared up, one consultant recommends the best approach for everyone is: "Assume you have no privacy at work."[25]

ATTRACTING A QUALITY WORKFORCE

The first responsibility of human resource management is to attract to the organization a high-quality workforce. An advertisement once run by the Motorola Corporation clearly identifies the goal of this aspect of HRM: "Productivity is learning how to hire the person who is right for the job." To attract the right people to its workforce, an organization must first know exactly what it is looking for—it must have a clear understanding of the jobs to be done and the talents required to do them well. Then it must have the systems in place to excel at employee recruitment and selection.

HUMAN RESOURCE PLANNING

Human resource planning is the process of analyzing an organization's human resource needs and determining how to best fill them. Effective and strategic human resource planning ensures that the best people are always in place when needed by the organization. The major elements in this process are shown in *Figure 12.2.*

Strategic human resource planning begins with a review of organizational mission, objectives, and strategies. This establishes a frame of reference for forecasting human resource needs and labor supplies. Ultimately, the planning process should help managers identify staffing requirements, assess the existing workforce, and determine what additions and/or replacements are required to meet future needs. GE Medical Systems uses a multigenerational staffing plan. For every new product plan there is a human resource plan associated with it—one that covers all generations of the product's anticipated life.[26]

The foundations for human resource planning are set by **job analysis**—the orderly study of job facts to determine just what is done, when, where, how, why, and by whom in existing or potential new jobs.[27] The job analysis provides useful information that can then be used to write and/or update **job descriptions.** These are written statements of job duties and responsibilities. The information in a job analysis can also be used to create **job specifications.** These are lists of the qualifications—such as education, prior experience, and skill requirements—needed by any person hired for or placed in a given job.

○ **Human resource planning** analyzes staffing needs and identifies actions to fill those needs.

○ **Job analysis** studies exactly what is done in a job, and why.

○ A **job description** details the duties and responsibilities of a job holder.

○ A **job specification** lists the qualifications required of a job holder.

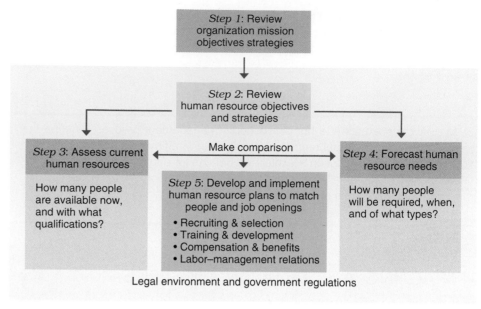

Figure 12.2 Steps in strategic human resource planning.

THE RECRUITING PROCESS

○ **Recruitment** is a set of activities designed to attract a qualified pool of job applicants.

Recruitment is a set of activities designed to attract a *qualified* pool of job applicants to an organization. Emphasis on the word "qualified" is important. Effective recruiting should bring employment opportunities to the attention of people whose abilities and skills meet job specifications. The three steps in a typical recruitment process are (1) advertisement of a job vacancy, (2) preliminary contact with potential job candidates, and (3) initial screening to create a pool of qualified applicants. In collegiate recruiting, for example, advertising is done by the firm posting short job descriptions in print or online through campus placement centers. Preliminary contact involves a short 20- to 30-minute interview, during which the candidate presents a résumé and briefly explains his or her job qualifications. Successful candidates at this stage are usually invited for further interviews during a formal visit to the organization.

External and Internal Recruitment

The collegiate recruiting example is one of *external recruitment* in which job candidates are sought from outside the hiring organization. Websites like HotJobs.com and Monster.com, newspapers, employment agencies, colleges, technical training centers, personal contacts, walk-ins, employee referrals, and even persons in competing organizations are all sources of external recruits. Labor markets and recruiting are increasingly global in the new economy. When Nokia, the Finnish mobile-phone maker, needed high-tech talent, it posted all job openings on a website and received thousands of résumés from all over the world. The head of Nokia's recruiting strategy said: "There are no geographical boundaries anymore."[28]

Internal recruitment seeks applicants from inside the organization. Most organizations have a procedure for announcing vacancies through newsletters, electronic bulletin boards, and the like. They also rely on managers to recommend subordinates as candidates for advancement. Internal recruitment creates opportunities for long-term career paths. Consider the story of Robert Goizueta. As CEO of Coca-Cola when he died, Goizueta owned over $1 billion of the company's stock. He made his way to the top over a 43-year career in the firm, an example of how loyalty and hard work can pay off.[29]

Both recruitment strategies offer potential advantages and disadvantages. External recruiting brings in outsiders with fresh perspectives. It also provides access to specialized expertise or work experience not otherwise available from insiders. Internal recruitment is usually less expensive. It also deals with persons whose performance records are well established. A history of serious internal recruitment also builds employees' loyalty and motivation, showing that one can advance by working hard and doing well when given responsibility.

www.iflyswa.com

The selection process at Southwest Airlines is rigorous. Even humor counts; it goes with the corporate culture. An interviewee may be asked to "tell a joke." It's a serious requirement—you can't work for the company if you can't pass the levity test.

Realistic Job Previews

In what may be called *traditional recruitment,* the emphasis is on selling the organization to job applicants. The emphasis is on the most positive features of the job and organization. Bias may even occur as the best features are exaggerated while negative features are avoided or even concealed. This form of recruitment may create unrealistic expectations that cause costly turnover when new hires become disillusioned and quit. The individual suffers a career disruption; the employer suffers lost productivity and the added costs of recruiting again.

The alternative is to provide **realistic job previews** that give the candidate all pertinent information about the job and organization without distortion and before the job is accepted.[30] Instead of "selling" only positive features, this approach tries to be open and balanced in describing the job and organization. Both favorable and unfavorable aspects are covered. The interviewer in a realistic job preview might use phrases such as: "Of course, there are some downsides. . . ." "Things don't always go the way we hope. . . ." "Something that you will want to be prepared for is. . . ." "We have found that some new hires had difficulty with. . . ." This type of conversation helps the candidate establish "realistic" job expectations and better prepare for the inevitable "ups and downs" of a new job. Higher levels of early job satisfaction and less inclination to leave prematurely are among the expected benefits.

○ **Realistic job previews** provide job candidates with all pertinent information about a job and organization.

HOW TO MAKE SELECTION DECISIONS

The process of **selection** involves choosing from a pool of applicants the person or persons who offer the greatest performance potential. Steps in a typical selection process are shown in *Figure 12.3.* They are (1) completion of a formal application form, (2) interviewing, (3) testing, (4) reference checks, (5) physical examination, and (6) final analysis and decision to hire or reject. The best employers exercise extreme care in making selection decisions, seeking the best fit between individual and organization.

○ **Selection** is choosing who to hire from a pool of qualified job applicants.

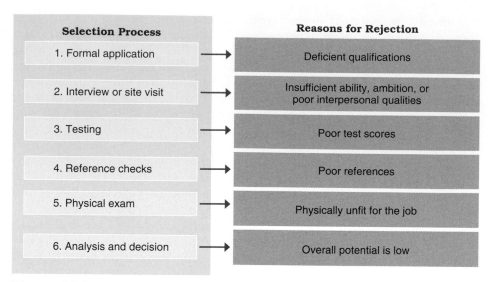

Figure 12.3 Steps in the selection process: the case of a rejected job applicant.

Application Forms

The application form declares the individual as a formal candidate for a job. It documents the applicant's personal history and qualifications. The personal résumé is often included with the job application. This important document should accurately summarize an applicant's special qualifications. As a job applicant, you should exercise great care in preparing your résumé for job searches. See the Student Portfolio section in the end-of-text Management Learning Workbook for advice. As a recruiter, you should also learn how to screen applications and résumés for insights that can help you make good selection decisions.

Interviews

Interviews are times in the selection process when both the job applicant and potential employer can learn a lot about one another. However, they can be difficult for both parties. Sometimes interviewers ask the wrong things, sometimes they talk too much, sometimes the wrong people do the interviewing, sometimes their personal biases prevent an applicant's capabilities from being fully considered. Interviewees fail, too. They may be unprepared; they may be poor communicators; they may lack interpersonal skills. An increasingly common and challenging interview setting for job applicants is highlighted in *Manager's Notepad 12.2*—the telephone interview.

Employment Tests

Testing is often used in the screening of job applicants. Some of the common employment tests are designed to identify intelligence, aptitudes, personality, and interests. Whenever tests are used, the goal should be to gather information that will help predict the applicant's eventual performance success. Like any selection device, tests should meet the criteria of

How to succeed in a telephone interview

- Be prepared ahead of time—study the organization; carefully list your strengths and capabilities.
- Take the call in private—make sure you are in a quiet room, with privacy and without the possibility of interruptions.
- Dress professionally—don't be casual; dressing right increases confidence and sets a tone for your side of the conversation.
- Practice your interview "voice"—your impression will be made quickly; how you sound counts; it even helps to stand up while you talk.
- Have reference materials handy—your résumé and other supporting documents should be within easy reach.
- Have a list of questions ready—don't be caught hesitating; intersperse your best questions during the interview.
- Ask what happens next—find out how to follow up by telephone, e-mail, etc.; ask what other information you can provide.

reliability and validity. **Reliability** means that the device is consistent in measurement; it returns the same results time after time. **Validity** means that there is a demonstrable relationship between a person's score or rating on a selection device and his or her eventual job performance. In simple terms, validity means that a good test score really does predict good performance.

New developments in testing extend the process into actual demonstrations of job-relevant skills and personal characteristics. An **assessment center** evaluates a person's potential by observing his or her performance in experiential activities designed to simulate daily work. A related approach is **work sampling,** which asks applicants to work on actual job tasks while being graded by observers on their performance. When Mercedes opened its new plant in Alabama, it set up job-specific exercises to determine who had the best of the required skills and attitudes.[31] One was a tire-changing test, with color-coded bolts and a set of instructions. As Charlene Paige took the test, she went slowly and carefully followed directions; two men with her changed the tires really fast. Charlene got the job and soon worked into a team leader position.[32]

o **Reliability** means a selection device gives consistent results over repeated measures.

o **Validity** means scores on a selection device have demonstrated links with future job performance.

o An **assessment center** examines how job candidates handle simulated work situations.

o In **work sampling** applicants are evaluated while performing actual work tasks.

Reference and Background Checks

Reference checks are inquiries to previous employers, academic advisors, coworkers, and/or acquaintances regarding the qualifications, experience, and past work records of a job applicant. Although they may be biased if friends are prearranged "to say the right things if called," reference checks are important. The Society for Human Resources Management estimates that 25 percent of job applications and résumés contain errors.[34] Reference checks can better inform the potential em-

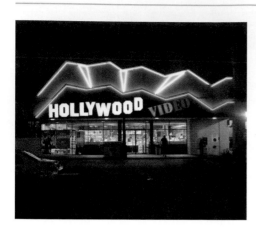

Computer kiosks screen job applicants

Computers do more than keep track of inventory and register customer transactions at Hollywood Video, a division of Hollywood Entertainment Corporation. Prospective employees use computers to answer queries regarding their qualifications, job history, and work habits. They may even take online tests that help match their capabilities with potential jobs. Many employers like the computerized approach as an efficient way to gather and screen applicants. Brad Triplett spent 20 minutes filling out his computerized application at a Hollywood Video store in Shawnee Mission, Kansas. The manager reviewed his profile the next day, and Triplett ended up with a job.[33]

ployer. They can also help add credibility to the candidate if they back up what is said in an application.

Physical Examinations

Many organizations ask job applicants to take a physical examination. This health check helps ensure that the person is physically capable of fulfilling job requirements. It may also be used as a basis for enrolling the applicant in health-related fringe benefits such as life, health, and disability insurance programs. A controversial development is drug testing, used for pre-employment health screening and even as a basis for continued employment at some organizations.

Final Decisions to Hire or Reject

The best selection decisions are most likely to be those involving extensive consultation among an applicant, future manager, or team leader and coworkers, as well as the human resource staff. Importantly, the emphasis in selection should be comprehensive and should focus on the person's capacity to perform well. Just as a "good fit" can produce long-term advantage, a "bad fit" can be the source of many long-term problems.

Learning check 3

Be sure you can • explain the difference between internal recruitment and external recruitment • discuss the value of realistic job previews to employers and job candidates • differentiate reliability and validity as two criteria of selection devices • illustrate the operation of an assessment center • discuss the importance of conducting background and reference checks

---

DEVELOPING A QUALITY WORKFORCE

When people join an organization, they must "learn the ropes" and become familiar with "the way things are done." It is important to help newcomers fit into the work environment in a way that furthers their development and performance potential. **Socialization** is the process of influencing the expectations, behavior, and attitudes of a new employee in a desirable way.[35]

○ **Socialization** systematically influences the expectations, behavior, and attitudes of new employees.

EMPLOYEE ORIENTATION

Socialization of newcomers begins with **orientation**—a set of activities designed to familiarize new employees with their jobs, coworkers, and key aspects of the organization as a whole. This includes clarifying mission and culture, explaining operating objectives and job expectations, and communicating policies and procedures. At the Disney World Resort in Buena Vista, Florida, each employee is carefully selected and trained to provide high-quality customer service as a "cast member." During orientation, newly hired employees are taught the corporate culture. They learn that everyone employed by the company, regardless of her or his specific job—be it entertainer, ticket seller, or groundskeeper—is there "to make the customer happy." The company's interviewers say that they place a premium on personality. "We can train for skills," says an HRM specialist. "We want people who are enthusiastic, who have pride in their work, who can take charge of a situation without supervision."[36]

○ **Orientation** familiarizes new employees with jobs, coworkers, and organizational policies and services.

The first six months of employment are often crucial in determining how well someone is going to fit in and perform over the long run. It is a time when the original expectations are tested and patterns are set for future relationships between an individual and employer. Unfortunately, orientation is sometimes neglected and newcomers are often left to fend for themselves. They may learn job and organizational routines on their own or through casual interactions with coworkers, and they may acquire job attitudes the same way.[37] The result is that otherwise well-intentioned and capable persons may learn the wrong things and pick up bad attitudes and habits. A good orientation, like Disney's, can set the stage for high performance, job satisfaction, and work enthusiasm.

REALITY CHECK 12.2

Threats to employee retention
A survey of employers by the Society for Human Resource Management revealed that higher salaries offered by others was the biggest threat to employee retention. Take the online "Reality Check" to learn more about the factors that can make it difficult to retain talented workers.

TRAINING AND DEVELOPMENT

Training is a set of activities that helps people acquire and improve job-related skills. This applies both to initial training of an employee and to upgrading or improving skills to meet changing job requirements. Progressive organizations invest in extensive training and development programs to ensure that their workers always have the capabilities needed to perform well.

○ **Training** provides learning opportunities to acquire and improve job-related skills.

On-the-Job Training

On-the-job training takes place in the work setting while someone is doing a job. A common approach is job rotation that allows people to spend time working in different jobs and thus expand the range of their job capabilities. Another is **coaching,** in which an experienced person provides performance advice to someone else. One form of coaching is **mentoring,** in which early-career employees are formally assigned as

○ **Coaching** occurs as an experienced person offers performance advice to a less-experienced person.

○ **Mentoring** assigns early career employees as protégés to more senior ones.

○ **Modeling** uses personal behavior to demonstrate performance expected of others.

protégés to senior persons. The mentoring relationship gives them regular access to advice on developing skills and getting better informed about the organization. **Modeling** is an informal type of coaching. It occurs when someone demonstrates through day-to-day personal behavior that which is expected of others. One way to learn managerial skills, for example, is to observe and practice the techniques displayed by good managers. Modeling is a very important influence on behavior in organizations. A good example is how the behaviors of senior managers help set the ethical culture and standards for other employees.

Off-the-Job Training

○ **Management development** is training to improve knowledge and skills in the management process.

Off-the-job training is accomplished outside the work setting. An important form is **management development,** designed to improve a person's knowledge and skill in the fundamentals of management. For example, *beginning managers* often benefit from training that emphasizes team leadership and communication; *middle managers* may benefit from training to better understand multifunctional viewpoints; *top managers* may benefit from advanced management training to sharpen their decision-making and negotiating skills, and to expand their awareness of corporate strategy and direction. At the Center for Creative Leadership, managers learn by participating in the Looking Glass simulation that models the pressures of daily work. The simulation is followed by extensive debriefings and discussions in which participants give feedback to one another. One participant commented, "You can look in the mirror but you don't see yourself. People have to say how you look."[38]

AROUND THE WORLD

Software maker takes on the world with employee support

Family friendliness is evident at Autodesk, Inc., a software maker and Internet portal that serves the world's top businesses. The firm was rated highly by its employees in a *Business Week* annual survey and is included on *Working Mother* magazine's Best Employers listing. The fact that you can bring dogs, cats, and even iguanas to work with coworkers' approval in some locations is a bit extreme. But the job flexibility offered by the firm isn't. It offers opportunities for lifestyle choices and balance between work and family. The company atmosphere is informal, employees are allowed to set their own work schedules, and almost half spend one day a week working from their homes. The firm's website says that its corporate strategy is advanced because of a special approach to "employee contentment—providing plenty of flexibility and freedom."[39]

○ A **performance management system** sets standards, assesses results, and plans for performance improvements.

PERFORMANCE MANAGEMENT SYSTEMS

An important part of human resource management is design and implementation of a successful **performance management system.** This is a system that ensures that performance standards and objectives are set, that performance is regularly assessed for accomplishments, and that actions are taken to improve future performance.

Purpose of Performance Appraisal

The process of formally assessing someone's work accomplishments and providing feedback is **performance appraisal.** It serves both evaluation and development purposes. The *evaluation purpose* is intended to let people know where they stand relative to performance objectives and standards. The *development purpose* is intended to assist in their training and continued personal development.[40]

The evaluation purpose of performance appraisal focuses on past performance and measures results against standards. Performance is documented for the record and to establish a basis for allocating rewards. The manager acts in a *judgmental role* in which he or she gives a direct evaluation of another person's accomplishments. The development purpose of performance appraisal, by contrast, focuses on future performance and the clarification of success standards. It is a way of discovering performance obstacles and identifying training and development opportunities. Here the manager acts in a *counseling role,* focusing on the other person's developmental needs.

Like employment tests, any performance appraisal method can fulfill these purposes only when the criteria of *reliability* and *validity* are met. To be reliable, the method should consistently yield the same result over time and/or for different raters; to be valid, it should be unbiased and measure only factors directly relevant to job performance. Both these criteria are especially important in today's complex legal environment. A manager who hires, fires, or promotes someone is increasingly called upon to defend such actions—sometimes in specific response to lawsuits alleging that the actions were discriminatory. At a minimum, written documentation of performance appraisals and a record of consistent past actions will be required to back up any contested evaluations.

○ **Performance appraisal** is the process of formally evaluating performance and providing feedback to a job holder.

Performance Appraisal Methods

Organizations use a variety of performance appraisal methods.[41] One of the simplest is a **graphic rating scale** in which appraisers complete checklists of traits or performance characteristics. A manager rates the individual on each item using a numerical score. Athough this approach is quick and easy to complete, its reliability and validity are questionable.

A more advanced approach is the **behaviorally anchored rating scale** (BARS), which describes actual behaviors that exemplify various levels of performance achievement in a job. Look at the case of a customer service representative illustrated in *Figure 12.4.* "Extremely poor" performance is clearly defined as rude or disrespectful treatment of a customer. Because performance assessments are anchored to specific descriptions of work behavior, a BARS is more reliable and valid than the graphic rating scale. The behavioral anchors can also be helpful in training people to master job skills of demonstrated performance importance. The city of Irving, Texas, used a BARS approach in redesigning its performance appraisal system. Many examples of different levels of

○ A **graphic rating scale** uses a checklist of traits or characteristics to evaluate performance.

○ A **behaviorally anchored rating scale** uses specific descriptions of actual behaviors to rate various levels of performance.

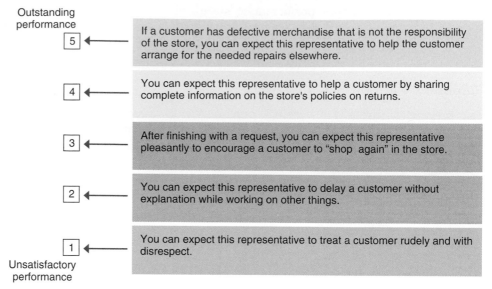

Outstanding performance

5 ← If a customer has defective merchandise that is not the responsibility of the store, you can expect this representative to help the customer arrange for the needed repairs elsewhere.

4 ← You can expect this representative to help a customer by sharing complete information on the store's policies on returns.

3 ← After finishing with a request, you can expect this representative pleasantly to encourage a customer to "shop again" in the store.

2 ← You can expect this representative to delay a customer without explanation while working on other things.

1 ← You can expect this representative to treat a customer rudely and with disrespect.

Unsatisfactory performance

Figure 12.4 Sample behaviorally anchored rating scale for performance appraisal.

○ The **critical-incident technique** keeps a log of someone's effective and ineffective job behaviors.

○ A **multiperson comparison** compares one person's performance with that of others.

job performance were written so that appraisers could pick the ones most representative of city workers' job behaviors.[42]

The **critical-incident technique** involves keeping a running log or inventory of effective and ineffective job behaviors. By creating a written record of positive and negative performance examples, this method documents success or failure patterns that can be specifically discussed with the individual. Using the case of the customer service representative again, a critical-incidents log might contain the following types of entries: *Positive example*—"Took extraordinary care of a customer who had purchased a defective item from a company store in another city"; *negative example*—"Acted rudely in dismissing the complaint of a customer who felt that a sale item was erroneously advertised."

Some performance management systems use **multiperson comparisons,** which formally compare one person's performance with that of one or more others. Such comparisons can be used on their own or in combination with some other method. They can also be done in different ways. In *rank ordering,* all persons being rated are arranged in order of performance achievement. The best performer goes at the top of the list, the worst performer at the bottom; no ties are allowed. In *paired comparisons,* each person is formally compared with every other person and rated as either the superior or the weaker member of the pair. After all paired comparisons are made, each person is assigned a summary ranking based on the number of superior scores achieved. In *forced distribution,* each person is placed into a frequency distribution that requires that a certain percentage fall into specific performance classifications, such as top 10 percent, next 40 percent, next 40 percent, and bottom 10 percent.

Not all performance appraisals are completed only by one's immediate boss. It is increasingly popular today to expand the role of a job's stakeholders in the appraisal process. The new workplace often involves use of *peer appraisal,* including in the process others who work regularly and directly with a job holder, and *upward appraisal,* including in the process subordinates reporting to the job holder. An even broader stakeholder approach is known as **360° feedback,** where superiors, subordinates, peers, and even internal and external customers are involved in the appraisal of a job holder's performance.[43]

○ **360° feedback** includes in the appraisal process superiors, subordinates, peers, and even customers.

Be sure you can • define the term socialization and describe its importance to organizations as part of the employee orientation process • differentiate coaching, mentoring, and modeling as on-the-job training approaches • explain the major types of performance appraisal methods—graphic rating scales, behaviorally anchored rating scales, critical-incident technique, and multiperson comparisons • discuss the strengths and weaknesses of each type

MAINTAINING A QUALITY WORKFORCE

It is not enough to attract and develop workers with the talents to achieve high-performance results for the short term only. They must be successfully retained, nurtured, and managed for long-term effectiveness. When adverse turnover occurs and talented workers leave to pursue other opportunities, the resulting costs for the employer can be staggering. When the Society for Human Resource Management surveyed employers to identify the most effective tools for maintaining a quality workforce, they found: good benefits—especially health care, competitive salaries, flexible work schedules and personal time off, and opportunities for training and development.[44]

CAREER DEVELOPMENT

In his book *The Age of Unreason,* British scholar and consultant Charles Handy discusses dramatic new developments in the world of work and careers. Specifically, Handy says: "The times are changing and we must change with them."[45] A **career** is a sequence of jobs and work pursuits that constitutes what a person does for a living. For many of us, a career begins on an anticipatory basis with our formal education. From there it progresses into an initial job choice and any number of subsequent choices that may involve changes in task assignments, employing organizations, and even occupations. A *career path* is a sequence of jobs held over time during a career. Career paths vary between those that are pursued internally with the same employers and those pursued externally among various employers. Although many organizations place great emphasis on making long-term career opportunities available to their employees, Handy believes that external career paths will be increasingly important in the future.

○ A **career** is a sequence of jobs that constitutes what a person does for a living.

 Career planning is the process of systematically matching career goals and individual capabilities with opportunities for their fulfillment. It involves answering such questions as "Who am I?," "Where do I want to go?," "How do I get there?" While some suggest that a career should be allowed to progress in a somewhat random but always opportunistic way, others view a career as something to be rationally planned and pursued in a logical step-by-step fashion. In fact, a well-managed career will probably

○ **Career planning** is the process of matching career goals and individual capabilities with opportunities for their fulfillment.

Systems design for work-life balance makes a difference

SAS Institute, headquartered in Cary, North Carolina, is the world's largest privately held software company. Its 9000+ employees in some 50 countries help develop, refine, and market unique business intelligence software and services used by top firms worldwide to improve strategic management. Led by CEO Jim Goodnight, SAS has operated since its founding on the guiding principle: "If you treat employees as if they make a difference to the company, they will make a difference to the company . . . satisfied employees create satisfied customers." The firm is designed to allow employees to integrate their personal needs with the opportunities and demands of a SAS career. Work-life programs include child-care centers, elder care support, health care clinics, wellness programs, fitness facilities, and more. SAS is well known for its repeat listings as one of *Fortune* magazine's "100 Best Companies to Work for in America."[50]

include elements of each. The carefully thought-out plan can point you in a general career direction; an eye for opportunity can fill in the details along the way.

When you think about adult life stages or transitions, you should recognize that sooner or later most people's careers level off. A **career plateau** is a position from which someone is unlikely to move to a higher level of work responsibility.[46] Three common reasons for career plateaus are personal choice, limited abilities, and lack of opportunity. For some, the plateau may occur at a point in life when it suits their individual needs. For others, such as employees within 10 to 15 years of retirement age, plateaus can be very frustrating. Progressive employers seek ways to engage them with new opportunities in lateral moves, mentoring assignments, and even overseas jobs. Susan Peters, vice president for executive development at GE, says: "Suddenly they come to a stage when they may have more flexibility to take a foreign assignment or do something they couldn't at a younger age."[47] She strongly believes in the value of broad experience and the willingness to pursue opportunities through lateral career moves.

> O A **career plateau** is a position from which someone is unlikely to move to a higher level of work responsibility.

WORK-LIFE BALANCE

"Hiring good people is tough," starts an article in the *Harvard Business Review*. The sentence finishes with "keeping them can be even tougher."[48] A very important retention issue given today's fast-paced and complicated lifestyles is **work-life balance**—how people balance the demands of careers with their personal and family needs. "Family" in this context includes not just children but also elderly parents and other relatives in need of care. Human resource practices that support a healthy work-life balance are increasingly valued, with the chapter case on the SAS Institute a good example.

> O **Work-life balance** involves balancing career demands with personal and family needs.

Included among work-life balance concerns are the unique needs of *single parents,* who must balance parenting responsibilities with a job, and *dual-career couples,* who must balance the career needs and opportunities of each partner. The special situations of both working mothers and working fathers are also being recognized.[49] Not surprisingly, the "family-friendliness" of an employer is now frequently and justifiably used as a screening criterion by job candidates. *Business Week, Working Mother,* and *Fortune* are among the magazines annually ranking employers on this criterion.

COMPENSATION AND BENEFITS

Good compensation and benefit systems attract qualified people to the organization and help retain them. **Base compensation** in the form of salary or hourly wages can help get the right people into jobs to begin with and keep them there by making outside opportunities less attractive. Unless an organization's prevailing wage and salary structure is competitive in the relevant labor markets, it will be difficult to attract and retain a staff of highly competent workers. Also important are **fringe benefits,** the additional nonwage or nonsalary forms of compensation. Benefit packages can constitute some 30 percent or more of a typical worker's earnings. They usually include various options on disability protection, health and life insurance, and retirement plans.

○ **Base compensation** is a salary or hourly wage paid to an individual.

○ **Fringe benefits** are non-monetary forms of compensation such as health insurance and retirement plans.

The ever-rising cost of fringe benefits, particularly employee medical benefits, is a major worry for employers. Some are attempting to gain control over health care costs by becoming more active in their employees' choices of health care providers and by encouraging healthy lifestyles. An increasingly common approach overall is **flexible benefits,** sometimes known as *cafeteria benefits,* which let the employee choose a set of benefits within a certain dollar amount. The growing significance of work-life balance in the new social contract is also reflected in a trend toward more **family-friendly benefits** that help employees better balance work and nonwork responsibilities. These include child care, elder care, flexible schedules, parental leave, and part-time employment options, among others. The best employers also offer **employee assistance programs** that help employees deal with troublesome personal problems. EAP programs may include assistance in dealing with stress, counseling on alcohol and substance abuse problems, referrals for domestic violence and sexual abuse, family and marital counseling, and advice on community resources.

○ **Flexible benefits** programs allow employees to choose from a range of benefit options.

○ **Family-friendly benefits** help employees achieve better work-life balance.

○ **Employee assistance programs** help employees cope with personal stresses and problems.

RETENTION AND TURNOVER

The several steps in the human resource management process both conclude and recycle with *replacement* decisions. These involve the management of promotions, transfers, terminations, layoffs, and retirements. Any replacement situation is an opportunity to review human resource plans, update job analyses, rewrite job descriptions and job specifications, and ensure that the best people are selected to perform the required tasks.

Some replacement decisions shift people between positions within the organization. *Promotion* is movement to a higher-level position; *transfer* is movement to a different job at a similar level of responsibility. Another set of replacement decisions relates to *retirement,* something most people look forward to . . . until it is close at hand. Then the prospect of being retired often raises fears and apprehensions. Many organizations offer special counseling and other forms of support for retiring employees, including advice on company benefits, money management, estate planning, and use of leisure time.

The most extreme replacement decisions involve *termination,* the involuntary and permanent dismissal of an employee. In some cases the termination is based on performance problems. The person involved is not meeting the requirements of the job or has violated key organizational policy. In other cases the termination may be due to financial conditions of the employer, such as those requiring downsizing or restructuring. The persons involved may be performing well but are being terminated as part of a workforce reduction. Where possible, organizations may provide outplacement services to help terminated employees find other jobs. In any and all cases, terminations should be handled fairly according to organizational policies and in full legal compliance. They should show respect for the person being dismissed, who may well find it hard to accept the decision.

IN PRACTICE

Human capital — what is a worker worth to a firm?

The Saratoga Institute states its goal as helping "companies around the world leverage Human Capital Intelligence to attract, retain, manage, and develop their people, helping them maximize the value of their human assets." Assume that you run a service firm. It has $1 million in revenues and earns $500,000 in profits before taxes. Operating expenses total $200,000; payroll and benefits costs are an additional $300,000. The question is: *What is your company's return on human capital?* Saratoga's answer is 1.67. For each $1 of investment in payroll and benefits, the human resources of the firm in this example returned $1.67 in value. Not bad as a measure of human capital performance. To get the answer, you deduct operating expenses plus payroll and benefits expenses from total revenue. This gives adjusted profit of $500,000. Then divide this by payroll and benefits costs to get 1.67.[51]

LABOR–MANAGEMENT RELATIONS

○ A **labor union** is an organization that deals with employers on the workers' collective behalf.

A final aspect of human resource management involves the role of organized labor. **Labor unions** are organizations to which workers belong that deal with employers on the workers' behalf.[52] Although they used to be associated primarily with industrial and business occupations, labor unions increasingly represent such public-sector employees as teachers, college professors, police officers, and government workers. They are important forces in the modern workplace both in the United States and around the world. About 13 percent of American workers belong to a union; the figures are over 30 percent for Canada and some 25 percent for Great Britain.[53]

○ A **labor contract** is a formal agreement between a union and employer about the terms of work for union members.

Labor unions act as a collective "voice" for members in dealing with employers. They serve as bargaining agents that negotiate legal contracts affecting many aspects of the employment relationship. These **labor contracts,** for example, typically specify the rights and obligations of employees and management with respect to wages, work hours, work rules, seniority, hiring, grievances, and other conditions of employment. All of this has implications for management. In a unionized work setting, the labor

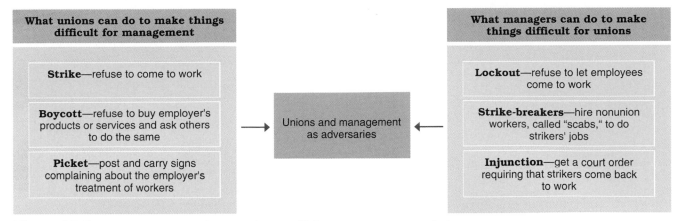

Figure 12.5 The traditional adversarial view of labor–management relations.

contract and its legal implications must be considered when making human resource management decisions.

The foundation of any labor and management relationship is **collective bargaining,** which is the process of negotiating, administering, and interpreting labor contracts. Labor contracts and the collective bargaining process—from negotiating a new contract to resolving disputes under an existing one—are major influences on human resource management in unionized work settings. They are also governed closely in the United States by a strict legal framework with three important foundations. The *National Labor Relations Act of 1935* (known as the *Wagner Act*) protects employees by recognizing their right to join unions and engage in union activities. It is enforced by the National Labor Relations Board (NLRB). The *Taft-Hartley Act of 1947* protects employers from unfair labor practices by unions and allows workers to decertify unions. And the *Civil Service Reform Act Title VII of 1978* clarifies the right of government employees to join and be represented by labor unions.

The collective bargaining process typically occurs in face-to-face meetings between labor and management representatives. During this time, a variety of demands, proposals, and counterproposals are exchanged. Several rounds of bargaining may be required before a contract is reached or a dispute over a contract issue is resolved. And, as you might expect, the process can lead to problems. In *Figure 12.5,* labor and management are viewed as "win-lose" adversaries destined to be in opposition and possessed of certain weapons with which to fight one another. If labor–management relations take this form, a lot of energy on both sides can be expended in prolonged conflict. This adversarial approach is, to some extent, giving way to a new and more progressive era of greater cooperation. Each side seems more willing to understand the need for cooperation and mutual adjustment to new and challenging times.

○ **Collective bargaining** is the process of negotiating, administering, and interpreting a labor contract.

Be sure you can • define the terms career plateau and work-life balance • discuss the significance of each term for the human resource management process • explain why compensation and benefits are important elements in human resource management • define the terms labor union, labor contract, and collective bargaining • compare the adversarial and cooperative approaches to labor–management relations

Learning check 5

CHAPTER 12 STUDY GUIDE

Where We've Been

BACK TO WORKING MOTHER

The opening example of Working Mother Media introduced a resource devoted to the support of mothers and their careers. It reminded you of the complexities of work-life balance in our complex environment and the resulting challenges faced by people and their employers. In this chapter you learned about the human resource management process, the legal environment that governs this process, and the managerial responsibilities through which decisions are made and actions taken to ensure that organizations always attract, develop, and maintain a talented workforce capable of creating high performance results.

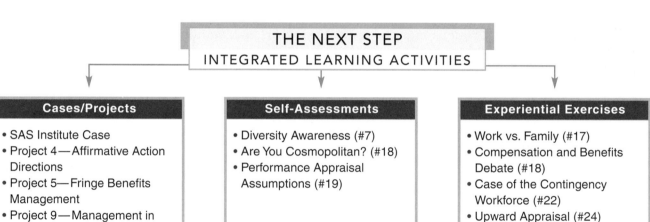

THE NEXT STEP
INTEGRATED LEARNING ACTIVITIES

Cases/Projects

- SAS Institute Case
- Project 4—Affirmative Action Directions
- Project 5—Fringe Benefits Management
- Project 9—Management in Popular Culture

Self-Assessments

- Diversity Awareness (#7)
- Are You Cosmopolitan? (#18)
- Performance Appraisal Assumptions (#19)

Experiential Exercises

- Work vs. Family (#17)
- Compensation and Benefits Debate (#18)
- Case of the Contingency Workforce (#22)
- Upward Appraisal (#24)

STUDY QUESTIONS SUMMARY

1. Why do people make the difference?

- Even in this age of information, high technology, and globalization, people are irreplaceable assets that make organizations work.
- Organizations with positive human resource policies and practices are gaining significant performance advantages.
- The challenges of complexity and uncertainty in highly competitive environments are best met by a diverse and talented workforce.
- The diversity advantage is gained only when the talents of all persons, regardless of personal characteristics, are respected and given the opportunity to be displayed.

2. What is strategic human resource management?

- The human resource management process involves attracting, developing, and maintaining a quality workforce.
- Human resource management becomes strategic when it is integrated into the organization's strategic leadership.
- Human resource management is influenced by a complex and changing legal environment.
- Equal employment opportunity guarantees people the right to employment and advancement without discrimination.
- Current legal issues in HRM include sexual harrasment, comparable worth, rights of

independent contractors, and employee privacy.

3. How do organizations attract a quality workforce?

- Human resource planning is the process of analyzing staffing needs and identifying actions to satisfy these needs over time.
- The purpose of human resource planning is to make sure the organization always has people with the right abilities available to do the required work.
- Recruitment is the process of attracting qualified job candidates to fill vacant positions.
- Realistic job previews provide candidates with accurate information on the job and organization.
- Managers use interviews, employment tests, and references to help make selection decisions; the use of assessment centers and work sampling is becoming more common.

4. How do organizations develop a quality workforce?

- Orientation is the process of formally introducing new employees to their jobs, performance expectations, and the organization.
- On-the-job training includes coaching, apprenticeship, modeling, and mentoring; off-the-job training includes formal programs, such as management development courses.

- Performance management systems establish work standards and the means for assessing performance results.
- Common performance appraisal methods are graphic rating scales, narratives, behaviorally anchored rating scales, and multiperson comparisons.

5. How do organizations maintain a quality workforce?

- Career planning systematically matches individual career goals and capabilities with opportunities for their fulfillment.
- Programs that address work-life balance and the complex demands of job and family responsibilities are increasingly important in human resource management.
- Compensation and benefits packages must be continually updated so that the organization stays competitive in labor markets.
- Whenever workers must be replaced through promotions, transfers, retirements, and/or terminations, the goal should be to treat everyone fairly while ensuring that remaining jobs are filled with the best personnel available.
- In collective bargaining situations, labor–management relations should be positively approached and handled with all due consideration of applicable laws.

KEY TERMS REVIEW

Labor contract (p. 314)	Performance management system (p. 308)	Socialization (p. 307)
Labor union (p. 314)		Strategic human resource management (p. 297)
Management development (p. 308)	Realistic job preview (p. 303)	
Mentoring (p. 307)	Recruitment (p. 302)	360° feedback (p. 311)
Modeling (p. 308)	Reliability (p. 305)	Training (p. 307)
Multiperson comparison (p. 310)	Selection (p. 303)	Validity (p. 305)
	Sexual harassment (p. 299)	Work sampling (p. 305)
Orientation (p. 307)		Work-life balance (p. 312)
Performance appraisal (p. 309)	Social contract (p. 294)	Workplace privacy (p. 300)

SELF-TEST 12

MULTIPLE-CHOICE QUESTIONS:

1. Human resource management is the process of _____, developing, and maintaining a high-quality workforce.
   (a) attracting (b) compensating (c) appraising (d) selecting

2. A _____ is a criterion that can be legally justified for use in screening candidates for employment.
   (a) job description (b) bona fide occupational qualification (c) job specification (d) BARS

3. _____ programs are designed to ensure equal employment opportunities for persons historically unrepresented in the workforce.
   (a) Realistic recruiting (b) External recruiting (c) Affirmative action (d) Employee assistance

4. An employment test that yields different results over time when taken by the same person should be replaced because it lacks _____.
   (a) validity (b) specificity (c) realism (d) reliability

5. The assessment center approach to employee selection relies heavily on _____.
   (a) pencil-and-paper tests (b) simulations and experiential exercises (c) 360° feedback (d) formal one-on-one interviews

6. _____ is a form of on-the-job training wherein an individual learns by observing others who demonstrate desirable job behaviors.
   (a) Case study (b) Work sampling (c) Modeling (d) Simulation

7. The first step in human resource planning is to _____.
   (a) forecast human resource needs (b) forecast labor supplies (c) assess the existing workforce (d) review organizational mission, objectives, and strategies

8. In the United States, the _____ Act of 1947 protects employers from unfair labor practices by unions.
   (a) Wagner (b) Taft-Hartley (c) Labor Union (d) Hawley-Smoot

9. Socialization of newcomers occurs during the _____ step of the staffing process.
   (a) recruiting (b) orientation (c) selecting (d) training

10. In human resource planning, a/an _____ is used to determine exactly what is done in an existing job.
    (a) critical-incident technique (b) assessment center (c) job analysis (d) multiperson comparison

11. In what is called the new "social contract" between employers and employees, the implications for the individual include accepting more personal responsibility for _____.
    (a) learning and mobility (b) salary negotiation (c) labor–management relations (d) socialization

12. The _____ purpose of performance appraisal is being addressed when a manager describes training options that might help an employee improve future performance.
    (a) development (b) evaluation (c) judgmental (d) legal

13. When a team leader is required to rate 10 percent of team members as "superior," 80 percent as "good," and 10 percent as "unacceptable" for their performance on a project, this is an example of the _____ approach to performance appraisal.
    (a) graphic (b) forced distribution (c) behaviorally anchored rating scale (d) realistic

14. An employee with family problems that are starting to interfere with work would be pleased to learn that his employer had a(n) _____ plan to help on such matters.
    (a) employee assistance (b) cafeteria benefits (c) comparable worth (d) collective bargaining

15. A manager who _____ is displaying a commitment to valuing human capital.
    (a) believes payroll costs should be reduced wherever possible (b) is always looking for new ways to replace people with machines (c) protects workers from stress by withholding from them information about the organization's performance (d) views people as assets to be nurtured and developed over time

SHORT-RESPONSE QUESTIONS:

16. How do internal recruitment and external recruitment compare in terms of advantages and disadvantages for the employer?

17. Why is orientation an important part of the staffing process?

18. What is the difference between the graphic rating scale and the BARS as performance appraisal methods?

19. How does mentoring work as a form of on-the-job training?

APPLICATION QUESTION:

20. Sy Smith is not doing well in his job. The problems began to appear shortly after Sy's job was changed from a manual to a computer-based operation. He has tried hard, but is just not doing well in learning to use the computer and meet performance expectations. As a 55-year-old employee with over 30 years with the company, Sy is both popular and influential among his work peers. Along with his performance problems, you have also noticed the appearance of some negative attitudes, including a tendency for Sy to sometimes "badmouth" the firm. As Sy's manager, what options would you consider in terms of dealing with the issue of his retention in the job and in the company? What would you do and why?

13

Leading

Planning Ahead →

After reading Chapter 13,
you should be able to
answer these questions
in your own words.

CHAPTER 13 study questions

1. **What is the nature of leadership?**

2. **What are the important leadership traits and behaviors?**

3. **What are the contingency theories of leadership?**

4. **What is transformational leadership?**

5. **What are current issues in leadership development?**

SOUTHWEST AIRLINES—EMPLOYEES ARE A FIRM'S MOST IMPORTANT CUSTOMERS

When most people think of Southwest Airlines, they think first of reasonable prices, second of success in a turbulent industry and a service spirit, and third of its well-known founder and retired CEO Herb Kelleher. Indeed, all points are on target. You can learn more about Kelleher and his leadership style by reading the Southwest Airlines case for this chapter. Before doing that, however, consider Colleen Barrett, Southwest's new president and CEO.

In an interview with *BizEd* magazine, Barrett indicates that the airline's success begins with its high-priority commitment to all employees. She says the firm has three types of customers: employees, passengers, and shareholders. Whereas many would consider it strange and perhaps even wrong to define employees as an organization's most important customers, Barret says it has a purpose: "If senior leaders regularly communicate with employees, if we're truthful and factual, if we show them that we care, and we do our best to respond to their needs, they'll feel good about their work environment and they'll be better at serving the passenger." Satisfied passengers, of course, are essential for business reputation and profits.

At Southwest, a strong and unique sense of mission helps leaders at all levels to rally themselves and others to everyday performance excellence. "We tell job applicants we're in the customer service business," says Barrett. "We just happen to provide airline transportation." That is a unique spin in an industry known for customer complaints and dissatisfaction.

Leadership development at Southwest is supported from the top, with everyone expected to be great at "TLC"—tender loving care for employees and customers. There are leadership classes and seminars, outside speakers, meetings with senior managers, roundtable discussions and brown-bag meetings with employees. Barrett describes herself as a mentor, willing to work with "anyone who seems to have a passion for what he or she does, or who has a desire to learn."[1]

Chapter 13 Learning Preview

In the chapter opening example of Colleen Barrett's leadership role at Southwest Airlines, you should note the importance of leading with vision and in a way that is consistent with the mission of the organization. Barrett is a classic example of a leader who invests herself in the responsibilities of leadership—fully, personally, and comprehensively. In this chapter you will learn about leadership concepts and the various approaches taken by scholars to understand leadership effectiveness. You will learn about the current issues in leadership development, and you will also be asked to reflect on your personal capacities to lead with excellence.

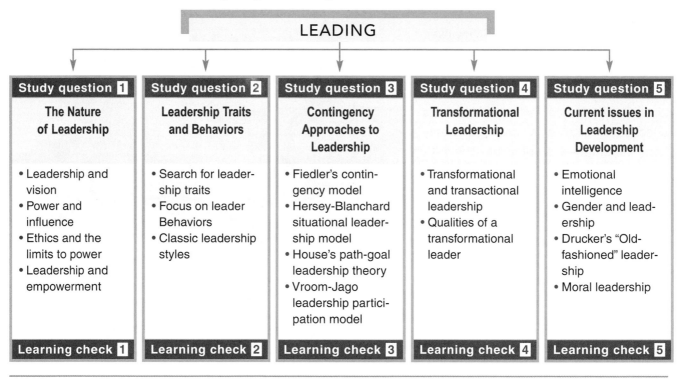

LEADING

Study question 1	Study question 2	Study question 3	Study question 4	Study question 5
The Nature of Leadership	**Leadership Traits and Behaviors**	**Contingency Approaches to Leadership**	**Transformational Leadership**	**Current issues in Leadership Development**
• Leadership and vision • Power and influence • Ethics and the limits to power • Leadership and empowerment	• Search for leadership traits • Focus on leader Behaviors • Classic leadership styles	• Fiedler's contingency model • Hersey-Blanchard situational leadership model • House's path-goal leadership theory • Vroom-Jago leadership participation model	• Transformational and transactional leadership • Qualities of a transformational leader	• Emotional intelligence • Gender and leadership • Drucker's "Old-fashioned" leadership • Moral leadership
Learning check 1	Learning check 2	Learning check 3	Learning check 4	Learning check 5

At Herman Miller, Inc., the innovative Michigan-based maker of office furniture, Max DePree, the firm's former chairperson and the son of its founder, tells the story of a millwright who worked for his father.[3] When the man died, DePree's father, wishing to express his sympathy to the family, went to their home. There he listened as the widow read some beautiful poems, which, he was surprised to learn, had been written by the millwright. To this day, DePree says, he and his father still wonder, "Was the man a poet who did millwright's work, or a millwright who wrote poetry?"

DePree summarizes the lesson of the story this way: "It is fundamental that leaders endorse a concept of persons. This begins with an understanding of the diversity of people's gifts, talents, and skills." When we recognize the unique qualities of others, we become less inclined to believe that we alone know what is best. By valuing and respecting people, we learn how to provide them with meaningful work and opportunities. This leadership lesson extends to all types and sizes of organizations. Great leaders bring out the best in people. Consultant and author Tom Peters says that the leader is "rarely—possibly never?—the best performer."[4] They don't have to be; they thrive through and by the successes of others.

THE NATURE OF LEADERSHIP

Warren Bennis, a respected scholar and consultant, claims that too many American corporations are "over-managed and under-led." The late Grace Hopper, another management expert and the first female admiral in the U.S. Navy, said, "You manage things; you lead people."[2] A glance at the shelves in your local bookstore will quickly confirm that **leadership**—the process of inspiring others to work hard to accomplish important tasks, is one of the most popular management topics. As shown in *Figure 13.1,* it is also one of the four functions that constitutes the management process. Planning sets the direction and objectives; organizing brings the resources together to turn plans into action; *leading* builds the commitments and enthusiasm for people to apply their talents to help accomplish plans; controlling makes sure things turn out right.

Managers today must lead under new and difficult conditions. The time frames for getting things accomplished are becoming shorter; leaders are expected to get things right the first time, with second chances few and far between; the problems to be resolved through leadership are complex, ambiguous, and multidimensional; leaders are expected to be long-term oriented even while meeting demands for short-term performance results.[5] Anyone aspiring to career success in leadership must rise to these challenges, and more, becoming good at communication, interpersonal relations, motivation, teamwork, and change—all topics in this final part of *Management 8/e.*

O **Leadership** is the process of inspiring others to work hard to accomplish important tasks.

LEADERSHIP AND VISION

"Great leaders," it is said, "get extraordinary things done in organizations by inspiring and motivating others toward a common purpose."[6] Frequently today, leadership is associated with **vision**—a future that one hopes to create or achieve in order to improve upon the present state of affairs. The term **visionary leadership** describes a leader who

O A **vision** is a clear sense of the future.

O **Visionary leadership** brings to the situation a clear sense of the future and an understanding of how to get there.

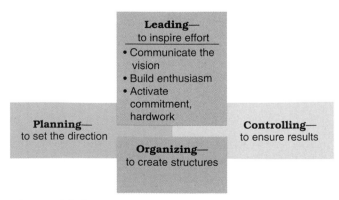

Figure 13.1 Leading viewed in relationship to the other management functions.

MANAGER'S NOTEPAD 13.1   Five principles of visionary leadership

- *Challenge the process:* Be a pioneer; encourage innovation and support people who have ideas.
- *Show enthusiasm:* Inspire others through personal enthusiasm to share in a common vision.
- *Help others to act:* Be a team player and support the efforts and talents of others.
- *Set the example:* Provide a consistent role model of how others can and should act.
- *Celebrate achievements:* Bring emotion into the workplace and rally "hearts" as well as "minds."

---

brings to the situation a clear and compelling sense of the future as well as an understanding of the actions needed to get there successfully.[7] But simply having the vision of a desirable future is not enough. Truly great leaders are extraordinarily good at turning their visions into accomplishments. This involves the ability to communicate the vision in such a way that others are willing to work hard to achieve it. Visionary leaders, simply put, inspire others to take the actions necessary to turn vision into reality. At General Electric, for example, an "A" leader is considered to be someone ". . . with vision and the ability to articulate that vision to the team, so vividly and powerfully that it also becomes their vision."[8]

Manager's Notepad 13.1 offers five principles for meeting the challenges of visionary leadership.[9] The suggestions go beyond a manager's responsibilities for making long-term plans and drafting budgets, putting structures in place, assigning people to jobs, and making sure that results are consistent with plans. Leading with vision means doing all these things and more. It means having a clear vision, communicating that vision to all concerned, and getting people motivated and inspired to pursue the vision in their daily work. Visionary leadership means bringing meaning to people's work, making what they do worthy and valuable.

POWER AND INFLUENCE

○ **Power** is the ability to get someone else to do something you want done or to make things happen the way you want.

The foundations of effective leadership lie in the way a manager uses power to influence the behavior of other people. **Power** is the ability to get someone else to do something you want done. It is the ability to make things happen the way you want them to.[10] Research recognizes that a need for power is essential to executive success.[11] But this need for power is not a desire to control for the sake of personal satisfaction; it is a desire to influence and control others for the good of the group or organization as a whole. This "positive" face of power is the foundation of effective leadership. *Figure 13.2* shows that leaders gain power from both the positions they hold and from their personal qualities.[12]

Sources of power...

Power of the POSITION: *Based on things managers can offer to others.*	Power of the PERSON: *Based on how managers are viewed by others.*
Rewards: "If you do what I ask, I'll give you a reward."	**Expertise**—as a source of special knowledge and information.
Coercion: "If you don't do what I ask, I'll punish you."	**Reference**—as a person with whom others like to identify.
Legitimacy: "Because I am the boss; you *must* do as I ask."	

Figure 13.2 Sources of position power and personal power used by managers.

Sources of Position Power

A manager's official status, or position, in the organization's hierarchy of authority is an important source of power. Although anyone holding a managerial position theoretically has this power, how well it is used will vary from one person to the next. Consequently, leadership success will vary as well. The three bases of *position power* are reward power, coercive power, and legitimate power.

Reward power is the ability to influence through rewards. It is the capability to offer something of value—a positive outcome—as a means of influencing the behavior of other people. This involves the control of rewards or resources such as pay raises, bonuses, promotions, special assignments, and verbal or written compliments. To mobilize reward power, a manager says, in effect, "If you do what I ask, I'll give you a reward."

○ **Reward power** is the capacity to offer something of value as a means of influencing other people.

CAREER CONNECTION

Public school leaders must make visions happen

At her Leadership Institute in New York City, founder Lorraine Monroe brings leadership to life in the "Monroe Doctrine"—"We can reform society only if every place we live—every school, workplace, church, and family—becomes a site of reform." Monroe has held a variety of responsible positions in New York City public schools and previously founded an experimental public high school in Harlem, the Frederick Douglas's Academy. Monroe's leadership principles start with what she calls the "heart of the matter": "Leadership is about making a vision happen. . . . The job of a good leader is to articulate a vision that others are inspired to follow. . . . That leader makes everybody in an organization understand how to make the vision active." Monroe's book *Nothing's Impossible: Leadership Lessons from the Front Lines* was praised by *Ms.* magazine as offering inspiration on every page.[13]

Coercive power is the ability to influence through punishment. It is the capacity to punish or withhold positive outcomes as a way to influence the behavior of other people. A manager may attempt to coerce someone by threatening him or her with verbal reprimands, pay penalties, and even termination. To mobilize coercive power, a manager says, in effect, "If you don't do what I want, I'll punish you."

○ **Coercive power** is the capacity to punish or withhold positive outcomes as a means of influencing other people.

○ **Legitimate power** is the capacity to influence other people by virtue of formal authority, or the rights of office.

Legitimate power is the ability to influence through authority—the right by virtue of one's organizational position or status to exercise control over persons in subordinate positions. It is the capacity to influence the behavior of other people by virtue of the rights of office. To mobilize legitimate power, a manager says, in effect, "I am the boss, therefore you are supposed to do as I ask."

PERSONAL MANAGEMENT

Leadership is an interpersonal process. You either lead well or poorly in large part due to your ability to relate well to other people. Furthermore, in today's high-performance work settings, with their emphasis on horizontal structures, cross-functional teams, and projects, leading requires skillful **NETWORKING**. Within teams, across functions and in day-to-day work encounters, the best leaders get things done because they build and maintain positive working relationships with others. In the social context of organizations, there is very little you can do by yourself; the vast majority of work gets done because people in your networks help you out. For some of us, networking is as natural as walking down the street. For others, it is a big challenge in the intimidating realm of interpersonal relationships. But even if you fall into this last category, the fact remains: To be a successful leader you need networking skills. Don't underestimate the challenge; be prepared for leadership. Do you have confidence in these networking skills?

- *Network identification*—knowing and finding the right people to work with.
- *Network building*—engaging others and relating to them in positive ways.
- *Network maintenance*—actively nurturing and supporting others in their work.

Get to know yourself better ➤
Complete Self-Assessments #20—**T-P Leadership Questionnaire,** #21-**T-T Leadership,** and #22—**Least Preferred CoWorker Scale,** from the Management Learning Workbook.

Sources of Personal Power

The unique personal qualities of a manager are further sources of power. In fact, a truly successful leader is very good at building and using the two bases of *personal power*— expert power and referent power.

Expert power is the ability to influence through special expertise. It is the capacity to influence the behavior of other people because of one's knowledge and skills. Expertise derives from the possession of technical understanding or information pertinent to the issue at hand. It is developed by acquiring relevant skills or competencies and by gaining a central position in relevant information networks. It is maintained by protecting one's credibility and not overstepping the boundaries of true expertise. When a manager uses expert power, the implied message is, "You should do what I want because of my special expertise or information."

Referent power is the ability to influence through identification. It is the capacity to influence the behavior of other people because they admire you and want to identify positively with you. Reference is a power derived from charisma or interpersonal attractiveness. It is developed and maintained through good interpersonal relations that encourage the admiration and respect of others. When a manager uses referent power, the implied message is: "You should do what I want in order to maintain a positive self-defined relationship with me."

Turning Power into Influence

To succeed at leadership, managers must both acquire all types of power and use them appropriately.[14] The best leaders understand that use of the various power bases results in quite different outcomes. When one relies on rewards and legitimacy to influence others, the likely outcome is temporary compliance. The follower will do what the leader requests, but only so long as the reward continues and/or the legitimacy persists. When one relies on coercion, compliance is also temporary and dependent on the continued threat of punishment. In this case, however, the compliance is often accompanied by resentment. The use of expert and

○ **Expert power** is the capacity to influence other people because of specialized knowledge.

reference power has the most enduring results, creating commitment rather than compliance. Followers respond positively because of internalized understanding or beliefs that create a long-lasting impact on behavior.

Position power and the compliance it generates are often insufficient for managers to achieve and sustain needed influence. Personal power and the resulting commitment are what often make the difference between leadership success and mediocrity. This is particularly true in today's horizontal organizations with their emphasis on teamwork and cooperation. Four points to keep in mind when building your managerial power are: (1) there is no substitute for expertise, (2) likable personal qualities are very important, (3) effort and hard work breed respect, and (4) personal behavior must match expressed values.[15]

In organizations, power and influence are also linked to where one fits and how one acts in the structures and networks of the workplace.[16] *Centrality* is important. Managers gain power by establishing networks of interpersonal contacts and getting involved in the information flows within them. They avoid becoming isolated. *Criticality* is important. To gain power, managers must take good care of others who are dependent on them. They support them exceptionally well by doing things that add value to the work setting. *Visibility* is also important. It helps to become known as an influential person in the organization. Managers gain power by performing well in formal presentations, on key task forces or committees, and in special assignments that display their talents and capabilities.

> o **Referent power** is the capacity to influence other people because of their desire to identify personally with you.

ETHICS AND THE LIMITS TO POWER

On the issue of ethics and the limits to power, it is always helpful to remember Chester Barnard's *acceptance theory of authority.* He identifies four conditions that determine whether a leader's directives will be followed and true influence achieved:[17] (1) The other person must truly understand the directive. (2) The other person must feel capable of carrying out the directive. (3) The other person must believe that the directive is in the organization's best interests. (4) The other person must believe that the directive is consistent with personal values.

In Chapter 3 it was noted that many ethical dilemmas begin when leaders and managers pressure followers to do questionable things. Using the acceptance theory of authority as a starting point, the ethical question a follower must always be prepared to ask is: "Where do I (or will I) draw the line; at what point do I (or will I) refuse to comply with requests?" Someday you may face a situation in which you are asked by someone in authority to do something that violates personal ethics and/or even the law. Can you . . . will you . . . when will you, say "no"? After all, as Barnard said, it is "acceptance" that establishes the limits of managerial power.

REALITY CHECK 13.1

How culture influences views of the "ideal" leader
Researchers asked workers across cultures if they preferred a *specifics leader,* focused on getting the job done, or an *integrated-whole leader,* focused on getting subordinates to work well together. Canadians preferred a specifics leader, Singaporeans didn't. Take the online "Reality Check" to learn more on leadership preferences across cultures.

LEADERSHIP AND EMPOWERMENT

At many points in this book we have talked about **empowerment,** the process through which managers enable and help others to gain power

> o **Empowerment** enables others to gain and use decision-making power.

MANAGER'S NOTEPAD   13.2

How to empower others

- Get others involved in selecting their work assignments and the methods for accomplishing tasks.
- Create an environment of cooperation, information sharing, discussion, and shared ownership of goals.
- Encourage others to take initiative, make decisions, and use their knowledge.
- When problems arise, find out what others think and let them help design the solutions.
- Stay out of the way; give others the freedom to put their ideas and solutions into practice.
- Maintain high morale and confidence by recognizing successes and encouraging high performance.

and achieve influence within the organization. Effective leaders empower others by providing them with the information, responsibility, authority, and trust to make decisions and act independently. They know that when people feel empowered to act, they tend to follow through with commitment and high-quality work. They also realize that power in organizations is not a "zero-sum" quantity; in order for someone to gain power, it isn't necessary for someone else to give it up. Indeed, today's high-performance organizations thrive by mobilizing power throughout all ranks of employees.

Max DePree of Herman Miller praises leaders who are willing to focus on what is best for the organization and "permit others to share ownership of problems—to take possession of the situation."[18] Lorraine Monroe of the School Leadership Academy says: " . . . a really great boss is not afraid to hire smart people. You want people who are smart about things you are not smart about."[19] Both are talking about leadership through empowerment—allowing and helping people to use their experience, knowledge, and judgment to make a real difference in daily workplace affairs. *Manager's Notepad 13.2* offers tips on how leaders can empower others.[20] Doing so requires respect for the talents and creativity of others. And it requires the confidence to let people work with initiative in responsible jobs, participate in decisions affecting their work, and make reasonable choices regarding their work-life balance.

Learning check 1

Be sure you can • define the term vision • explain the concept of visionary leadership • define the term power • illustrate three types of position power and discuss how managers use each • illustrate two types of personal power and discuss how managers use each • explain the implications of Barnard's acceptance theory of authority for ethical behavior in organizations • define the term empowerment • explain why managers benefit by empowering others

LEADERSHIP TRAITS AND BEHAVIORS

For centuries, people have recognized that some persons perform very well as leaders, whereas others do not. The question still debated is: "Why?" Historically, the issue of leadership success has been studied from the perspective of the trait, behavioral, and contingency approaches. Each takes a slightly different tack in attempting to explain both leadership effectiveness and identify the pathways to leadership development.

SEARCH FOR LEADERSHIP TRAITS

An early direction in leadership research involved the search for universal traits or distinguishing personal characteristics that would separate effective and ineffective leaders.[21] Sometimes called the *great person theory,* the notion was to identify successful leaders and then determine what made them great.

Briefly, the results of many years of research in this direction can be summarized as follows. Physical characteristics such as a person's height, weight, and physique make no difference in determining leadership success. On the other hand, certain personal traits do seem to differentiate leaders, although they must always be considered along with situational factors. A study of over 3400 managers, for example, found that followers rather consistently admired leaders who were honest, competent, forward-looking, inspiring, and credible.[22] In a comprehensive review of research to date, Shelley Kirkpatrick and Edwin Locke further identify these personal traits as being common among successful leaders.[23]

- *Drive:* Successful leaders have high energy, display initiative, and are tenacious.

◄———
Personal traits of successful leaders

- *Self-confidence:* Successful leaders trust themselves and have confidence in their abilities.
- *Creativity:* Successful leaders are creative and original in their thinking.
- *Cognitive ability:* Successful leaders have the intelligence to integrate and interpret information.
- *Business knowledge:* Successful leaders know their industry and its technical foundations.
- *Motivation:* Successful leaders enjoy influencing others to achieve shared goals.
- *Flexibility:* Successful leaders adapt to fit the needs of followers and demands of situations.
- *Honesty and integrity:* Successful leaders are trustworthy; they are honest, predictable, and dependable.

FOCUS ON LEADERSHIP BEHAVIORS

Researchers next turned their attention toward how leaders behave when working with followers. Work in this tradition investigated **leadership styles**—the recurring patterns of behaviors exhibited by leaders.[24] If the

○ **Leadership style** is the recurring pattern of behaviors exhibited by a leader.

best style could be identified, the implications were straightforward and practical: train leaders to become skilled at using it.

Most leader behavior research focused on two dimensions of leadership style: (1) concern for the task to be accomplished and (2) concern for the people doing the work. The terminology used to describe these dimensions varies among many studies. Concern for task is sometimes called "initiating structure," "job-centeredness," and "task orientation"; concern for people is sometimes called "consideration," "employee centeredness," and "relationship orientation." But regardless of the terminology, the behaviors characteristic of each dimension are quite clear. A *leader high in concern for task* plans and defines work to be done, assigns task responsibilities, sets clear work standards, urges task completion, and monitors performance results. By contrast, a *leader high in concern for people* acts warm and supportive toward followers, maintains good social relations with them, respects their feelings, is sensitive to their needs, and shows trust in them.

The results of leader behavior research at first suggested that followers of people-oriented leaders would be more productive and satisfied than those working for more task-oriented leaders.[25] Later results, however, suggested that truly effective leaders were high in both concern for people and concern for task. *Figure 13.3* describes one of the popular versions of this conclusion—the Leadership Grid® of Robert Blake and Jane Mouton.[26] This grid describes alternative leadership styles that managers display. It is designed to assist in the process of leadership development. The approach uses assessments (such as #20 in the Management Learning Workbook) to first determine where someone falls with respect to people and task concerns. Then a training program is designed to help shift the person's style in the preferred direction of becoming strong on both dimensions. Blake and Mouton called this preferred style *team management.* This leader shares decisions with subordinates, encourages participation, and supports the teamwork needed for high levels of task accomplishment. Today, this would be a manager who "empowers" others.

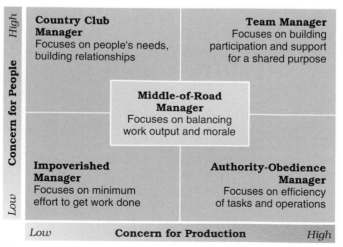

Figure 13.3 Managerial styles in Blake and Mouton's Leadership Grid.

CLASSIC LEADERSHIP STYLES

Even today, when people describe the leaders with whom they work, their vocabulary includes three classic styles of leadership from the behavioral leadership theories.[27] A leader with an **autocratic style** emphasizes task over people, keeps authority and information to himself or herself, and acts in unilateral command-and-control fashion. A leader with a **laissez-faire style** does just the opposite, showing little concern for task, letting the group make decisions, and acting with a "do the best you can and don't bother me" attitude. In contrast to both, a leader with a **democratic style** is committed to task and people, getting things done while sharing information, encouraging participation in decision making, and otherwise helping others develop their skills and capabilities. An important personal question, of course, is: "What type of leader are you?" And perhaps even more importantly: "How would the people with whom you work and study describe your style—autocratic, laissez-faire, or democratic?"

○ A leader with an **autocratic style** acts in unilateral command-and-control fashion.

○ A leader with a **laissez-faire style** displays a "do the best you can and don't bother me" attitude.

○ A leader with a **democratic style** encourages participation with an emphasis on both task accomplishment and development of people.

Be sure you can • contrast the trait and leader behavior approaches to leadership research • identify five personal traits common among successful leaders • illustrate leader behaviors consistent with a high concern for task • illustrate leader behaviors consistent with a high concern for people • explain the leadership development implications of Blake and Mouton's Leadership Grid • describe three classic leadership styles

Learning check 2

CONTINGENCY APPROACHES TO LEADERSHIP

As leadership research continued, scholars recognized the need to probe beyond leader behaviors and examine yet another question: "When and under what circumstances is a particular leadership style preferable to others?" They developed the following *contingency approaches,* which share the goal of understanding the conditions for leadership success in different situations.

FIEDLER'S CONTINGENCY MODEL

An early contingency leadership model developed by Fred Fiedler proposed that good leadership depends on a match between leadership style and situational demands.[28] Leadership style in Fiedler's model is measured on the *least-preferred coworker scale,* known as the LPC scale. It describes tendencies to behave either as a task-motivated (low LPC score) or relationship-motivated (high LPC score) leader. This "either/or" concept is important. Fiedler believes that leadership style is part of one's personality; therefore, it is relatively enduring and difficult to change. He doesn't place much hope in trying to train a task-motivated leader to behave in a relationship-motivated manner, or vice versa. Rather, Fiedler believes that the key to leadership success is putting our existing styles to work in situations for which they are the best "fit."

Get Connected!

Get your LPC leadership score online and in the *Management Learning Workbook* (assessment #22).

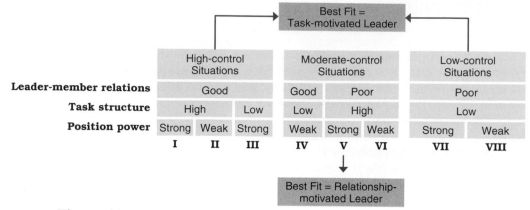

	High-control Situations			Moderate-control Situations			Low-control Situations	
Leader-member relations	Good			Good	Poor		Poor	
Task structure	High		Low	Low	High		Low	
Position power	Strong	Weak	Strong	Weak	Strong	Weak	Strong	Weak
	I	II	III	IV	V	VI	VII	VIII

Figure 13.4 Matching leadership style and situation: summary predictions from Fiedler's contingency theory.

This is true contingency leadership thinking with the goal of successfully matching one's style with situational demands.

Understanding Leadership Situations

In Fiedler's model, the amount of control a situation allows the leader is a critical issue in determining the correct style-situation fit. Three contingency variables are used to diagnose situational control. The *quality of leader-member relations* (good or poor) measures the degree to which the group supports the leader. The *degree of task structure* (high or low) measures the extent to which task goals, procedures, and guidelines are clearly spelled out. The *amount of position power* (strong or weak) measures the degree to which the position gives the leader power to reward and punish subordinates. *Figure 13.4* shows eight leadership situations that result from different combinations of these variables. They range from the most favorable situation of high control (good leader-member relations, high task structure, strong position power) to the least favorable situation of low control (poor leader-member relations, low task structure, weak position power).

Matching Leadership Style and Situation

Figure 13.4 also summarizes Fiedler's extensive research on the contingency relationships between situation control, leadership style, and leader effectiveness. Note that neither the task-oriented nor the relationship-oriented leadership style is effective all the time. Instead, each style appears to work best when used in the right situation. The results can be stated as two propositions. *Proposition 1* is that a task-oriented leader will be most successful in either very favorable (high-control) or very unfavorable (low-control) situations. *Proposition 2* is that a relationship-oriented leader will be most successful in situations of moderate control.

Assume, for example, that you are the leader of a team of bank tellers. The tellers seem highly supportive of you, and their job is clearly defined regarding what needs to be done. You have the authority to evaluate their performance and to make pay and promotion recommendations. This is a high-control situation consisting of good leader-mem-

www.gore.com

Empowerment is in at W. L. Gore & Associates, of Newark, Delaware. Everyone is an "associate" at Gore, and leaders achieve their positions by accomplishment and the support of others. "Leadership," says late founder Bill Gore, "is defined by what you do, not who you are."

ber relations, high task structure, and high position power. Figure 13.4 shows that a task-motivated leader would be most effective in this situation.

Now take another example. Suppose that you are chairperson of a committee asked to improve labor-management relations in a manufacturing plant. Although the goal is clear, no one can say for sure how to accomplish it. Task structure is low. Because committee members are free to quit any time they want, the chairperson has little position power. Because not all members believe the committee is necessary, poor leader-member relations are apparent. According to the figure, this low-control situation also calls for a task-motivated leader.

Finally, assume that you are the new head of a retail section in a large department store. Because you were selected over one of the popular sales clerks you now supervise, leader-member relations are poor. Task structure is high since the clerk's job is well defined. Your position power is low because the clerks work under a seniority system and fixed wage schedule. The figure shows that this moderate-control situation requires a relationship-motivated leader.

HERSEY-BLANCHARD SITUATIONAL LEADERSHIP MODEL

In contrast to Fiedler's notion that leadership style is hard to change, the Hersey-Blanchard situational leadership model suggests that successful leaders do adjust their styles. And they do so based on the *maturity* of followers, indicated by their readiness to perform in a given situation.[29] "Readiness," in this sense, is based on how able and willing or confident followers are to perform required tasks. As shown in *Figure 13.5*, the possible leadership styles that result from different combinations of task-oriented and relationship-oriented behaviors are as follows:

- *Delegating*—allowing the group to take responsibility for task decisions; a low-task, low-relationship style.

- *Participating*—emphasizing shared ideas and participative decisions on task directions; a low-task, high-relationship style.

Leadership styles in the Hersey-Blanchard situational model

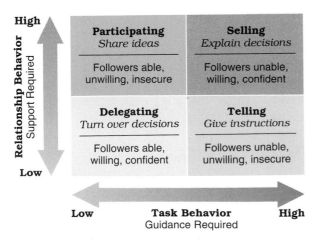

Figure 13.5 Leadership implications of the Hersey-Blanchard situational leadership model.

- *Selling*—explaining task directions in a supportive and persuasive way; a high-task, high-relationship style.
- *Telling*—giving specific task directions and closely supervising work; a high-task, low-relationship style.

Managers using this model must be able to implement the alternative leadership styles as needed. The *delegating style* works best in high-readiness situations of able and willing or confident followers; the *telling style* works best at the other extreme of low readiness, where followers are unable and unwilling or insecure. The *participating style* is recommended for low-to-moderate readiness (followers able but unwilling or insecure) and the *selling style* for moderate-to-high readiness (followers unable but willing or confident). Hersey and Blanchard further believe that leadership styles should be adjusted as followers change over time. The model also implies that if the correct styles are used in lower-readiness situations, followers will "mature" and grow in ability, willingness, and confidence. This allows the leader to become less directive as followers mature. Although the Hersey-Blanchard model is intuitively appealing, limited research has been accomplished on it to date.[30]

HOUSE'S PATH-GOAL LEADERSHIP THEORY

A third contingency leadership approach is the *path-goal theory* advanced by Robert House.[31] This theory suggests that an effective leader is one who clarifies paths through which followers can achieve both task-related and personal goals. The best leaders raise motivation and help followers move along these paths. They remove any barriers that stand in the way and provide appropriate rewards for task accomplishment. Path-goal theorists believe leaders should be flexible and move back and forth among four leadership styles to create positive "path-goal" linkages.

Leadership styles in the path-goal theory

- *Directive leadership*—letting subordinates know what is expected; giving directions on what to do and how; scheduling work to be done; maintaining definite standards of performance; clarifying the leader's role in the group.
- *Supportive leadership*—doing things to make work more pleasant; treating group members as equals; being friendly and approachable; showing concern for the well-being of subordinates.
- *Achievement-oriented leadership*—setting challenging goals; expecting the highest levels of performance; emphasizing continuous improvement in performance; displaying confidence in meeting high standards.
- *Participative leadership*—involving subordinates in decision making; consulting with subordinates; asking for suggestions from subordinates; using these suggestions when making a decision.

Path-Goal Predictions and Managerial Implications

The path-goal theory, summarized in *Figure 13.6,* advises managers to use leadership styles that fit situational needs. This means that the leader adds value by contributing things that are missing from the situation or that need strengthening; she or he specifically avoids redundant behaviors. For example, when team members are expert and competent at their tasks, it is unnecessary and even dysfunctional for the leader to tell them how to do things.

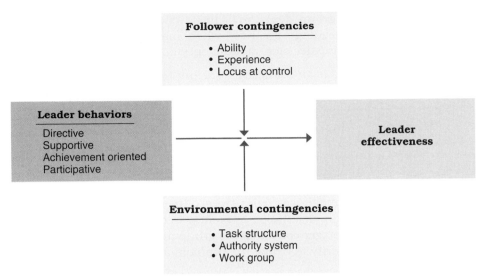

Figure 13.6 Contingency relationships in the path-goal leadership theory.

The important contingencies for making good path-goal leadership choices include follower characteristics (ability, experience, and locus of control) and work environment characteristics (task structure, authority system, and work group). For example, the match of leader behaviors and situation might take the following forms.[32] When *job assignments* are unclear, directive leadership is appropriate to clarify task objectives and expected rewards. When *worker self-confidence* is low, supportive leadership is appropriate to increase confidence by emphasizing individual abilities and offering needed assistance. When *performance incentives* are poor, participative leadership is appropriate to clarify individual needs and identify appropriate rewards. When *task challenge* is insufficient in a job, achievement-oriented leadership is appropriate to set goals and raise performance aspirations.

Substitutes for Leadership

Path-goal theory has also contributed to the recognition of what are called **substitutes for leadership**.[33] These are aspects of the work setting and the people involved that can reduce the need for a leader's personal involvement. In effect, they make leadership from the "outside" unnecessary because leadership is already provided from within the situation. Possible substitutes for leadership include *subordinate characteristics* such as ability, experience, and independence; *task characteristics* such as routineness and availability of feedback; and *organizational characteristics* such as clarity of plans and formalization of rules and procedures. When these substitutes are present, managers should avoid duplicating them. Instead, they should concentrate on other and more important things.

O **Substitutes for leadership** are factors in the work setting that direct work efforts without the involvement of a leader.

VROOM-JAGO LEADER-PARTICIPATION MODEL

The Vroom-Jago leader-participation model is designed to help a leader choose the decision-making method that best fits the problem being faced.[34] The key issue is on the amount of decision-making participation allowed followers. The broad choices are for the leader to make an **author-**

O An **authority decision** is made by the leader and then communicated to the group.

ity, consultative, or **group decision.**[35] In its current version, the model views a manager as leading effectively when making the right selection from among the following decision-making options.

Vroom-Jago decision-making choices

1. *Decide alone*—This is an authority decision; the manager decides how to solve the problem and communicates the decision to the group.
2. *Consult individually*—The manager makes the decision after sharing the problem and consulting individually with group members to get their suggestions.
3. *Consult with group*—The manager makes the decision after convening the group, sharing the problem, and consulting with everyone to get their suggestions.
4. *Facilitate*—The manager convenes the group, shares the problem, and then facilitates group discussion to make a decision.
5. *Delegate*—The manager convenes the group and delegates to group members the authority to define the problem and make a decision.

○ A **consultative decision** is made by a leader after receiving information, advice, or opinions from group members.

○ A **group decision** is made by group members themselves.

In true contingency fashion, no one decision method is considered by the Vroom-Jago model as universally superior to any others. Each of the five decision methods is appropriate in certain situations, and each has its advantages and disadvantages.[36] Leadership success results when the decision type correctly matches the characteristics of the problem to be solved. The key rules guiding the choice relate to: (1) *decision quality*— based on who has the information needed for problem solving; (2) *decision acceptance*—based on the importance of subordinate acceptance of the decision to its eventual implementation; and (3) *decision time*—based on the time available to make and implement the decision.

As shown in *Figure 13.7,* the more authority-oriented decisions work best when leaders personally have the expertise needed to solve the problem, they are confident and capable of acting alone, others are likely to accept and implement the decision they make, and little or no time is available for discussion. By contrast, the more group-oriented and participative decision methods are recommended when:

When participation works best

- The leader lacks sufficient expertise and information to solve this problem alone.
- The problem is unclear and help is needed to clarify the situation.
- Acceptance of the decision and commitment by others are necessary for implementation.
- Adequate time is available to allow for true participation.

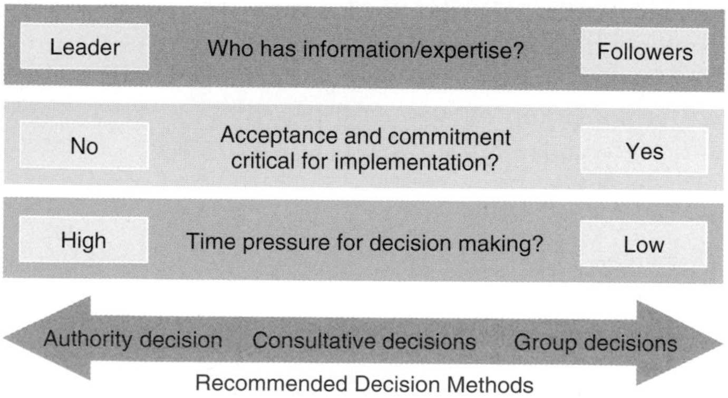

Leader	Who has information/expertise?	Followers
No	Acceptance and commitment critical for implementation?	Yes
High	Time pressure for decision making?	Low

Authority decision ← Consultative decisions → Group decisions

Recommended Decision Methods

Figure 13.7 Leadership implications of Vroom-Jago leader-participation model.

The more participative decision methods offer important benefits.[37] They help improve decision quality by bringing more information to bear on the problem. They help improve decision acceptance as participants gain understanding and become committed to the process. They also contribute to the development of leadership potential in others through the experience gained by active participation in the problem-solving process. However, there is a potential cost of lost efficiency. The greater the participation, the more time required for the decision process. Leaders do not always have sufficient time available; some problems must be resolved immediately. In such cases the authority decision may be the only option.[38]

| **Learning check 3** | *Be sure you can* • contrast the leader behavior and contingency approaches to leadership research • explain the relationship between leadership style and a person's score on Fiedler's least-preferred coworker scale • explain Fiedler's contingency thinking on matching leadership style and situation • identify the four leadership styles in the Hersey-Blanchard situational model • explain House's path-goal theory • illustrate the behaviors of directive, supportive, achievement-oriented, and participative leadership styles • define the term substitutes for • contrast the authority, consultative, and group decisions in the Vroom-Jago model • explain when more participative decisions work best |

TRANSFORMATIONAL LEADERSHIP

There is a great deal of interest today in "superleaders," persons whose visions and strong personalities have an extraordinary impact on others. They are often called **charismatic leaders** because of their special powers to inspire others in exceptional ways. Charisma was traditionally thought of as being limited to a few lucky persons who were born with it. Today, it is considered part of a broader set of special personal leadership that can be developed with foresight and practice.

O A **charismatic leader** develops special leader-follower relationships and inspires followers in extraordinary ways.

TRANSFORMATIONAL AND TRANSACTIONAL LEADERSHIP

Leadership scholars James MacGregor Burns and Bernard Bass suggest that the research and models we have discussed so far tend toward **transactional leadership**.[41] The impression is that if you learn the frameworks you can then apply them systematically to keep others moving forward to implement plans and achieve performance goals. Managers with this approach to leadership change styles, adjust tasks, and allocate rewards to achieve positive influence. Notably absent from this description is any evidence of "enthusiasm" and "inspiration," more emotional qualities that are characteristic of superleaders having charismatic appeal. Importantly, these are the very qualities that Burns and Bass associate with **transformational leadership**. This describes someone who is truly inspirational as a leader, who is personally excited about what they are doing, and who arouses others to seek extraordinary performance accomplishments. A transformational leader uses charisma and related qualities to raise aspi-

O **Transactional leadership** directs the efforts of others through tasks, rewards, and structures.

O **Transformational leadership** is inspirational and arouses extraordinary effort and performance.

Southwest Airlines
It takes a leader to make the leadership difference

Herb Kelleher led Southwest Airlines from a small startup in 1971 to one of America's premier airlines. And he did it with a difference—low fares, on-time performance, and . . . fun! It wasn't just a winning airline industry strategy—finding a market niche and sticking with it—that Kelleher's leadership brought to the firm. It was also a leadership style focused on building and sustaining a positive organizational culture. Kelleher's personal style has been described as "dynamic" and based on "humor and friendliness." Colleen Barrett, his successor as CEO, follows the model. Under her leadership the firm is still tops in maintaining employee loyalty. What is Kelleher's advice to Barrett and other would-be leaders? "Ask your employees what's important to them. Ask your customers what is important to them. Then do it."[42]

rations and shift people and organizational systems into new high-performance patterns. The presence of transformational leadership is reflected in followers who are enthusiastic about the leader and his or her ideas, who work very hard to support them, who remain loyal and devoted, and who strive for superior performance accomplishments.

The transactional and transformational leadership approaches are not mutually exclusive. On its own, transactional leadership is probably insufficient to meet fully the leadership challenges and demands of today's dynamic work environments. Rather, it is a foundation or building block for solid day-to-day leadership. But in a context of continuous and often large-scale change, the additional and inspirational impact of transformational leadership becomes essential. One way to describe this in a classroom situation is the following. Skill at transactional leadership will earn you a B, allowing you to routinely lead people quite well. Moving from B to A leadership however, requires additional excellence in transformational leadership.

QUALITIES OF A TRANSFORMATIONAL LEADER

The goal of excellence in transformational leadership offers a distinct management challenge, with important personal development implications. It is not enough to possess leadership traits, know the leadership behaviors, and understand leadership contingencies. Any manager must also be prepared to lead in an inspirational way and with a compelling personality. The transformational leader provides a strong sense of vision and a contagious enthusiasm that substantially raises the confidence, aspirations, and performance commitments of followers. The special qualities characteristic of transformational leaders include:[43]

> Attributes of transformational leaders

- *Vision*—having ideas and a clear sense of direction; communicating them to others; developing excitement about accomplishing shared "dreams."
- *Charisma*—using the power of personal reference and emotion to arouse others' enthusiasm, faith, loyalty, pride, and trust in themselves.

- *Symbolism*—identifying "heroes" and holding spontaneous and planned ceremonies to celebrate excellence and high achievement.
- *Empowerment*—helping others develop by removing performance obstacles, sharing responsibilities, and delegating truly challenging work.
- *Intellectual stimulation*—gaining the involvement of others by creating awareness of problems and stirring their imaginations.
- *Integrity*—being honest and credible, acting consistently out of personal conviction, and following through on commitments.

Be sure you can • define the terms transformational leadership and transactional leadership • explain when transformational leadership becomes essential • identify the special personal qualities of transformational leaders

Learning check 4

CURRENT ISSUES IN LEADERSHIP DEVELOPMENT

A number of issues and themes related to leadership development add further context to the many insights of this chapter. Of particular interest are research on both emotional intelligence and the relationship between gender and leadership, as well as practical discussions of the everyday work of a leader and the importance of ethical leadership in our society.

EMOTIONAL INTELLIGENCE

An area of leadership development that is currently very popular is **emotional intelligence,** first discussed in Chapter 1 as part of the essential human skills of managers. Popularized by the work of Daniel Goleman, "EI" is defined as "the ability to manage ourselves and our relationships effectively."[44] According to his research, emotional intelligence is an important influence on leadership effectiveness, especially in more senior management positions. In Goleman's words: "the higher the rank of the person considered to be a star performer, the more emotional intelligence capabilities showed up as the reason for his or her effectiveness."[45] This is a strong endorsement for considering whether or not EI is one of your leadership assets. Important too is Goleman's belief that emotional intelligence skills can be learned.

For purposes of research and training, Goleman breaks emotional intelligence down into five critical components.[46] He argues that each of us should strive for competency in each component and thereby maximize our ability to work well in relationships with others. The critical components of EI are the following.

1. *Self-awareness*—ability to understand our own moods and emotions, and to understand their impact on our work and on others.
2. *Self-regulation*—ability to think before we act and to control otherwise disruptive impulses.

○ **Emotional intelligence** is the ability to manage our emotions in social relationships.

Dimensions of emotional intelligence

3. *Motivation*—ability to work hard with persistence and for reasons other than money and status.
4. *Empathy*—ability to understand the emotions of others and to use this understanding to better relate to them.
5. *Social skill*—ability to establish rapport with others and to build good relationships and networks.

GENDER AND LEADERSHIP

One of the leadership themes of continuing interest deals with the question of whether gender influences leadership styles and/or effectiveness. Sara Levinson, President of NFL Properties, Inc., of New York, for example, once asked the all-male members of her management team: "Is my leadership style different from a man's?." "Yes," they replied, suggesting that the very fact that she was asking the question was evidence of the difference. They also indicated that her leadership style emphasized communication, and gathering ideas and opinions from others. When Levinson probed further by asking "Is this a distinctly 'female' trait?," they said that they thought it was.[47]

REALITY CHECK 13.2

How do women lead?
A study of the performance evaluations of 425 managers by Hagberg Consulting Group found women managers significantly outscoring men on their ability to motivate others. Take the online "Reality Check" to learn more about this study of male and female executives.

The evidence clearly supports the fact that both women and men can be effective leaders.[48] As suggested in the prior example, however, they may tend toward somewhat different styles.[49] Victor Vroom and his colleagues have investigated gender differences in respect to the leader-participation model discussed earlier.[50] They find women managers to be significantly more participative than their male counterparts. Other studies report that peers, subordinates, and supervisors of female leaders rate them higher than men on motivating others, fostering communication, listening to others, and producing high-quality work.[51] This style has been called *interactive leadership.*[52] Leaders with this style display behaviors typically considered democratic and participative—showing respect for others, caring for others, and sharing power and information with others. They focus on building consensus and good interpersonal relations through communication and involvement. The interactive style has qualities in common with the transformational leadership just discussed.[53] An interactive leader tends to use personal power, gaining influence over others through support, and interpersonal relationships. Men, by contrast, may tend toward more transactional approaches, relying more on directive and assertive behaviors, and using position power in a traditional "command and control" way.

Given the emphasis on shared power, communication, cooperation, and participation in the new-form organizations of today, these results are provocative. The interactive leadership style seems to be an excellent fit with the demands of a diverse workforce and the new workplace. As Harvard professor and consultant Rosabeth Moss Kanter says: "Women get high ratings on exactly those skills required to succeed in the Global Information Age, where teamwork and partnering are so important."[54] Gender issues aside, it seems clear that future leadership success for anyone will rest on one's capacity to lead through openness, positive relationships, support, and empowerment.

Faith Wohl: Leadership can make a family-friendly workplace

With three children and eight grandchildren, Faith Wohl built a career in business, government, and nonprofit leadership. As one of DuPont's first senior female managers, her goal was to make work compatible with families. She championed job sharing, flextime, day-care programs, and elder care. Blending leadership style with the demands of the corporate environment, she made communication a key to her success. She made data-filled presentations, held well-publicized meetings with employees, met frequently with managers, set up "work life" committees to solicit employee suggestions, and made sure the CEO regularly expressed his public support. As president of the Child Care Action Campaign, she led an organization devoted to "investment in child care by employers, state and local governments, schools and community organizations."[55]

DRUCKER'S "OLD-FASHIONED" LEADERSHIP

Peter Drucker offers a time-tested and very pragmatic view of leadership. It is based on what he refers to as a "good old-fashioned" look at the plain hard work it takes to be a successful leader. Consider, for example, his description of a telephone conversation with a potential consulting client. "We'd want you to run a seminar for us on how one acquires charisma," she said. Drucker's response was not what she expected. He advised her that there was more to leadership than the popular emphasis on personal "dash" or charisma. In fact, he said that "leadership . . . is work."[56]

Drucker's observations remind us that leadership effectiveness must have strong foundations. First, he believes that the basic building block of effective leadership is *defining and establishing a sense of mission*. A good leader sets the goals, priorities, and standards. A good leader keeps them all clear and visible, and maintains them. In Drucker's words, "The leader's first task is to be the trumpet that sounds a clear sound." Second, he believes in *accepting leadership as a responsibility rather than a rank*. Good leaders surround themselves with talented people. They are not afraid to develop strong and capable subordinates. And they do not blame others when things go wrong. As Drucker says, "The buck stops here" is still a good adage to remember. Third, he stresses the importance of *earning and keeping the trust of others*. The key here is the leader's personal integrity. The followers of good leaders trust them. This means that they believe the leader means what he or she says and that his or her actions will be consistent with what is said. In Drucker's words again, "Effective leadership . . . is not based on being clever; it is based primarily on being consistent."

MORAL LEADERSHIP

As discussed in Chapter 3, society today is unforgiving in its demands that organizations be run with **ethical leadership**—that is, leadership by

○ **Ethical leadership** is always "good" and "right" by moral standards.

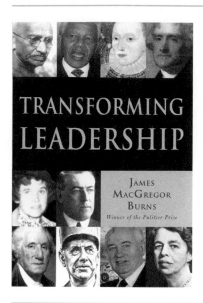

Great leadership is a moral resource to the world

In his book *Transforming Leadership: A New Pursuit of Happiness,* James MacGregor Burns explains that transformational leadership creates significant, even revolutionary, change in social systems. But he disassociates certain historical figures from this definition: Napoleon is out—too much order-and-obey in his style; Hitler is out—no moral foundations; Mao is out, too—no true empowerment of followers. Among Burns's positive role models from history are Gandhi, George Washington, and Eleanor Roosevelt. He firmly believes that great leaders follow agendas true to the wishes of followers. He gives the example of Franklin Delano Roosevelt who said: "If we do not have the courage to lead the American people where they want to go, someone else will." Burns also says that wherever in the world great leadership is found it will always have a moral anchor point.[57]

moral standards that meet the ethical test of being "good" and not "bad," of being "right" and not "wrong."[58] The expectation is that anyone in a leadership position will practice high ethical standards of behavior, help to build and maintain an ethical organizational culture, and both help and require others to behave ethically in their work. *Management 8/e* has communicated throughout an essential belief about success in work and in life: Long-term, sustainable success can only be built upon a foundation of solid ethical behavior. As a leader, you should not try to be ethical out of fear of being caught doing something wrong; you should want to be ethical because of the freedom and success that it brings. Ethical leaders have little to fear when the inevitable problems and traumas of daily work appear. They can act with confidence, always knowing that their actions are beyond reproach.

Ethical leadership begins with personal integrity, a concept fundamental to the notions of both transformational and good old-fashioned leadership. A leader with **integrity** is honest, credible, and consistent in putting values into action. When a leader has integrity, he or she earns the *trust* of followers. And when followers believe leaders are trustworthy, they are willing to commit themselves to behave in ways that live up to the leader's expectations. For managers in our high-pressure and competitive work environments, nothing can substitute for leadership strongly anchored in personal integrity. When viewed through the lens of what is truly the right thing to do, even the most difficult decisions become easier.

John W. Gardner talks with great insight about further "moral aspects" of leadership.[59] He does so with great respect for people and the talents that they bring with them to the workplace. "Most people in most organizations most of the time," Gardner writes, "are more stale than they know, more bored than they care to admit." Leaders, according to Gardner, have a moral obligation to build performance capacities by awakening the potential of each individual—to urge each person "to take the initiative in performing leader-like acts." He points out that high expectations tend to generate high performance. It is the leader's job to re-

○ **Integrity** in leadership is honesty, credibility, and consistency in putting values into action.

move "obstacles to our effective functioning—to help individuals see and pursue shared purposes."

The concept of **authentic leadership** advanced by Fred Luthans and Bruce Avolio is relevant in this same context.[60] Authentic leadership activates performance through the positive psychological states of confidence, hope, optimism, and resilience. It enhances self-awareness and self-development by the leader and by her or his associates. The resulting positive self-regulation helps authentic leaders to clearly frame moral dilemmas, transparently respond to them, and serve as ethical role models.[61] There is no doubt that ethical leadership has such authenticity and is also strongly anchored in a true commitment to people. This wisdom is evident in the advice from two exemplars featured in our early chapter examples, Max DePree of Herman Miller and Lorraine Monroe of the Leadership Institute.[62]

O **Authentic leadership** activates positive psychological states to achieve self-awareness and positive self-regulation.

"Nobody is common. Everybody has a right to be an insider."

Max DePree

"The real leader is a servant of the people she leads."

Lorraine Monroe

Be sure you can • explain how emotional intelligence contributes to leadership success • discuss alternative views of the relationship between gender and leadership • list Drucker's three essentials of good old-fashioned leadership • define the term integrity and discuss it as a foundation for moral leadership

Learning check 5

CHAPTER 13 STUDY GUIDE

Where We've Been

BACK TO SOUTHWEST AIRLINES

The opening example of Herb Kelleher and Colleen Barrett at Southwest Airlines introduced leadership in a unique and high-performance work environment. It suggested that great leadership enables and supports high performance throughout an organization or team, and it should remind you to search within for your leadership potential. In this chapter you learned about the trait and leader behavior approaches to leadership, as well as important contingency models is developed by Fiedler, Hersey-Blanchard, House, and Vroom-Jago. You also learned the difference between transformational and transactional leadership, and were introduced to current issues in leadership development, including emotional intelligence, gender differences, and moral foundations.

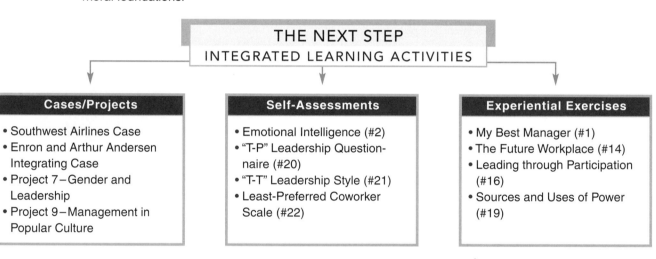

THE NEXT STEP
INTEGRATED LEARNING ACTIVITIES

Cases/Projects	Self-Assessments	Experiential Exercises
• Southwest Airlines Case • Enron and Arthur Andersen Integrating Case • Project 7 – Gender and Leadership • Project 9 – Management in Popular Culture	• Emotional Intelligence (#2) • "T-P" Leadership Questionnaire (#20) • "T-T" Leadership Style (#21) • Least-Preferred Coworker Scale (#22)	• My Best Manager (#1) • The Future Workplace (#14) • Leading through Participation (#16) • Sources and Uses of Power (#19)

STUDY QUESTIONS SUMMARY

1. What is the nature of leadership?

• Leadership is the process of inspiring others to work hard to accomplish important tasks.
• The ability to communicate a vision, a clear sense of the future, is increasingly considered to be an essential ingredient of effective leadership.
• Power is the ability to get others to do what you want them to do through leadership.
• Managerial power equals position power plus personal power.
• Sources of position power include rewards, coercion, and legitimacy or formal authority; sources of personal power include expertise and reference.
• Effective leaders empower others—that is, they help and allow others to make job-related decisions on their own.

2. What are the important leadership traits and behaviors?

• Early leadership research searched unsuccessfully for a set of personal traits that would always differentiate successful and unsuccessful leaders.

- Traits that do seem to have a positive impact on leadership include drive, integrity, and self-confidence.
- Research on leader behaviors focused on alternative leadership styles based on concerns for task and concerns for people.
- One suggestion of leader-behavior researchers is that effective leaders will be good at team-based or participative leadership that is high in both task and people concerns.

3. What are the contingency theories of leadership?

- Contingency leadership approaches point out that no one leadership style always works best; the best style is one that properly matches the demands of each unique situation.
- Fiedler's contingency model describes how situational differences in task structure, position power, and leader-member relations may influence which leadership style works best.
- House's path-goal theory points out that leaders should add value to situations by responding with supportive, directive, achievement-oriented, and/or participative styles as needed.
- The Hersey-Blanchard situational model recommends using task-oriented and people-oriented behaviors, depending on the "maturity" levels of followers.
- The Vroom-Jago leader-participation theory advises leaders to choose decision-making methods—individual, consultative, group—

that best fit the problems they are trying to solve.

4. What is transformational leadership?

- Charismatic leadership creates a truly inspirational relationship between leader and followers.
- Transactional leadership focuses on tasks, rewards, and structures to influence follower behavior.
- Transformational leaders use charisma and emotion to inspire others toward extraordinary efforts in support of change and performance excellence.

5. What are current issues in leadership development?

- Emotional intelligence, the ability to manage our relationships and ourselves effectively, is an important leadership capability.
- The interactive leadership style often associated with women emphasizes communication, involvement, and interpersonal respect, all things consistent with the demands of the new workplace.
- Drucker and others remind us leadership is "hard work" that always requires a personal commitment to consistently meeting high ethical and moral standards.

KEY TERMS REVIEW

SELF-TEST 13

MULTIPLE-CHOICE QUESTIONS:

1. Someone with a clear sense of the future and the actions needed to get there is considered a _____ leader.
   (a) task-oriented (b) people-oriented (c) transactional (d) visionary

2. Managerial power = _____ power × _____ power.
   (a) reward, punishment (b) reward, expert (c) legitimate, position (d) position, personal

3. A manager who says "Because I am the boss, you must do what I ask" is relying on _____ power.
   (a) reward (b) legitimate (c) expert (d) referent

4. The personal traits now considered important for managerial success include _____.
   (a) self-confidence (b) gender (c) age (d) personality

5. According to the Blake and Mouton model of leader behaviors, the most successful leader is one who acts with _____.
   (a) high initiating structure (b) high consideration (c) high concern for task and high concern for people (d) low job stress and high task goals

6. In Fiedler's contingency model, both highly favorable and highly unfavorable leadership situations are best dealt with by a _____ leader.
   (a) task-oriented (b) laissez-faire (c) participative (d) relationship-oriented

7. Directive leadership and achievement-oriented leadership are among the options in House's _____ theory of leadership.
   (a) trait (b) path-goal (c) transformational (d) life-cycle

8. Vision, charisma, integrity, and symbolism are all on the list of attributes typically associated with _____ leaders.
   (a) contingency (b) informal (c) transformational (d) transactional

9. _____ leadership theory suggests that leadership success is achieved by correctly matching leadership style with situations.
   (a) Trait (b) Fiedler's (c) Transformational (d) Blake and Mouton's

10. In the leader-behavior approaches to leadership, someone who does a very good job of planning work, setting standards, and monitoring results would be considered a(n) _____ leader.
    (a) task-oriented (b) control-oriented (c) achievement-oriented (d) employee-centered

11. When a leader assumes that others will do as she asks because they want to positively identify with her, she is relying on _____ power to influence their behavior.
    (a) expert (b) reference (c) legitimate (d) reward

12. The interactive leadership style often associated with women is characterized by _____.
    (a) inclusion and information sharing (b) use of rewards and punishments (c) command and control (d) emphasis on position power

13. A leader whose actions indicate an attitude of "do as you want and don't bother me" would be described as having a(n) _____ leadership style.
(a) autocratic (b) country club (c) democratic (d) laissez-faire

14. The critical contingency variable in the Hersey-Blanchard situational model of leadership is _____.
(a) followers' maturity (b) LPC (c) task structure (d) emotional intelligence

15. A leader who _____ would be described as achievement oriented in the path-goal theory.
(a) works hard to achieve high performance (b) sets challenging goals for others (c) gives directions and monitors results (d) builds commitment through participation

SHORT-RESPONSE QUESTIONS:

16. Why does a person need both position power and personal power to achieve long-term managerial effectiveness?

17. What is the major insight offered by the Vroom-Jago leader-participation model?

18. What are the three variables that Fiedler's contingency model uses to diagnose the favorability of leadership situations, and what does each mean?

19. How does Peter Drucker's view of "good old-fashioned leadership" differ from the popular concept of transformational leadership?

APPLICATION QUESTION:

20. When Marcel Henry took over as leader of a new product development team, he was both excited and apprehensive. "I wonder," he said to himself on the first day in his new assignment, "if I can meet the challenges of leadership." Later that day, Marcel shares this concern with you during a coffee break. Based on the insights of this chapter, how would you describe to him the implications for his personal leadership development of current thinking on transformational leadership and moral leadership?

www.wiley.com/college/schermerhorn

14 | Motivation—theory and practice

Planning Ahead
→
After reading Chapter 14,
you should be able to
answer these questions
in your own words.

CHAPTER 14 study questions

1. **What is motivation?**

2. **What are the different types of individual needs?**

3. **What are the process theories of motivation?**

4. **What role does reinforcement play in motivation?**

5. **What are the challenges of motivation in the new workplace?**

CHARLIE BUTCHER—MAKE PEOPLE YOUR TOP PRIORITY

Even when the "dot.com" firms and the "new economy" were making most of the news, the really smart analysts knew that there is still a lot to learn from "old economy" companies. One, the Butcher Company, a maker of floor care products, made headlines when its founder Charlie Butcher, at age 83, sold the firm to family-owned S.C. Johnson Company. Not a bad deal for Charlie and family, you might say. Well, yes, but the story is much deeper than that. You see, after Charlie sold the company, he shared $18 million of the proceeds with the firm's 325 employees. Not only that, he chose to sell to another family-owned firm so that he could do it. Says Charlie: "I knew if I went public, I would not be able to give out $18 million. Investors are very tight with their money."

The day after the sale, Charlie was at the plant handing out checks. The firm's president, Paul P. McClaughlin, said the employees ". . . just filled up with tears. They would just throw their arms around Charlie and give him a hug." But this wasn't anything new; Charlie had always been a believer in people. This was just another chance to confirm the theory that he'd been practicing for years—a belief that treating talented people well will create business success. "When people are happy in their jobs, they are at least twice as productive," Charlie says.

What did the $18 million add up to for Charlie's loyal Butcher Company workers? An average of $55,000 per person was the net return. Each of his employees received about $1.50 for every hour they had worked for the firm over the years.[1]

Get Connected!

What do you want from work? Don't settle for anything less than the best fit between opportunities in your work environment and personal goals.

Chapter 14 Learning Preview

The chapter opening example of the Butcher Company shows a unique example of management commitment to employees—considering each and every one an owner. There is no doubt that Charlie Butcher's style paid off over the years, as he grew his company to success. There's also no doubt that it did so well because of the motivation and accomplishments of the workers. In this chapter you will learn about the concept of motivation. You will examine the main content, process, and reinforcement theories that help to explain motivation to work. You will also gain an understanding of their practical implications.

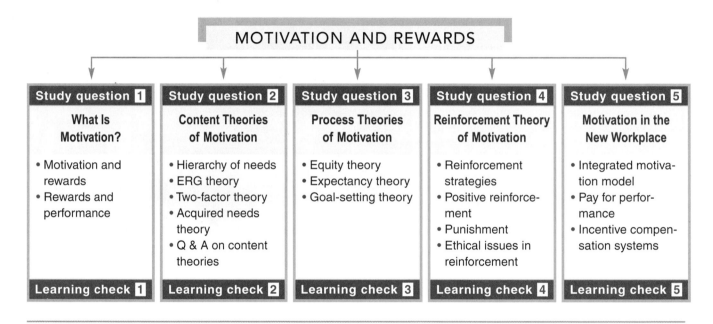

MOTIVATION AND REWARDS

Study question **1**	Study question **2**	Study question **3**	Study question **4**	Study question **5**
What Is Motivation?	**Content Theories of Motivation**	**Process Theories of Motivation**	**Reinforcement Theory of Motivation**	**Motivation in the New Workplace**
• Motivation and rewards • Rewards and performance	• Hierarchy of needs • ERG theory • Two-factor theory • Acquired needs theory • Q & A on content theories	• Equity theory • Expectancy theory • Goal-setting theory	• Reinforcement strategies • Positive reinforcement • Punishment • Ethical issues in reinforcement	• Integrated motivation model • Pay for performance • Incentive compensation systems
Learning check **1**	Learning check **2**	Learning check **3**	Learning check **4**	Learning check **5**

Why do some people work enthusiastically, often doing more than required to turn out an extraordinary performance? Why do others hold back and do the minimum needed to avoid reprimand or termination? How can a team leader or manager build a high-performance work setting? What can be done to ensure that the highest possible performance is achieved by every person in every job on every workday? These questions are, or should be, asked by managers in all work settings. Good answers begin with a true respect for people, with all of their talents and diversity, as the human capital of organizations. The best managers already know this. Like the opening example of Charlie Butcher, the work cultures they create invariably reflect an awareness that "productivity through people" is an irreplaceable foundation for long-term success. Consider these comments by those who know what it means to lead a high-performance organization.[2]

> *When people feel connected to something with a purpose greater than themselves, it inspires them to reach for levels they might not other-wise obtain. . . . Our business is based on human potential.*
>
> George Zimmer, founder and CEO of Men's Warehouse

No business goal is worth sacrificing your values. If you have to treat people poorly, or cut corners in your dealings with customers, forget it. . . . You can build an organization based on mutual loyalty . . . but you can't do it if you treat people as disposable.

Patrick Kelly, CEO of PSS World Medical

It's part of a soundly designed strategy. . . . If you hire adults and treat them like adults, then they'll behave like adults.

Jim Goodnight, CEO of SAS Institute

It is easy to say as a leader or write in a mission statement that "people are our most important asset." But the proof comes when actions back up the words. This means consistently demonstrating that one's organization is committed to people, that it offers a truly "motivational" work environment. Realistically, however, this task isn't always easy. The workplace often becomes complicated as the intricacies of human psychology come to play in daily events and situations. At a packaging plant in California, for example, senior executive Kevin Kelley learned that a supervisor was starting to retire on the job. The man had worked for 20 years and felt it was time to slow down. He was unresponsive to gentle nudging from coworkers and managers. But when Kelley politely confronted him with the facts, saying "we need your talent, your knowledge of those machines," the supervisor responded with new vigor and his work earned the praise of peers. Kelley believes in employee involvement and claims that one of the best motivators is information on the firm's competitive environment.

WHAT IS MOTIVATION?

The term **motivation** is used in management theory to describe forces within the individual that account for the level, direction, and persistence of effort expended at work. Simply put, a highly motivated person works hard at a job; an unmotivated person does not. A manager who leads through motivation does so by creating conditions under which other people feel consistently inspired to work hard. Obviously, a highly motivated workforce is indispensable to the achievement of sustained high-performance results.

○ **Motivation** accounts for the level, direction, and persistence of effort expended at work.

MOTIVATION AND REWARDS

A *reward* is a work outcome of positive value to the individual. A motivational work setting is rich in rewards for people whose performance accomplishments help meet organizational objectives. In management, it is useful to distinguish between two types of rewards, extrinsic and intrinsic. **Extrinsic rewards** are externally administered. They are valued outcomes given to someone by another person, typically, a supervisor or higher-level manager. Common workplace examples are pay bonuses, promotions, time off, special assignments, office fixtures, awards, verbal praise, and recognition. The motivational stimulus of these extrinsic rewards originates outside of the individual; the rewards are made available by another person or by the organizational system.[4]

○ An **extrinsic reward** is provided by someone else.

TAKE IT TO THE CASE

Fast cars, passion motivate top drivers

The fastest growing sport in American is stock car racing, and the largest stock car racing group is *NASCAR.* A marketing powerhouse, with races, merchandise, collectibles, apparel, and co-marketing tie-ins, NASCAR fields race cars that have been described as "200 mile-per-hour billboards." Legendary crew-chief Ray Evernham likes to point out that with the cars so similar, people—drivers and crews—make the difference. One of the rising stars on the NASCAR circuit is driver Ryan Newman, who started by racing season winning rookie of the year honors. Newman's passion for racing began just a few months shy of his fifth birthday when he started racing quarter-midgetcarts. His motivation grew over the years, bringing Newman to the point of likely becoming a NASCAR legend.[9]

○ An **intrinsic reward** occurs naturally during job performance.

Intrinsic rewards, by contrast, are self-administered. They occur "naturally" as a person performs a task and are, in this sense, built directly into the job itself. The major sources of intrinsic rewards are the feelings of competency, personal development, and self-control people experience in their work.[5] In contrast to extrinsic rewards, the motivational stimulus of intrinsic rewards is internal and does not depend on the actions of some other person. Being self-administered, they offer the great advantage and power of "motivating from within." An air traffic controller, for example, says: "I don't know of anything I'd rather be doing. I love working the airplanes."[6] At a small copper kettle manufacturer in northern Ohio, 50-year-old Steve Schifer makes timpani drum bowls. He says: "It gets in your blood and you can't get rid of it. It's something you can create with your hands and no one else can."[7]

REWARDS AND PERFORMANCE

Starbucks seems to have the recipe right—not just for coffee, but also for rewards and performance. The company offers a stock option plan to all its employees. Called "bean stock," the incentive plan offers employees stock options linked to their base pay. This means they can buy the company's stock at a fixed price in the future; if the market value is higher than the price of their option, they gain. Thus, they should be motivated to do things that help the firm perform best. CEO Howard Schulz says the plan has had a positive impact on attitudes and performance. The phrase "bean-stocking it" is even used by employees when they find ways to reduce costs or increase sales. Schulz is committed to the motivational value of this innovative reward plan.[8]

There are many possible ways to creatively and directly link rewards and performance in the new workplace, that is, to establish *performance-contingent rewards.* To take full advantage of the possibilities, however, managers must (1) respect diversity and individual differences to best understand what people want from work, and (2) allocate rewards in ways that satisfy the interests of both individuals and the organization. A variety of motivation theories provide insights into this complex process. The *content theories of motivation* help us to understand human needs and how people with different needs may respond to different work situations. The *process theories of motivation* describe how people give meaning to rewards and then make decisions on various work-related behaviors. The *reinforcement theory of motivation* focuses on the environment as a major source of rewards that influences human behavior.

Be sure you can • define the term motivation • differentiate extrinsic and intrinsic rewards • explain the concept of performance-contingent rewards • differentiate the basic approaches of the content, process, and reinforcement theories

Learning check 1

CONTENT THEORIES OF MOTIVATION

Most discussions of motivation begin with the concept of individual **needs**—the unfulfilled physiological or psychological desires of an individual. Content theories of motivation use individual needs to explain the behaviors and attitudes of people at work. Although each of the following theories discusses a slightly different set of needs, all agree that needs cause tensions that influence attitudes and behavior. Good managers and leaders establish conditions in which people are able to satisfy important needs through their work. They also eliminate work obstacles that interfere with the satisfaction of important needs.

○ A **need** is an unfulfilled physiological or psychological desire.

REALITY CHECK 14.1

Benefits that attract the best workers
Compensation and benefits are important sources of need satisfaction. Take the online "Reality Check" to learn more about benefit priorities in the American workforce.

HIERARCHY OF NEEDS THEORY

The theory of human needs developed by Abraham Maslow was introduced in Chapter 2 as an important foundation of the history of management thought. According to his hierarchy of human needs, **lower-order needs** include physiological, safety, and social concerns, and **higher-order needs** include esteem and self-actualization concerns.[10] Whereas lower-order needs are desires for social and physical well-being, the higher-order needs are desires for psychological development and growth.

Maslow uses two principles to describe how these needs affect human behavior. The *deficit principle* states that a satisfied need is not a motivator of behavior. People are expected to act in ways that satisfy deprived needs—that is, needs for which a "deficit" exists. The *progression principle* states that a need at one level does not become activated until the next-lower-level need is already satisfied. People are expected to advance step-by-step up the hierarchy in their search for need satisfactions. At the level of self-actualization, the more these needs are satisfied, the stronger they are supposed to grow. According to Maslow, a person should continue to be motivated by opportunities for self-fulfillment as long as the other needs remain satisfied.

○ **Lower-order needs** are physiological, safety, and social needs in Maslow's hierarchy.

○ **Higher-order needs** are esteem and self-actualization needs in Maslow's hierarchy.

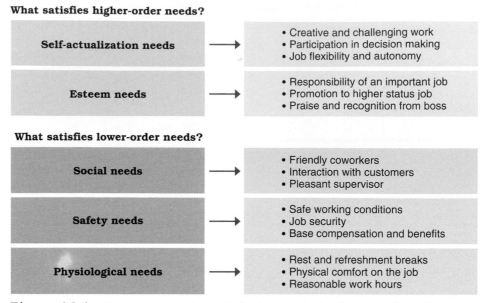

Figure 14.1 Opportunities for satisfaction in Maslow's hierarchy of human needs.

Although research has not verified the strict deficit and progression principles, Maslow's ideas are very helpful for understanding the needs of people at work and considering what can be done to satisfy them. His theory advises managers to recognize that deprived needs may result in negative attitudes and behaviors. By the same token, opportunities for need satisfaction may have positive motivational consequences. *Figure 14.1* illustrates how managers can use Maslow's ideas to better meet the needs of the people with whom they work. Notice that the higher-order self-actualization needs are served entirely by intrinsic rewards. The esteem needs are served by both intrinsic and extrinsic rewards. Lower-order needs are served solely by extrinisic rewards.

ERG THEORY

One of the most promising efforts to build on Maslow's work is the ERG theory proposed by Clayton Alderfer.[11] This theory collapses Maslow's five needs categories into three. *Existence needs* are desires for physiological and material well-being. *Relatedness needs* are desires for satisfying interpersonal relationships. *Growth needs* are desires for continued psychological growth and development. Alderfer's ERG theory also differs from Maslow's theory in other respects. ERG does not assume that lower-level needs must be satisfied before higher-level needs become activated; any or all types of needs can influence individual behavior at a given time. Alderfer also does not assume that satisfied needs lose their motivational impact. ERG theory contains a *frustration-regression principle* according to which an already-satisfied lower-level need can become reactivated and influence behavior when a higher-level need cannot be satisfied. Alderfer's approach offers an additional means for understanding human needs and their influence on people at work.

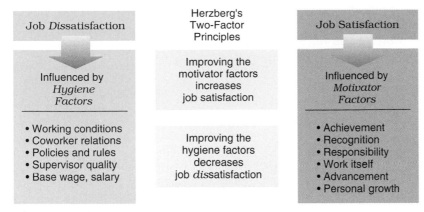

Figure 14.2 Herzberg's two-factor theory.

TWO-FACTOR THEORY

The two-factor theory of Frederick Herzberg was developed from a pattern identified in the responses of almost 4000 people to questions about their work.[12] When questioned about what "turned them on," they tended to identify things relating to the nature of the job itself. Herzberg calls these **satisfier factors.** When questioned about what "turned them off," they tended to identify things relating more to the work setting. Herzberg calls these **hygiene factors.**

As shown in *Figure 14.2,* the two-factor theory associates hygiene factors, or sources of job *dissatisfaction,* with aspects of *job context.* The *hygiene factors* include such things as working conditions, interpersonal relations, organizational policies and administration, technical quality of supervision, and base wage or salary. These factors contribute to more or less job dissatisfaction. Herzberg argues that improving them, such as by adding piped in music or implementing a no-smoking policy, can make people less dissatisfied with these aspects of their work. But this will not increase job satisfaction. That requires attention to an entirely different set of factors and managerial initiatives.

To improve motivation Herzberg advises managers to focus on the satisfier factors. By making improvements in *job content* he believes that job satisfaction and performance can be raised. The important *satisfier factors* include such things as a sense of achievement, feelings of recognition, a sense of responsibility, the opportunity for advancement, and feelings of personal growth.

Scholars have criticized Herzberg's theory as being method-bound and difficult to replicate.[13] For his part, Herzberg reports confirming studies in countries located in Europe, Africa, the Middle East, and Asia.[14] At the very least, the two-factor theory remains a useful reminder that there are two important aspects of all jobs: *job content,* what people do in terms of job tasks; and *job context,* the work setting in which they do it. Herzberg's advice to managers is still timely: (1) always correct poor context to eliminate actual or potential sources of job dissatisfaction; and (2) be sure to build satisfier factors into job content to maximize opportunities for job satisfaction. The two-factor theory also cautions managers not to expect too much by way of motivational im-

○ A **satisfier factor** is found in job content, such as a sense of achievement, recognition, responsibility, advancement, or personal growth.

○ A **hygiene factor** is found in the job context, such as working conditions, interpersonal relations, organizational policies, and salary.

provements from investments in things like special office fixtures, attractive lounges for breaks, and even high base salaries. Instead, it focuses attention on the nature of the job itself and on such things as responsibility and personal growth, as opportunities for higher-order need satisfaction.

ACQUIRED NEEDS THEORY

In the late 1940s, David McClelland and his colleagues began experimenting with the Thematic Apperception Test (TAT) as a way of examining human needs. The TAT asks people to view pictures and write stories about what they see. The stories are then content analyzed for themes that display individual needs.[15] From this research, McClelland identified three needs that are central to his approach to motivation. **Need for Achievement** is the desire to do something better or more efficiently, to solve problems, or to master complex tasks. **Need for Power** is the desire to control other people, to influence their behavior, or to be responsible for them. **Need for Affiliation** is the desire to establish and maintain friendly and warm relations with other people.

According to McClelland, people acquire or develop these needs over time as a result of individual life experiences. He also associates each need with a distinct set of work preferences. Managers are encouraged to recognize the strength of each need in themselves and in other people. Attempts can then be made to create work environments responsive to them. People high in the need for achievement, for example, like to put their competencies to work, they take moderate risks in competitive situations, and they are willing to work alone. As a result, the work preferences of high-need achievers include (1) individual responsibility for results, (2) achievable but challenging goals, and (3) feedback on performance.

Through his research McClelland concludes that success in top management is not based on a concern for individual achievement alone. It requires broader interests that also relate to the needs for power and affiliation. People high in the need for power are motivated to behave in ways that have a clear impact on other people and events. They enjoy being in control of a situation and being recognized for this responsibility. A person with a high need for power prefers work that involves control over other persons, has an impact on people and events, and brings public recognition and attention.

Importantly, McClelland distinguishes between two forms of the power need. *The need for "personal" power* is exploitative and involves manipulation for the pure sake of personal gratification. This type of power need is not successful in management. By contrast, the *need for "social" power* is the positive face of power. It involves the use of power in a socially responsible way, one that is directed toward group or organizational objectives rather than personal ones. This need for social power is essential to managerial leadership.

People high in the need for affiliation seek companionship, social approval, and satisfying interpersonal relationships. They take a special interest in work that involves interpersonal relationships, work that provides for companionship, and work that brings social approval. McClelland believes that people very high in the need for affiliation alone may not make the best managers; their desires for social approval and

---

○ **Need for Achievement** is the desire to do something better, to solve problems, or to master complex tasks.

○ **Need for Power** is the desire to control, influence, or be responsible for other people.

○ **Need for Affiliation** is the desire to establish and maintain good relations with people.

friendship may complicate decision making. There are times when managers and leaders must decide and act in ways that other persons may disagree with. To the extent that the need for affiliation interferes with someone's ability to make these decisions, managerial effectiveness will be sacrificed. Thus, the successful executive, in McClelland's view, is likely to possess a high need for social power that is greater than an otherwise strong need for affiliation.

QUESTIONS AND ANSWERS ON CONTENT THEORIES

Figure 14.3 shows how the human needs identified by Maslow, Alderfer, Herzberg, and McClelland compare with one another. Although the terminology varies, there is a lot of common ground. The insights of the theories can and should be used together to add to our understanding of human needs in the workplace. By way of summary, the following questions and answers further clarify the content theories and their managerial implications.[16]

"How many different individual needs are there?" Research has not yet identified a perfect list of individual needs at work. But, as a manager, you can use the ideas of Maslow, Alderfer, Herzberg, and McClelland to better understand the various needs that people may bring with them to the work setting. *"Can a work outcome or reward satisfy more than one need?"* Yes, work outcomes or rewards can satisfy more than one need. Pay is a good example. It is a source of performance feedback for the high need achiever. It can be a source of personal security for someone with strong existence needs. It can also be used indirectly to obtain things that satisfy social and ego needs. *"Is there a hierarchy of needs?"* Research does not support the precise five-step hierarchy of needs postulated by Maslow. It seems more legitimate to view human needs as operating in a flexible hierarchy, such as the one in Alderfer's ERG theory. However, it is useful to distinguish between the motivational properties of lower-order and higher-order needs. *"How important are the various needs?"* Research is inconclusive as to the importance of different needs. Individuals vary widely in this regard. They may also value needs differently at different times and at different ages or career

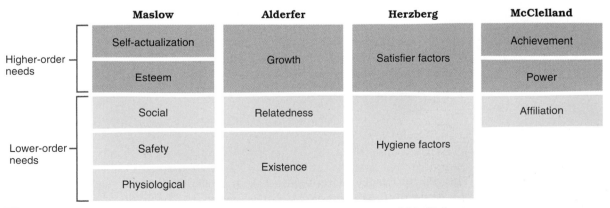

Figure 14.3 Comparison of Maslow's, Alderfer's, Herzberg's, and McClelland's motivation theories.

stages. This is another reason that managers should use the insights of all the content theories to understand the differing needs of people at work.

PROCESS THEORIES OF MOTIVATION

Although the details vary, each of the content theories can help managers better understand individual differences and deal positively with them. The process theories add to this understanding. The equity, expectancy, and goal-setting theories offer advice and insight on how people actually make choices to work hard or not, based on their individual preferences, the available rewards, and possible work outcomes.

CAREER CONNECTION

A company that protects workers from burnout

How would you like to work for a company that cares enough not to overwork you? Founded in 1991 by Roger Greene, Ipswitch, Inc. is a software firm with a difference. He reminds employees about the need to take time for personal affairs—not missing vacation time or using their personal days, for example. In an industry where employee turnover is very high, the Ipswitch culture pays off with turnover under 9 percent. Ipswitch pays higher salaries to keep attracting the best talent, rather than relying on the more risky stock options. As for the tendency of many people to work hard for 30 to 40 years and then retire to "have fun," Greene, says: "I'd much rather live life as it goes along and do neat things while you're working and enjoy every year of your life."[17]

EQUITY THEORY

The equity theory of motivation is best known in management through the work of J. Stacy Adams.[18] It is based on the logic of social comparisons and the notion that perceived inequity is a motivating state. That is, when people believe that they have been unfairly treated in comparison to others, they will be motivated to eliminate the discomfort and re-

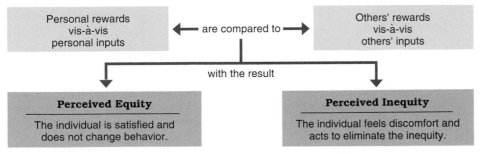

Figure 14.4 Equity theory and the role of social comparison.

store a sense of perceived equity to the situation. The classic example is pay. The equity question is: "In comparison with others, how fairly am I being compensated for the work that I do?" According to the equity theory, an individual who perceives that she or he is being treated unfairly in comparison to others will be motivated to act in ways that reduce the perceived inequity.

Figure 14.4 shows how the equity dynamic works in the form of input-to-outcome comparisons. These equity comparisons are especially common whenever managers allocate extrinsic rewards, things like compensation, benefits, preferred job assignments, and work privileges. The comparison points may be coworkers in the group, workers elsewhere in the organization, and even persons employed by other organizations. Perceived inequities occur whenever people feel that the rewards received for their work efforts are unfair given the rewards others appear to be getting. Adams predicts that people will try to deal with perceived negative inequity by:

- Changing their work inputs by putting less effort into their jobs.
- Changing the rewards received by asking for better treatment.
- Changing the comparison points to make things seem better.
- Changing the situation by leaving the job.

Research on equity theory has largely been accomplished in the laboratory. It is most conclusive with respect to perceived negative inequity. People who feel underpaid, for example, experience a sense of anger. This causes them to try and restore perceived equity to the situation by pursuing one or more of the actions described in the above list, such as reducing current work efforts to compensate for the missing rewards or even quitting the job.[19] There is also evidence that the equity dynamic occurs among people who feel overpaid. This time the perceived inequity is associated with a sense of guilt. The attempt to restore perceived equity may involve, for example, increasing the quantity or quality of work, taking on more difficult assignments, or working overtime.

A key point in the equity theory is that people behave according to their perceptions. What influences individual behavior is not the reward's absolute value or the manager's intentions; the recipient's perceptions determine the motivational outcomes. Rewards perceived as equitable should have a positive result on satisfaction and performance; those perceived as inequitable may create dissatisfaction and cause performance problems.

Informed managers anticipate perceived negative inequities whenever especially visible rewards such as pay or promotions are

← Possible responses to perceived inequity

allocated. Instead of letting equity dynamics get out of hand, they try to manage the perceptions. They carefully communicate the intended value of rewards being given, clarify the performance appraisals upon which they are based, and suggest appropriate comparison points.

In respect to pay, two equity situations mentioned earlier in the book are worth remembering. First is *gender equity.* It is well established that women on the average earn less than men. This difference is most evident in occupations traditionally dominated by men, such as the legal professions, but it also includes ones where females have traditionally held most jobs, such as teaching. Second is *comparable worth.* This is the concept that people doing jobs of similar value based on required education, training, and skills (such as nursing and accounting) should receive similar pay. Advocates of comparable worth claim that it corrects historical pay inequities and is a natural extension of the "equal-pay-for-equal-work" concept. Critics claim that "similar value" is too difficult to define and that the dramatic restructuring of wage scales would have a negative economic impact on society.

EXPECTANCY THEORY

Victor Vroom's expectancy theory of motivation asks a central question: What determines the willingness of an individual to work hard at tasks important to the organization?[20] In response, the theory indicates that "people will do what they can do when they want to do it." More specifically, Vroom suggests that the motivation to work depends on the relationships between the *three expectancy factors,* depicted in *Figure 14.5* and described here:

- **Expectancy**—a person's belief that working hard will result in a desired level of task performance being achieved (this is sometimes called effort-performance expectancy).
- **Instrumentality**—a person's belief that successful performance will be followed by rewards and other potential outcomes (this is sometimes called performance-outcome expectancy).

PERSONAL MANAGEMENT

It is very difficult to say that someone completely lacks **INITIATIVE.** Each of us has to display a certain amount of initiative just to survive each day. But the initiative of people at work varies greatly, just as it does among students. The issue for you becomes: Do you have the self-initiative to work hard and apply your talents to achieve high performance in school, in a job, on an assigned task? Don't hide from the answer. The way you work now in school or in a job is a good predictor of the future. Part of the key to initiative lies in a good person–job fit, finding the right job in the right career field. The rest, however, is all up to you. Only you can decide that you want to work really hard. Look at the following criteria for someone high in self-initiative. Consider how you behave as a student or in a job. Can you honestly say that each statement accurately describes you?

- Willing to look for problems, and fix them.
- Willing to do more than required, to work beyond expectations.
- Willing to help others when they are stuck or overwhelmed.
- Willing to try and do things better; not being comfortable with the status quo.
- Willing to think ahead; to craft ideas and make plans for the future.

Get to know yourself better ▶
Complete Self-Assessments #23—**Student Engagement Survey,** and #24—**Job Design Choices,** and Experiential Exercise #23—**Best Job Design,** from the Management Learning Workbook.

Three expectancy factors —→ • **Valence**—the value a person assigns to the possible rewards and other work-related outcomes.

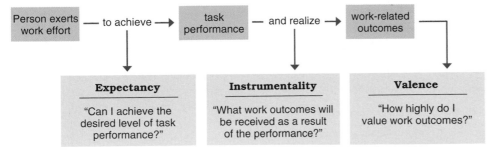

Figure 14.5 Elements in the expectancy theory of motivation.

In the expectancy theory motivation *(M)*, expectancy *(E)*, instrumentality *(I)*, and valence *(V)* are related to one another in a multiplicative fashion: $M = E \times I \times V$. In other words, motivation is determined by expectancy times instrumentality times valence. This multiplier effect has important managerial implications. Mathematically speaking, a zero at any location on the right side of the equation (that is, for *E*, *I*, or *V*) will result in zero motivation. Managers are thus advised to act in ways that: (1) maximize expectancy—people must believe that if they try, they can perform; (2) maximize instrumentality—people must perceive that high performance will be followed by certain outcomes; and (3) maximize and valence—people must value the outcomes. Not one of these factors can be left unattended.

Suppose, for example, that a manager is wondering whether or not the prospect of earning a promotion will be motivational to a subordinate. A typical assumption is that people will work hard to earn a promotion. But is this necessarily true? Expectancy theory predicts that a person's motivation to work hard for a promotion will be low if any one or more of the following three conditions apply. First, *if expectancy is low, motivation will suffer.* The person may feel that he or she cannot achieve the performance level necessary to get promoted. So why try? Second, *if instrumentality is low, motivation will suffer.* The person may lack confidence that a high level of task performance will result in being promoted. So why try? Third, *if valence is low, motivation will suffer.* The person may place little value on receiving a promotion. It simply isn't much of a reward. So, once again, why try?

As shown in *Figure 14.6*, the management implications of expectancy theory include being willing to work with each individual to maximize his or her expectancies, instrumentalities, and valences in ways that support organizational objectives. The theory reminds managers that different people answer the question "Why should I work hard today?" in different ways. The implication is that every person must be respected as an individual with unique needs, preferences, and concerns regarding work. Knowing this, a manager can try to customize work environments to best fit individual needs and preferences.

○ **Expectancy** is a person's belief that working hard will result in high task performance.

○ **Instrumentality** is a person's belief that various outcomes will occur as a result of task performance.

○ **Valence** is the value a person assigns to work-related outcomes.

GOAL-SETTING THEORY

The goal-setting theory described by Edwin Locke focuses on the motivational properties of task goals.[21] The basic premise is that task goals can be highly motivating *if* they are properly set and *if* they are well

To Maximize Expectancy

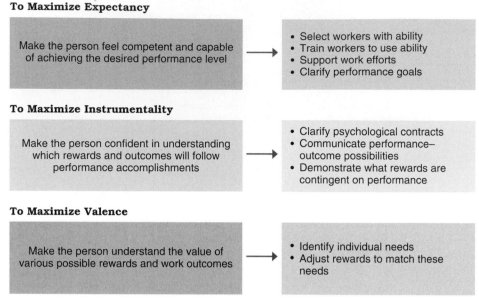

Figure 14.6 Managerial implications of expectancy theory.

managed. Goals give direction to people in their work. Goals clarify the performance expectations between a supervisor and subordinate, between coworkers, and across subunits in an organization. Goals establish a frame of reference for task feedback. Goals also provide a foundation for behavioral self-management.[22] In these and related ways, Locke believes goal setting can enhance individual work performance and job satisfaction.

To achieve the motivational benefits of goal setting, research by Locke and his associates indicates that managers and team leaders must work with others to set the right goals in the right ways. The keys in this respect largely relate to *goal specificity, goal difficulty, goal acceptance,* and *goal commitment.* These are among the goal-setting recommendations provided in *Manager's Notepad 14.1.* Participation is a major element in applying these concerts to unlock the motivational value of task goals. The concept of MBO, described in Chapter 8 on planning and controlling, is a good example. When done well, MBO brings supervisors and subordinates together in a joint and participative process of goal setting and performance review. Research indicates that a positive impact is most likely to occur when the participation in MBO (1) allows for increased understanding of specific and difficult goals and (2) provides for greater acceptance and commitment to them. Along with participation, the opportunity to receive feedback on goal accomplishment is also essential to motivation.

Managers should be aware of the participation options in goal setting. It may not always be possible to allow participation when selecting exactly which goals need to be pursued, but it may be possible to allow participation in the decisions about how to best pursue them. Furthermore, the constraints of time and other factors operating in some situations may not allow for participation. In these settings, Locke's research suggests that workers will respond positively to externally imposed goals if supervisors assigning them are trusted and

MANAGER'S NOTEPAD 14.1

How to make goal setting work for you

- *Set specific goals:* They lead to higher performance than more generally stated ones, such as "Do your best."
- *Set challenging goals:* When viewed as realistic and attainable, more difficult goals lead to higher performance than do easy goals.
- *Build goal acceptance and commitment:* People work harder for goals they accept and believe in; they resist goals forced on them.
- *Clarify goal priorities:* Make sure that expectations are clear as to which goals should be accomplished first and why.
- *Provide feedback on goal accomplishment:* Make sure that people know how well they are doing in respect to goal accomplishment.
- *Reward goal accomplishment:* Don't let positive accomplishments pass unnoticed; reward people for doing what they set out to do.

if workers believe they will be adequately supported in their attempts to achieve them.

Learning check 3

Be sure you can • explain the role of social comparison in Adams's equity theory • apply the equity theory to explain how people with felt negative inequity behave • define the terms expectancy, instrumentality, valence • explain the implications of Vrooms expectancy theory: $M = E \times I \times V$ • explain Locke's goal-setting theory • describe the fit between goal-setting theory and MBO

REINFORCEMENT THEORY OF MOTIVATION

The content and process theories are concerned with explaining "why" people do things in terms of satisfying needs, resolving felt inequities, and/or pursuing positive expectancies and task goals. Reinforcement theory, by contrast, views human behavior as determined by its environmental consequences. Instead of looking within the individual to explain motivation, it focuses on the external environment and the consequences it holds for the individual. The basic premises of reinforcement theory are based on what E. L. Thorndike called the **law of effect:** Behavior that results in a pleasant outcome is likely to be repeated; behavior that results in an unpleasant outcome is not likely to be repeated.[23]

> **The law of effect** states that behavior followed by pleasant consequences is likely to be repeated; behavior followed by unpleasant consequences is not.

REINFORCEMENT STRATEGIES

Psychologist B. F. Skinner popularized the concept of **operant conditioning** as the process of applying the law of effect to control behavior by ma-

> **Operant conditioning** is the control of behavior by manipulating its consequences.

nipulating its consequences.[24] You may think of operant conditioning as learning by reinforcement. In management the goal is to use reinforcement principles to systematically reinforce desirable work behavior and discourage undesirable work behavior.[25]

> **Positive reinforcement** strengthens a behavior by making a desirable consequence contingent on its occurrence.

> **Negative reinforcement** strengthens a behavior by making the avoidance of an undesirable consequence contingent on its occurrence.

> **Punishment** discourages a behavior by making an unpleasant consequence contingent on its occurrence.

> **Extinction** discourages a behavior by making the removal of a desirable consequence contingent on its occurrence.

Four strategies of reinforcement are used in operant conditioning. **Positive reinforcement** strengthens or increases the frequency of desirable behavior by making a pleasant consequence contingent on its occurrence. *Example:* A manager nods to express approval to someone who makes a useful comment during a staff meeting. **Negative reinforcement** increases the frequency of or strengthens desirable behavior by making the avoidance of an unpleasant consequence contingent on its occurrence. *Example:* A manager who has been nagging a worker every day about tardiness does not nag when the worker comes to work on time. **Punishment** decreases the frequency of or eliminates an undesirable behavior by making an unpleasant consequence contingent on its occurrence. *Example:* A manager issues a written reprimand to an employee whose careless work creates quality problems. **Extinction** decreases the frequency of or eliminates an undesirable behavior by making the removal of a pleasant consequence contingent on its occurrence. *Example:* A manager observes that a disruptive employee is receiving social approval from coworkers; the manager counsels coworkers to stop giving this approval.

Figure 14.7 shows how these four reinforcement strategies can be applied in management. The supervisor's goal in the example is to improve work quality as part of a TQM program. Notice how the supervisor can use each of the strategies to influence continuous improvement practices among employees. Note, too, that both positive and negative reinforcement strategies strengthen desirable behavior when it occurs. The punishment and extinction strategies weaken or eliminate undesirable behaviors.

POSITIVE REINFORCEMENT

Among the reinforcement strategies, positive reinforcement deserves special attention. It should be a central part of any manager's motiva-

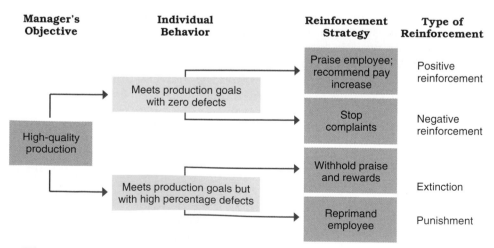

Figure 14.7 Applying reinforcement strategies: case of total quality management.

Guidelines for positive reinforcement . . . and punishment	MANAGER'S NOTEPAD 14.2

Positive Reinforcement:

- Clearly identify desired work behaviors.
- Maintain a diverse inventory of rewards.
- Inform everyone what must be done to get rewards.
- Recognize individual differences when allocating rewards.
- Follow the laws of immediate and contingent reinforcement.

Punishment:

- Tell the person what is being done wrong.
- Tell the person what is being done right.
- Make sure the punishment matches the behavior.
- Administer the punishment in private.
- Follow the laws of immediate and contingent reinforcement.

tional strategy. One of the best examples of how this approach has been used is the classic story of Mary Kay Cosmetics. Among Mary K's sales force the legendary pink Cadillac has been a sought-after prize by top performers for many years. More recently and to keep pace with changing times, the firm has added sport vehicles and other cars to the list of prizes. Of course, all are awarded with great ceremony at gala celebrations.[26]

There are two important laws of positive reinforcement. First, the *law of contingent reinforcement* states: For a reward to have maximum reinforcing value, it must be delivered only if the desired behavior is exhibited. Second, the *law of immediate reinforcement* states: The more immediate the delivery of a reward after the occurrence of a desirable behavior, the greater the reinforcing value of the reward. Managers should use these laws to full advantage in the everyday pursuit of the benefits of positive reinforcement. Several useful guidelines are presented in *Manager's Notepad 14.2.*

The power of positive reinforcement can be mobilized through a process known as **shaping.** This is the creation of a new behavior by the positive reinforcement of successive approximations to it. The timing of positive reinforcement can also make a difference in its impact. A *continuous reinforcement schedule* administers a reward each time a desired behavior occurs. An *intermittent reinforcement schedule* rewards behavior only periodically. In general, a manager can expect that continuous reinforcement will elicit a desired behavior more quickly than will intermittent reinforcement. Also, behavior acquired under an intermittent schedule will be more permanent than will behavior acquired under a continuous schedule. One way to succeed with a shaping strategy, for example, is to give reinforcement on a continuous basis until the desired behavior is achieved. Then an intermittent schedule can be used to maintain the behavior at the new level.

○ **Shaping** is positive reinforcement of successive approximations to the desired behavior.

PUNISHMENT

As a reinforcement strategy, punishment attempts to eliminate undesirable behavior by making an unpleasant consequence contingent with its occurence. To punish an employee, for example, a manager may deny a valued reward, such as verbal praise or merit pay, or administer an unpleasant outcome, such as a verbal reprimand or pay reduction. Like positive reinforcement, punishment can be done poorly or it can be done well. All too often, it is probably done poorly. If you look back to Manager's Notepad 14.2, it offers guidance on how to best handle punishment as a reinforcement strategy.

ETHICAL ISSUES IN REINFORCEMENT

The use of reinforcement techniques in work settings has produced many success stories of improved safety, decreased absenteeism and tardiness, and increased productivity.[27] But there are still debates over both the results and the ethics of controlling human behavior. Opponents are concerned that use of operant conditioning principles ignores the individuality of people, restricts their freedom of choice, and fails to recognize that people can be motivated by things other than extrinsic rewards. Advocates attack the criticisms straight on. They agree that reinforcement involves the control of behavior, but they argue that control is part of every manager's job. The real question, they say, is whether it is ethical not to control behavior well enough so that the goals of both the organization and the individual are well served. Even as research continues, the value of reinforcement techniques is undeniable. This is especially true when they are combined with the insights of the other motivation theories discussed in this chapter.[28]

Learning check 4

Be sure you can • define the terms law of effect and operant conditioning • illustrate how positive reinforcement, negative reinforcement, punishment, and extinction are used to influence work behavior • explain the reinforcement technique of shaping • describe how managers should use the laws of immediate and contingent reinforcement when allocating rewards

---

MOTIVATION AND THE NEW WORKFORCE

The changes taking place in organizations have been mentioned many times so far in *Management 8/e*—horizontal structures, primacy of people, importance of teamwork, high-performance goals, adaptability and speed, worker empowerment, and high technology. All these developments and more are creating new work environments in which people search for meaning, rewards, and valuable contributions. The workforce is changing as well. More work is being done by part-timers; there is an increasing divide between low-skill, low-pay workers and high-skill, high-pay workers; the number of older workers is growing; and volunteers are playing increasingly important roles in the nonprofit service organizations of communities. Managers must rise to the

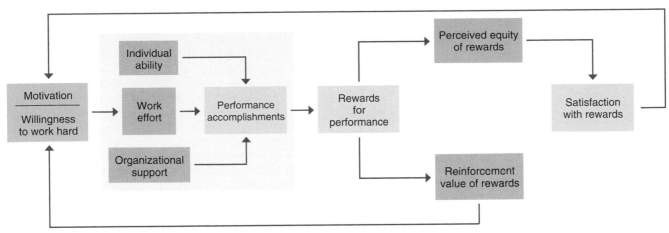

Figure 14.8 An integrated approach to motivational dynamics.

challenge of creating motivational environments in these new realities. The following integrated motivational model is a helpful point of reference. It pulls together the best insights from all motivation theories, allowing them to be applied to good advantage in a manager's unique circumstances.

INTEGRATED MODEL OF MOTIVATION

Figure 14.8 shows how each of the theoretical perspectives discussed so far can be combined into one model of motivational dynamics. In this figure motivation leads to effort that, when combined with appropriate individual abilities and organizational support, leads to performance. The motivational impact of any rewards received for this performance depends on equity and reinforcement considerations. Ultimately, satisfaction with rewards should lead to increased motivation to work hard in the future. Among the motivation issues that can be addressed within this integrating framework, perhaps none receives as much attention as com-

IN PRACTICE

Entrepreneur's idea just too good to fail

"I have this deep passion for entrepreneurs and what they do and what they add to society," says Charles Schwab. He should. As founder and Chairman of the financial services firm, Charles Schwab, he employs over 16,000 people. He started the $4 billion firm with an investment of $100,000 in 1975. When growing up he was dyslexic, but didn't know it. Believing that he "had to work harder than the other kids," he did just that. Schwab learned the values of hard work and commitment early in life. He also says that a sense of humility is an ever-present reminder that you can always try to do better. He strives to create a work environment in which employees work hard and are treated with respect, the same as customers. Says Schwab: "People love working because when they go home at night, they can feel good about themselves."[30]

pensation.[29] There are many advantages, both individual and organizational, to be gained from a truly motivational compensation scheme. But in practice, the link between motivation and compensation can be quite complicated.

PAY FOR PERFORMANCE

○ **Merit pay** awards pay increases in proportion to performance contributions.

The notion of paying people for their performance is consistent with the equity, expectancy, and reinforcement theories.[31] Formally defined, **merit pay** is a compensation system that awards pay increases in proportion to individual performance contributions. By allocating pay increases in this way managers are attempting to recognize and positively reinforce high performers. They are also attempting to remind low performers of their lack of achievement and send a signal that they must do better in the future. In principle it makes sense to reward people in proportion to their work contributions. But because of the difficulty of actually linking pay with performance in a contingent and equitable manner, merit pay does not always achieve the desired results.

A successful merit pay system must have a solid foundation in agreed-upon and well-defined "performance measures." Any weakness in the performance appraisal methods can undermine a merit pay system. There must also be consistency in applying merit pay at all levels of the organization. Failure to do so undermines the system's credibility. There is a lot of concern today, for example, that CEO pay isn't adequately linked to performance. Magazines like *Business Week* and *Fortune* regularly report on the issues. The impression of some is that CEOs are well rewarded no matter how well the company performs. A critical report by *Responsible Wealth* once cited a dramatic example. Honeywell CEO Michael Bonsignore made some $54 million in total compensation the same year that his firm laid off 11,600 workers worldwide.[32]

For these and related reasons, not everyone believes in merit pay. John Whitney, author of *The Trust Factor*, suggests that pay-for-performance may not work very well. While pointing out that market forces should determine base pay, Whitney believes that annual increases should be an equal percentage of base. This communicates a universal sense of importance to all employess. And it helps to avoid frustrations and complaints when merit increases are tied to performance differences. Says Whitney: "Quibbling over whether someone should get a 4.7% raise or 5.1% is a colossal waste of time.[33]

INCENTIVE COMPENSATION SYSTEMS

Organizations use a variety of incentive compensation systems. Examples include pay for knowledge, bonus pay plans, profit-sharing plans, gain-sharing plans, and employee stock ownership plans.[34] As you consider the descriptions that follow, however, remember that any incentive compensation system will work only as well as its implementation. The well-known compensation scholar and consultant Edward Lawler, for example, tells of this experience.[35] While consulting with a furniture manufacturing plant, he became convinced that a "gain sharing" incentive plan would be helpful and thus advised the plant manager on starting one. The manager proceeded only reluctantly, claiming: "These guys are already paid enough . . . they should be happy to have a job." Says Lawler: "Although the program was somewhat successful, the plant manager's continuing tendency to call it an 'employee bribe program' definitely limited its success."

Pay for Knowledge

Consistent with the emphasis on human capital, some organizations now emphasize paying for knowledge. A concept called **skills-based pay** pays workers according to the number of job-relevant skills they master. Federal Express uses this approach in its pay-for-knowledge reward system. The firm's customer-contact employees, for example, must periodically take and pass written job knowledge tests. Test scores are incorporated into the employee's performance appraisals, and pay can be increased for employees scoring high. Skills-based pay is common in self-managing teams where part of the "self-management" includes training and certification of coworkers in job skills.

○ **Skills-based pay** is a system of paying workers according to the number of job-relevant skills they master.

Bonus Pay

Bonus pay plans provide one-time or lump-sum payments to employees based on the accomplishment of specific performance targets or some other extraordinary contribution, such as an idea for a work improvement. They typically do not increase base salary or wages. Bonuses have been most common at the executive level, but they are now being used more extensively. Corning, for example, has tried rewarding individual achievements with on-the-spot bonuses of 3 to 6 percent of someone's pay. As director of risk management and prevention for the firm, Peter Maier gave about 40 percent of his subordinates individual bonuses in a

---

AROUND THE WORLD

A history of making pay-for-performance pay off

At Lincoln Electric, long known for its innovative approach to employee compensation, a pay-for-performance system includes a low base salary topped by bonuses tied to company profitability and individual performance ratings. To promote quality and to impart a sense of responsibility, employees are held accountable for each piece of work they produce. Pieces are "signed," or marked, so that defective ones are easily traced back to the worker. Rejects and returns are noted on employees' merit ratings. These ratings have direct impact on year-end bonuses. Lincoln's system isn't for everyone. And it's not problem-free. The firm still faces hard questions about its unique approach to incentives and how well it fits with the demands of globalization. When Lincoln embarked on international expansion that affected its profitability, domestic workers complained. They felt their bonuses were being threatened by things beyond their control—the costs of the firm's globalization drive.[39]

year. He says, "If someone has done a spiffy job, you need to recognize them.[36]

Profit Sharing

Profit-sharing plans distribute to some or all employees a proportion of net profits earned by the organization during a stated performance period. The exact amount typically varies according to the level of profits and each person's base compensation. At the marketing services firm Valassis Communications Inc., a member of *Fortune's* 100 Best Companies to Work For, every employee from the press operator right up to CEO is eligible for profit sharing that runs from 10 to 25 percent of pay. At Vatex America, a T-shirt and sweatshirt manufacturing firm, CEO Jerry Gorde started a profit-sharing program to help "democratize" the work environment. The program distributes 10 percent of pretax profits to employees each month and an additional amount at the end of the year. The exact share depends on an individual's monthly attendance, tardiness, and performance as rated by supervisors.[37]

www.sgi.com

At SGI, formerly known as Silicon Graphics, employees can receive "spirit" awards for things like "encouraging creativity" and "seeking solutions rather than blame." Winners get trips for two and year-long appointments to the management advisory group.

Gain Sharing

Gain-sharing plans extend the profit-sharing concept by allowing groups of employees to share in any savings or "gains" realized through their efforts to reduce costs and increase productivity. Specific formulas are used to calculate both the performance contributions and gain-sharing awards. The classic example is the Scanlon plan, which usually results in 75 percent of gains being distributed to workers and 25 percent being kept by the company. At East Alabama Medical Center, another of *Fortune's* 100 Best Companies, the mission focuses everyone's attention on caring for people. A gain-sharing plan directly supports that mission. It rewards employees with gain-sharing compensation for meeting patient satisfaction and financial goals. The CEO distributes the checks at a special annual ceremony.[38]

Employee Stock Ownership

Employee stock ownership plans involve employees in ownership through the purchase of stock in the companies that employ them. Whereas formal "ESOP" plans are often used as financing schemes to save jobs and prevent business closings, stock ownership by employees is an important performance incentive. It can be motivating to have an ownership share in one's place of employment. An approach to employee ownership through **stock options** gives the option holder the right to buy shares of stock at a future date at a fixed price. This links ownership directly with a performance incentive, since employees holding stock options presumably are motivated to work hard to raise the price of the firm's stock. When the price has risen they can exercise their options and buy the stock at a discount, thus realizing a financial gain. Stock options are most common in senior executive compensation, but their use is spreading to include lower-level employees.

○ **Stock options** give the right to purchase shares at a fixed price in the future.

The Hay Group reports that the most admired companies in America are also ones that offer stock options to a greater proportion of their work forces. Intel, Merck, and Kimberly-Clark are examples of global firms that allow all of their employees to have access to options.[40] One of the issues with stock options, however, is risk. If and when a company's shares perform poorly, the options are worth less; their motivational value is largely elminated. When the technology companies experienced a downturn in the stock market, for example, many employees were disappointed with incentive pay that was tied to stock options. One result is a resurgence of interest in cash bonuses. How would you like to someday receive a letter like this one once sent to two top executives by Amazon.com's chairman Jeff Bezos? "In recognition and appreciation of your contributions," his letter read, "Amazon.com will pay you a special bonus in the amount of $1,000,000."[41] Not bad for a performance incentive!

Be sure you can • construct an integrative model of motivation that includes ideas of the content, process, and reinforcement theories • apply this model to describe how pay-for-performance systems should work • differentiate among skill-based pay, bonus pay, profit sharing, gain sharing, and stock options as incentive compensation systems	**Learning check 5**

CHAPTER 14 STUDY GUIDE

Where We've Been

BACK TO THE BUTCHER COMPANY

The opening example of Charlie Butcher set a benchmark for leadership commitment to motivation and respect for the contributions of a firm's employees. The value extended by Charlie was returned manyfold in the form of sustained performance for his company. In this chapter you learned how content theories explain motivation in respect to human needs, and how equity and expectancy theories focus on the decisions people make to work or not to work hard. You learned the important principles underlying reinforcement theory and the special importance of positive reinforcement in the workplace. You also learned about the motivational issues in pay-for-performance and incentive compensation systems.

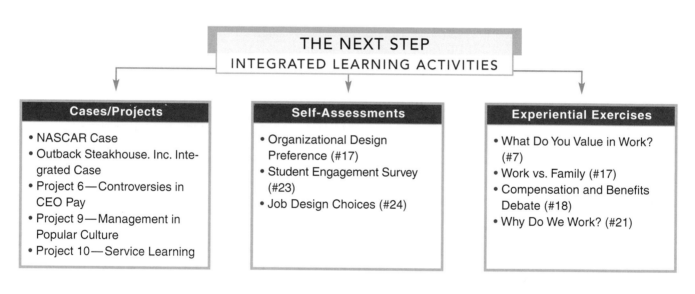

THE NEXT STEP

INTEGRATED LEARNING ACTIVITIES

Cases/Projects	Self-Assessments	Experiential Exercises
• NASCAR Case • Outback Steakhouse. Inc. Integrated Case • Project 6—Controversies in CEO Pay • Project 9—Management in Popular Culture • Project 10—Service Learning	• Organizational Design Preference (#17) • Student Engagement Survey (#23) • Job Design Choices (#24)	• What Do You Value in Work? (#7) • Work vs. Family (#17) • Compensation and Benefits Debate (#18) • Why Do We Work? (#21)

STUDY QUESTIONS SUMMARY

1. What is motivation?

• Motivation involves the level, direction, and persistence of effort expended at work; simply put, a highly motivated person works hard.

• Extrinsic rewards are given by another person; intrinsic rewards derive naturally from the work itself.

• To maximize the motivational impact of rewards, they should be allocated in ways that respond to individual needs.

• The three major types of motivation theories are the content, process, and reinforcement theories.

2. What are the different types of individual needs?

• Maslow's hierarchy of human needs suggests a progression from lower-order physiological, safety, and social needs to higher-order ego and self-actualization needs.

• Alderfer's ERG theory identifies existence, relatedness, and growth needs.

• Herzberg's two-factor theory points out the importance of both job content and job context to motivation and performance.

• McClelland's acquired needs theory identifies the needs for achievement, affiliation, and power, all of which may influence what a person desires from work.

3. What are the process theories of motivation?

- Adams's equity theory recognizes that social comparisons take place when rewards are distributed in the workplace.
- People who feel inequitably treated are motivated to act in ways that reduce the sense of inequity; perceived negative inequity may result in someone working less hard in the future.
- Vroom's expectancy theory states that Motivation = Expectancy × Instrumentality × Valence.
- Expectancy theory encourages managers to make sure that any rewards offered for motivational purposes are achievable, predictable and individually valued.
- Locke's goal-setting theory emphasizes the motivational power of goals; task goals should be specific rather than ambiguous, difficult but achievable, and set through participatory means.

4. What role does reinforcement play in motivation?

- Reinforcement theory recognizes that human behavior is influenced by its environmental consequences.

- The law of effect states that behavior followed by a pleasant consequence is likely to be repeated; behavior followed by an unpleasant consequence is unlikely to be repeated.
- Reinforcement strategies used by managers include positive reinforcement, negative reinforcement, punishment, and extinction.
- Positive reinforcement works best when applied according to the laws of contingent and immediate reinforcement.

5. What are the challenges of motivation in the new workplace?

- The insights of content, process, and reinforcement theories can be integrated in a model of motivational dynamics.
- Merit pay plans tie pay increases to performance accomplishments.
- Incentive compensation programs, such as bonuses, gain sharing, and profit sharing, allow workers to benefit materially from improved organizational profits and productivity.
- Pay-for-knowledge systems link pay to the mastery of job-relevant skills.

KEY TERMS REVIEW

Expectancy (p. 361)
Extinction (p. 364)
Extrinsic reward
(p. 351)
Higher-order needs
(p. 353)
Hygiene factor
(p. 355)
Instrumentality
(p. 361)
Intrinsic reward
(p. 352)
Law of effect (p. 363)

Lower-order needs
(p. 353)
Merit pay (p. 368)
Motivation (p. 351)
Need (p. 353)
Need for Achievement
(nAch) (p. 356)
Need for Affiliation
(nAff) (p. 356)
Need for Power (nPower)
(p. 356)
Negative reinforcement
(p. 364)

Operant conditioning
(p. 363)
Positive reinforcement
(p. 364)
Punishment (p. 364)
Satisfier factors
(p. 355)
Shaping (p. 365)
Skills-based pay
(p. 369)
Stock options
(p. 370)
Valence (p. 361)

SELF-TEST 14

MULTIPLE-CHOICE QUESTIONS:

1. Lower-order needs in Maslow's hierarchy correspond to _____ needs in ERG theory.
   (a) growth (b) affiliation (c) existence (d) achievement

2. A worker high in need for _____ power in McClelland's theory tries to use power for the good of the organization.
   (a) position (b) expert (c) personal (d) social

3. In the _____ theory of motivation, an individual who feels under-rewarded relative to a coworker might be expected to reduce his or her performance in the future.
   (a) ERG (b) acquired needs (c) two-factor (d) equity

4. Which of the following is a correct match?
   (a) McClelland—ERG theory (b) Skinner—reinforcement theory (c) Vroom—equity theory
   (d) Locke—expectancy theory

5. The expectancy theory of motivation says that: motivation = expectancy × _____ × _____.
   (a) rewards, valence (b) instrumentality, valence (c) equity, instrumentality (d) rewards, valence

6. The law of _____ states that behavior followed by a positive consequence is likely to be repeated, whereas behavior followed by an undesirable consequence is not likely to be repeated.
   (a) reinforcement (b) contingency (c) goal setting (d) effect

7. _____ is a positive reinforcement strategy that rewards successive approximations to a desirable behavior.
   (a) Extinction (b) Negative reinforcement (c) Shaping (d) Merit pay

8. A(n) _____ pay plan gives bonuses based on cost savings or productivity increases workers help to generate.
   (a) merit (b) gain-sharing (c) entrepreneurial (d) skills-based

9. In Herzberg's two-factor theory, base pay is considered a(n) _____ factor.
   (a) valence (b) satisfier (c) equity (d) hygiene

10. Jobs high in _____ rewards naturally provide workers with higher-order need satisfactions.
    (a) intrinsic (b) extrinsic (c) monetary (d) existence

11. When a team member shows what would be called strong ego needs in Maslow's hierarchy, the team leader should find ways to link work on the team task with _____.
    (a) compensation tied to group performance (b) individual praise and recognition for work well done (c) lots of social interaction with other team members (d) challenging individual performance goals

12. When someone has a high and positive "expectancy" in the expectancy theory of motivation, this means that the person _____.
    (a) believes he or she can meet performance expectations (b) highly values the rewards being offered (c) sees a relationship between high performance and the available rewards (d) believes that rewards are equitable

13. In goal-setting theory, the goal of "becoming more productive in my work" would not be considered a source of motivation since it fails the criterion of goal _____.
(a) acceptance (b) specificity (c) challenge (d) commitment

14. B. F. Skinner would argue that "getting a paycheck on Friday" reinforces a person for coming to work on Friday, but would not reinforce the person for doing an extraordinary job on Tuesday. This is because the Friday paycheck fails the law of _____ reinforcement.
(a) negative (b) continuous (c) immediate (d) intermittent

15. In the integrated model of motivation, a person will be satisfied with rewards only if they are _____.
(a) perceived as equitable (b) high in instrumentality (c) meeting growth needs (d) improving on hygiene factors

SHORT-RESPONSE QUESTIONS:

16. What preferences does a person high in the need for achievement bring to the workplace?

17. Why is participation important to goal-setting theory?

18. What is motivation to work?

19. What is the managerial significance of Herzberg's distinction between job content and job context factors?

APPLICATION QUESTION:

20. How can a manager combine the powers of goal setting and positive reinforcement to create a highly motivational work environment for a group of workers with high needs for achievement?

www.wiley.com/college/schermerhorn

15 | Individual behavior and performance

Planning Ahead

After reading Chapter 15, you should be able to answer these questions in your own words.

CHAPTER 15 study questions

1. How do we understand people at work?

2. What should we know about work attitudes and behavior?

3. What are the alternative approaches to job design.

4. How can jobs be enriched?

5. How can work be scheduled to improve work-life balance?

MONITOR COMPANY — *UNLOCK EVERYONE'S PERFORMANCE POTENTIAL*

Baston-based Monitor Company isn't just another of the world's top strategic management consulting firms. It's a firm with a difference, and a major part of that difference is a genuine respect for knowledge. Where is the knowledge located? In the minds of each and every one of the firm's 1000 + employees, as well as with their clients.

Essential to Monitor's talent development strategy is to provide people with a work enviornment that meets their needs, doesn't inhibit them with performance obstacles, and is full of learning opportunities. Says Alan Kantrow, chief knowledge officer for Monitor: "The employees we are trying to attract expect to have a series of careers. If Monitor can't provide outlets for their ambitions, they'll go elsewhere. So by design, all the roles, titles and clusters of activities are transitory."

Consulting jobs at Monitor are complex, and the deadlines are often tight. No one ever knows for sure who is the expert. Everyone has to work together, while depending on each other to do their best. The team that successfully helped Bermuda turn around its flagging tourism industry was headed by project coordinator Joseph Babiec. About the experience he says: "We were a team of equals. It didn't matter who was in Bermuda the longest. I worked for you. Then you worked for me."

It had to be that way. The team was dealing with different and sometimes warring government units, labor unions, outside investors, and industry representatives. Whereas strictly defined roles and a rigid hierarchy of authority would have made the task almost impossible, the knowledge-based approach of Monitor's consulting team worked wonders for the client, and did so quickly.

Monitor employees work for a firm dedicated to talent, a firm that states that part of its mission is "creating personal competitive advantage—in the form of unique skills and insights—for each of our employees."[1]

Get Connected!

How well do you fit in this new world of knowledge and talent? Make sure that any employer you choose has the job design, culture, and learning environment that are the best fit for you.

Chapter 15 Learning Preview

The chapter opening example of Monitor Company introduced life inside a professional consulting firm. Monitor consultants solve complex and ambiguous problems for client organizations. Although their work is intense and demanding, respect for talent and freedom to act add a high performance edge. In this chapter you will learn more about the meaning of work, quality of work life, job satisfaction, and individual performance. You will also learn about job designs and work arrangements that can improve the fit between work demands and individual capabilities.

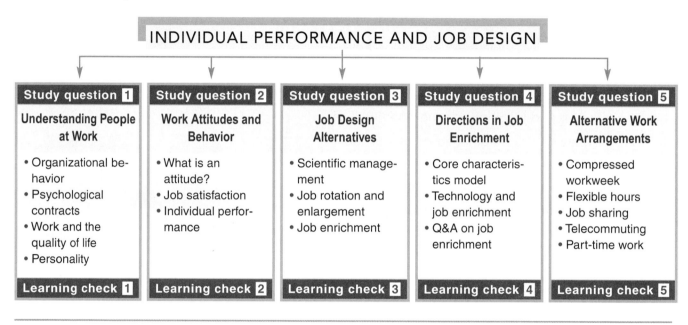

INDIVIDUAL PERFORMANCE AND JOB DESIGN

Study question 1	Study question 2	Study question 3	Study question 4	Study question 5
Understanding People at Work	**Work Attitudes and Behavior**	**Job Design Alternatives**	**Directions in Job Enrichment**	**Alternative Work Arrangements**
• Organizational behavior • Psychological contracts • Work and the quality of life • Personality	• What is an attitude? • Job satisfaction • Individual performance	• Scientific management • Job rotation and enlargement • Job enrichment	• Core characteristics model • Technology and job enrichment • Q&A on job enrichment	• Compressed workweek • Flexible hours • Job sharing • Telecommuting • Part-time work
Learning check 1	**Learning check 2**	**Learning check 3**	**Learning check 4**	**Learning check 5**

For managers in organizations of all types and sizes a critical pathway toward performance improvement is better mobilizing and unlocking the great potential of human talent.[2] The ideal situation is a loyal and talented workforce that is committed to organizational goals and highly motivated to work hard in their behalf. But saying this is one thing; achieving it is quite another. Even in the best of circumstances the management of human resources is a challenging task. In order for human capital to have an impact on organizational performance, it must be supported, nurtured, and allowed to work to its best advantage. All too often it is not, observe scholars Jeffrey Pfeffer and Charles O'Reilly. They believe that too many organizations underperform because they operate with great untapped "hidden value" in human resources; they fail to take full advantage of the talent they already have available.[3] They criticize organizations "with smart, motivated, hard-working, decent people who nevertheless don't perform very well because the company doesn't let them shine and doesn't really capitalize on their talent and motivation." O'Reilly and Pfeffer also praise true high-performance organizations as ones able to "produce extraordinary results from almost everybody."

UNDERSTANDING PEOPLE AT WORK

What do you think about when you see or hear the word "work"? Is it a "turn-on" or a "turn-off"? When Dolly Parton sang "Working 9 to 5; what a way to make a living," she reminded us of an unfortunate reality—that work is not a positive experience for everyone. But isn't this a shame? Some years ago, Karen Nussbaum founded an organization called "9 to 5" and devoted to improving women's salaries and promotion opportunities in the workplace.[4] She started the business after leaving her job as a secretary at Harvard University. Describing what she calls "the incident that put her over the edge," Nussbaum says, "One day . . . I was sitting at my desk at lunchtime, when most of the professors were out. A student walked into the office and looked me dead in the eye and said, 'Isn't *anyone* here?',"[4] Nussbaum founded 9 to 5 to support her personal commitment to "remake the system so that it does not produce these individuals."

Although expressed in different ways and through different media, Parton and Nussbaum direct our attention toward an unfortunate fact of life in the modern workplace—some people, too many people, work under conditions that fail to provide them with respect and satisfaction. A central premise of *Management 8/e* is that it doesn't have to be this way. People at work can both achieve high performance and experience job satisfaction. When managers value people and create jobs and high-quality work environments that respect people's needs and potential, everyone gains.

ORGANIZATIONAL BEHAVIOR

The present and following chapters on individuals, groups, and interpersonal dynamics will draw upon concepts and insights from **organizational behavior,** the study of individuals and groups in organizations. Called "OB" for short, it is an applied scientific discipline that seeks both to explain human behavior in organizations and to make practical suggestions for influencing it. Research in OB addresses such outcome or dependent variables as individual and team performance, job satisfaction, group morale, absenteeism, turnover, organizational citizenship, organizational commitment, and other matters of individual, organizational, and social consequence. The foundations of OB as a scientific discipline are as follows:[5]

○ **Organizational behavior** is the study of individuals and groups in organizations.

1. *An interdisciplinary body of knowledge*—OB draws insights from the social sciences and related areas.
2. *Use of scientific methods*—The knowledge base of OB is created by scientific methods using rigorous concepts and disciplined analysis.
3. *Focus on practical applications*—OB strives to make a positive difference by improving the performance of organizations and their members.
4. *Contingency thinking*—OB respects individual differences, seeking the best fits between management practices and situational complexities.

←
Major foundations of organizational behavior

One of the important contingency issues in OB is the notion of *person-job fit*, finding a good match of individual interests and capabilities with job characteristics. For example, Rich De Vault, a manager at Stryker Instruments, noticed that an employee's interpersonal talents weren't being well utilized. After DeVault moved him to another job that required good human relations skills, the employee saved Stryker $1 million in outsourcing fees. Says DeVault: "The look on his face when he's working is different—he's much more absorbed in what he's doing. His new position allows him to use his talents by coordinating a number of in-house and subcontractor resources. His enthusiasm stepped up as well as his impact."[6]

PSYCHOLOGICAL CONTRACTS

○ A **psychological contract** is the set of individual expectations about the employment relationship.

The effective management of person–job fit begins with the nature of the employment relationship itself. Work should provide a mutual and positive exchange of value between people and organizations. This sense of mutual benefit is reflected in the **psychological contract,** or set of expectations held by the individual about what will be given and received in the employment relationship.[7] The ideal work situation is one in which the exchange of values in the psychological contract is considered fair. When the psychological contract is unbalanced or broken, however, morale problems easily develop. This problem surfaced in Japan where workers historically enjoyed high job security and, in return, put in long work hours at great personal sacrifice. But when the Japanese economy experienced difficulty and companies cut back on job protections, worker morale declined. The psychological contract shared between workers and employers had been damaged.[8]

Figure 15.1 shows that a healthy psychological contract offers a balance between individual contributions made to the organization and inducements received in return. *Contributions* are work activities, such as effort, time, creativity, and loyalty, that make the individual a valuable human resource. *Inducements* are things the organization gives to the individual in exchange for these contributions. Typical inducements in-

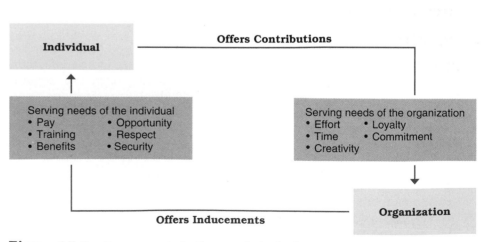

Figure 15.1 Components in the psychological contract.

clude pay, fringe benefits, training, opportunities for personal growth and advancement, and job security. Such inducements should be valued by employees and should make it worthwhile for them to work hard for the organization.

WORK AND THE QUALITY OF LIFE

The term "quality of work life" (QWL) was first used in Chapter 1 to describe the overall quality of human experiences in the workplace. Most people spend many hours a week, and many years of their lives, at work. What happens to them at work, how they are treated, and what their work is like are influences on their overall quality of life.[9] Our experiences at work can and often do spill over to affect our nonwork activities and lives, just as our nonwork experiences sometimes affect our attitudes and performance at work.

Anyone who serves as a manager must accept that the job carries a high level of social responsibility. Poor management practices can diminish a person's overall quality of life, not just the quality of work life; good management, by contrast, has the potential to enhance both. If you think this is an overstatement, consider a steel worker's compelling words once shared with the noted author Studs Terkel:[10]

> *When I come home, know what I do for the first twenty minutes? Fake it. I put on a smile. I got a kid three years old. Sometimes she says, "Daddy, where've you been?" I say, "Work." I could have told her I'd been in Disneyland. What's work to a three-year-old kid? If I feel bad, I can't take it out on the kid. Kids are born innocent of everything but birth. You can't take it out on your wife either. That is why you go to a tavern. You want to release it there rather than do it at home. What does an actor do when he's got a bad movie? I got a bad movie every day.*

Today's managers are expected to help create work environments within which people have positive experiences while performing to high levels of expectation. The themes of this chapter all relate in one way or another to this goal.

www.catalystwomen.org

Catalyst reports that many people use flexible hours as a screening criterion when searching for employment. They want freedom to "come in early, leave late, go to the school play or a soccer game," and to do so without fear of damaging their careers.

PERSONALITY TRAITS

"Of course he's a bad fit for the job; with a personality like that, he doesn't work well with others." "Put Shoshanna on the project; her personality is perfect for the intensity that we expect from the team." These are examples of everyday conversations about people at work, with the key word being **personality**—the combination or overall profile of characteristics that makes one person unique from every other. Individual personalities and variations among them are important managerial considerations in any work setting. It is common and helpful in this regard to understand what psychologists call the *Big Five personality traits.*[11]

○ **Personality** is the profile of characteristics making a person unique from others.

← Big Five personality traits

- **Extroversion**—The degree to which someone is outgoing, sociable, and assertive. An extrovert is comfortable and confident in interpersonal relationships; an introvert is more withdrawn and reserved.

- **Agreeableness**—The degree to which someone is good-natured, cooperative, and trusting. An agreeable person gets along well with

○ **Extroversion** is being outgoing, sociable, and assertive.

○ **Agreeableness** is being good-natured, cooperative, and trusting.

○ **Conscientiousness** is being responsible, dependable, and careful.

○ **Emotional stability** is being relaxed, secure, and unworried.

○ **Openness** is being curious, receptive to new ideas, and imaginative.

others; a disagreeable person is a source of conflict and discomfort for others.

• **Conscientiousness**—The degree to which someone is responsible, dependable, and careful. A conscientious person focuses on what can be accomplished and meets commitments; a person who lacks conscientiousness is careless, often trying to do too much and failing, or doing little.

• **Emotional stability**—The degree to which someone is relaxed, secure, and unworried. A person who is emotionally stable is calm and confident; a person lacking in emotional stability is anxious, nervous, and tense.

• **Openness**—The degree to which someone is curious, open to new ideas, and imaginative. An open person is broad-minded, receptive to new things, open to change; a person who lacks openness is narrow-minded, has few interests, and is resistant to change.

You can easily spot these personality traits in people with whom you work, study, and socialize. But don't forget that they also apply to you; others have impressions of your personality on these very same dimensions. In the social context of the workplace, managers must be able to understand and respond to these personality differences when making job assignments, building teams, and otherwise engaging in the daily give-and-take of work. Psychologists also use the Big Five to steer people in the direction of career choices that provide the best personality–job fits.

Figure 15.2 displays the Big Five along with five other personality dimensions that can make a further difference in how people work and how well they work together in organizations.[12] Scholars have a strong interest in **locus of control,** recognizing that some people believe they are in control of their destinies while others believe that what happens to them is beyond their control.[13] "Internals" are more self-confident and accept responsibility for their own actions, while "externals" are more prone to blame others and outside forces for what happens to them. Interestingly, research suggests that internals tend to be more satisfied and less alienated from their work.

○ **Locus of control** is the extent to which one believes that what happens is within one's control.

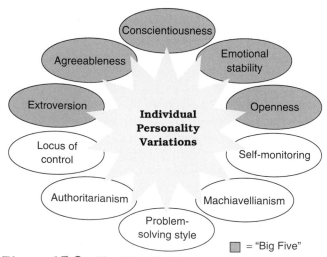

Figure 15.2 The "Big Five" and five more personality dimensions that influence human behavior at work.

Authoritarianism is the degree to which a person defers to authority and accepts status differences.[14] Someone with an authoritarian personality would tend to act rigidly and be control-oriented when in a leadership capacity; this same person would be subservient and follow the rules when in a follower capacity. The tendency of people with an authoritarian personality to obey orders can be problematic if they follow a supervisor's directives to the point of acting unethically—or even illegally.

In his 16th-century book *The Prince,* Niccolo Machiavelli gained lasting fame for giving advice on how to use power to achieve personal goals.[15] Machiavellianism describes the extent to which someone is emotionally detached and manipulative in using power.[16] A person with a "high-Mach" personality is usually viewed as exploitative and unconcerned about others, with the guiding rule being that the end justifies the means. A person with a "low-Mach" personality, by contrast, would be deferential in allowing others to exert power over them.

The psychologist Carl Jung pointed out that people display significant differences in **problem-solving styles,** or the way they gather and evaluate information for decision making.[17] Information is gathered by *sensation* (emphasizing details, facts, and routine) or by *intuition* (looking for the "big picture" and being willing to deal with various possibilities). Information is evaluated by *thinking* (using reason and analysis) or by *feeling* (responding to the feelings and desires of others). Because these differences are so extreme, it is not surprising that people approach their jobs in different ways and have difficulty at times working with one another. Many organizations use the Myers-Briggs Type Indicator, a 100-question survey instrument, to measure variations in problem-solving styles. Employees are trained to both understand their own problem-solving styles and to learn how to work more productively with people with different styles.

Finally, **self-monitoring** reflects the degree to which someone is able to adjust and modify behavior in response to the situation and external factors.[19] A person high in self-monitoring tends to be a learner, comfortable with feedback, and both willing and able to change. Because high self-monitors are flexible in changing behavior from one situation to the next, it may be hard to get a clear reading of where they stand. A person low in self-monitoring, by contrast, is predictable, tending to act consistently regardless of circumstances.

○ **Authoritarianism** is the degree to which a person tends to defer to authority.

PERSONAL MANAGEMENT

Your PROBLEM-SOLVING STYLE is likely to differ from those of people you study and work with. It is important to understand your style and learn about problems that can occur as styles clash when you work with others. Which of the four master problem-solving styles shown here best describes you?[18]

- *Sensation-Thinker:* STs take a realistic approach to problem solving, preferring "facts," clear goals, and certainty.
- *Intuitive-Thinker:* NTs are comfortable with abstraction and unstructured situations, tending to be idealistic and to avoid details.
- *Intuitive-Feeler:* NFs are insightful, like to deal with broad issues, and value flexibility and human relationships.
- *Sensation-Feeler:* SFs emphasize analysis using facts, while being open communicators and respectful of feelings and values.

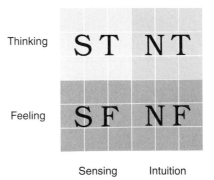

Thinking — ST NT

Feeling — SF NF

Sensing   Intuition

Get to know yourself better ▶
Complete Self-Assessments #25—**Cognitive Style**, and #26—**Internal-External Control**, from the Management Learning Workbook.

○ **Self-monitoring** is the degree to which someone is able to adjust behavior in response to external factors.

WORK ATTITUDES AND BEHAVIOR

At last report, Challis M. Lowe was one of only two African-American women among the five highest-paid executives in over 400 U.S. companies surveyed by the woman's advocacy and research organization Catalyst.[20] She became executive vice president at Ryder System after a 25-year career that included several changes of employers and lots of stressors—working-mother guilt, a failed marriage, gender bias on the job, and an MBA degree earned part-time. Through it all she says: "I've never let being scared stop me from doing something. Just because you haven't done it before doesn't mean you shouldn't try." That, simply put, is what we would call a can-do attitude!

WHAT IS AN ATTITUDE?

○ An **attitude** is a predisposition to act in a certain way.

An **attitude** is a predisposition to act in a certain way toward people and things in one's environment.[21] In the case of Challis Lowe, for example, she was predisposed to take risk and embrace challenges. This "positive" attitude influenced her behavior when dealing with the inevitable problems, choices, and opportunities of work and career. To fully understand attitudes, positive or negative, you must recognize their three components. First, the *cognitive component* reflects a belief or opinion. You might believe, for example, that your management course is very interesting. Second, the *affective or emotional component* of an attitude reflects a specific feeling. For example, you might feel very good about being a management major. Third, the *behavioral component* of an attitude reflects an intention to behave consistently with the belief and feeling. Using the same example again, you might say to yourself: "I am going to work hard and try to get an A in all my management courses."

Importantly, the intentions reflected in an attitude may or may not be confirmed in one's actual behavior. Despite having a positive attitude and all good intentions, the demands of family, friends, or leisure activities might use up the time you would otherwise need to devote to studying hard enough to get an A in your management courses. Thus, you might fail to live up to your own expectations. In fact, the psychological concept of **cognitive dissonance** describes the discomfort felt when one's attitude and behavior are inconsistent.[22] For most people, dissonance is very uncomfortable and results in changing the attitude to fit the behavior ("Oh, I really don't like management that much anyway"), changing future behavior to fit the attitude (dropping out of intramural sports to get extra study time), or rationalizing to force the two to be compatible ("Management is an okay major, but being a manager also requires the experience I'm gaining in my extracurricular activities").

○ **Cognitive dissonance** is discomfort felt when attitude and behavior are inconsistent.

At Panera the recipe for success is a positive attitude

When Ron Shaich opened a cookie store in Boston in 1980, even he didn't know that he was on an entrepreneurial pathway to business success. It wasn't long before he joined forces with a local French bakery to expand his product line in a new venture named Au Bon Pain. Finding a niche with fresh breads and high-quality meats, Au Bon Pain grew rapidly through the mid-1990s and then leveled off. Shaich wanted more. Sensing opportunity in the St. Louis Bread Company, a small new chain they had acquired and then renamed Panera, he went to Au Bon Pain's board with a proposal: sell Au Bon Pain and focus on Panera. The board said they thought he might be "washed up," but he didn't give in. After nine months they agreed. Panera took off like a rocket, growing to 500+ stores in less than four years. Shaich, with an ever-positive attitude toward opportunity, sees more growth ahead.[23]

JOB SATISFACTION

People hold attitudes about many things in the workplace—bosses, each other, tasks, policies, goals, and more. A comprehensive work attitude is **job satisfaction,** the degree to which an individual feels positive or negative about various aspects of work.[24] The evaluative points of reference in job satisfaction are such things as pay, coworkers, supervisor, work setting, advancement opportunities, and workload. In a poll of American workers, the *Wall Street Journal* asked this question: How satisfied are you with your current job? Interestingly, a majority were at least to some extent satisfied with their jobs. The responses were 37 percent completely satisfied, 47 percent somewhat satisfied, 10 percent somewhat dissatisfied, 4 percent completely dissatisfied, and 2 percent not sure.[25]

> **○ Job satisfaction** is the degree to which an individual feels positive or negative about a job.

In terms of consequences, researchers know that there is a strong relationship between job satisfaction and *absenteeism.* Workers who are more satisfied with their jobs are absent less often than those who are dissatisfied. There is also a relationship between job satisfaction and *turnover.* Satisfied workers are more likely to stay, and dissatisfied workers are more likely to quit their jobs. Both of these findings are important since absenteeism and turnover are costly in terms of the recruitment and training needed to replace workers, as well as in the productivity lost while new workers are learning how to perform up to expectations. One study reports that changing retention rates up or down results in magnified changes to corporate earnings. The author warns about the adverse impact on corporate performance of declining employee loyalty and "revolving door" defections.[26]

Closely related to job satisfaction are two other concepts with quality of work life implications. **Job involvement** is defined as the extent to which an individual is dedicated to a job. Someone with high job involvement, for example, would be expected to work beyond expectations to complete a special project. **Organizational commitment** is defined as the loyalty of an individual to the organization itself. Individuals with a high organizational commitment would identify strongly with the organization

> **○ Job involvement** is the extent to which an individual is dedicated to a job.

> **○ Organizational commitment** is the loyalty of an individual to the organization.

TAKE IT TO THE CASE

Craftwork, tradition, and time build grand pianos

Stop in at Steinway & Sons online and take their factory tour. You'll see how the finest in individual craftwork, the ingenuity of patented designs and methods, and the very best of teamwork still combine to build what may be the world's most famous pianos. The firm remains true to its history, dating to its founding in 1853 by Henry Englehard Steinway. Over half the firm's 114 patents were in place before 1900. The traditions of skilled craftspeople building handmade pianos continue today. Highly skilled workers bend and shape the very best wood using time-tested techniques, taking eight months to finish a concert grand. Skill, patience, the best materials, and modern organization allow the firm to produce some 5000 pianos a year worldwide.[28]

and take pride in considering themselves a member. In respect to the consequences again, a survey of 55,000 American workers by the Gallup Organization found evidence that attitudes reflecting job involvement and commitment correlated with higher profits for their employers. The four attitudes that counted most were believing one has the opportunity to do one's best every day, believing one's opinions count, believing fellow workers are committed to quality, and believing there is a direct connection between one's work and the company's mission.[27]

INDIVIDUAL PERFORMANCE

Somewhere in Michigan near a Ford Motor Company plant, the following sign once hung in a tavern: "I spend 40 hours a week here—am I supposed to work too?" The message behind these words is an important one in management: It is one thing for people to come to work and even to be satisfied with their jobs; it is quite another for them to work hard and achieve high performance. **Job performance** is measured as the quantity and quality of tasks accomplished by an individual or group. It is, so to speak, the "bottom line" for people at work. And the important managerial question becomes: What factors determine individual performance?

○ **Job performance** is the quantity and quality of tasks accomplished.

In answering this question, the following *Individual Performance Equation* is a good starting point: *Performance = Ability × Support × Effort.*[29] The logic of this equation is straightforward and very practical. If high performance is to be achieved in any work setting, the individual must possess the right abilities—creating the *capacity* to perform, work hard at the task—showing the *willingness* to perform, and have the necessary support—creating the *opportunity* to perform.[30] All three factors are important and necessary; failure to provide for any one or more is likely to cause performance losses.

Performance Begins with Ability

Ability establishes an individual's capacity to perform at a high level of accomplishment. As discussed in Chapter 12 on human resource management, proper employee selection brings people with the right abilities to a job; poor selection does not. Good training and development keep peoples' skills up to date and job relevant; poor or insufficient training does not. The best managers never let a job vacancy or training opportunity pass without giving it serious attention. The best managers make sure every day that all jobs under their supervision are staffed up to the moment with talented people.

Performance Requires Support

Even the most capable and hard-working individual will not achieve the highest performance levels unless proper support is available. Support creates a work environment rich in opportunities to apply one's talents to maximum advantage. To fully utilize their abilities workers need sufficient resources, clear goals and directions, freedom from unnecessary rules and job constraints, appropriate technologies, and performance feedback. Providing these and other forms of direct work support is a basic managerial responsibility. The best information on the need for support, of course, comes from the workers themselves. Wouldn't it be nice to hear more managers speak the following words in everyday conversations with their subordinates: "How can I help you today?"

REALITY CHECK 15.1

Job satisfaction across cultures
In an international survey of job satisfaction, workers from Switzerland scored the highest, with 82 percent of respondents saying they liked their jobs. Take the online "Reality Check" to learn more about how workers from other countries, including the United States, responded.

Performance Involves Effort

The willingness to work hard at a task is an essential component of the high-performance workplace. But the decision to exert work effort rests squarely with the individual alone; it is the ultimate test of the motivation theories discussed in Chapter 14. All any manager (or teacher, or parent) can do is attempt to create the conditions under which the answer to the all-important question—"Should I work hard today?"—is more often "Yes" than "No" And quite frankly, the most powerful and enduring "Yes" is the one driven by forces within the individual—intrinsic motivation—rather than by outside initiatives such as supervisory appeals, offers of monetary reward, or threats of punishment. Good managers understand this reality as they build jobs for people in organizations.

Be sure you can • define the terms attitude, job satisfaction, and job performance • list the three components of an attitude • explain cognitive dissonance • explain the potential consequences of high and low job satisfaction • explain the multiplication signs in the individual performance equation: $P = A \times S \times E$ • illustrate how managers can positively influence performance through each factor in this equation

Learning check 2

JOB DESIGN ALTERNATIVES

A **job** is a collection of tasks performed in support of organizational objectives. The process of **job design** is one of creating or defining jobs by assigning specific work tasks to individuals and groups. Job design uses

○ A **job** is the collection of tasks a person performs in support of organizational objectives.

○ **Job design** is the allocation of specific work tasks to individuals and groups.

the insights of motivation theories discussed in the last chapter to help accomplish two major goals—high levels of both job satisfaction and job performance. Jobs can and should be designed so that satisfaction and performance go hand in hand. This is in many ways an exercise in "fit." A good job design provides a good fit between the individual worker and the task requirements. *Figure 15.3* shows a continuum of job design alternatives—job simplification, job enlargement and rotation, and job enrichment.

SCIENTIFIC MANAGEMENT

○ **Job simplification** employs people in clearly defined and very specialized tasks.

○ **Automation** is the total mechanization of a job.

Job simplification involves standardizing work procedures and employing people in well-defined and highly specialized tasks. This is an extension of the scientific management approach discussed in Chapter 2. Simplified jobs are narrow in *job scope*—that is, the number and variety of different tasks a person performs. Many employees around the world earn their livings working at highly simplified tasks, often on assembly lines. The most extreme form of job simplification is **automation,** or the total mechanization of a job.

The logic of job simplification is straightforward. Because the jobs don't require complex skills, workers should be easier and quicker to train, less difficult to supervise, and easy to replace if they leave. Furthermore, because tasks are well defined, workers should become good at them while performing the same work over and over again. Consider the case of Cindy Vang, who works on an assembly line for Medtronics, Inc. She works in a dust-free room making a specialized medical component. She is certified on five of 14 job skills in her department. At any given time, however, she performs one of them, for example, feeding small devices by tweezers into special containers. It is tedious work without much challenge. But Vang says: "I like it." Importantly, she notes that the job doesn't interfere with her home life with a husband and three sons. Her economic needs are met in a low-stress job and comfortable work environment.[31]

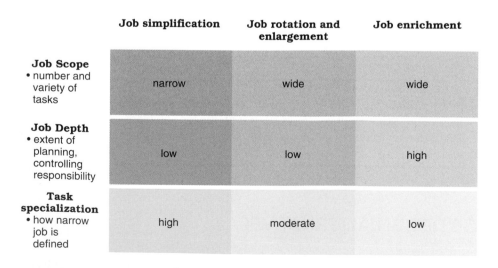

	Job simplification	Job rotation and enlargement	Job enrichment
Job Scope • number and variety of tasks	narrow	wide	wide
Job Depth • extent of planning, controlling responsibility	low	low	high
Task specialization • how narrow job is defined	high	moderate	low

Figure 15.3 A continuum of job design alternatives.

Job enrichment checklist

- *Check 1:* Remove controls that limit people's discretion in their work.
- *Check 2:* Grant people authority to make decisions about their work.
- *Check 3:* Make people understand their performance accountability.
- *Check 4:* Allow people to do "whole" tasks or complete units of work.
- *Check 5:* Make performance feedback available.

Situations don't always work out this well in highly simplified jobs. Productivity can suffer as unhappy workers drive up costs through absenteeism and turnover, and through poor performance caused by boredom and alienation. Although simplified jobs appeal to some people, disadvantages can develop with the structured and repetitive tasks.

JOB ROTATION AND JOB ENLARGEMENT

One way to move beyond simplification in job design is to broaden the scope through **job rotation,** increasing task variety by periodically shifting workers between jobs involving different task assignments. Job rotation can be done on a regular schedule; it can also be done periodically or occasionally. The latter approach is often used in training to inform people about jobs performed by others. Another way to broaden scope is **job enlargement,** increasing task variety by combining two or more tasks that were previously assigned to separate workers. Often these are tasks done immediately before or after the work performed in the original job. This is sometimes called *horizontal loading*—pulling prework and/or later work stages into the job.

○ **Job rotation** increases task variety by periodically shifting workers between different jobs.

○ **Job enlargement** increases task variety by combining into one job two or more tasks previously assigned to separate workers.

JOB ENRICHMENT

Frederick Herzberg, whose two-factor theory of motivation was discussed in Chapter 14, questions the motivational value of horizontally loading jobs through enlargement and rotation. "Why," he asks, "should a worker become motivated when one or more meaningless tasks are added to previously existing ones or when work assignments are rotated among equally meaningless tasks?" By contrast, he says, "If you want people to do a good job, give them a good job to do."[32] He argues that this is best done through **job enrichment,** the practice of expanding job content to create more opportunities for satisfaction.

In contrast to job enlargement and rotation, job enrichment focuses not just on job scope but also on *job depth*—that is, the extent to which task planning and evaluating duties are performed by the individual worker rather than the supervisor. Changes designed to increase job depth are sometimes referred to as *vertical loading.* Herzberg's recommendations for enriching jobs are found in *Manager's Notepad 15.1.*

○ **Job enrichment** increases job depth by adding work planning and evaluating duties normally performed by the supervisor.

Be sure you can • illustrate a job designed by scientific management • illustrate jobs designed by job rotation and job enlargement • illustrate a job designed by Herzberg's concept of job enrichment • explain the job satisfaction implications of job design by simplification, enlargement, rotation, and enrichment

DIRECTIONS IN JOB ENRICHMENT

Modern management theory takes job enrichment a step beyond the suggestions of Frederick Herzberg. Most importantly, it adopts a contingency perspective and recognizes that job enrichment may not be best for everyone. Among the directions in job design, the core characteristics model developed by J. Richard Hackman and his associates offers a way for managers to create jobs, enriched or otherwise, that best fit the needs of people and organizations.[33]

CORE CHARACTERISTICS MODEL

The model described in *Figure 15.4* offers a diagnostic approach to job enrichment. A job that is high in the five core characteristics is considered enriched; the lower a job scores on these characteristics, the less enriched it is. The *five core job characteristics* are:

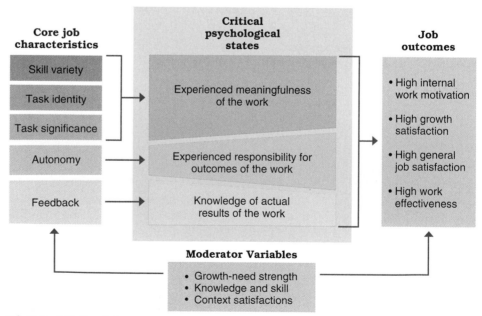

Figure 15.4 Job design and individual work outcomes using the core characterstics model.
Source: Reprinted by permission from J. Richard Hackman and Greg R. Oldham, *Work Redesign* (Reading, MA: Addison-Wesley, 1980), p. 90.

1. *Skill variety*—the degree to which a job requires a variety of different activities to carry out the work, and involves the use of a number of different skills and talents of the individual.

2. *Task identity*—the degree to which the job requires completion of a "whole" and identifiable piece of work, one that involves doing a job from beginning to end with a visible outcome.

3. *Task significance*—the degree to which the job has a substantial impact on the lives or work of other people elsewhere in the organization or in the external environment.

4. *Autonomy*—the degree to which the job gives the individual freedom, independence, and discretion in scheduling work and in choosing procedures for carrying it out.

5. *Feedback from the job itself*—the degree to which work activities required by the job result in the individual obtaining direct and clear information on his or her performance.

Five core job characteristics

According to this model, job satisfaction and performance are influenced by three critical psychological states: (1) experienced meaningfulness of the work; (2) experienced responsibility for the outcomes of the work; and (3) knowledge of actual results of work activities. These, in turn, are influenced by the presence or absence of the five core job characteristics. In true contingency fashion, however, the core characteristics will not affect all people in the same way. Generally speaking, people who respond most favorably to enriched jobs will have strong higher-order needs, appropriate job knowledge and skills, and be otherwise satisfied with job context. One of the key contingency or moderator variables in the model is **growth-need strength,** described in Alderfer's ERG theory (see Chapter 14) as the degree to which an individual seeks psychological growth in his or her work. The expectation is that people with strong growth needs will respond most positively to enriched jobs.

o **Growth-need strength** is the desire to achieve psychological growth in one's work.

When job enrichment is a good job design choice, Hackman and his colleagues recommend five ways to improve the core characteristics.

CAREER CONNECTION

Blending technology and talent to create high-performance products

At Boeing Company, technology and people were keys to the development of the 777 aircraft. Designs for the 777 airplanes utilized the latest computer-assisted and largely paperless techniques. Engineers worked out problems on powerful computers, including all the coordinating details of over 130,000 engineered parts and more than 3 million rivets, screws, and fasteners. But technology didn't and couldn't stand alone as a performance driver. It was part of a sociotechnical system in which the talents of people were activated. Engineers worked in a team structure where cross-functional "design-build" teams included representatives from all areas, whose contributions were essential. The teams were expected to resolve design and manufacturing problems before they interfered with production.[36]

First, you can *form natural units of work*. Make sure that the tasks people perform are logically related to one another and provide a clear and meaningful task identity. Second, try to *combine tasks*. Expand job responsibilities by pulling together into one larger job a number of smaller tasks previously done by others. Third, *establish client relationships*. Put people in contact with others who, as clients inside and/or outside the organization, use the results of their work. Fourth, *open feedback channels*. Provide opportunities for people to receive performance feedback as they work and to learn how performance changes over time. Fifth, *practice vertical loading*. Give people more control over their work by increasing their authority to perform the planning and controlling previously done by supervisors.

TECHNOLOGY AND JOB ENRICHMENT

○ A **sociotechnical system** integrates technology and human resources in high-performance systems.

On the important issue of technology, the managerial challenge is quite clear: Job design should proceed with the goal of increasing productivity through integrated **sociotechnical systems**.[34] These are job designs that use technology to best advantage while still treating people with respect and allowing their human talents to be applied to their fullest potential. The continuing inroads made by computers into the workplace are changing structures, workflows, and the mix of skills needed in many settings. Consider the special case of *robotics*—the use of computer-controlled machines to completely automate work tasks previously performed by hand. Such automation of work is the most extreme form of job simplification and has both its limits and critics. On the positive side, such technology offers an opportunity to take over many routine tasks previously assigned to individuals and thereby frees human talents for more enriched job assignments. In this and other ways, technology utilization and job enrichment can be complementary strategies.

QUESTIONS AND ANSWERS ON JOB ENRICHMENT

"Is it expensive to implement job enrichment?" Job enrichment can be costly. The cost grows as the required changes in technology, workflow, and other facilities become more complex.

"Will people demand more pay for doing enriched jobs?" Herzberg believes that if people are being paid truly competitive wages (i.e., if pay dissatisfaction does not already exist), the satisfactions of performing enriched tasks will be adequate compensation for the increased work involved. But any job-enrichment program should be approached with recognition that pay may be an issue for the people involved.[36]

"Should everyone's job be enriched?" No, contingency counts. The people most likely to respond favorably to job enrichment are those seeking higher-order or growth-need satisfactions at work and who have the levels of training, education, and ability required to perform the enriched job.

"What do the unions say about job enrichment?" Suffice it to say that the following comments made some years ago by one union official are still worth consideration. "Better wages, shorter hours, vested pensions, a

right to have a say in their working conditions, the right to be promoted on the basis of seniority, and all the rest. That's the kind of job enrichment that unions believe in."[37]

Be sure you can • list and describe the five core job characteristics • explain the relationship between these characteristics and job enrichment • explain how a person's growth needs, skills, and context satisfaction can affect their responses to these characteristics • apply the core characteristics model to a job situation and recommend ways to improve job satisfaction and performance • answer the question: Should everyone's job be enriched?

ALTERNATIVE WORK ARRANGEMENTS

Not only is the content of jobs changing for people in today's workplace, the context is changing too. Among the more significant developments is the emergence of a number of alternative ways for people to schedule their work time.[38] And "flexibility" is the key word. This is especially important as employers deal with work-life balance issues affecting today's highly diverse workforce. Many are finding that alternative work schedules can help attract and retain the best workers.

AROUND THE WORLD

Meet the craftswomen of the world

Did you know that one-quarter of the world's families are totally supported by women? Paola Gianturco didn't, until she heard the news from the United Nations Fourth World Conference on Women held in China. Since then she has traveled the world to learn more about the struggles of third-world women entrepreneurs. She met Muslim mirror embroiderers in a poor Indian village in the state of Gujarat, found women knitters in a Bolivian cooperative blessing loan money with confetti and beer, and watched Zulu women weave baskets in South Africa to be sold under a common brand name. Gianturco helps support women entrepreneurs through the Crafts Council, a nonprofit in Washington, D.C., with the mission "to improve the lives of the world's poor, especially women, by helping them develop sustainable micro enterprises, while preserving their cultures, beliefs, and environments."[39]

THE COMPRESSED WORKWEEK

A **compressed workweek** is any work schedule that allows a full-time job to be completed in less than the standard 5 days of 8-hour shifts.[40] Its most common form is the "4–40," that is, accomplishing 40 hours of work in four 10-hour days. One advantage of the 4–40 schedule is that the employee receives 3 consecutive days off from work each

○ A **compressed workweek** allows a full-time job to be completed in less than five days.

week. This benefits the individual through more leisure time and lower commuting costs. The organization should also benefit through lower absenteeism and any improved performance that may result. Potential disadvantages include increased fatigue and family adjustment problems for the individual, as well as increased scheduling problems, possible customer complaints, and union objections for the organization.

Positive examples of this approach to work scheduling are available. At USAA, a diversified financial services company that has been listed among the 100 best companies to work for in America, a large part of the firm's San Antonio workforce is on a four-day schedule, with some working Monday through Thursday and others working Tuesday through Friday. Company benefits include improved employee morale, lower overtime costs, less absenteeism, and less sick leave.[41]

FLEXIBLE WORKING HOURS

The term **flexible working hours,** also called *flexitime* of *flextime,* describes any work schedule that gives employees some choice in the pattern of their daily work hours. A sample flexible working schedule offers choices of starting and ending times, such as the program depicted in *Figure 15.5.* Employees in this example work 4 hours of "core" time, or the time they must be present at work. In this case, core time falls between 9 and 10 A.M. and 1 and 3 P.M. They are then free to choose another 4 work hours from "flextime" blocks. Such flexible schedules give employees greater autonomy while ensuring that they maintain work responsibility. Some may choose to come in earlier and leave earlier, while still completing an 8-hour day; others may choose to start later in the morning and leave later. In between these extremes are opportunities to attend to personal affairs, such as dental appointments, home emergencies, visits to children's schools, and so on.

○ **Flexible working hours** give employees some choice in daily work hours.

Flexible hours help organizations attract and retain talented employees whose lives are complicated by personal responsibilities. These include dual-career couples, single parents with child-care complications, and employees who are care providers for elderly parents. All top 100 companies in *Working Mother* magazine's list of best employers for work-

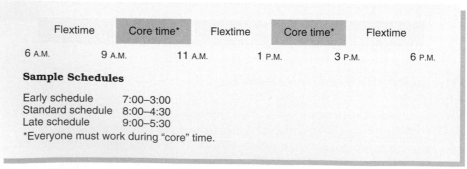

Figure 15.5 A sample flexible working hours schedule.

ing moms offer flexible scheduling. Reports indicate that flexibility in dealing with nonwork obligations reduces stress and unwanted job turnover.[42] At the women's sports apparel company Athleta, for example, a low turnover rate compared to the industry average is attributed to flexible scheduling.[42]

JOB SHARING

Another work scheduling alternative is **job sharing,** where one full-time job is split between two or more persons. This often involves each person working one-half day, but it can also be done on weekly or monthly sharing arrangements. Organizations benefit by employing talented people who would otherwise be unable to work. The qualified specialist who is also a parent may be unable to stay away from home for a full workday but may be able to work a half day. Job sharing allows two such persons to be employed as one, often to great benefit.

When such concerns about a new job sharing program were investigated at Lotus Development Corporation, not one of the initial nine teams of job sharers had to apologize to anybody. They were among the top performers in annual merit pay appraisals.[43]

Job sharing should not be confused with a more controversial concept called *work-sharing.* This involves an agreement between employees who face layoffs or terminations to cut back their work hours so they can all keep their jobs. Instead of losing 20 percent of a firm's workforce to temporary layoffs in an unexpected business downturn, for example, a work-sharing program would cut everyone's hours by 20 percent to keep them all employed. This allows employers to retain trained and loyal workers even when forced to temporarily economize by reducing labor costs. For employees whose seniority could protect them from layoff, the disadvantage is lost earnings. For those who would otherwise be terminated, however, it provides continued work—albeit with reduced earnings—and with a preferred employer. Some unions endorse this concept, and it is now legal in many states. It is prohibited in others, however, because of legal complications relating to unemployment compensation and benefits.

○ **Job sharing** splits one job between two people.

TELECOMMUTING

It is increasingly popular for people to work away from a fixed office location. **Telecommuting,** sometimes called *flexiplace,* is a work arrangement that allows at least a portion of scheduled work hours to be completed outside the office. Often this is facilitated by information technology that allows one to work from home while linked with customers and a central office. Telecommuting frees the jobholder from the normal constraints of commuting, fixed hours, special work attire, and even direct contact with supervisors. It is popular, for example, among computer programmers and is found increasingly in such diverse areas as marketing, financial analysis, and administrative services. New terms are even becoming associated with telecommuting practices. We speak of *hoteling* when telecommuters come to the central office and use temporary office facilities; we also refer to *virtual offices* that include everything from an office at home to a mobile workspace in an automobile.

○ **Telecommuting** involves using IT to work at home or outside the office.

MANAGER'S NOTEPAD 15.2 — How to make telecommuting work for you

- Treat telecommuting like any work day; keep regular hours.
- Limit nonwork distractions; set up private space dedicated to work.
- Establish positive routines and work habits; be disciplined.
- Report regularly to your boss and main office; don't lose touch.
- Seek out human contact; don't become isolated.
- Use technology: instant messaging, intranet links, net meetings.
- Keep your freedoms and responsibilities in balance.
- Reward yourself with time off; let flexibility be an advantage.

Overall, there is no doubt that telecommuting is here to stay as an important aspect of the continually developing new workplace. When asked what they like, telecommuters tend to report increased productivity, fewer distractions, the freedom to be your own boss, and the benefit of having more time for themselves. On the negative side, they cite working too much, having less time to themselves, difficulty separating work and personal life, and having less time for family.[44] Other considerations for the individual include feelings of isolation and loss of visibility for promotion. Managers, in turn, may be required to change their routines and procedures to accommodate the challenges of supervising people from a distance. One telecommuter's advice to others is: "You have to have self-discipline and pride in what you do, but you also have to have a boss that trusts you enough to get out of the way."[45] *Manager's Notepad 15.2* offers several guidelines for how to make telecommuting work for you.[46]

PART-TIME WORK

○ **Part-time work** is temporary employment for less than the standard 40-hour workweek.

○ **Contingency workers** are employed on a part-time and temporary basis to supplement a permanent workforce.

The growing use of temporary workers is another striking employment trend, and it has a controversial side. **Part-time work** is done on any schedule less than the standard 40-hour workweek and that does not qualify the individual as a full-time employee. Many employers rely on **contingency workers**—part-timers or *permatemps* who supplement the full-time workforce, often on a long-term basis. Such workers now constitute some 30 percent of the American workforce; over 90 percent of firms surveyed by the American Management Association use them.[47] No longer limited to the traditional areas of clerical services, sales personnel, and unskilled labor, these workers serve an increasingly broad range of employer needs. It is now possible to hire on a part-time basis everything from executive support, such as a chief financial officer, to such special expertise as engineering, computer programming, and market research. The Families and Work Institute reports that 33 percent of women and 28 percent of men would work part-time if they could afford it; the AARP reports also that 58 percent of baby boomers entering retirement would like to work part-time.[48]

Because part-time or contingency workers can be easily hired, contracted with, and/or terminated in response to changing needs, many employers like the flexibility they offer in controlling labor costs and dealing with cyclical demand. On the other hand, some worry that temporaries lack the commitment of permanent workers and often lower productivity. Perhaps the most controversial issue of the part-time work trend relates to the different treatment part-timers often receive from employers. They may be paid less than their full-time counterparts, and many do not receive important benefits, such as health care, life insurance, pension plans, and paid vacations.

Be sure you can • describe the compressed workweek, flexible work hours, job sharing, and telecommuting as alternative work schedules • discuss the potential advantages and disadvantages of each to both employers and employees • discuss the significance of part-time contingency workers in the economy

Learning check 5

CHAPTER 15 STUDY GUIDE

Where We've Been

BACK TO MONITOR COMPANY

The opening example of the Monitor Company showed how jobs and work environments can be designed to meet the needs of highly talented people. Monitor illustrates that designing jobs to fit people pays off in both job satisfaction and high levels of performance accomplishment. In this chapter you learned about psychological contracts, attitudes, personality, the nature of job satisfaction, and factors influencing individual performance. You learned alternative job design approaches, with specific attention to job enrichment. You also learned about alternative work arrangements available in the new workplace.

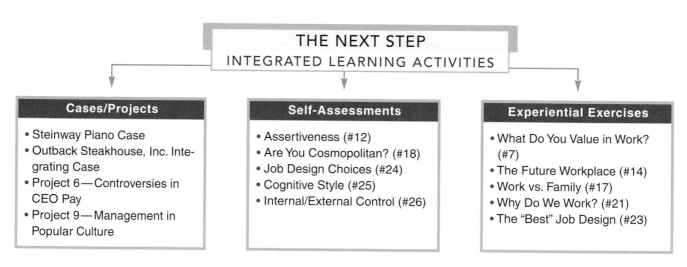

THE NEXT STEP
INTEGRATED LEARNING ACTIVITIES

Cases/Projects

- Steinway Piano Case
- Outback Steakhouse, Inc. Integrating Case
- Project 6—Controversies in CEO Pay
- Project 9—Management in Popular Culture

Self-Assessments

- Assertiveness (#12)
- Are You Cosmopolitan? (#18)
- Job Design Choices (#24)
- Cognitive Style (#25)
- Internal/External Control (#26)

Experiential Exercises

- What Do You Value in Work? (#7)
- The Future Workplace (#14)
- Work vs. Family (#17)
- Why Do We Work? (#21)
- The "Best" Job Design (#23)

STUDY QUESTIONS SUMMARY

1. How do we understand people at work?

- Organizational behavior is the study of individuals and groups in organizations.
- Work is an exchange of values between individuals and organizations.
- A healthy psychological contract occurs when a person's contributions—such as time and effort—and inducements—such as pay and respect—are in balance.
- What happens to people at work, their quality of work life, is an important influence on their quality of life overall.
- The Big Five personality factors are extroversion, agreeableness, conscientiousness, emotional stability, and openness.
- Additional personality dimensions of work significance are locus of control, authoritarianism, Machiavellianism, problem-solving style, and self-monitoring.

2. What should we know about work attitudes and behavior?

- An attitude is a predisposition to respond in a certain way to people and things.
- Cognitive dissonance occurs when a person's attitude and behavior are inconsistent.
- Job satisfaction is an important work attitude, reflecting a person's evaluation of the job, co-workers, and other aspects of the work setting.
- Job satisfaction influences such behaviors as work attendance and turnover, and is related to other attitudes such as job involvement and organizational commitment.

- The individual performance equation states: Performance = Ability × Support × Effort.

3. What are the alternative approaches to job design?

- Job design is the process of creating or defining jobs by assigning specific work tasks to individuals and groups.
- Jobs should be designed so workers enjoy high levels of both job performance and job satisfaction.
- Job simplification creates narrow and repetitive jobs consisting of well-defined tasks with many routine operations, such as the typical assembly-line job.
- Job enlargement allows individuals to perform a broader range of simplified tasks; job rotation allows individuals to shift among different jobs of similar skill levels.
- Job enrichment results in more meaningful jobs that give people more autonomy in decision making and broader task responsibilities.

4. How can jobs be enriched?

- The diagnostic approach to job enrichment involves analyzing jobs according to five core characteristics: skill variety, task identity, task significance, autonomy, and feedback.
- Jobs deficient in one or more of these core characteristics can be redesigned to improve their level of enrichment.

- Jobs can be enriched by forming natural work units, combining tasks, establishing client relationships, opening feedback channels, and vertically loading to give workers more planning and controlling responsibilities.
- Job enrichment does not work for everyone; it works best for people with strong growth-needs—the desire to achieve psychological growth in their work.

5. How can work be scheduled to improve work-life balance?

- Alternative work schedules can make work hours less inconvenient and enable organizations to respond better to individual needs and personal responsibilities.
- The compressed workweek allows 40 hours of work to be completed in only 4 days' time.
- Flexible working hours allow people to adjust the starting and ending times of their daily schedules.
- Job sharing allows two people to share one job.
- Telecommuting allows people to work at home or in mobile offices through computer links with their employers and/or customers.
- An increasing number of people work on part-time schedules as part of a contingency workforce.

KEY TERMS REVIEW

Agreeableness (p. 382)

Attitude (p. 384)

Authoritarianism (p. 383)

Automation (p. 388)

Cognitive dissonance (p. 384)

Compressed workweek (p. 393)

Conscientiousness (p. 382)

Contingency workers (p. 396)

Emotional stability (p. 382)

Extroversion (p. 382)

Flexible working hours (p. 394)

Growth-need strength (p. 391)

Job (p. 388)

Job design (p. 388)

Job enlargement (p. 389)

Job enrichment (p. 389)

Job involvement (p. 385)

SELF-TEST 15

MULTIPLE-CHOICE QUESTIONS:

1. Interest in organizational behavior on individual differences and good person–job fits reflects a commitment to _____.
    (a) sociotechnical systems (b) an interdisciplinary knowledge base (c) use of scientific methods (d) high quality of work life

2. A manager's job design goals should be to establish the conditions for workers to achieve high levels of both task performance and _____.
    (a) financial gain (b) social interaction (c) job satisfaction (d) job security

3. Vertical loading of a job is most associated with _____.
    (a) bringing prework into the job (b) bringing later work stages into the job (c) bringing higher-level or managerial work into the job (d) raising standards for high performance

4. The _____ strategy of job design allows workers to shift among a variety of jobs requiring essentially the same skills.
    (a) job simplification (b) job enlargement (c) job rotation (d) job sharing

5. The addition of more planning and evaluating responsibilities to a job is an example of the _____ job design strategy.
    (a) job enrichment (b) job enlargement (c) job rotation (d) job sharing

6. _____ is one of the core characteristics that should be improved upon in order to enrich a job.
    (a) Work-life balance (b) Task significance (c) Growth-need strength (d) Automation

7. Workers in a compressed workweek typically work 40 hours in _____ days.
    (a) 3 (b) 4 (c) 5 (d) a flexible number of

8. Another term used to describe part-time workers is _____.
    (a) contingency workers (b) virtual workers (c) flexible workers (d) secondary workers

9. _____ is where two workers split one job on an arranged work schedule; _____ is where a group of workers accept reduced individual work hours in order to avoid layoffs.
    (a) Job rotation, job sharing (b) Job sharing, work sharing (c) Job enrichment, job sharing (d) Job splitting, job reduction

10. Hoteling is a development associated with the growing importance of _____ in the new workplace.
    (a) personal wellness (b) telecommuting (c) compressed workweeks (d) Type A personalities

TRUE-FALSE QUESTIONS:

11. A person with a high _____ personality would be unemotional and willing to manipulate others to achieve personal goals.
    (a) extrovert (b) sensation-thinking (c) self-monitoring (d) Machiavellianism

12. Among the Big Five personality traits, _____ indicates someone who is responsible, dependable, and careful in respect to tasks.
    (a) authoritarianism (b) agreeableness (c) conscientiousness (d) emotional stability

13. The _____ component of an attitude indicates a person's belief about someone or something.
    (a) cognitive (b) emotional (c) affective (d) behavioral

14. The term used to describe the discomfort someone feels when his or her behavior is inconsistent with an expressed attitude is _____.
    (a) alienation (b) cognitive dissonance (c) job dissatisfaction (d) person–job imbalance

15. A manager who asks subordinates the question "How can I help you today?" will get answers useful in addressing the _____ factor in the Individual Performance Equation.
    (a) motivation (b) effort (c) support (d) ability

SHORT-RESPONSE QUESTIONS:

16. What is a "healthy" psychological contract?

17. What difference does growth-need strength make in the job enrichment process?

18. Which three of the Big Five personality traits do you believe most affect how well people work together in organizations, and why?

19. Why might an employer not want to offer employees the option of working on a compressed workweek schedule?

APPLICATION QUESTION:

20. Kurt Swenson has just attended a management development program in which the following equation was discussed: Performance = Ability × Support × Effort. As a plant manager, he is interested in implementing the concept. He plans to hold a meeting for all of his team leaders to explain the implications of this equation. If you were Kurt, how would you explain the importance of each performance factor—ability, support, effort—and how would you explain the significance of the multiplication signs in the equation?

16 | Teams and teamwork

Planning Ahead

After reading Chapter 16, you should be able to answer these questions in your own words.

CHAPTER 16 study questions

1. How do teams contribute to organizations?

2. What are current trends in the use of teams?

3. How do teams work?

4. How do teams make decisions?

5. What are the challenges of leading high-performance teams?

PIXAR ANIMATION STUDIOS—TEAMS ARE WORTH THE HARD WORK

Toy Story, Toy Story II, A Bug's Life, Monsters Inc., Finding Nemo—you surely recognize the names of these popular animated films. All, by the way, share a common heritage, being created, brought to life if you will, at Pixar Animation Studios. Working in partnership with Disney Studios, it pursues its dream of using computer animation to bring to the motion picture screen the finest of original stories.

To create the best animated films, Pixar's leadership, including CEO Steven Jobs of Apple Computer fame, knows it can only be as good as the talents of its team members. The firm does its best to attract great people and enthuse them with a challenging, satisfying, and rewarding workplace. The employment portion of its website declares: "Pixar provides an environment that is irresistible in its professional challenges, creative output and open, collaborative spirit." By all reports, the collaborative team spirit that drives the work culture also means "fun." The headquarters in Emeryville, California, has been described as a "fun house." Hallways are art galleries featuring employees' work; the lunchroom has a trattoria; roller scooters are allowed in the building; offices are outfitted to individual tastes.

In a setting that depends on creativity and teamwork, the building spaces and the culture encourage personal expression and interaction. CEO Jobs says: "Even though we use computers, our films are handmade, and we wanted the building to reflect that." So far it all seems to be working according to plans in Pixar's fun house. The firm's talented employees have won 15 Academy Awards, and the hits keep coming. Also, its technical teams have created three major proprietary software packages—Marionette, Ringmaster, and RenderMan—that are industry standards for excellence in animation. Watch for what will be coming next from Pixar's team![1]

Get Connected!

There's no doubt that you'll have to be good at teamwork in the new workplace. Are you prepared to lead teams? . . . to participate well as a member of teams? Just how good are your team skills?

Chapter 16 Learning Preview

In the chapter opening example of Pixar Animation Studios you were able to peek inside one of the award-winning companies in the movie business. You saw how important it is to build work environments that energize talent in an industry that thrives on creativity. At Pixar, teams and teamwork are essential parts of a high-performance system. In this chapter you will learn more about the nature of teams, the types of teams found in organizations, and new directions in the use of teams. You will learn about team effectiveness. You will also learn how norms, cohesion, decision making, communication, and group processes influence team accomplishments and the satisfactions of members.

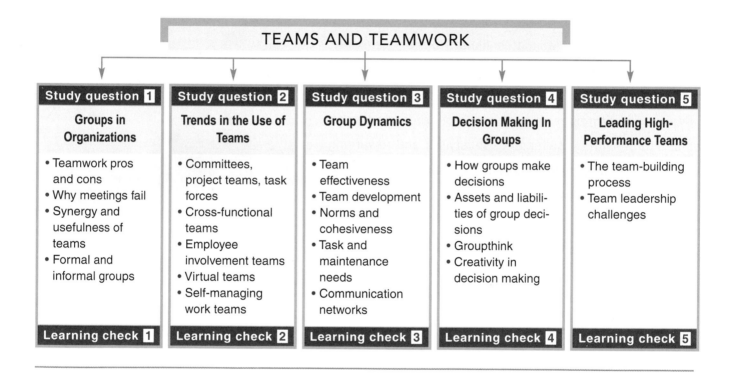

TEAMS AND TEAMWORK

Study question **1**	Study question **2**	Study question **3**	Study question **4**	Study question **5**
Groups in Organizations	**Trends in the Use of Teams**	**Group Dynamics**	**Decision Making In Groups**	**Leading High-Performance Teams**
• Teamwork pros and cons • Why meetings fail • Synergy and usefulness of teams • Formal and informal groups	• Committees, project teams, task forces • Cross-functional teams • Employee involvement teams • Virtual teams • Self-managing work teams	• Team effectiveness • Team development • Norms and cohesiveness • Task and maintenance needs • Communication networks	• How groups make decisions • Assets and liabilities of group decisions • Groupthink • Creativity in decision making	• The team-building process • Team leadership challenges
Learning check **1**	Learning check **2**	Learning check **3**	Learning check **4**	Learning check **5**

People have the need to work in teams. There is a desire to work with others and enjoy the benefits of your work and your successes together, these . . . satisfactions are as important today as they have ever been.

Andy Grove, former Chairman of Intel, Inc.

I learned a long time ago that in team sports or in business, a group working together can always defeat a team of individuals even if the individuals, by themselves, are better than your team . . . If you're going to empower people and you don't have teamwork, you're dead.

John Chambers, CEO of Cisco Systems

As these opening quotes suggest, the new workplace is rich in teams and teamwork.[2] To build high-performance organizations driven by speed, innovation, efficiency, spontaneity, and continuous change, the great potential of teams and teamwork must be harnessed. But even as we recognize that finding the best ways to utilize teams as performance resources is an important managerial task, we must also admit that it is not always easy to successfully lead through teamwork.

Just the words *"group"* and *"team"* elicit both positive and negative reactions in the minds of many people. Although it is said that "two heads are better than one," we are also warned that "too many cooks spoil the broth." The true skeptic can be heard to say: "A camel is a horse put together by a committee." Against this somewhat humorous background lies a most important point. Teams are both rich in performance potential and very complex in the way they work.[3] Consider, too, these realities. Many people prefer to work in teams rather than independently; over 60 percent of the average worker's time is spent in a team environment; even though most workers spend at least some time in teams, less than half receive training in group dynamics.[4]

TEAMS IN ORGANIZATIONS

Most tasks in organizations are well beyond the capabilities of individuals alone. Managerial success is always earned in substantial part through success at mobilizing, leading, and supporting people as they work together in groups. The new organizational designs and cultures require it, as does any true commitment to empowerment and employee involvement.[5] There is no doubt that teams are indispensable to the new workplace. The question for managers, and the guiding theme of this chapter, thus becomes: How do we make sure that teams and teamwork are utilized to everyone's best advantage?

Before proceeding, let's be specific about the terminology. A **team** is a small group of people with complementary skills, who work together to accomplish shared goals while holding themselves mutually accountable for performance results.[6] **Teamwork** is the process of people working together to accomplish these goals.

○ A **team** is a collection of people who regularly interact to pursue common goals.

○ **Teamwork** is the process of people actively working together to accomplish common goals.

TEAMWORK PROS AND CONS

Figure 16.1 shows four important roles that managers must perform in order to fully master the challenges of teams and teamwork. These roles, along with examples, are: (1) *supervisor*—serving as the appointed head of a formal work unit; (2) *facilitator*—serving as the peer leader and networking hub for a special task force; (3) *participant*—serving as

Supervisor   Network facilitator   Helpful participant   External coach

How managers get involved with teams and teamwork

Figure 16.1 Team and teamwork roles for managers.

a helpful contributing member of a project team; and (4) *coach*—serving as the external convenor or sponsor of a problem-solving team staffed by others.

Experience has taught all of us that serving in these roles isn't always easy and that things don't always work out as intended. Teams and teamwork are not problem-free. For example, who hasn't encountered **social loafing**—the presence of "free-riders" who slack off because responsibility is diffused in teams and others are present to do the work?[7] Things don't have to be this way. The time we spend in groups can be productive and satisfying, but to make it so we must understand the complex nature of groups and their internal dynamics.[8]

○ **Social loafing** is the tendency of some people to avoid responsibility by "free-riding" in groups.

An important management skill is knowing *when* a team is the best choice for a task. Another is knowing *how* to work with and manage the team to best accomplish that task. Take social loafing as an example. What can a leader or other concerned team member do when someone is free-riding? It's not easy, but the problem can be addressed. Actions can be taken to make individual contributions more visible, reward individuals for their contributions, make task assignments more interesting, and keep group size small so that free-riders are more visible to peer pressure and leader evaluation.[9]

Other problems are also common when we work in groups and teams. Personality conflicts and individual differences in work styles can disrupt the team. Tasks are not always clear. Ambiguous agendas and/or ill-defined problems can cause teams to work too long on the wrong things. Not everyone is always ready to work. Sometimes the issue is lack of motivation, but it may also be conflicts with other work deadlines and priorities. Low enthusiasm for group work may also be caused by a lack of team organization or progress, as well as by meetings that lack purpose and members who come unprepared. These and other difficulties can easily turn the great potential of teams into frustration and failure.

PERSONAL MANAGEMENT

No one can deny that teams are indispensable in today's organizations. And importantly, you cannot deny that a large part of your career success will depend on your skills at working in and leading teams. The question of the day is: Are you ready for truly valuable TEAM CONTRIBUTIONS? Consider this list of critical skills that you must have in order to contribute significantly to the success of work teams:

- Good at encouraging and motivating others.
- Good at accepting suggestions.
- Good at listening to different points of view.
- Good at communicating information and ideas.
- Good at persuasion.
- Good at conflict resolution and negotiating.
- Good at building consensus.
- Good at fulfilling commitments.

Ask yourself the tough questions. In your classes and/or at work, are you making these contributions to the teams in which you are asked to participate? Push the question even further. Ask others who know and work with you to assess your performance and contributions as a group member. What suggestions do they have for how you could improve your team contributions?

WHY MEETINGS FAIL

One of the best examples of group work in organizations is the ever-present meeting.[10] But what do you think when someone says: "Let's have a meeting." Are you ready, apprehensive, or even perturbed? Meetings are a hard fact of the workplace, especially in today's horizontal,

---

Seven sins of deadly meetings

1. People arrive late, leave early, and don't take things seriously.
2. The meeting is too long, sometimes twice as long as necessary.
3. People don't stay on topic; they digress and are easily distracted.
4. The discussion lacks candor; people are unwilling to tell the truth.
5. The right information isn't available, so decisions are postponed.
6. Nothing happens when the meeting is over; no one puts decisions into action.
7. Things never get better; the same mistakes are made meeting after meeting.

flexible, and team-oriented structures. But all too often, those who must attend do not view the call to yet another meeting enthusiastically. A survey by Office Team, for example, found that 27 percent of respondents viewed meetings as their biggest time wasters, ranking ahead of unnecessary interruptions.[11] "We have the most ineffective meetings of any company," says a technology executive. "We just seem to meet and meet and meet and we never seem to do anything," says another in the package delivery industry. "We realize our meetings are unproductive. A consulting firm is trying to help us. But we've got a long way to go," says yet another corporate manager.[12]

Consider the list of typical meeting problems described in *Manager's Notepad 16.1*.[13] You might even be able to add to the list from personal experience in student groups and work teams. But remember, in your career it will be important for you to make the most of meetings as a leader and as a member. Meetings can and should be places where information is shared, decisions get made, and people gain understanding of one another. And this can be accomplished without "wasting" time. The material in this chapter offers a useful knowledge base about group dynamics that can be helpful in making your meetings effective. But as with all group activities in organizations, good things don't happen by chance. People have to work hard and work together to make their meetings productive and rewarding.

REALITY CHECK 16.1

Meeting patterns around the world
Cultures vary and so do their approaches to meetings. In the United States, it is common for meetings to open informally, with a brief introduction, perhaps a cup of coffee, and even a light joke. Take the on-line "Reality Check" to learn more about meeting practices in other parts of the world.

SYNERGY AND THE USEFULNESS OF TEAMS

Synergy is the creation of a whole that is greater than the sum of its parts. Teamwork in our society makes available everything from aircraft to the Internet to music videos. It all happens because of synergy, the pooling of individual talents and efforts to create extraordinary results. Synergy occurs when a team uses its membership resources to the

○ **Synergy** is the creation of a whole greater than the sum of its individual parts.

fullest and thereby achieves through collective action far more than could otherwise be achieved. This is very good for organizations and it can also be very good for their members. Being part of a team can have a strong influence on individual attitudes and behaviors. When the experience is positive, working in and being part of a team helps satisfy important individual needs. Sometimes these are needs that may be difficult to meet in the regular work setting. Thus, in terms of both performance and satisfaction, the usefulness of teams is extensive. They offer:[14]

Usefulness of teams →

- More resources for problem solving.
- Improved creativity and innovation.
- Improved quality of decision making.
- Greater commitments to tasks.
- Higher motivation through collective action.
- Better control and work discipline.
- More individual need satisfaction.

FORMAL AND INFORMAL GROUPS

○ A **formal group** is officially recognized and supported by the organization.

The teams officially recognized and supported by the organization for specific purposes are **formal groups.** They are part of the formal structure and are created to fulfill a variety of essential operations. A good example is the work group consisting of a manager and subordinates, and responsible for the continuing performance of important tasks. Work groups exist in various sizes and go by different labels. They may be called *departments* (e.g., market research department), *units* (e.g., audit unit), *teams* (e.g., customer service team), or *divisions* (e.g., office products division), among other possibilities. In all cases, they are the building blocks of organization structures. Indeed, in Rensis Likert's classic view of organizations, they form an interlocking network of groups in which managers and leaders serve important "linking pin" roles.[15] Each manager or leader serves both as a superior in one work group and as a subordinate in the next-higher-level one.

○ An **informal group** is unofficial and emerges from relationships and shared interests among members.

Informal groups are also present and important in every organization. They are not recognized on organization charts and are not officially created to serve an organizational purpose. They emerge from natural or spontaneous relationships among people. Some informal groups are *interest groups* in which workers band together to pursue a common cause, such as better working conditions. Some emerge as *friendship groups* that develop for a wide variety of personal reasons, including shared nonwork interests. Others emerge as *support groups* in which the members basically help one another do their jobs.

Two points about informal groups are especially important for managers to understand. First, informal groups are not necessarily bad. Indeed, they can have a positive impact on work performance. The relationships and connections made possible by informal groups may actually help speed the workflow or allow people to "get things done" in ways not possible within the formal structure. Second, informal groups can help satisfy social needs that are otherwise thwarted or left unmet. Among other things, for example, informal groups often offer their members social satisfactions, security, support, and a sense of belonging.

Learning check 1

Be sure you can • define the terms team and teamwork • identify four roles managers perform in groups • discuss the implications of social loafing • explain how synergy works • differentiate formal and informal groups • explain the potential benefits of informal groups

TRENDS IN THE USE OF TEAMS

The trend toward greater empowerment in organizations is associated with new developments in the use of teams.[16] Committees, project teams, task forces and cross-functional teams are mainstream in the modern workplace. A variety of employee involvement teams, including quality circles, are also increasingly commonplace. And, developments in information technology are creating new opportunities for people to work together in computer-mediated or virtual teams.

COMMITTEES, PROJECT TEAMS AND TASK FORCES

A **committee** brings people together outside of their daily job assignments to work in a small team for a specific purpose. The task agenda is typically narrow, focused, and ongoing. For example, organizations usually have a variety of permanent or standing committees dedicated to a wide variety of concerns—such as diversity and compensation.[17] Committees are led by a designated head or chairperson who is held accountable for performance results.

○ A **committee** is designated to work on a special task on a continuing basis.

Project teams or **task forces** bring together people from various parts of an organization to work on common problems, but on a temporary rather than permanent basis. The task assignments for project teams and task forces are very specific; completion deadlines are also clearly defined; creativity and innovation are often very important once the project or task is completed and the team disbands. Project teams, for example, might be formed to develop a new product or service, redesign an office layout, or provide specialized consulting for a client.[18] Some guidelines for managing projects and task forces are found in *Manager's Notepad 16.2.*[19]

○ A **project team** or **task force** is convened for a specific purpose and disbands when its task is completed.

CROSS-FUNCTIONAL TEAMS

The **cross-functional team,** whose members come from different functional units, is indispensable to organizations that emphasize adaptation and horizontal integration.[20] Members of cross-functional teams work together on specific problems or tasks, and with the needs of the whole organization in mind. They are expected to share information, explore new ideas, seek creative solutions, and meet project deadlines. They are expected to knock down the "walls" that otherwise separate departments and people in the organization. At Tom's of Maine, for example, "Acorn Groups"—symbolizing the fruits of the stately oak tree—are used to help launch new products. They bring together members of all departments to work on new ideas from concept to finished product. The goal is to mini-

○ A **cross-functional team** operates with members who come from different functional units of an organization.

MANAGER'S NOTEPAD 16.2   Guidelines for managing projects and task forces

- Select appropriate team members who will be challenged by the assignment, who have the right skills, and who seem able to work well together.
- Clearly define the purpose of the team to ensure that members and important outsiders know what is expected, why, and on what timetable.
- Carefully select a team leader who has good interpersonal skills, can respect the ideas of others, and is willing to do what needs to be done.
- Periodically review progress to ensure that all team members feel collectively accountable for results, and that they receive performance feedback.

---

mize problems and maximize efficiency through cross-departmental cooperation.[21]

EMPLOYEE INVOLVEMENT TEAMS

○ An **employee involvement team** meets on a regular basis to help achieve continuous improvement.

○ A **quality circle** is a team of employees who meet periodically to discuss ways of improving work quality.

Another development in today's organizations is use of **employee involvement teams.** These are groups of workers who meet on a regular basis outside of their formal assignments, with the goal of applying their expertise and attention to continuous improvement. A popular form of employee involvement team is the **quality circle,** a group of workers that meets regularly to discuss and plan specific ways to improve work quality.[22] After receiving special training in problem solving, team processes, and quality issues, members of the quality circle try to come up with suggestions that can be implemented to raise productivity through quality improvements. Quality circles became popular in U.S. industry in part because of their place in Japanese management.

VIRTUAL TEAMS

○ Members of a **virtual team** work together and solve problems through computer-based interactions.

A newer form of group that is increasingly common in today's organizations is the **virtual team**—sometimes called a *computer-mediated group* or *electronic group network*.[23] This is a team of people who work together and solve problems largely through computer-mediated rather than face-to-face interactions. First discussed in Chapter 7 on information and decision making, the use of virtual teams is changing the way many committees, task forces, and other problem-solving teams function. Working in virtual environments, team members in dispersed locations can easily address problems and seek consensus on how to best deal with them. Virtual teams operate just like other teams in respect to what gets done; how

Teams help drive a greener company

Recycling car parts is the goal of the RAT pack at Ford Motor Company worldwide. The firm started Recycle Action Teams in the United States and Europe to find new ways to use recycled materials and to recycle as much as possible of the firm's products. Ford vehicles now are incorporating parts made from recycled tires, soda bottles, and even used carpeting from homes. They use over 4 billion pounds of recycled materials a year. A special project of Ford's environmental outreach and strategy program, RAT is a good example of applying team creativity and initiative to solve important problems. Ford also purchased a vehicle reclying facility in Florida as part of its initiative to expand the activity as part of its goal of reducing the amount of old auto parts that end up in landfills.[24]

Recycling gives autos "new life"

The automobile is one of the most highly recycled durable goods – second only to auto batteries. More than 75 percent of a vehicle is recycled after its useful life – including all metals, catalytic converters, batteries and many fluids. In addition, some familiar consumer products are finding a second life in today's cars and trucks. Recycled products now being used by Ford Motor Company include:

Source: Ford Motor Company

things get done, however, is different and this can be a source of both potential advantages and disadvantages.[25]

In terms of potential advantages, virtual teams can save time and travel expenses. They can allow members to work collectively in a time-efficient fashion, and without interpersonal difficulties that might otherwise occur—especially when the issues are controversial. A vice president for human resources at Marriott, for example, once called electronic meetings "the quietest, least stressful, most productive meetings you've ever had."[27] Virtual teams can also be easily expanded to include additional experts as needed, and the discussions and information shared among team members can be stored on-line for continuous updating and access. When problems do occur in virtual teams, they often arise because members have difficulty establishing good working relationships. Relations among team members can become depersonalized as the lack of face-to-face interaction limits the role of emotions and nonverbal cues in the communication process.[26]

Following some basic guidelines can help ensure that the advantages of virtual teams outweigh their disadvantages. The critical ingredients relate to the creation of positive impressions and the development of trust among team members with limited face-to-face meeting opportunities.[28]

- Virtual teams should begin with social messaging that allows members to exchange information about themselves to personalize the process.

- Virtual team members should be assigned clear roles so that they can focus while working alone and also know what others are doing.

- Virtual team members must join and engage the team with positive attitudes that support a willingness to work hard to meet team goals.

← Ingredients of successful virtual teams

SELF-MANAGING WORK TEAMS

In a growing number of organizations traditional work units consisting of first-level supervisors and their immediate subordinates are disappearing. They are being replaced with **self-managing work teams.** Sometimes called *autonomous work groups,* these are teams of workers whose jobs

○ Members of a **self-managing work team** have the authority to make decisions about how they share and complete their work.

have been redesigned to create a high degree of task interdependence and who have been given authority to make many decisions about how they go about doing the required work.[29]

Self-managing teams operate with participative decision making, shared tasks, and the responsibility for many of the managerial tasks performed by supervisors in more traditional settings. The "self-management" responsibilities include planning and scheduling work, training members in various tasks, sharing tasks, meeting performance goals, ensuring high quality, and solving day-to-day operating problems. In some settings, the team's authority may even extend to "hiring" and "firing" its members when necessary. A key feature is *multitasking,* in which team members each have the skills to perform several different jobs. As shown in *Figure 16.2,* typical characteristics of self-managing teams are as follows:

Characteristics of self-managing teams →

- Members are held collectively accountable for performance results.
- Members have discretion in distributing tasks within the team.
- Members have discretion in scheduling work within the team.
- Members are able to perform more than one job on the team.
- Members train one another to develop multiple job skills.
- Members evaluate one another's performance contributions.
- Members are responsible for the total quality of team products.

Within a self-managing team the emphasis is always on participation. The leader and members are expected to work together not only to do the required work but also to make the decisions that determine how it gets done. A true self-managing team emphasizes team decision making, shared tasks, high involvement, and collective responsibility for accomplished results. The expected advantages include better performance, de-

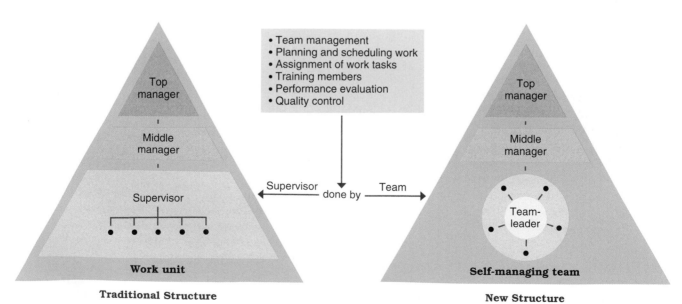

Figure 16.2 Organizational and management implications of self-managing work teams.

creased costs, and higher morale. Of course, these results are not guaranteed. Managing the transition to self-managing teams from more traditional work settings isn't always easy. The process requires leadership committed to both empowerment and a lot of support for these learning to work in new ways. As the concept of self-managing teams spreads globally, researchers are also examining the receptivity of different cultures to self-management concepts.[30] Such cultural dimensions as high-power distance and individualism, for example, may generate resistance that must be considered when implementing this and other team-based organizational practices.

HOW TEAMS WORK

Regardless of its form and purpose, any team must achieve three key results—perform tasks, satisfy members, and remain viable for the future.[31] On the *performance* side, a work group or team is expected to transform resource inputs (such as ideas, materials, and objects) into product outputs (such as a report, decision, service, or commodity) that have some value to the organization. The members of a team should also be able to experience *satisfaction* from both these performance results and their participation in the process. And, in respect to *future viability,* the team should have a social fabric and work climate that makes members willing and able to work well together in the future, again and again as needed.

WHAT IS AN EFFECTIVE TEAM?

An **effective team** is one that achieves and maintains high levels of task performance, member satisfaction, and viability for future action.[32] *Figure 16.3* shows how any team can be viewed as an open system that transforms various resource inputs into these outcomes. Among the important inputs are such things as the organizational setting, the nature of the task, the team size, and the membership characteristics.[33] Each of these factors influences the group process and helps set the stage for the accomplishment of group outcomes.

○ An **effective team** achieves high levels of task performance, membership satisfaction, and future viability.

Group Inputs

The *nature of the task* is always important. It affects how well a team can focus its efforts and how intense the group process needs to be to

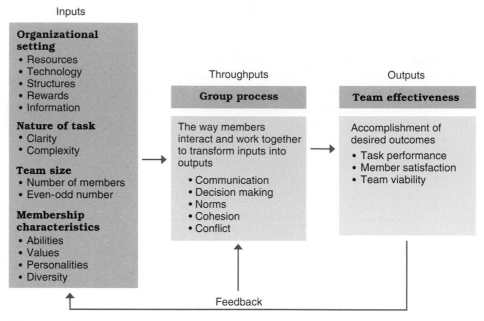

Figure 16.3 An open-systems model of work team effectiveness.

get the job done. Clearly defined tasks make it easier for team members to combine their work efforts. Complex tasks require more information exchange and intense interaction than do simpler tasks. The *organizational setting* can also affect how team members relate to one another and apply their skills toward task accomplishment. A key issue is the amount of support provided in terms of information, material resources, technology, organization structures, available rewards, and spatial arrangements. Increasingly, for example, organizations are being architecturally designed to directly facilitate teamwork. At SEI Investments, employees work in a large, open space without cubicles or dividers; each has a private set of office furniture and fixtures—but all on wheels; all technology easily plugs and unplugs from suspended power beams that run overhead. Project teams convene and disband as needed, and people easily meet and converse intensely with the ebb and flow of work all day.[34]

Team size affects how members work together, handle disagreements, and reach agreements. The number of potential interactions increases geometrically as teams increase in size, and communications become more congested. Teams larger than about six or seven members can be difficult to manage for the purpose of creative problem solving. When voting is required, teams with odd numbers of members help prevent "ties." In all teams, the *membership characteristics* are also important. Teams must have members with the right abilities, or skill mix, to master and perform tasks well. They must also have values and personalities that are sufficiently compatible for everyone to work well together.

○ **Group process** is the way team members work together to accomplish tasks.

Group Process

Although having the right inputs available to a team is important, it is not a guarantee of effectiveness. **Group process** counts too. This is the way the members of any team actually work together as they transform inputs into outputs. Also called *group dynamics,* the process aspects of any group or team include how members communicate with one another, make decisions, and handle conflicts, among other things. When the process breaks down and the internal dynamics fail in any way, team effectiveness can suffer. This *Team Effectiveness Equation* is a helpful reminder: Team effectiveness = quality of inputs + (process gains − process losses).

Team Diversity

Team diversity, in the form of different values, personalities, experiences, demographics, and cultures among the membership, can present significant group process challenges. The more homogeneous the team—the more similar the members are to one another—the easier it is to manage relationships. As team diversity increases, so too does the complexity of interpersonal relationships among members. But with the complications also come special opportunities. The more heterogeneous the team—the more diversity among members—the greater the variety of available ideas, perspectives, and experiences that can add value to problem solving and task performance.

In teamwork, as with organizations at large, the diversity lesson is very clear. There is a lot to gain when membership diversity is valued and well managed. The process challenge is to maximize the advantages of team diversity while minimizing its potential disadvantages. In the international arena, for example, research indicates that culturally diverse work teams have more difficulty learning how to work well together than do culturally homogeneous teams.[35] They tend to struggle more in the early stages of working together. But once the process challenges are successfully mastered, the diverse teams eventually prove to be more creative than the homogeneous ones.

www.rockport.com

When Angel Martinez was CEO of Rockport Co., he expanded the top management team to implement change and new performance norms. Says Martinez, "The easiest thing is getting rid of everyone, but that can create many more problems in the long run."

STAGES OF TEAM DEVELOPMENT

A synthesis of research on small groups suggests that there are five distinct phases in the life cycle of any team:[36]

1. *Forming*—a stage of initial orientation and interpersonal testing.
2. *Storming*—a stage of conflict over tasks and working as a team.
3. *Norming*—a stage of consolidation around task and operating agendas.
4. *Performing*—a stage of teamwork and focused task performance.
5. *Adjourning*—a stage of task completion and disengagement.

Stages of team development

Forming Stage

The forming stage involves the first entry of individual members into a team. This is a stage of initial task orientation and interpersonal testing. As individuals come together for the first time or two, they ask a number of questions: "What can or does the team offer me?" "What will I be asked to contribute?" "Can my needs be met while my efforts serve the task needs of the team?"

In the forming stage, people begin to identify with other members and with the team itself. They are concerned about getting acquainted, establishing interpersonal relationships, discovering what is considered acceptable behavior, and learning how others perceive the team's task. This may also be a time when some members rely on or become temporarily dependent on another member who appears "powerful" or especially "knowledgeable." Such things as prior experience with team members in other contexts and individual impressions of organization philosophies, goals, and policies may also affect member relationships in new work teams. Difficulties in the forming stage tend to be greater in more culturally and demographically diverse teams.

Storming Stage

The storming stage of team development is a period of high emotionality. Tension often emerges between members over tasks and interpersonal concerns. There may be periods of outright hostility and infighting. Coalitions or cliques may form around personalities or interests. Subteams form around areas of agreement and disagreement involving group tasks and/or the manner of operations. Conflict may develop as individuals compete to impose their preferences on others and to become influential in the group's status structure.

Important changes occur in the storming stage as task agendas become clarified and members begin to understand one another's interpersonal styles. Here attention begins to shift toward obstacles that may stand in the way of task accomplishment. Efforts are made to find ways to meet team goals while also satisfying individual needs. Failure in the storming stage can be a lasting liability, whereas success in the storming stage can set a strong foundation for later team effectiveness.

Norming Stage

Cooperation is an important issue for teams in the norming stage. At this point, members of the team begin to become coordinated as a working unit and tend to operate with shared rules of conduct. The team feels a sense of leadership, with each member starting to play useful roles. Most

Creative team workouts are designed to improve competitiveness

When Richard Ellenberger became CEO of Broadwing, Inc., he challenged employees with a novel approach to team development. He gave teams cardboard and tapes, and had them build boats to race one another in a swimming pool. His point? Get the workers thinking creatively and as a team. He sent 25 employees to NASCAR legend Richard Petty's racing school to learn to drive cars at over 120 mph. His point? Speed was essential to Broadwing's competitive strategy, and he wanted it to become part of the corporate culture. He held a company retreat at a Cincinnati aquarium and had sushi delivered for everyone. Employees ate sushi while staring at the live fish swimming in the aquarium. His point? This was supposed to inspire them to be more aggressive in attacking and trying to devour Broadwing's competition.[38]

interpersonal hostilities give way to a precarious balancing of forces as norming builds initial integration. Harmony is emphasized, but minority viewpoints may be discouraged.

In the norming stage, members are likely to develop initial feelings of closeness, a division of labor, and a sense of shared expectations. This helps protect the team from disintegration. Holding the team together may become even more important than successful task accomplishment.

Performing Stage

Teams in the performing stage are more mature, organized, and well functioning. This is a stage of total integration in which team members are able to deal in creative ways with both complex tasks and any interpersonal conflicts. The team operates with a clear and stable structure, and members are motivated by team goals.

The primary challenges of teams in the performing stage are to continue refining the operations and relationships essential to working as an integrated unit. Such teams need to remain coordinated with the larger organization and adapt successfully to changing conditions over time. A team that has achieved total integration will score high on the criteria of team maturity shown in *Figure 16.4*.[37]

Adjourning Stage

The final stage of team development is adjourning, when team members prepare to achieve closure and disband. Ideally, temporary committees, task forces, and project teams disband with a sense that important goals have been accomplished. This may be an emotional time, and disbandment should be managed with this possibility in mind. For members who

	Very poor			Very good	
1. Trust among members	1	2	3	4	5
2. Feedback mechanisms	1	2	3	4	5
3. Open communications	1	2	3	4	5
4. Approach to decisions	1	2	3	4	5
5. Leadership sharing	1	2	3	4	5
6. Acceptance of goals	1	2	3	4	5
7. Valuing diversity	1	2	3	4	5
8. Member cohesiveness	1	2	3	4	5
9. Support for each other	1	2	3	4	5
10. Performance norms	1	2	3	4	5
	Where you don't want to be			Where you do want to be	

Figure 16.4 Criteria for assessing the maturity of a team.

have worked together intensely for a period of time, breaking up the close relationships may be painful. In all cases, the team would like to disband with members feeling they would work with one another again sometime in the future. Members should be acknowledged for their contributions and praised for the group's overall success.

NORMS AND COHESIVENESS

○ A **norm** is a behavior, rule, or standard expected to be followed by team members.

A **norm** is a behavior expected of team members.[39] It is a "rule" or "standard" that guides their behavior. When violated, a norm may be enforced with reprimands and other sanctions. In the extreme, violation of a norm can result in a member being expelled from a team or socially ostracized by other members. The *performance norm,* which defines the level of work effort and performance that team members are expected to contribute, is extremely important. In general, work groups and teams with positive performance norms are more successful in accomplishing task objectives than are teams with negative performance norms. Other important team norms relate to such things as helpfulness, participation, timeliness, quality, and innovation.

Team leaders should help and encourage members to develop norms that support organizational objectives. During forming and storming steps of development, for example, norms relating to membership issues such as expected attendance and levels of commitment are important. By the time the stage of performing is reached, norms relating to adaptability and change become most relevant. Guidelines for *how to build positive group norms* are:[40]

How to build positive norms

- Act as a positive role model.
- Reinforce the desired behaviors with rewards.
- Control results by performance reviews and regular feedback.
- Train and orient new members to adopt desired behaviors.
- Recruit and select new members who exhibit the desired behaviors.
- Hold regular meetings to discuss progress and ways of improving.
- Use team decision-making methods to reach agreement.

○ **Cohesiveness** is the degree to which members are attracted to and motivated to remain part of a team.

Team members vary in the degree to which they accept and adhere to group norms. Conformity to norms is largely determined by the strength of group **cohesiveness,** the degree to which members are attracted to and motivated to remain part of a team.[41] Persons in a highly cohesive team value their membership and strive to maintain positive relationships with other team members. They experience satisfaction from team identification and interpersonal relationships. Because of this they tend to conform to the norms. Importantly, this can be good or bad for organizations; it depends on whether or not the performance norm is positive.

Look at *Figure 16.5.* When the performance norm of a team is positive, high cohesion and the resulting conformity to norms has a beneficial effect on overall team performance. This is a "best-case" scenario for both the manager and the organization. Competent team members work hard and reinforce one another's task accomplishments while experiencing satisfaction with the team. But when the performance norm is negative in a cohesive team, high conformity to the norm can have undesirable results. The figure shows this as a "worst-case" scenario where team performance suffers from restricted work efforts by members. Be-

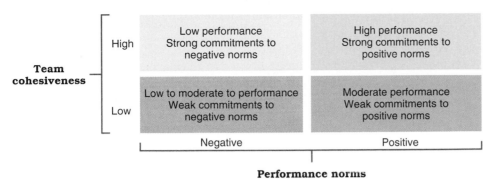

Figure 16.5 How cohesiveness and norms influence team performance.

tween these two extremes are mixed situations of moderate to low performance.

To achieve and maintain the best-case scenario shown in the figure managers should be skilled at influencing both the norms and cohesiveness of any team. They will want to build and maintain high cohesiveness in teams whose performance norms are positive. Guidelines on *how to increase cohesion* include:

- Induce agreement on team goals.
- Increase membership homogeneity.
- Increase interactions among members.
- Decrease team size.
- Introduce competition with other teams.
- Reward team rather than individual results.
- Provide physical isolation from other teams.

← How to increase team cohesiveness

TASK AND MAINTENANCE NEEDS

Research on the social psychology of groups identifies two types of activities that are essential if team members are to work well together over time.[42] **Task activities** contribute directly to the team's performance purpose, and **maintenance activities** support the emotional life of the team as an ongoing social system. Although the team leader or supervisor will often handle them, the responsibility for both types of activities should be shared and distributed among all team members. Any one can help lead a team by acting in ways that satisfy its task and maintenance needs. This concept of *distributed leadership in teams* makes every member continually responsible for both recognizing when task or maintenance activities are needed and taking actions to provide them.

Figure 16.6 offers useful insights on distributed leadership in teams. Leading through task activities involves making an effort to define and solve problems and advance work toward performance results. Without the relevant task activities, such as initiating agendas, sharing information, and others listed in the figure, teams will have difficulty accomplishing their objectives. Leading through maintenance activities, by contrast, helps strengthen and perpetuate the team as a social system. When the maintenance activities such as encouraging others and reducing tensions are performed well, good interpersonal relationships are

○ A **task activity** is an action taken by a team member that directly contributes to the group's performance purpose.

○ A **maintenance activity** is an action taken by a team member that supports the emotional life of the group.

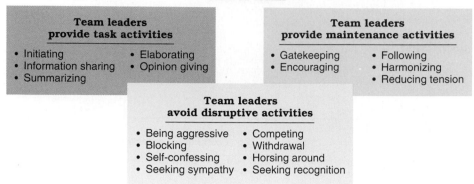

Figure 16.6 Distributed leadership helps teams meet task and maintenance needs.

achieved and the ability of the team to stay together over the longer term is ensured.

Both team task and maintenance activities stand in distinct contrast to the *dysfunctional activities* also described in Figure 16.6. Activities such as withdrawing and horsing around are usually self-serving to the individual member. They detract from, rather than enhance, team effectiveness. Unfortunately, very few teams are immune to dysfunctional behavior by members. Everyone shares in the responsibility for minimizing its occurrence and meeting the distributed leadership needs of a team by contributing functional task and maintenance behaviors.

COMMUNICATION NETWORKS

Figure 16.7 depicts three interaction patterns and communication networks that are common in teams.[43] When teams are interacting intensively and their members are working closely together on tasks, close coordination of activities is needed. This need is best met by a **decentralized communication network** in which all members communicate directly with one another. Sometimes this is called the *all-channel* or *star communication network*. At other times and in other situations team members work on tasks independently, with the required work being divided up among them. Activities are coordinated and results pooled by a central point of control. Most communication flows back and forth between individual members and this hub or center point. This creates a **centralized communication network** as shown in the figure. Sometimes this is called a *wheel* or *chain communication structure*. When teams are composed of subgroups experiencing issue-specific disagreements, such as a temporary debate over the best means to achieve a goal, the resulting interaction pattern often involves a *restricted communication network*. Here, polarized subgroups contest one another and may even engage in antagonistic relations. Communication between the subgroups is limited and biased, with negative consequences for group process and effectiveness.

The best teams use communication networks in the right ways, at the right times, and for the right tasks. Centralized communication networks

○ A **decentralized communication network** allows all members to communicate directly with one another.

○ In a **centralized communication network,** communication flows only between individual members and a hub or center point.

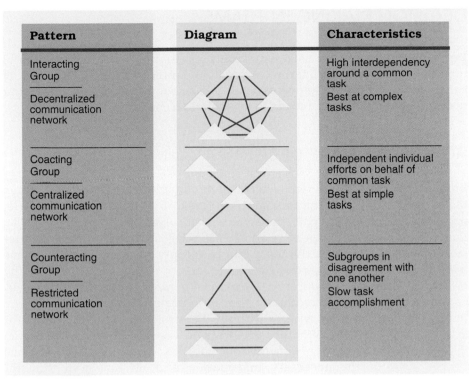

Pattern	Diagram	Characteristics
Interacting Group Decentralized communication network		High interdependency around a common task Best at complex tasks
Coacting Group Centralized communication network		Independent individual efforts on behalf of common task Best at simple tasks
Counteracting Group Restricted communication network		Subgroups in disagreement with one another Slow task accomplishment

Figure 16.7 Interaction patterns and communication networks in teams. *Source:* John R. Schermerhorn, Jr., James G. Hunt, and Richard N. Osborn, *Organizational Behavior,* 8th ed. (New York: Wiley, 2003), p. 347. Used by permission.

seem to work better on simple tasks.[44] These tasks require little creativity, information processing, and problem solving and lend themselves to more centralized control. The reverse is true for more complex tasks, where interacting groups do better. Here, the decentralized networks work well since they are able to support the more intense interactions and information sharing required to perform complicated tasks. When teams get complacent, the conflict among co-acting groups can be a source of creativity and critical evaluation. But when subgroups have difficulty communicating with one another, task accomplishment typically suffers for the short run at least.

Be sure you can • define the term group effectiveness • identify inputs that influence group effectiveness • define the term group process, and explain its influence on team effectiveness • discuss how membership diversity influences team effectiveness • list five stages of group development • illustrate how group members act in each stage • define the term group norm and list ways to build positive group norms • define the term cohesiveness and list ways to increase and decrease group cohesion • explain how norms and cohesiveness interact to influence group performance • differentiate task, maintenance, and disruptive activities by group members • describe how and when groups should use decentralized and centralized communication networks

Learning check 3

DECISION MAKING IN TEAMS

○ **Decision making** is the process of making choices among alternative courses of action.

Decision making, discussed extensively in Chapter 7, is the process of making choices among alternative possible courses of action. It is one of the most important group processes. It is also complicated by the fact that decisions in teams can be made in several different ways.

HOW TEAMS MAKE DECISIONS

Edgar Schein, a respected scholar and consultant, notes that teams make decisions by at least six methods: lack of response authority rule, minority rule, majority rule, consensus, and unanimity.[45] In *decision by lack of response,* one idea after another is suggested without any discussion taking place. When the team finally accepts an idea, all others have been bypassed and discarded by simple lack of response rather than by critical evaluation. In *decision by authority rule,* the leader, manager, committee head, or some other authority figure makes a decision for the team. This can be done with or without discussion and is very time efficient. Whether the decision is a good one or a bad one, however, depends on whether the authority figure has the necessary information and on how well this approach is accepted by other team members. In *decision by minority rule,* two or three people are able to dominate or "railroad" the team into making a mutually agreeable decision. This is often done by providing a suggestion and then forcing quick agreement by challenging the team with such statements as "Does anyone object? . . . Let's go ahead, then."

REALITY CHECK 16.2

Getting to group consensus

Everyone talks about group consensus, but we are often disappointed in our abilities to reach it. The truth of the matter is that consensus is only possible when the members of a team do the right things to make it possible. Do you know how to help move a team toward consensus? Take the online "Reality Check" to learn more about guidelines for reaching consensus.

One of the most common ways teams make decisions, especially when early signs of disagreement arise, is *decision by majority rule.* Here, formal voting may take place, or members may be polled to find the majority viewpoint. This method parallels the democratic political system and is often used without awareness of its potential problems. The very process of voting can create coalitions; that is, some people will be "winners" and others will be "losers" when the final vote is tallied. Those in the minority—the "losers"—may feel left out or discarded without having had a fair say. They may be unenthusiastic about implementing the decision of the "majority," and lingering resentments may impair team effectiveness in the future. There is no better example of the dynamics associated with close voting than the American presidential elections of 2000, and the great controversy over Bush/Gore vote tallies in Florida.

Teams are often encouraged to follow *decision by consensus.* This is where full discussion leads to one alternative being favored by most members and the other members agree to support it. When a consensus is reached, even those who may have opposed the chosen course of action know that they have been heard and have had an opportunity to influence the decision outcome. Such consensus does not require unanimity. But it does require that team members be able to argue, engage in reasonable conflict, and still get along with and respect one another.[46] And it requires that there be the opportunity for any dissenting members to know that they have been able to speak and that they have been listened to.

A *decision by unanimity* may be the ideal state of affairs. Here, all team members agree on the course of action to be taken. This is a logically perfect method for decision making in teams, but it is also extremely difficult to attain in actual practice. One of the reasons that teams sometimes turn to authority decisions, majority voting, or even minority decisions, in fact, is the difficulty of managing the team process to achieve consensus or unanimity.

ASSETS AND LIABILITIES OF GROUP DECISIONS

The best teams don't limit themselves to just one decision-making method. Instead, they vary methods to best fit the problems at hand, in true contingency management fashion. A very important team leadership skill is the ability to help a team choose the "best" decision method—one that provides for a timely and quality decision and one to which the members are highly committed. This reasoning is consistent with the Vroom–Jago leader-participation model discussed in Chapter 13.[47] You should recall that this model describes how leaders should utilize the full range of individual, consultative, and group decision methods as they resolve daily problems. To do this well, however, team leaders must understand the potential assets and potential liabilities of group decisions.[48]

The potential *advantages of group decision making* are significant. Because of this, the general argument is that team decisions should be sought whenever time and other circumstances permit. Team decisions make greater amounts of information, knowledge, and expertise available to solve problems. They expand the number of action alternatives that are examined; they help groups to avoid tunnel vision and tendencies to consider only a limited range of options. Team decisions increase the understanding and acceptance of outcomes by members. And importantly, team decisions increase the commitments of members to follow through to implement the decision once made. Simply put, team decisions can result in quality decisions that all members work hard to make successful.

The potential *disadvantages of group decision making* largely trace to the difficulties that can be experienced in group process. In a team deci-

---

High-tech runs with the support of teams

Teams of all types are in at Motorola plants around the world. In Penang, Malaysia, a team spirit rallies workers, who in one year submitted 41,000 suggestions for improvement and saved the firm some $2 million. The Malaysian practices have been exported to other Motorola locations. Says one manager who spent three years working there: "The whole plant in Penang had this craving for learning." Motorola's Total Customer Satisfaction Teams bring together diverse members to address a specific goal, such as reduction in cycle time, quality improvement, profit improvement, environmental leadership, or process improvement. Teams also are critical to outreach and community. A Workforce & Education Team in Arizona links Motorola workers with educators in the community in an attempt to strengthen the educational system so that graduates have the skills and capabilities needed to compete in tomorrow's workplace.[50]

sion there may be social pressure to conform. Individual members may feel intimidated or compelled to go along with the apparent wishes of others. There may be minority domination, where some members feel forced or "railroaded" to accept a decision advocated by one vocal individual or small coalition. Also, the time required to make team decisions can sometimes be a disadvantage. As more people are involved in the dialogue and discussion, decision making takes longer. This added time may be costly, even prohibitively so, in certain circumstances.[49]

GROUPTHINK

A high level of cohesiveness can sometimes be a disadvantage during decision making. Members of very cohesive teams feel so strongly about the group that they may not want to do anything that might detract from feelings of goodwill. This may cause them to publicly agree with actual or suggested courses of action, while privately having serious doubts about them. Strong feelings of team loyalty can make it hard for members to criticize and evaluate one another's ideas and suggestions. Unfortunately, there are times when desires to hold the team together at all costs and avoid disagreements may result in poor decisions.

○ **Groupthink** is a tendency for highly cohesive teams to lose their evaluative capabilities.

Psychologist Irving Janis calls this phenomenon **groupthink,** the tendency for highly cohesive groups to lose their critical evaluative capabilities.[51] You should be alert to spot the following *symptoms of groupthink* when they occur in your decision-making teams:

Symptoms of groupthink

- *Illusions of invulnerability:* Members assume that the team is too good for criticism or beyond attack.
- *Rationalizing unpleasant and disconfirming data:* Members refuse to accept contradictory data or to thoroughly consider alternatives.
- *Belief in inherent group morality:* Members act as though the group is inherently right and above reproach.
- *Stereotyping competitors as weak, evil, and stupid:* Members refuse to look realistically at other groups.
- *Applying direct pressure to deviants to conform to group wishes:* Members refuse to tolerate anyone who suggests the team may be wrong.
- *Self-censorship by members:* Members refuse to communicate personal concerns to the whole team.
- *Illusions of unanimity:* Members accept consensus prematurely, without testing its completeness.
- *Mind guarding:* Members protect the team from hearing disturbing ideas or outside viewpoints.

Groupthink can occur anywhere. In fact, Janis ties a variety of well-known historical blunders to the phenomenon, including the lack of preparedness of the United States's naval forces for the Japanese attack on Pearl Harbor, the Bay of Pigs invasion under President Kennedy, and the many roads that led to the United States's involvement in Vietnam. When and if you encounter groupthink, Janis suggests taking action along the lines shown in *Manager's Notepad 16.3.*

CREATIVITY IN TEAM DECISION MAKING

Among the potential benefits that teams can bring to organizations is increased creativity. Two techniques that are particularly helpful for creativ-

How to avoid groupthink

- Assign the role of critical evaluator to each team member; encourage a sharing of viewpoints.
- Don't, as a leader, seem partial to one course of action; do absent yourself from meetings at times to allow free discussion.
- Create subteams to work on the same problems and then share their proposed solutions.
- Have team members discuss issues with outsiders and report back on their reactions.
- Invite outside experts to observe team activities and react to team processes and decisions.
- Assign one member to play a "devil's advocate" role at each team meeting.
- Hold a "second-chance" meeting after consensus is apparently achieved to review the decision.

ity in decision making are brainstorming and the nominal group technique.[52] Both can now be pursued in computer-mediated or virtual team discussions, as well as in face-to-face formats.

In **brainstorming,** teams of 5 to 10 members meet to generate ideas. Brainstorming teams typically operate within these guidelines. *All criticism is ruled out*—judgment or evaluation of ideas must be withheld until the idea-generation process has been completed. *"Freewheeling" is welcomed*—the wilder or more radical the idea, the better. *Quantity is important*—the greater the number of ideas, the greater the likelihood of obtaining a superior idea. *Building on one another's ideas is encouraged*—participants should suggest how ideas of others can be turned into better ideas, or how two or more ideas can be joined into still another hybrid idea.

O **Brainstorming** engages group members in an open, spontaneous discussion of problems and ideas.

By prohibiting criticism, the brainstorming method reduces fears of ridicule or failure on the part of individuals. Ideally, this results in more enthusiasm, involvement, and a freer flow of ideas among members. But there are times when team members have very different opinions and goals. The differences may be so extreme that a brainstorming meeting might deteriorate into antagonistic arguments and harmful conflicts. In such cases, a **nominal group technique** could help. This approach uses a highly structured meeting agenda to allow everyone to contribute ideas without the interference of evaluative comments by others. Participants are first asked to work alone and respond in writing with possible solutions to a stated problem. Ideas are then shared in round-robin fashion without any criticism or discussion; all ideas are recorded as they are presented. Ideas are next discussed and clarified in round-robin sequence, with no evaluative comments allowed. Next, members individually and silently follow a written voting procedure that allows for all alternatives to be rated or ranked in priority order. Finally, the last two steps are repeated as needed to further clarify the process.

O The **nominal group technique** structures interaction among team members discussing problems and ideas.

Learning check 4

Be sure you can • illustrate how groups make decisions by authority rule, minority rule, majority rule, consensus, and unanimity • list advantages and disadvantages of group decision making • define the term groupthink • identify the symptoms of groupthink • illustrate how brainstorming and the nominal group techniques can improve creativity in decision making

LEADING HIGH-PERFORMANCE TEAMS

When we think of the word "team," sporting teams often come to mind. And we know these teams certainly have their share of problems. Members slack off or become disgruntled; even world-champion teams have losing streaks; and, the most highly talented players sometimes lose motivation, quibble with other team members, and lapse into performance slumps. When these things happen, the owners, managers, and players are apt to take corrective action to "rebuild the team" and restore what we have called team effectiveness. Work teams are teams in a similar sense. Even the most mature work team is likely to experience problems over time. When such difficulties arise, structured efforts at team building can help.

THE TEAM-BUILDING PROCESS

○ **Team building** is a sequence of collaborative activities to gather and analyze data on a team and make changes to increase its effectiveness.

Team building is a sequence of planned activities used to gather and analyze data on the functioning of a team, and to implement constructive changes to increase its operating effectiveness.[53] Most systematic approaches to team building follow the steps described in *Figure 16.8.* The cycle begins with awareness that a problem may exist or may develop within the team. Members then work together to gather and analyze data so that the problem is fully understood. Action plans are made by members and collectively implemented. Results are evaluated by team members working together. Any difficulties or new problems that are discovered serve to recycle the team-building process. Consider this added detail to the case featured in Figure 16.8.

www.worthington industries.com

At Worthington Industries, the innovative Ohio steelmaker, applicants for new positions must pass the team test. They interview with members of their potential teams and then must serve a 90-day probation period before being voted on by an employee council of coworkers.

> The consultant received a call from the hospital's director of personnel. He indicated that a new hospital president felt the top management team lacked cohesiveness and was not working well together as a team. The consultant agreed to facilitate a team-building activity that would include a day-long retreat at a nearby resort hotel. The process began when the consultant conducted interviews with the president and other members of the executive team. During the retreat, the consultant reported these results to the team as a whole. He indicated that the hospital's goals were generally understood by all but that they weren't clear enough to allow agreement on action priorities. Furthermore, he reported that interpersonal problems between the director of nursing services and the director of administration were making it difficult for the team to work together comfortably. These and other issues were addressed by the team at the retreat. Working sometimes in small subteams, and at other times together as a whole, they agreed first of all that action should be taken to clarify the hospital's overall mission and create a priority list of objectives for the current year. Led by the

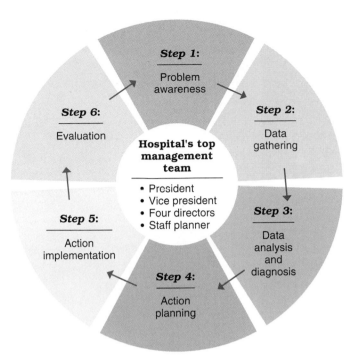

Figure 16.8 Steps in the team-building process: case of the hospital top management team.

president, activity on this task would involve all team members and was targeted for completion within a month. The president asked that progress on the action plans be reviewed at each of the next three monthly executive staff meetings. Everyone agreed.

This example introduces team building as a way to assess a work team's functioning and take corrective action to improve its effectiveness. It can and should become a regular work routine. There are many ways to gather data on team functioning, including structured and unstructured interviews, questionnaires, and team meetings. Regardless of the method used, the basic principle of team building remains the same. The process requires that a careful and collaborative assessment of the team's inputs, processes, and results be made. All members should participate in data gathering, assist in data analysis, and collectively decide on actions to be taken.

Sometimes teamwork can be improved when people share the challenges of unusual and even physically demanding experiences. On a fall day, for example, a team of employees from American Electric Power (AEP) went to an outdoor camp for a day of team-building activities. They worked on problems like how to get six members through a spider-web maze of bungee cords strung 2 feet above the ground. When her colleagues lifted Judy Gallo into their hands to pass her over the obstacle, she was nervous. But a trainer told the team this was just like solving a problem together at the office. The spider web was just another performance constraint like difficult policies or financial limits they might face at work. After "high-fives" for making it through the Web, Judy's team jumped tree stumps together, passed hula hoops while holding hands, and more. Says one team trainer, "We throw clients into situations to try and bring out the traits of a good team."[54]

TAKE IT TO THE CASE

Big Bertha's team hits a long ball

He is described as "a man of vision, yet very focused with the willingness to undertake challenges others couldn't—or wouldn't—with a work-hard ethic that inspired us all." Ely Callaway, founder of *Callaway Golf,* maker of the famous "Big Bertha" driver, certainly was special. The goal he infused in his firm is continuous improvement, doing better than competitors and the firm's own past work. Callaway remains self-described as committed to producing golf products that are "Demonstrably Superior and Pleasingly Different." The work environment at Callaway is different too, with a campus-like setting where employees can ride company bicycles building-to-building and the license on a corporate vice president's car reads WRK4FUN. Even as the firm has grown from a group of 5 in 1982 to over 2400 employees today, it strives for a family atmosphere and a comfortable, fun work culture. New members of the Callaway team are expected to have integrity, be honest and daring, and to work hard, with enthusiasm and a sense of personal accountability.[56]

SUCCESS FACTORS IN TEAMS

Among the many developments in the workplace today, the continuing effort to refine and apply creative team concepts is high on most executives' action agendas. But whether the group or team is working at the top, bottom, cross-functionally, or in direct customer service, high-performance results can't be left to chance. There are too many forces in the environment and group dynamics that can lead teams astray. Team success is only achieved through the special efforts of leaders and members alike. We know, for example, that high-performance teams generally share these characteristics.[55]

Characteristics of high-performance teams

• a clear and elevating goal

• a task-driven and results-oriented structure

• competent and committed members who work hard

• a collaborative climate

• high standards of excellence

• external support and recognition

• and strong, principled leadership

TEAM LEADERSHIP CHALLENGES

The last point on this list—the need for strong and principled leadership—may be the key to them all. In their book, *Teamwork: What Can Go Right/What Can Go Wrong,* Carl Larson and Frank LaFasto state: "The right person in a leadership role can add tremendous value to any collective effort, even to the point of sparking the outcome with an intangible kind of magic."[57] They further point out that leaders of high-performing teams share many characteristics with the "transformational leader" examined in Chapter 13.

Successful team leaders *establish a clear vision of the future.* This vision serves as a goal that inspires hard work and the quest for performance excellence; it creates a sense of shared purpose. Successful team leaders help to *create change.* They are dissatisfied with the status quo, influence team members toward similar dissatisfaction, and infuse the team with the motivation to change in order to become better. Finally, successful team leaders *unleash talent.* They make sure the team is staffed with members who have the right skills and abilities. And they make sure these people are highly motivated to use their talents to achieve the group's performance objectives.

The best leaders know that teams are hard work, but that they are also worth it. You don't get a high-performing team by just bringing a group of people together and giving them a shared name or title. Leaders of high-performance teams create supportive climates in which team members know what to expect from the leader and each other, and know what the leader expects from them. They empower team members. By personal example they demonstrate the importance of setting aside self-interests to support the team's goals. And, they view team building as an ongoing leadership responsibility. An important aspect of this responsibility is developing future leaders for the team. Joe Liemandt, founder and CEO of the software firm Trilogy, Inc., says: As Trilogy grew, one of the most important lessons we learned is that hiring for raw talent isn't enough. We had to build leaders. I believe you should always work to replace yourself."[58]

Be sure you can • define the term team building • illustrate how managers can use team building to improve group effectiveness • list three things that successful leaders do to create and maintain high-performance teams

Learning check 5

CHAPTER 16 STUDY GUIDE

Where We've Been

BACK TO PIXAR ANIMATION STUDIOS

The opening example of Pixar Animation Studios showed talented individuals working together in a highly creative setting. It also indicated that high performance by the firm depends on more than the presence of talented individuals; it requires that they be blended together into effective teams. In this chapter you learned about the nature of teams and different types of teams found in organizations. You learned about group effectiveness, the stages of team development, and the input factors that influence team performance. You also learned about group processes and how leaders build high-performing teams that sustain themselves with satisfied members.

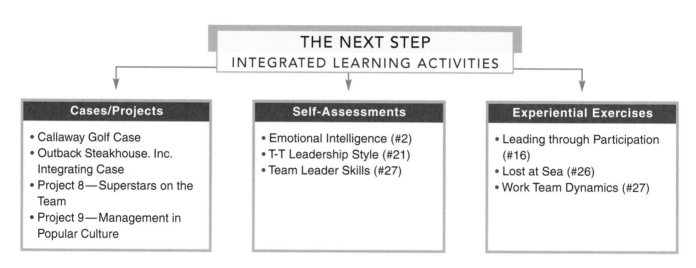

THE NEXT STEP
INTEGRATED LEARNING ACTIVITIES

Cases/Projects	Self-Assessments	Experiential Exercises
• Callaway Golf Case • Outback Steakhouse. Inc. Integrating Case • Project 8—Superstars on the Team • Project 9—Management in Popular Culture	• Emotional Intelligence (#2) • T-T Leadership Style (#21) • Team Leader Skills (#27)	• Leading through Participation (#16) • Lost at Sea (#26) • Work Team Dynamics (#27)

STUDY QUESTIONS SUMMARY

1. How do teams contribute to organizations?

- A team is a collection of people working together to accomplish a common goal.
- Organizations operate as interlocking networks of formal work groups, which offer many benefits to the organizations and to their members.
- Teams help organizations through synergy in task performance, the creation of a whole that is greater than the sum of its parts.
- Teams help satisfy important needs for their members, providing various types of job support and social satisfactions.
- Social loafing and other problems can limit the performance of teams.

2. What are current trends in the use of teams?

- Teams are important mechanisms of empowerment and participation in the workplace.
- Committees and task forces are used to facilitate operations and allow special projects to be completed with creativity.
- Cross-functional teams bring members together from different departments and help improve lateral relations and integration in organizations.
- Employee involvement teams, such as the quality circle, allow employees to provide important insights into daily problem solving.

- New developments in information technology are making virtual teams, or computer-mediated teams, more commonplace.
- Self-managing teams are changing organizations by allowing team members to perform many tasks previously reserved for their supervisors.

3. How do teams work?

- An effective team achieves high levels of task performance, member satisfaction, and team viability.
- Important team input factors include the organizational setting, nature of the task, size, and membership characteristics.
- A team matures through various stages of development, including forming, storming, norming, performing, and adjourning.
- Norms are the standards or rules of conduct that influence the behavior of team members; cohesion is the attractiveness of the team to its members.
- In highly cohesive teams, members tend to conform to norms; the best situation for a manager or leader is a team with positive performance norms and high cohesiveness.
- Distributed leadership in serving a team's task and maintenance needs helps in achieving long-term effectiveness.
- Effective teams make use of alternative communication networks to best complete tasks.

4. How do teams make decisions?

- Teams can make decisions by lack of response, authority rule, minority rule, majority rule, consensus, and unanimity.
- The potential advantages of group decision making include having more information available and generating more understanding and commitment.
- The potential liabilities to group making include social pressures to conform and greater time requirements.
- Groupthink is a tendency of members of highly cohesive teams to lose their critical evaluative capabilities and make poor decisions.
- Techniques for improving creativity in teams include brainstorming and the nominal group technique.

5. What are the challenges of leading high-performance teams?

- Team building helps team members develop action plans for improving the way they work together and the results they accomplish.
- The team-building process should be data based and collaborative, involving a high level of participation by all team members.
- High-performance work teams have a clear and shared sense of purpose as well as a strong internal commitment to its accomplishment.

KEY TERMS REVIEW

Brainstorming (p. 425)
Centralized communication network (p. 420)
Cohesiveness (p. 419)
Committee (p. 409)
Cross-functional team (p. 409)
Decentralized communication network (p. 420)
Decision making (p. 422)

Effective team (p. 413)
Employee involvement team (p. 410)
Formal group (p. 408)
Group process (p. 414)
Groupthink (p. 424)
Informal group (p. 408)
Maintenance activity (p. 419)
Nominal group technique (p. 425)

Norm (p. 418)
Project team (p. 409)
Quality circle (p. 410)
Self-managing work teams (p. 411)
Social loafing (p. 406)
Synergy (p. 407)
Task activity (p. 419)
Task force (p. 409)
Team (p. 405)
Team building (p. 426)
Teamwork (p. 405)
Virtual team (p. 410)

SELF-TEST 16

MULTIPLE-CHOICE QUESTIONS:

1. When a group of people is able to achieve more than what its members could by working individually, this is called _____.
   (a) social loafing (b) consensus (c) viability (d) synergy

2. In an organization operating with self-managing teams, the traditional role of _____ is replaced by the role of team leader.
   (a) chief executive officer (b) first-line supervisor (c) middle manager (d) general manager

3. An effective team is defined as one that achieves high levels of task performance, member satisfaction, and _____.
   (a) resource efficiency (b) team viability (c) consensus (d) creativity

4. In the open-systems model of teams, the _____ is an important input factor.
   (a) communication network (b) decision-making method (c) performance norm (d) set of membership characteristics

5. A basic rule of team dynamics states that the greater the _____ in a team, the greater the conformity to norms.
   (a) membership diversity (b) cohesiveness (c) task structure (d) competition among members

6. Groupthink is most likely to occur in teams that are _____.
   (a) large in size (b) diverse in membership (c) high performing (d) highly cohesive

7. Gatekeeping is an example of a _____ activity that can help teams work effectively over time.
   (a) task (b) maintenance (c) team-building (d) decision-making

8. Members of a team tend to become more motivated and able to deal with conflict during the _____ stage of team development.
   (a) forming (b) norming (c) performing (d) adjourning

9. One way for a manager to build positive norms within a team is to _____.
   (a) act as a positive role model (b) increase group size (c) introduce groupthink (d) isolate the team from others

10. When teams are highly cohesive, _____.
    (a) members are high performers (b) members tend to be satisfied with their team membership (c) members have positive norms (d) the group achieves its goals

11. A "quality circle" is an example of how organizations try to use _____ teams for performance advantage.
    (a) virtual (b) informal (c) employee involvement (d) self-managing

12. It would be common to find members of self-managing work teams engaged in _____.
    (a) social loafing (b) multitasking (c) centralized communication (d) decision by authority rule

13. The "team effectiveness equation" states: Team effectiveness = quality of inputs + (_____ − process losses).
    (a) process gains (b) leadership impact (c) membership ability (d) problem complexity

14. A _____ decision is one in which all members agree on the course of action to be taken.
(a) consensus (b) unanimity (c) majority (d) synergy

15. To increase the cohesiveness of a group, a manager would be best off _____.
(a) starting competition with other groups (b) increasing the group size (c) acting as a positive role model (d) introducing a new member

SHORT-RESPONSE QUESTIONS:

16. How can a manager improve team effectiveness by modifying inputs?

17. What is the relationship among a team's cohesiveness, performance norms, and performance results?

18. How would a manager know that a team is suffering from groupthink (give two symptoms) and what could the manager do about it (give two responses)?

19. What makes a self-managing team different from a traditional work team?

APPLICATION QUESTION:

20. Marcos Martinez has just been appointed manager of a production team operating the 11 P.M. to 7 A.M. shift in a large manufacturing firm. An experienced manager, Marcos is concerned that the team members really like and get along well with one another, but they also appear to be restricting their task outputs to the minimum acceptable levels. What could Marcos do to improve things in this situation and why should he do them?

www.wiley.com/college/schermerhorn

17

Communication and interpersonal skills

Planning Ahead

After reading Chapter 17, you should be able to answer these questions in your own words.

CHAPTER 17 study questions

1. What is the communication process?

2. How can communication be improved?

3. How does perception influence communication?

4. How can we deal positively with conflict?

5. How can we negotiate successful agreements?

CENTER FOR CREATIVE LEADERSHIP—LEAD THE WAY WITH COMMUNICATION

The importance of communication and interpersonal skills in leadership development is mainstream at the internationally regarded Center for Creative Leadership. Headquartered in Greensboro, North Carolina, the center's mission is: "to advance the understanding, practice and development of leadership for the benefit of society worldwide." A branch in Brussels, Belgium, expands the center's reach to European managers.

We know that leaders need to effectively communicate with diverse audiences and use interpersonal skills to engage and enthuse others in their work. But a lot of managers have difficulties doing so. The Center for Creative Leadership helps managers gain better insights into their interpersonal styles and build leadership skills for personal and organizational success. It has a global reputation for excellence and has been ranked #1 by *Business Week* for executive education in leadership.

Coaching for leadership development is an important initiative within the center. When Richard S. Herlich came to the Center, he had been recently promoted to director of marketing for his firm. "I thought I had the perfect style," he said. He learned through role-playing that others viewed him as an aloof and poor communicator. After returning to his job and meeting with his subordinates to discuss his style, Herlich became more involved in their work projects. Another participant, Robert Siddall, received feedback that he was too structured and domineering. Center instructors worked with him to develop more positive relationships and to display a more "coaching" style of management. After he returned to his job, Siddall's performance ratings went up and his relationships with coworkers improved. He says, "If I start screaming and yelling, they say—'Old Bob, old Bob.'" The Center for Creative Leadership was founded on the initiative of H. Smith Richardson, Jr., a successful executive. He believed: "What organizations needed was not just leadership for the present and the near future, but a kind of innovative leadership with a broader focus and a longer view. Such leadership would be concerned not with profits, markets and business strategies alone, but with the place of business in society."[1]

Chapter 17 Learning Preview

The chapter opening example of the Center for Leadership introduced an organization devoted to leadership training that makes a difference—a real difference in the behavior of leaders. The Center uses a variety of learning approaches to help participants better understand themselves and their behavior when working with other persons. In this chapter you will learn about the communication process, communication barriers, and ways to become effective in interpersonal communication. You will learn about perception and how it influences communication through stereotypes and other perceptual distortions. You will also learn about the processes of conflict and negotiation, and how they can be engaged in positive and successful ways.

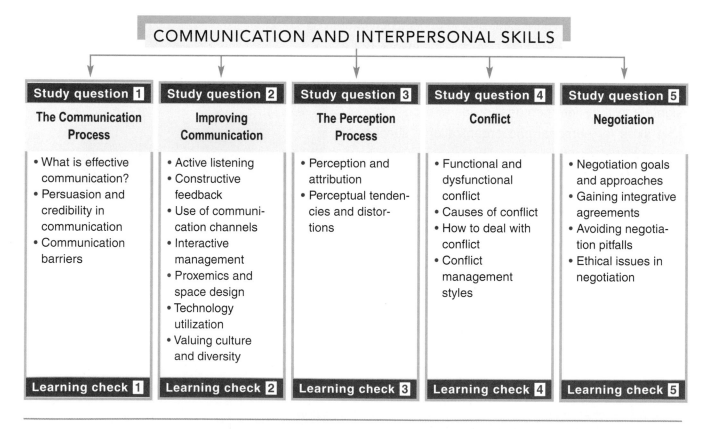

COMMUNICATION AND INTERPERSONAL SKILLS

Study question **1**	Study question **2**	Study question **3**	Study question **4**	Study question **5**
The Communication Process	**Improving Communication**	**The Perception Process**	**Conflict**	**Negotiation**
• What is effective communication? • Persuasion and credibility in communication • Communication barriers	• Active listening • Constructive feedback • Use of communication channels • Interactive management • Proxemics and space design • Technology utilization • Valuing culture and diversity	• Perception and attribution • Perceptual tendencies and distortions	• Functional and dysfunctional conflict • Causes of conflict • How to deal with conflict • Conflict management styles	• Negotiation goals and approaches • Gaining integrative agreements • Avoiding negotiation pitfalls • Ethical issues in negotiation
Learning check **1**	Learning check **2**	Learning check **3**	Learning check **4**	Learning check **5**

Anyone heading into the new workplace must understand that the work of managers and team leaders is highly interpersonal and communication intensive. Whether you work at the top building support for strategies and organizational goals or at lower levels interacting with others to support their work efforts and your own, communication and interpersonal skills are essential to your personal toolkit. Think back to the descriptions of managerial work by Henry Mintzberg, John Kotter, and others as discussed in Chapter 1. For Mintzberg, managerial success involves performing well as an information "nerve center," gathering information from and disseminating information to internal and external sources.[2] For Kotter, it depends largely on one's ability to build and maintain a complex web of interpersonal networks with insiders and outsiders so as to implement work priorities and agendas.[3] Says Pam Alexander, CEO of Ogilvy Public Relations Worldwide: "Relationships are the most powerful form of media. Ideas will only get you so far these days. Count on personal relationships to carry you further."[4]

The ability to communicate well both orally and in writing is a critical managerial skill and the foundation of effective leadership.[5] Through communication people exchange and share information with one another, and influence one another's attitudes, behaviors, and understandings. Communication allows managers to establish and maintain interpersonal relationships, listen to others, and otherwise gain the information needed to create an inspirational workplace. No manager can handle conflict, negotiate successfully, and succeed at leadership without being a good communicator. Any student portfolio should include adequate testimony to one's abilities to communicate well in interpersonal relationships, in various forms of writing and public speaking, and increasingly through the electronic medium of the computer.

THE COMMUNICATION PROCESS

Communication is an interpersonal process of sending and receiving symbols with messages attached to them. In more practical terms, the key elements in the communication process are shown in *Figure 17.1*. They include a *sender*, who is responsible for encoding an intended *message* into meaningful symbols, both verbal and nonverbal. The message is sent through a *communication channel* to a *receiver*, who then decodes or interprets its *meaning*. This interpretation, importantly, may or may not match the sender's original intentions. *Feedback*, when present, reverses the process and conveys the receiver's response back to the sender. Another way to view the communication process is as a series of questions. "Who?" (sender) "says what?" (message) "in what way?" (channel) "to whom?" (receiver) "with what result?" (interpreted meaning).

○ **Communication** is the process of sending and receiving symbols with meanings attached.

WHAT IS EFFECTIVE COMMUNICATION?

Effective communication occurs when the message is fully understood. The intended meaning of the sender and the interpreted meaning of the receiver are one and the same. However, the goal, effectiveness, in com-

○ In **effective communication** the intended meaning is fully understood by the receiver.

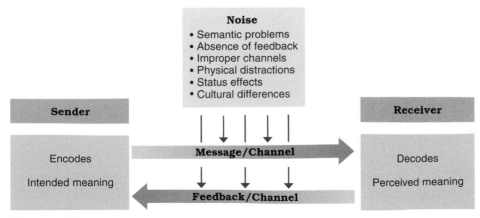

Figure 17.1 The interactive two-way process of interpersonal communication.

○ **Efficient communication** occurs at minimum cost.

munication is not always achieved. **Efficient communication** occurs at minimum cost in terms of resources expended. Time, in particular, is an important resource in the communication process. Picture your instructor taking the time to communicate individually with each student about this chapter. It would be virtually impossible. Even if it were possible, it would be costly. This is why managers often leave voice-mail messages and interact by e-mail rather than visit their subordinates personally. Simply put, these alternatives are more efficient ways to communicate than through one-on-one and face-to-face communications.

One problem is that efficient communications are not always effective. A low-cost approach such as an e-mail note to a distribution list may save time, but it does not always result in everyone getting the same meaning from the message. Without opportunities to ask questions and clarify the message, erroneous interpretations are possible. By the same token, an effective communication may not always be efficient. If a work team leader visits each team member individually to explain a new change in procedures, this may guarantee that everyone truly understands the change. But it may also be very costly in the demands it makes on the leader's time. A team meeting would be more efficient. In these and other ways, potential trade-offs between effectiveness and efficiency must be recognized in communication.

PERSUASION AND CREDIBILITY IN COMMUNICATION

Communication is not always just about sharing information or being "heard"; it often includes the desire of one party to influence or motivate the other in a desired way. Especially in management, one of the most important purposes of communication is **persuasion,** getting someone else to support the message being presented.[6]

○ **Persuasion** is presenting a message in a manner that casues the other person to support it.

Much of what happens in today's horizontal structures and organic designs is outside of the formal supervisor–subordinate relationship, and much of what happens within it is in the context of empowerment. Managers get things done by working with and persuading others who are their peers, teammates, coworkers. They get things done more by convincing than by order-giving. Furthermore, they must be able to persuade others over and over again in the dynamic and complex workplace; once is not enough.

In terms of the power bases discussed in Chapter 13 on leadership, personal powers of expertise and reference are essential to the art of effective persuasion. Scholar and consultant Jay Conger says that many managers "confuse persuasion with taking bold stands and aggressive arguing." He points out that this often leads to "counter persuasion" responses and to questions regarding the managers' credibility.[7] And without **credibility**—trust, respect and integrity in the eyes of others, he sees little chance that persuasion can be successful. Conger's advice is to build credibility for persuasive communication through expertise and relationships.

○ **Credibility** is trust, respect and integrity in the eyes of others.

To build *credibility through expertise,* you must be knowledgeable about the issue in question and/or have a successful track record in dealing with similar issues in the past. In a hiring situation where you are trying to persuade team members to select candidate A rather than B, for example, you had better be able to defend your reasons. And it will always be better if your past recommendations turned out to be good ones. To build *credibility through relationships,* you must have a good working relationship with the person to be persuaded. The iron rule of reference power should be remembered: It is always easier to get someone to do what you want if they like you. To return to the prior example, if you have to persuade your boss to support a special bonus package to attract candidates, a good relationship will add credibility to your request.

COMMUNICATION BARRIERS

Communication is a shared and two-way process that requires effort and skill on the part of both the sender and the receiver. **Noise,** as previously shown in Figure 17.1, is anything that interferes with the effectiveness of the communication process. For example, when Yoshihiro Wada was president of Mazda Corporation, he once met with representatives of the firm's American joint venture partner, Ford. But he had to use an interpreter. He estimated that 20 percent of his intended meaning was lost in the exchange between himself and the interpreter; another 20 percent was lost between the interpreter and the Americans, with whom he was ultimately trying to communicate.[9] In addition to the obvious problems when different languages are involved, common sources of noise in communication include poor choice of channels, poor written or oral expression, failure to recognize nonverbal signals, physical distractions, and status effects.

Poor Choice of Channels

A **communication channel** is the medium through which a message is conveyed from sender to receiver. Good managers choose the right communication channel, or combination of channels, to accomplish their intended purpose in a given situation.[10] In general, *written channels* are acceptable for simple messages that are easy to convey and for those that require extensive dissemination quickly. They are also important as documentation when formal policies or directives are being conveyed. *Spoken channels* work best for messages that are complex and difficult to convey, where immediate feedback to the sender is valuable. They are also more personal and can create a supportive, even inspirational, emotional climate.

Poor Written or Oral Expression

Communication will be effective only to the extent that the sender expresses a message in a way that can be clearly understood by the re-

MANAGER'S NOTEPAD　17.1　　How to make a successful presentation

- *Be prepared:* Know what you want to say; know how you want to say it; rehearse saying it.
- *Set the right tone:* Act audience centered; make eye contact; be pleasant and confident.
- *Sequence points:* State your purpose; make important points; follow with details; then summarize.
- *Support your points:* Give specific reasons for your points; state them in understandable terms.
- *Accent the presentation:* Use good visual aids; provide supporting "handouts" when possible.
- *Add the right amount of polish:* Attend to details; have room, materials, and arrangements ready to go.
- *Check your technology:* Check everything ahead of time; make sure it works and know how to use it.
- *Don't bet on the Internet:* Beware of plans to make real-time Internet visits; save sites on a disk and use a browser to open the file.
- *Be professional:* Be on time; wear appropriate attire; act organized, confident, and enthusiastic.

---

ceiver. This means that words must be well chosen and properly used to express the sender's intentions. Consider the following "bafflegab" found among some executive communications.

> *A business report said:* "Consumer elements are continuing to stress the fundamental necessity of a stabilization of the price structure at a lower level than exists at the present time." (*Translation:* Consumers keep saying that prices must go down and stay down.)

> *A manager said:* "Substantial economies were effected in this division by increasing the time interval between distribution of data-eliciting forms to business entities." (*Translation:* The division saved money by sending out fewer questionnaires.)

Both written and oral communication require skill. It isn't easy, for example, to write a concise letter or to express one's thoughts in a computer e-mail report. Any such message can easily be misunderstood. It takes practice and hard work to express yourself well. The same holds true for oral communication that takes place in telephone calls, face-to-face meetings, formal briefings, video conferences, and the like. *Manager's Notepad 17.1* identifies guidelines for an important communication situation—the executive briefing or formal presentation.[12]

Failure to Recognize Nonverbal Signals

○ **Nonverbal communication** takes place through gestures and body language.

Nonverbal communication takes place through such things as hand movements, facial expressions, body posture, eye contact, and the use of

Nobody communicated better than "Mr. Sam"

The late Sam Walton, Wal-Mart's founder, was a master communicator. Stopping once to visit a Memphis store, he called everyone to the front, saying, "Northeast Memphis, you're the largest store in Memphis, and you must have the best floor-cleaning crew in America. This floor is so clean, let's sit down on it." Kneeling casually and wearing his Wal-Mart baseball cap, Walton congratulated them on their fine work. "I thank you," he said. "The company is so proud of you we can hardly stand it," he said, reminding them of bonus checks recently given out. "But," he added, "you know that confounded Kmart is getting better, and so is Target. So what's our challenge?" Walton asked. "Customer service," he replied in answer to his own question. Walton's quality message was clear to everyone.[11]

interpersonal space. It can be a powerful means of transmitting messages. Eye contact or voice intonation can be used intentionally to accent special parts of an oral communication. The astute observer notes the "body language" expressed by other persons. At times our body may be "talking" for us even as we otherwise maintain silence. And when we do speak, our body may sometimes "say" different things than our words convey. A **mixed message** occurs when a person's words communicate one message while his or her actions, body language, appearance, or use of interpersonal space communicate something else. Watch how people behave in a meeting. A person who feels under attack may move back in a chair or lean away from the presumed antagonist, even while expressing verbal agreement. All of this is done quite unconsciously, but it sends a message to those alert enough to pick it up.

> O A **mixed message** results when words communicate one message while actions, body language, or appearance communicate something else.

Nonverbal channels probably play a more important part in communication than most people recognize. One researcher indicates that gestures alone may make up as much as 70 percent of communication.[13] In fact, a potential side effect of the growing use of electronic mail, computer networking, and other communication technologies is that gestures and other nonverbal signals that may add important meaning to the communication event are lost.

Physical Distractions

Any number of physical distractions can interfere with the effectiveness of a communication attempt. Some of these distractions, such as telephone interruptions, drop-in visitors, and lack of privacy, are evident in the following conversation between an employee, George, and his manager:

> Okay, George, let's hear your problem [phone rings, boss picks it up, promises to deliver a report "just as soon as I can get it done"]. Uh, now, where were we—oh, you're having a problem with your technician. She's [manager's secretary brings in some papers that need his immediate signature; secretary leaves] . . . you say she's overstressed lately, wants to leave. . . . I tell you what, George, why don't you [phone rings again, lunch partner drops by] . . . uh, take a stab at handling it yourself. . . . I've got to go now.[14]

www.alcoa.com

Alcoa's senior executives work in "cockpit offices" with special furniture and short, movable walls. This promotes interaction and spontaneous association. The offices include a common "coffee kitchen" complete with notepads for jotting down ideas that pop up in informal conversations.

Besides what may have been poor intentions in the first place, the manager in this example did not do a good job of communicating with George. This problem could be easily corrected. If George has something important to say, he should set aside adequate time for the meeting. Additional interruptions such as telephone calls and drop-in visitors could be eliminated by issuing appropriate instructions to the secretary. Many communication distractions can be avoided or at least minimized through proper planning.

Status Effects

"Criticize my boss? I don't have the right to." "I'd get fired." "It's her company, not mine." As suggested in these comments, the hierarchy of authority in organizations creates another potential barrier to effective communications. Consider the "corporate cover-up" once discovered at an electronics company. Product shipments were being predated and papers falsified to meet unrealistic sales targets set by the president. His managers knew the targets were impossible to attain, but at least 20 persons in the organization cooperated in the deception. It was months before the top found out. What happened in this case is **filtering**—the intentional distortion of information to make it appear favorable to the recipient.

The presence of such information filtering is often found in communications between lower and higher levels in organizations. Tom Peters, the popular management author and consultant, has called such information distortion "Management Enemy Number 1."[15] Simply put, it most often involves someone "telling the boss what he or she wants to hear." Whether the reason behind this is a fear of retribution for bringing bad news, an unwillingness to identify personal mistakes, or just a general desire to please, the end result is the same. The person receiving filtered communications can end up making poor decisions because of a biased and inaccurate information base.

O **Filtering** is the intentional distortion of information to make it appear most favorable to the recipient.

Learning check 1

Be sure you can • describe the communication process and identify its key components • differentiate effective and efficient communication • explain the role of credibility in persuasive communication • list the common sources of noise that create barriers to effective communication • illustrate how the barriers might affect communication between a team leader and team members • explain how mixed messages and filtering can interfere with communication in organizations

---

IMPROVING COMMUNICATION

A number of things can be done to overcome barriers and improve the process of communication. They include active listening, making constructive use of feedback, opening upward communication channels, understanding proxemics and the use of space, utilizing technology, and valuing diversity.

ACTIVE LISTENING

O **Active listening** helps the source of a message say what he or she really means.

Managers must be very good at listening. When people "talk," they are trying to communicate something. That "something" may or may not be what they are saying. **Active listening** is the process of taking action to help someone say exactly what he or she really means. It involves being sincere in listening

Ten steps to good listening

1. Stop talking.
2. Put the other person at ease.
3. Show that you want to listen.
4. Remove any potential distractions.
5. Empathize with the other person.
6. Don't respond too quickly; be patient.
7. Don't get mad; hold your temper.
8. Go easy on argument and criticism.
9. Ask questions.
10. Stop talking.

to find the full meaning of what is being said. It also involves being disciplined in controlling emotions and withholding premature evaluations or interpretations. There are five rules for becoming an active listener:[16]

1. *Listen for message content:* Try to hear exactly what content is being conveyed in the message.
2. *Listen for feelings:* Try to identify how the source feels about the content in the message.
3. *Respond to feelings:* Let the source know that her or his feelings are being recognized.
4. *Note all cues:* Be sensitive to nonverbal and verbal messages; be alert for mixed messages.
5. *Paraphrase and restate:* State back to the source what you think you are hearing.

◄——
Rules for active listening

Different responses to the following two questions contrast how a "passive" listener and an "active" listener might act in real workplace conversations. Question 1: "Don't you think employees should be promoted on the basis of seniority?" *Passive listener's response:* "No, I don't!" *Active listener's response:* "It seems to you that they should, I take it?" Question 2: "What does the supervisor expect us to do about these out-of-date computers?" *Passive listener's response:* "Do the best you can, I guess." *Active listener's response:* "You're pretty disgusted with those machines, aren't you?" These examples show how active listening can facilitate communication in difficult circumstances, rather than discourage it. *Manager's Notepad 17.2* offers more guidelines for good listening.

CONSTRUCTIVE FEEDBACK

The process of telling other people how you feel about something they did or said, or about the situation in general, is called **feedback.** The art of giving feedback is an indispensable skill, particularly for managers who must regularly give feedback to other people. Often this takes the form of performance feedback given as evaluations and appraisals. When poorly done, such feedback can be threatening to the recipient and cause resentment. When properly done, feedback—even performance criticism—can

○ **Feedback** is the process of telling someone else how you feel about something that person did or said.

be listened to, accepted, and used to good advantage by the receiver.[17] When Lydia Whitfield, a marketing vice president at Avaya, asked one of her managers for feedback she was surprised. He said: "You're angry a lot." Whitfield learned from the experience, saying: "What he and other employees saw as my anger, I saw as my passion."[18]

There are ways to help ensure that feedback is useful and constructive rather than harmful. To begin with, the sender must learn to recognize when the feedback he or she is about to offer will really benefit the receiver and when it will mainly satisfy some personal need. A supervisor who berates a computer programmer for errors, for example, actually may be angry about personally failing to give clear instruction in the first place. Also, a manager should make sure that any feedback is considered by recipient as understandable, acceptable, and plausible. *Guidelines for giving "constructive" feedback* include:[19]

Constructive feedback guidelines →

- Give feedback directly and with real feeling, based on trust between you and the receiver.
- Make sure that feedback is specific rather than general; use good, clear, and preferably recent examples to make your points.
- Give feedback at a time when the receiver seems most willing or able to accept it.
- Make sure the feedback is valid; limit it to things the receiver can be expected to do something about.
- Give feedback in small doses; never give more than the receiver can handle at any particular time.

USE OF COMMUNICATION CHANNELS

○ **Channel richness** is the capacity of a communication channel to effectively carry information.

Channel richness is the capacity of a communication channel to carry information in an effective manner.[20] *Figure 17.2* shows that face-to-face communication is very high in richness, enabling two-way interaction and real-time feedback. Formal reports and memos are very low in richness, due to impersonal one-way interaction with limited opportunity for feedback. Managers need to understand the limits of the possible channels and choose wisely when using them for communication.

INTERACTIVE MANAGEMENT

○ In **management by wandering around (MBWA)** managers spend time outside of their offices to meet and talk with workers at all levels.

Interactive management approaches use a variety of means to keep communication channels open between organizational levels. A popular choice is **management by wandering around (MBWA)**—dealing directly with subordinates by regularly spending time walking around and talking with

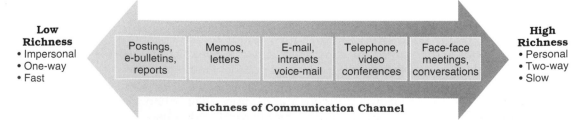

Figure 17.2 Channel richness and the use of communication media.

them about work-related matters. MBWA involves finding out for yourself what is going on in face-to-face communications. The basic objectives are to break down status barriers, increase the frequency of interpersonal contact, and get more and better information from lower-level sources. Of course, this requires a trusting relationship. Patricia Gallup, CEO of PC Connection, became known for her interactive style of leadership and emphasis on communication. By making herself available by e-mail and spending as much time as possible out of her office, she made MBWA part of her style.[21]

Management practices designed to open channels and improve upward communications have traditionally involved *open office hours,* whereby busy senior executives like Gallup set aside time in their calendars to welcome walk-in visits during certain hours each week. Today this approach can be expanded to include *online discussion forums* and "chat rooms" that are open at certain hours. Programs of regular *employee group meetings* are also helpful. Here, a rotating schedule of "shirtsleeve" meetings brings top managers into face-to-face contact with mixed employee groups throughout an organization. The face-to-face groups can be supplemented by *computer-mediated meetings* and *video conferences,* which serve similar purposes, overcoming time and distance limitations to communication. In some cases, a comprehensive communications program includes an *employee advisory council* composed of members elected by their fellow employees. Such councils meet with management on a regular schedule to discuss and react to new policies and programs that will affect employees.

When executives suspect that they are having communication problems, *communication consultants* can be hired to conduct interviews and surveys of employees on their behalf. Marc Brownstein, president of a public relations and advertising firm, for example, was surprised when managers in an anonymous survey complained that he was a poor listener and gave them insufficient feedback. They also felt poorly informed about the firm's financial health. In other words, poor communication was hurting staff morale. With help from consultants, Brownstein now holds more meetings and works more aggressively to share information and communicate regularly with the firm's employees.[22]

Another interactive approach that seeks to broaden the awareness of "bosses" regarding the feelings and perceptions of other people that they work closely with is **360-degree feedback,** discussed in Chapter 12.[23] This typically involves upward appraisals done by a manager's subordinates as well as additional feedback from peers, internal and external customers, and higher-ups. A self-assessment is also part of the process. The goal of 360-degree feedback is to provide the manager with information that can be used for constructive improvement. Managers who have participated in the process often express surprise at what they learn. Some have found themselves perceived as lacking vision, having bad tempers, and being bad listeners, lacking flexibility.[24]

www.scotts.org

The Scotts Company holds large meetings to thank employees for their work, tell them the results of the firm's financial performance, and celebrate teamwork. The food is good and plentiful, there is music and entertainment, and a lot of information is shared.

O **360° feedback** includes views of bosses, peers, and subordinates in performance appraisals.

PROXEMICS AND SPACE DESIGN

An important but sometimes neglected part of communication involves proxemics, or the use of space.[26] The distance between people conveys varying intentions in terms of intimacy, openness, and status. And the physical layout of an office is an often-overlooked form of nonverbal communication. Check it out. Offices with chairs available for side-by-side seating convey different messages from those where the manager's chair sits behind the desk and those for visitors sit facing it in front.

Research helps define managers' training and development needs

The American Management Association, or AMA, is a nonprofit organization devoted to improving management practices by offering a wide variety of training and educational services. The goal is to improve organizational performance through better management. One of the services provided by the AMA is research that can inform and help its members set self-improvement goals. A recent survey asked respondents to rate the members of their organization's senior management team on a variety of dimensions. Only 22.1 percent rated them as high on communicating information and direction. Most managers were rated average at best, and some 10 percent were considered low in this skill category. About the same percentage also considered the senior managers low in understanding people.[25]

REALITY CHECK 17.1

How private is office communication?
For most workers there is an increasing chance that their employers are monitoring their communication and performance. Electronic monitoring was up 45 percent in a survey by the American Management Association. Take the online "Reality Check" to learn more about the ways in which employers monitor employee communications.

Office or workspace architecture is an important influence on communication and behavior. Architects and consultants specializing in *organizational ecology* are helping executives build offices conducive to the intense communication needed today. When Sun Microsystems built its San Jose, California, facility, public spaces were designed to encourage communication among persons from different departments. Many meeting areas have no walls, and most of the walls that exist are glass. As manager of planning and research, Ann Bamesberger said: "We were creating a way to get these people to communicate with each other more." Importantly, the Sun project involved not only the assistance of expert architectural consultants, but also extensive inputs and suggestions from the employees themselves. The results seem to justify the effort. A senior technical writer, Terry Davidson, commented: "This is the most productive workspace I have ever been in."[27]

TECHNOLOGY UTILIZATION

When IBM surveyed employees to find out how they learned what was going on at the company, executives were not surprised that co-workers were perceived as credible and useful sources. But they were surprised that the firm's intranet ranked equally high. IBM's internal web sites were ranked higher than news briefs, company memos, and information from managers.[28] The new age of communication is one of e-mail, voice mail, instant messaging, teleconferencing, online discussions, videoconferencing, virtual or computer-mediated meetings, intranets and Web portals. And the many implications of technology utilization must be understood.

Technology offers the power of the *electronic grapevine,* speeding messages and information from person-to-person. When the members of a sixth-grade class in Taylorsville, North Carolina (population 1566) sent out the e-mail message "Hi! . . . We are curious to see where in the world our e-mail will travel," they were surprised. Over a half-million replies flooded in, overwhelming not only the students but the school's computer system.[29] Messages fly with equal speed and intensity around organizations.

The results can be both functional—when the information is accurate and useful, and dysfunctional—when the information is false, distorted, or simply based on rumor. Managers should be quick to correct misimpressions and inaccuracies; they should also positively utilize the electronic grapevines as ways to quickly transfer factual and relevant information among organizational members.

Knowing how and when to use e-mail may well be the biggest communication issue for people in organizations today. Purpose and privacy are two concerns. Employers are concerned that too much work time gets spent handling personal e-mail; employees are concerned that employers are eavesdropping on their e-mail messages. The best advice comes down to this: (1) find out the employer's policy on personal e-mail and follow it; (2) don't assume that you ever have e-mail privacy at work. Another major concern is e-mail workload, which can be overwhelming. At Intel, for example, managers discovered that some employees faced up to 300 e-mail messages a day and spent some 2.5 hours per day dealing with them. The firm initiated a training program to improve e-mail utilization and efficiency.[30] Tips on managing your e-mail include:[31]

- Read items only once.
- Take action immediately to answer, move to folders, or delete.
- Purge folders regularly of useless messages.
- Send group mail and use "reply to all" only when really necessary.
- Get off distribution lists without value to your work.
- Send short messages in the subject line, avoiding a full-text message.
- Put large files on websites, instead of sending as attachments.
- Use IM, instant messaging, as an e-mail alternative.
- Don't forget the basic rule of e-mail privacy: There isn't any.

← How to streamline your e-mail

VALUING CULTURE AND DIVERSITY

Workforce diversity and globalization are two of the most talked-about trends in modern society. Communicating under conditions of diversity, where the sender and receiver are part of different cultures, is certainly a significant challenge. Cross-cultural communication was first discussed in Chapter 5 on the global dimensions of management. It is useful to recall that a major source of difficulty is **ethnocentrism,** the tendency to consider one's culture superior to any and all others. Ethnocentrism can adversely affect communication in at least three major ways: (1) it may cause someone to not listen well to what others have to say; (2) it may cause someone to address or speak with others in ways that alienate them; and (3) it may lead to the use of inappropriate stereotypes when dealing with persons from another culture.[32]

○ **Ethnocentrism** is the tendency to consider one's culture superior to any and all others.

For years, cultural challenges have been recognized by international travelers and executives. But as we know, you don't have to travel abroad to come face to face with communication and cultural diversity. The importance of cross-cultural communication skills applies at home just as much as it does in a foreign country. Just going to work is a cross-cultural journey for most of us today. The workplace abounds with subcultures based on gender, age, ethnicity, race, and other factors. All are a source of different perspectives, experiences, values, and expectations that can complicate the communication process. When the sender and receiver are unable to empathize with one another's cultures they will have difficulties understanding when and why certain words, gestures, and messages are misinterpreted.

THE PERCEPTION PROCESS

○ **Perception** is the process through which people receive, organize, and interpret information from the environment.

Perception is the process through which people receive and interpret information from the environment. It is the way we form impressions about ourselves, other people, and daily life experiences. And it is the way we process information to make the decisions that ultimately guide our actions.[33] As shown in *Figure 17.3,* perception acts as a screen or filter through which information passes before it has an impact on communication, decision making, and action. Because perceptions are influenced by such things as cultural background, values, and other personal and situational circumstances, people can and do perceive the same things or situations differently. And importantly, people behave according to their perceptions.

PERCEPTION AND ATTRIBUTION

One of the ways in which perception exerts its influence is through *attribution,* the process of developing explanations for events. It is natural for people to try to explain what they observe and the things that happen to them. The fact that people can perceive the same things quite differently has an important influence on attributions and their ultimate influence on behavior.

○ Fundamental **attribution error** overestimates internal factors and underestimates external factors as influences on someone's behavior.

In social psychology, attribution theory describes how people try to explain the behavior of themselves and other people.[34] One of its significant applications is in the context of people's performance at work. Fundamental **attribution error** occurs when observers blame another person's performance failures more on internal factors relating to the individual than on external factors relating to the environment. In the case of someone who is producing poor-quality work, for example, a supervisor might

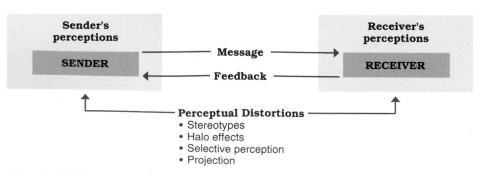

Figure 17.3 Perception and communication.

blame a lack of job skills or laziness—an unwillingness to work hard enough. In response the supervisor is likely to try to resolve the problem through training, motivation, or even replacement. The attribution error leads to the neglect of possible external explanations, for example, that the poor-quality work was caused by unrealistic time pressures or substandard technology. Opportunities to improve upon these factors through managerial action will thus be missed.

Another confounding aspect of perception and attribution occurs as a **self-serving bias.** This happens when individuals blame their personal failures or problems on external causes and attribute their successes to internal causes. You might think of this tendency the next time you "blame" your instructor for a poor course grade. The self-serving bias is harmful when it causes us to give insufficient attention to the need for personal change and development. While readily taking credit for successes, we are often too quick to focus on the environment to explain away our failures.

O **Self-serving bias** explains personal success by internal causes and personal failures by external causes.

PERCEPTUAL TENDENCIES AND DISTORTIONS

In addition to the attribution errors just discussed, a variety of perceptual tendencies and distortions can also influence communication and workplace behavior. Of particular interest are the use of stereotypes, halo effects, selective perception, and projection.

Stereotypes

A **stereotype** occurs when someone is identified with a group or category, and then oversimplified attributes associated with the group or category are used to describe the individual. We all use stereotypes and they are not always negative or ill-intended. But those based on such factors as gender, age, and race can, and unfortunately still do, bias the perceptions of people in some work settings.

The *glass ceiling,* mentioned in Chapter 1 as an invisible barrier to career advancement, still exists. Legitimate questions can be asked about *racial and ethnic stereotypes* and about the slow progress of minority managers into America's corporate mainstream.[35] In the world of international business, only about 13 percent of American managers sent abroad by their employers on work assignments are women. Why? A Catalyst study of opportunities for women in global business points to *gender stereotypes* that place women at a disadvantage to men for these types of opportunities. The tendency is to assume they lack the ability and/or willingness for working abroad.[36] Although employment barriers caused by gender stereotypes are falling, women may still suffer from false impressions and biases imposed on them. Even everyday behavior may be misconstrued. Consider this example: *Case—"He's* talking with coworkers." (*Interpretation:* He's discussing a new deal.); "*She's* talking with coworkers." (*Interpretation:* She's gossiping.)[37]

Ability stereotypes and *age stereotypes* also exist in the workplace. A candidate with a disability may be overlooked by a recruiter even though her skills are perfect for the job. A talented older worker may not be promoted because a manager assumes older workers are cautious and tend to avoid risk. For those employers who break through stereotypes to find the true value in people, the rewards are there. A Conference Board survey of workers 50 and older, for example, found that 72 percent felt they could

Student perceptions of teacher evaluations
There is always controversy over the use and value of student evaluations of teachers. Faculty tend to think that students give higher ratings to "easy" and "entertaining" professors. Take the online "Reality Check" to learn more about how students consider the accuracy of these perceptions.

O A **stereotype** is when attributes commonly associated with a group are assigned to an individual.

take on additional responsibilities, and two-thirds were interested in further training and development.[38]

Halo Effects

○ A halo effect occurs when one attribute is used to develop an overall impression of a person or situation.

A **halo effect** occurs when one attribute is used to develop an overall impression of a person or situation. When meeting someone new, for example, the halo effect may cause one trait, such as a pleasant smile, to result in a positive first impression. By contrast, a particular hairstyle or manner of dressing may create a negative reaction. Halo effects cause the same problem for managers as do stereotypes; that is, individual differences become obscured. This is especially significant in performance evaluations. One factor, such as a person's punctuality, may become the "halo" for a positive overall performance assessment. Even though the general conclusion seems to make sense, it may or may not be true in a given circumstance.

Selective Perception

○ Selective perception is the tendency to define problems from one's own point of view.

Selective perception is the tendency to single out for attention those aspects of a situation or person that reinforce or appear consistent with one's existing beliefs, values, or needs.[39] Information that makes us uncomfortable is screened out. What this often means in an organization is that people from different departments or functions—such as marketing and manufacturing—tend to see things from their own points of view and fail to recognize other points of view. Like the other perceptual distortions, selective perception can bias a manager's view of situations and individuals. One way to reduce its impact is to be sure to gather additional opinions from other people.

Projection

○ Projection is the assignment of personal attributes to other individuals.

Projection is the assignment of personal attributes to other individuals. A classic projection error is to assume that other persons share our needs, desires, and values. Suppose, for example, that you enjoy a lot of responsibility and challenge in your work. Suppose, too, that you are the newly appointed supervisor for people whose work you consider dull and routine. You might move quickly to start a program of job enrichment to help them experience more responsibility and challenge. This may not be a good decision. Instead of designing jobs to best fit their needs, you have designed their jobs to fit *yours*. In fact, your subordinates may be quite satisfied and productive doing jobs that, to you, seem routine. Such projection errors can be controlled through self-awareness and a willingness to communicate and empathize with other persons, that is, to try to see things through their eyes.

Be sure you can • define the term perception • describe its role in the communication process • explain the concepts of attribution error and self-serving bias • define the terms stereotype, halo effect, selective perception, and projection • illustrate how each of these perceptual tendencies can adversely affect work behavior

Learning check 3

CONFLICT

Among your communication and related interpersonal skills, the ability to deal with conflicts is critical. **Conflict** is a disagreement between people on substantive or emotional issues.[40] And, managers and leaders spend a lot of time dealing with conflicts of various forms. **Substantive conflicts** involve disagreements over such things as goals and tasks; the allocation of resources; the distribution of rewards, policies, and procedures; and job assignments. **Emotional conflicts** result from feelings of anger, distrust, dislike, fear, and resentment, as well as from personality clashes and relationship problems. Both forms of conflict can cause difficulties in the workplace. But when managed well, they can also be helpful in promoting creativity and high performance.

FUNCTIONAL AND DYSFUNCTIONAL CONFLICT

It is important to remember that not all conflict is bad and the absence of conflict is not always good. In Chapter 16, for example, the phenomenon of "groupthink" is associated with highly cohesive groups whose members make bad decisions because they are unwilling to engage in conflict. But whether or not conflict benefits people and organizations depends on two factors: (1) the intensity of the conflict and (2) how well the conflict is managed. The inverted "U" curve depicted in *Figure 17.4* shows that conflict of moderate intensity can be good for performance. This **functional conflict,** or *constructive conflict,* stimulates people toward greater work efforts, cooperation, and creativity. It helps groups achieve their goals. At very low or very high intensities **dysfunctional conflict,** or *destructive conflict,* occurs. This makes it difficult for groups to achieve their goals. Too much conflict is distracting and interferes with other more task-relevant activities; too little conflict may promote complacency and the loss of a creative, high-performance edge.

CAUSES OF CONFLICT

A number of antecedent conditions can make the eventual emergence of conflict very likely. *Role ambiguities* set the stage for conflict. Unclear job expectations and other task uncertainties increase the probability that some people will be working at cross-purposes, at least some of the time. *Resource scarcities* cause conflict. Having to share resources with others and/or compete directly with them for resource allocations creates a potential situation conflict, especially when resources are scarce. *Task interdependencies* cause conflict. When individuals or groups must depend on what others do to perform well themselves, conflicts often occur. *Competing objectives* are opportunities for conflict. When objectives are poorly set or reward systems are poorly designed, individuals and groups may come into conflict by working to one another's disadvantage. *Structural differentiation* breeds conflict. Dif-

○ **Conflict** is a disagreement over issues of substance and/or an emotional antagonism.

○ **Substantive conflict** involves disagreements over goals, resources, rewards, policies, procedures, and job assignments.

○ **Emotional conflict** results from feelings of anger, distrust, dislike, fear, and resentment as well as from personality clashes.

○ **Functional conflict** is constructive and helps task performance.

○ **Dysfunctional conflict** is destructive and hurts task performance.

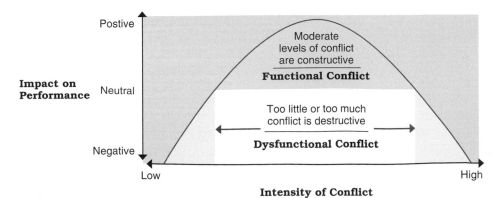

Figure 17.4 The relationship between conflict and performance.

ferences in organization structures and in the characteristics of the people staffing them may foster conflict because of incompatible approaches toward work. And *unresolved prior conflicts* tend to erupt in later conflicts. Unless a conflict is fully resolved, it may remain latent and later emerge as a basis for future conflicts over the same or related matters.

AROUND THE WORLD

International agency promotes labor rights worldwide

The International Labour Organization, known in the news as the ILO, is the only surviving entity from the 1919 Treaty of Versailles, which formed the League of Nations, the precursor to the United Nations. The ILO's mission is described as the "promotion of social justice and internationally recognized labor rights." In its recent report *Time for Equality at Work,* the ILO notes that work discrimination based on a person's religion, skin color, and gender occurs every day around the world. It also states that the elimination of such discrimination is essential to advance the values of human dignity, individual freedom, social justice, and social cohesion. It further states that the elimination of discrimination will not happen just because governments want it to happen; everyone— employers and workers—is responsible for championing equality at work.[41]

HOW TO DEAL WITH CONFLICT

When any one or more of these antecedent conditions are present, an informed manager expects conflicts to occur. And when they do, the conflicts then can either be "resolved," in the sense that the sources are corrected, or "suppressed," in that the sources remain but the conflict behaviors are controlled. Suppressed conflicts tend to fester and recur at a later time. True **conflict resolution** eliminates the underlying causes of conflict and reduces the potential for similar conflicts in the future.

Managers use various approaches to deal with conflicts between individuals or groups. There are times when *appealing to superordinate goals* can focus the attention on one mutually desirable end state. The appeal to higher-level goals offers all parties a common frame of reference against which to analyze differences and reconcile disagreements. Conflicts whose antecedents lie in the competition for scarce resources can be resolved by *making more resources available* to everyone. Although costly, this technique removes the reasons for the continuing conflict. By *changing the people,* that is, by replacing or transferring one or more of the conflicting parties, conflicts caused by poor interpersonal relationships can be eliminated. The same holds true for *altering the physical environment.* Facilities, work space, or workflows can be rearranged to physically separate conflicting parties and decrease opportunities for contact with one another.

The *integrating devices* introduced in Chapter 11 as ways to improve coordination in an organization can also be used to deal with conflicts. Using liaison personnel, special task forces, cross-functional teams, and even the matrix form of organization, can change interaction patterns and assist in conflict reduction. *Changing reward systems* may reduce competition between individuals and groups for rewards. Creating systems that reward cooperation can encourage behaviors and attitudes that promote teamwork

○ **Conflict resolution** is the removal of the substantial and/or emotional reasons for a conflict.

and reduce conflict. *Changing policies and procedures* may redirect behavior in ways that minimize the likelihood of known conflict-prone situations. Finally, *training in interpersonal skills* can help prepare people to communicate and work more effectively in situations where conflict is likely.

CONFLICT MANAGEMENT STYLES

Interpersonally, people respond to conflict through different combinations of cooperative and assertive behaviors.[42] *Cooperativeness* is the desire to satisfy another party's needs and concerns; *assertiveness* is the desire to satisfy one's own needs and concerns. *Figure 17.5* shows five interpersonal styles of conflict management that result from various combinations of the two.

- **Avoidance** or *withdrawl*—being uncooperative and unassertive; downplaying disagreement, withdrawing from the situation, and/or staying neutral at all costs.
- **Accommodation** or *smoothing*—being cooperative but unassertive; letting the wishes of others rule; smoothing over or overlooking differences to maintain harmony.
- **Competition** or *authoritative command*—being uncooperative but assertive; working against the wishes of the other party, engaging in win-lose competition, and/or forcing through the exercise of authority.
- **Compromise**—being moderately cooperative and assertive, bargaining for "acceptable" solutions in which each party wins a bit and loses a bit.
- **Collaboration** or *problem solving*—being cooperative and assertive; trying to fully satisfy everyone's concerns by working through differences; finding and solving problems so that everyone gains.[43]

The five conflict management styles should be selected and used with caution, and with the requirements of each unique conflict situation carefully considered.[44] Conflict management by *avoiding* or *accommodating* often creates **lose-lose conflict.** No one achieves her or his true desires and the underlying reasons for conflict often remain unaffected. Although a lose-lose conflict may appear settled or may even disappear for a while, it tends to recur in the future. Avoidance is an extreme form of nonatten-

Five conflict management styles

O **Avoidance** pretends that a conflict doesn't really exist.

O **Accommodation** or smoothing plays down differences and highlights similarities to reduce conflict.

O **Competition** or authoritative command uses force, superior skill, or domination to "win" a conflict.

O **Compromise** occurs when each party to the conflict gives up something of value to the other.

O **Collaboration** or problem solving involves working through conflict differences and solving problems so everyone wins.

O In **lose-lose conflict** no one achieves his or her true desires and the underlying reasons for conflict remain unaffected.

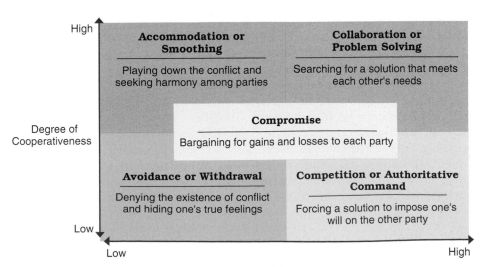

Figure 17.5 Alternative conflict management styles.

tion. Everyone withdraws and pretends that conflict doesn't really exist, hoping that it will simply go away. Accommodation plays down differences and highlights similarities and areas of agreement. Peaceful coexistence through a recognition of common interests is the goal. In reality, such smoothing may ignore the real essence of a conflict.

○ In **win-lose conflict** one party achieves its desires and the other party does not.

Competing and *compromising* tend to create **win-lose conflict.** Here, each party strives to gain at the other's expense. In extreme cases, one party achieves its desires to the complete exclusion of the other party's desires. Because win-lose methods fail to address the root causes of conflict, future conflicts of the same or a similar nature are likely to occur. In competition, one party wins, as superior skill or outright domination allows his or her desires to be forced on the other. This occurs in the form of authoritative command, where the forcing is accomplished by a higher-level supervisor who simply dictates a solution to subordinates. Compromise occurs when trade-offs are made such that each party to the conflict gives up and gains something of value. Because each party loses something, antecedents for future conflicts are established.

○ In **win-win conflict** the conflict is resolved to everyone's benefit.

Collaborating in true problem solving tries to reconcile underlying differences and is often the most effective conflict management style. It is a form of **win-win conflict** wherein issues are resolved to the mutual benefit of all conflicting parties. This is typically achieved by confronting the issues and through the willingness of everyone involved to recognize that something is wrong and needs attention. Win-win conditions are created by eliminating the underlying causes of the conflict. All relevant issues are raised and discussed openly. Win-win methods are clearly the most preferred of the interpersonal styles of conflict management.

Be sure you can • differentiate substantive and emotional conflict • differentiate functional and dysfunctional conflict • explain the common causes of conflict • list the possible approaches to conflict resolution • explain the conflict management styles of avoidance, accommodation, competition, compromise, and collaboration • discuss how these styles create lose-lose, win-lose, and win-win conflicts

Learning check 4

NEGOTIATION

○ **Negotiation** is the process of making joint decisions when the parties involved have different preferences.

Put yourself in the following situations. How would you behave, and what would you do? (1) You have been offered a promotion and would really like to take it. However, the pay raise being offered is less than you hoped. (2) You have enough money to order one new computer for your department. Two of your subordinates have each requested new computers.[45] These are but two examples of the many work situations that lead to **negotiation**—the process of making joint decisions when the parties involved have different preferences. Stated a bit differently, negotiation is a way of reaching agreement. People negotiate over salary, merit raises, performance evaluations, job assignments, work schedules, work locations, and many other considerations. All such negotiations are susceptible to conflict and test the communication and interpersonal skills of those involved.

NEGOTIATION GOALS AND APPROACHES

There are two important goals in negotiation. *Substance goals* are concerned with outcomes; they are tied to the content issues of the negotiation. *Relationship goals* are concerned with processes; they are tied to the way people work together while negotiating and how they (and any constituencies they represent) will be able to work together again in the future. Effective negotiation occurs when issues of substance are resolved and working relationships among the negotiating parties are maintained or even improved in the process. The three criteria of effective negotiation are: (1) *quality*—negotiating a "wise" agreement that is truly satisfactory to all sides; (2) *cost*—negotiating efficiently, using up minimum resources and time; and (3) *harmony*—negotiation in a way that fosters, rather than inhibits, interpersonal relationships.[46]

The way each party approaches a negotiation can have a major impact on the results.[47] **Distributive negotiation** focuses on "claims" made by each party for certain preferred outcomes. This can take a competitive form in which one party can gain only if the other loses. In such "win-lose" conditions, relationships are often sacrificed as the negotiating parties focus only on their respective self-interests. It may also become accommodative if the parties defer to one another's wishes simply "to get it over with." **Principled negotiation,** often called **integrative negotiation,** is based on a "win-win" orientation. The focus on substance is still important, but the interests of all parties are considered. The goal is to base the final outcome on the merits of individual claims and to try to find a way for all claims to be satisfied if at all possible. No one should "lose," and relationships should be maintained in the process.

> ○ **Distributive negotiation** focuses on "win-lose" claims made by each party for certain preferred outcomes.

> ○ **Principled/integrative negotiation** uses a "win-win" orientation to reach solutions acceptable to each party.

GAINING INTEGRATIVE AGREEMENTS

In their book *Getting to Yes,* Roger Fisher and William Ury point out that truly integrative agreements are obtained by following four negotiation rules:[48]

1. Separate the people from the problem.
2. Focus on interests, not on positions.
3. Generate many alternatives before deciding what to do.
4. Insist that results be based on some objective standard.

> ← Four rules of principled negotiation

Proper attitudes and good information are necessary foundations for integrative agreements. The attitudinal foundations involve the willingness of each negotiating party to trust, share information with, and ask reasonable questions of the other party. The informational foundations involve each party knowing what is really important to them and finding out what is really important to the other party. In addition, each should understand his or her personal **best alternative to a negotiated agreement (BATNA).** This is an answer to the question "What will I do if an agreement can't be reached?"

Figure 17.6 introduces a typical case of labor–management negotiations over a new contract and salary increase. This helps to illustrate ele-

> ○ **BATNA** is the best alternative to a negotiated agreement.

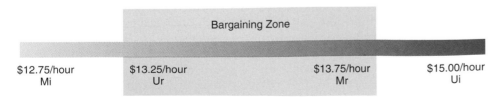

	Bargaining Zone		
$12.75/hour Mi	$13.25/hour Ur	$13.75/hour Mr	$15.00/hour Ui

Mi = Management's initial offer Mr = Management's maximum reservation point
Ur = Union's minimum reservation point Ui = Union's initial offer

Figure 17.6 The bargaining zone in classic two-party negotiation.

ments of classic two-party negotiation as they occur in many contexts.[49] To begin, look at the figure and case from the labor union's perspective. The union negotiator has told her management counterpart that the union wants a new wage of $15.00 per hour. This expressed preference is the union's *initial offer*. However, she also has in mind a *minimum reservation point* of $13.25 per hour. This is the lowest wage rate that she is willing to accept for the union. But the management negotiator has a different perspective. His *initial offer* is $12.75 per hour, and his *maximum reservation point*, the highest wage he is prepared eventually to offer to the union, is $13.75 per hour.

○ A **bargaining zone** is the area between one party's minimum reservation point and the other party's maximum reservation point.

In classic two-party negotiation of this type, the **bargaining zone** is defined as the zone between one party's minimum reservation point and the other party's maximum reservation point. The bargaining zone of $13.25 per hour to $13.75 per hour in this case is a "positive" one since the reservation points of the two parties overlap. If the union's minimum reservation point were greater than management's maximum reservation point, no room would exist for bargaining. Whenever a positive bargaining zone exists, there is room for true negotiation. A key task for any negotiator is to discover the other party's reservation point. Until this is known and each party becomes aware that a positive bargaining zone exists, it is difficult to proceed effectively.

AVOIDING NEGOTIATION PITFALLS

The negotiation process is admittedly complex, and negotiators must guard against at least four common pitfalls. The first is *falling prey to the myth of the "fixed pie."* This involves acting on the distributive assumption that in order for you to gain, the other person must give something up. Negotiating this way fails to recognize the integrative assumption that the "pie" can sometimes be expanded and/or utilized to everyone's advantage. A second negotiation error is *nonrational escalation of conflict.* The negotiator in this case becomes committed to previously stated "demands" and allows personal needs for "ego" and "face saving" to increase the perceived importance of satisfying them. The third error is *overconfidence and ignoring the other's needs.* The error negotiator becomes overconfident, believes his or her position is the only correct one, and fails to see the needs of the other party and the merits in its position. The fourth error is *too much "telling" and too little "hearing."* When committing the "telling" problem, parties to a negotiation don't really make themselves understood to each other. When committing the "hearing" problem they fail to listen sufficiently well to understand what each other is saying.[50]

DISPUTE RESOLUTION

○ In **mediation** a neutral party tries to help conflicting parties improve communication to resolve their dispute.

It may not always be possible to achieve integrative agreements. When disputes reach the point of impasse, mediation and arbitration can be useful. **Mediation** involves a neutral third party who tries to improve communication between negotiating parties and keep them focused on relevant issues. The *mediator* does not issue a ruling or make a decision but can take an active role in discussions. This may include making suggestions in an attempt to move the parties toward agreement. **Arbitration,** such as salary arbitration in professional sports, is a stronger form of dispute resolution. It involves a neutral third party, the *arbitrator,* who acts as a "judge" and issues a binding decision. This usually includes a formal hearing in which the arbitrator listens to both sides and reviews all facets

○ In **arbitration** a neutral third party issues a binding decision to resolve a dispute.

TAKE IT TO THE CASE

The United Nations
Conflict and negotiation are center stage when nations meet

On any given day, United Nations Secretary General Kofi A. Annan can be counted on to have his hands full. Full of conflict, that is. The UN, committed by mission to preserving peace through international cooperation and collective security, is often center stage when members of the community of 189 nations have disagreements with one another. Part of Annan's task is to help them peacefully resolve conflcts and together advance harmony and progress throughout the world. In addition to concerns for war and terrorism, one of Annan's current priorities is to gain endorsement by world business and labor leaders of a Global Compact supporting human rights, labor, and the environment. The compact is designed to unite them in practices "enabling all the world's people to share the benefits of globalization and embedding the global market in values and practices that are fundamental to meeting socio-economic needs."[51]

of the case before making a ruling. Some organizations formally provide for a process called *alternative dispute resolution*. This approach utilizes mediation and/or arbitration but only after direct attempts to negotiate agreements between the conflicting parties have failed. Often an *ombudsperson,* or designated neutral third party who listens to complaints and disputes, plays a key role in the process.

ETHICAL ISSUES IN NEGOTIATION

Managers, and anyone else involved in negotiation, should maintain high standards of ethical conduct even when engaged in a dynamic and challenging situation. The motivation to behave unethically sometimes arises from an undue emphasis on the profit motive. This may be experienced as a desire to "get just a bit more" or to "get as much as you can" from a negotiation. The motivation to behave unethically may also result from a sense of competition. This may be experienced as a desire to "win" a negotiation just for the sake of winning it, or in the misguided belief that someone else must "lose" in order for you to gain.

When unethical behavior occurs in negotiation, the persons involved may try to explain it away with inappropriate rationalizing: "It was really unavoidable," "Oh, it's harmless," "The results justify the means," or "It's really quite fair and appropriate."[51] Of course these excuses for questionable behavior are morally unacceptable. Such practices and viewpoints can also be challenged by the possibility that any short-run gains will be accompanied by long-run losses. Negotiators using unethical tactics will incur lasting legacies of distrust, disrespect, and dislike. They can also expect to be targeted for "revenge" in later negotiations.

Be sure you can • define the term negotiation • differentiate distributive and principled negotiation • list the four rules of principled negotiation • define the terms BATNA and bargaining zone • use these terms to illustrate a labor–management wage negotiation • describe the potential pitfalls in the negotiation process • differentiate mediation and arbitration in dispute resolution • discuss the ethical challenges of negotiation

Learning check 5

CHAPTER 17 STUDY GUIDE

Where We've Been

BACK TO CENTER FOR CREATIVE LEADERSHIP

The opening example of the Center for Creative Leadership confirmed once again that leadership begins with one's ability to work well with other people. In this chapter you learned about interpersonal communication, with an emphasis on dealing with barriers and achieving communication effectiveness. You learned about perception and how perceptual distortions can influence communication and behavior. You also learned about the processes of conflict and negotiation, including how each can be engaged positively in the work setting.

THE NEXT STEP
INTEGRATED LEARNING ACTIVITIES

Cases/Projects	Self-Assessments	Experiential Exercises
• The United Nations • Enron and Arthur Andersen Integrating Case • Project 7—Gender and Leadership • Project 10—Service Learning	• Emotional Intelligence (#2) • Assertiveness (#12) • Performance Appraisal Assumptions (#19) • Conflict Management Style (#28)	• What Managers Do (#2) • Upward Appraisal (#24) • How to Give, Take Criticism (#25) • Feedback and Assertiveness (#28)

STUDY QUESTIONS SUMMARY

1. What is the communication process?

- Communication is the interpersonal process of sending and receiving symbols with messages attached to them.
- Effective communication occurs when the sender and the receiver of a message both interpret it in the same way; efficient communication occurs when the message is sent at low cost for the sender.
- Persuasive communication results in the recipient acting as intended by the sender.
- Credibility earned by expertise and good relationships is essential to persuasive communication.
- Noise is anything that interferes with the effectiveness of communication; it is caused by poor utilization of channels, poor written or oral expression, physical distractions, and status effects.

2. How can communication be improved?

- Active listening, through reflecting back and paraphrasing, can help overcome barriers and improve communication.
- Interactive management through MBWA and use of structured meetings, suggestion systems and advisory councils can improve upward communication.
- Office architecture and physical space can be used and designed to improve communication in organizations.
- Information technology, such as e-mail and intranets can improve communication in organizations, but it is must be well used.

- The negative influences of ethnocentrism on communication can be offset by greater cross-cultural awareness and sensitivity.

3. How does perception influence communication?

- Perception acts as a filter through which all communication passes as it travels from one person to the next.
- Because people tend to perceive things differently, the same message may be interpreted quite differently by different people.
- Fundamental attribution error occurs when we blame others for performance problems while excluding possible external causes; self-serving bias occurs when in judging our own performance. we take personal credit for successes and blame failures on external factors.
- Stereotypes, projections, halo effects, and selective perception can distort perceptions and reduce communication effectiveness.

4. How can we deal positively with conflict?

- Conflict occurs as disagreements over substantive or emotional issues.
- Moderate levels of conflict are functional for performance and creativity; too little or too much conflict becomes dysfunctional.

- Conflict may be managed through structural approaches that involve changing people, goals, resources, or work arrangements.
- Personal conflict management styles include avoidance, accommodation, compromise, competition, and collaboration.
- True conflict resolution involves problem solving through a win-win collaborative approach.

5. How can we negotiate successful agreements?

- Negotiation is the process of making decisions in situations in which the participants have different preferences.
- Both substance goals, those concerned with outcomes, and relationship goals, those concerned with processes, are important in successful negotiation.
- Effective negotiation occurs when issues of substance are resolved and the process results in good working relationships.
- Distributive approaches to negotiation emphasize win-lose outcomes; Integrative approaches to negotiation emphasize win-win outcomes.
- Mediation and arbitration offer structured approaches to dispute resolution.

KEY TERMS REVIEW

360° feedback (p. 445)
Accommodation (p. 453)
Active listening (p. 442)
Arbitration (p. 456)
Attribution error (p. 448)
Avoidance (p. 453)
Bargaining zone (p. 456)
BATNA (p. 455)
Channel richness (p. 444)
Collaboration (p. 453)

Communication (p. 437)
Communication channel (p. 437)
Competition (p. 453)
Compromise (p. 453)
Conflict (p. 451)
Conflict resolution (p. 452)
Credibility (p. 438)
Distributive negotiation (p. 455)
Dysfunctional conflict (p. 451)

Effective communication (p. 437)
Efficient communication (p. 438)
Emotional conflict (p. 451)
Ethnocentrism (p. 447)
Feedback (p. 443)
Filtering (p. 442)
Functional conflict (p. 451)
Halo effect (p. 450)

Integrative negotiation (p. 455)

Lose-lose conflict (p. 453)

Management by wandering around (p. 444)

Mediation (p. 456)

Mixed message (p. 441)

Negotiation (p. 454)

Noise (p. 439)

Nonverbal communication (p. 440)

Perception (p. 448)

Persuasion (p. 438)

Principled negotiation (p. 455)

Projection (p. 450)

Selective perception (p. 450)

Self-serving bias (p. 449)

Stereotype (p. 449)

Substantive conflict (p. 451)

Win-lose conflict (p. 454)

Win-win conflict (p. 454)

SELF-TEST 17

MULTIPLE-CHOICE QUESTIONS:

1. The use of paraphrasing and reflecting back what someone else says in communication is characteristic of _____.
   (a) mixed messages (b) active listening (c) projection (d) lose-lose conflict

2. When the intended meaning of the sender and the interpreted meaning of the receiver are the same, communication is _____.
   (a) effective (b) persuasive (c) selective (d) efficient

3. Constructive feedback is _____.
   (a) general rather than specific (b) indirect rather than direct (c) given in small doses (d) given any time the sender is ready

4. When a manager uses e-mail to send a message that is better delivered in person, the communication process suffers from _____.
   (a) semantic problems (b) a poor choice of communication channels (c) physical distractions (d) information overload

5. _____ is a form of interactive management that helps improve upward communication.
   (a) Attribution (b) Mediation (c) MBWA (d) BATNA

6. Cross-cultural communication may run into difficulties because of _____, or the tendency to consider one's culture superior to others.
   (a) selective perception (b) ethnocentrism (c) mixed messages (d) projection

7. An appeal to superordinate goals is an example of a(n) _____ approach to conflict management.
   (a) avoidance (b) structural (c) dysfunctional (d) self-serving

8. The conflict management style with the greatest potential for true conflict resolution involves _____.
   (a) compromise (b) competition (c) smoothing (d) collaboration

9. When a person is highly cooperative but not very assertive in approaching conflict, the conflict management style is referred to as _____.
   (a) avoidance (b) authoritative (c) smoothing (d) collaboration

10. The three criteria of an effective negotiation are quality, cost, and _____.
    (a) harmony (b) timeliness (c) efficiency (d) effectiveness

11. In order to be truly and consistently persuasive when communicating with others in the workplace, a manager should build credibility by _____.
    (a) making sure the rewards for compliance are clear (b) making sure the penalties for noncompliance are clear (c) making sure that they know who is the boss (d) making sure that good relationships have been established with them

12. Among the 10 rules for good listening described in the chapter, _____ is both #1 and #10.
    (a) "Stop talking" (b) "Be patient" (c) "Ask questions" (d) "Empathize"

13. A manager who understands the importance of proxemics in communication would be likely to _____.
    (a) avoid sending mixed messages (b) arrange work spaces so as to encourage interaction (c) be very careful in the choice of written and spoken words (d) make frequent use of e-mail messages to keep people well informed

14. Self-serving bias is a form of attribution error that involves _____.
    (a) blaming yourself for problems caused by others (b) blaming the environment for problems you caused (c) choosing to communicate one-way instead of two-way (d) projecting one's values onto others

15. A conflict is most likely to be functional and have a positive impact on group performance when it is _____.
    (a) based on emotions (b) resolved by arbitration (c) caused by resource scarcities (d) of moderate intensity

SHORT-RESPONSE QUESTIONS:

16. Briefly describe what a manager would do to be an "active listener" when communicating with subordinates.

17. What is the difference between the halo effect and selective perception?

18. How do tendencies toward assertiveness and cooperativeness in conflict management result in win-lose, lose-lose, and win-win outcomes?

19. What is the difference between substance and relationship goals in negotiation?

APPLICATION QUESTION:

20. After being promoted to store manager for a new branch of a large department store chain, Harold Welsch was concerned about communication in the store. Six department heads reported directly to him, and 50 full-time and part-time sales associates reported to them. Given this structure, Harold worried about staying informed about all store operations, not just those coming to his attention as senior manager. What steps might Harold take to establish and maintain an effective system of upward communication in his store?

18 Change leadership

CHAPTER 18 study questions

Planning Ahead →

After reading Chapter 18, you should be able to answer these questions in your own words.

1. What are the challenges of strategic leadership and innovation?

2. What is the nature of organizational change?

3. How can planned organizational change be managed?

4. What is organization development?

5. How can stress be manged in a change environment?

HEWLETT-PACKARD—VISION AND LEADERSHIP CREATE TRANSFORMATIONS

It is hard to speak about change leadership these days without the name Carly Fiorina being mentioned. When she took over as CEO of Hewlett-Packard, she inherited a company with an entrenched organizational culture, a legacy of success, and challenging problems in a highly competitive industry. But problems represented opportunities for Fiorina, and she tackled them with both a vengeance and confidence. Her success and hard work earned her top spot on a recent *Fortune* magazine list of the 50 Most Powerful Women in Business.

If one word could be used to describe Fiorina's leadership at Hewlett-Packard, it would be "transformation." And in her quest to transform the firm she challenged old ways of thinking and resistance to change. With her vision a merger with Compaq became a top priority. Not even the opposition of William Hewlett, the son of one of the firm's founders, was able to stop her from reaching the goal.

Fiorina is often asked the question: "Does being a woman affect the way you run the company?" Her response is that gender is irrelevant, saying: "I have to do the job I've been asked to do to the best of my ability." That ability has manifested itself in tripling the cost savings she originally predicted before the merger with Compaq and a willingness to take on competition from Dell and others head on.

Change and innovation are a way of life at the new Hewlett-Packard. Even with over 140,000 employees, 42 factories in 30 countries, and a billion customers, there is no time for the firm or its CEO to stand still or rest on past laurels. The industry is being pressured like never before as more jobs migrate to overseas locations, innovation drives a continuous stream of new products, and globalization brings a rash of new international competitors. Fiorina understands the need for strategic change leadership, and she is both willing and capable in providing it. Looking back on the controversial merger with Compaq, she states: "I would do it again if I had to. We did it because tech was changing. If you're not leading, you're losing."[1]

Chapter 18 Learning Preview

In the chapter opening example of Carly Fiorina and Hewlett-Packard, you were introduced to challenges of strategic change leadership in a very dynamic and highly competitive industry. Fiorina's leadership capabilities extend beyond having a good sense of strategy and vision. They include the personal confidence and understanding needed to transform a huge global enterprise. In Chapter 18 you will learn about how strategic leadership supports change, creativity and innovation in organizations. You will learn about change leaders, change strategies, and resistance to change. You will learn about the process of organization development. You will also learn about the stress that comes with change in the workplace and how stress can be managed constructively.

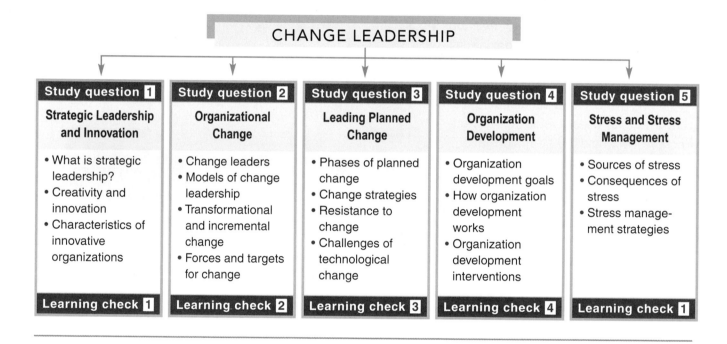

CHANGE LEADERSHIP

Study question **1**	Study question **2**	Study question **3**	Study question **4**	Study question **5**
Strategic Leadership and Innovation	**Organizational Change**	**Leading Planned Change**	**Organization Development**	**Stress and Stress Management**
• What is strategic leadership? • Creativity and innovation • Characteristics of innovative organizations	• Change leaders • Models of change leadership • Transformational and incremental change • Forces and targets for change	• Phases of planned change • Change strategies • Resistance to change • Challenges of technological change	• Organization development goals • How organization development works • Organization development interventions	• Sources of stress • Consequences of stress • Stress management strategies
Learning check **1**	Learning check **2**	Learning check **3**	Learning check **4**	Learning check **1**

When a group of Japanese students drove out of Tokyo one day, the event wouldn't have seemed remarkable to bystanders. But when they arrived some 900 kilometers later on the northern island of Hokkaido, Mitsubishi's president was sure pleased. The students' car, powered by a new engine technology, had made the trip without refueling! In fact, there was fuel to spare in the gas tank. It was an important breakthrough for the company. For a long time engineers had known the feat was technically possible, but they didn't know how to do it. Finally, through hard work, through a lot of information sharing and problem solving, and through learning, they found the answer.[2]

Novel answers to perplexing problems move people, organizations, and societies continuously ahead in our dynamic and very challenging world. We are living and working at a time when intellectual capital, knowledge management, and learning organizations are taking center stage. And rightfully so. Harvard scholars Michael Beer and Nitin Nohria observe: "The new economy has ushered in great business opportunities and great turmoil. Not since the Industrial Revolution have the stakes of dealing with change been so high. Most traditional organizations have accepted, in theory at least, that they must either change or die."[3] Speaking from the vantage point of a corporate leader always looking toward the future, John Chambers, CEO of Cisco Systems, would no doubt agree. "Companies that are successful will have cultures that thrive on change," he says, "even though change makes most people uncomfortable."[4]

Unfortunately and even though the watchwords of today continue to be *change, change,* and *change,* many organizations and too many leaders are slow in responding to the challenge. Creating positive change in organizations is not easy. Change involves risk, complexity, uncertainty, anxiety, and stress. Leading organizations on the pathways of change takes great understanding, discipline, and commitment to creativity and human ingenuity. In his book *The Circle of Innovation,* consultant Tom Peters warns that we must refocus the attention of managers and leaders away from past accomplishments and toward the role of innovation as the primary source of competitive advantage. Doing well in the past, simply put, is no guarantee of future success.[5] The future is the issue in this final chapter of *Management 8/e*—organizational futures, managerial futures, and your future. It is time to inquire into your readiness to master the challenges of change in the evolving new workplace.

STRATEGIC LEADERSHIP AND INNOVATION

At the World Economic Forum, a famous and futuristic think tank for global business, government, and civic leaders held in Davos, Switzerland, the popular buzzwords were "business webs," "value networks," "molecular organizations," and more. The following trends and possibilities were prominent among observations about the changing nature of business in the new economy.[6]

> *Companies that design and brand their own products, build and package them, and then deliver them to customers will soon no longer exist.*

> *Companies (now) have the ability to strip down their business to its essence, to focus on where the greatest value creation (and profits) lies.*

> *Extraneous functions can be eliminated through partnerships and newly supercharged forms of outsourcing.*

> *Instead of one big monolithic entity, companies start to look like clusters of distributed capabilities.*

There are those who might go so far as to say that the corporation as we have traditionally known it is dead, or at least dying. For sure the traditional forms, practices, and systems of the past are being replaced by dramatic new developments driven by the forces of information technology and the relentless pressures of global competitiveness. And this is all happening very, very fast. No leader in any organization, no matter how big or small and whether operating for-profit or not-for-profit, can fail to take notice.

WHAT IS STRATEGIC LEADERSHIP?

Although the points and details may differ, the conclusion reached by futurists is the same. The years ahead will be radically different from those

www.clorox.com

Top management at Clorox tries to avoid chasing new management fads. "You need to be fairly selective and consistent over time so you're not upsetting your organization over the tool of the month," says the vice president of strategy and planning. "When top management is linked to fads, confidence is easily undermined in the employee ranks."

MANAGER'S NOTEPAD 18.1 Six components of strategic leadership

1. Determining the organization's purpose or vision.
2. Exploiting and maintaining the organization's core competencies.
3. Developing the organization's human capital.
4. Sustaining an effective organizational culture.
5. Emphasizing and displaying ethical practices.
6. Establishing balanced organizational controls.

O A **learning organization** utilizes people, values, and systems to continuously change and improve its performance.

past. We and our organizations must be prepared not only to change, but to change continuously and successfully in the face of ever-present uncertainties. In earlier chapters we discussed the benefits of what Peter Senge calls **learning organizations**—ones that mobilize people, values, and systems to achieve continuous change and performance improvements driven by the lessons of experience.[7] This is the ideal; it is the target; it is what organizations should be like. It is what leaders everywhere should strive for as they help and move and push organizations forward into the complicated world of tomorrow.

O **Strategic leadership** creates the capacity for ongoing strategic change.

Scholars R. Duane Ireland and Michael Hitt describe **strategic leadership** as the "ability to anticipate, envision, maintain flexibility, think strategically, and work with others to initiate changes that will create a viable future for the organization."[8] Strategic leaders are change leaders who build learning organizations and keep them competitive even in difficult and uncertain times. The goal is to make a core competency out of the ability to successfully and continuously change. But this isn't just pushing change for the sake of change; the change must have a strategic and customer-driven purpose. Dawn Lepore, Vice chairman and CIO of the financial services firm Charles Schwab, says: "What we must have—and I do mean 'must'—is a core competence in reinventing ourselves as the needs of our customers change with the marketplace."[9] *Manager's Notepad 18.1* highlights strategic leadership components that best prepare managers to meet this challenge.[10]

CREATIVITY AND INNOVATION

O **Creativity** is the generation of a novel idea or unique approach that solves a problem or crafts an opportunity.

Sustainable competitive advantage in a change environment is earned in part through organizational cultures and human capital that unlock the full powers of creativity and innovation. **Creativity** is the generation of a novel idea or unique approach to solving problems or crafting opportunities.[11] It is one of the great assets of human capital. People have ideas; people possess ingenuity; people have the capacity to invent. Creativity is what allows us to turn technologies and other resources into unique processes and products that differentiate the accomplishments of any one organization from those of the next.

O **Innovation** is the process of taking a new idea and putting it into practice.

Creativity exerts its influence in organizations through **innovation,** the process of creating new ideas and putting them into practice.[12] Management consultant Peter Drucker calls innovation "an effort to create purposeful, focused change in an enterprise's economic or social potential."[13] Said a bit differently, it is the act of converting new ideas into usable applications with positive economic or social consequences. Consider two very different cxamples.

> Groove Neworks, Inc. The firm has been described as "Napster for business" and founder Ray Ozzie is sometimes called the "wizard of peer-to-peer computing." After watching his son play multiplayer games on the Web and his daughter send instant messages, Ozzie realized the potential and created new software devoted to "P2P" collaboration in business. Before this he had created Lotus Notes, now owned by IBM.[14]

> Grammeen Phone What happens when the digital age meets the developing world? Progress, at least if you are part of the Grammeen Bank network in Bangladesh. Most of the country's 68,000 villages have no phone service; the average annual income is about $200. That is changing through an innovative program. The grameen bank makes loans to women entrepreneurs to allow them to buy and operate a cellular telephone, each typically serving an entire village. The bank's goal is twofold: to receive an economic return on its investment and to contribute to economic development. The model is now spreading to serve the rural poor in other nations.[15]

Innovation in and by organizations occurs in two broad forms: (1) **process innovations,** which result in better ways of doing things; and (2) **product innovations,** which result in the creation of new or improved goods and services. The management of both requires active encouragement and support for *invention*—the act of discovery, and for *application*—the act of use. Managers need to be concerned about investing and building new work environments that stimulate creativity and an ongoing stream of new ideas. They must also make sure that good ideas for new or modified processes and products are actually implemented. One way to describe the full set of responsibilities for the innovation process is in these five steps, constituting what consultant Gary Hamel calls the *wheel of innovation.*[16]

O **Process innovations** result in better ways of doing things.

O **Product innovations** result in new or improved goods or services.

1. *Imagining*—thinking about new possibilities; making discoveries by ingenuity or communication with others; extending existing ways.
2. *Designing*—testing ideas in concept; discussing them with peers, customers, clients, or technical experts; building initial models, prototypes, or samples.
3. *Experimenting*—examining practicality and financial value through experiments and feasibility studies.
4. *Assessing*—identifying strengths and weaknesses, potential costs and benefits, and potential markets or applications, and making constructive changes.
5. *Scaling*—gearing up and implementing new processes; putting to work what has been learned; commercializing new products or services.

← Hamel's wheel of innovation

One of the major requirements of successful innovation is that the entire process meets real needs of the organization and its marketplace. New ideas alone are not sufficient to guarantee success in this setting; they must be relevant and they must be well implemented in order to

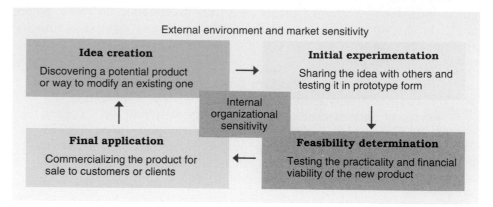

External environment and market sensitivity

Idea creation

Discovering a potential product or way to modify an existing one

Initial experimentation

Sharing the idea with others and testing it in prototype form

Internal organizational sensitivity

Final application

Commercializing the product for sale to customers or clients

Feasibility determination

Testing the practicality and financial viability of the new product

Figure 18.1 Process of commercializing innovation in organizations: the case of new product development.

○ **Commercializing innovation** turns ideas into economic value added.

improve organizational performance. In business, **commercializing innovation** is the process of turning new ideas into products or processes that can increase profits through greater sales or reduced costs.[17] For example, 3M Corporation generates over one-third of its revenues from products that didn't exist four years ago. The firm, for whom product innovation is a way of life, owes its success to the imagination of employees like Art Fry. He's the person whose creativity turned an adhesive that "wasn't sticky enough" into the blockbuster product known worldwide today as Post-It Notes.® *Figure 18.1* uses the example of new product development to highlight the various steps of commercializing innovation.

CHARACTERISTICS OF INNOVATIVE ORGANIZATIONS

Innovative organizations like 3M, Johnson & Johnson, Apple Computer, and others are great at mobilizing talent and intellectual capital to support creativity and entrepreneurship. Their managers at all levels are masters at actively leading the innovation process.[19] In highly innovative organizations, the *corporate strategy and culture support innovation.* The strategies of the organization, the visions and values of senior management, and the framework of policies and expectations emphasize an entrepreneurial spirit. Innovation is expected, failure is accepted, and the organization is willing to take risks. Johnson & Johnson's former CEO James Burke once said: "I try to give people the feeling that it's okay to fail, that it's important to fail." His key point is that managers should eliminate risk-averse climates and replace them with organizational cultures in which innovation is a norm.

In highly innovative organizations, *organization structures support innovation.* More and more large organizations are trying to capture the structural flexibility of smaller ones. They are striving for more organic operations that emphasize lateral communications and extensively use cross-functional teams and task forces. In particular, research and development, historically a separate and isolated function, is being integrated into a team setting. As Peter Drucker points out, "Successful innovations . . . are now being turned out by cross-functional teams with people from marketing, manufacturing, and finance participating in research work from the very beginning."[20]

Creativity is there for the asking—you just have to open up to it

It's a long way from Takashimiya's home base in Tokyo to the streets of Manhattan. But that doesn't stop Marita Wesley-Clough from carefully scanning the aisles of one of Japan's leading department stores. It's the first stop on Wesley-Clough's semiannual tour of New York's finest stores. "You can walk out of there renewed and refreshed," she says, "and not having bought a thing." Of course, buying isn't her main purpose; ideas are. Wesley-Clough is a trends expert for Hallmark Cards. Her job is to help keep creativity alive at the firm. On this trip to Takashimiya, it was color that caught her eye—"look at the color" she says, and the Zen-like quietness. All this will go in a report when she returns to Hallmark's home base of Kansas City, Missouri. "You have to get out of your own head and to let other ideas in" says Wesley-Clough. That's good advice for anyone interested in creativity.[18]

In highly innovative organizations, *top management supports innovation*. In the case of 3M, for example, many top managers have been the innovators and product champions in the company's past. They understand the innovation process, are tolerant of criticisms and differences of opinion, and take all possible steps to keep the goals clear and the pressure on. The key, once again, is to allow the creative potential of people to operate fully.

In highly innovative organizations, *the organization's staffing supports innovation*. Organizations need different kinds of people to support the innovation process. The critical innovation roles to be filled include:[21]

* *Idea generators*—people who create new insights from internal discovery or external awareness, or both.

* *Information gatekeepers*—people who serve as links between people and groups within the organization and with external sources.

* *Product champions*—people who advocate and push for change and innovation, and for the adoption of specific product or process ideas.

* *Project managers*—people who perform technical functions needed to keep an innovative project on track with necessary resource support.

* *Innovation leaders*—people who encourage, sponsor, and coach others to keep the innovation values, goals and energies in place.

← Innovation roles in organizations

Be sure you can • discuss the link between learning organizations and strategic leadership • define the terms creativity and innovation • list the five steps in Hamel's wheel of innovation • define the term commercializing innovation • list and explain the characteristics of innovative organizations • identify the critical innovation roles in organizations

ORGANIZATIONAL CHANGE

According to Peter Drucker, purposeful innovation should add value to organizations and society.[22] This positive message makes change sound almost a matter of routine, something readily accepted by everyone involved. But what are the realities of trying to systematically change organizations and the behaviors of people within them? When Angel Martinez became CEO of Rockport Company, for example, he sought to change traditional ways that were not aligned with future competition. Rather than embrace the changes he sponsored, employees resisted. Martinez said they "gave lip service to my ideas and hoped I'd go away."[23] Consider also what once happened at Bank of America after the company announced a large quarterly operating loss. Its new CEO at the time, Samuel Armacost, complained about the lack of "agents of change" among his top managers. Claiming that managers seemed more interested in taking orders than initiating change, he said: "I came away quite distressed from my first couple of management meetings. Not only couldn't I get conflict, I couldn't even get comment. They were all waiting to see which way the wind blew."[24]

CHANGE LEADERS

○ A **change leader** is a **change agent** who tries to change the behavior of another person or social system.

A **change leader** is a **change agent** who takes leadership responsibility for changing the existing pattern of behavior of another person or social system. Change agents make things happen, and part of every manager's job is to act as a change leader in the work setting. This requires being alert to situations or to people needing change, being open to good ideas and opportunities, and being ready and able to support the implementation of new ideas in actual practice. *Figure 18.2* contrasts a true "change leader" with a "status quo manager." The former is forward-looking, proactive, and embraces new ideas; the latter is backward-looking, reactive, and comfortable with habit. Obviously, the new workplace demands change leadership at all levels of management.

MODELS OF CHANGE LEADERSHIP

In Chapter 16 on teams and teamwork, we discussed the concept of distributed leadership in teams. The point was that every team member

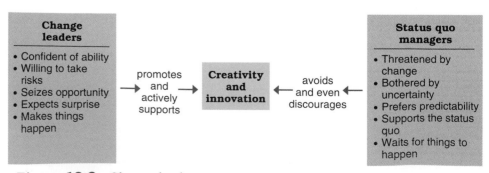

Figure 18.2 Change leaders versus status quo managers.

has the potential to lead by serving group needs for task and maintenance activities. The same notion applies when it comes to change leadership. The responsibilities for change leadership are ideally distributed and shared by all managers top to bottom in any organization.

Top-Down Change

In **top-down change,** senior managers initiate changes with the goal of comprehensive impact on the organization and its performance capabilities. This is the domain of strategic leadership as discussed earlier in the chapter. Importantly, however, reports indicate that some 70 percent or more of large-scale change efforts actually fail.[25] The most common reason is poor implementation. The success of top-down change is usually determined by the willingness of middle-level and lower-level workers to actively support top-management initiatives. Change programs have little chance of success without the support of those who must implement them. Any change that is driven from the top runs the risk of being perceived as insensitive to the needs of lower-level personnel. It can easily fail if implementation suffers from excessive resistance and insufficient commitments to change. Thus, it is not enough to simply mandate change from the top; action must be taken to earn the support of others throughout the organization.

○ In **top-down change,** the change initiatives come from senior management.

Bottom-Up Change

In **bottom-up change** the initiatives for change come from any and all parts of the organization, not just top management. This type of change is essential to organizational innovation and is very useful in terms of adapting operations and technologies to the changing requirements of work. It is made possible by management commitments to empowerment, involvement, and participation, as discussed in earlier chapters. For example, at Johnson Controls, Inc., Jason Moncer was given the nickname "Mr. Kaizen" by his coworkers.[26] The nickname refers to a Japanese practice of continuous improvement. Moncer earned it by offering many ideas for changes in his work area. At his plant, workers contributed over 200 suggestions that were implemented in just one year alone. The company is committed to the belief that workers should be encouraged to use their job knowledge and common sense to improve things. In other words, when the workers talk at Johnson Controls, managers listen.

○ In **bottom-up change,** change initiatives come from all levels in the organization.

Integrated Change Leadership

The most successful and enduring change leadership is that which can harness the advantages of both top-down and bottom-up change. Top-down initiatives may be needed to break traditional patterns and implement difficult economic adjustments; bottom-up initiatives are necessary to build institutional capability for sustainable change and organizational learning. When first taking over as CEO of General Electric in 1981, Jack Welch began an aggressive top-down restructuring that led to major workforce cuts and a trimmer organization structure. Once underway, however, this evolved into bottom-up change focusing

MANAGER'S NOTEPAD 18.2

How to lead transformational change

- Establish a sense of urgency for change.
- Form a powerful coalition to lead the change.
- Create and communicate a change vision.
- Empower others to move change forward.
- Celebrate short-term "wins" and recognize those who help.
- Build on success; align people and systems with new ways.
- Stay with it; keep the message consistent; champion the vision.

on employee involvement. He started a widely benchmarked program called Work-Out to invigorate a process of continuous reassessment and planned change.[28] In Work-Out sessions employees confront their managers in a "town meeting" format, with the manager in front listening to suggestions for removing performance obstacles and improving operations. The managers are expected to respond immediately to the suggestions and support positive change initiatives raised during the session.

REALITY CHECK 18.1

Why large-scale change efforts often fail

Most large-scale change efforts fail because senior executives fail to establish a sense of urgency throughout the organization. Take the online "Reality Check" to learn more about reasons for change failure.

○ **Reactive change** responds to events as or after they occur.

○ **Planned change** aligns the organization with anticipated future challenges.

○ A **performance gap** is a discrepancy between a desired and actual state of affairs.

○ **Transformational change** results in a major and comprehensive redirection of the organization.

TRANSFORMATIONAL AND INCREMENTAL CHANGE

Some changes occur spontaneously in organizations, largely in response to unanticipated events. These *unplanned changes* can be disruptive, such as a wildcat strike that results in a plant closure. But they can also be beneficial, such as an interpersonal conflict that results in a decision to try a new procedure or work process. Good managers do their best to take advantage of opportunities for such **reactive change,** doing a good job of responding to events as or after they occur. But the really great managers are not satisfied with being reactive. They are forward thinking and always alert to potential future problems and opportunities. They offer organizations proactive leadership that activates **planned change**—taking steps to best align the organization with anticipated future challenges.[29] They are always on the alert for **performance gaps,** or discrepancies between desired and actual states of affairs. Performance gaps may represent problems to be resolved or opportunities to be explored. In both cases, proactive change leaders take action in the present to deal with performance gaps in ways that improve future organizational performance.

There are two major types of planned organizational change. The first is radical or frame-breaking **transformational change**—that which results in a major and comprehensive redirection of the organization.[30] Transformational change is led from the top and designed to change the basic character of the organization. It results in fundamental shifts in strategies, culture, structures, and even the underlying sense of purpose or mission. A good example is the case of Hewlett-Packard described in the chapter opener. As you would expect, transformational change is intense, highly stressful, and very complex to achieve. *Manager's Notepad 18.2* offers several lessons learned from studies of large-scale transformational change in business.[31]

The second type of planned change in organizations is **incremental change.** Rather than radical transformation of an organization, this type of change bends and nudges existing systems and practices to better align them with emerging problems and opportunities. Leadership of incremental change focuses on building upon existing ways of doing things with the goal of improvement, doing them better in the future. Common incremental changes in organizations involve new products, new processes, new technologies, and new work systems. The quality concept of continuous improvement is closely linked with this notion of incremental change.

O **Incremental change** bends and adjusts existing ways to improve performance.

FORCES AND TARGETS FOR CHANGE

The impetus for organizational change, transformational or incremental, can arise from a variety of external forces.[32] These include globalization, market competition, local economic conditions, government laws and regulations, technological developments, market trends, and social forces and values, among others. As an organization's general and specific environments develop and change over time, the organization must adapt as well. Internal forces for change are important too. Indeed, any change in one part of the organization as a complex system—perhaps a change initiated in response to one or more of the external forces just identified—can often create the need for change in another part of the system. The common *organizational targets for change*—tasks, people, culture, technology, and structure—are highly interrelated:[33]

- *Tasks*—the nature of work as represented by organizational mission, objectives, and strategy, and the job designs for individuals and groups.
- *People*—the attitudes and competencies of the employees and the human resource systems that support them.
- *Culture*—the value system for the organization as a whole, and the norms guiding individual and group behavior.
- *Technology*—the operations and information technology used to support job designs, arrange workflows, and integrate people and machines in systems.
- *Structure*—the configuration of the organization as a complex system, including its design features and lines of authority and communications.

← Organizational targets for change

Learning check 2

Be sure you can • define the term change agent • discuss the pros and cons of top-down change and of bottom-up change • differentiate planned and unplanned change • differentiate transformational and incremental change • list common organizational targets for change

LEADING PLANNED CHANGE

The many complications of change in organizations begin with human nature. People tend to act habitually and in stable ways over time. They may not want to change even when circumstances require it. As a manager and change agent, you will need to recognize and deal with such tendencies in order to successfully lead planned change.

PHASES OF PLANNED CHANGE

Kurt Lewin, a noted psychologist, recommends that any planned change effort be viewed as a process with the three phases shown in *Figure 18.3*.[34] Lewin's three phases of planned change are: (1) *unfreezing*—preparing a system for change; (2) *changing*—making actual changes in the system; and (3) *refreezing*—stabilizing the system after change.

Unfreezing

In order for change to be successful, people must be ready for it. Planned change has little chance for long-term success unless people are open to doing things differently. **Unfreezing** is the stage in which a situation is prepared for change and felt needs for change are devel-

o **Unfreezing** is the phase during which a situation is prepared for change.

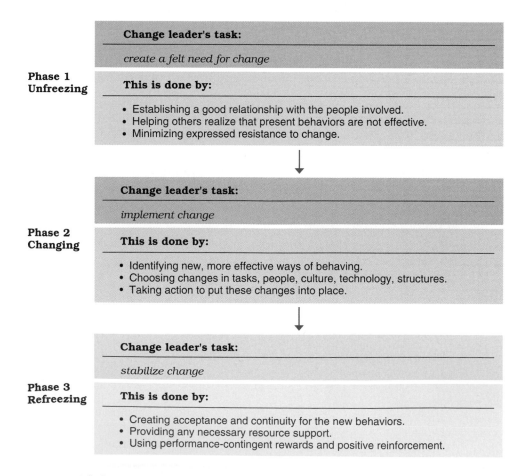

Phase 1 Unfreezing

Change leader's task:

create a felt need for change

This is done by:

- Establishing a good relationship with the people involved.
- Helping others realize that present behaviors are not effective.
- Minimizing expressed resistance to change.

Phase 2 Changing

Change leader's task:

implement change

This is done by:

- Identifying new, more effective ways of behaving.
- Choosing changes in tasks, people, culture, technology, structures.
- Taking action to put these changes into place.

Phase 3 Refreezing

Change leader's task:

stabilize change

This is done by:

- Creating acceptance and continuity for the new behaviors.
- Providing any necessary resource support.
- Using performance-contingent rewards and positive reinforcement.

Figure 18.3 Lewin's three phases of planned organizational change.

oped. It can be facilitated in several ways: through environmental pressures for change, declining performance, the recognition that problems or opportunities exist, and the observation of behavioral models that display alternative approaches. When handled well, conflict can be an important unfreezing force in organizations. It often helps people break old habits and recognize alternative ways of thinking about or doing things.

Changing

In the **changing** phase, something new takes place in a system and change is actually implemented. This is the point at which managers initiate changes in such organizational targets as tasks, people, culture, technology, and structure. This phase is ideally reached after unfreezing, with a good diagnosis of a problem and a careful examination of alternatives. However, Lewin believes that many change agents enter the changing phase prematurely, are too quick to change things, and therefore end up creating resistance to change. When managers implement change before people feel a need for it, there is an increased likelihood of failure.

○ **Changing** is the phase where a planned change actually takes place.

Refreezing

The final stage in the planned change process is **refreezing.** Here, the manager is concerned about stabilizing the change and creating the conditions for its long-term continuity. Refreezing is accomplished by linking change with appropriate rewards for performance, positive reinforcement, and necessary resource support. It is also important in this phase to evaluate results carefully, provide feedback to the people involved, and make any required modifications in the original change. When refreezing is done poorly, changes are too easily forgotten or abandoned with the passage of time. When it is done well, change should be more long lasting.

○ **Refreezing** is the phase at which change is stabilized.

CHANGE STRATEGIES

The act of actually changing or moving people to do things differently can be pursued in different ways. *Figure 18.4* summarizes three common change strategies known as force-coercion, rational persuasion, and shared power.[35] Managers, as change agents, should understand that each can have very different consequences.

Force-Coercion Strategies

A **force-coercion strategy** uses the power bases of legitimacy, rewards, and punishments as the primary inducements to change. A change agent that seeks to create change through force-coercion believes that people are basically motivated by self-interest and by what the situation offers in terms of potential personal gains or losses.[36] This change agent believes that people change only in response to such motives, tries to find out where their vested interests lie, and then puts the pressure on. Once a weakness is found, it is exploited.

○ A **force-coercion strategy** pursues change through formal authority and/or the use of rewards or punishments.

Change Strategy	Power Bases	Managerial Behavior	Likely Results
Force–Coercion Using position power to create change by decree and formal authority	Legitimacy Rewards Punishments	*Direct forcing* and unilateral action *Political maneuvering* and indirect action	Faster, but low commitment and only temporary compliance
Rational Persuasion Creating change through rational persuasion and empirical argument	Expertise	*Informational efforts* using credible knowledge, demonstrated facts, and logical argument	
Shared power Developing support for change through personal values and commitments	Reference	*Participative efforts* to share power and involve others in planning and implementing change	Slower, but high commitment and longer term internalization

Figure 18.4 Alternative change strategies and their leadership implications.

In a *direct forcing* strategy, the change agent takes direct and unilateral action to "command" that change take place. This involves the exercise of formal authority or legitimate power, offering special rewards and/or threatening punishment. In *political maneuvering,* the change agent works indirectly to gain special advantage over other persons and thereby make them change. This involves bargaining, obtaining control of important resources, forming alliances or granting small favors.

Any force-coercion strategy on its own produces limited results. Although it can be implemented rather quickly, most people respond to force-coercion out of fear of punishment or hope for a reward. This usually results in only temporary compliance with the change agent's desires. The new behavior continues only so long as the opportunity for rewards and punishments is present. For this reason, force-coercion is most useful as an unfreezing device that helps people break old patterns of behavior and gain initial impetus to try new ones. The example of General Electric's Work-Out program, noted earlier, applies here.[37] Jack Welch started Work-Out to create a forum for active employee empowerment of continuous change. But he didn't make the program optional; participation in Work-Out was mandatory from the start. Welch used his authority as leader to initiate the program because he was confident it would survive and prosper on its own—once it was experienced. Part of his commitment to change leadership was a willingness to use authority to unfreeze situations and get new things started.

Rational Persuasion Strategies

O A **rational persuasion strategy** pursues change through empirical data and rational argument.

Change agents using a **rational persuasion strategy** attempt to bring about change through persuasion backed by special knowledge, empirical data, and rational argument. A change agent following this strategy believes that people are inherently rational and are guided by reason in their actions and decision making. Once a specific course of action is demonstrated to be in a person's self-interest, the change agent assumes that reason and rationality will cause the person to adopt it. Thus, he or she uses information and facts to communicate the essential desirability of change.

The likely outcome of rational persuasion is eventual compliance with reasonable commitment. When successful, a rational persuasion strategy

TAKE IT TO THE CASE

The art of brand building keeps Disney center stage

Yes, brand building is an art form at the company that Walt Disney built. He began in 1922 with a firm called Laugh-O-Gram Films. It failed in 1923. But Walt didn't give up. Later that year he and brother Roy launched Disney Brothers Studio on $3,000. The company has changed a lot since then, now a global giant and a benchmark in organizational practices. It's all built with human talent and an eye to the future. But change is always be part of Disney's script. It's always ready. The firm's Professional Development Institute offers programs in leadership, service, and creativity that are highly valued within the firm and externally. "Join us," says the corporate electronic billboard advertising Disney careers. "We are a cast of thousands . . . our varied backgrounds, personalities and talents make us each an integral part of team Disney."[39]

helps both unfreeze and refreeze a change situation. Although slower than force-coercion, it tends to result in longer-lasting and more internalized change. To be successful, a manager using rational persuasion must convince others that the cost–benefit value of a planned change is high and that it will leave them better off than before. This power can come directly from the change agent if she or he has personal credibility as an "expert." If not, it can be obtained in the form of consultants and other outside experts, or from credible demonstration projects and benchmarks. The magic of Walt Disney World, for example, extends to more than family fun and holidays. Many firms use Disney as a benchmark to demonstrate to their own employees how changes can improve operations. A Ford vice president says, "Disney's track record is one of the best in the country as far as dealing with customers." The firm sends managers to Disney to learn about customer loyalty, hoping to drive customer service initiatives of their own.[38] In this sense the power of rational persuasion is straightforward: If it works for Disney, why can't it work for us?

Shared Power Strategies

A **shared power strategy** engages people in a collaborative process of identifying values, assumptions, and goals from which support for change will naturally emerge. The process is slow, but it is likely to yield high commitment. Sometimes called a *normative reeducative strategy,* this approach is based on empowerment and is highly participative in nature. It relies on involving others in examining personal needs and values, group norms, and operating goals as they relate to the issues at hand. Power is shared by the change agent and other persons as they work together to develop a new consensus to support needed change.

○ A **shared power strategy** pursues change by participation in assessing change needs, values and goals.

Managers using shared power as an approach to planned change need referent power and the skills to work effectively in groups. They must be comfortable allowing others to participate in making decisions that affect the planned change and the way it is implemented. Because it entails a high level of involvement, this strategy is often quite time consuming. But importantly, power sharing is likely to result in a longer-lasting and internalized change.

A change agent who shares power begins by recognizing that people have varied needs and complex motivations. He or she believes people behave as they do because of sociocultural norms and commitments to the expectations of others. Changes in organizations are understood to inevitably involve changes in attitudes, values, skills, and significant relationships, not just changes in knowledge, information, or intellectual rationales for action and practice. Thus, when seeking to change others, this change agent is sensitive to the way group pressures can support or inhibit change. In working with people, every attempt is made to gather their opinions, identify their feelings and expectations, and incorporate them fully into the change process.

The great "power" of sharing power in the change process lies with unlocking the creativity and experience of people within the system. Unfortunately, many managers are hesitant to engage this process for fear of losing control or of having to compromise on important organizational goals. Harvard scholar Teresa M. Amabile, however, points out that managers and change leaders should have the confidence to share power regarding means and processes, but not overall goals. "People will be more creative," she says, "if you give them freedom to decide how to climb particular mountains. You needn't let them choose which mountains to climb."[40]

RESISTANCE TO CHANGE

Hyatt Hotels uses surveys to check organzational climate and effectiveness. Employees are asked: "Tell us what you think of management." From this they create a General Morale Index that is closely watched by senior management.

Change typically brings with it resistance. When people resist change, furthermore, they are most often defending something important and that appears threatened. A change of work schedules for workers in ON Semiconductor's Rhode Island plant, for example, may not have seemed like much to top management. But to the workers it was significant enough to bring about an organizing attempt by the Teamster's Union. When management delved into the issues, they found that workers viewed changes in weekend work schedules as threatening to their personal lives. With inputs from the workers, the problem was resolved satisfactorily.[41]

There are any number of reasons why people in organizations may resist planned change. Some of the more common ones are shown in *Manager's Notepad 18.3.* Change agents and managers often view such resistance as something that must be "overcome" in order for change to be successful. But, resistance is better viewed as feedback that the informed change agent can use to plan or modify change to best fit situational needs and goals. When resistance appears, it usually means that something can be done to achieve a better "fit" among the planned change, the situation, and the people involved. Consider the implications of this conversation reported by Jim Stam, a shift work consultant with Circadian Technologies. *Manager*—"Come on, Jim, there must be one schedule that's the right schedule for this industry." *Jim*—"Yes, it's the one the people in the plant pick."[42]

Once resistance to change is recognized and understood, it can be dealt with in various ways.[43] Among the alternatives for effectively managing resistance, the *education and communication* approach uses discussions, presentations, and demonstrations to educate people beforehand about a change. *Participation and involvement* allow others to contribute ideas and help design and implement the change. The *facilitation and support* approach involves providing encouragement and training, actively listening to problems and complaints, and helping to overcome performance pressures. *Facilitation and agreement* provides incentives that appeal to those who are actively resisting or ready to resist. It also makes trade-offs in exchange for assurances that change will not be blocked. *Manipulation*

Why people may resist change

- *Fear of the unknown*—not understanding what is happening or what comes next.
- *Disrupted habits*—feeling upset when old ways of doing things can't be followed.
- *Loss of confidence*—feeling incapable of performing well under the new ways of doing things.
- *Loss of control*—feeling that things are being done "to" you rather than "by" or "with" you.
- *Poor timing*—feeling overwhelmed by the situation or that things are moving too fast.
- *Work overload*—not having the physical or psychic energy to commit to the change.
- *Loss of face*—feeling inadequate or humilated because it appears that the "old" ways weren't "good" ways.
- *Lack of purpose*—not seeing a reason for the change and/or not understanding its benefits.

---

and co-optation try to covertly influence others by providing information selectively and structuring events in favor of the desired change. *Explicit and implicit coercion* forces people to accept change by threatening resistors with a variety of undesirable consequences if they do not go along as asked. Obviously, the last two approaches carry great risk and potential for negative side effects.

IN PRACTICE

Mistakes can be turned into successes

Since its founding in 1914, Toro Company has created many innovative products for the landscaping and lawn-care markets. But success doesn't always come in a straight line. Once, when a new molding technique didn't work, Toro lost mower sales. Members of the engineering team responsible for the technique were called to the CEO's office. But instead of "pink slips," they were met with a party that included balloons and a cake. The celebration was in honor of the risk they had taken. Later, it was found that the technique could be used successfully in the production of other Toro products.[44]

CHALLENGES OF TECHNOLOGICAL CHANGE

Ongoing technological change is a way of life in today's organizations, but it also brings special challenges to change leaders. For the full advantages of new technologies to be realized, a good fit must be achieved with work needs, practices, and people. This, in turn, requires sensitivity to resistance and continual gathering of information so that appropriate adjustments can be made during the time a new technology is being implemented. The demands of managing technological change have been described using the analogy of contrasting styles between navigators from the Micronesian island of Truk and their European counterparts.[45]

> *The European navigator works from a plan, relates all moves during a voyage to the plan, and tries to always stay "on course." When something unexpected happens, the plan is revised systematically, and the new plan followed again until the navigator finds the ship to be off course. The Trukese navigator, by contrast, starts with an objective and moves off in its general direction. Always alert to information from waves, clouds, winds, etc., the navigator senses subtle changes in conditions and steers and alters the ship's course continually to reach the ultimate objective.*

Like the navigators of Truk, technological change may best be approached as an ongoing process that will inevitably require improvisation as things are being implemented. New technologies are often designed external to the organization in which they are to be used. The implications of such a technology for a local application may be difficult to anticipate and plan for ahead of time. A technology that is attractive in concept may appear complicated to the new users; the full extent of its benefits and/or inadequacies may not become known until it is tried. This, in turn, means that the change leader and manager should be alert to resistance, should continually gather and process information relating to the change, and should be willing to customize the new technology to best meet the needs of the local situation.[46]

Learning check 3

Be sure you can • identify Lewin's phases of planned change • discuss a change leader's action responsibilities for each phase • explain the force-coercion, rational persuasion, and shared power change strategies • discuss the pros and cons of each change strategy • list several reasons why people resist change • identify strategies for dealing with resistance to change • discuss the challenges of technological change

---

ORGANIZATION DEVELOPMENT

o **Organization development** is a comprehensive effort to improve an organization's ability to solve problems and improve performance.

There will always be times when the members of organizations should sit together and systematically reflect on strengths and weaknesses, performance accomplishments and failures, and the future. One way to ensure that this happens in a participative and action-oriented environment is through **organization development.** This is a comprehensive approach to planned organizational change that involves the application of behavioral science in a systematic and long-range effort to improve organizational effectiveness.[47] "OD" is an important way for leaders to share power to advance planned change agendas, foster creativity and innovation, and continuously improve organizational performance. Although it often involves the assistance of a consultant with special training, all managers can and should include OD in their change leadership agendas.

ORGANIZATION DEVELOPMENT GOALS

Two goals are pursued simultaneously in organization development. The *outcome goals of OD* focus on task accomplishments, while the *process goals of OD* focus on the way people work together. The second goal strongly differentiates OD from more general attempts at planned change in organizations. You may think of OD as a form of "planned change plus," with the "plus" meaning that change is accomplished in such a way that organization members develop a capacity for continued self-renewal. That is, OD tries to achieve change in ways that help organization members become more active and self-reliant in their ability to continue changing in the future. What also makes OD unique is its commitment to strong humanistic values and established principles of behavioral science. OD is committed to improving organizations through freedom of choice, shared power, and self-reliance, and by taking the best advantage of what we know about human behavior in organizations.

HOW ORGANIZATION DEVELOPMENT WORKS

Figure 18.5 presents a general model of OD and shows its relationship to Lewin's three phases of planned change. To begin the OD process successfully, any consultant or facilitator must first *establish a working relationship* with members of the client system. The next step is *diagnosis*—gathering and analyzing data to assess the situation and set appropriate change objectives. This helps with unfreezing as well as pinpointing appropriate directions for action. Diagnosis leads to active *intervention,* wherein change objectives are pursued through a variety of specific interventions, a number of which will be discussed shortly. Also essential to any OD effort is *evaluation.* This is the examination of the process to determine whether things are proceeding as desired and whether further action is needed. Eventually, the OD consultant or facilitator should *achieve a terminal relationship* that leaves the client able to function on its own. If OD has been well done, the system and its members should be better prepared to manage their ongoing need for self-renewal and development.

The success or failure of any OD program lies in part with the strength of its methodological foundations. As shown in *Figure 18.6,* these foundations rest on **action research**—the process of systematically collecting data on an organization, feeding it back to the members for action plan-

O **Action research** is a collaborative process of collecting data, using it for action planning, and evaluating the results.

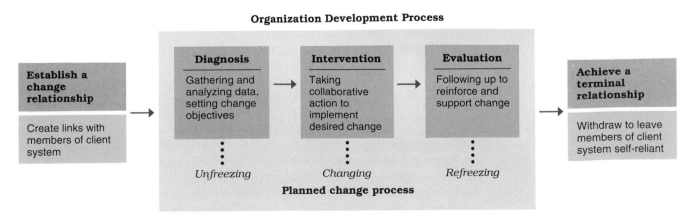

Figure 18.5 Organization development and the planned change process.

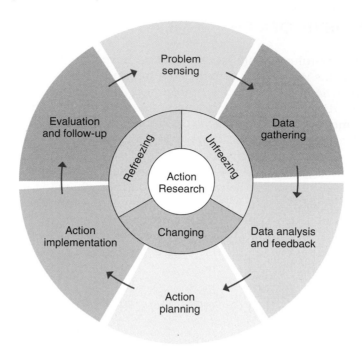

Figure 18.6 Action research as a foundation of organization development.

ning, and evaluating results by collecting more data and repeating the process as necessary. Action research is initiated when someone senses a performance gap and decides to analyze the situation to understand its problems and opportunities. Data gathering can be done in several ways. Interviews are a common means of gathering data in action research. Formal written surveys of employee attitudes and needs are also growing in popularity. Many such "climate," "attitude," or "morale" questionnaires have been tested for reliability and validity. Some have even been used so extensively that norms are available so that one organization can compare its results with those from a broad sample of counterparts.

ORGANIZATION DEVELOPMENT INTERVENTIONS

O An **OD intervention** is a structured activity that helps create change for organization development.

In many ways organization development is employee involvement in action. The process involves respect for people and commitments to their full participation in self-directed change efforts. The process is activated by a variety of **OD interventions** that directly facilitate participatory change. Importantly, these interventions are linked to concepts and ideas discussed elsewhere in this book and that are well represented in the practices and approaches of the new workplace.[48]

Individual Interventions

Organization development practitioners recognize that needs for personal growth and development are most likely to be satisfied in a supportive and challenging work environment. They also accept the premise that most people are capable of assuming responsibility for their own actions and of making positive contributions to organizational performance. Based on these principles, some of the more popular OD interventions designed to help improve individual effectiveness include the following:

- *Sensitivity training*—unstructured sessions (T-groups) where participants learn interpersonal skills and increased sensitivity to other people.
- *Management training*—structured educational opportunities for developing important managerial skills and competencies.
- *Role negotiation*—structured interactions to clarify and negotiate role expectations among people who work together.
- *Job redesign*—realigning task components to better fit the needs and capabilities of individuals.
- *Career planning*—structured advice and discussion sessions to help individuals plan career paths and personal development programs.

Individual OD interventions

Team Interventions

The team plays a very important role in organization development. OD practitioners recognize two principles in this respect. First, teams are viewed as important vehicles for helping people satisfy important needs. Second, it is believed that improved collaboration within and among teams can improve organizational performance. Selected OD interventions designed to improve team effectiveness include the following:

- *Team building*—structured experiences to help team members set goals, improve interpersonal relations, and become a better-functioning team.
- *Process consultation*—third-party observation and advice on critical team processes (e.g., communication, conflict, and decision making).
- *Intergroup team building*—structured experiences to help two or more teams set shared goals, reduce conflict, improve intergroup relations, and become better coordinated.

Team OD interventions

Organization-Wide Interventions

At the level of the total organization, OD practitioners operate on the premise that any changes in one part of the system will also affect other parts. The organization's culture is considered to have an important impact on member attitudes and morale. And it is believed that structures and jobs can be designed to bring together people, technology, and systems in highly productive and satisfying working combinations. Some of the OD interventions with an emphasis on overall organizational effectiveness include the following:

- *Survey feedback*—comprehensive and systematic data collection to identify attitudes and needs, analyze results, and plan for constructive action.
- *Confrontation meeting*—one-day intensive, structured meetings to gather data on workplace problems and plan for constructive actions.
- *Structural redesign*—realigning the organization structure to meet the needs of environmental and contextual forces.
- *Management by objectives*—Formalizing MBO throughout the organization to link individual, group, and organizational objectives.

Organization-wide OD interventions

Learning check 4   *Be sure you can* • define the term organization development • differentiate outcome and process goals of OD • explain the steps in the OD process • explain the role of action research in OD • list OD interventions focusing on individuals and on teams • list organization-wide OD interventions

STRESS AND STRESS MANAGEMENT

○ **Stress** is a state of tension experienced by individuals facing extraordinary demands, constraints, or opportunities.

With the ever-present and ever-changing demands of working in the new economy, it is not surprising that people are experiencing more stress in their daily lives. Formally defined, **stress** is a state of tension experienced by individuals facing extraordinary demands, constraints, or opportunities.[49] Any look toward your future work career would be incomplete without considering stress as a challenge that you are sure to encounter along the way—and a challenge you must be prepared to help others learn to deal with. In his book *The Future of Success,* for example, Robert Reich says that even though the new economy gives us much to celebrate, its "rewards are coming at the price of lives that are more frenzied, less secure, more economically divergent, more socially stratified."[50] At center stage in this milieu stand job stress and its implications for the managerial role. Consider this statement by a psychologist who worked with top-level managers having alcohol abuse problems: "All executives deal with stress. They wouldn't be executives if they didn't. Some handle it well, others handle it poorly."[51]

The world's "futurists" stay focused on the future

The early years of the 21st century have confirmed that no one can perfectly predict the future. But still, we need to look ahead. The *Futurist* magazine, published by the World Future Society, includes articles with forecasts and projections for a future shaped by the social and technological developments of our day. Its Top 10 Forecasts address issues ranging from gene therapy to worker dependence on employers to child malnutrition. The *impact wheel* is one of the recommended techniques to improve future thinking in organizations. Exercise participants write an idea on large paper, draw five or more possible "impacts" extending out from it like the spokes on a wheel, and discuss the likelihood and implications of each.[64]

SOURCES OF STRESS

○ A **stressor** is anything that causes stress.

Stressors are things that cause stress. Whether they originate directly from a change environment, other aspects of the work setting, or in personal and nonwork situations, stressors are have the potential to influence our work attitudes, behavior, job performance, and even health.

Work factors have an obvious potential to create job stress. Some 34 percent of workers in one survey said that their jobs were so stressful that they were thinking of quitting.[52] We often experience such stress in long hours of work, excessive e-mails, unrealistic work deadlines, difficult bosses or coworkers, unwelcome or unfamiliar work, and unrelenting change.[53] It is also associated with excessively high or low task demands, role conflicts or ambiguities, poor interpersonal relations, or career progress that is too slow or too fast. Stress tends to be high during periods of work overload, when office politics are common, and among persons working for organizations undergoing staff cutbacks and downsizing. Two of the common work-related stress syndromes are: (1) *set up to fail*—where the performance expectations are impossible or the support is totally inadequate to the task; and (2) *mistaken identity*—where the individual ends up in a job that doesn't at all match talents or that he or she simply doesn't like.[54]

A variety of *personal factors* are also sources of potential stress for people at work. Such individual characteristics as needs, capabilities, and personality can influence how one perceives and responds to work and change. Researchers, for example, identify a **Type A personality** that is high in achievement orientation, impatience, and perfectionism. Type A persons are likely to create stress in circumstances that others find relatively stress-free. Type A's, in this sense, bring stress on themselves. The stressful behavior patterns of *Type A personalities* include the following:[55]

- Always moving, walking, and eating rapidly.
- Acting impatient, hurrying others, disliking waiting.
- Doing, or trying to do, several things at once.
- Feeling guilty when relaxing.
- Trying to schedule more in less time.
- Using nervous gestures such as a clenched fist.
- Hurrying or interrupting the speech of others.

Finally, stress from *nonwork factors* can have spillover effects that affect people at work. Stressful life situations including such things as family events (e.g., the birth of a new child), economics (e.g., a sudden loss of extra income), and personal affairs (e.g., a preoccupation with a bad relationship) are often sources of emotional strain. Depending on the individual and his or her ability to deal with them, preoccupation with such situations can affect one's work and add to the stress of work-life conflicts.

○ A **Type A personality** is a person oriented toward extreme achievement, impatience, and perfectionism.

PERSONAL MANAGEMENT

It may strike you as odd to talk here about personal STRENGTH AND ENERGY. But the fact is that it isn't easy to work today. One national survey of American workers, for example, found 54 percent feeling overworked, 55 percent overwhelmed by their workloads, 56 percent not having enough time to complete their work, 59 percent not having enough time for reflection, and 45 percent having to do too many things at once.[27] At a minimum this reminds us that work in the 21st century can be very stressful. And just as to play tennis or some other sport, we have to get and stay in shape for work. This means building strength and energy to best handle the inevitable strains and anxieties of organizational changes, job pressures, and the potential conflicts between work demands and personal affairs.

- Is it hard to relax after a day in class?
- Does it take effort to concentrate in your spare time?
- Do you lay awake thinking and worrying about events of the day?
- Are you so tired that you are unable to join friends or family in a leisure activities?

Any "yes" answer indicates the need to do a better job of building and sustaining your capacities to handle heavy workloads. And if you think things are tough as a student, get ready. The real challenges lie ahead!

Get to know yourself better ▶
Complete Self-Assessments #29—**Stress Self-Test,** and #30—**Work-Life Balance,** from the Management Learning Workbook.

CONSEQUENCES OF STRESS

The discussion of stress so far may give the impression that it always acts as a negative influence on our lives. But like conflict, stress actually has two faces—one constructive and one destructive.[56] Consider the analogy of a violin.[57] When a violin string is too loose, the sound produced by even the most skilled player is weak and raspy. When the string is too tight, however, the sound gets shrill and the string might even snap. But when the tension on the string is just right, neither too loose or too tight, a most beautiful sound is created. With just enough stress, in other words, performance is optimized.

○ **Constructive stress** acts in a positive way to increase effort, stimulate creativity, and encourage diligence in one's work.

The same argument tends to hold in the workplace. **Constructive stress**, sometimes called *eustress,* acts in a positive way for the individual and/or the organization. It occurs in moderation and proves energizing and performance enhancing.[58] The stress is sufficient to encourage increased effort, stimulate creativity, and enhance diligence in one's work, while not overwhelming the individual and causing negative outcomes. Individuals with a Type A personality, for example, are likely to work long hours and to be less satisfied with poor performance. For them, challenging task demands imposed by a supervisor may elicit higher levels of task accomplishment. Even nonwork stressors such as new family responsibilities may cause them to work harder in anticipation of greater financial rewards.

Just like tuning the violin string, however, achieving the right balance of stress for each person and situation is difficult. The question is, "When is a little stress too much stress?" **Destructive stress,** or *distress,* is dysfunctional. It occurs as intense or long-term stress that, as shown in *Figure 18.7,* overloads and breaks down a person's physical and mental systems. Destructive stress can lead to **job burnout**—a form of physical and mental exhaustion that can be incapacitating both personally and in respect to one's work. Productivity can suffer as people react to very intense stress through turnover, absenteeism, errors, accidents, dissatisfaction, and reduced performance. Today as well, there is increased concern for another consequence of excessive stress, **workplace rage**—overtly aggressive behavior toward coworkers and the work setting in general. Lost tempers are a common example; the unfortunate extremes are tragedies involving physical harm to others.[59]

Medical research is also concerned that too much stress can reduce resistance to disease and increase the likelihood of physical and/or mental illness. It may contribute to health problems such as hypertension, ulcers, substance abuse, overeating, depression, and muscle aches, among others.[60] Also important to understand is that excessive work stress can have *spillover effects* on one's personal life. A study of dual-career couples found that one partner's work experiences can have psychological consequences for the other; as one's work stress increases, the partner is likely to experience stress too.[61] The bottom line is that any stress we experience at work is contagious; it can affect one's spouse, family, and friends. The wife of a company controller, for example, went through a time when her husband was stressed by a boss who was overly critical. "He was angry,

○ **Destructive stress** impairs the performance of an individual.

○ **Job burnout** is physical and mental exhaustion from work stress.

○ **Workplace rage** is aggressive behavior toward co-workers or the work setting.

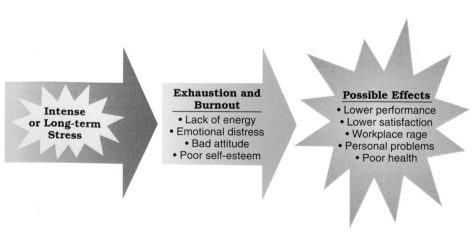

Figure 18.7 Potential negative consequences of a destructive job stress–burnout cycle.

really angry when he came home," she says. His mood affected her and their young child and created what she called "one of the worst times in our seven-year marriage."[62]

STRESS MANAGEMENT STRATEGIES

The best stress management is to prevent it from reaching excessive levels in the first place. Stressors emerging from personal and nonwork factors must be identified so that action can be taken to prevent them or minimize their negative consequences. Family difficulties, for example, may be relieved by a change of work schedule, or the anxiety they cause may be reduced by an understanding supervisor. Also, people sometimes need help in combating the tendency toward "working too much." They need to be reminded not to forgo vacations or not to work excessive overtime.

REALITY CHECK 18.2

What happens when stress turns into workplace rage?
There is a disturbing increase in incidents of workplace rage. Stress experienced at work can have a number of side effects, none more troubling than rage that becomes expressed as abuse of others. Take the online "Reality Check" to learn more about the most common expressions of workplace rage in our society.

Among the work factors with the greatest potential to cause excessive stress are role ambiguities, conflicts, and overloads. *Role clarification* through a management-by-objectives approach can work to good advantage here. By bringing the supervisor and subordinate together in face-to-face task-oriented communications, MBO offers an opportunity both to spot stressors and to take action to reduce or eliminate them. Another common stressor is a poor fit between individual abilities and job demands. In this case job redesign may be helpful to better configure task requirements. Alternatively, changing jobs altogether can help achieve a better person-job fit.

Personal wellness is a term used to describe the pursuit of one's physical and mental potential through a personal health-promotion program. This form of *preventative stress management* recognizes the individual's responsibility to enhance his or her personal health through a disciplined approach to such things as smoking, alcohol use, diet, exercise and physical-fitness. The essence of personal wellness is a lifestyle that reflects a true commitment to health. And it makes a great deal of sense. Those who aggressively maintain their personal wellness are better prepared to deal with the inevitable stresses of work, work-life conflicts, and organizational changes. Many employers are now sponsor wellness programs that help employees with such things as: smoking control, health risk appraisals, back care, stress management, exercise/physical fitness, nutrition education, high blood pressure control, and weight control. The expectations are that investments in wellness programs benefit both the organization and its employees.

○ **Personal wellness** is the pursuit of one's full potential through a personal-health promotion program.

Be sure you can • define the term stress • identify the common stressors found in work and in personal life • describe a person with a Type A personality • differentiate constructive and destructive stress • explain the destructive nature of job burnout and workplace rage • discuss personal wellness as a stress management strategy

Learning check 5

CHAPTER 18 STUDY GUIDE

Where We've Been

BACK TO HEWLETT-PACKARD

The opening example of Hewlett-Packard and CEO Carly Fiorina brought the issues of change leadership center stage in your study of management. In this chapter you learned about the challenges of strategic leadership and innovation. You learned the responsibilities of leading change, including understanding the phases of planned change, the nature of resistance to change, and the alternative change strategies. You also learned about organization development and how important it is to manage stress in work settings undergoing the pressures of change.

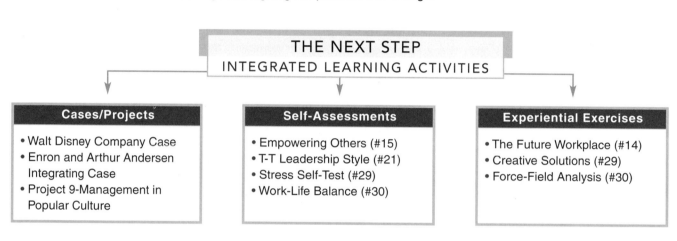

THE NEXT STEP
INTEGRATED LEARNING ACTIVITIES

Cases/Projects
- Walt Disney Company Case
- Enron and Arthur Andersen Integrating Case
- Project 9-Management in Popular Culture

Self-Assessments
- Empowering Others (#15)
- T-T Leadership Style (#21)
- Stress Self-Test (#29)
- Work-Life Balance (#30)

Experiential Exercises
- The Future Workplace (#14)
- Creative Solutions (#29)
- Force-Field Analysis (#30)

STUDY QUESTIONS SUMMARY

1. What are the challenges of strategic leadership and innovation?

- The future will be like our past—always unpredictable, very challenging, and full of continuous change.
- A learning organization is one in which people, values, and systems support innovation and continuous change based upon the lessons of experience.
- Organizations need strategic leaders who work with a strategic direction to initiate and successfully implement changes that help organizations perform well in changing environments.
- Innovation allows creative ideas to be turned into products and/or processes that benefit organizations and their customers.
- Highly innovative organizations tend to have supportive cultures, strategies, structures, staffing, and top management.

- The possible barriers to innovation in organizations include a lack of top-management support, excessive bureaucracy, short time horizons, and vested interests.

2. What is the nature of organizational change?

- Change leaders are change agents who take responsibility for helping to change the behavior of people and organizational systems.
- Managers should be able to spot change opportunities and lead the process of planned change in their areas of work responsibilities.
- Although organizational change can proceed with a top-down emphasis, inputs from all levels of responsibility are essential to achieve successful implementation.
- Transformational change is led from the top and makes radical changes in organizational

directions; incremental change is led from all levels and makes continuing adjustments to existing ways and practices.

- The many possible targets for change include organizational tasks, people, cultures, technologies, and structures.

3. How can planned organizational change be managed?

- Lewin three phases of planned change are: unfreezing—preparing a system for change; changing—making a change; and refreezing—stabilizing the system with a new change in place.
- Good change agents understand the nature of force-coercion, rational persuasion, and shared power change strategies.
- People resist change for a variety of reasons, including fear of the unknown and force of habit.
- Good change agents deal with resistance positively and in a variety of ways, including education, participation, facilitation, manipulation, and coercion.
- Success with technological change requires an openness to resistance and willingness to improvise as implementation proceeds.

4. What is organization development?

- Organization development (OD) is a comprehensive approach to planned organization change that uses principles of behavioral science to improve organizational effectiveness over the long term.
- Outcome goals of OD focus on improved task accomplishment; process goals of OD focus on improvements in the way people work together to accomplish important tasks.
- The OD process involves action research wherein people work together to collect and analyze data on system performance and decide what actions to take to improve things.
- OD interventions are structured activities that help people work together to accomplish change; they may be implemented at the individual, group, and/or organizational levels.

5. How can stress be managed in a change environment?

- Stress occurs as the tension accompanying extraordinary demands, constraints, or opportunities.
- Stress can be destructive or constructive; a moderate level of stress typically has a positive impact on performance.
- Stressors are found in a variety of work, personal, and nonwork situations.
- For some people, having a Type A personality creates stress as a result of continual feelings of impatience and pressure.
- Stress can be effectively managed through both prevention and coping strategies, including a commitment to personal wellness.

KEY TERMS REVIEW

Personal wellness (p. 487)	Reactive change (p. 472)	Top-down change (p. 471)
Planned change (p. 472)	Refreezing (p. 475)	Transformational change (p. 472)
Process innovations (p. 467)	Shared power strategy (p. 477)	Type A personality (p. 485)
Product innovations (p. 467)	Strategic leadership (p. 466)	Unfreezing (p. 474)
Rational persuasion strategy (p. 476)	Stress (p. 484) Stressor (p. 484)	Workplace rage (p. 486)

SELF-TEST 18

MULTIPLE-CHOICE QUESTIONS:

1. In organizations, product innovation (creating new goods or services) and _____ innovation (creating new ways of doing things) are important.
   (a) content (b) process (c) quality (d) task

2. The first step in Hamel's "wheel of innovation" is _____.
   (a) imagining (b) assessing (c) experimenting (d) scaling

3. An executive pursuing transformational change would give highest priority to which one of these change targets?
   (a) an out-of-date policy (b) the organizational culture (c) technology support for a new MIS (d) job designs for individuals in a customer service department

4. A manager using a force-coercion strategy will rely on the power of _____ to bring about change.
   (a) expertise (b) reference (c) rewards, punishments, or authority (d) information

5. The most participative of the planned change strategies is _____.
   (a) force-coercion (b) rational persuasion (c) shared power (d) command and control

6. Trying to covertly influence others, offering only selective information, and/or structuring events in favor of the desired change are ways of dealing with resistance by _____.
   (a) participation (b) manipulation and cooptation (c) force-coercion (d) facilitation

7. In organization development both _____ and _____ goals are important.
   (a) task, maintenance (b) management, labor (c) outcome, process (d) profit, market share

8. Sensitivity training and role negotiation are examples of organization development interventions at the _____ level.
   (a) individual (b) group (c) system-wide (d) organization

9. The concept of empowerment is most often associated with the _____ strategy of planned change.
   (a) market-driven (b) rational persuasion (c) direct forcing (d) normative-reeducative

10. Unfreezing occurs during the _____ step of organizational development.
    (a) diagnosis (b) intervention (c) evaluation (d) termination

11. The quality concept of continuous improvement is most consistent with the notion of _____.
(a) incremental change (b) transformational change (c) radical change (d) reactive change

12. True internalization and commitment to a planned change is most likely to occur when a manager uses a(n) _____ change strategy.
(a) education and communication (b) rational persuasion (c) manipulation and cooptation (d) shared power

13. Through _____, the stress people experience in their personal lives can create problems for them at work and the stress experienced at work can create problems for their personal lives.
(a) eustress (b) refreezing (c) spillover effects (d) action research

14. As a stress management strategy, MBO would be especially useful in helping people deal with _____.
(a) role ambiguities (b) workplace rage (c) personal wellness (d) resistance to change

15. Learning organizations that sustain themselves through positive change are made possible by strong and continuing _____.
(a) force-coercion (b) stress (c) strategic leadership (d) project management

SHORT-RESPONSE QUESTIONS:

16. What are the three phases of change described by Lewin, and what are their implications for change leadership?

17. What are the major differences in the potential outcomes of force-coercion, rational persuasion, and shared power strategies of planned change?

18. What does the statement "OD equals planned change plus" mean?

19. Why is it important for a manager to understand the Type A personality?

APPLICATION QUESTION:

20. As a newly appointed manager in any work setting, you are likely to spot many things that "could be done better" and to have many "new ideas" that you would like to implement. Based on the ideas presented in this chapter, how should you go about effecting successful planned change in such situations?

Cases for Critical THINKING

CASE 1

Apple Computer, Inc.: People and Design Create Apple's Future

- -

Apple Computer paradoxically exists as both one of America's greatest successes and one of its greatest failures to achieve potential. It ignited the personal computer industry in the 1970s,[1] bringing such behemoths as IBM and Digital Equipment almost to their knees. At the same time, Apple is an example of opportunities lost. It represents a fascinating microcosm of American business as it continues to utilize its strengths while reinventing itself.

Corporate History [2]

The history of Apple Computer is a history of passion among its founders, employees, and loyal users. A pair of Stevens, who from an early age had an interest in electronics, started it. Steven Wozniak and Steven Jobs initially utilized their skills at Hewlett Packard and Atari, respectively. Wozniak constructed his first personal computer, the Apple I, and, along with Jobs, created Apple Computer on April 1, 1976.

However, it wasn't until 1977 and the introduction of the Apple II, with its plastic case and color graphics, that Apple really took off. The addition of a floppy drive in early 1978 added to the popularity of the new computer. By 1980, the release of the Apple III found the company with several thousand employees and Steven Jobs at the helm.

Early on, Apple Computer exhibited an extreme emphasis on new and innovative styling in its computer offerings. Jobs took a personal interest in the development of new products, including the Lisa and the legendary MacIntosh, with its graphical interface and 3.5-inch floppy disk.

The passion that Apple is so famous for was clearly evident in the design of the MacIntosh (Mac). Project teams worked around the clock to develop the machine and its graphical user interface (GUI) operating system (Mac OS), based loosely on a design developed by the Xerox Palo Alto Research Center. The use of graphical icons to create simplified user commands was immensely popular.

When IBM entered the personal computer market, Jobs recognized the threat posed and realized that it was time for Apple to "grow up" and be run in a more business-like fashion. In early 1983, he persuaded John Sculley, then president of Pepsi-Cola, to join Apple as president. The two men clashed almost from the start, with Sculley eventually ousting Jobs from the company.

The launch of the Mac, with its increased speed from a Motorola chip and its expandability, reinvigorated Apple's sales once again. In tandem with the LaserWriter, the first affordable PostScript laser printer for the Mac, and Pagemaker, one of the first desktop publishing programs, the Mac was an ideal solution for inexpensive publishing.

However, by the 1990s IBM PCs and clones were saturating the personal computer market. In addition, Microsoft launched Windows 3.0, a greatly improved version of the Wintel operating system for use on IBM PCs and clones. While in 1991 Apple had contemplated licensing its Mac operating system to other computer manufacturers and making it run on Intel-based machines, the idea was nixed by then chief operating officer (COO) Michael Spindler.

Innovative Design to the Rescue

Apple continued to rely on innovative design to remain competitive. In the 1990s, Apple introduced a very popular notebook computer line, along with the unsuccessful Newton personal digital assistant. Sculley, having lost interest in the day-to-day operations of Apple, was eventually forced out and replaced with Michael Spindler.

Spindler oversaw a number of innovations, including the PowerMac family, the first Macs to be based on the PowerPC chip, an extremely fast processor that was co-developed with IBM and Motorola. The PowerPC processor allowed Macs to compete with, and in many cases surpass, the speed of Intel's newer processors. In addition, Apple finally licensed its operating system to a number of Mac-cloners, but never in significant numbers.

After a difficult time in the mid-1990s, Spindler was replaced with Gil Amelio, the former president of National Semiconductor. This set the stage for one of the most famous returns in corporate history.

Jobs's Return

After leaving Apple, Steven Jobs started NeXT computer, an advanced personal computer with a sleek, innovative design. However, with its proprietary software, the device never gained a large following. Jobs then co-founded Pixar computer-animation studios in the late 1980s. It co-produced a number of movies with Walt Disney Studios, including the popular *Toy Story*.[3]

In late 1996, Apple announced the purchase of NeXT and Jobs returned to Apple in an unofficial capacity as advisor to the president. However, when Gil Amelio resigned, Jobs accepted the role of "interim CEO" (i CEO) of Apple Computer and wasted no time in making his return felt.

Jobs announced an alliance with Apple's former rival, Microsoft. In exchange for $150 million in Apple stock, Microsoft and Apple would have a five-year patent cross-license for their graphical interface operating systems. He revoked licenses allowing the production of Mac clones and started offering Macs over the Web through the Apple Store.

In addition to many new product offerings, Jobs introduced the iMac, with a revolutionary see-through design that has proved popular among consumers. This was followed shortly by the iBook, a similar-type portable computer. Apple once again was viewed as an industry innovator, with its revolutionary designs and innovations.[4]

Unfortunately, Apple remains a relatively small player in the computer industry. While its products are wildly popular among a dedicated set of users, it still commands only a little over 5 percent of the total computer market. It remains locked in constant boom-or-bust cycles, dependent on its ability to turn out a stream of new product hits.

What Does the Future Hold?

Apple is faced with a stark reality: Can it continue to offer both hardware and software solutions in a rapidly changing technology environment? Its early decision to keep its technology proprietary, as opposed to IBM's decision to support an open architecture system, has proved to be a costly strategy to support in the long run.

Some argue that Apple should reinvent itself once again and this time concentrate on software. Apple is gradually admitting that it can no longer afford to fight the Wintel system, the combination of Microsoft's Windows operating system and the Intel processor. Apple's new product introductions fail to attract many present non-Mac users—just 15 percent of its revenues come from Wintel customers.[5]

Apple is betting that its new operating system, the Mac OS X, will be a big hit with computer users. It is the largest update in the operating system since it was first released in the mid-1980s. Recognizing the need to attract new Mac users rather than just recycle present Ap-

ple enthusiasts, Apple is emphasizing the compatibility of its system with Windows. "The transition to a Mac is easy in part because you'll continue to use the same applications you already know . . . Word, PowerPoint and Excel, . . . And, thanks to exclusive features, the Mac versions improve on their Windows counterparts. Office documents are fully compatible between Mac and Windows, so you can share everything from spreadsheets to presentations. . . . [T]he Mac is at home on PC networks . . . making the business of sharing files and printers with PCs entirely painless."[6]

Part of Apple's new corporate strategy, developed in the face of a massive slowdown in the technology industry, involves taking advantage of the explosion of personal electronic devices—CD players, MP3 players, digital cameras, DVD players, and so on —by initially building Mac-only applications that add value to those devices. Just as iMovies adds tremendous value to digital cameras, iDVD adds value to DVD players and iTunes adds value to CD and MP3 players. However, Apple recognizes the size of the PC market that is not being reached and has made iPod and iTunes into Windows-compatible products. In its first week, iTunes sold 1.5 million songs and captured 80 percent of the market share of legal music down-

loads. It is Apple's hope that making Apple products the "digital hub" of the new "digital lifestyle" will revitalize Apple's sales and guarantee the long-term security of the company.[7]

Apple is also eyeing the global market and in November 2003 opened its first store in Japan. With five floors of Apple products and applications located in Japan's Ginza, it offers an experience to rival that of the Sony store in the same shopping area. Apple is hoping to develop a global presence and to attract new users internationally.[8]

Review Questions

1. Why is Apple not a dominant provider of personal computers?
2. Evaluate Apple in the context of the new economy. Can Apple survive?
3. Should the firm enable its operating system to run on both Apple and PC systems?
4. What would you suggest Apple do to popularize the Apple computer line?

You Do the Research

1. Look at the Apple home page's Top 10 reasons to switch. What do these indicate about Apple's strategy?
2. Locate five sources on the Web that discuss Apple and the history of the personal computer market.

The Coca-Cola Company: Coke Gets Back to Business

With production facilities in over 200 countries in the world, there are few products as internationally recognized as the ubiquitous Coke bottle.[1] To put this in perspective, another American icon, McDonald's, has locations in only 119 countries.[2] As one of the world's best-known brands, Coca-Cola has capitalized on opportunities and thrived. However, the process has not been without some upheavals.

When Roberto Goizueta, its CEO for 17 years, passed away on October 18, 1997, after a short bout with lung cancer, the future looked uncertain. During Goizueta's tenure at Coca-Cola, the market value of the company had dramatically increased from $4 billion to nearly $150 billion. This made him one of the greatest value creators in history. While the appointment of CFO Douglas Ivester as his replacement did not immediately allay the concerns of the financial market, the value of Coke stock continued to increase until mid-1998. Since then, the value of the stock has declined and as of late November 2003, the market value of Coca-Cola was $115 billion. Douglas Daft, president and chief operating officer, with 30 years of Coke experience, replaced Ivester as chairman and CEO in 2000.[3] The question, then and now, on many investors' minds remains: "Can Coke recapture its previous growth pace and stock value without Goizueta's legendary leadership?"

Coca-Cola's Global Dominance

The larger a company is, the harder it is to continue to grow at a steady pace. This remains the major challenge facing the Coca-Cola Company. The U.S. market is already well developed, with an average consumption per person of one serving per day of Coke products in both 2001 and 2002. The European and Eurasian market grew slightly from 2001 to 2002, with average consumption increasing from one and a half to two servings per week. The Latin American, Asian, and African markets' consumption levels were unchanged from 2001 to 2002 at four servings per week, two servings per month, and three servings per month, respectively.[4] However, even given the much lower consumption rate internationally than in the United States, more than 70 percent of Coca-Cola's income is generated outside the United States. This is primarily due to population differentials.

Coca-Cola, recognizing the importance of international sales, has been very sensitive to local market conditions. Products are developed to meet the varied taste preferences of consumers. In fact, Coca-Cola produces more than 300 brands worldwide in addition to its flagship brands, Coke and Diet Coke. The bottling and distribution system is also adapted to local needs. For instance, all bottlers are local companies either independently owned or only partially owned by the Coca-Cola Company. In this way, Coca-Cola gains the benefits of intrinsic local knowledge. The distribution systems range from boats in Indonesia to four-legged power in the Andes to fleets of trucks in the United States. In each case, local conditions are considered. Coca-Cola prides itself on acting as a local citizen in a global marketplace.

Coke's Dominance

Coca-Cola has achieved its dominance in the global marketplace through its consistent loyalty to the Coke heritage and the image and standards that it conveys. Coca-Cola historically has not been a company noted for innovation; it was almost 100 years after the introduction of Coke that it introduced Diet Coke. After the disastrous introduction of New Coke, there was reluctance to tamper with Coke. As Douglas Daft, chairman and CEO, put it in his 2002 letter to share owners, "Responsibility for the world's most beloved and valuable brand requires extreme care in how, when, and why we extend it. We don't risk consumer loyalty to the brand or seek an artificial bump in volume by spinning out product after product to chase the latest fad."[5] However, 2002 represented a period of unprecedented innovation—Vanilla Coke, Diet Vanilla Coke, and Diet Coke with lemon attracted new consumers.

Historically, carbonated beverages have been the backbone of the Coca-Cola Company; in 2002 they accounted for 85 percent of sales. Coca-Cola acknowledgment of changing consumer tastes has fostered a continued expansion of its line of noncarbonated beverages. Growth in sales of noncarbonated beverages was 28 percent from 2001 to 2002. This growth has been fueled both internally and through acquisitions and licensing agreements. Coca-Cola is hoping to achieve profitability through economies of scale and by capitalizing on its existing distribution system.

The Coca-Cola Company has positioned itself for growth by moving key decision making closer to local markets and by fostering deeper connections to con-

sumers. It has also restructured, with a management team coordinating a new, nimble, and entrepreneurial network. As one of his first acts as CEO, Daft axed 6,000 employees, many of them middle and senior managers in Atlanta. The new structure reflects his continuing commitment to a leaner, more entrepreneurial organization. Under him, there is a 10-person executive management team composed of:

- President and chief operating officer of the Coca-Cola Company
- Senior vice president and chief marketing officer
- Senior vice president and worldwide public affairs and communications officer
- Executive vice president and chief financial officer
- Executive vice president and general counsel and secretary
- Five executive vice presidents of the Coca-Cola Company who are presidents and chief operating officers for North America; Europe, Eurasia, and the Middle East; Latin America; Asia; and Africa

Twenty-four division and operations presidents report to the chief operating officers. This group of individuals, along with Coca-Cola employees and partners worldwide, are responsible for implementing the six strategic priorities that are laid out in the 2002 Annual Report:[6]

1. "Accelerate carbonated soft-drink growth, led by Coca-Cola."
2. "Selectively broaden our family of beverage brands to drive profitable growth."
3. "Grow system profitability and capability together

with our bottling partners. Our drive for profitability throughout our system brought us even closer to our bottlers in 2002."
4. "Serve customers with creativity and consistency to generate growth across all channels."
5. "Direct investments to highest-potential areas across markets. Our business approach is tailored to each market based on its stage of development. In rural areas of China, we direct our efforts toward expanding availability of affordable packages, while in cities such as Shanghai and Beijing, we execute more sophisticated image-building promotions, activating points of purchase so that consumers have greater connections with our brands."
6. "Drive efficiency and cost effectiveness everywhere. We continue to drive efficiency throughout our system, establishing disciplined routines and gaining economies of scale in material and ingredient purchasing."

Will the restructuring and the new strategic initiatives help Coca-Cola achieve its mission of "benefiting and refreshing everyone it touches" and regain the growth and value experienced under Roberto Goizueta?

Review Questions

1. Apply Henri Fayol's five rules of management to the Coca-Cola case.
2. Consider the following quote from Coca-Cola's statement on diversity: "We embrace our commit-

ment to diversity in all its forms at The Coca-Cola Company as a core value. Diversity—of race, gender, sexual orientation, ideas, ways of living, cultures and business practices—provides the creativity and innovation essential to our economic well-being. Equally important is a highly motivated, healthy and productive workforce that achieves business success through superior execution and superb customer satisfaction."[7]

Relate this quote to the case and to the behavioral approaches to management.

3. How does Coca-Cola score on the eight attributes of performance excellence?

4. Do you think Douglas Daft will be successful in regaining the growth and value experienced under Roberto Goizueta?

You Do the Research

1. While stock prices have declined since 1998, what has happened to revenues and income over the same period?

2. What are Coca-Cola's underlying beliefs? See the following website: www2.coca-cola.com/ ourcompany/ ourbeliefs.html.

3. Read Coca-Cola's statement on diversity. What insights does it provide? See the following website: www2.coca-cola.com/ ourcompany/ourdiversity.html.

CASE 3

Tom's of Maine: At Tom's, "Doing Business" Means "Doing Good"

Tom's of Maine represents one of the first natural health care companies to distribute its products beyond the normal channels of health food stores. With its continued growth, the owners, Tom and Kate Chappell, still emphasize the values that got them started more than three decades ago. The experiences of Tom and Kate Chappell in meeting the challenges they have encountered provide considerable insight into how a small firm can stay true to its founding principles and continue to grow in a fiercely competitive environment.

Getting Tom's of Maine Going

For its first 15 years, Tom's of Maine looked a lot like many other new businesses. Tom and Kate Chappell had an idea they believed in and felt others would buy into as well. Based on this idea, and with financing from a small loan, the Chappells started the company in 1970. As is the case with many business startups, the company's first product was not successful. Its phosphate-free detergent was environmentally friendly

but, according to Tom Chappell, "it didn't clean so well."[1] Consumers did appear to be interested in "green," or environmentally friendly, products, however, and the fledgling company's next products, toothpaste and soap, were more successful.

All Tom's of Maine products were made with all-natural ingredients and were packaged using recycled materials whenever possible. New personal care products, including shampoo and deodorant, were developed

while avoiding the controversial practice of animal testing.[2] This refusal caused Tom's to wait seven years and spend about ten times the usual sum to get the American Dental Association's seal of approval for its fluoride toothpastes.

In 1992, Tom's deodorant accounted for 25 percent of its business. Chappell reformulated the product for ecological reasons (replacing petroleum with vegetable glycerin), but the new formulation "magnified the human bacteria that cause odor" in half its customers. After much agonizing, Chappell ordered the deodorant taken off the shelves at a cost of $400,000, or 30 percent of the firm's projected profits for the year. Dissatisfied consumers were sent refunds for the new product, along with a letter of apology.

Tom's of Maine recovered from this experience, but founder Tom Chappell was not happy. The company's products were a success in health food stores, and Chappell was beginning to think in terms of national distribution. He had hired a team of marketing people with experience at major companies. At the same time, he felt that something was missing; he was "tired of creating new brands and making money."[3]

One pivotal event was the introduction of baking soda toothpaste. The product was gritty and didn't have the sweet flavor typical of commercial toothpastes, and the marketing manager told Chappell, "In all candor I don't know how we're going to sell it."[4] Chappell insisted that the product be test-marketed. It proved to be a best-seller and was quickly copied by Arm and Hammer and Procter & Gamble.[5] It also appeared that the new product's sales potential had become more important to the company than the qualities of the product itself. "We were working for the numbers, and we got the numbers. But I was confused by success, unhappy with success" said Chappell.[6] He later wrote, "I had made a real go of something I'd started. What more could I do in life except make more money? Where was the purpose and direction for the rest of my life?"[7] As a result of this line of thinking, the successful businessman Tom Chappell entered Harvard Divinity School in the fall of 1986.[8]

Sharpening the Company's Focus

The years that Chappell spent as a part-time student at the divinity school brought him to a new understanding of his role. "For the first time in my career, I had the language I needed to debate my bean-counters" he explained.[9] He realized that his company was his ministry. "I'm here to succeed. But there's a qualifier. It's not to succeed at all costs, it's to succeed according to my principles."[10]

One tangible result was the development of a mission statement for the company that reflected both the company's business aspirations and its commitment to social responsibility. This document spelled out the values that would guide the company in the future. It covered the types of products ordered and the need for natural ingredients and high quality. It also included respect for employees and the need for meaningful work as well as fair pay. It pointed out the need to be concerned with the community and even the world. Finally, it called for Tom's of Maine "to be a profitable and successful company, while acting in a socially responsible manner."[11] Some of the company's programs were the result of decisions made by top management. The company began donating 10 percent of its pretax profits to charities ranging from arts organizations to environmental groups. These included funds donated to state and local curbside recycling programs as well as a pledge of $100,000 for the Rainforest Alliance.

The company also urged its employees to get involved in charitable causes. It set up a program that allowed employees to donate 5 percent of their work time to volunteer activities. Employees enthusiastically took advantage of the opportunity. When one employee began teaching art classes for emotionally disturbed children, others became interested, until almost all of the company's employees were involved.[12] Other employees worked in soup kitchens and homeless shelters. Employees formed their own teams to work on projects or used the company's matching service. Tom's even created the position of vice president of community life.

The volunteer program did have its costs, however. Other employees had to pitch in to cover volunteers' absences, which amounted to the equivalent of 20 days a month. However, Colleen Myers, the vice president of community life, believed that the volunteer activities were valuable to the company as well as the community. "After spending a few hours at a soup kitchen or a shelter, you're happy to have a job. It's a morale booster, and better morale translates pretty directly into better productivity."[13] Sometimes the company even benefited directly from these activities. Chappell explained, "The woman who headed up those art classes—she discovered she's a heck of a project manager. We found that out, too."[14]

Employee benefits were not strictly psychological. The company offered flexible four-day scheduling and subsidized day care. Even coffee breaks were designed with employee preferences in mind, providing them with fresh fruit. The company also helped individual employees earn their high school equivalency degrees and develop skills for new positions.[15]

By 1993, Tom's of Maine was moving beyond health food stores and into supermarkets and drugstores, where 70 percent of toothpaste is purchased. Even as Tom's product distribution expanded nationwide, the company's marketing strategy was low key. Katie Shisler, vice president of marketing, says: "We just tell them our story. We tell them why we have such a loyal base of consumers who vote with their dollars every day. A number of trade accounts appreciate our social responsibility and are willing to go out on a limb with us."[16] Tom Chappell agreed: "We're selling a lot more than toothpaste; we're selling a point of view—that nature is worth protecting."[17]

By the mid-1990s, Tom's of Maine was facing increasing competition. Its prices were similar to those of its national competitors for baking soda toothpaste but 20 to 40 percent higher for deodorant and mouthwash. Tom Chappell did not appear worried, however. He believed that "you have to understand from the outset that they have more in the marketing war chest than you. That's not the way you're going to get market share, you're going to get it by being who you are."[18] He explained his philosophy: "A small business obviously needs to distinguish itself from the commodities. If we try to act like commodities, act like a toothpaste, we give up our souls. Instead, we have to be peculiarly authentic in everything we do."[19] This authenticity is applied to both ingredients and advertising decisions. "When you start doing that customers are very aware of your difference. And they like the difference."[20]

Tom's of Maine: A Different Kind of Company?

Tom's of Maine distinguishes itself from other companies by stressing the "common good" in all of its endeavors. The company is passionately concerned about corporate wellness, customer wellness, product wellness, community and environmental wellness, and employee wellness. In late 2000 the company launched Tom's Online Wellness Store to make its full product line available to customers around the globe. Among other customer-oriented activities, Tom's utilizes the services of a wellness advisory council and provides wellness education. Tom's of Maine practices stewardship through its commitment to natural, sustainable, and responsible ingredients, products, and packaging. In embracing the philosophy of "doing well by doing good," Tom's has continued to produce impressive business results that attest to an ongoing stream of corporate wellness. In fiscal year 2001, Tom's sales exceeded $35 million, which directly reflects the continued strengthening of its various product lines.[21]

Throughout the 1990s Tom's of Maine was repeatedly recognized for providing a model of ethical business standards for others to follow. Among other awards, Tom and Kate Chappell have received the Corporate Conscience Award for Charitable Contributions from the Council of Economic Priorities, the New England Environmental Leadership Award, and the Governor's Award for Business Excellence.[22] Clearly, Tom's of Maine demonstrates that "common-good capitalism" can work and that businesses can be operated to simultaneously earn a profit and serve the common good. In an effort to pass these lessons on to other businesspeople, Tom Chappell has authored two books, *The Soul of a Business: Managing for Profit and the Common Good* and *Managing Upside Down: Seven Intentions for Values-Centered Leadership*, and created the Saltwater Institute, a nonprofit organization that provides training in the Seven Intentions.[23]

Chappell's Seven Intentions for seeking and achieving a values–profits balance are:

1. Connect with goodness. Non-work discussions with an upbeat spin usually draw people to common ground, away from hierarchical titles.
2. Know thyself, be thyself. Discovering and tapping people's passions, gifts and strengths generates creative energy.
3. Envision your destiny. The company is better served if its efforts are steered by strengths instead of following market whims.
4. Seek counsel. The journey is long, and assistance from others is absolutely necessary.
5. Venture out. The success of any business hinges

on pushing value-enhanced products into the market.

6. **Assess.** Any idea must be regularly reviewed and refined if necessary.

7. **Pass it on.** Since developing and incorporating values is a trial-and-error process, sharing ideas and soliciting feedback allows for future growth.[24]

Review Questions

1. Which way of thinking about ethical behavior best describes Tom's of Maine and its founder, Tom Chappell?
2. What potential dilemma did Tom Chappell face in the mid-1980s?
3. How important were Tom Chappell's personal views in helping Tom's of Maine to be successful?

You Do the Research

1. Should Tom's stay independent, or should it merge with a larger firm?
2. Can Chappell's approach to ethical management work at larger firms?
3. Find five Internet sites that discuss ethics and social responsibility, and identify an important ethical lesson or insight that is provided on each site.

CASE 4

United Parcel Service: UPS Hits the Road with Technology

United Parcel Service (UPS), the world's largest package distribution company, transports more than 4 billion parcels and documents annually. With more than 360,000 employees, 1,750 operating facilities, 2,000 daily flights, 88,000 vehicles, and the world's largest private communication system, UPS provides service in more than 200 countries.[1] How does UPS control such a vast and extended enterprise and still fulfill its commitment to serving the needs of the global marketplace?

Corporate History

In 1907, there was a great need in America for private messenger and delivery services. Only a few homes had private telephones, and luggage, packages, and personal messages had to be carried by hand. The U.S. Postal Service did not yet have the parcel post system. To help meet this need, an enterprising 19-year-old, James E. ("Jim") Casey, borrowed $100 from a friend and established the American Messenger Company in Seattle, Washington. Despite stiff competition, the company did well, largely because of Jim Casey's

strict policies on customer courtesy, reliability, round-the-clock service, and low rates. These principles, which guide UPS even today, are summarized by Jim's slogan: "Best Service and Lowest Rates."[2]

Obsessed with efficiency from the beginning, the company pioneered the concept of consolidated delivery—combining packages addressed to certain neighborhoods onto one delivery vehicle. In this way, manpower and motorized equipment could be used more efficiently. The 1930s brought more growth. By this time, UPS provided

delivery services in all major West Coast cities, and a foothold had been established on the other coast with a consolidated delivery service in the New York City area. Many innovations were adopted, including the first mechanical system for package sorting. During this time, accountant George D. Smith joined the firm and helped make financial cost control the cornerstone of all planning decisions. The name United Parcel Service was adopted—"United" to emphasize the unity of the company's operations in each city, "Parcel" to identify the nature of the business, and "Service" to indicate what was provided to customers.[3]

In 1953, UPS resumed air service, which had been discontinued during the Depression, offering two-day service to major cities on the East and West Coasts. Packages flew in the cargo holds of regularly scheduled airlines. Called UPS Blue Label Air, the service grew, until by 1978 it was available in every state, including Alaska and Hawaii. The demand for air parcel delivery increased in the 1980s, and federal deregulation of the airline industry created new opportunities for UPS. But deregulation caused change, as established airlines reduced the number of flights or abandoned routes altogether. To ensure dependability, UPS began to assemble its own jet cargo fleet—the largest in the industry. With growing demand for faster service, UPS entered the overnight air delivery business, and by 1985 UPS Next Day Air service was available in all 48 contiguous states and Puerto Rico. Alaska and Hawaii were added later. That same year, UPS entered a new era with international air package and document service, linking the United States and six European nations.

UPS Today

In 1988, UPS received authorization from the Federal Aviation Administration (FAA) to operate its own aircraft, thus officially becoming an airline. Recruiting the best people available, UPS merged a number of different organizational cultures and procedures into a seamless opera-

tion called UPS Airline. UPS Airline was the fastest-growing airline in FAA history, formed in little more than one year with all the necessary technology and support systems. UPS Airline has become one of the 10 largest airlines in the United States. UPS Airline features some of the most advanced information systems in the world to support flight planning, scheduling, and load handling.

Today, the UPS system moves more than 13.3 million packages and documents daily around the globe. UPS picks up from 1.8 million customers per day and delivers to 6.1 million customers per day. Packages are processed using advanced information technology and are transported by the company's own aircraft, chartered aircraft, and a fleet of delivery vehicles.[4] U.S. and international package delivery operations constitute a substantial segment of UPS's business. Another growing and important segment is the company's nonpackage unit, which focuses on supply chain solutions for UPS customers.[5] Today, UPS emphasizes its customer service orientation with the advertising slogan: "What can brown do for you?"

Innovations at UPS

Known for its technological innovations, UPS keeps its package delivery and nonpackage operations on the cutting edge. Tom Weidemeyer, chief operating officer, says that UPS likes to take the really long-term view about investments in its infrastructure. Technology at UPS spans an incredible

range, from specially designed package delivery vehicles to global computer and communications systems. For example, UPSnet is a global electronic data communications network that provides an information-processing pipeline for international package processing and delivery. UPSnet, which has more than 500,000 miles of communications lines and a satellite, links more than 1,300 distribution sites in 46 countries. The system tracks 821,000 packages daily.[6]

UPS Worldport™ is the latest example of technology being used to increase efficiency and quality in the company's package operations. Located in Louisville, Kentucky, Worldport is a 4-million-square-foot facility outfitted with "overhead cameras to read smart labels and process documents, small packages, and irregular-shaped objects with astounding speed. Equipped with more than 17,000 high speed conveyors, Worldport is capable of processing some 84 packages every second and can be expanded to handle nearly 140 packages per second—or more than 500,000 packages per hour."[7] Worldport can also consolidate more volume at a single location, thereby enabling the company to use larger and more efficient aircraft and streamlining sorting at regional hubs throughout the world.[8]

UPS Supply Chain Solutions—the company's nonpackage operation—is targeted toward a variety of supply chain challenges faced by customers, including but not limited to helping customers in managing overseas suppliers, post-sales servicing of parts logistics, and order processing. This operation also coordinates transportation, vendors, contracts, and shipments, and simplifies international trade and regulatory compliance.

UPS Supply Chain Solutions relies on a physical and virtual infrastructure for managing the flow of goods, information, and funds for different customers. For example, UPS developed an integrated supply chain with advanced automation to enable Honeywell to provide efficient and rapid order processing and delivery to the North American automotive aftermarket. Another supply chain solution was provided to TeddyCrafters, thereby enabling it to better manage the transportation and distribution of supplies from Asian and U.S. vendors. UPS designed a comprehensive inbound distribution system for TeddyCrafters that improved inventory management and provided for weekly restocking of the chain's retail stores. Still another supply chain challenge was solved for Tokyo Electron America. UPS implemented a field restocking network that provided real-time inventory management. In all these cases, and many others, UPS uses its own technological expertise in the transportation and distribution of documents and packages to help other companies achieve efficient, rapid, and low-cost solutions for all stages of their supply chains.[9]

Three Trends Driving the Industry

Frederick Smith of FedEx, a UPS competitor, identifies three trends driving the package delivery business: globalization, cost cutting, and Internet commerce. *Globalization* will cause the world express-transportation market to explode to more than $150 billion. While DHL Worldwide Express is a major player in the international market, UPS and Fed Ex are expanding at a rapid pace. Lee Hibbets of Air Cargo Management Group in Seattle states that: "FedEx is seen as more aggressive, whereas UPS is a little bit more methodical and long term." *Cost cutting* among customer firms—primarily by cutting inventory—fits into the package firms' delivery systems. Technology plays a significant part in package delivery companies' capabilities to assist customers in cutting their inventories. UPS and FedEx are competing fiercely in using technology to facilitate cost-cutting efforts. *Internet commerce*, the third trend, generates a huge need for shipping. Package delivery companies hope to capture the lion's share of the Internet commerce shipping business.[10]

It remains to be seen who will win out in the package delivery wars, but FedEx and UPS are both leaders in the market. Their ability to track packages around the world is a testament to the value of technology in the workplace. With technological innovations generating higher productivity, the future for package delivery remains bright. Moreover, with attention being given to the challenges of supply chain management, package delivery companies can apply their technological expertise in developing additional business opportunities.

Review Questions

1. Describe UPS's competitive advantage.
2. How does UPS approach customer relationship management?
3. How does technology enable UPS to be a quality-driven organization?

You Do the Research

1. Describe the general environmental factors that affect UPS and its competitors in the package delivery industry.
2. Identify the stakeholders for UPS, and explain how those stakeholders potentially influence the company.
3. Describe the organizational culture at UPS and the role that it plays in the company's success.

Harley-Davidson: Harley Style and Strategy Have Global Reach

With a celebration of almost legendary proportions, Harley-Davidson marked a century in business with a year-long International Road Tour from July 2002 to July 2003. The party finally culminated in August 2003 in hometown Milwaukee.[1] Brought back from near death, Harley-Davidson represents a true American success story. Reacting to global competition, Harley has been able to reestablish itself as the dominant maker of big bikes in the United States. However, success often breeds imitation, and Harley faces a mixture of domestic and foreign competitors encroaching on its market. Can it meet the challenge?

Harley-Davidson

When Harley-Davidson was founded in 1903, it was one of more than 100 firms producing motorcycles in the United States. The U.S. government became an important customer for the company's high-powered, reliable bikes, using them in both world wars. By the 1950s, Harley-Davidson was the only remaining American manufacturer.[2]

But British competitors were beginning to enter the market with faster, lighter-weight bikes. Honda Motor Company of Japan began marketing lightweight bikes in the United States, moving into middleweight vehicles in the 1960s. Harley initially tried to compete by manufacturing smaller bikes but had difficulty making them profitably. The company even purchased an Italian motorcycle firm, Aermacchi, but many of its dealers were reluctant to sell the small Aermacchi Harleys.[3]

American Machine and Foundry Co. (AMF) took over Harley in 1969, expanding its portfolio of recreational products. AMF increased production from 14,000 to 50,000 bikes per year. This rapid expansion led to significant problems with quality, and better-built Japanese motorcycles began to take over the market. Harley's share of its major U.S. market—heavyweight motorcycles—fell to 23 percent.[4]

In 1981, a group of 13 managers bought Harley-Davidson back from AMF and began to turn the company around with the rallying cry "The Eagle Soars Alone." As Richard Teerlink, former CEO of Harley, explained: "The solution was to get back to detail. The key was to know the business, know the customer, and pay attention to detail."[5] The key elements in this process were increasing quality and improving service to customers and dealers. Management kept the classic Harley style and focused on the company's traditional strength—heavyweight and super-heavyweight bikes.

In 1983, Harley-Davidson asked the International Trade Commission (ITC) for tariff relief on the basis that Japanese manufacturers were stockpiling inventory in the United States and providing unfair competition. The tariff relief was granted on April 1, 1983, and a tariff for five years was placed on all imported Japanese motorcycles that were 700cc or larger. In 1987, Harley petitioned the ITC to have the tariff lifted because the company felt capable and confident in its ability to compete with foreign imports. Also in 1983, the Harley Owners Group® (H.O.G.®) was formed. H.O.G. membership soared to more than 90,000 by 1989 and by 2003 exceeded 750,000 members.[6]

Once Harley's quality image had been restored, the company slowly began to expand production. The company made only 280 bikes per day in January 1992, increasing output to 345 bikes per day by the end of that year. Despite increasing demand, production was scheduled to reach only 420 per day, approximately 100,000 per year, by 1996.[7] However, in 1996 Harley recognized the demand and the first of many grander expansion plans began with the opening of a new distribution center in Franklin, Wisconsin. In 1997, Harley began production in new facilities in Milwaukee, Wisconsin, Menomonee Falls, Wisconsin, and Kansas City, Missouri. In 1998, a new assembly plant was opened in Manaus, Brazil and Harley acquired the remaining interest in Buell motorcycles. In 2001, expansions were announced for the Milwaukee, Wisconsin, Tomahawk, Wisconsin, and York, Pennsylvania plants.[8]

As indicated by the expansions, the popularity of the motorcycles continued to increase throughout the 1980s. The average Harley purchaser was in his late thirties, with an average household income of over $40,000. Teerlink didn't like the description of his customers as "aging" baby-boomers: "Our customers want the sense of adventure that they get on our bikes. . . . Harley-Davidson doesn't sell transportation, we sell transformation. We sell excitement, a way of life."[9] However, the average age and income of Harley riders has continued to increase. In 2002, the median age of a Harley rider was 47 and the median income was just under $80,000.[10]

Although the company had been exporting motorcycles ever since it was founded, it was not until the late 1980s that Harley-Davidson management began to think seriously about international markets. In 1987, the company acknowledged its ability to compete with foreign imports and started to consider competing more seriously in the international market. Traditionally, the company's ads had been translated word for word into foreign languages.

Now, ads were developed specifically for different markets, and rallies were adapted to fit local customs.[11] The company also began to actively recruit and develop dealers in Europe and Japan. It purchased a Japanese distribution company and built a large parts warehouse in Germany to support its European operations. Harley-Davidson continued to look for ways to expand its activities. Recognizing that German motorcyclists rode at high speeds—often more than 100 mph—the company began to study ways to give Harleys a smoother ride. It also began to emphasize accessories that would give riders more protection.[12]

The company also created a line of Harley accessories available through dealers or by catalog, all adorned with the Harley-Davidson logo. These jackets, caps, T-shirts, and other items became popular with nonbikers as well. In fact, the clothing and parts had a higher profit margin than the motorcycles; nonbike products made up as much as half of sales at some dealers.

International Efforts

Harley continues to make inroads in overseas markets. In 2002, Harley had 30 percent of the worldwide market for heavyweight motorcycles—chrome-laden cruisers, aerodynamic rocket bikes mostly produced by the Japanese, and oversize touring motorcycles. In the United States, Harley had the largest market share, 46.4 percent, followed by Honda with 20.2 percent. In Europe,

Harley ranked sixth, with only 6.6 percent of the market share behind Honda, Yamaha, BMW, Suzuki, and Kawasaki. However, in the Asia/Pacific market, where it might be expected that Japanese bikes would dominate, Harley had the largest market shares for 2000, 2001, and 2002. Harley had 21.3 percent of the market share compared to 19.2 percent for Honda.[13]

Harley motorcycles are among America's fastest-growing exports to Japan. Harley's Japanese subsidiary adapted the company's marketing approach to Japanese tastes, even producing shinier and more complete tool kits than available in the United States. Harley bikes have long been considered symbols of prestige in Japan. Before World War II, a small company called Rikuo built them under a licensing arrangement. Consistent with their U.S. counterparts, many Japanese enthusiasts see themselves as rebels on wheels.[14]

Another recent effort by Harley to expand its buyer base involves the development of its Blast motorcycle from its Buell division. Fifty percent of Blast sales are to women, raising the overall percentage of women buying Harleys from 2 percent in 1987 to 9 percent by 1999. That 9 percent figure remained constant through 2002. With 17 consecutive years of increased production as well as record revenues and earnings, the future for Harley appears bright.[15]

Review Questions

1. Describe Harley-David-son's international busi-

ness strategy. Would you consider Harley to be a multinational corporation?

2. If you were Harley's top management, in which regions of the world would you consider expanding?

3. Evaluate Harley-Davidson's decision not to produce overseas. What would be the advantages of overseas production? What problems might the company encounter if it does manufacture abroad?

4. Harley appears to have moved from providing a product (motorcycles) to providing a service (a way of life). Discuss how this movement from products to services may have affected the company.

You Do the Research

1. How successful have competitors been against Harley in the United States?

2. Should Harley alter its image as the U.S. population ages?

3. Should businesses like Harley receive protection from overseas competition? Can you find another instance where a company asked that a tariff against imports be eliminated early?

CASE 6

Domino's Pizza: Great Ideas Bring Domino's to Your Door

As of 2002, Domino's Pizza had more than 7,300 company-owned and franchised stores in the United States and more than 50 other countries. *Pizza Today* named it "Chain of the Year" for 2003. With sales in 2002 of more than 400 million pizzas and revenues of nearly $4 billion, it represents an impressive success story. Starting in 1960 with one store in Ypsilanti, Michigan, Tom Monaghan redefined the pizza industry and, in so doing, built a corporate powerhouse. It entered the international market in 1983 with its first store outside the United States, which was in Winnipeg, Canada. At the end of 2003, 2,500 of the stores were international and revenues generated in those stores exceeded $1 billion.[1] Could you be another Tom, given the chance?

The Domino Story

Tom Monaghan and his brother, James, borrowed $500 in 1960 to purchase "DomiNick's," a pizza store, in Ypsilanti, Michigan. The following year Tom bought out his brother's half interest for a used Volkswagen Beetle. In 1965, Tom changed the name of the establishment to "Domino's Pizza" and two years later opened the first franchise location in Ypsilanti.[2]

Growing up in orphanages, Tom dreamed of succeeding in a big way. In his first 13 years in the business, he worked 100-hour weeks, seven days a week. He only had one vacation, and that was for six days when he got married to his wife, Margie.[3] The following quote exhibits his high need to be the best at whatever he does:

I was distracted by some of the rewards of success, which was hurting my business. I put all of those distractions aside, and focused solely on Domino's Pizza. I decided to take a "millionaire's vow of poverty." I am focusing on God, family and Domino's Pizza.[4]

The pizza industry is highly fragmented, with more than 61,000 pizzerias and $30 billion in sales per year. More than 3 billion pizzas are sold each year in America, representing annual consumption of over 23 pounds of pizza per capita.[5] The issue for any pizzeria is how to create an advantage and differentiate its product.

Monaghan decided to concentrate only on pizzas and developed the strategy of delivering a hot pie in 30 minutes or less. He chose to locate his early franchises in college towns and near military bases, whose populations are both high consumers of pizzas. This strategy proved to be very successful, and Domino's passed 200 locations in the late 1970s.[6]

Monaghan is credited with developing many of the pizza practices now taken for granted within the industry, including dough trays, the corrugated pizza box, insulated bags to transport pizzas, and a unique system of internal franchising. "Tom Monaghan made pizza delivery what it is today," says Eric Marcus, a 46-unit Domino's franchisee based in Dayton, Ohio. "The one thing about Tom is that he knew what he wanted, and he knew how to stay focused on what he wanted. He had a vision that pizza should be delivered in 30 minutes or less."[7]

The 1980s proved to be a huge time for Domino's growth, as it closed out the decade with more than 5,000 locations and $2 billion in sales.[8] During that time, Monaghan purchased the Detroit Tigers baseball team and developed significant philanthropic activities in various Domino's communities.

However, the road to success was not entirely smooth, and Domino's did have to face hurdles and challenges along the way. In 1968, the firm's commissary and company headquarters were destroyed by fire. In 1976, Amstar Corp., maker of Domino Sugar, filed a trademark infringement lawsuit against the firm that was settled in Domino's favor in 1980. In 1993, responding to concerns for drivers' safety, the firm discontinued the "30-minute guarantee" and replaced it with the total satisfaction guarantee: "If for any reason you are dissatisfied with your Domino's Pizza dining experience, we will re-make your pizza or refund your money."[9]

In 1998, Monaghan sold "a significant" portion of his ownership in Domino's to Bain Capital Inc., a Massachusetts investment firm. While he remained on the board of directors, he was no longer engaged in the day-to-day activities of the firm. Instead, he wanted to devote his time to religious pursuits, including the building of educational facilities in Ann Arbor, Michigan.[10]

David Brandon, formerly of Procter & Gamble and Valassis Communications, was hired as president. In his first full year as president, Domino's achieved a 4.4 percent growth in sales. Now chairman and CEO, Brandon has been recognized as the visionary who led Domino's to win the coveted "Chain of the Year" award for 2003 given by *Pizza Today*. Jeremy White, editor-in-chief of the monthly trade publication, observed: "Domino's had an impressive year. Between solid product introductions, savvy advertising and a 'People First' mentality that has trickled down from Chairman and CEO Dave Brandon to store employees, the chain managed to post positive financial results in a time of economic instability."[11]

Domino's Future

With a history of innovations in the pizza industry, Domino's constantly looks for new ways to enhance customer value. *Pizza Today* honored the company for outstanding sales, strong leadership, innovation, brand image, and customer satisfaction.[12] In Domino's early years, Tom Monaghan set the stage for the company's later successes with his innovations and brand development strategies. He even recognized how important it was to adapt to local culture in order to achieve success overseas. "Culture comes first. Some early attempts to open Domino's stores internationally faltered because the company tried to establish in markets that had cultures unaccustomed to pizza or the convenience of home delivery. Understanding cultures and adapting to them was the first step in the process of global expansion."[13] Can Domino's continue to be innovators in the pizza business?

Monaghan displayed the drive and determination representative of many entrepreneurs in today's dynamic market. He had what it took to succeed. Could *you* do what Tom Monaghan did?

Review Questions

1. What allowed Tom Monaghan to develop Domino's into a worldwide enterprise?

2. Why do you think Tom Monaghan chose to get out of the day-to-day operations of Domino's?

3. How do you think the characters of Tom Monaghan and David Brandon differ? How are they similar?

Why was each the right person for the company at the time?

You Do the Research

1. What are pizza parlors presently doing to differentiate their products?

2. Look at the profiles of other successful entrepreneurs. Do they have some character attributes in common?

CASE 7

Kate Spade: Risk Turns Niches into Opportunities

After graduating from college in 1986, Katherine (Kate) Noel Brosnahan was employed by *Mademoiselle* magazine, working her way up to senior fashion editor/head of accessories before her departure in 1991. During this time, Kate concluded that the women's fashion accessories market lacked stylish, practical handbags. Kate, along with her then boyfriend and now husband, Andy Spade, saw an opportunity and capitalized on it.[1] How did Kate and Andy capitalize on this opportunity?

The Startup

Kate and Andy set out "to develop a well-edited line of fashionable, but not 'trendy' handbags."[2] Kate developed design sketches for six handbags with simple shapes that emphasized utility, color, and fabric. Kate also investigated production costs. Andy contributed the marketing expertise, drawing on his experience at several advertising agencies. In January 1993, Kate and Andy launched Kate Spade Handbags.[3]

Kate worked full time to get the new company firmly established while Andy initially worked only part time. From January 1993 until September 1996, Andy worked nights and weekends on behalf of the new company and continued to work full time for an advertising agency. Andy began working full time with Kate Spade Handbags in September 1996, becoming its president and creative director.

Early on, Kate and Andy recognized the crucial need for recruiting talented people to help them grow the business. In late 1993, Pamela Simotas joined the company to assist Kate with the sourcing of materials and the manufacturing of the handbags. In 1994, Elyce Arons joined the company to focus on sales and public relations. The addition of Simontas and Arons led to the creation of a partnership that now numbers seven persons, each of whom brings special expertise and talents to the company.[4]

Growing into the Future

Kate Spade's vision focused on developing product lines and appropriately positioning the company in both the domestic and global marketplace. Kate Spade's original design philosophy relied on simplicity, elegance, and enduring quality "to create products that combined great personal style with long-lasting utility." This design philosophy has been consistently applied to growing the company's product lines. In addition to the original six nylon tote bags, Kate Spade's product lines now include leather handbags and accessories, evening bags, baby bags, a luggage collection, shoes, glasses, paper products (e.g., personal organizers, address books, and journals), and beauty products. In 1999, Jack Spade, an accessories line for men, was launched under Andy's tutelage. Jack Spade products include messenger bags, briefcases, and utility bags, among other items.[5]

In mid-1996, Kate Spade opened its first retail shop in New York City's Soho neighborhood. Expansion of the retail operation soon followed, with stores being opened in Boston, Los Angeles, Greenwich, Manhasset, San Francisco, Georgetown, and Chicago. Numerous Kate Spade outlets now exist in several Japanese cities, including Tokyo, Kyoto, and Osaka. International distribution of Kate Spade products has also expanded to Australia, the Bahamas, Bermuda, Canada, England, Guam, Hong Kong, Ireland, Korea, the Philippines, Puerto Rico, Saipan, Singapore, and Taiwan. An e-commerce operation is currently under development.[6]

In just over a decade, Kate Spade has grown from the germ of an idea about how to fill a void in the women's fashion accessories market into a multi–product line business with distribution in several U.S. and international locations. A future challenge for Kate Spade is how to build on its phenomenal success of the past decade. Continued expansion will be a key element in accomplishing this. Growth of the fledgling Jack Spade business may be another important element of the company's continued growth. Perhaps the Jack Spade line will be the company's growth engine of the next decade? Kate and Andy Spade recognize that their biggest challenge in the future will be to continue differentiating themselves from their competition while creating a passionate following among customers who have numerous choices.[7]

Review Questions

1. Describe the key decisions that Kate and Andy faced in the startup of their company.
2. What were the key elements of Kate Spade's growth in the first decade of its operations? What specific business decisions were made in implementing these key elements of growth?
3. What key decisions will Kate Spade need to make during the second decade of its operations?

You Do the Research

1. What options are available to Kate Spade in developing an e-commerce operation?
2. How might Kate Spade utilize information technology to help fuel continuing global expansion?

CASE 8

Wal-Mart: Planning for Superstore Competition

Wal-Mart, first opened in 1962 by Sam Walton in Rogers, Arkansas, has become the largest retailer in the world, with more than 4,600 store locations and approximately 1.25 million associates worldwide. Despite the death of Sam Walton in 1992, Wal-Mart continues to be successful, reaching record annual sales of $244.5 billion and earnings of $8.0 billion in fiscal 2003.[1] Maintaining this phenomenal growth presents an important challenge to Wal-Mart's current leadership.

Carrying on Sam Walton's Legacy

In his 1990 letter to Wal-Mart stockholders, then-CEO David Glass laid out the company's philosophy: "We approach this new exciting decade of the '90s much as we did in the '80s—focused on only two main objectives, (a) providing the customers what they want, when they want it, all at a value, and (b) treating each other as we would hope to be treated, acknowledging our total dependency on our associate-partners to sustain our success."[2] Following in Sam Walton's footsteps, Glass believed that the traditional format of organization, employee commitment, cost control, carefully planned locations for new stores, and attention to customer needs and desires would enable Wal-Mart to enjoy continued success.

Wal-Mart grew by paying careful attention to its market niche of customers who were looking for quality at a bargain price. Customers did not have to wait for a sale to realize savings. Many of its stores were located in smaller towns, primarily throughout the South and Midwest. As Glass looked ahead at the 1990s, he recognized the opportunities and threats that confronted Wal-Mart. While the traditional geographical markets served by Wal-Mart were not saturated, growth in these areas was limited. Any strategy to achieve continuing growth would have to include expansion into additional geographical regions. Glass recognized that continued growth might also have to include new product lines and higher-priced products to allow existing stores to achieve year-to-year sales growth.

In 1993, the company added the 91-store Pace Membership Warehouse chain, which it had purchased from Kmart.[3] Competition was increasing as smaller regional chains such as Costco and Price Club merged and opened stores in many of the same markets as Wal-Mart.[4] The company began to experiment with one-stop shopping in 1987, when it opened Hypermart USA, a Wal-Mart/supermarket combination. Experimentation with different retailing formats continued in subsequent years.

Wal-Mart is now made up of five retail divisions and five specialty divisions. The retail divisions include Wal-Mart Stores, SAM's Clubs (membership warehouse clubs), Neighborhood Markets (selling groceries, pharmaceuticals, and general merchandise), International Division, and Walmart.com (an online version of the neighborhood Wal-Mart store). Three of the specialty divisions—Tire & Lube Express, Wal-Mart Optical, and Wal-Mart Pharmacy—are commonly operated in conjunction with the Wal-Mart Stores and Supercenters and SAM'S Club outlets.[5]

Wal-Mart subscribes to the corporate policy "buy American whenever possible." Nonetheless, it has a global procurement system that enables it to effectively coordinate its entire worldwide supply chain and to share its buying power and merchandise network with all its operations throughout the world.[6] The company has set up an extensive inventory control procedure based on a satellite communication system that links all stores with the Bentonville, Arkansas, headquarters. The satellite system is also used to transmit messages from headquarters, training materials, and communications among stores, and can even be used to track the company's delivery trucks. In addition, Wal-Mart has an online system that links the company's computer systems with its suppliers. Because of its use of innovative technology, Wal-Mart has gained a competitive advantage in the speed with which it delivers goods to its customers.

While each new Wal-Mart brings in new jobs, it can also bring detrimental effects to the community as well. A 1991 *Wall Street Journal* article noted that many small retailers are forced to close after Wal-Mart opens nearby.[7] In one Wisconsin town, even J.C. Penny lost 50 percent of its Christmas sales and closed down when Wal-Mart opened up. In an Iowa town, four clothing and shoe stores, a hardware store, a drug store, and a dime store all went out of business. In 1994, the voters in Greenfield, Massachusetts, forced Wal-Mart to withdraw its building plans by using a few simple rules of engagement. It also had to give up plans to build in Bath, Maine; Simi Valley, California; and two towns in Pennsylvania. Vermont successfully resisted all Wal-Mart plans to locate in that state.

Even Wal-Mart's "Bring it home to the USA" buying program produced controversy when an NBC news program found clothing that had been made abroad hanging on racks under a "Made in the USA" sign in 11 Wal-Mart stores. In addition, the program showed a tape of children sewing at a Wal-Mart supplier's factory in Bangladesh. Wal-Mart insisted that its supplier was obeying local labor laws, which allowed 14-year-olds to work. A company official had also paid a surprise visit to the factory and had not found any problems. Then-CEO David Glass stated: "I can't tell you today that illegal child labor hasn't happened someplace, somewhere. All we can do is try our best to prevent it."[8]

Meanwhile, Wal-Mart began considering international expansion. In March 1994, the company bought 122 Canadian Woolco stores, formerly owned by Woolworth Corp., the largest single purchase Wal-Mart had made.[9] This international expansion continued, and in 2003, Wal-Mart's international division was the second largest with respect to sales and earnings. The almost 1,200 international locations had $41 billion in sales and an operating profit of $2 billion.[10]

Sam's Cultural Legacy

Wal-Mart's success is built upon its culture. Rob Walton, the company's current chairman of the board, says: "Although Wal-Mart has grown large, we still focus daily on the culture and values established by my father, Sam Walton."[11] Sam Walton founded and built Wal-Mart around three basic beliefs: *respect for the individual, service to our customers*, and *striving for excellence*. Wal-Mart's slogan that "our people make the difference" reflects the company's respect for and commitment to its associates (employees). Diversity is also highly valued. Wal-Mart's philosophy of customer service emphasizes the lowest possible prices along with the best possible service to each and every customer. Lee Scott, Wal-Mart Stores' current president and CEO, observes: "Sam was never satisfied that prices were as low as they needed to be or that our product's quality was as high as they deserved—he believed in the concept of striving for excellence before it became a fashionable concept."[12]

Three critical elements in Wal-Mart's approach to customer service are the *sundown rule*, the *ten-foot rule*, and *every day low prices*. The *sundown rule* means Wal-Mart sets a standard of accomplishing tasks on the same day that the need arises—in short, responding to requests by sundown on the day it receives them. The *ten-foot rule* promises that if an employee comes within ten feet of a customer, the employee must look the customer in the eye and ask if the person would like to be helped.

Every day low prices is another important operating philosophy. Wal-Mart believes that by lowering markup, it will earn more because of increased volume, thereby bringing consumers added value for the dollar every day.[13]

While Wal-Mart has enjoyed phenomenal success, there is no guarantee that it will continue to do so in the future. As the company's 2003 Annual Report points out, preserving and advancing the *every day low prices* concept and helping thousands of new associates to embrace the customer-centered Wal-Mart culture are essential for the company to continue growing.[14]

Review Questions

1. What are Wal-Mart's key objectives?
2. How have Wal-Mart's managerial philosophies and principles enabled it to pursue these key objectives?
3. How do planning and controlling seem to be linked at Wal-Mart?

You Do the Research

1. Explain how the various elements of Sam Walton's cultural legacy contribute to the company's ethical orientation.
2. Sam Walton's 1992 book *Made in America* identifies 10 key factors in building a business. These factors are identified on the company's website, www.walmartstores.com. How do these factors relate to Wal-Mart's culture and success?

CASE 9

Virgin Group: Reaching for the Sky in a New Economy

- -

Sir Richard Branson has assembled a collection of companies under the umbrella brand of "Virgin." Branson has repeatedly confounded analysts with his ability to spot emerging trends and profit from them. One senior executive at Virgin describes the company as a "branded venture-capital firm."[1] Branson has continually redefined Virgin's business operations, branching out into a variety of ventures but always capitalizing on his exuberant entrepreneurial spirit.

Richard Branson: Young Entrepreneur

Born in 1950, Branson began his first entrepreneurial venture when he was a 16-year-old student at a boarding school. He founded a magazine called *Student* to address contemporary issues of the time, such as the Vietnam War and the Paris student uprising. While raising about $6,000 over a six-month period to fund the magazine, Branson recruited well-known celebrities—like Jean-Paul Sarte and Vanessa Redgrave, among others—to be interviewed in or to write for the publication.[2] Branson, with his brashness, extraordinary ambition, and passion for success, went on to become a billionaire entrepreneur.

The magazine was followed in 1970 with a venture into discount records. Branson and Company ran ads in a mail-order catalog, and an increasing number of individuals purchased discounted records from it. Then his group from the magazine found an old shop, cleaned it up, and started a discount record store. Searching for a name for the business, they came up with three options: "Slipped Disc," "Student," and "Virgin." Since they were all virgins at business, the name Virgin was selected.[3] It quickly became the largest discount music megastore chain in the world.

In 1972 Branson branched out into the music recording business with Virgin Records. His first recording artist, Mike Oldfield, released "Tubular Bells," which went on to sell more than 5 million copies. When punk rock became popular, Branson signed the Sex Pistols, a group no other recording studio would touch. Other groups included Genesis, Simple Minds, Culture Club, Phil Collins, and the Rolling Stones.

Moving on to Other Ventures

Other people might have been content with their early success, but Richard Branson was not finished. Running his business interests out of a houseboat on the Thames River, he launched Virgin Airways in 1984 (now Virgin Atlantic) with a single jumbo jet. Taking on British Airways, he sued them for alleged dirty tricks and won. The airline is famous for its offbeat perks, including massages and premium first-class service.

Branson also refuses to follow the industry leaders. As many airlines drop fares and cut service in order to compete for passengers, Branson keeps Virgin Atlantic focused on reasonable fares and unique customer service, including ice cream with movies, private bedrooms, showers, and exercise facilities.

Looking back on his various business ventures, Branson says, "I started the magazine because I had a passion for what I was doing. That's also why I went into the airline business, even though everybody I talked to told me that there was no money to be made there. I felt that I could make a difference. That's the best reason to go into business—because you feel strongly that you can change things."[4] Branson's business objectives from the start have been to be noticed, have fun, and make money by constantly starting new firms.[5]

Over the years, Virgin Group Ltd. has created more than 200 new businesses, employing more than 25,000 people, with revenues exceeding £3 billion (US$5 billion) annually.[6] Virgin Group

Ltd. currently has business interests in planes, trains, finance, soft drinks, music, mobile phones, holidays, cars, wines, publishing, bridal wear—and more.[7] Virgin doesn't represent a business so much as it represents a business-making machine.[8]

When Virgin starts a new business, it is based on solid research and analysis. The company reviews the industry and puts itself in the customer's shoes. Virgin asks several fundamental questions: "Is this an opportunity for restructuring a market and creating competitive advantage? What are the competitors doing? Is the customer confused or badly served? Is this an opportunity for building the Virgin brand? Can we add value? Will it interact with our other businesses? Is there an appropriate trade-off between risk and reward?"[9]

Not everything touched by Branson turns to gold. He was forced in the early 1990s to sell his beloved Virgin Records to Thorn EMI to secure the survival of his Virgin Airlines. As a result, Branson now employs a strategy of using wealthy partners to provide the bulk of the cash necessary to run a business, with Virgin providing the brand-name recognition in exchange for a controlling interest in the venture. Rather than mixing with investment bankers, he has a habit of keeping his companies private—preferring to sell off chunks of his empire to fund new business startups. His sale of a 49 percent share of Virgin Atlantic to Singapore Airlines for $979 million provided him the needed cash to plow into his Internet ventures.[10]

Although Virgin represents a late arrival to the Internet, Branson has attacked the venture with the same enthusiasm displayed in his previous business startups. Many of his business interests already had a presence on the Web, including Thetrainline.com, a joint venture with the British transport company Stagecoach. The site sells tickets for Britain's 23 train operators, has more than 1.8 million users and purchases of more than $2.5 million weekly, and is adding 55,000 new users each week.[11] By transferring an airline-type reservation system onto the Net, Virgin earns 9 percent of every ticket booked. Virgin will sell competitors' services right alongside its own. What Branson is hoping to do is leverage his presence into a "cyberbrand" with a premium presence on the Web.

"Virgin's approach to the Net has been very clever," claims Simon Knox, professor of brand marketing at the Cranfield University School of Management in Bedford. "Each launch of a new business builds upon the one before, rather than developing isolated branded businesses."[12] Others, like Michael Arnbjerg, with the market research firm IDC in Copenhagen, disagree. He argues that "Virgin can leverage its brand in certain market sectors, but that's not enough to become a major player."[13]

Expanding the Business Portfolio

The Virgin Group's main focus is on providing services rather than on producing products. To help fuel its services growth, Virgin actively seeks business proposals from the public via its website. "If you have a fantastic idea for us, then we're all ears! We're always on the lookout for fresh ideas to improve our current companies and to create brand new ones."[14]

In soliciting proposals, the company emphasizes that "Virgin is famous for its down-to-earth good value and service, so all new ideas will need to reflect these values. We also have a great sense of fun, and we like to do things just a little bit differently from the rest."[15] Virgin asks people who submit business proposals to address the following issues: the nature of the product or service idea; the business sector into which this idea fits; the idea or project's current stage of development; the proposal submitter's involvement in the project, as well as the role he/she/they would like to maintain; the reason for approaching Virgin and the anticipated role of Virgin in the project; and an assessment of the venture's potential.[16]

Virgin says that it respects the intellectual property rights of all new business proposals that it receives. The company notes, however, that it receives "hundreds of proposals which are often similar to those suggested by others, or to ideas which we have developed internally."[17] While only a few submitted proposals actually move forward in the business development process, the ones that are most likely to be successful are already well developed, have large-scale potential, and can be implemented quickly.[18]

What does the future hold for Sir Richard and the Virgin Group? If history is any predictor, the company's portfolio will continue to embrace a wide range of businesses that have the potential for providing quality service in a fun and different way.

Review Questions

1. What are the key strategic questions that the Virgin Group asks when starting a new business venture?

2. How has the Virgin Group established a competitive advantage?

3. How would you characterize the corporate strategy of Branson's Virgin Group?

4. What are the main advantages and disadvantages associated with Virgin's solicitation of business proposals from the public to help grow the business?

You Do the Research

1. Examine the range of businesses that fall under the Virgin Group's corporate umbrella. Does investment in these different businesses make sense from a business strategy perspective? Why or why not?

2. Do a SWOT analysis for Virgin Group Ltd.

3. How dependent is the success of Virgin on Richard Branson? If something happened to him, would the company be able to survive?

CASE 10

Krispy Kreme: Where Growth Is Really Sweet

At Krispy Kreme's 324th store opening in late October 2003, a crowd began gathering early outside the store. Close to 100 people huddled under a tent and umbrellas on that cold, rainy morning waiting for the store's opening. With the local media present, the store opened at 5:30 A.M. to the crowd's chanting "Doughnuts! Doughnuts!" One customer who had been in line since 3:00 A.M. admitted to getting up early to see presidents and governors—and now to purchase Krispy Kreme doughnuts. As admirable—or crazy—as this may seem, it's tame compared to the doughnut dedication shown by others. Some people will even camp out at the stores in the final days of construction and set up before the opening. Rob Perugini camped outside of the 324th Krispy Kreme for 17 days before the opening, breaking the old record of 13 days.[1] What does Krispy Kreme do to produce such devotion to its doughnuts?

The Founding and Early Growth of Krispy Kreme

Krispy Kreme Doughnuts, founded in 1937, has grown from a small doughnut shop in a rented building into "a leading branded specialty retailer, producing more than 5 million doughnuts a day and over 1.8 billion a year."[2] After purchasing a yeast-raised doughnut recipe from a French chef in New Orleans, Vernon Rudolph, Krispy Kreme's founder, began making doughnuts in a rented building in Winston-Salem, North Carolina, and selling them to local grocery stores. Soon Rudolph began selling hot doughnuts directly to customers.[3] In the ensuing years, Krispy Kreme grew into a small chain of stores, all using the same recipe. Product quality varied, however, and the company established a dry-mix plant and distribution system to ensure a consistent product. Krispy Kreme continued to expand and enjoyed steady growth until the mid-1970s, when the company was sold to Beatrice Foods subsequent to Rudolph's death.[4]

The sale to Beatrice Foods ushered in an era in which Krispy Kreme stores sold ice cream, sausage biscuits, and other food products in addition to doughnuts. Even the doughnut recipe was changed. Horrified by what was happening, a group of Krispy Kreme franchisees repurchased the company from Beatrice foods a few years later.[5]

With the 1982 repurchase, Krispy Kreme refocused on making the hot doughnut experience a company priority. The company continued expanding throughout the southeastern United States, and then in 1996 it opened its first unit outside the Southeast. This store was in New York City. In 1999, Krispy Kreme opened its first store in California. National expansion has accelerated rapidly since then. In December 2001, the company opened a store in Canada, its first outside the United States.[6]

Growth Through Excellence

Krispy Kreme has a strategic philosophy that is oriented toward growth through excellence. The company's strategic philosophy revolves around the following beliefs:

- "All products we make in our stores will have a taste and quality that are second to none."
- "The starting point in controlling product quality is controlling the quality and freshness of the ingredients."
- "We will be thoroughly prepared to execute growth initiatives when they become needed."
- "We view quality, service, and innovation as keys to creating and maintaining a competitive advantage."
- "We view our company as a set of capabilities, not just a product or brand."
- "We view our growth and success as a company as a natural result of the growth and success of our people."[7]

Krispy Kreme's growth has been partly fueled by the company's obsession with product consistency. Krispy Kreme strives for such consistency that a doughnut purchased anywhere in the world at any time will taste exactly the same. This is accomplished by testing all raw ingredients before delivery is accepted. If a test sample of a shipment does not meet the company's standards, the entire shipment is rejected. Krispy Kreme also makes sample doughnuts from every single 2,500-pound batch of mix to ensure that each batch is blended correctly.[8]

Krispy Kreme is more like a factory than a bakery. Krispy Kreme stores typically operate around the clock, producing doughnuts for walk-in customers as well as for wholesale purchase by supermarkets and grocery stores.[9]

National expansion through franchising has driven a good portion of Krispy Kreme's growth, particularly since the mid-1990s. Significant growth has occurred even though a Krispy Kreme franchise is the most costly food franchise available—being about five times the standard cost for most operations, as estimated by the International Franchise Association. A Krispy Kreme franchise, costing $2 million per location on average, is both extraordinarily difficult to obtain and in great demand. Krispy Kreme requires its franchisees to have "$5 million in net worth to apply and . . . ownership and operating experience with multi-unit food service operations."[10] Krispy Kreme also seeks "area developers"— franchisees who will open at least 10 stores in a region.

Krispy Kreme stores are high-volume operations with higher profit margins than other fast-food business. A typical McDonald's franchise has revenues of about $1.5 million annually and a typical Dunkin' Donuts averages about $744,000.[11] In fiscal 2001, Krispy Kreme franchisees had average revenue of $2.2 million per location. This jumped to $2.8 million in fiscal 2002 and $3 million in fiscal 2003. Company stores had even higher annual sales volume, reaching about $4 million in fiscal 2003.[12]

"Krispy Kreme now takes an ownership stake in all new franchisees, claiming anywhere from 33% to 75%," a strategy that increasingly is being adopted by other franchising companies. "The parent companies engage in such partnerships because they lead to higher earnings and faster expansion." Krispy Kreme takes an ownership stake even though franchisees "have the money and desire to open as many stores as the company will allow."[13]

While fueling growth, this joint-partnership strategy has not been a smooth road. A lawsuit over the terms of an alleged contract was filed by two franchisees in northern California. An equity fund that was formed by 35 Krispy Kreme executives to invest in franchise stores was disbanded in the aftermath of the Enron scandal so "that no individual's personal gain would conflict with the overall good of the company."[14]

Krispy Kreme's rapid growth has also been facilitated by its use of information technology. The company uses the Internet as well as a corporate intranet to aid national and international expansion. Using its information technology, Krispy Kreme has made more and more of its services and information accessible to corporate staff, stores, franchisees, and suppliers. The vast majority of orders from individual units are placed over the company's intranet. Using the Internet and intranet, individual stores from anywhere in the world can train employees around the clock.[15]

Krispy Kreme continues to expand into new markets, both in the United States and overseas. In fiscal 2003, the company entered 17 new U.S. markets as well as one in Canada. It also opened its first store outside of North America, which is in Sydney, Australia. At the end of fiscal 2003, the company is also preparing for a store opening in London. In addition, the company acquired Montana Mills Bread Company and successfully introduced Krispy Kreme Signature Coffees—an outgrowth of its earlier acquisition of Digital Java, Inc. Krispy Kreme has developed a roasting process for coffee beans that ensures the same high level of quality and consistency with its coffees as it has with its doughnuts.[16]

In line with its emphasis on product consistency, Krispy Kreme's opening of a new store engenders highly consistent customer behavior. A Krispy Kreme store opening attracts a lot of attention. The experience of James Consentino, a West Palm Beach, Florida, franchisee is typical on the morning of a store opening and in the ensuing days. "At 5:30 A.M. that morning, he'll let in a mob of people who've been waiting outside for hours for the warm doughnuts streaming from his ovens at a rate of 2,640 per hour. The event will probably be covered by a TV news crew—most Krispy Kreme openings are—and in his first week Consentino will take in almost as much in revenue as the typical Dunkin' Donuts store makes in a year."[17]

Review Questions

1. What are the key elements of Krispy Kreme's strategic philosophy? How do these elements relate to the organizing trend of balancing decentralization with centralization?
2. What type of organizational structure does Krispy Kreme appear to be using?
3. What is the potential for developing a network structure at Krispy Kreme?

You Do the Research

1. Based on its recent growth history, what would you predict for Krispy Kreme in the next five years? What type of organizational structure should be used to accommodate whatever growth you predict?
2. Suppose that you decide to exercise your entrepreneurial motivation and want to look into franchising opportunities. What key elements would you look for in a franchising relationship?
3. Does Krispy Kreme present a better franchise opportunity than those provided by other franchising companies? Why or why not?

BET Holdings: World-Class Entrepreneur Places BET on Future

Robert Johnson, born the ninth of ten children in Hickory, Mississippi, is a true rags-to-riches success story. His father, Archie, chopped wood while his mother taught school. Ultimately, their search for a better life led them to Freeport, Illinois, a predominantly white working-class neighborhood. Archie supplemented his factory jobs by operating his own junkyard on the predominantly black east side of town. Edna Johnson got a job at Burgess Battery, and although she eventually secured a job for her son, Robert, at the battery firm, he knew it wasn't for him.[1]

Robert Johnson's Journey to Becoming an Entrepreneur

Bobby Johnson showed an enterprising nature at an early age, delivering papers, mowing lawns, and cleaning out tents at local fairs. At Freeport High School, he was an honors student and entered the University of Illinois upon graduation. Virgil Hemphill, his freshman roommate, commented: "He was not overly slick, overly smooth. He was kind of innocent and naive. His strength was being able to talk to different types of people. I went to Freeport with him, and he could communicate with the regular people and with the suit-and-tie people."[2]

Johnson did well at Illinois, studying history, holding several work-study jobs, and participating in Kappa Alpha Psi, a black fraternity. After graduation in 1968, he was admitted to a two-year program at Princeton University's Woodrow Wilson School of Public and International Affairs. He had a full scholarship plus expenses but dropped out after the first semester to marry his college sweetheart, Sheila Crump, a former cheerleader and a gifted violinist. He eventually returned to Princeton to earn his master's degree in public administration in 1972.[3]

He moved on to Washington, D.C., to work at the Corporation for Public Broadcasting, followed by the Washington Urban League, where the director, Sterling Tucker, was leading the struggle for District home rule. Tucker appreciated Johnson's ability to think both "micro-ly and macro-ly" while still "thinking like a visionary" in pursuing larger goals.[4] Moving on to work for the Congressional Black Caucus, Johnson became impressed with the possibilities for black power that lay in television—and cable, in particular. In 1976, he began working as a lobbyist for the National Cable Television Association (NCTA), where he gained invaluable insight into the cable industry.

At the NCTA's 1979 convention, Johnson met Bob Rosencrans, president of UA-Columbia Cablevision. While Bob Johnson had a strong idea for providing cable programming to minority audiences, he had no satellite time. Rosencrans, on the other hand, was looking for programs to support his local franchises and to fill some unused slots on one of the cable TV satellites. "I just said, 'Bob, you're on. Let's go.' I don't think we even charged him. We knew he couldn't afford much, and for us, it was a plus because it gave us more ammunition to sell cable. The industry was not attracting minority customers."[5]

With $15,000 from a consulting contract that he received upon his departure from NCTA, Robert Johnson launched Black Entertainment Television (BET) at 11:00 P.M. on January 8, 1980. The first BET show was a 1974 African safari movie, *Visit to a Chief's Son*. Initially, BET aired for only two hours on Friday nights. The first show bounced off an RCA satellite and into 3.8 million homes served by Rosencrans's franchises. Johnson received his first crucial financing from John Malone of TCI in the form of a $380,000 loan plus $120,000 for a 20 percent ownership in BET.[6]

To raise capital in the 1980s, Johnson sold off pieces of BET to Time Inc.

and Taft Broadcasting for more than $10 million. However, controversy over programming followed Johnson from the start, with his heavy reliance on music videos (60 percent of total programming), gospel and religious programs, infomercials, and reruns of older shows such as *Sanford and Son* and *227*.[7] After a decade of learning the finer points of the cable industry, Johnson went public with BET.

BET suffered from low fees compared to other cable offerings. Early on BET was earning only 2 cents per subscriber, while major networks such as TNT and USA were getting 15 to 20 cents. Johnson won the battle for higher fees, which jumped from 2.5 cents to 5 cents in 1989 and eventually to 15.5 cents over the next five years.[8]

The Growth of BET Holdings

Robert Johnson had grand plans for BET, seeking to turn the enterprise into what marketers call an umbrella brand.[9] The firm published two national magazines that reached 250,000 readers: *Young Sisters and Brothers* for teens and *Emerge* for affluent adults, and it had interests in film production, electronic retailing, and radio.[10] The first BET Sound-Stage restaurant opened in suburban Washington and another in Disney World in Orlando. With Hilton as a partner, Johnson explored opening a casino in Las Vegas, Nevada.[11]

Johnson wanted to capture some of the black consumers' disposable income—valued at $425 billion annually. To do this, he partnered primarily with big names as such Disney, Hilton, Blockbuster, Microsoft, and others. "You simply cannot get big anymore by being 100 percent black-owned anything," Johnson claimed.[12] His Black Entertainment Television cable station provided the perfect medium to influence this increasingly affluent black audience.

BET, Inc. aims to become "the leading African-America multi-media entertainment company. BET is committed to establishing the most valued consumer brand within the African-American marketplace."[13] Black Entertainment Television, distinctly targeted toward serving the African-American community, remains at the core of the BET business empire. As of late 2003, Black Entertainment Television reached more than 74 million cable subscribers in the United States.[14] Included among this subscriber base are more than 90 percent of all black households that have cable hookups. BET's related digital cable businesses include BET on Jazz, BET Gospel, BET Classic Soul, BET International, and BET Hip Hop. BET Books publishes literature on African-American themes written by African-American authors. BET Pictures produces documentaries on African-American themes and made-for-TV movies. BET Interactive, a partnership among BET, Microsoft, Liberty Digital Media, News Corporation, and USA Networks, has the Internet portal BET.com, which is the leading online site for African-Americans.[15]

BET Holdings II, Inc. has grown into such a success story that Viacom, Inc. purchased it for $3 billion in November 2000. Robert Johnson remains as chairman and CEO of the Viacom subsidiary, reporting to Viacom's president and chief operating officer, Mel Karmazin.[16] Karmazin describes the acquisition of BET Holdings as "a strategically perfect fit. . . . Viacom is home to the industry's most creative and distinctive branded programming, the perfect environment for BET's television and online business to grow and prosper."[17]

Review Questions

1. Is a mechanistic organizational design or an organic organizational design more appropriate for BET? Explain your answer.
2. How might environment and strategy influence BET's organizational design?
3. As a multifaceted, multimedia entertainment company, what challenges regarding differentiation and integration does BET likely face?

You Do the Research

1. Was Robert Johnson correct in selling his BET Holdings II to Viacom?
2. Will BET Interactive become a major force on the Web?
3. What's next for Robert Johnson?

CASE 12

SAS Institute: Systems Help People Make a Difference

Founded in 1976 by Dr. James Goodnight and Dr. John Sall, both professors at North Carolina State University, SAS Institute, Inc. provides business intelligence (BI) software and services at more than 40,000 customer sites worldwide, including 90 percent of the *Fortune* 500 companies. SAS, which stands for "statistical analysis software," is headquartered in Cary, North Carolina. It is the world's largest privately held software company, having more than 100 offices worldwide with approximately 10,000 employees. With an unbroken record of growth and profitability, SAS had revenue of $1.18 billion in 2002 and invested about 25 percent of revenues into research and development.[1] The phenomenal success story of SAS is, in no small part, due to its human resources strategy, policies, and practices. How do the HR strategy, policies, and practices contribute so much to the success of SAS?

Human Resources Policies and Practices at SAS

Fast Company metaphorically describes the SAS Institute as a modern company that is like a kingdom in a fairy-tale land. "Although this company is thoroughly modern (endowed with advanced computers, the best child care, art on almost every wall, and athletic facilities that would make an NBA trainer drool), there is something fairy-tale-like about the place. The inhabitants are happy, productive, well rounded—in short, content in a way that's almost unheard-of today. They are loyal to the kingdom and to its king, who in turn is the model of a benevolent leader. The king—almost unbelievably—goes by the name Goodnight."[2]

SAS is strongly committed to its employees. The company strives to hire talented people and goes to extraordinarily lengths to ensure that they are satisfied. James Goodnight, the CEO of SAS, says: "We've made a conscious effort to ensure that we're hiring and keeping the right talent to improve our products and better serve our customers. To attract and retain that talent, it's essential that we maintain our high standards in regards to employee relations."[3]

SAS has been widely recognized for its work-life programs and emphasis on employee satisfaction. The company's various honors include being recognized by *Working Mothers* magazine as one of "100 Best Companies for Working Mothers" and by *Fortune* magazine as one of the "100 Best Companies to Work for in America." The *Working Mothers* recognition has been received 13 times, and the *Fortune* recognition has occurred for six consecutive years.[4]

SAS pays its employees competitively, targeted at the average for the software industry. It does not provide stock options like other companies in the industry.[5] Instead of relying on high salaries and stock options to attract and retain workers like many software companies do, SAS takes a very different approach. It focuses on providing meaningful and challenging work, and it encourages teamwork. SAS also provides a host of benefits that appeal to the employees and help keep them satisfied. As one employee who took a 10 percent pay cut to join SAS said: "It's better to be happy than to have a little more money."[6]

Employees are given the freedom, flexibility, responsibility, and resources to do their jobs, and they are also held accountable for results. Managers know what employees are doing and they work alongside them, writing computer code.[7] "The company employs very few external contractors and very few part-time staff, so there is a strong sense of teamwork throughout the organization."[8] SAS employees are clearly involved in their work. One employee, Kathy Passarella, notes: "When you walk down the halls here, it's rare that you hear people talking about anything but work."[9]

Included among the various employee benefits that SAS provides are an employee fitness and recreational center, an employee laundry service, a heavily subsidized employee cafeteria, live piano music in the employee cafeteria, subsidized on-site child care, and a free health center.[10] All of these benefits are geared toward employees having a better work experience and/or a better balance between their work lives and their personal lives. The company's commitment to work-life balance is evident in SAS's 35-hour workweek, which clearly recognizes the importance of employees' personal lives.[11]

In reflecting on the company's generous benefits package, David Russo, SAS's head of human resources, says: "To some people, this looks like the Good Ship Lollipop, floating down the stream. It's not. It's part of a soundly designed strategy." That strategy is intended "to make it impossible for people not to do their work."[12]

Extraordinary Employee Benefits: At What Cost?

While SAS goes to extraordinary lengths to ensure that employees are satisfied, the company expects and demands productivity and performance results in return. The owners of SAS want employees to be satisfied because they believe satisfied employees will be excellent performers and will provide exceptional service to the company's customers. "If you treat employees as if they make a difference to the company, they will make a difference to the company. . . . Satisfied employees create satisfied customers."[13] This viewpoint might be described as a form of enlightened realism and enlightened self-interest on the part of the company. Satisfied employees make for satisfied customers, and satisfied customers make for an ongoing stream of revenue and profits for SAS.

SAS's leaders recognize both the benefits and costs associated with keeping employees satisfied. One of the most significant benefits for SAS is a very low annual turnover rate, which is less than 4 percent, as compared to approximately 25 percent for the industry as a whole. This low turnover saves the company about $70 million annually in employee replacement costs.[14] On the cost side, of course, is the company's monetary outlay for the various programs. David Russo, the human resources director, argues that the employee replacement cost saving more than pays for the company's generous benefits. "That's the beauty of it," says Russo. "There's no way I could spend all the money we save."[15]

Perhaps of more concern on the "cost side" is the potential for employees failing to perform. In commenting on the company's performance expectations for employees, Goodnight says: "I like to be around happy people, but if they don't get that next release out, they're not going to be very happy."[16] Pondering the likelihood that SAS employees would take advantage of the company's relaxed atmosphere, John Sall, co-owner of SAS, observes: "I can't imagine that playing Ping-Pong would be more interesting than work."[17] David Russo adds some additional perspective. He says: "If you're out sick for six months, you'll get cards and flowers, and people will come to cook dinner for you. If you're out sick for six Mondays in a row, you'll get fired. We expect adult behavior."[18]

Clearly, human resource management at SAS is a two-way street. SAS has an HR strategy and related policies and practices that attract, motivate, and retain highly capable workers who make significant contributions to the ongoing success of the company. Goodnight and the other SAS leaders expect nothing less than superior performance from the employees, and they continue to get it. The employees are loyal and committed to the company, and they are productive—so loyal, committed, and productive, in fact, that only a small percentage of the employees ever leave once they have been hired at SAS. Having quality employees who want to stay—isn't this the human resources goal that should challenge all companies?

Review Questions

1. What is the basic management philosophy that governs employee relationship management at SAS Institute?
2. Explain how the SAS human resources strategy, policies, and practices affect the company's ability to attract, develop, and maintain a quality workforce.
3. What impact have the SAS human resources strategy, policies, and

practices had on the company's financial success?

You Do the Research

1. Compare SAS with Trilogy Software, a competitor in the computer software industry, in terms of approaches to attracting, developing, and maintaining a quality workforce.

2. Why does Trilogy take the approach that it does? Why does SAS take the approach that it does?

3. Would the SAS approach to attracting, developing, and maintaining a quality workforce be adaptable to any company in any industry? Why or why not?

CASE 13

Southwest Airlines: How Herb Kelleher Led the Way

The U.S. airline industry experienced problems in the early 1990s. From 1989 through 1993, the largest airlines, including American, United, Delta, and USAir, lost billions of dollars. Only Southwest Airlines remained profitable throughout that period. Herb Kelleher, co-founder of Southwest in 1971 and until recently its CEO, pointed out that "we didn't make much for a while there. It was like being the tallest guy in a tribe of dwarfs."[1] Nevertheless, Southwest Airlines has grown to the point of having operating revenue of $5.5 billion in 2002, which also was its 30th consecutive year of profitability. This is particularly noteworthy since Southwest flies to only 58 cities in 30 states, and its average flight length is 537 miles.[2] How did a little airline get to be so big? Its success is due to its core values, developed by Kelleher and carried out daily by the company's 35,000 employees. These core values are humor, altruism, and "luv" (the company's stock ticker symbol).[3]

Southwest Airlines's Unique Character and Success

One of the things that make Southwest Airlines so unique is its short-haul focus. The airline does not assign seats or sell tickets through the reservation systems used by travel agents. Many passengers buy tickets at the gate. The only foods served are peanuts, pretzels, and similar snacks, but passengers don't seem to mind. In fact, serving Customers (at Southwest, always written with a capital C) is the focus of the company's employees. When Colleen Barrett, currently Southwest's president and chief operating officer (COO), was the executive vice president for customers, she said, "We will never jump on employees for leaning too far toward the customer, but we come down on them hard for not using common sense."[4] Southwest's core values produce employees who are highly motivated and who care about the customers and about one another.

One way in which Southwest carries out this philosophy is by treating employees and their ideas with respect. As executive vice president, Colleen Barrett formed a "culture committee," made up of employees from different functional areas and levels. The committee continues and meets quarterly to come up with ideas for maintaining Southwest's corporate spirit and image. All managers, officers, and directors are expected to "get out in the field," meet and talk to employees, and understand their jobs. Employees are encouraged to use their creativity and sense of humor to make their jobs and the customers' experiences more enjoyable. Gate agents, for example, are given a book of games to play with waiting passengers when a flight is delayed. Flight agents might do an imitation of Elvis or Mr. Rogers while making announcements. Others have jumped out of the overhead luggage bins to surprise boarding passengers.[5]

Kelleher, currently chairman of the board and chairman of the executive committee, knows that not everyone would be happy as a Southwest employee: "What we are looking for, first and foremost, is a sense of humor. Then we are looking for people who have to excel to satisfy themselves and who work well in a collegial environment." He feels that the company can teach specific skills but that a compatible attitude is most important. When asked to prove that she had a sense of humor, Mary Ann Adams, hired in 1997 as a finance executive, recounted a practical joke in which she turned an unflattering picture of her boss into a screen saver for her department.[6]

To encourage employees to treat one another as well as they treat their customers, departments examine linkages within Southwest to see what their "internal customers" need. The provisioning department, for example, whose responsibility is to provide the snacks and drinks for each flight, selects a flight attendant as "customer of the month." The provisioning department's own board of directors makes the selection decision, as well as other departmental managerial decisions. Other departments have sent pizza and ice cream to their "internal customers." Employees write letters commending the work of other employees or departments, and these letters are valued as much as those from "external customers."

When problems do occur between departments, the employees work out solutions in supervised meetings.

Employees exhibit the same attitude of altruism and "luv" (Southwest's term for its relationship with its customers) toward other groups as well. A significant portion of Southwest employees volunteer their time at Ronald McDonald Houses throughout Southwest's service territory. When the company purchased a small regional airline, employees personally sent cards and company T-shirts to their new colleagues to welcome them to the Southwest family. They demonstrate similar caring toward the company itself. As gasoline prices rose during the period of the Gulf War in the early 1990s, many of the employees created the "Fuel from the Heart Program," donating fuel to the company by deducting the cost of one or more gallons from their paychecks.

Acting in the company's best interests is also directly in the interest of the employees. Southwest has a profit-sharing plan for all eligible employees; and unlike many of its competitors, Southwest consistently has profits to share. Employees can also purchase Southwest stock at 90 percent of market value; at least 13 percent of Southwest's employees own company stock. Although approximately 81 percent of employees are unionized, the company has a history of good labor relations.[7]

Southwest Airlines is a low-cost operator. According to Harvard University professor John Kotter, setting the standard for low costs in the airline industry does not mean Southwest is *cheap*. "Cheap is trying to get your prices down by nibbling costs off everything . . . [firms like Southwest Airlines] are thinking 'efficient,' which is very different. . . . They recognize that you don't necessarily have to take a few pennies off of everything. Sometimes you might even spend more."[8] By buying one type of plane—the Boeing 737—Southwest saves on both pilot training and maintenance costs. The *cheap* paradigm would favor used planes; Southwest's choice results in the youngest fleet of airplanes in the industry because the model favors high productivity over lower capital expenditures.

Southwest currently operates a fleet of 381 Boeing 737 jets with the configuration shown in the table below.[9]

By utilizing each plane an average of 12 hours per day, Southwest is able to make more trips with fewer planes than any other airline. Since May 1988, Southwest Airlines has won the monthly "Triple Crown" distinction of airline service—Best On-Time Record, Best Baggage Handling, and Fewest Customer Complaints—more than 30 times. From 1992 through 1996, Southwest won the annual "Triple Crown" every year.[10]

Type of 737	Number of Aircraft	Seats per Aircraft
737-200	26	122
737-300	194	137
737-500	25	122
737-700	136	137

Southwest's Ongoing Challenges

Despite its impressive record of success, Southwest Airlines has pressing concerns to address. Management worries about the effects on morale of limited opportunities for promotion. The company has created "job families" with different grade levels so that employees can work their way up within their job category. However, after five or six years employees begin to hit the maximum compensation level for their job category.

Another issue is how to maintain the culture of caring and fun while expanding rapidly into new markets. Southwest's success has been built with the enthusiasm and hard work of its employees; as Kelleher said, "The people who work here don't think of Southwest as a business. They think of it as a crusade."[11] Cultivating that crusading atmosphere is a continuing priority for the company.

As Herb Kelleher prepared to relinquish his role as Southwest's CEO, a major concern for investors was whether the company's success could be maintained because so much of Southwest's success was attributable to Kelleher's unique management and leadership style. Recent events, however, seem to demonstrate that Kelleher's successors—longtime Southwest employees Jim Parker (currently vice chairman of the board

and CEO) and Colleen Barrett (currently president and COO)—were well prepared to handle the challenges of maintaining Southwest's culture and success. As Barrett wrote in the company's *Spirit Magazine*: "Air travel changed forever two years ago, but our steadfast determination remains unbroken to provide the high-spirited Customer Service, low fares, and frequent nonstop flights that Americans want and need."[12] Not even terrorist attacks can derail the company that Herb Kelleher led to success. Southwest Airlines continues to be recognized by *Fortune* magazine as America's most admired airline as well as one of the most admired companies in America. In 2003 *Air Transport World* magazine selected Southwest as the "Airline for the Year." The reasoning: 30 consecutive years of profitability, while providing affordable fares for millions of passengers. Other recognitions of Southwest culture and success continue to pile up.[13]

2002 Fun Facts

- Southwest received 243,657 resumes and hired 5,042 new employees.
- Southwest booked approximately 83 million reservations.
- Southwest served 32.8 million cans of soda and juice and 11.7 million cans of water.
- Southwest served 162.4 million bags of peanuts.
- Southwest purchased 1.1 billion gallons of jet fuel.
- Southwest has 1,000 married couples working for the company.
- Southwest received requests for service from 140 destinations.[14]

Review Questions

1. What role has leadership played in the success of Southwest Airlines?
2. Explain the role of employee empowerment at Southwest Airlines and how it can act as a substitute for leadership.
3. Describe Kelleher's leadership style.
4. What is the key to Southwest's continued success under leaders other than Herb Kelleher?

You Do the Research

1. How did Herb Kelleher use power and exercise influence at Southwest Airlines?
2. Which of the leadership theories described in Chapter 13 seem to provide the most useful explanation for Herb Kelleher's success in leading Southwest Airlines?
3. Find examples that show how Herb Kelleher and other leaders at Southwest Airlines have acted with integrity. What lessons do these examples provide for future managers and leaders?

NASCAR: Fast Cars, Passion Motivate Top Drivers

In only his second full year of NASCAR Winston Cup Series racing, the young Ryan Newman was rapidly becoming a racing phenomenon. He had a spectacular 2002 racing season and was on target to surpass it in 2003. As of mid-October 2003, Newman had competed in 34 Winston Cup races, finishing among the top ten 19 times while winning eight pole positions and eight races.[1] Ryan Newman appears driven to succeed. What motivates someone like Ryan Newman?

Ryan Newman's Racing Passion

A self-admitted car buff, Ryan Newman loves to drive cars and work on them.[2] His passion for fast cars developed at an early age. Encouraged by his parents, he started racing quarter midgets when he was only four-and-a-half years old. Newman amassed more than 100 midget car victories. Later he raced midget cars and sprint cars, achieving extraordinary success there as well. He won Rookie of the Year honors in 1993 for the All-American Midget Series, in 1995 for the USAC National Midget Series, in 1996 for USAC Silver Crown Racing, and in 1999 for sprint cars.[3] In 2000, Newman began driving for the Penske Racing Team, competing in five Automobile Racing Club of America (ARCA) races and one NASCAR Winston Cup Series race. He won two of the ARCA races. In 2001, Newman competed in a total of 26 ARCA, Busch Grand National Series, and Winston Cup races, finishing in the top ten on 11 occasions with two first-place finishes.[4] In 2002, Newman raced full time in the Winston Cup Series, earning six pole positions, 22 top-ten finishes, 14 top-five finishes, and one first-place finish in 36 starts. Finishing in sixth place in the 2002 Winston Cup rankings, Newman won Rookie of the Year honors.[5]

In the off-season, Newman pursued his college degree in mechanical engineering at Purdue University, with the intent of gaining an advantage in his racing career. He crafted a plan of study that enabled him to focus on vehicle dynamics—vehicle design, materials strength, and so on—that would complement his interest in racing.[6]

Joining the Penske Racing Team

When Newman joined the Penske Racing Team in late 1999, the team's co-owners hired Buddy Baker, a former race car driver and subsequently a race car driving instructor, to work with Newman. Being very selective about the drivers he works with, Baker insisted on meeting Newman and his family before accepting the job offer. Baker says: "When I started talking to Ryan, I could feel the energy that he had, and the passion he had for the sport. Then, I met his dad, and right there I knew, OK, he's got a good background. His father's been with him in go-carts, midgets. He turned the wrenches for his son. It was an automatic fit for me." Baker thinks of Newman as though he were one of his own sons, both of whom briefly tried racing but neither of whom had a passion for it. Baker says that he never wanted to do anything but race, and Newman is just like him. Referring to Newman, Baker says: "From the time he was 5 years old until now, he's never wanted to be anything else."[7]

Referring to his pre–Winston Cup racing days, Newman says: "I always worked on my own cars and maintained them, did the set-ups, things like that. Obviously, I also drove them so I was always a hands-on, involved, seat of the pants driver." As a Winston Cup driver, Newman acknowledges that he misses working on the cars, "but when you have great guys doing that work, you don't feel like you have to do it yourself."[8] "For all my life, my family has been my crew. To come to an organization like Penske, and have so many more people behind you fighting for the same goals, it's like being in a bigger family. When you're with people you like, you have the confidence to do things well."[9]

Most of the people who work on Newman's crew are engineers, and all of them are computer whizzes—significant talents for building and maintaining today's race cars.[10] Newman and the crew, lead by Matt Borland, try to learn from the problem situations that they encounter so they can "keep the freak things from happening."[11]

Challenges of the 2033 Racing Season

In anticipation of the Daytona 500 near the beginning of the 2003 NASCAR season, Newman said: "I love racing at Daytona. Sure I won an ARCA race at Daytona, but I don't really have much experience there. It's a track that is just incredible to be at. The minute you drive through the tunnel, you feel overwhelmed." Newman enters every race with the attitude that he can and will win it.[12]

Newman had a spectacular crash at the Daytona 500 in which his car became airborne. He walked away sore but uninjured. When asked about the potential impact of the crash on him and the Penske racing team, Newman simply replied that such events make them fight back harder and stronger.[13] Just a few weeks later, a cut tire sent Newman into the wall at Talladega Superspeedway, triggering a fiery 27-

car wreck. Newman walked away uninjured.[14]

Newman's success seems to be part racing talent, part drive and determination, and part engineering expertise. In the Kansas 400 in early October 2003, Newman made his last pit stop with 79 laps remaining while many other drivers made pit stops with 65 laps to go. Newman won the race, his eighth Winston Cup victory of the 2003 season and his third in his last five outings. Some drivers questioned how Newman could have gone the 79 laps without refueling. Jeremy Mayfield, who finished third, said: "I'm not an engineer. But I know that if you've got 22 gallons of fuel in your car, and everybody's got the same length fuel line and everybody's got so much horsepower, it takes so much fuel to make that." Although hinting that Newman had cheated, Mayfield used the same type of car and a similar race strategy. Mayfield drove a Dodge, just like Newman and the second-place finisher. Mayfield also stayed out of the pits, just as Newman did.[15] Moreover, several other drivers made fuel stops with 78 laps to go and did not return to the pits for the remainder of the race.[16]

Driver Bill Elliot, who led on 115 laps of the race, was upset about the situation and refused to attend the post-race news conference. While asserting that it's very difficult to get both fuel mileage and power, Mike Ford, the crew chief for Elliot, nonetheless said any wrongdoing by Newman's team was purely speculative. Responding to the insinuation that cheating had occurred, Newman and his

crew chief, Matt Borland, maintained that no NASCAR rules were broken.[17]

In the ensuring days, Jeff Gordon and Tony Stewart, both Winston Cup champions, expressed suspicions about Newman's fuel usage. Other drivers and crew chiefs viewed Newman's critics as sore losers. Rookie driver Jamie McMurray commented: "Each time you win, somebody accuses you of cheating. That's just a sore loser. We want to be Ryan Newman. We want to go out and win eight races next year. We hope everybody accuses us of cheating." McMurray's veteran crew chief, Donnie Wingo, added: "I wouldn't take anything way from those guys. They've worked real hard. I don't think it's anything they're doing wrong that they shouldn't be doing." Veteran driver Bobby LaBonte pointed out that young drivers and crew chiefs, like Ryan Newman and Matt Borland, build their racing strategies around science and track position. Noting that technological advances have changed the competitive climate in racing, LaBonte said: "There are a lot of smart people working on race teams lately. You have people that are looking at all different ways to win races." Adamantly maintaining that he and his crew have done nothing wrong, Newman asserts that his racing team does the best job it can with what they have. "When there's an opportunity to try and stretch it to the end, we're going to try to stretch to the end," says Newman.[18]

Review Questions

1. What are the key factors that motivate Ryan Newman?

2. Using the fundamental ideas of the content theories of motivation, explain Ryan Newman's racing success.
3. How can the expectancy theory of motivation help in understanding Ryan Newman's passion for racing?
4. How can goal-setting theory help in understanding Ryan Newman's passion for racing?

5. Use equity theory to explain the various reactions to Ryan Newman's win at the Kansas 400 in early October 2003.

You Do the Research

1. What is passion in the context of work? In the context of a person's life outside of work?
2. What are you passionate about? How can you incorporate your true passion into your work-life?
3. Follow up on the controversy regarding Ryan Newman's win of the Kansas 400 in early October 2003. How did this controversy unfold? What are the motivational implications for Newman? For his racing crew? For other drivers and their crews?

CASE 15
Steinway & Sons: Craftwork, Tradition, and Time Build Grand Pianos

Steinway & Sons remains one of the best-known producers of concert pianos in the world. Throughout its great history, the company has shown a distinctive talent at innovation, as evidenced by its more than 100 patents, and is known for quality workmanship. In an age of mass production, Steinway continues to manufacture a limited number of hand-made pianos in a unique testament to individual craftsmanship. However, some rival piano makers have tried to challenge Steinway's dominance of the concert piano market.[1] Can Steinway continue its cherished ways, or will it need to adjust to new circumstances?

A Long and Golden History

German immigrant Henry Enghelhart Steinway founded Steinway & Sons in 1853. Henry was a master cabinetmaker who built his first piano in the kitchen of his home in Seesen, Germany. He had built 482 pianos by the time he established Steinway & Sons. The first piano produced by the company, number 483, was sold to a New York family for $500. It is now displayed at New York City's Metropolitan Museum of Art.

Steinway's unique quality became obvious early in the history of the firm, as proven by its winning gold medals in several American and European exhibitions in 1855. The company gained international recognition in 1867 at the Paris Exhibition when it was awarded the prestigious Grand Gold Medal of Honor for excellence in manufacturing and engineering.[2] Henry Steinway developed his pianos with emerging technical and scientific research, including the acoustical theories of the renowned physicist Herman von Helmhotz.

Steinway was owned in the 1970s by CBS, and many concert artists complained that the quality of the pianos had suffered as a result of that ownership. Pianists talked of the "Teflon controversy," when Steinway replaced some fabric innards with Teflon (it now coats the Teflon with fabric). Steinway was sold by CBS in 1985, and many experts voiced the opinion that Steinway's legendary quality was returning. Larry Fine, a piano expert, argued that "a Steinway has a kind of sustained, singing tone that a Yamaha doesn't have. Yamaha has a more brittle tone in the treble that some jazz pianists prefer."[3]

The Steinway Factory

Today, the making of a Steinway piano follows the Steinway tradition. Every grand piano takes more than a year to complete and incorporates more than 1,000 details that set a Steinway apart from its competitors. A tour of the Steinway factory is a trip back through time, as many of the manufacturing techniques have not changed since 1853. The key steps in the process of crafting a Steinway piano are described below.[4]

Using a method that was patented in 1878, the piano manufacturing process begins with the creation of the inner and outer piano rims that give a grand piano its distinctive shape—this is known as the piano case. Eighteen layers of hard-rock maple, each 22 feet in length, are laminated together and then formed into shape on a giant piano-shaped vise. The rim-bending team centers the wood on the vise and forces it into place with the aid of wood clamps.

Meanwhile the soundboard is formed by hand, being "expertly tapered by a craftsman to be slightly thinner at the edges so that it can vibrate properly once it is glued to the piano's inner rim." The bridge of the soundboard must be notched for the piano strings before the soundboard can be placed into the piano case. A highly skilled crafts-man, with years of training, performs this operation because precision is so essential to the quality of the piano's sound.

The veneer for a piano is cut from a single tree to ensure a uniform appearance of the wood finish. It is cut to size and matched for grain, to be applied subsequently to the designated piano.

A wooden brace assembly is then crafted to fit within the piano case and to help support the 340-pound cast-iron plate that provides the rigid and stable foundation for approximately 40,000 pounds of tension from the piano strings. This brace assembly is secured to the rim of the piano with fine carpentry joinery and maple dowels. The cast-iron plate is then fitted to the piano case and any needed adjustments are made before final installation of the plate.

After the soundboard and cast-iron plate are properly fitted in the piano case, the piano wires are installed, using both a machine-guided stringer and appropriate hand tools. Next, the felt hammers are formed into the proper shape, using glue and a copper forming tool. The felt hammers are then put on the hammershanks and dampers are installed to prevent unintentional vibration of the piano strings. A master technician painstakingly matches the damper felts to the strings; reaching underneath the piano while looking in mirrors, the master technician adjusts the levers that control each of the dampers.

Next, the keyboard is calibrated by inserting lead weights into the body of each key so that the pressure required to push a key down is the same for every key. Subsequently, a master voicer will adjust the tone quality of each key. This is done by sticking the hammer's felt with a small row of needles to reduce stiffness of the felt, resulting in a mellower tone, or by applying a small amount of lacquer to the felt to achieve the opposite effect. Finally, a tone regulator adjusts string tension by turning the tuning pins.

Steinway's process of making a grand piano is complex, requiring numerous processes and procedures that must be performed by highly skilled craftsmen. True craftsmen produce the world's finest-quality concert pianos. However, not everyone wants or can afford a Steinway piano. What has Steinway & Sons done to reach other markets while maintaining the Steinway reputation for product quality?

Expansion Beyond the Classic Steinway Pianos

In recent years, Steinway developed Boston Piano in an attempt to broaden its market. Steinway & Sons designed Boston pianos using the latest computer technology and then outsourced the manufacturing to Kawai, the second-largest Japanese piano maker. By transferring its quality and knowledge of building pianos to the Boston Piano operation, Steinway was able to open up a whole new market. The Boston Piano venture demonstrated that Steinway's core competence of hand craftsmanship could be applied in a newer, high-technology manner to a lower-priced market niche.[5]

In early 2001, Steinway & Sons introduced a third line of pianos, called the Essex, to complement its Steinway and Boston lines. The Essex line offers two grand and two upright models ranging in price from $5,200 to $17,800. With the Essex, Steinway now provides pianos for every level of musical ability and budget.[6]

The question remains: Can Steinway continue to operate in the way that has proved successful over the past 150 years? At the moment, the answer appears to be—YES.

Review Questions

1. The equation specifying that Performance = Ability × Support × Effort is known as the individual performance equation. Using this equation, explain the exceptional performance that is required of and exhibited by the craftsmen at Steinway.
2. Use the core job characteristics model to explain the implications of Steinway's piano manufacturing process for work motivation and behavior.
3. How does Steinway's piano manufacturing process exhibit the need for teamwork? How does this relate to job enrichment?

You Do the Research

1. How does Steinway continue its emphasis on craftsmanship in this age of mass production?
2. Can any of Steinway's processes be transferred to other companies?
3. What other consumer products appear to be using a Steinway approach to producing its products?

CASE 16

Callaway Golf: Big Bertha's Team Hits a Long Ball

"Callaway Golf Company designs, creates, builds and sells Demonstrably Superior and Pleasingly Different golf products. That means that any club, ball or putter in the Callaway Golf family must be a significant improvement not only upon the products of our competitors, but also our own."[1] How does Callaway Golf achieve its goals of manufacturing and distributing demonstrably superior and pleasingly different golf products?

Callaway's DSPD Philosophy

In 1982, after a long business career in textiles and wine making, Ely Callaway purchased and bought a 50 percent interest in Hickory Stick USA, a small pitching wedge and putter manufacturing operation. Callaway's goal was to build demonstrably superior and pleasingly different (DSPD) golf clubs. The DSPD philosophy was based on his previous business experiences and served as the primary guiding principle for Callaway Golf, the company that grew out of Hickory Stick.[2]

The DSPD philosophy provides an important foundation for Callaway Golf's corporate mission. According to the company's 2002 Annual Report, the mission is as follows: "Callaway Golf Company is driven to be a world class organization that designs, develops, makes and delivers demonstrably superior and pleasingly different golf products that incorporate breakthrough technologies, backs those products with noticeably superior customer service, and generates a return to our shareholders in excess of the cost of capital. We share every golfer's passion for the game, and commit our talents and technology to increasing the satisfaction and enjoyment all golfers derive from pursuing that passion."[3]

Implementing the DSPD Philosophy

Callaway Golf's numerous innovations "revolutionized the industry with friendly clubs that helped golfers of all abilities find more enjoyment and a few more great shots in their game."[4] These innovations included the 2-Ball putter and the HX aerodynamic cover pattern on golf balls. Perhaps the company's most publicized innovation was the Big Bertha Driver with a large stainless steel head.

Capitalizing on its design and manufacture of "demonstrably superior and pleasingly different golf products," Callaway Golf continued to grow. It went public with its stock in 1992, the year in which it also acquired Odyssey Putters. Callaway entered the golf ball market in 2000.[5] Today Callaway Golf is the "number one manufacturer of drivers, fairway woods, irons, and putters."[6]

Callaway Golf operates in 107 countries, building on Ely Callaway's vision of helping the average golfer to find more enjoyment from the game. Ely Callaway, now deceased, retired from the company in 2001. His vision continues to be carried out under the leadership of his handpicked successor, Ron Drapeu, and the various teams that are the backbone of Callaway's operations.[7]

Teamwork at Callaway Golf

Teamwork at Callaway Golf is built around five different teams: research and development, information systems, manufacturing, sales, and general/administrative. The *research and development team*—which draws on engineering, analytical, and computer skills from people trained in a wide range of industries—is responsible for designing, building prototypes, and testing the company's innovative, premium golf equipment. The *information systems team* uses various computer applications to supply the company's information needs around the clock. The *manufacturing team* uses the latest manufacturing and assembly techniques to achieve levels of efficiency, innovation, and safety that are at the top of the golf industry. Among other fields, the manufacturing team members have backgrounds in industrial, mechanical, electrical, and process engineering, as well as in chemistry and aerodynamics. The *sales team* spans the world to provide golf retailers with the latest innovations in golf equipment and the highest-quality service. The *general/administrative team*—consisting of accountants, legal experts, artists, human resource generalists, receptionists, writers, and others—helps to build and grow the company by supporting the activities of the other teams.[8]

While the members of these teams reflect considerable diversity of backgrounds, all of the team members share some common characteristics. Callaway Golf looks for "integrity, honesty, daring, enthusiasm, accountability and hard work" in its employees. In addition, the company seeks to keep a "healthy balance between career and play," recognizing that this results in "happier people who are more productive in every aspect of their lives."[9] Thus far, Callaway Golf has used both similarities and differences among it employees to forge five very effective teams. Will Callaway be able to maintain this balance in the future, or will diversity be sacrificed for commonality, or commonality for diversity?

Review Questions

1. What is the DSPD philosophy? Explain how the operations of the different teams reflect the DSPD philosophy.
2. What team member characteristics does Callaway Golf consider to be important? Why do these characteristics seem to be important?
3. Consider the question at the very end of the case: "Will Callaway be able to maintain this balance in the future, or will diversity be sacrificed for commonality, or commonality for diversity?" What is the most reasonable answer to this question? Why?

You Do the Research

1. Identify a competitor of Callaway Golf. How does Callaway Golf's DSPD philosophy compare to the fundamental management philosophy of the competitor? What managerial insights do you gain from making this comparison?
2. Use the Callaway Golf competitor that you identified for the

previous question. How does Callaway Golf's emphasis on teamwork compare to the competitor's approach to organizing and utilizing the talents of its employees? What insights about teamwork does this comparison provide?

The United Nations: Conflict and Negotiation in the Global Community

The United Nations (UN),[1] like its precursor the League of Nations, was established after a devastating World War in order to promote cooperation, peace, and security among countries. UN members are sovereign nations—the organization is not a world government and does not make laws. On October 24, 1945, the UN officially came into existence with 51 member countries. It now has over 190 members, including most countries in the world.

Members accept the obligations of the UN Charter, an international treaty that sets out basic principles of international relations. It is an organization that truly embraces the concepts of diversity, cooperation, and conflict resolution and prevention. However, the UN does much more than resolve conflict. Looking at the major headings on its home page, you find, in addition to peace and security, emphases on economic and social development, human rights, humanitarian affairs, and international law.

A World Order—How Does It Work?

The United Nations is made up of six main branches:

- The General Assembly: This body considers pressing international problems, and each member has one vote. Key decisions require a two-thirds majority; for others, a simple majority is sufficient. In recent years, in an effort to promote harmony, there has been a striving for consensus.
- The Security Council: The 15-member council has primary responsibility for maintaining international peace and security. Five of the member countries (China, France, the Russian Federation, the United Kingdom, and the United States of America) are permanent members; the other ten are elected for two-year terms. Under the UN charter, UN members are obligated to follow the Security Council's directives. Decisions require nine "yes" votes, and any permanent member can veto a decision. The Security Council tries to exhaust all possibilities for resolution prior to authorizing the use of force. The possibilities short of force include negotiation, mediation, reference to the International Court of Justice, and economic pressure.
- The Economic and Social Council: The 54-member council coordinates the economic and social work of the UN system. Members are elected for three-year terms.
- The Trusteeship Council: The council was formed to administer 11 trust territories. When the final territory became self-governing in 1994, the rules of procedure were changed. The current council is composed of the five permanent mem-

bers of the Security Council and meets only if needed.

- The International Court of Justice: Often called the World Court, this body is responsible for deciding disputes between countries when the countries agree to participate. The 15 judges, elected jointly by the General Assembly and Security Council, make decisions that those appearing before them are obligated to accept. It is based in The Hague and is the only UN body not headquartered in New York.
- The Secretariat: The Secretariat, the staff of the UN headed by the elected Secretary-General, handles the administrative work of the United Nations.

In addition, there are 14 other independent organizations, such as the International Monetary Fund and the World Health Organization, that are linked to the UN through cooperative agreements. These organizations, along with the UN's six branches, subunits, programs, and funds, form the UN system. The UN system promotes human rights, protects the environment, fights disease, fosters economic development, and reduces poverty, in addition to preserving world peace and security.

The UN offers the most opportunity in its ability to influence international public opinion. World conflicts are discussed on a world stage with a world audience. However, that does not guarantee that conflict can be prevented or that peacekeeping is a simple exercise.

In fact, one of its most inclusive experiences to date involved engaging in conflict.

The UN served as a focal point in arranging a coalition of nations to counter Iraq's invasion and occupation of Kuwait in the early 1990s. Thirty-four nations, under the auspices of the Security Council, provided the military forces necessary for Operation Desert Storm and drove Saddam Hussein's forces out of Kuwait. President George H. W. Bush's claim of a "New World Order" as a result of the outcome did not come to pass.

Peacekeeping can be a very dangerous enterprise and can be of short duration or last for decades. As of October 2003, 1,841 peacekeepers had died since the inception of the UN; 252 of those deaths occurred in 1993. In October 2003, there were thirteen peacekeeping missions in operation: two in Asia, three in the Middle East, three in Europe, and five in Africa. Two of those had been in operation for decades—the one at the India–Pakistan border began in 1949, and UN peacekeepers have been in Cyprus since 1964. It seems that the goal of durable peace may be hard to achieve.

Other Conflicts

While the Security Council has the primary responsibility for maintaining international peace and security, the Security Council itself is not entirely peaceful. After the September 11, 2001, terrorist attacks on the World Trade Center and the Pentagon, the Security Council speedily adopted a resolution that obligated member countries to ensure that terrorists would be brought to justice. However, the dissension among Security Council members regarding the ap-

propriate action to take against Iraq subsequent to September 11 was newsworthy and unresolved. Some members wished to continue to try to settle the matter peacefully through diplomatic means. However, in the end the United States and its allies took nonsanctioned action against Saddam Hussein. It remains to be seen whether this has caused an irreparable breach in relations or damaged the power and prestige of the UN. The UN Security Council has implicitly accepted the situation by adopting resolutions indicating their willingness to become involved in the process of stabilizing a postwar Iraq.

The structure of the Security Council, funding, and priorities are also a source of conflict within the UN. While the UN provides an infrastructure system that transcends national borders, thereby encouraging international solutions to world problems, many smaller countries argue against domination by the larger nations, particularly by the Security Council's permanent membership.

In reaction to pressure from a number of nations, including the United States, the UN launched a reform movement in the late 1990s. Discussions on financing, operations, and Security Council makeup continue, but many times to the frustration of the smaller countries. These frustrations are best expressed by quotations taken from the speeches made during the September 22 to October 7, 1997, debate of the General Assembly on UN reform.[2] The following quotes illustrate the frustration with the power of the Security Council, the use of the veto, and the lack of transparency in its actions:

If reform of the [Security] Council is to be truly comprehensive and consistent with the spirit and realities of our time, then we must seek to remove—or at least, as a first step, restrict—the use of the veto power. Democracy in the United Nations is a mockery if the voice of the majority is rendered meaningless by the narrow interests of the dominant few. (Minister for Foreign Affairs of Malaysia, HE Dato' Seri Abdullah bin Haji Ahmad Badawi)

We also believe that real reform of the Security Council should aim above all at ensuring that decision-making machinery and processes have the transparency, effectiveness and pluralism that must characterize every democratic institution. This includes, among other specific measures, the limitation of the veto power of the Council's permanent members, and for timelier and more effective action to prevent international conflicts at the request of any State Member of the Organization. (President of the Republic of Ecuador, HE Mr. Fabian Alarcon Rivera)

We would similarly like to see certain restrictions placed on the use of the veto. We understand that all efforts at restructuring and reform in the United Nations, however, should be focused on economic growth and development. In addition, my country is calling for

a reversal in the diminishing role of the General Assembly. The accountability of the Security Council to the General Assembly must be re-emphasized, and the General Assembly should more actively assert its role in the maintenance of international peace and security. (Chair of the delegation of Antigua and Barbuda, HE Mr. Patrick Albert Lewis)

In the era of democracy, transparency and proper management that we are claiming for our countries, there is nothing more normal than to insist, together, on the same values and principles in this Organization which unites us. (Minister for Foreign Affairs of Algeria, HE Mr. Ahmed Attaf)

Belgium, together with a number of like-minded countries that share the general concern with regard to strengthening the authority of the Security Council, . . . advocate[s] an increase in both permanent and non-permanent members, greater regional representativeness, enhanced Council efficiency and a limitation of the right of veto. The right of veto is incompatible with the general interest. It should be possible to modify the decision-making mechanism so as to avoid recourse to this instrument, which has become entirely obsolete. Belgium also pleads for more transparency and closer cooperation between the Security Council and countries contributing to

peacekeeping operations. (Minister for Foreign Affairs of Belgium, HE Mr. Erik Derycke)

Another source of dissension among UN members is the direction of the UN toward goals than are not so directly related to maintaining peace and security. The United States withheld its dues for a number of years in protest regarding UN policies and charges of administrative waste within its programs. The dissension concerning the funding and priorities of the UN is illustrated in the following quotes drawn from the same debate, in which implicit reference also is made to the United States and other member countries withholding of funds from the UN:[3]

The situation of the United Nations social sphere is the most worrisome. The greatest burden of the Organization's budgetary crisis has fallen upon the bodies involved, whose financing has dropped by many millions of dollars during the present decade. . . . In a world where 1.3 billion people still survive on less than a dollar a day, in a world where, for the price of one combat plane, 57,000 children in Africa can be fed for a year, it is impossible to conceive of a reform of the United Nations whose priority is not to strengthen the work of its institutions and programmes dedicated to social issues. (President of the Republic of Colombia, HE Mr. Ernesto Samper Pisano, also Chair of the Non-Aligned Movement)

. . . the eradication of poverty throughout the world should be the main goal of the international community's coordinated efforts in the coming years. The globalization of the economy cannot be limited to the use of cheap labour in the developing world, the proliferation of profitable investments and the exploitation of certain markets. It should also aim at providing coordinated and systematic assistance to immense populations whose only experience of globalization has been their poverty and frustration. (President of the Republic of Ecuador, HE Mr. Fabian Alarcon Rivera)

While we are deeply engaged in this process of reform we must not lose sight of the fundamental goals that impelled us to undertake it in the first place: to enhance the Organization's ability to foster development and to address the root causes of poverty and conflict. Reform should not become a euphemism for budget slashing or an excuse for certain Member States to renege on their financial obligations to the Organization. (Minister for Foreign Affairs of Indonesia, HE Mr. Ali Alatas)

Jamaica also endorses the need for measures to improve efficiency, and we have no quarrel with reform to streamline and rationalize the system. In welcoming these steps, we must however emphasize that reform is not synonymous with cost cutting. Reform is

not about doing less; it is about doing better. (Prime Minister of Jamaica, The Right Honourable Percival James Patterson)

The current financial situation has no link with the assessment system. The way to deal with it is by making full, timely and unconditional payments of the assessments the General Assembly assigns to Member States. . . . The financial crisis of the Organization should not lead us to take decisions that distort the spirit of reform we share. Carried to the extreme, this logic would call for the designation of Ted Turner as a permanent member of the Security Council, with the right of veto. By the way, we appreciate Mr. Turner's generosity. (Minister for Foreign Affairs of Mexico, HE Mr. Angel Gurria)

It cannot be justified that some countries unilaterally pay less than their legally binding share, or nothing at all. Non-payment is unacceptable. How can those of us who always make a point of paying in full and on time, without conditions, expect our citizens and taxpayers to continue financing free riders? (Minister for Foreign Affairs of Norway, HE Mr. Bjorn Tore Godal)

If the United Nations is to be reformed and made effective, then adequate financing is a matter of top priority. We therefore appeal to all Member States to pay their dues in full, on

time, and without conditions. (First Deputy Prime Minister and Minister for Foreign Affairs of Uganda, HE The Honourable Iriya Kategaya)

Reform should not become a euphemism for budget slashing or an excuse for certain Member States to renege on their financial obligations to the Organization. (Minister for Foreign Affairs of Indonesia, HE Mr. Ali Alatas)

It is apparent that considerable concern exists over the funding, the organization, and the role of the UN. But does that mean that it has failed?

The Future

Even in the face of frustration, it appears that most members continue to believe that the UN still represents the world's best opportunity to create a climate of communication and dispute resolution across national borders, and to promote worldwide well-being. They recognize that the UN has had notable success in a variety of areas, including both the Nuclear Non-Proliferation Treaty (1968) and the Comprehensive Nuclear-Test-Ban Treaty (1996), the promotion of democracy, the improvement of world health, and the resolution of conflicts within and between member nations. The Millennium Declaration of 2000 set out goals for the UN in key areas including, among others, peace, security and disarmament, economic development and poverty eradication, environmental protection, and human rights.

The following quotes,

drawn from the same debate as the previous quotes, illustrate the ongoing commitment to and belief in the UN as the best chance for effective international cooperation:[4]

The General Assembly is a unique body in international institutional machinery. In it, representativity is practically universal. States participate on an equal footing without regard for their size or power, and the ideal of international democracy attains its clearest expression, at least in formal terms. The decisions of this body have great moral and political force and accordingly, it is essential to formulate them better and make them more timely. (Minister for Foreign Affairs of Uruguay, HE Mr. Alvaro Ramos)

The United Nations has an irreplaceable role in a world that still combines forces of integration and cooperation with forces of disintegration and aggression. (Minister of External Relations of Brazil, HE Mr. Luiz Felipe Lampreia)

Where else but at the United Nations can we deal with the truly global issues such as the new security threats of uncivil society, environmental degradation, violations of human rights and poverty? Given the nature of these issues, unilateral, bilateral or even regional efforts are of course good, but not enough. Not even the most prosperous and powerful nations on earth can successfully solve them alone. Only the United Nations has a global mandate and global legitimacy. (Minister for Foreign Affairs of Finland, HE Ms. Tarja Kaarina Halonen, now president of Finland)

Will the members continue to support the UN, join forces, and seize the opportunities to revitalize the UN—a "unique and universal instrument for concerted action in pursuit of the betterment of humankind" as Kofi Annan requested[5]—or allow it to go the way of the League of Nations?

Review Questions

1. What is the difference between mediation and ne-

gotiation? Can you find an effective use of each by the UN?

2. Based on the quotes given, how would you classify the *General Debate on Reform* in terms of conflict management styles?

3. If reform does occur, how do you think the reform will be perceived—lose–lose, win–lose, or win–win?

4. What suggestions might you make to the UN to improve communication and conflict resolution?

You Do the Research

1. What does the most recent Security Council resolution about Iraq indicate regarding the UN's involvement in that area?

2. In how many peacekeeping operations is the UN currently involved?

3. Has there actually been any reform of the Security Council since the *General Debate on Reform* in 1997?

4. How many member countries are currently in arrears in their payments to the UN?

5. What are the current issues on the UN agenda?

The Walt Disney Company: The Art of Brand Building Keeps Disney Center Stage

----

The Walt Disney Company has evolved from a wholesome family-oriented entertainment company into a massive multimedia conglomerate. Not only is Disney a producer of media but it also distributes its and others' media products through a variety of channels; operates theme parks and resorts; and produces, sells, and licenses consumer products based on Disney characters and other intellectual property. CEO Michael Eisner has been instrumental in many of these changes. How can such extensive changes occur while trying to maintain the Disney brand?

Disney Through the Years

After his first film business failed, artist Walt Disney and his brother Roy started a film studio in Hollywood in 1923. The first Mickey Mouse cartoon, *Plane Crazy*, was completed in 1928. *Steamboat Willie*, the first cartoon with a soundtrack, was the third production. The studio's first animated feature film was *Snow White* in 1937, followed by *Fantasia* and *Pinocchio* in the 1940s. Disneyland, the theme park developed largely by Walt, opened in 1955 in Anaheim, California. The television series the *Mickey Mouse Club* was produced from 1955 to 1959, and the Disney weekly television series (under different names, including *The Wonderful World of Disney*) ran for 29 straight years.[1]

Walt Disney died in 1966 of lung cancer. Disney World in Orlando, Florida, opened in 1971, the same year that Roy Disney died. His son, Roy E., took over the organization. However, the creative leadership of brothers Walt and Roy Disney was noticeably absent. Walt's son-in-law, Ron Miller, became president in 1980. Many industry watchers felt that Disney had lost its creative energy and sense of direction because of lackluster corporate leadership and nepotism. In 1984, the Bass family, in alliance with Roy E. Disney, bought a controlling interest in the company. Their decision to bring in new CEO Michael Eisner from Paramount and a new president, Frank Wells, from Warner Bros., ushered in a new era in the history of Disney.[2]

Work the Brand

Michael Eisner has been involved in the entertainment industry from the start of his career (ironically, beginning at ABC television in the 1960s). He exhibits a knack for moving organizations from last place to first through a combination of hard work and timely decisions. For example, when he arrived at Paramount Pictures in 1976, it was dead last among the six major motion picture studios. During his reign as the company's president, Paramount moved into first place with blockbusters such as *Raiders of the Lost Ark*, *Trading Places*, *Beverly Hills Cop*, and *Airplane*, along with other megahits. By applying lessons he learned in television at ABC to keep costs down, he kept the average cost of a Paramount picture during his tenure at $8.5 million, while the industry average was $12 million.[3]

Eisner viewed Disney as a greatly underutilized franchise identifiable by millions throughout the world. In addition to reenergizing film production, Eisner wanted to extend the brand recognition of Disney products through a number of new avenues. Examples of his efforts over the years include the Disney Channel (cable), Tokyo Disneyland (Disney receives a management fee only), video distribution, Disney stores, Broadway shows (e.g., *Beauty and the Beast*), and additional licensing arrangements for the Disney characters.

However, in the early 1990s problems began emerging for Disney. An attempt to build a theme park in Virginia based on a Civil War theme was defeated by local political pressure. EuroDisney, the firm's theme park in France, resulted in over $500 million in losses for Disney due to miscalculations on attendance and concessions. In 1994, Eisner underwent emergency open-heart bypass surgery and Frank Wells, long working in the shadows of his boss but increasingly viewed as integral for the success of Disney, died in a helicopter crash. Eisner's choice to succeed Wells, Michael Ovitz from Creative Artists Agency, did not work out, and Ovitz soon left. Stories of Eisner's dictatorial management style brought succession worries to shareholders.

Capital Cities/ABC

Once again, Eisner ushered in a new era at Disney by announcing the $19 billion takeover of Capital Cities/ABC on July 31, 1995. The deal came in the same week as Westinghouse Electric Corporation's $5.4 billion offer for CBS Inc. Disney represented one of several consolidations of media conglomerates that increasingly control the distribution of entertainment programming in the United States. Disney ranked as the third-largest media conglomerate behind AOL Time Warner and Viacom.

Eisner appreciated the importance of both programming content and the distribution assets needed to deliver it.[4] As a result of many of Eisner's decisions, the Walt Disney Company has been transformed from a sleepy film production studio into a major entertainment giant, with its revenues of over $2 billion in 1987 increasing to $22 billion in 1997.[5] Its stock price has multiplied over 15 times, creating enormous wealth for both stockholders and executives of Disney.

One of the biggest questions arising from the ABC deal is whether Disney paid too dearly for declining network assets. Viewership among all the major networks was declining. According to Michael Jordan, the CEO of CBS, "the pure network television business is basically a low-margin to breakeven business."[6] The networks were squeezed by having to pay extravagantly for programming and were attracting an audience of older viewers who were scorned by advertisers.

However, another way to look at networks is as the lifeblood of the global, vertically integrated entertainment giants that own them and as loss leaders that act to promote their parent company's more lucrative operations. In this scenario, ABC acts as Disney's megaphone to tell the masses about Disney movies, theme parks, Disney-made shows, and toys. Another financial advantage occurs when the network owns and syndicates a hit show, something that could not be done before the networks were deregulated in the mid-1990s. By owning more of their own shows, the networks avoid the increasing licensing fees from the production companies.[7]

A potential risk is that a network will miss out on a hit by favoring its own shows. Disney has blocked out certain parts of the week for its own shows. Fox and Disney appear best situated to exploit their platforms, with Fox injecting new life into an old brand, and Disney providing diverse production assets to feed its network.[8] This strategy works as long as networks remain big. During the 1990s, however, network viewership declined; the various networks have cushioned this problem by investing more in their cable holdings.

Hard Times and Brand Investment

Not everything Disney touches turns to gold. For example, in early 2001, the company was forced to downscale its go.com Internet site as it continued to lose hundreds of millions of dollars.[9] Moreover, from fiscal 1998 through fiscal 2000, net income declined by half, from $1.85 billion to $920 million, while operating revenue grew from $22.98 billion to $25.4 billion.[10] In fiscal 2001 the company had a net loss of $158 million on operating revenue of $25.2 billion.[11]

Nonetheless, Disney remained committed to integrating its various operations into the greater Disney picture and to developing its brands. As Michael Eisner said in the late 1990s: "It sounds funny, but I am thinking about the millennium change. I've got to protect the Disney brand well into the future."[12]

As of fiscal 2002, the Walt Disney Company's businesses included *media networks*, *studio entertainment*, *Walt Disney parks and resorts*, and *consumer products.* Among the various *media network* holdings are (1) broadcasting networks such as ABC Television Network, Disney-owned and -operated television stations and radio stations, and Touchstone Television and Buena Vista productions, and (2) cable networks such as the ESPN-branded businesses, the Disney Channel, Toon Disney, SOAPnet, and a variety of online commerce, broadband, and wireless subscription services.[13] Disney's *studio entertainment* segment produces and/or acquires animated and live-action films, musical recordings, live stage plays, and animated television products.[14] *Walt Disney parks and resorts* include the company's theme park and resort operations (e.g., Walt Disney World, Disneyland, and the Disney Cruise Line) and ESPN Zone sports-theme restaurants, among others. Walt Disney parks and resorts also receives licensing royalties and/or management fees from the Paris and Tokyo Disneyland resorts.[15] The *consumer products* segment produces books and magazines, operates Disney retail stores, and licenses Disney's characters and other intellectual property to manufacturers, retailers, publishers, and promoters.[16]

The Walt Disney Company has been very careful in maintaining brand identity and family values. However, the company recognizes that not everything is a Disney cartoon. For example, when the company goes outside its tradition, it produces its films under the Pixar or Buena Vista labels. Such movies are still family oriented in a broadly defined manner but are not the typical Disney film.

In his letter to shareholders in Disney's 2002 annual report, Michael Eisner wrote: "The past years have been disappointing in terms of earnings and stock price, but they have also been an exciting period of investment in our key brands . . . investment that I am confident will pay off well in the years ahead."[17] The company's competitive advantage is rooted in "maintaining strong and differentiated brands, most notably the Disney and ESPN brands." These brands are powerful from a business perspective because they are unique, thereby differentiating the products, and they are relevant to consumers.[18] This competitive advantage has helped return the Walt Disney Company to financial success. In fiscal 2002, the Walt Disney Company's net income was $1.2 billion on operating revenue of $25.3 billion.

Review Questions

1. Examine the internal and external forces for change faced by Disney.
2. How have external forces in the entertainment industry affected Disney's need for change?
3. What changes do you foresee in the entertainment industry in the next five years?

You Do the Research

1. Disney has apparently turned it fortunes around. What are the prospects that the company will maintain this success in the future?
2. Has the Walt Disney Company really moved past its reputation as a children's movie and theme park provider?
3. Are media conglomerates headed for trouble?

Integrating CASES

Outback Steakhouse, Inc.
Fueling the Fast-Growth Company

- - - - - - - - - - - - - - - -

Marilyn L. Taylor, D.B.A., Gottlieb-Missouri, Distinguished Professor of
Business Strategy, Henry W. Bloch School of Business and Public
Administration, University of Missouri—Kansas City,
Kansas City, MO 64110

Krishnan Ramaya, Ph.D., Henry W. Bloch School of Business and
Public Administration, University of Missouri—Kansas City,
Kansas City, MO 64110

George M. Puia, Ph.D., School of Business,
Indiana State University, Terre Haute, IN 47809
Tel: (812) 237-2090

*Support for the development of this case and its accompanying video
were provided by*

Center for Entrepreneurial Leadership
Ewing Marion Kauffman Foundation
Kansas City, MO

- - - - - - - - - - - - - - - - - -

The authors express deep appreciation to the following individuals at the Ewing Marion Kauffman Foundation: Dr. Ray Smilor, vice president of the Center for Entrepreneurial Leadership Inc.; Ms. Pam Kearney, communications specialist, Communications Department; and Ms. Judith Cone, ETI professional with the Center for Entrepreneurial Leadership Inc. In addition, the authors wish also to express appreciation to Outback executives Chris Sullivan, chairman and CEO; Bob Basham, president and COO; Tim Gannon, sr. vice president; Bob Merritt, sr. vice president, CFO, and treasurer; Nancy Schneid, vice president of marketing; Ava Forney, assistant to the chairman and CEO; as well as the other Outback officers, executives, and employees who gave so enthusiastically and generously of their time, knowledge, and skills to make this case study possible.

Contact Person: George M. Puia, Ph.D.

Management cooperated in the field research for this case, which was written solely for the purpose of stimulating student discussion. Copyright © 1998 Case Research Journal, Marilyn Taylor, George Puia, Krishnan Ramaya.

Exhibits may be found in the Instructor's Manual.

Outback Steakhouse: Fueling the Fast-Growth Company

Since the company's initial public offering in June of 1991, Wall Street observers had continually predicted a downturn in the price of Outback's stock. Indeed, most analysts viewed Outback as just another fad in an intensely competitive industry where there are plenty of imitators. They continued to caution that Outback was in a saturated market and that the company could not continue growing at its existing pace. The December 1994 issue of *Inc.* magazine declared Outback's three founders as winners of the coveted Entrepreneur of the Year award. The company was profiled in 1994 and early 1995 by the business press as one of the biggest success stories in corporate America in recent years.[1]

At 5:00 P.M. on a Saturday in early 1995 in Brandon, a suburb outside Tampa, the lines had already begun to form in a strip mall outside Outback Steakhouse. Customers waited anywhere from half an hour to almost two hours for a table.

The firm's founders, Chris Sullivan, Bob Basham, and Tim Gannon, organized Outback in August 1987 with the expectation of building five restaurants and spending increased leisure time on the golf course and with their families. In 1988 the company had sales of $2.7 million from its two restaurants. By year-end 1994 the chain exceeded all of the founders' expectations, with over 200 restaurants and $549 million in systemwide sales (see Exhibits 1 and 2 for financial data) and had formed a joint venture partnership with Texas-based Carrabbas Italian Grill to enter the lucrative Italian restaurant segment, currently dominated by General Mills' Olive Garden. A 1994 national survey of the country's largest restaurant chains ranked Outback first in growth (52.9%), second by sales per unit ($3.3 million), sixth by market share (5.9%), and tenth by number of units (205), all of which was accomplished in less than six years (see Exhibit 3).[2]

The founders expected that Outback could grow into a 550–600-unit chain in the continental United States. During 1995 alone, the company expected to add 65 to 70 new restaurants, maintain overall sales growth comparable to 1994, and continue to increase its same-store sales. In spite of the company's past success and future plans, however, analysts and other industry observers questioned how long Outback could continue its astounding growth, whether the company could maintain its strong momentum while pursuing multiple major strategic thrusts to propel its growth, and whether and how the culture of the company could be maintained. Skepticism about Outback's continued growth was clearly evident in the way Wall Street analysts viewed the company. By the end of 1994, Outback's stock was one of the most widely held stocks on the short sellers' list.[3] Adjusted for stock splits, Outback's share price rose from $3.50 to almost $30 over a three-year period. Exhibits 4 and 5 provide information on Outback's stock performance as well as samples of analysts' perspectives on Outback's continued growth during 1994.

The French Restaurant Legacy

The French coined the term *restaurant*, meaning "a food that restores," and were the first to create a place that could be defined as a restaurant by modern standards.[4] Before the French Revolution most culinary experiences were the exclusive domain of the nobility. The French Revolution dispersed the nobility and their chefs. The chefs, denied the patronage of the nobles, scattered throughout Europe, taking the restaurant concept with them.

In contrast, American restaurants grew up in response to the need to serve the burgeoning 19th-century U.S. workforce. The rapid growth of U.S. cities, fueled by the influx of European immigrants, provided the initial impetus for the American restaurant industry. Initially, restaurants were single family-owned operations and consisted of two broad categories.[5] The first category, fine dining, had facilities that were affordable only to the wealthy and were located primarily in major cities. The second category catered primarily to industrial workers. This latter category included concepts such as lunch wagons and soda fountains, which later evolved into coffee shops and luncheonettes. These grew rapidly in response to the continuous expansion of urban areas. The American obsession with efficiency propelled yet another restaurant concept, the self-service restaurant, to become a central theme for 20th-century American restaurants.

Retail and theater chains emerged with the new century. The first large U.S. restaurant chain organization was the brainchild of Frederick Henry Harvey, an English immigrant.[6] After his Harvey House opened in 1876 in Topeka, Kansas, restaurant chains too quickly became part of the American scene.

The restaurant industry's $290 billion revenues in 1993 accounted for 4.3 percent of U.S. GDP.[7] The industry's 100 largest chains accounted for 40 percent of total industry sales. U.S. restaurants in the latter part of the twentieth century could broadly be classified into three segments—fast-food, casual dining, and fine dining. However, within these three broad categories were highly fragmented sub-segment markets. The fast-food segment was primarily catered to by major chains such as McDonald's, Wendy's, Burger King, Hardee's, and Kentucky Fried Chicken. Casual dining catered to the cost conscious and typically priced menu entrees between fastfood and fine dining restaurants. Fine dining establishments catered to affluent customers and were located primarily in major metropolitan areas. Fine dining establishments were mostly single-unit businesses. In the early 1990s 75 percent of all casual dining establishments were still mom-and-pop operations.[8] The industry was characterized by high failure rates. Approximately 75 percent of all establishments failed within the first year; 90 percent within five years. Failure in the restaurant industry was attributed to a plethora of factors, including undercapitalization, poor location, poor food quality, underestimation of the effort needed to be successful, the effect of changing demographics segments, and government regulations.[9]

Restaurant operations are highly labor-intensive businesses. However, aspiring restaurant owners often seriously underestimated their capitalization require-

ments, that is, the funds needed for leasehold improvements and equipment. Indeed, new restaurants are often seriously undercapitalized. The owners might also fail to plan for other startup funds such as the first year's working capital, preopening expenses, advertising, and inventory costs.

Location choice was another common error. A restaurant location had to attract sufficient traffic to sustain operations. The demographics required for appropriate fine dining restaurant sites were different from those required for casual dining establishments, which differed again from fast-food establishments such as McDonald's. The availability of suitable locations especially in major cities had become an important factor in the success or failure of restaurants.

Aspiring restaurant owners also often underestimated *the effort required* to make a restaurant successful. Running a restaurant was hard work and could easily involve 80 to 100 hours of work each week. *Changing demographics* affected not only location choices but also the theme and type of restaurant. What had once been easily definable segments had fundamentally changed. It had become increasingly difficult to clearly define targetable segments. *American Demographics* magazine referred to the current situation as "particle markets."[10] Examples of such particle markets included empty nesters, stepfamilies, the baby boomlet, immigrants, the disabled, savers, the affluent, the elderly, and others. The restaurant industry was also one of the country's most *regulated industries.* Myriad regulations on such issues as hygiene, fire safety, and the consumption of alcoholic beverages governed daily operations.

Still another requirement for a successful restaurant was the maintenance of consistent *food quality.* Maintaining a level of consistent food quality was challenging. Any variability in food quality was typically viewed as deficient.

Founding Outback Steakhouse—From Down Under to Where?

In March 1987 three friends—Chris Sullivan, Bob Basham, and Tim Gannon—opened their first two Outback restaurants in Tampa, Florida. Each of the three had started early in their careers in the restaurant industry—Chris as a busboy, Bob as a dishwasher, and Tim as a chef's assistant. Between them they had more than sixty years of restaurant experience, most in the casual dining segment. The three met when they went to work for Steak & Ale, a Pillsbury subsidiary, shortly after they completed college in the early 1970s. Chris and Bob went to executive roles in the Bennigan's restaurant group, part of the Steak & Ale group. The two men met their mentor and role model in casual dining legend Norman Brinker. Brinker had headed Pillsbury's restaurant subsidiary. When Brinker left Pillsbury to form Brinker International, Chris and Bob followed him. Among Brinker International's casual dining chains was Chili's. Brinker helped the two men finance a chain of 17 Chili's restaurants in Florida and Georgia. Chris and Bob described their contribution as "sweat equity."[11] Brinker was considered a leading pioneer in the development of the causal dining industry.[12] Brinker International, the restaurant holding company that Brinker created, was widely considered an industry barometer for the casual dining segment.

Brinker International, the parent company, acquired Chris and Bob's interest in the Chili's franchise for $3 million in Brinker stock. With about $1.5 million each, Chris and Bob turned their attention to a long-standing dream—their own entrepreneurial venture. They considered several options, finally settling on the idea of a startup venture consisting of a small chain of casual dining restaurants. Each of the two men brought special skills to the table—Chris in his overall strategic sense and Bob in his strong skills in operations and real estate.

In early fall 1987 the two men asked Tim Gannon to join Outback as its chief chef. Tim had left Steak & Ale in 1978 to play a significant entrepreneurial role in several restaurant chains and single-establishment restaurants, primarily in the New Orleans area. His last venture was a restaurant with Pete Fountain at the New Orleans World's Fair. The venture at the World's Fair had experienced early success and then suddenly encountered severe financial difficulties, leaving Tim with virtually no financial resources. In fact, when Gannon accepted Chris and Bob's invitation to join them, he had to sell his one remaining prized possession, a saddle, in order to buy gas money to travel from New Orleans to Tampa.

Tim brought with him recipes drawn from 25 years of experience. His first tutelage had been under a French chef in Aspen, Colorado. Concerning his initial teacher, Tim said:

I was an Art History major (who) found his way to Colorado to Aspen to ski. My first job was as a cook. That job became exciting because the man I worked for was a chef from Marseilles who had a passion for great foods. I grew to love the business. . . . I have made the restaurant industry my whole life.

Bob Basham especially wanted a restaurant concept that focused on steaks. The three men recognized that in the United States in-home consumption of beef had declined over the years, primarily because of health concerns. However, they also noted that the upscale steak houses and the budget steak houses were extremely popular in spite of all the concerns about red meat. That observation came from their market research, which Bob Basham described as follows:

We visited restaurants to see what people were eating. We talked to other people in the industry. Basically we observed and read trade magazines. That is the kind of research I am talking about. We did not hire a marketing research crew to go out and do a research project. It was more hands-on research . . . . the experts said people will eat less red meat, but we saw them lining up to get in. We believed in human behavior, not market research.

The partners concluded that people were cutting in-home red meat consumption but were still very interested in going out to a restaurant for a good steak. They saw an untapped opportunity between high-priced and budget steakhouses to serve quality steaks at an affordable price.

Outback operated in the dinner house category of the casual dining segment where 75 percent of all such establishments were family-owned and operated. The top fifteen dinner house chains accounted for approximately $9 billion dollars in total sales.[13] Dinner house chains usually had higher sales volumes than fast-food chains. However, dinner houses typically cost more to build and operate.[14]

The initial investment for Outback came from the sale of the Chili's restaurant franchise. Both men were able to forgo taking cash salaries from Outback for the company's first two years. Funding for the early restaurants came from their own resources, relatives, and the sale of limited partnerships. During 1990 the founders turned to venture capitalists for about $2.5 million. Just as the venture capital deal was materializing, Bob Merritt was hired as CFO. Trained as an accountant, Merrit had extensive experience with the financial side of the restaurant business. Prior to joining Outback, Merritt served as the vice president of finance for JB's Restaurants. Merritt had IPO experience, and the founders later decided a public offering was warranted. The company went public in June 1991. The market had a general aversion toward restaurant stocks during the mid- and late 1980s. However, Outback's share offering, contrary to expectations, traded at premium. CFO Merritt recalled his efforts to borrow funds in 1990 even after the venture-capital infusion:

In November 1990, Outback was really taking off . . . . The most significant limitation was capital . . . . So, I shaved off my beard—because Tampa is a fairly conservative community-and went from bank to bank. I spent every day trying to borrow. I think we were asking for $1.5M so that we could finance that year's crop of equipment packages for the restaurants. We basically met with dead ends . . . . [It was] very frustrating . . . . So Chris and I started talking about where the market was. One strategy, I felt, was to sell a little bit of the company to finance maybe 18 months of growth, get a track record in the Street and come back with another offering with credibility. [So] we priced the transaction at about a 20 percent discount relative to the highest-flying restaurant stock we could find and, of course, the stock traded up from 15 to 22 on the first day. At that point we were trading at a premium for restaurant stocks.

Outback's continuing success made possible two additional stock offerings during the following eighteen months. All together, a total of $68 million was raised. By the end of 1994, the founders owned almost 24 percent of the company, which was valued at approximately $250 million.

Outback's Strategy and Structure—"No rules—just right"

The Theme—"Cheerful, comfortable, enjoyable, and fun!"

The three partners debated for some time about the appropriate theme and name for their restaurants. They wanted a casual theme but felt that the western theme was overused by budget steak houses. Ultimately, they focused on an Australian theme. None of the partners had ever been to Australia, but U.S. attention was focused there. Bob Basham explained:

In late 1987–88 when we started there was a lot of hype about Australia. We had just lost the Americas Cup not long before that. They were celebrating their bicentennial. The movie Crocodile Dundee had just come out. [So, there] was a lot of interest in Australia when we were looking for a theme . . . that was probably one of our hardest decisions . . . (we) wanted to stay away from a western theme . . . . [We] started talking about Australia [which] is perceived as very casual and we wanted to be a casual steakhouse. It is a good marketing niche tool and we continue to take advantage of it in our ads.

Bob's wife, Beth, ultimately wrote the name "Outback" with her lipstick on a mirror. As Tim Gannon put it, the name epitomized:

[what] we wanted to convey. We wanted to be a hearty good-fun atmosphere and [the name] represents our personalities too. The three of us live robust, fun lives.

The founders of Outback were convinced that any enduring concept must place a heavy emphasis upon fun, family, quality food, and community. Bob Basham explained:

I don't care what business you are in, if you aren't having fun, you shouldn't be in that business . . . . Chris, Tim, and I have a lot of fun doing what we are doing, and we want our people to have a lot of fun doing what they are doing. We try to set it up so they can do that.

Tim, whom the other two partners described as being the "hospitality" part of the team, elaborated on the entertainment aspect of the Outback theme:

We are in the business of entertainment and the way we entertain is through flavors. Service is a big component of that. We want our customers—someone who comes in at 7 P.M. and waits until 9 P.M. and leaves at 10:30 P.M.—to view us as their entertainment. We owe it to them!

Outback employees who waited on customers typically handled only three tables at a time, and this allowed closer customer attention.

Choosing the Menu— "Kookaburra Wings, Victoria's Filet, Chocolate Thunder Down Under"

The company gave Australian theme names to many of the menu items. For example, Buffalo chicken wings were called "Kookabura wings," a filet mignon was called "Victoria's Filet,"

and a rich chocolate sauce dessert was titled, "Chocolate Thunder Down Under." The menu also included a wide variety of beverages, including a full liquor service featuring Australian beer and wine. The menu for the trio's casual dining operation featured specially seasoned steaks and prime rib and also included chicken, ribs, fish, and pasta entrees. Tim explained the menu selections for Outback:

At Outback we don't look at other menus or trends . . . . [The] best things I learned in a lifetime I put in the menu.

The company's house specialties included its "'Aussie-Tizers' . . . and delectable desserts."[15] The company's signature trademark quickly became its best-selling "Aussie-Tizer," the "Bloomin' Onion." The idea for a large single-hearted onion cut to resemble a blooming flower, dipped in batter, and fried was originally developed by a New Orleans chef from a picture in a Japanese book. Tim added seasonings and enlarged it to "Outback size." The company expected to serve nine million "Bloomin' Onions" in 1995.

The menu, attention to quality from suppliers, and the emphasis on exceeding customer expectations all contributed to the high food quality. At about 40 percent of total costs, Outback's food costs were among the highest in the industry. "If we didn't have the highest food costs in the industry," explained Bob Basham, "we would be worried."

Outback's founders paid particular attention to the flavor profiles of the food. As Bob Merritt put it:

One of the important reasons for our success is that we took basic American meat and potatoes and enhanced the flavor profile so that it fit with the aging population . . . . Just look at what McDonald's and Burger King did in their market segment. They tried to add things to their menu that were more flavorful. McDonald's put the Big Mac on their menu because they found that as people aged, they wanted more flavor. McDonald's could not address that customer need with an old cheeseburger which tastes like cardboard . . . . That's why Tex Mex is such a great segment. That's why Italian is such a great segment because Italian food tends to have higher flavor profiles. It's not happenstance. It's a science. There's too much money at risk in this business not to know what's going on with customer taste preferences.

The founders knew that as people age, their taste buds also age. Thus, they recognized that their baby-boomer customers, those born in the 1946 to 1964 period, would demand more flavor in their food.

The 1995 menu remained essentially the same in character as originally envisioned in 1987. The price range of appetizers was about $2 to $6 with entrees ranging between $8 and $17. The average check per person was approximately $15 to $16.[16] The changing of menu items was done with care. For example, a new item planned for 1995 was the rack of lamb. As Tim Gannon explained, the menu was an issue to which all three founders turned their attention:

Where we all come together is on the menu. Bob comes to the plate thinking how the kitchen can put this out and how it can be stored. Chris will look at it from how the customer is going to view it. Is it of value? I come to it from a flavor point of view. Is it an exciting dish? We all add something to the final decision.

Tim and the staff at the company's original restaurant located on Henderson Avenue in Tampa, Florida, undertook most of the company's R&D. The founders approved any menu changes only after paying careful attention to development. For example, Tim and the Henderson staff had worked for a number of months on the rack of lamb entree. Tim explained:

We have been working with it [the rack of lamb entree] for some time on the operational side trying to get the cook times down. The flavors are there. Chris is excited although it [the rack] is not a mainstream product. It is an upscale product for us . . . . We are still fine-tuning the operational side to be sure it is in balance with other things we are doing. We are serving 800 dinners a night, and you can't have a menu item that throws the chemistry of the kitchen off.

Quality Fanatics—"We won't tolerate less than the best"

Outback executives and restaurant managers were staunchly committed to the principle that good food required outstanding ingredients. Tim explained the com-

pany's attention to the suppliers:

I have been to every onion grower from Oregon, Idaho, and all the way to Mexico looking for a continuous supply of single-hearted onions. I talk to the growers . . . . If it's a product you serve, you cannot rely on the words of a distributor to say, "This is what we have." I have to get into the fields and see what they have. If I am going to take 50 percent of the crop like that, I have to get into the fields to know, to see, how the crop is developed. So that took me into the fields of Idaho to see what makes onions get that big and what makes double hearts because they are hard for us to use. We do that with everything, the species of shrimp, which boats have the ice, what's the best safety standards. [I go] with the guys who purchase the cattle and learn to look for what they look for . . . . That's the only way you can produce great food.

Supplier relationships were long-standing. The company made beef purchases centrally for the entire Outback system. The company's original menu was designed by Tim Gannon with help from Warren LeRuth, one of New Orleans's premier chefs. LeRuth recommended Bruss, a Chicago-based meatpacking company, as a source of high-quality beef. Tim explained why Bruss was such a great partner as a supplier:

We couldn't even get samples [from the others]. We were on a low budget at the time. This company believed in us. They sent us samples after samples . . . . Their cutters were more like craftsmen; the

sense of pride that the Chicago butchers have about their product is really what we wanted in our restaurants. Bruss was at about $37 million at the time. Today, they are at $100 million, and we represent $75 to $80 million of that. We've been a great partner for them as they have been for us.

In 1994 Outback had two major suppliers of beef, but Bruss continued to supply over half of the Outback restaurants. About 60 percent of Outback's menu items were red meat entrees, and its best-selling steak alone accounted for about 25 percent of entrees sold. The attention to quality extended, however, to all suppliers. Vanilla, used only for the whipped cream in just one dessert item, was the "real thing" from the island of Madagascar. Olive oil was imported from Tuscany and wheels of parmesan cheese from Italy. Tim explained the company policy:

. . . if any supplier replaces our order with a cheap imitation, I will know about it and they will not supply us anymore . . . . I will not tolerate anything less than the best.

The attention to quality and detail was also evidenced at the individual restaurant level. For example, croutons were made daily at each restaurant with 17 different seasonings, including fresh garlic and butter, and cut by hand into irregular shapes so that customers would recognize they were handmade.

In addition to his oversight of supplier quality, Tim Gannon also focused on continual training of the restaurant staff throughout the Outback system. He held about ten meetings a year in various parts of the country with staff members from various regional restaurants. Typically, about 50 kitchen managers and other kitchen staff attended these meetings. There was a presentation from a special guest with half of the group in the front of the restaurant. In the meantime, the other half of the group worked on "the basics" in the kitchen. Then the two groups exchanged places. Tim felt these meetings were critical for generating new ideas, sometimes from very new kitchen staff employees. For example, one new employee had urged attention to the dessert sauces. Discussion of this issue ultimately resulted in a reformulation of the sauces so that they did not so easily crystallize as well as the installation of the warmers that held the sauces at a constant temperature. This innovation allowed the restaurants to serve desserts more quickly.

The restaurant general managers also emphasized food quality. This commitment was illustrated by Joe Cofer, manager of the Henderson Street restaurant in Tampa, when he said:

We watch the food as it comes out of the kitchen, touching every single plate to make sure every single plate is perfect—that's our commitment to this restaurant [i.e.,] to watch the food. We can take care of every single table by watching the food. If we have a problem at a table, we go to talk to them.

Designing a Restaurant—"Bob Basham's Memorial Kitchen"

Facility design was also a critical component in quality food preparation. Bob Basham especially paid attention to kitchen design, so much so that Chris and Tim termed Outback's kitchen design Bob's "Memorial Kitchen." Fully 45 percent of Outback's restaurant unit was generally dedicated to the kitchen. Analysts and other industry observers had pointed out that Outback could enlarge the dining area and reduce wait times for customers. However, Bob Basham explained the logic behind the company's restaurant design:

Restaurants get busy on a Friday night or a Saturday night when most people go out to eat. That's when you are trying to make the best impression on people. [But] physically, the kitchen cannot handle the demand. So if you have standards in your operation of a 12-minute cook time . . . . [it's] impossible to execute that way. We all decided we would not have it happening in our restaurant. So we underdesigned the front of the house and overdesigned the back of the house. That has worked very, very well for us. To this day we limit the number [of tables]. Even in our busiest restaurants where people tell us we could be twice as big and do twice the sales, we still discipline ourselves to build our restaurants one size.

The interior design was a "subtle decor featuring blond woods, large booths and tables [with] Australian memorabilia—boomerangs,*

surfboards, maps, and flags."[17] A typical Outback occupied over 6,000 square feet, featuring a dining room and an island bar. The restaurant area had 30 to 35 tables and could seat about 160 patrons. The bar had about six to nine tables with seating for about 35.

Location Is Everything?—"You're going to put a restaurant where? For dinner only?!"

The company's first restaurant was located on a site that had held several restaurants before Bob and Chris leased it. Early Outback restaurants were all located in strip shopping centers or were retrofits of existing freestanding restaurant sites. When the company first started, lease costs for retrofits were lower than the cost of constructing and owning a building. Bob Basham explained the rationale behind Outback's location strategy:

. . . We call it our A-market B-location . . . . we didn't have enough money to go to the corner of Main and Main. So we felt that if we went to a great market [that] had great demographics that we needed, and got in what we called a B-location, that typically most restaurant companies would think of as a B-location, we felt we could be successful there if we executed great, and that strategy continues today.

However, as the company expanded into other parts of the country, the cost structure shifted. In 1993 the company developed a prototype that was being constructed in most new locations. The company devoted significant effort to site evaluation efforts that focused on area demographics, target population density, household income levels, competition, and specific site characteristics such as visibility, accessibility, and traffic volume.

Conventional wisdom in the restaurant industry suggested that facilities should be utilized as long as possible during the day. However, Outback restaurants were open daily for seven hours from 4:30 to 11:30 P.M. This dinner-only approach had been highly successful. The dinner-only concept had led to the effective utilization of systems, staff, and management. By not offering lunch, Outback avoided restaurant sites in high-traffic, high-cost city centers. Furthermore, the dinner-only theme minimized the strain on staff. Tips were typically much higher for dinner than for lunch or breakfast service. Outback restaurants averaged 3,800 customers per week and were usually filled shortly after opening. In an industry where a sales-to-investment ratio of 1.2;1 was considered strong, Outback's restaurants generated $2.10 in sales for every $1 invested in the facility.

Operating Structure— "No organization charts here"

Management remained informal in 1995. Corporate headquarters were located on the second floor of an unpretentious office building near the Tampa airport. The headquarters offices were about two miles from the original store on Henderson Boulevard. Headquarters staff numbered approximately 80. Corporate existed as a service center. As Bob Merritt put it:

We exist here to service the restaurants . . . . There is nothing I can do from Tampa, Florida, to make sure the customer has a great experience in Kansas City, nothing except to put in management people who have great attitudes, who like to take care of people, who are highly motivated economically, and make sure they have hired the best and most highly motivated people, and trained them to get the job done. It is absolutely our point of differentiation. You can get at the food and all the other stuff, but in the end what makes this company work is its decentralized nature and our willingness, particularly Chris and Bob's willingness, to live with the mistakes of their subordinates and look at those mistakes as opportunities to teach, not opportunities to discipline. That is the pervasive element of our corporate culture that makes it work.

There was no human resources department at corporate. However, Trudy Cooper, vice president for training and development, had been involved in the hiring of associates at most new restaurants until 1994. In 1994 Cooper added two coordinators who helped with new restaurant openings. One of the coordinators supervised training in the front operations and the other supervised the kitchen. Each selected 15 other high-quality employees from restaurants throughout the system to work on a temporary, one to one basis with the new employees during an opening. The two coordinators and the special training staff all returned to their home restaurant assignments once an opening was completed.

Training at a new restaurant site took place over a two-week period. Outback absorbed all the costs related to an opening into the marketing/advertising budget. The restaurant staff had four practice nights. On the first night, a Friday, the guests were family members of the staff. On the second and third nights, Saturday and Sunday, the invited guests were community members, including construction workers, vendors, and other VIP guests. The fourth night, Monday, was charity night. Trudy Cooper described a new restaurant opening:

We have those people on site for about two weeks. We have classroom sessions, then a food show and a wine show. We do a mock night. We do two nights of role play. We do a night with the media followed by a charity function. All of the proceeds go to charity. It is $10 a person for heavy hors d'oeuvres and an open bar. We make quite a bit of money on that night for the charity chosen by the restaurant manager.

Local press representatives were invited to a special briefing session an hour in advance of the opening night. All the proceeds from opening night went to a charity of the restaurant manager's choice.

A typical Outback restaurant staff consisted of a general manager, one assistant manager, and a kitchen manager plus 50 to 70 hourly employees, many of whom worked part-time. Job candidates for the restaurant staff were required to pass an aptitude test that assessed basic skills such as making change at the till. Every applicant interviewed with two managers. A friendly and outgoing disposition was a critical job requirement. The company also used psychological profile tests to better understand an applicant's personality.

Outback placed a great degree of emphasis upon learning and personal growth throughout the company. Trudy Cooper called it "Our learn-teach-learn approach." Chris Sullivan further explained:

I was given the opportunity to make a lot of mistakes and learn, and we try to do that today. We try to give our people a lot of opportunity to make some mistakes, learn, and go on.

"Every worker an owner . . . "

The three founders keenly remembered their early desire to own their own restaurant. Consequently, Outback provided ownership opportunities at three levels in the organization: at the individual restaurant level; through multiple store arrangements (joint venture and franchise opportunities); and through the newly formed employee stock ownership plan.

Top management selected the joint venture partners and franchisees. As franchisee Hugh Connerty put it, "There is no middle management here. All franchisees report directly to the president." Franchisees and joint venture partners in

turn hired the general managers at each restaurant. All of the operating partners and general managers were required to complete a comprehensive 12-week training course that emphasized the company's operating strategy, procedures, and standards.

From the beginning, the founders wanted ownership opportunities for each restaurant general manager and formed the limited partner arrangement. Each restaurant general manager committed to a five-year contract and invested $25,000 for a 10 percent stake in the restaurant. Initially, the arrangement was in the form of a limited partnership. However, the company was in the process of converting all agreements to general partnerships backed with liability insurance.

Under the program, the restaurant general manager received a base salary of $45,000 plus 10 percent of the pre-rent "cash flow" from the restaurant. "Pre-rent" cash flow for Outback restaurants was calculated monthly and defined as earnings before taxes, interest, and depreciation.[18] Each manager's name appeared over the restaurant door with the designation, "Proprietor." An average Outback generated $3.2 million in sales and a pre-rent "cash flow" of $736,000. Average total compensation for managing partners exceeded $100,000, including an average $73,600 share of the restaurant profits. If the manager chose to leave the company at the end of a five-year period, Outback bought out the manager's ownership. If managers chose to stay with Outback, they could sign up for five additional years at

the same restaurant or invest another $25,000 in a new store. After the company went public in 1991, the company began to give restaurant managers nonqualified stock options at the time they became managing partners. The options vested at the end of five years. Each manager received about 4,000 shares of stock over the five-year period. Outback's attractive arrangements for restaurant general managers resulted in a 1994 management turnover of 5 percent compared to 30 percent to 40 percent industry-wide.

By early 1995, eleven stores had celebrated their five-year anniversaries (see Exhibit 3). Of the eleven managers, two had left the company. One later returned. Four had gone on to new stores in which they invested $25,000 with the same repeat deal. Five stayed with their same stores, renewing their contract with additional options that would vest at the end of the second five-year period. Joe Cofer, manager of the Henderson Street Outback in Tampa, indicated how his position as general manager of the restaurant affected his life:

I have been with the Outback for about 4 1/2 years now. I started out as a manager. Sixteen months ago I was offered a partnership in the Henderson store. I grew up in Tampa, right down the street, and have lived here nearly my whole life. So when they offered me this store, it was perfect . . . . If you walk in the restaurant and look at the name on the sign, some people I went to high school with say, "How in the heck did this happen?" . . . . The other organization [I worked for] had long hours when you were open from 11:30 in the morning until 1 or 2 in the evening. Those hours have a tendency to burn people out . . . . At Outback, from the [supplier] level all the way down to the dishwasher level we all work as a team. That is another difference between Outback and the organization I used to work for . . . . Here at Outback we don't have those rules and regulations . . . Chris always claims he plays a lot of golf in the daytime and has a lot of fun . . . . He will come up to you and ask, "Are you having fun?" [We say] "Oh, we're having a great time." He says, "Okay, that's the way you need to run this stuff."

Multiple-store ownership occurred through franchises, joint venture partnership arrangements, and sometimes a combination. The founders' original plan did not include franchises. However, in 1990 a friend who owned several restaurants in Kentucky asked to put Outback franchises in two of his restaurants that had not done very well. The founders reluctantly awarded the KY franchise. The two franchised restaurants quickly became successful. Under a franchise arrangement, the franchisees paid 3 percent of gross revenues to Outback.

After the IPO the company began to form joint venture partnerships with individuals who had strong operating credentials but not a lot of funds to invest. Under a joint venture arrangement a joint venture partner invested $50,000 and in return received a $50,000 base salary, plus 10 percent of the "cash flow" generated by the restaurants in his/her group

after the restaurant general managers were paid their 10 percent. Therefore, a joint venture partner who operated ten Outbacks generating $600,000 each would end up with $54,000 per unit or $540,000 total plus the $50,000 base. Since Outback's general managers were experienced restaurateurs, the joint venture partners focused primarily on area development, including site research for new locations and hiring and training new managers. The company instituted its employee stock ownership plan in 1993 for employees at the restaurant level. At the time the ESOP was established, all employees received stock proportional to their time in service. Each employee received a yearly statement. The stock ownership program required no investment from the employees and vested after five years.

Advertising and Promotion—"We have always established that Outback is quality product at a great value"

Vice president of marketing Nancy Schneid came to Outback in 1990. Before working for Outback, Schneid had been first a media buyer in a large advertising agency and then an advertising sales representative for Tampa's dominant radio station. She met Chris and Bob while she was at the radio station and they were running their Chili's franchise. Although Chili's advertising strategy did not usually include radio advertising, Chris and Bob chose to use a significant level of local radio advertising.

Nancy was well aware of Chris and Bob's success with Chili's. When they established Outback, she became an early investor in the form of a limited partnership. She explained how the radio station she worked with was able to help the three entrepreneurs with advertising:

When they first opened Outback they were struggling. Our radio station was expensive to advertise on . . . . So I made an opportunity for them to go on radio on a morning show that had a 35 percent share of the market and an afternoon show that had a 28 percent share of the market. That gave them the opportunity to tell the Tampa Bay community about the concept [which was] in a very B location on Henderson. Tim Gannon came at 5:00 A.M. and set up a cooking station downstairs. He cooked and ran food upstairs while Chris and Bob talked to the DJ. They basically owned the morning show.

Outback used very little print media. Print advertisements typically appeared only if a charity or sports event offered space as part of its package. Thus, Outback ads might appear in the American Cancer Magazine or a golf tournament program. Billboards were used to draw customers to specific restaurant locations. TV advertising began in 1991 after the local advertising agency, the West Group in Tampa, was selected. The company produced about three or four successful TV advertisements per year. Although not a company spokesman, well-known model Rachel Hunter had participated in several of the ads and had become identified with Outback.

Hunter's New Zealand origin was generally interpreted by audiences to be Australian.

Except for the development of the TV advertisements, advertising and marketing efforts were decentralized. As VP Schneid put it:

We are very much micro-managers when it comes to the spending of our media dollars . . . . We are very responsive to the needs of the community, for example, Big Sisters and Brothers . . . . [Our advertising, marketing, and community involvement efforts] help us build friends and an image of great food at a great price.

Community Involvement—"We have been rewarded . . . out of proportion to our needs, and we want to give some of that back"

Central to Outback's operating strategy was a high degree of visibility and involvement in the community. Outback sponsored the Outback Bowl that first aired on ESPN on New Year's afternoon 1996. In addition, the company was involved in a number of charity golf tournaments with a unique format involving food preparation and service at each hole. Community involvement involved not only top management but everyone at Outback. Each new store opening involved community participation and community service to charities. Other community involvement took various forms. The Tampa-based corporate staff included a full-time special events person with a staff

that catered to charity as well as for-profit events in the Tampa area. For many charity events Outback provided the food while staff donated their time.

For example, a black-tie dinner for 400 was scheduled for May 1995 at Tampa's Lowry Park Zoo, a special interest of Outback's three top executives.

Every local restaurant managing partner was likely to have a Little League or other sports sponsorship. Basham explained:

We are really involved in the community . . . . I think you have to give back. We have been very, very fortunate, we have been rewarded . . . out of proportion to our needs, and we want to give some of that back to the community . . . . I think if more people did that we would have a lot less problems in this country than we have right now . . . . I have certainly been rewarded out of proportion to any contribution I feel I have made, and I just feel I should give something back. That goes throughout our company.

The Founders' Relationship—"The three of us kind of stay on each other, challenging each other, kid each other a lot, but more than anything support each other to make this thing work"

The three founders contributed in different ways to running the company. Each shared his perspective on his own as well the others' roles. Chris gave his view of the trio:

. . . Bob and I became corporate-type restaurant people, and sometimes that is more systems-oriented and not so much hospitality-oriented. Tim really brought that to our success. But more than that, he is easy to get along with. He absolutely gets done what needs to get done. He needs a little prodding. Bob and I need a little prodding. So the three of us kind of stay on each other, kid each other a lot, but more than anything support each other to make this thing work.

Bob explained the synergy among the three:

We have been together eight years. I think we have a balance between our strengths and our weaknesses. There are some things Chris does extremely well that I don't do well. There are things that Tim puts into the formula that Chris and I could not do as well as he does, and hopefully there are some things that I do well that they would need. I think just the three of us have synergies together that have really worked very positively for us. We kind of all feed off of each other . . . . Right now, each one of us has a different role in the company. I concentrate on operations, the people side of the business, the day-to-day going-on of the business.

I think Chris has a little more of the strategic overview of the company, keeps us going in the direction we need to be going. He is very good at seeing things long-term. Tim is our food guy. Tim makes sure that we can all have a lot of fun. He has a lot of fun in his work. So we have a balance there. We all contribute and it all works.

Tim gave his perspective on how he fit in:

. . . My challenge: How do I fit in? . . . Partnerships of three are always hard but it has worked very well. I now understand my role and have been treated well . . . . [There is] nothing in life greater than having a great partnership . . . . We meet all the time. I never make a menu decision without them, Chris has eyes for the guest and Bob has eyes for the employee . . . . A lot of organizations bust up at the top, not bottom! I only want to work with Outback.

Competition— "We have all we need of the greatest kind of flattery"

A number of competitors in casual dining's steak dinner house subsegment had begun to make their presence felt. The most formidable competition was the Wichita, Kansas-based Lone Star Steakhouse & Saloon. However, there was also a growing set of players with a formula involving rustic buildings and beef value items that began operations in early 1990 and 1991. These included Sizzler International's Buffalo Ranch, Shoney's Barbwire, S&A Restaurant Corp.'s Montana Steak Co., and O'Charley Logan's Roadhouse. In addition, a number of chains had added or upgraded steak menu items in reaction to Outback.

Chris Sullivan explained his view of competition and what Outback had to do:

Our competitors-there are a lot . . . [We] can't run way from it—it's a fact. I think a lot of companies get in trouble because they start worrying about what the competitor is doing and they react to that. We really ask our people and we talk about—just go out and execute and do what you do best. The customers will decide . . . If we continue to do what we have been doing, we feel very, very confident that we will continue to be successful regardless of the number of competitors out there because with our situation, our setup, and the proprietors we have in our restaurants, I don't think there is anybody who can compete with us.

Outback's Future Outlook

The company as a whole was optimistic about its future. Wall Street analysts were skeptical, however. Citing the numerous entrants into the industry, they argued that casual dining operators such as Outback were close to saturation and questioned whether the firm could withstand the intense competitive pressures characteristic of the industry. However, Outback's management was unperturbed by Wall Street concerns or by the increasing competition. Joe Cofer summarized the management attitude:

I've heard so many times, "I love coming to your restaurant because your staff is so upbeat, they are so happy." They are always great people to have work for you. People just love the people here . . . . I see us as a McDonald's of the future, but a step up. I don't think anybody can come close to our efficiency because it is so simplistic and everyone is so laid back about it from the owners on down. And we are having such fun, making so much money. No one wants to go anywhere. I will never work for another company as long as I live . . . . You have that feeling mixed with the great food. I don't think anyone is a threat . . . . You have a very good investment with the stock. The stock has split three times in the last three years . . . . This is just going to split more and more and more. I'm just going to hold on to it forever. Hopefully, it will be my retirement.

The company intended to drive its future growth through a four-pronged strategy: (1) continuous expansion within the United States with an additional 300 to 350 Outback concept stores, (2) the rollout of Carrabbas Italian franchise as its second system of restaurants, (3) development of additional restaurant themes, and (4) international franchising. Chris Sullivan explained:

. . . We can do 500 to 600 restaurants, and possibly more over the next five years . . . . Our Italian concept, Carrabbas, that is in its infancy stage right now . . . has the potential to have the same kind of growth pattern that we have had in Outback . . . . We will continue to focus on Outback and continue to build that because we have a lot of work left there. Develop Carrabbas and use that as our next growth vehicle and continue to look . . . for a third leg on that stool, and who knows what is going to be hot in a couple of years.

. . . The world is becoming one big market, and we want to be in place so we don't miss that opportunity. There are some problems, some challenges with it, but at this point there have been some casual restaurants chains that have gone [outside the United States] and their average unit sales are way, way above the sales level they enjoyed in the United States. So the potential is there . . . . We are real excited about the future internationally.

In the face of the dire predictions from industry observers and analysts, Outback CEO Chris Sullivan put his organization's plans quite simply: "We want to be the major player in the casual dining segment."[19]

Enron and Arthur Andersen: Beyond the Debacles

During the last decade of the 20th century, Enron Corp. became a major player in the energy sector of the economy and a growing force in other businesses, with total revenues across all businesses of US$101 billion in 2000. Even with the company's expansion into non-energy commodities, energy represented Enron's primary business venture. On November 9, 2001, the merger of Enron and Dynegy Corp. was announced. The merger soon unraveled as Enron's questionable accounting practices and financial dealings—in particular, highly irregular partnership arrangements—were discovered. Enron, with recorded revenues of approximately $140 billion during the first three quarters of 2001, experienced a catastrophic collapse in the market value of its stock.

The merger was called off. Enron sued Dynegy and Dynegy countersued Enron, with each accusing the other of wrongdoing. In early December 2001, Enron filed for bankruptcy. Just days before this filing, 500 of the company's employees were paid $55.7 million in bonuses. More than 4,000 Enron employees were fired at the time of the bankruptcy filing. (1) Moreover, numerous companies around the world suffered significant losses as a result of the Enron debacle.

The Demise of Arthur Andersen

In mid-December 2001, the U.S. Congress initiated hearings on the Enron debacle. Executives from Arthur Andersen, Enron's auditor, testified about possible illegal acts and violations of securities laws by Enron officials as well as about Andersen's role in the situation. In January 2002, the U.S. Justice Department initiated a criminal investigation into the debacle. This investigation uncovered evidence of destruction by Andersen employees of documents related to Enron's questionable activities. David Duncan, head of Andersen's audit team for Enron, was fired and later admitted to ordering the shredding of Enron-related documents shortly after learning of the Justice Department's investigation. Enron fired Andersen as its auditor. Subsequently, Andersen was charged with obstruction of justice, stood trial, and was found guilty. Numerous auditing clients severed ties with Arthur Andersen, and the accounting firm was virtually destroyed. (2) An appeal to the Fifth U.S. Court of Appeals was pending at the time of writing this case update.

The Bankruptcy Aftermath at Enron

Meanwhile, bizarre events related to Enron continued to unfold. A former Enron executive committed suicide, apparently in remorse over the Enron debacle. The *Powers Report*, prepared by a special committee of Enron's board of directors, blamed Enron executives as well as the auditors, lawyers, and board members for the improper partnerships. In testimony before Congress, key Enron executives either denied responsibility for what had happened or asserted Fifth Amendment privilege against self-incrimination. Jeffrey Skilling, former Enron CEO, testified that the company was in "great shape" when he left his position. He also asserted that he was the victim of "outrageous lies" and insisted that he was not responsible in any way for Enron's collapse. Kenneth Lay, Enron's former chairman, asserted his Fifth Amendment rights shortly after resigning from Enron's board of directors. (3)

Sherron Watkins, Enron's vice president of corporate development, was one of the few beacons of proper behavior in carrying out her responsibilities. Being aware of the questionable partnerships and the off-balance-sheet accounting, Watkins sensed the doom Enron was facing. She told her boss, Kenneth Lay, and a friend at Arthur Andersen, who then told Andersen's head Enron auditor, David Duncan. In testimony before Congress, Watkins said she believed that Lay was probably duped by Skilling and others. (4)

In the ensuing months, several Enron executives were charged with various criminal acts, including fraud, money laundering, and insider trading. Former Enron executive David Delainey, closely connected to former CEO Jeff Skilling, pled guilty to one count of insider trading and paid almost $8 million in fines. He also agreed to cooperate in the government's Enron investigations. (5) Lea Fastow, former assistant treasurer at Enron and the wife of Andrew Fastow, Enron's former chief financial officer, was charged with six criminal counts, including conspiracy to commit wire fraud, money laundering, and four counts of filing false tax returns. When a plea bargain agreement fell through, she pled not guilty to all counts. (6)

Ben Glisan, Enron's former treasurer, was charged with two dozen counts of money laundering, fraud, and conspiracy. He pled guilty to one count of conspiracy to commit fraud in exchange for the other charges being dropped. Glisan received a prison term, three years of post-prison supervision, and financial penalties of more than a $1 million. Glisan admitted that Enron was a "house of cards." Glisan was a close associate of Andrew Fastow, former Enron chief financial officer, who faced almost 100 counts of money laundering, fraud, and conspiracy. At the time of writing, Fastow maintained his innocence. (7)

As of late 2003, Enron was still struggling to work its way out of bankruptcy. Enron's creditors sought permission from a federal bankruptcy judge to sue more than three dozen former Enron executives, Arthur Andersen, and three law firms for negligence and failure to fulfill their duties as corporate officers. A final report by Enron's bankruptcy examiner in late November 2003 concluded that Kenneth Lay and Jeffrey Skilling had breached their fiduciary duties and might be liable for repaying millions of dollars to Enron. Lay and Skilling, of course, disputed the bankruptcy examiner's findings. (8)

Culture and Leadership: The Seeds of Enron's Demise

Enron's collapse did not happen overnight; it was long in the making, dating from the early 1990s. Along with the company's rapid growth came the development of a corporate culture and leadership that was obsessed with stock prices, bonuses, and exotic accounting practices.

Rich Kinder, Enron's chief operating officer (COO) from 1990 to 1996, was obsessed with stock prices and earning targets. He focused his attentions on operations and cash flow, and would "terrify people if they didn't meet their goals." (9) Then when Jeff Skilling took over from Kinder, there was still an obsession with stock prices but a drastic "flip-flop" in the method for maintaining Enron's favorable stock prices.

Skilling seemingly paid little attention to expenses or day-to-day operations, instead delegating those responsibilities. Skilling was concerned about expanding both revenues and profit margins. To accomplish this, Enron began an extensive program of buying, expanding, and launching businesses in both energy and non-energy domains. To help run these businesses, Skilling sought the best and brightest new hires, ones who would be "ruthless traders." Skilling wanted people who could prosper in a "go-go, high-achievement environment." Unfortunately, there was insufficient monitoring of these new hires to ensure that they learned the fundamentals of good management. (10)

Under Skilling, a very rigorous and threatening evaluation process was instituted for all Enron employees. Known as "rank and yank," Enron's employees annually ranked their fellow employees on a 1 (best) to 5 (worst) scale. Each of the company's divisions was arbitrarily forced to give the lowest ranking to one-fifth of its employees. These employees were then fired. Employees often downgraded their peers in order to enhance their own positions in the company. (11)

Enron's bonus program was another major contributor to the company's demise. "Those who closed major deals were paid up to 3 percent of the value of the entire deal, payable when it was struck, not when the project actually began earning money." (12) The bonus program encouraged the use of non-standard accounting practices and the inflation of deals on the company's books. Deal inflation within the company became sufficiently widespread that "more effort was put into hiding the consequences than owning up to the problem." (13) In fact, four partnerships were created solely for the purpose of hiding losses.

The company was very decentralized and de-emphasized teamwork—each division and business unit was kept separate from the other businesses. Consequently, very few people in the Enron organization knew much of what was going on in the company from a "big picture"

perspective. Basically, people heading their divisions and business units knew what was happening in their part of the company but not throughout the company. Fostering this decentralized operation, which also lacked sufficient operational and financial controls, was "a distracted, hands-off chairman, a compliant board of directors and an impotent staff of accountants, auditors and lawyers." (14)

Into the Future

The Enron and Arthur Andersen debacles have destroyed businesses and many people's lives—and most likely will continue to do so for some time in the future. The ethical failures of both Enron and Arthur Andersen have sent shock waves through the global business community, among employees of both small and large corporations, and among private citizens. After a two-year ride on a "roller coaster of volatility," the discovery of ethically bizarre decisions and actions seem all too frequent and commonplace. All of these events should leave us wondering: "What enduring lessons for humanity will these debacles end up providing?"

Questions for Integrative Thinking

1. Explain the collapse of Enron in terms of failures of the four functions of management—planning, organizing, leading, and controlling.
2. What managerial initiatives and actions might

have prevented Enron's collapse?
3. Why was Arthur Andersen affected so drastically by the Enron debacle? What should (or could) Andersen have done differently?
4. What key lessons regarding ethics and social responsibility have the Enron and Arthur Andersen debacles provided?

Research Questions for Keeping Current

New evidence in the Enron and Arthur Andersen debacles unfolds with great frequency. An excellent source of current as well as archived information about Enron as well as Arthur Andersen's relationship to Enron is the *Houston Chronicle*—http://www.chron.com/content/chronicle/special/01/enron/. Search its pages for information that keeps you abreast of this unfolding saga. The following questions are intended to provide some useful focus when conducting your search:

1. What is the current status of Enron Corp. with respect to its attempt to recover from bankruptcy?
2. What is the current legal status of key Enron executives who have been accused of involvement in Enron's misdeeds?
3. What is the current status of Arthur Andersen?
4. What useful lessons for businesses and business-people continue to emerge in the aftermath of the Enron and Arthur Andersen debacles?

ACTIVE LEARNING

PROJECTS

PROJECT 1

Diversity Lessons—"What Have We Learned?"

QUESTION

What are the current "facts" in terms of progress for minorities and women in the workplace? What lessions of diversity have been learned? What are the "best" employers doing?

Possible Research Directions

- Examine case studies of employers reported as having strong diversity programs. What do they have in common? What do they do differently?
- Find out what we know about how well people of different racial, ethnic, gender, life-style, and generational groups work together. What are the common problems, if any? What concerns do managers and workers have?

- Get specific data on how the "glass ceiling" affects the careers of women and minorities in various occupational settings. Analyze the data and develop the implications.
- Take a critical look at the substance of diversity training programs. What do these programs try to accomplish, and how? Are they working or not, and how do we know?

PROJECT 2

Corporate Social Responsibility—"What's the Status?"

QUESTION

Where do businesses stand today with respect to the criteria for evaluating social responsibility discussed in the textbook?

Possible Research Directions

- Create a scale that could be used to measure the social responsibility performance of an organization. Review the scholarly research in this area, but also include your own ideas and expectations.
- Use your scale to research and evaluate the "status" of major organizations and local ones on social responsibility performance. How well are they doing? Would you use them as models of social responsibility for others to follow, or not?
- Conduct research to identify current examples of the "best" and the "worst" organizations in terms of performance or social responsibility criteria. Pursue this investigation on an (a) international, (b) national, and/or (c) local scale.

PROJECT 3

Globalization—"What Are the Pros and Cons?"

QUESTION

"Globalization" is frequently in the news. You can easily read or listen to both advocates and opponents. What is the bottom line? Is globalization good or bad, and for whom?

Possible Research Directions

- What does the term "globalization" mean? Review various definitions and find the common ground.

- Read and study the scholarly arguments about globalization. Summarize what the scholars say about the forces and consequences of globalization in the past, present, and future.
- Examine current events relating to globalization. Summarize the issues and arguments. What is the positive side of globalization? What are the negatives that some might call its "dark" side?
- Consider globalization from the perspective of your local community or one of its major employers. Is globalization a threat or an opportunity, and why?
- Take a position on globalization. State what you believe to be the best course for government and business leaders to take. Justify your position.

PROJECT 4

Affirmative Action Directions—"Where Do We Go from Here?"

QUESTION

Consultant R. Roosevelt Thomas argues that it is time to "move beyond affirmative action" and learn how to "manage diversity." There are a lot of issues that may be raised in this context—issues of equal employment opportunity, hiring quotas, reverse discrimination, and others. What is the status of affirmative action today?

Possible Research Directions

- Read articles by Thomas and others. Make sure you are clear on the term "affirmative action" and its legal underpinnings. Research the topic, identify the relevant laws, and make a history line to chart its development over time.
- Examine current debates on affirmative action. What are the issues? How are the "for" and "against" positions being argued?
- Identify legal cases where reverse discrimination has been charged. How have they been resolved and with what apparent human resource management implications?
- Look at actual organizational policies on affirmative action. Analyze them and identify the common ground. Prepare a policy development guideline for use by human resource managers.
- As you ponder these issues and controversies be sure to engage different perspectives. Talk to and read about people of different "majority" and "minority" groups. Find out how they view these things—and why.

PROJECT 5

Fringe Benefits—"How Can They Be Managed"

QUESTION

Employers complain that the rising cost of "fringe benefits" is a major concern. Is this concern legitimate? If so, how can fringe benefits be best managed?

Possible Research Directions

- Find out exactly what constitutes "fringe benefits" as part of the typical compensation package. Look in the literature and also talk to local employers. Find out what percentage of a typical salary is represented in fringe benefits.
- Find and interview two or three human resource managers in your community. Ask them to describe their fringe benefits programs and how they manage fringe benefits costs. What do they see happening in the future? What do they recommend? Talk to two or three workers from different employers in your community. Find out how things look to them and what they recommend.
- Pick a specific benefit such as health insurance. What are the facts? How are employers trying to manage the rising cost of health insurance? What are the implications for workers?
- Examine the union positions on fringe benefits. How is this issue reflected in major labor negotiations. What are the results of major recent negotiations?
- Look at fringe benefits from the perspective of temporary, part-time, or contingent workers. What do they get? What do they want? How are they affected by rising costs?

PROJECT 6

CEO Pay—"Is It Too High?"

QUESTION

What is happening in the area of executive compensation? Are CEOs paid too much? Are they paid for "performance," or are they paid for something else?

Possible Research Directions

- Check the latest reports on CEO pay. Get the facts and prepare a briefing report as if you were writing a short informative article for

Fortune magazine. The title of your article should be "Status Report: Where We Stand Today on CEO Pay."

- Address the pay-for-performance issue. Do corporate CEOs get paid for performance or for something else? What do the researchers say? What do the business periodicals say? Find some examples to explain and defend your answers to these questions.
- Take a position: Should a limit be set on CEO pay? If no, why not? If yes, what type of limit do we set? Who, if anyone, should set these limits—Congress, company boards of directors, or someone else?
- Examine the same issues in the university setting. Are university presidents paid too much?

PROJECT 7

Gender and Leadership—"Is There a Difference?"

QUESTION

Do men and women lead differently?

Possible Research Directions

- Review the discussion on gender and leadership in the textbook, Chapter 13. Find and read the articles cited in the endnotes. Then, update this literature by finding and reading the most recent scholarly findings and reports.
- Interview managers from organizations in your local community. Ask them the question. Ask them to give you specific examples to justify their answers. Look for patterns and differences. Do male managers and female managers answer the question similarly?
- Interview workers from organizations in your local community. Ask them the question. Ask them to give you specific examples to justify their answers. Look for patterns and differences. Do male workers and female workers answer the question similarly? Do the same for students—pressing them to share insights and examples from their experiences in course study groups and student organizations.
- Summarize your findings. Describe the implications of your findings in terms of leadership development for both men and women.

PROJECT 8

Superstars on the Team—"What Do They Mean?"

QUESTION

Do we want a "superstar" on our team?

Possible Research Directions

- Everywhere you look—in entertainment, in sports, and in business—a lot of attention these days goes to the superstars. What is the record of teams and groups with superstars? Do they really outperform the rest?
- What is the real impact of a superstar's presence on a team or in the workplace? What do they add? What do they cost? Consider the potential costs of having a superstar on a team in the equation: Benefits − Costs = Value. What is the bottom line of having a superstar on the team?
- Interview the athletic coaches on your campus. Ask them the question. Compare and contrast their answers. Interview players from various teams. Do the same for them.
- Develop a set of guidelines for creating team effectiveness for a situation where a superstar is present. Be thorough and practical. Can you give advice good enough to ensure that a superstar always creates super performance for the team or work group or organization?

PROJECT 9

Management in Popular Culture—"Seeing Ourselves Through Our Pastimes"

QUESTION

What management insights are found in popular culture and reflected in our everyday living?

Possible Research Directions

- Listen to music. Pick out themes that reflect important management concepts and theories. Put them together in a multi-media report that presents your music choices and describes their messages about management and working today.
- Watch television. Look again for the management themes. In a report, describe what popular television programs have to say about management and working. Also consider TV advertisements. How do they use and present workplace themes to help communicate their messages?
- Read the comics, also looking for management themes. Compare and contrast management and working in two or three popular comic strips.
- Read a best-selling novel. Find examples of management and work themes in the novel. Report on what the author's characters and their experiences say about people at work.
- Watch a film or video. Again, find examples of management and work themes. In a report describe the message of the movie in respect to management and work today.

Note: These ideas are borrowed from the extensive work in this area by my colleague Dr. Robert (Lenie) Holbrook of Ohio University.

Service Learning in Management—"Learning from Volunteering"

QUESTION

What can you learn about management and leadership by working as a volunteer for a local community organization?

Possible Research Directions

- Explore service learning opportunities on your campus. Talk to your instructor about how to add a service learning component to your management course.
- List the nonprofit organizations in your community that might benefit from volunteers. Contact one or more of them and make inquiries as to how you might help them. Do it, and then report back on what you learned as a result of the experience that is relevant to management and leadership.
- Locate the primary schools in your community or region. Contact the school principals and ask how you might be able to help teachers working with first- through sixth-grade students. Do it, and then report back on what you learned with respect to personal management and leadership development.
- For either the nonprofit organization or the primary school, form a group of students who share similar interests in service learning. Volunteer as a group to help the organization and prepare a team report on what you learned.
- Take the initiative. Create service learning ideas of your own—to be pursued individually or as part of a team. While working as a volunteer always keep your eyes and ears open for learning opportunities. Continually ask—"What is happening here in respect to: leadership, morale, motivation, teamwork, conflict, interpersonal dynamics, organization culture and structures, and more?"

eXperiential

EXERCISES

My Best Manager

Preparation

Working alone, make a list of the *behavioral attributes* that describe the *best* manager you have ever worked for. This could be someone you worked for in a full-time or part-time job, summer job, volunteer job, student organization, or whatever. If you have trouble identifying an actual manager, make a list of behavioral attributes of the type of manager you would most like to work for in your next job.

Instructions

Form into groups as assigned by your instructor, or work with a nearby classmate.

Share your list of attributes and listen to the lists of others. Be sure to ask questions and make comments on items of special interest. Work together to create a master list that combines the unique attributes of the "best" managers experienced by members of your group. Have a spokesperson share that list with the rest of the class.

Source: Adapted from John R. Schermerhorn, Jr., James G. Hunt, and Richard N. Osborn, *Managing Organizational Behavior,* 3rd ed. (New York: Wiley, 1988), pp. 32–33. Used by permission.

What Managers Do

Preparation

Think about the questions that follow. Record your answers in the spaces provided.

1. How much of a typical manager's time would you expect to be allocated to these relationships? (total should = 100%)

___% of time working with
    subordinates
___% of time working with boss
___% of time working with peers and
    outsiders

2. How many hours per week does the average manager work? ___ hours

3. What amount of a manager's time is typically spent in the following activities? (total should = 100%)

___% in scheduled meetings
___% in unscheduled meetings
___% doing desk work
___% talking on the telephone
___% walking around the organization/
    work site

Instructions

Talk over your responses with a nearby classmate. Explore the similarities and differences in your answers. Be prepared to participate in a class discussion led by your instructor.

Defining Quality

Preparation

Write your definition of the word *quality* here. QUALITY =

Instructions

Form groups as assigned by your instructor. (1) Have each group member present a definition of the word *quality*. After everyone has presented, come up with a consensus definition of *quality*. That is, determine and write down one definition of the word with which every member can agree. (2) Next, have the group assume the position of top manager in each of the following organizations. Use the group's *quality* definition to state for each a *quality objective* that can guide the behavior of members in producing high-"quality" goods and/or services for customers or clients. Elect a spokesperson to share group results with the class as a whole.

Organizations:

a. A college of business administration

b. A community hospital

c. A retail sporting goods store

d. A fast-food franchise restaurant

e. A United States post office branch

f. A full-service bank branch

g. A student-apartment rental company

h. A used textbook store

i. A computer software firm

What Would the Classics Say?

Preparation

Consider this situation:

Six months into his new job, Bob, a laboratory worker, is performing just well enough to avoid being fired. When hired he was carefully selected and had the abilities required to do the job really well. At first Bob was enthusiastic about his new job, but now he isn't performing up to this high potential. Fran, his supervisor, is concerned and wonders what can be done to improve this situation.

Instructions

Assume the identify of one of the following persons: Frederick Taylor, Henri Fayol, Max Weber, Abraham Maslow, Chris Argyris. As-

sume that *as this person* you have been asked by Fran for advice on the management situation just described. Answer these questions as you think your assumed identity would respond. Be prepared to share your answers in class and to defend them based on the text's discussion of this person's views.

1. As *(your assumed identity)*, what are your basic beliefs about good management and organizational practices?

2. As *(your assumed identity)*, what do you perceive may be wrong in this situation that would account for Bob's low performance?

3. As *(your assumed identity)*, what could be done to improve Bob's future job perfor-

The Great Management History Debate

Preparation

Consider the question "What is the best thing a manager can do to improve productivity in her or his work unit?"

Instructions

The instructor will assign you, individually or in a group, to one of the following positions. Complete the missing information as if you were the management theorist referred to. Be prepared to argue and defend your position before the class.

• Position A: "Mary Parker Follett offers the best insight into the question. Her advice would be to . . . " (advice to be filled in by you or the group).

• Position B: "Max Weber's ideal bureaucracy offers the best insight into the question. His advice would be to . . . " (advice to be filled in by you or the group).

• Position C: "Henri Fayol offers the best insight into the question. His advice would be to . . . " (advice to be filled in by you or the group).

• Position D: "The Hawthorne studies offer the best insight into the question. Elton Mayo's advice would be to . . . " (advice to be filled in by you or the group).

Confronting Ethical Dilemmas

Preparation

Read and indicate your response to each of the situations below.

a. Ron Jones, vice president of a large construction firm, receives in the mail a large envelope marked "personal." It contains a competitor's cost data for a project that both firms will be bidding on shortly. The data are accompanied by a note from one of Ron's subordinates saying: "This is the real thing!" Ron knows that the data could be a major advantage to his firm in preparing a bid that can win the contract. *What should he do?*

b. Kay Smith is one of your top-performing subordinates. She has shared with you her desire to apply for promotion to a new position just announced in a different division of the company. This will be tough on you since recent budget cuts mean you will be unable to replace anyone who leaves, at least for quite some time. Kay knows this and in all fairness has asked your permission before she submits an application. It is rumored that the son of a good friend of your boss is going to apply for the job. Although his credentials are less impressive than Kay's, the likelihood is that he will get the job if she doesn't apply. *What will you do?*

c. Marty Jose got caught in a bind. She was pleased to represent her firm as head of the local community development committee. In fact, her supervisor's boss once held this position and told her in a hallway conversation, "Do your best and give them every support possible." Going along with this, Marty agreed to pick up the bill (several hundred dollars) for a dinner meeting with local civic and business leaders. Shortly thereafter, her supervisor informed everyone that the entertainment budget was being eliminated in a cost-saving effort. Marty, not wanting to renege on supporting the community development committee, was able to charge the dinner bill to an advertising budget. Eventually, an internal auditor discovered the mistake and reported it to you, the personnel director. Marty is scheduled to meet with you in a few minutes. *What will you do?*

Instructions

Working alone, make the requested decisions in each of these incidents. Think carefully about your justification for the decision. Meet in a group assigned by your instructor. Share your decisions and justifications in each case with other group members. Listen to theirs. Try to reach a group consensus on what to do in each situation and why. Be prepared to share the group decisions, and any dissenting views, in general class discussion.

What Do You Value in Work?

Preparation

Rank order the nine items in terms of how important (9 = most important) they would be to you in a job.

How important is it to you to have a job that:
___ Is repsected by other people?
___ Encourages continued development of knowledge and skills?
___ Provides job security?
___ Provides a feeling of accomplishment?
___ Provides the opportunity to earn a high income?
___ Is intellectually stimulating?
___ Rewards good performance with recognition?

___ Provides comfortable working conditions?

___ Permits advancement to high administrative responsibility?

Instructions

Form into groups as designated by your instructor. Within each group, the *men in the group* will meet to develop a consensus ranking of the items as they think the *women* in the Beutell and Brenner survey ranked them. The reasons for the rankings should be shared and discussed so they are clear to everyone. The *women in the group* should not participate in this ranking task. They should listen to the discussion and be prepared to comment later in class discussions. A spokesperson for the men in the group should share the group's rankings with the class.

Optional Instructions

Form into groups as designated by your instructor but with each group consisting entirely of men or women. Each group should meet and decide which of the work values members of the *opposite* sex ranked first in the Beutell and Brenner survey. Do this again for the work value ranked last. The reasons should be discussed, along with the reasons why each of the other values probably was not ranked first . . . or last. A spokesperson for each group should share group results with the rest of the class.

Source: Adapted from Roy J. Lewicki, Donald D. Bowen, Douglas T. Hall, and Francine S. Hall, *Experiences in Management and Organizational Behavior,* 3rd ed. (New York: Wiley, 1988), pp.23–26. Used by permission.

EXERCISE 8

Which Organizational Culture Fits You?

Instructions

Indicate which one of the following organizational cultures you feel most comfortable working in.

1. A culture that values talent, entrepreneurial activity, and performance over commitment; one that offers large financial rewards and individual recognition.

2. A culture that stresses loyalty, working for the good of the group, and getting to know the right people; one that believes in "generalists" and step-by-step career progress.

3. A culture that offers little job security; one that operates with a survival mentality, stresses that every individual can make a difference, and focuses attention on "turnaround" opportunities.

4. A culture that values long-term relationships; one that emphasizes systematic career development, regular training, and advancement based on gaining functional expertise.

Interpretation

These labels identify the four different cultures: 1 = "the baseball team," 2 = "the club," 3 = "the fortress," and 4 = "the academy."

Discuss results in work groups assigned by your instructor. To some extent, your future career success may depend on working for an organization in which there is a good fit between you and the prevailing corporate culture. This exercise can help you learn how to recognize various cultures, evaluate how well they can serve your needs, and recognize how they may change with time. A risk taker, for example, may be out of place in a "club" but fit right in with a "baseball team." Someone who wants to seek opportunities wherever they may occur may be out of place in an "academy" but fit right in with a "fortress."

Source: Developed from Carol Hymowitz, "Which Corporate Culture Fits You?" *Wall Street Journal* (July 17, 1989), p. B1.

Beating the Time Wasters

Preparation

1. Make a list of all the things you need to do tomorrow. Prioritize each item in terms of *how important it is to create outcomes that you can really value.* Use this classification scheme:

(A) Most important, top priority
(B) Important, not top priority
(C) Least important, low priority

Look again at all activities you have classified as B. Reclassify any that are really A's or C's. Look at your list of A's. Reclassify any that are really B's or C's. Double-check to make sure you are comfortable with your list of C's.

2. Make a list of all the "time wasters" that often interfere with your ability to accomplish everything you want to on any given day.

Instructions

Form into groups as assigned by the instructor. Have all group members share their lists and their priority classifications. Members should politely "challenge" each other's classifications to make sure that only truly "high-priority" items receive an A rating. They might also suggest that some C items are of such little consequence that they might not be worth doing at all. After each member of the group revises his or her "to do" list based on this advice, go back and discuss the time wasters identified by group members. Develop a master list of time wasters and what to do about them. Have a group spokesperson be prepared to share discussion highlights and tips on beating common time wasters with the rest of the class.

Source: Developed from Roy J. Lewicki, Donald D. Bowen, Douglas T. Hall, and Francine S. Hall, *Experiences in Management and Organizational Behavior*, 3rd ed. (New York: Wiley, 1988), pp. 314–16.

Personal Career Planning

Preparation

Complete the following three activities, and bring the results to class. Your work should be in a written form suitable for your instructor's review.

Step 1: *Strengths and Weaknesses Inventory* Different occupations require special talents, abilities, and skills if people are to excel in their work. Each of us, you included, has a repertoire of existing strengths and weaknesses that are "raw materials" we presently offer a potential employer. Of course, actions can (and should!) be taken over time to further develop current strengths and to turn weaknesses into strengths. Make a list identifying your most important strengths and weaknesses at the moment in relation to the career direction you are most likely to pursue upon graduation. Place a * next to each item you consider most important to address in your courses and student activities *before* graduation.

Step 2. *Five-Year Career Objectives* Make a list of 3 to 5 career objectives that are appropriate given your list of personal strengths and weaknesses. Limit these objectiveness to ones that can be accomplished within 5 years of graduation.

Step 3. *Five-Year Career Action Plans* Write a specific action plan for accomplishing each of the 5 objectives. State exactly what you will do, and by when, in order to meet each objective. If you will need special support or assistance, identify it *and* state how you will obtain it. Remember, an outside observer should be able to read your action plan for each objective and end up feeling confident that (a) he or she knows exactly what you are going to do and (b) why.

Instructions

Form into groups as assigned by the instructor. Share your career-planning analysis with the group; listen to those of others. Participate in a discussion that examines any common patterns and major differences among group members. Take advantage of any opportunities to gather feedback and advice from others. Have one group member be prepared to summarize the group discussion for the class as a whole. Await further class discussion led by the instructor.

Source: Developed in part from Roy J. Lewicki, Donald D. Bowen, Douglas T. Hall, and Francine S. Hall, *Experiences in Management and Organizational Behavior,* 3rd ed. (New York: Wiley, 1988), pp. 261–67. Used by permission.

EXERCISE 11

Decision-Making Biases

Instructions

How good are you at avoiding potential decision-making biases? Test yourself by answering the following questions:

1. Which is riskier:
(a) driving a car on a 400-mile trip?
(b) flying on a 400-mile commercial airline flight?

2. Are there more words in the English language:
(a) that begin with *r*?
(b) that have *r* as the third letter?

3. Mark is finishing his MBA at a prestigious university. He is very interested in the arts and at one time considered a career as a musician. Is Mark more likely to take a job:
(a) in the management of the arts?
(b) with a management consulting firm?

4. You are about to hire a new central-region sales director for the fifth time this year. You predict that the next director should work out reasonably well since the last four were "lemons" and the odds favor hiring at least one good sales director in five tries. Is this thinking
(a) correct?
(b) incorrect?

5. A newly hired engineer for a computer firm in the Boston metropolitan area has 4 years' experience and good all-round qualifications. When asked to estimate the starting salary for this employee, a chemist with very little knowledge about the profession or industry guessed an annual salary of $35,000. What is your estimate?
$ ___ per year

Scoring

Your instructor will provide answers and explanations for the assessment questions.

Interpretation

Each of the preceding questions examines your tendency to use a different judgmental heuristic. In his book *Judgment in Managerial Decision Making,* 3rd ed. (New York: Wiley, 1994), pp. 6-7, Max Bazerman calls these heuristics "simplifying strategies, or rules of thumb" used in making decisions. He states, "In general, heuristics are helpful, but their use can sometimes lead to severe errors. . . . If we can make managers aware of the potential adverse impacts of using heruistics, they can then decide when and where to use them." This assessment offers an initial insight into your use of such heuristics. An informed decision maker understands the heuristics, is able to recognize when they appear, and eliminates any that may inappropriately bias decision making.

Test yourself further. Write next to each item the name of the judgmental heuristic that you think applies (see Chapter 7).

Source: Incidents from Max H. Bazerman, *Judgment in Managerial Decision Making,* 3rd ed. (New York: Wiley, 1994), pp. 13–14. Used by permission.

Strategic Scenarios

Preparation

In today's turbulent environments, it is no longer safe to assume that an organization that was highly successful yesterday will continue to be so tomorrow—or that it will even be in existence. Changing times exact the best from strategic planners. Think about the situations currently facing the following well-known organizations. Think, too, about the futures they may face.

McDonald's
Apple Computer
Yahoo.com
L.L. Bean
Delta Airlines
National Public Radio

Instructions

Form into groups as assigned by your instructor. Choose one or more organizations from the prior list (as assigned) and answer for the organization the following questions:

1. What in the future might seriously threaten the success, perhaps the very existence, of this organization? (As a group develop at least three such *future scenarios*.)

2. Estimate the probability (0 to 100 percent) of each future scenario occurring.

3. Develop a strategy for each scenario that will enable the organization to successfully deal with it.

Thoroughly discuss these questions within the group and arrive at your best possible consensus answers. Be prepared to share and defend your answers in general class discussion.

Source: Suggested by an exercise in John F. Veiga and John N. Yanouzas, *The Dynamics of Organization Theory: Gaining a Macro Perspective* (St. Paul, MN: West, 1979), pp. 69–71.

The MBO Contract

Listed below are performance objectives from an MBO contract for a plant manager.

a. To increase deliveries to 98% of all scheduled delivery dates

b. To reduce waste and spoilage to 3% of all raw materials used

c. To reduce lost time due to accidents to 100 work days/year

d. To reduce operating cost to 10% below budget

e. To install a quality-control system at a cost of less than $53,000

f. To improve production scheduling and increase machine utilization time to 95% capacity

g. To complete a management development program this year

h. To teach a community college course in human resource management

1. Study this MBO contract. In the margin write one of the following symbols to identify each objective as an improvement, maintenance, or personal development objective.

  I = Improvement objective

M = Maintenance objective

  P = Personal development objective

2. Assume that this MBO contract was actually developed and implemented under the following circumstances. After each statement, write "yes" if the statement reflects proper MBO procedures and write "no" if it reflects poor MBO procedures.

(a) The president drafted the 8 objectives and submitted them to Atkins for review.

(b) The president and Atkins thoroughly discussed the 8 objectives in proposal form before they were finalized.

(c) The president and Atkins scheduled a meeting in 6 months to review Atkins's progress on the objectives.

(d) The president didn't discuss the objectives with Atkins again until the scheduled meeting was held.

(e) The president told Atkins his annual raise would depend entirely on the extent to which these objectives were achieved.

3. Share and discuss your responses to parts 1 and 2 of the exercise with a nearby classmate. Reconcile any differences of opinion by referring back to the chapter discussion of MBO. Await further class discussion.

EXERCISE 14

The Future Workplace

Instructions

Form groups as assigned by the instructor. Brainstorm to develop a master list of the major characteristics you expect to find in the future workplace in the year 2020. Use this list as background for completing the following tasks:

1. Write a one-paragraph description of what the typical "Workplace 2020 *manager's"* workday will be like.

2. Draw a "picture" representing what the "Workplace 2020 organization" will look like.

Choose a spokesperson to share your results with the class as a whole *and* explain their implications for the class members.

EXERCISE 15

Dots and Squares Puzzle

1. Shown here is a collection of 16 dots. Study the figure to determine how many "squares" can be created by connecting the dots.

2. Draw as many squares as you can find in the figure while making sure a dot is at every corner of every square. Count the squares and write this number in the margin to the right of the figure.

3. Share your results with those of a classmate sitting nearby. Indicate the location of squares missed by either one of you.

4. Based on this discussion, redraw your figure to show the maximum number of possible squares. Count them and write this number to the left of the figure.

5. Await further class discussion led by your instructor.

Leading Through Participation

Preparation

Read each of the following vignettes. Write in the margin whether you think the leader should handle the situation with an individual decision (I), consultative decision (C), or group decision (G).

Vignette I

You are a general supervisor in charge of a large team laying an oil pipeline. It is now necessary to estimate your expected rate of progress in order to schedule material deliveries to the next field site. You know the nature of the terrain you will be traveling and have the historical data needed to compute the mean and variance in the rate of speed over the type of terrain. Given these two variables, it is a simple matter to calculate the earliest and latest times at which materials and support facilities will be needed at the next site. It is important that your estimate be reasonably accurate; underestimates result in idle supervisors and workers, and overestimates result in materials being tied up for a period of time before they are to be used. Progress has been good, and your 5 supervisors along with the other members of the gang stand to receive substantial bonuses if the project is completed ahead of schedule.

Vignette II

You are supervising the work of 12 engineers. Their formal training and work experience are very similar, permitting you to use them interchangeably on projects. Yesterday, your manager informed you that a request had been received from an overseas affiliate for 4 engineers to go abroad on extended loan for a period of 6 to 8 months. He argued and you agreed that for a number of reasons this request should be filled from your group. All your engineers are capable of handling this assignment, and from the standpoint of present and future projects there is no particular reason that any one should be retained over any other. The problem is complicated by the fact that the overseas assignment is in what is generally regarded in the company as an undesirable location.

Vignette III

You are the head of a staff unit reporting to the vice president of finance. He has asked you to provide a report on the firm's current portfolio including recommendations for changes in the *selection criteria* currently employed. Doubts have been raised about the efficiency of the existing system in the current market conditions, and there is considerable dissatisfaction with prevailing rates of return. You plan to write the report, but at the moment you are quite perplexed about the approach to take. Your own specialty is the bond market, and it is clear to you that a detailed knowledge of the equity market, which you lack, would greatly enhance the value of the report. Fortunately, 4 members of your staff are specialists in different segments of the equity market. Together, they possess a vast amount of knowledge about the intricacies of investment. However, they seldom agree on the best way to achieve anything when it comes to the stock market. Whereas they are obviously conscientious as well as knowlegeable, they have major differences when it comes to investment philosophy and strategy. The report is due in 6 weeks, You have already begun to familiarize yourself with the firm's current portfolio and have been provided by management with a specific set of constraints that any portfolio must satisfy. Your immediate problem is to come up with some alternatives to the firm's present practices and select the most promising ones for detailed analysis in your report.

Vignette IV

You are on the division manager's staff and work on a wide variety of problems of both an administrative and technical nature. You have been given the assignment of developing a universal method to be used in each of the 5 plants in the division for manually reading equipment registers, recording the readings, and transmitting the scoring to a centralized information system. All plants are located in a relatively small geographical region. Until now there has been a high error rate in the reading and/or transmittal of the data. Some locations have considerably higher error rates than others, and the methods used to record and transmit the data vary between plants. It is probable, therefore, that part of the error variance is a function of specific local conditions rather than anything else, and this will complicate the establishment of any system common to all plants. You have the information on error rates but no information on the local practices that generate these errors or on the local conditions that necessitate the different practices. Everyone would benefit from an improvement in the quality of the data because it is used in a number of important decisions. Your contacts with the plants are through the quality control supervisors responsible for collecting the data. They are a conscientious group committed to doing their jobs well but are highly sensitive to interference on the part of higher management in their own operations. Any solution that does not receive the active support of the various plant supervisors is unlikely to reduce the error rate significantly.

Instructions

Form groups as assigned by the instructor. Share you choices with other group members and try to achieve a consensus on how the leader should best handle each situation. Refer back to the discussion of the Vroom-Jago "leader-participation" theory presented in Chapter 13. Analyze each vignette according to their ideas. Do you come to any different conclusions? If so, why? Nominate a spokesperson to share your results in general class discussion.

Source: Victor H. Vroom and Arthur G. Jago, *The New Leadership* (Englewood Cliffs, NJ: Prentice Hall, 1988). Used by permission.

EXERCISE 17

Work vs. Family—You Be the Judge

1. Read the following situation.

Joanna, a single parent, was hired to work 8:15 A.M. to 5:30 P.M. weekdays selling computers for a firm. Her employer extended her workday until 10 P.M. weekdays and from 8:15 A.M.–5:30 P.M. on Saturdays. Joanna refused to work the extra hours, saying that she had a six-year old son and that so many work hours would lead to neglect. The employer said this was a special request during a difficult period and that all employees needed to share in helping out during the "crunch." Still refusing to work the extra hours, Joanna was fired. She sued the employer.

2. You be the judge in this case. Take an individual position on the following questions:

Should Joanna be allowed to work only the hours agreed to when she was hired? Or is the employer correct in asking all employees, regardless of family status, to work the extra hours? Why?

3. Form into groups as assigned by the instructor. Share your responses to the questions and try to develop a group consensus. Be sure to have a rationale for the position the group adopts. Appoint a spokesperson who can share results with the class. Be prepared to participate in open class discussion.

Source: This case scenario is from Sue Shellenbarger, "Employees Challenge Policies on Family and Get Hard Lessons," *Wall Street Journal* (December 17, 1997), p. B1.

EXERCISE 18

Compensation and Benefits Debate

Preparation

Consider the following quotations.

On compensation: "A basic rule of thumb should be—pay at least as much, and perhaps a bit more, in base wage or salary than what competitors are offering."

On benefits: "When benefits are attractive or at least adequate, the organization is in a better position to employ highly qualified people."

Instructions

Form groups as assigned by the instructor. Each will be given *either* one of the preceding position statements *or* one of the following alternatives.

On compensation: "Given the importance of controlling costs, organizations can benefit by paying as little as possible for labor."

On benefits: "Given the rising cost of health-care and other benefit programs and the increasing difficulty many organizations have staying in business, it is best to minimize paid benefits and let employees handle more of the cost on their own."

Each group should prepare to debate a counterpoint group on its assigned position. After time is allocated to prepare for the debate, each group will present its opening positions. Each will then be allowed one rebuttal period to respond to the other group. General class discussion on the role of compensation and benefits in the modern organization will follow.

EXERCISE 19

Sources and Uses of Power

Preparation

Consider *the way you have behaved* in each of the situations described below. They may be from a full-time or part-time job, student organization or class group, sports team, or whatever. If you do not have an experience of the type described, try to imagine yourself in one; think about how you would expect yourself to behave.

1. You needed to get a peer to do something you wanted that person to do but were worried he or she didn't want to do it.

2. You needed to get a subordinate to do something you wanted her or him to do but were worried the subordinate didn't want to do it.

3. You needed to get your boss to do something you wanted him or her to do but were worried the boss didn't want to do it.

Instructions

Form into groups as assigned by the instructor. Start with situation 1 and have all members of the group share their approaches. Determine what specific sources of power (see Chapter 13) were used. Note any patterns in group members' responses. Discuss what is required to be successful in this situation. Do the same for situations 2 and 3. Note any special differences in how situations 1, 2, and 3 should be or could be handled. Choose a spokesperson to share results in general class discussion.

After Meeting/Project Review

After participating in a meeting or a group project, complete the following assessment.

1. How satisfied are *you* with the outcome of the meeting project?

   Note at all   Totally
   satisfied   satisfied
     1   2   3   4   5   6   7

2. How do you think *other members of the meeting/project group would rate you* in terms of your *influence* on what took place?

   No   Very high
   influence   influence
      1   2   3   4   5   6   7

3. In your opinion, how *ethical* is any decision that was reached.

   Highly   Highly
   *un*ethical   ethical
      1   2   3   4   5   6   7

4. To what extent did you feel "*pushed into*" going along with the decision.

   Not pushed
     into it   Very pushed
     at all   into it
      1   2   3   4   5   6   7

5. How *committed* are *you* to the agreements reached?

   Not at all   Highly
   committed   committed
     1   2   3   4   5   6   7

6. Did you understand what was expected of you as a member of the meeting or project group?

   Not at all   Perfectly
   clear   clear
     1   2   3   4   5   6   7

7. Were participants in the meeting/project group discussions listening to each other?

   Never   Always
     1   2   3   4   5   6   7

8. Were participants in the meeting/project group discussions honest and open in communicating with one another?

   Never   Always
     1   2   3   4   5   6   7

9. Was the meeting/project completed efficiently?

   Not at all   Very much
      1   2   3   4   5   6   7

10. Was the outcome of the meeting/project something that you felt proud to be a part of?

    Not   Very
    at all   much
      1   2   3   4   5   6   7

Instructions

In groups (actual meeting/ project group or as assigned by the instructor) share results and discuss their implications (a) for you, and (b) for the effectiveness of meetings and group project work in general.

Source: Developed from Roy J. Lewicki, Donald D. Bowen, Douglas T. Hall, and Francine S. Hall, *Experiences in Management and Organizational Behavior,* 4th ed. (New York: Wiley, 1997), pp. 195–197.

Why Do We Work?

Preparation

Read the following "ancient story."

In days of old a wandering youth happened upon a group of men working in a quarry. Stopping by the first man, he said, "What are you doing?" The worker grimaced and groaned as he replied, "I am trying to shape this stone, and it is backbreaking work." Moving to the next man, he repeated the question. This man showed little emotion as he answered, "I am shaping a stone for a building." Moving to the third man, our traveler heard him singing as he worked. "What are you doing?" asked the youth. "I am helping to build a cathedral," the man proudly replied.

Instructions

In groups assigned by your instructor, discuss this short story. Ask and answer the question: "What are the lessons of this ancient story for (a) workers and (b) managers of today?" Ask members of the group to role-play each of the stonecutters, respectively, while they answer a second question asked by the youth: "Why are you working?" Have someone in the group be prepared to report and share the group's responses with the class as a whole.

Source: Developed from Brian Dumaine, "Why Do We Work," *Fortune* (December 26, 1994), pp. 196–204.

The Case of the Contingency Workforce

Preparation

Part-time and contingency work is a rising percentage of the total employment in the United States. Go to the library and read about the current use of part-time and contingency workers in business and industry. Ideally, go to the Internet, enter a government database, and locate some current statistics on the size of the contingent labor force, the proportion that is self-employed and part-time, and the proportion of part-timers who are voluntary and involuntary.

Instructions

In your assigned work group, pool the available information on the contingency workforce. Discuss the information. Discuss one another's viewpoints on the subject as well as its personal and social implications. Be prepared to participate in a classroom "dialogue session" in which your group will be asked to role-play one of the following positions:

a. Vice president for human resources of a large discount retailer hiring contingency workers.

b. Owner of a local specialty music shop hiring contingency workers.

c. Recent graduate of your college or university working as a contingency employee at the discount retailer in (a).

d. Single parent with two children in elementary school, working as a contingency employee of the music shop in (b).

The question to be answered by the (a) and (b) groups is "What does the contingency workforce mean to me?" The question to be answered by the (c) and (d) groups is "What does being a contingency worker mean to me?"

The "Best" Job Design

Preparation

Use the left-hand column to rank the following job characteristics in the order most important *to you* (1 = highest to 10 = lowest). Then use the right-hand column to rank them in the order in which you think they are most important *to others*.

___ Variety of tasks   ___
___ Performance feedback   ___
___ Autonomy/freedom in work   ___
___ Working on a team   ___
___ Having responsibility   ___
___ Making friends on the job   ___
___ Doing all of a job, not part   ___
___ Importance of job to others   ___
___ Having resources to do well   ___
___ Flexible work schedule   ___

Instructions

Form work groups as assigned by your instructor. Share your rankings with other group members. Discuss where you have different individual preferences and where your impressions differ from the preferences of others. Are there any major patterns in your group—for either the "personal" or the "other" rankings? Develop group consensus rankings for each column. Designate a spokesperson to share the group rankings and results of any discussion with the rest of the class.

Source: Developed from John M. Ivancevich and Michael T. Matteson, *Organizational Behavior and Management*, 2nd ed. (Homewood, IL: BPI/Irwin, 1990), p. 500. Used by permission.

Upward Appraisal

Instructions

Form into work groups as assigned by the instructor. The instructor will then leave the room. As a group, complete the following tasks:

1. Within each group create a master list of comments, problems, issues, and concerns about the course experience to data that members would like to communicate with the instructor.

2. Select one person from the group to act as spokesperson and give your feedback to the instructor when he or she returns to the classroom.

3. The spokespersons from each group should meet to decide how the room should be physically arranged (placement of tables, chairs, etc.) for the feedback session. This should allow the spokespersons and instructor to communicate while they are being observed by other class members.

4. While the spokespersons are meeting, members remaining in the groups should discuss what they expect to observe during the feedback session.

5. The classroom should be rearranged. The instructor should be invited in.

6. Spokespersons should deliver feedback to the instructor while observers make notes.

7. After the feedback session is complete, the instructor will call on observers for comments, ask the spokespersons for their reactions, and engage the class in general discussion about the exercise and its implications.

Source: Developed from Eugene Owens, "Upward Appraisal: An Exercise in Subordinate's Critique of Superior's Performance," *Exchange: The Organizational Behavior Teaching Journal*, vol. 3 (1978), pp. 41–42.

How to Give, and Take, Criticism

Preparation

The "criticism session" may well be the toughest test of a manager's communication skills. Picture Setting 1—you and a subordinate meeting to review a problem with the subordinate's performance. Now picture Setting 2—you and your boss meeting to review a problem with *your* performance. Both situations require communication skills in giving and receiving feedback. Even the most experienced person can have difficulty, and the situations can end as futile gripe sessions that cause hard feelings. The question is "How can such 'criticism sessions' be handled in a positive manner that encourages improved performance . . . and good feelings?"

Instructions

Form into groups as assigned by the instructor. Focus on either Setting 1 or Setting 2, or both as also assigned by the instructor. First, answer the question from the perspective assigned. Second, develop a series of action guidelines that could best be used to handle situations of this type. Third, prepare and present a mini-management training session to demonstrate the (a) unsuccessful and (b) successful use of these guidelines.

If time permits, outside of class prepare a more extensive management training session that includes a videotape demonstration of your assigned criticism setting being handled first poorly and then very well. Support the videotape with additional written handouts and an oral presentation to help your classmates better understand the communication skills needed to successfully give and take criticism in work settings.

Lost at Sea

Consider This Situation

You are adrift on a private yacht in the South Pacific when a fire of unknown origin destroys the yacht and most of its contents. You and a small group of survivors are now in a large raft with oars. Your location is unclear, but you estimate that you are about 1,000 miles south-southwest of the nearest land. One person has just found in her pockets 5 $1 bills and a packet of matches. Everyone else's pockets are empty. The items at the right are available to you on the raft.

	A	B	C
Sextant	___	___	___
Shaving mirror	___	___	___
5 gallons water	___	___	___
Mosquito netting	___	___	___
1 survival meal	___	___	___
Maps of Pacific Ocean	___	___	___
Flotable seat cushion	___	___	___
2 gallons oil-gas mix	___	___	___
Small transistor radio	___	___	___
Shark repellent	___	___	___
20 square feet black plastic	___	___	___
1 quart 20-proof rum	___	___	___
15 feet nylon rope	___	___	___
24 chocolate bars	___	___	___
Fishing kit	___	___	___

Instructions

1. *Working alone*, rank in Column **A** the 15 items in order of their importance to your survival ("1" is most important and "15" is least important).

2. *Working in an assigned group*, arrive at a "team" ranking of the 15 items and record this ranking in Column **B.** Appoint one person as group spokesperson to report your group rankings to the class.

3. *Do not write in Column **C** until further instructions are provided by your instructor.*

Source: Adapted from "Lost at Sea: A Consensus-Seeking Task," in *The 1975 Handbook for Group Facilitators.* Used with permission of University Associates, Inc.

EXERCISE 27

Work Team Dynamics

Preparation

Think about your course work group, a work group you are involved in for another course, or any other group suggested by the instructor. Indicate how often each of the following statements accurately reflects your experience in the group. Use this scale:

1 = Always 2 = Frequently 3 = Sometimes
4 = Never

___ **1.** My ideas get a fair hearing.

___ **2.** I am encouraged to give innovative ideas and take risks.

___ **3.** Diverse opinions within the group are encouraged.

___ **4.** I have all the responsibility I want.

___ **5.** There is a lot of favoritism shown in the group.

___ **6.** Members trust one another to do their assigned work.

___ **7.** The group sets high standards of performance excellence.

___ **8.** People share and change jobs a lot in the group.

___ **9.** You can make mistakes and learn from them in this group.

___ **10.** This group has good operating rules.

Instructions

Form groups as assigned by your instructor. Ideally, this will be the group you have just rated. Have all group members share their ratings, and make one master rating for the group as a whole. Circle the items over which there are the biggest differences of opinion. Discuss those items and try to find out why they exist. In general, the better a group scores on this instrument, the higher its creative potential. If everyone has rated the same group, make a list of the five most important things members can do to improve its operations in the future. Nominate a spokesperson to summarize the group discussion for the class as a whole.

Source: Adapted from William Dyer, *Team Building,* 2nd ed. (Reading, MA: Addison-Wesley, 1987), pp. 123–125.

EXERCISE 28

Feedback and Assertiveness

Preparation

Indicate the degree of discomfort you would feel in each situation below by circling the appropriate number:

1. high discomfort
2. some discomfort
3. undecided
4. very little discomfort
5. no discomfort

1 2 3 4 5 **1.** Telling an employee who is also a friend that she or he must stop coming to work late.

1 2 3 4 5 **2.** Talking to an employee about his or her performance on the job.

1 2 3 4 5 **3.** Asking an employee if she or he has any comments about your rating of her or his performance.

1 2 3 4 5 **4.** Telling an employee who has problems in dealing with other employees that he or she should do something about it.

1 2 3 4 5 **5.** Responding to an employee who is upset over your rating of his or her performance.

1 2 3 4 5 **6.** An employee's becoming emotional and defensive when you tell her or him about mistakes on the job.

1 2 3 4 5 **7.** Giving a rating that indicates improvement is needed to an employee who has failed to meet minimum requirements of the job.

1 2 3 4 5 **8.** Letting a subordinate talk during an appraisal interview.

1 2 3 4 5 **9.** An employee's challenging you to justify your evaluation in the middle of an appraisal interview.

1 2 3 4 5 **10.** Recommending that an employee be discharged.

1 2 3 4 5 **11.** Telling an employee that you are uncomfortable with the role of having to judge his or her performance.

1 2 3 4 5 **12.** Telling an employee that her or his performance can be improved.

1 2 3 4 5 **13.** Telling an employee that you will not tolerate his or her taking extended coffee breaks.

1 2 3 4 5 **14.** Telling an employee that you will not tolerate her or his making personal telephone calls on company time.

Instructions

Form three-person teams as assigned by the instructor. Identify the 3 behaviors with which they indicate the most discomfort. Then each team member should practice performing these behaviors with another member, while the third member acts as an observer. Be direct, but try to perform the behavior in an appropriate way. Listen to feedback from the observer and try the behaviors again, perhaps with different members of the group. When finished, discuss the exercise overall. Be prepared to participate in further class discussion.

Source: Feedback questionnaire is from Judith R. Gordon, *A Diagnostic Approach to Organizational Behavior.* 3rd ed. (Boston: Allyn & Bacon, 1991), p. 298. Used by permission.

EXERCISE 29

Creative Solutions

Instructions

Complete these 5 tasks while working alone. Be prepared to present and explain your responses in class.

1. Divide the following shape into four pieces of exactly the same size.

2. Without lifting your pencil from the paper, draw no more than 4 lines that cross through all of the following dots.

3. Draw the design for a machine that will turn the pages of your textbook so you can eat a snack while studying.

4. Why would a wheelbarrow ever be designed this way?

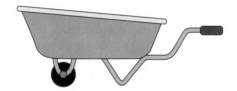

5. Turn the following into words.

(a) ___ program

(b) r\e\a\d\i\n\g

(c) ECNALG

(d)   j
         u
      yousme
         t

(e) stand
      i

Optional Instructions

After working alone, share your responses with a nearby classmate or with a group. See if you can develop different and/or better solutions based on this exchange of ideas.

_____

Source: Ideas 2 and 5 found in Russell L. Ackoff, *The Art of Problem Solving* (New York: Wiley, 1978); ideas 1 and 4 found in Edward De Bono, *Lateral Thinking: Creativity Step by Step* (New York: Harper & Row, 1970); source for 5 is unknown.

EXERCISE 30

Force-Field Analysis

1. Form into your class discussion groups.

2. Review the concept of force-field analysis—the consideration of forces driving in support of a planned change and forces resisting the change.

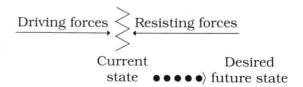

Driving forces ⟩ Resisting forces

Current state ●●●●● › Desired future state

3. Use this force-field analysis worksheet in the assignment:

List of Driving Forces (those supporting the change)

_____   . . . list as many as you can think of

List of Resisting Forces (those working against the change)

_____   . . . list as many as you can think of

4. Apply force-field analysis and make your lists of driving and resisting forces for one of the following situations:

(a) Due to rapid advances in web-based computer technologies, the possibility exists that the course you are presently taking could be in part offered online. This would mean a reduction in the number of required class sessions but an increase in students' responsibility for completing learning activities and assignments through computer mediation.

(b) A new owner has just taken over a small walk-in-and-buy-by-the-slice pizza shop in a college town. There are presently eight employees, three of whom are full-time and five of whom are part-timers. The shop is presently open seven days a week from 10:30 A.M. to 10:30 P.M. each day. The new owner believes there is a market niche available for late-night pizza and would like to stay open each night until 2 A.M.

(c) A situation assigned by the instructor.

5. Choose the three driving forces that are most significant to the proposed change. For each force develop ideas on how it could be further increased or mobilized in support of the change.

6. Choose the three resisting forces that are most significant to the proposed change. For each force develop ideas on how it could be reduced or turned into a driving force.

7. Be prepared to participate in a class discussion led by the instructor.

Self

Assessments

A 21st-Century Manager?

Instructions

Rate yourself on the following personal characteristics. Use this scale.

S = Strong, I am very confident with this one.
G = Good, but I still have room to grow.
W = Weak, I really need work on this one.
U = Unsure, I just don't know.

1. *Resistance to stress:* The ability to get work done even under stressful conditions.

2. *Tolerance for uncertainty:* The ability to get work done even under ambiguous and uncertain conditions.

3. *Social objectivity:* The ability to act free of racial, ethnic, gender, and other prejudices or biases.

4. *Inner work standards:* The ability to personally set and work to high performance standards.

5. *Stamina:* The ability to sustain long work hours.

6. *Adaptability:* The ability to be flexible and adapt to changes.

7. *Self-confidence:* The ability to be consistently decisive and display one's personal presence.

8. *Self-objectivity:* The ability to evaluate personal strengths and weaknesses and to understand one's motives and skills relative to a job.

9. *Introspection:* The ability to learn from experience, awareness, and self-study.

10. *Entrepreneurism:* The ability to address problems and take advantage of opportunities for constructive change.

Scoring

Give yourself 1 point for each S, and 1/2 point for each G. Do not give yourself points for W and U responses. Total your points and enter the result here [PMF = ___].

Interpretation

This assessment offers a self-described *profile of your management foundations (PMF)*.

Are you a perfect 10, or is your PMF score something less than that? There shouldn't be too many 10s around. Ask someone who knows you to assess you on this instrument. You may be surprised at the differences between your PMF score as you described it and your PMF score as described by someone else. Most of us, realistically speaking, must work hard to grow and develop continually in these and related management foundations. This list is a good starting point as you consider where and how to further pursue the development of your managerial skills and competencies. The items on the list are recommended by the American Assembly of Collegiate Schools of Business (AACSB) as the skills and personal characteristics that should be nurtured in college and university students of business administration. Their success— and yours—as 21st-century managers may well rest on (1) an initial awareness of the importance of these basic management foundations and (2) a willingness to strive continually to strengthen them throughout the work career.

Source: See *Outcome Measurement Project,* Phase I and Phase II Reports (St. Louis: American Assembly of Collegiate Schools of Business, 1986 and 1987).

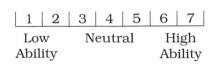

Emotional Intelligence

Instructions

Rate yourself on how well you are able to display the abilities for each item listed below. As you score each item, try to think of actual situations in which you have been called upon to use the ability. Use the following scale.

1	2	3	4	5	6	7
Low Ability		Neutral		High Ability		

1 2 3 4 5 6 7 **1.** Identify changes in physiological arousal.

1 2 3 4 5 6 7 **2.** Relax when under pressure in situations.

1 2 3 4 5 6 7 **3.** Act productively when angry.

1 2 3 4 5 6 7 **4.** Act productively in situations that arouse anxiety.

1 2 3 4 5 6 7 **5.** Calm yourself quickly when angry.

1 2 3 4 5 6 7 **6.** Associate different physical cues with different emotions.

1 2 3 4 5 6 7 **7.** Use internal "talk" to affect your emotional states.

1 2 3 4 5 6 7 **8.** Communicate your feelings effectively.

1 2 3 4 5 6 7 **9.** Reflect on negative feelings without being distressed.

1 2 3 4 5 6 7 **10.** Stay calm when you are the target of anger from others.

1 2 3 4 5 6 7 **11.** Know when you are thinking negatively.

1 2 3 4 5 6 7 **12.** Know when your "self-talk" is instructional.

1 2 3 4 5 6 7 **13.** Know when you are becoming angry.

1 2 3 4 5 6 7 **14.** Know how you interpret events you encounter.

1 2 3 4 5 6 7 **15.** Know what senses you are currently using.

1 2 3 4 5 6 7 **16.** Accurately communicate what you experience.

1 2 3 4 5 6 7 **17.** Identify what information influences your interpretations.

1 2 3 4 5 6 7 **18.** Identify when you experience mood shifts.

1 2 3 4 5 6 7 **19.** Know when you become defensive.

1 2 3 4 5 6 7 **20.** Know the impact your behavior has on others.

1 2 3 4 5 6 7 **21.** Know when you communicate incongruently.

1 2 3 4 5 6 7 **22.** "Gear up" at will.

1 2 3 4 5 6 7 **23.** Regroup quickly after a setback.

1 2 3 4 5 6 7 **24.** Complete long-term tasks in designated time frames.

1 2 3 4 5 6 7 **25.** Produce high energy when doing uninteresting work.

1 2 3 4 5 6 7 **26.** Stop or change ineffective habits.

1 2 3 4 5 6 7 **27.** Develop new and more productive patterns of behavior.

1 2 3 4 5 6 7 **28.** Follow words with actions.

1 2 3 4 5 6 7 **29.** Work out conflicts.

1 2 3 4 5 6 7 **30.** Develop consensus with others.

1 2 3 4 5 6 7 **31.** Mediate conflict between others.

1 2 3 4 5 6 7 **32.** Exhibit effective interpersonal communication skills.

1 2 3 4 5 6 7 **33.** Articulate the thoughts of a group.

1 2 3 4 5 6 7 **34.** Influence others, directly or indirectly.

1 2 3 4 5 6 7 **35.** Build trust with others.

1 2 3 4 5 6 7 **36.** Build support teams.

1 2 3 4 5 6 7 **37.** Make others feel good.

1 2 3 4 5 6 7 **38.** Provide advice and support to others, as needed.

1 2 3 4 5 6 7 **39.** Accurately reflect people's feelings back to them.

1 2 3 4 5 6 7 **40.** Recognize when others are distressed.

1 2 3 4 5 6 7 **41.** Help others manage their emotions.

1 2 3 4 5 6 7 **42.** Show empathy to others.

1 2 3 4 5 6 7 **43.** Engage in intimate conversations with others.

1 2 3 4 5 6 7 **44.** Help a group to manage emotions.

1 2 3 4 5 6 7 **45.** Detect incongruence between others' emotions or feelings and their behaviors.

Scoring

This instrument measures six dimensions of your emotional intelligence. Find your scores as follows.

Self-awareness—Add scores for items 1, 6, 11, 12, 13, 14, 15, 16, 17, 18, 19, 20, 21
Managing emotions—Add scores for items 1, 2, 3, 4, 5, 7, 9, 10, 13, 27
Self-motivation—Add scores for items 7, 22, 23, 25, 26, 27, 28
Relating well—Add scores for items 8, 10, 16, 19, 20, 29, 30, 31, 32, 33, 34, 35, 36, 37, 38, 39, 42, 43, 44, 45
Emotional mentoring—Add scores for items 8, 10, 16, 18, 34, 35, 37, 38, 39, 40, 41, 44, 45

Interpretation

The prior scoring indicates your self-perceived abilities in these dimensions of emotional intelligence. To further examine your tendencies, go back for each dimension and sum the number of responses you had that were 4 and lower (suggesting lower ability), and sum the number of responses you had that were 5 or better (suggesting higher ability). This gives you an indication by dimension of where you may have room to grow and develop your emotional intelligence abilities.

Source: Scale from Hendrie Weisinger, *Emotional Intelligence at Work* (San Francisco: Jossey-Bass, 1998), pp. 214–15. Used by permission.

ASSESSMENT 3

Learning Tendencies

Instructions

In each of the following pairs, distribute 10 points between the two statements to best describe how you like to learn. For example:

___3___ (a) I like to read.
___7___ (b) I like to listen to lectures.

1. _____ (a) I like to learn through working with other people and being engaged in concrete experiences.

_____ (b) I like to learn through logical analysis and systematic attempts to understand a situation.

2. _____ (a) I like to learn by observing things, viewing them from different perspectives, and finding meaning in situations.

_____ (b) I like to learn by taking risks, getting things done, and influencing events through actions taken.

Scoring

Place "dots" on the following graph to record the above scores: "Doing" = 2b. "Watching" = 1b. "Feeling" = 1a. "Thinking" = 2a. Connect the dots to plot your learning tendencies.

Interpretation

This activity provides a first impression of your learning tendencies or style. Four possible learning styles are identified on the graph—convergers, accommodators, divergers, and assimilators. Consider the following descriptions for their accuracy in describing you. For a truly good reading on your learning tendencies, ask several others to com-

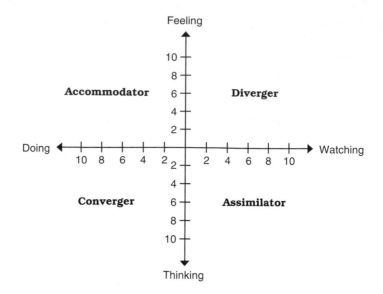

plete the Step 1 questions for you, and then assess how their results compare with your own perceptions.

Convergers—combined tendencies toward abstract conceptualization (thinking) and active experimentation (doing). They like to learn in practical situations. They prefer to deal with technical issues and solve problems through systematic investigation of alternatives. Good at experimentation, finding new ways of doing things, making decisions.

Accommodators—combine concrete experience (feeling) with active experimentation (doing). They like to learn from hands-on experience. They prefer "gut" responses to problems rather than systematic analysis of alternatives. Good at influencing others, committing to goals, seeking opportunities.

Divergers—combine concrete experience (feeling) with reflective observation (watching). They like to learn from observation. They prefer to participate in brainstorming and imaginative information gathering. Good at listening, imagining, and being sensitive to feelings.

Assimilators—combine abstract conceptualization (thinking) with reflective observation (watching). They like to learn through information. They prefer ideas and concepts to people and value logical reasoning. Good at organizing information, building models, and analyzing data.

Source: Developed from David A. Kolb, "Learning Style Inventory" (Boston, MA: McBer & Company, 1985); see also his article "On Management and the Learning Process," in David A. Kolb, Irwin M. Rubin, and James M. McIntyre, eds., *Organizational Psychology: A Book of Readings,* 2nd ed. (Englewood Cliffs, NJ: Prentice-Hall, 1974), pp. 27–42.

ASSESSMENT 4

What Are Your Managerial Assumptions?

Instructions

Read the following statements. Use the space in the margins to write "Yes" if you agree with the statement, or "No" if you disagree with it.

Force yourself to take a "yes" or "no" position. Do this for every statement.

1. Are good pay and a secure job enough to satisfy most workers?

2. Should a manager help and coach subordinates in their work?

3. Do most people like real responsibility in their jobs?

4. Are most people afraid to learn new things in their jobs?

5. Should managers let subordinates control the quality of their work?

6. Do most people dislike work?

7. Are most people creative?

8. Should a manager closely supervise and direct the work of subordinates?

9. Do most people tend to resist change?

10. Do most people work only as hard as they have to?

11. Should workers be allowed to set their own job goals?

12. Are most people happiest off the job?

13. Do most workers really care about the organization they work for?

14. Should a manager help subordinates advance and grow in their jobs?

Scoring

Count the number of "yes" responses to items 1, 4, 6, 8, 9, 10, 12; write that number here as [X = ___]. Count the number of "yes" responses to items 2, 3, 5, 7, 11, 13, 14; write that score here [Y = ___].

Interpretation

This assessment sheds insight into your orientation toward Douglas McGregor's Theory X (your "X" score) and Theory Y (your "Y" score) assumptions. You should review the discussion of McGregor's thinking in Chapter 2 and consider further the ways in which you are likely to behave toward other people at work. Think, in particular, about the types of "self-fulfilling prophecies" you are likely to create.

ASSESSMENT 5

Terminal Values Survey

Instructions

Rate each of the following values in terms of its importance to you. Think about each value *in terms of its importance as a guiding principle in your life.* As you work, consider each value in relation to all the other values listed in the survey.

Terminal Values

1. A comfortable life

1	2	3	4	5	6	7
Of lesser importance				Of greater importance		

2. An exciting life

1	2	3	4	5	6	7
Of lesser importance				Of greater importance		

3. A sense of accomplishment

1	2	3	4	5	6	7
Of lesser importance				Of greater importance		

4. A world at peace

1	2	3	4	5	6	7

Of lesser importance   Of greater importance

5. A world of beauty

1	2	3	4	5	6	7

Of lesser importance   Of greater importance

6. Equality

1	2	3	4	5	6	7

Of lesser importance   Of greater importance

7. Family security

1	2	3	4	5	6	7

Of lesser importance   Of greater importance

8. Freedom

1	2	3	4	5	6	7

Of lesser importance   Of greater importance

9. Happiness

1	2	3	4	5	6	7

Of lesser importance   Of greater importance

10. Inner harmony

1	2	3	4	5	6	7

Of lesser importance   Of greater importance

11. Mature love

1	2	3	4	5	6	7

Of lesser importance   Of greater importance

12. National security

1	2	3	4	5	6	7

Of lesser importance   Of greater importance

13. Pleasure

1	2	3	4	5	6	7

Of lesser importance   Of greater importance

14. Salvation

1	2	3	4	5	6	7

Of lesser importance   Of greater importance

15. Self-respect

1	2	3	4	5	6	7

Of lesser importance   Of greater importance

16. Social recognition

1	2	3	4	5	6	7

Of lesser importance   Of greater importance

17. True friendship

1	2	3	4	5	6	7

Of lesser importance   Of greater importance

18. Wisdom

1	2	3	4	5	6	7

Of lesser importance   Of greater importance

Interpretation

Terminal values reflect a person's preferences concerning the "ends" to be achieved. They are the goals individuals would like to achieve in their lifetimes.

Different value items receive different weights in this scale. (Example: "A comfortable life" receives a weight of "5" while "Freedom" receives a weight of "1.") Your score on Personal Values has your Social Values score subtracted from it to determine your Terminal Values score.

Scoring

To score this instrument, you must multiply your score for each item times a "weight"—e.g. (#3 × 5) = your new question 3 score.

1. Calculate your Personal Values Score as: (#1 × 5) + (#2 × 4) + (#3 × 4) + (#7) + (#8) + (#9 × 4) + (#10 × 5) + (#11 × 4) + (#13 × 5) + (#14 × 3) + (#15 × 5) + (#16 × 3) + (#17 × 4) + (#18 × 5)

2. Calculate your Social Values Score as: (#4 × 5) + (#5 × 3) + (#6 × 5) + (#12 × 5)

3. Calculate your Terminal Values Score as: Personal Values − Social Values

---

Source: Adapted from James Weber, "Management Value Orientations: A Typology and Assessment," *International Journal of Value Based Management*, vol. 3, no. 2 (1990), pp. 37–54.

- - - - - - - - - - - - **ASSESSMENT 6** -

Instrumental Values Survey

Instructions

Rate each of the following values in terms of its importance to you. Think about each value *in terms of its importance as a guiding principle in your life*. As you work, consider each value in relation to all the other values listed in the survey.

Instrumental Values

1. Ambitious	1	2	3	4	5	6	7
	Of lesser importance				Of greater importance		
2. Broadminded	1	2	3	4	5	6	7
	Of lesser importance				Of greater importance		
3. Capable	1	2	3	4	5	6	7
	Of lesser importance				Of greater importance		

4. Cheerful

1	2	3	4	5	6	7
Of lesser importance				Of greater importance		

5. Clean

1	2	3	4	5	6	7
Of lesser importance				Of greater importance		

6. Courageous

1	2	3	4	5	6	7
Of lesser importance				Of greater importance		

7. Forgiving

1	2	3	4	5	6	7
Of lesser importance				Of greater importance		

8. Helpful

1	2	3	4	5	6	7
Of lesser importance				Of greater importance		

9. Honest

1	2	3	4	5	6	7
Of lesser importance				Of greater importance		

10. Imaginative

1	2	3	4	5	6	7
Of lesser importance				Of greater importance		

11. Independent

1	2	3	4	5	6	7
Of lesser importance				Of greater importance		

12. Intellectual

1	2	3	4	5	6	7
Of lesser importance				Of greater importance		

13. Logical

1	2	3	4	5	6	7
Of lesser importance				Of greater importance		

14. Loving

1	2	3	4	5	6	7
Of lesser importance				Of greater importance		

15. Obedient

1	2	3	4	5	6	7
Of lesser importance				Of greater importance		

16. Polite

1	2	3	4	5	6	7
Of lesser importance				Of greater importance		

17. Responsible

1	2	3	4	5	6	7
Of lesser importance				Of greater importance		

18. Self-controlled

1	2	3	4	5	6	7
Of lesser importance				Of greater importance		

Interpretation

Instrumental Values are defined as the "means" for achieving desired ends. They represent how you might go about achieving your important end states, depending on the relative importance you attach to the instrumental values.

Different value items receive different weights in this scale. (Example: "Ambitious" receives a weight of "5" while "Obedient" receives a weight of "1.") Your score on Competence Values has your Moral Values score subtracted from it to determine your Instrumental Values score.

Scoring

To score this instrument, you must multiply your score for each item times a "weight"—e.g. (#3 $\times$ 5) = your new question 3 score.

1. Calculate your Competence Values Score as: (#1 $\times$ 5) + (#2 $\times$ 2) + (#3 $\times$ 5) + (#10 $\times$ 5) + (#11 $\times$ 5) + (#12 $\times$ 5) + (#13 $\times$ 5) + (#17 $\times$ 4)

2. Calculate your Moral Values Score as: (#4 $\times$ 4) + (#5 $\times$ 3) + (#6 $\times$ 2) + (#7 $\times$ 5) + (#8 $\times$ 5) + (#9 $\times$ 2) + (#14 $\times$ 5) + (#15) + (#16 $\times$ 3)

3. Calculate your Instrumental Values Score as: Competence Values– Moral Values

Source: Adapted from James Weber, "Management Value Orientations: A Typology and Assessment," *International Journal of Value Based Management*, vol. 3, no. 2 (1990), pp. 37–54.

ASSESSMENT 7

Diversity Awareness

Instructions

Complete the following questionnaire.

Diversity Awareness Checklist

Consider where you work or go to school as the setting for the following questions. Indicate "O" for often, "S" for sometimes, and "N" for never in response to each of the following questions as they pertain to the setting.

___ **1.** How often have you heard jokes or remarks about other people that you consider offensive?

___ **2.** How often do you hear men "talk down" to women in an attempt to keep them in an inferior status?

___ **3.** How often have you felt personal discomfort as the object of sexual harassment?

___ **4.** How often do you work or study with African Americans or Hispanics?

___ **5.** How often have you felt disadvantaged because members of ethnic groups other than yours were given special treatment?

___ **6.** How often have you seen a woman put in an uncomfortable situation because of unwelcome advances by a man?

___ **7.** How often does it seem that African Americans, Hispanics, Caucasians, women, men, and members of other minority demographic groups seem to "stick together" during work breaks or other leisure situations?

___ **8.** How often do you feel uncomfortable about something you did and/or said to someone of the opposite sex or a member of an ethnic or racial group other than yours?

___ **9.** How often do you feel efforts are made in this setting to raise the level of cross-cultural understanding among people who work and/or study together?

___ **10.** How often do you step in to communicate concerns to others when you feel actions and/or words are used to the disadvantage of minorities?

Scoring

There are no correct answers for the Diversity Awareness Checklist.

Interpretation

In the diversity checklist, the key issue is the extent to which you are "sensitive" to diversity issues in the workplace or university. Are you comfortable with your responses? How do you think others in your class responded? Why not share your responses with others and examine different viewpoints on this important issue?

Source: Items for the WV Cultural Awareness Quiz selected from a longer version by James P. Morgan, Jr., and published by University Associates, 1987. Used by permission.

ASSESSMENT 8

Global Readiness Index

Instructions

Rate yourself on each of the following items to establish a baseline measurement of your readiness to participate in the global work environment.

Rating Scale

1 = Very Poor
2 = Poor
3 = Acceptable
4 = Good
5 = Very Good

___ **1.** I understand my own culture in terms of its expectations, values, and influence on communication and relationships.

___ **2.** When someone presents me with a different point of view, I try to understand it rather than attack it.

___ **3.** I am comfortable dealing with situations where the available information is incomplete and the outcomes unpredictable.

___ **4.** I am open to new situations and am always looking for new information and learning opportunities.

___ **5.** I have a good understanding of the attitudes and perceptions toward my culture as they are held by people from other cultures.

___ **6.** I am always gathering information about other countries and cultures and trying to learn from them.

___ **7.** I am well informed regarding the major differences in government, political, and economic systems around the world.

___ **8.** I work hard to increase my understanding of people from other cultures.

___ **9.** I am able to adjust my communication style to work effectively with people from different cultures.

___ **10.** I can recognize when cultural differences are influencing working relationships and adjust my attitudes and behavior accordingly.

Interpretation

To be successful in the 21st-century work environment, you must be comfortable with the global economy and the cultural diversity that it holds. This requires a *global mindset* that is receptive to and respectful of cultural differences, *global knowledge* that includes the continuing quest to know and learn more about other nations and cultures, and *global work skills* that allow you to work effectively across cultures.

Scoring

The goal is to score as close to a perfect "5" as possible on each of the three dimensions of global readiness. Develop your scores as follows.

Items $(1 + 2 + 3 + 4)/4$
= ___ Global Mindset Score
Items $(5 + 6 + 7)/3$
= ___ Global Knowledge Score
Items $(8 + 9 + 10)/3$
= ___ Global Work Skills Score

_____

Source: Developed from "Is Your Company Really Global?", *Business Week* (December 1, 1997).

ASSESSMENT 9

Time Orientation

Instructions

This instrument examines your tendencies to favor "monochronic" or "polychronic" time orientations. Rate your tendencies for each item below using the following scale.

Rating Scale:

1 = Almost never   2 = Seldom
3 = Sometimes   4 = Usually
       5 = Almost always

___ **1.** I like to do one thing at a time.

___ **2.** I have a strong tendency to build lifetime relationships.

___ **3.** I concentrate on the job at hand.

___ **4.** I base the level of promptness on the particular relationship.

___ **5.** I take time commitments (deadlines, schedules) seriously.

___ **6.** I borrow and lend things often and easily.

___ **7.** I am committed to the job.

___ **8.** Intimacy with family and friends is more important than respecting their privacy.

___ **9.** I adhere closely to plans.

___ **10.** I put obligations to family and friends before work concerns.

___ **11.** I am concerned about not disturbing others (follow rules of privacy).

___ **12.** I change plans often and easily.

___ **13.** I emphasize promptness in meetings.

___ **14.** I am committed to people and human relationships.

___ **15.** I show great respect for private property (seldom borrow or lend).

___ **16.** I am highly distractible and frequently interrupt what I am doing.

___ **17.** I am comfortable with short-term relationships.

___ **18.** I like to do many things at once.

Scoring

To obtain your *monochronic time orientation* score, sum results for items 1, 3, 5, 7, 9, 11, 13, 15, 17. To obtain your *polychronic time orientation* score, sum results for items 2, 4, 6, 8, 10, 12, 14, 16, 18.

Interpretation

A person high in monochronic time orientation approaches time in a linear fashion with things dealt with one at a time in an orderly fashion. Time is viewed as a precious commodity, not to be wasted; this person values punctuality and promptness.

A person high in polychronic time orientation tends to do a number of things at once, intertwining them together in a dynamic process that considers changing circumstances. Commitments are viewed as objectives, but capable of adjustment when necessary.

Cultural differences in orientations toward time can be observed. Tendencies toward monochronic time orientation are common to North America and northern European cultures. Tendencies toward polychronic time orientation are common in cultures of the Middle East, Asia, and Latin America.

Source: Adapted from J. Ned Seelye and Alan Seelye-James. *Culture Clash* (Lincolnwood, IL: NTC Business Books, 1996).

- -

ASSESSMENT 10

Entrepreneurship Orientation

Instructions

Answer the following questions.

1. What portion of your college expenses did you earn (or are you earning)?
(a) 50 percent or more
(b) less than 50 percent
(c) none

2. In college, your academic performance was/is
(a) above average.
(b) average.
(c) below average.

3. What is your basic reason for considering opening a business?
(a) I want to make money.
(b) I want to control my own destiny.
(c) I hate the frustration of working for someone else.

4. Which phrase best describes your attitude toward work?
(a) I can keep going as long as I need to; I don't mind working for something I want.
(b) I can work hard for a while, but when I've had enough, I quit.

(c) Hard work really doesn't get you anywhere.

5. How would you rate your organizing skills?
(a) superorganized
(b) above average
(c) average
(d) I do well to find half the things I look for.

6. You are primarily a(n)
(a) optimist.
(b) pessimist.
(c) neither.

7. You are faced with a challenging problem. As you work, you realize you are stuck. You will most likely
(a) give up.
(b) ask for help.
(c) keep plugging; you'll figure it out.

8. You are playing a game with a group of friends. You are most interested in
(a) winning.
(b) playing well.
(c) making sure that everyone has a good time.
(d) cheating as much as possible.

9. How would you describe your feelings toward failure?
(a) Fear of failure paralyzes me.
(b) Failure can be a good learning experience.
(c) Knowing that I might fail motivates me to work even harder.
(d) "Damn the torpedoes! Full speed ahead."

10. Which phrase best describes you?
(a) I need constant encouragement to get anything done.
(b) If someone gets me started, I can keep going.
(c) I am energetic and hard-working—a self-starter.

11. Which bet would you most likely accept?
(a) a wager on a dog race
(b) a wager on a racquetball game in which you play an opponent
(c) Neither. I never make wagers.

12. At the Kentucky Derby, you would bet on
(a) the 100-to-1 long shot.
(b) the odds-on favorite.
(c) the 3-to-1 shot.
(d) none of the above.

Scoring

Give yourself 10 points for each of the following answers: 1a, 2a, 3c, 4a, 5a, 6a, 7c, 8a, 9c, 10c, 11b, 12c; total the scores and enter the results here [I = ___]. Give yourself 8 points for each of the following answers: 3b, 8b, 9b; total the scores and enter the results here [II = ___]. Give yourself 6 points for each of the following answers; 2b, 5b; total the scores and enter the results here [III = ___]. Give yourself 5 points for this answer: 1b; enter the result here [IV = ___]. Give yourself 4 points for this answer: 5c; enter the result here [V = ___]. Give yourself 2 points for each of the following answers: 2c, 3a, 4b, 6c, 9d, 10b, 11a, 12b; total the scores and enter the results here [VI = ___]. Any other scores are worth 0 points. Total your summary scores for I + II + III + IV + V + VI and enter the result here [EP = ___].

Interpretation

This assessment offers an impression of your *entrepreneurial profile*, or EP. It compares your characteristics with those of typical entrepreneurs. Your instructor can provide further information on each question as well as some additional insights into the backgrounds of entrepreneurs. You may locate your EP score on the following grid.

100 + = Entrepreneur extraordinaire
80–99 = Entrepreneur
60–79 = Potential entrepreneur
 0–59 = Entrepreneur in the rough

Source: Instrument adapted from Norman M. Scarborough and Thomas W. Zimmerer, *Effective Small Business Management*, 3rd ed. (Columbus: Merrill, 1991), pp. 26–27. Used by permission.

ASSESSMENT 11

Your Intuitive Ability

Instructions

Complete this survey as quickly as you can. Be honest with yourself. For each question, select the response that most appeals to you.

1. When working on a project, do you prefer to
(a) be told what the problem is but be left free to decide how to solve it?
(b) get very clear instructions about how to go about solving the problem before you start?

2. When working on a project, do you prefer to work with colleagues who are
(a) realistic?
(b) imaginative?

3. Do you most admire people who are
(a) creative?
(b) careful?

4. Do the friends you choose tend to be
(a) serious and hard working?
(b) exciting and often emotional?

5. When you ask a colleague for advice on a problem you have, do you
(a) seldom or never get upset if he or she questions your basic assumptions?
(b) often get upset if he or she questions your basic assumptions?

6. When you start your day, do you
(a) seldom make or follow a specific plan?
(b) usually first make a plan to follow?

7. When working with numbers do you find that you
(a) seldom or never make factual errors?
(b) often make factual errors?

8. Do you find that you
(a) seldom daydream during the day and really don't enjoy doing so when you do it?
(b) frequently daydream during the day and enjoy doing so?

9. When working on a problem, do you
(a) prefer to follow the instructions or rules when they are given to you?
(b) often enjoy circumventing the instructions or rules when they are given to you?

10. When you are trying to put something together, do you prefer to have
(a) step-by-step written instructions on how to assemble the item?
(b) a picture of how the item is supposed to look once assembled?

11. Do you find that the person who irritates you *the most* is the one who appears to be
(a) disorganized?
(b) organized?

12. When an unexpected crisis comes up that you have to deal with, do you
(a) feel anxious about the situation?
(b) feel excited by the challenge of the situation?

Scoring

Total the number of "a" responses circled for questions 1, 3, 5, 6, 11; enter the score here [A = ___]. Total the number of "b" responses for questions 2, 4, 7, 8, 9, 10, 12; enter the score here [B = ___]. Add your "a" and "b" scores and enter the sum here [A + B = ___]. This is your *intuitive score*. The highest possible intuitive score is 12; the lowest is 0.

Interpretation

In his book *Intuition in Organizations* (Newbury Park, CA: Sage, 1989), pp. 10–11, Weston H. Agor states, "Traditional analytical techniques . . . are not as useful as they once were for guiding major decisions. . . . If you hope to be better prepared for tomorrow, then it only seems logical to pay some attention to the use and development of intuitive skills for decision making." Agor developed the preceding survey to help people assess their tendencies to use intuition in decision making. Your score offers a general impression of your strength in this area. It may also suggest a need to further develop your skill and comfort with more intuitive decision approaches.

Source: AIM Survey (El Paso, TX: ENFP Enterprises, 1989). Copyright ©1989 by Weston H. Agor. Used by permission.

ASSESSMENT 12

Assertiveness

Instructions

This instrument measures tendencies toward aggressive, passive, and assertive behaviors in work situations. For each statement below, decide which of the following answers best fits you.

1 = Never true
2 = Sometimes true

3 = Often true
4 = Always true

___ **1.** I respond with more modesty than I really feel when my work is complimented.

___ **2.** If people are rude, I will be rude right back.

___ **3.** Other people find me interesting.

___ **4.** I find it difficult to speak up in a group of strangers.

___ **5.** I don't mind using sarcasm if it helps me make a point.

___ **6.** I ask for a raise when I feel I really deserve it.

___ **7.** If others interrupt me when I am talking, I suffer in silence.

___ **8.** If people criticize my work, I find a way to make them back down.

___ **9.** I can express pride in my accomplishments without being boastful.

___ **10.** People take advantage of me.

___ **11.** I tell people what they want to hear if it helps me get what I want.

___ **12.** I find it easy to ask for help.

___ **13.** I lend things to others even when I don't really want to.

___ **14.** I win arguments by dominating the discussion.

___ **15.** I can express my true feelings to someone I really care for.

___ **16.** When I feel angry with other people, I bottle it up rather than express it.

___ **17.** When I criticize someone else's work, they get mad.

___ **18.** I feel confident in my ability to stand up for my rights.

Scoring

Obtain your scores as follows:

Aggressiveness tendency score—Add items 2, 5, 8, 11, 14, and 17
Passive tendency score—Add items 1, 4, 7, 10, 13, and 16
Assertiveness tendency score—Add items 3, 6, 9, 12, 15, and 18

Interpretation

The maximum score in any single area is 24. The minimum score is 6. Try to find someone who knows you well. Have this person complete the instrument also as it relates to you. Compare his or her impression of you with your own score. What is this telling you about your behavior tendencies in social situations?

_____

Source: From Douglas T. Hall, Donald D. Bowen, Roy J. Lewicki, and Francine S. Hall, *Experiences in Management and Organizational Behavior,* 2nd ed. (New York: Wiley, 1985). Used by permission.

ASSESSMENT 13

Time Management Profile

Instructions

Complete the following questionnaire by indicating "Y" (yes) or "N" (no) for each item. Force yourself to respond yes or no. Be frank and allow your responses to create an accurate picture of how you tend to respond to these kinds of situations.

___ **1.** When confronted with several items of similar urgency and importance, I tend to do the easiest one first.

___ **2.** I do the most important things during that part of the day when I know I perform best.

___ **3.** Most of the time I don't do things someone else can do; I delegate this type of work to others.

___ **4.** Even though meetings without a clear and useful purpose upset me, I put up with them.

___ 5. I skim documents before reading them and don't complete any that offer a low return on my time investment.

___ 6. I don't worry much if I don't accomplish at least one significant task each day.

___ 7. I save the most trivial tasks for that time of day when my creative energy is lowest.

___ 8. My workspace is neat and organized.

___ 9. My office door is always "open"; I never work in complete privacy.

___ 10. I schedule my time completely from start to finish every workday.

___ 11. I don't like "to do" lists, preferring to respond to daily events as they occur.

___ 12. I "block" a certain amount of time each day or week that is dedicated to high-priority activities.

Scoring

Count the number of "Y" responses to items 2, 3, 5, 7, 8, 12. [Enter that score here ___.] Count the number of "N" responses to items 1, 4, 6, 9, 10, 11. [Enter that score here ___.] Add together the two scores.

Interpretation

The higher the total score, the closer your behavior matches recommended time management guidelines. Reread those items where your response did not match the desired one. Why don't they match? Do you have reasons why your behavior in this instance should be different from the recommended time management guideline? Think about what you can do (and how easily it can be done) to adjust your behavior to be more consistent with these guidelines. For further reading, see Alan Lakein, *How to Control Your Time and Your Life* (New York: David McKay, no date), and William Oncken, *Managing Management Time* (Englewood Cliffs, NJ: Prentice Hall, 1984).

Source: Suggested by a discussion in Robert E. Quinn, Sue R. Faerman, Michael P. Thompson, and Michael R. McGrath, *Becoming a Master Manager: A Contemporary Framework* (New York: Wiley, 1990), pp. 75–76.

ASSESSMENT 14

Facts and Inferences

Preparation

Read the following report:

Often, when we listen or speak, we don't distinguish between statements of fact and those of inference. Yet, there are great differences between the two. We create barriers to clear thinking when we treat inferences (guesses, opinions) as if they are facts. You may wish at this point to test your ability to distinguish facts from inferences by taking the accompanying fact-inference test based on those by Haney (1973).

Instructions

Carefully read the following report and the observations based on it. Indicate whether you think the observations are true, false, or doubtful on the basis of the information presented in the report. Write T if the observation is definitely true, F if the observation is definitely false, and ? if the observation may be either true or false. Judge each observation in order. Do not reread the observations after you have indicated your judgment, and do not change any of your answers.

A well-liked college instructor had just completed making up the final examinations and had turned off the lights in the office. Just then a tall, broad figure with dark glasses appeared and demanded the examination. The professor opened the drawer. Everything in the drawer was picked up, and the individual ran down the corridor. The president was notified immediately.

___ **1.** The thief was tall, broad, and wore dark glasses.

___ **2.** The professor turned off the lights.

___ **3.** A tall figure demanded the examination.

___ **4.** The examination was picked up by someone.

___ **5.** The examination was picked up by the professor.

___ **6.** A tall, broad figure appeared after the professor turned off the lights in the office.

___ **7.** The man who opened the drawer was the professor.

___ **8.** The professor ran down the corridor.

___ **9.** The drawer was never actually opened.

___ **10.** Three persons are referred to in this report.

When told to do so by your instructor, join a small work group. Now, help the group complete the same task by making a consensus decision on each item. Be sure to keep a separate record of the group's responses and your original individual responses.

Scoring

Your instructor will read the correct answers. Score both your individual and group responses.

Interpretation

To begin, ask yourself if there was a difference between your answers and those of the group for each item. If so, why? Why do you think people, individually or in groups, may answer these questions incorrectly? Good planning depends on good decision making by the people doing the planning. Being able to distinguish "facts" and understand one's "inferences" are important steps toward improving the planning process. Involving others to help do the same can frequently assist in this process.

Source: Joseph A. Devito, *Messages: Building Interpersonal Communication Skills,* 3rd ed. (New York: HarperCollins, 1996), referencing William Haney, *Communicational Behavior: Text and Cases,* 3rd ed. (Homewood, IL: Irwin, 1973). Reprinted by permission.

ASSESSMENT 15

Empowering Others

Instructions

Think of times when you have been in charge of a group—this could be a full-time or part-time work situation, a student work group, or whatever. Complete the following questionnaire by recording how you feel about each statement according to this scale:

1 = Strongly disagree 2 = Disagree 3 = Neutral 4 = Agree 5 = Strongly agree

When in charge of a group, I find that:

___ **1.** Most of the time other people are too inexperienced to do things, so I prefer to do them myself.

___ **2.** It often takes more time to explain things to others than to just do them myself.

___ **3.** Mistakes made by others are costly, so I don't assign much work to them.

___ **4.** Some things simply should not be delegated to others.

___ **5.** I often get quicker action by doing a job myself.

___ **6.** Many people are good only at very specific tasks and so can't be assigned additional responsibilities.

___ **7.** Many people are too busy to take on additional work.

___ **8.** Most people just aren't ready to handle additional responsibilities.

___ **9.** In my position, I should be entitled to make my own decisions.

Scoring

Total your responses: enter the score here [___].

Interpretation

This instrument gives an impression of your *willingness to delegate.* Possible scores range from 9 to 45. The higher your score, the more willing you appear to be to delegate to others. Willingness to delegate is an important managerial characteristic: It is essential if you—as a manager—are to "empower" others and give them opportunities to assume responsibility and exercise self-control in their work. With the growing importance of empowerment in the new workplace, your willingness to delegate is worth thinking about seriously. Be prepared to share your results and participate in general class discussion.

_____

Source: Questionnaire adapted from L. Steinmetz and R. Todd, *First Line Management,* 4th ed. (Homewood, IL: BPI/Irwin, 1986), pp. 64–67. Used by permission.

ASSESSMENT 16

Turbulence Tolerance Test

Instructions

The following statements were made by a 37-year-old manager in a large, successful corporation. How would you like to have a job with these characteristics? Using the following scale, choose your response to the left of each statement.

0 = This feature would be very unpleasant for me.
1 = This feature would be somewhat unpleasant for me.
2 = I'd have no reaction to this feature one way or another.
3 = This would be enjoyable and acceptable most of the time.
4 = I would enjoy this very much; it's completely acceptable.

___ **1.** I regularly spend 30 to 40 percent of my time in meetings.

___ **2.** Eighteen months ago my job did not exist, and I have been essentially inventing it as I go along.

___ **3.** The responsibilities I either assume or am assigned consistently exceed the authority I have for discharging them.

___ **4.** At any given moment in my job, I have on the average about a dozen phone calls to be returned.

___ **5.** There seems to be very little relation in my job between the quality of my performance and my actual pay and fringe benefits.

___ **6.** About 2 weeks a year of formal management training is needed in my job just to stay current.

___ **7.** Because we have very effective equal employment opportunity (EEO) in my company and because it is thoroughly multinational, my job consistently brings me into close working contact at a professional level with people of many races, ethnic groups and nationalities, and of both sexes.

___ **8.** There is no objective way to measure my effectiveness.

___ **9.** I report to three different bosses for different aspects of my job, and each has an equal say in my performance appraisal.

___ **10.** On average about a third of my time is spent dealing with unexpected emergencies that force all scheduled work to be postponed.

___ **11.** When I have to have a meeting of the people who report to me, it takes my secretary most of a day to find a time when we are all available, and even then, I have yet to have a meeting where everyone is present for the entire meeting.

___ **12.** The college degree I earned in preparation for this type of work is now obsolete, and I probably should go back for another degree.

___ **13.** My job requires that I absorb 100–200 pages of technical materials per week.

___ **14.** I am out of town overnight at least 1 night per week.

___ **15.** My department is so interdependent with several other departments in the company that all distinctions about which departments are responsible for which tasks are quite arbitrary.

___ **16.** In about a year I will probably get a promotion to a job in another division that has most of these same characteristics.

___ **17.** During the period of my employment here, either the entire company or the division I worked in has been reorganized every year or so.

___ **18.** While there are several possible promotions I can see ahead of me, I have no real career path in an objective sense.

___ **19.** While there are several possible promotions I can see ahead of me, I think I have no realistic chance of getting to the top levels of the company.

___ **20.** While I have many ideas about how to make things work better, I have no direct influence on either the business policies or the personnel policies that govern my division.

___ **21.** My company has recently put in an "assessment center" where I and all other managers will be required to go through an extensive battery of psychological tests to assess our potential.

___ **22.** My company is a defendant in an antitrust suit, and if the case comes to trial, I will probably have to testify about some decisions that were made a few years ago.

___ **23.** Advanced computer and other electronic office technology is continually being introduced into my division, necessitating constant learning on my part.

___ **24.** The computer terminal and screen I have in my office can be monitored in my bosses' offices without my knowledge.

Scoring

Add up all of your scores and then divide the total by 24. This is your "Turbulence Tolerance Test" (TTT) score.

Interpretation

This instrument gives an impression of your tolerance for managing in turbulent times—something likely to characterize the world of work well into the new century. In general, the higher your TTT score, the more comfortable you seem to be with turbulence and change—a positive sign.

For comparison purposes, the average TTT scores for some 500 MBA students and young managers was 1.5-1.6. The test's author suggests TTT scores may be interpreted much like a grade point average in which 4.0 is a perfect "A". On this basis, a 1.5 is below a "C"! How did you do?

Source: Peter B. Vail, *Managing as a Performance Art: New Ideas for a World of Chaotic Change* (San Francisco: Jossey-Bass, 1989), pp. 8–9. Used by permission.

Organizational Design Preference

Instructions

In the margin near each item, write the number from the following scale that shows the extent to which the statement accurately describes your views.

5 = strongly agree
4 = agree somewhat
3 = undecided
2 = disagree somewhat
1 = strongly disagree

I prefer to work in an organization where

1. goals are defined by those in higher levels.

2. work methods and procedures are specified.

3. top management makes important decisions.

4. my loyalty counts as much as my ability to do the job.

5. clear lines of authority and responsibility are established.

6. top management is decisive and firm.

7. my career is pretty well planned out for me.

8. I can specialize.

9. my length of service is almost as important as my level of performance.

10. management is able to provide the information I need to do my job well.

11. a chain of command is well established.

12. rules and procedures are adhered to equally by everyone.

13. people accept the authority of a leader's position.

14. people are loyal to their boss.

15. people do as they have been instructed.

16. people clear things with their boss before going over his or her head.

Scoring

Total your scores for all questions. Enter the score here [___].

Interpretation

This assessment measures your preference for working in an organization designed along "organic" or "mechanistic" lines (see Chapter 11). The higher your score (above 64), the more comfortable you are with a mechanistic design; the lower your score (below 48), the more comfortable you are with an organic design. Scores between 48 and 64 can go either way. This organizational design preference represents an important issue in the new workplace. Indications are that today's organizations are taking on more and more organic characteristics. Presumably, those of us who work in them will need to be comfortable with such designs.

Source: John F. Veiga and John N. Yanouzas. *The Dynamics of Organization Theory: Gaining a Macro Perspective* (St. Paul, MN: West, 1979), pp. 158–60. Used by permission.

Are You Cosmopolitan?

Instructions

Answer the following questions.

1. You believe it is the right of the professional to make his or her own decisions about what is to be done on the job.
Strongly disagree 1 2 3 4 5 Strongly agree

2. You believe a professional should stay in an individual staff role regardless of the income sacrifice.
Strongly disagree 1 2 3 4 5 Strongly agree

3. You have no interest in moving up to a top administrative post.
Strongly disagree 1 2 3 4 5 Strongly agree

4. You believe that professionals are better evaluated by professional colleagues than by management.
Strongly disagree 1 2 3 4 5 Strongly agree

5. Your friends tend to be members of your profession.
Strongly disagree 1 2 3 4 5 Strongly agree

6. You would rather be known or get credit for your work outside rather than inside the company.
Strongly disagree 1 2 3 4 5 Strongly agree

7. You would feel better making a contribution to society than to your organization.
Strongly disagree 1 2 3 4 5 Strongly agree

8. Managers have no right to place time and cost schedules on professional contributors.
Strongly disagree 1 2 3 4 5 Strongly agree

Scoring

Add your score for each item to get a total score between 8 and 40.

Interpretation

A "cosmopolitan" identifies with the career profession, and a "local" identifies with the employing organization. A score of 30–40 suggests a "cosmopolitan" work orientation, 10–20 a "local" orientation, and 20–30 a "mixed" orientation.

Source: Developed from Joseph A. Raelin, _The Clash of Cultures, Managers and Professionals_, (Boston: Harvard Business School Press, 1986).

Performance Appraisal Assumptions

Instructions

In each of the following pairs of statements, check off the statement that best reflects your assumptions about performance evaluation.

Performance evaluation is

1. (a) a formal process that is done annually.
(b) an informal process done continuously.

2. (a) a process that is planned for subordinates.
(b) a process that is planned with subordinates.

3. (a) a required organizational procedure.
(b) a process done regardless of requirements.

4. (a) a time to evaluate subordinates' performance.

(b) a time for subordinates to evaluate their manager.

5. (a) a time to clarify standards.
(b) a time to clarify the subordinate's career needs.

6. (a) a time to confront poor performance.
(b) a time to express appreciation.

7. (a) an opportunity to clarify issues and provide direction and control.
(b) an opportunity to increase enthusiasm and commitment.

8. (a) only as good as the organization's forms.
(b) only as good as the manager's coaching skills.

Scoring

There is no formal scoring for this assessment, but there may be a pattern to your responses. Check them again.

Interpretation

In general, the "a" responses represent a more traditional approach to performance appraisal that emphasizes its *evaluation* function. This role largely puts the supervisor in the role of documenting a subordinate's performance for control and administrative purposes. The "b" responses represent a more progressive approach that includes a strong emphasis on the *counseling* or *development* role. Here, the supervisor is concerned with helping the subordinate do better and with learning from the subordinate what he or she needs to be able to do better. There is more of an element of reciprocity in this role. It is quite consistent with new directions and values emerging in today's organizations.

Source: Developed in part from Robert E. Quinn, Sue R. Faerman, Michael P. Thompson, and Michael R. McGrath, *Becoming a Master Manager: A Contemporary Framework* (New York: Wiley, 1990), p. 187. Used by permission.

ASSESSMENT 20

"T-P" Leadership Questionnaire

Instructions

The following items describe aspects of leadership behavior. Respond to each item according to the way you would most likely act if you were the leader of a work group. Circle whether you would most likely behave in the described way: always (A), frequently (F), occasionally (O), seldom (S), or never (N).

A F O S N **1.** I would most likely act as the spokesperson of the group.

A F O S N **2.** I would encourage overtime work.

A F O S N **3.** I would allow members complete freedom in their work.

A F O S N **4.** I would encourage the use of uniform procedures.

A F O S N **5.** I would permit the members to use their own judgment in solving problems.

A F O S N **6.** I would stress being ahead of competing groups.

A F O S N **7.** I would speak as a representative of the group.

A F O S N **8.** I would push members for greater effort.

A F O S N **9.** I would try out my ideas in the group.

A F O S N **10.** I would let the members do their work the way they think best.

A F O S N **11.** I would be working hard for a promotion.

A F O S N **12.** I would tolerate postponement and uncertainty.

A F O S N **13.** I would speak for the group if there were visitors present.

A F O S N **14.** I would keep the work moving at a rapid pace.

A F O S N **15.** I would turn the members loose on a job and let them go to it.

A F O S N **16.** I would settle conflicts when they occur in the group.

A F O S N **17.** I would get swamped by details.

A F O S N **18.** I would represent the group at outside meetings.

A F O S N **19.** I would be reluctant to allow the members any freedom of action.

A F O S N **20.** I would decide what should be done and how it should be done.

A F O S N **21.** I would push for increased performance.

A F O S N **22.** I would let some members have authority which I could otherwise keep.

A F O S N **23.** Things would usually turn out as I had predicted.

A F O S N **24.** I would allow the group a high degree of initiative.

A F O S N **25.** I would assign group members to particular tasks.

A F O S N **26.** I would be willing to make changes.

A F O S N **27.** I would ask the members to work harder.

A F O S N **28.** I would trust the group members to exercise good judgment.

A F O S N **29.** I would schedule the work to be done.

A F O S N **30.** I would refuse to explain my actions.

A F O S N **31.** I would persuade others that my ideas are to their advantage.

A F O S N **32.** I would permit the group to set its own pace.

A F O S N **33.** I would urge the group to beat its previous record.

A F O S N **34.** I would act without consulting the group.

A F O S N **35.** I would ask that group members follow standard rules and regulations.

Interpretation

Score the instrument as follows.

a. Write a "1" next to each of the following items if you scored them as S (seldom) or N (never).
8, 12, 17, 18, 19, 30, 34, 35

b. Write a "1" next to each of the following items if you scored them as A (always) or F (frequently).
1, 2, 3, 4, 5, 6, 7, 9, 10, 11, 13, 14, 15, 16, 20, 21, 22, 23, 24, 25, 26, 27, 28, 29, 31, 32, 33

c. Circle the "1" scores for the following items, and then add them up to get your TOTAL "P" SCORE = ___.
3, 5, 8, 10, 15, 18, 19, 22, 23, 26, 28, 30, 32, 34, 35

d. Circle the "1" scores for the following items, and then add them up to get your TOTAL "T" SCORE = ___.
1, 2, 4, 6, 7, 9, 11, 12, 13, 14, 16, 17, 20, 21, 23, 25, 27, 29, 31, 33

e. Record your scores on the following graph to develop an indication of your tendencies toward task-oriented leadership, people-oriented leadership, and shared leadership. Mark your T and P scores on the appropriate lines, then draw a line between these two points to determine your shared leadership score.

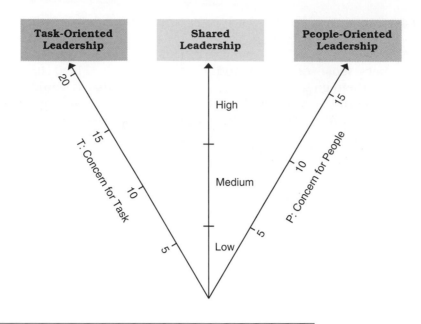

Source: Modified slightly from "T-P Leadership Questionnaire," University Associates, Inc., 1987. Used by permission.

- -

ASSESSMENT 21

"T-T" Leadership Style

Instructions

For each of the following 10 pairs of statements, divide 5 points between the two according to your beliefs or perceptions of yourself or according to which of the two statements characterizes you better. The 5 points may be divided between the a and b statements in any one of the following ways: 5 for a, 0 for b; 4 for a, 1 for b; 3 for a, 2 for b; 1 for a, 4 for b; 0 for a, 5 for b, but not equally (2-1/2) between the two. Weigh your choices between the two according to which one characterizes you or your beliefs better.

1. (a) As leader I have a primary mission of maintaining stability.
(b) As leader I have a primary mission of change.

2. (a) As leader I must cause events.
(b) As leader I must facilitate events.

3. (a) I am concerned that my followers are rewarded equitably for their work.
(b) I am concerned about what my followers want in life.

4. (a) My preference is to think long range: What might be.
(b) My preference is to think short range: What is realistic.

5. (a) As a leader I spend considerable energy in managing separate but related goals.
(b) As a leader I spend considerable energy in arousing hopes, expectations, and aspirations among my followers.

6. (a) Although not in a formal classroom sense, I believe that a significant part of my leadership is that of teacher.
(b) I believe that a significant part of my leadership is that of facilitator.

7. (a) As leader I must engage with followers on an equal level of morality.
(b) As leader I must represent a higher morality.

8. (a) I enjoy stimulating followers to want to do more.
(b) I enjoy rewarding followers for a job well done.

9. (a) Leadership should be practical.
(b) Leadership should be inspirational.

10. (a) What power I have to influence others comes primarily from my ability to get people to identify with me and my ideas.
(b) What power I have to influence others comes primarily from my status and position.

Scoring

Circle your points for items 1b, 2a, 3b, 4a, 5b, 6a, 7b, 8a, 9b, 10a and add up the total points you allocated to these items; enter the score here [T = ___]. Next, add up the total points given to the uncircled items 1a, 2b, 3a, 4b, 5a, 6b, 7a, 8b, 9a, 10b; enter the score here [T = ___].

Interpretation

This instrument gives an impression of your tendencies toward "transformational" leadership (your T score) and "transactional" leadership (your T score). You may want to refer to the discussion of these concepts in Chapter 13. Today, a lot of attention is being given to the transformational aspects of leadership—those personal qualities that inspire a sense of vision and the desire for extraordinary accomplishment in followers. The most successful leaders of the future will most likely be strong in both "T"s.

_____

Source: Questionnaire by W. Warner Burke, Ph.D. Used by permission.

ASSESSMENT 22

Least-Preferred Coworker Scale

Instructions

Think of all the different people with whom you have ever worked—in jobs, in social clubs, in student projects, or whatever. Next think of the *one person* with whom you could work *least* well—that is, the person with whom you had the most difficulty getting a job done. This is the one person—a peer, boss, or subordinate—with whom you would least want to work. Describe this person by circling numbers at the appropriate points on each of the following pairs of bipolar adjectives. Work rapidly. There are no right or wrong answers.

Pleasant	8 7 6 5 4 3 2 1	Unpleasant
Friendly	8 7 6 5 4 3 2 1	Unfriendly
Rejecting	1 2 3 4 5 6 7 8	Accepting
Tense	1 2 3 4 5 6 7 8	Relaxed
Distant	1 2 3 4 5 6 7 8	Close
Cold	1 2 3 4 5 6 7 8	Warm
Supportive	8 7 6 5 4 3 2 1	Hostile
Boring	1 2 3 4 5 6 7 8	Interesting
Quarrelsome	1 2 3 4 5 6 7 8	Harmonious
Gloomy	1 2 3 4 5 6 7 8	Cheerful
Open	8 7 6 5 4 3 2 1	Guarded
Backbiting	1 2 3 4 5 6 7 8	Loyal
Untrustworthy	1 2 3 4 5 6 7 8	Trustworthy
Considerate	8 7 6 5 4 3 2 1	Inconsiderate
Nasty	1 2 3 4 5 6 7 8	Nice
Agreeable	8 7 6 5 4 3 2 1	Disagreeable
Insincere	1 2 3 4 5 6 7 8	Sincere
Kind	8 7 6 5 4 3 2 1	Unkind

Scoring

This is called the "least-preferred coworker scale" (LPC). Compute your LPC score by totaling all the numbers you circled; enter that score here [LPC = ___].

Interpretation

The LPC scale is used by Fred Fiedler to identify a person's dominant leadership style (see Chapter 13). Fiedler believes that this style is a relatively fixed part of one's personality and is therefore difficult to change. This leads Fiedler to his contingency views, which suggest that the key to leadership success is finding (or creating) good "matches" between style and situation. If your score is 73 or above, Fiedler considers you a "relationship-motivated" leader; if your score is 64 or below, he considers you a "task-motivated" leader. If your score is between 65 and 72, Fiedler leaves it up to you to determine which leadership style is most like yours.

Source: Fred E. Fiedler and Martin M. Chemers, *Improving Leadership Effectiveness: The Leader Match Concept,* 2nd ed. (New York: Wiley, 1984). Used by permission.

ASSESSMENT 23

Student Engagement Survey

Instructions

Use the following scale to indicate the degree to which you agree with the following statements:

1—No agreement
2—Weak agreement
3—Some agreement
4—Considerable agreement
5—Very strong agreement

1. Do you know what is expected of you in this course?

2. Do you have the resources and support you need to do your coursework correctly?

3. In this course, do you have the opportunity to do what you do best all the time?

4. In the last week, have you received recognition or praise for doing good work in this course?

5. Does your instructor seem to care about you as a person?

6. Is there someone in the course who encourages your development?

7. In this course, do your opinions seem to count?

8. Does the mission/purpose of the course make you feel your study is important?

9. Are other students in the course committed to doing quality work?

10. Do you have a best friend in the course?

11. In the last six sessions, has someone talked to you about your progress in the course?

12. In this course, have you had opportunities to learn and grow?

Scoring

Score the instrument by adding up all your responses. A score of 0–24 suggests you are "actively disengaged" from the learning experience; a score of 25–47 suggests you are "moderately engaged"; a score of 48–60 indicates you are "actively engaged."

Interpretation

This instrument suggests the degree to which you are actively "engaged" or "disengaged" from the learning opportunities of your course. It is a counterpart to a survey used by the Gallup Organization to measure the "engagement" of American workers. The Gallup results are surprising—indicating that up to 19 percent of U.S. workers are actively disengaged, with the annual lost productivity estimated at some $300 billion per year. One has to wonder: What are the costs of academic disengagement by students?

Source: This survey was developed from a set of "Gallup Engagement Questions" presented in John Thackray, "Feedback for Real," _Gallup Management Journal_ (March 15, 2001), retrieved from http://gmj.gallup.com/management_articles/employee_engagement/article.asp?i = 238&p = 1, June 5, 2003; data reported from James K. Harter, "The Cost of Disengaged Workers," Gallup Poll (March 13, 2001).

ASSESSMENT 24

Job Design Choices

Instructions

People differ in what they like and dislike about their jobs. Listed below are 12 pairs of jobs. For each pair, indicate which job you would prefer. Assume that everything else about the jobs is the same—pay attention only to the characteristics actually listed for each pair of jobs. If you would prefer the job in Column A, indicate how much you prefer it by putting a check mark in a blank to the left of the Neutral point. If you prefer the job in Column B, check one of the blanks to the right of Neutral. Check the Neutral blank only if you find the two jobs equally attractive or unattractive. Try to use the Neutral blank sparingly.

Column A

Column B

1. A job that offers little or no challenge.

Strongly prefer A | Neutral | Strongly prefer B

A job that requires you to be completely isolated from coworkers.

2. A job that pays well.

Strongly prefer A | Neutral | Strongly prefer B

A job that allows considerable opportunity to be creative and innovative.

3. A job that often requires you to make important decisions.

Strongly prefer A | Neutral | Strongly prefer B

A job in which there are many pleasant people to work with.

4. A job with little security in a somewhat unstable organization.

Strongly prefer A | Neutral | Strongly prefer B

A job in which you have little or no opportunity to participate in decisions that affect your work.

5. A job in which greater responsibility is given to those who do the best work.

Strongly   Neutral   Strongly
prefer A   prefer B

A job in which greater responsibility is given to loyal employees who have the most *seniority*.

6. A job with a supervisor who sometimes is highly critical.

Strongly   Neutral   Strongly
prefer A   prefer B

A job that does not require you to use much of your talent.

7. A very routine job.

Strongly   Neutral   Strongly
prefer A   prefer B

A job in which your coworkers are not very friendly.

8. A job with a supervisor who respects you and treats you fairly.

Strongly   Neutral   Strongly
prefer A   prefer B

A job that provides constant opportunities for you to learn new and interesting things.

9. A job that gives you a real chance to develop yourself personally.

Strongly   Neutral   Strongly
prefer A   prefer B

A job with excellent vacation and fringe benefits.

10. A job in which there is a real chance you could be laid off.

Strongly   Neutral   Strongly
prefer A   prefer B

A job that offers very little chance to do challenging work.

11. A job that gives you little freedom and independence to do your work in the way you think best.

Strongly   Neutral   Strongly
prefer A   prefer B

A job with poor working conditions.

12. A job with very satisfying teamwork.

Strongly   Neutral   Strongly
prefer A   prefer B

A job that allows you to use your skills and abilities to the fullest extent.

Interpretation

People differ in their need for psychological growth at work. This instrument measures the degree to which you seek growth-need satisfaction. Score your responses as follows:

For items 1, 2, 7, 8, 11, and 12 give yourself the following points for each item:

1	2	3	4	5	6	7

Strongly   Neutral   Strongly
prefer A   prefer B

For items 3, 4, 5, 6, 9, and 10 give yourself the following points for each item:

7	6	5	4	3	2	1

Strongly   Neutral   Strongly
prefer A   prefer B

Add up all of your scores and divide by 12 to find the average. If you score above 4.0, your desire for growth-need satisfaction through work tends to be high and you are likely to prefer an enriched job. If you score below 4.0, your desire for growth-need satisfaction through work tends to be low and you are likely to not be satisfied or motivated with an enriched job.

Source: Reprinted by permission from J. R. Hackman and G. R. Oldham, *The Job Diagnostic Survey: An Instrument for the Diagnosis of Jobs and the Evaluation of Job Redesign Projects, Technical Report 4* (New Haven, CT: Yale University, Department of Administrative Sciences, 1974).

Cognitive Style

Instructions

A. This assessment is designed to get an impression of your cognitive style, based on the work of psychologist Carl Jung. For each of the following 12 pairs, place a "1" next to the statement that best describes you. Do this for each pair even though the description you chose may not be perfect.

1. ___ (a) I prefer to learn from experience.
   ___ (b) I prefer to find meanings in facts and how they fit together.

2. ___ (a) I prefer to use my eyes, ears, and other senses to find out what is going on.
   ___ (b) I prefer to use imagination to come up with new ways to do things.

3. ___ (a) I prefer to use standard ways to deal with routine problems.
   ___ (b) I prefer to use novel ways to deal with new problems.

4. ___ (a) I prefer to learn from experience.
   ___ (b) I prefer to find meanings in facts and how they fit together.

5. ___ (a) I am patient with details but get impatient when they get complicated.
   ___ (b) I am impatient and jump to conclusions but am also creative, imaginative, and inventive.

6. ___ (a) I enjoy using skills already mastered more than learning new ones.
   ___ (b) I like learning new skills more than practicing old ones.

7. ___ (a) I prefer to decide things logically.
   ___ (b) I prefer to decide things based on feelings and values.

8. ___ (a) I like to be treated with justice and fairness.
   ___ (b) I like to be praised and to please other people.

9. ___ (a) I sometimes neglect or hurt other people's feelings without realizing it.

___ (b) I am aware of other people's feelings.

10. ___ (a) I give more attention to ideas and things than to human relationships.
    ___ (b) I can predict how others will feel.

11. ___ (a) I do not need harmony; arguments and conflicts don't bother me.
    ___ (b) I value harmony and get upset by arguments and conflicts.

12. ___ (a) I am often described as analytical, impersonal, unemotional, objective, critical, hard-nosed, rational.
    ___ (b) I am often described as sympathetic, people-oriented, unorganized, uncritical, understanding, ethical.

B. Sum your scores as follows, and record them in the space provided. (Note that the Sensing and Feeling scores will be recorded as negatives.)

$(-$ ___ $)$ *Sensing (S Type)* $= 1a + 2a + 3a + 4a$
$+ 5a + 6a$

$($ ___ $)$ *Intuitive (N Type)* $= 1b + 2b + 3b +$
$4b + 5b + 6b$

$($ ___ $)$ *Thinking (T Type)* $= 7a + 8a + 9a +$
$10a + 11a + 12a$

$(-$ ___ $)$ *Feeling (F Type)* $= 7b + 8b + 9b +$
$10b + 11b + 12b$

C. Plot your scores on the following graph. Place an "X" at the point that indicates your suggested problem-solving style.

Interpretation

This assessment examines cognitive style through the contrast of personal tendencies toward information gathering (sensation vs. intuition) and information evaluation (feeling vs. thinking) in one's approach to problem solving. The result is a classification of four master cognitive styles, with the following characteristics. Read the descriptions and consider the implications of your suggested style, including how well you might work with persons whose styles are very different.

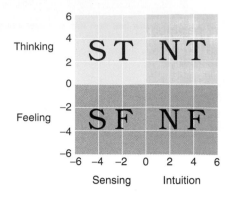

Sensation Thinkers: STs tend to emphasize the impersonal rather than the personal and take a realistic approach to problem solving. They like hard "facts," clear goals, certainty, and situations of high control.

Intuitive Thinkers: NTs are comfortable with abstraction and unstructured situations. They tend to be idealistic, prone toward intellectual and theoretical positions; they are logical and impersonal but also avoid details.

Intuitive Feelers: NFs prefer broad and global issues. They are insightful and tend to avoid details, being comfortable with intangibles; they value flexibility and human relationships.

Sensation Feelers: SFs tend to emphasize both analysis and human relations. They tend to be realistic and prefer facts; they are open communicators and sensitive to feelings and values.

Source: Developed from Donald Bowen, "Learning and Problem-Solving: You're Never Too Jung," in Donald D. Bowen, Roy J. Lewicki, Donald T. Hall, and Francine S. Hall, eds., *Experiences in Management and Organizational Behavior,* 4th ed. (New York: Wiley, 1997), pp. 7–13; and John W. Slocum, Jr., "Cognitive Style in Learning and Problem Solving," ibid., pp. 349–353.

ASSESSMENT 26

Internal/External Control

Instructions

Circle either "a" or "b" to indicate the item you most agree with in each pair of the following statements.

1. (a) Promotions are earned through hard work and persistence.
(b) Making a lot of money is largely a matter of breaks.

2. (a) Many times the reactions of teachers seem haphazard to me.
(b) In my experience I have noticed that there is usually a direct connection between how hard I study and the grades I get.

3. (a) The number of divorces indicates that more and more people are not trying to make their marriages work.
(b) Marriage is largely a gamble.

4. (a) It is silly to think that one can really change another person's basic attitudes.
(b) When I am right I can convince others.

5. (a) Getting promoted is really a matter of being a little luckier than the next guy.
(b) In our society an individual's future earning power is dependent upon his or her ability.

6. (a) If one knows how to deal with people, they are really quite easily led.
(b) I have little influence over the way other people behave.

7. (a) In my case the grades I make are the results of my own efforts; luck has little or nothing to do with it.
(b) Sometimes I feel that I have little to do with the grades I get.

8. (a) People like me can change the course of world affairs if we make ourselves heard.
(b) It is only wishful thinking to believe that one can really influence what happens in society at large.

9. (a) Much of what happens to me is probably a matter of chance.
(b) I am the master of my fate.

10. (a) Getting along with people is a skill that must be practiced.

(b) It is almost impossible to figure out how to please some people.

Scoring

Give 1 point for 1b, 2a, 3a, 4b, 5b, 6a, 7a, 8a, 9b, 10a.

8–10 = high *internal* locus of control

6–7 = moderate *internal* locus of control

5 = mixed locus of control

3–4 = moderte *external* locus of control

Interpretation

This instrument offers an impression of your tendency toward in *internal locus of control or external locus of control.* Persons with a high internal locus of control tend to believe they have control over their own destinies. They may be most responsive to opportunities for greater self-control in the workplace. Persons with a high external locus of control tend to believe that what happens to them is largely in the hands of external people or forces. They may be less comfortable with self-control and more responsive to external controls in the workplace.

Source: Instrument from Julian P. Rotter, "External Control and Internal Control," *Psychology Today* (June 1971), p. 42. Used by permission.

ASSESSMENT 27

Team Leader Skills

Instructions

Consider your experience in groups and work teams. Ask: "What skills do I bring to team leadership situations?" Then, complete the following inventory by rating yourself on each item using this scale.

1 = Almost Never
2 = Seldom
3 = Sometimes
4 = Usually
5 = Almost Always

1 2 3 4 5 **1.** I facilitate communications with and among team members between team meetings.

1 2 3 4 5 **2.** I provide feedback/coaching to individual team members on their performance.

1 2 3 4 5 **3.** I encourage creative and "out-of-the-box" thinking.

1 2 3 4 5 **4.** I continue to clarify stakeholder needs/expectations.

1 2 3 4 5 **5.** I keep team members' responsibilities and activities focused within the team's objectives and goals.

1 2 3 4 5 **6.** I organize and run effective and productive team meetings.

1 2 3 4 5 **7.** I demonstrate integrity and personal commitment.

1 2 3 4 5 **8.** I have excellent persuasive and influence skills.

1 2 3 4 5 **9.** I respect and leverage the team's cross-functional diversity.

1 2 3 4 5 **10.** I recognize and reward individual contributions to team performance.

1 2 3 4 5 **11.** I use the appropriate decision-making style for specific issues.

1 2 3 4 5 **12.** I facilitate and encourage border management with the team's key stakeholders.

1 2 3 4 5 **13.** I ensure that the team meets its team commitments.

1 2 3 4 5 **14.** I bring team issues and problems to the team's attention and focus on constructive problem solving.

1 2 3 4 5 **15.** I provide a clear vision and direction for the team.

Scoring

The inventory measures seven dimensions of team leadership. Add your scores for the items listed next to each dimension below to get an indication of your potential strengths and weaknesses.

1,9	Building the Team
2,10	Developing People
3,11	Team Problem Solving/Decision Making
4,12	Stakeholder Relations
5,13	Team Performance
6,14	Team Process
7,8,15	Providing Personal Leadership

Interpretation

The higher the score, the more confident you are on the particular skill and leadership capability. When considering the score, ask yourself if others would rate you the same way. Consider giving this inventory to people who have worked with you in teams and have them rate you. Compare the results to your self-assessment. Also, remember that it is doubtful that any one team leader is capable of exhibiting all the skills listed above. More and more, organizations are emphasizing "top-management teams" that blend a variety of skills, rather than depending on the vision of the single, heroic leader figure. As long as the necessary leadership skills are represented within the membership, it is more likely that the team will be healthy and achieve high performance. Of course, the more skills you bring with you to team leadership situations, the better.

Source: Developed from Lynda McDermott, Nolan Brawley, and William Waite, *World-Class Teams: Working across Borders* (New York: Wiley, 1998).

ASSESSMENT 28

Conflict Management Styles

Instructions

Think of how you behave in conflict situations in which your wishes differ from those of one or more other persons. In the space to the left of each of the following statements, write the number from the following scale that indicates how likely you are to respond that way in a conflict situation.

1 = very unlikely   2 = unlikely
3 = likely   4 = very likely

___ **1.** I am usually firm in pursuing my goals.

___ **2.** I try to win my position.

___ **3.** I give up some points in exchange for others.

___ **4.** I feel that differences are not always worth worrying about.

___ **5.** I try to find a position that is intermediate between the other person's and mine.

___ **6.** In approaching negotiations, I try to be considerate of the other person's wishes.

___ **7.** I try to show the logic and benefits of my positions.

___ **8.** I always lean toward a direct discussion of the problem.

___ **9.** I try to find a fair combination of gains and losses for both of us.

___ **10.** I attempt to work through our differences immediately.

___ **11.** I try to avoid creating unpleasantness for myself.

___ **12.** I try to soothe the other person's feelings and preserve our relationship.

___ **13.** I attempt to get all conerns and issues immediately out in the open.

___ **14.** I sometimes avoid taking positions that would create controversy.

___ **15.** I try not to hurt others' feelings.

Scoring

Total your scores for items 1, 2, 7; enter that score here [*Competing* = ___]. Total your scores for items 8, 10, 13; enter that score here [*Collaborating* = ___]. Total your scores for items 3, 5, 9; enter that score here [*Compromising* = ___]. Total your scores for items 4, 11, 14; enter that score here [*Avoiding* = ___]. Total your scores for items 6, 12, 15; enter that score here [*Accommodating* = ___].

Interpretation

Each of the scores above corresponds to one of the conflict management styles discussed in Chapter 16. Research indicates that each style has a role to play in management but that the best overall conflict management approach is collaboration; only it can lead to problem solving and true conflict resolution. You should consider any patterns that may be evident in your scores and think about how to best handle the conflict situations in which you become involved.

Source: Adapted from Thomas-Kilmann, *Conflict Mode Instrument.* Copyright © 1974, Xicom, Inc., Tuxedo, NY 10987. Used by permission.

ASSESSMENT 29

Stress Self-Test

Instructions

Complete the following questionnaire. Circle the number that best represents your tendency to behave on each bipolar dimension.

Am casual about appointments	1 2 3 4 5 6 7 8	Am never late
Am not competitive	1 2 3 4 5 6 7 8	Am very competitive
Never feel rushed	1 2 3 4 5 6 7 8	Always feel rushed
Take things one at a time	1 2 3 4 5 6 7 8	Try to do many things at once
Do things slowly	1 2 3 4 5 6 7 8	Do things fast
Express feelings	1 2 3 4 5 6 7 8	"Sit on" feelings
Have many interests	1 2 3 4 5 6 7 8	Have few interests but work

Scoring

Total the numbers circled for all items, and multiply this by 3; enter the result here [___].

Interpretation

This scale is designed to measure your personality tendency toward Type A or Type B behaviors. As described in Chapter 16, a Type A personality is associated with high stress. Persons who are Type A tend to bring stress on themselves even in situations where others are relatively stress-free. This is an important characteristic to be able to identify in yourself and in others.

Points	Personality
120+	A+
106 – 119	A
100 – 105	A–
90 – 99	B+
below 90	B

Source: Adapted from R. W. Bortner. "A Short Rating Scale as a Potential Measure of Type A Behavior," *Journal of Chronic Diseases,* vol. 22 (1966), pp. 87–91. Used by permission.

ASSESSMENT 30

Work-Life Balance

Instructions

Complete this inventory by circling the number that indicates the extent to which you agree or disagree with each of the following statements.

1. How much time do you spend on nonwork-related activities such as taking care of family, spending time with friends, participating in sports, enjoying leisure time?
Almost none/never   1 2 3 4 5   Very much/always

2. How often do family duties and nonwork responsibilities make you feel tired out?
Almost none/never   1 2 3 4 5   Very much/always

3. How often do you feel short of time for family-related and nonwork activities?
Almost none/never   1 2 3 4 5   Very much/always

4. How difficult is it for you to do everything you should as a family member and friend to others?
Almost none/never   1 2 3 4 5   Very much/always

5. I often feel that I am being run ragged, with not enough time in a day to do everything and do it well.
Completely disagree   1 2 3 4 5   Completely agree

6. I am given entirely too much work to do.
Strongly disagree   1   2   3   4   5   Strongly agree

7. How much conflict do you feel there is between the demands of your job and your family, and nonwork activities life?
Not at all/never   1   2   3   4   5   A lot/very often

8. How much does your job situation interfere with your family life?
Not at all/never   1   2   3   4   5   A lot/very often

9. How much does your family life and nonwork activities interfere with your job?
Not at all/never   1   2   3   4   5   A lot/very often
Submit Response Reset Fields

Scoring

1. Family Demand Score: Total items #1, #2, #3, #4 and divide by 4.

2. Work Demand Score: Total items #5, #6 and divide by 2.

3. Work-Family Conflict Score: Total items #7, #8, #9 and divide by 3.

Your responses to items 1–4 are totaled and divided by 4, giving you the Life Demand score. Your responses to items 5–6 are totaled and divided by 2, resulting in your Work Demand score. Responses to items 7–9 are summed and divided by 3, giving your Work-Life conflict score.

Interpretation

Compare yourself to these scores from a sample of Chinese and American workers.

	U.S.	Chinese	Your Scores
Life Demand	3.53	2.58	4
Work Demand	2.83	2.98	4
Work-Life Conflict	2.53	2.30	4.67

Are there any suprises in this comparison?

Work-life conflict is defined as "a form of interrole conflict in which the role pressures from the work and family nonwork domains are mutually noncompatible in some respect." Demands of one role make it difficult to satisfy demands of the others.

Source: Based on Nini Yang, Chao. D. Chen, Jaepil Choi, and Yimin Zou, "Sources of Work-Family Conflict: A Sino–U.S. Comparison of the Effects of Work and Family Demands," *Academy of Management Journal*, vol. 43, no. 1, pp. 113–123.

STUDENT Portfolio BUILDER

John R. Schermerhorn, Jr.

OHIO UNIVERSITY

What Is a Student Portfolio?

A *Student Portfolio* is a paper or electronic collection of documents that summarizes your academic and personal accomplishments in a way that effectively communicates with academic advisors and potential employers.[1] At a minimum, your portfolio should include the following:

Minimum components of a Student Portfolio

- an up-to-date professional résumé.
- a listing of courses in your major and related fields of study.
- a listing of your extra-curricular activities and any leadership positions.
- documentation of your career readiness in terms of skills and learning outcomes.

The purpose of a Student Portfolio is twofold—academic assessment and career readiness.

1. *Academic Assessment Goal* The Student Portfolio serves as an on-going academic assessment tool that documents your learning and academic accomplishments. As you progress through a curriculum, the portfolio depicts the progress you are making in acquiring the skills and competencies necessary to be successful in lifelong career pursuits. Over time, your portfolio will become increasingly sophisticated in the range and depth of learning and accomplishments that are documented. A well-prepared Student Portfolio is a very effective way of summarizing your academic achievements in consultation with both faculty advisors and professors.

2. *Career Readiness Goal* The Student Portfolio serves as an important means of communicating your résumé and credentials to potential employers, as you search for both internship and full-time job opportunities. The portfolio is an effective career tool that offers value far beyond the standard résumé. Potential employers can readily examine multiple aspects of your accomplishments and skill sets in order to make a desired match. A professional and complete portfolio allows potential employers to easily review your background and range of skills and capabilities. It may convey your potential to a much greater depth and with a more positive impression than a traditional résumé. There is no doubt that a professional and substantive portfolio can help set you apart from the competition and attract the interest of employers.

Planning Your Student Portfolio

Your Student Portfolio should document, in a progressive and clear manner, your credentials and academic work. As you progress through the curriculum in your major and supplementary fields of study, the portfolio should be refined and materials added to display your most up-to-date skills, competencies, and accomplishments. Use of the *Management 8/e* Skill and Outcome Assessment Framework, described shortly, will help you to do this. At my university we ask students to utilize the

[1] The value and use of Student Portfolios are described by David S. Chappell and John R. Schermerhorn, Jr., in "Using Electronic Student Portfolios in Management Education: A Stakeholder Perspective," *Journal of Management Education*, vol. 23 (1999), pp. 651–62; and, "Electronic Student Portfolios in Management Education" in Robert deFelippi and Charles Wrankel (eds.), *Educating Managers with Tomorrow's Technology* (Information Age Press, 2003), pp. 101–129.

portfolio to store their coursework. We then review it periodically with them as part of our department's formal advising and outcome assessment programs.

The closer you get to graduation, the entries in your portfolio should become more specific to your job and career goals. In this way, your portfolio becomes a dynamic and evolving career tool with value far beyond that of the standard résumé. I recommend that my students plan their portfolios to serve two immediate career purposes: (1) obtain a professional internship for the junior/senior year period, and (2) obtain their initial full-time job after graduation. A typical student of ours begins his or her portfolio as a sophomore and then refines and adds to it throughout the program of study.

Résumé Writing Guide

The first thing that should go into your Student Portfolio is a professional résumé. Don't worry about how sophisticated or complete it is at first. The important things are to (1) get it started and (2) continue to build it as your experience grows. You will be surprised at how complete it will become with systematic attention and a personal commitment to take full advantage of the professional development opportunities available to you.

The following example should help get you started. It shows both a professional format and the types of things that can and should be included. I have also annotated the sample to show how an internship recruiter or potential employer might respond when reading the résumé for the first time. Wouldn't you like to have such positive reactions to the accomplishments and experiences documented in your résumé?

Interview Preparation Guide

You will know that your Student Portfolio was worthwhile and successful when it helps you land a preferred internship or your first-choice job. But the portfolio only helps get you to the point of a formal interview. The next step is doing well in it. In order to prepare for this step in the recruiting process, consider the following tips on job interviewing.[2]

- *Research the organization* — Make sure you read their recent literature, including annual reports, scan current news reports, and examine the industry and their major competitors.

- *Prepare to answer common interview questions* — Sample questions include: What do you really want to do in life? What do you consider your greatest strengths and weaknesses? How can you immediately contribute to our organization? Why did you choose your college or university? What are your interests outside of work? What was your most rewarding college experience? How would one of your professors describe you? What do you see yourself doing five years from now?

- *Dress for success* — Remember that impressions count, and first impressions often count the most. If you aren't sure what to wear or how to look, get advice from your professors and from career counselors at your college or university.

---

[2] This section and the tips were recommended by my colleague Dr. Robert Lenie Holbrook of Ohio University.

Résumé Sample

Note: The annotations indicate positive reactions by a prospective employer to the information being provided.

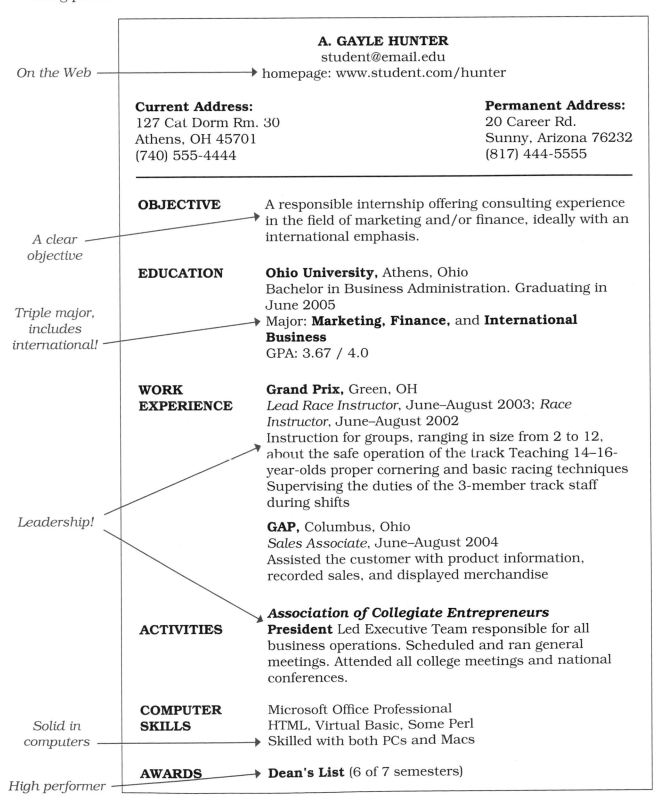

On the Web

A. GAYLE HUNTER
student@email.edu
homepage: www.student.com/hunter

Current Address:
127 Cat Dorm Rm. 30
Athens, OH 45701
(740) 555-4444

Permanent Address:
20 Career Rd.
Sunny, Arizona 76232
(817) 444-5555

OBJECTIVE

A clear objective

A responsible internship offering consulting experience in the field of marketing and/or finance, ideally with an international emphasis.

EDUCATION

Triple major, includes international!

Ohio University, Athens, Ohio
Bachelor in Business Administration. Graduating in June 2005
Major: **Marketing, Finance,** and **International Business**
GPA: 3.67 / 4.0

WORK EXPERIENCE

Grand Prix, Green, OH
Lead Race Instructor, June–August 2003; *Race Instructor,* June–August 2002
Instruction for groups, ranging in size from 2 to 12, about the safe operation of the track Teaching 14–16-year-olds proper cornering and basic racing techniques Supervising the duties of the 3-member track staff during shifts

Leadership!

GAP, Columbus, Ohio
Sales Associate, June–August 2004
Assisted the customer with product information, recorded sales, and displayed merchandise

ACTIVITIES

Association of Collegiate Entrepreneurs
President Led Executive Team responsible for all business operations. Scheduled and ran general meetings. Attended all college meetings and national conferences.

COMPUTER SKILLS

Solid in computers

Microsoft Office Professional
HTML, Virtual Basic, Some Perl
Skilled with both PCs and Macs

AWARDS

High performer

Dean's List (6 of 7 semesters)

- *Dine for success*—There are no interview "time-outs" for refreshments or meals. The interview is always on. Make sure that you know how to dine in the presence of others. If you don't, get help before the interview.

- *Follow-up*—After the interview, send a "thank you" letter, ideally no longer than a week later. In the letter be sure to mention specific things about the organization that are important/insightful to you, and take the opportunity to clarify again where and how you believe you would fit as a valuable employee. Be prompt in providing any additional information requested during the interview.

Skill and Outcome Assessment Framework

Skill and outcome assessment is an increasingly important part of management education. It allows you to document key academic accomplishments and career readiness for faculty review and for review by potential employers. Following guidelines of the AACSB, the International Association for Management Education, I suggest integrating into your portfolio specific documentation of your accomplishments in the following six areas of professional development.

Six components of the Skill and Outcome Assessment Framework

1. *Communication*—Demonstrates ability to share ideas and findings clearly in written and oral expression, and with technology utilization.

2. *Leadership*—Demonstrates ability to influence and support others to perform complex and ambiguous tasks.

3. *Teamwork*—Demonstrates ability to work effectively as a team member and as a team leader.

4. *Critical Thinking*—Demonstrates ability to gather and analyze information for creative problem solving.

5. *Self-Management*—Demonstrates ability to evaluate oneself, modify behavior, and meet obligations.

6. *Professionalism*—Demonstrates ability to sustain a positive impression, instill confidence, and advance in a career.

The many learning resources and activities in this *Management Learning Workbook* — cases, projects, exercises, and self-assessments— relate to these skills and outcome assessment areas. There is no better time than the present to start participating in the learning experiences and documenting your results and accomplishments in your student portfolio.

Getting Started with Your *Student Portfolio*

The basic Student Portfolio consists of (1) a professional résumé and (2) a compendium of coursework samples that displays your career readiness skills and capabilities.

Communication - Demonstrates ability to share ideas and findings clearly in written and oral expression.

- Writing
- Oral presentation
- Giving and receiving feedback
- Technology utilization

Leading - Demonstrates ability to influence and support others to perform complex and ambiguous tasks.

- Diversity awareness
- Global awareness
- Project management
- Strategic leadership

Teamwork - Demonstrates ability to work effectively as a team member and a team leader.

- Team contribution
- Team leadership
- Conflict management
- Negotiation and consensus building

Critical Thinking - Demonstrates ability to gather and analyze information for creative problem solving.

- Problem solving
- Judgment and decision making
- Information gathering/interpretation
- Creativity and innovation

Self-Management - Demonstrates ability to evaluate oneself, modify behavior, and meet obligations.

- Ethical understanding/behavior
- Personal flexibility
- Tolerance for ambiguity
- Performance responsibility

Professionalism - Demonstrates ability to sustain a positive impression, instill confidence, and advance in a career.

- Personal presence
- Personal initiative
- Career management
- Unique "value added"

Portfolio Format

The easiest way to organize a paper portfolio is with a three-ring binder. This binder should be professional in appearance and have an attractive cover page that clearly identifies it as your student portfolio. The binder should be indexed with dividers that allow a reader to easily browse the résumé and other materials to gain a complete view of your special credentials.

In today's age of information technology and electronic communication, it is also highly recommended that you develop an online or *electronic portfolio*. This format allows you to communicate easily and effectively through the Internet with employers offering potential internship and job placements. An online version of your student portfolio can be displayed either on your personal website or on one provided by your university. Once you have created an electronic portfolio, it is easy to maintain. It is also something that will impress reviewers and help set you apart from the competition. At the very least, the use of an electronic portfolio communicates to potential employers that you are a full participant in this age of information technology.

Career Development Plan—A Portfolio Project

A very good way to enhance your Student Portfolio is by completing the following project as part of your introductory management course, or on your own initiative. Called the "Career Development Plan," the objective of this project is to identify professional development opportunities that you can take advantage of while in college and to advance your personal career readiness.

Deliverable: Write and file in your Student Portfolio a two-part career development memorandum that is written in professional format and addressed to your instructor or to "prospective employer." The memorandum should do the following.

- *Part A.* Answer the question: "What are my personal strengths and weaknesses as a potential manager?"

    It is recommended that you utilize the *Management 8/e* Skill & Outcome Assessment Framework in structuring your analysis. It is also recommended that you support your answer in part by analysis of results from your work with a selection of experiential exercises and self-assessments from this workbook. You can also supplement the analysis with other relevant personal insights.

- *Part B.* Answer the question: "How can I best take advantage of opportunities remaining in my undergraduate experience to improve my managerial potential?"

    Make this answer as specific as possible. Describe a clear plan of action that encompasses the time available to you between now and graduation. This plan should include summer and intercession activities, as well as academic and extracurricular experiences. Your goal should be to build a résumé and complete portfolio that will best present you as a skilled and valuable candidate for the entry-level job that you would like in your chosen career field.

Evaluation: Your career development memorandum should be professional and error-free, and meet the highest standards of effective written communication. It should be sufficiently analytical in Part A to show serious consideration of your personal strengths and weaknesses in managerial potential at this point in time. It should be sufficiently detailed and in-depth in Part B so that you can objectively evaluate your progress step-by-step between now and graduation. Overall, it should be a career development plan you can be proud to formally include in your Student Portfolio. It should serve as a positive indicator of your professionalism.

Sample Portfolio Components

The following samples are taken from portfolios built by my students. They document a range of accomplishments and capabilities. As with the sample résumé presented earlier, I have shown them here with illustrative comments (written in red) that indicate how a prospective employer might react when reading them in print or viewing them online. As you look at these samples, ask: "How can I best display my course and academic accomplishments to document my learning and career readiness?"

Written Assignment in French

La Conception de L'Amour Pendant toute L'Histoire

Second language skill!! →

La conception de l'amour pendant toute l'histoire est tres interresant de voir. Pendant l'histoire, les formes de l'mouront ont change un peu, mais l'idee le plus de base reste la meme. Dans les ouvrages au XVIeme siecle, on peut trouver les idees de l'amour qui sont semblable a la conception de l'amour dans notre societe moderne. Avec un comparaison entre la poesie de Louise Labe et Ronsard au XVIeme siecle, et le film Indochine, que Regis Wargnier a realise a 1992, on peut voir la conception de l'amour pendant l'histoire.

International Virtual Teamwork Project

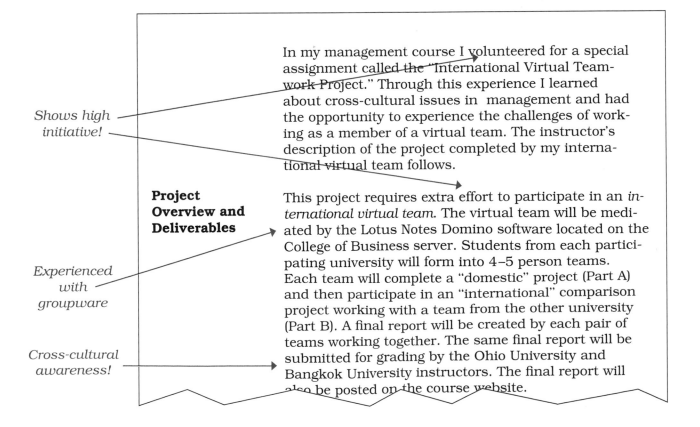

Shows high initiative! —

In my management course I volunteered for a special assignment called the "International Virtual Teamwork Project." Through this experience I learned about cross-cultural issues in management and had the opportunity to experience the challenges of working as a member of a virtual team. The instructor's description of the project completed by my international virtual team follows.

Project Overview and Deliverables

Experienced with groupware —

Cross-cultural awareness! —

This project requires extra effort to participate in an *international virtual team*. The virtual team will be mediated by the Lotus Notes Domino software located on the College of Business server. Students from each participating university will form into 4–5 person teams. Each team will complete a "domestic" project (Part A) and then participate in an "international" comparison project working with a team from the other university (Part B). A final report will be created by each pair of teams working together. The same final report will be submitted for grading by the Ohio University and Bangkok University instructors. The final report will also be posted on the course website.

Self-Test Answers

Chapter 1

1. d
2. c
3. a
4. b
5. a
6. a
7. c
8. a
9. b
10. b
11. c
12. a
13. b
14. c
15. c
16. Managers must value people and respect subordinates as mature, responsible, adult human beings. This is part of their ethical and social responsibility as persons to whom others report at work. The work setting should be organized and managed to respect the rights of people and their human dignity. Included among the expectations for ethical behavior would be actions to protect individual privacy, provide freedom from sexual harassment, and offer safe and healthy job conditions. Failure to do so is socially irresponsible. It may also cause productivity losses due to dissatisfaction and poor work commitments.
17. The manager is held accountable by her boss for performance results of her work unit. The manager must answer to her boss for unit performance. By the same token, the manager's subordinates must answer to her for their individual performance. They are accountable to her.
18. If the glass ceiling effect operates in a given situation, it would act as a hidden barrier to advancement beyond a certain level. Managers controlling promotions and advancement opportunities in the firm would not give them to African-American candidates, regardless of their capabilities. Although the newly hired graduates may progress for a while, sooner or later their upward progress in the firm would be halted by this invisible barrier.
19. Kenichi Ohmae uses the term "borderless world" to describe how more businesses are operating on a global scale. Globalization means that the countries and peoples of the world are increasingly interconnected and that business firms increasingly cross national boundaries in acquiring resources, getting work accomplished, and selling their products. This internationalization of work will affect most everyone in the new economy. People will be working with others from different countries, working in other countries, and certainly buying and using products and services produced in whole or in part in other countries. As countries become more interdependent economically, products are sold and resources purchased around the world, and business strategies increasingly target markets in more than one country.
20. One approach to this question is through the framework of essential management skills offered by Katz. At the first level of management, technical skills are important and I would feel capable in this respect. However, I would expect to learn and refine these skills through my work experiences. Human skills, the ability to work well with other people, will also be very important. Given the diversity anticipated for this team, I will need good human skills. Included here would be my emotional intelligence, or ability to understand my emotions and those of others when I am interacting with them. I will also have a leadership responsibility to help others on the team develop and utilize these skills so that the team itself can function effectively. Finally, I would expect opportunities to develop my conceptual or analytical skills in anticipation of higher-level appointments. In terms of personal development, I should recognize that the conceptual skills will increase in importance relative to the technical skills as I move upward in management responsibility. The fact that the members of the team will be diverse, with some of different demographic and cultural backgrounds from my own, will only increase the importance of my abilities in the human skills area. It will be a challenge to embrace and value differences to create the best work experience for everyone and to fully value everyone's potential contributions to the au-

dits we will be doing. Conceptually I will need to understand the differences and try to utilize them to solve problems faced by the team, but in human relationships I will need to excel at keeping the team spirit alive and everyone committed to working well together over the life of our projects.

Chapter 2

1. d
2. b
3. b
4. a
5. c
6. a
7. a
8. b
9. c
10. c
11. a
12. d
13. c
14. c
15. a
16. Theory Y assumes that people are capable of taking responsibility and exercising self-direction and control in their work. The notion of self-fulfilling prophecies is that managers who hold these assumptions will act in ways that encourage workers to display these characteristics, thus confirming and reinforcing the original assumptions. The emphasis on greater participation and involvement in the modern workplace is an example of Theory Y assumptions in practice. Presumably, by valuing participation and involvement, managers will create self-fulfilling prophecies in which workers behave this way in response to being treated with respect. The result is a positive setting where everyone gains.
17. According to the deficit principle, a satisfied need is not a motivator of behavior. The social need will only motivate if it is deprived or in deficit. According to the progression principle, people move step by step up Maslow's hierarchy as they strive to satisfy needs. For example, once the social need is satisfied, the esteem need will be activated.
18. Contingency thinking takes an "if–then" approach to situations. It seeks to modify or adapt management approaches to fit the needs of each situation. An example would be to give more customer contact responsibility to workers who want to satisfy social needs at work, while giving more supervisory responsibilities to those who want to satisfy their esteem or ego needs.
19. The external environment is the source of the resources an organization needs to operate. In order to continue to obtain these resources, the organization must be successful in selling its goods and services to customers. If customer feedback is negative, the organization must make adjustments or risk losing the support needed to obtain important resources.
20. A bureaucracy operates with a strict hierarchy of authority, promotion based on competency and performance, formal rules and procedures, and written documentation. Enrique can do all of these things in his store, since the situation is probably quite stable and most work requirements are routine and predictable. However, bureaucracies are quite rigid and may deny employees the opportunity to make decisions on their own. Enrique must be careful to meet the needs of the workers and not to make the mistake—identified by Argyris—of failing to treat them as mature adults. While remaining well organized, the store manager should still be able to help workers meet higher-order esteem and self-fulfillment needs as well as assume responsibility as would be consistent with McGregor's Theory Y assumptions.

Chapter 3

1. b
2. a
3. d
4. c
5. c
6. d
7. b
8. a
9. c
10. b
11. d
12. c
13. a
14. c
15. d
16. The individualism view is that ethical behavior is that which best serves long-term interests. The justice view is that ethical behavior is fair and equitable in its treatment of people.
17. The rationalizations are believing that: (1) the behavior is not really illegal, (2) the behavior is really in everyone's best interests, (3) no one will find out, and (4) the organization will protect you.
18. The socioeconomic view of corporate social responsibility argues that socially responsible behavior is in a firm's long-run best interests. It should be good for profits, it creates a positive public image, it helps avoid government regulation, it meets public expectations, and it is an ethical obligation.
19. Government agencies implement and enforce laws that are passed to regulate business activities. They act in the public's behalf to ensure compliance with laws on such matters as occupational safety and health, consumer protection, and environmental protection.
20. The manager could make a decision based on any one of the strategies. As an obstructionist, the manager may assume that Bangladesh needs the business and that it is a local matter as to who will be employed to make the gloves. As a defensive strategy, the manager may decide to require the supplier to meet the minimum employment requirements under Bangladeshi law. Both of these approaches represent cultural relativism. As an accommodation strategy, the

manager may require that the supplier go beyond local laws and meet standards set by equivalent laws in the United States. A proactive strategy would involve the manager in trying to set an example by operating in Bangladesh only with suppliers who not only meet local standards but also actively support the education of children in the communities in which they operate. These latter two approaches would be examples of universalism.

Chapter 4

1. a
2. c
3. b
4. b
5. d
6. c
7. c
8. a
9. b
10. a
11. a
12. b
13. a
14. d
15. b
16. Possible operating objectives reflecting a commitment to competitive advantage through customer service include: (1) providing high-quality goods and services, (2) producing at low cost so that goods and services can be sold at low prices, (3) providing short waiting times for goods and services, and (4) providing goods and services meeting unique customer needs.
17. External customers are the consumers or clients in the specific environment who buy the organization's goods or use its services. Internal customers are found internally in the workflows among people and subsystems in the organization. They are individuals or groups within the organization who utilize goods and services produced by others also inside the organization.
18. The core culture of the organization consists of the values

that shape and direct the behavior of members. Examples would be "honesty" and "quality" in everything that people do. Value-based management actively models such core values, communicates them, and encourages others to live up to them in their work. Responsibility for value-based management is shared by all managers from senior executives to first-level supervisors and team leaders.

19. Subcultures are important in organizations because of the many aspects of diversity found in the workforce. Although working in the same organization and sharing the same organizational culture, members differ in subculture affiliations based on such aspects as gender, age, and ethnic differences, as well as in respect to occupational and functional affiliations. It is important to understand how subculture differences may influence working relationships. For example, a 40-year-old manager of 20-year-old workers must understand that the values and behaviors of the younger workforce may not be totally consistent with what she or he believes in, and vice versa.
20. I disagree with this statement since a strong organizational or corporate culture can be a positive influence on any organization, large or small. Also, issues of diversity, inclusiveness, and multiculturalism apply as well. In fact, such things as a commitment to pluralism and respect for diversity should be part of the core values and distinguishing features of the organization's culture. The woman working for the large company is mistaken in thinking that the concepts do not apply to her friend's small business. In fact, the friend as owner and perhaps founder of the business should be working hard to establish the values and other elements that will create a strong and continuing culture and respect

for diversity. Employees of any organization should have core organizational values to serve as reference points for their attitudes and behavior. The rites and rituals of everyday organizational life are also important ways to recognize positive accomplishments and add meaning to the employment relationships. It may even be that the friend's roles as creator and sponsor of the corporate culture and diversity leader are more magnified in the small-business setting. As the owner and manager, she is visible every day to all employees. How she acts will have a great impact on any "culture" that is established in her business.

Chapter 5

1. c
2. b
3. b
4. d
5. b
6. a
7. a
8. c
9. a
10. d
11. d
12. a
13. c
14. d
15. c
16. The North American Free Trade Agreement, NAFTA, provides the framework for Mexico, the United States, and Canada to free the flows of investments, products, and workers across their borders. This agreement creates a large consumer market and is an opportunity for business in all three countries to take full advantage of the entire North American region as a resource and customer base.
17. The relationship between an MNC and a host country should be mutually beneficial. Sometimes, however, host countries complain that MNCs take unfair advantage of them and do not include them in the benefits of their international

operations. The complaints against MNCs include taking excessive profits out of the host country, hiring the best local labor, not respecting local laws and customs, and dominating the local economy. Engaging in corrupt practices is another important concern.

18. The power-distance dimension of national culture reflects the degree to which members of a society accept status and authority inequalities. Since organizations are hierarchies with power varying from top to bottom, the way power differences are viewed from one setting to the next is an important management issue. Relations between managers and subordinates or team leaders and team members will be very different in high-power-distance cultures than in low-power-distance ones. The significance of these differences is most evident in international operations when a manager from a high-power-distance culture has to perform in a low-power-distance one, or vice versa. In both cases, the cultural differences can cause problems as the manager deals with local workers.

19. For each region of the world you should identify a major economic theme or issue or element. For example: Europe—the European Union should be discussed for its economic significance to member countries and to outsiders; the Americas—NAFTA should be discussed for its current implications as well as potential significance once Chile and other nations join; Asia—the Asia-Pacific Economic Forum should be identified as a platform for growing regional economic cooperation among a very economically powerful group of countries; Africa—the new nonracial democracy in South Africa should be cited as a stimulus to broader outside investor interest in Africa.

20. Kim must recognize that the cultural differences between the United States and Japan may affect the success of group-oriented work practices such as quality circles and work teams. The United States was the most individualistic culture in Hofstede's study of national cultures; Japan is much more collectivist. Group practices such as the quality circle and teams are natural and consistent with the Japanese culture. When introduced into a more individualistic culture, these same practices might cause difficulties or require some time for workers to get used to. At the very least, Kim should proceed with caution, discuss ideas for the new practices with the workers before making any changes, and then monitor the changes closely so that adjustments can be made to improve them as the workers gain familiarity with them and have suggestions of their own.

Chapter 6

1. d
2. a
3. b
4. b
5. b
6. a
7. d
8. a
9. b
10. a
11. b
12. d
13. c
14. b
15. a
16. Entrepreneurship is rich with diversity. It is an avenue for business entry and career success that is pursued by many women and members of minority groups. Data show almost 40 percent of U.S. businesses are owned by women. Many report leaving other employment because they had limited opportunities. For them, entrepreneurship made available the opportunities for career success that they lacked. Minority-owned businesses are one of the fastest-growing sectors, with the growth rates highest for Hispanic-owned, Asian-owned, and African-American-owned businesses in that order.

17. The three stages in the life cycle of an entrepreneurial firm are birth, breakthrough, and maturity. In the birth stage, the leader is challenged to get customers, establish a market, and find the money needed to keep the business going. In the breakthrough stage, the challenges shift to becoming and staying profitable, and managing growth. In the maturity stage, a leader is more focused on revising/maintaining a good business strategy and more generally managing the firm for continued success and possibly more future growth.

18. The limited partnership form of small business ownership consists of a general partner and one or more "limited partners." The general partner(s) play an active role in managing and operating the business; the limited partners do not. All contribute resources of some value to the partnership for the conduct of the business. The advantage of any partnership form is that the partners may share in profits, but their potential for losses is limited by the size of their original investments.

19. This is the realm of "intrapreneurship," or entrepreneurship that takes place within the context of a large organization. One of the ways to stimulate entrepreneurship in such settings is to make it a valued part of the culture—in other words, to reward entrepreneurial behavior, not discourage it. Another way is to set up entrepreneurial units, sometimes called skunkworks, that are allowed to operate free from any constraints of the larger organization. The creative teamwork in these units can be a major force for entrepreneurship.

20. My friend is right—it takes a lot of forethought and planning

to prepare the launch of a new business venture. In response to the question of how to ensure that I am really being customer-focused, I would ask and answer for myself the following questions. In all cases I would try to frame my business model so that the answers are realistic but still push my business toward a strong customer orientation. The "customer" questions might include: "Who are my potential customers? What market niche am I shooting for? What do the customers in this market really want? How do these customers make purchase decisions? How much will it cost to produce and distribute my product/service to these customers? How much will it cost to attract and retain customers?" Following an overall executive summary, which includes a commitment to this customer orientation, I would address the following areas in writing up my initial business plan. The plan would address such areas as company description—mission, owners, and legal form—as well as an industry analysis, product and services description, marketing description and strategy, staffing model, financial projections with cash flows, and capital needs.

Chapter 7

1. c
2. a
3. c
4. c
5. c
6. a
7. c
8. b
9. a
10. b
11. a
12. c
13. a
14. d
15. a
16. An optimizing decision is one that represents the absolute "best" choice of alternatives. It is selected from a set of all known alternatives. A satisficing decision selects the first alternative that offers a "satisfactory" choice, not necessarily the absolute best choice. It is selected from a limited or incomplete set of alternatives.
17. The ethics of a decision can be checked with the "spotlight" question: "How would you feel if your family found out?" "How would you feel if this were published in the local newspaper?" Also, one can test the decision by evaluating it on four criteria. (1) Utility—does it satisfy all stakeholders? (2) Rights—does it respect everyone's rights? (3) Justice—is it consistent with fairness and justice? (4) Caring—does it meet responsibilities for caring?
18. A manager using systematic thinking is going to approach problem solving in a logical and rational fashion. The tendency will be to proceed in a linear step-by-step fashion, handling one issue at a time. A manager using intuitive thinking will be more spontaneous and open in problem solving. He or she may jump from one stage in the process to the other and deal with many different things at once.
19. It almost seems contradictory to say that one can prepare for crisis, but it is possible. The concept of crisis management is used to describe how managers and others prepare for unexpected high-impact events that threaten an organization's health and well-being. Crisis management involves both anticipating possible crises and preparing teams and plans ahead of time for how to handle them if they do occur. Many organizations today, for example, are developing crisis management plans to deal with terrorism and computer "hacking" attacks.
20. This is what I would say: Continuing developments in information technology are changing the work setting for most employees. An important development for the traditional white-collar worker falls in the area of office automation—the use of computers and related technologies to facilitate everyday office work. In the "electronic office" of today and tomorrow, you should be prepared to work with and take full advantage of the following: smart workstations supported by desktop computers; voice messaging systems whereby computers take dictation, answer the telephone, and relay messages; database and word processing software systems that allow storage, access, and manipulation of data as well as the preparation of reports; electronic mail systems that send mail and data computer to computer; electronic bulletin boards for posting messages; and computer conferencing and videoconferencing that allow people to work with one another every day over great distances. These are among the capabilities of the new workplace. To function effectively, you must be prepared not only to use these systems to full advantage but also to stay abreast of new developments as they become available.

Chapter 8

1. d
2. a
3. b
4. d
5. b
6. d
7. c
8. c
9. c
10. d
11. a
12. d
13. d
14. d
15. a
16. The five steps in the formal planning process are: (1) Define your objectives, (2) determine where you stand relative to objectives, (3) develop premises about future conditions, (4) identify and choose among ac-

tion alternatives to accomplish objectives, (5) implement action plans and evaluate results.

17. Benchmarking is the use of external standards to help evaluate one's own situation and develop ideas and directions for improvement. The bookstore owner/manager might visit other bookstores in other towns which are known for their success. By observing and studying the operations of those stores and then comparing her store to them, the owner/manager can develop plans for future action.

18. Douglas McGregor's concept of Theory Y involves the assumption that people can be trusted to exercise self-control in their work. This is the essence of internal control—people controlling their own work by taking personal responsibility for results. If manager's approach work with McGregor's Theory Y assumptions, they will, according to him, promote more self-control or internal control by people at work.

19. A progressive discipline system works by adjusting the discipline to fit the severity and frequency of the inappropriate behavior. In the case of a person who comes late to work, for example, progressive discipline might involve a verbal warning after 3 late arrivals, a written warning after 5, and a pay-loss penalty after 7. In the case of a person who steals money from the business, there would be immediate dismissal after the first such infraction.

20. I would begin the speech by describing MBO as an integrated planning and control approach. I would also clarify that the key elements in MBO are objectives and participation. Any objectives should be clear, measurable, and time-defined. In addition, these objectives should be set with the full involvement and participation of the employees; they should not be set by the manager and then told to the employees. Given this, I would describe how each business manager should jointly set objectives with each of his or her employees and jointly review progress toward their accomplishment. I would suggest that the employees should work on the required activities while staying in communication with their managers. The managers, in turn, should provide any needed support or assistance to their employees. This whole process could be formally recycled at least twice per year.

Chapter 9

1. a
2. b
3. c
4. c
5. d
6. b
7. c
8. a
9. b
10. c
11. d
12. b
13. d
14. a
15. c
16. A corporate strategy sets long-term direction for an enterprise as a whole. Functional strategies set directions so that business functions such as marketing and manufacturing support the overall corporate strategy.
17. A SWOT analysis is useful during strategic planning. It involves the analysis of organizational strengths and weaknesses, and of environmental opportunities and threats.
18. An e-business strategy uses the Internet to help achieve sustainable competitive advantage. This can be done through B2B strategies that link businesses electronically with one another in business-to-business relationships. A good example is B2B in supply chain management, where suppliers are linked by the Internet and extranets to customers' information systems. They follow sales and track inventories in real time and ship new orders as needed. The B2C approach is more of a retailing model linking businesses to customers. An example is Amazon.com, which uses online sales and online customer interaction to sell its products.

19. Strategic leadership is the ability to enthuse people to participate in continuous change, performance enhancement, and the implementation of organizational strategies. The special qualities of the successful strategic leader include the ability to make trade-offs, create a sense of urgency, communicate the strategy, and engage others in continuous learning about the strategy and its performance responsibilities.

20. Porter's competitive strategy model involves the possible use of three alternative strategies: differentiation, cost leadership, and focus. In this situation, the larger department store seems better positioned to follow the cost leadership strategy. This means that Kim may want to consider the other two alternatives. A differentiation strategy would involve trying to distinguish Kim's products from those of the larger store. This might involve a "made in America" theme or an emphasis on leather or canvas or some other type of clothing material. A focus strategy might specifically target college students and try to respond to their tastes and needs rather than those of the the larger community population. This might involve special orders and other types of individualized service for the college student market.

Chapter 10

1. b
2. a
3. b
4. a
5. b
6. c
7. b

8. b
9. b
10. a
11. a
12. a
13. c
14. c
15. b
16. The product structure organizes work around a product; the division or unit would be headed by a product manager or executive. The geographical structure organizes work by area or location; different geographical regions would be headed by regional managers or executives.
17. The functional structure is prone to problems of internal coordination. One symptom may be that the different functional areas, such as marketing and manufacturing, are not working well together. This structure is also slow in responding to changing environmental trends and challenges. If the firm finds that its competitors are getting to market faster with new and better products, this is another potential indicator that the functional structure is not supporting operations properly.
18. A network structure often involves one organization "contracting out" aspects of its operations to other organizations that specialize in them. The example used in the text was of a company that contracted out its mailroom services. Through the formation of networks of contracts, the organization is reduced to a core of essential employees whose expertise is concentrated in the primary business areas. The contracts are monitored and maintained in the network to allow the overall operations of the organization to continue even though they are not directly accomplished by full-time employees.
19. By reducing levels of management, the organization may benefit from lower overhead costs. It can also benefit as lower levels find they are in closer and more frequent contact with higher levels, and vice versa. Communication should flow more readily and quickly up and down the chain of command, as there are fewer levels to pass through. This should also mean that decisions are made more quickly.
20. Faisal must first have confidence in the two engineers—he must trust them and respect their capabilities. Second, he must have confidence in himself—trusting his own judgment to give up some work and allow these others to do it. Third, he should follow the rules of effective delegation. These include being very clear on what must be accomplished by each engineer. Their responsibilities should be clearly understood. He must also give them the authority to act in order to fulfill their responsibility, especially in relationship to the other engineers. And he must not forget his own final accountability for the results. He should remain in control and, through communication, make sure that work proceeds as planned.

Chapter 11

1. b
2. d
3. b
4. a
5. c
6. b
7. a
8. b
9. b
10. c
11. b
12. c
13. c
14. a
15. b
16. The term "contingency" is used in management to indicate that management strategies and practices should be tailored to fit the unique needs of individual situations. There is no universal solution that fits all problems and circumstances. Thus, in organizational design, contingency thinking must be used to identify and implement particular organizational points in time. What works well at one point in time may not work well in another as the environment and other conditions change.
17. The environment is an important influence on organizational design. The more complex, variable, and uncertain the elements in the general and specific environments, the more difficult it is for the organization to operate. This calls for more organic designs. In general, stable and more certain environments allow for mechanistic designs since operations can be more routine and predictable.
18. Differentiation and integration are somewhat conflicting in organizational design. As differentiation increases—that is, as more differences are present in the complexity of the organization—more integration is needed to ensure that everything functions together to the betterment of the whole organization. However, the greater the differentiation, the harder it is to achieve integration. Thus, when differentiation is high, organization design tends to shift toward the use of more complex horizontal approaches to integration and away from the vertical ones such as formal authority and rules or policies. In horizontal integration, the focus is on such things as cross-functional teams and matrix structures.
19. The focus of process reengineering is on reducing costs and streamlining operations efficiency while improving customer service. This is accomplished by closely examining core business processes through the following sequence of activities: (1) identify the core processes; (2) map them in a workflows diagram; (3) evaluate all tasks involved; (4) seek ways to eliminate unnecessary tasks; (5) seek ways to eliminate delays, errors, and misunderstandings in the workflows; and (6) seek efficiencies in how work is shared

and transferred among people and departments.

20. This situation involves the basic contingency notion of organizational design. There is no one best way to design an organization, and different designs serve organizations well under different circumstances. The first person is most likely working for an organization facing rather routine and known environmental demands. This allows for the organizational design to become more vertical and mechanistic, focusing as it does on predictable problems and outcomes. The individuals who remain in such a design are probably compatible with the internal climate of such an organization and thus find it a good "fit," resulting in reasonable levels of job satisfaction. By contrast, the second person probably works for an organization facing uncertain challenges in a dynamic environment, with the result that it is by design a more adaptive or flexible structure emphasizing horizontal rather than vertical operations. In this case, the design fits the demands of the environment, and it is also most likely to satisfy those individuals who remain with it over time. Thus we have a good demonstration of two aspects of contingency factors in organizational design: the environment-structure-performance fit and the structure-individual fit.

Chapter 12

1. a
2. b
3. c
4. d
5. b
6. c
7. d
8. b
9. b
10. c
11. a
12. a
13. b
14. a
15. d

16. Internal recruitment deals with job candidates who already know the organization well. It is also a strong motivator because it communicates to everyone the opportunity to advance in the organization through hard work. External recruitment may allow the organization to obtain expertise not available internally. It also brings in employees with new and fresh viewpoints who are not biased by previous experience in the organization.

17. Orientation activities introduce a new employee to the organization and the work environment. This is a time when the individual may develop key attitudes and when performance expectations will also be established. Good orientation communicates positive attitudes and expectations and reinforces the desired organizational culture. It formally introduces the individual to important policies and procedures that everyone is expected to follow.

18. The graphic rating scale simply asks a supervisor to rate an employee on an established set of criteria, such as quantity of work or attitude toward work. This leaves a lot of room for subjectivity and debate. The behaviorally anchored rating scale asks the supervisor to rate the employee on specific behaviors that had been identified as positively or negatively affecting performance in a given job. This is a more specific appraisal approach and leaves less room for debate and disagreement.

19. Mentoring is when a senior and experienced individual adopts a newcomer or more junior person with the goal of helping him or her develop into a successful worker. The mentor may or may not be the individual's immediate supervisor. The mentor meets with the individual and discusses problems, shares advice, and generally supports the individual's attempts to grow and perform. Mentors are considered very useful for persons newly ap-

pointed to management positions.

20. As Sy's supervisor, you face a difficult but perhaps expected human resource management problem. Not only is Sy influential as an informal leader, he also has considerable experience on the job and in the company. Even though he is experiencing performance problems using the new computer system, there is no indication that he doesn't want to work hard and continue to perform for the company. Although retirement is an option, Sy may also be transferred, promoted, or simply terminated. The latter response seems unjustified and may cause legal problems. Transferring Sy, with his agreement, to another position could be a positive move; promoting Sy to a supervisory position in which his experience and networks would be useful is another possibility. The key in this situation seems to be moving Sy out so that a computer-literate person can take over the job, while continuing to utilize Sy in a job that better fits his talents. Transfer and/or promotion should be actively considered both in his and in the company's interest.

Chapter 13

1. d
2. d
3. b
4. a
5. c
6. a
7. b
8. c
9. b
10. a
11. b
12. a
13. d
14. a
15. b

16. Position power is based on reward, coercion or punishment, and legitimacy or formal authority. Managers, however, need to have more power than

that made available to them by the position alone. Thus, they have to develop personal power through expertise and reference. This personal power is essential in helping managers to get things done beyond the scope of their position power alone.

17. Leader-participation theory suggests that leadership effectiveness is determined in part by how well managers or leaders handle the many different problem or decision situations that they face every day. Decisions can be made through individual or authority, consultative, or group-consensus approaches. No one of these decision methods is always the best; each is a good fit for certain types of situations. A good manager or leader is able to use each of these approaches and knows when each is the best approach to use in various situations.

18. (1) Position power—how much power the leader has in terms of rewards, punishments, and legitimacy. (2) Leader–member relations—the quality of relationships between the leader and followers. (3) Task structure—the degree to which the task is clear and well defined, or open ended and more ambiguous.

19. Drucker says that good leaders have more than the "charisma" or "personality" being popularized in the concept of transformational leadership. He reminds us that good leaders work hard to accomplish some basic things in their everyday activities. These include: (1) establishing a clear sense of mission, (2) accepting leadership as a responsibility, not a rank, and (3) earning and keeping the respect of others.

20. In his new position, Marcel must understand that the transactional aspects of leadership are not sufficient to guarantee him long-term leadership effectiveness. He must move be-

yond the effective use of task-oriented and people-oriented behaviors and demonstrate through his personal qualities the capacity to inspire others. A charismatic leader develops a unique relationship with followers in which they become enthusiastic, highly loyal, and high achievers. Marcel needs to work very hard to develop positive relationships with the team members. He must emphasize in those relationships high aspirations for perform-ance accomplishments, en-thusiasm, ethical behavior, integrity and honesty in all dealings, and a clear vision of the future. By working hard with this agenda and by allowing his personality to positively express itself in the team setting, Marcel should make continuous progress as an effective and moral leader.

Chapter 14

1. c
2. d
3. d
4. b
5. b
6. d
7. c
8. b
9. d
10. a
11. b
12. a
13. b
14. c
15. a
16. People high in need for achievement will prefer work settings and jobs in which they have (1) challenging but achievable goals, (2) individual responsibility, and (3) performance feedback.
17. Participation is important to goal-setting theory because, in general, people tend to be more committed to the accomplishment of goals they have helped to set. When people participate in the setting of goals, they also understand them better. Participation in goal setting improves goal acceptance and understanding.

18. Motivation is formally defined as the forces within an individual that account for the level, direction, and persistence of effort expended at work. Thus a person who is highly motivated will work hard. This does not necessarily mean that person will be a high performer. High performance also depends on ability and support, not just effort due to high motivation.

19. Herzberg suggests that job content factors are the satisfiers or motivators. Based in the job itself, they represent such things as responsibility, sense of achievement, and feelings of growth. Job context factors are considered sources of dissatisfaction. They are found in the job environment and include such things as base pay, technical quality of supervision, and working conditions. Whereas improvements in job context make people less dissatisfied, improvements in job content are considered necessary to motivate them to high-performance levels.

20. It has already been pointed out in the answer to question 16 that a person with a high need for achievement likes moderately challenging goals and performance feedback. Participation of both manager and subordinate in goal setting offers an opportunity to choose goals to which the subordinate will respond and which also will serve the organization. Furthermore, through goal setting, the manager and individual subordinates can identify performance standards or targets. Progress toward these targets can be positively reinforced by the manager. Such reinforcements can serve as indicators of progress to someone with high need for achievement, thus responding to their desires for performance feedback.

Chapter 15

1. a
2. c

3. c
4. c
5. a
6. b
7. b
8. a
9. b
10. b
11. d
12. c
13. a
14. b
15. c
16. A psychological contract is the individual's view of the inducements he or she expects to receive from the organization in return for his or her work contributions. The contract is healthy when the individual perceives that the inducements and contributions are fair and in a state of balance.
17. Growth-need strength helps determine which individuals are good candidates for job enrichment. A person high in growth-need strength seeks higher-order satisfaction of ego and self-fulfilment needs at work. These are needs to which job enrichment can positively respond. A person low in growth-need strength may not respond well to the demands and responsibilities of an enriched job.
18. All the Big Five personality traits are relevant to the workplace. To give some basic examples, consider the following. Extroversion suggests whether or not a person will reach out to relate and work well with others. Agreeableness suggests whether or not a person is open to the ideas of others and willing to go along with group decisions. Conscientiousness suggests whether someone can be depended on to meet commitments and perform agreed-upon tasks. Emotional stability suggests whether or not someone will be relaxed and secure, or uptight and tense, in work situations. Openness suggests whether someone will be open to new ideas or resistant to change.

19. The compressed workweek, or 4–40 schedule, offers employees the advantage of a three-day weekend. However, it can cause problems for the employer in terms of ensuring that operations are covered adequately during the normal five workdays of the week. Labor unions may resist, and the compressed workweek will entail more complicated work scheduling. In addition, some employees find that the schedule is tiring and can cause family adjustment problems.
20. The high-performance equation states: Performance = Ability × Support × Effort. The multiplication signs are important. They indicate that each of the performance factors must be high and positive in order for high performance to occur. That is, neither ability nor effort can be neglected by Kurt or any of the managers/team leaders in his plant. Furthermore, the factors are straightforward in their managerial implications. Ability is an issue of proper selection, training, and development of all employees. Support involves providing capable employees with such things as clear goals, appropriate technology, helpful structures, and an absence of performance obstacles such as poor rules and procedures. Effort involves making sure that the environment is motivating and offers varied intrinsic as well as extrinsic rewards. Only by giving direct and serious attention to each of these factors can Kurt and his management team take full advantage of the insights of the high-performance equation.

Chapter 16

1. d
2. b
3. b
4. d
5. b
6. d

7. b
8. c
9. a
10. b
11. c
12. b
13. a
14. b
15. a
16. Input factors can have a major impact on group effectiveness. In order to best prepare a group to perform effectively, a manager should make sure that the right people are put in the group (maximize available talents and abilities), that these people are capable of working well together (membership characteristics should promote good relationships), that the tasks are clear, and that the group has the resources and environment needed to perform up to expectations.
17. A group's performance can be analyzed according to the interaction between cohesiveness and performance norms. In a highly cohesive group, members tend to conform to group norms. Thus, when the performance norm is positive and cohesion is high, we can expect everyone to work hard to support the norm—high performance is likely. By the same token, high cohesion and a low performance norm will act similarly—low performance is likely. With other combinations of norms and cohesion, the performance results will be more mixed.
18. The textbook lists several symptoms of groupthink along with various strategies for avoiding groupthink (see Manager's Notepad 16.3). For example, a group whose members censure themselves from contributing "contrary" or "different" opinions and/or whose members keep talking about outsiders as "weak" or the "enemy" may be suffering from groupthink. This may be avoided or corrected, for example, by asking someone to be the "devil's advocate" for a meeting and by inviting-in an

outside observer to help gather different viewpoints.

19. In a traditional work group, the manager or supervisor directs the group. In a self-managing team, the members of the team provide self-direction. They plan, organize, and evaluate their work, share tasks, and help one another develop skills; they may even make hiring decisions. A true self-managing team does not need the traditional "boss" or supervisor, since the team as a whole takes on the supervisory responsibilities.

20. Marcos is faced with a highly cohesive group whose members conform to a negative or low-performance norm. This is a difficult situation that is ideally resolved by changing the performance norm. In order to gain the group's commitment to a high-performance norm, Marcos should act as a positive role model for the norm. He must communicate the norm clearly and positively to the group. He should not assume that everyone knows what he expects of them. He may also talk to the informal leader and gain his or her commitment to the norm. He might carefully reward high-performance behaviors within the group. He may introduce new members with high-performance records and commitments. And he might hold group meetings in which performance standards and expectations are discussed, with an emphasis on committing to new high-performance directions. If his attempts to introduce a high-performance norm fail, Marcos may have to take steps to reduce group cohesiveness so that individual members can pursue higher-performance results without feeling bound by group pressures to restrict their performance.

Chapter 17

1. b
2. a
3. c
4. b
5. c
6. b
7. b
8. d
9. c
10. a
11. d
12. a
13. b
14. b
15. d
16. The manager's goal in active listening is to help the subordinate say what he or she really means. To do this, the manager should carefully listen for the content of what someone is saying, paraphrase or reflect back what the person appears to be saying, remain sensitive to nonverbal cues and feelings, and not be evaluative.

17. The halo effect occurs when a single attribute of a person, such as the way he or she dresses, is used to evaluate or form an overall impression of the person. Selective perception occurs when someone focuses in a situation on those aspects that reinforce or are most consistent with his or her existing values, beliefs, or experiences.

18. Win-lose outcomes are likely when conflict is managed through high-assertiveness and low-cooperativeness styles. In this situation of competition, the conflict is resolved by one person or group dominating another. Lose-lose outcomes occur when conflict is managed through avoidance (where nothing is resolved) and possibly when it is managed through compromise (where each party gives up something to the other). Win-win outcomes are associated mainly with problem solving and collaboration in conflict management, which is a result of high assertiveness and high cooperativeness.

19. In a negotiation, both substance and relationship goals are important. Substance goals relate to the content of the negotiation. A substance goal, for example, may relate to the final salary agreement between a job candidate and a prospective employer. Relationship goals relate to the quality of the interpersonal relationships among the negotiating parties. Relationship goals are important because the negotiating parties most likely have to work together in the future. For example, if relationships are poor after a labor–management negotiation, the likelihood is that future problems will occur.

20. Harold can do a number of things to establish and maintain a system of upward communication for his department store branch. To begin, he should, as much as possible, try to establish a highly interactive style of management based upon credibility and trust. Credibility is earned through building personal power through expertise and reference. With credibility, he might set the tone for the department managers by using MBWA—"managing by wandering around." Once this pattern is established, trust will build between him and other store employees, and he should find that he learns a lot from interacting directly with them. Harold should also set up a formal communication structure, such as bimonthly store meetings, where he communicates store goals, results, and other issues to the staff, and in which he listens to them in return. An e-mail system whereby Harold and his staff could send massages to one another from their workstation computers would also be beneficial.

Chapter 18

1. b
2. a
3. b
4. c
5. c
6. b
7. c

8. a
9. d
10. a
11. a
12. d
13. c
14. a
15. c
16. Lewin's three phases of planned change are: Unfreezing—preparing a system for change; changing—moving or creating change in a system; and refreezing—stabilizing and reinforcing change once it has occurred.
17. In general, managers can expect that others will be more committed and loyal to changes that are brought about through shared power strategies. Rational persuasion strategies can also create enduring effects if they are accepted. Force-coercion strategies tend to have temporary effects only.
18. The statement that "OD equals planned change plus" basically refers to the fact that OD tries both to create change in an organization and to make the organization members capable of creating such change for themselves in the future.
19. The Type A personality is characteristic of people who bring stress on themselves by virtue of personal characteristics. These tend to be compulsive individuals who are uncomfortable waiting for things to happen, who try to do many things at once, and who generally move fast and have difficulty slowing down. Type A personalities can be stressful for both the individuals and the people around them. Managers must be aware of Type A personality tendencies in their own behavior and among others with whom they work. Ideally, this awareness will help the manager take precautionary steps to best manage the stress caused by this personality type.
20. In any change situation, it is important to remember that successful planned change occurs only when all three phases of change—unfreezing, changing, and refreezing—have been taken care of. Thus, I would not rush into the changing phase. Rather, I would work with the people involved to develop a felt need for change based on their ideas and inputs as well as mine. Then I would proceed by supporting the changes and helping to stabilize them into everyday routines. I would also be sensitive to any resistance and respect that resistance as a signal that something important is being threatened. By listening to resistance, I would be in a position to better modify the change to achieve a better fit with the people and the situation. Finally, I would want to take maximum advantage of the shared power strategy, supported by rational persuasion, and with limited use of force-coercion (if it is used at all). By doing all of this, I would like my staff to feel empowered and committed to constructive improvement through planned change.

Glossary

A

Above-average returns exceed what could be earned from alternative investments of equivalent risk.

Accommodation or **smoothing** plays down differences and highlights similarities to reduce conflict.

An **accommodative strategy** of social responsibility tries to satisfy prevailing economic, legal, and ethical performance criteria.

Accountability is the requirement to show performance results to a supervisor.

Action research is a collaborative process of collecting data, using it for action planning, and evaluating the results.

Active listening involves taking action to help the source of a message say what he or she really means.

An **adaptive organization** operates with a minimum of bureaucratic features and encourages worker empowerment and teamwork.

The **administrative decision model** describes how managers act in situations of limited information and bounded rationality.

An **administrator** is a manager who works in a public or nonprofit organization.

An **affirmative action** program tries to increase employment opportunities for women and minorities.

An **after-action review** formally reviews results to identify lessons learned in a completed project, task force, or special operation.

Aggreeableness is being good-natured, cooperative, and trusting.

An **analyzer strategy** seeks the stability of a core business while selectively responding to opportunities for innovation and change.

An **angel investor** is a wealthy individual willing to invest in return for equity in a new venture.

APEC, Asia-Pacific Economic Cooperation is a platform for regional economic alliances among Asian and Pacific Rim countries.

Applications software allows the user to perform a variety of information-based tasks without writing unique computer programs.

An **apprenticeship** is a special form of training that involves a formal assignment to serve as understudy or assistant to a person who already has the desired job skills.

Arbitration is the process by which parties to a dispute agree to abide by the decision of a neutral and independent third party, called an arbitrator.

The **Asian-Pacific Economic Forum (APEC)** is a platform for regional economic cooperation among Asian and Pacific Rim countries.

An **assessment center** is a selection technique that engages job candidates in a series of experimental activities over a 1- or 2-day period.

An **attitude** is a predisposition to act in a certain way.

Attribution error overestimates internal factors and underestimates external factors as influences on someone's behavior.

Authentic leadership activates high self-awareness and self-regulated positive behavior in one's self and others.

Authoritarianism is the degree to which a person tends to defer to authority.

Authority is the right to assign tasks and direct the activities of subordinates in ways that support accomplishment of the organization's purpose.

An **authority decision** is a decision made by the leader and then communicated to the group.

A leader with an **autocratic style** acts in unilateral command-and-control fashion.

Automation is the total mechanization of a job.

Avoidance involves pretending that a conflict doesn't really exist or hoping that a conflict will simply go away.

B

A **B2C business strategy** uses IT to link businesses with customers.

A **bargaining zone** is the area between one party's minimum reservation point and the other party's maximum reservation point.

Base compensation is a salary or hourly wage paid to an individual.

BATNA is the "best alternative to a negotiated agreement," or what can be done if an agreement cannot be reached.

The **BCG matrix** ties strategy formulation to an analysis of business opportunities according to market growth rate and market share.

The **behavioral decision model** describes decision making with limited information and bounded rationality.

A **behaviorally anchored rating scale (BARS)** is a performance appraisal method that uses specific descriptions of actual behaviors to rate various levels of performance.

Benchmarking is a process of comparing operations and performance with other organizations known for excellence.

Best practices are things that lead to superior performance.

Bona fide occupational qualifications are EEO exceptions justified by individual capacity to perform a job.

A **bonus pay plan** provides cash bonuses to employees based on the achievement of specific performance targets.

In **bottom-up change,** change initiatives come from all levels in the organization.

Bottom-up planning begins with ideas developed at lower management levels, which are modified as they are passed up the hierarchy to top management.

A **boundaryless organization** eliminates internal boundaries among parts and external boundaries with the external environment.

Brainstorming is a group technique for generating a large quantity of ideas by free-wheeling contributions made without criticism.

Break-even analysis calculates where sales revenues cover costs.

A **budget** is a plan that commits resources to projects or programs; a formalized way of allocating resources to specific activities.

Bureaucracy is a rational and efficient form of organization founded on logic, order, and legitimate authority.

Business incubators offer space, shared services, and advice to help small businesses get started.

A **business plan** describes the direction for a new business and the financing needed to operate it.

A **business strategy** identifies the intentions of a division or strategic business unit to compete in its special product and /or service domain.

C

A **career** is a sequence of jobs that constitute what a person does for a living.

Career planning is the process of systematically matching career goals and individual capabilities with opportunities for their fulfillment.

A **career plateau** is a position from which someone is unlikely to move to a higher level of work responsibility.

A **career portfolio** documents academic and personal accomplishments for external review.

Centralization is the concentration of authority for most decisions at the top level of an organization.

In a **centralized communication network** communication flows only between individual members and a hub or center point.

A **certain environment** offers complete information on possible action alternatives and their consequences.

The **chain of command** links all persons with successively higher levels of authority.

A **change agent** is a person or group that takes leadership responsibility for changing the existing pattern of behavior of another person or social system.

Changing is the central phase in the planned change process in which a planned change actually takes place.

Channel richness is the capacity of a communication channel to effectively carry information.

A **charismatic leader** is a leader who develops special leader-follower relationships and inspires followers in extraordinary ways.

Child labor is the full-time employment of children for work otherwise done by adults.

A **CIO** is a senior executive responsible for IT and its utilization throughout an organization.

The **classical decision model** describes how managers ideally make decisions using complete information.

Coaching is the communication of specific technical advice to an individual.

A **code of ethics** is a written document that states values and ethical standards intended to guide the behavior of employees.

Coercive power is the capacity to punish or withhold positive outcomes as a means of influencing other people.

Cognitive dissonance is discomfort felt when attitude and behavior are inconsistent.

Cohesiveness is the degree to which members are attracted to and motivated to remain part of a team.

Collaboration or **problem solving** involves working through conflict differences and solving problems so everyone wins.

Collective bargaining is the process of negotiating, administering, and interpreting a labor contract.

A **combination strategy** involves stability, growth, and retrenchment in one or more combinations.

Commercializing innovation turns ideas into economic value added.

A **committee** is a formal team designated to work on a special task on a continuing basis.

Communication is the process of sending and receiving symbols with meanings attached.

A **communication channel** is the medium through which a message is sent.

Comparable worth holds that persons performing jobs of similar importance should be paid at comparable levels.

Comparative management is the study of how management practices differ systematically from one country and/or culture to the next.

Competition or **authoritative command** uses force, superior skill, or domination to "win" a conflict.

A **competitive advantage** is a special edge that allows an organization to deal with market and environmental forces better than its competitors.

A **compressed workweek** is any work schedule that allows a full-time job to be completed in less than the standard 5 days of 8-hour shifts.

Compromise occurs when each party to the conflict gives up something of value to the other.

Computer competency is the ability to understand and use computers to advantage.

Growth through **concentration** is within the same business area.

A **conceptual skill** is the ability to think analytically and solve complex problems to the benefit of everyone involved.

A **concurrent control** or *steering control* is a control that acts in anticipation of problems and focuses primarily on what happens during the work process.

Conflict is a disagreement over issues of substance and/or an emotional antagonism.

Conflict resolution is the removal of the reasons—substantial and/or emotional—for a conflict.

Conscientiousness is being responsible, dependable, and careful in work.

Constructive stress acts in a positive way to increase effort, stimulate creativity, and encourage diligence in one's work.

A **consultative decision** is a decision made by a leader after receiving information, advice, or opinions from group members.

Contingency planning identifies alternative courses of action that can be taken if and when circumstances change with time.

Contingency thinking maintains that there is no one best way to manage; what is best depends on the situation.

Contingency workers are employed a part-time and temporary basis to supplement a permanent workforce.

Continuous improvement involves always searching for new ways to improve operations quality and performance.

In **continuous-process production** raw production materials continuously move through an automated system.

A **control chart** is a method for quality control in which work results are displayed on a graph that clearly delineates upper control limits and lower control limits.

Controlling is the process of measuring performance and taking action to ensure desired results.

A **core competency** is a special strength that gives an organization a competitive advantage.

Core values are underlying beliefs shared by members of the organization and that influence their behavior.

Corporate culture is the predominant value system for the organization as a whole.

Corporate governance is the system of control and performance monitoring of top management.

Corporate social responsibility is an obligation of an organization to act in ways that serve both its own interests and the interests of its many external publics.

A **corporate strategy** sets long-term direction for the total enterprise.

A **corporation** is a legal entity that exists separately from its owners.

Corruption involves illegal practices to further one's business interests.

A **cost leadership strategy** is a corporate competitive strategy that seeks to achieve lower costs than competitors by improving efficiency of production, distribution, and other organizational systems.

Cost-benefit analysis involves comparing the costs and benefits of each potential course of action.

Creativity is the generation of a novel idea or unique approach that solves a problem or crafts an opportunity.

Credibility is trust and respect in the eyes of others.

A **crisis** is an unexpected problem that can lead to disaster if not resolved quickly and appropriately.

Crisis management is preparation for the management of crises that threaten an organization's health and well-being.

A **critical-incident technique** is a performance appraisal method that involves a running log of effective and ineffective job behaviors.

A **cross-functional team** is a team structure in which members from different functional departments work together as needed to solve problems and explore opportunities.

Cultural relativism suggests there is no one right way to behave; ethical behavior is determined by its cultural context.

Culture is a shared set of beliefs, values, and patterns of behavior common to a group of people.

Culture shock is the confusion and discomfort a person experiences when in an unfamiliar culture.

Currency risk is possible loss because of fluctuating exchange rates.

Customer relationship management strategically tries to build lasting relationships and add value to customers.

A **customer structure** is a divisional structure that groups together jobs and activities that serve the same customers or clients.

A **cybernetic control system** is a control system that is entirely self-contained in its performance monitoring and correction capabilities.

Cycle time is the elapsed time between the receipt of an order and the delivery of a finished good or service.

D

Data are raw facts and observations.

Debt financing involves borrowing money that must be repaid over time with interest.

Decentralization is the dispersion of authority to make decisions throughout all levels of the organization.

A **decentralized communication network** allows all members to communicate directly with one another.

A **decision** is a choice among alternative courses of action for dealing with a "problem."

Decision making is the process of making choices among alternative possible courses of action.

The **decision-making process** begins with identification of a problem and ends with evaluation of implemented solutions.

A **decision support system** allows managers to interact with the computer to utilize information for solving structured and semistructured problems.

A **defender strategy** is a corporate competitive strategy that emphasizes existing products and current market share without seeking growth.

A **defensive strategy** of social responsibility seeks to protect the organization by doing the minimum legally required to satisfy social expectations.

Delegation is the process of distributing and entrusting work to other persons.

Departmentalization is the process of grouping together people and jobs under common supervisors to form various work units or departments.

Design for disassembly is the design of products with attention to how their component parts will be used when product life ends.

Design for manufacturing is creating a design that lowers production costs and improves quality in all stages of production.

Destructive stress impairs the performance of an individual.

Differentiation is the degree of differences that exist among people, departments, or other internal components of an organization.

A **differentiation strategy** is a corporate strategy that seeks competitive advantage through uniqueness, by developing goods and/or services that are clearly different from those offered by the competition.

Discipline is the act of influencing behavior through reprimand.

Discrimination is an active form of prejudice that disadvantages people by denying them full benefits of organizational membership.

A **distinctive competence** is a special strength that gives an organization a competitive advantage in its operating domain.

Distributive justice concerns the degree to which people are treated the same regardless of individual characteristics such as ethnicity, race, gender, or age.

Distributive negotiation focuses on "win-lose" claims

made by each party for certain preferred outcomes.

Growth through **diversification** is by acquisition of or investment in new and different business areas.

The term **diversity** describes race, gender, age, and other individual differences.

Divestiture sells off parts of the organization to focus attention and resources on core business areas.

A **divisional structure** groups together people who work on the same product, work with similar customers, or work in the same area or processes.

Downsizing decreases the size of operations with the intent to become more streamlined.

A **dual-career couple** is one in which both adult partners are employed.

Dysfunctional conflict is destructive and hurts task performance.

E

An **e-business strategy** strategically uses the Internet to gain competitive advantage.

The **economic order quantity (EOQ)** method orders a fixed number of items every time an inventory level falls to a predetermined point.

Effective communication occurs when the intended meaning of the source and the perceived meaning of the receiver are identical.

An **effective group** is a group that achieves and maintains high levels of both task performance and membership satisfaction over time.

Effective negotiation occurs when issues of substance and working relationships among the negotiating parties are maintained or even improved in the process.

An **effective team** achieves high levels of both task performance and membership satisfaction.

Efficient communication is communication that occurs at minimum cost in terms of resources expended.

Electronic commerce or *e-business* uses information technology to support online commercial transactions.

An **emergent strategy** develops over time as managers learn from and respond to experience.

Emotional conflict results from feelings of anger, distrust, dislike, fear, and resentment as well as from personality clashes.

Emotional intelligence is the ability to manage ourselves and our relationships effectively.

Emotional stability is being relaxed, secure, and unworried.

Employee assistance programs help employees cope with personal stresses and problems.

An **employee Involvement team** meets on a regular basis to use its talents to help solve problems and achieve continuous improvement.

An **employee stock ownership plan** (ESOP) allows employees to share ownership of their employing organization through the purchase of stock.

Employment discrimination occurs when non–job relevant criteria are used for hiring and job placements.

Empowerment distributes decision-making power throughout an organization.

An **enterprise-wide network** is a set of computer-communication links that connect a diverse set of activities throughout an organization.

An **entrepreneur** is willing to pursue opportunities in situations others view as problems or threats.

Entrepreneurship is dynamic, risk-taking, creative, and growth-oriented behavior.

Environmental uncertainty is a lack of complete information about the environment.

Environmentalism is the expression and demonstration of public concern for conditions of the natural or physical environment.

Equal employment opportunity (EEO) is the right to employment and advancement without regard to race, sex, religion, color, or national origin.

Equity financing involves exchanging ownership shares for outside investment monies.

Escalating commitment is the tendency to continue to pursue a course of action even though it is not working.

Ethical behavior is accepted as "right' or "good' in the context of a governing moral code.

An **ethical dilemma** is a situation with a potential course of action that, although offering potential benefit or gain, is also unethical.

The attempt to externally impose one's ethical standards on other cultures is criticized as a form of **ethical imperialism.**

Ethical leadership is always "good" and "right" by moral standards.

Ethics set moral standards as to what is good or bad, or right or wrong in one's conduct.

Ethics training seeks to help people better understand the ethical aspects of decision making and to incorporate high ethical standards into their daily behavior.

Ethnocentric attitudes consider practices of the home country as the best.

Ethnocentrism is the tendency to consider one's culture as superior to all others.

The **euro** is the new common European currency.

The **European Union (EU)** is a political and economic alliance of European countries that have agreed to support mutual economic growth and to lift barriers that previously limited cross-border trade and business development.

Eustress is stress that is constructive for an individual and helps her or him achieve a positive balance with the external environment.

An **expatriate** lives and works in a foreign country.

Expectancy is a person's belief that working hard will result in high task performance.

Expert power is the capability to influence other people because of specialized knowledge.

An **expert system** is a computer program designed to analyze and solve problems at the level of the human expert.

Exporting is the process of producing products locally and selling them abroad in foreign markets.

External control is control that occurs through direct supervision or administrative systems, such as rules and procedures.

An **external customer** is the customer or client who buys or uses the organization's goods and/or services.

Extinction discourages a behavior by making the removal of a desirable consequence contingent on the occurrence of the behavior.

Extranets are computer networks that use the public Internet for communication between the organization and its environment.

An **extrinsic reward** is a reward given as a motivational stimulus to a person, usually by a superior.

Extroversion is being outgoing, sociable, and assertive.

F

A **family business** is owned and controlled by members of a family.

Family-friendly benefits help employees achieve better work-life balance.

Feedback is the process of telling someone else how you feel about something that person did or said or about the situation in general.

A **feedback control** or *postaction control* is a control that takes place after an action is completed.

A **feedforward control** or *preliminary control* ensures that proper directions are set and that the right resources are available to accomplish them before the work activity begins.

Filtering is the intentional distortion of information to make it appear most favorable to the recipient.

First-line managers oversee single units and pursue short-term performance objectives consistent with the plans of middle- and top-management levels.

A **first-mover advantage** comes from being first to exploit a niche or enter a market.

A **flexible benefits** program allows employees to choose from a range of benefit options within certain dollar limits.

A **flexible budget** allows the allocation of resources to vary in proportion with various levels of activity.

Fiexible manufacturing involves the ability to change manufacturing processes quickly and efficiently to produce different products or modifications of existing ones.

Flexible working hours are work schedules that give employees some choice in the pattern of daily work hours.

A **focus strategy** is a corporate competitive strategy that concentrates attention on a special market segment to serve its needs better than the competition.

A **focused cost leadership strategy** seeks the lowest costs of operations within a special market segment.

A **focused differentiation strategy** offers a unique product to a special market segment.

A **force-coercion strategy** attempts to bring about change through formal authority and/or the use of rewards or punishments.

Forecasting attempts to predict outcomes; it involves a projection into the future based on historical data combined in some scientific manner.

A **formal group** is created by the formal authority within the organization.

Formal structure is the structure of the organization in its pure or ideal state.

Framing error occurs when a problem is solved in the context in which it is perceived or presented.

A **franchise** is when one business owner sells to another the right to operate the same business in another location.

Fringe benefits are additional nonmonetary forms of compensation (e.g., health plans, retirement plans) provided to an organization's workforce.

The **functional chimneys problem** is a lack of communication and coordination across functions.

Functional conflict is constructive and helps task performance.

A **functional group** is a formally designated work group consisting of a manager and subordinates.

Functional managers are responsible for one area of activity, such as finance, marketing, production, personnel, accounting, or sales.

A **functional strategy** guides activities within one specific area of operations.

A **functional structure** is an organizational structure that groups together people with similar skills who perform similar tasks.

A **functional team** is a formally designated work team with a manager or team leader.

G

A **gain-sharing plan** allows employees to share in any savings or "gains" realized through their efforts to reduce costs and increase productivity.

In the **General Agreement on Tariffs and Trade (GATT)** and **World Trade Organization (WTO)** member nations agree to ongoing negotiations and reducing tariffs and trade restrictions.

The **general environment** is comprised of the cultural, economic, legal–political, and educational conditions in the locality in which an organizational operates.

General managers are responsible for complex organizational units that include many areas of functional activity.

Geocentric attitudes value talent and best practices from all over the world.

A **geographical structure** is a divisional structure that groups together jobs and activities being performed in the same location or geographical region.

The **glass ceiling effect** is an invisible barrier that limits the advancement of women and minorities to higher-level responsibilities in organizations.

The **global economy** is an economic perspective based on worldwide interdependence of resource supplies, product markets, and business competition.

A **global manager** works successfully across international boundaries.

Global sourcing is a process of purchasing materials or components in various parts of the world and then assembling them at home into a final product.

Globalization is the worldwide interdependence of resource flows, product markets, and business competition.

A **globalization strategy** adopts standardized products and advertising for use worldwide.

A **grapevine** is a common informal communication network.

A **graphic rating scale** is a performance appraisal method that uses a checklist of traits or characteristics thought to be related to high-performance outcomes in a given job.

A **group** is a collection of people who regularly interact with one another over time in respect to the pursuit of one or more common goals.

Group cohesiveness is the degree to which members are attracted to and motivated to remain part of a group.

A **group decision** is a decision made with the full participation of all group members.

A **group decision-support system** facilitates group efforts at solving complex problems while utilizing computerized information systems.

Group dynamics are forces operating in groups that affect task performance and membership satisfaction.

A **group norm** is a behavior, rule, or standard expected to be followed by group members.

Group process is the way team members work together to accomplish tasks.

Groupthink is a tendency for highly cohesive teams to lose their evaluative capabilities.

Groupware is a software system that allows people from different locations to work together in computer-mediated collaboration.

A **growth strategy** involves expansion of the organization's current operations.

Growth-need strength is an individual's desire to achieve a sense of psychological growth in her or his work.

H

A **halo effect** occurs when one attribute is used to develop an overall impression of a person or situation.

The **Hawthorne effect** is the tendency of persons singled out for special attention to perform as expected.

Heuristics are strategies for simplifying decision making.

High-context cultures rely on nonverbal and situational cues as well as spoken or written words in communication.

Higher-order needs, in Maslow's hierarchy, are esteem and self-actualization needs.

Human capital is the economic value of people with job-relevant abilities, knowledge, ideas, energies, and commitments.

The **human relations movement** is based on the viewpoint that managers who use good human relations in the workplace will achieve productivity.

Human resource maintenance is a team's ability to maintain its social fabric so that members work well together.

Human resource management is the process of attracting, developing, and maintaining a talented and energetic workforce.

Human resource planning is the process of analyzing staffing needs and identifying actions to fill those needs over time.

Human resources are the people, individuals, and groups that help organizations produce goods or services.

A **human skill** is the ability to work well in cooperation with other people.

A **hygiene factor** is a factor in the work setting, such as working conditions, interpersonal relations, organizational policies, and administration, supervision, and salary.

I
___

Importing is the process of acquiring products abroad and selling them in domestic markets.

Incremental change bends and adjusts existing ways to improve performance.

Independent contractors are hired on temporary contracts and are not part of the organization's official workforce.

An **individual decision** is made when a manager chooses a preferred course of action without consulting others.

The **individualism view** is a view of ethical behavior based on the belief that one's primary commitment is to the advancement of long-term self-interests.

An **informal group** is not offically created and emerges based on relationships and shared interests among members.

Informal learning occurs as people interact informally throughout the workday.

Informal structure is the undocumented and officially unrecognized structure that coexists with the formal structure of an organization.

Information is data made useful for decision making.

Information competency is the ability to utilize computers and information technology to locate, retrieve, evaluate, organize, and analyze information for decision making.

An **information system** collects, organizes, and distributes data regarding activities occurring inside and outside an organization.

Information technology is computer hardware, software, networks, and databases supporting information utilization.

Innovation is the process of taking a new idea and putting it into practice as part of the organization's normal operating routines.

An **input standard** is a standard that measures work efforts that go into a performance task.

Inside-out planning focuses planning on internal strengths and trying to do better than what one already does.

Instant messaging is instantaneous communication between people online at the same time.

Instrumental values are preferences regarding the means for accomplishing desired ends.

Instrumentality is a person's belief that various work-related outcomes will occur as a result of task performance.

Integration is the level of coordination achieved among subsystems in an organization.

Integrity in leadership is honesty, credibility, and consistency in putting values into action.

Intellectual capital is the collective brainpower or shared knowledge of a workforce.

Intensive technology focuses the efforts and talents of many people with high interdependence to serve clients.

Interactional justice is the degree to which others are treated with dignity and respect.

Internal control is self-control that occurs through self-discipline and the personal exercise of individual or group responsibility.

An **internal customer** is someone who uses or depends on the work of another person or group within the organization.

An **international business** conducts commercial transactions across national boundaries.

International management involves the conduct of business or other operations in foreign countries.

Intranets are computer networks that allow persons within an organization to share databases and communicate electronically.

Intrapreneurship is entrepreneurial behavior displayed by people or subunits within large organizations.

An **intrinsic** or **natural reward** is a reward that occurs naturally as a person performs a task or job.

Intuitive thinking occurs when someone approaches problems in a flexible and spontaneous fashion.

Inventory consists of materials or products kept in storage.

An **IPO** is an initial selling of shares of stock to the public and for trading on a stock exchange.

ISO certification is granted by the International Standards

Organization to indicate that a business meets a rigorous set of quality standards.

ISO 14000 offers a set of certification standards for responsible environmental policies.

J

A **job** is the collection of tasks a person performs in support of organizational objectives.

Job analysis is an orderly study of job requirements and facets that can influence performance results.

Job burnout is physical and mental exhaustion that can be incapacitating personally and in respect to work.

A **job description** is a written statement that details the duties and responsibilities of any person holding a particular job.

Job design is the allocation of specific work tasks to individuals and groups.

Job enlargement is a job-design strategy that increases task variety by combining into one job two or more tasks that were previously assigned to separate workers.

Job enrichment is a job-design strategy that increases job depth by adding to a job some of the planning and evaluating duties normally performed by the supervisor.

Job involvement is defined as the extent to which an individual is dedicated to a job.

Job performance is the quantity and quality of task accomplishment by an individual or group.

Job rotation is a job-design strategy that increases task variety by periodically shifting workers among jobs involving different tasks.

Job satisfaction is the degree to which an individual feels positively or negatively about various aspects of the job, including assigned tasks, work setting, and relationships with coworkers.

Job scope is the number and combination of tasks an individual or group is asked to perform.

Job sharing is an arrangement that splits one job between two people.

Job simplification is a job-design strategy that involves standardizing work procedures and employing people in clearly defined and very specialized tasks.

A **job specification** is a list of the qualifications required of any job occupant.

A **joint venture** is a form of international business that establishes operations in a foreign country through joint ownership with local partners.

The **justice view** considers ethical behavior as that which treats people impartially and fairly according to guiding rules and standards.

Just-in-time scheduling (JIT) schedules materials to arrive at a workstation or facility "just in time" to be used.

K

Keiretsu is a Japanese term describing alliances or business groups that link together manufacturers, suppliers, and finance companies with common interests.

Knowledge management is the process of utilizing organizational knowledge to achieve competitive advantage.

A **knowledge worker** is someone whose knowledge is a critical asset to employers.

L

A **labor contract** is a formal agreement between a union and the employing organization that specifies the rights and obligations of each party with respect to wages, work hours, work rules, and other conditions of employment.

A **labor union** is an organization to which workers belong and that deals with employers on their collective behalf.

Thorndike's **law of effect** states that behavior followed by pleasant consequences is likely to be repeated, whereas behavior followed by unpleasant consequences is not likely to be repeated.

Leadership is the process of inspiring others to work hard to accomplish important tasks.

Leadership style is the recurring pattern of behaviors exhibited by a leader.

Leading is the process of arousing enthusiasm and directing human resource efforts toward organizational goals.

Lean production involves streamlining systems and implementing new technologies to allow work to be performed with fewer workers and smaller inventories.

Learning is any change in behavior that occurs as a result of experience.

A **learning organization** utilizes people, values, and systems to continuously change and improve its performance based on the lessons of experience.

Legitimate power is the capability to influence other people by virtue of formal authority or the rights of office.

A **licensing agreement** occurs when a firm pays a fee for the rights to make or sell another company's products.

Lifelong learning is continuous learning from daily experiences and opportunities.

Line managers have direct responsibility for activities

making direct contributions to the production of the organization's basic goods or services.

Lobbying expresses opinions and preferences to government officials.

Locus of control is the extent to which one believes that what happens is in one's control.

In **long-linked technology** a client moves from point to point during service delivery.

In **lose-lose conflict** no one achieves his or her true desires and the underlying reasons for conflict remain unaffected.

Low-context cultures emphasize communication via spoken or written words.

Lower-order needs, in Maslow's hierarchy, are physiological, safety, and social needs.

M

Machiavellianism is the extent to which someone is manipulative in using power to achieve goals.

A **maintenance activity** is an action taken by a team member that supports the emotional life of the group.

Management is the process of planning, organizing, leading, and controlling the use of resources to accomplish performance goals.

Management by exception focuses managerial attention on substantial differences between actual and desired performance.

Management by objectives (MBO) is a process of joint objective setting between a superior and subordinate.

In **management by wandering around (MBWA)** workers at all levels talk with bosses about a variety of work-related matters.

Management development is training to improve knowledge and skills in the fundamentals of management.

A **management information system (MIS)** collects, organizes, and distributes data in such a way that the information meets managers' needs.

Management science or **operations research** is a scientific approach to management that uses mathematical techniques to analyze and solve problems.

A **manager** is a person in an organization who is responsible for the work performance of one or more other persons.

Managerial competency is a skill or personal characteristic that contributes to high performance in a management job.

Managing diversity is building an inclusive work environment that allows everyone to reach their full potential.

Maquiladoras are foreign manufacturing plants that operate in Mexico with special privileges.

Mass customization involves manufacturing individualized products quickly and with the production efficiencies once only associated with mass production of uniform products.

Mass production is the production of a large number of one or a few products with an assembly-line type of system.

A **master budget** is a comprehensive short-term budget for an organization as a whole.

A **matrix structure** is an organizational form that combines functional and divisional departmentation to take best advantage of each.

A **mechanistic design** is highly bureaucratic, with centralized authority, many rules and procedures, a clearcut division of labor, narrow spans of controls, and formal coordination.

Mediating technology links together parties seeking a mutually beneficial exchange of values.

In **mediation** a neutral party engages in substantive discussions with conflicting parties in the hope that the dispute can be resolved.

Mentoring is the act of sharing experiences and insights between a seasoned and a junior manager.

Merit pay is a system of awarding pay increases in proportion to performance contributions.

Middle managers report to top-level management, oversee the work of several units, and implement plans consistent with higher-level objectives.

The **mission** of an organization is its reason for existing as a supplier of goods and/or services to society.

A **mixed message** results when a person's words communicate one message while actions, body language, or appearance communicate something else.

Modeling demonstrates through personal behavior that which is expected of others.

In a **monochronic culture** people tend to do one thing at a time.

The **moral-rights view** is a view of ethical behavior that seeks to respect and protect the fundamental rights of people.

Most favored nation status gives a trading partner most favorable treatment for imports and exports.

Motion study is the science of reducing a task to its basic physical motions.

Motivation is a term used in management theory to describe forces within the individual that account for the level, direction, and persistence of effort expended at work.

A **multicultural organization** is based on pluralism and operates with respect for diversity in the workplace.

Multidimensional thinking is the capacity to view many problems at once, in relationship to one another, and across long and short time horizons.

A **multidomestic strategy** customizes products and advertising to best fit local needs.

A **multinational corporation (MNC)** is a business firm with extensive international operations in more than one foreign country.

A **multiperson comparison** is a performance appraisal method that involves comparing one person's performance with that of one or more other persons.

N

NAFTA is the **North American Free Trade Agreement** linking Canada, the United States, and Mexico in a regional economic alliance.

A **narrative approach** to performance appraisal method uses a written essay description of a person's job performance.

Nationalization is when a government seizes ownership of foreign assets.

A **need** is a physiological or psychological deficiency a person feels the compulsion to satisfy.

Need for Achievement (nAch) is the desire to do something better or more efficiently, to solve problems, or to master complex tasks.

Need for Affiliation (nAff) is the desire to establish and maintain good relations with people.

Need for Power (nPower) is the desire to control, influence, or be responsible for other people.

Negative reinforcement strengthens a behavior by making the avoidance of an undesirable consequence contingent on the occurrence of the behavior.

Negotiation is the process of making joint decisions when the parties involved have different preferences.

A **network** is a system of computers that are linked together to allow users to easily transfer and share information.

A **network structure** is an organizational structure that consists of a central core with "networks" of outside suppliers of essential business services.

Noise is anything that interferes with the effectiveness of the communication process.

The **nominal group technique** is a group technique for generating ideas by following a structured format of individual response, group sharing without criticism, and written balloting.

A **nonprogrammed decision** is unique and specifically tailored to a problem at hand.

Nonverbal communication is communication that takes place through channels such as body language and the use of interpersonal space.

A **norm** is a behavior, rule, or standard expected to be followed by team members.

O

Objectives are the specific results or desired end states that one wishes to achieve.

An **obstructionist strategy** avoids social responsibility and reflects mainly economic priorities.

An **OD intervention** is a structured activity initiated by consultants or managers that directly assists in a comprehensive organizational development program.

An **open system** interacts with its environment and transforms resource inputs into outputs.

Openness is being curious, receptive to new ideas, and imaginative.

Operant conditioning is the process of controlling behavior by manipulating its consequences.

An **operating budget** is a budget that assigns resources to a responsibility center on a short-term basis.

Operating objectives are specific results that organizations try to accomplish.

An **operational plan** is a plan of limited scope that addresses those activities and resources required to implement strategic plans.

Operations management is a branch of management theory that studies how organizations transform resource inputs into product and service outputs.

An **optimizing decision** results when a manager chooses an alternative that gives the absolute best solution to a problem.

An **organic design** is decentralized with fewer rules and procedures, more open divisions of labor, wide spans of control, and more personal coordination.

An **organization** is a collection of people working together in a division of labor to achieve a common purpose.

An **organization chart** is a diagram that describes the basic arrangement of work positions within an organization.

Organization development (OD) is the application of behavioral science knowledge in a long-range effort to improve an organization's ability to cope with change in its external environment and increase its internal problem-solving capabilities.

Organization structure is the system of tasks, reporting relationships, and communication that links people and groups together to accomplish tasks that serve the organizational purpose.

Organizational behavior is the study of individuals and groups in organizations.

Organizational commitment is defined as the loyalty of an individual to the organization.

Organizational communication is the process through which information is exchanged through interactions among people inside an organization.

Organizational culture is the system of shared beliefs and values that develops within an organization and guides the behavior of its members.

Organizational design is the process of creating structures that best organize resources to serve mission and objectives.

Organizational ecology is the study of how building design may influence communication and productivity.

Organizational effectiveness is sustainable high performance in accomplishing mission and objectives.

The **organizational life cycle** is the evolution of an organization over time through different stages of growth.

Organizational stakeholders are directly affected by the behavior of the organization and hold a stake in its performance.

Organizing is the process of arranging people and resources to work toward a common purpose.

Orientation consists of activities through which new employees are made familiar with their jobs, their coworkers, and the policies, rules, objectives, and services of the organization as a whole.

An **output standard** is a standard that measures performance results in terms of quantity, quality, cost, or time.

Outside-in planning uses analysis of the external environment and makes plans to take advantage of opportunities and avoid problems.

Outsourcing is when a business function is contracted to an outside supplier.

P

Participatory planning is the inclusion in the planning process of as many people as possible from among those who will be affected by plans and/or asked to help implement them.

A **partnership** is when two or more people agree to contribute resources to start and operate a business together.

Part-time work is work done on a basis that classifies the employee as "temporary" and requires less than the standard 40-hour workweek.

Peer-to-peer file sharing connects PCs directly to one another over the Internet without the support of a central server.

Perception is the process through which people receive, organize, and interpret information from the environment.

Performance appraisal is a process of formally evaluating performance and providing feedback on which performance adjustments can be made.

Performance effectiveness is an output measure of a task or goal accomplishment.

Performance efficiency is a measure of the resource cost associated with goal accomplishment.

A **performance gap** is a discrepancy between the desired and actual state of affairs.

A **performance management system** sets standards, assesses results, and plans actions to improve future performance.

A **performance norm** identifies the level of work effort and performance expected of group members.

Personal staff are "assistant-to" positions that provide special administrative support to higher-level positions.

Personal wellness is the pursuit of one's physical and mental potential through a personal-health promotion program.

Personality is the profile of characteristics making a person unique from others.

Persuasion is presenting a message in a manner that causes the other person to support it.

A **plan** is a statement of intended means for accomplishing a desired result.

Planned change involves action to align the organization with anticipated future challenges.

Planning is the process of setting objectives and determining what should be done to accomplish them.

A **policy** is a standing plan that communicates broad guidelines for making decisions and taking action.

Political action committees collect money for donation to political campaigns.

Political risk is the possible loss of investment or control over a foreign asset because of political changes in the host country.

Political-risk analysis forecasts how political events may impact foreign investments.

Polycentric attitudes assume locals know the best ways to manage in their countries.

In a **polychronic culture** time is used to accomplish many different things at once.

A **portfolio planning** approach seeks the best mix of investments among alternative business opportunities.

Positive reinforcement strengthens a behavior by making a desirable consequence contingent on the occurrence of the behavior.

Power is the ability to get someone else to do something you want done or to make things happen the way you want.

Prejudice is the holding of negative, irrational attitudes toward individuals because of their group identity.

Principled negotiation or **integrative negotiation** uses a "win-win" orientation to reach solutions acceptable to each party.

Privatization is the selling of state-owned enterprises into private ownership.

A **proactive strategy** meets all the criteria of social responsibility, including discretionary performance.

A **problem** is a difference between an actual situation and a desired situation.

Problem solving is the process of identifying a discrepancy between an actual and desired state of affairs and then taking action to resolve it.

Problem-solving style is the way people gather and evaluate information for decision making.

A **problem symptom** is a sign of the presence of a performance deficiency or opportunity that should trigger a manager to act.

Procedural justice concerns the degree to which policies and rules are fairly administered.

A **procedure** or **rule** is a standing plan that precisely describes what actions are to be taken in specific situations.

A **process** is a group of related tasks creating something of value to a customer.

Process innovations result in better ways of doing things.

Process reengineering systematically analyzes work processes to design new and better ones.

A **process structure** groups jobs and activities that are part of the same processes.

Process value analysis identifies and evaluates core processes for their performance contributions.

Product innovations result in new or improved goods or services.

Product life cycle is the series of stages a product or service goes through in the "life" of its marketability.

A **product structure** is an organizational structure that groups together jobs and activities working on a single product or service.

Productivity is a summary measure of the quantity and quality of work performance with resource utilization considered.

A **profit-sharing plan** distributes a proportion of net profits to employees during a stated performance period.

The **program evaluation and review technique (PERT)** is a means for identifying and controlling the many separate events involved in the completion of projects.

A **programmed decision** applies a solution from past experience to the problem at hand.

Progressive discipline is the process of tying reprimands in the form of penalties or punishments to the severity of the employee's infractions.

Project management makes sure that activities required to complete a project are accomplished on time and correctly.

Project managers coordinate complex projects with task deadlines and people with many areas of expertise.

A **project schedule** is a single-use plan for accomplishing a specific set of tasks.

Project teams are convened for a particular task or project and disband once it is completed.

Projection is the assignment of personal attributes to other individuals.

Projects are one-time activities that have clear beginning and end points.

A **prospector strategy** is a corporate competitive strategy that involves pursuing innovation and new opportunities in the face of risk and with the prospects of growth.

Protectionism is a call for tariffs and favorable treatments to protect domestic firms from foreign competition.

Proxemics is the use of interpersonal space, such as in the process of interpersonal communication.

A **psychological contract** is the shared set of expectations held by an individual and the organization, specifying what each expects to give and receive from the other in the course of their working relationship.

Punishment discourages a behavior by making an unpleasant consequence contingent on the occurrence of that behavior.

Q

Quality is a degree of excellence, often defined as the ability to meet customer needs 100 percent of the time.

A **quality circle** is a group of employees who meet periodically to discuss ways of improving the quality of their products or services.

Quality control involves checking processes, material, products, or services to ensure that they meet high standards.

Quality of work life (QWL) is the overall quality of human experiences in the workplace.

R

A **rational persuasion strategy** attempts to bring about change through persuasion backed by special knowledge, empirical data, and rational argument.

Reactive change responds to events as or after they occur.

A **reactor strategy** is a corporate competitive strategy that involves simply responding to competitive pressures in order to survive.

Realistic job previews are attempts by the job interviewer to provide the job candidate with all pertinent information about a prospective job and the employing organization, without distortion and before a job offer is accepted.

A **reason strategy** of influence relies on personal power and persuasion based on data, needs, and/or values.

A **reciprocity strategy** of influence involves the mutual exchange of values and a search for shared positive outcomes.

Recruitment is a set of activities designed to attract a qualified pool of job applicants to an organization.

Referent power is the capability to influence other people because of their desires to identify personally and positively with the power source.

Refreezing is the final stage in the planned change process during which the manager is concerned with stabilizing the change and creating the conditions for its long-term continuity.

Reliability refers to the ability of an employment test to yield the same result over time if taken by the same person.

Replacement is the management of promotions, transfers, terminations, layoffs, and retirements.

Responsibility is the obligation to perform that results from accepting assigned tasks.

Restructuring changes the scale and/or mix of operations to gain efficiency and improve performance.

A **retrenchment strategy** involves slowing down, cutting back, and seeking performance improvement through greater efficiencies in operations.

A **retribution strategy** of influence relies on position power and results in feelings of coercion or intimidation.

A **reward** is a work outcome of positive value to the individual.

Reward power is the capability to offer something of value—a positive outcome—as a means of influencing other people.

A **risk environment** is a problem environment in which information is lacking, but some sense of the "probabilities" associated with action alternatives and their consequences exists.

Robotics is the use of computer-controlled machines to completely automate work tasks previously performed by hand.

A **role** is a set of activities expected of a person in a particular job or position within the organization.

Role ambiguity occurs when a person in a role is uncertain about what others expect in terms of his or her behavior.

Role conflict occurs when the person in a role is unable to respond to the expectations held by others.

Role overload occurs when too many role expectations are being communicated to a person at a given time.

Role underload occurs when a person is underutilized or asked to do too little and/or to do things that fail to challenge her or his talents and capabilities.

S

A **satisficing decision** involves choosing the first satisfactory alternative that comes to your attention.

A **satisfier factor** is a factor in job content, such as a sense of achievement, recognition, responsibility, advancement, or personal growth, experienced as a result of task performance.

Scenario planning identifies alternative future "scenarios" and makes plans to deal with each.

Scientific management involves developing a science for every job, including rules of motion and standardized work instruments, careful selection and training of workers, and proper supervisory support for workers.

Selection is the process of choosing from a pool of applicants the person or persons who best meet job specifications.

Selective perception is the tendency to define problems from one's own point of view or to single out for attention things consistent with one's existing beliefs, values, or needs.

A **self-fulfilling prophecy** occurs when a person acts in ways in order to confirm another's expectations.

A **self-managing work team,** sometimes called an autonomous work group, is a group of workers whose jobs have been redesigned to create a high degree of task interdependence and who have been given authority to make decisions about how they go about the required work.

Self-monitoring is the degree to which someone is able to adjust behavior in response to external factors.

Self-serving bias explains personal success by internal causes and personal failures by external causes.

Semantic barriers are verbal and nonverbal symbols that are poorly chosen and expressed, creating barriers to successful communication.

Sexual harassment occurs as behavior of a sexual nature that affects a person's employment situation.

Shaping is positive reinforcement of successive approximations to the desired behavior.

A **shared power strategy** is a participative change strategy that relies on involving others to examine values, needs, and goals in relationship to an issue at hand.

Simultaneous systems operate when mechanistic and organic designs operate together in an organization.

A **single-use plan** is used only once.

A **skill** is the ability to translate knowledge into action that results in the desired performance.

Skills-based pay is a system of paying workers according to the number of job-relevant skills they master.

Skunkworks are teams allowed to work creatively together, free of constraints from the larger organization.

Small-batch production is the production of a variety of custom products that are tailor-made, usually with considerable craftsmanship, to fit customer specifications.

A **small business** has fewer than 500 employees, is independently owned and operated, and does not dominate its industry.

Small Business Development Centers offer guidance and support to small business owners in how to set up and run a business operation.

The **social contract** reflects expectations in the employee-employer relationship.

Social loafing is the tendency of some people to avoid responsibility by "free-riding" in groups.

A **social responsibility audit** is a systematic assessment and reporting of an organization's commitments and accomplishments in areas of social responsibility.

Socialization is the process of systematically changing the expectations, behavior, and attitudes of a new employee in a manner considered desirable by the organization.

A **sociotechnical system** designs jobs so that technology and human resources are well integrated in high-performance systems with maximum opportunities for individual satisfaction.

A **sole proprietorship** is an individual pursuing business for a profit.

Span of control is the number of subordinates reporting directly to a manager.

Specialized staff are positions that perform a technical service or provide special problem-solving expertise for other parts of the organization.

A **specific environment** is comprised of the actual organizations and persons with whom the focal organization must interact in order to survive and prosper.

A **stability strategy** maintains the present course of action.

Staff managers use special technical expertise to advise and support the efforts of line workers.

Stakeholders are the persons, groups, and institutions directly affected by an organization's performance.

A **standing plan** is used more than once.

Statistical quality control is the use of statistical techniques to assist in the quality control process.

A **stereotype** results when an individual is assigned to a group or category and then the attributes commonly associated with the group or category are assigned to the individual in question.

In a **strategic alliance** organizations join together in partnership to pursue an area of mutual interest.

A **strategic business unit (SBU)** is a separate operating division that represents a major business area and operates with some autonomy vis-à-vis other similar units in the organization.

A **strategic constituencies analysis** is the review and analysis of the interests of external stakeholders of an organization.

Strategic human resource management mobilizes human capital to implement organizational strategies.

Strategic intent focuses and applies organizational energies on a unifying and compelling goal.

Strategic leadership enthuses people to continuously change, refine, and improve strategies and their implementation.

Strategic management is the managerial responsibility for leading the process of formulating and implementing strategies that lead to longer-term organizational success.

Strategic opportunism is the ability to remain focused on long-term objectives by being flexible in dealing with short-term problems and opportunities as they occur.

A **strategic plan** is comprehensive and addresses longer-term needs and directions of the organization.

A **strategy** is a comprehensive plan or action orientation that sets critical direction and guides the allocation of resources for an organization to achieve long-term objectives.

Strategy formulation is the process of creating strategies.

Strategy implementation is the process of putting strategies into action.

Stress is a state of tension experienced by individuals facing extraordinary demands, constraints, or opportunities.

A **stressor** is anything that causes stress.

A **structured problem** is familiar, straightforward, and clear in its information requirements.

Subcultures within organizations are common to groups of people with similar values and beliefs based upon shared personal characteristics.

Substantive conflict is disagreement over such things as goals; the allocation of resources; distribution of rewards, policies, and procedures; and job assignments.

Substitutes for leadership are factors in the work setting that move work efforts toward organizational objectives without the direct involvement of a leader.

A **subsystem** is a work unit or smaller component within a larger organization.

A **succession plan** describes how the leadership transition and related financial matters will be handled.

The **succession problem** is the issue of who will run the business when the current head leaves.

Supply chain management strategically links all operations dealing with resource supplies.

Survivor syndrome is the stress experienced by people who fear for their jobs after having "survived" large layoffs and staff cutbacks in an organization.

Sustainable career advantage is a combination of personal attributes that allows you to consistently outperform others in meeting needs of employers.

Sustainable development meets the needs of the present without hurting future generations.

Sweatshops employ workers at very low wages, for long hours, and in poor working conditions.

A **SWOT analysis** sets the stage for strategy formulation by analyzing organizational strengths and weaknesses and environmental opportunities and threats.

A **symbolic leader** uses symbols to establish and maintain a desired organizational culture.

Synergy is the creation of a whole that is greater than the sum of its individual parts.

A **system** is a collection of inter-related parts working together for a purpose.

Systematic thinking occurs when someone approaches problems in a rational and analytical fashion.

T

A **task activity** is an action taken by a group member that contributes directly to the group's performance purpose.

A **task force** is a formal team convened for a specific purpose and expected to disband when that purpose is achieved.

Task goals are performance targets for individuals and/or groups.

A **team** is a collection of people who regularly interact to pursue common goals.

Team building is a sequence of collaborative activities to gather and analyze data on a team and make changes to increase its effectiveness.

Team leaders and **supervisors** report to middle managers and directly supervise non-managerial workers.

A **team structure** is an organizational structure through which permanent and temporary teams are created to improve lateral relations and solve problems throughout an organization.

Teamwork is the process of people working together in groups to accomplish common goals.

A **technical skill** is the ability to use a special proficiency or expertise in one's work.

The **technological imperative** states that technology is a major influence on organizational structure.

Technology is the combination of equipment, knowledge, and work methods that allows an organization to transform inputs into outputs.

Telecommuting or **flexiplace** involves working at home or other places using computer links to the office.

Terminal values are preferences about desired end states.

Theory X is a set of managerial assumptions that people in general dislike work, lack ambition, are irresponsible and resistant to change, and prefer to be led than to lead.

Theory Y is a set of managerial assumptions that people in general are willing to work and accept responsibility and are capable of self-direction, self-control, and creativity.

Theory Z is a term that describes a management framework used by American firms following Japanese examples.

In **top-down change,** the change initiatives come from senior management.

Top-down planning begins with broad objectives set by top management.

Top managers are the highest-level managers and work to ensure that major plans and objectives are set and accomplished in accord with the organization's purpose.

Total quality management (TQM) is managing with an organization-wide commitment to continuous work improvement, product quality, and meeting customer needs completely.

Training involves a set of activities that provide learning opportunities through which people can acquire and improve job-related skills.

A **trait** is a relatively stable and enduring personal characteristic of an individual.

Transactional leadership is leadership that orchestrates and directs the efforts of others through tasks, rewards, and structures.

Transformational change results in a major and comprehensive redirection of the organization.

Transformational leadership is the ability of a leader to get people to do more than they originally expected to do in support of large-scale innovation and change.

A **transnational corporation** is an MNC that operates worldwide on a borderless basis.

A **transnational strategy** seeks efficiencies of global operations with attention to local markets.

A **Type A personality** is a person oriented toward extreme achievement, impatience, and perfectionism and who may find stress in circumstances others find relatively stress-free.

360-degree feedback is an upward communication approach that involves upward appraisals done by a manager's subordinates, as well as additional feedback from peers, internal and external customers, and higher-ups.

U

An **uncertain environment** is a problem environment in which information is so poor that it is difficult even to assign probabilities to the likely outcomes of known alternatives.

Unfreezing is the initial phase in the planned change process during which the manager prepares a situation for change.

Universalism suggests that ethical standards apply across all cultures.

Unplanned change occurs spontaneously or at random and without a change agent's direction.

An **unstructured problem** involves ambiguities and information deficiencies.

The **upside-down pyramid** puts customers at the top, served by workers whose managers support them.

The **utilitarian view** considers ethical behavior as that which delivers the greatest good to the greatest number of people.

V

Valence is the value a person assigns to work-related outcomes.

Validity refers to the ability of an employment test to measure exactly what it is intended to relative to the job specification.

A **value chain** is the sequence of activities that transform materials into finished products.

Value-based management actively develops, communicates, and enacts shared values in an organization.

Values are broad beliefs about what is or is not appropriate behavior.

Venture capitalists make large investments in new ventures in return for an equity stake in the business.

Growth through **vertical integration** is by acquiring suppliers or distributors.

A **virtual meeting** is a meeting conducted by a computer-mediated process of information sharing and decision making.

The **virtual office** enables workers to "commute" via computer networks, fax machines, and express mail delivery service.

A **virtual organization** is a shifting network of strategic alliances that are engaged as needed.

A **virtual team** is a group of people who work together and solve problems through computer-based rather than face-to-face interactions.

Vision is a term used to describe a clear sense of the future.

Visionary leadership brings to the situation a clear sense of the future and an understanding of how to get there.

W

A **whistleblower** exposes the misdeeds of others in organizations.

A **wholly owned subsidiary** is a local operation completely owned by a foreign firm.

A **win-lose conflict** occurs when one party achieves its desires at the expense and exclusion of the other party's desires.

A **win-win conflict** occurs when conflict is resolved to the mutual benefit of all concerned parties.

A **work process** is a related group of tasks that together create a value for the customer.

Work-at-home involves accomplishing a job while spending all or part of one's work time in the home.

Work-life balance involves balancing career demands with personal and family needs.

Workflow is the movement of work from one point to another in a system.

Workforce diversity is a term used to describe demographic differences (age, gender, race and ethnicity, and able-bodiedness) among members of the workforce.

Workplace privacy is the right to privacy while at work.

Workplace rage is overtly aggressive behavior toward coworkers or the work setting.

In the **World Trade Organization (WTO)** member nations agree to negotiate and resolve disputes about tariffs and trade restrictions.

Z

A **zero-based budget** allocates resources to a project or activity as if it were brand new.

Endnotes

Chapter 1 Notes

[1]"Monster.com Growth Continues with 8 Million Job Seeker Accounts; Monster.com Dominates the Online Career Space, Ranked #1 According to Media Metrix," *Business Wire* (June 20, 2000) See also www.monster.com.

[2]Information from the *Fast Company* website: www.fastcompany.com.

[3]Charles O'Reilly III and Jeffrey Pfeffer, *Hidden Value: How Great Companies Achieve Extraordinary Results with Ordinary People* (Boston: Harvard Business School Press, 2000), p. 2.

[4]For a research perspective see Denise M. Rousseau, "Organizational Behavior in the New Organizational Era," *Annual Review of Psychology*, vol. 48 (1997), pp. 515–46; for a consultant's perspective see Tom Peters, *The Circle of Innovation* (New York: Knopf, 1997); and Joan Magretta, *Managing in the New Economy* (Boston: Harvard Business School Press, 1999).

[5]See Kevin Kelly, *New Rules for a New Economy: 10 Radical Strategies for a Connected World* (New York: Penguin, 1999).

[6]Max DePree's books include *Leadership Is an Art* (New York: Dell, 1990) and *Leadership Jazz* (New York: Dell, 1993). See also Herman Miller's home page at www.hermanmiller.com.

[7]Thomas A. Stewart, *Intellectual Capital: The Wealth of Organizations* (New York: Bantam, 1998).

[8]See Peter F. Drucker, *The Changing World of the Executive* (New York: T.T. Times Books, 1982), and *The Profession of Management* (Cambridge, MA: Harvard Business School Press, 1997); and Francis Horibe, *Managing Knowledge Workers: New Skills and Attitudes to Unlock the Intellectual Capital in Your Organization* (New York: Wiley, 1999).

[9]Information from Jamie Smyth, "Xerox's Chief Copies Good Practices Not Past Mistakes," *Irish Times* (March 21, 2003), p. 24.

[10]Kenichi Ohmae's books include *The Borderless World: Power and Strategy in the Interlinked Economy* (New York: Harper, 1989); *The End of the Nation State* (New York: Free Press, 1996); and *The Invisible Continent: Four Strategic Imperatives of the New Economy* (New York: Harper, 1999).

[11]For a discussion of globalization see Thomas L. Friedman, *The Lexus and the Olive Tree: Understanding Globalization* (New York: Bantam Doubleday Dell, 2000); and John Micklethwait and Adrian Woolridge, *A Future Perfect: The Challenges and Hidden Promise of Globalization* (New York: Crown, 2000.

[12]Alfred E. Eckes, Jr., and Thomas W. Zeiler, *Globalization and the American Century* (Cambridge, UK: Cambridge University Press, 2003), pp. 1, 2.

[13]Michael E. Porter, *The Competitive Advantage of Nations: With a New Introduction* (New York: Free Press, 1998).

[14]See, for example, Carl Shapiro and Hal R. Varian, *Information Rules: A Strategic Guide to the Network Economy* (Cambridge, MA: Harvard Business School Press, 1998).

[15]*Workforce 2000: Work and Workers for the 21st Century* (Indianapolis: Towers Perrin/Hudson Institute, 1987).

[16]Richard W. Judy and Carol D'Amico (eds.), *Workforce 2020: Work and Workers for the 21st Century* (Indianapolis: Hudson Institute, 1997).

[17]See Richard D. Bucher, *Diversity Consciousness: Opening Our Minds to People, Cultures, and Opportunities* (Upper Saddle River, NJ: Prentice-Hall, 2000).

[18]See, for example Yochi J. Dreazen and Jess Bravin, "Bias Suit Against Microsoft Aims at 'Flat' Workplace," *Wall Street Journal* (January 4, 2001), p. A10.

[19]For a discussion of diversity issues, see R. Roosevelt Thomas, "From Affirmative Action to Affirming Diversity," *Harvard Business Review* (March–April 1990), pp. 107–17; and *Beyond Race and Gender: Unleashing the Power of Your Total Workforce by Managing Diversity* (New York: AMACOM, 1992).

[20]Quotations from Thomas, op cit. (1990); and *Business Week* (August 8, 1990), p. 50, emphasis added.

[21]Survey results reported in Rebecca Gomez, "Women Execs Increasing in Number, Survey Finds," *Columbus Dispatch* (November 19, 2002), p. D12.

[22]Sue Shellenbarger, "Number of Women Managers Rises," *Wall Street Journal* (September 30, 2003), p. D2; "Women of Color," Working Mother Media website: www.workingmother.com/pr.chicago1.shtml.

[23]Information from "Racism in Hiring Remains, Study Says," *Columbus Dispatch* (January 17, 2003), p. B2.

[24]Stephanie N. Mehta, "What Minority Employees Really Want," *Fortune* (July 10, 2000), pp. 181–86.

[25]For background see Taylor Cox, Jr., "The Multicultural Organization," *Academy of Management Executive*, vol. 5 (1991), pp. 34–47; and *Cultural Diversity in Organizations: Theory, Research and Practice* (San Francisco: Berrett-Koehler, 1993).

[26]For discussions of the glass ceiling effect see Ann M. Morrison, Randall P. White, and Ellen Van Velso, *Breaking the Glass Ceiling* (Reading, MA: Addison-Wesley, 1987); Anne E. Weiss, *The Glass Ceiling: A Look at Women in the Workforce* (New York: Twenty First Century, 1999); and Debra E. Meyerson and Joyce K. Fletcher, "A Modest Manifesto for Shattering the Glass Ceiling," *Harvard Business Review* (January–February 2000).

[27]Judith B. Rosener, "Women Make Good Managers, So What?" *Business Week* (December 11, 2000), p. 24.

[28]Portions adapted from John W. Dienhart and Terry Thomas, "Ethical Leadership: A Primer on Ethical Responsibility in Management," in John R. Schermerhorn, Jr., (ed.), *Management*, 7th ed. (New York: Wiley, 2002).

[29]Judy and D'Amico, op cit.

[30]Credo selection from www.jnj.com.

[31]Charles Handy, *The Age of Unreason* (Cambridge, MA: Harvard Business School Press, 1990).

[32]"Is Your Job Your Calling?" *Fast Company* (February–March 1998), p. 108.

[33]Tom Peters, "The New Wired World of Work," *Business Week* (August 28, 2000), pp. 172–73.

[34]Robert Reich, "The Company of the Future," *Fast Company* (November 1998), p. 124ff.

[35]Developed from Peters, op cit. (2000).

[36]For an overview of organizations and organization theory see W. Richard Scott, *Organizations; Rational, Natural and Open Systems,* 4th ed. (Englewood Cliffs, NJ: Prentice-Hall, 1998).

[37]Ronald B. Lieber, "Why Employees Love These Companies," *Fortune* (January 12, 1998), pp. 72–74; and David Whitford, "A Human Place to Work," *Fortune* (January 8, 2001), pp. 108–20. See also www.medtronic.com.

[38]For a discussion of organizations as systems, see Scott, op cit. and Lane Tracy, *The Living Organization* (New York: Quorum Books, 1994).

[39]Developed in part from Jay A. Conger, *Winning 'em Over: A New Model for Managing in the Age of Persuasion* (New York: Simon & Chuster, 1998), pp. 180–81; Stewart D. Friedman, Perry Christensen, and Jessica De- Groot, "Work and Life: The End of the Zero-Sum Game," *Harvard Business Review* (November–December 1998), pp. 119–29; Chris Argyris, "Empowerment: The Emperor's New Clothers," *Harvard Business Review* (May–June 1998), pp. 98–105, and John A. Byrne, "Management by Web," *Business Week* (August 28, 2000), pp. 84–98.

[40]Philip B. Crosby, *Quality Is Still Free: Making Quality Certain in Uncertain Times* (New York: McGraw-Hill, 1995). For a comprehensive review see Robert E. Cole and W. Richard Scott (eds.), *The Quality Movement & Organization Theory* (Thousand Oaks, CA: Sage, 2000).

[41]"Apple," *Business Week* (July 31, 2000), pp. 102–13, "Apple Wins with Design," *Business Week* (July 31. 2000), pp. 144 and "Apple Putting Hopes on New MacIntosh Line," *New York Times* (January 10, 2001), p. C7.

[42]Jeffrey Pfeffer and John F. Veiga, "Putting People First for Organizational Success," *Academy of Management Executive,* vol. 13 (May 1999), pp. 37–48; and Jeffrey Pfeffer, *The Human Equation: Building Profits by Putting People First* (Boston: Harvard Business School Press, 1998).

[43]"Workweek," *Wall Street Journal* (January 9, 2001), p. 1.

[44]Henry Mintzberg, "The Manager's Job: Folklore and Fact," *Harvard Business Review,* vol. 53 (July–August 1975), p. 61. See also his book *The Nature of Managerial Work* (New York: Harper & Row, 1973, and Harper-Collins, 1997).

[45]Hal Lancaster, "Middle Managers Are Back—But Now They're 'High-Impact' Players," *Wall Street Journal* (April 14, 1998), p. B1.

[46]Information from David Whitford, "A Human Place to Work," *Fortune* (January 8, 2001), pp. 108–20.

[47]Lancaster, op cit.

[48]For a perspective on the first-level manager's job, see Leonard A. Schlesinger and Janice A. Klein, "The First-Line Supervisor: Past, Present and Future," pp. 370–82, in Jay W. Lorsch (ed.), *Handbook of Organizational Behavior* (Englewood Cliffs, NJ: Prentice-Hall, 1987). Research reported in "Remember Us?" *Economist* (February 1, 1992), p. 71.

[49]Whitford, op cit.

[50]Stewart D. Friedman, Perry Christensen, and Jessica De Groot, "Work and Life: The End of the Zero-Sum Game," *Harvard Business Review* (November–December 1998), pp. 119–29.

[51]For a classic study see Thomas A. Mahoney, Thomas H. Jerdee, and Stephen J. Carroll, "The Job(s) of Management," *Industrial Relations,* vol. 4 (February 1965), pp. 97–110.

[52]This running example is developed from information from "Accountants Have Lives, Too, You Know," *Business Week* (February 23, 1998), pp. 88–90, and the Ernst & Young website: www.ey.com.

[53]Mintzberg, op cit. (1973/1997), p. 30.

[54]See, for example, John R. Veiga and Kathleen Dechant, "Wired World Woes: www.help," *Academy of Management Executive,* vol. 11 (August 1997), pp. 73–79.

[55]See Mintzberg, op cit (1973/1997); and Henry Mintzberg, "Covert Leadership: The Art of Managing Professionals," *Harvard Business Review* (November–December 1998), pp. 140–47; and, Jonathan Gosling and Henry Mintzberg, "The Five Minds of a Manager," *Harvard Business Review* (November, 2003), pp. 1–9.

[56]Mintzberg, op cit. (1973/1997), p. 60.

[57]For research on managerial work see Morgan W. McCall, Jr., Ann M. Morrison, and Robert L. Hannan, *Studies of Managerial Work: Results and Methods. Technical Report #9* (Greensboro, NC:

Center for Creative Leadership, 1978), pp. 7–9. See also John P. Kotter, "What Effective General Managers Really Do," *Harvard Business Review* (November–December 1982), pp. 156–57.

[58]Kotter, op cit. p. 164. See also his book *The General Managers* (New York: Free Press, 1986); and David Barry, Catherine Durnell Crampton, and Stephen J. Carroll, "Navigating the Garbage Can: How Agendas Help Managers Cope with Job Realities," *Academy of Management Executive,* vol. 11 (May 1997), pp. 43–56.

[59]To read more on the Johari Window, see R. P. Esposito, H. McAdoo, and L. Scher, "The Johari Window Test: A Research Note," *Journal of Humanistic Psychology,* vol. 18, no. 1 (1978), pp. 79–81.

[60]Robert L. Katz, "Skills of an Effective Administrator," *Harvard Business Review* (September–October 1974), p. 94.

[61]Hendrie Weisinger, *Emotional Intelligence at Work* (San Francisco: Jossey-Bass, 2000).

[62]See Daniel Goleman's books *Emotional Intelligence* (New York: Bantam, 1995) and *Working with Emotional Intelligence* (New York: Bantam, 1998); and his articles "What Makes a Leader," *Harvard Business Review* (November–December 1998), pp. 93–102, and "Leadership That Makes a Difference," *Harvard Business Review* (March–April 2000), pp. 79–90, quote from p. 80.

[63]Richard E. Boyatzis, *The Competent Manager: A Model for Effective Performance* (New York: Wiley, 1982). See also Jon P. Briscoe and Douglas T. Hall, "Grooming and Picking Leaders Using Competency Frameworks: Do They Work?" *Organizational Dynamics* (Autumn 1999), pp. 37–52.

Chapter 2 Notes

[1]Quote from "How Good Is Googol?" *The Economist* (November 1, 2003). Additional information from corporate website: www.google.com/corporate/history.html.

[2]Pauline Graham, *Mary Parker Follett—Prophet of Management: A Celebration of Writings from the 1920s* (Boston: Harvard Business School Press, 1995).

[3]For a timeline of twentieth-century management ideas see "75 Years of Management Ideas and Practices: 1922–1997," *Harvard Business Review,* supplement (September–October 1997).

[4]A thorough review and critique of the history of management thought, including management in ancient civilizations, is provided by Daniel A. Wren, *The Evo-*

lution of Management Thought, 4th ed. (New York: Wiley, 1993).

[5]For a timeline of major people and themes see "75 Years of Management," op.cit.

[6]For a sample of this work see Henry L. Gantt, *Industrial Leadership* (Easton, MD: Hive, 1921; Hive edition published in 1974); Henry C. Metcalfe and Lyndall Urwick (eds.), *Dynamic Administration: The Collected Papers of Mary Parker Follett* (New York: Harper & Brothers, 1940); James D. Mooney, *The Principles of Administration,* rev. ed. (New York: Harper & Brothers, 1947); Lyndall Urwick, *The Elements of Administration* (New York: Harper & Brothers, 1943); and *The Golden Book of Management* (London: N. Neame, 1956).

[7]References on Taylor's work are from Frederick W. Taylor, *The Principles of Scientific Management* (New York: W. W. Norton, 1967), originally published by Harper & Brothers in 1911. See Charles W. Wrege and Amedeo G. Perroni, "Taylor's Pig-Tale: A Historical Analysis of Frederick W. Taylor's Pig Iron Experiments," *Academy of Management Journal,* vol. 17 (March 1974), pp. 6-27, for a criticism; see Edwin A. Lock, "The Ideas of Frederick W. Taylor: An Evaluation," *Academy of Management Review,* vol. 7 (1982), p. 14, for an examination of the contemporary significance of Taylor's work. See also the biography, Robert Kanigel, *The One Best Way* (New York: Viking, 1997).

[8]Kanigel, op cit.

[9]See Frank B. Gilbreth, *Motion Study* (New York: Van Nostrand, 1911).

[10]Available in the English language as Henri Fayol, *General and Industrial Administration* (London: Pitman, 1949); subsequent discussion is based on M. B. Brodie, *Fayol on Administration* (London: Pitman, 1949).

[11]Information from Justin Martin, "Mercedes: Made in Alabama," *Fortune* (July 7, 1997), pp. 150-158; and "A Plant Grows in Alabama," *Mercedes Momentum* (Spring 1998), pp. 56-61.

[12]M. P. Follett, *Freedom and Coordination* (London: Management Publications Trust, 1949).

[13]Judith Garwood, "A Review of *Dynamic Administration: The Collected Papers of Mary Parker Follett,*" *New Management,* vol. 2 (1984), pp. 61-62; eulogy from Richard C. Cabot, *Encyclopedia of Social Work,* vol. 15, "Follett, Mary Parker," p. 351.

[14]Information from "Honesty Top Trait for Chair," *Columbus Dispatch* (January 15, 2003), p. G1.

[15]A. M. Henderson and Talcott Parsons (eds. and trans.), *Max Weber: The Theory of Social Economic Organization* (New York: Free Press, 1947).

[16]Ibid., p. 337.

[17]The Hawthorne studies are described in detail in F. J. Roethlisberger and William J. Dickson, *Management and the Worker* (Cambridge, MA: Harvard University Press, 1966); and G. Homans, *Fatigue of Workers* (New York: Reinhold, 1941). For an interview with three of the participants in the relay-assembly test-room studies, see R. G. Greenwood, A. A. Bolton, and R. A. Greenwood, "Hawthorne a Half Century Later: 'Relay Assembly Participants Remember'," *Journal of Management,* vol. 9 (1983), pp. 217-31.

[18]Information from corporate website: www.fourseasons.com/about us/.

[19]The criticisms of the Hawthorne studies are detailed in Alex Carey, "The Hawthorne Studies: A Radical Criticism," *American Sociological Review,* vol. 32 (1967), pp. 403-16; H. M. Parsons, "What Happened at Hawthorne?" *Science,* vol. 183 (1974), pp. 922-32; and B. Rice, "The Hawthorne Defect: Persistence of a Flawed Theory," *Psychology Today,* vol. 16 (1982), pp. 70-74. See also Wren, op cit.

[20]This discussion of Maslow's theory is based on Abraham H. Maslow, *Eupsychian Management* (Homewood, IL: Richard D. Irwin, 1965); and Abraham H. Maslow, *Motivation and Personality,* 2nd ed. (New York: Harper & Row, 1970).

[21]Information from Terry Stephan, "Honing Her Kraft," *Northwestern* (Winter 2000), pp. 22-25.

[22]Douglas McGregor, *The Human Side of Enterprise* (New York: McGraw-Hill, 1960).

[23]See Gary Heil, Deborah F. Stevens, and Warren G. Bennis, *Douglas McGregor on Management: Revisiting the Human Side of Enterprise* (New York: Wiley, 2000).

[24]Quote from Allan H. Church, Executive Commentary, *Academy of Management Executive* (February 2002), p. 74.

[25]Chris Argyris, *Personalitly and Organization* (New York: Harper & Row, 1957).

[26]The ideas of Ludwig von Bertalanffy contributed to the emergence of this systems perspective on organizations. See his article, "The History and Status of General Systems Theory," *Academy of Management Journal,* vol. 15 (1972), pp. 407-26. This viewpoint is further developed by Daniel Katz and Robert L. Kahn in their classic book, *The Social Psychology of Organizations* (New York: Wiley, 1978). For an integrated systems view see Lane Tracy, *The Living Organization* (New York: Quorum Books, 1994). For an overview, see W. Richard Scott, *Organizations: Rational, Natural, and Open Systems,* 4th ed. (Upper Saddle River, NJ: Prentice-Hall, 1998).

[27]Chester I. Barnard, *Functions of the Executive* (Cambridge, MA: Harvard University Press, 1938).

[28]See discussion by Scott, op cit., pp. 66-68.

[29]Peter F. Drucker, "The Future That Has Already Happened," *Harvard Business Review,* vol. 75 (September–October 1997), pp. 20-24. See also Shaker A. Zahra "An Interview with Peter Drucker," *Academy of Management Executive,* vol. 17 (2003), p. 9-12.

[30]For an overview, see Scott, op cit., pp. 95-97.

[31]For the classics see W. Edwards Deming, *Quality, Productivity, and Competitive Position* (Cambridge, MA: MIT Press, 1982); and Joseph M. Juran, *Quality Control Handbook,* 3rd ed. (New York: McGraw-Hill, 1979).

[32]Jay R. Gailbraith, "Designing the Networked Organization: Leveraging Size and Competencies" in Susan Albers Mohrman, Jay R. Galbraith, Edward E. Lawler III and Associates *Tomorrow's Organization: Crafting Winning Capabilities in a Dynamic World* (San Francisco: Jossey-Bass, 1998), pp. 92-94.

[33]Thomas J. Peters and Robert H. Waterman, Jr., *In Search of Excellence: Lessons from America's Best-Run Companies* (New York: Harper & Row, 1982). For a retrospective see William C. Bogner, "Tom Peters on the Real World of Business" and "Robert Waterman on Being Smart and Lucky," *Academy of Management Executive,* vol. 16 (2002), pp. 40-50.

[34]William Ouchi, *Theory Z: How American Businesses Can Meet the Japanese Challenge* (Reading, MA: Addison-Wesley, 1981); and Richard Tanner Pascale and Anthony G. Athos, *The Art of Japanese Management: Applications for American Executives* (New York: Simon & Schuster, 1981).

[35]Ouchi, op cit.; see also the review by J. Bernard Keys, Luther Tray Denton, and Thomas R. Miller, "The Japanese Management Theory Jungle-Revisited," *Journal of Management,* vol. 20 (1994), pp. 373-402.

[36]Peter Senge, *The Fifth Discipline* (New York: Harper, 1990).

[37]John Gardner, *No Easy Victories* (New York: Harper & Row, 1968).

[38]Information from Ann Harrington, "Coke Denied: Prevention Is the Best Defense," *Fortune* (July 10, 2000), p. 188.

[39]Peter F. Drucker, "Looking Ahead: Implications of the Present," *Harvard Business Review* (September–October, 1997), pp. 18–32.

[40]Quote from Ralph Z. Sorenson, "A Lifetime of Learning to Manage Effectively," *Wall Street Journal* (February 28, 1983), p. 18.

Endnotes—Chapter 3

[1]Information from corporate website, including "timeline": www.benandjerrys.com.

[2]Adapted from Terry Thomas, John W. Dienhart, and John R. Schermerhorn, Jr., "Leading Toward Ethical Behavior in Business," working paper, 2003.

[3]For more on the WorldCom debacle see Susan Pulliam, "A Staffer Ordered to Commit Fraud Balked, Then Caved," *Wall Street Journal* (June 23, 2003), pp. A1, A6; for more on the Andersen saga see Barbara Ley Toffler, *Final Accounting: Ambition, Greed and the Fall of Arthur Andersen* (New York: Broadway Books, 2003).

[4]See the discussion by Lynn Sharpe Paine, "Managing for Organizational Integrity," *Harvard Business Review* (March–April 1994), pp. 106–117.

[5]This quote is from an interview with Jana Matthews for the magazine of her alma mater, Earlham College. See "Business as an Ethical Activity," *Earlhamite* (Winter 2003), pp. 14–15.

[6]Desmond Tutu, "Do More Than Win," *Fortune* (December 30, 1991), p. 59.

[7]For an overview, see Linda K. Trevino and Katherine A. Nelson, *Managing Business Ethics*, 3rd ed. (New York: Wiley, 2003).

[8]Ibid.

[9]Milton Rokeach, *The Nature of Human Values* (New York: Free Press, 1973). See also W. C. Frederick and J. Weber, "The Values of Corporate Executives and Their Critics: An Empirical Description and Normative Implications," in W. C. Frederick and L. E. Preston (eds.), *Business Ethics: Research Issues and Empirical Studies* (Greenwich, CT: JAI Press, 1990).

[10]Tom Chappell, *The Soul of a Business: Managing for Profit and for the Common Good* (New York: Bantam Books, 1993); and information from corporate website: www.tomsofmaine.com/mission/stewardship_content.htm.

[11]See Gerald F. Cavanagh, Dennis J. Moberg, and Manuel Velasquez, "The Ethics of Organizational Politics," *Academy of Management Review*, vol. 6 (1981), pp. 363–74; Justin G. Locknecker, Joseph A. McKinney, and Carlos W. Moore, "Egoism and Independence: Entrepreneurial Ethics,"*Organizational Dynamics* (winter 1988), pp. 64–72; and Justin G. Locknecker, Joseph A. McKinney, and Carlos W. Moore, "The Generation Gap in Business Ethics," *Business Horizons* (September–October 1989), pp. 9–14.

[12]Raymond L. Hilgert, "What Ever Happened to Ethics in Business and in Business Schools," *The Diary of Alpha Kappa Psi* (April 1989), pp. 4–8.

[13]Jerald Greenburg, "Organizational Justice: Yesterday, Today, and Tomorrow," *Journal of Management*, vol. 16, (1990) pp. 399–432; and Mary A. Konovsky, "Understanding Procedural Justice and Its Impact on Business Organizations," *Journal of Management*, vol. 26 (2000), pp. 489–511.

[14]Interactional justice is described by Robert J. Bies, "The Predicament of Injustice: The Management of Moral Outrage," in L. L. Cummings & B. M. Staw (eds.). *Research in Organizational Behavior*, vol. 9 (Greenwich, CT: JAI Press, 1987), pp. 289–319. The example is from Carol T. Kulik & Robert L. Holbrook, "Demographics in Service Encounters: Effects of Racial and Gender Congruence on Perceived Fairness," *Social Justice Research* vol. 13 (2000), pp. 375–402.

[15]Robert D. Haas, "Ethics—A Global Business Challenge," *Vital Speeches of the Day* (June 1, 1996), pp. 506–9.

[16]Thomas Donaldson, "Values in Tension: Ethics Away from Home," *Harvard Business Review*, vol. 74 (September–October 1996), pp. 48–62.

[17]Thomas Donaldson and Thomas W. Dunfee, "Towards a Unified Conception of Business Ethics: Integrative Social Contracts Theory," *Academy of Management Review*, vol. 19 (1994), pp. 252–85.

[18]Developed from Donaldson, op cit.

[19]Reported in Barbara Ley Toffler, "Tough Choices: Managers Talk Ethics," *New Management*, vol. 4 (1987), pp. 34–39. See also Barbara Ley Toffler, *Tough Choices: Managers Talk Ethics* (New York: Wiley, 1986).

[20]See discussion by Trevino and Nelson, op cit., pp. 47–62.

[21]Information from Steven N. Brenner and Earl A. Mollander, "Is the Ethics of Business Changing?" *Harvard Business Review*, vol. 55 (January–February 1977).

[22]Saul W. Gellerman, "Why 'Good' Managers Make Bad Ethical Choices," *Harvard Business Review*, vol. 64 (July–August, 1986), pp. 85–90.

[23]Survey results from Del Jones, "48% of Workers Admit to Unethical or Illegal Acts," *USA Today* (April 4, 1997), p. A1.

[24]Reported in Adam Smith, "Wall Street's Outrageous Fortunes," *Esquire* (April 1987), p. 73.

[25]The Body Shop came under scrutiny over the degree to which its business practices actually live up to this charter and the company's self-promoted green image. See, for example, John Entine, "Shattered Image," *Business Ethics* (September–October 1994), pp. 23–28.

[26]Information from Thomas Teal, "Not a Fool, Not a Saint," *Fortune* (November 11, 1996), pp. 201–4; quote from Shelley Donald Coolidge, *The Christian Science Monitor* (March 28, 1996).

[27]Information on this case from William M. Carley, "Antitrust Chief Says CEOs Should Tape All Phone Calls to Each Other," *Wall Street Journal* (February 15, 1983), p. 23; "American Air, Chief End Antitrust Suit, Agree Not to Discuss Fares with Rivals," *Wall Street Journal* (July 15, 1985), p. 4; "American Airlines Loses Its Pilot," *Economist* (April 18, 1998), p. 58.

[28]Alan L. Otten, "Ethics on the Job: Companies Alert Employees to Potential Dilemmas," *Wall Street Journal* (July 14, 1986), p. 17; and "The Business Ethics Debate," *Newsweek* (May 25, 1987), p. 36.

[29]See "Whistle-Blowers on Trial," *Business Week* (March 24, 1997), pp. 172–78; and "NLRB Judge Rules for Massachusetts Nurses in Whistle-Blowing Case," *American Nurse* (January–February 1998), p. 7.

[30]For a review of whistleblowing, see Marcia P. Micelli and Janet P. Near, *Blowing the Whistle* (Lexington, MA: Lexington Books, 1992); see also Micelli and Near, "Whistleblowing: Reaping the Benefits," *Academy of Management Executive*, vol. 8 (August 1994), pp. 65–72.

[31]Information from James A. Waters, "Catch 20.5: Mortality as an Organizational Phenomenon," *Organizational Dynamics*, vol. 6 (spring 1978), pp. 3–15.

[32]Information from Ethics Resource Center, "Major Survey of America's Workers Finds Substantial Improvements in Ethics": www.ethics.org/releases/nr_20030521_nbes.html.

[33]Robert D. Gilbreath, "The Hollow Executive," *New Management*, vol. 4 (1987), pp. 24–28.

[34]Information from "Gifts of Gab: A Start-up's Social Conscience Pays Off," *Business Week* (February 5, 2001), p. F38.

[35]Developed from recommendations of the Government Accountability Project reported in "Blowing the Whistle without Paying the Piper."

[36]Information from www.josephsoninstitute.org/MED/MED-2sixpillars.htm.

[37]Information from corporate website: www.gapinc.com/community sourcing/vendor_conduct.htm.

[38]For a good review see Robert H. Miles, *Managing the Corporate Social Environment* (Englewood Cliffs, NJ: 1987).

[39]See Thomas Donaldson and Lee Preston, "The Stakeholder Theory of the Corporation," *Academy of Management Review,* vol. 20 (January 1995), pp. 65–91.

[40]Mary Miller, "Ben Cohen's Hot Fudge Venture Fund," *Business Ethics,* vol. 16 (January–February 2002), p. 6.

[41]Information from "The Socially Correct Corporate," *Fortune* special advertising section (July 24, 2000), pp. S32–S34; Joseph Pereiva, "Doing Good and Doing Well at Timberland," *Wall Street Journal* (September 9, 2003), pp. B1, B10.

[42]Quote from corporate website: http//www.tomsofmaine.com.

[43]See Joel Makower: Putting Social Responsibility to Work for Your Business and the World (New York: Simon & Schuster, 1994), pp. 17–18.

[44]The historical framework of this discussion is developed from Keith Davis, "The Case for and against Business Assumption of Social Responsibility," *Academy of Management Journal* (June 1973), pp. 312–22; Keith Davis and William Frederick, *Business and Society: Management: Public Policy, Ethics,* 5th ed. (New York: McGraw-Hill, 1984). The debate is also discussed by Makower, op. cit., pp. 28–33. See also, "Civics 101," *Economist* (May 11, 1996), p. 61.

[45]The Friedman quotation is from Milton Friedman, *Capitalism and Freedom* (Chicago: University of Chicago Press, 1962); the Samuelson quotation is from Paul A. Samuelson, "Love That Corporation," *Mountain Bell Magazine* (spring 1971). Both are cited in Davis, op. cit.

[46]Davis and Frederick, Quoted in op. cit.

[47]See James K. Glassman, "When Ethics Meet Earnings," *International Herald Tribune* (May 24–25, 2003), p. 15.

[48]See Makower, op cit. (1994), pp. 71–75; and Sandra A. Waddock and Samuel B. Graves, "The Corporate Social Performance-Financial Performance Link," *Strategic Management Journal* (1997), pp. 303–19.

[49]Davis, op cit.

[50]Information from the Global Social Responsibility Resource Center, Business for Social Responsibility website: www.bsr.org/resourcecenter/index.html.

[51]The "compliance–conviction" distinction is attributed to Mark Goyder in Martin Waller, "Much Corporate Responsibility Is Box-Ticking," *The Times Business* (July 8, 2003), p. 21.

[52]Archie B. Carroll, "A Three-Dimensional Model of Corporate Performance," *Academy of Management Review,* vol. 4 (1979), pp. 497–505. Carroll's continuing work in this area is most recently reported in Mark S. Schwartz and Archie B, Carroll, "Corporate Social Responsibility: A Three Domain Approach, "*Business Ethics Quarterly,* vol. 13 (2003), pp. 503–530.

[53]Elizabeth Gatewood and Archie B. Carroll, "The Anatomy of Corporate Social Response," *Business Horizons,* vol. 24 (September–October 1981), pp. 9–16.

[54]Information from www.cepaa.org/AboutSAI/.

[55]Judith Burns, "Everything You Wanted to Know About Corporate Governance… But Didn't Know to Ask," *The Wall Street Journal* (October 27, 2003), p. R6.

[56]See for example "Pay for Performance Report," Institute of Management and Administration, (December, 2003).

Chapter 4 Notes

[1]Information from David Rocks, "Reinventing Herman Miller," *Business Week e.biz* (April 3, 2000), pp. E88–E96; www.hermanmiller.com.

[2]Robert Reich, *The Future of Success* (New York: Knopf, 2001), p. 7.

[3]Quote from *The New Blue* (IBM Annual Report, 1997), p. 8.

[4]Reich, op cit.

[5]See Michael E. Porter, *Competitive Strategy: Techniques for Analyzing Industries and Competitors* (New York: Free Press, 1980), and *Competitive Advantage: Creating and Sustaining Superior Performance* (New York: Free Press, 1986); also, Richard A. D'Aveni, *Hyper-Competition: Managing the Dynamics of Strategic Maneuvering* (New York: Free Press, 1994).

[6]Information from *The Vermont Teddy Bear Company Gazette,* vol. 4 (summer 1993); and www.vtbear.com.

[7]Joseph M. Juran, "Made in U.S.A.: A Renaissance in Quality," *Harvard Business Review* (July–August 1993), pp. 42–50.

[8]Michael Porter, *The Competitive Advantage of Nations* (New York: Free Press, 1989).

[9]See Richard D. Bucher, *Diversity Consciousness: Opening Our Minds to People, Cultures, and Opportunities* (Upper Saddle River, NJ: Prentice-Hall, 2000), p. 201.

[10]Information from "Ivory Tower: How an MBA Can Bend Your Mind," *Business Week* (April 1, 2002), p. 12.

[11]James D. Thompson, *Organizations in Action* (New York: McGraw-Hill, 1967); and Robert B. Duncan, "Characteristics of Organizational Environments and Perceived Environmental Uncertainty," *Administrative Science Quarterly,* vol. 17 (1972), pp. 313–27. For discussion of the implications of uncertainty see Hugh Courtney, Jane Kirkland, and Patrick Viguerie, "Strategy Under Uncertainty," *Harvard Business Review* (November–December 1997), pp. 67–79.

[12]Quote from *The Vermont Teddy Bear Company Gazette,* op cit., p. 3.

[13]Quotation from a discussion by Richard J. Shonberger and Edward M. Knod Jr., *Operations Management: Serving the Customer,* 3rd ed. (Plano, TX: Business Publications, 1988), p. 4.

[14]Rosabeth Moss Kanter, "Transcending Business Boundaries: 12,000 World Managers View Change," *Harvard Business Review* (May–June 1991), pp. 151–64.

[15]Reported in Jennifer Steinhauer, "The Undercover Shoppers," *New York Times* (February 4, 1998), pp. C1, C2.

[16]Information from "How Marriott Never Forgets a Guest," *Business Week* (February 21, 2000), p. 74.

[17]Roger D. Blackwell and Kristina Blackwell, "The Century of the Consumer: Converting Supply Chains into Demand Chains," *Supply Chain Management Review* (fall 1999).

[18]See Joseph M. Juran, *Quality Control Handbook,* 3rd ed. (New York: McGraw-Hill, 1979) and "The Quality Trilogy: A Universal Approach to Managing for Quality," in H. Costin (ed.), *Total Quality Management* (New York: Dryden, 1994); W. Edwards Derning, *Out of Crisis* (Cambridge, MA: MIT Press, 1986) and "Deming's Quality Manifesto," *Best of Business Quarterly,* vol. 12 (winter 1990–1991), pp. 6–10. See also Howard S. Gitlow and Shelly J. Gitlow, *The Deming Guide to Quality and Competitive Position* (Englewood Cliffs, NJ: Prentice-Hall, 1987); and Juran, op cit. (1993).

[19]See information on the Malcolm Baldrige National Quality Award at: www.quality.nist.gov/bcpg; see also, "Does the Baldrige Award Really Work? *Harvard Business Review* (January–February 1992), pp. 126–47.

[20]Philip B. Crosby, *Quality Is Free* (New York: McGraw-Hill, 1979); *The Eternally Successful Organization* (New York: McGraw-Hill, 1988); and *Quality Is Still Free: Making Quality Certain in Uncertain Times* (New York: McGraw-Hill, 1995).

[21]Rafael Aguay, *Dr. Deming: The American Who Taught the Japanese About Quality* (New York: Free Press, 1997); and W. Edwards Deming, op cit. (1986).

[22]See Edward E. Lawler III, Susan Albers Mohrman, and Gerald E. Ledford, Jr., *Employee Involvement and Total Quality Management: Practices and Results in Fortune 1000 Companies* (San Franoisco: Jossey-Bass, 1992).

[23]Edward E. Lawler III and Susan Albers Mohrman, "Quality Circles After the Fad," *Harvard Business Review* (January–February 1985), pp. 65–71.

[24]Quotes from Arnold Kanarick, "The Far Side of Quality Circles." *Management Review,* vol. 70 (October 1981), pp. 16–17.

[25]See B. Joseph Pine II, Bart Victor, and Andrew C. Boynton, "Making Mass Customization Work," *Harvard Business Review* (September–October 1993), pp. 108–19; and "The Agile Factory: Custom-made, Direct from the Plant," *Business Week,* special report on "21st Century Capitalism" (January 23, 1995), pp. 158–59; and Justin Martin, "Give 'Em *Exactly* What They Want," *Fortune* (November 10, 1997), p. 283.

[26]Edgar H. Schein, "Organizational Culture," *American Psychologist,* vol. 45 (1990), pp. 109–19. See also Schein's *Organizational Culture and Leadership,* 2nd ed. (San Francisco: Jossey-Bass, 1997); and *The Corporate Culture Survival Guide* (San Francisco: Jossey-Bass, 1999).

[27]James Collins and Jerry Porras, *Built to Last* (New York: Harper Business, 1994).

[28]Schein, op.cit. (1997); Terrence E. Deal and Alan A. Kennedy, *Corporate Cultures: The Rites and Rituals of Corporate Life* (Reading, MA: Addison-Wesley, 1982); and Ralph Kilmann, *Beyond the Quick Fix* (San Francisco: Jossey-Bass, 1984).

[29]In their book *Corporate Culture and Performance* (New York: Macmillan, 1992), John P. Kotter and James L. Heskett make the point that strong cultures have the desired effects over the long term only if they encourage adaptation to a changing environment. See also Collins and Porras, op cit. (1994).

[30]This is a simplified model developed from Schein, op cit. (1997).

[31]James C. Collins and Jerry I. Porras, "Building Your Company's Vision," *Harvard Business Review* (September–October 1996), pp. 65–77.

[32]This case is reported in Jenny C. McCune, "Making Lemonade," *Management Review* (June 1997), pp. 49–53.

[33]Ralph H. Kilmann, Mary J. Saxton, and Roy Serpa, "Issues in Understanding and Changing Corporate Culture," *California Management Review,* vol. 28 (1986), pp. 87–94.

[34]Information from Michael Allen, "Endeavor Bets on Latin American Entrepreneurs," *Wall Street Journal* (April 15, 2002), p. B4.

[35]See Mary Kay Ash, *Mary Kay: You Can Have It All* (New York: Roseville, CA: Prima Publishing, 1995).

[36]Lee Gardenswartz and Anita Rowe, *Managing Diversity: A Complete Desk Reference and Planning Guide* (Chicago: Irwin, 1993).

[37]R. Roosevelt Thomas, Jr., *Beyond Race and Gender* (New York: AMACOM, 1992), p. 10; see also R. Roosevelt Thomas, Jr., "From 'Affirmative Action' to 'Affirming Diversity,'" *Harvard Business Review,* (November–December 1990), pp. 107–17; R. Roosevelt Thomas, Jr., with Marjorie I. Woodruff, *Building a House for Diversity* (New York: AMACOM, 1999).

[38]Thomas Kochan, Katerina Bezrukova, Robin Ely, Susan Jackson, Aparna Joshi, Karen Jehn, Jonathan Leonard, David Levine, and David Thomas, "The Effects of Diversity on Business Performance: Report of the Diversity Research Network," reported in SHRM Foundation Research Findings, retrieved from www.shrm.org/foundation/findings.asp. Full article published in *Human Resource Management* (2003).

[39]Gardenswartz and Rowe, op cit., p. 220+.

[40]Taylor Cox, Jr., *Cultural Diversity in Organizations* (San Francisco: Berrett Koehler, 1994).

[41]Joseph A. Raelin, *Clash of Cultures* (Cambridge, MA: Harvard Business School Press, 1986).

[42]Geert Hofstede, *Culture's Consequences* (Beverly Hills: Sage, 1982).

[43]See Anthony Robbins and Joseph McClendon III, *Unlimited Power: A Black Choice* (New York: Free Press, 1997), and Augusto Failde and William Doyle, *Latino Success: Insights from America's Most Powerful Latino Executives* (New York: Free Press, 1996).

[44]See, for example, the discussion in Ron Zembke, Claire Raines, and Bob Filipczak, *Generations at Work: Managing the Clash of Veterans, Boomers, Xers, and Nexters in Your Workplace* (New York: AMACOM, 1999); and Brian O'Reilly, "Meet the Future: It's Your Kids," *Fortune* (July 24, 2000), pp. 144–64.

[45]Barbara Benedict Bunker, "Appreciating Diversity and Modifying Organizational Cultures: Men and Women at Work," Chapter 5 in Suresh Srivastva and David L. Cooperrider, *Appreciative Management and Leadership* (San Francisco: Jossey-Bass, 1990).

[46]See Gary N. Powell, *Women & Men in Management* (Thousand Oaks, CA: Sage, 1993) and Cliff Cheng (ed.), *Masculinities in Organizations* (Thousand Oaks, CA: Sage, 1996). For added background, see also Sally Helgesen, *Everyday Revolutionaries: Working Women and the Transformation of American Life* (New York: Doubleday, 1998).

[47]Stephanie N. Mehta, "What Minority Employees Really Want," *Fortune* (July 10, 2000), pp. 181–86.

[48]Ibid.

[49]Information from Marjorie Valbrun, "More Muslims Claim They Suffer Job Bias," *Wall Street Journal* (April 15, 2003), pp. B1, B8.

[50]Information from "The Bugs in Microsoft Culture," *Fortune* (January 8, 2001), p. 128.

[51]Information from Kimberly Blanton, "U.S. Downturn Undermines Gains by Blacks in Labor Market," *International Herald Tribune* (May 24–25, 2003), p. 12.

[52]Data reported in "How to Enable the Disabled," *Business Week* (November 6, 2000), p. 36.

[53]This section is based on ideas set forth by Thomas, op cit. (1992); and Thomas and Woodruff, op cit. (1999).

[54]Thomas, op cit. (1992), p. 17.

[55]Thomas and Woodruff, op cit. (1999), pp. 211–26.

[56]Based on ibid., pp. 11–12.

[57]Survey reported in "The Most Inclusive Workplaces Generate the Most Loyal Employees," *Gallup Management Journal* (December 2001), retrieved from http://gmj.gallup.com/press_room/release.asp?i = 117.

[58]"Diversity Today: Corporate Recruiting Practices in Inclusive Workplaces," *Fortune* (June 12, 2000), p. S4.

Chapter 5 Notes

[1]Information from corporate website: www.limited.com; quotes from

www.limited.com/feature.jsp and www.limited.com/who/index.jsp. See also Les Wekner, "How I Conquered the Women's Retail Clothing Industry (and an Ulcer), *Fortune Small Business* (September, 2003), pp. 40–43.

[2]Information from Lindsay Whipp and Kae Inoue, "Japan Carmakers to Expand U.S. Output," *International Herald Tribune* (May 23, 2003), p. B3.

[3]See Kenichi Ohmae, *The Evolving Global Economy* (Cambridge, MA: Harvard Business School Press, 1995).

[4]For a discussion of globalization see Thomas L. Friedman. *The Lexus and the Olive Tree: Understanding Globalization* (New York: Bantam Doubleday Dell, 2000); and John Micklethwait and Adrian Woodridge, *A Future Perfect: The Challenges and Hidden Promise of Globalization* (New York: Crown, 2000).

[5]Rosabeth Moss Kanter, *World Class: Thinking Locally in the Global Economy* (New York: Simon & Schuster, 1995), preface.

[6]See the discussion by Alfred E. Eckes, Jr., and Thomas W. Zeiler, *Globalization and the American Century* (Cambridge, UK: Cambridge University Press, 2003).

[7]Quote from Jeffrey E. Garten, "The Mind of the CEO," *Business Week* (February 5, 2001), p. 106.

[8]The *Economist* is a good weekly source of information on Europe. See www.economist.com.

[9]A monthly publication that covers the *maquiladora* industries is the *Twin Plant News* (El Paso, Texas); see website at: www.twin-plant-news.com/.

[10]Information from Rich Teerlink, "Harley's Leadership U-Turn," *Harvard Business Review* (March–April 2000), pp. 3–4. See also Rich Teerlink and Lee Ozley, *More Than a Motorcycle: The Leadership Journey at Harley-Davidson* (Cambridge, MA: Harvard Business School Press 2000); and corporate website: www.harley-davidson.com/company.asp.

[11]For an overview of business in China see John Studdard and James G. Shiro, *The New Silk Road: Secrets of Business Success in China Today* (New York: Wiley, 2000). Export data from "Surviving the Onslaught," *Wall Street Journal* (October 6, 2003), p. B1.

[12]Information from Hiawatha Bray, "Philippines Vies for 'Back-Office' Operations," *International Herald Tribune* (May 23, 2003), p. 14.

[13]The *Economist* is a good weekly source of information on Africa. See www.economist.com.

[14]Bray, op cit.

[15]James A. Austin and John G. McLean, "Pathways to Business Success in Sub-Saharan Africa," *Journal of African Finance and Economic Development,* vol. 2 (1996), pp. 57–76.

[16]Information from "International Business: Consider Africa," *Harvard Business Review,* vol. 76 (January–February 1998), pp. 16–18.

[17]Information from Africa information website: www.mbendi.co.za/orsadc.htm.

[18]See "Inside View: South Africa," *New York Times* (September 18, 2000), pp. A15–A17.

[19]Quotes from Mort Rosenblum, "Turnaround: Once a Basket Case, Mozambique Now a Free-Market Example," *Columbus Dispatch* (December 14, 1997), p. 4c.

[20]Quote from John A. Byrne, "Visionary vs. Visionary," *Business Week* (August 28, 2000), p. 210.

[21]First reported in *Business Week* (February 29, 1988), pp. 63–66; further information on corporate website: www.falconproducts.com/.

[22]Developed from Anthony J. F. O'Rcilly, "Establishing Successful Joint Ventures in Developing Nations: A CEO's Perspective," *Columbia Journal of World Business* (spring 1988), pp. 65–71; and "Best Practices for Global Competitiveness," *Fortune* (March 30, 1998), pp. S1–S3, special advertising section.

[23]Whipp and Inoue, op cit.

[24]Quoted from "Own Words: Percy Barnevik, ABB and Investor," *Financial Times Limited,* 1998.

[25]Information from Karby Leggett, "U.S. Auto Makers Find Promise—and Peril—in China," *Wall Street Journal* (June 19, 2003), p. B1.

[26]See Peter F. Drucker, "The Global Economy and the Nation-State," *Foreign Affairs,* vol. 76 (September–October 1997), pp. 159–71.

[27]Adapted from R. Hall Mason. "Conflicts between Host Countries and Multinational Enterprise," *California Management Review,* vol. 17 (1974), pp. 6, 7.

[28]For a good overview, see Randall E. Stros, *Bulls in the China Shop and Other Sino-American Business Encounters* (New York: Pantheon, 1991); as well as Studdard and Shir, op cit.

[29]For an interesting discussion of one company's experience in China see Jim Mann, *Beijing Jeep: A Case Study of Western Business in China* (Boulder, CO: Westview Press, 1997).

[30]Information from corporate website: www.nikeBiz.com/labor/toc_monitoring.html.

[31]"An Industry Monitors Child Labor," *New York Times* (October 16, 1997), pp. B1, B9; and Rugmark International website: www.rugmark.de.

[32]Definition from World Commission on Environment and Development, *Our Common Future* (Oxford: Oxford University Press, 1987); reported on International Institute for Sustainable Development website: www.iisdl.iisd.ca.

[33]Examples reported in Neil Chesanow, *The World-Class Executive* (New York: Rawson Associates, 1985).

[34]Based on Barbara Benedict Bunker, "Appreciating Diversity and Modifying Organizational Cultures: Men and Women at Work," in Suresh Srivastva and David L. Cooperrider (eds.), *Appreciative Management and Leadership: The Power of Positive Thought and Action in Organizations* (San Francisco: Jossey-Bass, 1990), pp. 127–49.

[35]For a good overview of the practical issues, see Richard D. Lewis, *The Cultural Imperative: Global Trends in the 21st Century* (Yarmouth, ME: Intercultural Press, 2002); and Martin J. Gannon, *Understanding Global Cultures* (Thousand Oaks, CA: Sage, 1994).

[36]Information from Ronald B. Lieber, "Flying High, Going Global," *Fortune* (July 7, 1997), pp. 195–197.

[37]See Gary P. Ferraro, "The Need for Linguistic Proficiency in Global Business," *Business Horizons* (May–June 1996), pp. 39–46; quote from Carol Hymowitz, "Companies Go Global, but Many Managers Just Don't Travel Well," *Wall Street Journa* (August 15, 2000), p. B1.

[38]Edward T. Hall, *Beyond Culture* (New York: Doubleday, 1976).

[39]Edward T. Hall, *The Silent Language* (New York: Anchor Books, 1959); *The Hidden Dimension* (New York: Anchor Books, 1969).

[40]Hall, op cit., (1959).

[41]Lady Borton, "Learning to Work with Viet Nam," *The Academy of Management Executive,* vol. 14 (December 2000), pp. 20–31.

[42]Edward T. Hall, *Hidden Differences* (New York: Doubleday, 1990).

[43]Both examples from Hymowitz, op. cit.

[44]Geert Hofstede, *Culture's Consequences* (Beverly Hills: Sage, 1984).

[45]This dimension is explained more thoroughly by Geert Hofstede et al., *Masculinity and Feminity: The Taboo Dimension of National Cultures* (Thousand Oaks, CA.: Sage, 1998).

[46]For an introduction to the fifth dimension, see Geert Hofstede and

Michael H. Bond, "The Confucius Connection: From Cultural Roots to Economic Growth," *Organizational Dynamics,* vol. 16 (1988), pp. 4–21, which presents comparative data from Bond's "Chinese Values Survey."

[47]Michael Schuman, "How Interbrew Blended Disparate Ingredients in Korean Beer Venture," *Wall Street Journal* (July 24, 2000), pp. A1, A6.

[48]Fons Trompenaars, *Riding the Waves of Culture: Understanding Cultural Diversity in Business* (London: Nicholas Brealey Publishing, 1993).

[49]See Robert B. Reich, "Who Is Them?" *Harvard Business Review* (March–April 1991), pp, 77–88.

[50]"Going International: Willett Systems Limited," *Fortune* (February 16, 1998), p. S6, special advertising section.

[51]Information from Mark Niquette, "Honda's 'Bold Move' Paid Off," *Columbus Dispatch* (November 16, 2002), pp. C1, C2.

[52]Mark Clifford and Majeet Kripalani, "Different Countries, Adjoining Cubicles," *Business Week* (August 28, 2000), pp. 182–184.

[53]Information from Gail Edmondson, "See the World, Erase Its Borders," *Business Week* (August 28, 2000), pp. 113–14.

[54]For a perspective on the role of women in expatriate managerial assignments, see Marianne Jelinek and Nancy J. Adler, "Women: World-Class Managers for Global Competition" *Academy of Management Executive* (February 1988), pp. 11–19.

[55]Geert Hofstede, "Motivation, Leadership, and Organization," p. 43. See also Hofstede's "Cultural Constraints in Management Theories," *Academy of Management Review,* vol. 7 (1993), pp. 81–94.

[56]The classics are William Ouchi, *Theory Z: How American Businesses Can Meet the Japanese Challenge* (Reading, MA: Addison-Wesley, 1981), and Richard Tanner Pascale and Anthony G. Athos, *The Art of Japanese Management: Applications for American Executives* (New York: Simon & Schuster, 1981). See also J Bernard Keys, Luther Tray Denton, and Thomas R. Miller, "The Japanese Management Theory Jungle—Revisited," *Journal of Management,* vol. 20 (1994), pp. 373–402.

[57]For a good discussion, see Chapters 4 and 5 in Miriam Erez and P. Christopher Early, *Culture, Self-Identity, and Work* (New York: Oxford University Press, 1993).

[58]For a good discussion of the historical context of Japanese management practices see Makoto Ohtsu, *Inside Japanese Business: A Narrative History 1960–2000* (Armonk, NY: M.E. Sharpe, 2002), pp. 39–41.

[59]Lewis, op. cit.

[60]Information from Ohtsu, op. cit.

[61]Quote from Kenichi Ohmae, "Japan's Admiration for U.S. Methods Is an Open Book," *Wall Street Journal* (October 10, 1983), p. 21. See also his book *The Borderless World: Power and Strategy in the Interlinked Economy,* (New York, Harper, 1989).

[62]See for example Mzamo P. Mangaliso, "Building Competitive Advantage from *ubuntu:* Management lessons from South Africa," *Academy of Management Executive,* vol. 15 (2001), pp. 23–33.

[63]Geert Hofstede, "A Reply to Goodstein and Hunt," *Organizational Dynamics,* vol. 10 (summer 1981), p. 68.

[64]This discussion is based on Howard V. Perlmutter, "The Tortuous Evolution of the Multinational Corporation," *Columbia Journal of World Business,* vol. 4 (January–February, 1969).

Chapter 6 Notes

[1]Information from "Women Business Owners Receive First-Ever Micro Loans Via the Internet," *Business Wire* (August 9, 2000); Jim Hopkins, "Non-Profit Loan Group Takes Risks on Women in Business," *USA Today* (August 9, 2000), p. 2B; and "Women's Group Grants First Loans to Entrepreneurs," *Columbus Dispatch* (August 10, 2000), p. B2.

[2]Speech at the Llyod Greif Center for Entrepreneurial Studies, Marshall School of Business, University of Southern California, 1996.

[3]Information from the corporate websites and from The Entrepreneur's Hall of Fame: www.ltbn.com/halloffame.html.

[4]For a review and discussion of the entrepreneurial mind see Jeffry A. Timmons, *New Venture Creation: Entrepreneurship for the 21st Century* (New York: Irwin/McGraw-Hill, 1999), pp. 219–25.

[5]See the review by Robert D. Hisrich and Michael P. Peters, *Entrepreneurship,* 4th ed. (New York: Irwin/McGraw-Hill, 1998), pp. 67–70; and Paulette Thomas, "Entrepreneurs' Biggest Problems and How They Solve Them," *Wall Street Journal Reports* (March 17, 2003), pp. R1, R2.

[6]Based on research summarized by Hisrich and Peters, op. cit., pp. 70–74.

[7]Information from Jim Hopkins, "Serial Entrepreneur Strikes Again at Age 70," *USA Today* (August 15, 2000).

[8]Timothy Butler and James Waldroop, "Job Sculpting: The Art of Retaining Your Best People," *Harvard Business Review* (September–October 1999), pp. 144–52.

[9]Hopkins, op cit.

[10]Information from Janet Whitman, "How Do You Handle Extraordinary Growth?" *Wall Street Journal Reports* (March 17, 2003), p. R3.

[11]Data from *Paths to Entrepreneurship: New Directions for Women in Business* (New York: Catalyst, 1998) as summarized on the National Foundation for Women Business Owners website: www.nfwbo.org/key.html.

[12]Ibid.

[13]National Foundation for Women Business Owners, *Women Business Owners of Color: Challenges and Accomplishments* (1998).

[14]"New Report of Growth of Minority-Owned Businesses," news release SBA 99–116 ADVO (April 15, 1999).

[15]This list is developed from Timmons, op. cit, pp. 47–48; and Hisrich and Peters, op. cit., pp. 67–70.

[16]*The Facts About Small Business 1999* (Washington, DC: U.S. Small Business Administration, Office of Advocacy).

[17]See U.S. Small Business Administration website: www.sba.gov; and *Statistical Abstract of the United States* (Washington, DC: U.S. Census Bureau, 1999).

[18]Information reported in "The Rewards," *Inc. State of Small Business* (May 20–21, 2001), pp. 50–51.

[19]Information from "Got Spanish?" *Business Week Frontier* (August 14, 2000), p. F12; and "Cultivating Creativity," Interview by National Association of Female Executives (August 2000): www.nafe.com.

[20]"Small Business Expansions in Electronic Commerce," U.S. Small Business Administration, Office of Advocacy (June 2000).

[21]Information from Will Christensen, "Rod Spencer's Sports-Card Business Has Migrated Cyberspace Marketplace," *Columbus Dispatch* (July 24, 2000), p. F1.

[22]Julia Angwin, "Used-Car Auctioneers, Dealers Meet Online," *The Wall Street Journal* (November 20, 2003), pp. B1, B13, and "Renaissance in Cyberspace," *The Wall Street Journal* (November 20, 2003), p. B1.

[23]See "Join the Globetrotters: More Small Businesses Are Hustling to Ex-

port," *Business Week Frontier* (November 8, 1999), p. F10.

[24]Data reported by The Family Firm Institute: www.ffi.org/looking/factsfb.html.

[25]Conversation from the case "Am I My Uncle's Keeper?" by Paul I. Karofsky (Northeastern University Center for Family Business) and published at: www.fambiz.com/contprov.cfm? ContProvCode=NECFB&ID=140.

[26]*Survey of Small and Mid-Sized Businesses: Trends for 2000* (Arthur Andersen, 2000).

[27]Ibid.

[28]Information from Scott Williams, "Program to Help Firms Enter the Internet Marketplace," *Hispanic Business* (August 2000); and information on the program website: www.usmcoc.org/wiringdescription.html.

[29]See U.S. Small Business Administration website: www.sba.gov.

[30]George Gendron, "The Failure Myth," *Inc.* (January 2001), p. 13.

[31]Based on Norman M. Scarborough and Thomas W. Zimmerer, *Effective Small Business Management* (Englewood Cliffs, NJ: Prentice-Hall, 2000), pp. 25–30; and Scott Clark, "Most Small-Business Failures Tied to Poor Management," *Business Journal* (April 10, 2000).

[32]See, for example, John L. Nesheim, *High Tech Start Up* (New York: Free Press, 2000).

[33]Discussion based on "The Life Cycle of Entrepreneurial Firms," in Ricky Griffin (ed.), *Management*, 6th ed. (New York: Houghton Mifflin, 1999), pp. 309–10; and Neil C. Churchill and Virginia L. Lewis, "The Five Stages of Small Business Growth," *Harvard Business Review* (May–June 1993), pp. 30–50.

[34]Developed from William S. Sahlman, "How to Write a Great Business Plan," *Harvard Business Review* (July–August 1997), pp. 98–108.

[35]Marcia H. Pounds, "Business Plan Sets Course for Growth," *Columbus Dispatch* (March 16, 1998), p. 9; see also firm website: www.calcustoms.com.

[36]Standard components of business plans are described in many text sources such as Linda Pinson and Jerry Jinnett, *Anatomy of a Business Plan: A Step-by-Step Guide to Starting Smart, Building the Business, and Securing Your Company's Future*, 4th ed. (Dearbern Trade, 1999), and Scarborough and Zimmerer, op. cit.; and on websites such as: American Express Small Business Services, Business Town.com., and BizplanIt.com.

[37]See James D. Krasner and Michel Soignet, "Strategic Vision Drives Domino's Pizza Distribution," *Logistics Management* (spring 1997) and available at www.manufacturing.net/magazine/logistic/archives/1997/scmr/11pizza.htm; quotes from the corporate website: www.dominos.com.

[38]"You've Come a Long Way Baby," *Business Week Frontier* (July 10, 2000).

[39]Information from David J. Dent, "The Next Black Power Movement: The Boom in African-American Entrepreneurship Isn't Just a Business Story. It's Also a Logical Extension of the Civil Rights Struggle. Here's Why," *Fortune Small Business* (May 2, 2003): www.fortune.com/fortune/smallbusiness/articles/0,15114,449148,00.html.

[40]Gifford Pinchot III, *Intrapreneuring, or Why You Don't Have to Leave the Corporation to Become an Entrepreneur* (New York: Harper & Row, 1985).

[41]Information from John A. Byrne, "Management by Web," *Business Week* (August 28, 2000), pp. 84–97.

[42]Story originally reported by Christopher Farrell, "When Bureaucrats Are a Boon," *Business Week*, Enterprise issue (September 1, 1997), pp. ENT4-6; for current progress see company website: www.mambodesign.com/index.html.

Chapter 7 Notes

[1]Information from http://history.sandiego.edu/gen/recording/motown.html, www.history-of-rock.com/motown_records.htm, www.motown.com/classicmotown.

[2]See Alvin Toffler, *Powershift* (New York: Bantam Books, 1990); and www.tofflerassociates.com/index1.htm.

[3]"E-Meetings Redefine Productivity," *Fortune*, Special Advertising Section (February 5, 2001), p. S2.

[4]Peter F. Drucker, "Looking Ahead: Implications of the Present," *Harvard Business Review* (September–October 1997), pp. 18–32. See also Shaker A. Zahra, "An Interview with Peter Drucker," *Academy of Management Executive*, vol. 17 (August 2003), pp. 9–12.

[5]Thomas A. Stewart, *Intellectual Capital: The Wealth of Organizations* (New York: Doubleday, 1997).

[6]Information from Robert W. Bly, "Does Your 'Second Generation' Site Get a Passing Grade?" (September 8, 2000), www.dotcom.com.

[7]See Robert Spector, *Amazon.com: get Big Fast* (New York: Harper Collins, 2002).

[8]See Susan G. Cohen and Don Mankin, "The Changing Nature of Work: Managing the Impact of Information Technology," Chapter 6 in Susan Albers Mohrman, Jay R. Galbraith, Edward E. Lawler III and Associates, *Tomorrow's Organization: Crafting Winning Capabilities in a Dynamic World* (San Francisco: Jossey-Bass, 1988), pp. 154–78.

[9]See "Technology: The Best Way to Go," *Wall Street Journal Reports* (September 15, 2003).

[10]Drucker, op. cit., "Looking Ahead" (1997) p. 22.

[11]Information from John A. Byrne, "Visionary vs. Visonary," *Business Week* (August 28, 2000), pp. 210–14.

[12]Jaclyn Fierman, "Winning Ideas from Maverick Managers," *Fortune* (February 6, 1995), pp. 66–80.

[13]Information from Pui-Wing Tam, ". . . Communication with Employees," *Wall Street Journal* (September 15, 2003), pp. R4, R10.

[14]Ann Zimmerman, "To Sell Goods to Wal-Mart, Get on the Net," *Wall Street Journal* (November 21, 2003), pp. B1, B6.

[15]Henry Mintzberg, *The Nature of Managerial Work* (New York: HarperCollins, 1997).

[16]For scholarly reviews, see Dean Tjosvold, "Effects of Crisis Orientation on Managers' Approach to Controversy in Decision Making," *Academy of Management Journal,* vol. 27 (1984), pp. 130–38; and Ian I. Mitroff, Paul Shrivastava, and Firdaus E. Udwadia, "Effective Crisis Management," *Academy of Management Executive,* vol. 1 (1987), pp. 283–92.

[17]Developed from Anna Muoio, "Where There's Smoke It Helps to Have a Smoke Jumper," *Fast Company,* vol. 33, p. 290.

[18]See David Greisling, *I'd Like to Buy the World a Coke: The Life and Leadership of Roberto Goizueta* (New York: Wiley, 1998).

[19]See Hugh Courtney, Jane Kirkland, and Patrick Viguerie, "Strategy Under Uncertainty," *Harvard Business Review* (November–December 1997), pp. 67–79.

[20]For information see D'Artagnan story at company website: www.d'artagnan.com.

[21]For a good discussion, see Watson H. Agor, *Intuition in Organizations: Leading and Managing Productively* (Newbury Park, CA: Sage, 1989); Herbert A. Simon, "Making Management Decisions: The Role of Intuition and Emotion," *Academy of Management Executive,* vol. 1 (1987), pp. 57–64; Orlando Behling and Norman L. Eckel, "Making Sense Out of Intuition," *Academy of Manage-*

ment Executive, vol. 5 (1991), pp. 46–54.

[22]Daniel J. Isenberg, "How Senior Managers Think," *Harvard Business Review,* vol. 62 (November–December 1984), pp. 81–90.

[23]Daniel J. Isenberg, "The Tactics of Strategic Opportunism," *Harvard Business Review,* vol. 65 (March–April 1987), pp. 92–97.

[24]See George P. Huber, *Managerial Decision Making* (Glenview, IL: Scott, Foresman 1975). For a comparison, see the steps in Xerox's problemsolving process as described in David A. Garvin, "Building a Learning Organization," *Harvard Business Review* (July–August 1993), pp. 78–91; and the Josephson model for ethical decision making described at www.josephsoninstitute.org/MED/MED-4sevensteppath.htm.

[25]Peter F. Drucker, *Innovation and Entrepreneurship: Practice and Principles* (New York: Harper & Row, 1985).

[26]For a sample of Simon's work, see Herbert A. Simon, *Administrative Behavior* (New York: Free Press, 1947); James G. March and Herbert A. Simon, *Organizations* (New York: Wiley, 1958); Herbert A. Simon, *The New Science of Management Decision* (New York: Harper, 1960).

[27]Information from Carol Hymowitz, "Independent Program Puts College Students on Leadership Paths," *Wall Street Journal* (January 14, 2003), p. B1.

[28]This presentation is based on the work of R. H. Hogarth, D. Kahneman, A. Tversky, and others, as discussed in Max H. Bazerman, *Judgment in Managerial Decision Making,* 3rd ed. (New York: Wiley, 1994).

[29]Barry M. Staw, "The Escalation of Commitment to a Course of Action," *Academy of Management Review,* vol. 6 (1981), pp. 577–87; and Barry M. Staw and Jerry Ross, "Knowing When to Pull the Plug," *Harvard Business Review,* vol. 65 (March–April 1987), pp. 68–74.

[30]The classic work is Norman R. Maier, "Assets and Liabilities in Group Problem Solving," *Psychological Review,* vol. 74 (1967), pp. 239–49.

[31]Information from Bart Boehlert, "Kate Spade and Her Hip Handbags," *Urban Desires* 1996, http://desires.com/2.1/Style/Spade/spade.html; "Kate and Andy Spade," *Fortune Small Business* (September 2003), pp. 51–57; and company website: www.katespade.com.

[32]Maier, op. cit.

[33]Josephson, op. cit.

[34]Based on Gerald F. Cavanagh, *American Business Values,* 4th ed. (Upper Saddle River, NJ: Prentice-Hall, 1998).

[35]Peter F. Drucker, "The Future That Has Already Happened," *Harvard Business Review,* vol. 75 (September–October 1997), pp. 20–24; and Peter F. Drucker, Esther Dyson, Charles Handy, Paul Daffo, and Peter M. Senge, "Looking Ahead: Implications of the Present," *Harvard Business Review,* vol. 75 (September–October, 1997).

[36]See, for example, Thomas H. Davenport and Laurence Prusak, *Working Knowledge: How Organizations Manage What They Know* (Cambridge, MA: Harvard Business School Press, 1997).

[37]Information and quote from corporate website:www.wipro.com.

[38]Steven E. Prokesch, "Unleashing the Power of Learning," *Harvard Business Review* (September–October 1997), pp. 147–68.

[39]Peter Senge, *The Fifth Discipline* (New York: Harper, 1990).

[40]Prokesch, op cit.

Chapter 8 Notes

[1]Information from corporate website: www.kinkos.com/about_us.

[2]Gary Hamel, *Leading the Revolution* (Boston: Harvard Business School Press, 2000).

[3]Quote from "Today's Companies Won't Make It, and Gary Hamel Knows Why," *Fortune* (September 4, 2000), p. 386–87.

[4]T. J. Rodgers, with William Taylor and Rick Foreman, "No Excuses Management," *World Executive's Digest* (May 1994) pp. 26–30.

[5]Eaton Corporation Annual Report, 1985.

[6]Henry Mintzberg, "The Manager's Job: Folklore and Fact," *Harvard Business Review,* vol. 53 (July–August 1975), pp. 54–67; and Henry Mintzberg, "Planning on the Left Side and Managing on the Right," *Harvard Business Review,* vol. 54 (July–August 1976), pp. 46–55.

[7]Information from Ameet Sachdev, "Business Schools Study Best Approach to Ethics," *Columbus Dispatch* (April 20, 2003), p. B1.

[8]Quote from Stephen Covey and Roger Merrill, "New Ways to Get Organized at Work," *USA Weeknd* (February 6–8, 1998), p. 18. Books by Stephen R. Covey include: *The 7 Habits of Highly Effective People: Powerful Lessons in Personal Change* (New York: Fireside, 1990), and Stephen R. Covey and Sandra Merril Covey, *The 7 Habits of Highly Effective Families: Building a Beautiful Family Culture in a Turbulent World* (New York: Golden Books, 1996).

[9]For a classic study, see Stanley Thune and Robert House, "Where Long-Range Planning Pays Off," *Business Horizons,* vol. 13 (1970), pp. 81–87. For a critical review of the literature, see Milton Leontiades and Ahmet Teel, "Planning Perceptions and Planning Results," *Strategic Management Journal,* vol. 1 (1980), pp. 65–75; and J. Scott Armstrong, "The Value of Formal Planning for Strategic Decisions," *Strategic Management Journal,* vol. 3 (1982), pp. 197–211. For special attention to the small business setting, see Richard B. Robinson Jr., John A. Pearce II, George S. Vozikis, and Timothy S. Mescon, "The Relationship Between Stage of Development and Small Firm Planning and Performance," *Journal of Small Business Management,* vol. 22 (1984), pp. 45–52; and Christopher Orphen, "The Effects of Long-Range Planning on Small Business Performance: A Further Examination," *Journal of Small Business Management,* vol. 23 (1985), pp. 16–23. For an empirical study of large corporations, see Vasudevan Ramanujam and N. Venkatraman, "Planning and Performance: A New Look at an Old Question," *Business Horizons,* vol. 30 (1987), pp. 19–25.

[10]Quotes from *Business Week* (August 8, 1994), pp. 78–86.

[11]See William Oncken, Jr., and Donald L. Wass, "Management Time: Who's Got the Monkey?" *Harvard Business Review,* vol. 52 (September–October 1974), 75–80, and featured as an HBR classic, *Harvard Business Review* (November–December 1999).

[12]Survey results from "Hurry Up and Decide," *Business Week* (May 14, 2001), p. 16.

[13]See Elliot Jaques, *The Form of Time* (New York: Russak & Co., 1982). For an executive commentary on his research, see Walter Kiechel III, "How Executives Think," *Fortune* (December 21, 1987), pp. 139–44.

[14]See Henry Mintzberg, "Rounding Out the Manager's Job," *Sloan Management Review* (fall 1994), pp. 1–25.

[15]Information from "Avoiding a Time Bomb: Sexual Harassment," *Business Week.* Enterprise issue (October 13, 1997), pp. ENT20–21.

[16]For a thorough review of forecasting, see J. Scott Armstrong, *Long-Range Forecasting,* 2nd ed. (New York: Wiley, 1985).

[17]Information from Associated Press, "Cola Jihad Bubbling in Europe," *Columbus Dispatch* (February 11, 2003), pp. C1, C2.

[18]The scenario-planning approach is described in Peter Schwartz, *The Art of the Long View* (New York: Doubleday/Currency, 1991); and Arie de Geus, *The Living Company: Habits for Survival in a Turbulent Business Environment* (Boston, MA: Harvard Business School Press, 1997).

[19]Ibid.

[20]See, for example, Robert C. Camp, *Business Process Benchmarking* (Milwaukee: ASQ Quality Press 1994); Michael J. Spendolini, *The Benchmarking Book* (New York: AMACOM, 1992); and Christopher E. Bogan and Michael J. English, *Benchmarking for Best Practices: Winning Through Innovative Adaptation* (New York: McGraw-Hill, 1994).

[21]"How Classy Can 7-Eleven Get?" *Business Week* (September 1, 1997), pp. 74–75; and Kellie B. Gormly, "7-Eleven Moving Up a Grade," *Columbus Dispatch* (August 3, 2000), pp. C1–C2.

[22]"The Renewal Factor: Friendly Fact, Congenial Controls," *Business Week* (September 14, 1987), p. 105.

[23]Rob Cross and Lloyd Baird, "Technology Is Not Enough: Improving Performance by Building Institutional Memory," *Sloan Management Review* (spring 2000), p. 73.

[24]Information from Leon E. Wynter, "Allstate Rates Managers on Handling Diversity," *Wall Street Journal* (October 1, 1997), p. B1.

[25]Information from Thomas Petzinger, Jr., "How a Ski Maker on a Slippery Slope Regained Control," *Wall Street Journal* (October 3, 1997), p. 3; see also corporate web site: www.volantsports.com.

[26]Information from Raju Narisetti, "For IBM, a Groundbreaking Sales Chief," *Wall Street Journal* (January 19, 1998), pp. B1, B5.

[27]Based on discussion by Harold Koontz and Cyril O'Donnell, *Essentials of Management* (New York: McGraw-Hill, 1974), pp. 362–65; see also Cross and Baird, op.cit.

[28]Information from Louis Lee, "I'm Proud of What I've Made Myself Into—What I've Created," *Wall Street Journal* (August 27, 1997), pp. B1, B5; and Jim Collins, "Bigger, Better, Faster," *Fast Company,* vol. 71 (June 2003), p. 74; www.fastcompany.com/magazine/71/walmart.html.

[29]See John F. Love, *McDonald's: Behind the Arches* (New York: Bantam Books, 1986); and Ray Kroc and Robert Anderson, *Grinding It Out: The Making of McDonald's* (New York: St. Martin's Press, 1990).

[30]Douglas McGregor, *The Human Side of Enterprise* (New York: McGraw-Hill, 1960).

[31]See Dale D. McConkey, *How to Manage by Results,* 3rd ed. (New York: AMACOM, 1976); Stephen J. Carroll, Jr., and Henry J. Tosi, Jr., *Management by Objectives: Applications and Research* (New York: Macmillan, 1973); and Anthony P. Raia, *Managing by Objectives* (Glenview, IL: Scott, Foresman, 1974).

[32]For a discussion of research, see Carroll and Tosi, op.cit.; Raia, op.cit; and Steven Kerr, "Overcoming the Dysfunctions of MBO," *Management by Objectives,* vol. 5, no. 1 (1976). Information in part from Dylan Loeb McClain, "Job Forecast: Internet's Still Hot," *New York Times* (January 30, 2001), p. 9.

[33]McGregor, op.cit.

[34]The work on goal setting and motivation is summarized in Edwin A. Locke and Gary P. Latham, *Goal Setting: A Motivational Technique That Works!* (Englewood Cliffs, NJ: Prentice-Hall, 1984).

[35]The "hot stove rules" are developed from R. Bruce McAfee and William Poffenberger, *Productivity Strategies: Enhancing Employee Job Performance* (Englewood Cliffs, NJ: Prentice-Hall, 1982), pp. 54–55. They are originally attributed to Douglas McGregor, "Hot Stove Rules of Discipline," in G. Strauss and L. Sayles, eds., *Personnel: The Human Problems of Management,* (Englewood Cliffs, NJ: Prentice-Hall, 1967).

[36]Information from Karen Carney, "Successful Performance Measurement: A Checklist," *Harvard Management Update* (No. U9911B), 1999.

Chapter 9 Notes

[1]Information from "Starbucks: Making Values Pay," *Fortune* (September 29, 1997), pp. 261–72; Howard Schultz and Dori Jones Yang, *Pour Your Heart into It* (San Francisco: Hyperion, 1997); and www.starbucks.com.

[2]Jim Collins, "Bigger, Better, Faster," *Fast Company,* vol. 71 (June 2003), p. 74; and www.fastcompany.com/magazine/71/walmart.html.

[3]Keith H. Hammond, "Michael Porter's Big Ideas," *Fast Company* (March 2001), pp. 150–56.

[4]Gary Hamel and C. K. Prahalad, "Strategic Intent," *Harvard Business Review* (May–June 1989), pp. 63–76.

[5]Information and quotes from Marcia Stepanek, "How Fast Is Net Fast?" *Business Week E-Biz* (November 1, 1999), pp. EB52–EB54.

[6]For research support, see Daniel H. Gray, "Uses and Misuses of Strategic Planning," *Harvard Business Review,* vol. 64 (January–February 1986), pp. 89–97.

[7]Information and quotes from John Shepler, "Richard Branson's Virgin Success," http://www.johnshepler.com/articles/branson.html and corporate website: www.virgin.com.

[8]Hammond, op cit., p. 153.

[9]Michael A. Hitt, R. Duane Ireland, and Robert E. Hoskisson, *Strategic Management: Competitiveness and Globalization* (Minneapolis: West, 1997), p. 5.

[10]See Michael E. Porter, *Competitive Strategy: Techniques for Analyzing Industries and Competitors* (New York: Free Press, 1980), and *Competitive Advantage: Creating and Sustaining Superior Performance* (New York: Free Press, 1986); and Richard A. D'Aveni, *Hyper-Competition: Managing the Dynamics of Strategic Maneuvering* (New York: Free Press, 1994).

[11]D'Aveni, op cit.

[12]Example from "Memorable Memo: McDonald's Sends Operators to War on Fries," *Wall Street Journal* (December 18, 1997), p. B1.

[13]Peter F. Drucker, "Five Questions," *Executive Excellence* (November 6, 1994), pp. 6–7.

[14]Peter F. Drucker, *Management: Tasks, Responsibilities, Practices* (New York: Harper & Row, 1973), p. 122.

[15]Ibid.

[16]See Laura Nash, "Mission Statements—Mirrors and Windows," *Harvard Business Review* (March–April 1988), pp. 155–56; James C. Collins and Jerry I. Porras, "Building Your Company's Vision," *Harvard Business Review* (September–October 1996), pp. 65–77; and James C. Collins and Jerry I. Porras, *Built to Last: Successful Habits of Visionary Companies* (New York: Harper Business, 1997).

[17]Gary Hamel, *Leading the Revolution* (Boston, MA: Harvard Business School Press, 2000), pp. 72–73.

[18]For a discussion of nonprofit organization mission statements, see Peter F. Drucker, "Self-Assessment: The First Action Requirement of Leadership," Drucker Foundation Self-Assessment Tool, www.pfdf.org/leaderbook.

[19]Terrence E. Deal and Allen A. Kennedy, *Corporate Cultures: The Rites and Rituals of Corporate Life* (Reading, MA: Addison-Wesley, 1982), p. 22. For more on organizational culture see Edgar H. Schein, *Organizational Culture and Leadership,* 2nd ed. (San Francisco: Jossey-Bass, 1997).

[20]Peter F. Drucker's views on organizational objectives are expressed in his classic books: *The Practice of Management* (New York: Harper & Row, 1954), and *Management: Tasks, Responsibilities, Practices* (New York: Harper & Row, 1973). For a more recent commentary, see his article, "Management: The Problems of Success," *Academy of Management Executive,* vol. 1 (1987), pp. 13–19.

[21]C. K. Prahalad and Gary Hamel, "The Core Competencies of the Corporation," *Harvard Business Review* (May–June 1990), pp. 79–91; see also Hitt et al., op. cit., pp. 99–103.

[22]For a discussion of Michael Porter's approach to strategic planning, see his books *Competitive Strategy* and *Competitive Advantage:* his article, "What Is Strategy? *Harvard Business Review* (November–December, 1996), pp. 61–78; and Richard M. Hodgetts' interview "A Conversation with Michael E. Porter: A Significant Extension Toward Operational Improvement and Positioning," *Organizational Dynamics* (summer 1999), pp. 24–33.

[23]The four grand strategies were originally described by William F. Glueck, *Business Policy: Strategy Formulation and Management Action,* 2nd ed. (New York: McGraw-Hill, 1976).

[24]Hitt et al., op cit., p. 197.

[25]See William McKinley, Carol M. Sanchez, and A. G. Schick, "Organizational Downsizing: Constraining, Cloning, Learning," *Academy of Management Executive,* vol. 9 (August 1995), pp. 32–44.

[26]Kim S. Cameron, Sara J. Freeman, and A. K. Mishra, "Best Practices in White-Collar Downsizing: Managing Contradictions," *Academy of Management Executive,* vol. 4 (August 1991), pp. 57–73.

[27]This strategy classification is found in Hitt et al., op. cit.; the attitudes are from a discussion by Howard V. Perlmutter, "The Tortuous Evolution of the Multinational Corporation," *Columbia Journal of World Business,* vol. 4 (January–February 1969).

[28]See Michael E. Porter, "Strategy and the Internet," *Harvard Business Review* (March 2001), pp. 63–78.

[29]Information from Michael Rappa, *Business Models on the Web* (www.ecommerce.ncsu.edu/business_models.html. February 6, 2001).

[30]Hammond, op. cit.

[31]D'Aveni, op. cit.

[32]D'Aveni, op. cit.

[33]Porter, op cit. (1980), (1986), (1996).

[34]Information from www.polo.com.

[35]Information from Suzanne Steel, "Quality in Bloom," *Business Today* (August 22, 1994), pp. 1–2.

[36]Richard G. Hammermesh, "Making Planning Strategic," *Harvard Business Review,* vol. 64 (July–August 1986), pp. 115–120; and Richard G. Hammermesh, *Making Strategy Work* (New York: Wiley, 1986).

[37]See Gerald B. Allan, "A Note on the Boston Consulting Group Concept of Competitive Analysis and Corporate Strategy," Harvard Business School, Intercollegiate Case Clearing House, ICCH9-175-175 (Boston: Harvard Business School, June 1976).

[38]The adaptive model is described in Raymond E. Miles and Charles C. Snow's book. *Organizational Strategy, Structure, and Process* (New York: McGraw-Hill, 1978); and their articles, "Designing Strategic Human Resources Systems," *Organizational Dynamics,* vol. 13 (summer 1984), pp. 36–52, and "Fit, Failure, and the Hall of Fame," *California Management Review,* vol. 26 (spring 1984), pp. 10–28.

[39]Information and quotes from www.ebay.com/community/aboutebay/index.html.

[40]James Brian Quinn, "Strategic Change: Logical Incrementalism," *Sloan Management Review,* vol. 20 (fall 1978), pp. 7–21.

[41]Henry Mintzberg, *The Nature of Managerial Work* (New York: Harper & Row, 1973); and John R. P. Kotter, *The General Managers* (New York: Free Press, 1982).

[42]Henry Mintzberg, "Planning on the Left Side and Managing on the Right," *Business Review,* vol. 54 (July–August 1976), pp. 46–55; Henry Mintzberg and James A. Waters, "Of Strategies, Deliberate and Emergent," *Strategic Management Journal,* vol. 6 (1985), pp. 257–72; Henry Mintzberg, "Crafting Strategy," *Harvard Business Review,* vol. 65 (July–August 1987), pp. 66–75.

[43]For research support, see Daniel H. Gray, "Uses and Misuses of Strategic Planning," *Harvard Business Review,* vol. 64 (January–February 1986), pp. 89–97.

[44]For a discussion of corporate governance issues, see Hugh Sherman and Rajeswararao Chaganti, *Corporate Governance and the Timeliness of Change* (Westport, CT: Quorum Books, 1998).

[45]See Carol Hyowitz, "GE Chief Is Charting His Own Strategy, Focusing on Technology," *Wall Street Journal* (September 23, 2003), p. B1.

[46]See R. Duane Ireland and Michael A. Hitt, "Achieving and Maintaining Strategic Competitiveness in the 21st Century," *Academy of Management Executive,* vol. 13 (1999), pp. 43–57.

[47]Hammond, op. cit.

[48]Michael Dell quotes from Matt Murray, "As Huge Companies Keep Growing, CEOs Struggle to Keep Pace," *Wall Street Journal* (February 8, 2001), pp. A1, A6.

[49]Jon R. Katzenbach, "The Myth of the Top Management Team," *Harvard Business Review* (November–December 1997), pp. 82–91.

Chapter 10 Notes

[1]Information from Richard Teitelbaum, "The Wal-Mart of Wall Street," *Fortune* (October 13, 1997), pp. 128–30; and "Edward Jones: The Last Not-Com Brokerage," *Industry Standard* (August 7, 2000); online: www.thestandard.com/article/display/0.1151.17432.000.html.

[2]Henry Mintzberg and Ludo Van der Heyden, "Organigraphs: Drawing How Companies Really Work," *Harvard Business Review* (September–October 1999), pp. 87–94.

[3]See, for example, Charles O'Reilly III and Jeffrey Pfeffer, *Hidden Value: How Great Companies Achieve Extraordinary Results with Ordinary People* (Boston: Harvard Business School Press, 2000); Jeffrey Pfeffer and John F. Veiga, "Putting People First for Organizational Success," *Academy of Management Executive,* vol. 13 (May 1999), pp. 37–48; Jeffrey Pfeffer, *The Human Equation: Building Profits by Putting People First* (Boston: Harvard Business School Press, 1998); Jeffrey Pfeffer, "When It Comes to 'Best Practices'—Why Do Smart Organizations Occasionally Do Dumb Things?" *Organizational Dynamics,* vol. 25 (summer 1996), pp. 33–44; and Michael Beer, "How to Develop an Organization Capable of Sustained High Performance: Embrace the Drive for Results—Capability Development Paradox," *Organizational Dynamics,* vol. 29 (spring 2001), pp. 233–247.

[4]The classic work is Alfred D. Chandler, *Strategy and Structure* (Cambridge, MA: MIT Press, 1962).

[5]See Alfred D. Chandler, Jr., "Origins of the Organization Chart," *Harvard Business Review* (March–April 1988), pp. 156–57.

[6]Information and quotes from Maggie Jackson, "Work's Lessons Occurring in Unexpected Places," *Rockland Journal-News* (January 7, 1998), pp. 4A, 4E.

[7]See David Krackhardt and Jeffrey R. Hanson, "Informal Networks: The Company Behind the Chart," *Harvard Business Review* (July–August 1993), pp. 104–11.

[8]See Kenneth Noble, "A Clash of Styles: Japanese Companies in the U.S." *New York Times* (January 25, 1988), p. 7.

[9]For a discussion of departmentalization, see H. I. Ansoff and R. G. Bradenburg, "A Language for Organization Design," *Management Science,* vol. 17 (August 1971), pp. B705–B731; Mariann Jelinek, "Organization Structure: The Basic Conformations," in Mariann Jelinek, Joseph A. Litterer, and Raymond E. Miles, eds., *Organizations by Design: Theory and Practice* (Plano, TX: Business Publications, 1981), pp. 293–302; Henry Mintzberg, "The Structuring of Organizations," in James Brian Quinn, Henry Mintzberg, and Robert M. James (eds.), *The Strategy Process: Concepts, Contexts, and Cases* (Englewood Cliffs, NJ: Prentice-Hall, 1988), pp. 276–304.

[10]Robert L. Simison, "Jaguar Slowly Sheds Outmoded Habits," *Wall Street Journal* (July 26, 1991), p. A6; and Richard Stevenson, "Ford Helps Jaguar Get Back Old Sheen," *International Herald Tribune* (December 14, 1994), p. 11.

[11]These alternatives are well described by Mintzberg, op cit.

[12]The focus on process is described in Michael Hammer, *Beyond Reengineering* (New York: Harper Business, 1996).

[13]Ibid.

[14]Excellent reviews of matrix concepts are found in Stanley M. Davis and Paul R. Lawrence, *Matrix* (Reading, MA: Addison-Wesley, 1977); Paul R. Lawrence, Harvey F. Kolodny, and Stanley M. Davis, "The Human Side of the Matrix," *Organizational Dynamics,* vol. 6 (1977), pp. 43–61; and Harvey F. Kolodny, "Evolution to a Matrix Organization," *Academy of Management Review,* vol. 4 (1979), pp. 543–53.

[15]Davis and Lawrence, op cit.

[16]Information and quotes from corporate website and www.intel.com/ireland/about/pressroom/2003/january/012203ir.htm.

[17]Developed from Frank Ostroff, *The Horizontal Organization: What the Organization of the Future Looks Like and How It Delivers Value to Customers* (New York: Oxford University Press, 1999).

[18]The nature of teams and teamwork is described in Jon R. Katzenbach and Douglas K. Smith, "The Discipline of Teams," *Harvard Business Review* (March–April 1993), pp. 111–20.

[19]Susan Albers Mohrman, Susan G. Cohen, and Allan M. Mohrman, Jr., *Designing Team-Based Organizations* (San Francisco: Jossey-Bass, 1996).

[20]See Glenn M. Parker, *Cross-Functional Teams* (San Francisco: Jossey-Bass, 1995).

[21]Information from William Bridges, "The End of the Job," *Fortune* (September 19, 1994), pp. 62–74; Alan Deutschman, "The Managing Wisdom of High-Tech Superstars," *Fortune* (October 17, 1994), pp. 197–206.

[22]See the discussion by Jay R. Galbraith, "Designing the Networked Organization: Leveraging Size and Competencies," in Susan Albers Mohrman, Jay R. Galbraith, Edward E. Lawler III and Associates, *Tomorrow's Organizations: Crafting Winning Strategies in a Dynamic World* (San Francisco: Jossey-Bass, 1998), pp. 76–102. See also Rupert F. Chisholm, *Developing Network Organizations: Learning from Practice and Theory* (Reading, MA: Addison-Wesley, 1998).

[23]See Jerome Barthelemy, "The Seven Deadly Sins of Outsourcing," *Academy of Management Executive,* vol. 17 (2003), pp. 87–98.

[24]Information in part from Thomas Petzinger, Jr., "June Holley Brings a Touch of Italy to Appalachian Effort," *Wall Street Journal* (October 24, 1997), p. B1.

[25]See Ron Ashkenas, Dave Ulrich, Todd Jick, and Steve Kerr, *The Boundaryless Organization: Breaking the Chains of Organizational Structure* (San Francisco: Jossey-Bass, 1996.

[26]Robert Slater, *Jack Welch and the GE Way: Management Insights and Leadership Secrets from the Legendary CEO* (New York: 1998); and "Jack the Job-Killer Strikes Again," *Business Week* (February 12, 2001), p. 12.

[27]Information from "Scott Livengood and the Tasty Tale of Krispy Kreme," *BizEd* (May/June 2003), pp. 16–20

[28]Information from John A. Byrne, "Management by Web," *Business Week* (August 28, 2000), pp. 84–97.

[29]See the collection of articles by Cary L. Cooper and Denise M. Rousseau, eds., *The Virtual Organization: Vol. 6, Trends in Organizational Behavior* (New York: Wiley, 2000).

[30]David Van Fleet, "Span of Management Research and Issues," *Academy of Management Journal,* vol. 26 (1983), pp. 546–52.

[31]Developed from Roger Fritz, *Rate Your Executive Potential* (New York: Wiley, 1988), pp. 185–86; Roy J. Lewicki, Donald D. Bowen, Douglas T. Hall, and Francine S. Hall, *Experiences in Management and Organizational Behavior,* 3rd ed. (New York: Wiley, 1988), p. 144.

[32]See George P. Huber, "A Theory of Effects of Advanced Information Technologies on Organizational Design, Intelligence, and Decision Making," *Academy of Management Review,* vol. 15 (1990), pp. 67–71.

Chapter 11 Notes

[1]Information from www.kpmg.com.

[2]Described by Andrew Ross Sorkin, "Gospel According to St. Luke's," *New York Times* (February 12, 1998), pp. C1, C7; see also corporate website: www.stlukes.co.uk.

[3]Information and quotes from corporate website and Judith Rehak, "A Swiss Giant Awakens with a Start," *International Herald Tribune* (May 3–4, 2003), pp. 13, 14. http://pages.ebay.com/community/aboutebay/index.html.

[4]For a discussion of organization theory see W. Richard Scott. *Organizations: Rational, Natural, and Open Systems,* 4th ed. (Upper Saddle River, NJ: Prentice-Hall, 1998).

[5]For a classic work see Jay R. Galbraith, *Organizational Design* (Reading, MA: Addison Wesley, 1977).

[6]This framework is based on Harold J. Leavitt, "Applied Organizational Change in Industry," in James G. March, *Handbook of Organizations* (New York: Rand McNally, 1965), pp. 1144–70; and Edward E. Lawler III, *From the Ground Up: Six Principles for the New Logic Corporation* (San Francisco: Jossey-Bass Publishers, 1996), pp. 44–50.

[7]See the discussion in Gaerth Jones, *Organizaional Theory and Design,* 3rd ed. (Upper Saddle River, NJ: Prentice-Hall, 2001).

[8]See the discussion in James L. Gibson, John M. Ivancevich, and James H. Donnelly, Jr., *Organizations: Behavior, Structure, Processes,* 5th ed. (Homewood, IL: Richard D. Irwin, 1991).

[9]Information from "BET.com Ranked #1 in Unique Visitors Among African American Sites," *PR Newswire* (June 6, 2000); www.Bet,com.

[10]Max Weber, *The Theory of Social and Economic Organization,* A. M. Henderson, trans., and H. T. Parsons (New York: Free Press, 1947).

[11]For classic treatments of bureaucracy, see Alvin Gouldner, *Patterns of Industrial Bureaucracy* (New York: Free Press, 1954); and Robert K. Merton, *Social Theory and Social Structure* (New York: Free Press, 1957).

[12]Tom Burns and George M. Stalker, *The Management of Innovation* (London: Tavistock, 1961; republished by Oxford University Press, London, 1994).

[13]See Henry Mintzberg, *Structure in Fives: Designing Effective Organizations* (Englewood Cliffs, NJ: Prentice-Hall, 1983).

[14]Information from Thomas Petzinger, Jr., "Self-Organization Will Free Employees to Act Like Bosses," *Wall Street Journal* (January 3, 1997), p. B1.

[15]See Rosabeth Moss Kanter, *The Changing Masters* (New York: Simon & Schuster, 1983). Quotation from Rosabeth Moss Kanter and John D. Buck, "Reorganizing Part of Honeywell: From Strategy to Structure," *Organizational Dynamics,* vol. 13 (winter 1985), p. 6.

[16]See for example, Jay R. Galbraith, Edward E. Lawler III, and Associates, *Organizing for the Future* (San Francisco: Jossey-Bass Publishers, 1993); and Susan Albers Mohrman, Jay R. Galbraith, Edward E. Lawler III, and Associates, *Tomorrow's Organizations: Crafting Winning Strategies in a Dynamic World* (San Francisco: Jossey-Bass, 1998).

[17]Peter Senge, *The Fifth Discipline: The Art and Practice of the Learning Organization* (New York: Doubleday, 1994).

[18]Information from organizational website: www.mayoclinic.org.

[19]A classic treatment of environment and organizational design is found in James D. Thompson, *Organizations in Action* (New York: McGraw-Hill, 1967). See also Scott, op.cit., pp. 264–69.

[20]Alfred D. Chandler, Jr., *Strategy and Structure: Chapter in the History of American Industrial Enterprise* (Cambridge, MA: MIT Press, 1962).

[21]See, for example, Danny Miller, "Configurations of Strategy and Structure: Towards a Synthesis," *Strategic Management Journal,* vol. 7 (1986), pp. 233–49.

[22]Joan Woodward, *Industrial Organization: Theory and Practice* (London: Oxford University Press, 1965; republished by Oxford University Press, 1994).

[23]This classification is from Thompson, op. cit.

[24]Information from Timothy Aeppel, "At a Job Shop, It's the Year of Living Cautiously," *Wall Street Journal* (February 8, 2001), pp. B1, B4.

[25]See Peter M. Blau and Richard A. Schoennerr, *The Structure of Organizations* (New York: Basic Books, 1971); and Scott, op.cit., pp. 259–63.

[26]D. E. Gumpert, "The Joys of Keeping the Company Small," *Harvard Business Review* (July–August 1986); pp. 6–8, 12–14.

[27]John R. Kimberly and Robert H. Miles, *The Organizational Life Cycle* (San Francisco: Jossey-Bass, 1980).

[28]Kim Cameron, Sarah J. Freeman, and Naneil K. Mishra, "Best Practices in White-Collar Downsizing: Managing Contradictions," *Academy of Management Executive,* vol. 5 (August 1991), pp. 57–73.

[29]See Gifford Pinchot III, *Intrapreneuring: Or Why You Don't Have to Leave the Corporation to Become an Entrepreneur* (New York: Harper & Row, 1985).

[30]Information from Simon London, "Enterprise Drives Home the Service Ethic," *Financial Times* (June 2, 2003), p. 7.

[31]See Jay Lorsch and John Morse, *Organizations and Their Members: A Contingency Approach* (New York: Harper & Row, 1974); and, Scott, op.cit., pp. 263–64.

[32]"The Rebirth of IBM," *The Economist* (June 6, 1998), pp. 65–68.

[33]Paul R. Lawrence and Jay W. Lorsch, *Organizations and Environment* (Boston: Division of Research, Graduate School of Business Administration, Harvard University, 1967).

[34]Burns and Stalker, op cit.

[35]See Jay R. Galbraith, op.cit., and Susan Albers Mohrman, "Integrating Roles and Structure in the Lateral Organization," chapter 5 in Jay R. Galbraith, Edward E. Lawler III, and Associates, *Organizing for the Future* (San Francisco: Jossey-Bass Publishers, 1993).

[36]For a good discussion of coordination and integration approaches, see Scott, op.cit., pp. 231–39.

[37]Michael Hammer and James Champy, *Reengineering the Corporation: A Manifesto for Business Revolution,* rev. ed. (New York: Harper Business, 1999).

[38]Michael Hammer, *Beyond Reengineering* (New York: Harper Business, 1997).

[39]Ibid., p. 5; see also the discussion of processes in Gary Hamel, *Leading the Revolution* (Boston, MA: Harvard Business School Press, 2000).

[40]Thomas M. Koulopoulos, *The Workflow Imperative* (New York: Van Nostrand Reinhold, 1995); Hammer, *Beyond Reengineering,* op cit. (1997).

[41]Paul Roberts, "Humane Technology—PeopleSoft," *Fast Company,* vol. 14 (1998), p. 122.

[42]Ronni T. Marshak, "Workflow Business Process Reengineering," special advertising section, *Fortune* (1997).

[43]A similar example is found in Hammer, op cit.(1997), pp. 9, 10.

[44]Ibid., pp. 28–30.

[45]Ibid., p. 29.

[46]Ibid., p. 27.

[47]Quote from Hammer and Company website: www.hammerandco.com/WhatIsAProcessOrgFrames.html.

Chapter 12 Notes

[1]Information and quotes from corporate website: www.workingwoman.com.

[2]Robert Reich, *The Future of Success* (New York: Knopf, 2000).

[3]Robert B. Reich, "The Company of the Future," *Fast Company* (November 1998), pp. 124ff;

[4]See Jeffrey Pfeffer, *The Human Equation: Building Profits by Putting People First* (Boston: Harvard University Press, 1998).

[5]See, for example, Charles Handy, *The Age of Unreason* (Cambridge, MA: Harvard Business School Press, 1990); and Tom Peters, "The Brand Called *You,*" *Fast Company* (August 1997), pp. 83ff.

[6]Pfeffer, op cit., p. 292.

[7]Jeffrey Pfeffer and John F. Veiga, "Putting People First for Organizational Success," *Academy of Management Executive,* vol. 13 (May 1999), pp. 37–48.

[8]Ibid; and Pfeffer, op.cit.

[9]James N. Baron and David M. Kreps, *Strategic Human Resources: Frameworks for General Managers* (New York: Wiley, 1999).

[10]R. Roosevelt Thomas, Jr., *Beyond Race and Gender* (New York: AMACOM, 1992).

[11]Lawrence Otis Graham, *Proversity: Getting Past Face Value and Finding the Soul of People* (New York: Wiley, 1997).

[12]See also R. Roosevelt Thomas, Jr.'s books, op. cit. and (with Marjorie I. Woodruff) *Building a House for Diversity* (New York: AMACOM, 1999); and Richard D. Bucher, *Diversity Consciousness* (Englewood Cliffs, NJ: Prentice-Hall, 2000).

[13]Thomas, op. cit., p. 4.

[14]Quote from William Bridges, "The End of the Job," *Fortune* (September 19, 1994), p. 68.

[15]See Baron and Kreps, op. cit.

[16]Quotes from Kris Maher, "Human-Resources Directors Are Assuming Strategic Roles," *Wall Street Journal* (June 17, 2003), p. B8.

[17]Ibid.

[18]Information from "SHRM Code of Ethical and Professional Standards in Human Resource Management," retrieved from www.shrm.org/ethics/code-of-ethics.asp.

[19]For a discussion of affirmative action see R. Roosevelt Thomas, Jr. "From 'Affirmative Action' to 'Affirming Diversity,'" *Harvard Business Review* (November–December 1990), pp. 107–17; and Thomas, op. cit. (1998).

[20]See the discussion by David A. DeCenzo and Stephen P. Robbins, *Human*

Resource Management, 6th ed. (New York: Wiley, 1999), pp. 66–68 and 81–83.

[21]Ibid., pp. 77–79.

[22]Information from "There Are Questions You Shouldn't Answer," *New York Times* (January 30, 2001), p. 2.

[23]See discussion by DeCenzo and Robbins, op cit., pp. 79–90.

[24]See Frederick S. Lane, *The Naked Employee: How Technology is Compromising Workplace Privacy* (New York: Amacon, 2003).

[25]Quote from George Myers, "Bookshelf," *Columbus Dispatch* (June 9, 2003), p. E6.

[26]Information from Thomas A. Stewart, "In Search of Elusive Tech Workers," *Fortune* (February 16, 1998), pp. 171–72.

[27]See Ernest McCormick, "Job and Task Analysis," in Marvin Dunnette (ed.), *Handbook of Industrial and Organizational Psychology* (Chicago: Rand McNally, 1976), pp. 651–96.

[28]Information from Gautam Naik, "India's Technology Whizzes Find Passage to Nokia," *Wall Street Journal* (August 1, 2000), p. B1.

[29]See David Greising, *I'd Like to Buy the World a Coke: The Life and Leadership of Roberto Goizueta* (New York: Wiley, 1998).

[30]See John P. Wanous, *Organizational Entry: Recruitment, Selection, and Socialization of Newcomers* (Reading, MA: Addison-Wesley, 1980), pp. 34–44.

[31]Information from Justin Martin, "Mercedes: Made in Alabama," *Fortune* (July 7, 1997), pp. 150–58.

[32]Information from Kemba J. Dunham, "The Jungle: Focus on Recruitment, Pay and Getting Ahead," *Wall Street Journal* (September 23, 2003), p. B8.

[33]Information from Matt Richtel, "Online Revolution's Latest Twist: Computers Screening Job Applicants," *New York Times* (February 6, 2000), p. 10. See also Stacy Forster, ". . . Recruit New Workers," *Wall Street Journal* (September 15, 2003), p. R8.

[34]Reported in "Would You Hire This Person Again?" *Business Week,* Enterprise issue (June 9, 1997), pp. ENT32.

[35]For a scholarly review, see John Van Maanen and Edgar H. Schein, "Toward a Theory of Socialization," in Barry M. Staw (ed.), *Research in Organizational Behavior,* vol. 1 (Greenwich, CT: JAI Press, 1979), pp. 209–64; for a practitioner's view, see Richard Pascale, "Fitting New Employees into the Company Culture," *Fortune* (May 28, 1984), pp. 28–42.

[36]Quote from Ronald Henkoff, "Finding, Training, and Keeping the Best Service Workers," *Fortune* (October 3, 1994), pp. 110–22.

[37]This involves the social information processing concept as discussed in Gerald R. Salancik and Jeffrey Pfeffer, "A Social Information Processing Approach to Job Attitudes and Task Design," *Administrative Science Quarterly,* vol. 23 (June 1978); pp. 224–53.

[38]Quote from Peter Petre, "Games That Teach You to Manage," *Fortune* (October 29, 1984), pp. 65–72; see also, the "Looking Glass" description on the Center for Creative Leadership website: www.ccl.org.

[39]Information from David Coburn, "Balancing Home, Work Still Big Concern," *Columbus Dispatch* (February 16, 1998), pp. 8, 9; quotes from corporate website: www.autodesk.com.

[40]See Larry L. Cummings and Donald P. Schwab, *Performance in Organizations: Determinants and Appraisal* (Glenview, IL: Scott, Foresman, 1973).

[41]Dick Grote, "Performance Appraisal Reappraised," *Harvard Business Review Best Practice* (1999), Reprint F00105.

[42]Ibid.

[43]See Mark R. Edwards and Ann J. Ewen, *360-Degree Feedback: The Powerful New Tool for Employee Feedback and Performance Improvement* (New York: AMACOM, 1996).

[44]Information from "What Are the Most Effective Retention Tools?" *Fortune* (October 9, 2000), p. S7.

[45]Charles Handy, *The Age of Unreason* (Cambridge, MA: Harvard Business School Press, 1990), p. 55.

[46]See Thomas P. Ference, James A. F. Stoner, and E. Kirby Warren, "Managing the Career Plateau," *Academy of Management Review,* vol. 2 (October 1977), pp. 602–12.

[47]Information and quote from Carol Hymowitz, "Baby Boomers Seek New Ways to Escape Career Claustrophobia," *Wall Street Journal* (June 24, 2003), p. B1.

[48]Timothy Butler and James Waldroop, "Job Sculpting: The Art of Retaining Your Best People," *Harvard Business Review* (September–October 1999), pp. 144–52.

[49]See Betty Friedan, *Beyond Gender: The New Politics of Work and the Family* (Washington, DC: Woodrow Wilson Center Press, 1997); and James A. Levine, *Working Fathers: New Strategies for Balancing Work and Family* (Reading, MA: Addison-Wesley, 1997).

[50]Information and quotes from corporate website: www.sas.com.

[51]Information from Dennis Berman, "What's a Worker Worth?" *Business Week Frontier* (October 11, 1999), p. F4; additional information from corporate website: www.saratoga-institute.com.

[52]For reviews see Richard B. Freeman and James L. Medoff, *What Do Unions Do?* (New York: Basic Books, 1984); Charles C. Heckscher, *The New Unionism* (New York: Basic Books, 1988); and Barry T. Hirsch, *Labor Unions and the Economic Performance of Firms* (Kalamazoo, MI: W.E. Upjohn Institute for Employment Research, 1991).

[53]Yochi J. Dreazen, "Percentage of U.S. Workers in a Union Sank, to Record Low of 13.5% Last Year," *Wall Street Journal* (January 19, 2001), p. A2.

Chapter 13 Notes

[1]Information and quotes from Sharon Shinn, "Luv, Colleen," *BizEd* (March–April 2003), pp. 18–23; corporate website: www.southwestairlines.com.

[2]Quotations from Marshall Loeb, "Where Leaders Come From," *Fortune* (September 19, 1994), pp. 241–42; Genevieve Capowski, "Anatomy of a Leader: Where Are the Leaders of Tomorrow?" *Management Review* (March 1994), pp. 10–17. For additional thoughts, see Warren Bennis, *Why Leaders Can't Lead* (San Francisco: Jossey-Bass, 1996).

[3]Max DePree, "An Old Pro's Wisdom: It Begins with a Belief in People," *New York Times* (September 10, 1989), p. F2; Max DePree, *Leadership Is an Art* (New York: Doubleday, 1989); David Woodruff, "Herman Miller: How Green Is My Factory," *Business Week* (September 16, 1991), pp. 54–56; and Max DePree, *Leadership Jazz* (New York: Doubleday, 1992).

[4]Tom Peters, "Rule #3: Leadership Is Confusing as Hell," *Fast Company* (March 2001), pp. 124–40.

[4]Abraham Zaleznick, "Leaders and Managers: Are They Different?" *Harvard Business Review* (May–June 1977), pp. 67–78.

[5]See Jean Lipman-Blumen, *Connective Leadership: Managing in a Changing World* (New York: Oxford University Press, 1996), pp. 3–11.

[6]James M. Kouzes and Barry Z. Posner, "The Leadership Challenge," *Success* (April 1988), p. 68. See also their books *The Leadership Challenge: How to Get Extraordinary Things Done in Organizations* (San Francisco: Jossey-Bass, 1987), and *Credibility: How Leaders Gain and Lose It; Why People Demand It* (San Francisco: Jossey-Bass, 1996); *En-*

couraging the Heart: A Leader's Guide to Rewarding and Recognizing Others (San Francisco: Jossey-Bass, 1999).

[7]Burt Nanus, Visionary Leadership: Creating a Compelling Sense of Vision for Your Organization (San Francisco: Jossey-Bass, 1992).

[8]Quotation from General Electric Company Annual Report 1997, p. 5. For more on Jack Welch's leadership approach at GE see Jack Welch & the GE Way (New York: McGraw-Hill, 1998).

[9]See Kouzes and Posner, op cit. and James C. Collins and Jerry I. Porras, "Building Your Company's Vision," Harvard Business Review, (September–October 1996), pp. 65–77.

[10]Rosabeth Moss Kanter, "Power Failure in Management Circuits," Harvard Business Review (July–August 1979), pp. 65–75.

[11]For a good managerial discussion of power, see David C. McClelland and David H. Burnham, "Power Is the Great Motivator," Harvard Business Review, (March-April 1976), pp. 100–10.

[12]The classic treatment of these power bases is John R. P. French Jr. and Bertram Raven, "The Bases of Social Power," in Darwin Cartwright, ed., Group Dynamics: Research and Theory (Evanstion, IL: Row, Peterson, 1962), pp. 607–13. For managerial applications of this basic framework, see Gary Yukl and Tom Taber, "The Effective Use of Managerial Power, "Personnel, vol. 60 (1983), pp. 37–49; and Robert C. Benfari, Harry E. Wilkinson, and Charles D. Orth, "The Effective Use of Power," Business Horizons, vol. 29 (1986), pp. 12–16. Gary A. Yukl, Leadership in Organizations, 4th ed. (Englewood Cliffs, NJ: Prentice-Hall, 1998), includes "information" as a separate, but related, power source.

[13]Lorraine Monroe, "Leadership Is About Making Vision Happen—What I Call 'Vision Acts,'" Fast Company (March 2001), p. 98; School Leadership Academy website: www.lorrainemonroe.com.

[14]Based on David A. Whetten and Kim S. Cameron, Developing Management Skills, 2nd ed. (New York: Harper-Collins, 1991), pp. 281–97.

[15]Ibid., p. 282.

[16]Ibid.

[17]Chester A. Barnard, Functions of the Executive (Cambridge, MA: Harvard University Press, 1938).

[18]DePree, op cit.

[19]Monroe, op cit.

[20]Jay A. Conger, "Leadership: The Art of Empowering Others," Academy of Management Executive, vol. 3 (1989), pp. 17–24.

[21]The early work on leader traits is well represented in Ralph M. Stogdill, "Personal Factors Associated with Leadership: A Survey of the Literature," Journal of Psychology, vol. 25 (1948), pp. 35–71. See also Edwin E. Ghiselli, Explorations in Management Talent (Santa Monica, CA: Goodyear, 1971); and Shirley A. Kirkpatrick and Edwin A. Locke, "Leadership: Do Traits Really Matter?" Academy of Management Executive (1991), pp. 48–60.

[22]See also John W. Gardner's article, "The Context and Attributes of Leadership," New Management, vol. 5 (1988), pp. 18–22; John P. Kotter, The Leadership Factor (New York: Free Press, 1988); and Bernard M. Bass, Stogdill's Handbook of Leadership (New York: Free Press, 1990).

[23]Kirkpatrick and Locke, op cit. (1991).

[24]See, for example, Jan P. Muczyk and Bernie C. Reimann, "The Case for Directive Leadership," Academy of Management Review, vol. 12 (1987), pp. 637–47.

[25]See Bass, op cit.

[26]Robert R. Blake and Jane Srygley Mouton, The New Managerial Grid III (Houston: Gulf Publishing, 1985).

[27]This terminology comes from the classic studies by Kurt Lewin and his associates at the University of Iowa. See, for example, K. Lewin and R. Lippitt, "An Experimental Approach to the Study of Autocracy and Democracy: A Preliminary Note," Sociometry, vol. 1 (1938), pp. 292–300; K. Lewin, "Field Theory and Experiment in Social Psychology: Concepts and Methods," American Journal of Sociology, vol. 44 (1939), pp. 86–896; and K. Lewin, R. Lippitt, and R. K. White, "Patterns of Aggressive Behavior in Experimentally Created Social Climates," Journal of Social Psychology, vol. 10 (1939), pp. 271–301.

[28]For a good discussion of this theory, see Fred E. Fiedler, Martin M. Chemers, and Linda Mahar, The Leadership Match Concept (New York: Wiley, 1978); Fiedler's current contingency research with the cognitive resource theory is summarized in Fred E. Fiedler and Joseph E. Garcia, New Approaches to Effective Leadership (New York: Wiley, 1987).

[29]Paul Hersey and Kenneth H. Blanchard, Management and Organizational Behavior (Englewood Cliffs, NJ: Prentice-Hall, 1988). For an interview with Paul Hersey on the origins of the model, see John R. Schermerhorn Jr., "Situational Leadership: Conversations with Paul Heresy," Mid-American Journal of Business (fall 1997), pp. 5–12.

[30]See Claude L. Graeff, "The Situational Leadership Theory: A Critical View," Academy of Management Review, vol. 8 (1983), pp. 285–91.

[31]See, for example, Robert J. House, "A Path-Goal Theory of Leader Effectiveness," Administrative Sciences Quarterly, vol. 16 (1971), pp. 321–38; Robert J. House and Terrence R. Mitchell, "Path-Goal Theory of Leadership," Journal of Contemporary Business (Autumn 1974), pp. 81–97; the path-goal theory is reviewed by Bass, op cit., and Yukl, op cit. A supportive review of research is offered in Julie Indvik, "Path-Goal Theory of Leadership; A Meta-Analysis," in John A. Pearce II and Richard B. Robinson Jr. eds., Academy of Management Best Paper Proceedings (1986), pp. 189–92.

[32]See the discussions of path-goal theory in Yukl, op cit.; and Bernard M. Bass, "Leadership: Good, Better, Best," Organizational Dynamics (winter 1985), pp. 26–40.

[33]See Steven Kerr and John Jermier, Substitutes for Leadership: Their Meaning and Measurement Organizational Behavior and Human Performance, vol. 22 (1978), pp. 375–403; Jon P. Howell and Peter W. Dorfman, "Leadership and Substitutes for Leadership among Professional and Nonprofessional Workers," Journal of Applied Behavioral Science," vol. 22 (1986), pp. 29–46.

[34]Victor H. Vroom and Arthur G. Jago, The New Leadership: Managing Participation in Organizations (Englewood Cliffs, NJ: Prentice-Hall, 1988). This is based on earlier work by Victor H. Vroom, "A New Look in Managerial Decision-Making," Organizational Dynamics (spring 1973), pp. 66–80; and Victor H. Vroom and Phillip Yetton, Leadership and Decision-Making (Pitts-burgh: University of Pittsburgh Press, 1973).

[35]For a related discussion see Edgar H. Schein, Process Consultation Revisited: Building the Helping Relationship (Reading, MA: Addison-Wesley, 1999).

[36]Vroom and Jago, op. cit.

[37]For a review see Yukl, op cit.

[38]See the discussion by Victor H. Vroom, "Leadership and the Decision Making Process," Organizational Dynamics, vol. 28 (2000), pp. 82–94.

[39]Among the popular books addressing this point of view are Warren Bennis and Burt Nanus, Leaders: The Strategies for Taking Charge (New York: Harper Business 1997); Max DePree, Leadership Is an Art, op. cit.; Kotter, The Leadership Factor, op. cit.; Kouzes and Posner, The Leadership Challenge, op cit.

[40]See, for example, Jay A. Conger, "Inspiring Others: The Language of Leadership," *Academy of Management Executive,* vol. 5 (1991), pp. 31–45.

[41]The distinction was originally made by James McGregor Burns, *Leadership* (New York: Harper & Row, 1978) and was further developed by Bernard Bass, *Leadership and Performance Beyond Expectations* (New York: Free Press, 1985) and Bernard M. Bass, "Leadership: Good, Better, Best," *Organizationational Dynamics* (winter 1985), pp. 26–40.

[42]Information from "We Weren't Just Airborne Yesterday," http://www.tfly.swa.com/about_swa/airborne.html; quote from http://www.kelleher.html (11/24/2000).

[43]This list is based on Kouzes and Posner, op cit.; Gardner, op cit.

[44]Daniel Goleman, "Leadership That Gets Results," *Harvard Business Review* (March–April 2000), pp. 78–90. See also his books *Emotional Intelligence* (New York: Bantam Books, 1995) and *Working with Emotional Intelligence* (New York: Bantam Books, 1998).

[45]Daniel Goleman, "What Makes a Leader?" *Harvard Business Review* (November–December 1998), pp. 93–102.

[46]Goleman, op cit. (1998).

[47]Information from "Women and Men, Work and Power," *Fast Company,* Issue 13 (1998), p. 71.

[48]A. H. Eagley, S. J. Daran, and M. G. Makhijani, "Gender and the Effectiveness of Leaders: A Meta-Analysis," *Psychological Bulletin,* vol. 117 (1995), pp. 125–45.

[49]Research on gender issues in leadership is reported in Sally Helgesen, *The Female Advantage: Women's Ways of Leadership* (New York: Doubleday, 1990); Judith B. Rosener, "Ways Women Lead," *Harvard Business Review* (November–December 1990), pp. 119–25; and Alice H. Eagly, Steven J. Karau, and Blair T. Johnson, "Gender and Leadership Style Among School Principals: A Meta Analysis," *Administrative Science Quarterly,* vol. 27 (1992), pp. 76–102; Jean Lipman-Blumen, *Connective Leadership: Managing in a Changing World* (New York: Oxford University Press, 1996); and Alice H. Eagley, Mary C. Johannesen-Smith, and Marloes L. van Engen, "Transformational, Transactional and Laissez-Faire Leadership: A Meta-Analysis of Women and Men, *Psychological Bulletin,* Vol. 124 (4), 2003: pp. 569–591.

[50]Vroom, op cit. (2000).

[51]Data reported by Rochelle Sharpe, "As Women Rule," *Business Week* (November 20, 2000), p. 75.

[52]Rosener, op cit. (1990).

[53]For debate on whether some transformational leadership qualities tend to be associated more with female than male leaders, see "Debate: Ways Women and Men Lead," *Harvard Business Review* (January–February 1991), pp. 150–60.

[54]Quote from "As Leaders, Women Rule," *Business Week* (November 20, 2000), pp. 75–84. Rosabeth Moss Kanter is the author of *Men and Women of the Corporation,* 2nd ed. (New York: Basic Books, 1993).

[55]Joseph Weber, "Meet DuPont's In-House Conscience," *Business Week* (June 24, 1991), pp. 62–65; and Marilyn Gardner, "A Voice for Children and Families Will Soon Fall Silent," *Christian Science Monitor* (April 23, 2003): retrieved from: www.csmonitor.com.

[56]Peter F. Drucker, "Leadership: More Doing than Dash," *Wall Street Journal* (January 6, 1988), p. 16. For a compendium of writings on leadership sponsored by the Drucker Foundation, see Frances Hesselbein, Marshall Goldsmith, and Richard Beckhard, *Leader of the Future* (San Francisco: Jossey-Bass, 1997).

[57]James MacGregor Burns, *Transforming Leadership: A New Pursuit of Happiness* (New York: Atlantic Monthly Press, 2003); information from Christopher Caldwell, book review, *International Herald Tribune* (April 29, 2003), p. 18.

[58]Based on the discussion by John W. Dienhart and Terry Thomas, "Ethical Leadership: A Primer on Ethical Responsibility" in John R. Schermerhorn, Jr., *Management,* 7th ed. (New York: Wiley, 2003).

[59]Gardner, op cit.

[60]Fred Luthans and Bruce Avolio, "Authentic Leadership: A Positive Development Approach", in K. S. Cameron, J. E. Dutton, and R. E. Quinn (eds.), *Positive Organizational Scholarship* (San Francisco, Berrett-Koehler, 2003) pp. 241–258.

[61]Doug May, Adrian Chan, Timothy Hodges and Bruce Avolio point out ("Developing the Moral Component of Authentic Leadership", *Organizational Dynamics,* 2003, vol. 32, pp. 247–60).

[62]De Pree, op cit. (1989), School Leadership Academy web site, http://www.lorrainemonroe.com/.

Chapter 14 Notes

[1]Information and quotes from Julie Flaherty, "A Parting Gift from the Boss Who Cared," *New York Times* (September 28, 2000), pp. C1, C25; Business Wire Press Release, "Employees of the Butcher Company Share over $18 Million as Owner Shares Benefits of Success" (September 21, 2000).

[2]Quotes from Charles O'Reilly III and Jeffrey Pfeffer, *Hidden Value: How Great Companies Achieve Extraordinary Results Through Ordinary People* (Boston, MA: Harvard Business School Press, 2000), pp. 5–6.

[3]Example taken from Kevin Kelley, "I'm the Boss, That's Why," *Business Week,* Enterprise issue (June 9, 1997), p. ENT 32.

[4]For a comprehensive treatment of extrinsic rewards, see Bob Nelson, *1001 Ways to Reward Employees* (New York: Workman Publishing, 1994).

[5]For a research perspective, see Edward Deci, *Intrinsic Motivation* (New York: Plenum, 1975); Edward E. Lawler III, "The Design of Effective Reward Systems," in Jay W. Lorsch (ed.), *Handbook of Organizational Behavior* (Englewood Cliffs, NJ: Prentice-Hall, 1987), pp. 255–71.

[6]Michael Maccoby's book, *Why Work: Leading the New Generation* (New York: Simon & Schuster, 1988), deals extensively with this point of view.

[7]Example from Frank Hinchey, "Tops in Copper," *Columbus Dispatch* (August 27, 2000), pp. G1, G2.

[8]Information from Ellen Graham, "Work May Be a Rat Race, But It's Not a Daily Grind," *Wall Street Journal,* (September 19, 1997), pp. R1, R4. The story of Starbucks is told in Howard Schulz and Dori Jones Yang, *Pour Your Heart Into It: How Starbucks Built a Company One Cup at a Time* (New York: Hyperion, 1999).

[9]"Ryan Newman Biography," http://www.penskeracing.com/newman.

[10]See Abraham H. Maslow, *Eupsychian Management* (Homewood, IL: Richard D. Irwin, 1965); Abraham H. Maslow, *Motivation and Personality,* 2d ed. (New York: Harper & Rw, 1970). For a research perspective, see Mahmoud A. Wahba and Lawrence G. Bridwell, "Maslow Reconsidered: A Review of Research on the Need Hierarchy," *Organizational Behavior and Human Performance,* vol. 16 (1976), pp. 212–40.

[11]See Clayton P. Alderfer, *Existence, Relatedness, and Growth* (New York: Free Press, 1972).

[12]The complete two-factor theory is in Frederick Herzberg, Bernard Mausner, and Barbara Block Synderman, *The Motivation to Work,* 2d ed. (New York: Wiley, 1967); Frederick Herzberg, "One More Time: How Do You Motivate Employees?" *Harvard Business Review* (January–February 1968), pp. 53–62,

and reprinted as an *HBR classic* (September–October 1987), pp. 109–20.

[13]Critical reviews are provided by Robert J. House and Lawrence A. Wigdor, "Herzberg's Dual-Factor Theory of Job Satisfaction and Motivation: A Review of the Evidence and a Criticism," *Personnel Psychology,* vol. 20 (winter 1967), pp. 369–89; Steven Kerr, Anne Harlan, and Ralph Stogdill, "Preference for Motivator and Hygiene Factors in a Hypothetical Interview Situation," *Personnel Psychology,* vol. 27 (winter 1974), pp. 109–24.

[14]Frederick Herzberg, "Workers' Needs: The Same around the World," *Industry Week* (September 21, 1987), pp. 29–32.

[15]For a collection of McClelland's work, see David C. McClelland, *The Achieving Society* (New York: Van Nostrand, 1961); "Business Drive and National Achievement," *Harvard Business Review,* vol. 40 (July–August 1962), pp. 99–112; David C. McClelland and David H. Burnham, "Power is the Great Motivator," *Harvard Business Review* (March–April 1976), pp. 100–10; David C. McClelland, *Human Motivation* (Glenview, IL: Scott, Foresman, 1985); David C. McClelland and Richard E. Boyatsis, "The Leadership Motive Pattern and Long-Term Success in Management," *Journal of Applied Psychology,* vol. 67 (1982), pp. 737–43.

[16]Developed originally from a discussion in Edward E. Lawler III, *Motivation in Work Organizations* (Monterey, CA: Brooks/Cole Publishing, 1973), pp. 30–36.

[17]Information from Eleena De Lisser, Start-Up Attracts Staff with a Ban on Midnight Oil," *Wall Street Journal* (August 23, 2000), pp. B1, B6; and corporate website: www.ipswitch.com.

[18]See, for example, J. Stacy Adams, "Toward an Understanding of Inequity," *Journal of Abnormal and Social Psychology,* vol. 67 (1963), pp. 422–36; J. Stacy Adams, "Inequity in Social Exchange," in vol. 2, L. Berkowitz, (ed.), *Advances in Experimental Social Psychology,* (New York: Academic Press, 1965), pp. 267–300.

[19]See, for example, J. W. Harder, "Play for Pay: Effects of Inequity in a Pay-for-Performance Context," *Administrative Science Quarterly,* vol. 37 (1992), pp. 321–35.

[20]Victor H. Vroom, "Work and Motivation (New York: Wiley, 1964; republished by Jossey-Bass, 1994).

[21]The work on goal-setting theory is well summarized in Edwin A. Locke and Gary P. Latham, *Goal Setting: A Motivational Technique That Works!* (Englewood Cliffs, NJ: Prentice Hall, 1984). See also Edwin A. Locke, Kenneth N. Shaw, Lisa A. Saari, and Gary P. Latham, "Goal Setting and Task Performance 1969–1980," *Psychological Bulletin,* vol. 90 (1981), pp. 125–52; Mark E. Tubbs, "Goal Setting: A Meta-Analytic Examination of the Empirical Evidence," *Journal of Applied Psychology,* vol. 71 (1986), pp. 474–83; and Terence R. Mitchell, Kenneth R. Thompson, and Jane George-Falvy, "Goal Setting: Theory and Practice," Chapter 9 in Cary L. Cooper and Edwin A. Locke (eds.), *Industrial and Organizational Psychology: Linking Theory with Practice* (Malden, MA: Blackwell Business, 2000), pp. 211–249.

[22]Gary P. Latham and Edwin A. Locke, "Self-Regulation Through Goal Setting," *Organizational Behavior and Human Decision Processes,* vol. 50 (1991), pp. 212–47.

[23]E. L. Thorndike, *Animal Intelligence* (New York: Macmillan, 1911), p. 244.

[24]See B. F. Skinner, *Walden Two* (New York: Macmillan, 1948); *Science and Human Behavior* (New York: Macmillan, 1953); *Contingencies of Reinforcement* (New York: Appleton-Century-Crofts, 1969).

[25]OB mod is clearly explained in Fred Luthans and Robert Kreitner, *Organizational Behavior Modification* (Glenview, IL: Scott, Foresman, 1975) and Fred Luthans and Robert Kreitner, *Organizational Behavior Modification and Beyond* (Glenview, IL: Scott, Foresman, 1985); see also Fred Luthans and Alexander D. Stajkovic, "Reinforce for Performance: The Need to Go Beyond Pay and Even Rewards," *Academy of Management Executive,* vol. 13 (1999), pp. 49–57.

[26]For the Mary Kay story and philosophy see Mary Kay Ash, *Many Kay on People Management* (New York: Warner Books, 1985); see also information at the corporate website: http://www.marykay.com.

[27]For a good review, see Lee W. Frederickson (ed.), *Handbook of Organizational Behavior Management* (New York: Wiley-Inerscience, 1982); Luthans and Kreitner, op cit. (1985); and Andrew D. Stajkovic and Fred Luthans, "A Meta-Analysis of the Effects of Organizational Behavior Modification on Task Performance 1975–95," *Academy of Management Journal,* vol. 40 (1997), pp. 1122–49.

[28]Edwin A. Locke, "The Myths of Behavior Mod in Organizations," *Academy of Management Review,* vol. 2 (October 1977), pp. 543–53.

[29]For a discussion of compensation and performance, see Rosabeth Moss Kanter, "The Attack on Pay," *Harvard Business Review,* vol. 65 (March–April 1987), pp. 60–67; Edward E. Lawler III, *Strategic Pay* (San Francisco: Jossey-Bass, 1990).

[30]Information from "Charles Schwab," Fortune Small Business (September, 2003), pp. 104–115.

[31]Karthryn M. Bartol and Cathy C. Durham, "Incentives: Theory and Practice," Chapter 1 in Cooper and Locke, op cit. (2000).

[32]As CEO Pay Rockets Higher, Shareholders Urge Companies to Share the Rewards More Widely," report by *Responsible Wealth* (April 5, 2000); www.responsiblewealth.org/press/CEO_shareholder.html.

[33]Information from Jaclyn Fierman, "The Perilous New World of Fair Pay," *Fortune* (June 13, 1994), pp. 57–61.

[34]Tove Helland Hammer, "New Developments in Profit Sharing, Gain Sharing, and Employee Ownership," chapter 12 in John P. Campbell and Richard J. Campbell (eds.), *Productivity in Organizations: New Perspective form Industrial and Organizational Psychology* (San Francisco: Jossey-Bass, 1988).

[35]Edward E. Lawler III, *From the Ground Up: Six Principles for Building the New Logic Corporation* (San Francisco: Jossey-Bass, 1996), pp. 217–18. See also Lawler's *Rewarding Excellence* (San Francisco: Jossey-Bass, 2000).

[36]Jaclyn Fierman, "The Perilous New World of Fair Pay," *Fortune* (June 13, 1994), pp. 57–61.

[37]Amanda Bennett, "Paying Workers to Meet Goals Spreads, but Gauging Performance Proves Tough," *Wall Street Journal* (September 10, 1991), p. B1; "Pay to Live On, Stock to Grow On," *Fortune* (January 8, 2001), p. 151.

[38]See Carl F. Frost, John H. Wakeley, and Robert A. Ruh, *The Scanlon Plan for Organizational Development* (Lansing, MI: Michigan State University Press, 1996).

[39]See *Restoring Competitive Luster to American Industry: An Agenda for Success* (Cleveland, OH: Lincoln Electric Company), Barnaby J. Feder, "Carrots, Sticks, and Growing Pains," *International Herald Tribune* (September 8, 1994), pp. 9, 10; corporate website: www.lincolnelectric.com.

[40]Information from www.intel.com and Stock Ownership for Everyone," Hewitt Associates November 27, 2000): www.hewitt.com/hewitt/business/talent/subtalent/con_bckg_global.htm.

[41]Information from Susan Pulliam, "New Dot-Com Mantra: 'Just Pay Me in Cash, Please,'" *Wall Street Journal* (November 28, 2000), p. C1.

Chapter 15 Notes

[1]Information from Neil Gross, "Mining a Company's Mother Lode of Talent," *Business Week* (August 8, 2000), pp. 135–37; corporate website: www.monitor.com.

[2]Jeffrey Pfeffer and John F. Veiga, "Putting People First for Organizational Success," *Academy of Management Executive,* vol. 13 (1999), pp. 37–48; see also Jeffrey Pfeffer, *The Human Equation: Building Profits by Putting People First* (Boston: Harvard University Press, 1998).

[3]Charles O'Reilly III and Jeffrey Pfeffer *Hidden Value: How Great Companies Achieve Extraordinary Results Through Ordinary People* (Boston: MA: Harvard Business School Publishing, 2000), quotes from p. 2.

[4]This example is reported in *Esquire* (December 1986), p. 243. Emphasis is added to the quotation. *Note:* Nussbaum became director of the Labor Department's Women's Bureau during the Clinton administration and subsequently moved to the AFL CIO as head of the Women's Bureau.

[5]See John R. Schermerhorn, Jr., James G. Hunt, and Richard N. Osborn, *Organizational Behavior,* 8th ed. (New York: Wiley 2003).

[6]Steve Crabtree, "Stryker's Investment in Talent Pays Off," *Gallup Management Journal* (June 12, 2003). Retrieved from http://gmj.gallup.com/ip/article.asp?i = 346.

[7]John P. Kotter, "The Psychological Contract: Managing the Joining Up Process," *California Management Review,* vol. 15 (spring 1973), 91–99; Denise Rousseau (ed.), *Psychological Contracts in Organizations* (San Francisco: Jossey-Bass, 1995); Denise Rousseau, "Changing the Deal While Keeping the People," *Academy of Management Executive,* vol. 10 (1996), pp. 50–59; and Denise Rousseau and Rene Schalk (eds.), *Psychological Contracts in Employment: Cross-Cultural Perspectives* (San Francisco: Jossey-Bass, 2000).

[8]Linda Grant, "Unhappy in Japan," *Fortune* (January 13, 1997), p. 142.

[9]For a thought provoking discussion of this issue, see Ben Hamper, *Rivethead: Tales from the Assembly Line* (New York: Warner, 1991).

[10]Studs Terkel, *Working* (New York: Avon Books, 1975).

[11]See M. R. Barrick and M. K. Mount, "The Big Five Perosnality Dimensions and Job Performance: A Meta-Analysis," *Personnel Psychology,* vol. 44 (1991), pp. 1–26.

[12]This discussion based in part on Schermerhorn. et. al, op cit., pp. 54–60.

[13]J. B. Rotter, "Generalized Expectancies for Internal Versus External Control of Reinforcement," *Psychological Monographs,* vol. 80 (1966), pp. 1–28.

[14]T. W. Adorno, E. Frenkel-Brunswick, D. J. Levinson, and R. N. Sanford, *The Authoritarian Personality* (New York: Harper & Row, 1950).

[15]Niccolo Machiavelli, *The Prince,* trans. George Bull (Middlesex, UK: Penguin, 1961).

[16]Richard Christie and Florence L. Geis, *Studies in Machiavellianism* (New York: Academic Press, 1970).

[17]I. Briggs-Myers, *Introduction to Type* (Palo Alto, CA: Consulting Psychologists Press, 1980). For management applications and research, see William L. Gardner and Mark J. Martinko, "Using the Myers-Briggs Type Indicator to Study Managers: A Literature Review and Research Agenda," *Journal of Management,* vol. 22 (1996), pp. 45–83.

[18]Developed from Donald Bowen, "Learning and Problem-Solving: You're Never Too Jung," in Donald D. Bowen, Roy J. Lewicki, Donald T. Hall, and Francine S. Hall, *Experiences in Management and Organizational Behavior,* 4th ed. (New York: Wiley 1997), pp. 7–13.

[19]See M. Snyder, *Public Appearances/Private Realities: The Psychology of Self-Monitoring* (New York: Freeman, 1987).

[20]Information and quote from Joann S. Lublin, "How One Black Woman Lands Her Top Jobs: Risks and Networking," *Wall Street Journal* (March 4, 2003), p. B1.

[21]Martin Fishbein and Icek Ajzen, *Belief, Attitude, Intention and Behavior: An Introduction to Theory and Research* (Reading, MA: Addison-Wesley, 1973).

[22]See Leon Festinger, *A Theory of Cognitive Dissonance* (Palo Alto, CA: Stanford University Press, 1957).

[23]Information from "Panera CEO's Recipe: Learn from the Past, Anticipate Trends," *Wall Street Journal* (June 10, 2003), p. B1.

[24]For an overview Charles N. Greene, "The Satisfaction-Performance Controversy," *Business Horizons,* vol. 15 (1982), pp. 31+; Michelle T. Iaffaldano and Paul M. Muchinsky, "Job Satisfaction and Job Performance: A Meta Analysis," *Psychological Bulletin,* vol. 97 (1985), pp. 251–273; Paul E. Spector, *Job Satisfaction* (Thousand Oaks, CA: Sage, 1997); and Timothy A. Judge and Allan H. Church, "Job Satisfaction: Research and Practice," Chapter 7 in Cary L. Cooper and Edwin A. Locke (eds.), *Industrial and Organizational Psychology: Linking Theory with Practice* (Malden, MA: Blackwell Business, 2000).

[25]Linda Grant, "Happy Workers, High Returns," *Fortune* (January 12, 1998), p. 81.

[26]Data reported in "When Loyalty Erodes, So Do Profits," *Business Week* (August 13, 2001), p. 8.

[27]Information from Sue Shellenbarger, "Employers Are Finding It Doesn't Cost Much to Make a Staff Happy," *Wall Street Journal* (November 19, 1997), p. B1. See also, "Job Satisfaction on the Decline," The Conference Board (July, 2002).

[28]Information from James Barron, "Mystery at Steinway," *International Herald Tribune* (May 12, 2003), p. 2; see also www.steinway.com.

[29]The Individual Performance Equation and its management and research implications are discussed in William L. Gardner and John R. Schermerhorn, Jr., "Strategic Operational Leadership and the Management of Supportive Work Environments," in Robert L. Phillips and James G. Hunt, eds., *Leadership: A Multi-Organizational-Level Perspective* (Beverly Hills, CA: Sage, 1992); Thomas N. Martin, John R. Schermerhorn, Jr., and Lars L. Larson, "Motivational Consequences of a Supportive Work Environment," in M. L. Maehr and C. Ames, eds., *Advances in Motivation and Achievement: Motivation Enhancing Environments,* Vol. 6 (Greenwich, CT: JAI Press, 1989); John R. Schermerhorn, Jr., "Team Development of High Performance Management," *Training & Development Journal,* vol. 40 (1986), pp. 38–41; and John R. Schermerhorn, Jr., William L. Gardner, and Thomas N. Martin, "Management Dialogues: Turning on the Marginal Performer, *Organizational Dynamics* (Summer 1990), pp. 47–59.

[30]See Melvin Blumberg and Charles D. Pringle, "The Missing Opportunity in Organizational Research: Some Implications for a Theory of Work Motivation," *Academy of Management Review,* vol. 7 (1982), pp. 560–69.

[31]Information from David Whitford, "A Human Place to Work," *Fortune* (January 8, 2001), pp. 108–20.

[32]See Frederick Herzberg, Bernard Mausner, and Barbara Block Synderman, *The Motivation to Work,* 2d ed. (New York: Wiley, 1967). The quotation is from Frederick Herzberg, "One More Time: Employees?" *Harvard Business Review* (January–February 1968), pp. 53–62, and reprinted as an HBR Classic in (September–October 1987), pp. 109–20.

[33]For a complete description of the core characteristics model, see J. Richard

Hackman and Greg R. Oldham, *Work Redesign* (Reading, MA: Addison-Wesley, 1980).

[34]See Richard E. Walton, *Up and Running: Integrating Information Technology and the Organization* (Boston, MA: Harvard Business School Press, 1989); Richard Walton, "From Control to Commitment in the Workplace," *Harvard Business Review* (March–April 1985), pp. 77–94; and William A. Pasmore, *Designing Effective Organizations: A Sociotechnical Systems Perspective* (New York: Wiley, 1988).

[35]See Karl Sabbagh, *21st Century Jet: The Making and Marketing of the Boeing 777* (New York: Scribner, 1996).

[36]Paul J. Champagne and Curt Tausky, "When Job Enrichment Doesn't Pay," *Personnel,* vol. 3 (January–February 1978), pp. 30–40.

[37]Quote from William W. Winipsigner, "Job Enrichment: A Union View," in Karl O. Magnusen (ed.), *Organizational Design, Development, and Behavior: A Situational View,* (Glenview, IL: Scott, Foresman, 1977), p. 22.

[38]Barney Olmsted and Suzanne Smith, *Creating a Flexible Workplace: How to Select and Manage Alternative Work Options* (New York: American Management Association, 1989).

[39]Information from www.craftscenter. org/about/board.

[40]See Allen R. Cohen and Herman Gadon, *Alternative Work Schedules: Integrating Individual and Organizational Needs* (Reading, MA: Addison-Wesley, 1978), p. 125; Simcha Ronen and Sophia B. Primps, "The Compressed Work Week as Organizational Change: Behavioral and Attitudinal Outcomes," *Academy of Management Review,* vol. 6 (1981), pp. 61–74.

[41]Information from Lesli Hicks, "Workers, Employers Praise Their Four-Day Workweek," *Columbus Dispatch* (August 22, 1994), p. 6; and Walsh, op cit. (2001).

[42]Business for Social Responsibility Resource Center: www.bsr.org/resourcecenter (January 24, 2001); Anusha Shrivastava, "Flextime is now key Benefit for Mom-Friendly Employers," *The Columbus Dispatch* (September 23, 2003), p. C2; Sue Shellenbarger, "Number of Women Managers Rises," *The Wall Street Journal* (September 30, 2003), p. D2.

[43]"Networked Workers," *Business Week* (October 6, 1997), p. 8; and Diane E. Lewis, "Flexible Work Arrangements as Important as Salary to Some," *Columbus Dispatch* (May 25, 1998), p. 8.

[44]For a review see Wayne F. Cascio, "Managing a Virtual Workplace," *Academy of Management Executive,* vol. 14 (2000), pp. 81–90.

[45]Quote from Phil Porter, "Telecommuting Mom Is Part of a National Trend," *Columbus Dispatch* (November 29, 2000), pp. H1, H2.

[46]These guidelines are collected from a variety of sources, including: The Southern California Telecommuting Partnership: www.socalcommute.org/telecom. htm; ISDN Group; www.isdnzone.com/ telcom/tips.

[47]See "Report on the American Workforce 1999" (Washington: U.S. Bureau of Labor Statistics); "1999 AMA Survey of Contingent Workers" (New York: American Management Association, 1999).

[48]Data and example from Sue Shellenbarger, "Employees Are Seeking Fewer Hours; Maybe Bosses Should Listen," *Wall Street Journal,* (February 21, 2001), p. B1.

Chapter 16 Notes

[1]Information from Brent Schlender, "Pixar's Fun House," *Fortune* (July 23, 2001); corporate website: http:// www.pixar.com.

[2]Grove quote from John A. Bryne, "Visionary vs. Visionary," *Business Week* (August 28, 2000), pp. 210–14; Chambers quote from Charles O'Reilly III and Jeffrey Pfeffer, *Hidden Value: How Great Companies Achieve Extraordinary Results Through Ordinary People* (Boston, MA: Harvard Business School Publishing, 2000), p. 4.

[3]See Edward E. Lawler III, *From the Ground Up: Six Principles for Building the New Logic Corporation* (San Francisco: Jossey-Bass, 1996), pp. 131+.

[4]Cited in Lynda C. McDermott, Nolan Brawley, and William A. Waite, *World-Class Teams: Working Across Borders* (New York: Wiley, 1998), p. 5.

[5]See, for example, Edward E. Lawler III, Susan Albers Mohrman, and Gerald E. Ledford Jr., *Employee Involvement and Total Quality Management: Practices and Results in Fortune 1000 Companies* (San Francisco: Jossey-Bass, 1992); Susan A. Mohrman, Susan A. Cohen and Monty A. Mohrman, *Designing Team-based Organizations: New Forms for Knowledge Work* (San Francisco: Jossey-Bass, 1995).

[6]Jon R. Katzenbach and Douglas K. Smith, *The Wisdom of Teams: Creating the High Performance Organization* (Boston: Harvard Business School Press, 1993).

[7]A classic work is Bib Latane, Kipling Williams, and Stephen Harkins, "Many Hands Make Light the Work: The Causes and Consequences of Social Loafing, *Journal of Personality and Social Psychology,* vol. 37 (1978), pp. 822–32.

[8]See Marvin E. Shaw, *Group Dynamics: The Psychology of Small Group Behavior,* 2d ed. (New York: McGraw-Hill, 1976); Harold J. Leavitt, "Suppose We Took Groups More Seriously," in Eugene L. Cass and Frederick G. Zimmer (eds.), *Man and Work in Society* (New York: Van Nostrand Reinhold, 1975), pp. 67–77.

[9]John M. George, "Extrinsic and Intrinsic Origins of Perceived Social Loafing in Organizations," *Academy of Management Journal* (March, 1992), pp. 191–202; and W. Jack Duncan, "Why Some People Loaf in Groups While Others Loaf Alone," *Academy of Management Executive,* vol. 8 (1994), pp. 79–80.

[10]For insights on how to conduct effective meetings see Mary A. De Vries, *How to Run a Meeting* (New York: Penguin, 1994).

[11]Survey reported in "Meetings Among Top Ten Time Wasters," *San Francisco Business Times* (April 7, 2003): www. bizjournals.com/sanfrancisco/stories/ 2003/04/07/daily21.html.

[12]Quotes from Eric Matson, "The Seven Sins of Deadly Meetings," *Fast Company* (April/May, 1996), p. 122.

[13]Developed from ibid.

[14]See Leavitt, op cit.

[15]The "linking pin" concept is introduced in Rensis Likert, *New Patterns of Management* (New York: McGraw-Hill, 1962).

[16]See discussion by Susan G. Cohen and Don Mankin, "The Changing Nature of Work," in Susan Albers Mohrman, Jay R. Galbraith, Edward E. Lawler III, and Associates, *Tomorrow's Organization: Crafting, Winning Capabilities in a Dynamic World* (San Francisco: Jossey-Bass, 1998), pp. 154–78.

[17]Information from "Diversity: America's Strength," special advertising section, *Fortune* (June 23, 1997); American Express corporate communication (1998).

[18]See Susan D. Van Raalte, "Preparing the Task Force to Get Good Results," *S.A.M. Advanced Management Journal,* vol. 47 (winter, 1982), pp. 11–16; Walter Kiechel III, "The Art of the Corporate Task Force," *Fortune* (January 28, 1991), pp. 104–6.

[19]Developed from ibid.

[20]Mohrman et al., op cit.

[21]Information from Jenny C. McCune, "Making Lemonade," *Management Review* (June, 1997), pp. 49–53.

22For a good discussion of quality circles, see Edward E. Lawler III and Susan A. Mohrman, "Quality Circles After the Fad," *Harvard Business Review* vol. 63 (January–February, 1985), pp. 65–71; Edward E. Lawler III and Susan Albers Mohrman, "Employee Involvement, Reengineering, and TQM: Focusing on Capability Development," in Mohrman. et al. (1998), pp. 179–208.

23See Wayne F. Cascio, "Managing a Virtual Workplace," *Academy of Management Executive,* vol. 14 (2000), pp. 81–90.

24Information from "Ford Team Find Ways to Recycle Car Parts," *Columbus Dispatch* (December 20, 1997), p. G1; and corporate web site:

25See Sheila Simsarian Webber, "Virtual Teams: A Meta-Analysis,": http://www.shrm.org/foundation/findings.asp.

26R. Brent Gallupe and William H. Cooper, "Brainstorming Electronically," *Sloan Management Review* (winter, 1997), pp. 11–21; Cascio, op cit.

27William M. Bulkeley, "Computerizing Dull Meetings Is Touted as an Antidote to the Mouth That Bored," *Wall Street Journal* (January 28, 1992), pp. B1, B2.

28Cascio, op cit.

29See, for example, Paul S. Goodman, Rukmini Devadas, and Terri L. Griffith Hughson, "Groups and Productivity: Analyzing the Effectiveness of Self-Managing Teams," Chapter 11 in John R. Campbell and Richard J. Campbell, *Productivity in Organizations* (San Francisco: Jossey-Bass, 1988); Jack Orsbrun, Linda Moran, Ed Musslewhite, and John H. Zenger, with Craig Perrin, *Self-Directed Work Teams: The New American Challenge* (Homewood, IL: Business One Irwin, 1990); Dale E. Yeatts and Cloyd Hyten, *High Performing Self-Managed Work Teams* (Thousand Oaks, CA: Sage, 1997).

30Bradley L. Kirkman and Debra L. Shapiro, "The Impact of Cultural Values on Employee Resistance to Teams: Toward of Model of Globalized Self-Managing Work Team Effectiveness," *Academy of Management Review,* vol. 22 (1997), pp. 730–57.

31For a discussion of effectiveness in the context of top management teams, see Edward E. Lawler III, David Finegold, and Jay A. Conger, "Corporate Boards: Developing Effectiveness at the Top," in Mohrman, op cit. (1998), pp. 23–50.

32For a review of research on group effectiveness, see J. Richard Hackman, "The Design of Work Teams," in Jay W. Lorsch (ed.), *Handbook of Organizational Behavior* (Englewood Cliffs, NJ: Prentice-Hall, 1987), pp. 315–42; and J. Richard Hackman, Ruth Wageman, Thomas M. Ruddy, and Charles L. Ray, "Team Effectiveness in Theory and Practice," Chapter 5 in Cary L. Cooper and Edwin A. Locke, *Industrial and Organizational Psychology: Linking Theory with Practice* (Malden, MA: Blackwell, 2000).

33Ibid; Lawler et al., op cit., 1998.

34Example from "Designed for Interaction," *Fortune* (January 8, 2001), p. 150.

35See Warren Watson, "Cultural Diversity's Impact on Interaction Process and Performance," *Academy of Management Journal,* vol. 16 (1993); and Christopher Earley and Elaine Mosakowski, "Creating Hybrid Team Structures: An Empirical Test of Transnational Team Functioning," *Academy of Management Journal,* vol. 5 (February, 2000), pp. 26–49.

36J. Steven Heinen and Eugene Jacobson, "A Model of Task Group Development in Complex Organizations and a Strategy of Implementation," *Academy of Management Review,* vol. 1 (1976), pp. 98–111; Bruce W. Tuckman, "Developmental Sequence in Small Groups," Psychological Bulletin, vol. 63 (1965), pp. 384–99; Bruce W. Tuckman and Mary Ann C. Jensen, "Stages of Small-Group Development Revisited," *Group & Organization Studies,* vol. 2 (1977), pp. 419–27.

37See for example, Edgar Schein, *Process Consultation* (Reading, MA: Addison-Wesley, 1988); and Linda C. McDermott, Nolan Brawley, and William A. Waite, *World-Class Teams: Working Across Borders* (New York: Wiley, 1998).

38Information from James Hannah, "Exec Touts Rigorous Retreats," *Columbus Dispatch* (October 8, 2000), p. G2.

39For a good discussion, see Robert F. Allen and Saul Pilnick, "Confronting the Shadow Organization: How to Detect and Defeat Negative Norms," *Organizational Dynamics* (Spring 1973), pp. 13–16.

40See Schein, op cit., pp. 76–79.

41Marvin E. Shaw, *Group Dynamics: The Psychology of Small Group Behavior* (New York: McGraw-Hill, 1976).

42A classic work in this area is K. Benne and P. Sheets, *Journal of Social Issues,* vol. 2 (1948), pp. 42–47; see also, Likert, op cit., pp. 166–69; Schein, op cit. pp. 49–56.

43Based on John R. Schermerhorn Jr., James G. Hunt, and Richard N. Osborn, *Organizational Behavior,* 7th ed. (New York: Wiley, 2000), pp. 345–46.

44Research on communication networks is found in Alex Bavelas, "Communication Patterns in Task-Oriented Groups," *Journal of the Acoustical Society of America,* vol. 22 (1950), pp. 725–30; Shaw, op cit.

45Schein, op cit., pp. 69–75.

46See Kathleen M. Eisenhardt, Jean L. Kahwajy, and L. J. Bourgeois III, "How Management Teams Can Have a Good Fight," *Harvard Business Review* (July–August 1997), pp. 77–85.

47Victor H. Vroom and Arthur G. Jago, *The New Leadership: Managing Participation in Organizations* (Englewood Cliffs, NJ: Prentice Hall, 1988); Victor H. Vroom, "A New Look in Managerial Decision-Making," *Organizational Dynamics* (spring 1973), pp. 66–80; Victor H. Vroom and Phillip Yetton, *Leadership and Decision-Making* (Pittsburgh: University of Pittsburgh Press, 1973).

48Norman F. Maier, "Assets and Liabilities in Group Problem Solving," *Psychological Review,* vol. 74 (1967), pp. 239–49.

49Ibid.

50Information from "Importing Enthusiasm," *Business Week* (November 7, 1994); and corporate web site: www.Motorola.com/General/inside.html.

51See Irving L. Janis, "Groupthink," *Psychology Today* (November 1971), pp. 43–46; *Victims of Groupthink,* 2d ed. (Boston: Houghton Mifflin, 1982).

52These techniques are well described in Andre L. Delbecq. Andrew H. Van de Ven, and David H. Gustafson, Group Techniques for Program Planning (Glenview, IL: Scott, Foresman, 1975).

53A very good overview is provided by William D. Dyer, *Team-Building* (Reading MA: Addison-Wesley, 1977).

54Dennis Berman, "Zap! Pow! Splat!" *Business Week,* Enterprise issue (February 9, 1998), p. ENT22.

55Katzenbach and Smith, op cit; see also Jon R. Katzenbach, "The Myth of the Top Management Team," *Harvard Business Review,* vol. 75 (November–December 1997), pp. 83–91.

56Information from www.callawaygolf.com.

57Carl E. Larson and Frank M. J. LaFasto, *Team Work: What Must Go Right/What Can Go Wrong* (Newbury Park, CA: Sage, 1990).

58Quote from "Teach Your Leaders that Their Main Priority Is to Energize and Grow Their Team Around Themselves," *Fast Company* (March, 2001), p. 95.

Chapter 17 Notes

1Quotes from *Business Week* (July 8, 1991), pp. 60–61; for additional information see center's website: www.ccl.org.

[2]Henry Mintzberg, *The Nature of Managerial Work* (New York: Harper & Row, 1973).

[3]John P. Kotter, "What Effective General Managers Really Do," *Harvard Business Review,* vol. 60 (November–December 1982), pp. 156–57; and *The General Managers* (New York: Macmillan, 1986).

[4]"Relationships Are the Most Powerful Form of Media," *Fast Company* (March 2001), p. 100.

[5]See Mintzberg, op cit., Kotter, op. cit.

[6]Jay A. Conger, *Winning 'Em Over: A New Model for Managing in the Age of Persuasion* (New York: Simon & Schuster, 1998), pp. 24–79.

[7]This discussion developed from ibid.

[8]Survey information from "What Do Recruiters Want?" *BizEd* (November–December 2002), p. 9; "Much to Learn, Professors Say," *USA Today* (July 5, 2001), p. 8D; and AMA Fast-Response Survey, "The Passionate Organization" (September 26–29, 2000).

[9]*Business Week* (February 10, 1992), pp. 102–8.

[10]See Robert H. Lengel and Richard L. Daft, "The Selection of Communication Media as an Executive Skill," *Academy of Management Executive,* vol. 2 (August 1988), pp. 225–32.

[11]Quotations from John Huey, "America's Most Successful Merchant," *Fortune* (September 23, 1991), pp. 46–59; see also Sam Walton and John Huey, *Sam Walton: Made in America: My Story* (New York: Bantam Books, 1993).

[12]See also Eric Matson, "Now That We Have Your Complete Attention," *Fast Company* (February–March 1997), pp. 124–32.

[13]David McNeill, *Hand and Mind: What Gestures Reveal about Thought* (Chicago: University of Chicago Press, 1992).

[14]Adapted from Richard V. Farace, Peter R. Monge, and Hamish M. Russell, *Communicating and Organizing* (Reading, MA: Addison-Wesley, 1977), pp. 97–98.

[15]Tom Peters and Nancy Austin, *A Passion for Excellence* (New York: Random House, 1985).

[16]This discussion is based on Carl R. Rogers and Richard E. Farson, "Active Listening" (Chicago: Industrial Relations Center of the University of Chicago, n.d.).

[17]A useful source of guidelines is John J. Gabarro and Linda A. Hill, "Managing Performance," Note 9-96-022 (Boston, MA: Harvard Business School Publishing, n.d.).

[18]Information from Carol Hymowitz, "Managers See Feedback from Their Staffers as Most Valuable," *Wall Street Journal,* (August 22, 2000), p. B1.

[19]Developed from John Anderson, "Giving and Receiving Feedback," in Paul R. Lawrence, Louis B. Barnes, and Jay W. Lorsch (eds.), *Organizational Behavior and Administration,* 3d ed. (Homewood, IL: Richard D. Irwin, 1976), p. 109.

[20]See Lengel and Daft, op cit. (1988).

[21]Information from Esther Wachs Book, "Leadership for the Millennium," *Working Woman* (March 1998), pp. 29–34.

[22]Information from Hilary Stout, "Self-Evaluation Brings Change to a Family's Ad Agency," *Wall Street Journal* (January 6, 1998), p. B2.

[23]See Richard Lepsinger and Antoinette D. Lucia, *The Art and Science of 360° Feedback* (San Francisco: Jossey-Bass, 1997).

[24]Brian O'Reilly, "360° Feedback Can Change Your Life," *Fortune* (October 17, 1994), pp. 93–100.

[25]Information from American Management Association, "The Passionate Organization Fast-Response Survey," September 25–29, 2000, and organization website: http://www.amanet.org/aboutama/index.htm.

[26]A classic work on proxemics is Edward T. Hall's book, *The Hidden Dimension* (Garden City, NY: Doubleday, 1986).

[27]Mirand Wewll, "Alternative Spaces Spawning Desk-Free Zones," *Columbus Dispatch* (May 18, 1998), pp. 10–11.

[28]Information from Susan Stellin, "Intranets Nurture Companies from the Inside," *New York Times* (January 21, 2001), p. C4.

[29]Example from Heidi A. Schuessler, "Social Studies Class finds How Far E-Mail Travels," *New York Times* (February 22, 2001), p. D8.

[30]Alison Overholt, "Intel's got (Too Much) Mail; *Fortune* (March, 2001), pp. 56–58.

[31]Developed from *Working Woman* (November 1995), p. 14; and Elizabeth Weinstein, "Help! I'm Drowing in E-Mail!" *Wall Street Journal* (January 10, 2002), pp. B1, B4.

[32]See Edward T. Hall, *The Silent Language* (New York: Doubleday, 1973).

[33]See H. R. Schiffman, *Sensation and Perception: An Integrated Approach,* 3d ed. (New York: Wiley, 1990).

[34]A good review is E. L. Jones (ed.), *Attribution: Perceiving the Causes of Behavior* (Morristown, NJ: General Learning Press, 1972). See also John H. Harvey and Gifford Weary, "Current Issues in Attribution Theory and Research," *Annual Review of Psychology,* vol. 35 (1984), pp. 427–59.

[35]See, for example, Stephan Thernstrom and Abigail Thernstrom, *American in Black and White* (New York: Simon & Schuster, 1997); and David A. Thomas and Suzy Wetlaufer, "A Question of Color: A Debate on Race in the U.S. Workplace," *Harvard Business Review* (September–October 1997), pp. 118–32.

[36]Information from "Misconceptions About Women in the Global Arena Keep Their Numbers Low," Catalyst study: www.catalystwomen.org/home.html.

[37]These examples are from Natasha Josefowitz, *Paths to Power* (Reading, MA: Addison-Wesley, 1980), p. 60. For more on gender issues see Gary N. Powell (ed.), *Handbook of Gender and Work* (Thousand Oaks, CA: Sage, 1999).

[38]Survey reported in Kelly Greene, "Age Is Still More Than a Number," *Wall Street Journal* (April 10, 2003), p. D2.

[39]The classic work is Dewitt C. Dearborn and Herbert A. Simon, "Selective Perception: A Note on the Departmental Identification of Executives," *Sociometry,* vol. 21 (1958), pp. 140–44. See also, J. P. Walsh, "Selectivity and Selective Perception: Belief Structures and Information Processing, *Academy of Management Journal,* vol. 24 (1988), pp. 453–70.

[40]Richard E. Walton, *Interpersonal Peacemaking: Confrontations and Third-Party Consultation* (Reading, MA: Addison-Wesley, 1969), p. 2.

[41]Information from ILO website: http://www.ilo.org/public/english/index.htm and http://www.ilo.org/public/english/standards/decl/publ/reports/report4.htm.

[42]See Kenneth W. Thomas, "Conflict and Conflict Management," in M. D. Dunnett (ed.), *Handbook of Industrial and Organizational Behavior* (Chicago; Rand McNally, 1976), pp. 889–935.

[43]See Robert R. Blake and Jane Strygley Mouton, "The Fifth Achievement," *Journal of Applied Behavioral Science,* vol. 6 (1970), pp. 413–27; Alan C. Filley, *Interpersonal Conflict Resolution* (Glenview, IL: Scott, Foresman, 1975).

[44]This discussion is based on Filley, op cit.

[45]Portions of this treatment of negotiation originally adapted from John R. Schermerhorn Jr., James G. Hunt, and Richard N. Osborn, *Managing Organizational Behavior,* 4th ed. (New York: Wiley, 1991), pp. 382–87. Used by permission.

[46]See Roger Fisher and William Ury; *Getting to Yes: Negotiating Agreement Without Giving In* (New York: Penguin, 1983); James A. Wall, Jr., *Negotiation:*

Theory and Practice (Glenview, IL: Scott, Foresman, 1985); and William L. Ury, Jeanne M. Brett, and Stephen B. Goldberg, *Getting Disputes Resolved* (San Francisco: Jossey-Bass, 1997).

[47]Fisher and Ury, op cit.

[48]Ibid.

[49]Developed from Max H. Bazerman, *Judgment in Managerial Decision Making*, 4th ed. (New York: Wiley, 1998), Chapter 7.

[50]Fisher and Ury, op cit.

[51]Information from the United Nations website: www.un.org/News/ossg/sg/pages/sg_biography.html (February 22, 2001).

[52]Roy J. Lewicki and Joseph A. Litterer, *Negotiation* (Homewood, IL: Irwin, 1985).

Chapter 18 Notes

[1]Information and quotes from Amy Taso and Jane Black, "Where Will Carly Fiorina Take HP?" *Business Week Online* (June 11, 2003); Dan Thanh Dang, "Hewlett-Packard Chief Speaks to University of Maryland Students, Executives," *The Baltimore Sun, Maryland* (October 11, 2003), retrieved from Knight Ridder/Tribune Business News.

[2]Information from "On the Road to Innovation," in special advertising section. "Charting the Course: Global Business Sets Its Goals," *Fortune* (August 4, 1997).

[3]Michael Beer and Nitin Nohria, "Cracking the Code of Change," *Harvard Business Review* (May–June 2000), pp. 133–41.

[4]Quote from John A. Byrne, "Visionary vs. Visionary," *Business Week* (August 28, 2000), p. 210.

[5]Tom Peters, *The Circle of Innovation* (New York: Knopf, 1997).

[6]Quotes from David Kirkpatrick, "From Davos, Talk of Death," *Fortune* (March 5, 2001), pp. 180–82.

[7]Peter Senge, *The Fifth Discipline* (New York: Harper, 1990).

[8]R. Duane Ireland and Michael A. Hitt, "Achieving and Maintaining Strategic Competitiveness in the 21st Century: The Role of Strategic Leadership," *Academy of Management Executive* (February 1999), pp. 43–57.

[9]Byrne, op. cit.

[10]Developed from Ireland & Hitt, op. cit.

[11]See, for example, Roger von Oech, *A Whack on the Side of the Head* (New York: Warner Books, 1983) and *A Kick in the Seat of the Pants* (New York: Harper & Row, 1986).

[12]See Peter F. Drucker, "The Discipline of Innovation," *Harvard Business Review* (November-December 1998), pp. 3–8.

[13]Peter F. Drucker, *Management: Tasks, Responsibilities, and Practices* (New York: Harper & Row, 1973), p. 797.

[14]Information from David Kirkpatrick, Software's Humble Wizard Does It Again," *Fortune* (February 19, 2001), pp. 137–42.

[15]Information from "Providing Rural Phone Service Profitably in Poor Countries," *Business Week* (December 18, 2000), special advertising section.

[16]Based on Gary Hamel, *Leading the Revolution* (Boston, MA: Harvard Business School Press, 2000), pp. 293–95.

[17]Based on Edward B. Roberts, "Managing Invention and Innovation," *Research Technology Management* (January-February 1988), pp. 1–19, and Hamel, op cit.

[18]Information from Craig Wilson, "Hallmark Hits the Mark," *USA Today* (June 14, 2001), pp. D1, D2.

[19]This discussion is stimulated by James Brian Quinn, "Managing Innovation Controlled Chaos," *Harvard Business Review*, Vol. 63 (May–June 1985). Selected quotations and examples from Kenneth Labich. "The Innovators," *Fortune*, (June 6, 1988), pp. 49–64.

[20]Peter F. Drucker, "Best R&D Is Business Driven," *Wall Street Journal*, (February 10, 1988), p. 11.

[21]See Roberts, op cit.

[22]Drucker, op cit., 1998.

[23]Reported in Carol Hymowitz, "Task of Managing Changes in Workplace Takes a Careful Hand," *Wall Street Journal* (July 1, 1997), p. B1.

[24]Reported in G. Christian Hill and Mike Tharp, "Stumbling Giant—Big Quarterly Deficit Stuns BankAmerica, Adds Pressure on Chief," *Wall Street Journal*, (July 18, 1985), pp. 1–16.

[25]Beer and Nohria, op cit.; and "Change Management, An inside Job," *Economist* (July 15, 2000), p. 61.

[26]Reported in Robert Rose, "Kentucky Plant Workers Are Cranking Out Good Ideas," *Wall Street Journal* (August 13, 1996), p. B1.

[27]Survey results from "Too Much Work, Too Little Time," *Business Week* (July 16, 2001), p. 12.

[28]Beer & Nohria, op. cit.

[29]For a review of scholarly work on organizational change, see Arthur G. Bedian, "Organizational Change: A Review of Theory and Research," *Journal of Management*, vol. 25 (1999), pp. 293–315.

[30]For a discussion of alternative types of change, see David A. Nadler and Michael L. Tushman, *Strategic Organizational Design* (Glenview, II: Scott, Foresman, 1988); John P. Kotter, "Leading Change: Why Transformations Efforts Fail," *Harvard Business Review* (March–April 1995), pp 59–67; and W. Warner Burke, *Organization change* (Thousand Oaks, CA.: Sage, 2002).

[31]Based on Kotter, op. cit.

[32]See Edward E. Lawler III, "Strategic Choices for Changing Organizations," chapter 12 in Allan M. Mohrman Jr., Susan Albers Mohrman, Gerald E. Ledford Jr., Thomas G. Cummings, Edward E. Lawler III, and Associates, *Large Scale Organizational Change* (San Francisco; Jossey-Bass, 1989).

[33]The classic description of organizations on these terms is by Harold J. Leavitt, "Applied Organizational Change in Industry: Structural, Technological and Humanistic Approaches," in James G. March (ed.), *Handbook of Organizations* (Chicago: Rand McNally, 1965), pp. 1144–70.

[34]Kurt Lewin, "Group Decision and Social Change," in G. E. Swanson, T. M. Newcomb and E. L. Hartley (eds.), *Readings in Social Psychology* (New York: Holt, Rinehart, 1952), pp. 459–73.

[35]This discussion is based on Robert Chin and Kenneth D. Benne, "General Strategies for Effecting Changes in Human Systems," in Warren G. Bennis, Kenneth D. Benne, Robert Chin, and Kenneth E. Corey (eds.), *The Planning of Change*, 3rd ed. (New York: Holt, Rinehart; 1969), pp. 22–45.

[36]The change agent descriptions here and following are developed from an exercise reported in J. William Pfeiffer and John E. Jones, *A Handbook of Structured Experiences for Human Relations Training*, vol. 2 (La Jolla, CA: University Associates, 1973).

[37]Ram N. Aditya, Robert J. House, and Steven Kerr, "Theory and Practice of Leadership: Into the New Millennium," Chapter 6 in Cary L. Cooper and Edwin A. Locke, *Industrial and Organizational Psychology: Linking Theory with Practice* (Malden, MA: Blackwell, 2000).

[38]Information from Mike Schneider, Disney Teaching Exces Magic of Customer Service," *Columbus Dispatch* (December 17, 2000), p. G9.

[39]Ibid.

[40]Teresa M. Amabile, "How to Kill Creativity, *Harvard Business Review*, (September–October, 1998), pp. 77–87.

[41]Sue Shellenbarger, "Some Employers Find Way to Ease Burden of Changing Shifts," *Wall Street Journal* (March 25, 1998), p. B1.

[42]Ibid.

[43]John P. Kotter and Leonard A. Schlesinger, "Choosing Strategies for Change," *Harvard Business Review*, vol. 57 (March–April 1979); 109–12.

[44]Example from *Fortune* (December, 1991), pp. 56–62; additional information from corporate website: www.toro.com.

[45]Wanda J. Orlikowski and J. Debra Hofman, "An Improvisational Model for Change Management: The Case of Groupware Technologies," *Sloan Management Review* (winter 1997), pp. 11–21.

[46]Ibid.

[47]Overviews of organization development are provided by W. Warner Burke, *Organization Development: A Normative View* (Reading, MA: Addison-Wesley, 1987); William Rothwell, Roland Sullivan, and Gary N. McLean, *Practicing Organization Development* (San Francisco: Jossey-Bass, 1995); and Wendell L. French and Cecil H. Bell Jr., *Organization Development*, 6th ed. (Englewood Cliffs, NJ: Prentice-Hall, 1998).

[48]See French and Bell, op. cit.

[49]See Arthur P. Brief, Randall S. Schuler, and Mary Van Sell, *Managing Job Stress* (Boston: Little, Brown, 1981), pp. 7, 8.

[50]Robert B. Reich, *The Future of Success* (New York: Knopf, 2000), p. 8.

[51]Michael Weldholz, "Stress Increasingly Seen as Problem with Executives More Vulnerable," *Wall Street Journal*, (September 28, 1982), p. 31.

[52]Sue Shellenbarger, "Do We Work More or Not? Either Way, We Feel Frazzled," *Wall Street Journal*, (July 30, 1997), p. B1.

[53]See, for example, "Desk Rage," *Business Week* (November 27, 2000), p. 12.

[54]Carol Hymowitz, "Impossible Expectations and Unfulfilling Work Stress Managers, Too," *Wall Street Journal*, (January 16, 2001), p. B1.

[55]The classic work is Meyer Friedman and Ray Roseman, *Type A Behavior and Your Heart* (New York: Knopf, 1974).

[56]See Hans Selye, *Stress in Health and Disease* (Boston: Butterworth, 1976).

[57]Carol Hymowitz, "Can Workplace Stress Get *Worse*?" *Wall Street Journal*, (January 16, 2001), pp. B1, B3.

[58]See Steve M. Jex, *Stress and Job Performance* (San Francisco: Jossey-Bass, 1998).

[59]The extreme case of "workplace violence" is discussed by Richard V. Denenberg and Mark Braverman, *The Violence-Prone Workplace* (Ithaca, NY: Cornell University Press, 1999).

[60]See Daniel C. Ganster and Larry Murphy, "Workplace Interventions to Prevent Stress-Related Illness: Lessons from Research and Practice," Chapter 2 in Cooper and Locke (eds.), op cit. (2000).

[61]Reported in Sue Shellenbarger, "Finding Ways to Keep a Partner's Job Stress from Hitting Home," *Wall Street Journal*, (November 29, 2000), p. B1.

[62]Quote from Shellenbarger, op. cit.

[63]See John M. Ivancevich and Michael T. Matteson, "Optimizing Human Resources: A Case for Preventive Health and Stress Management," *Organizational Dynamics*, vol. 9 (Autumn 1980), pp. 6–8. See also John M. Ivancevich, Michael T. Matteson, and Edward P. Richards III, "Who's Liable for Stress on the Job?" *Harvard Business Review* (March–April 1985), pp. 60–71.

[64]Information from "Tea Leaves, Entrails, and Crystal Balls," *Business Week Frontier* (December 4, 2000), p. F26; and World Future Society website: www.wfs.org.

Photo Credits

Name Index

Subject Index